나의 토익 ~~KB086756~~ 달성기

TEST 1을 풀고난 후, 점수에 따라 자신의 수준에 맞는 학습 플랜을 선택하세요.

☐ [800점 이상] 2주 완성 학습 플랜
☐ [600~795점] 3주 완성 학습 플랜
☐ [595점 이하] 4주 완성 학습 플랜

※ 일 단위의 상세 학습 플랜은 p.24~25에 있습니다.

각 TEST를 마친 후, 해당 TEST의 점수를 ·로 표시하여 자신의 점수 변화를 확인하세요.

Listening

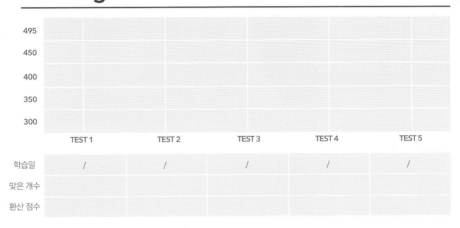

	TEST 1	TEST 2	TEST 3	TEST 4	TEST 5
학습일	/	/	/	/	/
맞은 개수					
환산 점수					

Reading

	TEST 1	TEST 2	TEST 3	TEST 4	TEST 5
학습일	/	/	/	/	/
맞은 개수					
환산 점수					

※ 점수 환산표는 p.244~245에 있습니다.

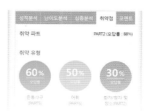

한 권으로 끝내는

해커스
토익

실전 LC+RC

모의고사 + 해설집

1

해커스 어학연구소

무료 토익 · 토스 · 오픽 · 지텔프 자료
Hackers.co.kr

단 한 권으로
'토익 실전 감각'을
높이세요.

토익 시험을 효과적으로 준비하려면
무엇보다도 충분한 실전 문제 풀이 연습을 통해
'토익 실전 감각'을 길러야 합니다.

≪한 권으로 끝내는 해커스 토익 실전 LC+RC 1≫(최신개정판)은
여러분이 토익 시험의 문항 유형을 빠르게 익히고,
단 한 권으로 실전에 대비할 수 있도록 돕기 위해 탄생했습니다.

**다양한 부가 학습자료로
약점 보완!**

**정확한 해석·해설로
정답과 오답의 근거 확실히 파악!**

**LC·RC 실전 모의고사 5회분으로
실전 감각 UP!**

Contents

책의 특징 및 활용 방법   6

토익 소개   10

파트별 출제 유형 및 전략   12

수준별 맞춤 학습 플랜   24

정답   238

점수 환산표   244

Answer Sheet   247

📖 **문제집[본책]**

TEST 1

LISTENING TEST   28

READING TEST   40

TEST 2

LISTENING TEST   70

READING TEST   82

TEST 3

LISTENING TEST   112

READING TEST   124

TEST 4

LISTENING TEST   154

READING TEST   166

TEST 5

LISTENING TEST   196

READING TEST   208

해설집 [책 속의 책]

TEST 1

LISTENING TEST 정답·스크립트·해석·해설   2
READING TEST 정답·해석·해설   24

TEST 2

LISTENING TEST 정답·스크립트·해석·해설   44
READING TEST 정답·해석·해설   66

TEST 3

LISTENING TEST 정답·스크립트·해석·해설   85
READING TEST 정답·해석·해설   107

TEST 4

LISTENING TEST 정답·스크립트·해석·해설   126
READING TEST 정답·해석·해설   148

TEST 5

LISTENING TEST 정답·스크립트·해석·해설   167
READING TEST 정답·해석·해설   189

 단어암기자료(HackersIngang.com)

 받아쓰기&쉐도잉 워크북(HackersIngang.com)

 온라인 실전모의고사(Hackers.co.kr)

책의 특징 및 활용 방법

01 LC · RC 실전 모의고사 5회분으로 실전 감각을 높이세요.

토익 시험에 대비해 실전 감각을 높이기 위해서는 LC와 RC의 모든 파트에 익숙해져야 합니다. ≪한 권으로 끝내는 해커스 토익 실전 LC+RC 1≫은 LC와 RC 실전 모의고사를 각 5회분씩 수록하여, 한 권의 교재로 토익 LC와 RC 문제 풀이 연습을 끝낼 수 있도록 구성했습니다.

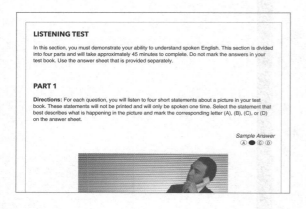

Listening Test

실제 토익 시험의 출제 경향을 완벽하게 반영한 **LC 실전 모의고사 5회분**을 수록하였습니다. 교재에 수록된 실전 문제들을 풀어보며 빠르게 실전 감각을 쌓을 수 있습니다.

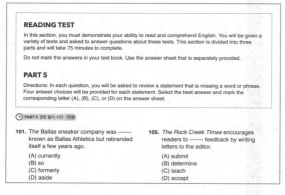

Reading Test

실제 토익 시험의 출제 경향을 완벽하게 반영한 **RC 실전 모의고사 5회분**을 수록하였습니다. 교재에 수록된 실전 문제들을 풀어보며 빠르게 실전 감각을 쌓을 수 있습니다.

Answer Sheet

교재 뒤에 수록된 Answer Sheet를 활용하여, 답안지 마킹까지 실제 시험처럼 연습해봄으로써 시간 관리 방법을 익히고, 실전 감각을 보다 극대화할 수 있습니다.

02 정확한 해석·해설로 정답과 오답의 근거를 확실히 파악하세요.

문제 풀이 후, 해석·해설을 확인하며 정답과 오답의 근거를 확실하게 정리하는 것이 중요합니다. ≪한 권으로 끝내는 해커스 토익 실전 LC+RC 1≫은 모든 문제에 대한 정확한 해석과 해설을 수록하여, 틀린 문제의 원인을 파악하고 보완할 수 있도록 구성했습니다.

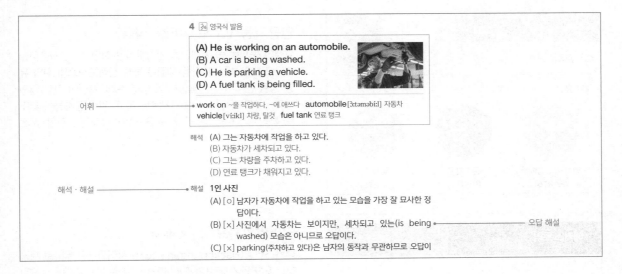

해석·해설
모든 지문 및 문제에 대한 정확한 해석을 통해 해석이 잘되지 않는 문장의 구조를 확실하게 익힐 수 있으며, 해설을 통해 자신이 어떤 과정으로 정답을 선택했는지 되짚어볼 수 있습니다.

오답 해설
오답 보기가 오답이 되는 이유까지 상세하게 설명하여 틀린 문제의 원인을 파악하고 보완할 수 있습니다.

어휘
지문 및 문제에서 사용된 단어와 표현을 의미와 함께 수록하여 문제를 복습할 때 일일이 사전을 찾는 불편을 덜 수 있습니다.

책의 특징 및 활용 방법

03 다양한 부가 학습자료로 약점을 보완하세요.

문제 풀이 후, 자신의 약점이 무엇인지를 파악하고 다양한 학습자료를 이용하여 이를 보완하는 것이 중요합니다. ≪한 권으로 끝내는 해커스 토익 실전 LC+RC 1≫은 자신의 약점을 보완하여 목표 점수에 좀 더 쉽게 도달할 수 있도록 다양한 부가 학습자료를 제공하고 있습니다.

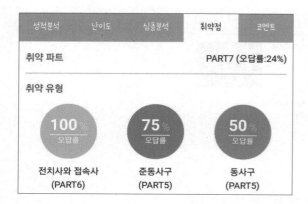

인공지능 1:1 토익어플 '빅플'

교재의 문제를 풀고 답안을 입력하기만 하면, 인공지능 어플 '해커스토익 빅플'이 **자동 채점은 물론 성적분석표와 취약 유형 심층 분석까지 제공**합니다. 이를 통해, 자신이 가장 많이 틀리는 취약 유형이 무엇인지 확인하고, 관련 문제들을 추가로 학습하며 취약 유형을 집중 공략하여 약점을 보완할 수 있습니다.

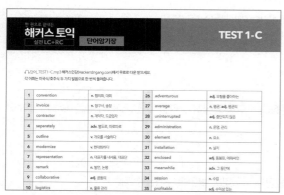

단어암기자료(PDF & MP3)

해커스인강(HackersIngang.com) 사이트에서 무료로 제공하는 **단어암기자료(PDF & MP3)**를 활용하여, 교재에 수록된 테스트의 중요 단어와 표현을 복습하고 암기할 수 있습니다.

받아쓰기 & 쉐도잉 워크북(PDF & MP3)

해커스인강(HackersIngang.com) 사이트에서 무료로 제공하는 **받아쓰기 & 쉐도잉 워크북(PDF & MP3)**을 활용하여, 교재에 수록된 핵심 문장을 복습하고 LC 점수를 향상할 수 있는 기본 실력을 갖출 수 있습니다.

정답 ANSWER KEYS

▌TEST 1

LISTENING TEST					READING TEST				
1 (B)	2 (A)	3 (D)	4 (A)	5 (D)	101 (C)	102 (B)	103 (D)	104 (A)	105 (A)
6 (C)	7 (C)	8 (D)	9 (C)	10 (C)	106 (D)	107 (A)	108 (A)	109 (C)	110 (A)
11 (A)	12 (A)	13 (C)	14 (A)	15 (A)	111 (A)	112 (D)	113 (B)	114 (D)	115 (C)
16 (A)	17 (A)	18 (B)	19 (B)	20 (C)	116 (D)	117 (B)	118 (A)	119 (D)	120 (D)
21 (D)	22 (A)	23 (A)	24 (C)	25 (C)	121 (D)	122 (C)	123 (B)	124 (A)	125 (B)
26 (A)	27 (C)	28 (B)	29 (B)	30 (B)	126 (C)	127 (C)	128 (B)	129 (B)	130 (D)
31 (D)	32 (A)	33 (C)	34 (D)	35 (B)	131 (D)	132 (B)	133 (A)	134 (C)	135 (A)
36 (D)	37 (B)	38 (B)	39 (D)	40 (A)	136 (A)	137 (D)	138 (C)	139 (B)	140 (D)
41 (B)	42 (C)	43 (A)	44 (B)	45 (C)	141 (C)	142 (A)	143 (D)	144 (B)	145 (D)
46 (D)	47 (D)	48 (A)	49 (D)	50 (D)	146 (A)	147 (B)	148 (A)	149 (A)	150 (D)
51 (C)	52 (B)	53 (C)	54 (B)	55 (C)	151 (B)	152 (D)	153 (A)	154 (D)	155 (C)
56 (A)	57 (B)	58 (D)	59 (B)	60 (B)	156 (B)	157 (D)	158 (D)	159 (B)	160 (D)
61 (D)	62 (B)	63 (D)	64 (D)	65 (C)	161 (D)	162 (C)	163 (D)	164 (B)	165 (A)

정답녹음 MP3

해커스인강(HackersIngang.com) 사이트에서 무료로 제공하는 **정답녹음 MP3**를 활용하여, 문제 풀이 후 보다 편리하게 채점할 수 있습니다.

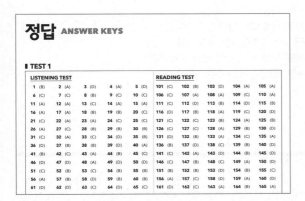

무료 온라인 실전모의고사

해커스토익(Hackers.co.kr) 사이트에서 제공하는 **온라인 실전모의고사**를 추가로 풀어보며 실전 감각을 키울 수 있습니다.

방대한 무료 학습자료

해커스토익(Hackers.co.kr) 사이트에서 토익 적중 예상특강을 비롯한 **방대하고 유용한 토익 학습자료**를 무료로 이용할 수 있습니다.

토익 소개

토익이란 무엇인가?

TOEIC은 Test Of English for International Communication의 약자로 영어가 모국어가 아닌 사람들을 대상으로 언어 본래의 기능인 '커뮤니케이션' 능력에 중점을 두고 일상생활 또는 국제 업무 등에 필요한 실용영어 능력을 평가하는 시험입니다. 토익은 일상 생활 및 비즈니스 현장에서 필요로 하는 내용을 평가하기 위해 개발되었고 다음과 같은 실용적인 주제들을 주로 다룹니다.

- 협력 개발: 연구, 제품 개발
- 재무 회계: 대출, 투자, 세금 회계, 은행 업무
- 일반 업무: 계약, 협상, 마케팅, 판매
- 기술 영역: 전기, 공업 기술, 컴퓨터, 실험실
- 사무 영역: 회의, 서류 업무
- 물품 구입: 쇼핑, 물건 주문, 대금 지불

- 식사: 레스토랑, 회식, 만찬
- 문화: 극장, 스포츠, 피크닉
- 건강: 의료 보험, 병원 진료, 치과
- 제조: 생산 조립 라인, 공장 경영
- 직원: 채용, 은퇴, 급여, 진급, 고용 기회
- 주택: 부동산, 이사, 기업 부지

토익 파트별 구성

구성		내용	문항 수	시간	배점
Listening Test	Part 1	사진 묘사	6문항(1번–6번)	45분	495점
	Part 2	질의 응답	25문항(7번–31번)		
	Part 3	짧은 대화	39문항, 13지문(32번–70번)		
	Part 4	짧은 담화	30문항, 10지문(71번–100번)		
Reading Test	Part 5	단문 빈칸 채우기(문법/어휘)	30문항(101번–130번)	75분	495점
	Part 6	장문 빈칸 채우기(문법/어휘/문장 고르기)	16문항, 4지문(131번–146번)		
	Part 7	지문 읽고 문제 풀기(독해)	54문항, 15지문(147번–200번)		
		– 단일 지문(Single Passage)	– 29문항, 10지문(147번–175번)		
		– 이중 지문(Double Passages)	– 10문항, 2지문(176번–185번)		
		– 삼중 지문(Triple Passages)	– 15문항, 3지문(186번–200번)		
Total	7 Parts		200문항	120분	990점

토익, 접수부터 성적 확인까지

1. 토익 접수

접수 기간 확인		사진(jpg 형식) 준비		인터넷/애플리케이션 접수
· 접수 기간을 TOEIC위원회 인터넷 사이트(www.toeic.co.kr) 혹은 공식 애플리케이션에서 확인합니다.	→	· 접수 시, jpg 형식의 사진 파일이 필요하므로 미리 준비해둡니다.	→	· TOEIC위원회 홈페이지 또는 애플리케이션의 시험 접수 창에서 절차에 따라 정보를 입력합니다.

2. 토익 응시

준비물

| 신분증 | 연필&지우개 | 시계 | 수험번호를 적어 둔 메모 | 오답노트 & 단어암기장 |

* 시험 당일 신분증이 없으면 시험에 응시할 수 없으므로, 반드시 ETS에서 요구하는 신분증(주민등록증, 운전면허증, 공무원증 등)을 지참해야 합니다.
  ETS에서 인정하는 신분증 종류는 TOEIC위원회 인터넷 사이트(www.toeic.co.kr)에서 확인 가능합니다.

시험 진행 순서

정기시험/추가시험 (오전)	추가시험 (오후)	진행 내용
AM 09:30 – 09:45	PM 2:30 – 2:45	답안지 작성 및 오리엔테이션
AM 09:45 – 09:50	PM 2:45 – 2:50	쉬는 시간
AM 09:50 – 10:10	PM 2:50 – 3:10	신분 확인 및 문제지 배부
AM 10:10 – 10:55	PM 3:10 – 3:55	듣기 평가(Listening Test)
AM 10:55 – 12:10	PM 3:55 – 5:10	독해 평가(Reading Test)

* 추가시험은 토요일 오전 또는 오후에 시행되므로 이 사항도 꼼꼼히 확인합니다.
* 당일 진행 순서에 대한 더 자세한 내용은 해커스토익(Hackers.co.kr) 사이트에서 확인할 수 있습니다.

3. 성적 확인

성적 발표일	시험일로부터 약 10일 이후 낮 12시 (성적 발표 기간은 회차마다 상이함)
성적 확인 방법	TOEIC위원회 인터넷 사이트(www.toeic.co.kr) 혹은 공식 애플리케이션
성적표 수령 방법	우편 수령 또는 온라인 출력 (시험 접수 시 선택) *온라인 출력은 성적 발표 즉시 발급 가능하나, 우편 수령은 약 7일가량의 발송 기간이 소요될 수 있음

파트별 출제 유형 및 전략

Part 1 사진 묘사 (6문제)

- Part 1은 주어진 4개의 보기 중에서 사진의 상황을 가장 잘 묘사한 보기를 선택하는 파트입니다.
- 문제지에는 사진만 제시되고 음성에서는 4개의 보기를 들려줍니다.

문제 형태

[문제지]

1.

[음성]

Number 1.

Look at the picture marked number one in your test book.

(A) A woman is serving a meal.
(B) A woman is washing a bowl.
(C) A woman is pouring some water.
(D) A woman is preparing some food.

출제 경향 및 대비 전략

사람 중심 사진이 가장 많이 출제됩니다!

사물 및 풍경 사진
28%

사람 중심 사진
72%

Part 1에서는 사람 중심 사진이 평균 4~5개로 가장 많이 출제됩니다.

핵심 대비 전략

보기를 듣기 전에 사진 유형을 확인하고 관련 표현을 미리 연상합니다.
보기를 듣기 전에 사람의 유무 및 수에 따라 사진 유형을 확인하고, 사람의 동작/상태 또는 사물의 상태/위치와 관련된 표현들을 미리 연상하면 보기를 훨씬 명확하게 들을 수 있어 정답 선택이 쉬워집니다.

○, ×, △를 표시하면서 오답을 걸러내는 연습을 합니다.
○, ×, △ 표시를 하지 않으면 다른 보기 내용과 혼동하기 쉬우므로, 보기를 듣고 ○, ×, △를 표시하면서 문제를 풀어야 헷갈리는 오답 보기를 확실히 제거하고 정답을 정확하게 선택할 수 있습니다.

Part 2 질의 응답 (25문제)

- Part 2는 주어진 질문이나 진술에 가장 적절한 응답을 선택하는 파트입니다.
- 문제지에는 질문과 보기가 제시되지 않으며 음성에서는 질문과 3개의 보기를 들려줍니다.

문제 형태

[문제지]	[음성]
7. Mark your answer on your answer sheet.	Number 7. Where is the nearest park? **(A) There's one on Lincoln Avenue.** (B) No, I don't drive. (C) I'm nearly finished.

출제 경향 및 대비 전략

의문사 의문문이 가장 많이 출제됩니다!

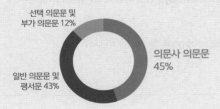

선택 의문문 및
부가 의문문 12%

의문사 의문문
45%

일반 의문문 및
평서문 43%

Part 2에서는 의문사 의문문이 평균 11~12개로 가장 많이 출제됩니다. 다음으로는 일반 의문문 및 평서문이 평균 10~11개, 선택 의문문 및 부가 의문문이 평균 3~4개 출제됩니다.

핵심 대비 전략

질문의 첫 단어는 절대 놓치지 않고 듣습니다.
Part 2에서 평균 11~12문제 정도 출제되는 의문사 의문문은 첫 단어인 의문사만 들어도 대부분 정답을 선택할 수 있습니다. 단, 부가 의문문은 평서문 뒤에 덧붙여진 'isn't it'이나 'right', 선택 의문문은 질문 중간에 접속사 'or'를 듣고 그 유형을 파악해야 합니다.

○, ×, △를 표시하면서 오답을 걸러내는 연습을 합니다.
○, ×, △ 표시를 하지 않으면 다른 보기 내용과 혼동하기 쉬우므로, 보기를 듣고 ○, ×, △를 표시하면서 문제를 풀어야 헷갈리는 오답 보기를 확실히 제거하고 정답을 정확하게 선택할 수 있습니다.

Part 3 짧은 대화 (39문제)

- Part 3는 2~3명의 대화를 듣고 이와 관련된 3개의 문제의 정답을 선택하는 파트입니다.
- 문제지에는 하나의 질문과 4개의 보기로 구성된 39문제가 제시되고, 일부 문제는 시각 자료가 함께 제시되기도 합니다. 음성으로는 하나의 대화와 이에 대한 3개의 문제의 질문을 들려줍니다.

문제 형태

[문제지]

32. What did the woman do during lunchtime?

(A) Spoke with a supervisor
(B) Called an important client
(C) Visited another company
(D) Finished a report

33. Why does the woman say, "But I have to meet with a Sorel representative on Friday"?

(A) To confirm an appointment
(B) To explain a mistake
(C) To express concern
(D) To change a deadline

34. What do the men suggest the woman do?

(A) Deal with a complaint
(B) Work on another project
(C) Review their proposals
(D) Meet them after work

[음성]

Questions 32 through 34 refer to the following conversation with three speakers.

W: George, Jerry . . . I'm sorry I couldn't make it for lunch today. My boss wanted to talk with me about the advertising campaign for Sorel Incorporated. This is a big project, and I'm a little nervous about it.

M1: Don't worry. You're a hard worker. And our clients never complain about your work.

W: But I have to meet with a Sorel representative on Friday. I'm not sure if I'll be able to create a proposal in time.

M2: Why don't we all go to a café after work? We can help you come up with some ideas.

M1: Yeah. We're happy to help.

Number 32. What did the woman do during lunchtime?

Number 33. Why does the woman say, "But I have to meet with a Sorel representative on Friday"?

Number 34. What do the men suggest the woman do?

출제 경향 및 대비 전략

3인 대화가 매회 2지문 출제됩니다!

2인 대화 + 시각 자료
23%

3인 대화
15%

2인 대화 62%

> Part 3에서는 3인 대화가 매회 2개 출제됩니다. 대화에 2명이 등장하는 2인 대화는 매회 8개로 가장 많이 출제되고, 2인 대화와 시각 자료가 함께 제시되는 지문도 매회 3개 출제됩니다.

핵심 대비 전략

대화를 듣기 전에 반드시 문제를 먼저 읽어야 합니다.
질문의 핵심 어구를 미리 읽으면 대화의 어느 부분을 중점적으로 들어야 할지 전략을 세울 수 있습니다. 시각 자료가 제시된 문제라면, 문제와 시각 자료를 함께 확인하면서 시각 자료의 종류와 내용을 파악합니다. 의도 파악 문제라면, 제시된 인용어구를 먼저 확인하고 해당 인용어구가 사용될 수 있는 문맥을 미리 예측합니다.

대화를 들으면서 동시에 정답을 선택해야 합니다.
문제를 읽을 때 세워놓은 전략에 따라, 대화를 들으면서 3개 문제의 정답을 선택해야 합니다. 즉, 대화를 들려주는 음성이 끝날 때에는 3개 문제의 정답 선택도 완료되어 있어야 합니다.

대화의 초반은 반드시 들어야 합니다.
Part 3에서는 대화의 초반에 언급된 내용 중 80% 이상이 문제로 출제되며, 특히 주제 및 목적 문제나 화자 및 장소 문제처럼 전체 대화 관련 문제에 대한 정답의 단서는 대부분 대화의 초반에 언급됩니다. 대화 초반의 내용을 듣지 못하면 대화 후반에서 언급된 특정 표현을 사용한 오답을 정답으로 선택하는 오류를 범할 수 있으므로 주의해야 합니다.

3인이 등장하는 대화에 유의합니다.
3인 대화에서 같은 성별의 화자 2명은 다른 국적의 발음으로 구분되므로, 미국·영국·호주·캐나다식 발음을 듣고 화자를 구분하여 대화의 문맥을 정확하게 파악하는 연습을 합니다.

Part 4 짧은 담화 (30문제)

- Part 4는 담화를 듣고 이와 관련된 3개의 문제의 정답을 선택하는 파트입니다.
- 문제지에는 하나의 질문과 4개의 보기로 구성된 30문제가 제시되고, 일부 문제는 시각 자료가 함께 제시되기도 합니다. 음성으로는 하나의 담화와 이에 대한 3개의 문제의 질문을 들려줍니다.

문제 형태

[문제지]

Lunch Specials	
Item	Price
Panini Sandwich	$7
Spaghetti	$6
Dinner Specials	
Item	Price
Lasagna	$9
Grilled Chicken	$11

71. What did the speaker do yesterday?

    (A) Raised dish prices
    (B) Attended a staff gathering
    (C) Met with customers
    (D) Sent menu information

72. Look at the graphic. Which meal will come with a complimentary beverage?

    (A) Panini Sandwich
    (B) Spaghetti
    (C) Lasagna
    (D) Grilled Chicken

73. What will the speaker probably do next?

    (A) Arrange some tables
    (B) Stock some ingredients
    (C) Hand out a list
    (D) Print a coupon

[음성]

Questions 71 through 73 refer to the following talk and menu.

As many of you already know, our restaurant's menu will be updated soon. I sent everyone an e-mail with the details yesterday, but I'll go over the main changes quickly now. First, the prices of our dinner menu items have been reduced by 10 percent to attract more evening customers. Also, we will provide a complimentary coffee or soft drink with one of our lunch specials . . . uh, the cheaper one. Some new dishes will be offered as well. I will now pass around a list of these dishes and the ingredients they will contain. Please study it so you'll be able to answer diners' questions.

Number 71. What did the speaker do yesterday?

Number 72. Look at the graphic. Which meal will come with a complimentary beverage?

Number 73. What will the speaker probably do next?

출제 경향 및 대비 전략

지문의 세부적인 내용을 묻는 문제가 가장 많이 출제됩니다!

전체 지문 관련
문제 23%

세부 사항 관련 문제
77%

> Part 4에서는 지문의 세부 사항을 묻는 문제가 평균 22~23개로 가장 많이 출제됩니다. 세부 사항을 묻는 문제 중 지도나 표 등의 시각 자료를 보고 푸는 시각 자료 문제도 매회 2개 출제됩니다.

핵심 대비 전략

지문을 듣기 전에 반드시 문제를 먼저 읽고, 시각 자료의 내용을 파악해야 합니다.
질문의 핵심 어구를 미리 읽으면 담화의 어느 부분을 중점적으로 들어야 할지 전략을 세울 수 있습니다. 시각 자료가 제시된 문제라면, 문제와 시각 자료를 함께 확인하면서 시각 자료의 종류와 내용을 파악합니다. 의도 파악 문제라면, 제시된 인용어구를 먼저 확인하고 해당 인용어구가 사용될 수 있는 문맥을 미리 예측합니다.

지문을 들으면서 동시에 정답을 선택해야 합니다.
문제를 읽을 때 세워놓은 전략에 따라, 지문을 들으면서 3개 문제의 정답을 선택해야 합니다. 즉, 지문을 들려주는 음성이 끝날 때에는 3개 문제의 정답 선택도 완료되어 있어야 합니다.

지문의 초반은 반드시 들어야 합니다.
Part 4에서는 지문의 초반에 언급된 내용 중 80% 이상이 문제로 출제되며, 특히 주제 및 목적 문제나 화자·청자 및 장소 문제처럼 전체 지문 관련 문제에 대한 정답의 단서는 대부분 지문의 초반에 언급됩니다. 지문 초반의 내용을 듣지 못할 경우, 더 이상 문제와 관련된 내용이 언급되지 않아 정답 선택이 어려워질 수 있으므로 주의해야 합니다.

Part 5 단문 빈칸 채우기 (30문제)

- Part 5는 한 문장의 빈칸에 알맞은 문법 사항이나 어휘를 4개의 보기 중에서 골라 채우는 파트입니다.
- Part 7 문제 풀이에 시간이 모자라지 않으려면 각 문제를 20~22초 내에, 총 30문제를 약 11분 내에 끝내야 합니다.

문제 형태

1. 문법

101. Kathleen Wilson is a recent graduate who ------- three months ago to help the marketing team with graphic design.

(A) hired　　　　　　　　　　　　　　　(B) hiring
(C) was hired　　　　　　　　　　　　(D) is hiring

2. 어휘

102. In spite of the bad weather and traffic delays, Mr. Chandra showed up ------- for his coworker's housewarming party.

(A) gradually　　　　　　　　　　　　(B) intensely
(C) considerably　　　　　　　　　　(D) punctually

출제 경향 및 대비 전략

문법 문제가 가장 많이 출제됩니다!

어휘 문제 33%

문법 문제 67%

> Part 5에서는 문법 요소와 그 쓰임을 묻는 문법 문제가 평균 20~21개로 가장 많이 출제됩니다. 문맥에 어울리는 어휘를 선택하는 어휘 문제는 평균 9~10개가 출제됩니다.

핵심 대비 전략

보기를 보고 문법 문제인지, 어휘 문제인지를 파악합니다.
hired, hiring, was hired, is hiring처럼 보기가 어근은 같지만 형태가 다른 단어들로 주로 구성되어 있다면 문법 문제이고, 보기가 gradually, intensely, considerably, punctually처럼 같은 품사의 다양한 어휘들로 구성되어 있으면 어휘 문제입니다.

파악한 문제 유형에 따라 빈칸 주변이나 문장의 전체적인 구조 및 문맥을 통해 정답을 선택합니다.
문법 문제는 문제 유형에 따라 빈칸 주변이나 문장의 전체적인 구조를 통해 빈칸에 적합한 문법적 요소를 정답으로 선택합니다. 만약 구조만으로 풀 수 없는 경우, 문맥을 확인하여 정답을 선택합니다. 어휘 문제는 그 문맥에 가장 적합한 어휘를 정답으로 선택합니다.

Part 6 장문 빈칸 채우기 (16문제)

- Part 6는 한 지문 내의 4개의 빈칸에 알맞은 문법 사항이나 어휘 및 문장을 4개의 보기 중에서 골라 채우는 파트입니다.
- Part 7 문제 풀이에 시간이 모자라지 않으려면 각 문제를 25~30초 내에, 총 16문제를 약 8분 내에 끝내야 합니다.

문제 형태

Questions 131-134 refer to the following e-mail.

-------. As you know, you are in charge of driving our visitor from Fennel Corporation, Mr. Palmer. He will be
131.
here as scheduled from May 16 to 20. However, his arrival time from Dublin has been moved back four hours
because he ------- a quick stop in New York. This means you do not need to be at the airport until 2 P.M. on
132.
the 16th. Also, the factory tour ------- he was supposed to take on Monday morning has been canceled. He'll
133.
have a breakfast meeting with the plant manager instead at the Oberlin Hotel. Attached is a revised -------.
134.
Please let me know as soon as you've confirmed these adjustments.

Helen Cho, Client relations Ctrek Apparel

131. (A) Regretfully, Mr. Palmer will no longer be
needing our services.
(B) I'm writing to inform you of a few
changes concerning our client.
(C) The following are some details about the
new factory manager.
(D) Finally, I have received the new schedule for
your flight to Dublin.

132. (A) will be made   **(B) is making**
(C) had made   (D) has been making

133. (A) this   (B) what
(C) when   **(D) that**

134. **(A) itinerary**   (B) estimate
(C) transcript   (D) inventory

출제 경향 및 대비 전략

알맞은 문장 고르기 문제가 4문항 출제됩니다!

어휘 문제 29%
알맞은 문장 고르기 25%
문법 문제 46%

> Part 6에서는 빈칸에 알맞은 문장을 고르는 문제가 매회 4개 출제됩니다. 문법 요소와 그 쓰임을 묻는 문법 문제가 평균 7~8개로 가장 많이 출제되며, 문맥에 어울리는 어휘를 선택하는 어휘 문제는 평균 4~5개가 출제됩니다.

핵심 대비 전략

빈칸이 포함된 문장, 또는 앞뒤 문장이나 전체 지문의 구조 및 문맥을 통해 정답을 선택합니다.
빈칸 주변이나 문장의 구조 및 문맥을 파악해야 하는 문제가 출제됩니다. 만약 빈칸이 포함된 문장만으로 정답 선택이 어려울 경우, 반드시 앞뒤 문장이나 전체 지문의 구조 및 문맥을 파악하여 문맥에 가장 잘 어울리는 보기를 정답으로 선택해야 합니다.

파트별 출제 유형 및 전략

Part 7 지문 읽고 문제 풀기 (54문제)

- Part 7은 제시된 지문과 관련된 질문들에 대해 4개의 보기 중에서 가장 적절한 답을 선택하는 파트입니다.
- 독해 지문은 단일 지문(Single Passage), 이중 지문(Double Passages), 삼중 지문(Triple Passages)으로 나뉘며, 단일 지문에서 29문제, 이중 지문에서 10문제, 삼중 지문에서 15문제가 출제됩니다.
- Part 7의 모든 문제를 제한 시간 내에 풀려면 한 문제를 약 1분 내에 풀어야 합니다.

문제 형태

1. 단일 지문(Single Passage)

Questions 149-150 refer to the following text message chain.

Natasha Lee	4:08 P.M.

Robert, about the sponsorship packages for the Shoreland Music Festival, do you want to go for the Platinum package? It allows us to broadcast commercials during the event.

Robert Brown	4:09 P.M.

That would give us good exposure. Plus, we can put up company banners at the venue.

Natasha Lee	4:10 P.M.

That's right. So, should I go ahead and sign us up? The deadline is this Friday.

Robert Brown	4:10 P.M.

Well, we can't spend any more than $6,000 on this. How much is it?

Natasha Lee	4:12 P.M.

More than that. How about the Gold sponsorship package then? It costs $5,250, and festival announcers will mention our company over the loudspeakers throughout the day.

Robert Brown	4:13 P.M.

That sounds OK to me. Send me all the details once you're done.

---

149. In which department do the writers most likely work?

(A) Accounting
(B) Marketing
(C) Customer service
(D) Human resources

150. At 4:12 P.M., what does Ms. Lee most likely mean when she writes, "More than that"?

(A) She believes that registering after the deadline is acceptable.
(B) She acknowledges that a cost exceeds a budgeted amount.
(C) She would like to receive some additional sponsorship benefits.
(D) She doubts that $6,000 is their maximum spending allowance.

---

2. 이중 지문(Double Passages)

Questions 176-180 refer to the following e-mail and online form.

To	Jennifer Ellis <jenniferellis@jagmail.com>
From	Travis Whitman <traviswhitman@mywebpress.com>
Date	November 1
Subject	Action Needed on Your Account

Dear Ms. Ellis,

Your MyWebPress account is due to renew in 10 days. You have the option to pay for another year at the rate of $29.99, or you may choose the three-year option at $79.99. We also offer a premium version of MyWebPress that enables many more features and design templates. One year of the higher level software costs $49.99 while the three-year package price is $129.99.

These special prices are only available if your renewal form is received by November 10.

Thank you,

Travis Whitman

MyWebPress Subscription Renewal Form   Date: November 8

Please fill out all information to process your renewal request and payment.

Account Name	Jennifer Ellis		Account Number	83402839

Please choose your renewal option:

	One Year	Three Years
MyWebPress Standard	☐ $29.99	☐ $79.99
MyWebPress Premium	■ $49.99	☐ $129.99
Pre-made Forms Add-On	☐ $5.99	☐ $8.99
Graphic Design Add-On	☐ $12.99	☐ $18.99

Payment Information:

Credit Card Type	☐ Bankster	■ SureCredit	☐ YPay	Card Number	2934 4992 0041
Expiration Date	November 30			Security Code	557

176. What is indicated about Ms. Ellis?

(A) She is using a new credit card for payment.
(B) She failed to meet a deadline set by MyWebPress.
(C) She chose an upgraded version of her original plan.
(D) She added some security features to her package.

...

3. 삼중 지문(Triple Passages)

Questions 186-190 refer to the following Web page, form, and e-mail.

Laurel Art Center

Upcoming Events

Summer Sounds Fest • Concert featuring local musicians • June 5, from noon to 10 P.M. • Tickets go on sale May 15	**Spectacular Vistas** • Exhibit of watercolor paintings by local landscape artist Samantha Davey • Opens 6 P.M., July 3, at the Campbell Gallery • Refreshments provided by Gordon's Café
Exploring Wood • Seminar conducted by Paula Sue • Thursday July 6 from 10:00 P.M. to 4 P.M. • $25 for eight classes (participants must bring safety glasses and a pair of work gloves)	**Annual Craft Show** • Our biggest event of the year, featuring handi-crafts made by talented local artists • August 5, 10 A.M. to 4 P.M. • Admission is $5 for adults and $2 for seniors • Includes a buffet lunch from Kostas Mediterranean Kitchen

To join our mailing list, click here.

Laurel Art Center

Registration Form

Name	Ella Chung	Date	June 12
Telephone	555-3205	Address	108 Spruce Drive Hendersonville, TN 37075
E-mail	ellachung@mymail.net		
Event title	Exploring Wood		
Payment method			

☐ Cash (Please pay two weeks in advance to reserve your slot)
■ Credit card: Liberty Bancard 2347-8624-5098-5728

To	Melissa Hamada <m.hamada@laurelart.org>
From	Hector Villa <h.villa@laurelart.org>
Subject	Catering
Date	June 21

Dear Melissa,

As we discussed yesterday afternoon, Kostas Mediterranean Kitchen had to back out of catering our August 5 event due to a scheduling conflict. However, I've received confirmation that Asian Flavors can take their place. Please update our Web site to reflect this change.

Hector Villa
Activities director, Laurel Art Center

186. What is suggested about Ms. Chung?

(A) She is a member of the Laurel Art Center.
(B) She will be attending an upcoming exhibit.
(C) She is expected to bring gear to an activity.
(D) She will be charged $5 for admission to an event.

187. Which event will Asian Flavors be catering?

(A) Summer Sounds Fest
(B) Spectacular Vistas
(C) Exploring Wood
(D) Annual Craft Show

...

출제 경향 및 대비 전략

다중 지문이 매회 5개 출제됩니다!

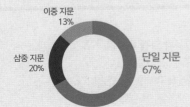

이중 지문
13%

삼중 지문
20%

단일 지문
67%

> Part 7에서는 이중 지문이 매회 2개, 삼중 지문이 매회 3개가 출제됩니다. 단일 지문은 매회 10개로 가장 많이 출제됩니다.

핵심 대비 전략

지문의 종류나 글의 제목을 먼저 확인하여 지문의 개괄적인 내용을 추측해야 합니다.
지문 맨 위에 지문을 소개하는 문장을 통해 언급된 지문의 종류를 확인하거나 글의 제목을 읽어서 지문이 어떤 내용을 담고 있을지 추측하며 문제를 풀도록 합니다.

질문을 먼저 읽고, 질문의 핵심 어구와 관련된 정답의 단서를 지문에서 확인해야 합니다.
질문을 읽고 질문의 핵심 어구를 파악한 후, 핵심 어구와 관련된 내용이 언급된 부분을 지문에서 찾아 정답의 단서를 확인합니다. 이중 지문이나 삼중 지문과 같은 연계 지문의 경우, 처음 확인한 단서만으로 정답을 선택할 수 없으면 첫 번째 단서와 관련된 두 번째 단서를 다른 지문에서 찾아야 합니다.

정답의 단서를 그대로 언급했거나 바꾸어 표현한 보기를 정답으로 선택해야 합니다.
정답의 단서를 그대로 언급했거나 패러프레이징한 보기를 정답으로 선택해야 합니다. 이중 지문이나 삼중 지문과 같은 연계 지문의 경우에는 두 개의 지문에 언급된 각각의 단서를 종합하여 정답을 선택해야 하는 경우도 있습니다.

수준별 맞춤 학습 플랜

TEST 1을 풀어본 뒤, 교재 뒤에 수록된 점수 환산표(p.244~245)에서 자신의 환산 점수를 확인하고 환산 점수에 맞는 학습 플랜을 선택하세요. 매일 박스에 체크하며 공부하고, 해설집과 다양한 부가 학습자료를 활용해 각 테스트를 꼼꼼하게 리뷰하세요.

800점 이상 학습 플랜 2주 동안 문제 풀이와 리뷰를 번갈아 하며 빠르게 실전 감각을 높이는 플랜

· 첫날에는 자신에게 맞는 학습 플랜을 고르기 위해, TEST 1을 풀어봅니다.
· 2주 동안 격일로 하루는 모의고사 1회분을 풀고, 다음 날 리뷰합니다.
· 각 테스트를 마친 후, 테스트 뒤에 수록된 Review 체크리스트를 활용하면 더욱 꼼꼼히 리뷰할 수 있습니다.

	1st Day	2nd Day	3rd Day	4th Day	5th Day
1st week	TEST 1 풀기 ☐	TEST 1 리뷰 ☐	TEST 2 풀기 ☐	TEST 2 리뷰 ☐	TEST 3 풀기 ☐
2nd week	TEST 3 리뷰 ☐	TEST 4 풀기 ☐	TEST 4 리뷰 ☐	TEST 5 풀기 ☐	TEST 5 리뷰 ☐

* 2주 완성의 경우 위의 표를 따르고, 1주 단기 완성을 원할 경우 위의 표에서 이틀 분량을 하루에 걸쳐서 학습하세요.

600~795점 학습 플랜 3주 동안 심화 학습을 통해 약점을 완벽하게 보완하는 플랜

· 첫날에는 자신에게 맞는 학습 플랜을 고르기 위해, TEST 1을 풀어봅니다.
· 3주 동안 첫째 날에는 모의고사 1회분을 풀고, 둘째 날에는 틀린 문제 위주로 해설집과 함께 리뷰합니다. 셋째 날에는 각 테스트에 해당하는 부가 학습자료와 함께 심화 학습을 합니다.
· 각 테스트를 마친 후, 테스트 뒤에 수록된 Review 체크리스트를 활용하면 더욱 꼼꼼히 리뷰할 수 있습니다.

	1st Day	2nd Day	3rd Day	4th Day	5th Day
1st week	TEST 1 풀기 ☐	TEST 1 리뷰 ☐	TEST 1 심화 학습 ☐	TEST 2 풀기 ☐	TEST 2 리뷰 ☐
2nd week	TEST 2 심화 학습 ☐	TEST 3 풀기 ☐	TEST 3 리뷰 ☐	TEST 3 심화 학습 ☐	TEST 4 풀기 ☐
3rd week	TEST 4 리뷰 ☐	TEST 4 심화 학습 ☐	TEST 5 풀기 ☐	TEST 5 리뷰 ☐	TEST 5 심화 학습 ☐

595점 이하 학습 플랜 4주 동안 각 영역을 꼼꼼하게 리뷰하여 실력을 향상시키는 플랜

· 첫날에는 자신에게 맞는 학습 플랜을 고르기 위해, TEST 1을 풀어봅니다.
· 4주 동안 첫째 날에는 리스닝 모의고사 1회분을 풀고 둘째 날에 리뷰, 셋째 날에는 리딩 모의고사 1회분을 풀고 넷째 날에 리뷰합니다. 학습 플랜의 마지막 날에는 그간 공부한 내용을 총 복습합니다.
· 각 테스트를 마친 후, 테스트 뒤에 수록된 Review 체크리스트를 활용하면 더욱 꼼꼼히 리뷰할 수 있습니다.

	1st Day	2nd Day	3rd Day	4th Day	5th Day
1st week	TEST 1 풀기 ☐	TEST 1 LC 리뷰 ☐	TEST 1 RC 리뷰 ☐	TEST 2 LC 풀기 ☐	TEST 2 LC 리뷰 ☐
2nd week	TEST 2 RC 풀기 ☐	TEST 2 RC 리뷰 ☐	TEST 3 LC 풀기 ☐	TEST 3 LC 리뷰 ☐	TEST 3 RC 풀기 ☐
3rd week	TEST 3 RC 리뷰 ☐	TEST 4 LC 풀기 ☐	TEST 4 LC 리뷰 ☐	TEST 4 RC 풀기 ☐	TEST 4 RC 리뷰 ☐
4th week	TEST 5 LC 풀기 ☐	TEST 5 LC 리뷰 ☐	TEST 5 RC 풀기 ☐	TEST 5 RC 리뷰 ☐	총 복습 ☐

무료 토익 · 토스 · 오픽 · 지텔프 자료
Hackers.co.kr

TEST 1

LISTENING TEST

Part 1
Part 2
Part 3
Part 4

READING TEST

Part 5
Part 6
Part 7

Review 체크리스트

잠깐! 테스트 전 아래 사항을 꼭 확인하세요.

휴대전화의 전원을 끄셨나요? 예 ☐
Answer Sheet(p.247), 연필, 지우개, 시계를 준비하셨나요? 예 ☐
Listening MP3를 들을 준비가 되셨나요? 예 ☐

모든 준비가 완료되었으면 목표 점수를 떠올린 후 테스트를 시작합니다.
테스트를 마친 후, Review 체크리스트(p.68)를 보며 자신이 틀린 문제를 반드시 복습합니다.

※ TEST 1을 통해 본인의 실력을 평가해본 후, 본인에게 맞는 학습플랜(p.24~p.25)으로 본 교재를 효율적으로 학습해 보세요.

🎧 TEST 1.mp3
실전용 · 복습용 문제풀이 MP3 무료 다운로드 및 스트리밍 바로듣기 (HackersIngang.com)
* 실제 시험장의 소음까지 재현해 낸 고사장 소음/매미 버전 MP3, 영국식 · 호주식 발음 집중 MP3, 고속 버전 MP3까지 구매
하면 실전에 더욱 완벽히 대비할 수 있습니다.

무료MP3 바로듣기

LISTENING TEST

In this section, you must demonstrate your ability to understand spoken English. This section is divided into four parts and will take approximately 45 minutes to complete. Do not mark the answers in your test book. Use the answer sheet that is provided separately.

PART 1

Directions: For each question, you will listen to four short statements about a picture in your test book. These statements will not be printed and will only be spoken one time. Select the statement that best describes what is happening in the picture and mark the corresponding letter (A), (B), (C), or (D) on the answer sheet.

Sample Answer
Ⓐ ● Ⓒ Ⓓ

The statement that best describes the picture is (B), "The man is sitting at the desk." So, you should mark letter (B) on the answer sheet.

1.

2.

GO ON TO THE NEXT PAGE

3.

4.

5.

6.

GO ON TO THE NEXT PAGE ➡

PART 2

Directions: For each question, you will listen to a statement or question followed by three possible responses spoken in English. They will not be printed and will only be spoken one time. Select the best response and mark the corresponding letter (A), (B), or (C) on your answer sheet.

7. Mark your answer on your answer sheet.

8. Mark your answer on your answer sheet.

9. Mark your answer on your answer sheet.

10. Mark your answer on your answer sheet.

11. Mark your answer on your answer sheet.

12. Mark your answer on your answer sheet.

13. Mark your answer on your answer sheet.

14. Mark your answer on your answer sheet.

15. Mark your answer on your answer sheet.

16. Mark your answer on your answer sheet.

17. Mark your answer on your answer sheet.

18. Mark your answer on your answer sheet.

19. Mark your answer on your answer sheet.

20. Mark your answer on your answer sheet.

21. Mark your answer on your answer sheet.

22. Mark your answer on your answer sheet.

23. Mark your answer on your answer sheet.

24. Mark your answer on your answer sheet.

25. Mark your answer on your answer sheet.

26. Mark your answer on your answer sheet.

27. Mark your answer on your answer sheet.

28. Mark your answer on your answer sheet.

29. Mark your answer on your answer sheet.

30. Mark your answer on your answer sheet.

31. Mark your answer on your answer sheet.

PART 3

Directions: In this part, you will listen to several conversations between two or more speakers. These conversations will not be printed and will only be spoken one time. For each conversation, you will be asked to answer three questions. Select the best response and mark the corresponding letter (A), (B), (C), or (D) on your answer sheet.

32. Why is the woman calling?

(A) To inquire about a job's requirements
(B) To postpone a job interview
(C) To ask whether her résumé was received
(D) To accept an offer of a position

33. What experience does the woman have?

(A) She worked as a research assistant.
(B) She studied business in college.
(C) She was employed as an intern.
(D) She volunteered for a charitable event.

34. What does the man suggest that the woman do?

(A) Read the description of a job online
(B) Come to the office for an in-person interview
(C) Obtain a reference letter from an employer
(D) Send in an application by a due date

35. Where most likely does the conversation take place?

(A) On a bus
(B) On an airplane
(C) On a train
(D) On a boat

36. What problem does the man mention?

(A) A password is incorrect.
(B) A lamp is not working.
(C) A connection is slow.
(D) A service is unavailable.

37. What does the man say he will do?

(A) Read a magazine
(B) Watch a show
(C) Reenter a password
(D) Move to another location

38. Why is making a survey necessary?

(A) A new advertisement was released.
(B) Some workers have quit.
(C) Customers have complained about a service.
(D) Cafeteria menu items will be added.

39. What does the woman offer to do?

(A) Take over an assignment
(B) Assist with an interview
(C) Talk to a supervisor
(D) Send a document

40. What does the woman remind Mark to do?

(A) Change some information
(B) Submit an evaluation
(C) Review an opinion
(D) Inquire about a facility

41. What is the conversation mainly about?

(A) The process for ordering a book
(B) An upcoming literary reading
(C) The shift schedule at a bookstore
(D) An award ceremony for writers

42. What does the woman mean when she says, "You can read yours last"?

(A) There will not be a long wait.
(B) There will be a time for questions.
(C) There will not be a schedule issue.
(D) There will be enough time for dinner.

43. According to the woman, what will the participants do after an event?

(A) Receive some refreshments
(B) Read a new issue of a journal
(C) Take a group photo
(D) Purchase books at a discount

GO ON TO THE NEXT PAGE

44. Why is the man visiting?

(A) To inquire about renting a building
(B) To perform a repair
(C) To reset an alarm
(D) To set up a boiler system

45. What does the woman thank the man for?

(A) Opening up a basement
(B) Identifying a problem
(C) Responding very rapidly
(D) Giving her free service

46. What does the woman say the man will receive?

(A) A floor plan
(B) Some contact information
(C) Pictures of some equipment
(D) A security pass

47. Where does the conversation most likely take place?

(A) At a clothing shop
(B) At a hair salon
(C) At a car wash
(D) At an appliance store

48. What is the man's main priority?

(A) Finding a cost-effective option
(B) Using his gift card
(C) Purchasing from a specific brand
(D) Utilizing some eco-friendly materials

49. What is mentioned about the Lexpro?

(A) It features personalized settings.
(B) It has been discontinued.
(C) It requires more energy.
(D) It was recently released.

50. What problem does the man mention?

(A) He did not receive a statement.
(B) A bank application is unavailable.
(C) An unusual purchase was made with his card.
(D) He cannot use his credit card.

51. What information does the woman request from the man?

(A) His date of birth
(B) His telephone number
(C) His address
(D) His credit card number

52. According to the woman, what will happen later today?

(A) A Web site will be updated.
(B) A card will become usable.
(C) A purchase will be canceled.
(D) A new card will arrive in the mail.

53. What is the man surprised by?

(A) The reduced sales of merchandise
(B) The reputation established by a company
(C) The success of a marketing strategy
(D) The price for a service

54. What does the man agree about?

(A) Creating a plan for a new project
(B) Employing an expert
(C) Contacting another company
(D) Increasing the advertising budget

55. Why does the woman say, "He has been working in that field for five years"?

(A) To highlight the need for experience
(B) To justify a candidate recommendation
(C) To explain the reason for a salary increase
(D) To suggest a transfer to another branch

56. What will happen tomorrow morning?

(A) A fashion show will be held.
(B) A store will be reopened.
(C) A magazine will be published.
(D) A work shift schedule will be posted.

57. What industry do the speakers most likely work in?

(A) Advertising
(B) Journalism
(C) Manufacturing
(D) Education

58. What does the woman reassure the man about?

(A) Assignments will not be delayed.
(B) Hard work will not be ignored.
(C) There will not be a crowd.
(D) A busy period will not last long.

---

59. What does the man inquire about?

(A) A mobile phone service plan
(B) The location of a product
(C) The features of a device
(D) A current sales promotion

60. Why was the man unaware of a situation?

(A) He was visiting other stores.
(B) He did not work in the morning.
(C) He had been waiting in line.
(D) He took the day off.

61. What does the woman give the man information about?

(A) A repair service
(B) A store's return policy
(C) A sales tax increase
(D) A recycling program

Café	Building 1	Grocery store	Building 2	Convenience store
Western Ave.				
Restaurant	Building 4	Bicycle shop		Building 3

62. Look at the graphic. Where will the barber shop be located?

(A) Building 1
(B) Building 2
(C) Building 3
(D) Building 4

63. According to the man, what is an advantage of the building?

(A) It does not require utility payments.
(B) It contains a large back room.
(C) It does not cost much per month.
(D) It is near public transportation.

64. How will the man recruit employees?

(A) By speaking to acquaintances
(B) By posting a sign on the building
(C) By contacting a staffing agency
(D) By putting ads in publications

GO ON TO THE NEXT PAGE

Friday				
	8 A.M.	9 A.M.	10 A.M.	11 A.M.
Carter	Conference call		Sales Meeting	HR Training
Delilah	Out of office			
Edgar		Conference call		
Frances			Out of office	

65. What does the man ask the woman to do?

(A) Approve a merger
(B) Create a new schedule
(C) Notify some employees
(D) Proofread an announcement

66. Look at the graphic. When will the department heads participate in a meeting?

(A) At 8 A.M.
(B) At 9 A.M.
(C) At 10 A.M.
(D) At 11 A.M.

67. Why is the woman's assistant unavailable right now?

(A) He is on a break.
(B) He only works part time.
(C) He is writing an e-mail.
(D) He is undergoing training.

68. Where most likely does the conversation take place?

(A) At a clothing store
(B) At a dry cleaner
(C) At a gift shop
(D) At a tailoring business

69. What does the woman ask the man about?

(A) His favorite color
(B) His preferred size
(C) His shopping budget
(D) His membership card

70. Look at the graphic. Why isn't this coupon valid for a purchase?

(A) It does not meet the minimum cost.
(B) It has already expired.
(C) It cannot be used with gift cards.
(D) It is for another location.

PART 4

Directions: In this part, you will listen to several short talks by a single speaker. These talks will not be printed and will only be spoken one time. For each talk, you will be asked to answer three questions. Select the best response and mark the corresponding letter (A), (B), (C), or (D) on your answer sheet.

71. What problem does the speaker mention?

    (A) A distribution system is causing complaints.
    (B) A product's quality is inconsistent.
    (C) A manufacturing plant is too small.
    (D) A store has discontinued a brand.

72. What solution does the speaker suggest?

    (A) Establishing a new factory
    (B) Rethinking a packaging design
    (C) Switching out some ingredients
    (D) Changing an affiliated company

73. What does the speaker ask the listeners to do?

    (A) Taste a new yogurt flavor
    (B) Look up information
    (C) Visit a store location
    (D) Clear a production floor

74. What caused the park project to take longer than planned?

    (A) Lack of materials
    (B) Insufficient funding
    (C) Work additions
    (D) Inclement weather

75. What does the mayor expect to happen?

    (A) Some economic activity will increase.
    (B) Some people will move to a neighborhood.
    (C) Some areas will become more expensive.
    (D) Some tourist attractions will be rebuilt.

76. What will happen next week?

    (A) An installation will be finished.
    (B) A ceremony will take place.
    (C) Invitations will be sent out.
    (D) Residents' opinions will be heard.

77. What promotion is the company currently offering?

    (A) Free installation
    (B) Upgraded battery packs
    (C) A coupon for 50 percent off
    (D) An extended warranty

78. Who is the advertisement intended for?

    (A) Battery manufacturers
    (B) Homeowners
    (C) Utility providers
    (D) Energy professionals

79. Why should the listeners contact the company?

    (A) To get tips on reducing electricity usage
    (B) To cancel a utility account
    (C) To receive a discount code
    (D) To talk about some options

80. Where does the speaker most likely work?

    (A) At a repair shop
    (B) At an electronics retailer
    (C) At an office supply store
    (D) At a manufacturing facility

81. Why does the speaker say, "It's a popular item"?

    (A) To recommend a product
    (B) To turn down an additional discount
    (C) To apologize for a delay
    (D) To encourage a quick decision

82. What should the listener do to buy a product?

    (A) Phone an employee
    (B) Make a reservation
    (C) Visit the customer service desk
    (D) Go to another branch

GO ON TO THE NEXT PAGE

83. What event is most likely taking place?

(A) A movie premier
(B) A theater opening
(C) A film festival
(D) A fundraiser

84. Who is Robert Willis?

(A) A festival organizer
(B) An investor
(C) A critic
(D) A crew member

85. What is *Off the Highway* about?

(A) Wildlife in the Midwest
(B) The history of an event
(C) A recent musical collaboration
(D) Living in a small town

---

86. What is being announced?

(A) A new album
(B) A special guest
(C) A contest result
(D) A tour schedule

87. What does the speaker mean when she says, "Ultima Records was surprised by the response"?

(A) Record sales increased significantly.
(B) Many people participated in an event.
(C) A Web site crashed due to increased traffic.
(D) Tickets sold out immediately.

88. What should the listeners do to learn about an upcoming promotion?

(A) Subscribe to a podcast
(B) Visit a Web site
(C) Send a text message
(D) Join a fan club

---

89. Who most likely is the speaker?

(A) A business owner
(B) A sales manager
(C) A landscape architect
(D) A maintenance worker

90. What will the listeners receive in a few minutes?

(A) A catalog of cleaning supplies
(B) A list of places to work
(C) A sign for a park
(D) An inventory of goods

91. What does the speaker ask Mr. Sandoval to do?

(A) Check a weather forecast
(B) Oversee a planting project
(C) Create a schedule for employees
(D) Confirm the stock of materials

---

92. Where is the tour taking place?

(A) At a hotel lobby
(B) At a university campus
(C) At a research facility
(D) At a photography museum

93. What will happen during the tour?

(A) A movie will be screened.
(B) Some scientists will be interviewed.
(C) The professor will give a speech.
(D) An instrument will be demonstrated.

94. What does the speaker imply when he says, "A recording of the tour will be available on our Web site"?

(A) Participation in the tour is not mandatory.
(B) There is an online forum for exchanging comments.
(C) The listeners do not have to take notes.
(D) Registration on the Web site is recommended.

Item	Quantity
Airway Headset (IB875747)	10
Blockland Paper Box (IB374665)	4
Officepro Pen, black (IB323722)	40
Blockland Pad, large	20

95. Look at the graphic. Which is the best-selling item in the company's new line?

(A) Item 1
(B) Item 2
(C) Item 3
(D) Item 4

96. What does the speaker say customers like most about the bag?

(A) The fabric
(B) The sizes
(C) The design
(D) The color

97. What most likely will the listeners do next?

(A) Review some proposals
(B) Look at competing products
(C) Compare product materials
(D) Check sales figures

98. Why is the speaker calling?

(A) To request a payment
(B) To accept a change
(C) To point out an opportunity
(D) To inquire about shipping

99. Look at the graphic. Which quantity number needs to change to get a discount?

(A) 10
(B) 4
(C) 40
(D) 20

100. What does the speaker say about the business?

(A) It is running low on stock.
(B) It specializes in electronics.
(C) It is introducing a new product.
(D) It can offer expedited delivery.

This is the end of the Listening test. Turn to PART 5 in your test book.

GO ON TO THE NEXT PAGE

READING TEST

In this section, you must demonstrate your ability to read and comprehend English. You will be given a variety of texts and asked to answer questions about these texts. This section is divided into three parts and will take 75 minutes to complete.

Do not mark the answers in your test book. Use the answer sheet that is separately provided.

PART 5

Directions: In each question, you will be asked to review a statement that is missing a word or phrase. Four answer choices will be provided for each statement. Select the best answer and mark the corresponding letter (A), (B), (C), or (D) on the answer sheet.

🕐 **PART 5 권장 풀이 시간** **11분**

---

101. The Ballas sneaker company was ------- known as Ballas Athletics but rebranded itself a few years ago.

(A) currently
(B) so
(C) formerly
(D) aside

102. The factory employees ------- to reread the operating system handbook.

(A) had directed
(B) were directed
(C) direct
(D) directed

103. The science convention will be held in September ------- the event's major sponsor has withdrawn its support.

(A) if only
(B) so that
(C) above all
(D) even though

104. The invoices from contractors are copied and filed separately ------- tax purposes.

(A) for
(B) at
(C) like
(D) in

105. *The Rock Creek Times* encourages readers to ------- feedback by writing letters to the editor.

(A) submit
(B) determine
(C) teach
(D) accept

106. Mr. Holly was the first salesperson hired by the firm and had to develop ------- own methods for selling.

(A) himself
(B) he
(C) his
(D) him

107. Fox Books sells a wide ------- of genres, ranging from fiction and poetry to history and philosophy.

(A) variety
(B) version
(C) knowledge
(D) position

108. The mayor of London outlined plans ------- some of the city's older metro lines.

(A) to modernize
(B) modernized
(C) have been modernized
(D) should have modernized

109. The Gage National Park recommends that hikers bring food and water ------- a compass.

(A) such as
(B) in case of
(C) along with
(D) seeing as

110. The company's project was announced by a marketing ------- at yesterday's press conference.

(A) representative
(B) representing
(C) representation
(D) represented

111. The invited speaker will have five minutes to give ------- remarks at the start of the seminar.

(A) most
(B) equal
(C) brief
(D) busy

112. The teams at Stranton Tech work ------- to identify problems and find appropriate solutions.

(A) collaborator
(B) collaborative
(C) collaboration
(D) collaboratively

113. The airline will be adding several new routes to South America to meet passengers' growing -------.

(A) cost
(B) demand
(C) attempt
(D) insight

114. ------- the elevator is fixed, residents of 110 Halpert Street will have to use the stairs.

(A) Then
(B) Only
(C) Since
(D) Until

115. Kemper Shipping is in ------- with a major US retailer to handle all of its logistics in the Middle East.

(A) negotiated
(B) negotiation
(C) negotiate
(D) negotiator

116. The institute will be unable to advance its research without obtaining ------- support from a funding agency.

(A) plain
(B) compact
(C) mere
(D) external

117. ------- extensive rainfall in Memphis, the city is dealing with widespread flood damage.

(A) Between
(B) After
(C) Aboard
(D) Except

118. Across the board, ------- personnel are required to wear identification badges issued by the company while working on the premises.

(A) all
(B) every
(C) each
(D) both

119. An investigation by the company's engineers ------- that the equipment's automatic control system had failed.

(A) chose
(B) requested
(C) revealed
(D) revised

120. Starting next week, Donald Peters will assume a ------- role at Zwingli Bank.

(A) supervises
(B) supervise
(C) supervisors
(D) supervisory

GO ON TO THE NEXT PAGE

121. The Web site gives recommendations to help people decide ------- smartphone will best suit their needs.

(A) whom
(B) whether
(C) which
(D) another

122. ------- production challenges earlier this year, the launch of the new Ecroon laptop was on schedule.

(A) With
(B) Owing to
(C) In spite of
(D) Because of

123. Dynaline has the ------- rating of any photo-editing application based on thousands of user reviews.

(A) high
(B) highest
(C) highly
(D) higher

124. Mr. Stewart was not allowed to return the items because he did not bring a -------.

(A) receipt
(B) guidance
(C) report
(D) procedure

125. Everyone who saw the film in a theater was ------- impressed with its spectacular special effects.

(A) ever
(B) quite
(C) last
(D) same

126. Anuman Foods opened its second international location in Hanoi this year, ------- its presence in Southeast Asia.

(A) expand
(B) expands
(C) expanding
(D) had expanded

127. ------- Mr. Hill nor Ms. Jackson had the qualifications to become head of regional sales.

(A) Not only
(B) Either
(C) Neither
(D) Other

128. The supermarket regularly issues coupons offering generous ------- on selected items.

(A) deals
(B) excuses
(C) shares
(D) chances

129. Ms. Chung dropped her car off at the repair shop and was asked to pick it up one week -------.

(A) left
(B) later
(C) more
(D) nowadays

130. ------- the recession is over, the travel industry is expected to recover.

(A) Despite
(B) Rather than
(C) In order that
(D) Now that

PART 6

Directions: In this part, you will be asked to read four English texts. Each text is missing a word, phrase, or sentence. Select the answer choice that correctly completes the text and mark the corresponding letter (A), (B), (C), or (D) on the answer sheet.

PART 6 권장 풀이 시간 8분

Questions 131-134 refer to the following article.

Martindale's Celebrates Anniversary

December 12—This week, Martindale's celebrates its 20th year as a fine dining restaurant.

Trained in France, chef and owner Joyce Martindale had always dreamed of having a

restaurant in downtown Elkhart, but it took several long years to realize her dream. She

------- opened her restaurant with the help of family and friends who believed in her vision.
131.

Today, Martindale's has become one of the best restaurants in Elkhart. -------.
132.

The restaurant ------- a selection of familiar French and American dishes, and these are
133.

prepared using only the freshest ingredients. First-time visitors should make it a point to try

the restaurant's -------. These include the steak dinner and roast chicken, which are among
134.

the favorite dishes of longtime customers.

---

131. (A) instead
(B) likewise
(C) frequently
(D) finally

132. (A) She has several favorite restaurants that she visits often.
(B) It has even been recognized with various prestigious awards.
(C) Reservations for groups can also be made through the application.
(D) Visitors who are early can take a seat near the entrance while they wait.

133. (A) features
(B) featured
(C) has featured
(D) will feature

134. (A) diversions
(B) activities
(C) specialties
(D) performances

GO ON TO THE NEXT PAGE

Questions 135-138 refer to the following notice.

AC Ambrose Farms Notice

AC Ambrose has decided to adopt a new ------- this year on its farms. We will be using the
135.
new HT509 robots made by Larkin Tech to speed up the packing process. Currently, it takes

teams an average of one hour to pack 1,000 pounds of produce for shipment. The robots

can complete the same job in 30 minutes. Thus, we expect the robots to ------- our
136.
productivity.

The robots will be delivered by the end of this month. ------- will be set up over a two-day
137.
period at all of our locations. Workers will be temporarily relocated so that our packing

operations can continue uninterrupted. Once the robots are ready, the manufacturer will be

sending over some people to train selected staff members on using the robots. -------.
138.

---

135. (A) approach
(B) approaching
(C) approachable
(D) approaches

136. (A) involve
(B) double
(C) repeat
(D) measure

137. (A) Mine
(B) That
(C) Other
(D) These

138. (A) The orientation for new employees will take place in the conference room.
(B) We may experience some delays in shipping the requested items.
(C) You will be notified if you are chosen as one of the participants.
(D) The group's work performance has improved significantly in the last year.

To: All Staff <staff@brandesson.com>
From: Beverly Castro <b.castro@brandesson.com>
Subject: Software update
Date: October 8

Dear Staff,

We've upgraded our Torrino administration software. The program has some elements that

you may find -------. For instance, it makes organizing work schedules and arranging
       139.
meetings easier.

Now, the software must be installed on your individual computers, which could take time.

-------, I've asked the IT staff to perform the installations over the weekend. They will start on
140.
Friday after 6 P.M. -------. When you return on Monday, just let me know if you're unable
       141.
------- the program for any reason.
142.

Beverly Castro
Office Manager

139. (A) confusing
    (B) useful
    (C) enclosed
    (D) unfamiliar

140. (A) Similarly
    (B) Meanwhile
    (C) On the other hand
    (D) For this reason

141. (A) Always remember to sign in when you
        arrive at work in the morning.
    (B) You can sign up for the training
        session by contacting the
        administrator.
    (C) Please leave your computers on for
        them at the end of the day.
    (D) It should not take you more than a few
        minutes to find your password.

142. (A) to access
    (B) access
    (C) accessing
    (D) having accessed

GO ON TO THE NEXT PAGE

Questions 143-146 refer to the following press release.

LISBON (May 7)—Flores Leather Goods will begin ------- shoes and handbags this summer.
143.
The 50-year-old company is in the process of adding to the types of products it sells. It

currently only offers wallets and belts. The move comes as the company ------- a shift in
144.
consumer tastes and preferences over the last few years. "Revenues from our wallets and

belts have been significantly -------," explains CEO and founder Mario Flores. "We need to
145.
adjust to changes in the market if we want to become profitable." -------. Watch straps and
146.
backpacks are some of the products that the company is developing.

143. (A) sale
(B) sold
(C) sell
(D) selling

144. (A) seeing
(B) has seen
(C) seen
(D) will see

145. (A) enhanced
(B) boosted
(C) canceled
(D) diminished

146. (A) The new location will be opening sometime in the fall.
(B) Users voted for their favorite one in an online poll.
(C) The company hopes to offer even more products in the future.
(D) Items without a proof of purchase may not be returned or exchanged.

PART 7

Directions: In this part, you will be asked to read several texts, such as advertisements, articles, instant messages, or examples of business correspondence. Each text is followed by several questions. Select the best answer and mark the corresponding letter (A), (B), (C), or (D) on your answer sheet.

PART 7 권장 풀이 시간 **54분**

Questions 147-148 refer to the following advertisement.

fleetz Office Warehouse

At Fleetz Office Warehouse, we carry a full range of office furniture suitable for every budget and style. Choose from our extensive lineup of products made by top manufacturers from around the world. Looking for great savings? Then you may be interested in our own brand of office furniture, EZwerks, which includes everything from chairs and desks to conference tables and filing cabinets. Ever since our CEO introduced the brand on a television program, EZwerks has been popular with business owners throughout San Antonio.

Stop by any of our four locations in the city to see why Fleetz Office Warehouse ranks high among customers for quality, affordability, and convenience. Visit www.fleetzoffice.com for a complete catalog of products. This month only, enjoy a 20 percent discount on single or bulk purchases when you sign up as a member in our Fleetz Rewards loyalty program.

147. What made EZwerks popular with business owners?

(A) It uses high-quality materials.
(B) It was featured on a television show.
(C) It gives discounts on large orders.
(D) It could be purchased in installments.

148. What is NOT true about Fleetz Office Warehouse?

(A) It has several branches in a city.
(B) It sells its own brand of products.
(C) It receives new items every month.
(D) It operates a membership program.

GO ON TO THE NEXT PAGE

Questions 149-150 refer to the following text-message chain.

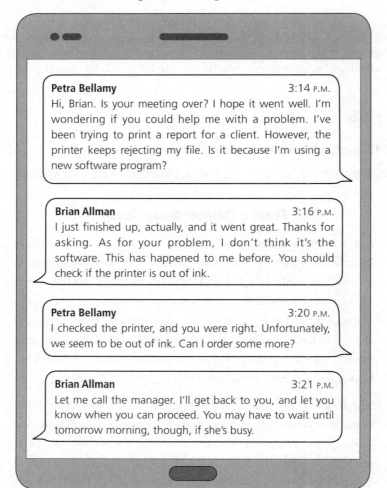

Petra Bellamy   3:14 P.M.

Hi, Brian. Is your meeting over? I hope it went well. I'm wondering if you could help me with a problem. I've been trying to print a report for a client. However, the printer keeps rejecting my file. Is it because I'm using a new software program?

Brian Allman   3:16 P.M.

I just finished up, actually, and it went great. Thanks for asking. As for your problem, I don't think it's the software. This has happened to me before. You should check if the printer is out of ink.

Petra Bellamy   3:20 P.M.

I checked the printer, and you were right. Unfortunately, we seem to be out of ink. Can I order some more?

Brian Allman   3:21 P.M.

Let me call the manager. I'll get back to you, and let you know when you can proceed. You may have to wait until tomorrow morning, though, if she's busy.

---

149. What is Ms. Bellamy's problem?

(A) She is unable to print out a document.
(B) Her proposal was rejected by a client.
(C) She is not familiar with a program.
(D) Her manager left unclear instructions.

150. At 3:21 P.M., what does Mr. Allman most likely mean when he writes, "Let me call the manager"?

(A) A product's availability must be confirmed.
(B) Access to a storeroom is restricted.
(C) A supplier has not replied to a message.
(D) Approval is needed to order an item.

Announcement for Riverbend Apartments Tenants

We are pleased to announce that Riverbend Apartments will be conducting work on the tenant parking lot. This will involve making necessary repairs, repaving the surface of the lot, and upgrading lighting and security features. Work will commence next week on April 11 and is expected to last until the end of the month. To ensure everyone's safety, the entire parking lot will be closed while work is in progress. We recommend that those with vehicles park at the Center Street Parking Garage until the renovations are complete. We apologize for any inconvenience this may cause. In compensation for fees that may be incurred, Riverbend Apartments will waive the $50 parking fee that is normally included with the rent for next month. For inquiries, please contact the building management team at 555-7731. Thank you for your patience and understanding.

151. What is the purpose of the announcement?

(A) To apologize for noise caused by construction work
(B) To provide information about upcoming improvements
(C) To thank residents for contributing funds to a project
(D) To inform tenants of increased parking lot rates

152. What can be inferred about tenants?

(A) They should expect to receive a statement in the mail.
(B) Some of them will pay less than usual in May.
(C) They have complained about the condition of the parking lot.
(D) Some of them will need to apply for new parking permits.

GO ON TO THE NEXT PAGE

StatBook
Make your dream project a reality

StatBook can help you turn your creative idea for a book project into a reality. Whether you want to print a personalized photo book to share with family and friends or publish a written work and sell it to the public, StatBook can help you realize your goal at an affordable price.

StatBook gives you complete control of your project from start to finish. Moreover, we offer software-based editing tools and assistance with design. When your book is ready to print, StatBook guarantees quick production and delivery of the finished work. Visit our Web site at www.statbook.com to view pricing or to get a quote based on your number of copies.

*Special November deal: Print a minimum of 2,000 copies, and we will upgrade the paper at no extra charge to the highest quality that we offer.

153. What is stated about StatBook?

(A) It specializes in producing audio books.
(B) It has an online application for smartphones.
(C) It offers discounts for students.
(D) It allows customers to publish their own work.

154. What is being offered in November?

(A) A discount on membership
(B) An upgrade on some paper
(C) A free set of holiday cards
(D) A limited trial of a service

MIDDLETON BANK WIRE TRANSFER REQUEST FORM

Please note that the wire transfer cutoff time is 3:00 P.M.

Customer Information	
Customer Name	Antoine Ducharme
Account Number	118825622042
Address	1432 Rue de Phare, Quebec, Canada

Wire Transfer Information			
Amount	$3,800 USD	Date	July 7

Purpose of Wire Transfer: To pay for the purchase of a painting
*The beneficiary will receive the amount in their local currency.

Beneficiary Information	
Beneficiary Name	Salles Gallery
Bank and Account Number	Carrousel Credit Union — 227722662243
Address	8 Rue de Moulinet, Paris, France

Customer Authorization

I acknowledge that all information provided is correct and authorize Middleton Bank to transfer funds. Furthermore, I understand that if any details provided are incorrect, the transfer may be delayed or rejected.

Signature: *Antoine Ducharme*
Phone Number: 555-6012

Wire Transfer Fee

___ $15 Domestic   ___ $25 International   X Waived*

*Wire fees are waived for VIP customers.

---

155. What is indicated about Salles Gallery?

(A) It will cover the transfer fees.
(B) It opened a location in Canada.
(C) It sold a painting to Mr. Ducharme.
(D) It will ship an artwork to France.

156. What is true about Mr. Ducharme's transaction?

(A) It will require a change of currency.
(B) It will be completed the following day.
(C) It will be repeated every month.
(D) It will need a manager's signature.

157. What is mentioned about Mr. Ducharme?

(A) He recently attended an event in Paris.
(B) He sent money on behalf of a business.
(C) He is a VIP customer of Middleton Bank.
(D) He has an account with Carrousel Credit Union.

GO ON TO THE NEXT PAGE

Questions 158-160 refer to the following e-mail.

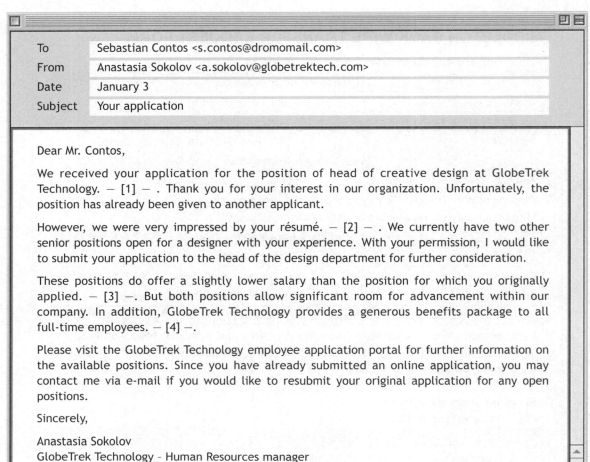

To   Sebastian Contos <s.contos@dromomail.com>

From   Anastasia Sokolov <a.sokolov@globetrektech.com>

Date   January 3

Subject   Your application

Dear Mr. Contos,

We received your application for the position of head of creative design at GlobeTrek Technology. — [1] — . Thank you for your interest in our organization. Unfortunately, the position has already been given to another applicant.

However, we were very impressed by your résumé. — [2] — . We currently have two other senior positions open for a designer with your experience. With your permission, I would like to submit your application to the head of the design department for further consideration.

These positions do offer a slightly lower salary than the position for which you originally applied. — [3] —. But both positions allow significant room for advancement within our company. In addition, GlobeTrek Technology provides a generous benefits package to all full-time employees. — [4] —.

Please visit the GlobeTrek Technology employee application portal for further information on the available positions. Since you have already submitted an online application, you may contact me via e-mail if you would like to resubmit your original application for any open positions.

Sincerely,

Anastasia Sokolov
GlobeTrek Technology – Human Resources manager

---

158. What is true about Mr. Contos?

(A) He worked at GlobeTrek Technology before.

(B) He has an advanced degree in business.

(C) He has no experience in the field of technology.

(D) He recently applied to be a department head.

159. What information can be found on the Web site?

(A) A list of openings

(B) An interview schedule

(C) A map of company facilities

(D) A team member's e-mail address

160. In which of the positions marked [1], [2], [3], and [4] does the following sentence best belong?

"We provide comprehensive health care and three weeks of paid vacation each year."

(A) [1]

(B) [2]

(C) [3]

(D) [4]

Questions 161-163 refer to the following Web page.

Hartwell Café

Home | Reserve a Table | View our Menu | Contact Us

Looking for fresh, healthy food in the Sheffield area? Look no further than the Hartwell Café! We opened three months ago and are proud to be Sheffield's newest organic restaurant!

All of our food is farm-fresh and free of artificial preservatives, dyes, and flavorings. We use only all-natural ingredients! Choose from a wide selection of vegetarian options and dairy-free, nut-free, and soy-free dishes. If you have special dietary needs, contact us and we will be happy to oblige. To reach out to our staff with a special request, just use the online contact form here.

We also have an ongoing promotion. Post a photo of yourself at the restaurant on our social media page and receive a free soup or salad with your next meal.

161. What is mentioned about Hartwell Café?

(A) It used to be known by another name.
(B) It does not offer custom meals.
(C) It has recently opened another branch.
(D) It does not use artificial dyes in its food.

162. The word "just" in paragraph 2, line 4, is closest in meaning to

(A) fairly
(B) carefully
(C) simply
(D) accurately

163. What will customers get if they participate in a promotion?

(A) A choice of side dish
(B) A complimentary beverage
(C) A discount on an entrée
(D) A gift card for future use

GO ON TO THE NEXT PAGE

Questions 164-167 refer to the following e-mail.

To: Eliza Kemper <e.kemper@usgrandtours.us>
From: David Sims <david.sims@bridgeporttravelexpo.com>
Subject: Expo
Date: August 1

Dear Ms. Kemper,

I'm writing to confirm that we received the $300 deposit you submitted to participate as a vendor at the Bridgeport Travel Expo on September 1 and 2. I apologize for the delay. We attracted a record number of applicants, so contacting everyone took longer than normal. Your tour company will be a great addition to this year's lineup.

The deposit will cover any damage that may occur at the venue as a result of negligence. Any repair or cleaning costs will be deducted from it. Otherwise, it will be returned within five business days of the end of the event. The payment of $1,200 for the booth rental is due on August 28.

Please note the following requirements:
- Uniform exterior signs will be provided for each booth, but vendors may display other signs within the booth itself.
- Every item or service for sale must be preapproved by the organizers. No food or beverages are permitted to be sold.
- Never leave personal belongings unattended. You must leave these items in your assigned storage lockers.
- Vendors are responsible for cleaning inside and around the booth.

If you have questions or additional material to submit, please e-mail me directly.

Sincerely,

David Sims
Event Coordinator
Bridgeport Travel Expo

---

164. What is the purpose of the e-mail?

(A) To inform organizers of a sponsorship proposal
(B) To affirm participation in an event
(C) To request payment of a deposit
(D) To advertise a promotional opportunity

165. What is implied about the expo?

(A) The number of applicants reached an all-time high.
(B) The exhibition has been extended by three days.
(C) The vendors represent different industries.
(D) The venue was moved to a larger location.

166. What is indicated about the deposit?

(A) It must be paid on September 1.
(B) It costs half as much as a booth rental.
(C) It could be used to pay for damage.
(D) It will be returned on the last day of the event.

167. What is Ms. Kemper NOT required to do?

(A) Maintain her area's cleanliness
(B) Obtain approval for items sold
(C) Create a design for exterior booth's sign
(D) Place personal items in a locker

Keptics Envisions a Plastic-Free Future

February 8—Keptics, the global consumer goods corporation headquartered in Seattle, has just announced the launch of a pilot program to evaluate the market for a new line of eco-friendly cleaning products. — [1] —. The products will use sustainable packaging designed to reduce plastic waste and pollution. The three-month program will begin in Seattle on March 1.

To participate, customers must sign up online for the Keptics Up program. — [2] —. Participants will receive a shipment from Keptics that includes samples of its home cleaning products packaged in refillable containers. Once a container's contents are consumed, customers can order a refill from Keptics or visit one of several planned locations to refill it themselves. — [3] —.

According to Keptics CEO Fiona Simpleton, the program will be limited to Seattle so that the company can keep a close watch on costs. — [4] —. However, if it succeeds, it could be introduced to other cities across the US by early next year.

168. What is Keptics planning to do?

(A) Test a new product line
(B) Start an environmental group
(C) Update its brand design
(D) Introduce a rewards program

169. What will some Keptics customers receive?

(A) An event invitation
(B) An online voucher
(C) A set of samples
(D) A regular pickup service

170. Why is Keptics only launching a program in Seattle?

(A) It needs to get permission from other cities.
(B) It wants to monitor associated costs.
(C) It is using ingredients only found locally.
(D) It is trying to avoid competing with other firms.

171. In which of the positions marked [1], [2], [3], and [4] does the following sentence best belong?

"These locations will be announced in the coming weeks."

(A) [1]
(B) [2]
(C) [3]
(D) [4]

GO ON TO THE NEXT PAGE

Questions 172-175 refer to the following online chat discussion.

Jang-mi Bae	[2:09 P.M.]	Any news regarding a new office location? We have to extend our lease here next month if we don't find something.
Paul Knox	[2:11 P.M.]	I saw one yesterday that I think would work perfectly. It's in a building called Janus Tower.
Edward Watts	[2:12 P.M.]	What are the amenities like? Does it have a gym? Assigned parking?
Paul Knox	[2:15 P.M.]	It has those things and more. It also has a brand-new heating and cooling system, so that should save us on renovation costs. The only potential issue is that it's above our budget at $6,500 a month. That's $700 more than we pay now.
Barbara Thompkins	[2:16 P.M.]	We've had a good year. If utilities are included and it has everything we need, I say we should definitely consider it.
Jang-mi Bae	[2:16 P.M.]	Valid point. Still, I'd like to see it. Could you schedule a visit, Paul? I'm free on Friday.
Paul Knox	[2:18 P.M.]	Sure thing. Let me check the real estate agency's mobile app for a phone number.
Paul Knox	[2:20 P.M.]	OK. I called the realtor and she confirmed she can meet us on Friday at 11 A.M. We can all go to Janus Tower together in my car.
Edward Watts	[2:21 P.M.]	Great. I'm available at that time, too.
Barbara Thompkins	[2:21 P.M.]	I'm going to be out all day visiting a client.
Paul Knox	[2:24 P.M.]	You can also see the office on video through the mobile application. Anyone who can't come can do that instead.

172. What is true about Janus Tower?

(A) It includes a workout facility.
(B) It contains inexpensive units.
(C) It is located near public transportation.
(D) It is owned by the city.

173. At 2:16 P.M., what does Ms. Bae most likely mean when she writes, "Valid point"?

(A) She agrees that the company can accommodate a higher budget.
(B) She thinks that a group should consider a potential problem.
(C) She feels that other employees should be consulted about a decision.
(D) She believes that asking for a realtor's help would be wise.

174. How many people will be accompanying the realtor on Friday?

(A) One
(B) Two
(C) Three
(D) Four

175. According to the online chat discussion, what can people do on a mobile application?

(A) Get directions to a building
(B) See video of an office space
(C) Find alternatives within a price range
(D) Schedule a visit to a location

GO ON TO THE NEXT PAGE

Come to Surf Shack

Located on Malibu Beach, Surf Shack invites travelers and locals alike to come and enjoy spectacular views of the ocean. What started as a surfers' paradise for a few friends has developed into a surfing school, equipment shop, and restaurant. Surf Shack serves excellent cuisine and drinks while you enjoy the sunset and listen to the waves. This is truly a special experience that is not to be missed. It is why radio station Malibu 102.5 has named us the top attraction in the area.

Surf Shack has a tradition of offering fresh smoothies daily with ingredients that have been sustainably sourced. We are currently running a two-for-one special on the following combinations.

- Monday & Tuesday: Banana and Strawberry
- Wednesday & Thursday: Pineapple and Coconut
- Friday & Saturday: Apple and Pear
- Sunday: Tropical Mix

Call us at 555-9691 to reserve a beach table today.

Surf Shack

About	Restaurant	Surfing	Shop	Location	Reviews

Name: Katerina Stokov
Rating: 2/5

I went to Surf Shack recently while visiting Los Angeles on vacation. I visited with some local friends who had never been there before. We didn't think that the place was well-known to tourists, so we were looking forward to enjoying a relatively quiet afternoon at a lovely beachside location. We even chose to go on a Tuesday as that is supposedly when they are least busy.

When we arrived, we were shocked to find that the place was crowded with tourists. We were lucky to get a beach table at the restaurant considering we hadn't reserved one. I ordered the smoothie that was on special offer, and it turned out to be delicious. Still, the service was slow, and the tables were not very clean. Overall, especially because of the crowds, my experience was not very good, and I cannot recommend the place to anyone.

176. In the advertisement, the word "serves" in paragraph 1, line 3, is closest in meaning to

(A) tests
(B) performs
(C) provides
(D) accepts

177. What is stated about Surf Shack?

(A) It merged with a local sports school.
(B) It was recommended by a radio station.
(C) It changes the menu seasonally.
(D) It is owned by former surf champions.

178. According to the advertisement, how can customers reserve a table?

(A) By sending an e-mail
(B) By making a phone call
(C) By using a mobile app
(D) By visiting a Web site

179. Which smoothie special did Ms. Stokov most likely order?

(A) Banana and Strawberry
(B) Pineapple and Coconut
(C) Apple and Pear
(D) Tropical Mix

180. Why was Ms. Stokov dissatisfied with Surf Shack?

(A) The servers were unfriendly.
(B) The food was flavorless.
(C) The view was not as advertised.
(D) The location was crowded.

GO ON TO THE NEXT PAGE

Questions 181-185 refer to the following notice and article.

NOTICE from Holton Centre

The Holton Centre will be closed on September 19 for the annual Stafford Literary Festival. Over 200 publishers and 350 writers from around the UK are expected to attend. It will feature talks by the best of today's British authors. Among those invited are the authors of *East Kingdom* and *The Gate*, both of which were released to spectacular critical acclaim.

Throughout the day, writers will also be giving lectures and participating in group discussions. In the main lobby, publishing houses will have booths set up where visitors can buy the latest titles at a discount. Once the festival concludes, an after-party will be held in the Lewistown Hotel, during which attendees will have the opportunity to mingle with noted writers and get their books signed. General admission is $40, including the after-party, and author lectures cost an additional $10 to attend.

Margaret Davidson, a Bold New Literary Voice
By Charles Hagan

With *The Gate*, Margaret Davidson has become one of my favourite young writers. A 30-year-old correspondent at *New Music Monthly* magazine, Ms. Davidson has been a well-known journalist for some time, but I wasn't inclined to read her book until I heard her give a hilarious talk at the Stafford Literary Festival. I'm happy to report that she's as good a writer as she is a speaker. In *The Gate*, she writes about the experiences that drew her to music journalism in the first place, hearing R&B at the age of five and beginning to play bass at 12. The book is divided into three sections, one focusing on her early years, the second focusing on her time playing in a band as a teenager, and the final section on her career as a music journalist. At the end of the book are excerpts from her writings at *New Music Monthly*, ranging from incisive reviews of new hip-hop albums to a humorous account of travelling with the punk group Stone Age.

181. What is suggested about the Stafford Literary Festival?

(A) It takes place twice a year.
(B) It focuses on authors from one country.
(C) It is geared mostly towards fiction writers.
(D) It has not received much publicity.

182. What can people NOT do at the festival?

(A) Receive free copies of certain titles
(B) Listen to authors' lectures
(C) Interact with writers in attendance
(D) Collect authors' signatures

183. What is mentioned about Ms. Davidson?

(A) She has written two novels.
(B) She signed a book for Mr. Hagan.
(C) Her work was well received by critics.
(D) Her career has changed many times.

184. What can be inferred about Mr. Hagan?

(A) He is a well-known music journalist.
(B) He paid an extra fee to see Ms. Davidson speak.
(C) He used to play in a band.
(D) He stayed at the Lewistown Hotel.

185. In the article, the word "drew" in paragraph 1, line 5 is closest in meaning to

(A) attracted
(B) presented
(C) created
(D) allowed

GO ON TO THE NEXT PAGE

Rick Houseman
119 Willow Drive
Queensland, NZ 0600

Dear Mr. Houseman,

My name is Matilda Gleeson, and I am writing on behalf of the Alumni Office at Queensland University. We are reaching out to selected graduates of Queensland University to see if they would be willing to contribute short professional biographies for our Web site. Given that you are a high-profile conservationist, we think that you would be a good example of a successful Queensland University graduate.

If you are interested, please send us a short biography of 100 words or less describing your career. In addition, we would appreciate it if you sent samples of papers you have published, newspaper articles written about you, and a photograph of yourself taken in the last five years. Please submit these to gleeson22@qland.nz. Thank you, and I look forward to hearing from you.

Sincerely,

Matilda Gleeson
Alumni Office, Queensland University

TO: Matilda Gleeson <gleeson22@qland.nz>
FROM: Rick Houseman <rick.houseman@qlandwildlife.nz>
SUBJECT: Alumni bio
DATE: May 29
ATTACHMENTS: file1, file2, file3

Dear Ms. Gleeson,

Thank you for contacting me regarding the alumni biographies. I've attached all of the items you requested except for the last one. I will send this to you tomorrow. I've also made a small donation to the Alumni Fund for the maintenance of the school library.

When you add my biography to the Web site, could you let me know by sending me a link to the page? I'd like to share it with some friends and family. Also, I may need to update the biography soon. I am currently in talks with the New Zealand Conservation Commission to serve as their assistant chair. All that is left is to undergo a panel interview. I will let you know in the following days whether I get the position so that you can update my biography on your Web site.

Best regards,

Rick Houseman

QUEENSLAND UNIVERSITY

Home | Admissions | Campus Life | **Alumni** | Announcements | Help

ALUMNI PROFILES

Rick Houseman

Since graduating from Queensland University's undergraduate program 10 years ago, Rick Houseman has worked to advance the world's body of knowledge about science. He has a doctorate from the prestigious National Academy of Natural Sciences and has published extensive research on New Zealand's wildlife. Most recently, he worked to ensure the passage of new legislation that designated parts of the country as protected wildlife areas to help preserve the habitats of unique animals like the kiwi bird. Presently, he is the assistant chair of the New Zealand Conservation Commission.

186. Why did Ms. Gleeson write Mr. Houseman the letter?

(A) To ask him for a donation
(B) To offer him a position
(C) To remind him about an event
(D) To request some information

187. What will Mr. Houseman send tomorrow?

(A) A short article
(B) A photograph
(C) A personal profile
(D) A research paper

188. What does Mr. Houseman ask Ms. Gleeson to do?

(A) Add a link to his personal Web page in his biography
(B) Give him an update on the school's operations
(C) Notify him when a post is made
(D) Add him to an alumni e-mail list

189. According to the post on the Web page, what did Mr. Houseman do most recently?

(A) Appeared in a TV program
(B) Joined a university faculty
(C) Helped pass a new law
(D) Applied for a doctorate program

190. What is indicated about Mr. Houseman?

(A) He dropped out of a graduate program at Queensland University.
(B) He has worked at a library in the Queensland area.
(C) He wrote a college thesis on the kiwi bird.
(D) He passed a panel interview for a new position.

GO ON TO THE NEXT PAGE

Questions 191-195 refer to the following memo, survey, and report.

TO: Customer Relations Staff
FROM: Nick Christman, Customer Relations Manager
SUBJECT: YourPage at Three Years
DATE: March 22

As of today, YourPage has been operating for three straight years. Over the course of that period, our user base has grown exponentially. In just the past two months, in fact, we have experienced a 500 percent increase in users, making us the fastest-growing social networking site. That means it's time we conducted a survey of our customers to see how their experience with our site has been. We want to hear from people who have been using it for a while, so let's send survey requests to users who made YourPage profiles over a year ago. These should also be people whose activity is fairly regular. As an incentive for taking the survey, we could offer to enter their names into a raffle for prizes. The prizes could be brand-new electronic devices from one of the companies we are affiliated with.

YourPage: Survey

Name: Pauline Carson
Date: April 12

On a scale of 1 to 5, with 5 being the best, how would you rank your experience with YourPage?
☐ 1　　☐ 2　　☐ 3　　☒ 4　　☐ 5

How frequently do you check YourPage?
  I usually check it repeatedly throughout the day. I do this whenever I am bored or want to catch up on what my friends are doing.

How often do you post messages, pictures, or other content on your page?
  I don't post that frequently. I would say I post maybe once or twice a week. However, I do like to comment on other people's posts.

How did you hear about YourPage?
  Through some friends

What would you like YourPage to improve?
  I think the design of the profile pages is a little cluttered, with a lot of different information mixed up together.

YourPage: Survey Results

Throughout the month of April, we sent over 5,000 survey requests to various active users of YourPage. Those who took the survey were entered into a raffle for Silver Plus smartphones, which were distributed to 10 winners. Roughly 1,000 people responded to our requests. The vast majority (88 percent) ranked their experience with the site as either a 4 or 5 on a scale of 1 to 5, with 5 being the highest. However, there were some common criticisms, including that the site shut down fairly frequently and that profile pages were difficult to navigate because of the confusing layout. Going forward, it is important we address these problems by fixing errors in the computer code that cause pages to shut down and reformatting the pages with the convenience of users in mind.

191. What is the purpose of the memo?

(A) To praise employees for their work
(B) To report a change in leadership
(C) To ask for suggestions for improvements
(D) To make a proposal to gather information

192. What does Mr. Christman indicate about YourPage?

(A) It is used mainly by teenagers.
(B) It attracted 100 new users in the past few months.
(C) It is rapidly becoming more popular.
(D) It was launched a year ago.

193. What can be inferred about Ms. Carson?

(A) She has used YourPage for over a year.
(B) She finds YourPage very easy to use.
(C) She is not eligible to win a raffle prize.
(D) She did not submit the survey on time.

194. What is implied about Silver Plus?

(A) It produces software for companies.
(B) It has been having technical issues.
(C) It created a survey for YourPage.
(D) It has a partnership with YourPage.

195. What does the report recommend doing?

(A) Advertising the site in foreign countries
(B) Fixing a Web site's persistent problems
(C) Offering additional rewards for more feedback
(D) Conducting a more in-depth survey

GO ON TO THE NEXT PAGE

The 4th Boston Leadership Summit Is Going Live

Jefferson Bank is proud to announce that it has secured the participation of two keynote speakers for its fourth annual summit, which is scheduled for January 17 and 18. The CEO of SpitalGround, Susanne Coerver, will talk about how her innovative company is changing the health-care sector and how she manages her company in a competitive environment. Henry Moss, chief executive of Moss Tech, will close the summit with insights into what it takes to become a successful entrepreneur.

For the first time, the Boston Leadership Summit will also be streamed live through an online application, enabling it to reach a wider audience. A ticket to participate online is $220 for both days. However, customers of Jefferson Bank are invited to virtually join the event to learn about leadership skills, partake in workshops, and interact with other online visitors free of charge. Find the nearest Jefferson Bank branch, and become a customer in time for the summit.

To	Allison Cruise <a.cruise@jeffersonbank.com>
From	Preston Ali <p.ali@mosstechorg.com>
Subject	Summit
Date	December 28

Dear Ms. Cruise,

I am sorry to inform you that Mr. Moss will not be able to attend the summit as planned due to an unforeseen business matter. He asked me to send his regrets, especially since he had such an enjoyable time speaking at last year's event.

That said, Mr. Moss can recommend someone to take his place. She is the CEO of Galacomms, a software services company that she and Mr. Moss started together some years ago. I can send you her contact details once we receive confirmation of her availability. You can expect an update before the end of the week. Once again, please accept our apologies for this inconvenience.

Sincerely,

Preston Ali
Executive Assistant
Moss Tech

To: Leonard Vega <l.vega@jeffersonbank.com>
From: Allison Cruise <a.cruise@jeffersonbank.com>
Subject: Summit
Date: January 9

Leonard,

I need you to go to the summit location two days earlier than originally planned. Please go ahead and book a new flight if you have to.

As you know, there has been a change to our speaker lineup, and this change must be reflected in all printed materials posted at the venue. For your reference, the new speaker's name is Fiona Murphy, and she is the CEO of Galacomms. While you're at the venue, please test the setup for the live stream to ensure that everything runs smoothly.

Thanks for your help, and let me know if you have any questions.

Alison

196. What is NOT true about a summit?

(A) It has been put on before.
(B) It is expanding its audience reach.
(C) It is being hosted by a financial institution.
(D) It will focus on the health-care industry.

197. What are Jefferson Bank customers encouraged to do?

(A) Stream some content for free
(B) Take advantage of higher savings interest rates
(C) Enter a contest to win a cash prize
(D) Visit a branch location for some merchandise

198. What does Mr. Ali suggest about Mr. Moss?

(A) He was invited to speak at another event.
(B) He was in Boston the year before.
(C) He will be watching a speech online.
(D) He plans to retire from his company.

199. What is mentioned about Fiona Murphy?

(A) She requested a change of schedule.
(B) She is a customer of Jefferson Bank.
(C) She needs confirmation of a flight booking.
(D) She started a company with Mr. Moss.

200. What does Ms. Cruise ask Mr. Vega to do?

(A) Test a live stream connection
(B) Revise a speaker contract
(C) Find a new event venue
(D) Prepare an internal newsletter

This is the end of the test. You may review Parts 5, 6, and 7 if you finish the test early.

Review 체크리스트

TEST 1을 푼 다음, 아래 체크리스트에 따라 틀린 문제를 리뷰하고 박스에 완료 여부를 표시하세요.
만약 시험까지 얼마 남지 않았다면, 초록색으로 표시된 항목이라도 꼭 확인하세요.

☐ 틀린 문제의 경우, 다시 풀어봤다.

☐ 틀린 문제의 경우, 스크립트/해석을 확인하며 지문/문제의 내용을 정확하게 파악했다.

☐ 해설을 통해 각 문제의 정답과 오답의 근거가 무엇인지 정확하게 파악했다.

☐ Part 1과 Part 2에서 틀린 문제의 경우, 선택한 오답의 유형이 무엇이었는지 확인하고 같은
   함정에 빠지지 않도록 정리해두었다.

☐ Part 3와 Part 4의 각 문제에서 사용된 패러프레이징을 확인했다.

☐ Part 5와 Part 6의 경우, 틀린 문제에서 사용된 문법 포인트 또는 정답 및 오답 어휘를 정리
   했다.

☐ Part 6의 알맞은 문장 고르기 문제의 경우, 지문 전체를 정확하게 해석하며 전체 글의 흐름
   과 빈칸 주변 문맥을 정확하게 파악하는 연습을 했다.

☐ Part 7에서 질문과 보기의 키워드를 찾아 표시하며 지문에서 정답의 근거가 되는 문장이나
   구절을 찾아보고, 문제에서 사용된 패러프레이징을 확인했다.

☐ Part 1~Part 4는 받아쓰기 & 쉐도잉 워크북을 활용하여, TEST에 수록된 핵심 문장을 받아
   쓰고 따라 읽으며 복습했다.

☐ Part 1~Part 7은 단어암기자료를 활용하여, TEST에 수록된 핵심 어휘와 표현을 암기했다.

많은 양의 문제를 푸는 것도 중요하지만, 틀린 문제를 제대로 리뷰하는 것도 중요합니다.
틀린 문제를 한 번 더 꼼꼼히 리뷰한다면, 빠른 시간 내에 효과적으로 목표 점수를 달성할 수 있습니다.

TEST 2

LISTENING TEST

Part 1
Part 2
Part 3
Part 4

READING TEST

Part 5
Part 6
Part 7

Review 체크리스트

잠깐! 테스트 전 아래 사항을 꼭 확인하세요.

휴대전화의 전원을 끄셨나요? 예 ☐
Answer Sheet(p.249), 연필, 지우개, 시계를 준비하셨나요? 예 ☐
Listening MP3를 들을 준비가 되셨나요? 예 ☐

모든 준비가 완료되었으면 목표 점수를 떠올린 후 테스트를 시작합니다.
테스트를 마친 후, Review 체크리스트(p.110)를 보며 자신이 틀린 문제를 반드시 복습합니다.

🎧 TEST 2.mp3
실전용·복습용 문제풀이 MP3 무료 다운로드 및 스트리밍 바로듣기 (HackersIngang.com)
* 실제 시험장의 소음까지 재현해 낸 고사장 소음/매미 버전 MP3, 영국식·호주식 발음 집중 MP3, 고속 버전 MP3까지 구매
  하면 실전에 더욱 완벽히 대비할 수 있습니다.

무료MP3 바로듣기

LISTENING TEST

In this section, you must demonstrate your ability to understand spoken English. This section is divided into four parts and will take approximately 45 minutes to complete. Do not mark the answers in your test book. Use the answer sheet that is provided separately.

PART 1

Directions: For each question, you will listen to four short statements about a picture in your test book. These statements will not be printed and will only be spoken one time. Select the statement that best describes what is happening in the picture and mark the corresponding letter (A), (B), (C), or (D) on the answer sheet.

Sample Answer
Ⓐ ● Ⓒ Ⓓ

The statement that best describes the picture is (B), "The man is sitting at the desk." So, you should mark letter (B) on the answer sheet.

1.

2.

GO ON TO THE NEXT PAGE

3.

4.

5.

6.

GO ON TO THE NEXT PAGE

PART 2

Directions: For each question, you will listen to a statement or question followed by three possible responses spoken in English. They will not be printed and will only be spoken one time. Select the best response and mark the corresponding letter (A), (B), or (C) on your answer sheet.

7. Mark your answer on your answer sheet.

8. Mark your answer on your answer sheet.

9. Mark your answer on your answer sheet.

10. Mark your answer on your answer sheet.

11. Mark your answer on your answer sheet.

12. Mark your answer on your answer sheet.

13. Mark your answer on your answer sheet.

14. Mark your answer on your answer sheet.

15. Mark your answer on your answer sheet.

16. Mark your answer on your answer sheet.

17. Mark your answer on your answer sheet.

18. Mark your answer on your answer sheet.

19. Mark your answer on your answer sheet.

20. Mark your answer on your answer sheet.

21. Mark your answer on your answer sheet.

22. Mark your answer on your answer sheet.

23. Mark your answer on your answer sheet.

24. Mark your answer on your answer sheet.

25. Mark your answer on your answer sheet.

26. Mark your answer on your answer sheet.

27. Mark your answer on your answer sheet.

28. Mark your answer on your answer sheet.

29. Mark your answer on your answer sheet.

30. Mark your answer on your answer sheet.

31. Mark your answer on your answer sheet.

PART 3

Directions: In this part, you will listen to several conversations between two or more speakers. These conversations will not be printed and will only be spoken one time. For each conversation, you will be asked to answer three questions. Select the best response and mark the corresponding letter (A), (B), (C), or (D) on your answer sheet.

32. Why did the man call?

(A) To ask about an interview
(B) To accept a job offer
(C) To arrange a meeting
(D) To discuss a project

33. Why has there been a delay?

(A) An application form was not submitted.
(B) Some team members are on vacation.
(C) A hiring committee has yet to meet.
(D) Some documents are being reviewed.

34. What will a human resources staff member probably do tomorrow morning?

(A) Give candidates a tour
(B) Contact applicants
(C) Look over a résumé
(D) Advertise a position

35. What most likely is the woman's profession?

(A) Author
(B) Publisher
(C) Photographer
(D) Performer

36. What does the man mean when he says, "I'm free today and tomorrow"?

(A) He will perform a task.
(B) He will extend a deadline.
(C) He will update a schedule.
(D) He will take a day off.

37. What will the woman do in the afternoon?

(A) Attend a workshop
(B) Give a presentation
(C) Visit an office
(D) Join an online meeting

38. What is the problem?

(A) Customers have decreased.
(B) A business has closed.
(C) Guests have complained.
(D) Food quality has gone down.

39. What does the man suggest?

(A) Introducing new entrées
(B) Reducing prices
(C) Hiring more staff
(D) Offering free appetizers

40. What do the women say about their restaurant?

(A) It just moved to the neighborhood.
(B) It recently changed its recipes.
(C) It offers inexpensive dishes.
(D) It plans to open a second location.

41. What will take place next week?

(A) A travel fair
(B) A store opening
(C) A hotel convention
(D) A trade show

42. What are the speakers mainly discussing?

(A) Flight schedules
(B) Accommodation options
(C) Event venues
(D) Exhibit dates

43. Why does the man say, "The company will reimburse me up to $250 per night"?

(A) To reject a suggestion
(B) To address a concern
(C) To make an offer
(D) To respond to a complaint

GO ON TO THE NEXT PAGE

44. What is the man's problem?

(A) An employee is not available.
(B) A highway is not accessible.
(C) A vehicle is not functioning.
(D) A garage is not open.

45. What does the woman agree to do?

(A) Forward a message
(B) Clear some snow
(C) Send a worker
(D) Contact emergency personnel

46. What does the woman inquire about?

(A) If a truck can be towed
(B) Whether traffic has been blocked
(C) What caused a delay
(D) When the man must be picked up

47. What does the man ask the woman to do?

(A) Provide transportation
(B) Select a destination
(C) Make a purchase
(D) Verify information

48. What happened this morning?

(A) A bus was damaged.
(B) An event was rescheduled.
(C) A mechanic was hired.
(D) An appointment was confirmed.

49. What is mentioned about Bob Granger?

(A) He is a professional driver.
(B) He has a large automobile.
(C) He is an event organizer.
(D) He knows a retreat location well.

50. What problem does the man mention?

(A) An assignment was not completed.
(B) A document has been lost.
(C) A device is not working.
(D) An office is currently in use.

51. What did the woman do earlier today?

(A) Tested a projector
(B) Charged a battery
(C) Lost a phone
(D) Joined a conference

52. What does the man ask the woman about?

(A) The location of an outlet
(B) The length of a power cord
(C) The size of a room
(D) The height of a table

53. According to the woman, what is prepared every year?

(A) Some financial documents
(B) An industry conference
(C) Some training programs
(D) An investment plan

54. What is mentioned about Opus Investments?

(A) It is a well-known firm.
(B) It is on the ninth floor.
(C) It is a new company.
(D) It is relocating employees.

55. What does the woman offer to do?

(A) Set up a meeting with supervisors
(B) Guide a colleague to a work space
(C) Arrange seats for an office gathering
(D) Give a tour of a production facility

56. What is the woman's problem?

(A) She cannot watch a presentation.
(B) She is unable to attend a function.
(C) She cannot rent some equipment.
(D) She is unfamiliar with a venue.

57. Why is the Dumont Conference Center closed this week?

(A) It is being renovated.
(B) Its lobby is being cleaned.
(C) It is being prepared for an event.
(D) Its audio system is being upgraded.

58. How can the woman get the information she requires?

(A) By meeting with an investor
(B) By attending a workshop
(C) By calling a coworker
(D) By visiting a Web site

---

59. What does the man need assistance with?

(A) Finding a seat
(B) Returning a purchase
(C) Booking a trip
(D) Selecting a product

60. Who most likely is the woman?

(A) A tour guide
(B) A boat captain
(C) A customer
(D) A salesperson

61. What will the man most likely do next?

(A) Examine some vehicles
(B) Visit another store
(C) Watch a demonstration
(D) Order some food

Printer Room	Room 1	Room 2	Room 3	Staircase
Elevator	Room 4	Break Room	Storage Room	

62. Who most likely is Mr. Zimmerman?

(A) A department head
(B) An intern
(C) A receptionist
(D) A sales manager

63. Look at the graphic. Where will a meeting be held?

(A) Room 1
(B) Room 2
(C) Room 3
(D) Room 4

64. What will the woman receive shortly?

(A) A beverage
(B) A document
(C) A room key
(D) A pass code

Room Type	Regular Price
Standard	$250
Premium	$270
Deluxe	$300
Regal	$350

65. What does the man ask the woman for?

(A) A refund
(B) A statement
(C) A new room
(D) A discount

66. Why is the man surprised?

(A) He was expecting a different price.
(B) His room was in bad condition.
(C) His credit card was declined.
(D) He is being charged for late check-out.

67. Look at the graphic. Which type of room did the man stay in?

(A) Standard
(B) Premium
(C) Deluxe
(D) Regal

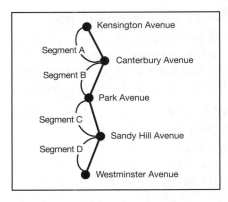

68. What did the woman recently do?

(A) Relocated to a new city
(B) Accepted a job offer
(C) Visited a government office
(D) Purchased a transit pass

69. Look at the graphic. Which segment is temporarily closed?

(A) Segment A
(B) Segment B
(C) Segment C
(D) Segment D

70. What will the woman most likely do next?

(A) Go to a bus stop
(B) Inspect a construction site
(C) Take a taxi
(D) Reschedule an appointment

PART 4

Directions: In this part, you will listen to several short talks by a single speaker. These talks will not be printed and will only be spoken one time. For each talk, you will be asked to answer three questions. Select the best response and mark the corresponding letter (A), (B), (C), or (D) on your answer sheet.

71. What type of business is being advertised?

(A) An interior design firm
(B) A cleaning company
(C) A real estate agency
(D) A home appliance retailer

72. What can the listeners receive until May 12?

(A) A product sample
(B) A free consultation
(C) A gift certificate
(D) A discounted service

73. Why should the listeners visit the Web site?

(A) To make a payment
(B) To schedule an appointment
(C) To download a coupon
(D) To complete a questionnaire

74. What is the speaker mainly discussing?

(A) An updated policy
(B) A refunded ticket
(C) A misplaced item
(D) A canceled flight

75. What should Ms. Freeman do to receive compensation?

(A) Submit some paperwork
(B) Provide a ticket
(C) Speak with a baggage handler
(D) Return a damaged product

76. What will the speaker most likely do next?

(A) Inspect a suitcase
(B) Go to an office
(C) Confirm a payment
(D) Send an e-mail

77. Where most likely are the listeners?

(A) At a retirement party
(B) At a writing workshop
(C) At an art exhibit
(D) At an award ceremony

78. What does the speaker imply when he says, "You've probably heard her name"?

(A) Jill Holloway was mentioned before.
(B) Jill Holloway has attended previous events.
(C) Jill Holloway won an award recently.
(D) Jill Holloway is famous.

79. What will the listeners most likely do next?

(A) Discuss a book
(B) Register for a seminar
(C) Take a brief break
(D) Listen to a speech

80. What is the speaker mainly talking about?

(A) A product review
(B) A marketing strategy
(C) A job opening
(D) A work schedule

81. Who most likely is Mindy Lineman?

(A) A company executive
(B) A business consultant
(C) A job applicant
(D) A recent hire

82. Why does the speaker say, "our time is almost up"?

(A) A gathering has to be rescheduled.
(B) A deadline is quickly approaching.
(C) A meeting is about to finish.
(D) A task has yet to be completed.

GO ON TO THE NEXT PAGE

83. According to the speaker, what should be done first?

(A) Make a delivery
(B) Examine a product
(C) Confirm a date
(D) Issue a refund

84. Why should the listeners contact a supervisor?

(A) To report that an item is damaged
(B) To check if a request was processed
(C) To receive some paperwork
(D) To provide a reason for a return

85. What should the listeners ask customers to do?

(A) Complete a form
(B) Make a purchase
(C) Cancel a payment
(D) Sign a contract

86. What is the broadcast mainly about?

(A) A traffic jam
(B) A local event
(C) A new restaurant
(D) A school competition

87. What are the listeners advised to do?

(A) Use public transportation
(B) Avoid a major highway
(C) Sign up early for an event
(D) Make a charitable donation

88. Who will the listeners hear from next?

(A) A weather forecaster
(B) A business owner
(C) A local politician
(D) A popular chef

89. Why did the speaker call?

(A) To place an order for products
(B) To continue a conversation
(C) To extend a deadline
(D) To ask for some advice

90. What has the speaker already done?

(A) Delivered some samples
(B) Turned down a business offer
(C) Contacted some retailers
(D) Reviewed a price list

91. Why should a presentation be prepared?

(A) To share information about products
(B) To introduce a recent hire
(C) To describe a new service
(D) To explain a shipping process

92. Who most likely is Judith Frost?

(A) A literary critic
(B) A novelist
(C) A program host
(D) A film director

93. What is mentioned about *Bright Lights*?

(A) It is part of a collection.
(B) It will be made into a movie.
(C) It has been featured in an article.
(D) It has not been published yet.

94. What does the speaker mean when he says, "Many people will likely be disappointed"?

(A) A guest has canceled an interview.
(B) Availability of tickets to a book signing is limited.
(C) A recent movie has received poor reviews.
(D) Some events will take place at a later time.

Horgen Cultural Center
Lecture Series

Time	Topic
9 A.M.	Salary negotiations
11 A.M.	Corporate branding
4 P.M.	Financial crimes
6 P.M.	Panel discussions

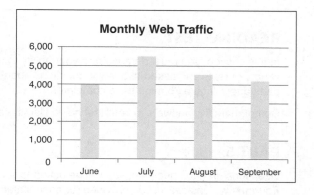

95. Look at the graphic. When will Ms. Parkerson most likely speak?

(A) At 9 A.M.
(B) At 11 A.M.
(C) At 4 P.M.
(D) At 6 P.M.

96. What does the speaker say about Ms. Parkerson?

(A) She has not signed a contract.
(B) Her lecture will be recorded.
(C) Her payment will not change.
(D) She is the event's keynote speaker.

97. What are the listeners asked to do?

(A) Review a lecture
(B) Post a notice
(C) Print some handouts
(D) Open a ticket booth

98. What kind of business does the speaker most likely work for?

(A) A research firm
(B) A travel agency
(C) An online retailer
(D) A shipping company

99. Look at the graphic. When did the company run a television advertisement?

(A) In June
(B) In July
(C) In August
(D) In September

100. What does the speaker ask the listeners to do?

(A) Reduce costs
(B) Provide suggestions
(C) Review feedback
(D) Contact customers

This is the end of the Listening test. Turn to PART 5 in your test book.

READING TEST

In this section, you must demonstrate your ability to read and comprehend English. You will be given a variety of texts and asked to answer questions about these texts. This section is divided into three parts and will take 75 minutes to complete.

Do not mark the answers in your test book. Use the answer sheet that is separately provided.

PART 5

Directions: In each question, you will be asked to review a statement that is missing a word or phrase. Four answer choices will be provided for each statement. Select the best answer and mark the corresponding letter (A), (B), (C), or (D) on the answer sheet.

🕐 PART 5 권장 풀이 시간 11분

101. To attract young consumers, promoting new products online is more ------- than advertising on television.

(A) effects
(B) effectively
(C) effecting
(D) effective

102. Twins Excursions employs licensed guides who ------- tours in five different languages.

(A) conduct
(B) receive
(C) inspect
(D) distribute

103. The employee handbook provides information on how personnel may take advantage of ------- medical benefits.

(A) they
(B) their
(C) them
(D) themselves

104. Upon request, official receipts can be issued for all ------- to the Global Awareness Foundation.

(A) contributions
(B) contributed
(C) contributes
(D) contribute

105. Director Phillip Anderson's movie *Silent Moon* received a ------- for the Best Film Award this year.

(A) nomination
(B) subscription
(C) destination
(D) creation

106. The Seattle Food Convention was a success, attracting over 1,000 chefs ------- a large number of amateur cooks.

(A) nor
(B) and
(C) but
(D) only

107. During peak shopping seasons, Johnson's Sportswear provides additional staff training to ensure an ------- workforce.

(A) experienced
(B) experiencing
(C) experiences
(D) experience

108. Only staff employed for more than 15 years are ------- to receive an Excellent Worker Award.

(A) accountable
(B) modified
(C) entitled
(D) important

109. The new recruitment process ------- all future job candidates to submit their résumés via e-mail.

(A) requirement
(B) requires
(C) require
(D) requiring

110. The recent economic downturn does not ------- mean that the unemployment rate will increase.

(A) necessarily
(B) expectedly
(C) hesitantly
(D) consciously

111. As a result of ------- from environmentally conscious residents, the local government is constructing bicycle lanes throughout the town.

(A) encouragingly
(B) encourages
(C) encouraged
(D) encouragement

112. The Foley Dental Clinic requests that patients reconfirm an appointment at least two days ------- its scheduled date.

(A) prior to
(B) provided that
(C) among
(D) since

113. After sending her manuscript to dozens of publishers, Susan James was finally ------- a contract by Spring Books.

(A) offered
(B) offer
(C) offers
(D) offering

114. Peramo Co.'s management was ------- to upgrade its computer systems because of the high cost.

(A) reluctant
(B) unanticipated
(C) acceptable
(D) vulnerable

115. After Telestar Computing secures funding, it ------- a large team of developers to carry out its expansion plans.

(A) is recruited
(B) recruited
(C) will recruit
(D) was recruiting

116. Passengers on the canceled flight received a full refund and a $500 voucher as ------- for their inconvenience.

(A) compensation
(B) presentation
(C) motivation
(D) admiration

117. The ------- reason for the negative reviews of the Central Highland Gym is the poor condition of the pool.

(A) principal
(B) considerate
(C) secure
(D) beneficial

118. A recent poll indicates that residents are ------- of City Council's plan to raise taxes for a new park.

(A) supporting
(B) supportive
(C) supported
(D) supports

119. Mr. Cruise ------- apologized for having misspoken during his speech to the company shareholders.

(A) quickness
(B) quickly
(C) quicken
(D) quickened

120. The Killiam Public Library will be hosting a ------- of lectures by local authors over the summer.

(A) gathering
(B) means
(C) series
(D) conclusion

GO ON TO THE NEXT PAGE

121. ------- an agreement is reached, representatives from both corporations will sign the contract.

(A) Not only
(B) In order to
(C) Due to
(D) As soon as

122. As a regional manager, Ms. Nissim reports ------- to the company's board of directors.

(A) directly
(B) directed
(C) directs
(D) directing

123. Bolton Enterprises decided to rent office space for its new branch ------- purchasing a building.

(A) about
(B) on behalf of
(C) regarding
(D) instead of

124. For the best results, give ------- time to recover between workouts.

(A) your
(B) yours
(C) yourself
(D) itself

125. Northpoint Cellular is investing heavily in new wireless technologies to ------- other well-established firms.

(A) surpassing
(B) surpass
(C) surpassed
(D) surpasses

126. Renewable energy has grown more affordable in recent years, and ------- more consumers are choosing to try it.

(A) otherwise
(B) therefore
(C) once
(D) instead

127. Joel Hardwick's second novel received ------- reviews from critics, who praised its realistic dialog and believable characters.

(A) defective
(B) renewable
(C) artificial
(D) favorable

128. The number of subscribers to *Edible Magazine* has increased steadily, ------- that of all other culinary publications.

(A) exceeds
(B) exceedingly
(C) exceeded
(D) exceeding

129. Sales ------- weeks three and four of the promotion will be monitored to determine whether it should be extended.

(A) above
(B) next
(C) during
(D) beside

130. CanAir's frequent flyer program is designed ------- passengers who regularly fly with the airline.

(A) reward
(B) rewarding
(C) to reward
(D) rewards

PART 6

Directions: In this part, you will be asked to read four English texts. Each text is missing a word, phrase, or sentence. Select the answer choice that correctly completes the text and mark the corresponding letter (A), (B), (C), or (D) on the answer sheet.

🕐 **PART 6 권장 풀이 시간** 8분

Questions 131-134 refer to the following letter.

Ms. Victoria Collins
645 Keystone Avenue
Bellevue, WA 98007

Dear Ms. Collins,

When you were in our shop for a consultation last week, you ------- that you will need a
                                                             131.
unique outfit for the Bellevue Fine Art Society's charity dinner.

We just received an ------- of pieces from designer Eleanor Harris's summer collection. In
                    132.
particular, we have a blue evening dress that you might be interested in. This item is

exclusive to our shop, but it is a size small. -------.
                                               133.
You said that the dinner is being ------- in May. The weather will be warm by then, so a light
                                  134.
dress such as this one will be perfect for the event. Please let me know when you are

available to stop by.

Miranda Hudson
The Dot Boutique

---

131. (A) mentioning
(B) mentionable
(C) mentioned
(D) mentions

132. (A) assortment
(B) estimate
(C) invitation
(D) announcement

133. (A) We are concerned that the dress is too formal.
(B) Clothes can sometimes shrink when placed in a dryer.
(C) Minor alterations can be done to ensure a great fit.
(D) It is sold at popular retail stores around the country.

134. (A) represented
(B) discussed
(C) canceled
(D) held

GO ON TO THE NEXT PAGE ➤

Questions 135-138 refer to the following memo.

Date: December 10
To: All staff
From: Jonathan Carter, COO
Subject: Policy change

To encourage greater efficiency, management has decided to change how staff ------- are
135.

carried out next year. Beginning in January, team members must participate in a -------
136.

assessment every year. This process will involve examining all aspects of their performance.

Employees ------- bonuses based on the results. Additional information about the new
137.

system has been included in the updated version of the employee manual. -------.
138.

If you have any questions, please contact Director of Personnel Dave Stewart.

135. (A) interviews
(B) assignments
(C) registrations
(D) evaluations

136. (A) thorough
(B) temporary
(C) voluntary
(D) selective

137. (A) have been receiving
(B) received
(C) will receive
(D) were receiving

138. (A) This process has already improved
performance.
(B) This document will be distributed next
week.
(C) Some members have not yet been
assessed.
(D) However, these results were not very
surprising.

Vacancies for Cooks at Quinn Grill

We are a fine dining establishment with an excellent reputation, and we have been in

business for over five years. Our customer base ------- rapidly during this period due to word
139.

of mouth and positive reviews from critics. ------- we are expanding our main dining room,
140.

we are in need of experienced cooks. All applicants must have at least two years of

experience working in a restaurant. This should include cooking a broad range of dishes.

-------. Our ideal candidate will be able to handle a high-pressure environment, collaborate
141.

with other members of a team, and work ------- hours, including weekends and holidays.
142.

Please send your application letter, résumé, and reference letters to Sophia Quinn at

squinn@quinngrill.com.

139. (A) grows
(B) had grown
(C) has grown
(D) will grow

140. (A) Because
(B) Then
(C) As if
(D) Unless

141. (A) Everyone passed the mandatory food
safety course.
(B) We also have several other specific
requirements.
(C) The results of the interview will be
posted soon.
(D) Guests must be shown to their tables
immediately.

142. (A) flexibility
(B) flexibleness
(C) flexible
(D) flexibly

GO ON TO THE NEXT PAGE

Questions 143-146 refer to the following letter.

Sandra Ericta
Landlord, Bristol Apartments
355 Main Street
San Francisco, CA 95125

Dear Ms. Ericta,

This letter serves as notice that I will be vacating Unit 307 of Bristol Apartments on
September 30. I am giving you the ------- 30 days' notice according to my rental contract.
143.
I realize that I have an ------- to leave the apartment in good condition. Otherwise, I will lose
144.
my security deposit. Please let me know when you are available to inspect the unit and
confirm that everything is -------. I would like my deposit returned to me on September 30,
145.
after I have moved out and handed you the key. -------.
146.

Thank you.

Sincerely,
John Schroeder

143. (A) requesting
(B) request
(C) requests
(D) requested

144. (A) occupation
(B) obligation
(C) inquiry
(D) option

145. (A) capable
(B) challenging
(C) satisfactory
(D) appreciative

146. (A) Tenants are prohibited from making copies of the key.
(B) An incorrect amount must have been transferred.
(C) I will provide my bank account details on the same day.
(D) It will not be possible for me to move my furniture today.

PART 7

Directions: In this part, you will be asked to read several texts, such as advertisements, articles, instant messages, or examples of business correspondence. Each text is followed by several questions. Select the best answer and mark the corresponding letter (A), (B), (C), or (D) on your answer sheet.

PART 7 권장 풀이 시간 **54분**

Questions 147-148 refer to the following advertisement.

Have you just moved into a new apartment or house? Do you need some help fixing up your home? If so, then you are in luck as you can just call:

Harold and Sons
Serving the greater Centerville area
555-2398

We provide a wide range of services, including:
Basic home repairs
Appliance, lighting, and fixture installation
Wallpaper pasting and wall painting
Furniture arrangement
Tile laying

Harold Clark started his business 25 years ago, and now his sons Robert and William work with him to provide their home services to local residents. The family's experience and professionalism is beyond comparison. If you call in the month of June, Harold and Sons will install a ceiling fan or light fixture for free with the purchase of any service.

147. What most likely does Harold and Sons do?

(A) Designs wallpaper patterns for home interiors
(B) Moves furniture from one house to another
(C) Conducts residential maintenance tasks
(D) Specializes in installing office lighting

148. What can customers receive in June?

(A) A gift certificate
(B) A complimentary service
(C) A product sample
(D) A new company catalog

GO ON TO THE NEXT PAGE

Questions 149-150 refer to the following text message chain.

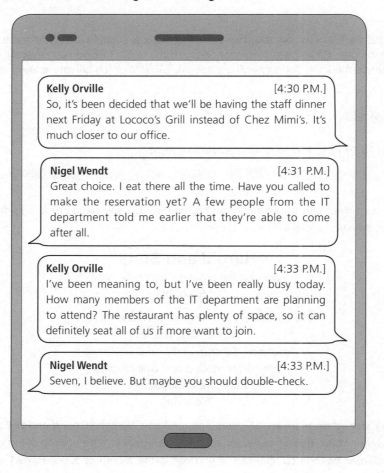

Kelly Orville [4:30 P.M.]
So, it's been decided that we'll be having the staff dinner next Friday at Lococo's Grill instead of Chez Mimi's. It's much closer to our office.

Nigel Wendt [4:31 P.M.]
Great choice. I eat there all the time. Have you called to make the reservation yet? A few people from the IT department told me earlier that they're able to come after all.

Kelly Orville [4:33 P.M.]
I've been meaning to, but I've been really busy today. How many members of the IT department are planning to attend? The restaurant has plenty of space, so it can definitely seat all of us if more want to join.

Nigel Wendt [4:33 P.M.]
Seven, I believe. But maybe you should double-check.

149. What is NOT true about Lococo's Grill?

(A) It can host corporate gatherings.
(B) It is frequently visited by Mr. Wendt.
(C) It is nearer to a workplace than Chez Mimi's.
(D) It requires reservations on weekends.

150. At 4:33 P.M., what does Ms. Orville most likely mean when she writes, "I've been meaning to"?

(A) She plans to invite members of another department.
(B) She does not know how many staff will attend.
(C) She intends to let employees know about a change.
(D) She has not contacted a restaurant.

Medallion Helps New Employees Adapt

Earlier this year, Medallion Corporation created a staff mentoring program to develop the skills of its employees. — [1] —. The program, called Medallion Mentoring, pairs newly hired workers with senior-level managers, who provide advice about day-to-day tasks as well as career growth strategies. — [2] —. Human resources coordinators assign mentors to new workers and schedule two one-hour sessions per week. — [3] —. Additionally, all mentors in the program must fulfill this time requirement.

Although it took a while to get this program off the ground, participation is gradually increasing. This year, human resources coordinators aim to have 200 mentors companywide. — [4] —. Medallion Corporation Chairperson Sally Kay said, "There is a lot more interest in this program now, so there will be no problem finding enough supervisors to volunteer as mentors."

151. What is suggested about the Medallion Mentoring program?

(A) It was featured on a business Web site.
(B) It requires quarterly recruiting efforts.
(C) It is not supported by upper management.
(D) It was established less than 12 months ago.

152. What are mentors required to do?

(A) Meet a minimum number of necessary hours
(B) Volunteer for two hours a day after work
(C) Get together with family members of mentored staff
(D) Have regular counseling sessions with a coordinator

153. In which of the positions marked [1], [2], [3], and [4] does the following sentence best belong?

"This goal is expected to be achieved by October."

(A) [1]
(B) [2]
(C) [3]
(D) [4]

Questions 154-155 refer to the following e-mail.

To: Leah Young <leahyoung@journeyon.com>
From: Evan Harris <evanharris@smartmail.com>
Date: May 9
Subject: Travel insurance
Attachment: Receipt, Police Report

Dear Ms. Young,

I am writing to request reimbursement for an unexpected expense. Recently, I traveled to Mexico on vacation. I insured my trip through Journey on Travel Insurance. My policy number is 4533906.

I booked a room at Hotel Fiesta in Cozumel for five nights. On the second day of my visit, someone gained access to my room and took my laptop computer. The hotel manager gave me a refund for the remaining three nights, but this doesn't come close to covering the cost of purchasing a replacement computer.

From my understanding, I am entitled to up to $5,000 of insurance coverage from your company in this type of situation. The total cost of my laptop was $2,300. I have attached copies of my receipt for the computer and the police report.

Sincerely,
Evan Harris

154. Why did Mr. Harris write the e-mail?

(A) To ask for compensation
(B) To make a reservation
(C) To criticize a hotel
(D) To cancel a payment

155. According to the e-mail, what happened at Hotel Fiesta?

(A) A guest was overcharged for a room.
(B) An electronic device was stolen.
(C) A personal computer was damaged.
(D) A refund request was denied.

Questions 156-157 refer to the following Web page.

Great Deals of Delta
Your source for special deals at area businesses

We work with shops, restaurants, travel companies, salons, spas, and home service businesses to create a one-stop shop for Delta area consumers. You won't find this many deals in any other place. Find a great deal today!

Product or Service SEARCH

Business SEARCH

This Web site has been provided by *The Delta Times* Newspaper.

Home	Shopping	**Home Services**	Personal Services

Great Deal #1:
Hammerhead Window Washing
-$40 off your first residential window cleaning service

Great Deal #2:
Scrub Masters Tile and Air Vent Cleaning
-Order both services and receive 20 percent off the regular price

Great Deal #3:
Bloom's Yards
-Six months of weekly lawn care services, prepaid, at 25 percent off

Great Deal #4:
Swift Swipe Carpet Cleaning
-Receive a one-time cleaning service for rugs in up to five rooms for 10 percent off

More on the next page. Click here! >>>

156. What is the purpose of the Web page?

(A) To compare the costs of similar services
(B) To provide reviews of local services
(C) To introduce new enterprises
(D) To advertise business discount offers

157. How much of a discount is being offered on landscaping services?

(A) 10 percent
(B) 20 percent
(C) 25 percent
(D) 40 percent

GO ON TO THE NEXT PAGE

Questions 158-160 refer to the following letter.

April 12

Chad Steiner
1420 Elm Street, Suite 32
Madison, WI 53705

Dear Mr. Steiner,

This letter has been sent to all residents of Singing Vines Apartments. As you know, the spaces in this building's parking lot are reserved for tenants. However, we have received several complaints about visitors ignoring this regulation. Starting next week, we will be checking all automobiles parked in our lot. If a resident parking pass is not displayed in the window, we will have the vehicle removed.

Please inform your guests that they can park on Elm Street in front of the building for free at any time of the day. Parking is also allowed on Boulder Avenue and Park Road, but there is an hourly charge. Note that a city rule prohibits parking on Devon Boulevard, which runs along the west side of the building.

If you have any questions or concerns, please feel free to contact me.

Sincerely,
Rachel Solomon
Building manager, Singing Vines Apartments

158. What problem does Ms. Solomon mention?

(A) A building is not being cleaned.
(B) A fee has been increased.
(C) An automobile has been scratched.
(D) A rule is not being followed.

159. What will happen next week?

(A) Passes will be issued.
(B) Vehicles will be examined.
(C) Tenants will be contacted.
(D) Apartments will be renovated.

160. Where are visitors not allowed to park?

(A) On Elm Street
(B) On Boulder Avenue
(C) On Park Road
(D) On Devon Boulevard

Questions 161-163 refer to the following e-mail.

To:	Marcy Sizemore <marcysizemore@fullerchemical.com>
From:	Shane Ellis <shaneellis@quantumlaboratories.com>
Date:	January 14
Subject:	Congratulations
Attachment:	Résumé

Hi Marcy,

It has been nearly 10 years since we last worked together, but when I recently saw an article in *Science News Monthly* about your promotion to vice president of research and development at Fuller Chemical, I remembered our early days working together as research assistants for LabSure Corporation. I knew that with your talent and work ethic, you would be successful. Congratulations on your promotion.

As you may know, I am the director of quality assurance for Quantum Laboratories. We have a very talented researcher that will be leaving our company to seek out other employment opportunities. While we are sad to lose her, I would like to recommend her to you in case you have a suitable opening at your company. You will find that she has an impressive educational background and a great deal of experience in the field of biological research. I have attached her résumé for you to review.

Even if you don't have a position open, would you mind meeting her to offer career advice? If you are willing to help, please let me know. Thank you, and I wish you all the best at your new position.

Regards,

Shane Ellis

161. Why did Mr. Ellis write the e-mail?

(A) To request help with a research project
(B) To announce his promotion
(C) To offer an investment opportunity
(D) To recommend a potential employee

162. How do Ms. Sizemore and Mr. Ellis know each other?

(A) They attended the same conference.
(B) They used to be coworkers.
(C) They met through a shared acquaintance.
(D) They went to the same school.

163. What does Mr. Ellis suggest that Ms. Sizemore do?

(A) Apply for a position
(B) Propose a candidate
(C) Have a meeting
(D) Contact a client

GO ON TO THE NEXT PAGE

Questions 164-167 refer to the following online chat discussion.

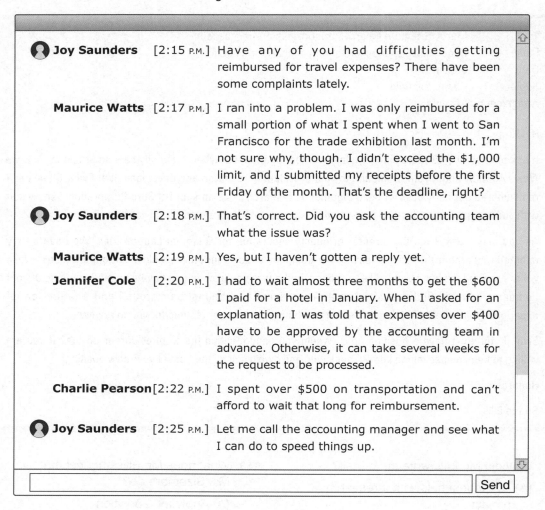

Joy Saunders [2:15 P.M.] Have any of you had difficulties getting reimbursed for travel expenses? There have been some complaints lately.

Maurice Watts [2:17 P.M.] I ran into a problem. I was only reimbursed for a small portion of what I spent when I went to San Francisco for the trade exhibition last month. I'm not sure why, though. I didn't exceed the $1,000 limit, and I submitted my receipts before the first Friday of the month. That's the deadline, right?

Joy Saunders [2:18 P.M.] That's correct. Did you ask the accounting team what the issue was?

Maurice Watts [2:19 P.M.] Yes, but I haven't gotten a reply yet.

Jennifer Cole [2:20 P.M.] I had to wait almost three months to get the $600 I paid for a hotel in January. When I asked for an explanation, I was told that expenses over $400 have to be approved by the accounting team in advance. Otherwise, it can take several weeks for the request to be processed.

Charlie Pearson [2:22 P.M.] I spent over $500 on transportation and can't afford to wait that long for reimbursement.

Joy Saunders [2:25 P.M.] Let me call the accounting manager and see what I can do to speed things up.

164. What is mentioned about Mr. Watts?

(A) He is a member of the accounting team.
(B) He will transfer to another branch soon.
(C) He helped organize a trade show.
(D) He went on a business trip recently.

165. At 2:18 P.M., what does Ms. Saunders most likely mean when she writes, "That's correct"?

(A) The accounting department usually copies receipts.
(B) A deadline falls on the first Friday of every month.
(C) The $1,000 limit cannot be exceeded for any reason.
(D) A team member explained her expenses properly.

166. How much did Ms. Cole spend on accommodations in January?

(A) $400
(B) $500
(C) $600
(D) $1,000

167. What can be inferred about Ms. Saunders?

(A) She will purchase some airline tickets.
(B) She approved a reimbursement request.
(C) She will contact a department manager.
(D) She submitted a complaint to management.

January 28

Eugene Lee
66 Westing Road
Wilmington, DE 19801

Dear Mr. Lee,

At the Hoyle Community Theater, we strive to provide the best performing arts experience possible. As a nonprofit organization, we depend on the support of the community. Therefore, we ask that our patrons periodically make donations. — [1] —.

Enclosed is an envelope into which you can place your donation. — [2] —. Any amount would be greatly appreciated. Substantial benefits are available to those who contribute $100 or more. — [3] —.

And to show gratitude to our loyal patrons, we're planning on staging some of our most ambitious performances yet this year. — [4] —. In March, we'll be putting on a play by the famed Kenyan playwright David Kobo called *Searching for the Homeland*. And in June, we'll be holding a three-week-long performance of a new play by local playwright Steve Weller. Then, this autumn we're going to be performing a series of classical Greek tragedies.

As the only theater in Wilmington that offers free performances, we are supported by people like you. So, thank you for your continued dedication.

Sincerely,

Kathryn Little
Director, Hoyle Community Theater

168. What is the purpose of the letter?

(A) To solicit money from a patron
(B) To advertise a new theater
(C) To announce a schedule change
(D) To seek actors for a performance

169. What is mentioned about *Searching for the Homeland*?

(A) It will run for three weeks.
(B) It is based on a Greek tragedy.
(C) It is being directed by Steve Weller.
(D) It was written by a well-known artist.

170. What is indicated about the Hoyle Community Theater?

(A) It is located outside of Wilmington.
(B) It hires student actors for performances.
(C) It does not charge money for admission.
(D) It is closed on weekends and national holidays.

171. In which of the positions marked [1], [2], [3], and [4] does the following sentence best belong?

"These include gift cards to restaurants in the area and tickets to local concerts."

(A) [1]
(B) [2]
(C) [3]
(D) [4]

GO ON TO THE NEXT PAGE

Road Closures

Please note that certain sections of King Street, Queen Street, and Dundas Avenue will be closed in March and April. These closures are necessary to perform required work on parts of these roads that were damaged during the long winter. The roads are all major routes through the city, and they should not be left in their current condition.

Please note the following schedule:

- March 6 to March 20 – King Street will be closed between Bathurst Street and University Avenue.
- March 21 to April 3 – Queen Street will be closed between Ossington Avenue and Kensington Avenue.
- April 4 to April 18 – Dundas Avenue will be closed between University Avenue and Young Street.

We suggest using Royce Avenue and Church Street as detours for all of the routes listed above. If you decide to use smaller residential streets, please remember to observe the reduced speed limit at all times.

Thank you for your patience and understanding.

The Toronto Public Works Committee

172. Why are some roads being closed?

(A) To allow a festival to take place
(B) To repair them after the winter
(C) To construct new sidewalks
(D) To expand them by adding lanes

173. The word "condition" in paragraph 1, line 5, is closest in meaning to

(A) requirement
(B) district
(C) state
(D) task

174. Which road will NOT be closed?

(A) Queen Street
(B) King Street
(C) Dundas Avenue
(D) Royce Avenue

175. What are some drivers asked to do?

(A) Follow the speed limit
(B) Only travel along main roads
(C) Contact a committee for information
(D) Use a toll booth to access a road

GO ON TO THE NEXT PAGE

Questions 176-180 refer to the following memo and form.

To: All employees
From: Chase Milton
Date: December 3
Subject: Employee holiday gift
Attachment: Gift choice card

Dear employees,

As you know, the holidays are fast approaching. To thank everyone for their hard work this year, Carrigan Foods will provide each employee with a turkey, ham, or basket of vegetarian food. The meat products will be available on December 12, while the baskets will be ready on December 16.

Please keep in mind that each employee is allowed to select only one gift. To indicate your choice, fill out the attached card and turn it in to your manager before December 6. We have also included the option of sending one of these items to a local food bank that provides meals to the homeless in case you do not wish to receive anything.

We hope you enjoy your gift and the coming holiday.

Sincerely,
Chase Milton
President, Carrigan Foods

Carrigan Foods
Employee Gift Choice Card

Check the label on the food product you receive for storage instructions. All items must be kept refrigerated or frozen. It is recommended that you pick up your gift from the administration office when your shift has ended so that you do not have to leave it in your office or car for a long period of time.

If you will not be working on the day your gift is scheduled to be distributed, please arrange to have a coworker get it for you. Note that we cannot hold food items past their designated pickup days. Those that are not taken will be given to the food bank.

- -

Name: <u>Selena Kim</u>
Employee ID Number: <u>1002532</u>
Division: <u>Marketing</u>
Phone Extension: <u>7457</u>

Please pick one of the following options:
■ Frozen turkey
□ Frozen ham
□ Vegetarian basket

I would like to give my gift to a food bank: Yes □ No ■

176. What is Carrigan Foods planning to do?

(A) Organize a holiday dinner
(B) Show appreciation to its employees
(C) Offer a class on cooking techniques
(D) Send gift cards to some customers

177. In the memo, the word "select" in paragraph 2, line 1, is closest in meaning to

(A) vote
(B) choose
(C) assign
(D) prefer

178. According to the form, what are employees advised to do?

(A) Contact a local food bank
(B) Go to a storage area immediately
(C) Claim an item after finishing work
(D) Schedule a pickup time in advance

179. When will Ms. Kim most likely receive her gift?

(A) December 3
(B) December 6
(C) December 12
(D) December 16

180. What information is NOT requested on the form?

(A) Item preference
(B) Phone number
(C) Pickup time
(D) Department name

GO ON TO THE NEXT PAGE

15TH ANNUAL BOOK SALE

The Carlton Library on Ferris Street is holding its 15th Annual Book Sale on Friday, August 2. Bring any books you have lying around to the staff at the front desk. Our staff will check these books to make sure that they don't have any torn pages, water damage, or writing in the margins. And if they are in good condition, we'll buy them at reasonable prices.

Also, we have a huge selection of used books on sale on the library's second floor. These include everything from translations of ancient poetry to contemporary bestsellers. All paperbacks are $5, and all hardcover books are $12. In addition, we are selling a variety of library merchandise, including tote bags for $8, backpacks for $20, and planners for $11.

The proceeds from all sales will be donated to the Appleton Institute, a charitable organization that provides tutoring to children. For more information about the Book Sale event, visit www.carltonsale.org.

TO: <questions@appleton.org>
FROM: Sally Fisher <sallyfisher44@fastmail.com>
SUBJECT: Volunteer opportunities
DATE: August 4
ATTACHMENT: Résumé

To Whom It May Concern,

Two days ago, I bought a $5 item at the Carlton Library's book sale event and received a flyer for the Appleton Institute. I had never heard of your organization before, but after reading over the flyer, I became very interested in the services you provide.

I am a former high school English teacher who has recently retired. However, I am looking to continue doing educational work in some capacity. I have extensive experience mentoring people who struggle with reading and writing, and I highly enjoy that kind of work. Therefore, I was wondering if your organization has any volunteer or part-time work opportunities.

I am available on most days of the week, although on Thursdays I perform charity work at a community center. I have attached my résumé to this e-mail. I look forward to hearing from you soon.

Sincerely,

Sally Fisher

181. According to the notice, what will library staff NOT check used books for?

(A) Damage from moisture
(B) Ripped pages
(C) Notes next to the text
(D) A missing cover

182. What will the money raised by the book sale be used for?

(A) Supporting a nonprofit organization
(B) Renovating a reading room
(C) Funding public schools
(D) Marketing new magazines

183. What did Ms. Fisher purchase at the Carlton Library?

(A) A backpack
(B) A paperback
(C) A hardcover
(D) A planner

184. What does Ms. Fisher say about her professional experience?

(A) She has worked at the Appleton Institute before.
(B) She published books to help struggling readers.
(C) She was employed as an educator.
(D) She has provided English tutoring at a library.

185. Why is Ms. Fisher not available on Thursdays?

(A) Because her language class was rescheduled
(B) Because she works at a bookstore
(C) Because her book club has weekly meetings
(D) Because she has a volunteer position

GO ON TO THE NEXT PAGE

RB BANK

Open an investment account with RB Bank and take advantage of our special offer. Get 60 days of free trading and a cash incentive when you deposit $2,500 or more.*

- $100 incentive + free trades with deposit of $2,500 to $49,999
- $250 incentive + free trades with deposit of $50,000 to $99,999
- $500 incentive + free trades with deposit of $100,000 to $249,999
- $750 incentive + free trades with deposit of $250,000 or more

Why choose RB Bank?
- Fair pricing with no hidden fees
- Educational resources for every investor
- Various investment types to choose from
- Round-the-clock support from financial advisers
- Easy-to-use trading software for desktop and mobile devices

* Offer is valid until April 30. Standard trading fee is $9.99. For inquiries, call 555-2975, e-mail info@rbbank.com, or visit one of our 60 branches nationwide.

To: Beth Viola <b.viola@ambercrafts.com>
From: Ron Campbell <r.campbell@rbbank.com>
Subject: Your account
Date: April 21

Dear Ms. Viola,

Thank you for opening an investment account with RB Bank. Your deposit of $50,000 was received yesterday. Please note that it will take approximately 60 days for your cash bonus to be released.

Regarding your other inquiry, there are a couple of options available for business owners who wish to borrow money. The first is the SBA Loan. This is for companies with fewer than 50 employees. Up to $100,000 may be borrowed at a 4.9 percent interest rate. The other option is the CTA Loan. It can only be applied for by firms with 50 employees or more. For this loan, up to $500,000 is available to the borrower at a 3.9 percent interest rate. Please visit our Web site for additional information about these loan programs and instructions on how to apply.

Sincerely,

Ron Campbell
Financial adviser

Loan Application Form

Company Information
Company Name: Amber Crafts
Owner: Beth Viola
Address: 527 Fairfax Avenue, Roanoke, VA 24016
Telephone: 555-2308
E-mail: b.viola@ambercrafts.com

Loan Type: SBA Loan
☑ Check here if you have read the RB Bank Privacy Agreement.

Please note that you must include a copy of your company's business license with your application.

186. What is NOT mentioned about RB Bank?

(A) It charges the lowest fees in the industry.
(B) It has a range of investment options.
(C) It offers 24-hour financial support.
(D) It provides learning materials for investors.

187. How much cash will Ms. Viola receive for opening an investment account?

(A) $100
(B) $250
(C) $500
(D) $750

188. According to the e-mail, what is an advantage of the CTA Loan over the SBA Loan?

(A) A more generous signup bonus
(B) A lower interest rate
(C) A longer borrowing period
(D) A less complex application process

189. What is implied about Amber Crafts?

(A) Its owner is looking for investors.
(B) It recently opened another branch.
(C) Its products are sold in multiple countries.
(D) It employs fewer than 50 workers.

190. What has Ms. Viola been asked to provide?

(A) Personnel records
(B) Financial statements
(C) An operating permit
(D) A legal contract

GO ON TO THE NEXT PAGE

About Empire Group

Within just 25 years, Empire Group has become a leader in property development, with experience in construction and financing.

Currently, Empire Group carries out commercial and residential construction projects in 45 cities, including New York, San Francisco, and Los Angeles. Over the past two years, it has established an international presence with offices and residential buildings in Malaysia, Canada, and Germany. Furthermore, the group has built 32 hotels in the US that are run by major operators like Blackwood and Le Clare.

Empire Group's most recent expansion has been into Australia. As in other places, its initial aim in Australia is to increase its workforce in cities that have a large population of upper-income residents.

Empire Group Australia is seeking qualified candidates to fill several full-time positions. To apply, e-mail your résumé to jobs@empiregroup.au.

Executive assistant
• Two positions (Brisbane and Melbourne)
• Duties involve providing administrative support
• Must be willing to travel
• College graduates preferred with 2+ years of experience in a business organization

Human resources worker
• Two positions (Melbourne and Perth)
• Duties include handling employee-related matters and assisting with recruiting
• Must hold a degree in human resources management with 3+ years of related experience
• Priority given to candidates with professional certification

Contracts specialist
• Four positions (Sydney and Perth)
• Duties include managing supplier relationships and negotiating commercial contracts
• Must have a business degree with 5+ years of real estate experience

Marketing associate
• Two positions (Brisbane and Perth)
• Duties include conducting research and developing advertising campaigns
• Must be proficient in office software and adept at presentations
• Must be college graduates with 3+ years of real estate work experience

Empire Group Australia

www.empiregroup.au

July 14

Dear Ms. Chen,

Thank you for your application and for participating in the interview. Unfortunately, we have decided to give the job to another applicant. Although you met our basic requirements in terms of experience and education, the applicant we selected has several certificates that you have not yet received.

We wish you well in your continued job search and encourage you to apply for other positions at Empire Group in the future. The company is still in its early stages in Australia and has further plans for growth, particularly in your city of Melbourne.

Warmly,

Leonora Mitchell
Recruiting specialist

---

191. What is indicated about Empire Group?

(A) It began as a financial services firm.
(B) Most of its offices are in Europe.
(C) It builds commercial and residential structures.
(D) Some of hotels it built will open next month.

192. What can be inferred about the city of Brisbane?

(A) It has the highest number of available job openings.
(B) It is the site of Empire Group's Australian headquarters.
(C) It has many residents with high incomes.
(D) It is the location of an upcoming real estate exposition.

193. What is true about the advertised marketing positions?

(A) They feature incentives for exceeding sales goals.
(B) They are only open to candidates with marketing degrees.
(C) They involve occasional overseas travel.
(D) They require good computer skills.

194. Why did Ms. Mitchell write the letter?

(A) To congratulate a successful applicant
(B) To invite a candidate to an interview
(C) To reject a job applicant
(D) To request details about work history

195. Which position did Ms. Chen most likely apply for?

(A) Executive assistant
(B) Human resources worker
(C) Contracts specialist
(D) Marketing associate

GO ON TO THE NEXT PAGE

www.pps.org

Support the Philadelphia Preservation Society (PPS)

Thanks to the work of the Philadelphia Preservation Society, Philadelphia boasts one of the largest ongoing collections of public art in the country. People from all backgrounds can enjoy access to these works at any time for free.

Here are some ways that you can support our mission to preserve public art for everyone:
- Join as a **PPS individual member** and receive advance invitations to PPS special events.
- Become a **PPS corporate partner** and attend our semiannual banquets at no cost to your business.
- Make a one-time donation for any amount by clicking <u>here</u>. Get a free PPS coffee mug when you donate.

To	Marilyn Johnson <m.johnson@pps.org>
From	Dixie Piper <d.piper@solomon.edu>
Subject	Class activity
Date	May 2

Dear Ms. Johnson,

I recently signed up as an individual member of the Philadelphia Preservation Society and am interested in bringing my 6th grade art class on one of the self-guided tours listed in your brochure. Ideally, I'd like to lead the students on a tour near a lake or river, where they can make sketches of what they see. We could do the activity on a Friday from 9 A.M. to 12 P.M. and end with a picnic lunch. Also, I'd prefer to rent bikes for this activity since one of your self-guided tours seemed to have that option. Please let me know what you think so that I can draw up a concrete plan.

Thank you,

Dixie Piper

Self-Guided Tours at the Philadelphia Preservation Society

Self-guided tours are a great way to experience Philadelphia's public art! Try one of the tours organized by the Philadelphia Preservation Society below.

Nature Center
2-hour trip
View fascinating works of contemporary public art set amid 28,000 square meters of well-tended greenery. (Grounds are open on weekdays only from 9 A.M. to 3 P.M.)

Philadelphia Museum of Art
1-hour trip
The area around the museum is home to a large collection of sculptures. For more art, stop in at the museum itself. (The area outside the museum is closed to the public on Mondays.)

Kelly Drive

2.5-hour trip

Take a leisurely trip along the Schuylkill River, passing a number of outdoor sculptures on the way. (Bike rentals available at Floyd Hall.)

Visit www.pps.org for details.

Rittenhouse Square

1-hour trip

See several historic sculptures in Rittenhouse Square, a lovely park dating back to Philadelphia's founding.

---

196. What most likely does the Philadelphia Preservation Society do?

(A) Offers art lessons to local students
(B) Manages a city's tourist industry
(C) Funds the maintenance of modern buildings
(D) Maintains artwork for public enjoyment

197. What is being offered to those who give a donation?

(A) A membership discount
(B) A complimentary item
(C) An information booklet
(D) A free trial class

198. What is suggested about Ms. Piper?

(A) She will receive invitations to PPS events.
(B) She recently participated in a field trip.
(C) She secured some funding for her organization.
(D) She will make a one-time donation to PPS.

199. Which tour is Ms. Piper interested in?

(A) Nature Center
(B) Kelly Drive
(C) Philadelphia Museum of Art
(D) Rittenhouse Square

200. What is indicated about the self-guided tours?

(A) Each one takes an hour to complete.
(B) They are discounted for students and groups.
(C) All of them are suitable for bikers.
(D) Some of them are unavailable on certain days of the week.

This is the end of the test. You may review Parts 5, 6, and 7 if you finish the test early.

점수 환산표 p.244 / 정답·해석·해설 [책 속의 책] p.44

▌다음 페이지에 있는 Review 체크리스트에 따라 틀린 문제를 다시 점검해보세요.

´Review 체크리스트

TEST 2를 푼 다음, 아래 체크리스트에 따라 틀린 문제를 리뷰하고 박스에 완료 여부를 표시하세요.
만약 시험까지 얼마 남지 않았다면, 초록색으로 표시된 항목이라도 꼭 확인하세요.

☐ 틀린 문제의 경우, 다시 풀어봤다.

☐ 틀린 문제의 경우, 스크립트/해석을 확인하며 지문/문제의 내용을 정확하게 파악했다.

☐ 해설을 통해 각 문제의 정답과 오답의 근거가 무엇인지 정확하게 파악했다.

☐ Part 1과 Part 2에서 틀린 문제의 경우, 선택한 오답의 유형이 무엇이었는지 확인하고 같은 함정에 빠지지 않도록 정리해두었다.

☐ Part 3와 Part 4의 각 문제에서 사용된 패러프레이징을 확인했다.

☐ Part 5와 Part 6의 경우, 틀린 문제에서 사용된 문법 포인트 또는 정답 및 오답 어휘를 정리했다.

☐ Part 6의 알맞은 문장 고르기 문제의 경우, 지문 전체를 정확하게 해석하며 전체 글의 흐름과 빈칸 주변 문맥을 정확하게 파악하는 연습을 했다.

☐ Part 7에서 질문과 보기의 키워드를 찾아 표시하며 지문에서 정답의 근거가 되는 문장이나 구절을 찾아보고, 문제에서 사용된 패러프레이징을 확인했다.

☐ Part 1~Part 4는 받아쓰기 & 쉐도잉 워크북을 활용하여, TEST에 수록된 핵심 문장을 받아쓰고 따라 읽으며 복습했다.

☐ Part 1~Part 7은 단어암기자료를 활용하여, TEST에 수록된 핵심 어휘와 표현을 암기했다.

많은 양의 문제를 푸는 것도 중요하지만, 틀린 문제를 제대로 리뷰하는 것도 중요합니다.
틀린 문제를 한 번 더 꼼꼼히 리뷰한다면, 빠른 시간 내에 효과적으로 목표 점수를 달성할 수 있습니다.

TEST 3

LISTENING TEST

Part **1**
Part **2**
Part **3**
Part **4**

READING TEST

Part **5**
Part **6**
Part **7**

Review 체크리스트

잠깐! 테스트 전 아래 사항을 꼭 확인하세요.

휴대전화의 전원을 끄셨나요? 예 ☐
Answer Sheet(p.251), 연필, 지우개, 시계를 준비하셨나요? 예 ☐
Listening MP3를 들을 준비가 되셨나요? 예 ☐

모든 준비가 완료되었으면 목표 점수를 떠올린 후 테스트를 시작합니다.
테스트를 마친 후, Review 체크리스트(p.152)를 보며 자신이 틀린 문제를 반드시 복습합니다.

무료MP3 바로듣기

🎧 TEST 3.mp3
실전용·복습용 문제풀이 MP3 무료 다운로드 및 스트리밍 바로듣기 (HackersIngang.com)
* 실제 시험장의 소음까지 재현해 낸 고사장 소음/매미 버전 MP3, 영국식·호주식 발음 집중 MP3, 고속 버전 MP3까지 구매
  하면 실전에 더욱 완벽히 대비할 수 있습니다.

LISTENING TEST

In this section, you must demonstrate your ability to understand spoken English. This section is divided into four parts and will take approximately 45 minutes to complete. Do not mark the answers in your test book. Use the answer sheet that is provided separately.

PART 1

Directions: For each question, you will listen to four short statements about a picture in your test book. These statements will not be printed and will only be spoken one time. Select the statement that best describes what is happening in the picture and mark the corresponding letter (A), (B), (C), or (D) on the answer sheet.

Sample Answer

The statement that best describes the picture is (B), "The man is sitting at the desk." So, you should mark letter (B) on the answer sheet.

1.

2.

GO ON TO THE NEXT PAGE ➡

3.

4.

5.

6.

GO ON TO THE NEXT PAGE

PART 2

Directions: For each question, you will listen to a statement or question followed by three possible responses spoken in English. They will not be printed and will only be spoken one time. Select the best response and mark the corresponding letter (A), (B), or (C) on your answer sheet.

7. Mark your answer on your answer sheet.

8. Mark your answer on your answer sheet.

9. Mark your answer on your answer sheet.

10. Mark your answer on your answer sheet.

11. Mark your answer on your answer sheet.

12. Mark your answer on your answer sheet.

13. Mark your answer on your answer sheet.

14. Mark your answer on your answer sheet.

15. Mark your answer on your answer sheet.

16. Mark your answer on your answer sheet.

17. Mark your answer on your answer sheet.

18. Mark your answer on your answer sheet.

19. Mark your answer on your answer sheet.

20. Mark your answer on your answer sheet.

21. Mark your answer on your answer sheet.

22. Mark your answer on your answer sheet.

23. Mark your answer on your answer sheet.

24. Mark your answer on your answer sheet.

25. Mark your answer on your answer sheet.

26. Mark your answer on your answer sheet.

27. Mark your answer on your answer sheet.

28. Mark your answer on your answer sheet.

29. Mark your answer on your answer sheet.

30. Mark your answer on your answer sheet.

31. Mark your answer on your answer sheet.

PART 3

Directions: In this part, you will listen to several conversations between two or more speakers. These conversations will not be printed and will only be spoken one time. For each conversation, you will be asked to answer three questions. Select the best response and mark the corresponding letter (A), (B), (C), or (D) on your answer sheet.

32. What are the speakers working on?
    (A) A vehicle design
    (B) A window display
    (C) A publication cover
    (D) A business Web site

33. What does the woman ask the man about?
    (A) When a document should be printed
    (B) Why an image must be removed
    (C) Whether a draft requires more changes
    (D) Who will attend a meeting

34. What will the speakers most likely do next?
    (A) Select a design
    (B) Visit an office
    (C) Purchase a car
    (D) Examine a vehicle

35. Where do the speakers most likely work?
    (A) At an office supplies store
    (B) At a dining venue
    (C) At a grocery store
    (D) At a flower shop

36. Why is the man behind schedule?
    (A) A coworker is unavailable.
    (B) An order was changed.
    (C) An event was moved ahead.
    (D) A delivery is late.

37. What does the woman offer to do?
    (A) Get some supplies
    (B) Talk to a client
    (C) Set up an appointment
    (D) Remove some packages

38. What did the woman do this morning?
    (A) Read a message
    (B) Visited another department
    (C) Reviewed some receipts
    (D) Sent an e-mail

39. What is mentioned about the company?
    (A) It will move to another building.
    (B) It will expand its parking lot.
    (C) It will reimburse employees for a fee.
    (D) It will hold a special event for clients.

40. What is the woman concerned about?
    (A) The cost of a pass
    (B) The location of a facility
    (C) The amount of a fine
    (D) The size of a garage

41. Where does the woman work?
    (A) At a clothing shop
    (B) At a fitness facility
    (C) At a furniture store
    (D) At a magazine company

42. What does the man want to know?
    (A) The price of a product
    (B) The location of a shop
    (C) The reason for a call
    (D) The purpose for a project

43. According to the woman, what will expire soon?
    (A) A coupon
    (B) A publication subscription
    (C) A membership
    (D) A lease contract

GO ON TO THE NEXT PAGE

44. What does the man say about the seminar?

(A) It took place at a hotel.
(B) It was attended by few people.
(C) It was sponsored by Actercorp.
(D) It focused on digital publishing.

45. What does the man want the woman to give to him?

(A) Some contact details
(B) A registration form
(C) Some directions
(D) A media file

46. What does the man ask for?

(A) Creating a new account
(B) Going to a lecture series
(C) Using another e-mail address
(D) Delivering an item in person

47. What does the man mean when he says, "I've always been interested in exotic cuisine"?

(A) He wants another option.
(B) He is not worried about cost.
(C) He has never tasted Thai food.
(D) He prefers an advertised deal.

48. What does the woman give to the man?

(A) Coupons
(B) Schedules
(C) Brochures
(D) Tickets

49. What most likely will the woman do next?

(A) Check a reservation system
(B) Update a tour timetable
(C) Reboot a computer
(D) Send out a book

50. What problem does the woman mention?

(A) A facility is short on supplies.
(B) A hotel reservation was lost.
(C) A room location is noisy.
(D) A bill is inaccurate.

51. What is suggested about Room 240?

(A) It has been reserved for tonight.
(B) It is the only available room.
(C) It has been recently renovated.
(D) It is located at the end of the hall.

52. What does the man offer to do?

(A) File a formal complaint
(B) Request a repair
(C) Find a supervisor
(D) Provide a free upgrade

53. Where is the conversation most likely taking place?

(A) At a production facility
(B) At a retail outlet
(C) At a financial institution
(D) At a travel agency

54. Why does the man say, "That program was just launched last week"?

(A) To express concern about a request
(B) To explain a mistake
(C) To promote a new service
(D) To apologize for a delay

55. What does the man ask the woman to do?

(A) Provide a credit card
(B) Return at a later time
(C) Try on other merchandise
(D) Complete a document

56. Where does the conversation most likely take place?

(A) At a manufacturing facility
(B) At a coffee shop
(C) At an exposition center
(D) At a fitness center

57. What does the man's new assignment consist of?

(A) Demonstrating a new tool
(B) Erecting a booth
(C) Organizing some drinks
(D) Checking the temperature

58. What will Ms. Jones do next?

(A) Provide some work clothes
(B) Print some manuals
(C) Prepare a payment
(D) Taste a new beverage

59. What does the woman say about the report?

(A) It was created by her supervisor.
(B) It should be submitted this week.
(C) It includes inaccurate information.
(D) It must be printed for a gathering.

60. What does the woman want to do?

(A) Make some copies
(B) Do some calculations
(C) Post a file to a Web site
(D) Rearrange some figures

61. According to the man, what can the woman find online?

(A) Registration forms
(B) Assistance with a program
(C) Information about an order
(D) Sample software

Presentation Schedule	
Speakers	Time
John Foreman	9:00 A.M. – 10:30 A.M.
Harry Garcia	10:30 A.M. – 12:00 P.M.
Fred Jones	1:30 P.M. – 3:00 P.M.
Peter Wright	3:00 P.M. – 4:30 P.M.

62. What are the speakers mainly discussing?

(A) Event venues
(B) Presentation schedules
(C) A deadline for an application
(D) A topic for a conference

63. Look at the graphic. Who will arrive from Boston?

(A) John Foreman
(B) Harry Garcia
(C) Fred Jones
(D) Peter Wright

64. What does the woman ask the man to do?

(A) Send out extra invitations
(B) Contact speakers
(C) Meet with a venue manager
(D) Extend a deadline

GO ON TO THE NEXT PAGE

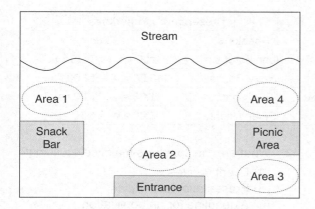

65. What did the woman recently do?

(A) Installed a new door
(B) Read a notification
(C) Requested a lawn care service
(D) Called the maintenance person

66. Why is the man worried?

(A) Officials have rejected a request.
(B) A city plan could have a negative impact.
(C) A play area has been closed down.
(D) Maintenance work has not been completed.

67. Look at the graphic. Where do the children usually play?

(A) Area 1
(B) Area 2
(C) Area 3
(D) Area 4

68. Why was the woman surprised?

(A) A company stopped production of a device.
(B) A speaker system is too expensive.
(C) A product is relatively unpopular.
(D) A business announced a recall.

69. Look at the graphic. What aspect will most likely be addressed immediately?

(A) Price
(B) Sound quality
(C) Portability
(D) Design

70. What will the man probably do this afternoon?

(A) Meet with a director
(B) Talk with some customers
(C) Copy some charts
(D) Test a new product

PART 4

Directions: In this part, you will listen to several short talks by a single speaker. These talks will not be printed and will only be spoken one time. For each talk, you will be asked to answer three questions. Select the best response and mark the corresponding letter (A), (B), (C), or (D) on your answer sheet.

71. Where most likely are the listeners?

    (A) At a community center
    (B) At an employment agency
    (C) At a financial institution
    (D) At a government office

72. What did Mr. Hernandez do in New York?

    (A) Interviewed an employee
    (B) Conducted a workshop
    (C) Received an award
    (D) Founded a business

73. What will the listeners probably do this evening?

    (A) Attend an employee orientation
    (B) Meet at a dining establishment
    (C) Drive to a convention center
    (D) Take a training course

74. Why has there been a flight cancellation?

    (A) The aircraft has a mechanical issue.
    (B) The weather conditions are too severe.
    (C) A security problem has occurred.
    (D) An airport has lost power.

75. What will be provided to certain passengers?

    (A) Accommodation vouchers
    (B) Discounted fares
    (C) Seat upgrades
    (D) Full refunds

76. According to the speaker, where is a service desk located?

    (A) By a check-in counter
    (B) Near a gate
    (C) Across from a cafeteria
    (D) Next to a ticketing office

77. What type of business is Spark?

    (A) A real estate office
    (B) An instrument store
    (C) A music academy
    (D) A consulting firm

78. What does the speaker say about Spark's staff?

    (A) They are familiar with different kinds of music.
    (B) They have 10 years of experience.
    (C) They are on site seven days a week.
    (D) They offer individual lessons.

79. How can the listeners receive a discount?

    (A) By calling a hotline
    (B) By visiting a facility
    (C) By going to a Web page
    (D) By e-mailing a salesperson

80. Who most likely is Gregory Smyth?

    (A) A company executive
    (B) A government official
    (C) A medical professional
    (D) A university professor

81. Why does the speaker say, "The city cut our funding by 30 percent"?

    (A) To request some donations
    (B) To announce a schedule change
    (C) To provide the reason for a closure
    (D) To suggest some savings methods

82. What will happen next?

    (A) A speaker will take the stage.
    (B) A fitness class will begin.
    (C) A budget will be released.
    (D) A charity drive will be discussed.

GO ON TO THE NEXT PAGE

83. What is the speaker mainly discussing?

(A) A design flaw
(B) Sales performance
(C) Advertising strategies
(D) A department expansion

84. According to the speaker, what did On Point Solutions do?

(A) Manufactured parts
(B) Managed some funding
(C) Distributed some goods
(D) Developed a campaign

85. Why will a meeting be held this afternoon?

(A) To discuss customer feedback
(B) To test a device feature
(C) To plan a new product line
(D) To review financial analyses

86. What is the main purpose of the talk?

(A) To request that employees work late
(B) To explain a store policy
(C) To inform staff about an outing
(D) To describe a task

87. What happened yesterday?

(A) A promotion ended.
(B) A misplaced item was found.
(C) An employee was hired.
(D) A storage area was organized.

88. What does the speaker imply when he says, "You've all done this before"?

(A) A mistake has been made.
(B) A procedure should be familiar.
(C) A project will be completed quickly.
(D) A change is about to be announced.

89. Who is Philip Calandra?

(A) A corporate board member
(B) A departmental manager
(C) A training instructor
(D) A computer technician

90. What does the speaker ask the listeners to do first?

(A) Pass out some brochures
(B) Sign an attendance sheet
(C) Download an employee manual
(D) Visit a Web site

91. What does the speaker recommend?

(A) Deleting an account
(B) Registering for a seminar
(C) Watching a video
(D) Completing a survey

92. Where does the speaker probably work?

(A) At a call center
(B) At an employment agency
(C) At a chemical plant
(D) At a beauty shop

93. Why does the speaker say, "The person who provided you the service is no longer working here"?

(A) To suggest more staff members need to be hired
(B) To guarantee a problem will not occur again
(C) To show some services are no longer available
(D) To recommend an appointment be rescheduled

94. What will the listener most likely receive?

(A) Financial compensation
(B) Additional training
(C) A complimentary item
(D) In-home services

Mountain Music Festival - Schedule	
Saturday	9:00 P.M. – The Early Birds 11:00 P.M. – Open Source
Sunday	7:00 P.M. – Green Wave 9:00 P.M. – The Black Hats 11:00 P.M. – Cherry Blossom

Chicago Continental Suites	
Room	**Type of bed(s)**
Master Room	1 single regular-sized bed
Deluxe Room	1 king-sized bed
Premium Room	2 regular-sized beds
Gold Room	2 king-sized beds

95. What does the speaker say about the festival?

(A) It was organized by a musician.
(B) It is a charity event.
(C) It is held every year.
(D) It was moved to a new site.

96. What did the listener most likely ask about?

(A) Equipment
(B) Accommodations
(C) Fees
(D) Transportation

97. Look at the graphic. Which band will perform first on Saturday night?

(A) Open Source
(B) Green Wave
(C) The Black Hats
(D) Cherry Blossom

98. What does the speaker say about the Chicago Restaurant Convention?

(A) It provides a good chance to market a product.
(B) It requires attendees to pay a large admission fee.
(C) It is becoming more popular each year.
(D) It attracts attendees from around the world.

99. In which field does the speaker most likely work?

(A) Hospitality
(B) Commercial real estate
(C) Appliance manufacturing
(D) Restaurant management

100. Look at the graphic. Which type of suite are employees staying in?

(A) Master Room
(B) Deluxe Room
(C) Premium Room
(D) Gold Room

This is the end of the Listening test. Turn to PART 5 in your test book.

GO ON TO THE NEXT PAGE

READING TEST

In this section, you must demonstrate your ability to read and comprehend English. You will be given a variety of texts and asked to answer questions about these texts. This section is divided into three parts and will take 75 minutes to complete.

Do not mark the answers in your test book. Use the answer sheet that is separately provided.

PART 5

Directions: In each question, you will be asked to review a statement that is missing a word or phrase. Four answer choices will be provided for each statement. Select the best answer and mark the corresponding letter (A), (B), (C), or (D) on the answer sheet.

PART 5 권장 풀이 시간 11분

101. MYK Inc. ------- opposed the government's plan to regulate the opening hours of restaurants and cafés.

(A) strongest
(B) stronger
(C) strength
(D) strongly

102. No one ------- the manager can deactivate the store's alarm system.

(A) within
(B) except
(C) across
(D) since

103. The researchers experienced some minor difficulties with the new program, but ------- were able to complete their projects.

(A) most
(B) no
(C) each
(D) another

104. Staff members are required to obtain ------- before ordering additional office supplies.

(A) distribution
(B) confession
(C) situation
(D) permission

105. Investors complained that ------- could not access information about the company's financial status.

(A) they
(B) their
(C) them
(D) themselves

106. Parker and Dean is the only local law firm ------- attorneys deal with both civil and criminal legal cases.

(A) what
(B) whose
(C) whom
(D) which

107. The patient asked Dr. Marple for a ------- to an eye specialist.

(A) referral
(B) refers
(C) refer
(D) referred

108. With its spectacular scenery and mild climate, Santa Rosa is a very ------- location for a resort.

(A) contributing
(B) promising
(C) proposing
(D) collecting

109. Southwest College ------- degrees in a wide variety of fields, from engineering to philosophy.

(A) grants
(B) will be granted
(C) granting
(D) is granted

110. Please submit the expense report to the accounting department ------- meeting with Ms. Thompson.

(A) before
(B) around
(C) in front of
(D) along

111. The prolonged drought caused the water level in the reservoir to fall ------- than it ever had before.

(A) low
(B) lower
(C) lowly
(D) lowest

112. Peter Lee spent the past year ------- searching for new ways to market his software to young consumers.

(A) continually
(B) continuous
(C) continue
(D) continual

113. The main role of the department supervisor is to ------- employees toward achieving the company's stated goals.

(A) adopt
(B) guide
(C) initiate
(D) establish

114. Please note that applicants will be notified of the company's decision ------- approximately two weeks.

(A) at
(B) to
(C) in
(D) on

115. As you requested, your Web site's design will be ------- to include brighter colors and larger images.

(A) partnered
(B) practiced
(C) altered
(D) relieved

116. Perot Petrochemicals signed a contract ------- oil and natural gas to the utility company.

(A) supply
(B) supplied
(C) to supply
(D) be supplied

117. Our latest television's product manual ------- to print by the end of next week.

(A) is ready
(B) will be ready
(C) has been ready
(D) was being ready

118. We will ------- send marketing team members to our stores to assist with promotional events.

(A) periodically
(B) absently
(C) mistakenly
(D) formerly

119. At the campaign event, the politician was busy meeting local citizens and ------- her policies.

(A) explain
(B) is explained
(C) explaining
(D) to explain

120. All fees must be received no more than one month ------- a bill has been issued for a course.

(A) even if
(B) over
(C) after
(D) soon

GO ON TO THE NEXT PAGE

121. The city council is relocating bus stops throughout the region to make them more ------- to local residents.

(A) increased
(B) adverse
(C) constructive
(D) accessible

122. The keynote speaker at the Detroit Accounting Convention discussed ------- the new tax regulations would affect the automobile industry.

(A) who
(B) whatever
(C) then
(D) how

123. ------- animals is prohibited in all of the country's national parks and conservation areas.

(A) Feed
(B) Fed
(C) Feeding
(D) Feeds

124. Factories constructed near residential areas must comply ------- strict environmental rules.

(A) into
(B) for
(C) on
(D) with

125. The company ------- the new Italian restaurant is known for its high-quality work.

(A) built
(B) build
(C) building
(D) builds

126. Once the financial assessment is -------, it will be sent to the legal department at Newfield Electronics.

(A) nominated
(B) consumed
(C) finalized
(D) misplaced

127. ------- the merger between Corus Corporation and Overland Resources is expected to take government officials several weeks.

(A) Approve
(B) Approved
(C) Approving
(D) Approval

128. The renovations of the Portman Building will be carried out on the weekend to ------- their effect on office operations.

(A) subtract
(B) minimize
(C) disturb
(D) consider

129. Record low temperatures were reported ------- the country during the severe winter storm.

(A) across
(B) under
(C) upon
(D) wide

130. Although Steven Harris has published books on a variety of topics, his ------- focus is European history.

(A) main
(B) cooperative
(C) convenient
(D) previous

Directions: In this part, you will be asked to read four English texts. Each text is missing a word, phrase, or sentence. Select the answer choice that correctly completes the text and mark the corresponding letter (A), (B), (C), or (D) on the answer sheet.

PART 6 권장 풀이 시간 8분

Questions 131-134 refer to the following e-mail.

To: Linda Shute <lshute@plustech.com>
From: Stanley Robinson <srobinson@midwayexhibitions.com>
Subject: Office Supplies Trade Show
Date: April 23

Hello Ms. Shute,

I am writing to inform you that ------- a recent cancellation, we have room for one more
131.
exhibition booth at our Office Supplies Trade Show. I recall how disappointed you were

about missing last month's application deadline, but you now have a second chance to

register. However, you must indicate your interest as quickly as possible. You ------- to pay
132.
a fee of $250 to participate. -------.
133.
I strongly encourage you to participate. This is an event ------- a growing following over the
134.
years and should draw a record number of visitors again this year.

Stanley Robinson
Customer Relations

131. (A) in spite of
(B) opposite
(C) due to
(D) as long as

132. (A) will need
(B) needing
(C) needed
(D) to need

133. (A) This can be done either by bank transfer or by visiting our office.
(B) The booth was widely visited throughout the show.
(C) There are several openings available for exhibitors.
(D) The deadline for registration has been adjusted significantly.

134. (A) will attract
(B) is attracting
(C) being attracted
(D) which has attracted

GO ON TO THE NEXT PAGE

Questions 135-138 refer to the following article.

A Flextime System for Edge Technologies
By Sarah Peterson

June 11—CEO of Edge Technologies Gerald McCarthy announced that his company will be adopting a flextime system. Once ------- fully puts this system into practice, all employees
            135.
will have the option of adjusting their daily work schedules. For example, a staff member who comes in at 7:00 A.M. instead of 9:00 A.M. will be able to leave two hours earlier.

-------. Everyone must continue to work an eight-hour day at the office.
 136.
The stated goal of the new system is to have all employees develop a better work-life

balance. -------, Mr. McCarthy hopes that his company will experience improved morale. The
      137.
policy ------- as a response to increased competitiveness among technology companies in
     138.
terms of employee work benefits.

---

135. (A) it
(B) they
(C) someone
(D) him

136. (A) Employees are free to make up the missing hours from home.
(B) The store will still be open on weekends.
(C) Schedules will no longer change on a weekly basis.
(D) The total hours worked each day will remain the same.

137. (A) Instead
(B) Nevertheless
(C) In this way
(D) Despite that

138. (A) is creating
(B) was created
(C) creates
(D) has created

Tree Doctor

A tree can live a long time if it is taken care of well. ------- the life of your trees, you need to
139.
give them proper care. The staff members at Tree Doctor have ------- knowledge of tree
140.
management. This is because they are all certified professionals with a great deal of

experience. Our experts can visit your property to evaluate the condition of your trees.

-------. And if you are considering planting new trees, they can advise you on which ones you
141.
plan to add ------- in your soil well. To learn more about our services and to book an
142.
appointment, visit www.treedoctor.com.

139. (A) Prolonged
(B) To prolong
(C) Prolonging
(D) Prolong

140. (A) prior
(B) clever
(C) extensive
(D) partial

141. (A) As a result, they were familiar with a variety of treatments.
(B) Certain trees have already been removed from the yard.
(C) Some fertilizers are harmful to many species.
(D) Specifically, they will check for diseased branches and roots.

142. (A) will grow
(B) are growing
(C) grew
(D) have been growing

GO ON TO THE NEXT PAGE

Questions 143-146 refer to the following e-mail.

To: Belle Rogers <brogers@smail.com>
From: Aaron Cooper <aaroncooper@moneyphase.com>
Subject: Welcome!
Date: January 31

Dear Ms. Rogers,

On behalf of our entire company, I would like to welcome you as a new -------. We are thrilled
143.
that you have chosen our company for assistance with managing your investment portfolio.

We know that ------- your finances takes time, patience, and effort. There are a wide variety
144.
of investment options to choose from, and selecting the right ones requires guidance. You

can be assured that we will provide you with expert advice.

Please let me know when it would be convenient to hold our first meeting. -------. Please
145.
either contact me at 555-1221 ------- reply to this e-mail. Once again, we welcome you and
146.
hope that our relationship will be a successful one!

Sincerely yours,

Aaron Cooper

Investment Analyst

---

143. (A) customer
(B) owner
(C) vendor
(D) student

144. (A) transferring
(B) decreasing
(C) planning
(D) canceling

145. (A) We are sure that these suggestions
will increase your profits.
(B) We appreciate the financial advice you
have e-mailed to us.
(C) We will discuss your short- and
long-term financial goals at that time.
(D) We think it is necessary to reschedule
our appointment.

146. (A) for
(B) and
(C) or
(D) but

PART 7

Directions: In this part, you will be asked to read several texts, such as advertisements, articles, instant messages, or examples of business correspondence. Each text is followed by several questions. Select the best answer and mark the corresponding letter (A), (B), (C), or (D) on your answer sheet.

PART 7 권장 풀이 시간 **54분**

Questions 147-148 refer to the following notice.

Brandenburg's Third Annual Winter Festival Ceremony will be held on December 2. Decorations will be placed along Muller Way, ice sculptures will appear along Hastings Avenue, and the ice rink at the intersection of Rossellini Drive and Peters Street will be open to skaters from 8 A.M. to 6 P.M. The main event of the night will be the lighting of the large pine tree on Sterner Way, which will take place at 10 P.M. Afterward, the Brandenburg Brass Band will play a variety of holiday songs. The lights will stay up until New Year's Day, and they will be removed the next day by employees of the city park service.

147. What is NOT a feature of the Winter Festival Ceremony?

(A) The performance of some music
(B) The decoration of Peters Street
(C) The operation of a skating rink
(D) The lighting of a tree

148. What will happen immediately after New Year's Day?

(A) Some ice sculptures will be removed.
(B) A city park will reopen.
(C) Some lights will be taken down.
(D) A ceremony will be held.

GO ON TO THE NEXT PAGE

Questions 149-150 refer to the following letter.

May 12

John Simon
772 North Avenue
Tucson, AZ 85701

Dear Mr. Simon,

Thank you for agreeing to speak at the dinner in Flagstaff organized by the Foundation for World Cultures. Everyone is excited to hear about the studies you've conducted about the ancient cultures of the Andes Mountains region. Because you're the keynote speaker at the event, you'll be giving your speech right after our organization's president, Ernesto Paramo. Following that, Will Meyer, a university student, will show a video he made about a recent trip to Colombia, and then dinner will be served. The closing speech will be given by Robert Shelling, who runs the Flagstaff Cultural Institute.

Your name has been added to our guest list, so all you need to do is show up at the door. We look forward to having you.

Sincerely,
Roberto Marquez

149. Who most likely is Mr. Simon?

(A) The head of an organization
(B) A workshop organizer
(C) A filmmaker
(D) A researcher

150. Who will precede Mr. Simon?

(A) Ernesto Paramo
(B) Will Meyer
(C) Robert Shelling
(D) Roberto Marquez

Questions 151-152 refer to the following text messages.

Tony Webb   [1:15 P.M.]
Did you hear that Dave Jonson is leaving next week?

Laura Hughes   [1:17 P.M.]
Yeah. When he and I were out for lunch earlier today, he mentioned that he had accepted an offer of a new job.

Tony Webb   [1:19 P.M.]
He's not the only one. Will the company hire more staff soon?

Laura Hughes   [1:21 P.M.]
Yeah. Human resources will interview applicants for our department next week. I've agreed to help with the training for newly hired employees.

Tony Webb   [1:21 P.M.]
Good. It's about time. It's been really hard to meet all of our marketing deadlines with so few people.

Laura Hughes   [1:22 P.M.]
I know. Everyone on my staff has been worried about that. Anyway, I'll let you know if I hear more.

151. What is NOT true about Ms. Hughes?

(A) She recently went to eat with a colleague.
(B) She will prepare new employees for a job.
(C) She was offered a position at another company.
(D) She is a member of the marketing department.

152. At 1:19 P.M., what does Mr. Webb most likely mean when he writes, "He's not the only one"?

(A) A task will be assigned to someone else.
(B) A training document must be updated.
(C) Several applicants have been selected.
(D) Other team members have resigned.

GO ON TO THE NEXT PAGE

Questions 153-154 refer to the following e-mail.

TO: Mitchell O'Connor <moconnor@fastmail.com>
FROM: Playback Streaming <support@playback.com>
SUBJECT: *Secrets of Paris*
DATE: September 19

Dear Mr. O'Connor,

Thank you for using Playback Streaming, the number one streaming service for media content. Our records indicate that you recently watched the documentary *Secrets of Paris*, directed by Sam Marshall and first aired on the HistoryNow Channel. We always encourage our customers to write reviews of what they've watched. To do this, simply click the button beneath the video you want to comment on. As a special incentive, those who review 100 items or more are awarded the status of "premium user," making them eligible to receive $50 worth of complimentary movies and TV shows.

Once again, thank you for using our service.

Sincerely,

Playback Streaming Customer Support

153. What is indicated about *Secrets of Paris*?
  (A) It is based on a famous book.
  (B) It received an award for best director.
  (C) It was first shown on a history channel.
  (D) It is available to buy at an additional cost.

154. What can customers receive if they write 100 reviews?
  (A) A DVD copy of a movie
  (B) Extra membership points
  (C) A yearlong subscription
  (D) Free media content

EXPLORE THE BRINKLEY SCIENCE CENTER

You don't need an excuse to visit the Brinkley Science Center, a three-story museum dedicated to sharing the wonders of science with the public. At our facility, you can view exhibits on everything from sound waves and tornadoes to soil and distant planets. So, bring all of your friends and family members!

MUSEUM HOURS
Tuesday-Friday: 9 A.M. to 5 P.M.
Saturday-Sunday: 9 A.M. to 6 P.M.
Closed on Mondays

TICKET PRICES
$10 general admission
$8 for students
$6 for people over 65 years old
Free admission for students attending Brinkley College
Free admission for children under age six
On the first Tuesday of every month, all residents of Brinkley are admitted for free. Proof of residence required.

DIRECTIONS
By car: From Interstate 20, take Exit 60 onto Grant Road. Then, turn left onto Lessing Way. The center will be on your left.
By subway: From Exit 2 of Havel Street Station, turn right onto Wallace Avenue. Continue for 100 meters and then turn right onto Lessing Way. The center will be on your right.
By bus: Buses 80 and 125 both stop right outside the center.

---

155. What is stated about the Brinkley Science Center?

(A) It has a special children's area.
(B) It attracts lots of international visitors.
(C) It has a weather-related exhibit.
(D) It is closed on holidays.

156. Who is never charged for admission?

(A) Senior citizens
(B) Parents of children under age six
(C) Students at Brinkley College
(D) Residents of Brinkley

157. Where is the Brinkley Science Center most likely located?

(A) On Grant Road
(B) On Havel Street
(C) On Wallace Avenue
(D) On Lessing Way

GO ON TO THE NEXT PAGE

Questions 158-160 refer to the following job advertisement.

Heimart Seeking Full-time Store Associate

Heimart is a leading European retailer that specializes in offering home goods and appliances at affordable prices. — [1] —. After the success of our first American stores in New York, Chicago, and Los Angeles, we are looking to fill positions at new locations in other major US cities.

As a store associate, you will be responsible for carrying out routine tasks, such as unloading new stock, filling shelves, and keeping the store clean and orderly at all times. — [2] —. Depending on performance, opportunities to try other roles may be offered. You could learn how to handle the register, work in customer service, and more. — [3] —.

Applicants must be 21 or older and have previous experience in a similar role. Employees should be willing to work on a flexible schedule. — [4] —. Successful candidates will receive a competitive hourly wage, health benefits, regular bonuses, and continuous job training.

To apply, e-mail jobs@heimart.com.

158. What is stated about Heimart?

(A) It is launching its first American store.
(B) It carries a variety of office furniture.
(C) It is offering a home delivery service.
(D) It has job openings in several cities.

159. What is a responsibility of the store associate?

(A) Arranging schedules
(B) Finding product suppliers
(C) Maintaining cleanliness
(D) Delivering orders

160. In which of the positions marked [1], [2], [3], and [4] does the following sentence best belong?

"This includes early morning and night shifts on occasion."

(A) [1]
(B) [2]
(C) [3]
(D) [4]

To: All Brumfield Co. employees
From: Fred Sears, human resources manager
Date: May 10
Subject: Renovations

As you may be aware, Brumfield Co. will be undergoing a month-long renovation of its fourth floor starting next week. This creates a space problem for the marketing department employees currently working there. We initially looked into seating them in various available workstations on the other floors of the building. However, after some consideration, we concluded that this was not a good idea. Our marketers are required to do a lot of speaking over the telephone, so arranging them in this way would be bothersome to other department members whose jobs require silence.

Therefore, we have decided to create a temporary work area for the team in the main conference room on the second floor of the building. The IT department will set up the necessary computers and printers there tomorrow. The smaller meeting room on the third floor next to the employee break room will be the only one available for members of other departments to use for the next month or so.

Thank you.

161. What is mentioned about Brumfield Co.?

(A) It is expanding its marketing team.
(B) It will remodel its office.
(C) It will relocate its IT department.
(D) It is upgrading its computers.

162. Why will marketing staff not be spread out over several floors?

(A) They must work together on most assignments.
(B) They are preparing an important presentation.
(C) They would be disruptive to other workers.
(D) They need to discuss projects with one another.

163. What can be inferred about the main conference room?

(A) It will be unavailable to some staff members.
(B) It is located next to the printer room.
(C) It was refurbished last month.
(D) It has been used as an employee lounge.

GO ON TO THE NEXT PAGE

Questions 164-167 refer to the following text message chain.

Carol Medina	[11:41 A.M.]	I'm planning the company's annual year-end party. I could really use some help.
Annie Sanders	[11:42 A.M.]	I'd be happy to lend a hand. What would you like me to do?
Carol Medina	[11:43 A.M.]	I still haven't found a place to hold the party. Could you look for a suitable banquet hall? We need to book one for December 22.
Annie Sanders	[11:43 A.M.]	Sure. How many people will be attending this year?
Carol Medina	[11:44 A.M.]	It's hard to say. Each employee is allowed to invite a guest. So, we should contact all of the employees and ask them whether they intend to bring someone to the party.
Vincent Bryce	[11:45 A.M.]	I can do that now. I'll just send an e-mail to everyone in the company. I'll let both of you know the number of guests to expect by lunch tomorrow.
Annie Sanders	[11:46 A.M.]	Perfect. What about food? Would you like me to look for catering companies as well?
Carol Medina	[11:47 A.M.]	No need. Bellwood Fine Foods has excellent menu options and reasonable prices. We've used them often over the past six years.

164. Why did Ms. Medina contact her coworkers?

(A) To announce an upcoming event
(B) To ask for advice on food
(C) To request assistance with a task
(D) To express interest in a project

165. What does Ms. Sanders agree to do?

(A) Confirm attendance
(B) Contact a caterer
(C) Find a venue
(D) Send invitations

166. At 11:47 A.M., what does Ms. Medina most likely mean when she writes, "No need"?

(A) She will ask about changing a menu.
(B) She is aware of the number of guests.
(C) She has already checked a hall's availability.
(D) She will use a particular catering company.

167. What is suggested about Bellwood Fine Foods?

(A) It specializes in parties for small groups.
(B) It has been in business for several years.
(C) It offers a limited number of menu options.
(D) It recently reduced its prices.

Construction News

East Parsons, June 3—At a press conference today, Transportation Commissioner Claudia Rittora announced that a new subway line—the Green Line—will be undergoing construction beginning in September. The line will provide service to the suburban neighborhoods of Peterson and Forest Falls. It will include stops at Pew Street, Jackson Avenue, and Crispin Boulevard, after which it will merge with the Red Line that runs downtown. — [1] —.

Ms. Rittora said that the decision to build a subway line in the suburbs was made in response to the many complaints that have been made by people who must commute to the city. — [2] —. There are only a few buses that go to the outlying neighborhoods, and they all run at infrequent intervals. There used to be a tram line that extended to the outer suburbs, with stops along Jackson Avenue and Wellford Street. However, it was very costly to operate, and not many people used it. — [3] —.

The new subway line should be more successful because the population of the suburban areas has greatly increased. — [4] —. The Green Line will operate 24 hours a day, seven days a week, and trains will reach stations every 10 minutes. Those wishing to learn more can go to www. eastparsonscity.gov.

168. The word "merge" in paragraph 1, line 5, is closest in meaning to

(A) join
(B) pile
(C) return
(D) trade

169. Why will the new subway line be constructed?

(A) To reduce commuting times for people living downtown
(B) To address some dissatisfaction from outlying areas
(C) To accommodate residents in a newly built community
(D) To compensate for the cancellation of bus services

170. What is stated about the tram line?

(A) It was operational 24 hours per day.
(B) It was owned by a private company.
(C) It was expensive to build.
(D) It was used by few people.

171. In which of the positions marked [1], [2], [3], and [4] does the following sentence best belong?

"As a result, the city decided to end this service 20 years ago."

(A) [1]
(B) [2]
(C) [3]
(D) [4]

GO ON TO THE NEXT PAGE

Questions 172-175 refer to the following form.

THE NORTHWEST LEDGER

NAME: Mohammed Abbar
SUBSCRIPTION: ■ Daily   □ Weekly   □ Semiweekly
ADDRESS: 155 Winateka Lane, Tacoma, WA 98401

I WOULD LIKE TO:
□ Change my subscription   ■ Cancel my subscription

IF CHANGING YOUR SUBSCRIPTION, PLEASE SELECT A PLAN:
□ Daily   □ Weekly   □ Semiweekly

IF CANCELING, PLEASE PROVIDE A REASON:
□ I am moving to a different address.
□ I cannot afford the subscription fee.
□ I am dissatisfied with the quality of the content.
■ Other

IF OTHER, PLEASE SPECIFY:

I used to rely on *The Northwest Ledger* for my daily local news. But in recent years, I have been getting news from TacomaToday.com and other Web sites instead. In addition, I'm busier than before, so I'm less likely to sit down and read a large newspaper.

SUGGESTIONS FOR IMPROVING *THE NORTHWEST LEDGER*:

Your paper mostly provides coverage of national sports leagues. I think there should be more stories devoted to our local league baseball and hockey teams. There should also be more restaurant reviews.

Once you submit this form, your service will be changed or discontinued. To confirm that this has been done, you will receive a letter at the address you have indicated above. If you do not receive this letter, please contact us at subscriptions@northwestledger.com.

172. Why did Mr. Abbar fill out the form?

(A) To sign up for a weekly mailing
(B) To stop getting a newspaper
(C) To change his mailing address
(D) To complain about some articles

173. What can be inferred about Mr. Abbar?

(A) He recently moved to Tacoma.
(B) He enjoys reading fiction publications.
(C) He wants to renew a subscription.
(D) He prefers online news sources.

174. What is implied about *The Northwest Ledger*?

(A) It does not have a reviews section.
(B) It has limited local sports sections.
(C) It is not published on a daily basis.
(D) It has an online version.

175. What will Mr. Abbar most likely receive?

(A) A confirmation letter
(B) A gift card
(C) A full refund
(D) A complimentary book

GO ON TO THE NEXT PAGE

Questions 176-180 refer to the following e-mail and product description.

TO: Angelica Lucci <angelica@craincameras.com>
FROM: Brad Farley <brad@craincameras.com>
SUBJECT: Product Descriptions
DATE: January 28

Dear Angelica,

I've been assigned to write our new Selector digital camera's publicity materials—specifically, the text that will appear next to photographs of the product on our online shopping site. However, I'm having a little trouble with certain aspects of this assignment. I'd like to focus on the features of this camera that were not included in our previous model, the ProViewer. Since you're the product manager for both camera models, could you help me with this? For example, I want to know if the ProViewer included face-detection technology. Also, did it have a four-gigabyte storage capacity? If not, I will highlight these features in the Selector's product description. I'm also a little confused about the new video feature for the Selector. Can you tell me a bit more about that? Please let me know the answers to my questions when you have a moment. Thanks!

Best Regards,

Brad Farley

THE NEW SELECTOR DIGITAL CAMERA FROM CRAIN CAMERAS

Perfect for professional and amateur photographers alike, the new Selector camera is outstanding in every way. As with our earlier models, the Selector can store up to four gigabytes of photographs and be used in a variety of lighting conditions. However, we've added **many new features** to make it more versatile, accessible, and sophisticated.

- The Selector has **face-detection technology** that automatically adjusts the focus to produce the clearest images of human faces.
- We've upgraded the battery life so that the Selector can **last for up to 20 hours** without needing to be recharged.
- The Selector can **shoot videos of up to 30 minutes in length**. Because these videos have a high resolution, they are very detailed. They can also be converted into various formats using almost any video-editing software.

Moreover, all units come with a foldout tripod on which the camera can be mounted. The tripod is adjustable, allowing you to shoot from both low and high angles.

176. Why did Mr. Farley write the e-mail?

(A) To ask for information about a product
(B) To follow up on a customer inquiry
(C) To request that a document be proofread
(D) To suggest a marketing strategy

177. In the product description, the word "outstanding" in paragraph 1, line 1, is closest in meaning to

(A) obvious
(B) overdue
(C) superior
(D) meaningful

178. What is suggested about the ProViewer?

(A) It can store up to four gigabytes of data.
(B) It is highly popular among professionals.
(C) It was released about one year ago.
(D) It automatically focuses on objects.

179. What does the product description say about the Selector's video feature?

(A) It can be added for an extra charge.
(B) It requires a certain software program.
(C) It sends footage to an online account.
(D) It allows for filming of half-hour videos.

180. According to the product description, what does the Selector come with?

(A) An extra battery
(B) An adjustable tripod
(C) A carrying case
(D) A selection of lenses

GO ON TO THE NEXT PAGE

NOTICE to Residents of West Carver

This week, several streets will be closed for the three-day Puerto Rican Culture Festival:

- **The 100 to 800 blocks of Madeline Street** will be closed **from 8 A.M. to 12 P.M. on Friday, July 2,** for a Puerto Rican parade with dancers and a marching band.

- **The 200 to 500 blocks of MacDunn Avenue** will be closed **from 11 A.M. to 5 P.M. on Saturday, July 3,** for a performance of traditional music.

- **The 300 to 600 blocks of Harrison Street** will be closed **from 2 P.M. to 10 P.M. on Sunday, July 4,** for a fun and games day featuring a waterslide and other carnival rides.

More activities, including singing, dancing, and a raffle for gifts, will be held in **Carver Park on July 3 and 4 between 9 A.M. and 11 P.M.**

If you have any disabilities that make it difficult to walk around town, we encourage you to contact a government representative at services@sanmiguel.gov. Arrangements will be made to bring you to the event that you are interested in.

TO: Lucy Garcia <lgarcia@puertoricanfestival.com>
FROM: Michael Gomez <mgomez@fastmail.com>
SUBJECT: Some questions
DATE: July 3

Dear Ms. Garcia,

My name is Michael Gomez, and I'm a resident of the West Carver neighborhood. Yesterday, I heard a large parade passing down the street my house is situated on and searched online to find out what it was. As I am a former resident of Puerto Rico, I'm interested in helping local residents celebrate my heritage. Are you still accepting volunteers? I can put up posters around the neighborhood, guide attendees to certain events, or set up tents for activities. I also have a truck, so I can pick up and drop off supplies. Please let me know if there's any way I can assist with this event.

I look forward to hearing from you.

Sincerely,

Michael Gomez

181. What is NOT an attraction listed on the notice?

(A) A musical performance
(B) A water ride
(C) A prize drawing
(D) A food tasting event

182. When should residents contact a government official?

(A) When they cannot purchase a ticket
(B) When they cannot get to a location on foot
(C) When they want to learn more about a party
(D) When they want to see videos of an event

183. What is indicated about Mr. Gomez?

(A) He has given a performance before.
(B) His family members are visiting West Carver.
(C) His house is located on Madeline Street.
(D) He will move to a new neighborhood.

184. Why does Mr. Gomez want to volunteer at the festival?

(A) He previously lived in Puerto Rico.
(B) He has some extra decorations in storage.
(C) He enjoys cooking traditional cuisine.
(D) He wants to work for a nonprofit organization.

185. What does Mr. Gomez offer to do?

(A) Transport items in his vehicle
(B) Post advertisements online
(C) Block off certain streets
(D) Clean up trash in a park

GO ON TO THE NEXT PAGE

Opal Museum of Art
Visitor Notice

Visitors to the Opal Museum of Art have three parking options: the Fairfield Lot, the Morrison Lot, and the Gosling Garage. The Morrison Lot offers the closest access to the museum's front entrance, while the Gosling Garage is nearest to our event hall.

Make sure to take a parking ticket from an automated machine. Fees are payable by credit card or cash at one of these machines upon leaving. To receive a discount as a museum member, scan your Opal Museum of Art membership card at a machine in the Gosling Garage.

Period	Non-member Fee	Member Fee
Less than 1 hour	$10	$8
1-2 hours	$12	$10
2-3 hours	$14	$12
3-4 hours	$16	$14
4 or more hours	$20	$18

For any inquiries, please call the museum's administrative office at 555-6698.

Ms. Kerry Fulton,
As a longtime member of the **Opal Museum of Art**
You are formally invited to
Dinner with the Artist
A quarterly event hosted at **Crystal Hall**
On Friday, June 5, 5-10 P.M.

This spring, our museum will hold a five-hour dinner event introducing internationally acclaimed sculptor Alexandra Galanos and her latest exhibit, *Crossing the Road*, which will be unveiled in the Alabaster Wing on June 12. Dinner will be brought out promptly at 8 P.M., followed by a speech from Ms. Galanos and then announcements from museum director Darrell Finn.

We hope that you have an enjoyable time at this event. Thank you for your continued support of the museum.

June 12

Darrell Finn
Opal Museum of Art, Director's Office
400 Morrison Avenue
Trenton, NJ 08618

Dear Mr. Finn,

I want to commend you on the success of last week's event. Your speech was inspiring and made me proud to be a member of your organization.

Also, I want to mention that I attended the opening of Ms. Galanos's exhibit today. I was impressed with not only the sculptural pieces but also the renovations that were made in the area where the exhibition was held.

Thank you, and I look forward to future museum events.

Sincerely,

Kerry Fulton

186. What is the purpose of the information?

(A) To present options for parking
(B) To announce some new charges
(C) To give some safety reminders
(D) To promote museum memberships

187. What is indicated about Gosling Garage?

(A) It is the most expensive parking option.
(B) It has a device for scanning cards.
(C) It is closest to the museum's entrance.
(D) It was recently closed for a city event.

188. What is mentioned about Ms. Galanos?

(A) She has visited the Opal Museum of Art before.
(B) She will conduct some classes on sculpture.
(C) She has signed a contract with Mr. Finn.
(D) She will make some remarks at a gathering.

189. How much did Ms. Fulton pay for parking if she stayed for the entire event?

(A) $10
(B) $14
(C) $18
(D) $20

190. According to the letter, what was Ms. Fulton impressed with on June 12?

(A) Ms. Galanos's informative lecture
(B) The repainted Crystal Hall
(C) Mr. Finn's tour of the facility
(D) The improved Alabaster Wing

GO ON TO THE NEXT PAGE

Questions 191-195 refer to the following Web page, e-mail, and review.

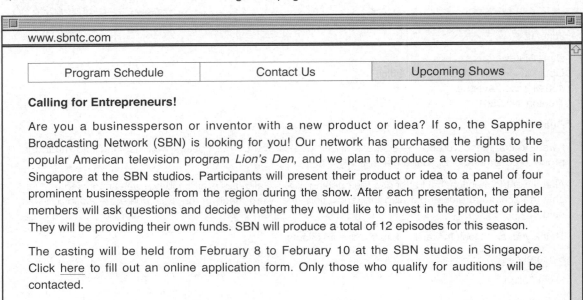

www.sbntc.com

| Program Schedule | Contact Us | Upcoming Shows |

Calling for Entrepreneurs!

Are you a businessperson or inventor with a new product or idea? If so, the Sapphire Broadcasting Network (SBN) is looking for you! Our network has purchased the rights to the popular American television program *Lion's Den*, and we plan to produce a version based in Singapore at the SBN studios. Participants will present their product or idea to a panel of four prominent businesspeople from the region during the show. After each presentation, the panel members will ask questions and decide whether they would like to invest in the product or idea. They will be providing their own funds. SBN will produce a total of 12 episodes for this season.

The casting will be held from February 8 to February 10 at the SBN studios in Singapore. Click here to fill out an online application form. Only those who qualify for auditions will be contacted.

TO   Susan Tsang <susantsang@rubydevelopments.com>
FROM   Dennis Ping <dping@sbntc.com>
SUBJECT *Lion's Den Asia*
DATE   January 29

Dear Ms. Tsang,

I am so pleased that you are interested in appearing on our program as an investor. We have already hired company presidents Chanchai Akkarat and Deepa Sidhu for the show. Mi-young Choi, the CEO of Trinity Manufacturing, is considering taking the fourth spot but still has to see if her work schedule can be adjusted to join the show.

Production starts at the beginning of April, but I would like to meet with you and the other members of our panel before then to discuss your responsibilities in more detail. Therefore, I will require you to attend a meeting with us at our downtown Singapore office on March 28.

Thanks so much again for agreeing to be part of our program!

Regards,

Dennis Ping
Producer, *Lion's Den Asia*

> http://www.couchtvreviewer.com/realitytv/lionsdenasia/
>
> **TELEVISION PROGRAM:** *Lion's Den Asia* **NETWORK:** SBN
> **BROADCAST TIME:** 8 P.M. on Wednesdays **REVIEWER:** Abdul Hassan
>
> I am a big fan of the original *Lion's Den* show. So, when I heard an Asian edition was being produced, I was very excited. I have watched the first six episodes of the show, and they have not disappointed me. Host Rajiv Sunder is very charming, and all the panel members are really interesting. Mi-young Choi is especially clever, often asking presenters unexpected questions. And Chanchai Akkarat adds some humor to the otherwise serious program. I also appreciate that Susan Tsang makes frequent offers to the show's entrepreneur participants. In contrast, I'm a bit worried that panel member Deepa Sidhu has only offered to be an investor for three of the entrepreneurs so far. I think she should be more open to investing her money. But overall, I find this version of the show to be as satisfying as the American one.

191. What is NOT true about *Lion's Den*?

(A) It features regional entrepreneurs.
(B) It was first broadcast in Singapore.
(C) It holds auditions for show participants.
(D) It involves presentations by contestants.

192. Why did Mr. Ping arrange a meeting for March 28?

(A) To secure approval for some ideas
(B) To negotiate compensation for presenters
(C) To introduce investors to a production team
(D) To discuss the obligations of panel members

193. What did Ms. Choi probably do?

(A) Made schedule changes to appear on a show
(B) Interviewed some businesspeople for panel positions
(C) Negotiated the purchase of a local television network
(D) Partnered with an associate in a manufacturing firm

194. What is indicated about Mr. Hassan?

(A) He was contacted by e-mail for an audition.
(B) He has not seen half of the episodes of *Lion's Den Asia*.
(C) He thinks *Lion's Den Asia* was less entertaining than the original.
(D) He personally met with one of participating investors before.

195. Which panel member does Mr. Hassan express concern about?

(A) Chanchai Akkarat
(B) Susan Tsang
(C) Mi-young Choi
(D) Deepa Sidhu

GO ON TO THE NEXT PAGE

The Richmond Sun

Healthy Fast Food is On Its Way

Fredericksburg, July 9—The country's first organic fast food restaurant, Fresh Goods, opens next month on Interstate 95. Proprietor Libby Hawkins hopes it will be the first of several hundred to serve quick, healthy, and affordable meals to travelers.

Ms. Hawkins has been a supporter of organic products since she started running her own farm 20 years ago. Today, her farm is one of Virginia's biggest producers of milk and cheese. A frequent traveler herself, she decided to open Fresh Goods when she noticed the lack of healthy dishes sold at rest stops.

Currently, she is working on establishing a network of farms that will supply organic ingredients for Fresh Goods. Participating farmers can expect to receive organic certification and fair prices for their products. However, to ensure the freshness of ingredients, farms that will be part of this network can be no farther than 50 miles from the restaurant.

Fourth Annual Culpeper Harvest Festival
Friday, September 8, to Sunday, September 10

SEPTEMBER 8: DISCUSSION
5 P.M. • Spotswood Inn Coffeehouse, 215 Davis Street
With Emmett Ashby, Director for the Virginia Food Cooperative (VFC)
More details at www.vfc.org

SEPTEMBER 9: FARM TOURS
11 A.M. - 1 P.M. • Westover Farms, 15384 Mill Road
1 - 3 P.M. • Whisper Hill Field, 899 Yowell Drive
3 - 5 P.M. • Salt Cedar Hatchery, 11452 Maple Lane

SEPTEMBER 10: FARMER'S MARKET
Followed by the Great Meal, a community meal prepared with locally grown ingredients
Anyone can bring dishes to share (optional)
2 - 4:30 P.M. • Farmer's Market
5 P.M. • Great Meal
Both the Farmer's Market and the Great Meal will be held
at Kingsbrook Park, 308 Chandler Street

To	Marvin Cooper <m.cooper@harrisonburg.net>
From	Libby Hawkins <l.hawkins@freshgoods.com>
Subject	Meeting
Date	August 29

Dear Mr. Cooper,

Thank you for recently becoming a member of my network of farms and deciding to supply chicken for my restaurant. Also, regarding the inquiry you e-mailed me about, I would be happy to meet with you at the upcoming Culpeper Harvest Festival. I won't be able to join the tour of your farm, the Salt Cedar Hatchery, but I can spare some time the following day before the Great Meal to stop by your booth at the Farmer's Market. If there is a problem, you can call me at 555-2498. Thanks, and I'll see you soon!

Sincerely,
Libby Hawkins

196. What is stated about Ms. Hawkins's farm?

(A) It is expected to expand next year.
(B) It is located near Interstate 95.
(C) It produces dairy products.
(D) It supplies restaurants nationwide.

197. What caused Ms. Hawkins to open her restaurant?

(A) An article published in a food industry magazine
(B) The unavailability of healthy food options at some locations
(C) A recommendation from one of her former colleagues
(D) The need to find a market for her products

198. What is true about the Culpeper Harvest Festival?

(A) It is usually held twice a year.
(B) It will last for one week.
(C) It is sponsored by the government.
(D) It will feature local food.

199. Where does Ms. Hawkins want to meet Mr. Cooper?

(A) At the Spotswood Inn
(B) At Kingsbrook Park
(C) At Salt Cedar Hatchery
(D) At Westover Farms

200. What can be inferred about Mr. Cooper?

(A) He will serve some dishes at the Great Meal.
(B) His facility has been operating for more than 10 years.
(C) He is participating in a festival for the first time.
(D) His farm is within 50 miles of Fresh Goods.

This is the end of the test. You may review Parts 5, 6, and 7 if you finish the test early.

점수 환산표 p.244 / 정답·해석·해설 [책 속의 책] p.85

▌다음 페이지에 있는 Review 체크리스트에 따라 틀린 문제를 다시 점검해보세요.

Review 체크리스트

TEST 3를 푼 다음, 아래 체크리스트에 따라 틀린 문제를 리뷰하고 박스에 완료 여부를 표시하세요.
만약 시험까지 얼마 남지 않았다면, 초록색으로 표시된 항목이라도 꼭 확인하세요.

☐ 틀린 문제의 경우, 다시 풀어봤다.

☐ 틀린 문제의 경우, 스크립트/해석을 확인하며 지문/문제의 내용을 정확하게 파악했다.

☐ 해설을 통해 각 문제의 정답과 오답의 근거가 무엇인지 정확하게 파악했다.

☐ Part 1과 Part 2에서 틀린 문제의 경우, 선택한 오답의 유형이 무엇이었는지 확인하고 같은
  함정에 빠지지 않도록 정리해두었다.

☐ Part 3와 Part 4의 각 문제에서 사용된 패러프레이징을 확인했다.

☐ Part 5와 Part 6의 경우, 틀린 문제에서 사용된 문법 포인트 또는 정답 및 오답 어휘를 정리
  했다.

☐ Part 6의 알맞은 문장 고르기 문제의 경우, 지문 전체를 정확하게 해석하며 전체 글의 흐름
  과 빈칸 주변 문맥을 정확하게 파악하는 연습을 했다.

☐ Part 7에서 질문과 보기의 키워드를 찾아 표시하며 지문에서 정답의 근거가 되는 문장이나
  구절을 찾아보고, 문제에서 사용된 패러프레이징을 확인했다.

☐ Part 1~Part 4는 받아쓰기 & 쉐도잉 워크북을 활용하여, TEST에 수록된 핵심 문장을 받아
  쓰고 따라 읽으며 복습했다.

☐ Part 1~Part 7은 단어암기자료를 활용하여, TEST에 수록된 핵심 어휘와 표현을 암기했다.

많은 양의 문제를 푸는 것도 중요하지만, 틀린 문제를 제대로 리뷰하는 것도 중요합니다.
틀린 문제를 한 번 더 꼼꼼히 리뷰한다면, 빠른 시간 내에 효과적으로 목표 점수를 달성할 수 있습니다.

한 권으로 끝내는
해커스 토익 실전 LC+RC 1

TEST 4

LISTENING TEST

Part 1
Part 2
Part 3
Part 4

READING TEST

Part 5
Part 6
Part 7

Review 체크리스트

잠깐! 테스트 전 아래 사항을 꼭 확인하세요.

휴대전화의 전원을 끄셨나요? 예 □
Answer Sheet(p.253), 연필, 지우개, 시계를 준비하셨나요? 예 □
Listening MP3를 들을 준비가 되셨나요? 예 □

모든 준비가 완료되었으면 목표 점수를 떠올린 후 테스트를 시작합니다.
테스트를 마친 후, Review 체크리스트(p.194)를 보며 자신이 틀린 문제를 반드시 복습합니다.

🎧 TEST 4.mp3
실전용·복습용 문제풀이 MP3 무료 다운로드 및 스트리밍 바로듣기 (HackersIngang.com)
* 실제 시험장의 소음까지 재현해 낸 고사장 소음/매미 버전 MP3, 영국식·호주식 발음 집중 MP3, 고속 버전 MP3까지 구매
  하면 실전에 더욱 완벽히 대비할 수 있습니다.

무료MP3 바로듣기

LISTENING TEST

In this section, you must demonstrate your ability to understand spoken English. This section is divided into four parts and will take approximately 45 minutes to complete. Do not mark the answers in your test book. Use the answer sheet that is provided separately.

PART 1

Directions: For each question, you will listen to four short statements about a picture in your test book. These statements will not be printed and will only be spoken one time. Select the statement that best describes what is happening in the picture and mark the corresponding letter (A), (B), (C), or (D) on the answer sheet.

Sample Answer
Ⓐ ● Ⓒ Ⓓ

The statement that best describes the picture is (B), "The man is sitting at the desk." So, you should mark letter (B) on the answer sheet.

1.

2.

GO ON TO THE NEXT PAGE →

3.

4.

5.

6.

GO ON TO THE NEXT PAGE ➡

PART 2

Directions: For each question, you will listen to a statement or question followed by three possible responses spoken in English. They will not be printed and will only be spoken one time. Select the best response and mark the corresponding letter (A), (B), or (C) on your answer sheet.

7. Mark your answer on your answer sheet.

8. Mark your answer on your answer sheet.

9. Mark your answer on your answer sheet.

10. Mark your answer on your answer sheet.

11. Mark your answer on your answer sheet.

12. Mark your answer on your answer sheet.

13. Mark your answer on your answer sheet.

14. Mark your answer on your answer sheet.

15. Mark your answer on your answer sheet.

16. Mark your answer on your answer sheet.

17. Mark your answer on your answer sheet.

18. Mark your answer on your answer sheet.

19. Mark your answer on your answer sheet.

20. Mark your answer on your answer sheet.

21. Mark your answer on your answer sheet.

22. Mark your answer on your answer sheet.

23. Mark your answer on your answer sheet.

24. Mark your answer on your answer sheet.

25. Mark your answer on your answer sheet.

26. Mark your answer on your answer sheet.

27. Mark your answer on your answer sheet.

28. Mark your answer on your answer sheet.

29. Mark your answer on your answer sheet.

30. Mark your answer on your answer sheet.

31. Mark your answer on your answer sheet.

PART 3

Directions: In this part, you will listen to several conversations between two or more speakers. These conversations will not be printed and will only be spoken one time. For each conversation, you will be asked to answer three questions. Select the best response and mark the corresponding letter (A), (B), (C), or (D) on your answer sheet.

32. Who most likely is the man?

(A) A cashier
(B) A receptionist
(C) A pharmacist
(D) A doctor

33. What does the man offer to do?

(A) Write a note
(B) Send a text message
(C) Prescribe a medicine
(D) Postpone an appointment

34. What is mentioned about the woman?

(A) She expects to arrive late.
(B) She hurt her back last month.
(C) Her condition has improved.
(D) Her payment was not received.

35. Where does the man most likely work?

(A) At a law office
(B) At a financial institution
(C) At a retail outlet
(D) At a security firm

36. What is mentioned about the woman's credit card?

(A) It has a regular fee.
(B) It offers cash back rewards.
(C) It was charged for a hotel stay.
(D) It is valid for one year.

37. Why does the woman say, "I've had this card for over a year"?

(A) To request a replacement
(B) To express satisfaction with a service
(C) To question a charge
(D) To ask for a free gift

38. What are the speakers mainly discussing?

(A) A software upgrade
(B) A productivity decline
(C) A product launch
(D) An office improvement

39. What does the woman say about the office lights?

(A) They are too strong.
(B) They use too much electricity.
(C) They were poorly installed.
(D) They are out of date.

40. What will happen next Thursday?

(A) A light will be repaired.
(B) A new space will be opened.
(C) A regular meeting will be held.
(D) A budget cut will be announced.

41. What was delivered yesterday?

(A) A replacement part
(B) An electronic device
(C) A personal letter
(D) A product list

42. What does the woman ask the man about?

(A) The date of a product launch
(B) The price of a publication
(C) The size of an item
(D) The weight of a tablet

43. What does the man offer to do?

(A) Share some financial details
(B) Call back at a later time
(C) Check with a supervisor
(D) Propose other model options

GO ON TO THE NEXT PAGE

44. According to the man, what must the speakers do?

(A) Write a report
(B) Give a presentation
(C) Review an account
(D) Set up a projector

45. Why is the woman concerned?

(A) She is not confident about a task.
(B) She is not able to attend a meeting.
(C) She misplaced a document.
(D) She made a calculation error.

46. What will the speakers do this evening?

(A) Look over some figures
(B) Meet with supervisors
(C) Stay late at work
(D) Reserve seats for a seminar

---

47. What is the conversation mainly about?

(A) A company dinner
(B) A house showing
(C) A volunteer event
(D) A private gathering

48. According to the man, what is located on Folgers Drive?

(A) A department store
(B) A workplace
(C) A residence
(D) A supermarket

49. What does the man ask Kelly to bring?

(A) Books
(B) Gifts
(C) Dessert
(D) Beverages

---

50. Why is the woman traveling to Frankfurt?

(A) To visit a relative
(B) To inspect a facility
(C) To meet a designer
(D) To attend a conference

51. What does the man ask the woman to do?

(A) Speak with a manager
(B) Go to another branch
(C) Remove a protective tag
(D) Provide proof of purchase

52. What will the woman most likely do in half an hour?

(A) Schedule an appointment
(B) Get on a shuttle bus
(C) Return to a retail outlet
(D) Board a plane

---

53. What is the woman considering?

(A) Accepting a summer job
(B) Working as a tour guide
(C) Taking a trip overseas
(D) Changing travel plans

54. Why does the man recommend the Peru Adventure package?

(A) It includes a luxury hotel room.
(B) It will save her some money.
(C) It offers more flexibility.
(D) It will come with a complimentary gift.

55. According to the man, what benefit does a membership provide?

(A) Travel insurance
(B) Reduced rates
(C) Free guidebooks
(D) Additional destinations

---

56. Who most likely is the man?

(A) A delivery person
(B) A personal assistant
(C) A computer programmer
(D) An office manager

57. What does the woman tell the man to do?

(A) Send a package to a new address
(B) Check the contents of a box
(C) Stop by a service counter
(D) Put a shipment on a desk

58. What will the woman most likely do next?

(A) Write her signature on a document
(B) Look over a list of purchased goods
(C) Contact the original sender
(D) Place another hardware order

---

59. What did the man do earlier in the week?

(A) Talked with a team leader
(B) Went on a business trip
(C) Participated in a workshop
(D) Requested a promotion

60. Why were interviews conducted?

(A) A manager will resign.
(B) A branch will expand.
(C) A department is understaffed.
(D) A job offer was turned down.

61. Why does the man say, "she has requested a transfer to our Vancouver office"?

(A) To explain why an option is unavailable
(B) To stress the importance of a position
(C) To recommend another location
(D) To encourage the woman to make a decision

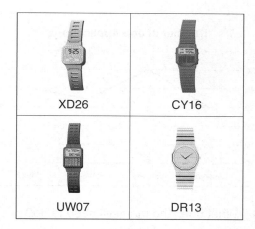

XD26	CY16
UW07	DR13

62. Look at the graphic. Which model was most recently released?

(A) XD26
(B) CY16
(C) UW07
(D) DR13

63. What problem does the woman mention?

(A) Reviews of new watches were negative.
(B) Inventory of an item is running low.
(C) Production in the factory has been shut down.
(D) A supervisor is having trouble finding staff.

64. Why does the man expect sales to increase?

(A) Some items have been put on sale.
(B) Watches are becoming more popular.
(C) An outside marketing firm was hired.
(D) The holiday season is approaching.

GO ON TO THE NEXT PAGE

TEST 4

인강으로 끝내는 해커스 토익 실전 LC+RC 1

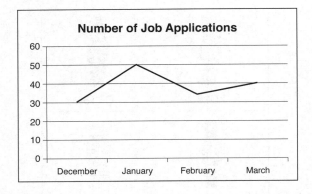

Number of Job Applications

65. What does the man still need to do?

(A) Post an advertisement
(B) Prepare for an interview
(C) Contact recent applicants
(D) Train new employees

66. According to the woman, why is a hiring decision urgent?

(A) A meeting is approaching.
(B) A project is on hold.
(C) A key staff member quit.
(D) A team was reorganized.

67. Look at the graphic. When were job openings advertised on the Web site?

(A) In December
(B) In January
(C) In February
(D) In March

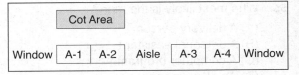

68. Where most likely are the speakers?

(A) At a ferry port
(B) At an airport
(C) At a train station
(D) At a bus stop

69. What does the man give to the woman?

(A) A credit card
(B) A missing-item form
(C) Some luggage
(D) Some identification

70. Look at the graphic. Which seat will the man be given?

(A) A-1
(B) A-2
(C) A-3
(D) A-4

PART 4

Directions: In this part, you will listen to several short talks by a single speaker. These talks will not be printed and will only be spoken one time. For each talk, you will be asked to answer three questions. Select the best response and mark the corresponding letter (A), (B), (C), or (D) on your answer sheet.

71. Why is the facility closed?

    (A) A holiday is being celebrated.
    (B) A building is being repaired.
    (C) A device needs to be inspected.
    (D) A system needs to be updated.

72. According to the speaker, what can the listeners do during a closure?

    (A) Return books
    (B) Pick up materials
    (C) Renew library cards
    (D) Go to other branches

73. How should the listeners address urgent issues?

    (A) By meeting with an employee
    (B) By dialing a number
    (C) By filling out an online form
    (D) By sending an e-mail

74. Who most likely is the speaker?

    (A) A computer repairperson
    (B) A research analyst
    (C) A corporate trainer
    (D) A sales representative

75. What does the speaker say about NextBook?

    (A) It was updated several months ago.
    (B) It takes a while to load on computers.
    (C) It was approved by a president.
    (D) It requires a special code to access.

76. What will an assistant pass out?

    (A) Application forms
    (B) Training materials
    (C) Office equipment
    (D) Electronic devices

77. Who most likely is John Harris?

    (A) A journalist
    (B) A weather forecaster
    (C) A snow plow operator
    (D) A public official

78. What is mentioned about the Harborview Bridge?

    (A) It is the site of an accident.
    (B) It is frozen over.
    (C) It is the only way to get downtown.
    (D) It is completely clear of snow.

79. What does the speaker imply when she says, "you may want to reconsider"?

    (A) An event might be postponed.
    (B) A traffic light is not working properly.
    (C) An alternative route should be taken.
    (D) A recent report has not been confirmed.

80. What does the speaker say will happen next week?

    (A) A manufacturing plant will open.
    (B) A beverage line will be released.
    (C) A TV commercial will be completed.
    (D) A client will come to an office.

81. What did the speaker ask the research team to do?

    (A) Begin surveying customers
    (B) Make corrections to a report
    (C) Share some results online
    (D) Prepare a brief presentation

82. Why should the listeners contact the speaker?

    (A) To ask questions
    (B) To coordinate schedules
    (C) To confirm attendance
    (D) To volunteer for a job

GO ON TO THE NEXT PAGE

83. What does Mr. Kramer have a lot of experience doing?

(A) Selling insurance products
(B) Managing employees
(C) Addressing customer complaints
(D) Handling business mergers

84. What does the speaker mention about Mr. Kramer?

(A) He would like to give a talk.
(B) He has lived in another country.
(C) He refused other offers.
(D) He will hire an assistant.

85. What will probably take place next Friday?

(A) A language class
(B) A trade fair
(C) A sales meeting
(D) An informal gathering

---

86. Who most likely are the listeners?

(A) Corporate presidents
(B) Bank tellers
(C) Company stakeholders
(D) Magazine editors

87. What is inferred about *BizSurprise*?

(A) It publishes monthly issues.
(B) It wants to interview a CEO.
(C) It sponsors business fairs.
(D) It has to hire more writers.

88. What does the speaker ask Ms. Harvey to do?

(A) Present an award
(B) Make a speech
(C) Applaud for a winner
(D) Take her seat

---

89. Who most likely is the speaker?

(A) A radio host
(B) A city employee
(C) A tour guide
(D) An advertising executive

90. Why does the speaker say, "It is tourist season, after all"?

(A) To indicate why there are many tour buses near a park
(B) To note that repairs must be finished by a certain date
(C) To explain why there is a lot of trash in parks
(D) To recommend holding a promotional event

91. What does the speaker suggest?

(A) Handing out trash bags
(B) Running some advertisements
(C) Recruiting temporary staff
(D) Speaking to a cleaning company

---

92. According to the speaker, what has to be approved?

(A) Time off
(B) Additional work hours
(C) A product design
(D) Management changes

93. Who most likely is Brittany Jacobs?

(A) A personnel employee
(B) A sales representative
(C) A photography expert
(D) A training instructor

94. What does the speaker mean when he says, "we have only five people"?

(A) An important decision cannot be agreed upon.
(B) A company will hire more workers soon.
(C) Some help is needed to complete a task.
(D) Some employees should work overtime.

Viva Rentals

Type	Capacity	Daily Rate
Sports car	2 people	$32.00
Sedan	4 people	$22.00
SUV	6 people	$28.00
Minivan	8 people	$34.00

	Building A		City Library
Building B	City Hall	Ocean Avenue	Building C
Oak Street			
Department Store	Building D		Subway Station

95. Why is the speaker calling?

(A) To confirm a reservation
(B) To offer a special deal
(C) To reply to some questions
(D) To give a store location

96. Look at the graphic. Which vehicle will the listener most likely choose?

(A) Sports car
(B) Sedan
(C) SUV
(D) Minivan

97. What is the listener instructed to do?

(A) Return a vehicle on time
(B) Make an online booking
(C) Verify some travel dates
(D) Submit a form in person

98. What is the broadcast mainly about?

(A) A corporate acquisition
(B) A property purchase
(C) An event place
(D) A land development

99. What will happen on June 3?

(A) A company will relocate.
(B) A project will start.
(C) An executive will retire.
(D) An office will reopen.

100. Look at the graphic. Which building did Western Development rent?

(A) Building A
(B) Building B
(C) Building C
(D) Building D

This is the end of the Listening test. Turn to PART 5 in your test book.

GO ON TO THE NEXT PAGE

READING TEST

In this section, you must demonstrate your ability to read and comprehend English. You will be given a variety of texts and asked to answer questions about these texts. This section is divided into three parts and will take 75 minutes to complete.

Do not mark the answers in your test book. Use the answer sheet that is separately provided.

PART 5

Directions: In each question, you will be asked to review a statement that is missing a word or phrase. Four answer choices will be provided for each statement. Select the best answer and mark the corresponding letter (A), (B), (C), or (D) on the answer sheet.

PART 5 권장 풀이 시간 11분

101. Sanders Industries recently ------- high-tech machinery that will allow it to double its output.

(A) to purchase
(B) purchase
(C) purchased
(D) purchases

102. ------- of the staff members surveyed is pleased with the expansion of the retirement program.

(A) Each
(B) All
(C) Other
(D) Their own

103. The heavy snowfall delayed the train's ------- by more than four hours.

(A) depart
(B) departed
(C) departs
(D) departure

104. The Shoreline Restaurant is ------- busy, as the area is filled with tourists year-round.

(A) less
(B) always
(C) exactly
(D) soon

105. Most new businesses fail within five years, but ------- go on to become very successful.

(A) any
(B) these
(C) some
(D) every

106. Ms. Wang had her home ------- by a real estate agent before offering it for sale.

(A) performed
(B) appeared
(C) assessed
(D) outlined

107. There are 30 seats ------- for the recipients' family and coworkers at the awards ceremony.

(A) reserve
(B) reserved
(C) reserving
(D) reservation

108. In order to maintain your account security, ------- at least one number and one letter in your password.

(A) include
(B) included
(C) including
(D) to include

109. Findera Construction took advantage of ------- growth in Vietnam's housing market to raise its international profile.

(A) best
(B) rapid
(C) original
(D) adverse

110. Many critics praised director John Parker for the ------- ending to his most recent action movie.

(A) thrilled
(B) thrillers
(C) thrilling
(D) thrills

111. The upcoming sale at Westside Electronics ------- shoppers a great deal of money on televisions.

(A) save
(B) saved
(C) saving
(D) will save

112. RubioTech recalled the new computer model after discovering that it contained ------- components.

(A) functional
(B) adjustable
(C) portable
(D) defective

113. Before ------- Carla Evans to schedule an interview, Mr. Harris verified the information on her résumé.

(A) contact
(B) contacts
(C) contacted
(D) contacting

114. Those planning to attend the conference need ------- at least seven days in advance.

(A) register
(B) to register
(C) registering
(D) registered

115. TriGem Chemicals admitted that it had ------- shipped the client's order to the wrong address.

(A) generously
(B) mutually
(C) productively
(D) accidentally

116. Product deliveries must be completed within three days according to the terms of the -------.

(A) figure
(B) contract
(C) research
(D) concept

117. Sales of the XL550 Tablet increased ------- 15 percent after a new version of the operating system was released.

(A) for
(B) on
(C) along
(D) by

118. The number of visitors to Ice River National Park in October was ------- higher than in the previous month.

(A) very
(B) much
(C) more
(D) so

119. The company's executive cafeteria will be ------- into an employee lounge during the renovations.

(A) converted
(B) convinced
(C) consented
(D) concealed

120. It is ------- whether countries can continue increasing the size of their economies while limiting fossil fuel use.

(A) debate
(B) debates
(C) debating
(D) debatable

GO ON TO THE NEXT PAGE

121. Poole Automotive ------- planned to expand overseas but decided to focus on increasing domestic sales instead.

(A) negatively
(B) currently
(C) initially
(D) rarely

122. At only $50 per night, the Warren Inn is considered a bargain ------- the many hotels in the area.

(A) before
(B) toward
(C) onto
(D) among

123. Applicants who are ------- in finding out more about the firm's benefits package should visit our Web site.

(A) obsessed
(B) displayed
(C) interested
(D) stimulated

124. To ------- its latest microwave from previous models, Langford Appliances launched a major marketing campaign.

(A) concentrate
(B) handle
(C) designate
(D) differentiate

125. The retailers' association selected the Debran Center for the meeting based on its members' ------- for a central location.

(A) performance
(B) preference
(C) collection
(D) exception

126. ------- he had decided to find a new job, Mr. Cooper made appointments with several recruitment agencies.

(A) Once
(B) During
(C) Soon
(D) Next

127. Pacer Industries purchased a factory in China ------- produces a wide range of electronic components.

(A) it
(B) that
(C) what
(D) whether

128. Recent polls suggest that most employees would take a pay cut if they could work ------- hours.

(A) shortly
(B) shorter
(C) shorten
(D) shortest

129. The Paxton Hotel offers a 20 percent discount to anyone ------- stays there more than four nights per month.

(A) who
(B) whom
(C) which
(D) whose

130. Donations from the Lumour Corporation ------- funding for the National Museum of Ancient Art.

(A) notify
(B) interpret
(C) provide
(D) confront

PART 6

Directions: In this part, you will be asked to read four English texts. Each text is missing a word, phrase, or sentence. Select the answer choice that correctly completes the text and mark the corresponding letter (A), (B), (C), or (D) on the answer sheet.

PART 6 권장 풀이 시간 8분

Questions 131-134 refer to the following article.

A Franchise or an Independent Business?

April 11—A difficult decision that an entrepreneur faces is whether to open a franchise or an independent business. -------. A franchise owner does not have to spend years developing
131.
brand recognition and receives support from the headquarters. On the other hand, people

who open an independent business have more freedom to select products and can decide

how to set ------- prices. Another factor to consider is the initial investment. ------- running a
132.   133.
franchise only requires a small initial investment, some profits must be paid to the corporate

headquarters. In contrast, an independent business owner will have high startup costs but

------- all the profits.
134.

---

131. (A) Most people prefer to shop at international chains.
(B) Many companies lose money in their first year of operation.
(C) Some brands on the market are significantly overpriced.
(D) Both choices have advantages and disadvantages.

132. (A) themselves
(B) them
(C) they
(D) their

133. (A) Except
(B) Just as
(C) Although
(D) Even

134. (A) estimate
(B) waste
(C) eliminate
(D) keep

GO ON TO THE NEXT PAGE

Questions 135-138 refer to the following announcement.

To all customers:

We are pleased to announce that Hamby-Russ has merged with Carmona Incorporated.

------- the start of the month, our headquarters in Seattle began operating under the name
135.
Hamby-Russ & Carmona.

-------. During this time, both companies negotiated extensively to develop a strategy for
136.
providing shoppers with the best recreational products available. As for our organizational

structure, it is being adjusted. However, we will ------- all our original employees. As a result,
137.
you will be able to work with the same salespeople that you had before. Our phone numbers

will also remain unchanged. Do not ------- to contact our administrative team at 555-3438
138.
with any questions.

---

135. (A) While
    (B) At
    (C) Down
    (D) Into

136. (A) We determined it would be best to
    cease operations entirely.
    (B) The spring shopping season is our
    busiest time of the year.
    (C) This merger had been planned for
    nearly 10 months.
    (D) An announcement will be made when
    an agreement is finalized.

137. (A) maintain
    (B) transfer
    (C) replace
    (D) dismiss

138. (A) hesitate
    (B) be hesitated
    (C) to hesitate
    (D) hesitating

For a recent trip to Miami, I arranged a car ------- through EZ Auto. I chose this company
139.
because it has lower daily rates for travelers than its competitors. However, when I arrived

at the EZ Auto branch near the airport, the SUV I had reserved was unavailable. -------.
140.
As there was a truck on the lot, I asked to rent it instead. But I ------- that I would have to pay
141.
the full price for the larger vehicle, which was higher than that of the SUV. The EZ Auto staff

should have provided me with an upgrade at no additional charge to compensate for their

mistake. Therefore, I have decided not ------- this company's services again in the future.
142.

139. (A) repair
(B) rental
(C) inspection
(D) delivery

140. (A) They had no record of my request for a navigation system.
(B) Unfortunately, there were no other vehicles.
(C) Apparently, there was a mistake with the date.
(D) I had already asked for a refund.

141. (A) was informed
(B) informed
(C) informing
(D) was informing

142. (A) to use
(B) using
(C) used
(D) use

GO ON TO THE NEXT PAGE

Questions 143-146 refer to the following memo.

From: Diane Langston, Sales Manager
To: All Employees
Date: September 23
Subject: Fall Marathon Street Closures

The annual Renfield Fall Marathon takes place this Friday. Be aware that some ------- streets
143.
may be closed during the event. Both Sandy Brook Road and the parking garage next to our

building will be ------- from 9 A.M. to 2 P.M. So if you normally drive to work, you should make
144.
other plans. -------. It is only a five-minute walk from the office. You can also take the bus to
145.
Davis Lane, which is two blocks from here. You can look up all the bus routes online. -------
146.
more assistance, you can let me know.

143. (A) neighborly
(B) neighbors
(C) neighborhood
(D) neighborliness

144. (A) safe
(B) vulnerable
(C) inaccessible
(D) acceptable

145. (A) If you can telecommute, I recommend
doing so.
(B) Luckily, we only experienced a
temporary inconvenience.
(C) The office will open after the marathon
is finished.
(D) For instance, there is a garage on
29th Street you can use.

146. (A) Do you need
(B) Should you need
(C) As you are needed
(D) When you are needed

PART 7

Directions: In this part, you will be asked to read several texts, such as advertisements, articles, instant messages, or examples of business correspondence. Each text is followed by several questions. Select the best answer and mark the corresponding letter (A), (B), (C), or (D) on your answer sheet.

🕐 **PART 7 권장 풀이 시간 54분**

Questions 147-148 refer to the following online review.

https://www.oakridge.com/customerreviews

Customer Name: Ruth Bell
Rating: ★
Date: April 3
Product: Lucas Coffee Table

I ordered a coffee table from Oakridge Furniture on February 10. Overall, I am happy with this piece of furniture. The design is very stylish and modern, and the table is just the right size for the living room of my new apartment. It was also very easy to assemble. The reason that I am giving this company only one star out of a possible five is that my order took much longer than expected to arrive. I was originally told it would be delivered on March 8, but it wasn't dropped off at my house until March 26. I guess there was a technical error with the company's distribution system that resulted in the table being shipped to the wrong address. I should have been offered an apology for this mistake and maybe even a discount, but I never was. Therefore, I don't think I'll be shopping at Oakridge Furniture again.

147. What is indicated about Ms. Bell?

(A) She was unable to assemble a table.
(B) She will return a piece of furniture.
(C) She moved into a new residence.
(D) She is looking for a new apartment.

148. Why did Ms. Bell give the company a poor review?

(A) An item is no longer in stock.
(B) An apology letter was sent too late.
(C) A package was damaged in transit.
(D) A delivery did not arrive on schedule.

GO ON TO THE NEXT PAGE

Questions 149-150 refer to the following text messages.

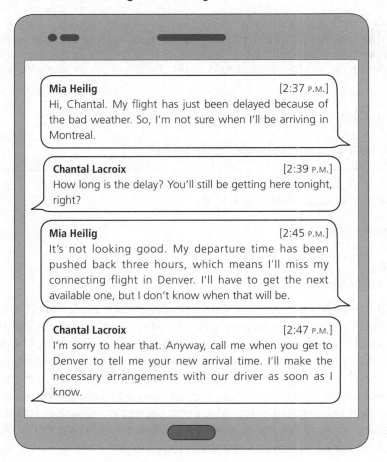

Mia Heilig [2:37 P.M.]
Hi, Chantal. My flight has just been delayed because of the bad weather. So, I'm not sure when I'll be arriving in Montreal.

Chantal Lacroix [2:39 P.M.]
How long is the delay? You'll still be getting here tonight, right?

Mia Heilig [2:45 P.M.]
It's not looking good. My departure time has been pushed back three hours, which means I'll miss my connecting flight in Denver. I'll have to get the next available one, but I don't know when that will be.

Chantal Lacroix [2:47 P.M.]
I'm sorry to hear that. Anyway, call me when you get to Denver to tell me your new arrival time. I'll make the necessary arrangements with our driver as soon as I know.

149. What is true about Ms. Heilig?

(A) She departed from Montreal.
(B) She will pick up Ms. Lacroix.
(C) She will take multiple flights.
(D) She contacted Ms. Lacroix from Denver.

150. At 2:45 P.M., what does Ms. Heilig most likely mean when she writes, "It's not looking good"?

(A) She cannot exchange a ticket.
(B) She may not receive a refund.
(C) She cannot contact a driver.
(D) She may not arrive tonight.

Video Marketing Enterprise
372 Highland Avenue
Mobile, AL 36575
555-8230

At Video Marketing Enterprise, we offer various video production services for your business, including idea generation, script writing, casting, directing, filming, and editing.

We produce videos for organizations of all types and sizes. Contact us if you need videos for marketing campaigns, product demonstrations, or training workshops. We employ a variety of professionals who are knowledgeable about all steps of the video-making process. Not to mention, our filming equipment and stage props are of the highest quality available.

From November 1 to December 31, we are offering a special winter deal for small business owners. For just $2,000, we will create a 30-second video for your company. Then, our online marketing team will give you tips on how to promote your video on social media sites. This will ensure that your advertisement is viewed by a large audience without your having to pay for costly airtime on television networks. For more information about this deal or our company in general, visit our Web site at www.videomarketingenterprise.com.

151. What is indicated about Video Marketing Enterprise?

(A) It has only a few staff members.
(B) It conducts workshops for filmmakers.
(C) It provides a wide range of services.
(D) It sells video production equipment.

152. What will happen from November 1 to December 31?

(A) A Web site will be updated.
(B) A business will be expanded.
(C) A promotion will be held.
(D) A social media platform will be launched.

TO   All Instructors
FROM   Adam Fitzpatrick <afitzpatrick@hardingbusinessinstitute.com>
SUBJECT   Update
DATE   June 17

Hello everybody,

As you probably know, the basement of the Farley Building was flooded last night as a result of yesterday's typhoon. Therefore, we are temporarily moving all classes that meet in the basement to the Sherman Center next door. Here is a list of temporary room assignments:

CLASS	INSTRUCTOR	ROOM
Attracting Investors to Your Start-up	Mark Helling	200
Branding 101	Jesse Weiner	205
Advanced Financial Accounting	Helen Boucher	207
Marketing with Social Media	Megan Davis	210

Your class times will remain the same, and your students will be notified of the situation by e-mail this afternoon. Alfred King, the Farley Building's manager, informed me that the flooded rooms will be cleaned out and repaired over the next three days. He said they will be available for use again next Monday.

Please contact me if you have any questions.

Best regards,

Adam Fitzpatrick
President, Harding Business Institute

153. According to the memo, what happened on June 16?

(A) A storm took place.
(B) Some classes were canceled.
(C) Some exams were corrected.
(D) A lecturer went on vacation.

154. What did Mr. King tell Mr. Fitzpatrick?

(A) The second floor of the Sherman Center is open.
(B) A class on marketing can meet as scheduled.
(C) The water damage is too expensive to repair.
(D) The Farley Building basement will be usable next week.

NOTICE

The Bristol City Council, in support of Mayor Thomas Anderson's recycling initiative, has agreed to conclude its contract with Sanders Waste Management by the end of the year. From that point on, all waste will be handled by Perry Waste and Recycling.

As a result of this recycling initiative, Bristol residents will be asked to separate their trash beginning January 1. Regular trash will be placed in black bins, while metal, glass, and paper will be placed in green bins. The new bins will be delivered this week, along with a detailed pamphlet. Residents are advised to review the printed guidelines carefully.

155. What is the purpose of the notice?

(A) To call for a council meeting
(B) To express support for a project
(C) To announce a service change
(D) To report on a program's success

156. What is stated about the recycling initiative?

(A) It will take effect the following year.
(B) It was proposed by the previous mayor.
(C) It will be managed by a council member.
(D) It is part of a larger campaign.

157. What are Bristol residents encouraged to do?

(A) Dispose of trash more often
(B) Use one type of bin
(C) Attend a city council meeting
(D) Read a document

Questions 158-161 refer to the following article.

On the Loose Again Set to Premiere at Goldwin Theater

On the Loose Again, the sequel to the popular comedy *On the Loose*, will premiere at Goldwin Theater on May 16. The stars of both films—Max Walter and Elena Marconi—will be in attendance, and a brief photo shoot will take place before the movie screens. The red carpet event will begin as soon as the theater opens, and the film will be shown one hour later, from 6 p.m. to 8 p.m. Immediately following the film will be a question and answer session with the cast and crew. Finally, an autograph signing will take place at 8:30 p.m.

On the Loose Again continues where the previous film ended. It features an escaped criminal and his wife as they travel across the American South attempting to avoid the police. Director Jamie Moya, who has also produced numerous popular television series, including *Above Ground* and *Special Investigations*, replaced Richard Weber, the director of the original movie. As the first movie did quite well, *On the Loose Again* is expected to draw large crowds. Those wishing to obtain tickets to the premiere should buy them well in advance by going to www. goldwintheater.com/tickets or calling 555-3716.

---

158. What is true about *On the Loose Again*?

(A) It is the third film in a series.
(B) It is especially popular among teenagers.
(C) It features the same actors as the first movie.
(D) It has received positive reviews.

159. The word "shown" in paragraph 1, line 6, is closest in meaning to

(A) exposed
(B) reported
(C) performed
(D) presented

160. What is mentioned about Mr. Moya?

(A) He was the director of *On the Loose*.
(B) He is known for his work in television.
(C) He is a friend of Ms. Marconi.
(D) He wrote the script for *On the Loose Again*.

161. What does the article advise people to do?

(A) Get to the theater by 8 P.M.
(B) Purchase tickets early
(C) Participate in a photo shoot
(D) Enter a raffle online

Questions 162-165 refer to the following online chat discussion.

Robin Underwood [8:30 P.M.] Hi, everyone. I think I've come up with a way to attract new gym members.

Franklin Bates [8:31 P.M.] I'm glad. We've lost a lot of customers to the fitness center that recently opened down the street. What's your plan?

Robin Underwood [8:33 P.M.] We can waive one month's fee for new members who sign up for a six-month membership and two months' fees if it's an annual membership.

Norma Flores [8:34 P.M.] Lots of other gyms have similar promotions. Maybe we need to do more.

Robin Underwood [8:35 P.M.] That's why I'm also planning to encourage our existing members to recommend us to their friends. Members who get someone else to sign up here will receive a free gym bag as a gift.

Franklin Bates [8:37 P.M.] That will probably work. Would you like me to add this information to our Web site? The first exercise class I teach isn't until 1:00 P.M. tomorrow, so I'll have time to do it before lunch.

Robin Underwood [8:38 P.M.] That would be great. Norma, could you put up some notices in the gym about this new policy?

Norma Flores [8:38 P.M.] Sure. I'll also notify the other employees so that they can tell our customers.

162. What is mentioned about the gym where Ms. Underwood works?

(A) It opened a second branch.
(B) It has a new competitor.
(C) It will move to another location.
(D) It offers two-month memberships.

163. At 8:34 P.M., what does Ms. Flores most likely mean when she writes, "Lots of other gyms have similar promotions"?

(A) She wants to imitate an offer.
(B) She agrees with a suggestion.
(C) She is doubtful about a plan.
(D) She needs to check on some details.

164. What will some existing members be eligible to receive?

(A) A gift certificate
(B) A fee reduction
(C) A membership upgrade
(D) A complimentary item

165. What will Mr. Bates most likely do tomorrow morning?

(A) Print some notices
(B) Lead a fitness class
(C) Update a Web site
(D) Meet with employees

GO ON TO THE NEXT PAGE

Questions 166-168 refer to the following information.

Workplace Health Research Association

www.whra.org

The Workplace Health Research Association (WHRA) is holding its Fifth Annual Workplace Health Conference on October 10 and 11 at the WHRA Institute. An alliance of research groups, WHRA has made the well-being of employees its primary goal.

This year's conference will offer participants the latest information on how sleep, nutrition, and exercise affect productivity in the workplace. Additional details about lecture topics and presenters will be finalized and posted on www.whra.org/events on August 7.

To register, please fill out the online registration form. If you are a member of WHRA, you will receive 30 percent off the total cost of attending on both days. Please be prepared to provide your membership number at the time of registration. If you would like to apply for membership, please visit the site's membership page.

Registration begins on August 1 and ends on September 15. Should you need to cancel your registration, please send an e-mail to rebecca.smith@whra.org by September 21. After this date, no refunds will be granted. For questions and inquiries, you may write to fifthconference@whra.org.

---

166. What is suggested about the WHRA?

(A) It will start a new research project.
(B) It was established recently.
(C) It operates offices overseas.
(D) It has hosted conferences before.

167. What is NOT mentioned about the event?

(A) Attendees may qualify for a discount.
(B) A program will be posted online.
(C) A membership is required to attend.
(D) Participants can register on a Web site.

168. By what date should participants register?

(A) August 1
(B) August 7
(C) September 15
(D) September 21

Questions 169-171 refer to the following article.

Stanton Rental Property Demand Continues to Rise

As the job market in Stanton has been good for the past 10 years, the need for rental housing has climbed steadily upward. — [1] —. People who work in the downtown business district want to live in the city, and a market survey has shown that they would rather rent apartments than take out large loans to own expensive downtown real estate. — [2] —. Developers have taken advantage of this trend, constructing high-rise apartment buildings in and around the district. — [3] —. Although many new apartment complexes have been built, monthly rental fees continue to rise due to high demand for units in Stanton. — [4] —. Real estate experts predict that the pattern will continue for a few more years before demand is satisfied.

169. What is the article mainly about?

(A) The popularity of multi-story buildings
(B) High rental housing demand in an area
(C) The declining price of urban real estate
(D) Forecasted patterns of growth in the suburbs

170. What is suggested about Stanton's rental housing market?

(A) It has already reached its peak.
(B) It is expected to slow down considerably.
(C) It will maintain its current growth for a while.
(D) It is being affected by high unemployment.

171. In which of the positions marked [1], [2], [3], and [4] does the following sentence best belong?

"However, the rising costs have not prevented people from renting."

(A) [1]
(B) [2]
(C) [3]
(D) [4]

GO ON TO THE NEXT PAGE

Date: May 5
To: All staff
From: Joel Smith, Human Resources Director
Subject: Employee benefits

Hello everyone,

There has been much discussion among the managers about the company's benefits package. When Smartech first opened, we could only provide basic health insurance to employees. — [1] —.

Since the company was founded three years ago, however, we have experienced significant revenue growth. — [2] —. Therefore, we have decided to improve our staff benefits package. Starting July 1, basic dental care will be provided. — [3] —. Employees will also have the option of paying extra for more dental insurance coverage. To take advantage of this, simply fill out an application and bring it to the human resources department.

An updated employee manual with information about this benefit change will be sent to all staff members next week. — [4] —. If you have any questions, please feel free to e-mail me at j.smith@smartech.com or to stop by my office. Thank you.

Best wishes,

Joel Smith

172. What is NOT mentioned about Smartech?

(A) Its revenues have increased.
(B) It has provided health insurance since its founding.
(C) Its employees receive annual bonuses.
(D) It was established three years ago.

173. How can employees acquire additional insurance coverage?

(A) By contacting a supervisor
(B) By choosing an option online
(C) By submitting a medical report
(D) By paying an additional charge

174. What will happen next week?

(A) A policy will be implemented.
(B) A document will be distributed.
(C) A contract will be negotiated.
(D) A staff meeting will be scheduled.

175. In which of the positions marked [1], [2], [3], and [4] does the following sentence best belong?

"This will cover the costs of regular checkups and cleaning but not major dental work."

(A) [1]
(B) [2]
(C) [3]
(D) [4]

GO ON TO THE NEXT PAGE

Launch Technologies Recalls Laptops

At a press conference on May 13, Launch Technologies CEO Jasmine Hong stated that the company has issued a recall for two of its laptops—the Edge XL and the Glide 780. Over 750,000 units of these models have been sold over the past year, making this recall larger than any others the company has ever had before.

According to Ms. Hong, the Edge XL has a defective power cable. This component is prone to overheating when the computer is running, in some cases causing the laptop to catch on fire. "Although there have been only a few reported instances of this, we take the safety of our customers very seriously. That is why we are asking everyone who purchased this laptop to return it immediately," said Ms. Hong. The company decided to recall the Glide 780 at the same time because it has a faulty hard drive that causes it to shut down unexpectedly.

Customers who own either model are eligible to receive a full refund and a $200 voucher that can be used for any Launch Technologies product.

Product Return Form
Launch Technologies
2839 Cumberland Road
Wheeling, WV 26003

■ **Customer Information**

Date: May 14

Name: Garret Brewer
Phone Number: 555-4119

E-mail: gbrewer@breweraccounting.com
Home address: 990 Park Road, Suite 314, Columbus, OH 43203

Product Name	Quantity	Reason
Edge XL	7	Product recalled by manufacturer

■ **Comments**

I purchased these computers to be used by the staff working at the company I own. Obviously, having to return them is a significant inconvenience. I would like my refund request to be processed by May 16 so that I can order replacements immediately. The amount owed to me should be refunded to the corporate credit card that I used to make the original purchase. If you require additional information, you can reach me at the number provided above. Thank you.

176. In the article, the word "issued" in paragraph 1, line 3, is closest in meaning to

(A) decided
(B) distributed
(C) recognized
(D) announced

177. What can be inferred about Launch Technologies?

(A) It has released a laptop within the past month.
(B) It has recalled products previously.
(C) It was established over a decade ago.
(D) It has recently hired a new CEO.

178. What will buyers of the Edge XL and the Glide 780 receive?

(A) A free software program
(B) A discount on a computer accessory
(C) Complimentary repair services
(D) Credit for a future purchase

179. Who most likely is Mr. Brewer?

(A) A product inspector
(B) A business owner
(C) A computer technician
(D) A factory worker

180. What is indicated about the devices purchased by Mr. Brewer?

(A) They came with replacement components.
(B) They turn off without warning.
(C) They become hot while being operated.
(D) They require hard drive upgrades.

GO ON TO THE NEXT PAGE

Captain Jack's Seafood

About	Menu	Location	Reviews

Located on Bridgeport Beach, Captain Jack's Seafood was founded over a decade ago by Jack Hoult, a local fisherman who dreamed of opening his own seafood restaurant. This restaurant faced a lot of competition from nearby seafood establishments in its early years. However, Mr. Hoult's dedication to providing fresh, well-prepared dishes has made Captain Jack's Seafood a popular eatery. In fact, *Food & Drink Magazine* has named Captain Jack's Seafood in many of its articles as the best seafood restaurant in Bridgeport.

Captain Jack's Seafood is known for its signature seafood dishes like lobster and crab cakes. And its delicious drinks are favorites among locals. Try one of several daily specials offered at reasonable prices:

Thursdays – Crab Cakes	**Fridays** – Fish and Chips
Saturdays – Fried Squid	**Sundays** – Lobster

Arrive before 6 P.M., and you will also receive a coupon for your next visit. Reservations are recommended. To book a table, call 555-2243.

Captain Jack's Seafood

About	Menu	Location	Reviews

Name: Carmen Vasquez
Rating: ★★★☆☆

I went to Captain Jack's Seafood last week expecting to be amazed. My friends had told me it was the greatest seafood place in town and that there was a large selection of items on the menu. When I got there, however, there was a 30-minute wait, despite it being only 5 P.M. on Thursday. After standing outside the restaurant for a while, I was finally seated. But it took another 10 minutes for a waiter to give me a menu. I ordered a cocktail and the special of the day, and then the waiter disappeared for another 40 minutes before bringing me my food.

Overall, I would give Captain Jack's Seafood three stars. The food and beverages were excellent, and the atmosphere was very welcoming. But the staff members need to learn how to address their customers' needs more quickly and efficiently.

181. What is stated about Captain Jack's Seafood?

(A) Its menu was changed recently.
(B) It has been recognized by a publication.
(C) Its chefs are mostly fishermen.
(D) It has multiple locations.

182. According to the Web page, what do locals especially enjoy at Captain Jack's Seafood?

(A) Nice surrounding views
(B) Tasty beverages
(C) Polite waiters
(D) Healthy food choices

183. What dish did Ms. Vasquez most likely order?

(A) Crab Cakes
(B) Fish and Chips
(C) Fried Squid
(D) Lobster

184. What can be inferred about Ms. Vasquez?

(A) She subscribes to a food magazine.
(B) She sat at an outdoor table.
(C) She recently moved to Bridgeport.
(D) She received a coupon for future use.

185. In the online review, the word "address" in paragraph 2, line 3, is closest in meaning to

(A) comply
(B) record
(C) talk to
(D) deal with

GO ON TO THE NEXT PAGE

Questions 186-190 refer to the following e-mails and schedule.

To	Tom Gonzales <t.gonzales@gomail.com>
From	Cecilia Wiggins <c.wiggins@topsmile.net>
Subject	Sudden change
Date	May 25

Dear Mr. Gonzales,

I regret to inform you that Dr. Makata will not be available on the date you requested for your oral health checkup. I realize that you made this appointment on April 12. However, Dr. Makata was asked to fill in for a colleague and will be at a conference in El Paso on the day scheduled for you. She is not due back in the office until June 16. Could we possibly move your appointment to the following week? I could schedule an appointment for your preferred time of 10 A.M. Please let me know.

Sincerely,

Cecilia Wiggins

15th Southern Regional Dental Conference
June 12 to 14, Bamba Hotel, El Paso, Texas

Schedule for Saturday, June 14

Time	Event	Location	Speaker
8:00 – 11:30 A.M.	Workshop: Dental Photography and Digital Processing	Javelina Hall	Dr. Stephen Gentry
9:00 – 11:30 A.M.	Lecture: Material Selection for Dental Surgery	Oryx Room	Dr. Warren Francis
11:30 A.M. – 1:30 P.M.	Lunch Break		
1:30 – 2:30 P.M.	Workshop: Excellence in Patient Customer Service	Javelina Hall	Dr. Janine Kirst
1:30 – 3:00 P.M.	Meeting: Financial Strategies for New Dentists	Oryx Room	Dr. Heather Wallace
2:00 – 4:30 P.M.	Lecture: Issues Surrounding Patient Insurance	Finch Room	Dr. Noemi Makata

Note: Members may attend any lecture or meeting free of charge. However, a fee may be charged for attending a workshop. All fees may be refunded in the event of cancellation.

To: Kyle Green <k.green@srdc.org>
From: Larry Ayala <l.ayala@bamba.com>
Subject: Your concern
Date: June 13

Dear Mr. Green,

We asked our engineers to check the air conditioner in Javelina Hall. Unfortunately, it will need repairs, and the earliest these can be done is tomorrow morning. I apologize for the inconvenience, but this means we will have to cancel the event for the Southern Regional Dental Conference being held in that hall before lunchtime tomorrow. By the way, I spoke to Ms. Lopez regarding your concern about the temperature of the buffet food. She will make sure that any dishes left out are kept warm until the lunch break ends. If you need further assistance, you may contact me at my mobile phone number, 555-4106.

Warmly,

Larry Ayala
Bamba Hotel

186. Who most likely is Ms. Wiggins?

(A) A facility owner
(B) An event coordinator
(C) A conference speaker
(D) A clinic receptionist

187. When was Mr. Gonzales supposed to meet with Dr. Makata?

(A) On April 12
(B) On May 25
(C) On June 14
(D) On June 16

188. What is NOT mentioned about Dr. Makata?

(A) She will return to work on June 16.
(B) She will be present at a morning workshop.
(C) She will be filling in for an associate.
(D) She will speak at an event.

189. What can be inferred about the Southern Regional Dental Conference?

(A) Dr. Francis's lecture will be canceled.
(B) Its lunch will have additional meal options.
(C) Dr. Kirst's event might be delayed.
(D) Some of its workshop participants will be refunded.

190. What is Mr. Green's concern?

(A) A room might be too crowded.
(B) Some food will become cold.
(C) A manager will be unreachable.
(D) Some materials might be distributed late.

GO ON TO THE NEXT PAGE

Thumping Thursdays at the Billings Hotel

Join us after work at Gordon's Grill for great music, food, and wine! Grab a chair on the veranda or take a seat on the lawn while enjoying live music. We are open for dinner from 5 P.M. to 10 P.M. The dates and musicians for live music performances are noted below. All performances will run from 6 P.M. to 8 P.M., if the weather permits. Per city regulations, alcoholic beverages are not allowed on the lawn. Go to www. billingshotel.com for more details.

July 10: Mister Misty	August 14: Roxy Blues
July 17: Elder Lake	August 21: Terry Crank
July 24: Roxy Blues	August 28: Mister Misty
July 31: Mister Misty	September 4: Roxy Blues
August 7: Elder Lake	September 11: Mister Misty

To	Walt Galvin <galvinw@stompmail.com>
From	Pauline Eagan <eaganp@bluemail.com>
Subject	Possible shows
Date	July 4

Walt,

Do you remember when I left my business card with Dena Harris, the event director at the Billings Hotel? Well, she contacted me today to ask if you and your fellow members of Deacon Delta would be willing to play at a hotel event called Thumping Thursdays. Apparently, she had originally booked Roxy Blues, but they backed out when they were invited to play at a blues festival in Edinburgh. She'd like you to cover all of their timeslots. Currently, I only have your band scheduled to perform on Friday nights at the Cowhead Lounge, so you'll have plenty of time for these performances. I've already told Ms. Harris that Deacon Delta is available for the event, so please confirm that you can take the job.

Pauline

TRIP TALES
www.triptales.com

Home > Accommodations Reviews > Billings Hotel Reviews

Mississippi Dreaming ★★★★☆
Posted September 20 by Isabel Calhoun

I stayed at this hotel earlier this month for three nights and four days while attending a friend's wedding that was held there. The rooms were basic but comfortable and included free Wi-Fi. The breakfast buffet at the Polk Room was decent, though I much preferred the food at the hotel's other restaurant, Gordon's Grill. The hotel also had a great blues band called Mister Misty on the first night I ate there. Nearby, there was plenty to do and see. My only complaint about this entire trip was getting woken up at 8 A.M. by construction noise outside my window. I discovered later that this happened because the hotel is building a new wing. Overall, the hotel offered good value and great fun, and I highly recommend it to other travelers, particularly those who enjoy blues music.

191. According to the flyer, what could cause organizers to cancel a musical event?

(A) City regulations
(B) Inclement weather
(C) Ongoing renovations
(D) Another event reservation

192. Who most likely is Ms. Eagan?

(A) An event director
(B) A restaurant owner
(C) A band manager
(D) An amateur musician

193. What is indicated about Deacon Delta?

(A) It may have to reschedule a concert in Edinburgh.
(B) It has performed with Roxy Blues in the past.
(C) It auditioned for a spot at a music festival.
(D) It might be scheduled for three shows at the Billings Hotel.

194. When did Ms. Calhoun probably see Mister Misty's performance?

(A) On July 10
(B) On August 28
(C) On September 4
(D) On September 11

195. What did Ms. Calhoun dislike about the Billings Hotel?

(A) The way her room was decorated
(B) The small selection of food items on offer
(C) The disturbances caused by some work
(D) The distance from tourist attractions

GO ON TO THE NEXT PAGE

Improve Your Self-Care with the Glider

The Glider is a multifunctional massage tool that works on all body parts. High-frequency vibrations release stress and pain and assist with physical recovery. The Glider is also a smart device, recording statistics on its use and providing live information and program suggestions. The Glider syncs with the Glider online application, which functions as your daily wellness tracker.

The Glider is already being used by professional athletes and in sports clinics. Order your device today, and become one of the thousands of satisfied customers. If you are a first-time customer, you will receive 10 percent off the Glider. Check out www.gliderdevice.net. We also welcome wholesale accounts. This September, become a wholesale partner and receive 20 percent off your order.

Glider
www.gliderdevice.net

| Home | I | Shop | I | About | I | **Partnerships** | I | Help |

Wholesale Information
The Glider is available for wholesale orders. Use and promote the device at your health clinic, workout studio, or sports organization. Apart from promoting the device on-site, we recommend that you feature it on your social media page. Uploading a promotional post about the device will entitle you to receive free accessories.

For inquiries, please contact Brianna Perez directly at b.perez@gliderdevice.net. You will be instructed by her personally on how to use the device correctly. This is a free service offered to any new wholesale account.

Pursuit Pilates Employee Notice
Week of September 14

Pursuit Pilates became an official wholesale partner of the Glider massage device last week. Through personal experience, I can say that this machine is highly effective and that our clients would benefit from using it regularly.

In connection with this development, each instructor is being asked to attend a workshop on September 30 at 7 P.M. A Glider representative will instruct us directly on the correct use of the device. Please download the accompanying Glider software application before the workshop. Lastly, I would like everyone to encourage our clients to purchase a Glider device from our studio directly. We will have a display model at reception that they can try before buying.

196. What is true about the Glider?

(A) It is the latest model in a series.
(B) It was designed by a fitness professional.
(C) It provides live feedback to users.
(D) It comes with a 30-day money-back warranty.

197. What are wholesale customers encouraged to do?

(A) Promote a device on social media
(B) Place an order on a regular basis
(C) Obtain an official certificate
(D) Sign a two-year commitment

198. What can be inferred about Pursuit Pilates?

(A) It holds online classes.
(B) It has purchased other massage tools before.
(C) It received a 20 percent discount.
(D) It had an increase in membership.

199. What is suggested about Brianna Perez?

(A) She has a degree in software engineering.
(B) She is one of the cofounders of Glider.
(C) She agreed to a meeting on September 30.
(D) She regularly works out at Pursuit Pilates.

200. What are employees at Pursuit Pilates asked to do?

(A) Download a program
(B) Install a device
(C) Attend a sales meeting
(D) Instruct a new team member

This is the end of the test. You may review Parts 5, 6, and 7 if you finish the test early.

Review 체크리스트

TEST 4를 푼 다음, 아래 체크리스트에 따라 틀린 문제를 리뷰하고 박스에 완료 여부를 표시하세요.
만약 시험까지 얼마 남지 않았다면, 초록색으로 표시된 항목이라도 꼭 확인하세요.

☐ 틀린 문제의 경우, 다시 풀어봤다.

☐ 틀린 문제의 경우, 스크립트/해석을 확인하며 지문/문제의 내용을 정확하게 파악했다.

☐ 해설을 통해 각 문제의 정답과 오답의 근거가 무엇인지 정확하게 파악했다.

☐ Part 1과 Part 2에서 틀린 문제의 경우, 선택한 오답의 유형이 무엇이었는지 확인하고 같은
   함정에 빠지지 않도록 정리해두었다.

☐ Part 3와 Part 4의 각 문제에서 사용된 패러프레이징을 확인했다.

☐ Part 5와 Part 6의 경우, 틀린 문제에서 사용된 문법 포인트 또는 정답 및 오답 어휘를 정리
   했다.

☐ Part 6의 알맞은 문장 고르기 문제의 경우, 지문 전체를 정확하게 해석하며 전체 글의 흐름
   과 빈칸 주변 문맥을 정확하게 파악하는 연습을 했다.

☐ Part 7에서 질문과 보기의 키워드를 찾아 표시하며 지문에서 정답의 근거가 되는 문장이나
   구절을 찾아보고, 문제에서 사용된 패러프레이징을 확인했다.

☐ Part 1~Part 4는 받아쓰기 & 쉐도잉 워크북을 활용하여, TEST에 수록된 핵심 문장을 받아
   쓰고 따라 읽으며 복습했다.

☐ Part 1~Part 7은 단어암기자료를 활용하여, TEST에 수록된 핵심 어휘와 표현을 암기했다.

많은 양의 문제를 푸는 것도 중요하지만, 틀린 문제를 제대로 리뷰하는 것도 중요합니다.
틀린 문제를 한 번 더 꼼꼼히 리뷰한다면, 빠른 시간 내에 효과적으로 목표 점수를 달성할 수 있습니다.

TEST 5

LISTENING TEST

Part 1
Part 2
Part 3
Part 4

READING TEST

Part 5
Part 6
Part 7

Review 체크리스트

잠깐! 테스트 전 아래 사항을 꼭 확인하세요.

휴대전화의 전원을 끄셨나요? 예 ☐
Answer Sheet(p.255), 연필, 지우개, 시계를 준비하셨나요? 예 ☐
Listening MP3를 들을 준비가 되셨나요? 예 ☐

모든 준비가 완료되었으면 목표 점수를 떠올린 후 테스트를 시작합니다.
테스트를 마친 후, Review 체크리스트(p.236)를 보며 자신이 틀린 문제를 반드시 복습합니다.

🎧 TEST 5.mp3
실전용·복습용 문제풀이 MP3 무료 다운로드 및 스트리밍 바로듣기 (HackersIngang.com)
* 실제 시험장의 소음까지 재현해 낸 고사장 소음/매미 버전 MP3, 영국식·호주식 발음 집중 MP3, 고속 버전 MP3까지 구매
하면 실전에 더욱 완벽히 대비할 수 있습니다.

무료MP3 바로듣기

LISTENING TEST

In this section, you must demonstrate your ability to understand spoken English. This section is divided into four parts and will take approximately 45 minutes to complete. Do not mark the answers in your test book. Use the answer sheet that is provided separately.

PART 1

Directions: For each question, you will listen to four short statements about a picture in your test book. These statements will not be printed and will only be spoken one time. Select the statement that best describes what is happening in the picture and mark the corresponding letter (A), (B), (C), or (D) on the answer sheet.

Sample Answer
Ⓐ ● Ⓒ Ⓓ

The statement that best describes the picture is (B), "The man is sitting at the desk." So, you should mark letter (B) on the answer sheet.

1.

2.

GO ON TO THE NEXT PAGE

3.

4.

5.

6.

GO ON TO THE NEXT PAGE

PART 2

Directions: For each question, you will listen to a statement or question followed by three possible responses spoken in English. They will not be printed and will only be spoken one time. Select the best response and mark the corresponding letter (A), (B), or (C) on your answer sheet.

7. Mark your answer on your answer sheet.

8. Mark your answer on your answer sheet.

9. Mark your answer on your answer sheet.

10. Mark your answer on your answer sheet.

11. Mark your answer on your answer sheet.

12. Mark your answer on your answer sheet.

13. Mark your answer on your answer sheet.

14. Mark your answer on your answer sheet.

15. Mark your answer on your answer sheet.

16. Mark your answer on your answer sheet.

17. Mark your answer on your answer sheet.

18. Mark your answer on your answer sheet.

19. Mark your answer on your answer sheet.

20. Mark your answer on your answer sheet.

21. Mark your answer on your answer sheet.

22. Mark your answer on your answer sheet.

23. Mark your answer on your answer sheet.

24. Mark your answer on your answer sheet.

25. Mark your answer on your answer sheet.

26. Mark your answer on your answer sheet.

27. Mark your answer on your answer sheet.

28. Mark your answer on your answer sheet.

29. Mark your answer on your answer sheet.

30. Mark your answer on your answer sheet.

31. Mark your answer on your answer sheet.

PART 3

Directions: In this part, you will listen to several conversations between two or more speakers. These conversations will not be printed and will only be spoken one time. For each conversation, you will be asked to answer three questions. Select the best response and mark the corresponding letter (A), (B), (C), or (D) on your answer sheet.

32. What is the woman's problem?
   (A) She forgot to make a reservation.
   (B) She lost a personal belonging.
   (C) She left her wallet at home.
   (D) She is unhappy with a meal.

33. What does the woman want the man to do?
   (A) Move her to another table
   (B) Talk to some workers
   (C) Remove a charge from a bill
   (D) Bring her a lunch menu

34. What will the woman most likely do next?
   (A) Take a seat
   (B) Return to work
   (C) Describe an item
   (D) Place an order

35. What has been replaced?
   (A) Some seating
   (B) A reception desk
   (C) Some lobby tables
   (D) A filing cabinet

36. What did the company recently do?
   (A) Applied for a loan
   (B) Sent back merchandise
   (C) Increased profits
   (D) Hired employees

37. What does the woman agree to do?
   (A) Summarize a meeting
   (B) Contact some clients
   (C) Suggest some ideas
   (D) Look over a budget

38. What is the man's problem?
   (A) He cannot contact a client.
   (B) He has a scheduling conflict.
   (C) He forgot about an appointment.
   (D) He missed a deadline.

39. Why does the man say, "Your team created it"?
   (A) To remind her that she agreed to help
   (B) To indicate that she is familiar with a project
   (C) To commend her for being a valued employee
   (D) To show her that there is a problem

40. What will the woman most likely do next?
   (A) Meet with a CEO
   (B) Cancel a project
   (C) Visit a factory
   (D) Review a document

41. What are the speakers mainly discussing?
   (A) Expenses for a retreat
   (B) Parking spaces for vans
   (C) Directions to a camp
   (D) Transportation to an event

42. What does the woman want to know about?
   (A) How much a shuttle bus will cost
   (B) Whether an employee has a van
   (C) Who will drive a rental vehicle
   (D) Where a parking garage is located

43. What will the man most likely do next?
   (A) Take a bus ride
   (B) Make a phone call
   (C) Register for an event
   (D) Compare some prices

GO ON TO THE NEXT PAGE

44. What is the conversation mainly about?

(A) Selecting a hotel room
(B) Preparing for a vacation
(C) Choosing an activity
(D) Paying for a trip

45. What is mentioned about Rachel?

(A) She went to the spa.
(B) She is interested in surfing lessons.
(C) She lives in Hawaii.
(D) She has a meeting at 11 o'clock.

46. What does the man give to the woman?

(A) A suitcase
(B) A souvenir
(C) A key
(D) A brochure

47. Who most likely is the man?

(A) A cleaning business owner
(B) A store bookkeeper
(C) A delivery truck driver
(D) A café manager

48. What was sent with a shipment?

(A) Sample goods
(B) A revised bill
(C) Office supplies
(D) A special coupon

49. What does the man ask the woman to do?

(A) Write an e-mail
(B) Send some packages
(C) Use a voucher
(D) Return some products

50. Where most likely is the conversation taking place?

(A) At a bookstore
(B) At a library
(C) At a publishing expo
(D) At a broadcasting studio

51. What does the woman say about *Voting for Peanuts*?

(A) It was released after *The Old Bride*.
(B) It is shelved behind the help desk.
(C) It was publicized in the media.
(D) It was written by a talk show host.

52. Why does the man say, "I heard it was popular"?

(A) To express excitement
(B) To indicate a lack of surprise
(C) To explain a decision
(D) To recommend a new book

53. What does the man say about *Help Yourself*?

(A) It was filmed this year.
(B) It is playing at a local theater.
(C) It features a well-known actor.
(D) It deals with food choices.

54. What type of service do the speakers most likely offer?

(A) Product advertising
(B) Nutritional consulting
(C) Video sales
(D) Career advice

55. What does the man suggest?

(A) Viewing a documentary
(B) Waiting in another room
(C) Filming a commercial
(D) Uploading materials online

56. What is the conversation mainly about?

(A) Launching a campaign
(B) Saving money on utilities
(C) Preventing environmental pollution
(D) Trying a new water source

57. In which department does the man work?

(A) Accounting
(B) Shipping
(C) Human Resources
(D) Maintenance

58. What do the women decide to do?

(A) Reschedule a meeting
(B) Collect some deliveries
(C) Order a new system
(D) Get some price quotes

---

59. What is the woman trying to do?

(A) Plan some entertainment
(B) Convince a friend to join her
(C) Promote a community event
(D) Get tickets to a museum

60. What does the man recommend?

(A) Having a picnic in the park
(B) Visiting a shopping center
(C) Watching a performance
(D) Taking a countryside tour

61. What does the man say he will do?

(A) Inquire about a building address
(B) Share an online link
(C) Confirm performance times
(D) List some attractions

> **Helga's Dry Cleaning**
> Helga Kim, Facility Owner
>
> **Phone Number**: 555-6922
> **Daily Hours**: 9 A.M.–7 P.M.
> **Street Address**: 37 Pine Road
> **E-mail Address**: helga@cleanwiz.net

62. Why is the woman visiting the shop?

(A) To verify an amount
(B) To make a complaint
(C) To select some materials
(D) To collect some items

63. Look at the graphic. What information contains an error?

(A) Phone Number
(B) Street Address
(C) Daily Hours
(D) E-mail Address

64. What will take 10 minutes to be completed?

(A) Cleaning some garments
(B) Fixing a photocopier
(C) Filling out a form
(D) Printing new cards

GO ON TO THE NEXT PAGE

Room	Maximum Capacity
Majesty Hall	100 people
Throne Hall	150 people
Scepter Hall	200 people
Royalty Hall	250 people

65. Why is the woman calling?

(A) To sign up for an event
(B) To inquire about a conference speaker
(C) To ask about a facility's location
(D) To update a reservation

66. Look at the graphic. Which room did the woman originally book?

(A) Majesty Hall
(B) Throne Hall
(C) Scepter Hall
(D) Royalty Hall

67. What does the woman request?

(A) Additional food
(B) Presentation equipment
(C) An updated list of rooms
(D) Extra guest passes

	Bronze Plan	Silver Plan	Gold Plan	Platinum Plan
free domestic calls	v	v	v	v
free international calls				v
unlimited texts		v	v	v
unlimited internet			v	v

68. Why does the woman want to change her service plan?

(A) She has established new business relationships.
(B) She needs an additional phone line.
(C) She wants to upgrade to a smart phone.
(D) She is going on an international business trip.

69. Look at the graphic. Which plan does the man recommend?

(A) Bronze Plan
(B) Silver Plan
(C) Gold Plan
(D) Platinum Plan

70. What will the man probably do next?

(A) Provide a free gift
(B) Collect a payment
(C) Update an account
(D) Make a telephone call

PART 4

Directions: In this part, you will listen to several short talks by a single speaker. These talks will not be printed and will only be spoken one time. For each talk, you will be asked to answer three questions. Select the best response and mark the corresponding letter (A), (B), (C), or (D) on your answer sheet.

71. What was supposed to be discussed tomorrow?
    (A) A work schedule
    (B) A project cancellation
    (C) A job opportunity
    (D) A sales proposition

72. Why must a meeting be postponed?
    (A) A family matter needs to be handled.
    (B) A flight was overbooked.
    (C) A worker is traveling overseas.
    (D) An office manager is feeling ill.

73. What does the speaker ask the listener to do?
    (A) Stop by her office
    (B) Contact her assistant
    (C) Call her mobile phone
    (D) Send her an e-mail

74. What is still taking place?
    (A) A running race
    (B) A sign installation
    (C) Building construction
    (D) Bridge repairs

75. What will probably happen within the hour?
    (A) A further update will be provided.
    (B) A community event will begin.
    (C) Cars will be moved from an area.
    (D) A hospital will reopen.

76. What does the speaker recommend?
    (A) Using a different route
    (B) Starting a commute early
    (C) Taking public transport
    (D) Avoiding an intersection

77. What is the company planning to do?
    (A) Relocate its headquarters
    (B) Order some chemicals
    (C) Open a new plant
    (D) Transfer some employees

78. Why does the speaker say, "Actually, it's near a residential area"?
    (A) To dismiss a potential concern
    (B) To highlight a convenient location
    (C) To suggest moving a facility
    (D) To point out a complicating factor

79. What is the speaker concerned about?
    (A) Financial costs
    (B) Environmental pollution
    (C) A production schedule
    (D) A government policy

80. What is the speaker mainly discussing?
    (A) Advice on working relationships
    (B) Guidance for job seekers
    (C) Selecting a career path
    (D) Pursuing job training

81. What does the speaker imply when he says, "You'd be surprised"?
    (A) A document includes few errors.
    (B) A process has become more complicated.
    (C) A requirement is relatively new.
    (D) A problem can easily occur.

82. According to the speaker, what can leave a bad impression?
    (A) Long cover letters
    (B) Insufficient experience
    (C) Spelling mistakes
    (D) Inappropriate attire

GO ON TO THE NEXT PAGE

83. Who most likely is the speaker?

(A) A facility manager
(B) A government official
(C) A professional athlete
(D) A corporate investor

84. What will the CRT Center be used for?

(A) Charity auctions
(B) Sporting events
(C) Industry conventions
(D) Community gatherings

85. What is mentioned about Kent Berkley?

(A) He oversaw some construction.
(B) He recently met with a mayor.
(C) He supported a project.
(D) He plans to give a talk.

---

86. Who most likely is the listener?

(A) A concert organizer
(B) A music instructor
(C) A school secretary
(D) A store owner

87. What is the main purpose of the message?

(A) To respond to a question
(B) To book a performer
(C) To sign up for a class
(D) To get a suggestion

88. Why does the speaker say, "I'm flexible"?

(A) He has an open schedule.
(B) He has no brand preference.
(C) He is available to take a course.
(D) He is a fan of different performers.

---

89. Where most likely are the listeners?

(A) At a recruitment interview
(B) At a trade show
(C) At a retirement celebration
(D) At a holiday party

90. According to the speaker, why was a campaign significant?

(A) It attracted foreign media attention.
(B) It won an award.
(C) It used new technology.
(D) It helped grow a business.

91. What does the speaker say she values the most?

(A) The dedication of her employees
(B) The purpose of her project
(C) Her overseas experience
(D) Her relationships with coworkers

---

92. What is the report mainly about?

(A) Establishing an additional school
(B) Training some teachers
(C) Appointing a new principal
(D) Expanding current curriculum

93. What did Yolanda Moya announce yesterday?

(A) The location of an office
(B) The size of a program
(C) The cost of a development
(D) The length of a project

94. What is mentioned about some parents?

(A) They do not want kids to be relocated.
(B) They voted on an issue last week.
(C) They accept a government plan.
(D) They think expenses should be lowered.

Product Specification	
Product Weight	**Price**
20 lbs	$2,000
25 lbs	$1,750
28 lbs	$1,000
35 lbs	$2,200

95. What kind of product is being demonstrated?

(A) A cleaning appliance
(B) A digital printer
(C) A musical instrument
(D) A flat screen television

96. According to the speaker, what is on the front panel?

(A) A display screen
(B) Control buttons
(C) A power switch
(D) Warning indicators

97. Look at the graphic. How much does the TouchFone 1000 cost?

(A) $2,000
(B) $1,750
(C) $1,000
(D) $2,200

PRODUCTION LINE

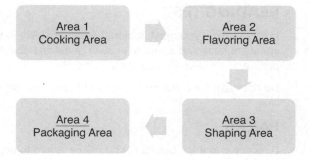

98. What is a characteristic of Dwyers' Sweets?

(A) It produces 100 types of candy.
(B) It has opened a second location.
(C) It operates a century-old facility.
(D) It has remained a family-owned business.

99. Look at the graphic. Where will the tour group go next?

(A) Area 1
(B) Area 2
(C) Area 3
(D) Area 4

100. What will the listeners receive after the tour?

(A) Samples of candy
(B) A list of best sellers
(C) Locations of international stores
(D) A set of gift vouchers

This is the end of the Listening test. Turn to PART 5 in your test book.

GO ON TO THE NEXT PAGE

READING TEST

In this section, you must demonstrate your ability to read and comprehend English. You will be given a variety of texts and asked to answer questions about these texts. This section is divided into three parts and will take 75 minutes to complete.

Do not mark the answers in your test book. Use the answer sheet that is separately provided.

PART 5

Directions: In each question, you will be asked to review a statement that is missing a word or phrase. Four answer choices will be provided for each statement. Select the best answer and mark the corresponding letter (A), (B), (C), or (D) on the answer sheet.

PART 5 권장 풀이 시간 11분

101. Visitors must present ------- when entering the research facility or accessing sensitive areas.

(A) identification
(B) identity
(C) identified
(D) identifying

102. Orex Enterprises' ------- focus is still fashion, although it has expanded into the restaurant business.

(A) high
(B) multiple
(C) primary
(D) outside

103. Mr. Kurtz was extremely ------- with the contract negotiations, which resulted in a 15 percent salary increase.

(A) pleased
(B) pleasing
(C) please
(D) pleasure

104. Only ------- who submit a résumé through the company's Web site will be considered for the intern position.

(A) neither
(B) that
(C) those
(D) which

105. Pete's Produce is well-known for ------- selling organic fruit and vegetables.

(A) exclusively
(B) exclusion
(C) exclude
(D) exclusive

106. By the time SolarTech opened its first factory in Europe, it ------- facilities in America and Asia already.

(A) is establishing
(B) has established
(C) establishes
(D) had established

107. Staff members at Flemwell Department Store ------- work overtime during the busy holiday season.

(A) routed
(B) routine
(C) routines
(D) routinely

108. Air East passengers are advised to use the automated check-in machines ------- the airport.

(A) upon
(B) throughout
(C) between
(D) almost

109. Customers can ------- unexpected fees by applying for a cellular plan that provides unlimited texting and data usage.

(A) prepare
(B) shorten
(C) comply
(D) avoid

110. Employees must contact the human resources department ------- request a leave of absence.

(A) after all
(B) in order to
(C) as for
(D) just

111. Under the ------- of the lease agreement, the tenant must give a month's notice before moving out.

(A) terms
(B) rights
(C) causes
(D) signs

112. This Wednesday is ------- the name of Zoltek Engineering's new CEO will be announced.

(A) when
(B) what
(C) why
(D) who

113. Athletes ------- more than 50 countries participated in the World Tennis Tournament held last year in Guangzhou.

(A) representing
(B) represented
(C) represents
(D) representation

114. The continued ------- of residents from rural to urban areas has created a housing shortage in Manila.

(A) arrangement
(B) relocation
(C) environment
(D) discovery

115. Details about the upcoming training workshop will begin to ------- following the announcement.

(A) compile
(B) include
(C) appoint
(D) emerge

116. All discussions regarding the potential company merger have been put on hold ------- the first week of February.

(A) about
(B) towards
(C) until
(D) except

117. Mr. Ross was considered an ------- candidate for the marketing position because he lacked professional experience.

(A) inadequately
(B) inadequacy
(C) inadequate
(D) inadequateness

118. Although participation in HPS Company's social responsibility committee is purely -------, employee involvement is very high.

(A) precise
(B) voluntary
(C) significant
(D) persistent

119. New boxes placed by the library's main entrance allow patrons ------- materials even after the facility has closed.

(A) return
(B) returned
(C) returning
(D) to return

120. Because *SharpBiz* Magazine is published -------, readers get updates on essential business news four times per year.

(A) quarterly
(B) properly
(C) constantly
(D) recently

GO ON TO THE NEXT PAGE

121. According to recent surveys, advertisements on television have a greater ------- on consumers than those found in newspapers and magazines.

(A) influence
(B) influential
(C) influenced
(D) have influenced

122. Edgecom will issue a statement today ------- the status of the company's overseas expansion.

(A) behind
(B) beyond
(C) regarding
(D) within

123. Customers who exceed the monthly mobile data allocation will ------- additional charges.

(A) replace
(B) incur
(C) switch
(D) possess

124. Mayfield Footwear's summer sale will be a good ------- for shoppers to purchase a variety of new shoes.

(A) opportunity
(B) contribution
(C) appearance
(D) restoration

125. Software products from Digital Age can be refunded within one month of purchase ------- they are accompanied by an original receipt.

(A) on behalf of
(B) although
(C) so that
(D) as long as

126. The revised environmental regulations ------- at reducing the amount of greenhouse gases emitted by local factories.

(A) aims
(B) aiming
(C) to aim
(D) are aimed

127. ------- did the buyers like the price of the house, but they also appreciated its location.

(A) Neither
(B) Not only
(C) Either
(D) Such as

128. To qualify for financial -------, students must submit a funding request each term.

(A) assistance
(B) assisted
(C) to assist
(D) assistant

129. Nesbit Software ------- its sales projections as it expects revenues to decrease this year.

(A) overtook
(B) connected
(C) reduced
(D) complimented

130. The ------- laptop model released by Core Electronics was much more popular with customers than its latest one.

(A) various
(B) relative
(C) customary
(D) previous

PART 6

Directions: In this part, you will be asked to read four English texts. Each text is missing a word, phrase, or sentence. Select the answer choice that correctly completes the text and mark the corresponding letter (A), (B), (C), or (D) on the answer sheet.

PART 6 권장 풀이 시간　8분

Questions 131-134 refer to the following e-mail.

To: Allan White <a.white@trytek.com>
From: Joseph Winfield <j.winfield@trytek.com>
Date: March 12
Subject: Orientation Seminar

Dear Allan,

I'm glad to report that the planning of our orientation seminar for new interns is proceeding smoothly. However, one important detail remains unresolved. We still need to schedule a short presentation by someone from the marketing department, but I have not heard from anyone who would ------- in the seminar. -------. So, please let everyone know that the
　　　　　　　　　　　　131.　　　　　　　　　　**132.**
presenter will talk about the interns' ------- duties for only 10 minutes. -------, you should
　　　　　　　　　　　　　　　　　　　　133.　　　　　　　　　　　　　　　　**134.**
remind everyone that contributors to the seminar will receive $200 as compensation for their time and effort.

Thank you very much,

Joe

131. (A) have liked participating
　　　(B) have liked to participate
　　　(C) like participating
　　　(D) like to participate

132. (A) Presenters have already begun
　　　　　rehearsing their speeches.
　　　(B) Staff members might think that it will
　　　　　take too much time.
　　　(C) New members have also joined to talk
　　　　　about their experiences.
　　　(D) Participation is mandatory for
　　　　　specified employees.

133. (A) anxious
　　　(B) momentary
　　　(C) regular
　　　(D) ongoing

134. (A) Unfortunately
　　　(B) In addition
　　　(C) Namely
　　　(D) Nevertheless

GO ON TO THE NEXT PAGE

Questions 135-138 refer to the following advertisement.

Madison Woodworks
Established 1987

Planning to ------- your home or office? Complement your new interior with finely crafted
135.

items from Madison Woodworks. For over 30 years, we have supplied quality handmade

goods to homes and businesses throughout Chesterfield County. Whether you like

traditional or contemporary styles, you are sure to find something in our store to enjoy for

years to come. If you prefer more ------- items, consult one of our in-house designers about
136.

creating a unique table, desk, or chair. Stop by our store today at 627 Stockport Lane in

Manchester. Take advantage of discounts on all ready-made ------- until the end of July. You
137.

can also view our catalog online. -------.
138.

135. (A) leave
(B) renovate
(C) finance
(D) promote

136. (A) personalize
(B) personalizes
(C) personalizing
(D) personalized

137. (A) fabric
(B) gadgets
(C) furniture
(D) structures

138. (A) A team of technicians has been
scheduled to inspect the product in
your home.
(B) The items can be replaced if you
provide us with this warranty card.
(C) Use the included instruction manual
and a few simple tools to assemble it.
(D) Go to www.madisonwoodworks.com
to browse our entire collection.

To: All staff
From: Jason Fraser, Human resources
Date: August 5
Subject: Professional development classes

Management is happy to announce that, beginning this fall, staff members of Hearthstone

Appliances will be ------- to receive financial support for academic courses related to their
139.

areas of responsibility. Participating employees will be reimbursed for 50 percent of their

total tuition fees. -------.
140.

Only employees ------- a class delivered by an approved educational institution may receive
141.

funding. In addition, there are some other restrictions that may prevent certain individuals

from participating. -------, we strongly recommend scheduling a meeting with a human
142.

resources representative before registering for a class.

139. (A) eligible
(B) prominent
(C) social
(D) preferable

140. (A) This amount will be paid upon
successful completion of their chosen
programs.
(B) District managers are required to lead
at least 20 hours of instruction.
(C) Employees of the school will receive
discounts on textbooks and other
materials.
(D) Applications for the job opening will be
collected by the human resources
department.

141. (A) take
(B) takes
(C) taking
(D) taken

142. (A) Likewise
(B) Afterward
(C) Consequently
(D) For instance

GO ON TO THE NEXT PAGE

Questions 143-146 refer to the following announcement.

PEN AND PAPER: ANNOUNCING OUR OPENING DAY

Come and celebrate our grand opening with us on November 1. Pen and Paper is a retail

------- supplying all kinds of business equipment, stationery, and other office supplies.
143.

We are certain that whatever you require for your workspace, you will be able to ------- at our
144.

store. Just tell our staff members what you are looking for, and they'll provide you with a

range of options to choose from. In addition to binding services, we also perform a variety of

print jobs, such as brochures and business cards.

We'll have all kinds of giveaways for any customer who ------- our store on that day. Plus, the
145.

100th customer will receive a $100 gift card. -------. So, make sure to join us at 550 Emerald
146.

Avenue for this special event!

---

143. (A) establish
(B) establishes
(C) established
(D) establishment

144. (A) find
(B) deliver
(C) repair
(D) exchange

145. (A) was entered
(B) enters
(C) enter
(D) entering

146. (A) It can be used for anything inside our store.
(B) The opening will be attended by our company's CEO.
(C) Our store's renovations have been completed.
(D) We will announce the winner of the prize tomorrow.

PART 7

Directions: In this part, you will be asked to read several texts, such as advertisements, articles, instant messages, or examples of business correspondence. Each text is followed by several questions. Select the best answer and mark the corresponding letter (A), (B), (C), or (D) on your answer sheet.

🕐 **PART 7 권장 풀이 시간** **54분**

Questions 147-148 refer to the following questionnaire.

Petra's Grill

It is our mission to provide you with the best dining experience possible, so we welcome customer feedback. Please fill out this short questionnaire and place it in the box beside the exit. Thank you!

Were you provided with prompt service?
---Yes   -**X**-No

How would you rate the quality of your meal?
---Excellent   -**X**-Very good   ---Satisfactory   ---Terrible

What was your main meal?
Roast chicken and a green salad with Italian dressing

Was the food worth the price?
-**X**-Yes   ---No

How frequently do you visit Petra's Grill?
---Often   ---Occasionally   ---Rarely   -**X**-This was my first visit

Comments
I think my next visit here will be better as I'll make sure to come when it's less busy. My server was dealing with a number of other tables and, although she was friendly and polite, it took a very long time for her to notice me and bring over a menu.

---

147. What can be inferred from the questionnaire?

(A) The restaurant primarily serves Italian cuisine.
(B) The customer intends to eat at Petra's Grill a second time.
(C) The dining area was recently remodeled.
(D) The menu was changed to reflect customer feedback.

148. What problem did the customer have at the restaurant?

(A) The food was cold when it arrived.
(B) There were no tables immediately available.
(C) It took a while to be acknowledged by a server.
(D) The items listed on the menu were overpriced.

GO ON TO THE NEXT PAGE

Questions 149-151 refer to the following notice.

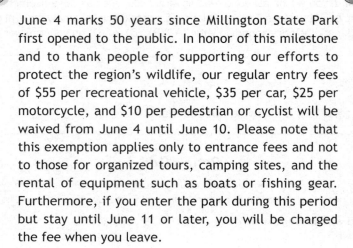

June 4 marks 50 years since Millington State Park first opened to the public. In honor of this milestone and to thank people for supporting our efforts to protect the region's wildlife, our regular entry fees of $55 per recreational vehicle, $35 per car, $25 per motorcycle, and $10 per pedestrian or cyclist will be waived from June 4 until June 10. Please note that this exemption applies only to entrance fees and not to those for organized tours, camping sites, and the rental of equipment such as boats or fishing gear. Furthermore, if you enter the park during this period but stay until June 11 or later, you will be charged the fee when you leave.

149. What is the topic of the notice?

(A) Changes to a facility's parking regulations
(B) An organization's environmental efforts
(C) Temporary free admission to a recreational area
(D) An anniversary banquet held at a state park

150. How much does it cost to enter the park on a bicycle?

(A) $10
(B) $25
(C) $35
(D) $55

151. What is suggested about Millington State Park?

(A) It charges guests based on the number of people in a car.
(B) Its organized tours are discounted for large groups.
(C) It regularly asks for financial support from the public.
(D) Its visitors can stay for multiple days.

Questions 152-153 refer to the following text message chain.

Brad Lee   9:34 A.M.
I just received a call from a tenant in one of the properties we manage. She's in Unit 202 of the Plaza Tower on Fifth Street.

Sara Godfrey   9:35 A.M.
Is she upset about the noise from the renovation work in the lobby? I've gotten a lot of complaints from the residents of that building this week.

Brad Lee   9:36 A.M.
No, that's not it. She was offered a position with a firm in Seattle. The job starts next week, so she will have to move out of the apartment this month. But she signed a one-year lease agreement. She wants to know if she will have to pay a penalty.

Sara Godfrey   9:38 A.M.
That depends. She has until the end of the month to find a new tenant. Otherwise, she will have to pay.

Brad Lee   9:39 A.M.
Actually, she mentioned that her brother was interested in the apartment. I'll tell him to fill out an application this week. Then, I'll speak with the owner.

152. What is indicated about the Plaza Tower?

(A) It is owned by a company in Seattle.
(B) It was built less than a year ago.
(C) It has several vacant apartments.
(D) It is currently being remodeled.

153. At 9:38 A.M., what does Ms. Godfrey most likely mean when she writes, "That depends"?

(A) An agreement has not yet been signed.
(B) A building owner has been difficult to reach.
(C) A penalty will be waived if a new tenant is found.
(D) A unit might not be available after a certain date.

GO ON TO THE NEXT PAGE

Questions 154-156 refer to the following e-mail.

To: Diana Mansfield <dmans@timemail.com>
From: Herbal Greens Customer Support <cs@herbalgreens.com>
Date: August 2
Subject: Membership

Dear Ms. Mansfield,

We noticed that you have placed several orders with us over the last few months, but you have not yet signed up for a membership on our Web site. — [1] —. While it is still possible to buy our products without registering, there are numerous reasons to become a member.

First of all, you will no longer be required to enter your shipping address, telephone number, and credit card details each time you make a purchase. — [2] —. You will also receive updates on our weekly promotions, allowing you to see great deals you would otherwise not know about. — [3] —. Furthermore, only members can build up loyalty credit. If you join, you will earn 10 percent of the total amount you spend whenever you place an order. You can put this credit toward the cost of your next purchase or let it accumulate to use at a later time. — [4] —.

Creating an account takes less than two minutes and costs nothing. We encourage you to take advantage of Herbal Greens' membership benefits by signing up today.

Clay Lewis
Herbal Greens Customer Support

154. What is the purpose of the e-mail?

(A) To explain how to set up an online account
(B) To convince a customer to become a member
(C) To ask a client to change a password
(D) To describe a membership upgrade benefit

155. What is NOT mentioned about loyalty credit?

(A) It can be used to purchase items.
(B) It can only be earned by members of a Web site.
(C) It expires after a certain amount of time.
(D) It is acquired each time an order is paid for.

156. In which of the positions marked [1], [2], [3], and [4] does the following sentence best belong?

"This information will be automatically inputted into the necessary fields when you are ready to check out."

(A) [1]
(B) [2]
(C) [3]
(D) [4]

Tam Bakery – The Best Cakes in Town!

Are you planning a birthday, wedding, or other important event? If you want the perfect cake to celebrate your special occasion, visit Tam Bakery on the corner of Harbor Street and Elm Avenue. Our talented cake designers can create works of art that are both affordable and delicious. They will work closely with you to ensure that the cake you receive is the one you envisioned. What's more, we use only the best ingredients and offer both vegan and low-fat options as well. From May 15 to June 15, we are reducing the prices of all custom cakes by 10 percent to celebrate our 10th anniversary. So, don't delay—stop by soon to begin planning your perfect cake.

For more information about Tam Bakery and the products we offer, visit our Web site at www.tambakery.com.

157. What is NOT mentioned about Tam Bakery's cakes?

(A) They can be made with high-quality ingredients.
(B) They can be planned by a customer.
(C) They can be purchased at a discount.
(D) They can be delivered to an event venue.

158. What is indicated about Tam Bakery?

(A) It sells merchandise online.
(B) It will be opening another branch.
(C) It has been in business for a number of years.
(D) It includes recipes on its Web site.

GO ON TO THE NEXT PAGE

Questions 159-162 refer to the following article.

September 7—A spokesperson for Brytwells Department Store announced today that, for the first time in 31 years, the company will change its logo. The classic red and yellow design that customers are so familiar with is being replaced by a more modern one. This is part of a wider effort to update the company's image by CEO Marcus Cathwell, who moved up into his position when Jackson Stevens retired two months ago.

For more than two decades now, Brytwells has faced stiff competition from new department stores offering more variety at cheaper prices. Several store closures have resulted each year, and another five are set to cease operations within the next 12 months. Mr. Cathwell acknowledges that the Brytwells brand is long overdue for an update and says he feels confident that the new logo will fit in well with the other changes being made to the company. These include a new contemporary store layout and the introduction of 15 clothing brands for young people.

Brytwells locations in the northeastern region of the nation, where Brytwells opened its initial store, will be the first to begin using the logo in October. Other Brytwells stores across the country will adopt the new corporate image before the end of autumn.

159. What is the article mainly about?

(A) An idea for a new store's logo
(B) The closure of a national chain
(C) Changes to a corporate symbol
(D) Competition among retailers

160. What is mentioned about Mr. Cathwell?

(A) He created a floor plan.
(B) He was hired in March.
(C) He was recently promoted.
(D) He founded a company.

161. What will most likely happen next year?

(A) Brytwells will launch a new Web site.
(B) Brytwells will lower prices at all locations.
(C) A number of Brytwells stores will close down.
(D) The CEO of Brytwells will resign from his position.

162. What is NOT mentioned about Brytwells?

(A) It will begin selling more products for young people.
(B) Its original branch will relocate.
(C) It opened its first store in the northeast.
(D) It has branches throughout the country.

NOTICE

Hopewell Productions will be filming a scene from *A New Life* on July 8. This feature-length film stars Christina Harvey and Mike Mann and is being directed by Herbert Mercer.

Anyone over the age of 18 is invited to audition as an extra. The casting call for extras will take place at West Newton High School on July 1 from noon until 8 P.M., and all participants must bring a driver's license, a passport, or some other type of official photo identification.

Extras will be used primarily as crowd members for a short sequence that takes place in a mall. The shoot will take 10 to 12 hours and involve a lot of standing and waiting around. Food will be provided, and a raffle for small prizes will be held at the end. The pay will be $9 an hour.

163. According to the notice, what is Hopewell Productions encouraging people to do?

(A) Work on a catering crew
(B) Set up equipment
(C) Conduct tours of a set
(D) Appear in a scene

164. What should participants bring to West Newton High School?

(A) A bank statement
(B) A résumé and cover letter
(C) A form of identification
(D) A recording of a performance

165. What is mentioned about the shoot?

(A) It will last for several days.
(B) It will include a prize drawing.
(C) It will mostly take place outside.
(D) It will start at noon.

GO ON TO THE NEXT PAGE

Questions 166-169 refer to the following e-mail.

To: Pingvillian Hotel Reservations <rsvn@pingvillianhotel.com>
From: Alice Rolstin <alirol@alertmail.com>
Date: September 10
Subject: Our stay

To Whom It May Concern,

I am writing in regard to the reservation I made for a room at your hotel through the online travel agency Frewel.com. I have a couple of requests. — [1] —. First of all, my husband and I will require a late check-in. We should be landing in Chiang Mai at 11:30 P.M. on September 17. I believe we will arrive at the hotel by midnight if the information on your Web page is accurate. — [2] —.

In addition, you'll see that we are supposed to check out on September 25th. However, our flight home was changed, and we will be departing at 8:30 P.M. on the 24th. — [3] —. Since we won't be spending the night of the 25th at your hotel as originally planned, I was wondering if we could cancel our reservation for the final day and check out at about 6:00 P.M. on the 24th instead. — [4] —. I know your check-out time is noon, but if we could stay until it is time for us to get a taxi to the airport, it would really be helpful.

Thank you for your time, and I am looking forward to our stay at Pingvillian Hotel.

Alice Rolstin

---

166. What is true about Ms. Rolstin?

(A) She made a reservation through a Web site.
(B) She will arrive at the hotel earlier than scheduled.
(C) She will be staying in Chiang Mai until next month.
(D) She has booked two rooms at the Pingvillian Hotel.

167. The word "originally" in paragraph 2, line 3, is closest in meaning to

(A) uniquely
(B) completely
(C) differently
(D) initially

168. What does Ms. Rolstin ask for?

(A) A compensation voucher
(B) A late check-out time
(C) A drive to the airport
(D) An additional night

169. In which of the positions marked [1], [2], [3], and [4] does the following sentence best belong?

"It says getting a taxi from the airport only takes about 15 to 20 minutes."

(A) [1]
(B) [2]
(C) [3]
(D) [4]

Construction of Wastewater Treatment Center Still in Doubt

A proposal by the local government to build a wastewater treatment center in Komlossy has been met with some uncertainty from the public. If municipal water-quality officials approve this construction project, residential and commercial property owners in the area will have to pay higher taxes to cover the cost. It is estimated that the system will cost $52 million to construct and a subsequent $420,000 a month to operate and maintain. Although some taxpayers are reluctant to stop using the far cheaper system currently in use, the majority feel that the new one is worth the added cost. At the very least, it will not permit any contaminants to enter nearby rivers and lakes, as the old one does. The issue will be discussed in depth at Komlossy's Water Quality Control Board meeting on November 6.

170. What is suggested about the current wastewater system?

(A) It contributes to water pollution.
(B) It is very expensive to operate.
(C) It was installed last year.
(D) It is preferred by most residents.

171. According to the article, what will occur in November?

(A) Construction of a new city facility will begin.
(B) Citizens will vote on whether to build a sewage system.
(C) A municipal matter will be examined at a gathering.
(D) A new citywide tax will be implemented.

GO ON TO THE NEXT PAGE

Questions 172-175 refer to the following online chat discussion.

Soomin Park [6:38 p.m.] There has been a change of plans. Ms. Lawson just texted me to say she will no longer be requiring our services on June 4. Her wedding date has been moved to September 16, and she wants our studio to do the photography for her ceremony and reception on that day instead.

Lauren Jean [6:41 p.m.] That is going to be a problem. I am covering another client's event all day then. Also, we don't have any jobs booked for June 4 now.

Taylor Morgan [6:43 p.m.] Is her wedding still going to be at the same place and time on September 16? If so, I can do it. I'll be free all afternoon.

Soomin Park [6:44 p.m.] Thanks, Taylor. The time and venue are the same as previously requested. I told Ms. Lawson that if we get another booking for June 4, we will transfer her deposit to her bill for September 16. If not, she will lose the deposit.

Lauren Jean [6:45 p.m.] That makes sense. We turned down several other prospective clients who wanted to hire us for that day. Now that I think about it, a few of them may still need a photographer.

Soomin Park [6:45 p.m.] Really? If you have any time, please get in touch with them.

Send

172. Why did Ms. Lawson contact Ms. Park?

(A) To arrange a photo shoot at a studio
(B) To negotiate a reduced rate
(C) To notify her of a location change
(D) To reschedule an appointment

173. What can be inferred about Ms. Lawson's wedding?

(A) It will be held at an outdoor venue.
(B) It will be photographed by Mr. Morgan.
(C) It has been paid for in full.
(D) It will occur a month from now.

174. What will happen if the studio cannot make a booking for June 4?

(A) Ms. Park will draft a new contract.
(B) Ms. Jean will be free to attend a wedding.
(C) Ms. Lawson will lose some money she paid.
(D) Mr. Morgan will be unable to access a venue.

175. At 6:45 P.M., what does Ms. Jean most likely mean when she writes, "That makes sense"?

(A) She wants to complain about other clients.
(B) She plans to check an account.
(C) She thinks a decision is reasonable.
(D) She feels a deposit should be refunded.

GO ON TO THE NEXT PAGE

Watertown Music Festival

From Saturday, June 5 through Sunday, June 6, the city of Watertown is hosting an event that every music lover will surely enjoy! The Watertown Music Festival will be a two-day celebration featuring vocalists from the surrounding region, including Kayla Swank, Sienna Hanson, and Tristan Woodlawn. Performances will be given on multiple stages that have been set up both outside and within the Morton Arena. Tickets will grant access to all performance areas and dining facilities. Adults will be charged $30 for entry, and children under the age of 10 can come for free.

The festival is sponsored by New Wave, a music and book retailer that has been in business for nearly 30 years. Be sure not to miss New Wave's booth next to the complex's entrance for a chance to win backstage passes to a concert on Darrell Lane's nationwide tour. For more information and to purchase tickets, visit www.watertownmusicfest.com.

Local Festival a Major Hit

By Marcus Cooper

June 10—The Watertown Music Festival, which occurred earlier this month, was a major event for the city. This year, musical artists drew in more than 20,000 audience members over two days. What helped make this possible was the change of venue. This June's location allowed more space for additional stages to be installed than Westfield Arena did last year.

Local restaurant owner, Nancy Welsh, said that the festival was incredibly popular with her entire family. "There was plenty of space for my three young kids to run around, and I had lots of fun enjoying all of the great music," Ms. Welsh noted. "I even took part in a prize giveaway sponsored by New Wave, which resulted in me winning backstage passes to a concert I was already planning on attending in August!"

For those who did not make it this June, keep up to date with information on next year's event by downloading the festival's smartphone application.

176. What is mentioned about the Watertown Music Festival?

(A) It has been held for more than a decade.
(B) It will have indoor and outdoor performance areas.
(C) It will feature international celebrities.
(D) It has been delayed due to another event.

177. In the advertisement, the word "grant" in paragraph 1, line 8, is closest in meaning to

(A) permit
(B) sign
(C) research
(D) request

178. What is indicated about the Westfield Arena?

(A) It is used as a festival venue every year.
(B) It will be closed down for the summer.
(C) It is less spacious than Morton Arena.
(D) It will be renovated to include a dining area.

179. Which performer does Ms. Welsh plan to see in August?

(A) Kayla Swank
(B) Darrell Lane
(C) Sienna Hanson
(D) Tristan Woodlawn

180. What is stated about the smartphone application?

(A) It will undergo some design changes this June.
(B) It was downloaded by Ms. Welsh's kids.
(C) It will include details about a subsequent festival.
(D) It was introduced in a local magazine last year.

GO ON TO THE NEXT PAGE

TEST 5

인강으로 끝내는 해커스 토익 실전 LC+RC 1

Sales Contract

This contract represents the sale of a used car by City Street Motors of Danville (represented by Blaine Ritter) to Grace Huang on November 5. All parties have agreed to the sale as outlined in this agreement. The contract remains valid unless terminated by both the buyer and the seller.

Make and Model: Merriton Motors, Juniper
Exterior and Interior Colors: Blue, Gray
Vehicle Identification Number: XCN138004832738
Sales Price: $14,000
Payment Method: ■ Cash   □ Check   □ Credit card

The seller has released all information regarding the car's accident and repair history. The buyer has agreed to purchase the car as is and, once the agreement is signed, will not be able to cancel the deal due to any defect found. The seller will provide two keys for the car and recent automobile inspection records to the buyer at the time of signing, along with an official receipt for the sale of the automobile.

Signature of Seller's Representative _____
Signature of Buyer _____

To: Blaine Ritter <blaineritter@citystreetmotors.com>
From: Grace Huang <gracehuang@huangdesign.com>
Date: November 2
Subject: Contract Review

Dear Mr. Ritter,

Thank you for writing the contract for the Juniper sedan. I am excited to purchase such a nice car. My old car cannot be repaired, making me especially eager to have the new one. I have a question to ask about the contract. When we talked yesterday, we agreed to meet on November 6. But the contract says that the sale date is November 5. Shouldn't this date be corrected? Please make the change and have the corrected document ready before I arrive.

I plan to visit your location at 10:00 A.M. A friend of mine is dropping me off there, so I do not need a ride from you, although I appreciate your offer. I will stop by the bank on the way to City Street Motors so that I'll be prepared to make the payment when I arrive.

Thank you for your assistance, and I look forward to meeting with you on November 6.

Sincerely,
Grace Huang

181. Where does Blaine Ritter most likely work?

(A) At a car dealership
(B) At a rental agency
(C) At a law office
(D) At a vehicle parts store

182. According to the form, what will the seller NOT provide?

(A) An insurance form
(B) Inspection results
(C) A set of keys
(D) Proof of payment

183. What is indicated about Ms. Huang's current vehicle?

(A) It needs to be painted.
(B) It requires a new component.
(C) It is unfixable.
(D) It is too small.

184. What problem does Ms. Huang have with the contract?

(A) A name is misspelled.
(B) A signature is missing.
(C) A date is incorrect.
(D) A price is inaccurate.

185. Why most likely will Ms. Huang visit a bank on November 6?

(A) To pick up some checks
(B) To send a wire transfer
(C) To withdraw some money
(D) To apply for a credit card

GO ON TO THE NEXT PAGE

Questions 186-190 refer to the following Web page, e-mail, and text message.

http://www.fairviewest.com/home

| **HOME** | PROPERTIES | HOME DESIGNS | BOOK VISIT |

Discover Your Dream Home at Fairview Estates!

Fairview Estates, located in beautiful Portland, is now open for business! Check out our beautiful properties and arrange for a tour by clicking on "BOOK VISIT."

Fairview Estates includes two-, three-, and four-bedroom homes. View pictures of our show homes by clicking on "HOME DESIGNS" above. Each home comes with a kitchen, dining area, living room, and two full bathrooms. All homes have indoor garages. The two-bedroom units include a single-vehicle space, while the others have garages that can accommodate two cars. And the complex has a 24-hour security guard available to ensure the safety of you and your loved ones.

An annual management fee of $865 per home is charged for the maintenance of the grounds.

TO   Fairview Estates Management Office <inquiries@fairviewest.com>
FROM   Mona Sawyer <monasawyer@genmail.com>
SUBJECT   Visit booking
DATE   March 2

Hello,

I have been offered a new position and I have to move from my current place here in Chicago. I have just completed the sale of my house, and I am looking to purchase a new one. I will be arriving on March 8, and I am interested in seeing your property and touring your show homes. My husband and I have two children, so we require three bedrooms. But please show us the four-bedroom unit as well because we are considering turning the extra bedroom into a home office. I do hope to hear from you soon as we need to find a place quickly. You can reply to this e-mail or send me a text message at 555-2833.

Regards,

Mona Sawyer

From: Andrew Kraft (555-5121)

To: Mona Sawyer (555-2833)

Received: March 10, 2:10 P.M.

I just want to let you know some of the details for our appointment tomorrow. I'll meet with you at the administrative office at 10 A.M. I think this time will be OK for you since you mentioned you need to stop by your accounting office at 8 A.M. After we go through the paperwork, I'll provide you with the keys and security codes to your new four-bedroom home. To ensure there is no delay, could you please make sure to bring a copy of your bank loan agreement with you? Thanks.

186. What is NOT true about Fairview Estates?

(A) Its units all have indoor spaces for parking.
(B) It allows visitors to make reservations to view homes.
(C) Its grounds are only protected by a security guard at night.
(D) It requires tenants to pay for the cost of maintenance.

187. Why will Ms. Sawyer relocate?

(A) Her family has outgrown their current residence.
(B) She recently accepted an accounting job.
(C) Her husband requires a larger home office.
(D) She is overpaying for her residence in Chicago.

188. Why does Ms. Sawyer wish to see the four-bedroom show home?

(A) She needs an additional parking spot.
(B) She is thinking about setting up a work space.
(C) She is planning to have many guests.
(D) She wants a large play area for her children.

189. What is indicated about Ms. Sawyer's chosen home?

(A) It includes a garage for multiple vehicles.
(B) It currently has tenants living in it.
(C) It is situated next to the complex's main entrance.
(D) It comes with a small storage closet.

190. What does Mr. Kraft request?

(A) A signed housing contract
(B) An initial deposit
(C) A financial document copy
(D) An apartment access code

GO ON TO THE NEXT PAGE

New Leaf Grocers: Natural Produce at Affordable Prices!

Maintaining a healthy diet that is low in processed or genetically modified foods, and free of pesticides can be a challenge! Reading all the information on labels is time-consuming, and researching which products are natural and organic can be tedious. Well, that is a problem of the past now that New Leaf Grocers is here in Kingston. We operate a full-service grocery store with one major difference—we guarantee that only natural, organic products are sold in our establishment. Our strict requirements for products allow you to rest assured that whatever you buy in our store is safe for you and your family. Check out our weekly specials and other offers at www.newleafgrocers.com! Or visit us from 8 A.M. through 8 P.M. Mondays through Fridays, and 11 A.M. to 6 P.M. on weekends at 694 Victoria Street.

TO	Rob Dawson <robdawson@selectcereals.com>
FROM	Ariana Septus <arianas@newleafgrocers.com>
SUBJECT	Order
DATE	May 2
ATTACHMENT	Order form

Dear Mr. Dawson,

I very much enjoyed meeting with you at your company booth during the Eco-Food Fair in Las Vegas. I have shared some of the samples of the Select Cereals products you gave me with my colleagues, and they enjoyed them as well. As food items from Select Cereals meet all the criteria for merchandise sold at New Leaf Grocers, we would like to test out your cereals with customers and place an initial order. We are interested in regular delivery of the product we requested the greatest amount of on the attached order form. Future shipments will be for the same amount, and we'd like them to arrive during the last week of each month. And should your other products prove popular with our shoppers, we would be open to placing regular orders for them also.

Thanks for your time, and let me know if you require any further information.

Regards,

Ariana Septus

SELECT CEREALS
Order Form

Customer Name: Ariana Septus
Company: New Leaf Grocers
Payment method: Company Check

Phone: (613) 555-2039
E-mail: arianas@newleafgrocers.com
Shipping address: 694 Victoria Street, Kingston ON

ITEM	COST PER CASE*	QUANTITY OF CASES	TOTAL COST
Bran Cereal with Blueberries	$24.00	2	$48.00
Oat Cereal with Honey	$20.00	3	$60.00
Corn Cereal with Fruit and Nuts	$24.00	2	$48.00
Multigrain Cereal with Raisins	$22.00	4	$88.00

SUBTOTAL: $244.00
SALES TAX: $24.40
SHIPPING AND HANDLING: $56.00
TOTAL AMOUNT DUE: $324.40

*Each case contains 5 boxes of cereal. You may pay with a credit card or by bank transfer. Payment by company check is also acceptable, but the order will not ship until the check has been cleared by your bank and the money has been deposited in our account.

191. According to the advertisement, what can be found on the store's Web site?

(A) Directions to the establishment
(B) A calendar of holiday closures
(C) Details on special promotions
(D) A list of product ingredients

192. What is suggested about Select Cereals?

(A) It hopes to expand its range of organic products.
(B) Its food items are only sold in specialty stores.
(C) It participates in a Las Vegas food fair every year.
(D) Its products are made from naturally grown ingredients.

193. What is indicated about Mr. Dawson?

(A) He represented his company at a food industry event.
(B) He mailed some product samples to his colleagues.
(C) He filled out purchase forms during a business trip.
(D) He is a regular supplier for New Leaf Grocers.

194. Which product will Select Cereals deliver to New Leaf Grocers regularly?

(A) Bran Cereal with Blueberries
(B) Oat Cereal with Honey
(C) Corn Cereal with Fruit and Nuts
(D) Multigrain Cereal with Raisins

195. According to the order form, what is implied about New Leaf Grocers?

(A) It wants more corn cereals than oat cereals.
(B) Its receipts are delivered to customers by e-mail.
(C) It will not have to pay for shipping fees on its next order.
(D) Its order will be sent after a payment has been processed.

GO ON TO THE NEXT PAGE

Questions 196-200 refer to the following article, e-mail, and letter.

Government Considering Incentive Plan

By Evan Proust
January 3

Several New South Wales government officials held discussions yesterday and proposed a new tax incentive program. They said that if it is authorised, this program will exempt residential building and manufacturing facility owners from paying taxes on repair costs for solar panels. However, a 12 percent tax will continue to be charged for the sale of any unused energy generated by the panels.

The program will be voted on by the department of environmental protection before the end of January. Should the program be approved, residence and business owners will be able to apply for enrollment on the department's Web site.

TO: Patty Kindale <patkin@eastonmanufacturing.co.au>
FROM: Rich Ward <richward@eastonmanufacturing.co.au>
SUBJECT: New assignment
DATE: February 10

Patty,

I'm writing regarding the matter we discussed last week. I'd like you to prepare the documentation we need to apply for the recently approved tax incentive program for each of our properties using solar power panels. The requirements for application may differ according to the type of facility, so please double-check those details on the department of environmental protection's Web page. I understand this is potentially a lot of work, but it really is important that we enroll in this program as soon as possible. I have also asked Jerry Headley and Brianne O'Neil to assist you with these preparations. I would like to have all of the application documents ready by the end of Friday, if possible. If that simply isn't enough time, please indicate a more reasonable deadline for this work. And should you need extra help with this task, I can have my assistant Vera Santos help you out as well.

Thanks,

Rich

March 28

Rich Ward
Accounting Division Manager
Easton Manufacturing
44 Grahame Street
Blaxland, NSW 2774

Dear Mr. Ward,

This letter serves to verify that your company's applications for the government's newly implemented solar energy tax benefit program have been approved. You will qualify for tax benefits for each of your manufacturing facilities from April 1.

I did notice, however, that three of your buildings have an excess amount of energy generated by solar panels, which you have been selling to local firms. Please keep in mind that the tax incentive program's policy regarding this practise has not changed.

Thank you for taking part in this program and for helping New South Wales in its clean and safe production of energy.

Sincerely yours,

Fred Dionne
Department of environmental protection

196. According to the article, what did government officials do yesterday?

(A) Created new guidelines for government offices
(B) Rejected a proposal to remove taxes on solar panels
(C) Proposed a deal to purchase solar panels for a community
(D) Discussed a plan that benefits some property owners

197. What is indicated about the tax incentive program?

(A) It was authorised by the government in January.
(B) It only applies to privately owned businesses.
(C) It has attracted foreign manufacturers to the region.
(D) It can be applied for starting from next year.

198. What does Mr. Ward offer to do for Ms. Kindale?

(A) Provide additional funding for a project
(B) Assign Vera Santos to a task
(C) Send some helpful documents
(D) Ask Jerry Headley to inspect a facility

199. Why was the letter written?

(A) To announce the results of a study
(B) To approve a construction proposal
(C) To confirm eligibility for a program
(D) To verify receipt of a tax payment

200. What is suggested about some of Easton Manufacturing's facilities?

(A) They may be charged a 12 percent tax.
(B) They are in need of more electricity than anticipated.
(C) They cut back on production levels on February 10.
(D) They require renovation before resuming operations.

This is the end of the test. You may review Parts 5, 6, and 7 if you finish the test early.

′Review 체크리스트

TEST 5를 푼 다음, 아래 체크리스트에 따라 틀린 문제를 리뷰하고 박스에 완료 여부를 표시하세요.
만약 시험까지 얼마 남지 않았다면, 초록색으로 표시된 항목이라도 꼭 확인하세요.

☐ 틀린 문제의 경우, 다시 풀어봤다.

☐ 틀린 문제의 경우, 스크립트/해석을 확인하며 지문/문제의 내용을 정확하게 파악했다.

☐ 해설을 통해 각 문제의 정답과 오답의 근거가 무엇인지 정확하게 파악했다.

☐ Part 1과 Part 2에서 틀린 문제의 경우, 선택한 오답의 유형이 무엇이었는지 확인하고 같은
   함정에 빠지지 않도록 정리해두었다.

☐ Part 3와 Part 4의 각 문제에서 사용된 패러프레이징을 확인했다.

☐ Part 5와 Part 6의 경우, 틀린 문제에서 사용된 문법 포인트 또는 정답 및 오답 어휘를 정리
   했다.

☐ Part 6의 알맞은 문장 고르기 문제의 경우, 지문 전체를 정확하게 해석하며 전체 글의 흐름
   과 빈칸 주변 문맥을 정확하게 파악하는 연습을 했다.

☐ Part 7에서 질문과 보기의 키워드를 찾아 표시하며 지문에서 정답의 근거가 되는 문장이나
   구절을 찾아보고, 문제에서 사용된 패러프레이징을 확인했다.

☐ Part 1~Part 4는 받아쓰기 & 쉐도잉 워크북을 활용하여, TEST에 수록된 핵심 문장을 받아
   쓰고 따라 읽으며 복습했다.

☐ Part 1~Part 7은 단어암기자료를 활용하여, TEST에 수록된 핵심 어휘와 표현을 암기했다.

많은 양의 문제를 푸는 것도 중요하지만, 틀린 문제를 제대로 리뷰하는 것도 중요합니다.
틀린 문제를 한 번 더 꼼꼼히 리뷰한다면, 빠른 시간 내에 효과적으로 목표 점수를 달성할 수 있습니다.

한 권으로 끝내는
해커스 토익 실전 LC+RC 1

정답
점수 환산표
ANSWER SHEET

정답 ANSWER KEYS

TEST 1

LISTENING TEST					READING TEST				
1 (B)	**2** (A)	**3** (D)	**4** (A)	**5** (D)	**101** (C)	**102** (B)	**103** (D)	**104** (A)	**105** (A)
6 (C)	**7** (C)	**8** (B)	**9** (C)	**10** (C)	**106** (C)	**107** (A)	**108** (A)	**109** (C)	**110** (A)
11 (A)	**12** (A)	**13** (C)	**14** (A)	**15** (A)	**111** (C)	**112** (D)	**113** (B)	**114** (D)	**115** (B)
16 (A)	**17** (A)	**18** (B)	**19** (B)	**20** (C)	**116** (D)	**117** (B)	**118** (A)	**119** (C)	**120** (D)
21 (C)	**22** (A)	**23** (A)	**24** (C)	**25** (C)	**121** (C)	**122** (C)	**123** (B)	**124** (A)	**125** (B)
26 (A)	**27** (C)	**28** (B)	**29** (B)	**30** (B)	**126** (C)	**127** (C)	**128** (A)	**129** (B)	**130** (D)
31 (C)	**32** (A)	**33** (C)	**34** (D)	**35** (B)	**131** (D)	**132** (B)	**133** (A)	**134** (C)	**135** (A)
36 (D)	**37** (B)	**38** (B)	**39** (D)	**40** (A)	**136** (B)	**137** (D)	**138** (C)	**139** (B)	**140** (D)
41 (B)	**42** (C)	**43** (A)	**44** (B)	**45** (C)	**141** (C)	**142** (A)	**143** (D)	**144** (B)	**145** (D)
46 (D)	**47** (D)	**48** (A)	**49** (D)	**50** (D)	**146** (C)	**147** (D)	**148** (C)	**149** (A)	**150** (D)
51 (C)	**52** (B)	**53** (C)	**54** (B)	**55** (B)	**151** (C)	**152** (B)	**153** (D)	**154** (B)	**155** (C)
56 (A)	**57** (B)	**58** (D)	**59** (B)	**60** (B)	**156** (A)	**157** (C)	**158** (D)	**159** (A)	**160** (D)
61 (D)	**62** (D)	**63** (C)	**64** (D)	**65** (C)	**161** (D)	**162** (C)	**163** (A)	**164** (B)	**165** (A)
66 (B)	**67** (A)	**68** (A)	**69** (D)	**70** (C)	**166** (C)	**167** (C)	**168** (A)	**169** (C)	**170** (B)
71 (A)	**72** (D)	**73** (B)	**74** (D)	**75** (A)	**171** (C)	**172** (A)	**173** (A)	**174** (C)	**175** (B)
76 (B)	**77** (A)	**78** (B)	**79** (D)	**80** (B)	**176** (C)	**177** (B)	**178** (B)	**179** (A)	**180** (D)
81 (D)	**82** (C)	**83** (C)	**84** (D)	**85** (D)	**181** (B)	**182** (A)	**183** (C)	**184** (B)	**185** (A)
86 (C)	**87** (B)	**88** (A)	**89** (D)	**90** (B)	**186** (D)	**187** (B)	**188** (C)	**189** (C)	**190** (D)
91 (D)	**92** (C)	**93** (D)	**94** (C)	**95** (B)	**191** (D)	**192** (C)	**193** (A)	**194** (D)	**195** (B)
96 (C)	**97** (A)	**98** (C)	**99** (A)	**100** (D)	**196** (D)	**197** (A)	**198** (B)	**199** (D)	**200** (A)

TEST 2

LISTENING TEST					READING TEST				
1 (D)	**2** (D)	**3** (B)	**4** (C)	**5** (A)	**101** (D)	**102** (A)	**103** (B)	**104** (A)	**105** (A)
6 (B)	**7** (B)	**8** (A)	**9** (B)	**10** (C)	**106** (B)	**107** (A)	**108** (C)	**109** (B)	**110** (A)
11 (C)	**12** (C)	**13** (A)	**14** (C)	**15** (B)	**111** (D)	**112** (A)	**113** (A)	**114** (A)	**115** (C)
16 (C)	**17** (A)	**18** (C)	**19** (B)	**20** (A)	**116** (A)	**117** (A)	**118** (B)	**119** (B)	**120** (C)
21 (A)	**22** (A)	**23** (C)	**24** (B)	**25** (A)	**121** (D)	**122** (A)	**123** (D)	**124** (C)	**125** (B)
26 (B)	**27** (A)	**28** (B)	**29** (A)	**30** (C)	**126** (B)	**127** (D)	**128** (D)	**129** (C)	**130** (C)
31 (A)	**32** (A)	**33** (D)	**34** (B)	**35** (A)	**131** (C)	**132** (A)	**133** (C)	**134** (D)	**135** (D)
36 (A)	**37** (D)	**38** (A)	**39** (B)	**40** (C)	**136** (A)	**137** (C)	**138** (B)	**139** (C)	**140** (A)
41 (D)	**42** (B)	**43** (B)	**44** (C)	**45** (C)	**141** (B)	**142** (C)	**143** (D)	**144** (B)	**145** (C)
46 (B)	**47** (A)	**48** (A)	**49** (B)	**50** (C)	**146** (C)	**147** (C)	**148** (B)	**149** (D)	**150** (D)
51 (B)	**52** (A)	**53** (A)	**54** (A)	**55** (B)	**151** (D)	**152** (A)	**153** (D)	**154** (A)	**155** (B)
56 (D)	**57** (A)	**58** (C)	**59** (D)	**60** (D)	**156** (D)	**157** (C)	**158** (D)	**159** (B)	**160** (D)
61 (A)	**62** (A)	**63** (D)	**64** (A)	**65** (B)	**161** (D)	**162** (B)	**163** (C)	**164** (D)	**165** (B)
66 (A)	**67** (B)	**68** (A)	**69** (A)	**70** (C)	**166** (C)	**167** (C)	**168** (A)	**169** (D)	**170** (C)
71 (B)	**72** (D)	**73** (B)	**74** (C)	**75** (A)	**171** (C)	**172** (B)	**173** (C)	**174** (D)	**175** (A)
76 (D)	**77** (B)	**78** (D)	**79** (D)	**80** (B)	**176** (B)	**177** (B)	**178** (C)	**179** (C)	**180** (C)
81 (D)	**82** (C)	**83** (C)	**84** (A)	**85** (A)	**181** (D)	**182** (A)	**183** (B)	**184** (C)	**185** (D)
86 (B)	**87** (A)	**88** (B)	**89** (B)	**90** (C)	**186** (A)	**187** (B)	**188** (B)	**189** (D)	**190** (C)
91 (A)	**92** (B)	**93** (A)	**94** (D)	**95** (D)	**191** (C)	**192** (C)	**193** (D)	**194** (C)	**195** (B)
96 (C)	**97** (B)	**98** (B)	**99** (A)	**100** (B)	**196** (D)	**197** (B)	**198** (A)	**199** (B)	**200** (D)

정답 ANSWER KEYS

TEST 3

LISTENING TEST

1 (D)	**2** (D)	**3** (A)	**4** (D)	**5** (A)
6 (B)	**7** (A)	**8** (A)	**9** (C)	**10** (B)
11 (A)	**12** (C)	**13** (B)	**14** (C)	**15** (B)
16 (B)	**17** (C)	**18** (A)	**19** (A)	**20** (C)
21 (B)	**22** (C)	**23** (B)	**24** (C)	**25** (C)
26 (B)	**27** (A)	**28** (C)	**29** (C)	**30** (A)
31 (A)	**32** (C)	**33** (C)	**34** (B)	**35** (D)
36 (A)	**37** (A)	**38** (A)	**39** (C)	**40** (B)
41 (A)	**42** (C)	**43** (C)	**44** (A)	**45** (D)
46 (C)	**47** (A)	**48** (C)	**49** (A)	**50** (C)
51 (B)	**52** (D)	**53** (B)	**54** (B)	**55** (D)
56 (C)	**57** (C)	**58** (A)	**59** (B)	**60** (D)
61 (B)	**62** (B)	**63** (A)	**64** (B)	**65** (B)
66 (B)	**67** (D)	**68** (C)	**69** (B)	**70** (A)
71 (C)	**72** (B)	**73** (B)	**74** (A)	**75** (A)
76 (B)	**77** (B)	**78** (A)	**79** (B)	**80** (A)
81 (A)	**82** (A)	**83** (B)	**84** (D)	**85** (A)
86 (D)	**87** (D)	**88** (B)	**89** (B)	**90** (D)
91 (C)	**92** (D)	**93** (B)	**94** (A)	**95** (B)
96 (B)	**97** (B)	**98** (A)	**99** (C)	**100** (B)

READING TEST

101 (D)	**102** (B)	**103** (A)	**104** (D)	**105** (A)
106 (B)	**107** (A)	**108** (B)	**109** (A)	**110** (A)
111 (B)	**112** (A)	**113** (B)	**114** (C)	**115** (C)
116 (C)	**117** (B)	**118** (A)	**119** (C)	**120** (C)
121 (D)	**122** (D)	**123** (C)	**124** (D)	**125** (C)
126 (C)	**127** (C)	**128** (B)	**129** (A)	**130** (A)
131 (C)	**132** (A)	**133** (A)	**134** (D)	**135** (A)
136 (D)	**137** (C)	**138** (B)	**139** (B)	**140** (C)
141 (D)	**142** (A)	**143** (A)	**144** (C)	**145** (C)
146 (C)	**147** (B)	**148** (C)	**149** (D)	**150** (A)
151 (B)	**152** (A)	**153** (C)	**154** (B)	**155** (C)
156 (C)	**157** (D)	**158** (D)	**159** (C)	**160** (D)
161 (B)	**162** (C)	**163** (A)	**164** (C)	**165** (C)
166 (D)	**167** (B)	**168** (A)	**169** (B)	**170** (D)
171 (C)	**172** (B)	**173** (D)	**174** (B)	**175** (A)
176 (A)	**177** (C)	**178** (A)	**179** (D)	**180** (B)
181 (D)	**182** (B)	**183** (C)	**184** (A)	**185** (A)
186 (A)	**187** (B)	**188** (D)	**189** (C)	**190** (D)
191 (B)	**192** (D)	**193** (A)	**194** (B)	**195** (D)
196 (C)	**197** (B)	**198** (D)	**199** (B)	**200** (D)

TEST 4

LISTENING TEST

1 (D)	**2** (A)	**3** (C)	**4** (A)	**5** (B)
6 (C)	**7** (C)	**8** (C)	**9** (A)	**10** (C)
11 (A)	**12** (B)	**13** (A)	**14** (C)	**15** (C)
16 (C)	**17** (C)	**18** (B)	**19** (C)	**20** (B)
21 (A)	**22** (A)	**23** (A)	**24** (B)	**25** (B)
26 (B)	**27** (B)	**28** (B)	**29** (A)	**30** (B)
31 (B)	**32** (B)	**33** (A)	**34** (C)	**35** (B)
36 (A)	**37** (C)	**38** (D)	**39** (A)	**40** (C)
41 (D)	**42** (C)	**43** (B)	**44** (B)	**45** (A)
46 (C)	**47** (D)	**48** (C)	**49** (D)	**50** (D)
51 (D)	**52** (B)	**53** (C)	**54** (C)	**55** (B)
56 (A)	**57** (D)	**58** (A)	**59** (B)	**60** (A)
61 (A)	**62** (D)	**63** (B)	**64** (D)	**65** (A)
66 (B)	**67** (B)	**68** (B)	**69** (D)	**70** (D)
71 (B)	**72** (A)	**73** (B)	**74** (C)	**75** (D)
76 (B)	**77** (D)	**78** (B)	**79** (C)	**80** (D)
81 (D)	**82** (A)	**83** (B)	**84** (B)	**85** (D)
86 (C)	**87** (A)	**88** (B)	**89** (B)	**90** (C)
91 (B)	**92** (B)	**93** (A)	**94** (C)	**95** (C)
96 (C)	**97** (B)	**98** (A)	**99** (B)	**100** (B)

READING TEST

101 (C)	**102** (A)	**103** (D)	**104** (B)	**105** (C)
106 (C)	**107** (B)	**108** (A)	**109** (B)	**110** (C)
111 (D)	**112** (D)	**113** (D)	**114** (B)	**115** (D)
116 (B)	**117** (D)	**118** (B)	**119** (A)	**120** (D)
121 (C)	**122** (D)	**123** (C)	**124** (D)	**125** (B)
126 (A)	**127** (B)	**128** (B)	**129** (A)	**130** (C)
131 (D)	**132** (D)	**133** (C)	**134** (D)	**135** (B)
136 (C)	**137** (A)	**138** (A)	**139** (B)	**140** (C)
141 (A)	**142** (A)	**143** (C)	**144** (C)	**145** (D)
146 (B)	**147** (C)	**148** (D)	**149** (C)	**150** (D)
151 (C)	**152** (C)	**153** (A)	**154** (D)	**155** (C)
156 (A)	**157** (D)	**158** (C)	**159** (D)	**160** (B)
161 (B)	**162** (B)	**163** (C)	**164** (D)	**165** (C)
166 (D)	**167** (C)	**168** (C)	**169** (B)	**170** (C)
171 (D)	**172** (C)	**173** (D)	**174** (B)	**175** (C)
176 (D)	**177** (B)	**178** (D)	**179** (B)	**180** (C)
181 (B)	**182** (B)	**183** (A)	**184** (D)	**185** (D)
186 (D)	**187** (C)	**188** (B)	**189** (D)	**190** (B)
191 (B)	**192** (C)	**193** (D)	**194** (D)	**195** (C)
196 (C)	**197** (A)	**198** (C)	**199** (C)	**200** (A)

정답 ANSWER KEYS

TEST 5

LISTENING TEST

1 (D)	**2** (A)	**3** (D)	**4** (B)	**5** (A)
6 (B)	**7** (C)	**8** (B)	**9** (B)	**10** (B)
11 (C)	**12** (C)	**13** (A)	**14** (B)	**15** (B)
16 (A)	**17** (A)	**18** (C)	**19** (C)	**20** (B)
21 (C)	**22** (C)	**23** (C)	**24** (B)	**25** (B)
26 (A)	**27** (B)	**28** (C)	**29** (A)	**30** (A)
31 (B)	**32** (B)	**33** (B)	**34** (C)	**35** (A)
36 (C)	**37** (A)	**38** (B)	**39** (B)	**40** (D)
41 (D)	**42** (B)	**43** (B)	**44** (C)	**45** (A)
46 (D)	**47** (D)	**48** (A)	**49** (B)	**50** (A)
51 (C)	**52** (B)	**53** (D)	**54** (B)	**55** (A)
56 (D)	**57** (A)	**58** (D)	**59** (A)	**60** (C)
61 (B)	**62** (D)	**63** (B)	**64** (D)	**65** (D)
66 (A)	**67** (A)	**68** (A)	**69** (D)	**70** (C)
71 (D)	**72** (A)	**73** (B)	**74** (D)	**75** (C)
76 (A)	**77** (C)	**78** (D)	**79** (B)	**80** (B)
81 (D)	**82** (C)	**83** (A)	**84** (B)	**85** (C)
86 (B)	**87** (D)	**88** (B)	**89** (C)	**90** (D)
91 (D)	**92** (A)	**93** (D)	**94** (C)	**95** (C)
96 (B)	**97** (A)	**98** (C)	**99** (B)	**100** (A)

READING TEST

101 (A)	**102** (C)	**103** (A)	**104** (C)	**105** (A)
106 (D)	**107** (D)	**108** (B)	**109** (D)	**110** (B)
111 (A)	**112** (A)	**113** (A)	**114** (B)	**115** (D)
116 (C)	**117** (C)	**118** (B)	**119** (D)	**120** (A)
121 (A)	**122** (C)	**123** (B)	**124** (A)	**125** (D)
126 (D)	**127** (B)	**128** (A)	**129** (C)	**130** (D)
131 (D)	**132** (B)	**133** (C)	**134** (B)	**135** (B)
136 (D)	**137** (C)	**138** (D)	**139** (A)	**140** (A)
141 (C)	**142** (C)	**143** (D)	**144** (A)	**145** (B)
146 (A)	**147** (B)	**148** (C)	**149** (C)	**150** (A)
151 (D)	**152** (D)	**153** (C)	**154** (B)	**155** (C)
156 (B)	**157** (D)	**158** (C)	**159** (C)	**160** (C)
161 (C)	**162** (B)	**163** (D)	**164** (C)	**165** (B)
166 (A)	**167** (D)	**168** (B)	**169** (B)	**170** (A)
171 (C)	**172** (D)	**173** (B)	**174** (C)	**175** (C)
176 (B)	**177** (A)	**178** (C)	**179** (B)	**180** (C)
181 (A)	**182** (A)	**183** (C)	**184** (C)	**185** (C)
186 (C)	**187** (B)	**188** (B)	**189** (A)	**190** (C)
191 (C)	**192** (C)	**193** (A)	**194** (D)	**195** (D)
196 (D)	**197** (A)	**198** (B)	**199** (C)	**200** (A)

무료 토익·토스·오픽·지텔프 자료
Hackers.co.kr

점수 환산표

※ 점수 환산표는 해커스토익 사이트 유저 데이터를 근거로 제작되었으며, 주기적으로 업데이트되고 있습니다. 해커스토익(Hackers.co.kr) 사이트에서 최신 경향을 반영하여 업데이트된 점수환산기를 이용하실 수 있습니다. (토익 > 토익게시판 > 토익점수환산기)

LISTENING

아래 점수 환산표로 자신의 토익 리스닝 점수를 예상해 봅니다.

정답수	예상 점수	정답수	예상 점수	정답수	예상 점수
100	495	66	305	32	135
99	495	65	300	31	130
98	495	64	295	30	125
97	495	63	290	29	120
96	490	62	285	28	115
95	485	61	280	27	110
94	480	60	275	26	105
93	475	59	270	25	100
92	470	58	265	24	95
91	465	57	260	23	90
90	460	56	255	22	85
89	455	55	250	21	80
88	450	54	245	20	75
87	445	53	240	19	70
86	435	52	235	18	65
85	430	51	230	17	60
84	425	50	225	16	55
83	415	49	220	15	50
82	410	48	215	14	45
81	400	47	210	13	40
80	395	46	205	12	35
79	390	45	200	11	30
78	385	44	195	10	25
77	375	43	190	9	20
76	370	42	185	8	15
75	365	41	180	7	10
74	355	40	175	6	5
73	350	39	170	5	5
72	340	38	165	4	5
71	335	37	160	3	5
70	330	36	155	2	5
69	325	35	150	1	5
68	315	34	145	0	5
67	310	33	140		

READING

아래 점수 환산표로 자신의 토익 리딩 점수를 예상해 봅니다.

정답수	예상 점수	정답수	예상 점수	정답수	예상 점수
100	495	66	305	32	125
99	495	65	300	31	120
98	495	64	295	30	115
97	485	63	290	29	110
96	480	62	280	28	105
95	475	61	275	27	100
94	470	60	270	26	95
93	465	59	265	25	90
92	460	58	260	24	85
91	450	57	255	23	80
90	445	56	250	22	75
89	440	55	245	21	70
88	435	54	240	20	70
87	430	53	235	19	65
86	420	52	230	18	60
85	415	51	220	17	60
84	410	50	215	16	55
83	405	49	210	15	50
82	400	48	205	14	45
81	390	47	200	13	40
80	385	46	195	12	35
79	380	45	190	11	30
78	375	44	185	10	30
77	370	43	180	9	25
76	360	42	175	8	20
75	355	41	170	7	20
74	350	40	165	6	15
73	345	39	160	5	15
72	340	38	155	4	10
71	335	37	150	3	5
70	330	36	145	2	5
69	320	35	140	1	5
68	315	34	135	0	5
67	310	33	130		

무료 토익·토스·오픽·지텔프 자료
Hackers.co.kr

Answer Sheet

TEST 1

LISTENING (PART I~IV)

READING (PART V~VII)

맞은 문제 개수: ___ / 200

시험시간: **120분** (LC 45분, RC 75분)

자르는 선

무료 토익·토스·오픽·지텔프 자료
Hackers.co.kr

Answer Sheet

TEST 2

LISTENING (PART I~IV)

READING (PART V~VII)

맞은 문제 개수: _____ / 200

자르는 선

무료 토익 · 토스 · 오픽 · 지텔프 자료
Hackers.co.kr

Answer Sheet

TEST 3

LISTENING (PART I~IV)

시험시간: **120분** (LC 45분, RC 75분)

READING (PART V~VII)

단안지 마킹은 연필을 사용하시기 바랍니다.

맞은 문제 개수: ____ / 200

절취선

무료 토익·토스·오픽·지텔프 자료
Hackers.co.kr

Answer Sheet

TEST 4

LISTENING (PART I~IV)

1	2	3	4	5	6	7	8	9	10	11	12	13	14	15	16	17	18	19	20
21	22	23	24	25	26	27	28	29	30	31	32	33	34	35	36	37	38	39	40
41	42	43	44	45	46	47	48	49	50	51	52	53	54	55	56	57	58	59	60
61	62	63	64	65	66	67	68	69	70	71	72	73	74	75	76	77	78	79	80
81	82	83	84	85	86	87	88	89	90	91	92	93	94	95	96	97	98	99	100

시험시간: **120분** (LC 45분, RC 75분)

READING (PART V~VII)

101	102	103	104	105	106	107	108	109	110	111	112	113	114	115	116	117	118	119	120
121	122	123	124	125	126	127	128	129	130	131	132	133	134	135	136	137	138	139	140
141	142	143	144	145	146	147	148	149	150	151	152	153	154	155	156	157	158	159	160
161	162	163	164	165	166	167	168	169	170	171	172	173	174	175	176	177	178	179	180
181	182	183	184	185	186	187	188	189	190	191	192	193	194	195	196	197	198	199	200

단어지 마킹은 **연필**을 사용하시기 바랍니다.

맞은 문제 개수: _____ / 200

무료 토익·토스·오픽·지텔프 자료
Hackers.co.kr

Answer Sheet

TEST 5

LISTENING (PART I~IV)

Questions 1–100, answer choices (A) (B) (C) (D)

READING (PART V~VII)

Questions 101–200, answer choices (A) (B) (C) (D)

맞은 문제 개수: _____ / 200

답안지 마킹은 연필을 사용하시기 바랍니다.

시험시간: **120분** (LC 45분, RC 75분)

무료 토익·토스·오픽·지텔프 자료
Hackers.co.kr

토익 초보도 부담 없이 **실전 훈련 2주 완성!**

한 권으로 끝내는

해커스 토익

실전 LC+RC
모의고사 + 해설집

1

개정 2판 4쇄 발행 2024년 8월 12일

개정 2판 1쇄 발행 2023년 4월 21일

지은이	해커스 어학연구소
펴낸곳	㈜해커스 어학연구소
펴낸이	해커스 어학연구소 출판팀
주소	서울특별시 서초구 강남대로61길 23 ㈜해커스 어학연구소
고객센터	02-537-5000
교재 관련 문의	publishing@hackers.com
동영상강의	HackersIngang.com
ISBN	978-89-6542-591-5 (13740)
Serial Number	02-04-01

외국어인강 1위, 해커스인강
HackersIngang.com

해커스인강

· 해커스 토익 스타강사의 **본 교재 인강**
· 단기 리스닝 점수 향상을 위한 **받아쓰기&쉐도잉 워크북**
· 들으면서 외우는 **단어암기장 및 단어암기 MP3**
· 빠르고 편리하게 채점하는 **정답녹음 MP3**

영어 전문 포털, 해커스토익
Hackers.co.kr

해커스토익

· 최신 출제경향이 반영된 **온라인 실전모의고사**
· **매월 적중예상특강** 및 실시간 토익시험 정답확인/해설강의
· **매일 실전 LC/RC 문제** 및 토익 기출보카 TEST, 토익기출 100단어 등 다양한 무료 학습 콘텐츠

헤럴드 선정 2018 대학생 선호브랜드 대상 '대학생이 선정한 외국어인강' 부문 1위

한 권으로 끝내는

해커스 토익

실전 LC+RC

1

해설집

해커스 어학연구소

한 권으로 끝내는
해커스
토익
실전 LC+RC

1

해설집

해커스 어학연구소

TEST 1

LISTENING TEST p.28

1 (B)	2 (A)	3 (D)	4 (A)	5 (D)
6 (C)	7 (C)	8 (B)	9 (C)	10 (C)
11 (A)	12 (A)	13 (C)	14 (A)	15 (A)
16 (A)	17 (A)	18 (C)	19 (B)	20 (C)
21 (C)	22 (A)	23 (A)	24 (C)	25 (C)
26 (A)	27 (C)	28 (B)	29 (B)	30 (B)
31 (C)	32 (A)	33 (C)	34 (D)	35 (B)
36 (D)	37 (B)	38 (B)	39 (D)	40 (A)
41 (B)	42 (C)	43 (A)	44 (B)	45 (C)
46 (D)	47 (D)	48 (A)	49 (C)	50 (D)
51 (C)	52 (B)	53 (C)	54 (B)	55 (B)
56 (A)	57 (B)	58 (D)	59 (B)	60 (B)
61 (D)	62 (D)	63 (C)	64 (C)	65 (C)
66 (B)	67 (A)	68 (A)	69 (D)	70 (C)
71 (A)	72 (A)	73 (B)	74 (D)	75 (C)
76 (B)	77 (A)	78 (B)	79 (D)	80 (C)
81 (D)	82 (C)	83 (C)	84 (C)	85 (C)
86 (C)	87 (B)	88 (A)	89 (D)	90 (B)
91 (D)	92 (C)	93 (D)	94 (C)	95 (B)
96 (C)	97 (A)	98 (C)	99 (A)	100 (D)

READING TEST p.40

101 (C)	102 (B)	103 (D)	104 (A)	105 (A)
106 (C)	107 (A)	108 (A)	109 (C)	110 (A)
111 (C)	112 (D)	113 (B)	114 (D)	115 (B)
116 (D)	117 (B)	118 (A)	119 (C)	120 (D)
121 (C)	122 (C)	123 (B)	124 (A)	125 (B)
126 (C)	127 (C)	128 (A)	129 (B)	130 (D)
131 (D)	132 (B)	133 (A)	134 (D)	135 (A)
136 (B)	137 (D)	138 (C)	139 (B)	140 (D)
141 (C)	142 (A)	143 (D)	144 (B)	145 (D)
146 (C)	147 (B)	148 (C)	149 (A)	150 (D)
151 (B)	152 (B)	153 (C)	154 (B)	155 (C)
156 (A)	157 (C)	158 (C)	159 (A)	160 (C)
161 (D)	162 (C)	163 (A)	164 (B)	165 (A)
166 (C)	167 (C)	168 (A)	169 (C)	170 (B)
171 (C)	172 (A)	173 (A)	174 (C)	175 (B)
176 (C)	177 (B)	178 (B)	179 (A)	180 (D)
181 (B)	182 (A)	183 (C)	184 (B)	185 (B)
186 (D)	187 (B)	188 (C)	189 (C)	190 (D)
191 (D)	192 (C)	193 (A)	194 (D)	195 (B)
196 (D)	197 (A)	198 (B)	199 (D)	200 (A)

PART 1

1 캐나다식 발음

(A) The man is putting on a scarf.
(B) The man is sitting on a bike.
(C) The man is wearing a helmet.
(D) The man is using a bicycle rack.

bicycle rack 자전거 보관대

해석 (A) 남자가 스카프를 두르고 있다.
(B) 남자가 자전거에 앉아 있다.
(C) 남자가 헬멧을 쓰고 있다.
(D) 남자가 자전거 보관대를 이용하고 있다.

해설 **1인 사진**
(A) [×] putting on(두르고 있다)은 남자의 동작과 무관하므로 오답이다. 옷·모자·구두 등을 이미 입은 상태를 나타내는 wearing과 입고 있는 중이라는 동작을 나타내는 putting on을 혼동하지 않도록 주의한다.
(B) [○] 남자가 자전거에 앉아 있는 모습을 가장 잘 묘사한 정답이다.
(C) [×] 사진에 헬멧(helmet)이 없고, 남자가 헬멧을 쓰고 있는 상태가 아니므로 오답이다.
(D) [×] 사진에 자전거 보관대(bicycle rack)가 없으므로 오답이다. 사진에 있는 자전거(bicycle)를 사용하여 혼동을 주었다.

2 호주식 발음

(A) She is cleaning a room.
(B) She is watching television.
(C) She is wiping a countertop.
(D) There is a flowerpot on the floor.

wipe[waip] 닦다 countertop[káuntərtùp] 주방용 조리대
flowerpot[fláuərpàt] 화분

해석 (A) 그녀는 방을 청소하고 있다.
(B) 그녀는 텔레비전을 보고 있다.
(C) 그녀는 주방용 조리대를 닦고 있다.
(D) 바닥에 화분이 있다.

해설 **1인 사진**
(A) [○] 여자가 방을 청소하고 있는 모습을 가장 잘 묘사한 정답이다.
(B) [×] watching television(텔레비전을 보고 있다)은 여자의 동작과 무관하므로 오답이다. 사진에 있는 television(텔레비전)을 사용하여 혼동을 주었다.
(C) [×] 사진에 주방용 조리대(countertop)가 없으므로 오답이다. She is wiping(그녀는 닦고 있다)까지만 듣고 정답으로 선택하지 않도록 주의한다.
(D) [×] 화분이 바닥에 있는 것이 아니라 선반 위에 있으므로 오답이다. 사진에 있는 flowerpot(화분)을 사용하여 혼동을 주었다.

3 3ª 미국식 발음

> (A) A man is pushing a cart.
> (B) Some people are putting items in a bag.
> (C) A woman is paying for some groceries.
> (D) Two men are on opposite sides of a register.

pay for (대가를) 지불하다 grocery[gróusəri] 식료품
be on opposite sides of ~의 맞은편에 있다
register[rédʒistər] 금전 등록기

해석 (A) 한 남자가 카트를 밀고 있다.
　　(B) 몇몇 사람들이 가방에 물건들을 넣고 있다.
　　(C) 한 여자가 식료품의 값을 지불하고 있다.
　　(D) 두 남자가 금전 등록기의 맞은편에 있다.

해설 **2인 이상 사진**
　　(A) [×] 사진에 카트를 밀고 있는(pushing a cart) 남자가 없으므로 오답이다.
　　(B) [×] putting items in a bag(가방에 물건들을 넣고 있다)은 사람들의 동작과 무관하므로 오답이다.
　　(C) [×] 사진에 값을 지불하고 있는(paying for) 여자가 없으므로 오답이다.
　　(D) [○] 두 남자가 금전 등록기의 맞은편에 있는 모습을 가장 잘 묘사한 정답이다.

4 3ª 영국식 발음

> (A) He is working on an automobile.
> (B) A car is being washed.
> (C) He is parking a vehicle.
> (D) A fuel tank is being filled.

work on ~을 작업하다, ~에 애쓰다 automobile[ɔ̀ːtəməbíːl] 자동차
vehicle[víːikl] 차량, 탈것 fuel tank 연료 탱크

해석 (A) 그는 자동차에 작업을 하고 있다.
　　(B) 자동차가 세차되고 있다.
　　(C) 그는 차량을 주차하고 있다.
　　(D) 연료 탱크가 채워지고 있다.

해설 **1인 사진**
　　(A) [○] 남자가 자동차에 작업을 하고 있는 모습을 가장 잘 묘사한 정답이다.
　　(B) [×] 사진에서 자동차는 보이지만, 세차되고 있는(is being washed) 모습은 아니므로 오답이다.
　　(C) [×] parking(주차하고 있다)은 남자의 동작과 무관하므로 오답이다. 사진에 있는 차량(vehicle)을 사용하여 혼동을 주었다.
　　(D) [×] 사진에서 연료 탱크가 채워지고 있는지(is being filled) 확인할 수 없으므로 오답이다.

5 3ª 호주식 발음

> (A) They are carrying a toolbox.
> (B) An antenna is being installed.
> (C) They are painting some boards.
> (D) A roof is being constructed.

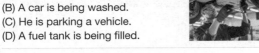

toolbox[미 túːlbɑːks, 영 túːlbɔks] 공구함 antenna[ænténə] 안테나, 첨탑
install[inst5ːl] 설치하다 roof[ruːf] 지붕
construct[kənstrʌ́kt] 건설하다

해석 (A) 그들은 공구함을 옮기고 있다.
　　(B) 안테나가 설치되고 있다.
　　(C) 그들은 몇몇 판자를 페인트칠하고 있다.
　　(D) 지붕이 건설되고 있다.

해설 **2인 이상 사진**
　　(A) [×] carrying(옮기고 있다)은 사람들의 동작과 무관하므로 오답이다. 사진에 있는 공구(tool)를 사용하여 혼동을 준 오답이다.
　　(B) [×] 사진에서 안테나가 설치되고 있는지(is being installed) 확인할 수 없으므로 오답이다.
　　(C) [×] painting(페인트칠하고 있다)은 사람들의 동작과 무관하므로 오답이다.
　　(D) [○] 지붕이 건설되고 있는 모습을 가장 잘 묘사한 정답이다.

6 3ª 미국식 발음

> (A) Food has been set out on a patio.
> (B) Some chairs have been stacked up.
> (C) Some pictures are mounted on the wall.
> (D) A window has been left open.

set out (음식·식기 등을) 차려내다 patio[pǽtiòu] 테라스, 베란다
stack[stæk] 쌓다, 쌓이다 mount[maunt] 고정시키다, 설치하다

해석 (A) 음식이 테라스에 차려져 있다.
　　(B) 몇몇 의자들이 쌓여 있다.
　　(C) 몇몇 그림들이 벽에 고정되어 있다.
　　(D) 창문이 열려 있다.

해설 **사물 및 풍경 사진**
　　(A) [×] 사진의 장소가 테라스(patio)가 아니므로 오답이다.
　　(B) [×] 사진에서 의자들은 보이지만, 쌓여 있는(have been stacked up) 모습은 아니므로 오답이다.
　　(C) [○] 몇몇 그림들이 벽에 고정되어 있는 모습을 가장 잘 묘사한 정답이다.
　　(D) [×] 사진에서 창문은 보이지만, 열려 있는(has been left open) 모습은 아니므로 오답이다.

PART 2

7 3ª 캐나다식 발음 → 호주식 발음

> Which spreadsheet software are you using?
> (A) To manage financial data.
> (B) Sure, you can use it.
> (C) It's called Organizer Plus.

financial data 재무 자료

해석 당신은 어떤 스프레드시트 소프트웨어를 사용하고 있나요?
　　(A) 재무 자료를 관리하기 위해서요.
　　(B) 물론이죠, 그것을 사용하셔도 돼요.
　　(C) 그것은 Organizer Plus라고 불려요.

해설 **Which 의문문**
　　(A) [×] 질문의 software(소프트웨어)와 관련 있는 data(자료)를 사용하여 혼동을 준 오답이다.
　　(B) [×] 질문의 using을 use로 반복 사용하여 혼동을 준 오답이다.
　　(C) [○] Organizer Plus라고 불린다며, 사용하고 있는 소프트웨어를 언급했으므로 정답이다.

8 🎧 영국식 발음 → 캐나다식 발음

Who paid the consultant for the program?
(A) A visit was scheduled for 2 P.M.
(B) The manager of our department.
(C) They'll take place next Tuesday.

pay for ~의 대금을 지불하다 be scheduled for ~으로 일정이 잡히다
take place 열리다, 일어나다

해석 프로그램의 대금을 누가 컨설턴트에게 지불했나요?
(A) 방문은 오후 2시로 일정이 잡혀 있었어요.
(B) 우리 부서의 부장님이요.
(C) 그것들은 다음 주 화요일에 열릴 거예요.

해설 Who 의문문
(A) [x] 프로그램의 대금을 누가 컨설턴트에게 지불했는지를 물었는데, 이와 관련 없는 방문이 오후 2시로 일정이 잡혀 있었다는 내용으로 응답했으므로 오답이다.
(B) [o] 우리 부서의 부장님이라며, 대금을 지불한 사람을 언급했으므로 정답이다.
(C) [x] 프로그램의 대금을 누가 컨설턴트에게 지불했는지를 물었는데, 이와 관련 없는 그것들이 다음 주 화요일에 열릴 것이라는 내용으로 응답했으므로 오답이다.

9 🎧 미국식 발음 → 호주식 발음

I placed an order for baked chicken about 20 minutes ago.
(A) Just place it on the table over there.
(B) Do you need help cooking it?
(C) Unfortunately, it's not ready yet.

bake[beik] 굽다 unfortunately[ʌnfɔ́ːrtʃənətli] 유감스럽게도

해석 저는 약 20분 전에 구운 치킨을 주문했어요.
(A) 그냥 저기 있는 탁자 위에 그것을 두세요.
(B) 당신은 그것을 요리하는 데 도움이 필요하신가요?
(C) 유감스럽게도, 아직 준비가 되지 않았어요.

해설 평서문
(A) [x] 질문의 placed를 place로 반복 사용하여 혼동을 준 오답이다.
(B) [x] 질문의 chicken(치킨)과 관련 있는 cooking(요리하는 것)을 사용하여 혼동을 준 오답이다.
(C) [o] 유감스럽게도 아직 준비가 되지 않았다며, 주문의 진행 상황을 전달했으므로 정답이다.

10 🎧 캐나다식 발음 → 영국식 발음

Have you ever been to the Bridgeport Museum of Art?
(A) The sculpture in the main hall.
(B) Museum hours are listed online.
(C) Yes. I go at least twice a year.

sculpture[skʌ́lptʃər] 조각품 list[list] 기재하다, 기입하다
at least 적어도, 최소한

해석 당신은 Bridgeport 미술관에 가본 적이 있나요?
(A) 메인 홀에 있는 조각품이요.
(B) 박물관 관람 시간은 온라인에 기재되어 있어요.
(C) 네. 저는 적어도 일 년에 두 번은 가요.

해설 조동사 의문문
(A) [x] 질문의 Museum of Art(미술관)와 관련 있는 sculpture(조각품)를 사용하여 혼동을 준 오답이다.
(B) [x] 질문의 Museum을 반복 사용하여 혼동을 준 오답이다.
(C) [o] Yes로 미술관에 가본 적이 있음을 전달한 후, 적어도 일 년에 두 번은 간다는 부연 설명을 했으므로 정답이다.

11 🎧 호주식 발음 → 영국식 발음

Didn't your sales surpass those of Uvic Inc. last quarter?
(A) Yes. We came out on top.
(B) At the quarterly report meeting.
(C) All items are 20 percent off.

sales[seilz] 매출, 판매량
surpass[미 sərpǽs, 영 səpɑ́ːs] 뛰어넘다, 능가하다
quarter[미 kwɔ́ːrtər, 영 kwɔ́ːtə] 분기
come out on top (경쟁에) 이기다
quarterly[kwɔ́ːrtərli] 분기별의

해석 지난 분기에 당신네 매출이 Uvic사의 것을 뛰어넘지 않았나요?
(A) 네. 저희가 이겼어요.
(B) 분기별 보고 회의에서요.
(C) 모든 품목은 20퍼센트 할인돼요.

해설 부정 의문문
(A) [o] Yes로 Uvic사의 매출을 뛰어넘었음을 전달한 후, 자신들이 이겼다는 부연 설명을 했으므로 정답이다.
(B) [x] quarter – quarterly의 유사 발음 어휘를 사용하여 혼동을 준 오답이다.
(C) [x] 질문의 sales(매출, 판매량)와 관련 있는 items(품목)를 사용하여 혼동을 준 오답이다.

12 🎧 캐나다식 발음 → 호주식 발음

Where will the annual retreat for employees be held next month?
(A) The same resort we went to last year.
(B) More than 300 employees will attend.
(C) I'll hold on to that for you.

annual[ǽnjuəl] 연례의, 매년의 retreat[ritríːt] 야유회
the same 바로 그, 아주 같은
hold on to (남을 위해) ~을 맡아 주다, 보관하다

해석 다음 달에 직원들을 위한 연례 야유회는 어디에서 열릴 것인가요?
(A) 우리가 작년에 갔던 바로 그 리조트에서요.
(B) 300명이 넘는 직원들이 참석할 거예요.
(C) 제가 당신을 위해 그것을 맡아 드릴게요.

해설 Where 의문문
(A) [o] 우리가 작년에 갔던 바로 그 리조트라며, 연례 야유회가 열릴 장소를 간접적으로 전달했으므로 정답이다.
(B) [x] 질문의 employees를 반복 사용하여 혼동을 준 오답이다.
(C) [x] 질문의 held를 hold로 반복 사용하여 혼동을 준 오답이다.

13 🎧 미국식 발음 → 영국식 발음

Could you send me an update on the current state of the market?
(A) Inside the supermarket.
(B) Sure, send it to me later.

(C) I'll get that to you in a minute.

---

state[steit] 상태, 형편 in a minute 금방, 즉각

해석 현재 시장 상태에 대한 업데이트를 제게 보내주실 수 있나요?
   (A) 슈퍼마켓 안이요.
   (B) 물론이죠, 그것을 나중에 제게 보내주세요.
   (C) 제가 금방 당신에게 그것을 가져다줄게요.

해설 **요청 의문문**
   (A) [×] market - supermarket의 유사 발음 어휘를 사용하여 혼동
      을 준 오답이다.
   (B) [×] 질문의 send를 반복 사용하여 혼동을 준 오답이다.
   (C) [○] 금방 그것을 가져다주겠다는 말로, 현재 시장 상태에 대한 업
      데이트를 보내줄 수 있음을 전달했으므로 정답이다.

14 🎧 호주식 발음 → 미국식 발음

When are you planning to take your vacation?
(A) I've booked my trip for August.
(B) A luxurious spa.
(C) The train ticket for Barcelona.

---

book[buk] 예약하다 luxurious[lʌɡʒúriəs] 호화로운, 사치스러운

해석 당신은 언제 휴가를 갈 계획인가요?
   (A) 저는 8월에 여행을 예약했어요.
   (B) 호화로운 스파요.
   (C) 바르셀로나행 기차표요.

해설 **When 의문문**
   (A) [○] 8월에 여행을 예약했다며, 휴가를 가는 시기를 언급했으므로
      정답이다.
   (B) [×] 질문의 vacation(휴가)과 관련 있는 spa(스파)를 사용하여 혼
      동을 준 오답이다.
   (C) [×] 질문의 vacation(휴가)과 관련 있는 train ticket(기차표)를 사
      용하여 혼동을 준 오답이다.

15 🎧 호주식 발음 → 영국식 발음

Mark ran the marathon this year, didn't he?
(A) He skipped it due to an injury.
(B) I don't like running long races.
(C) The course has many hills.

---

skip[skip] 건너뛰다 injury[índʒəri] 부상

해석 Mark는 올해 마라톤을 뛰었어요, 그렇지 않나요?
   (A) 그는 부상 때문에 그것을 건너뛰었어요.
   (B) 저는 장거리 경주를 뛰는 것을 좋아하지 않아요.
   (C) 그 코스는 많은 언덕이 있어요.

해설 **부가 의문문**
   (A) [○] 그가 부상 때문에 그것을 건너뛰었다는 말로, Mark가 올해 마
      라톤을 뛰지 않았음을 전달했으므로 정답이다.
   (B) [×] 질문의 ran을 running으로 반복 사용하여 혼동을 준 오답이
      다.
   (C) [×] 질문의 marathon(마라톤)과 관련 있는 course(코스)를 사용
      하여 혼동을 준 오답이다.

16 🎧 캐나다식 발음 → 호주식 발음

We should buy a microwave for the apartment.
(A) I'll search online for cheap ones.   ○

(B) I usually cook for my family.
(C) The apartment is out of our price range.

---

microwave[máikrouwèiv] 전자레인지 price range 가격대, 가격폭

해석 우리는 아파트를 위해 전자레인지를 사야 해요.
   (A) 제가 온라인에서 싼 것들을 찾아볼게요.
   (B) 저는 보통 저희 가족을 위해 요리를 해요.
   (C) 그 아파트는 우리의 가격대를 벗어나요.

해설 **평서문**
   (A) [○] 온라인에서 싼 것들을 찾아보겠다는 말로, 전자레인지를 사야
      한다는 의견에 동의했으므로 정답이다.
   (B) [×] 질문의 microwave(전자레인지)와 관련 있는 cook(요리하다)
      을 사용하여 혼동을 준 오답이다.
   (C) [×] 질문의 apartment를 반복 사용하여 혼동을 준 오답이다.

17 🎧 영국식 발음 → 캐나다식 발음

How much will the construction of an additional
manufacturing facility cost?
(A) We are waiting for a quote.
(B) It will take weeks to manufacture.
(C) Due to a large tax incentive.

---

construction[kənstrʌ́kʃən] 건설, 건축 additional[ədíʃənl] 추가적인
manufacturing[mænjufǽktʃəriŋ] 제조의 facility[fəsíləti] 시설, 설비
quote[미 kwout, 영 kwɔut] 견적액, 시세
incentive[inséntiv] 혜택, 장려책

해석 추가적인 제조 시설의 건설은 얼마나 많은 비용이 들까요?
   (A) 우리는 견적액을 기다리고 있어요.
   (B) 제조하는 데 몇 주가 걸릴 거예요.
   (C) 큰 세금 혜택 때문에요.

해설 **How 의문문**
   (A) [○] 견적액을 기다리고 있다는 말로, 건설이 얼마나 많은 비용이 들
      지 모른다는 간접적인 응답을 했으므로 정답이다.
   (B) [×] manufacturing - manufacture의 유사 발음 어휘를 사용
      하여 혼동을 준 오답이다.
   (C) [×] 질문의 cost(비용이 들다)와 관련 있는 tax incentive(세금 혜
      택)를 사용하여 혼동을 준 오답이다.

18 🎧 미국식 발음 → 캐나다식 발음

When will the new network system be installed?
(A) Don't forget to install the update.
(B) No later than next Friday.
(C) This weekend's networking event was canceled.

---

no later than 늦어도 ~까지

해석 새로운 네트워크 시스템은 언제 설치될 것인가요?
   (A) 업데이트를 설치하는 것을 잊지 마세요.
   (B) 늦어도 다음 주 금요일까지요.
   (C) 이번 주말의 교류 행사가 취소되었어요.

해설 **When 의문문**
   (A) [×] 질문의 installed를 install로 반복 사용하여 혼동을 준 오답이
      다.
   (B) [○] 늦어도 다음 주 금요일까지라며, 새로운 네트워크 시스템이 설
      치될 시점을 언급했으므로 정답이다.
   (C) [×] network - networking의 유사 발음 어휘를 사용하여 혼동
      을 준 오답이다.

Anna's wedding is on Saturday morning at the Renaissance Hotel.
(A) Two double rooms.
(B) Are you planning to attend the ceremony?
(C) It had many guests.

attend [əténd] 참석하다   ceremony [sérəmòuni] 행사, 의식

해석 Anna의 결혼식은 토요일 아침에 르네상스 호텔이에요.
  (A) 2인실 두 개요.
  (B) 당신은 그 행사에 참석할 계획인가요?
  (C) 많은 손님들이 있었어요.

해설 **평서문**
  (A) [×] 질문의 Hotel(호텔)과 관련 있는 double rooms(2인실)를 사용하여 혼동을 준 오답이다.
  (B) [○] 행사에 참석할 계획인지를 되물어, 결혼식에 대한 상대방의 참석 여부를 묻는 정답이다.
  (C) [×] 질문의 wedding(결혼식)과 관련 있는 guests(손님들)를 사용하여 혼동을 준 오답이다.

The advertising campaign for this product costs a lot, right?
(A) They make great quality products.
(B) Yes, she's an advertising manager.
(C) It'll be worth it in the long run.

quality [미 kwɑ́ləti, 영 kwɔ́liti] 고급의, 훌륭한
worth [미 wəːrθ, 영 wəːθ] 가치가 있는   in the long run 장기적으로

해석 이 제품의 광고 캠페인은 비용이 많이 들죠, 그렇죠?
  (A) 그들은 훌륭한 고급 제품들을 만들어요.
  (B) 네, 그녀는 광고 관리자예요.
  (C) 장기적으로 그것은 그럴 만한 가치가 있을 거예요.

해설 **부가 의문문**
  (A) [×] 질문의 product를 products로 반복 사용하여 혼동을 준 오답이다.
  (B) [×] 질문의 advertising을 반복 사용하여 혼동을 준 오답이다.
  (C) [○] 장기적으로 그것은 그럴 만한 가치가 있을 거라는 말로, 광고 캠페인은 비용이 많이 든다는 것을 간접적으로 전달했으므로 정답이다.

Didn't Rachel submit her monthly plan already?
(A) I'm going to be away for a month.
(B) I've already checked your submission.
(C) No. I'll send an e-mail to remind her.

be away 부재중이다   submission [səbmíʃən] 제출
remind [rimáind] 다시 한번 알려 주다

해석 Rachel이 이미 월간 계획서를 제출하지 않았나요?
  (A) 저는 한 달 동안 부재중일 거예요.
  (B) 저는 이미 당신의 제출을 확인했어요.
  (C) 아니요. 제가 그녀에게 다시 한번 알려 주기 위해 이메일을 보낼게요.

해설 **부정 의문문**
  (A) [×] monthly – month의 유사 발음 어휘를 사용하여 혼동을 준 오답이다.
  (B) [×] 질문의 already를 반복 사용하고, submit – submission의 유사 발음 어휘를 사용하여 혼동을 준 오답이다.
  (C) [○] No로 Rachel이 월간 계획서를 제출하지 않았음을 전달한 후, 그녀에게 다시 한번 알려 주기 위해 이메일을 보내겠다는 부연 설명을 했으므로 정답이다.

Should we stay for the award ceremony or leave after your speech?
(A) It's entirely up to you.
(B) Two speakers were placed on stage.
(C) Let's leave it as it is.

speech [spiːtʃ] 연설   entirely [미 intáiərli, 영 intáiəli] 전적으로, 완전히

해석 저희는 시상식 동안 머물러야 하나요, 아니면 당신의 연설 후에 떠나야 하나요?
  (A) 그건 전적으로 당신에게 달려 있어요.
  (B) 두 명의 연사들이 무대 위에 배치되었어요.
  (C) 그것을 그대로 둡시다.

해설 **선택 의문문**
  (A) [○] 그건 전적으로 상대방에게 달려 있다는 말로, 시상식 동안 머무는 것과 연설 후에 떠나는 것 둘 다 상관없음을 간접적으로 전달했으므로 정답이다.
  (B) [×] 질문의 speech(연설)와 관련 있는 speakers(연사들)를 사용하여 혼동을 준 오답이다.
  (C) [×] 질문의 leave를 반복 사용하여 혼동을 준 오답이다.

The rent for this unit is only $400 per month.
(A) That's quite affordable for the area.
(B) Yes, we can just go to a rental car place.
(C) Payment is due on the first of the month.

rent [rent] 임대료   unit [júːnit] 한 가구, 단위
affordable [미 əfɔ́ːrdəbl, 영 əfɔ́ːdəbl] 저렴한
payment [péimənt] 지불, 지급   due [djuː] (돈을) 지불해야 하는

해석 이 가구의 임대료는 한 달에 단지 400달러예요.
  (A) 그것은 그 지역에서 꽤 저렴해요.
  (B) 네, 우리는 그냥 자동차 대여 장소로 가면 돼요.
  (C) 지불은 그달 첫날에 해야 해요.

해설 **평서문**
  (A) [○] 그것은 그 지역에서 꽤 저렴하다며, 가구의 임대료에 대한 의견을 제시했으므로 정답이다.
  (B) [×] rent – rental의 유사 발음 어휘를 사용하여 혼동을 준 오답이다.
  (C) [×] 질문의 rent(임대료)와 관련 있는 Payment(지불)를 사용하여 혼동을 준 오답이다.

How can I register for the management basics course?
(A) It's pretty easy to distinguish the material.
(B) A management position will open soon.

(C) I'll give you a hand with that.

register[미 rédʒistər, 영 rédʒistə] 등록하다
distinguish[distíŋgwiʃ] 구별하다, 구분하다, 분류하다
material[mətíəriəl] 자료 open[óupən] 공석인 give a hand 도와주다

해석 제가 경영 기초 수업을 어떻게 등록할 수 있나요?
(A) 자료를 구별하는 것은 꽤 쉬워요.
(B) 관리직이 곧 공석일 거예요.
(C) 제가 그것을 도와드릴게요.

해설 How 의문문
(A) [×] 질문의 course(수업)와 관련 있는 material(자료)을 사용하여 혼동을 준 오답이다.
(B) [×] 질문의 management를 반복 사용하여 혼동을 준 오답이다.
(C) [○] 자신이 그것을 도와주겠다는 말로, 경영 기초 수업을 등록하는 방법을 알려주겠다는 간접적인 응답을 했으므로 정답이다.

25 [3해] 미국식 발음 → 호주식 발음

Would you mind bringing this package to Mr. Smith?
(A) Please don't mind the noise.
(B) You can wrap it with this paper.
(C) He's not at his desk right now.

package[pǽkidʒ] 소포, 택배 wrap[ræp] 포장하다

해석 이 소포를 Mr. Smith에게 가져다주시겠어요?
(A) 그 소리는 신경 쓰지 마세요.
(B) 당신은 그것을 이 종이로 포장하셔도 돼요.
(C) 그는 지금 그의 자리에 없어요.

해설 요청 의문문
(A) [×] 질문의 mind를 반복 사용하여 혼동을 준 오답이다.
(B) [×] 질문의 package(소포)와 관련 있는 wrap(포장하다)을 사용하여 혼동을 준 오답이다.
(C) [○] 그가 지금 그의 자리에 없다는 말로, 소포를 Mr. Smith에게 가져다주라는 요청을 간접적으로 거절한 정답이다.

26 [3해] 캐나다식 발음 → 미국식 발음

Have you heard about the new hotel development across the street?
(A) It's all anyone is talking about.
(B) You can use the crosswalk.
(C) You have to develop your driving skills.

crosswalk[krɔ́:swɔ:k] 횡단보도
develop[divéləp] 발달시키다, 진전시키다

해석 길 건너편 새로운 호텔 개발에 대해 들어본 적 있나요?
(A) 그건 모두가 이야기하고 있는 것이에요.
(B) 당신은 횡단보도를 이용하실 수 있어요.
(C) 당신은 운전 기술을 발달시켜야 해요.

해설 조동사 의문문
(A) [○] 그건 모두가 이야기하고 있는 것이라는 말로, 길 건너편 새로운 호텔 개발에 대해 들어본 적이 있음을 간접적으로 전달했으므로 정답이다.
(B) [×] across – crosswalk의 유사 발음 어휘를 사용하여 혼동을 준 오답이다.
(C) [×] development – develop의 유사 발음 어휘를 사용하여 혼동을 준 오답이다.

27 [3해] 미국식 발음 → 캐나다식 발음

Are you coming to my accounting seminar?
(A) I'll check the account.
(B) He's going with his colleagues.
(C) As long as I finish my work in time.

accounting[əkáuntiŋ] 회계 account[əkáunt] 계좌
colleague[미 káli:g, 영 kɔ́li:g] 동료

해석 당신은 제 회계 세미나에 오실 건가요?
(A) 제가 계좌를 확인해 볼게요.
(B) 그는 그의 동료들과 함께 갈 거예요.
(C) 제가 일을 제시간에 끝내기만 하면요.

해설 Be동사 의문문
(A) [×] accounting – account의 유사 발음 어휘를 사용하여 혼동을 준 오답이다.
(B) [×] 질문의 coming(오는)과 관련 있는 going(가는)을 사용하여 혼동을 준 오답이다.
(C) [○] 일을 제시간에 끝내기만 하면이라는 말로, 회계 세미나에 갈지 모른다는 간접적인 응답을 했으므로 정답이다.

28 [3해] 미국식 발음 → 호주식 발음

Where did you place the document I gave you this morning?
(A) We replaced the printer.
(B) It must be on my desk.
(C) During the morning team meeting.

document[미 dákjumənt, 영 dɔ́kjumənt] 서류
replace[ripléis] 교체하다

해석 제가 오늘 아침에 당신께 드린 서류를 어디에 두었나요?
(A) 우리는 프린터를 교체했어요.
(B) 그것은 제 책상 위에 있음이 틀림없어요.
(C) 아침 팀 회의 동안에요.

해설 Where 의문문
(A) [×] place – replaced의 유사 발음 어휘를 사용하여 혼동을 준 오답이다.
(B) [○] 그것이 자신의 책상 위에 있음이 틀림없다며, 서류의 위치를 언급했으므로 정답이다.
(C) [×] 질문의 morning을 반복 사용하여 혼동을 준 오답이다.

29 [3해] 호주식 발음 → 미국식 발음

Andy, who owns the property on the corner?
(A) That's the proper way to do it.
(B) It's a city property.
(C) I live a few blocks down.

property[미 prápərti, 영 prɔ́pəti] 부동산, 재산
proper[prápər] 적절한, 알맞은

해석 Andy, 길모퉁이에 있는 부동산을 누가 소유하고 있나요?
(A) 그게 그것을 하는 적절한 방법이에요.
(B) 그것은 시의 부동산이에요.
(C) 저는 몇 블록 아래에 살아요.

해설 Who 의문문
(A) [×] property – proper의 유사 발음 어휘를 사용하여 혼동을 준 오답이다.

(B) [o] 그것은 시의 부동산이라며, 길모퉁이에 있는 부동산을 소유하
고 있는 대상을 언급했으므로 정답이다.
(C) [×] 질문의 corner(길모퉁이)와 관련 있는 blocks(블록)를 사용하
여 혼동을 준 오답이다.

30 🎧 영국식 발음 → 캐나다식 발음

Why are there maintenance workers in the lobby?
(A) We'll maintain the current deadline.
(B) The air-conditioning system broke down.
(C) We can work on it together.

maintenance[méintənəns] 정비, 유지
maintain[meintéin] 지키다, 유지하다
current[미 kə́ːrənt, 영 kʌ́rənt] 현재의   break down 고장 나다

해석   로비에 왜 정비사들이 있나요?
(A) 우리는 현재의 마감일을 지킬 거예요.
(B) 공기 조절 장치가 고장 났어요.
(C) 우리는 그것을 함께 할 수 있어요.

해설   **Why 의문문**
(A) [×] maintenance – maintain의 유사 발음 어휘를 사용하여 혼
동을 준 오답이다.
(B) [o] 공기 조절 장치가 고장 났다며, 로비에 정비사들이 있는 이유
를 언급했으므로 정답이다.
(C) [×] workers – work의 유사 발음 어휘를 사용하여 혼동을 준 오
답이다.

31 🎧 영국식 발음 → 미국식 발음

Did you find a suitable candidate for the marketing
position?
(A) I voted for the other candidate.
(B) I don't think a suit is necessary.
(C) I e-mailed you a résumé.

suitable[súːtəbl] 적합한   candidate[kǽndidèit] 지원자, 후보자
vote[vout] 투표하다   necessary[nésəsèri] 필수적인

해석   당신은 마케팅 직에 적합한 지원자를 찾았나요?
(A) 저는 다른 후보자에게 투표했어요.
(B) 저는 정장이 필수적이라고 생각하지 않아요.
(C) 제가 이력서를 당신께 이메일로 보냈어요.

해설   **조동사 의문문**
(A) [×] 질문의 candidate(지원자)를 '후보자'라는 의미로 반복 사용
하여 혼동을 준 오답이다.
(B) [×] suitable – suit의 유사 발음 어휘를 사용하여 혼동을 준 오답
이다.
(C) [o] 이력서를 상대방에게 이메일로 보냈다며, 마케팅 직에 적합한
지원자를 찾았음을 간접적으로 전달했으므로 정답이다.

PART 3

32-34 🎧 미국식 발음 → 캐나다식 발음

Questions 32-34 refer to the following conversation.

W: Hi. ³²I wanted to inquire about the job advertisement
for a secretary you posted on your Web site. Does
that require a college degree? It wasn't clear in the
advertisement.

M: You don't have to be a college graduate, but we
would prefer it if you were at least working towards
a degree. We would also like you to have some
experience in a secretarial role.
W: Well . . . I'm studying for a bachelor's now at
Queen College. ³³I don't have any experience in
a secretarial role, but I completed an internship at
Artest Industries.
M: That's OK. We'd be happy to read your application.
³⁴Be sure to submit it by Tuesday, which is the
deadline.

inquire[미 inkwáiər, 영 inkwáiə] 문의하다
job advertisement 구인 광고   secretary[sékrətèri] 비서
graduate[grǽdʒuət] 졸업자   work towards ~을 지향하여 노력하다
secretarial[sèkrətɛ́əriəl] 비서직의   bachelor[bǽtʃələr] 학사 (학위)
internship[íntəːrnʃip] 인턴 연수 기간   be happy to 기꺼이 ~하다
application[æ̀pləkéiʃən] 지원서   be sure to 반드시 ~하도록 하다
submit[səbmít] 제출하다   deadline[dédlain] 마감일, 기한

해석
32-34번은 다음 대화에 관한 문제입니다.

여: 안녕하세요. ³²저는 웹사이트에 당신이 올린 비서 구인 광고에 대해 문의
하고 싶었어요. 그것이 대학 학위를 필요로 하나요? 그것이 광고에서 명
확하지 않았어요.
남: 당신은 대학 졸업생일 필요는 없지만, 적어도 학위를 지향해서 노력하고
있다면 저희는 그것을 더 선호해요. 저희는 또한 당신이 비서직에 약간의
경험이 있기를 바라요.
여: 음... 저는 지금 Queen 대학에서 학사 학위를 위해 공부하고 있어요.
³³저는 비서직 경험은 없지만, Artest Industries사에서 인턴 연수 기간
을 마쳤어요.
남: 괜찮아요. 저희는 당신의 지원서를 기꺼이 읽어볼게요. ³⁴반드시 그것을
화요일까지 제출하도록 하세요, 그때가 마감일이에요.

32 목적 문제

해석   여자는 왜 전화를 하고 있는가?
(A) 직무의 요구 조건에 대해 문의하기 위해
(B) 면접을 연기하기 위해
(C) 그녀의 이력서가 수령되었는지 묻기 위해
(D) 일자리 제의를 수락하기 위해

해설   전화의 목적을 묻는 문제이므로, 대화의 초반을 반드시 듣는다. 여
자가 "I wanted to inquire about the job advertisement for a
secretary you posted on your Web site. Does that require a
college degree?"라며 웹사이트에 남자가 올린 비서 구인 광고에 대
해 문의하고 싶었다고 한 후, 그것이 대학 학위를 필요로 하는지를 물
었다. 따라서 (A)가 정답이다.

어휘   requirement[미 rikwáiərmənt, 영 rikwáiəmənt] 요구 조건, 자격
postpone[미 poustpóun, 영 pəustpə́un] 연기하다
résumé[미 rézumèi, 영 rézjuːmèi] 이력서

33 특정 세부 사항 문제

해석   여자는 어떤 경험을 가지고 있는가?
(A) 연구 보조원으로 일했다.
(B) 대학에서 경영학을 공부했다.
(C) 인턴으로 근무했다.
(D) 자선 행사에 자원했다.

해설   여자의 말에서 질문의 핵심 어구(experience)가 언급된 주변을 주의
깊게 듣는다. 여자가 "I don't have any experience in a secretarial
role, but I completed an internship at Artest Industries."라며
비서직 경험은 없지만 Artest Industries사에서 인턴 연수 기간을 마

쳤다고 한 말을 통해 여자가 인턴으로 근무했음을 알 수 있다. 따라서 (C)가 정답이다.

패러프레이징
completed an internship 인턴 연수 기간을 마쳤다 →
was employed as an intern 인턴으로 근무했다

어휘 research assistant 연구 보조원
volunteer[미 vὰ:ləntíər, 영 vɔ̀ləntíə] 자원하다
charitable[tʃǽrɪtəbl] 자선의

34 제안 문제

해석 남자는 여자에게 무엇을 하라고 제안하는가?
(A) 온라인에서 직무에 대한 설명을 읽는다.
(B) 개인 면접을 위해 사무실에 방문한다.
(C) 고용주로부터 추천서를 얻는다.
(D) 마감일까지 지원서를 제출한다.

해설 남자의 말에서 제안과 관련된 표현이 언급된 내용을 주의 깊게 듣는다.
남자가 "Be sure to submit it[application] by Tuesday, which is
the deadline."이라며 반드시 지원서를 마감일인 화요일까지 제출하
라고 하였다. 따라서 (D)가 정답이다.

패러프레이징
submit 제출하다 → Send in 제출하다
deadline 마감일 → due date 마감일

어휘 description[dɪskrípʃən] 설명 in-person interview 개인 면접
obtain[əbtéin] 얻다, 획득하다 reference letter 추천서
due date 마감일

35-37 ③ 영국식 발음 → 캐나다식 발음

Questions 35-37 refer to the following conversation.

W: Good morning, sir. ³⁵I'm the head flight attendant,
Sarah. My colleague says you're having a problem.
M: Yes. ³⁵/³⁶I purchased the onboard Wi-Fi package,
³⁶but I can't get it working. I followed the
instructions on the seat-back screen, and my
phone connects after I enter the password. ³⁶But
it says that there is no Internet service available.
W: Oh, I'm sorry. There are sometimes problems with
the system right after departure, and then the Wi-Fi
system needs to be rebooted. I'll go do that now.
It should be back up and running in 10 minutes or
so.
M: OK. That will be fine. ³⁷I'll just watch one of the
shows on the screen in the meantime. Thank you
so much for your help.

head[hed] 수석의; 지도적 지위 flight attendant 승무원
colleague[미 ká:liːɡ, 영 kɔ́liːɡ] 동료 onboard[ánbɔ̀ːrd] 기내의
instruction[instrʌ́kʃən] 지시, 설명
departure[미 dipá:rtʃər, 영 dipá:tʃə] 출발 reboot[riːbúːt] 재시동하다
up and running (완전히 제대로) 작동되는, 작동 중인 or so ~ 정도, ~ 쯤
in the meantime 그동안에, 그 사이에

해석
35-37번은 다음 대화에 관한 문제입니다.

여: 좋은 아침입니다, 손님. ³⁵저는 수석 승무원 Sarah입니다. 제 동료가 말하
길 손님께서 문제를 겪고 있으시다고요.
남: 네. ³⁵/³⁶제가 기내 와이파이 패키지를 구매했는데, ³⁶그것을 작동시킬 수
없어요. 저는 좌석 등받이 화면의 지시에 따랐고, 비밀번호를 입력한 후
제 전화기가 연결되었어요. ³⁶하지만 그것은 이용 가능한 인터넷 서비스
가 없다고 나와요.

여: 아, 죄송합니다. 때로로 출발 직후 시스템에 문제가 있고, 그러면 와이파
이 시스템이 재시동되어야 합니다. 제가 지금 가서 그것을 하겠습니다.
10분 정도 뒤에 다시 작동될 것입니다.
남: 네. 괜찮겠네요. ³⁷저는 그동안에 화면에 나오는 쇼들 중 하나를 좀 볼게
요. 도와주셔서 정말 감사해요.

35 장소 문제

해석 대화는 어디에서 일어나고 있는 것 같은가?
(A) 버스에서
(B) 비행기에서
(C) 기차에서
(D) 배 위에서

해설 대화에서 장소와 관련된 표현을 놓치지 않고 듣는다. 여자가 "I'm the
head flight attendant, Sarah."라며 자신이 수석 승무원 Sara라고
하자, 남자가 "I purchased the onboard Wi-Fi package"라며 자
신이 기내 와이파이 패키지를 구매했다고 한 말을 통해 비행기에서 대
화가 일어나고 있음을 알 수 있다. 따라서 (B)가 정답이다.

36 문제점 문제

해석 남자는 무슨 문제를 언급하는가?
(A) 비밀번호가 틀리다.
(B) 전등이 작동하지 않는다.
(C) 연결이 느리다.
(D) 서비스를 이용할 수 없다.

해설 남자의 말에서 부정적인 표현이 언급된 주변을 주의 깊게 듣는다. 남
자가 "I purchased the onboard Wi-Fi package, but I can't get
it working."이라며 자신이 기내 와이파이 패키지를 구매했는데 그것
을 작동시킬 수 없다고 한 후, "But it says that there is no Internet
service available."이라며 그것은 이용 가능한 인터넷 서비스가 없다
고 나온다고 하였다. 따라서 (D)가 정답이다.

어휘 connection[kənékʃən] 연결
unavailable[ʌ̀nəvéiləbl] 이용할 수 없는

37 다음에 할 일 문제

해석 남자는 무엇을 할 것이라고 말하는가?
(A) 잡지를 읽는다.
(B) 쇼를 시청한다.
(C) 비밀번호를 다시 입력한다.
(D) 다른 위치로 이동한다.

해설 대화의 마지막 부분을 주의 깊게 듣는다. 남자가 "I'll just watch one
of the shows on the screen in the meantime."이라며 그동안에
화면에 나오는 쇼들 중 하나를 좀 보겠다는 것을 통해 남자가 쇼를 시
청할 것임을 알 수 있다. 따라서 (B)가 정답이다.

어휘 magazine[mǽɡəzíːn] 잡지 location[미 loukéiʃən, 영 ləukéiʃən] 위치

38-40 ③ 캐나다식 발음 → 호주식 발음 → 영국식 발음

Questions 38-40 refer to the following conversation with three speakers.

M1: Tom and Marla, ³⁸I need to work on an employee
satisfaction survey for management as several
employees have resigned recently. But the
problem is . . . I am not sure where I should start.
M2: Well, I've never made one, but Marla, you worked
on an employee survey before, didn't you?
W: Yes. ³⁹I did the last one, and I still have it in my
files. I can send it to you if you like.
M1: Great! That would be very helpful.

W: But . . . ⁴⁰Mark, you'll have to change the details in it. It only asked about satisfaction with our facilities.

satisfaction [sæ̀tisfǽkʃən] 만족(도)
survey [미 sə́ːrvei, 영 sə́ːvei] (설문) 조사
management [mǽnidʒmənt] 관리 resign [rizáin] 사직하다
detail [díteil] 세부 내용 facility [fəsíləti] 시설

해석
38-40번은 다음 세 명의 대화에 관한 문제입니다.

남1: Tom과 Marla, ³⁸최근에 여러 직원들이 사직했기 때문에 저는 관리를 위해 직원 만족도 설문 조사를 해야 해요. 하지만 문제는... 제가 어디서부터 시작해야 할지 확실하지 않다는 거예요.
남2: 글쎄요, 저는 그것을 만든 적이 없지만, Marla, 당신은 이전에 직원 설문 조사를 했죠, 그렇지 않나요?
여: 네. ³⁹저는 지난번 것을 했는데, 아직 제 파일에 그것을 가지고 있어요. 당신이 원하면 제가 당신께 그것을 보내드릴 수 있어요.
남1: 좋아요! 그것은 매우 도움이 될 거예요.
여: 하지만... ⁴⁰Mark, 당신은 그 안의 세부 내용을 바꿔야 할 거예요. 그것은 단지 우리의 시설에 대한 만족에 대해서만 물었어요.

38 이유 문제

해석 설문조사를 하는 것이 왜 필요한가?
(A) 새로운 광고가 나왔다.
(B) 몇몇 근무자들이 그만두었다.
(C) 고객들이 서비스에 대해 불평했다.
(D) 구내식당 메뉴 항목이 추가될 것이다.

해설 질문의 핵심 어구(survey)가 언급된 주변을 주의 깊게 듣는다. 남자1이 "I need to work on an employee satisfaction survey for management as several employees have resigned recently"라며 최근에 여러 직원들이 사직했기 때문에 관리를 위해 직원 만족도 설문 조사를 해야 한다고 하였다. 따라서 (B)가 정답이다.

패러프레이징
several employees have resigned 여러 직원들이 사직했다 → Some workers have quit 몇몇 근무자들이 그만두었다

어휘 release [rilíːs] 나오다, 발표하다 quit [kwit] 그만두다
complain [kəmpléin] 불평하다

39 제안 문제

해석 여자는 무엇을 해주겠다고 제안하는가?
(A) 업무를 인계한다.
(B) 면접을 돕는다.
(C) 관리자에게 이야기한다.
(D) 문서를 보낸다.

해설 여자의 말에서 제안과 관련된 표현이 포함된 문장을 주의 깊게 듣는다. 여자가 "I did the last one[employee survey], and I still have it in my files. I can send it to you if you like."라며 지난번 직원 설문 조사를 했는데 아직 자신의 파일에 그것을 가지고 있다며 원하면 보내줄 수 있다고 하였다. 따라서 (D)가 정답이다.

어휘 take over 인계하다 assignment [əsáinmənt] 업무
supervisor [미 súːpərvàizər, 영 súːpəvaizə] 관리자
document [미 dákjumənt, 영 dɔ́kjumənt] 문서, 서류

40 특정 세부 사항 문제

해석 여자는 Mark에게 무엇을 하라고 상기시키는가?
(A) 몇몇 정보를 변경한다.
(B) 평가서를 제출한다.
(C) 의견을 검토한다.
(D) 시설에 대해 문의한다.

해설 여자의 말에서 질문의 핵심 어구(remind Mark to do)와 관련된 내용을 주의 깊게 듣는다. 여자가 "Mark, you'll have to change the details in it[employee survey]"이라며 Mark에게 설문 조사 안의 세부 내용을 바꿔야 할 것이라고 하였다. 따라서 (A)가 정답이다.

패러프레이징
details 세부 내용 → information 정보

어휘 evaluation [ivæ̀ljuéiʃən] 평가(서) review [rivjúː] 검토하다

41-43 🎧 영국식 발음 → 호주식 발음

Questions 41-43 refer to the following conversation.

W: Hey, Kevin. This is Mary from the Book Corner on Second Avenue. I really enjoyed your poems in *The Kentucky Quarterly* last month. ⁴¹Are you interested in reading them at our bookstore's poetry reading this Thursday?
M: That'd be great. ⁴²When does the reading start? I get off work at 6, and it will take about 30 minutes to get there.
W: ⁴²It starts at 5:30. But if you want to participate, I won't put you in an early time slot. You can read yours last. ⁴²Then, you'll have enough time to make it. ⁴³We'll have some snacks and drinks after the reading.

poem [póuəm] (한 편의) 시, 운문 reading [ríːdiŋ] 낭독(회)
poetry [미 póuətri, 영 póuətri] (집합적) 시, 시가
participate [미 pɑːrtísəpeit, 영 pɑːtísipeit] 참여하다 time slot 시간대

해석
41-43번은 다음 대화에 관한 문제입니다.

여: 안녕하세요, Kevin. 저는 2번가에 있는 Book Corner의 Mary예요. 지난달 *The Kentucky Quarterly*지에 있는 당신의 시를 정말로 음미했어요. ⁴¹이번 주 목요일에 저희 서점의 시 낭독회에서 그것들을 낭독하는 데 관심이 있으신가요?
남: 그거 정말 좋을 것 같네요. ⁴²낭독회가 언제 시작하나요? 저는 6시에 퇴근해서, 거기에 도착하는 데 30분 정도 걸릴 거예요.
여: ⁴²5시 30분에 시작해요. 하지만 당신이 참여하고 싶다면, 당신을 이른 시간대에 넣지 않을게요. 당신은 당신의 것을 마지막에 읽을 수 있어요. ⁴²그러면, 당신은 도착하기에 충분한 시간이 있을 거예요. ⁴³우리는 낭독 후에 약간의 간식과 음료를 먹을 거예요.

41 주제 문제

해석 대화는 주로 무엇에 대한 것인가?
(A) 책을 주문하는 과정
(B) 곧 있을 문학 낭독회
(C) 서점의 교대 일정
(D) 작가들을 위한 시상식

해설 대화의 주제를 묻는 문제이므로, 대화의 초반을 반드시 듣는다. 여자가 "Are you interested in reading them[poems] at our bookstore's poetry reading this Thursday?"라며 이번 주 목요일에 서점의 시 낭독회에서 시를 낭독하는 데 관심이 있는지 물은 후, 시 낭독회에 대한 내용으로 지문이 이어지고 있다. 따라서 (B)가 정답이다.

패러프레이징
poetry reading 시 낭독회 → literary reading 문학 낭독회

어휘 process [미 prάses, 영 prə́uses] 과정
upcoming [ʌ́pkʌ̀miŋ] 곧 있을, 다가오는 literary [lítərəri] 문학의
shift [ʃift] 교대(조)

42 의도 파악 문제

해석 여자는 "당신은 당신의 것을 마지막에 읽을 수 있어요"라고 말할 때 무엇을 의도하는가?
(A) 오랜 대기가 없을 것이다.
(B) 질문할 시간이 있을 것이다.
(C) 일정 문제는 없을 것이다.
(D) 저녁 식사를 위한 충분한 시간이 있을 것이다.

해설 질문의 인용어구(You can read yours last)가 언급된 주변을 주의 깊게 듣는다. 남자가 "When does the reading start? I get off work at 6, and it will take about 30 minutes to get there."라며 낭독회가 언제 시작하는지 물으며 6시에 퇴근해서 그곳에 도착하는 데 30분 정도 걸릴 것이라고 하자, 여자가 "It starts at 5:30. But if you want to participate, I won't put you in an early time slot."이라며 5시 30분에 시작한다며 참여하고 싶다면 이른 시간대에 넣지 않겠다고 한 후, "Then, you'll have enough time to make it."이라며 그러면 도착하기에 충분한 시간이 있을 것이라고 하였으므로 일정 문제가 없을 것임을 알 수 있다. 따라서 (C)가 정답이다.

43 다음에 할 일 문제

해석 여자에 따르면, 참석자들은 행사 후에 무엇을 할 것인가?
(A) 약간의 다과를 받는다.
(B) 잡지의 신간 호를 읽는다.
(C) 단체 사진을 찍는다.
(D) 할인하여 책을 구입한다.

해설 여자의 말에서 질문의 핵심 어구(the participants do after an event)와 관련된 내용을 주의 깊게 듣는다. 여자가 "We'll have some snacks and drinks after the reading."이라며 낭독 후에 약간의 간식과 음료를 먹을 것이라고 하였다. 따라서 (A)가 정답이다.

패러프레이징
some snacks and drinks 약간의 간식과 음료 →
some refreshments 약간의 다과

어휘 participant[미 pɑːrtísəpənt, 영 pɑːtísipənt] 참석자
refreshment[rifréʃmənt] 다과, 간식
journal[dʒə́ːrnl] (학회·전문 기관 등의) 잡지 at a discount 할인하여

44-46 🎧 캐나다식 발음 → 미국식 발음

Questions 44-46 refer to the following conversation.

M: Hello, I'm Steven from Water Mates Services. ⁴⁴We received a call about a broken pipe in this building. I'm here to fix it.

W: Oh, yes. I called you earlier. ⁴⁵Thank you for coming so quickly. There's a problem with one of the pipes coming out of the boiler. Do you have any idea how long it will take to repair?

M: If the pipe is easy to access, it should take less than 30 minutes. However, I can't guarantee that because I don't know the actual situation.

W: OK. That is fine. Wait here for one second while I call the security guard. ⁴⁶He will give you an access card for the building.

pipe[paip] 배관 earlier[ə́ːrliər] 이전에, 앞서 access[ǽkses] 접근하다
guarantee[gærəntíː] 장담하다, 보장하다 actual[ǽktʃuəl] 현재의, 현실의
security guard 경비원 access card 출입 관리 카드

해석
44-46번은 다음 대화에 관한 문제입니다.

남: 안녕하세요, Water Mates 서비스의 Steven이에요. ⁴⁴저희는 이 건물의

부러진 배관에 관한 전화를 받았어요. 저는 그것을 고치러 여기에 왔어요.
여: 아, 네. 제가 이전에 전화했어요. ⁴⁵이렇게 빨리 와주셔서 감사해요. 보일러에서 나오는 배관들 중 하나에 문제가 있어요. 혹시 수리하는 데 얼마나 걸릴지 아시나요?
남: 배관이 접근하기 쉽다면, 30분도 안 걸릴 거예요. 하지만, 저는 현재 상황을 모르기 때문에 그것을 장담할 수 없어요.
여: 네. 괜찮아요. 제가 경비원을 부를 동안 여기서 잠깐만 기다려 주세요. ⁴⁶그가 당신에게 건물 출입 관리 카드를 드릴 거예요.

44 목적 문제

해석 남자는 왜 방문하고 있는가?
(A) 건물을 임차하는 것에 대해 문의하기 위해
(B) 수리를 이행하기 위해
(C) 경보 장치를 다시 맞추기 위해
(D) 보일러 시스템을 설정하기 위해

해설 대화의 목적을 묻는 문제이므로, 대화의 초반을 반드시 듣는다. 남자가 "We received a call about a broken pipe in this building. I'm here to fix it."이라며 이 건물의 부러진 배관에 관한 전화를 받고 그것을 고치러 여기에 왔다고 하였다. 따라서 (B)가 정답이다.

패러프레이징
fix 고치다 → perform a repair 수리를 이행하다

어휘 rent[rent] 임차하다 perform[미 pərfɔ́ːrm, 영 pəfɔ́ːm] 이행하다
reset[risét] 다시 맞추다 alarm[əlɑ́ːrm] 경보 장치 set up 설정하다

45 특정 세부 사항 문제

해석 여자는 남자에게 무엇에 대해 감사하는가?
(A) 지하실을 개방한 것
(B) 문제를 발견한 것
(C) 매우 빠르게 응답한 것
(D) 그녀에게 무료 서비스를 제공한 것

해설 질문의 핵심 어구(thank)가 언급된 주변을 주의 깊게 듣는다. 여자가 "Thank you for coming so quickly."라며 빨리 와줘서 감사하다고 하였다. 따라서 (C)가 정답이다.

패러프레이징
quickly 빨리 → rapidly 빠르게

어휘 basement[béismənt] 지하실
identify[미 aidéntəfài, 영 aidéntifài] 발견하다, 식별하다
respond[미 rispánd, 영 rispɔ́nd] 응답하다 rapidly[rǽpidli] 빠르게

46 특정 세부 사항 문제

해석 여자는 남자가 무엇을 받을 것이라고 말하는가?
(A) 평면도
(B) 몇몇 연락 정보
(C) 몇몇 장비의 사진
(D) 보안 출입증

해설 질문의 핵심 어구(receive)와 관련된 내용을 주의 깊게 듣는다. 여자가 "He[security guard] will give you an access card for the building."이라며 경비원이 남자에게 건물 출입 관리 카드를 줄 것이라고 하였다. 따라서 (D)가 정답이다.

패러프레이징
access card 출입 관리 카드 → security pass 보안 출입증

어휘 floor plan 평면도 security[미 sikjúərəti, 영 sikjúəriti] 보안의; 보안
pass[미 pæs, 영 pɑːs] 출입증, 통행증

Questions 47-49 refer to the following conversation with three speakers.

M: Excuse me. ⁴⁷I am interested in getting a new washing machine. Do you have any on sale at the moment?

W1: Yes, ⁴⁷we have several models discounted for a limited time. Do you also need a dryer?

M: Not necessarily. ⁴⁸My priority is getting the washer at a good price.

W1: OK, then I'll introduce you to my associate Laura. She can help you. Laura, could you point out some of our economical washers for this customer?

W2: Certainly, please follow me . . . ⁴⁹I personally have this Lexpro model, which the manufacturer recently launched. It is highly effective and also energy and water-efficient. It will save you time and money in the long run.

---

washing machine 세탁기　on sale 할인 중인
not necessarily 반드시 ~인 것은 아니다　priority [praiɔ́:rəti] 우선순위
associate [əsóuʃièit] 동료, 친구　point out 알려 주다, 가리키다
economical [미 ìːkənámikl, 영 ìːkənɔ́mikl] 실속 있는, 알뜰한
personally [미 pə́ːrsənəli, 영 pə́ːsənəli] 개인적으로
launch [lɔːntʃ] 출시하다, 시작하다

해석

47-49번은 다음 세 명의 대화에 관한 문제입니다.

남: 실례합니다. ⁴⁷저는 새 세탁기를 사는 것에 관심이 있어요. 지금 할인 중인 것이 있나요?

여1: 네, ⁴⁷저희는 한정된 기간 동안 할인되는 몇 가지 모델들이 있어요. 건조기도 필요하신가요?

남: 반드시 그런 건 아니에요. ⁴⁸제 우선순위는 좋은 가격에 세탁기를 구하는 거예요.

여1: 네, 그러면 제가 제 동료 Laura를 손님께 소개해 드릴게요. 그녀가 손님을 도울 수 있어요. Laura, 이 손님을 위해 몇몇의 실속 있는 세탁기들을 알려 줄래요?

여2: 그럼요, 저를 따라오세요... ⁴⁹저는 개인적으로 Lexpro 모델을 가지고 있는데, 이것을 업체가 최근에 출시했어요. 이것은 매우 효과적이고 에너지와 물도 적게 들어요. 이것은 장기적으로 손님께 시간과 돈을 절약해 줄 거예요.

47 장소 문제

해석 대화는 어디에서 일어나고 있는 것 같은가?
(A) 옷 가게에서
(B) 미용실에서
(C) 세차장에서
(D) 가전제품 상점에서

해설 대화에서 장소와 관련된 표현을 놓치지 않고 듣는다. 남자가 "I am interested in getting a new washing machine. Do you have any on sale at the moment?"라며 새 세탁기를 사는 것에 관심이 있다고 하며 지금 할인 중인 것이 있는지 물어보자, 여자1이 "we have several models discounted for a limited time"이라며 한정된 기간 동안 할인되는 몇 가지 모델들이 있다고 하였다. 이를 통해 가전제품 상점에서 대화가 일어나고 있음을 알 수 있다. 따라서 (D)가 정답이다.

어휘 **hair salon** 미용실　**appliance** [əpláiəns] 가전제품

48 특정 세부 사항 문제

해석 남자의 주요 우선순위는 무엇인가?
(A) 비용 효율적인 선택지를 찾는 것
(B) 그의 상품권을 사용하는 것
(C) 특정 브랜드에서 구매하는 것
(D) 몇몇 친환경 물질을 이용하는 것

해설 질문의 핵심 어구(priority)가 언급된 주변을 주의 깊게 듣는다. 남자가 "My priority is getting the washer at a good price."라며 자신의 우선순위는 좋은 가격에 세탁기를 구하는 것이라고 하였다. 따라서 (A)가 정답이다.

패러프레이징
at a good price 좋은 가격에 → cost-effective 비용 효율적인

어휘 **cost-effective** 비용 효율적인　**option** [ápʃən] 선택지
gift card 상품권　**specific** [미 spisífik, 영 spəsífik] 특정한, 구체적인
utilize [júːtəlàiz] 이용하다, 활용하다　**eco-friendly** 친환경적인
material [mətíəriəl] 물질, 재료

49 언급 문제

해석 Lexpro에 대해 언급된 것은?
(A) 개인 맞춤형 설정을 특징으로 삼는다.
(B) 생산이 중단되었다.
(C) 더 많은 에너지를 필요로 한다.
(D) 최근에 출시되었다.

해설 질문의 핵심 어구(Lexpro)가 언급된 주변을 주의 깊게 듣는다. 여자2가 "I personally have this Lexpro model, which the manufacturer recently launched."라며 자신이 개인적으로 Lexpro 모델을 가지고 있다고 하며 이것을 업체가 최근에 출시했다고 하였다. 따라서 (D)가 정답이다.

패러프레이징
launched 출시했다 → was ~ released 출시되었다

어휘 **feature** [미 fíːtʃər, 영 fíːtʃə] 특징으로 삼다
personalized [pə́ːrsənəlàizd] 개인 맞춤형의
discontinue [dìskəntínjuː] (생산을) 중단하다

Questions 50-52 refer to the following conversation.

W: Thank you for calling Sky Card. How may I help you?

M: Hi. My name is Aiden Sellers. ⁵⁰I'm calling because when I tried using my credit card today, the salesperson told me it was suspended. Can you tell me why?

W: Sure. I can check your account. ⁵¹To verify your identity, can you tell me where you live and the last four digits of your social security number?

M: 122 Oak Lane, Houston, and 5729.

W: OK, let's see. It looks like we suspended your account because there was an unusual purchase of $1,000.

M: Oh. Actually, I bought a television for my new house.

W: In that case, ⁵²I'll reactivate your account. It should be working again by the end of the day.

---

credit card 신용카드　salesperson [séilzpə̀ːrsn] 판매원
suspend [səspénd] 정지하다, 중단하다　verify [vérəfài] 확인하다, 증명하다
identity [aidéntəti] 신원, 정체성　digit [dídʒit] 숫자
social security number 사회 보장 번호(출생과 함께 공식적으로 부여되는 개인 신원 번호)

unusual[ʌnjúːʒuəl] 이례적인, 예외적인 in that case 그렇다면
reactivate[riӕktiveit] 다시 활성화하다, 재가동하다

해석

50-52번은 다음 대화에 관한 문제입니다.

여: Sky 카드사에 전화해 주셔서 감사합니다. 어떻게 도와드릴까요?

남: 안녕하세요. 제 이름은 Aiden Sellers입니다. 50제가 오늘 신용카드를 사용하려고 했을 때, 판매원이 제게 그것이 정지됐다고 말해서 전화해요. 제게 이유를 말씀해주실 수 있나요?

여: 물론이죠. 제가 고객님의 계좌를 확인해볼게요. 51고객님의 신원을 확인하기 위해, 고객님께서 사는 곳과 사회 보장 번호의 마지막 네 개 숫자를 말씀해주시겠어요?

남: 122번지 Oak로, 휴스턴, 그리고 5729예요.

여: 네, 제가 한 번 보겠습니다. 1,000달러의 이례적인 구매가 있어서 저희가 고객님의 계좌를 정지했던 것으로 보입니다.

남: 아. 사실, 저는 새로운 집을 위해 텔레비전을 샀어요.

여: 그렇다면, 52제가 고객님의 계좌를 다시 활성화해 드리겠습니다. 그것은 오늘이 끝날 무렵에 다시 작동할 것입니다.

50 문제점 문제

해석 남자는 무슨 문제를 언급하는가?
(A) 명세서를 받지 못했다.
(B) 은행 애플리케이션을 이용할 수 없다.
(C) 그의 카드로 이례적인 구매가 이루어졌다.
(D) 그의 신용카드를 사용할 수 없다.

해설 남자의 말에서 부정적인 표현이 언급된 주변을 주의 깊게 듣는다. 남자가 "I'm calling because when I tried using my credit card today, the salesperson told me it was suspended."라며 오늘 신용카드를 사용하려고 했을 때 판매원이 자신에게 그것이 정지됐다고 말해서 전화한다고 하였다. 따라서 (D)가 정답이다.

어휘 statement[stéitmənt] 명세서, 진술

51 특정 세부 사항 문제

해석 여자는 남자로부터 무슨 정보를 요청하는가?
(A) 그의 생년월일
(B) 그의 전화번호
(C) 그의 주소
(D) 그의 신용카드 번호

해설 대화에서 여자의 말을 주의 깊게 듣는다. 여자가 남자에게 "To verify your identity, can you tell me where you live ~?"라며 신원을 확인하기 위해 남자가 사는 곳을 말해줄 수 있는지 물었다. 따라서 (C)가 정답이다.

패러프레이징
where ~ live 사는 곳 → address 주소

52 다음에 할 일 문제

해석 여자에 따르면, 오늘 늦게 무슨 일이 일어날 것인가?
(A) 웹사이트가 업데이트될 것이다.
(B) 카드가 사용할 수 있게 될 것이다.
(C) 구매가 취소될 것이다.
(D) 새 카드가 우편으로 도착할 것이다.

해설 여자의 말에서 질문의 핵심 어구(later today)와 관련된 내용을 주의 깊게 듣는다. 여자가 "I'll reactivate your account. It should be working again by the end of the day."라며 남자의 계좌, 즉 신용 카드 계좌를 다시 활성화해 주겠다고 한 후, 오늘이 끝날 무렵에 다시 작동할 것이라고 한 말을 통해 오늘 늦게 카드가 사용할 수 있게 될 것임을 알 수 있다. 따라서 (B)가 정답이다.

패러프레이징
later today 오늘 늦게 → by the end of the day 오늘이 끝날 무렵

어휘 usable[júːzəbl] 사용할 수 있는

53-55 📻 캐나다식 발음 → 영국식 발음

Questions 53-55 refer to the following conversation.

M: Our social media channels drove sales up by 20 percent last month. 53I'm surprised that our advertising campaign was as effective as it was.

W: That makes me happy. I always thought we had to be more active on those platforms. 54As we are getting more followers quickly, we should hire a professional to manage our accounts.

M: 54I agree with you. Could you take care of that?

W: Well, 55I know someone who is qualified. It's my former coworker Luke. He has been working in that field for five years.

M: That's great. Ask him if he'd be interested in the position.

drive up (값 따위)를 끌어올리다
advertising[미 ӕdvərtàiziŋ, 영 ӕdvətàiziŋ] 광고
effective[iféktiv] 효과적인 active[ӕktiv] 적극적인
professional[prəféʃənl] 전문가 manage[mӕnidʒ] 관리하다
take care of ~을 처리하다
qualify[미 kwάːlifai, 영 kwɔ́lifai] 자격을 갖추다
former[fɔ́ːrmər] 이전의 coworker[kóuwə̀ːrkər] 동료
field[fiːld] 분야

해석

53-55번은 다음 대화에 관한 문제입니다.

남: 우리 소셜 미디어 채널들은 지난달에 매출을 20퍼센트 끌어올렸어요. 53저는 우리의 광고 캠페인이 그만큼 효과적이었다는 것이 놀라워요.

여: 그건 저를 기쁘게 하네요. 저는 항상 우리가 그 플랫폼들에서 더 적극적이어야 한다고 생각했어요. 54우리는 더 많은 팔로워들을 빠르게 얻고 있기 때문에, 계정들을 관리할 전문가를 고용해야 해요.

남: 54저는 당신에게 동의해요. 당신이 그것을 처리해 줄 수 있나요?

여: 음, 55저는 자격이 있는 사람을 알아요. 그건 제 이전 동료 Luke예요. 그는 그 분야에서 5년 동안 일해오고 있어요.

남: 잘됐네요. 그 자리에 관심이 있는지 그에게 물어봐 주세요.

53 특정 세부 사항 문제

해석 남자는 무엇에 놀라는가?
(A) 상품의 감소된 판매량
(B) 회사에 의해 확립된 명성
(C) 마케팅 전략의 성공
(D) 서비스의 가격

해설 질문의 핵심 어구(surprised)가 언급된 주변을 주의 깊게 듣는다. 남자가 "I'm surprised that our advertising campaign was as effective as it was."라며 자신들의 광고 캠페인이 그만큼 효과적이었다는 것이 놀랍다고 하였다. 따라서 (C)가 정답이다.

패러프레이징
advertising campaign was ~ effective 광고 캠페인이 효과적이었다
→ The success of a marketing strategy 마케팅 전략의 성공

어휘 reputation[rèpjutéiʃən] 명성, 평판
establish[istӕbliʃ] 확립하다, 설립하다
strategy[strӕtədʒi] 전략

54 특정 세부 사항 문제

해석 남자는 무엇에 대해 동의하는가?

(A) 새 프로젝트를 위한 계획을 만드는 것
(B) 전문가를 고용하는 것
(C) 다른 회사에 연락하는 것
(D) 광고 예산을 증액하는 것

해설 질문의 핵심 어구(agree)가 언급된 주변을 주의 깊게 듣는다. 여자가 "As we are getting more followers quickly, we should hire a professional to manage our accounts."라며 자신들이 더 많은 팔로워들을 빠르게 얻고 있기 때문에 계정들을 관리할 전문가를 고용해야 한다고 하자, 남자가 "I agree with you."라며 여자에게 동의한다고 하였다. 따라서 (B)가 정답이다.

패러프레이징
hire a professional 전문가를 고용하다 → Employing an expert 전문가를 고용하는 것

어휘 employ[implɔ́i] 고용하다   expert[미 ékspə:rt, 영 ékspə:t] 전문가
budget[bʌ́dʒit] 예산

55 의도 파악 문제

해석 여자는 왜 "그는 그 분야에서 5년 동안 일해오고 있어요"라고 말하는가?
(A) 경험의 필요성을 강조하기 위해
(B) 후보 추천을 정당화하기 위해
(C) 급여 인상의 이유를 설명하기 위해
(D) 다른 지점으로의 전근을 제안하기 위해

해설 질문의 인용어구(He has been working in that field for five years)가 언급된 주변을 주의 깊게 듣는다. 여자가 "I know someone who is qualified. It's my former coworker Luke."라며 자격이 있는 사람을 알고 있다며 그건 자신의 이전 동료 Luke라고 한 말을 통해 여자가 후보 추천을 정당화하기 위함임을 알 수 있다. 따라서 (B)가 정답이다.

어휘 highlight[háilait] 강조하다   justify[dʒʌ́stifai] 정당화하다
recommendation[rèkəməndéiʃən] 추천   salary[sǽləri] 급여
transfer[trǽnsfər] 전근, 이송   branch[brænʧ] 지점

56-58 🎙 미국식 발음 → 호주식 발음

Questions 56-58 refer to the following conversation.

W: I was just sent an invitation from a public relations firm. ⁵⁶There will be a Jack Farmer fashion show tomorrow morning.
M: ⁵⁷Do you want me to write about it? I could come with you and take some notes.
W: Yes. ⁵⁷It would be great if you could write something about the collection. I am expecting some colorful garments from Jack's new line. I also have to attend the opening of the Mara Flex store on 5th avenue after his show.
M: ⁵⁷/⁵⁸Fashion week is always the busiest time of year for our magazine.
W: Right. ⁵⁸But don't worry. Fashion week will end soon.

take notes 기록하다, 필기를 하다   colorful[kʌ́lərfəl] 색채가 풍부한
garment[gá:rmənt] 의상, 옷   line[lain] 제품, 상품
opening[미 óupəniŋ, 영 óupəniŋ] 개점, 개막
fashion week 패션 위크(디자이너들이 작품을 발표하는 주간)

해석
56-58번은 다음 대화에 관한 문제입니다.
여: 저는 홍보 회사로부터 방금 초대장을 받았어요. ⁵⁶내일 아침에 Jack Farmer 패션쇼가 있을 거예요.

남: ⁵⁷당신은 제가 그것에 대해 글을 쓰기를 바라나요? 제가 당신과 같이 가서 기록을 좀 할 수 있어요.
여: 네. ⁵⁷당신이 컬렉션에 대해 무언가를 써줄 수 있다면 좋을 거예요. 저는 Jack의 신제품에서 몇몇의 색채가 풍부한 의상들을 기대하고 있어요. 저는 또한 그의 쇼 이후 5번가에 있는 Mara Flex 매장 개점에 참석해야 해요.
남: ⁵⁷/⁵⁸패션 위크는 항상 우리 잡지사의 일 년 중 가장 바쁜 시기네요.
여: 맞아요. ⁵⁸하지만 걱정하지 마세요. 패션 위크는 곧 끝날 거예요.

56 다음에 할 일 문제

해석 내일 아침에 무슨 일이 일어날 것인가?
(A) 패션쇼가 개최될 것이다.
(B) 매장이 다시 열릴 것이다.
(C) 잡지가 발행될 것이다.
(D) 근무 교대 일정표가 게시될 것이다.

해설 질문의 핵심 어구(tomorrow morning)가 언급된 주변을 주의 깊게 듣는다. 여자가 "There will be a Jack Farmer fashion show tomorrow morning."이라며 내일 아침에 Jack Farmer 패션쇼가 있을 것이라고 한 말을 통해 내일 아침에 패션쇼가 개최될 것임을 알 수 있다. 따라서 (A)가 정답이다.

어휘 reopen[미 ri:óupən, 영 ri:óupən] 다시 열다, 다시 시작하다
publish[pʌ́bliʃ] 발행하다, 출간하다
post[미 poust, 영 pəust] 게시하다, 기록하다

57 화자 문제

해석 화자들은 어떤 산업에서 일하는 것 같은가?
(A) 광고
(B) 언론
(C) 제조
(D) 교육

해설 지문에서 신분 및 직업과 관련된 표현을 놓치지 않고 듣는다. 남자가 "Do you want me to write about it(fashion show)."이라며 여자에게 자신이 패션쇼에 대해 글을 쓰기를 바라는지 묻자, 여자가 "It would be great if you could write something about the collection."이라며 남자가 컬렉션에 대해 무언가를 써줄 수 있다면 좋을 것이라고 했고, 남자가 "Fashion week is always the busiest time of year for our magazine."이라며 패션 위크가 항상 자신들의 잡지사의 일 년 중 가장 바쁜 시기라고 한 말을 통해 화자들이 언론 산업에서 일한다는 것을 알 수 있다. 따라서 (B)가 정답이다.

어휘 industry[índəstri] 산업   journalism[dʒə́:rnəlizm] 언론계
education[èdʒukéiʃən] 교육

58 특정 세부 사항 문제

해석 여자는 무엇에 대해 남자를 안심시키는가?
(A) 업무가 지연되지 않을 것이다.
(B) 노력이 무시되지 않을 것이다.
(C) 인파가 없을 것이다.
(D) 바쁜 시기가 오래 지속되지 않을 것이다.

해설 질문의 핵심 어구(reassure)와 관련된 내용을 주의 깊게 듣는다. 남자가 "Fashion week is always the busiest time of year for our magazine."이라며 패션 위크가 항상 자신들의 잡지사의 일 년 중 가장 바쁜 시기라고 하자, 여자가 "But don't worry. Fashion week will end soon."이라며 남자에게 걱정하지 말라고 한 후, 패션 위크가 곧 끝날 것이라고 하였다. 이를 통해 여자가 바쁜 시기는 오래 지속되지 않을 것이라고 남자를 안심시키는 것을 알 수 있다. 따라서 (D)가 정답이다.

패러프레이징
will end soon 곧 끝날 것이다 → will not last long 오래 지속되지 않을 것이다

어휘　**reassure**[rì:əʃúr] 안심시키다　**hard work** 노력
ignore[ignɔ́:r] 무시하다, 간과하다　**crowd**[kraud] 인파, 군중
period[píəriəd] 시기, 시간　**last**[미 læst, 영 lɑ:st] 지속되다

59-61 🎧 캐나다식 발음 → 영국식 발음

Questions 59-61 refer to the following conversation.

M: Rachel, ⁵⁹a customer is looking for the new Truna phone that was released today. Do you know where it is?

W: Oh, it is already sold out. There was a line of people waiting for it around the block this morning when we opened.

M: Ah, ⁶⁰I didn't know because my shift started at noon. I will tell him to visit another store.

W: It'll be the same thing elsewhere. You should put the customer on our wait list.

M: Good idea.

W: ⁶¹Don't forget to mention that if he has an older Truna phone, we can recycle that one for him. He will then get a discount on the new one.

---

look for ~을 찾다　**be sold out** 매진되다
elsewhere[élshwɛər] 어느 곳이나　**wait list** 대기자 명단
recycle[ri:sáikl] 재활용하다　**discount on** ~에 대한 할인

해석
59-61번은 다음 대화에 관한 문제입니다.

남: Rachel, ⁵⁹한 고객이 오늘 출시된 새로운 Truna 휴대폰을 찾고 있어요. 그것이 어디에 있는지 아세요?

여: 아, 그것은 이미 매진되었어요. 오늘 아침 우리가 문을 열었을 때 그것을 기다리는 사람들이 블록을 돌아서 줄을 서 있었어요.

남: 아, ⁶⁰제 근무 시간이 정오에 시작해서 몰랐어요. 제가 그에게 다른 가게를 방문하라고 말할게요.

여: 어느 곳이나 똑같을 거예요. 당신은 그 고객을 우리의 대기자 명단에 올려놓아야 해요.

남: 좋은 생각이에요.

여: ⁶¹만약 그가 이전의 Truna 휴대폰을 가지고 있다면, 우리는 그를 위해 그 것을 재활용해줄 수 있음을 언급하는 것을 잊지 마세요. 그러면 그는 새로운 것에 대한 할인을 받을 거예요.

59 특정 세부 사항 문제

해석　남자는 무엇에 대해 물어보는가?
(A) 휴대폰 서비스 요금제
(B) 제품의 위치
(C) 장치의 특징
(D) 현재의 판매 홍보 활동

해설　대화에서 남자의 말을 주의 깊게 듣는다. 남자가 여자에게 "a customer is looking for the new Truna phone that was released today. Do you know where it is?"라며 한 고객이 오늘 출시된 새로운 Truna 휴대폰을 찾고 있는데 그것이 어디에 있는지 아는지 물었다. 따라서 (B)가 정답이다.

어휘　**plan**[plæn] 요금제, 제도　**feature**[미 fí:tʃər, 영 fí:tʃə] 특징
device[diváis] 장치
promotion[미 prəmóuʃən, 영 prəméuʃən] 홍보 활동

60 이유 문제

해석　남자는 왜 상황을 알지 못했는가?
(A) 다른 가게들을 방문하고 있었다.
(B) 아침에 일하지 않았다.

(C) 줄을 서서 기다리고 있었다.
(D) 쉬는 날이었다.

해설　질문의 핵심 어구(unaware of a situation)와 관련된 내용을 주의 깊게 듣는다. 남자가 "I didn't know because my shift started at noon"이라며 자신의 근무 시간이 정오에 시작해서 몰랐다고 한 말을 통해 남자가 아침에 일하지 않았음을 알 수 있다. 따라서 (B)가 정답이다.

패러프레이징
was ~ unaware 알지 못했다 → **didn't know** 몰랐다

어휘　**unaware of** ~을 알지 못하는　**wait in line** 줄을 서서 기다리다
day off 쉬는 날, 휴일

61 특정 세부 사항 문제

해석　여자는 남자에게 무엇에 대한 정보를 주는가?
(A) 수리 서비스
(B) 상점의 반품 정책
(C) 판매세 인상
(D) 재활용 프로그램

해설　여자의 말을 주의 깊게 듣는다. 여자가 남자에게 "Don't forget to mention that if he has an older Truna phone, we can recycle that one for him."이라며 만약 고객이 이전의 Truna 휴대폰을 가지고 있다면 그를 위해 그것을 재활용해줄 수 있음을 언급하는 것을 잊지 말라고 하였다. 따라서 (D)가 정답이다.

어휘　**return policy** 반품 정책　**sales tax** 판매세
recycling[ri:sáikliŋ] 재활용

62-64 🎧 미국식 발음 → 호주식 발음

Questions 62-64 refer to the following conversation and map.

W: ⁶²Have you found a location for your new barber shop yet?

M: Actually, I have. ⁶²It's on Western Avenue, right between a restaurant and a bicycle shop. It meets all my needs. Here's a picture of the space.

W: Oh, that seems spacious. And it's in an excellent part of town. Have you signed the lease?

M: I'm signing it next Thursday. ⁶³The rent is pretty cheap. It's just $2,000 per month. ⁶⁴The problem will be finding employees, so I'm posting job ads in newspapers.

W: Good idea. I'm sure you'll get a lot of responses. Let me know how that goes.

---

barber shop 이발소　**meet**[mi:t] 충족시키다
spacious[spéiʃəs] 넓은, 널찍한　**sign**[sain] 서명하다
lease[li:s] 임대 계약서　**response**[미 rispáns, 영 rispɔ́ns] 반응, 응답

해석
62-64번은 다음 대화와 지도에 관한 문제입니다.

여: ⁶²당신의 새 이발소를 위한 자리를 벌써 찾았나요?

남: 실은, 찾았어요. ⁶²Western가에 있어요, 식당과 자전거 가게 바로 사이에요. 그것은 제 모든 요구를 충족시켜요. 공간의 사진이 여기 있어요.

여: 아, 그건 넓어 보이네요. 그리고 마을의 아주 훌륭한 지역에 있네요. 당신은 임대 계약서에 서명했나요?

남: 저는 다음 주 목요일에 그것에 서명할 거예요. ⁶³임대료가 꽤 저렴해요. 한 달에 단지 2,000달러예요. ⁶⁴문제는 직원들을 구하는 것이 될 거라서, 저는 신문에 구인 광고를 올리고 있어요.

여: 좋은 생각이에요. 많은 반응들이 있을 것이라고 확신해요. 그것이 어떻게

진행되는지 제게 알려주세요.

카페 ☕	건물 1	식료품 가게	건물 2	편의점
Western가				
식당	62건물 4	자전거 가게 🚲	건물 3	

62 시각 자료 문제

해석 시각 자료를 보아라. 이발소는 어디에 위치할 것인가?
(A) 건물 1
(B) 건물 2
(C) 건물 3
(D) 건물 4

해설 제시된 지도의 정보를 확인한 후 질문의 핵심 어구(barber shop)가 언급된 주변을 주의 깊게 듣는다. 여자가 "Have you found a location for your new barber shop yet?"이라며 남자에게 새 이발소를 위한 자리를 벌써 찾았는지 묻자, 남자가 "It's on Western Avenue, right between a restaurant and a bicycle shop."이라며 Western가에 있으며 식당과 자전거 가게 바로 사이라고 하였으므로 이발소는 건물 4에 위치할 것임을 지도에서 알 수 있다. 따라서 (D)가 정답이다.

63 특정 세부 사항 문제

해석 남자에 따르면, 그 건물의 장점은 무엇인가?
(A) 공공요금 지불을 요구하지 않는다.
(B) 큰 뒷방을 포함한다.
(C) 한 달에 많은 비용이 들지 않는다.
(D) 대중교통과 가깝다.

해설 남자의 말에서 질문의 핵심 어구(advantage of the building)와 관련된 내용을 주의 깊게 듣는다. 남자가 "The rent is pretty cheap."이라며 임대료가 꽤 저렴하다고 하였다. 따라서 (C)가 정답이다.

패러프레이징
is ~ cheap 저렴하다 → does not cost much 많은 비용이 들지 않는다

어휘 advantage[미 ædvǽntidʒ, 영 ədváːntidʒ] 장점
utility[juːtíləti] 공공요금 contain[kəntéin] 포함하다
back room 뒷방 public transportation 대중교통

64 방법 문제

해석 남자는 어떻게 직원들을 모집할 것인가?
(A) 지인들에게 말함으로써
(B) 건물에 표지판을 게시함으로써
(C) 채용업체에 연락함으로써
(D) 출판물에 광고를 냄으로써

해설 질문의 핵심 어구(recruit employees)와 관련된 내용을 주의 깊게 듣는다. 남자가 "The problem will be finding employees, so I'm posting job ads in newspapers."라며 문제는 직원들을 구하는 것이 될 거라서 신문에 구인 광고를 올리고 있다고 하였다. 따라서 (D)가 정답이다.

패러프레이징
posting job ads in newspapers 신문에 구인 광고를 올리는 것 → putting ads in publications 출판물에 광고를 냄

어휘 recruit[rikrúːt] 모집하다, 채용하다
acquaintance[əkwéintəns] 지인, 아는 사람
staffing agency 채용업체
publication[미 pʌ̀bləkéiʃən, 영 pʌ̀blikéiʃən] 출판물, 간행물

65-67 🎙 호주식 발음 → 영국식 발음

Questions 65-67 refer to the following conversation and schedule.

M: Leslie, we are going to announce our merger on Friday afternoon. 65I'd like to have a meeting with all of our department heads to discuss it in the morning. Could you ask everyone to be present?
W: OK. 66What time do you think we should hold the meeting?
M: Hmm . . . Friday is usually pretty busy. 66It looks like Carter has the busiest schedule in the morning, so let's do it when he is available.
W: 67I'll ask my assistant to send out an e-mail this afternoon when he gets back to the office. He's having lunch in the cafeteria now.

announce[ənáuns] 발표하다 merger[mə́ːrdʒər] 합병
discuss[diskʌ́s] 논의하다, 토론하다 present[préznt] 참석한

해석
65-67번은 다음 대화와 일정표에 관한 문제입니다.

남: Leslie, 우리는 금요일 오후에 우리의 합병을 발표할 거예요. 65저는 오전에 그것에 대해 논의하기 위해 우리의 모든 부서장들과 회의를 하고 싶어요. 모두에게 참석할 것을 요청해 주시겠어요?
여: 알겠어요. 66우리가 회의를 몇 시에 해야 한다고 생각하시나요?
남: 흠... 요금일은 보통 꽤 바빠요. 66Carter가 오전에 가장 바쁜 일정이 있는 것 같으니, 그가 시간이 있을 때 해요.
여: 67제 조수가 사무실로 돌아오면 제가 오늘 오후에 이메일을 보내라고 할게요. 그는 지금 구내식당에서 점심을 먹고 있어요.

금요일				
	오전 8시	66오전 9시	오전 10시	오전 11시
Carter	전화 회의		영업 회의	HR 교육
Delilah	부재			
Edgar		전화 회의		
Frances			부재	

65 요청 문제

해석 남자는 여자에게 무엇을 하라고 요청하는가?
(A) 합병을 승인한다.
(B) 새 일정표를 만든다.
(C) 몇몇 직원들에게 통지한다.
(D) 공고를 교정한다.

해설 남자의 말에서 요청과 관련된 표현이 언급된 다음을 주의 깊게 듣는다. 남자가 여자에게 "I'd like to have a meeting with all of our department heads to discuss it[merger] in the morning. Could you ask everyone to be present?"라며 자신이 오전에 합병에 대해 논의하기 위해 모든 부서장들과 회의를 하고 싶어 모두에게 참석할 것을 요청해 줄 수 있는지 물었다. 따라서 (C)가 정답이다.

어휘 approve[əprúːv] 승인하다
notify[미 nóutifai, 영 nə́utifai] 통지하다, 알리다
proofread[prúːfriːd] 교정하다

66 시각 자료 문제

해석 시각 자료를 보아라. 부서장들은 언제 회의에 참석할 것인가?
(A) 오전 8시에
(B) 오전 9시에

(C) 오전 10시에
(D) 오전 11시에

해설　제시된 일정표의 정보를 확인한 후 질문의 핵심 어구(department heads participate in a meeting)와 관련된 내용을 주의 깊게 듣는다. 여자가 "What time do you think we should hold the meeting?"이라며 자신들이 회의, 즉 부서장들과의 회의를 몇 시에 해야 한다고 생각하는지 묻자, 남자가 "It looks like Carter has the busiest schedule in the morning, so let's do it when he is available."이라며 Carter가 오전에 가장 바쁜 일정이 있는 것 같으니 그가 시간이 있을 때 하자고 하였으므로, 부서장들은 오전 9시에 회의에 참석할 것임을 일정표에서 알 수 있다. 따라서 (B)가 정답이다.

67 이유 문제

해석　여자의 조수는 왜 지금 부재중인가?
(A) 휴식 중이다.
(B) 시간제로만 일한다.
(C) 이메일을 쓰고 있다.
(D) 교육을 받고 있다.

해설　질문의 핵심 어구(assistant unavailable right now)와 관련된 내용을 주의 깊게 듣는다. 여자가 "I'll ask my assistant to send out an e-mail this afternoon when he gets back to the office. He's having lunch in the cafeteria now."라며 자신의 조수가 사무실로 돌아오면 오늘 오후에 이메일을 보내라고 하겠다고 하며 그가 지금 구내식당에서 점심을 먹고 있다고 하였다. 따라서 (A)가 정답이다.

어휘　be on a break 휴식 중이다
undergo[미 ʌ̀ndərɡóu, 영 ʌ̀ndəɡə́u] 받다, 겪다, 경험하다

68-70 [2인] 캐나다식 발음 → 미국식 발음

Questions 68-70 refer to the following conversation and coupon.

M: Hello. ⁶⁸I would like to buy that black sweater.
W: Certainly. ⁶⁸However, that's actually our last one. You can buy the one on display if you don't mind.
M: That doesn't matter to me. I'll take it.
W: OK. It'll be $85. ⁶⁹Do you have a Centralix Clothes customer loyalty program card?
M: Yes. Here it is. And ⁷⁰here is a gift card to pay for my purchase. Also, I'd like to use this coupon. It says it can be applied to purchases made in June at this location.
W: I'm sorry. ⁷⁰This coupon can't be used for this purchase.
M: Oh, OK. That's no problem.

on display 진열된, 전시된
matter[미 mǽtər, 영 mǽtə] 중요하다, 문제가 되다
loyalty[lɔ́iəlti] 충성도　gift card 상품권　apply[əplái] 적용하다
location[미 loukéiʃən, 영 ləukéiʃən] 지점, 장소

해석

68-70번은 다음 대화와 쿠폰에 관한 문제입니다.

남: 안녕하세요. ⁶⁸저는 저 검은색 스웨터를 사고 싶어요.
여: 알겠어요. ⁶⁸그런데, 그것이 사실 저희의 마지막 것이에요. 손님께서 괜찮으시다면 진열된 것을 구입하실 수 있어요.
남: 그건 제게 중요치 않아요. 제가 그걸 살게요.
여: 네. 85달러가 될 거예요. ⁶⁹Centralix Clothes 고객 충성도 프로그램 카드를 가지고 있으신가요?
남: 네. 여기요. 그리고 ⁷⁰제 구입품에 대해 지불할 상품권이 여기 있어요. 또한, 저는 이 쿠폰도 사용하고 싶어요. 이 지점에서 6월에 이루어진 구매에

적용될 수 있다고 쓰여 있어요.
여: 죄송해요. ⁷⁰이 쿠폰은 이번 구매에 사용될 수 없어요.
남: 아, 알겠어요. 문제없어요.

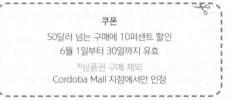

쿠폰
50달러 넘는 구매에 10퍼센트 할인
6월 1일부터 30일까지 유효
⁷⁰상품권 구매 제외
Cordoba Mall 지점에서만 인정

68 장소 문제

해석　대화는 어디에서 일어나고 있는 것 같은가?
(A) 의류점에서
(B) 세탁소에서
(C) 선물 가게에서
(D) 양복점에서

해설　대화에서 장소와 관련된 표현을 놓치지 않고 듣는다. 남자가 "I would like to buy that black sweater."라며 저 검은색 스웨터를 사고 싶다고 하자, 여자가 "However, that's actually our last one. You can buy the one on display if you don't mind."라며 그것이 사실 마지막 것이라며 남자가 괜찮다면 진열된 것을 구입할 수 있다고 한 말을 통해 의류점에서 대화가 일어나고 있음을 알 수 있다. 따라서 (A)가 정답이다.

어휘　clothing store 의류점　tailoring[téiləriŋ] 양복업, 재봉업

69 특정 세부 사항 문제

해석　여자는 남자에게 무엇에 대해 묻는가?
(A) 그의 가장 좋아하는 색상
(B) 그의 선호하는 사이즈
(C) 그의 쇼핑 예산
(D) 그의 멤버십 카드

해설　대화에서 여자의 말을 주의 깊게 듣는다. 여자가 남자에게 "Do you have a Centralix Clothes customer loyalty program card?"라며 Centralix Clothes 고객 충성도 프로그램 카드를 가지고 있는지 물었다. 따라서 (D)가 정답이다.

패러프레이징
customer loyalty program card 고객 충성도 프로그램 카드 → membership card 멤버십 카드

70 시각 자료 문제

해석　시각 자료를 보아라. 이 쿠폰은 왜 구매에 유효하지 않은가?
(A) 최소 비용을 충족하지 않는다.
(B) 이미 만료되었다.
(C) 상품권과 함께 사용될 수 없다.
(D) 다른 지점용이다.

해설　제시된 쿠폰의 정보를 확인한 후 질문의 핵심 어구(isn't ~ valid for a purchase)와 관련된 내용을 주의 깊게 듣는다. 남자가 "here is a gift card to pay for my purchase. Also, I'd like to use this coupon."이라며 구입품에 대해 상품권으로 지불하겠다고 하며 쿠폰도 사용하고 싶다고 하자, 여자가 "This coupon can't be used for this purchase."라며 이 쿠폰이 이번 구매에 사용될 수 없다고 하였으므로, 쿠폰이 상품권 구매에 제외된다는 것을 쿠폰에서 알 수 있다. 따라서 (C)가 정답이다.

어휘　minimum[mínəməm] 최소인
expire[미 ikspáiər, 영 ikspáiə] 만료되다　for ~ 용의

PART 4

71-73 [2회] 캐나다식 발음

Questions 71-73 refer to the following excerpt from a meeting.

71Let's discuss our distribution issue. Some of the stores that carry our yogurt have complained that they are not getting enough products. **Therefore, they are faced with partially empty shelves. Our production facility is not the problem. We produce enough yogurt to consistently restock our wholesale partners.** 72I was thinking we should change our partner distribution company as it is the reason for the delays. 73Please look into new companies and get estimates. **And then share what you find later.**

---

distribution[미 dìstrəbjúːʃən, 영 dìstribjúːʃən] 유통, 분배
carry[kǽri] 취급하다, 팔고 있다 **complain**[kəmpléin] 불평하다, 항의하다
partially[미 páːrʃəli, 영 páːʃəli] 부분적으로
consistently[kənsístəntli] 지속적으로
restock[rìːstáːk] 재고를 다시 채우다
wholesale[미 hóulseil, 영 hóulseil] 도매의, 대량의 **look into** 조사하다
estimate[éstəmeit] 견적(서)

해석
71-73번은 다음 회의 발췌록에 관한 문제입니다.

71우리의 유통 문제에 대해 논의해 봅시다. 우리의 요구르트를 취급하는 가게들 중 일부는 충분한 제품들을 받지 못하고 있다고 불평했습니다. 그래서, 그들은 부분적으로 비어있는 선반의 문제에 직면해 있습니다. 우리의 생산 시설은 문제가 아닙니다. 우리는 도매 동업자들에게 지속적으로 재고를 다시 채울 수 있는 충분한 요구르트를 생산합니다. 72저는 그것이 지연에 대한 이유이기 때문에 우리의 협력 유통 회사를 바꿔야 한다고 생각하고 있었습니다. 73새로운 회사들을 조사하고 견적을 받아보십시오. 그러고 나서 여러분이 찾은 것을 이후에 공유해 주세요.

71 특정 세부 사항 문제

해석 화자는 무슨 문제를 언급하는가?
(A) 유통 시스템이 불평을 야기하고 있다.
(B) 제품의 품질이 일정하지 않다.
(C) 제조 공장이 너무 작다.
(D) 가게가 브랜드를 단종했다.

해설 질문의 핵심 어구(problem)와 관련된 내용을 주의 깊게 듣는다. "Let's discuss our distribution issue. Some of the stores that carry our yogurt have complained that they are not getting enough products."라며 유통 문제에 대해 논의해 보자고 한 후, 자신들의 요구르트를 취급하는 가게들 중 일부가 충분한 제품들을 받지 못하고 있다고 불평했다고 하였다. 따라서 (A)가 정답이다.

어휘 **inconsistent**[ìnkənsístənt] 일정하지 않은
plant[plænt] 공장 **discontinue**[dìskəntínjuː] 중단하다, 그만두다

72 제안 문제

해석 화자는 어떤 해결책을 제안하는가?
(A) 새 공장을 설립하는 것
(B) 포장 디자인을 재고하는 것
(C) 몇몇 재료들을 변경하는 것
(D) 제휴된 회사를 바꾸는 것

해설 지문의 중후반에서 제안과 관련된 표현이 포함된 문장을 주의 깊게 듣는다. "I was thinking we should change our partner

---

distribution company as it is the reason for the delays."라며 그것이 지연에 대한 이유이기 때문에 협력 유통 회사를 바꿔야 한다고 생각하고 있었다고 하였다. 따라서 (D)가 정답이다.

패러프레이징
partner ~ company 협력 회사 → affiliated company 제휴된 회사

어휘 **establish**[istǽbliʃ] 설립하다, 확립하다 **rethink**[riːθíŋk] 재고하다
switch out 변경하다 **ingredient**[ingríːdiənt] 재료
affiliated[əfílièitid] 제휴된, 연합된

73 요청 문제

해석 화자는 청자들에게 무엇을 하라고 요청하는가?
(A) 새로운 요구르트 맛을 시식한다.
(B) 정보를 찾아본다.
(C) 가게 지점을 방문한다.
(D) 생산 작업장을 정리한다.

해설 지문의 중후반에서 요청과 관련된 표현이 포함된 문장을 주의 깊게 듣는다. "Please look into new companies and get estimates."라며 새로운 회사들을 조사하고 견적을 받아보라고 하였다. 따라서 (B)가 정답이다.

어휘 **flavor**[미 fléivər, 영 fléivə] 맛 **look up** 찾아보다 **floor**[flɔːr] 작업장, 층

74-76 [2회] 미국식 발음

Questions 74-76 refer to the following news report.

This is KMIA, and I'm Lisa Barker. 74The mayor just announced the completion of the River East Park Project. After a two-month delay due to bad weather, the path along the riverfront is now open to pedestrians. However, the bike lanes will not be completed until later this month. The mayor has made projects like these a cornerstone of her city-improvement efforts. 75She insists that the park will create new economic opportunities for local vendors and provide more greenery in the area. 76The official ribbon cutting will be held at the park next Monday at 10 A.M. and everyone is welcome.

---

mayor[méiər] 시장 **completion**[kəmplíːʃən] 완료, 완성
delay[diléi] 지연, 연기 **path**[pæθ] 길, 오솔길
riverfront[rívərfrʌnt] 강변 지대, 강가 **pedestrian**[pədéstriən] 보행자
cornerstone[kɔ́ːrnərstòun] 토대 **effort**[미 éfərt, 영 éfət] 노력
insist[insíst] 주장하다 **opportunity**[미 àpərtjúːnəti, 영 ɔ̀pətjúːnəti] 기회
vendor[미 véndər, 영 véndə] 상인 **greenery**[gríːnəri] 녹지, 푸른 나무
ribbon cutting 개관식, 개통식 **welcome**[wélkəm] 마음대로 ~해도 좋은

해석
74-76번은 다음 뉴스 보도에 관한 문제입니다.

KMIA이고, 저는 Lisa Barker입니다. 74시장이 방금 River East 공원 프로젝트의 완료를 발표했습니다. 좋지 않은 날씨로 인한 두 달의 지연 후에, 강변 지대의 길은 현재 보행자들에게 개방되었습니다. 하지만, 자전거 도로는 이번 달 말이 되어서야 완공될 것입니다. 시장은 이러한 프로젝트들을 그녀의 도시 개선 노력의 토대로 삼았습니다. 75그녀는 그 공원이 지역 상인들에게 새로운 경제적 기회를 창출하고 그 지역에 더 많은 녹지를 제공할 것이라고 주장합니다. 76공식적인 개관식은 다음 주 월요일 오전 10시에 공원에서 열릴 것이며 모두 마음대로 오셔도 좋습니다.

74 특정 세부 사항 문제

해석 무엇이 공원 프로젝트를 계획했던 것보다 더 오래 걸리게 했는가?
(A) 자재의 부족
(B) 불충분한 자금

(C) 작업 추가
(D) 악천후

해설 질문의 핵심 어구(take longer than planned)와 관련된 내용을 주의 깊게 듣는다. "The mayor just announced the completion of the River East Park Project. After a two-month delay due to bad weather"라며 시장이 방금 River East 공원 프로젝트의 완료를 발표했으며 좋지 않은 날씨로 인해 두 달의 지연이 있었다고 하였다. 따라서 (D)가 정답이다.

패러프레이징
bad weather 좋지 않은 날씨 → Inclement weather 악천후

어휘 lack[læk] 부족, 결핍 insufficient[insəfíʃənt] 불충분한 funding[fʌ́ndiŋ] 자금, 재정 지원 addition[ədíʃən] 추가, 부가 inclement weather 악천후

75 특정 세부 사항 문제

해석 시장은 무슨 일이 일어날 것이라고 예상하는가?
(A) 일부 경제 활동이 증대될 것이다.
(B) 몇몇 사람들은 인근으로 이사할 것이다.
(C) 일부 지역은 더 비싸질 것이다.
(D) 몇몇 관광 명소들이 재건될 것이다.

해설 질문의 핵심 어구(mayor expect to happen)와 관련된 내용을 주의 깊게 듣는다. "She[mayor] insists that the park will create new economic opportunities for local vendors"라며 시장은 그 공원이 지역 상인들에게 새로운 경제적 기회를 창출할 것이라고 주장한다고 하였다. 따라서 (A)가 정답이다.

어휘 neighborhood[néibərhùd] 인근, 주변 tourist attraction 관광 명소 rebuild[ribíld] 재건하다

76 다음에 할 일 문제

해석 다음 주에 무슨 일이 일어날 것인가?
(A) 설치가 완료될 것이다.
(B) 기념식이 열릴 것이다.
(C) 초대장이 발송될 것이다.
(D) 주민들의 의견이 들어질 것이다.

해설 질문의 핵심 어구(next week)와 관련된 내용을 주의 깊게 듣는다. "The official ribbon cutting will be held at the park next Monday at 10 A.M."이라며 공식적인 개관식이 다음 주 월요일 오전 10시에 공원에서 열릴 것이라고 하였다. 따라서 (B)가 정답이다.

패러프레이징
The ~ ribbon cutting will be held 개관식이 열릴 것이다 → A ceremony will take place 기념식이 열릴 것이다

어휘 installation[instəléiʃən] 설치 take place 열리다, 발생하다 resident[rézidənt] 주민

77-79 [2w] 영국식 발음

Questions 77-79 refer to the following advertisement.

Do you want to save money and help the environment at the same time? Then contact Action Energy today. 77We're currently offering a 20 percent discount and free installation on all orders of new solar power packages. 78Our systems include everything that you need to power your home, from the rooftop solar panels to the batteries. With our help, you can cut your monthly electric bill by 50 percent or more and reduce your reliance on fossil fuels that are polluting the environment. 79Call 555-8000 to discuss our products with a professional energy consultant and find the ⟳

one that best suits your needs.

environment[inváiərənmənt] 환경
currently[미 kə́:rəntli, 영 kʌ́rəntli] 현재 installation[instəléiʃən] 설치
solar power 태양열 발전
power[미 páuər, 영 páuə] 전력을 공급하다; 에너지
rooftop[미 rú:ftɑ:p, 영 rú:ftɔp] 옥상 cut[kʌt] 줄이다, 삭감하다
reliance[riláiəns] 의존, 신뢰 pollute[pəlú:t] 오염시키다
suit[su:t] 맞다, 어울리게 하다

해석
77-79번은 다음 광고에 관한 문제입니다.

여러분은 돈을 아끼면서 동시에 환경을 돕고 싶나요? 그렇다면 오늘 Action 에너지사에 연락하세요. 77저희는 현재 새로운 태양열 발전 패키지의 모든 주문에 대해 20퍼센트 할인과 무료 설치를 제공하고 있습니다. 78저희의 시스템은 옥상의 태양 전지판에서부터 배터리에 이르기까지, 여러분의 집에 전력을 공급하는 데 필요한 모든 것을 포함합니다. 저희의 도움으로, 여러분은 매월 전기 요금을 50퍼센트 이상 줄일 수 있고 환경을 오염시키는 화석 연료에 대한 의존도를 줄일 수 있습니다. 79555-8000으로 전화하셔서 전문 에너지 상담가와 저희 제품에 대해 논의하시고 여러분의 요구에 가장 잘 맞는 것을 찾으세요.

77 특정 세부 사항 문제

해석 회사는 현재 무슨 판촉을 제공하고 있는가?
(A) 무료 설치
(B) 업그레이드된 배터리 팩
(C) 50퍼센트 할인 쿠폰
(D) 연장된 보증

해설 질문의 핵심 어구(promotion ~ currently offering)와 관련된 내용을 주의 깊게 듣는다. "We're currently offering a 20 percent discount and free installation on all orders of new solar power packages."라며 현재 새로운 태양열 발전 패키지의 모든 주문에 대해 20퍼센트 할인과 무료 설치를 제공하고 있다고 하였다. 따라서 (A)가 정답이다.

어휘 extend[iksténd] 연장하다 warranty[wɔ́:rənti] 보증(서)

78 청자 문제

해석 광고는 누구를 위한 것인가?
(A) 배터리 제조업체들
(B) 주택 소유주들
(C) 공공시설 공급자들
(D) 에너지 전문가들

해설 지문에서 신분 및 직업과 관련된 표현을 놓치지 않고 듣는다. "Our systems include everything that you need to power your home, from the rooftop solar panels to the batteries."라며 자신들의 시스템이 옥상의 태양 전지판에서부터 배터리에 이르기까지 집에 전력을 공급하는 데 필요한 모든 것을 포함한다고 한 말을 통해 광고가 주택 소유주들을 위한 것임을 알 수 있다. 따라서 (B)가 정답이다.

어휘 be intended for ~를 위한 것이다
homeowner[미 hóumounər, 영 hə́umaunə] 주택 소유주
utility[ju:tíləti] 공공시설 provider[미 prəváidər, 영 prəváidə] 공급자
professional[prəféʃənl] 전문가

79 이유 문제

해석 청자들은 왜 회사에 연락해야 하는가?
(A) 전기 사용량을 줄이는 것에 대한 조언을 얻기 위해
(B) 공공 요금 계정을 해지하기 위해
(C) 할인 코드를 받기 위해
(D) 몇몇 선택지에 대해 이야기하기 위해

해설 질문의 핵심 어구(contact the company)와 관련된 내용을 주의

깊게 듣는다. "Call 555-8000 to discuss our products with a professional energy consultant and find the one that best suits your needs."라며 전화해서 전문 에너지 상담가와 제품에 대해 논의하고 요구에 가장 잘 맞는 것을 찾으라고 하였다. 따라서 (D)가 정답이다.

어휘 **tip**[tip] 조언 **electricity**[ilèktrísəti] 전기 **usage**[júːsidʒ] 사용량

80-82 〔캐나다식 발음〕

Questions 80-82 refer to the following telephone message.

Hello, Ms. Johnson. This is Arthur calling from Technical Innovations. ⁸⁰I wanted to let you know that we now have the hard drive you requested last month in stock. The manufacturer was behind schedule. ⁸¹I've put one aside for you in case they sell out again. However, we can only hold it for three days. It's a popular item. ⁸²To purchase it, just stop by the customer service desk at any time during store hours and tell them that you have an item on reserve. If you no longer need the item, please let us know so that we can put it back on the sales floor. Our number is 555-2840.

have ~ in stock ~의 재고가 있다 **behind schedule** 예정보다 늦게 **put aside for** ~를 위해 따로 남겨두다 **in case** ~할 경우에 대비해서 **hold**[미 hould, 영 həuld] 가지고 있다, 보유하다 **stop by** (잠시) 들르다 **store hours** 영업 시간 **sales floor** 매장

해석

80-82번은 다음 전화 메시지에 관한 문제입니다.

안녕하세요, Ms. Johnson. 저는 Technical Innovations에서 전화드리는 Arthur입니다. ⁸⁰저는 고객님께서 지난달에 요청하신 하드 드라이브를 저희가 지금 재고로 보유하고 있음을 알려드리고자 합니다. 제조업체가 예정보다 늦었습니다. ⁸¹그것들이 다시 매진될 경우에 대비해서 제가 고객님을 위해 하나를 따로 남겨두었습니다. 하지만, 저희는 그것을 3일 동안만 가지고 있을 수 있습니다. 그것은 인기 있는 제품입니다. ⁸²그것을 구매하시려면, 영업 시간 중 아무 때나 고객 서비스 데스크에 들러서 예약된 제품이 있다고 말씀하시기만 하면 됩니다. 만약 고객님께서 그 제품이 더 이상 필요하지 않으시다면, 저희가 그것을 다시 매장에 놓을 수 있도록 저희에게 알려주십시오. 저희 번호는 555-2840입니다.

80 화자 문제

해석 화자는 어디에서 일하는 것 같은가?
(A) 수리점에서
(B) 전자제품 소매점에서
(C) 사무용품 가게에서
(D) 제조시설에서

해설 대화에서 신분 및 직업과 관련된 표현을 놓치지 않고 듣는다. "I wanted to let you know that we now have the hard drive you requested last month in stock."이라며 지난달에 요청한 하드 드라이브를 지금 재고로 보유하고 있음을 알려고자 한다는 말을 통해 화자가 전자제품 소매점에서 일한다는 것을 알 수 있다. 따라서 (B)가 정답이다.

어휘 **retailer**[ríːteilər] 소매점, 유통업체 **office supply** 사무용품

81 의도 파악 문제

해석 화자는 왜 "그것은 인기 있는 제품입니다"라고 말하는가?
(A) 제품을 추천하기 위해
(B) 추가적인 할인을 거절하기 위해

(C) 지연에 대해 사과하기 위해
(D) 빠른 결정을 장려하기 위해

해설 질문의 인용어구(It's a popular item)가 언급된 주변을 주의 깊게 듣는다. "I've put one[hard drive] aside for you in case they sell out again. However, we can only hold it for three days."라며 하드 드라이브가 다시 매진될 경우에 대비해서 하나를 따로 남겨두었다고 한 후, 하지만 그것을 3일 동안만 가지고 있을 수 있다고 한 말을 통해 빠른 결정을 장려하기 위함임을 알 수 있다. 따라서 (D)가 정답이다.

어휘 **turn down** 거절하다
apologize[미 əpáːlədʒàiz, 영 əpɔ́lədʒàiz] 사과하다
encourage[미 inkɔ́ːridʒ, 영 inkʌ́ridʒ] 장려하다, 격려하다

82 특정 세부 사항 문제

해석 청자는 제품을 구매하기 위해 무엇을 해야 하는가?
(A) 직원에게 전화한다.
(B) 예약을 한다.
(C) 고객 서비스 데스크를 방문한다.
(D) 다른 지점으로 간다.

해설 질문의 핵심 어구(buy a product)와 관련된 내용을 주의 깊게 듣는다. "To purchase it[item], just stop by the customer service desk at any time during store hours"라며 제품을 구매하려면 영업 시간 중 아무 때나 고객 서비스 데스크에 들르라고 하였다. 따라서 (C)가 정답이다.

패러프레이징
stop by 들르다 → Visit 방문하다

83-85 〔호주식 발음〕

Questions 83-85 refer to the following speech.

I would like to thank the judges for awarding *Off the Highway* the Best Documentary of the Year Award. I can't say how much this means to me. ⁸³I've been coming to this festival for over 20 years, and I consider it the most important film event of the year. ⁸⁴I also want to thank my amazing crew, especially Robert Willis, our sound engineer. He was a tireless, enthusiastic collaborator. Finally, ⁸⁵I want to thank all the amazing people of New Bridge, Iowa, who gave interviews to our crew about growing up in that little town. I couldn't be more grateful.

judge[dʒʌdʒ] 심사위원, 심판 **award**[미 əwɔ́ːrd, 영 əwɔ́ːd] 상을 주다; 상
crew[kruː] 팀 **tireless**[táiərlis] 지칠 줄 모르는
enthusiastic[inθùːziǽstik] 열정적인
collaborator[kəlǽbərèitər] 협력자 **grateful**[gréitfəl] 감사하는

해석

83-85번은 다음 연설에 관한 문제입니다.

저는 *Off the Highway*에 올해의 최고 다큐멘터리상을 주신 심사위원분들께 감사드리고 싶습니다. 저는 이것이 제게 얼마나 많은 것을 의미하는지 말할 수 없습니다. ⁸³저는 이 축제에 20년 넘게 참석해오고 있고, 이것이 일 년 중 가장 중요한 영화 행사라고 생각합니다. ⁸⁴저는 또한 저의 굉장한 팀, 특히 저희 음향 엔지니어인 Robert Willis께 감사드리고 싶습니다. 그는 지칠 줄 모르는, 열정적인 협력자였습니다. 마지막으로, ⁸⁵저는 아이오와 주 New Bridge의 모든 대단한 사람들께 감사드리고 싶은데, 그들은 작은 마을에서 자라는 것에 대해 저희 팀에 인터뷰해주었습니다. 저는 이보다 더 감사할 수 없습니다.

83 특정 세부 사항 문제

해석 무슨 행사가 열리고 있는 것 같은가?

(A) 영화 개봉
(B) 극장 개관식
(C) 영화제
(D) 모금 행사

해설 질문의 핵심 어구(event)와 관련된 내용을 주의 깊게 듣는다. "I've been coming to this festival for over 20 years, and I consider it the most important film event of the year."라며 자신이 이 축제에 20년 넘게 참석해오고 있으며 이것이 일 년 중 가장 중요한 영화 행사라고 생각한다고 하였다. 따라서 (C)가 정답이다.

어휘 **premier**[미 príːmiər, 영 prémiə(r)] (영화의) 개봉, (연극의) 초연
fundraiser[fʌ́ndrèizər] 모금 행사

84 특정 세부 사항 문제

해석 Robert Willis는 누구인가?
(A) 축제 주최자
(B) 투자자
(C) 비평가
(D) 팀 구성원

해설 질문 대상(Robert Willis)의 신분 및 직업과 관련된 표현을 놓치지 않고 듣는다. "I also want to thank my amazing crew, especially Robert Willis, our sound engineer."라며 Robert Willis가 팀의 음향 엔지니어라고 하였다. 따라서 (D)가 정답이다.

어휘 **organizer**[ɔ́ːrgənàizər] 주최자, 조직자 **investor**[invéstər] 투자자
critic[krítik] 비평가

85 특정 세부 사항 문제

해석 *Off the Highway*는 무엇에 관한 것인가?
(A) 중서부의 야생 동물
(B) 행사의 역사
(C) 최신의 음악적 협업
(D) 작은 마을에서 사는 것

해설 질문의 핵심 어구(Off the Highway)와 관련된 내용을 주의 깊게 듣는다. "I want to thank all the amazing people of New Bridge, Iowa, who gave interviews to our crew about growing up in that little town"이라며 아이오와 주 New Bridge의 모든 대단한 사람들에게 감사하고 싶은데 그들이 작은 마을에서 자라는 것에 대해 팀에 인터뷰, 즉 *Off the Highway*를 위한 인터뷰해주었다고 하였다. 따라서 (D)가 정답이다.

패러프레이징
growing up in ~ little town 작은 마을에서 자라는 것 → Living in a small town 작은 마을에서 사는 것

어휘 **wildlife**[wáildlaif] 야생 동물
collaboration[kəlæbəréiʃn] 협업, 공동 작업

86-88 [3w] 미국식 발음

Questions 86-88 refer to the following podcast.

Welcome to the *Listening Together Podcast*. Today, our topic is modern jazz. Before we start, [86]we're going to announce the winner of the trip to the Greely Brothers concert. [87]More than 50,000 listeners registered for the special event. Our one lucky winner is June Sharp of Hamilton, Ontario. She and a guest will receive a fully paid trip to the concert, including tickets, airfare, and hotel, thanks to the generosity of our sponsor, Ultima Records. [87]Because of the great interest in the contest, we're already working together on another event. Actually, Ultima Records was

surprised by the response. And [88]be sure to subscribe to the podcast so you don't miss details about our next giveaway.

register[미 rédʒistər, 영 rédʒistə] 등록하다 **airfare**[érfer] 항공 요금
generosity[dʒènərάːsəti] 관대함, 아량
sponsor[미 spάnsər, 영 spɔ́nsə] 후원 업체, 후원자
interest[미 íntərəst, 영 íntrəst] 관심
response[미 rispάns, 영 rispɔ́ns] 반응, 대답
subscribe[səbskráib] 구독하다 **giveaway**[gívəwei] 경품

해석
86-88번은 다음 팟캐스트에 관한 문제입니다.

Listening Together 팟캐스트에 오신 것을 환영합니다. 오늘, 저희의 주제는 현대 재즈입니다. 시작하기 전에, [86]Greely Brothers 콘서트로의 여행에 대한 우승자를 발표하겠습니다. [87]50,000명이 넘는 청취자들이 특별한 행사에 등록했습니다. 우리의 유일한 행운의 승자는 온타리오 주 해밀턴의 June Sharp입니다. 그녀와 한 명의 손님은 저희의 후원 업체인 Ultima 레코드사의 관대함 덕분에 표, 항공 요금, 호텔을 포함하여 전액 지불된 콘서트로의 여행을 받을 것입니다. [87]대회에 대한 굉장한 관심 때문에, 저희는 이미 다른 행사를 함께 진행하고 있습니다. 사실, Ultima 레코드사는 반응에 놀랐습니다. 그리고 [88]여러분은 다음 경품에 대한 자세한 내용을 놓치지 않도록 반드시 팟캐스트를 구독하세요.

86 주제 문제

해석 무엇이 공지되고 있는가?
(A) 새 앨범
(B) 특별 손님
(C) 경연 결과
(D) 여행 일정

해설 공지되고 있는 것을 묻는 문제이므로, 지문의 초반을 반드시 듣는다. "we're going to announce the winner of the trip to the Greely Brothers concert"라며 Greely Brothers 콘서트로의 여행에 대한 우승자를 발표하겠다고 하였다. 따라서 (C)가 정답이다.

어휘 **contest**[kάːntest] 경연, 대회

87 의도 파악 문제

해석 화자는 "Ultima 레코드사는 반응에 놀랐습니다"라고 말할 때 무엇을 의도하는가?
(A) 음반 매출이 상당히 증가했다.
(B) 많은 사람들이 행사에 참여했다.
(C) 증가된 소통량으로 인해 웹사이트가 갑자기 기능을 멈췄다.
(D) 표들이 즉시 매진되었다.

해설 질문의 인용어구(Ultima Records was surprised by the response)가 언급된 주변을 주의 깊게 듣는다. "More than 50,000 listeners registered for the special event."라며 50,000명이 넘는 청취자들이 특별한 행사에 등록했다고 한 후, "Because of the great interest in the contest, we're already working together on another event."라며 대회에 대한 굉장한 관심 때문에 이미 다른 행사를 함께 진행하고 있다고 한 말을 통해 많은 사람들이 행사에 참여했음을 알 수 있다. 따라서 (B)가 정답이다.

어휘 **significantly**[signífikəntli] 상당히
crash[kræʃ] (시스템·프로그램이) 갑자기 기능을 멈추다
traffic[trǽfik] (전산망을 통한 정보의) 소통량
immediately[imíːdiətli] 즉시

88 특정 세부 사항 문제

해석 청자들은 곧 있을 홍보 활동에 대해 알기 위해 무엇을 해야 하는가?
(A) 팟캐스트를 구독한다.
(B) 웹사이트를 방문한다.

(C) 문자 메시지를 보낸다.
(D) 팬클럽에 가입한다.

해설 질문의 핵심 어구(upcoming promotion)와 관련된 내용을 주의 깊게 듣는다. "be sure to subscribe to the podcast so you don't miss details about our next giveaway"라며 다음 경품에 대한 자세한 내용을 놓치지 않도록 반드시 팟캐스트를 구독하라고 하였다. 따라서 (A)가 정답이다.

패러프레이징
upcoming promotion 곧 있을 홍보 활동 → next giveaway 다음 경품

어휘 join[dʒɔin] 가입하다

89-91 ⟨영⟩ 영국식 발음

Questions 89-91 refer to the following announcement.

> [89]I've just come back from meeting with the community center manager, and she instructed me to get the park ready for visitors as soon as possible. People will be flocking to the park as the weather warms up over the coming weeks. So, this Friday, we will go around the park and check that everything is in order. [89]We will do minor repairs, replant where necessary, and clean up. To ensure a thorough job, each of you will be responsible for a specific area. [90]I will hand out a copy of location assignments in a few minutes. [91]Mr. Sandoval, could you please check the storeroom to make sure we have enough supplies for the job?

flock[flɑːk] 모이다, 떼지어 가다   replant[riplǽnt] 옮겨 심다, 이식하다
ensure[미 inʃúər, 영 inʃɔ́ː] 보장하다   thorough[미 θɔ́ːrou, 영 θʌrə] 철저한
be responsible for ~을 담당하다, 맡다
specific[미 spisífik, 영 spəsífik] 특정한, 구체적인
hand out 나눠주다, 분배하다   storeroom[stɔ́ːruːm] 저장실

해석
89-91번은 다음 공지에 관한 문제입니다.

[89]저는 주민자치 센터 관리자와의 회의에서 막 돌아왔는데, 그녀는 제게 가능한 한 빨리 공원이 방문객들에게 준비되도록 해달라고 지시했습니다. 앞으로 몇 주 동안 날씨가 따뜻해지면 사람들이 공원으로 몰려들 것입니다. 그래서, 이번 주 금요일에, 우리는 공원을 돌아다니며 모든 것이 정상적으로 작동하는지 점검할 것입니다. [89]우리는 경미한 수리를 하고, 필요한 경우 식물을 옮겨 심고, 청소를 할 것입니다. 철저한 작업을 보장하기 위해, 여러분 각자가 특정 구역을 담당하게 될 것입니다. [90]잠시 후에 위치 배정 사본을 나눠드리겠습니다. [91]Mr. Sandoval, 작업을 위해 충분한 물품이 있는지 확실히 할 수 있도록 저장실을 확인해 주시겠어요?

89 화자 문제
해석 화자는 누구인 것 같은가?
(A) 사업체 소유주
(B) 영업부장
(C) 조경사
(D) 정비 직원

해설 지문에서 신분 및 직업과 관련된 표현을 놓치지 않고 듣는다. "I've just come back from meeting with the community center manager, and she instructed me to get the park ready for visitors as soon as possible."이라며 주민자치 센터 관리자와의 회의에서 막 돌아왔는데 그녀는 가능한 한 빨리 공원이 방문객들에게 준비되도록 해달라고 지시했다고 한 후, "We will do minor repairs, replant where necessary, and clean up."이라며 경미한 수리를 하고 필요한 경우 식물을 옮겨 심고 청소를 할 것이라고 한 말을 통해 화자가 정비 직원임을 알 수 있다. 따라서 (D)가 정답이다.

어휘 landscape architect 조경사

90 특정 세부 사항 문제
해석 청자들은 몇 분 후에 무엇을 받을 것인가?
(A) 청소 용품 카탈로그
(B) 일할 장소들의 목록
(C) 공원 표지판
(D) 상품 재고 목록

해설 질문의 핵심 어구(in a few minutes)가 언급된 주변을 주의 깊게 듣는다. "I will hand out a copy of location assignments in a few minutes."라며 잠시 후에 위치 배정 사본을 나눠주겠다고 하였다. 따라서 (B)가 정답이다.

어휘 inventory[미 ínvəntɔːri, 영 ínvəntri] 재고 목록   goods[gudz] 상품

91 요청 문제
해석 화자는 Mr. Sandoval에게 무엇을 하라고 요청하는가?
(A) 일기예보를 확인한다.
(B) 식재 프로젝트를 감독한다.
(C) 직원 일정표를 만든다.
(D) 용구 재고를 확인한다.

해설 지문의 중후반에서 요청과 관련된 표현이 포함된 문장을 주의 깊게 듣는다. "Mr. Sandoval, could you please check the storeroom to make sure we have enough supplies for the job?"이라며 Mr. Sandoval에게 작업을 위해 충분한 물품이 있는지 확실히 할 수 있도록 저장실을 확인해달라고 하였다. 따라서 (D)가 정답이다.

패러프레이징
supplies 물품 → materials 용구

어휘 weather forecast 일기예보
oversee[미 ðuvərsíː, 영 ðuvəsíː] 감독하다
planting[plǽntiŋ] 식재, 심기

92-94 ⟨캐⟩ 캐나다식 발음

Questions 92-94 refer to the following tour information.

> Hi, everyone. My name is Neil Cantwell, and [92]I'm the public relations manager here at Los Angeles's Black Hill Observatory. I understand you're here for a class on astrophysics, so I'm going to go into more detail than usual about this place and how our instruments work. Our first stop will be the main lobby, where we have various pictures of the stars and planets our astronomers took. Then [93]we'll proceed to the main dome, where we'll demonstrate the telescope. We'll stay there for about 30 minutes and then finish the tour outside. Oh, [94]you won't need those pads and pens. A recording of the tour will be available on our Web site.

public relations 홍보   observatory[əbzɔ́ːrvətɔːri] 천문대, 관측소
astrophysics[æstroufíziks] 천체 물리학, 우주 물리학
go into detail 자세하게 설명하다   instrument[ínstrəmənt] 기구
various[미 vɛ́əriəs, 영 vɛ́əriəs] 다양한   planet[plǽnit] 행성
astronomer[əstrɑ́nəmər] 천문학자
proceed to ~으로 향하다, ~에 이르다
demonstrate[démənstreit] 시연하다, 설명하다
telescope[téləskòup] 망원경   recording[rikɔ́ːrdiŋ] 녹화, 녹음, 기록

해석
92-94번은 다음 관광 안내에 관한 문제입니다.

안녕하세요, 여러분. 제 이름은 Neil Cantwell이고, [92]여기 로스앤젤레스의 Black Hill 천문대의 홍보 관리자입니다. 저는 여러분이 천체물리학 수업을

위해 이곳에 온 것으로 알고 있으므로, 이 장소 및 저희 기구들이 작동하는 방법에 대해 평소보다 더 자세하게 설명할 것입니다. 우리의 첫 번째 목적지는 메인 로비가 될 것인데, 이곳에는 저희 천문학자들이 찍은 별들과 행성들의 다양한 사진들이 있습니다. 그 뒤에 ⁹³우리는 메인 돔으로 향할 것이며, 그곳에서 우리는 망원경을 시연할 것입니다. 우리는 거기서 30분 정도 머문 다음에 밖에서 투어를 마칠 겁니다. 아, ⁹⁴여러분은 그 메모장과 펜이 필요하지 않을 것입니다. 투어 녹화는 저희 웹사이트에서 이용할 수 있을 겁니다.

92 장소 문제

해석 투어는 어디에서 열리고 있는가?
(A) 호텔 로비에서
(B) 대학교 캠퍼스에서
(C) 연구 시설에서
(D) 사진 박물관에서

해설 지문에서 장소와 관련된 표현을 놓치지 않고 듣는다. "I'm the public relations manager here at Los Angeles's Black Hill Observatory. I understand you're here for a class on astrophysics, so I'm going to go into more detail than usual about this place and how our instruments work."라며 자신이 여기 로스앤젤레스의 Black Hill 천문대의 홍보 관리자라고 한 후, 청자들이 천체물리학 수업을 위해 이곳에 온 것으로 알고 있으므로 이 장소 및 기구들이 작동하는 방법에 대해 평소보다 더 자세하게 설명할 것이라고 한 말을 통해 투어가 연구 시설에서 열리고 있음을 알 수 있다. 따라서 (C)가 정답이다.

패러프레이징
Observatory 천문대 → research facility 연구 시설

어휘 university[jùːnəvə́ːrsəti] 대학교   research facility 연구 시설

93 특정 세부 사항 문제

해석 투어 중에 무슨 일이 일어날 것인가?
(A) 영화가 상영될 것이다.
(B) 몇몇 과학자들이 인터뷰될 것이다.
(C) 교수가 연설을 할 것이다.
(D) 기구가 시연될 것이다.

해설 질문의 핵심 어구(during the tour)와 관련된 내용을 주의 깊게 듣는다. "we'll proceed to the main dome, where we'll demonstrate the telescope"라며 메인 돔으로 향할 것이며 그곳에서 망원경을 시연할 것이라고 하였다. 따라서 (D)가 정답이다.

패러프레이징
telescope 망원경 → instrument 기구

어휘 screen[skriːn] 상영하다   give a speech 연설하다

94 의도 파악 문제

해석 화자는 "투어 녹화는 저희 웹사이트에서 이용할 수 있을 겁니다"라고 말할 때 무엇을 의도하는가?
(A) 투어 참가는 필수적이지 않다.
(B) 의견 교환을 위한 온라인 포럼이 있다.
(C) 청자들은 필기를 할 필요가 없다.
(D) 웹사이트에서 등록이 권고된다.

해설 질문의 인용어구(A recording of the tour will be available on our Web site)가 언급된 주변을 주의 깊게 듣는다. "you won't need those pads and pens"라며 청자들에게 그 메모장과 펜이 필요하지 않을 것이라고 한 말을 통해 청자들이 필기를 할 필요가 없음을 알 수 있다. 따라서 (C)가 정답이다.

어휘 participation[미 paːrtìsipéiʃn, 영 paːtìsipéiʃn] 참가, 참여
mandatory[미 mǽndətɔːri, 영 mǽndətəri] 필수적인
exchange[ikstʃéindʒ] 교환하다
comment[미 kάment, 영 kɔ́ment] 의견
registration[rèdʒistréiʃən] 등록

95-97 🎧 미국식 발음

Questions 95-97 refer to the following talk and presentation slide.

We've received a lot of positive feedback about our new line of bags. While they've all sold well, ⁹⁵the backpack is clearly the star of the lineup. Its sales are nearly double those of all the other bags combined. It has also received the best customer reviews online. ⁹⁶They all mentioned that the bag's design made it perfect for both casual and formal settings. To build on its popularity, I'd like to offer some other varieties of it. ⁹⁷Let's look at some of my plans to modify it to increase its sales even further.

positive[pɑ́zətiv] 긍정적인   feedback[fíːdbæk] 의견, 반응
star[staːr] 주역, 주연   double[dʌ́bl] 두 배의
combine[kəmbáin] 합치다, 결합하다   casual[kǽʒuəl] 평상복의
formal[미 fɔ́ːrməl, 영 fɔ́ːməl] 정장의, 공식적인   build on ~을 기반으로 하다
popularity[pὰpjulǽrəti] 인기   variety[vəráiəti] 변형, 다양성
modify[미 mάːdəfài, 영 mɔ́difai] 변형하다, 수정하다
further[fə́ːrðər] 더, 더 나아가

해석
95-97번은 다음 담화와 발표 슬라이드에 관한 문제입니다.

우리는 우리의 새로운 가방 제품에 대해 많은 긍정적인 의견을 받았습니다. 그것들이 모두 잘 팔린 반면에, ⁹⁵배낭은 분명히 라인업의 주역입니다. 그것의 매출은 다른 모든 가방들을 합친 것의 거의 두 배입니다. 그것은 또한 온라인에서 최고의 고객 평가를 받았습니다. ⁹⁶고객 평가 모두는 그 가방의 디자인이 평상복과 정장 둘 다를 완벽하게 만든다고 언급했습니다. 그것의 인기를 기반으로 하기 위해, 저는 그것의 몇 가지 다른 변형을 제공하고 싶습니다. ⁹⁷매출을 훨씬 더 늘리기 위해 그것을 변형할 저의 몇몇 방안들을 살펴보시겠습니다.

제품 1	⁹⁵제품 2
제품 3	제품 4

95 시각 자료 문제

해석 시각 자료를 보아라. 회사의 신제품 중 가장 잘 팔리는 제품은 무엇인가?
(A) 제품 1
(B) 제품 2
(C) 제품 3
(D) 제품 4

해설 제시된 발표 슬라이드의 정보를 확인한 후 질문의 핵심 어구(best-selling item)와 관련된 내용을 주의 깊게 듣는다. "the backpack is clearly the star of the lineup. Its sales are nearly double those of all the other bags combined."라며 배낭이 분명히 라인업의 주역이며 그것의 매출이 다른 모든 가방들을 합친 것의 거의 두 배라고 하였으므로, 신제품 중 가장 잘 팔리는 제품은 제품 2임을 발표 슬라이드에서 알 수 있다. 따라서 (B)가 정답이다.

어휘 best-selling 가장 잘 팔리는

96 특정 세부 사항 문제

해석 화자는 고객들이 그 가방에 대해 무엇을 가장 좋아한다고 말하는가?
(A) 소재
(B) 사이즈
(C) 디자인
(D) 색상

해설 질문의 핵심 어구(customers like most about the bag)와 관련된 내용을 주의 깊게 듣는다. "They[customer reviews] all mentioned that the bag's design made it perfect for both casual and formal settings."라며 고객 평가 모두는 그 가방의 디자인이 평상복과 정장 둘 다를 완벽하게 만든다고 언급했다고 하였다. 따라서 (C)가 정답이다.

어휘 fabric[fǽbrik] 소재, 직물

97 다음에 할 일 문제

해석 청자들은 다음에 무엇을 할 것 같은가?
(A) 몇몇 제안서를 검토한다.
(B) 경쟁 제품을 살펴본다.
(C) 제품 소재를 비교한다.
(D) 매출 수치를 확인한다.

해설 지문의 마지막 부분을 주의 깊게 듣는다. "Let's look at some of my plans to modify it to increase its sales even further."라며 매출을 훨씬 더 늘리기 위해 그것을 변형한 몇몇 방안들을 살펴보겠다고 하였다. 따라서 (A)가 정답이다.

패러프레이징
look at some of ~ plans 몇몇 방안들을 살펴보다 → Review some proposals 몇몇 제안서를 검토하다

어휘 review[rivjú:] 검토하다 proposal[미 prəpóuzəl, 영 prəpáuzəl] 제안서 compare[미 kəmpɛ́ər, 영 kəmpéə] 비교하다 sales figures 매출 수치

98-100 [3에] 호주식 발음

Questions 98-100 refer to the following telephone message and order form.

Hello, Ms. Reynolds. This is Brad Pressley calling from Officepro Wholesale regarding an order you just placed. While looking at your order, I noticed that it included some phone accessories. ⁹⁸/⁹⁹I wanted to let you know about a quantity discount on the Airway headsets. ⁹⁹If you purchase two more, you will get one more for free. It might be useful to have some extra pairs on hand. Let me know if you would like to add those. ¹⁰⁰We are ready to expedite the shipment, so you should receive everything within two business days.

regarding[rigά:rdiŋ] ~과 관련하여
notice[미 nóutis, 영 nə́utis] 알아차리다
quantity[kwά:ntəti] 수량, 양 useful[jú:sfəl] 유용한
extra[ékstrə] 여분의 pair[pɛər] 한 쌍, 한 벌
on hand 소유하고 있는, 수중에 expedite[ékspədàit] 신속히 처리하다
shipment[ʃípmənt] 배송 business day 영업일

해석
98-100번은 다음 전화 메시지와 주문 양식에 관한 문제입니다.

안녕하세요, Ms. Reynolds. 방금 고객님께서 하신 주문과 관련하여 Officepro 도매에서 전화드리는 Brad Pressley라고 합니다. 고객님의 주문을 살펴보면서, 저는 그것이 몇 가지 휴대폰 액세서리를 포함하고 있다는 것을 알아차렸습니다. ⁹⁸/⁹⁹저는 고객님께 Airway 헤드셋의 수량 할인에 대

해 알려드리고자 합니다. ⁹⁹만약 고객님께서 두 개를 더 구매하시면, 무료로 한 개를 더 받게 될 것입니다. 여분의 한 쌍을 더 소유하고 있는 것이 유용할 것입니다. 만약 귀하께서 그것들을 추가하고 싶으시다면 제게 알려주십시오. ¹⁰⁰저희는 배송을 신속하게 처리할 준비가 되어 있으니, 귀하께서는 2영업일 이내에 모든 것을 받으실 것입니다.

물품	수량
⁹⁹Airway 헤드셋 (IB875747)	10
Blockland 종이 상자(IB374665)	4
Officepro 펜, 검은색 (IB323722)	40
Blockland 메모장, 대형	20

98 목적 문제

해석 화자는 왜 전화를 하고 있는가?
(A) 지불을 요청하기 위해
(B) 변경 사항을 받아들이기 위해
(C) 기회를 언급하기 위해
(D) 배송에 대해 문의하기 위해

해설 전화의 목적을 묻는 문제이므로, 지문의 초반을 반드시 듣는다. "I wanted to let you know about a quantity discount on the Airway headsets."라며 Airway 헤드셋의 수량 할인에 대해 알려주고자 한다는 말을 통해 화자가 기회를 언급하기 위해 전화하고 있음을 알 수 있다. 따라서 (C)가 정답이다.

어휘 point out 언급하다, 가리키다

99 시각 자료 문제

해석 시각 자료를 보아라. 할인을 받기 위해 어느 수량이 바뀌어야 하는가?
(A) 10
(B) 4
(C) 40
(D) 20

해설 제시된 주문 양식의 정보를 확인한 후 질문의 핵심 어구(discount)가 언급된 주변을 주의 깊게 듣는다. "I wanted to let you know about a quantity discount on the Airway headsets. If you purchase two more, you will get one more for free."라며 Airway 헤드셋의 수량 할인에 대해 알려주고자 하며 만약 두 개를 더 구매하면 무료로 한 개를 더 받게 될 것이라고 하였으므로, 할인을 받기 위해 Airway 헤드셋의 수량 10이 바뀌어야 함을 주문 양식에서 알 수 있다. 따라서 (A)가 정답이다.

100 언급 문제

해석 화자는 업체에 대해 무엇을 말하는가?
(A) 재고가 고갈되고 있다.
(B) 전자제품을 전문으로 한다.
(C) 신제품을 소개하고 있다.
(D) 신속히 처리되는 배송을 제공할 수 있다.

해설 질문의 핵심 어구(business)와 관련된 내용을 주의 깊게 듣는다. "We[Officepro Wholesale] are ready to expedite the shipment"라며 Officepro 도매에서는 배송을 신속하게 처리할 준비가 되어 있다고 하였다. 따라서 (D)가 정답이다.

어휘 run low 고갈되다 specialize in ~을 전문으로 하다

PART 5

101 부사 어휘 고르기

해설 'Ballas 스니커즈 운동화 회사는 이전에 Ballas Athletics로 알려져 있었다'라는 문맥이므로 (C) formerly(이전에, 예전에)가 정답이다. (A) currently는 '현재, 지금', (B) so는 '매우', (D) aside는 '따로, 별도

로'라는 의미이다.

해석 Ballas 스니커즈 운동화 회사는 이전에 Ballas Athletics로 알려져 있었으나 몇 년 전에 브랜드 이미지를 새롭게 하였다.

어휘 **be known as** ~으로 알려져 있다
rebrand v. 브랜드 이미지를 새롭게 하다

102 태에 맞는 동사 채우기

해설 문장에 동사가 없으므로 모든 보기가 정답의 후보이다. 주어(The factory employees)와 동사(direct)가 '직원들이 지시받다'라는 수동의 의미를 가지므로 수동태 동사 (B) were directed가 정답이다.

해석 그 공장 직원들은 운영 체제 안내서를 다시 읽도록 지시받았다.

어휘 **operating system** 운영 체제 **handbook** n. 안내서
direct v. 지시하다

103 부사절 접속사 채우기

해설 이 문장은 필수성분(The science convention ~ in September)을 갖춘 완전한 절이므로 ____ the event's major sponsor ~ its support는 수식어 거품으로 보아야 한다. 이 수식어 거품은 동사(has withdrawn)가 있는 거품절이므로, 거품절을 이끌 수 있는 부사절 접속사 (A), (B), (D)가 정답의 후보이다. '비록 행사의 주요 후원 업체가 후원을 철회했지만 그 과학 협의회는 9월에 열릴 것이다'라는 의미가 되어야 하므로 (D) even though(비록 ~이지만)가 정답이다. (A) if only는 '~하기만 했더라면', (B) so that은 '~할 수 있도록'이라는 의미이므로 이 문맥에 어울리지 않는다. 부사 (C)는 절과 절을 연결할 수 없으므로 답이 될 수 없다.

해석 비록 행사의 주요 후원 업체가 후원을 철회했지만 그 과학 협의회는 9월에 열릴 것이다.

어휘 **convention** n. 협의회, 대회 **sponsor** n. 후원 업체, 후원자
withdraw v. 철회하다, 기권하다 **support** n. 후원, 지원

104 전치사 채우기

해설 '청구서는 조세 용도로 복사되고 별도로 보관된다'라는 의미를 만드는 (A) for(~용의, ~의 대상으로)가 정답이다. (B) at은 '~에', (C) like는 '~처럼, ~과 같이', (D) in은 '~에, ~에서'라는 의미이다.

해석 계약자들로부터의 청구서는 조세 용도로 복사되고 별도로 보관된다.

어휘 **invoice** n. 청구서, 송장 **contractor** n. 계약자, 도급업자
separately adv. 별도로, 따로따로 **purpose** n. 용도, 의도

105 동사 어휘 고르기

해설 'The Rock Creek Times지는 독자들이 의견을 제출하도록 권장한다'라는 문맥이므로 (A) submit(제출하다)가 정답이다. (B) determine은 '결정하다', (C) teach는 '가르치다', (D) accept는 '받아들이다, 수락하다'라는 의미이다.

해석 The Rock Creek Times지는 독자들이 편집장에게 편지를 씀으로써 의견을 제출하도록 권장한다.

어휘 **encourage** v. 권장하다, 장려하다 **editor** n. 편집장, 편집자

106 격에 맞는 인칭대명사 채우기

해설 명사구(own methods) 앞에서 형용사처럼 쓰일 수 있는 인칭대명사는 소유격이므로 (C) his(그의)가 정답이다.

해석 Mr. Holly는 그 회사에 의해 고용된 첫 판매원이었고 판매를 위한 그의 고유한 방식을 발달시켜야 했다.

어휘 **salesperson** n. 판매원, 외판원 **own** adj. 고유한, 자기 자신의
method n. 방식, 방법

107 명사 관련 어구 완성하기

해설 'Fox Books사는 매우 여러 가지의 장르를 판매한다'라는 문맥에서 빈칸 앞의 부정관사(a)와 뒤의 전치사(of)와 함께 쓰여 '여러 가지의'라는 의미의 어구를 이루는 (A) variety가 정답이다. (a variety of: 여러 가지의) (B) version은 '버전, 변형', (C) knowledge는 '지식', (D) position은 '위치, 자리'라는 의미이다.

해석 Fox Books사는 범위가 소설과 시에서 역사와 철학에 이르는 매우 여러 가지의 장르를 판매한다.

어휘 **range from A to B** 범위가 A에서 B에 이르다 **fiction** n. 소설
poetry n. 시 **philosophy** n. 철학

108 to 부정사 채우기

해설 명사 plans를 뒤에서 꾸밀 수 있는 to 부정사 (A)와 과거분사 (B)가 정답의 후보이다. '그 도시의 오래된 지하 철도 노선 중 일부를 현대화할 계획'이라는 문맥으로 보아 목적어(some of ~ metro lines)를 취하면서 명사(plans)를 뒤에서 꾸밀 수 있는 to 부정사 (A) to modernize가 정답이다. 과거분사 (B) modernized는 뒤에 목적어를 취할 수 없으므로 답이 될 수 없다. 참고로, plan은 to 부정사를 취하는 명사이다.

해석 런던 시장은 그 도시의 오래된 지하 철도 노선 중 일부를 현대화할 계획의 개요를 서술했다.

어휘 **mayor** n. 시장 **outline** v. 개요를 서술하다 **metro line** 지하 철도 노선
modernize v. 현대화하다

109 전치사 채우기

해설 '나침반과 함께 음식과 물을 가져오다'라는 의미가 되어야 하므로 (C) along with(~과 함께)가 정답이다. (A) such as는 '~과 같은', (B) in case of는 '~의 경우에'라는 의미이다.

해석 Gage 국립 공원은 도보 여행자들에게 나침반과 함께 음식과 물을 가져오도록 권한다.

어휘 **hiker** n. 도보 여행자 **compass** n. 나침반

110 가산 명사와 불가산 명사 구별하여 채우기

해설 빈칸 앞에 부정관사(a)가 있고 '회사의 프로젝트가 마케팅 대표자에 의해 발표되었다'라는 의미가 되어야 하므로 가산 명사 (A) representative(대표자, 대리인)가 정답이다. 불가산 명사 (C)는 부정관사(a)와 함께 쓰일 수 없다. 분사 (B)와 (D)가 빈칸 앞의 명사 marketing(마케팅)을 수식하는 구조로 본다 하더라도 marketing은 불가산 명사이므로 부정관사(a)와 함께 쓰일 수 없다.

해석 회사의 프로젝트는 어제의 기자 회견에서 마케팅 대표자에 의해 발표되었다.

어휘 **press conference** 기자 회견
representation n. 대표자를 내세움, 대표단

111 형용사 어휘 고르기

해설 '초청된 연사는 잠시 동안의 발언을 하기 위해 5분의 시간을 가질 것이다'라는 문맥이므로 (C) brief(잠시 동안의, 짧은)가 정답이다. (A) most는 '(수·양·정도·액수가) 가장 많은', (B) equal은 '동일한, 같은', (D) busy는 '바쁜'이라는 의미이다.

해석 초청된 연사는 세미나의 시작 때 잠시 동안의 발언을 하기 위해 5분의 시간을 가질 것이다.

어휘 **remark** n. 발언, 논평

112 부사 자리 채우기

해설 동사(work)를 꾸미기 위해서는 부사가 와야 하므로 부사 (D) collaboratively(협력해서)가 정답이다. 명사 (A)와 (C), 형용사 (B)는 동사를 꾸밀 수 없다. 명사 (C)가 동사(work)의 목적어 역할을 하는 것으로 본다 하더라도 work in collaboration with someone의 형태로 쓰여야 하므로 답이 될 수 없다.

해석 Stranton Tech사의 팀들은 문제를 발견하고 적절한 해결책을 찾기 위해 협력해서 일한다.

어휘 **identify** v. 발견하다, 확인하다 **appropriate** adj. 적절한
solution n. 해결책, 해법 **collaborator** n. 공동 연구자, 협력자
collaborative adj. 공동의 **collaboration** n. 공동 작업

113 짝을 이루는 표현

해설 '승객들의 증가하는 수요를 충족시키기 위해 노선을 추가할 것이다'라는 문맥이므로 빈칸 앞의 meet과 함께 '수요를 충족시키다'라는 의미의 어구 meet demand를 만드는 명사 (B) demand(수요)가 정답이다. (A) cost는 '값, 비용', (C) attempt는 '시도', (D) insight는 '통찰력'이라는 의미이다.

해석 그 항공사는 승객들의 증가하는 수요를 충족시키기 위해 남아메리카 대륙으로의 몇몇 새로운 노선을 추가할 것이다.

어휘 **airline** n. 항공사 **route** n. 노선 **passenger** n. 승객

114 부사절 접속사 채우기

해설 이 문장은 필수성분(residents ~ the stairs)을 갖춘 완전한 절이므로 ____ the elevator is fixed는 수식어 거품으로 보아야 한다. 이 수식어 거품은 동사(is fixed)가 있는 거품절이므로, 거품절을 이끌 수 있는 부사절 접속사 (C)와 (D)가 정답의 후보이다. '엘리베이터가 고쳐질 때까지 계단을 이용해야 할 것이다'라는 의미가 되어야 하므로 (D) Until(~할 때까지)이 정답이다. (C) Since는 '~한 이래로, ~이기 때문에'라는 의미이므로 이 문맥에 어울리지 않는다. 부사 (A)와 (B)는 절과 절을 연결할 수 없다.

해석 엘리베이터가 고쳐질 때까지, 110번지 Halpert가의 주민들은 계단을 이용해야 할 것이다.

115 사람명사 추상명사 구별하여 채우기

해설 전치사(in)와 전치사(with) 사이에 올 수 있는 것은 명사이므로 명사 (B)와 (D)가 정답의 후보이다. 'Kemper Shipping은 소매상과 교섭 중이다'라는 의미이므로 추상명사 (B) negotiation(교섭, 협상)이 정답이다. 사람명사 (D) negotiator(교섭자)는 어색한 의미를 만들기 때문에 답이 될 수 없다. 참고로, negotiation은 be in negotiation with(~와 교섭 중이다)의 형태로 자주 쓰임을 알아둔다.

해석 Kemper Shipping은 중동에 있는 모든 물류 관리를 처리하기 위해 주된 미국 소매상과 교섭 중이다.

어휘 **retailer** n. 소매상 **handle** v. 처리하다, 다루다 **logistics** n. 물류 관리

116 형용사 어휘 고르기

해설 '기금 지원 기관으로부터의 외부적인 지원 획득이 없다면 연구를 진행시키지 못할 것이다'라는 문맥이므로 (D) external(외부적인)이 정답이다. (A) plain은 '분명한, 있는 그대로의', (B) compact는 '소형의, 간편한', (C) mere는 '단순한, 순전한'이라는 의미이다.

해석 그 협회는 기금 지원 기관으로부터의 외부적인 지원 획득이 없다면 연구를 진행시키지 못할 것이다.

어휘 **advance** v. 진행시키다, 진전시키다 **obtain** v. 획득하다, 얻다

117 전치사 채우기

해설 '엄청난 강우 후에 그 도시는 광범위한 수해에 대처하고 있다'라는 의미가 되어야 하므로 (B) After(~ 후에)가 정답이다. (A) Between은 '~ 사이에', (C) Aboard는 '~을 타고', (D) Except는 '~을 제외하고는'이라는 의미이다.

해석 멤피스에서의 엄청난 강우 후에, 그 도시는 광범위한 수해에 대처하고 있다.

어휘 **extensive** adj. (수량·규모·정도 따위가) 엄청난, 큰
rainfall n. 강우(량) **deal with** ~을 대처하다, 다루다
widespread adj. 광범위한, 널리 퍼진 **flood damage** 수해

118 수량 표현 채우기

해설 빈칸 뒤의 복수 가산 명사(personnel)를 꾸밀 수 있는 (A)와 (D)가 정답의 후보이다. '회사 전반에 걸쳐 모든 직원들은 신분 확인 명찰을 착용하도록 요구된다'라는 문맥이므로 수량 표현 (A) all(모든)이 정답이다. (D) both(둘 다의)를 쓸 경우 '회사 전반에 걸쳐 둘 다의 직원들은 신분 확인 명찰을 착용하도록 요구된다'라는 어색한 의미가 된다. (B) every와 (C) each는 단수 가산 명사와 함께 쓰여야 한다.

해석 회사 전반에 걸쳐, 모든 직원들은 구내에서 일하는 동안 회사에서 발급된 신분 확인 명찰을 착용하도록 요구된다.

어휘 **across the board** (회사·산업 등의) 전반에 걸쳐
identification badge 신분 확인 명찰 **issue** v. 발급하다, 교부하다
premise n. 구내, 부지

119 동사 어휘 고르기

해설 '조사는 장비의 자동 제어 장치가 실패했음을 밝혔다'라는 문맥이므로 reveal의 과거형 (C) revealed(밝히다)가 정답이다. (A)의 choose는 '택하다, 고르다', (B)의 request는 '요청하다, 요구하다', (D)의 revise는 '변경하다'라는 의미이다.

해석 그 회사의 기술자들에 의한 조사는 장비의 자동 제어 장치가 실패했음을 밝혔다.

어휘 **investigation** n. 조사, 수사 **automatic** adj. 자동의

120 형용사 자리 채우기

해설 명사(role)를 꾸미기 위해서는 형용사가 와야 하므로 형용사 (D) supervisory(지휘 감독의)가 정답이다. 동사 (A)와 (B), 명사 (C)는 형용사 자리에 올 수 없다.

해석 다음 주부터, Donald Peters는 Zwingli 은행에서 지휘 감독의 역할을 떠맡을 것이다.

어휘 **assume** v. (책임·임무 등을) 떠맡다 **supervisor** n. 감독관, 관리자

121 명사절 접속사 채우기

해설 동사(decide)의 목적어 역할을 하는 명사절(____ smartphone ~ their needs)을 이끌 수 있는 명사절 접속사 (A), (B), (C)가 정답의 후보이다. 빈칸 뒤에 명사(smartphone)가 있고, '어느 스마트폰이 그들의 필요에 가장 적합할 것인지'라는 의미가 되어야 하므로 smartphone과 함께 명사절의 주어 역할을 하는 의문형용사 (C) which가 정답이다. 의문대명사 (A) whom은 명사절을 이끌며, 그 자체가 명사절의 주어, 목적어, 보어 역할을 하므로 뒤에 주어, 목적어 또는 보어가 없는 불완전한 절이 와야 한다. 명사절 접속사 (B)가 절(The Web site ~ decide)과 절(smartphone ~ their needs)을 연결하는 것으로 본다 하더라도 smartphone은 가산 명사이므로 앞에 관사(a/the)가 와야 하므로 답이 될 수 없다. 수량 표현 (D) another는 명사절을 이끌 수 없다.

해석 그 웹사이트는 어느 스마트폰이 그들의 필요에 가장 적합할 것인지 사람들이 결정하도록 돕는 추천을 제공한다.

어휘 **recommendation** n. 추천, 권고

122 전치사 채우기

해설 '올해 초의 생산 문제에도 불구하고'라는 의미가 되어야 하므로 (C) In spite of(~에도 불구하고)가 정답이다. (A) With는 '~와 함께, ~을 가지고', (B) Owing to와 (D) Because of는 '~ 때문에'라는 의미이다.

해석 올해 초의 생산 문제에도 불구하고, 새로운 Ecroon 노트북 컴퓨터의 출시는 예정대로 되었다.

어휘 **challenge** n. 문제, 난제 **on schedule** 예정대로

123 최상급 표현 채우기

해설 빈칸 뒤의 명사(rating)를 꾸밀 수 있는 것은 형용사이므로 형용사 (A), (B), (D)가 정답의 후보이다. '모든 사진 편집 애플리케이션 중에

서 가장 높은 평점을 가진다'라는 의미가 되어야 하고 빈칸 앞에 정관사(the)가 있으므로 형용사 high(높은)의 최상급 (B) highest가 정답이다. 원급 (A)와 비교급 (D)는 최상급 표현과 함께 쓰일 수 없다. 부사 (C)는 형용사 자리에 올 수 없다.

해석 수천 개의 사용자 후기에 근거하여 Dynaline은 모든 사진 편집 애플리케이션 중에서 가장 높은 평점을 가진다.

어휘 rating n. 평점, 평가 based on ~에 근거하여

124 명사 어휘 고르기

해설 '영수증을 가지고 오지 않았기 때문에 그 물건들을 반품하도록 허용되지 않았다'라는 문맥이므로 (A) receipt(영수증)가 정답이다. (B) guidance는 '지도, 안내', (C) report는 '보고', (D) procedure는 '절차, 방법'이라는 의미이다.

해석 Mr. Stewart는 영수증을 가지고 오지 않았기 때문에 그 물건들을 반품하도록 허용되지 않았다.

어휘 be allowed to ~하도록 허용되다

125 강조 부사 채우기

해설 '화려한 특수 효과에 상당히 감명을 받았다'라는 의미가 되어야 하므로 부사 (B) quite(상당히, 꽤)가 정답이다. (A) ever는 '언제든, 항상', (C) last는 '마지막에, 최근에', (D) same은 주로 the와 함께 'the same'의 형태로 '똑같이'라는 의미이다.

해석 극장에서 그 영화를 본 모든 사람은 그것의 화려한 특수 효과에 상당히 감명을 받았다.

어휘 spectacular adj. 화려한, 환상적인 special effect 특수 효과

126 분사구문 채우기

해설 이 문장은 주어(Anuman Foods), 동사(opened), 목적어(its second international location)를 갖춘 완전한 절이므로, ____ its presence in Southeast Asia는 수식어 거품으로 보아야 한다. 따라서 수식어 거품이 될 수 있는 현재분사 (C) expanding이 정답이다. 동사 (A), (B), (D)는 수식어 거품이 될 수 없다.

해석 Anuman Foods사는 올해 하노이에 두 번째 국제적인 지점을 열며, 동남아시아에서 그것의 존재를 확장하였다.

어휘 presence n. 존재, 실재 expand v. 확장하다, 확대하다

127 상관접속사 채우기

해설 상관접속사 nor와 맞는 짝인 (C) Neither가 정답이다. 참고로, neither A nor B가 명사구(Mr. Hill)와 명사구(Ms. Jackson)를 연결하고 있다.

해석 Mr. Hill과 Ms. Jackson은 둘 다 지역 영업부장이 되기 위한 조건을 가지고 있지 않았다.

어휘 qualification n. 조건, 자격 regional adj. 지역의, 지방의

128 명사 어휘 고르기

해설 '엄선된 상품들에 대한 풍성한 할인 혜택'이라는 문맥이므로 (A) deals(할인 혜택)가 정답이다. (B)의 excuse는 '변명, 핑계', (C)의 share는 '몫, 부담', (D)의 chance는 '기회'라는 의미이다.

해석 그 슈퍼마켓은 엄선된 상품들에 대한 풍성한 할인 혜택을 제공하는 쿠폰을 정기적으로 발행한다.

어휘 issue v. 발행하다, 발급하다 generous adj. 풍성한, 많은 selected adj. 엄선된, 선택된

129 시간 부사 채우기

해설 '일주일 뒤에 그것을 찾으러 오도록 요청받았다'라는 의미가 되어야 하므로 (B) later(~ 후에, 나중에)가 정답이다. (A) left는 '왼쪽에, 좌측에', (C) more는 '(더) 많이', (D) nowadays는 '요즈음에는'이라는

의미이다.

해석 Ms. Chung은 정비소에 그녀의 차를 맡겼고 일주일 뒤에 그것을 찾으러 오도록 요청받았다.

어휘 repair shop 정비소

130 부사절 접속사 채우기

해설 이 문장은 필수성분(the travel industry ~ recover)을 갖춘 완전한 절이므로 ____ the recession is over는 수식어 거품으로 보아야 한다. 이 수식어 거품은 동사(is)가 있는 거품절이므로, 거품절에 올 수 있는 부사절 접속사 (B), (C), (D)가 정답의 후보이다. '불경기가 끝나므로 여행 산업이 회복될 것으로 기대된다'라는 의미가 되어야 하므로 이유를 나타내는 부사절 접속사 (D) Now that(~이므로, ~이니까)이 정답이다. (B) Rather than(~보다는)과 (C) In order that(~할 수 있도록)을 쓰면 각각 '불경기가 끝나기보다는/끝날 수 있도록 여행 산업이 회복될 것으로 기대된다'라는 어색한 의미를 만들기 때문에 답이 될 수 없다.

해석 불경기가 끝나므로, 여행 산업이 회복될 것으로 기대된다.

어휘 recession n. 불경기, 침체 recover v. 회복되다, 되찾다

PART 6

131-134번은 다음 기사에 관한 문제입니다.

Martindale's가 기념일을 맞이하다

12월 12일—이번 주, Martindale's가 고급 식당으로서 20주년을 맞이한다. 프랑스에서 교육을 받은, 요리사이자 주인인 Joyce Martindale은 항상 Elkhart 시내에 레스토랑을 갖는 것을 꿈꿔왔지만, 그녀의 꿈을 실현하는 것은 오랜 시간이 걸렸다. [131]그녀는 마침내 그녀의 통찰력을 믿어준 가족과 친구들의 도움으로 식당을 열었다. 오늘날, Martindale's는 Elkhart에서 최고의 식당들 중 하나가 되었다. [132]그것은 다양한 권위 있는 상으로 인정받기도 했다.

[133]그 식당은 여러 친숙한 프랑스식과 미국식 요리를 특징으로 하고, 이것들은 가장 신선한 재료들만을 사용하여 준비된다. [134]처음 오는 손님들은 반드시 식당의 전문 요리를 시도해 봐야 한다. 이것들은 스테이크 저녁 식사와 구운 치킨을 포함하는데, 오랜 고객들의 가장 좋아하는 요리들 중 하나이다.

celebrate v. 맞이하다, 축하하다 anniversary n. 기념일 realize v. 실현하다, 달성하다 vision n. 통찰력 a selection of 다양한 ingredient n. 재료, 성분 roast adj. 구운 longtime adj. 오랜

131 부사 어휘 고르기 주변 문맥 파악

해설 '그녀는 ____ 가족과 친구들의 도움으로 식당을 열었다'라는 문맥이므로 모든 보기가 정답의 후보이다. 빈칸이 있는 문장만으로 정답을 고를 수 없으므로 주변 문맥이나 전체 문맥을 파악한다. 앞 문장에서 'Joyce Martindale은 항상 Elkhart 시내에 레스토랑을 갖는 것을 꿈꿔왔지만 그녀의 꿈을 실현하는 것은 오랜 시간이 걸렸다'(Joyce Martindale had always dreamed of having a restaurant in downtown Elkhart, but it took several long years to realize her dream)라고 했으므로 그녀가 마침내 가족과 친구들의 도움으로 식당을 열었던 것임을 알 수 있다. 따라서 (D) finally가 정답이다.

어휘 instead adv. 대신에 likewise adv. 게다가, 더욱이 frequently adv. 자주, 빈번히

132 알맞은 문장 고르기

해석 (A) 그녀가 자주 방문하는 몇몇 인기 식당들이 있다.
(B) 그것은 다양한 권위 있는 상으로 인정받기도 했다.
(C) 단체 예약도 애플리케이션을 통해 이루어질 수 있다.

(D) 일찍 온 손님들은 기다리는 동안 출입구 주변에 있는 자리에 앉으면 된다.

해설 빈칸에 들어갈 알맞은 문장을 고르는 문제이므로 주변 문맥 또는 전체 문맥을 파악한다. 앞 문장 'Today, Martindale's has become one of the best restaurants in Elkhart.'에서 오늘날 Martindale's는 Elkhart에서 최고의 식당들 중 하나가 되었다고 했으므로, 빈칸에는 그것이 다양한 권위 있는 상으로 인정받기도 했다는 내용이 들어가야 함을 알 수 있다. 따라서 (B)가 정답이다.

어휘 **recognize** v. 인정하다, 인식하다 **prestigious** adj. 권위 있는

133 올바른 시제의 동사 채우기
해설 그 식당은 여러 친숙한 프랑스식과 미국식 요리를 특징으로 하고, 이것들은 가장 신선한 재료들만을 사용하여 준비된다는 현재의 상황을 언급하는 문맥이므로 현재 시제 (A) features가 정답이다.

어휘 **feature** v. 특징으로 하다, 특별히 포함하다

134 명사 어휘 고르기 주변 문맥 파악
해설 '처음 오는 손님들은 반드시 식당의 ____을 시도해 봐야 한다'라는 문맥이므로 모든 보기가 정답의 후보이다. 빈칸이 있는 문장만으로 정답을 고를 수 없으므로 주변 문맥이나 전체 문맥을 파악한다. 뒤 문장에서 '이것들은 스테이크 저녁 식사와 구운 치킨을 포함하는데 오랜 고객들의 가장 좋아하는 요리들 중 하나이다(These include the steak dinner and roast chicken, which are among the favorite dishes of longtime customers.)'라고 했으므로 처음 오는 손님들은 반드시 식당의 전문 요리를 시도해 봐야 한다는 것임을 알 수 있다. 따라서 (C) specialties(전문 요리)가 정답이다.

어휘 **diversion** n. 전환 **activity** n. 활동 **performance** n. 공연, 연주회

135-138번은 다음 공고에 관한 문제입니다.

AC Ambrose 농장 공고

135AC Ambrose는 올해 농장들에 새로운 접근법을 도입하기로 결정했습니다. 저희는 포장 공정의 속도를 높이기 위해 Larkin Tech사에 의해 제작된 새로운 HT509 로봇들을 사용할 것입니다. 현재, 팀들이 배송을 위해 1,000파운드의 농산물을 포장하는 데 평균 한 시간이 걸립니다. 그 로봇들은 같은 작업을 30분 안에 완료할 수 있습니다. 136따라서, 저희는 로봇들이 저희의 생산성을 두 배가 되게 할 것을 기대합니다.

로봇들은 이번 달 말까지 배송될 것입니다. 137이것들은 이틀의 기간에 걸쳐 우리의 모든 지점에 설치될 것입니다. 근로자들은 포장 작업이 중단되지 않은 채 계속될 수 있도록 일시적으로 재배치될 것입니다. 일단 로봇들이 준비되면, 제조업체는 일부 인력을 파견하여 로봇들을 사용하는 것에 대해 선별된 직원들에게 교육을 할 것입니다. 138만약 당신이 참가자들 중 한 명으로 선정되면 통지를 받을 것입니다.

adopt v. 도입하다, 채택하다 **average** n. 평균; adj. 평균의
produce n. 농산물 **productivity** n. 생산성
temporarily adv. 일시적으로 **relocate** v. 재배치하다
uninterrupted adj. 중단되지 않은

---

135 가산 명사와 불가산 명사 구별하여 채우기
해설 빈칸 앞의 형용사(new)의 꾸밈을 받을 수 있는 것은 명사이므로 명사 (A)와 (D)가 정답의 후보이다. 빈칸 앞에 부정관사 a가 있으므로 단수 명사 (A) approach(접근법)가 정답이다. (B)는 동명사일 경우 부정관사 a 다음에 올 수 없고, 현재분사일 경우 명사 자리에 올 수 없다. 형용사 (C)는 명사 자리에 올 수 없다.

136 동사 어휘 고르기 전체 문맥 파악
해설 '따라서 로봇들이 생산성을 ____ 것을 기대한다'라는 문맥이므로 (B) double(두 배가 되게 하다)과 (D) measure(측정하다)가 정답의 후보

이다. 빈칸이 있는 문장만으로 정답을 고를 수 없으므로 주변 문맥이나 전체 문맥을 파악한다. 앞부분에서 '현재 팀들이 배송을 위해 1,000파운드의 농산물을 포장하는 데 평균 한 시간이 걸린다(Currently, it takes teams an average of one hour to pack 1,000 pounds of produce for shipment.)'라고 했고, 앞 문장에서 '그 로봇들은 같은 작업을 30분 안에 완료할 수 있다(The robots can complete the same job in 30 minutes.)'고 했으므로 로봇들이 생산성을 두 배가 되게 할 것을 기대한다는 것임을 알 수 있다. 따라서 (B) double이 정답이다.

어휘 **involve** v. 포함시키다 **repeat** v. 반복하다

137 명사와 수/인칭 일치된 대명사 채우기 주변 문맥 파악
해설 '____은 이틀의 기간에 걸쳐 모든 지점에 설치될 것이다'라는 문맥이므로 (A), (B), (D)가 정답의 후보이다. 빈칸이 있는 문장만으로 정답을 고를 수 없으므로 주변 문맥이나 전체 문맥을 파악한다. 앞 문장에서 로봇들(The robots)이 이번 달 말까지 배송될 것이라고 했으므로 빈칸에 들어갈 대명사가 가리키게 되는 것은 robots이다. 따라서 복수 사물명사(robots)를 가리키는 대명사 (D) These가 정답이다.

138 알맞은 문장 고르기
해석 (A) 신입 직원들을 위한 오리엔테이션은 회의실에서 진행될 것입니다.
(B) 저희는 요청받은 물품들을 배송하는 데 약간의 지연을 겪을 수도 있습니다.
(C) 만약 당신이 참가자들 중 한 명으로 선정되면 통지를 받을 것입니다.
(D) 그 단체의 업무 성과는 작년에 상당히 향상되었습니다.

해설 빈칸에 들어갈 알맞은 문장을 고르는 문제이므로 주변 문맥 또는 전체 문맥을 파악한다. 앞 문장 'Once the robots are ready, the manufacturer will be sending over some people to train selected staff members on using the robots.'에서 일단 로봇들이 준비되면 제조업체는 일부 인력을 파견하여 로봇들을 사용하는 것에 대해 선별된 직원들에게 교육을 할 것이라고 했으므로, 빈칸에는 만약 참가자들 중 한 명으로 선정되면 통지를 받을 것이라는 내용이 들어가야 함을 알 수 있다. 따라서 (C)가 정답이다.

어휘 **performance** n. 성과, 수행 **significantly** adv. 상당히, 크게

139-142번은 다음 이메일에 관한 문제입니다.

수신: 모든 직원 <staff@brandesson.com>
발신: Beverly Castro <b.castro@brandesson.com>
제목: 소프트웨어 업데이트
날짜: 10월 8일

직원분들께,

저희는 저희의 Torrino 운영 소프트웨어를 업그레이드했습니다. 139그 프로그램은 여러분이 유용하다고 느낄만한 몇몇 요소들을 가지고 있습니다. 예를 들어, 이것은 업무 일정을 정리하고 회의를 더 쉽게 마련하게 합니다.

이제, 그 소프트웨어는 여러분의 개인 컴퓨터에 설치되어야 하는데, 이는 시간이 걸릴 수 있습니다. 140이러한 이유로, 저는 IT 직원들에게 주말 동안 설치를 수행해 달라고 요청했습니다. 그들은 금요일 오후 6시 이후에 시작할 것입니다. 141그들을 위해 퇴근할 때 여러분의 컴퓨터를 켜두세요. 142여러분이 월요일에 돌아오면, 어떤 이유로든 여러분이 프로그램에 접근할 수 없다면 저에게 알려주십시오.

Beverly Castro 드림
사무실 관리자

administration n. 운영, 관리 **element** n. 요소
organize v. 정리하다, 조직하다 **arrange** v. 마련하다, 배치하다
individual adj. 개인의, 각각의 **installation** n. 설치

---

139 형용사 어휘 고르기 주변 문맥 파악

해설 '그 프로그램은 _____ 하다고 느낄만한 몇몇 요소들을 가지고 있다'라는 문맥이므로 (A) confusing(혼란스러운), (B) useful(유용한), (D) unfamiliar(익숙하지 않은)가 정답의 후보이다. 빈칸이 있는 문장만으로 정답을 고를 수 없으므로 주변 문맥이나 전체 문맥을 파악한다. 뒤 문장에서 '예를 들어, 이것은 업무 일정을 정리하고 회의를 더 쉽게 마련하게 한다(For instance, it makes organizing work schedules and arranging meetings easier.)'고 했으므로 그 프로그램이 유용하다고 느낄만한 몇몇 요소들을 가지고 있음을 알 수 있다. 따라서 (B) useful이 정답이다.

어휘 enclosed adj. 동봉된, 에워싸인

140 접속부사 채우기 주변 문맥 파악

해설 빈칸이 콤마와 함께 문장의 맨 앞에 온 접속부사 자리이므로, 앞 문장과 빈칸이 있는 문장의 의미 관계를 파악하여 정답을 선택한다. 앞 문장에서 그 소프트웨어는 개인 컴퓨터에 설치되어야 하는데 이는 시간이 걸릴 수 있다고 했고, 빈칸이 있는 문장에서는 IT 직원들에게 주말 동안 설치를 수행해 달라고 요청했다고 했으므로, 앞에서 말한 내용에 따른 결과를 언급하는 내용의 문장에서 사용되는 (D) For this reason(이러한 이유로)이 정답이다.

어휘 similarly adv. 유사하게, 같게 meanwhile adv. 그동안에 on the other hand 한편

141 알맞은 문장 고르기

해석 (A) 여러분이 아침에 회사에 도착하면 항상 로그인할 것을 기억하세요.
(B) 여러분은 관리자에게 연락함으로써 교육 수업을 등록할 수 있습니다.
(C) 그들을 위해 퇴근할 때 여러분의 컴퓨터를 켜두세요.
(D) 여러분의 비밀번호를 찾는 데 몇 분이 넘게 걸리게 하진 않을 것입니다.

해설 빈칸에 들어갈 알맞은 문장을 고르는 문제이므로 주변 문맥 또는 전체 문맥을 파악한다. 앞 문장 'They[IT staff] will start on Friday after 6 P.M.'에서 IT 직원들이 금요일 오후 6시 이후에 시작할 것이라고 했으므로 빈칸에는 그들을 위해 퇴근할 때 컴퓨터를 켜두라는 내용이 들어가야 함을 알 수 있다. 따라서 (C)가 정답이다.

어휘 session n. 수업 administrator n. 관리자

142 to 부정사를 취하는 형용사

해설 빈칸 앞의 형용사 unable(~할 수 없는)은 to 부정사를 취하는 형용사이므로 to 부정사 (A) to access가 정답이다. 명사 또는 동사 (B), 현재분사 (C), 현재분사를 포함하는 (D)는 to 부정사 자리에 올 수 없다.

어휘 access v. 접근하다

143-146번은 다음 보도 자료에 관한 문제입니다.

리스본(5월 7일)—143Flores 가죽 제품사는 올여름부터 신발과 핸드백을 팔기 시작할 것이다. 50년 된 이 회사는 판매하는 제품 종류를 추가하는 과정에 있다. 이것은 현재 지갑과 벨트만 판매한다. 144그 움직임은 회사가 지난 몇 년 동안 소비자의 취향과 선호도의 변화를 보면서 이루어지고 있다. 145대표이사이자 창립자 Mario Flores는 "지갑과 벨트로 인한 수익이 크게 감소했습니다."라고 설명한다. "만약 저희가 수익성 있어지기를 원한다면 저희는 시장에서 변화에 적응해야 합니다." 146회사는 앞으로 훨씬 더 많은 제품들을 제공하고 싶어 한다. 시곗줄과 배낭은 그 회사가 개발하고 있는 제품들 중 일부이다.

shift n. 변화 taste n. 취향, 기호 preference n. 선호, 애호
revenue n. 수익, 수입 adjust v. 적응하다 profitable adj. 수익성 있는

143 동명사 채우기

해설 동사(begin)의 목적어 자리에는 명사 (A)와 동명사 (D)가 올 수 있다. 명사(shoes and handbags)를 목적어로 취하면서 동사의 목적어 자리에 올 수 있는 동명사 (D) selling이 정답이다. 명사 앞에 다른 명사가 연결이나 전치사 없이 바로 올 수 없으므로 명사 (A)는 답이 될 수 없다.

144 시간 표현과 일치하는 시제의 동사 채우기

해설 현재 완료 시간 표현인 over the last few years가 왔으므로 과거에 시작된 일이 현재까지 계속되는 일을 나타내는 현재 완료 시제 (B) has seen이 정답이다.

145 동사 어휘 고르기 주변 문맥 파악

해설 '지갑과 벨트로 인한 수익이 크게 _____'라는 문맥이므로 (A) enhanced(강화하다), (B) boosted(증가시키다), (D) diminished(감소하다)가 정답의 후보이다. 빈칸이 있는 문장만으로 정답을 고를 수 없으므로 주변 문맥이나 전체 문맥을 파악한다. 뒤 문장에서 '만약 수익성 있어지기를 원한다면 시장에서 변화에 적응해야 한다(We need to adjust to changes in the market if we want to become profitable.)'고 했으므로 지갑과 벨트로 인한 수익이 크게 감소했음을 알 수 있다. 따라서 (D) diminished가 정답이다.

146 알맞은 문장 고르기

해석 (A) 새 지점은 가을의 어느 때쯤에 열릴 것이다.
(B) 사용자들은 온라인 투표에서 그들의 가장 좋아하는 것에 투표했다.
(C) 회사는 앞으로 훨씬 더 많은 제품을 제공하고 싶어 한다.
(D) 구매 증빙이 없는 상품들은 반품 혹은 교환이 되지 않을 수도 있다.

해설 빈칸에 들어갈 알맞은 문장을 고르는 문제이므로 주변 문맥 또는 전체 문맥을 파악한다. 뒤 문장 'Watch straps and backpacks are some of the products that the company is developing.'에서 시곗줄과 배낭은 그 회사가 개발하고 있는 제품들 중 일부라고 했으므로, 빈칸에는 회사가 앞으로 훨씬 더 많은 제품들을 제공하고 싶어 한다는 내용이 들어가야 함을 알 수 있다. 따라서 (C)가 정답이다.

어휘 vote v. 투표하다 poll n. 투표, 여론조사 proof n. 증빙, 증거

PART 7

147-148번은 다음 광고에 관한 문제입니다.

Fleetz Office Warehouse사

Fleetz Office Warehouse사에서, 저희는 모든 예산과 스타일에 적합한 폭넓은 사무용 가구를 취급합니다. 전 세계 최고의 제조업체들에 의해 만들어진 광범위한 제품 라인업에서 선택하세요. 엄청난 절약을 바라시나요? 그렇다면 여러분은 148-B저희의 자체 사무용 가구 브랜드인 EZwerks에 관심이 있을 것인데, 이것은 의자와 책상에서부터 회의 테이블과 서류함에 이르기까지의 모든 것을 포함합니다. 147저희 대표이사가 텔레비전 프로그램에서 브랜드를 소개한 이후로, EZwerks는 샌안토니오 전역의 사업주들에게 인기가 있습니다.

148-A시내에 있는 네 지점들 중 하나에 들러서 Fleetz Office Warehouse사가 왜 품질, 저렴함 및 편의성에 대해 고객들 사이에서 높은 순위를 차지하는지를 알아보세요. 제품의 전체 카탈로그를 위해서는 www.fleetzoffice.com을 방문하세요. 이번 달에만, 148-D여러분이 Fleetz 보상 로열티 프로그램에 회원으로 가입하는 경우 단 한 개 또는 대량 구매에 20퍼센트의 할인을 누려보세요.

a full range of 폭넓은 extensive adj. 광범위한
look for ~을 바라다, 기대하다
rank high among ~ 사이에 높은 지위를 점하다
affordability n. 저렴함, 감당할 수 있는 비용 bulk adj. 대량의

147 육하원칙 문제

문제 무엇이 EZWerks를 사업주들에게 인기 있게 만들었는가?
(A) 고품질의 재료를 사용한다.
(B) 텔레비전 쇼에 출연했다.
(C) 대량 주문에 할인해준다.
(D) 할부로 구매될 수 있다.

해설 무엇(What)이 EZWerks를 사업주들에게 인기 있게 만들었는지를 묻는 육하원칙 문제이다. 질문의 핵심 어구인 EZwerks popular with business owners와 관련하여, 'Ever since our CEO introduced the brand on a television program, EZwerks has been popular with business owners throughout San Antonio.'에서 대표이사가 텔레비전 프로그램에서 브랜드를 소개한 이후로 EZwerks가 샌안토니오 전역의 사업주들에게 인기가 있다고 했으므로 (B)가 정답이다.

어휘 installment n. 할부

148 Not/True 문제

문제 Fleetz Office Warehouse사에 대해 사실이 아닌 것은?
(A) 한 도시에 여러 개의 지점을 가지고 있다.
(B) 자체 브랜드의 제품들을 판매한다.
(C) 매달 새로운 물건들을 받는다.
(D) 회원제 프로그램을 운영한다.

해설 질문의 핵심 어구인 Fleetz Office Warehouse와 관련된 내용을 지문에서 찾아 보기와 대조하는 Not/True 문제이다. (A)는 'Stop by any of our four locations in the city'에서 시내에 있는 네 지점들 중 하나에 들르라고 했으므로 지문의 내용과 일치한다. (B)는 'our own brand of office furniture, EZwerks, which includes everything from chairs and desks to conference tables and filing cabinets'에서 자체 사무용 가구 브랜드인 EZwerks는 의자와 책상에서부터 회의 테이블과 서류함에 이르기까지의 모든 것을 포함한다고 했으므로 지문의 내용과 일치한다. (C)는 지문에 언급되지 않은 내용이다. 따라서 (C)가 정답이다. (D)는 'enjoy a 20 percent discount ~ when you sign up as a member in our Fleetz Rewards loyalty program'에서 Fleetz 보상 로열티 프로그램에 회원으로 가입하는 경우 20퍼센트의 할인을 누려보라고 했으므로 지문의 내용과 일치한다.

어휘 branch n. 지점 operate v. 운영하다

149-150번은 다음 메시지 대화문에 관한 문제입니다.

Petra Bellamy	오후 3시 14분

안녕하세요, Brian. 당신의 회의가 끝났나요? 잘 되었다면 좋겠네요. 저는 당신이 문제에 대해 저를 도와줄 수 있는지 궁금해하고 있었어요. ¹⁴⁹저는 고객을 위해 보고서를 인쇄하려고 애쓰고 있었어요. 하지만, 인쇄기는 제 파일을 계속 거부하네요. 이건 제가 새로운 소프트웨어 프로그램을 사용하고 있기 때문인가요?

Brian Allman	오후 3시 16분

실은, 방금 끝났는데, 잘 되었어요. 물어봐 줘서 고마워요. 당신의 문제에 대해 말하자면, 저는 그것이 소프트웨어라고 생각하지 않아요. 이전에 저에게 이 일이 일어났어요. 당신은 인쇄기에 잉크가 부족한지 확인해야 해요.

Petra Bellamy	오후 3시 20분

제가 인쇄기를 확인해봤는데, 당신이 맞았어요. 안타깝게도, ¹⁵⁰우린 잉크가 다 떨어진 것 같아요. 좀 더 주문해도 되나요?

Brian Allman	오후 3시 21분

¹⁵⁰제가 관리자에게 전화해볼게요. ¹⁵⁰제가 당신에게 다시 연락해서, 당신이 언제 진행할 수 있는지 알려드릴게요. 하지만, 만약 그녀가 바쁘다면, 당신은 내일 아침까지 기다려야 할 수도 있어요.

---

client n. 고객 reject v. 거부하다, 거절하다 as for ~에 대해서 말하자면 get back to ~에게 (나중에) 다시 연락하다 proceed v. 진행하다

149 육하원칙 문제

문제 Ms. Bellamy의 문제는 무엇인가?
(A) 서류를 출력할 수 없다.
(B) 그녀의 제안은 고객에 의해 거절당했다.
(C) 프로그램에 익숙하지 않다.
(D) 그녀의 관리자는 불명확한 지시를 남겼다.

해설 Ms. Bellamy의 문제가 무엇(What)인지를 묻는 육하원칙 문제이다. 질문의 핵심 어구인 Ms. Bellamy's problem과 관련하여, 'I've been trying to print a report for a client. However, the printer keeps rejecting my file.'(3:14 P.M.)에서 Ms. Bellamy가 고객을 위해 보고서를 인쇄하려고 애쓰고 있었지만 인쇄기가 파일을 계속 거부한다고 했으므로 (A)가 정답이다.

패러프레이징
report 보고서 → document 서류

어휘 proposal n. 제안 unclear adj. 불명확한 instruction n. 지시, 명령

150 의도 파악 문제

문제 오후 3시 21분에, Mr. Allman이 "Let me call the manager"라고 썼을 때, 그가 의도한 것 같은 것은?
(A) 제품의 사용 가능 여부가 확인되어야 한다.
(B) 창고 접근은 제한된다.
(C) 공급업체가 메시지에 응답하지 않았다.
(D) 물품을 주문하기 위해서는 승인이 요구된다.

해설 Mr. Allman이 의도한 것 같은 것을 묻는 문제이므로, 질문의 인용어구(Let me call the manager)가 언급된 주변 문맥을 확인한다. 'we seem to be out of ink. Can I order some more?'(3:20 P.M.)에서 Ms. Bellamy가 잉크가 다 떨어진 것 같다며 좀 더 주문해도 되는지 묻자, Mr. Allman이 'Let me call the manager'(제가 관리자에게 전화해볼게요)라고 한 후, 'I'll get back to you, and let you know when you can proceed.'(3:21 P.M.)에서 자신이 Ms. Bellamy에게 다시 연락해서 언제 진행할 수 있는지 알려주겠다고 한 것을 통해, 물품을 주문하기 위해서는 승인이 요구된다는 것을 알 수 있다. 따라서 (D)가 정답이다.

어휘 confirm v. 확인하다 access n. 접근 restrict v. 제한하다 reply v. 응답하다 approval n. 승인

151-152번은 다음 공고에 관한 문제입니다.

Riverbend 아파트 주민들을 위한 공고

저희는 ¹⁵¹Riverbend 아파트가 거주자 주차장에 작업을 진행할 것임을 알려드리게 되어 기쁩니다. ¹⁵¹이는 필수적인 수리를 하는 것, 주차장 지면을 재포장하는 것, 그리고 조명 및 보안 기능 업그레이드하는 것을 포함할 것입니다. ¹⁵²작업은 다음 주 4월 11일에 시작될 것이며 이달 말까지 계속될 것으로 예상됩니다. 모두의 안전을 지키기 위해, 전체 주차장은 작업이 진행되는 동안 폐쇄될 것입니다. ¹⁵²저희는 수리가 완료될 때까지 차량을 가지고 계신 분들은 Center Street 주차장에 주차하는 것을 추천해 드립니다. 저희는 이것이 발생시킬 어떠한 불편함에 대해서라도 사과드립니다. ¹⁵²발생될 수도 있는 요금에 대한 보상으로, Riverbend 아파트는 통상 임대료와 함께 포함되는 50달러의 주차 요금을 다음 달에 면제해 드릴 것입니다. 문의 사항에 대해서는, 555-7731로 건물 관리팀에게 연락해주십시오. 여러분의 인내심과 이해에 감사드립니다.

---

tenant n. 주민, 거주자 conduct v. 진행하다, 수행하다 involve v. 포함하다 repave v. 재포장하다 surface n. 지면, 표면 security n. 보안, 경비 commence v. 시작되다 ensure v. 지키다 compensation n. 보상 incur v. 발생시키다, 처하게 되다 waive v. 면제하다 patience n. 인내심

151 목적 찾기 문제

문제 공고의 목적은 무엇인가?
(A) 공사 작업으로 인해 발생되는 소음에 대해 사과하기 위해
(B) 곧 있을 개량 공사에 대한 정보를 제공하기 위해
(C) 프로젝트에 기금을 기부해 준 주민들에게 감사하기 위해
(D) 인상된 주차장 요금을 주민들에게 알리기 위해

해설 공고의 목적을 묻는 목적 찾기 문제이다. 'Riverbend Apartments will be conducting work on the tenant parking lot. This will involve making necessary repairs, repaving the surface of the lot, and upgrading lighting and security features.'에서 Riverbend 아파트는 거주자 주차장에 작업을 진행할 것이고 이는 필수적인 수리를 하는 것, 주차장 지면을 재포장하는 것, 그리고 조명 및 보안 기능 업그레이드하는 것을 포함할 것이라고 했으므로 (B)가 정답이다.

> 패러프레이징
> making ~ repairs, repaving the surface ~, and upgrading ~ features 수리를 하는 것, 지면을 재포장하는 것, 그리고 기능 업그레이드하는 것
> → improvements 개량 공사

어휘 improvement n. 개량 (공사), 개선 contribute v. 기부하다, 기여하다

152 추론 문제

문제 주민들에 대해 추론될 수 있는 것은?
(A) 우편으로 명세서를 받을 것을 예상해야 한다.
(B) 그들 중 일부는 5월에 평소보다 더 적게 지불할 것이다.
(C) 주차장의 상태에 대해 불평해왔다.
(D) 그들 중 일부는 새로운 주차 허가증을 신청해야 할 것이다.

해설 질문의 핵심 어구인 tenants에 대해 추론하는 문제이다. 'Work will commence next week on April 11 and is expected to last until the end of the month.'에서 작업이 다음 주 4월 11일에 시작될 것이며 이달 말까지 계속될 것으로 예상된다고 했고, 'We recommend that those with vehicles park at the Center Street Parking Garage until the renovations are complete.', 'In compensation for fees that may be incurred, Riverbend Apartments will waive the $50 parking fee that is normally included with the rent for next month.'에서 수리가 완료될 때까지 차량을 가지고 있는 사람들은 Center Street 주차장에 주차하는 것을 추천하며 발생될 수도 있는 요금에 대한 보상으로 통상 임대료와 함께 포함되는 50달러의 주차 요금을 다음 달에 면제해줄 것이라고 했으므로 주민들 중 일부는 5월에 평소보다 더 적게 지불할 것임을 추론할 수 있다. 따라서 (B)가 정답이다.

어휘 statement n. 명세서 condition n. 상태, 환경 permit n. 허가(증)

153-154번은 다음 광고에 관한 문제입니다.

> ### StatBook사
> #### 여러분의 꿈의 프로젝트를 현실로 만드세요
>
> StatBook사는 여러분이 책 프로젝트에 대한 창의적인 아이디어를 현실이 되게 하는 데 도움을 줄 수 있습니다. ¹⁵³⁻ᴰ여러분이 가족 및 친구들과 공유하기 위해 개인화된 사진 책을 인쇄하기를 원하든지 또는 저작물을 출판하여 대중에게 판매하기를 원하든지, StatBook사는 여러분이 저렴한 가격에 목표를 실현하는 것을 도와줄 수 있습니다.
>
> StatBook사는 여러분에게 시작부터 끝까지 여러분의 프로젝트에 대한 온전한 지휘권을 줍니다. 게다가, 저희는 소프트웨어 기반의 편집 도구와 디자인 지원을 제공합니다. 여러분의 책이 인쇄할 준비가 되면, StatBook사는 완성된 작품의 빠른 생산과 배송을 보장합니다. 가격을 확인하거나 사본의 권 수에 따른 견적을 받으려면 저희 웹사이트 www.statbook.com을 방문하십시오.
>
> *¹⁵⁴11월 특별 거래: 최소 2,000권의 사본을 인쇄하면, 추가 비용 ⊙

없이 저희가 제공하는 가장 높은 품질로 종이를 업그레이드해 드립니다.

> reality n. 현실 creative adj. 창의적인, 창조적인
> personalize v. 개인화하다 written work 저작물
> public n. 대중, 일반 사람들 control n. 지휘(권), 통제력
> assistance n. 지원 guarantee v. 보장하다 quote n. 견적
> deal n. 거래 minimum n. 최소 (한도), 최소량

153 Not/True 문제

문제 StatBook사에 대해 언급된 것은?
(A) 오디오북 제작을 전문으로 한다.
(B) 스마트폰을 위한 온라인 애플리케이션을 가지고 있다.
(C) 학생들에게 할인을 제공한다.
(D) 고객들이 자신의 작품을 출판하게 해준다.

해설 질문의 핵심 어구인 StatBook과 관련된 내용을 지문에서 찾아 보기와 대조하는 Not/True 문제이다. (A), (B), (C)는 지문에 언급되지 않은 내용이다. (D)는 'Whether you want to print a personalized photo book to share with family and friends or publish a written work and sell it to the public, StatBook can help you realize your goal ~.'에서 가족 및 친구들과 공유하기 위해 개인화된 사진 책을 인쇄하기를 원하든지 또는 저작물을 출판하여 대중에게 판매하기를 원하든지 StatBook사가 목표를 실현하는 것을 도와줄 수 있다고 했으므로 지문의 내용과 일치한다. 따라서 (D)가 정답이다.

어휘 specialize in ~을 전문으로 하다

154 육하원칙 문제

문제 11월에 무엇이 제공될 것인가?
(A) 회원권 할인
(B) 용지 업그레이드
(C) 무료 연하장 세트
(D) 서비스의 제한된 체험

해설 11월에 무엇(What)이 제공될 것인지를 묻는 육하원칙 문제이다. 질문의 핵심 어구인 November와 관련하여, 'Special November deal: Print a minimum of 2,000 copies, and we will upgrade the paper at no extra charge to the highest quality that we offer.'에서 11월 특별 거래로 최소 2,000권의 사본을 인쇄하면 추가 비용 없이 자신들이 제공하는 가장 높은 품질로 종이를 업그레이드해준다고 했으므로 (B)가 정답이다.

어휘 holiday card 연하장, 홀리데이 카드 trial n. 체험, 실험

155-157번은 다음 양식에 관한 문제입니다.

> #### MIDDLETON 은행 전자 송금 요청 양식
> ¹⁵⁶⁻ᴮ전자 송금 마감 시간은 오후 3시임을 유의해 주세요.

¹⁵⁶⁻ᴬ고객 정보	
¹⁵⁵고객 이름	Antoine Ducharme
계좌 번호	118825622042
¹⁵⁶⁻ᴬ주소	1432번지 Phare 거리, 퀘벡, 캐나다

전자 송금 정보			
금액	3,800 미국 달러	일자	7월 7일

¹⁵⁵전자 송금 목적: 그림 구매 대금을 지불하기 위해
*¹⁵⁶⁻ᴬ수취인은 금액을 현지 통화로 받을 것입니다.

¹⁵⁶⁻ᴬ수취인 정보	
¹⁵⁵/¹⁵⁷⁻ᴰ수취인 이름	Salles 미술관
¹⁵⁷⁻ᴰ은행 및 계좌 번호	Carrousel 신용 조합 — 227722662243
¹⁵⁶⁻ᴬ주소	8번지 Moulinet 거리, 파리, 프랑스

⊙

155 추론 문제

문제   Salles 미술관에 대해 암시되는 것은?
(A) 이체 수수료를 부담할 것이다.
(B) 캐나다에 지점을 열었다.
(C) Mr. Ducharme에게 그림을 팔았다.
(D) 프랑스로 예술 작품을 배송할 것이다.

해설   질문의 핵심 어구인 Salles Gallery에 대해 추론하는 문제이다. 'Customer Name, Antoine Ducharme', 'Purpose of Wire Transfer: To pay for the purchase of a painting', 'Beneficiary Name, Salles Gallery'에서 Mr. Ducharme이 그림 구매 대금을 지불하기 위해 Salles 미술관에 전자 송금을 요청했으므로 Salles 미술관이 Mr. Ducharme에게 그림을 팔았다는 것을 추론할 수 있다. 따라서 (C)가 정답이다.

어휘   **cover** v. 부담하다, 담당하다   **artwork** n. 예술 작품, 미술품

156 Not/True 문제

문제   Mr. Ducharme의 거래에 대해 사실인 것은?
(A) 통화의 변경을 필요로 할 것이다.
(B) 다음날 완료될 것이다.
(C) 매달 반복될 것이다.
(D) 관리자의 서명이 필요할 것이다.

해설   질문의 핵심 어구인 Mr. Ducharme's transaction과 관련된 내용을 지문에서 찾아 보기와 대조하는 Not/True 문제이다. (A)는 'Customer Information'과 'Address, 1432 Rue de Phare, Quebec, Canada'에서 고객의 주소가 캐나다 퀘벡이고, 'The beneficiary will receive the amount in their local currency.'에서 수취인은 금액을 현지 통화로 받을 것이라고 했고, 'Beneficiary Information', 'Address, 8 Rue de Moulinet, Paris, France'에서 수취인의 주소가 프랑스 파리이므로 지문의 내용과 일치한다. 따라서 (A)가 정답이다. (B)는 'the wire transfer cutoff time is 3:00 P.M.'에서 전자 송금 마감 시간이 오후 3시라고 했으나 고객이 송금을 요청한 시간은 알 수 없으므로 지문의 내용과 일치하지 않는다. (C)와 (D)는 지문에 언급되지 않은 내용이다.

157 Not/True 문제

문제   Mr. Ducharme에 대해 언급된 것은?
(A) 최근에 파리에서의 행사에 참석했다.
(B) 사업체를 대표해서 돈을 보냈다.
(C) Middleton 은행의 VIP 고객이다.
(D) Carrousel 신용 조합에 계좌를 가지고 있다.

해설   질문의 핵심 어구인 Mr. Ducharme과 관련된 내용을 지문에서 찾아 보기와 대조하는 Not/True 문제이다. (A)와 (B)는 지문에 언급되지 않은 내용이다. (C)는 '_ X _ Waived*'와 '*Wire fees are waived for

VIP customers.'에서 VIP 고객들에게는 송금 수수료가 면제된다고 했는데 Mr. Ducharme에게 송금 수수료가 면제되었으므로 지문의 내용과 일치한다. 따라서 (C)가 정답이다. (D)는 'Beneficiary Name, Salles Gallery', 'Bank and Account Number, Carrousel Credit Union — 227722662243'에서 Carrousel 신용 조합에 계좌를 가지고 있는 것은 Salles 미술관이므로 지문의 내용과 일치하지 않는다.

어휘   **on behalf of** ~을 대표하여

158-160번은 다음 이메일에 관한 문제입니다.

position n. 직책, 직위   **organization** n. 조직   **open** adj. 공석인
permission n. 허락, 승인   **further** adj. 추가적인
consideration n. 고려, 숙고   **room** n. 여지
advancement n. 승진, 발전   **benefits package** 복리 후생 제도

158 Not/True 문제

문제   Mr. Contos에 대해 사실인 것은?
(A) 이전에 GlobeTrek Technology사에서 일했다.
(B) 경영학에 고급 학위가 있다.
(C) 기술 분야에 경력이 없다.
(D) 최근에 부서장에 지원했다.

해설   질문의 핵심 어구인 Mr. Contos와 관련된 내용을 지문에서 찾아 보기와 대조하는 Not/True 문제이다. (A), (B), (C)는 지문에 언급되지 않은 내용이다. (D)는 'Dear Mr. Contos'와 'We received your application for the position of head of creative design at GlobeTrek Technology.'에서 GlobeTrek Technology사의 창의적인 디자인 부장 직책에 대한 Mr. Contos의 지원서를 받았다고 했으므로 지문의 내용과 일치한다. 따라서 (D)가 정답이다.

어휘   **advanced degree** (학사 위의) 고급 학위

159 육하원칙 문제

문제   웹사이트에서 찾을 수 있는 정보는 무엇인가?
(A) 공석 목록
(B) 면접 일정

(C) 회사 시설 지도
(D) 팀원의 이메일 주소

해설 웹사이트에서 찾을 수 있는 정보가 무엇(What)인지를 묻는 육하원칙 문제이다. 질문의 핵심 어구인 Web site와 관련하여, 'Please visit the GlobeTrek Technology employee application portal for further information on the available positions.'에서 채용 가능한 직책에 대한 추가 정보를 위해 GlobeTrek Technology사의 직원 지원 포털 사이트를 방문하라고 했으므로 (A)가 정답이다.

패러프레이징
Web site 웹사이트 → portal 포털 사이트
information on the available positions 채용 가능한 직책에 대한 정보 → A list of openings 공석 목록

어휘 opening n. 공석, 빈자리

160 문장 위치 찾기 문제

문제 [1], [2], [3], [4]로 표시된 위치 중, 다음 문장이 들어갈 곳으로 가장 적절한 것은?

"저희는 매년 종합적인 건강 관리와 3주간의 유급 휴가를 제공합니다."

(A) [1]
(B) [2]
(C) [3]
(D) [4]

해설 지문의 흐름상 주어진 문장이 들어가기에 가장 적절한 곳을 고르는 문제이다. We provide comprehensive health care and three weeks of paid vacation each year에서 매년 종합적인 건강 관리와 3주간의 유급 휴가를 제공한다고 했으므로, 주어진 문장 앞에 복지 제도와 관련된 내용이 있을 것임을 예상할 수 있다. [4] 의 앞 문장인 'GlobeTrek Technology provides a generous benefits package to all full-time employees'에서 GlobeTrek Technology사는 모든 정규직 직원들에게 후한 복리 후생 제도를 제공한다고 했으므로, [4]에 주어진 문장이 들어가면 후한 복리 후생 제도인 종합적인 건강 관리와 3주간의 유급 휴가를 매년 제공한다는 내용을 설명하는 자연스러운 문맥이 된다는 것을 알 수 있다. 따라서 (D)가 정답이다.

어휘 comprehensive adj. 종합적인

161-163번은 다음 웹페이지에 관한 문제입니다.

Hartwell 카페

| 홈 | 자리 예약하기 | 메뉴 보기 | 문의 |

Sheffield 지역에서 신선하고, 건강한 음식을 찾고 계신가요? Hartwell 카페만 보세요! 저희는 3개월 전에 문을 열었고 Sheffield의 최신 유기농 음식점이 된 것을 자랑스러워합니다!

161-D저희의 모든 음식은 농장 직송이며 인공 방부제, 염료, 향료가 없습니다. 저희는 모두 천연 원료만으로 만든 재료만 사용합니다! 다양한 채식주의자 선택지와 유제품이 함유되지 않은, 견과류가 없는, 콩이 없는 요리 중에서 선택하세요. 161-B만약 여러분이 특별한 식이요법의 요구가 있다면, 저희에게 연락하시면 기꺼이 도와드리겠습니다. 특별한 요청사항을 가지고 저희 직원에게 연락을 취하려면, 162그저 여기 온라인 연락 양식을 이용하시면 됩니다.

163저희는 또한 계속 진행 중인 판촉 활동이 있습니다. 식당에서의 본인 사진을 저희의 소셜 미디어 페이지에 올려서 여러분의 다음 식사에 무료 수프나 샐러드를 받아보세요.

---

organic adj. 유기농의 farm-fresh adj. 농장 직송인, 산지 직송인
artificial adj. 인공적인 preservative n. 방부제 dye n. 염료
flavoring n. 향료 all-natural adj. 천연 원료만으로 만든
dietary adj. 식이요법의 oblige v. 돕다, (도움 등을) 베풀다
reach out 연락을 취하다 ongoing adj. 계속 진행 중인

161 Not/True 문제

문제 Hartwell 카페에 대해 언급된 것은?

(A) 다른 이름으로 알려져 있곤 했다.
(B) 맞춤 식사를 제공하지 않는다.
(C) 최근에 또 다른 지점을 열었다.
(D) 음식에 인공 염료를 사용하지 않는다.

해설 질문의 핵심 어구인 Hartwell Café와 관련된 내용을 지문에서 찾아 보기와 대조하는 Not/True 문제이다. (A)는 지문에 언급되지 않은 내용이다. (B)는 'If you have special dietary needs, contact us and we will be happy to oblige.'에서 특별한 식이요법의 요구가 있다면 연락하면 기꺼이 도와주겠다고 했으므로 지문의 내용과 일치하지 않는다. (C)는 지문에 언급되지 않은 내용이다. (D)는 'All of our food is farm-fresh and free of artificial preservatives, dyes, and flavorings.'에서 모든 음식은 농장 직송이며 인공 방부제, 염료, 향료가 없다고 했으므로 지문의 내용과 일치한다. 따라서 (D)가 정답이다.

어휘 custom adj. 맞춤의

162 동의어 찾기 문제

문제 2문단 네 번째 줄의 단어 "just"는 의미상 –와 가장 가깝다.

(A) 꽤
(B) 신중하게
(C) 그저
(D) 정확하게

해설 just를 포함한 구절 'just use the online contact form here'에서 just는 '그저'라는 뜻으로 사용되었다. 따라서 (C)가 정답이다.

163 육하원칙 문제

문제 고객들이 판촉 활동에 참여한다면 무엇을 받을 것인가?

(A) 곁들임 요리 선택
(B) 무료 음료
(C) 주요리에 대한 할인
(D) 나중의 사용을 위한 상품권

해설 고객들이 판촉 활동에 참여한다면 무엇(What)을 받을 것인지를 묻는 육하원칙 문제이다. 질문의 핵심 어구인 participate in a promotion과 관련하여, 'We also have an ongoing promotion. Post a photo of yourself at the restaurant on our social media page and receive a free soup or salad with your next meal.'에서 계속 진행 중인 판촉 활동으로 식당에서의 자신의 사진을 소셜 미디어 페이지에 올려서 다음 식사에 무료 수프나 샐러드를 받아보라고 했으므로 (A)가 정답이다.

패러프레이징
a free soup or salad 무료 수프나 샐러드 → side dish 곁들임 요리

어휘 side dish 곁들임 요리 complimentary adj. 무료의
entrée n. 주요리

164-167번은 다음 이메일에 관한 문제입니다.

수신: Eliza Kemper <e.kemper@usgrandtours.us>
발신: David Sims <david.sims@bridgeporttravelexpo.com>
제목: 박람회
날짜: 8월 1일

Ms. Kemper께,

9월 1일과 2일에 있는 164Bridgeport 여행 박람회에 판매자로서 참여하기 위해 164/166-B제출하신 보증금 300달러를 받았음을 확인해 드리고자 이메일을 씁니다. 지연에 대해 사과드립니다. 165저희가 기록적인 수의 지원자들을 유치해서, 모두에게 연락하는 것이 평소보다 더 오래 걸렸습니다. 귀하의 여행사는 올해 라인업에 큰 보탬이 될 것입니다.

166-C보증금은 부주의의 결과로 행사 장소에서 발생할 수 있는 모든 손해를 부담할 것입니다. 어떠한 수리 또는 청소 비용이라도 그것에서 공제될 것입니다. 그렇지 않으면, 166-D이것은 행사 종료일로부터 영업일 기준 5일 이내에 반환될 것입니다. 166-B부스 대여에 대한 대금 1,200달러 지불은 8월 28일에 해야 합니다.

다음 요건에 유의하시기 바랍니다:
· 167-C똑같은 외부 간판이 각 부스에 제공될 것인데, 판매자들은 부스 자체의 내부에 다른 간판을 진열할 수 있습니다.
· 167-B모든 판매용 품목이나 서비스는 주최 측에 의해 사전 승인을 받아야 합니다. 음식이나 음료는 판매가 허가되지 않습니다.
· 167-D개인 소지품을 방치된 채로 두지 마십시오. 여러분은 이러한 물품들을 할당된 보관함에 두어야 합니다.
· 167-A판매자들은 부스 내부와 주변을 청소할 책임이 있습니다.

여러분이 질문이 있거나 제출할 추가 자료가 있으시다면, 저에게 직접 이메일을 보내주시기 바랍니다.

David Sims 드림
행사 책임자
Bridgeport 여행 박람회

---

confirm v. 확인하다 deposit n. 보증금 vendor n. 판매자
addition n. 보탬, 보태는 것 cover v. 부담하다, 담당하다
negligence n. 부주의, 태만 deduct v. 공제하다
due adj. (돈을) 지불해야 하는 requirement n. 요건, 필요 조건
uniform adj. 똑같은, 동일한 exterior adj. 외부의 sign n. 간판
organizer n. 주최자 belonging n. 소지품
unattended adj. 방치된, 내버려 둔 assigned adj. 할당된
coordinator n. (기획·진행 따위의) 책임자

164 목적 찾기 문제

문제 이메일의 목적은 무엇인가?
(A) 주최자들에게 후원 제안을 알리기 위해
(B) 행사에 참가를 확인하기 위해
(C) 보증금의 지불을 요청하기 위해
(D) 홍보 기회를 광고하기 위해

해설 이메일의 목적을 묻는 목적 찾기 문제이므로 지문의 앞부분을 주의 깊게 확인한다. 'I'm writing to confirm that we received the $300 deposit you submitted to participate as a vendor at the Bridgeport Travel Expo'에서 Bridgeport 여행 박람회에 판매자로서 참여하기 위해 제출한 보증금 300달러를 받았음을 확인해주기 위해 이메일을 쓴다고 했으므로 (B)가 정답이다.

어휘 sponsorship n. 후원, 지원 affirm v. 확인하다

165 추론 문제

문제 박람회에 대해 암시되는 것은?
(A) 지원자의 수가 사상 최고치에 이르렀다.
(B) 박람회는 3일 연장되었다.
(C) 판매자들은 서로 다른 산업들을 대표한다.
(D) 행사 장소가 더 큰 장소로 옮겨졌다.

해설 질문의 핵심 어구인 expo에 대해 추론하는 문제이다. 'We [Bridgeport Travel Expo] attracted a record number of applicants, so contacting everyone took longer than normal.'에서 Bridgeport 여행 박람회가 기록적인 수의 지원자들을 유치해서 모두에게 연락하는 것이 평소보다 더 오래 걸렸다고 했으므로 (A)가 정답이다.

어휘 represent v. 대표하다, 나타내다

166 Not/True 문제

문제 보증금에 대해 언급된 것은?
(A) 9월 1일에 지불되어야 한다.

(B) 부스 임대료의 절반 가격이다.
(C) 손해를 배상하는 데 쓰일 수 있다.
(D) 행사의 마지막 날에 반환될 것이다.

해설 질문의 핵심 어구인 deposit과 관련된 내용을 지문에서 찾아 보기와 대조하는 Not/True 문제이다. (A)는 지문에 언급되지 않은 내용이다. (B)는 'we received the $300 deposit you submitted'와 'The payment of $1,200 for the booth rental is due on August 28.'에서 보증금은 부스 임대료의 1/4 가격이므로 지문의 내용과 일치하지 않는다. (C)는 'The deposit will cover any damage that may occur at the venue as a result of negligence.'에서 보증금은 부주의의 결과로 행사 장소에서 발생할 수 있는 모든 손해를 부담할 것이라고 했으므로 지문의 내용과 일치한다. 따라서 (C)가 정답이다. (D)는 'it[deposit] will be returned within five business days of the end of the event'에서 보증금은 행사 종료일로부터 영업일 기준 5일 이내에 반환될 것이라고 했으므로 지문의 내용과 일치하지 않는다.

패러프레이징
cover ~ damage 손해를 부담하다 → pay for damage 손해를 배상하다

어휘 pay for ~을 배상하다

167 Not/True 문제

문제 Ms. Kemper가 하도록 요구되는 것이 아닌 것은?
(A) 그녀의 구역의 청결함을 유지한다.
(B) 판매 품목에 대한 승인을 받는다.
(C) 외부 부스 간판의 디자인을 만든다.
(D) 개인 물품을 보관함에 넣는다.

해설 질문의 핵심 어구인 Ms. Kemper ~ required to do와 관련된 내용을 지문에서 찾아 보기와 대조하는 Not/True 문제이다. (A)는 'Vendors are responsible for cleaning inside and around the booth.'에서 판매자들은 부스 내부와 주변을 청소할 책임이 있다고 했으므로 지문의 내용과 일치한다. (B)는 'Every item or service for sale must be preapproved by the organizers.'에서 모든 판매용 품목이나 서비스는 주최 측에 의해 사전 승인을 받아야 한다고 했으므로 지문의 내용과 일치한다. (C)는 'Uniform exterior signs will be provided for each booth'에서 똑같은 외부 간판이 각 부스에 제공될 것이라고 했으므로 지문의 내용과 일치하지 않는다. 따라서 (C)가 정답이다. (D)는 'Never leave personal belongings unattended. You must leave these items in your assigned storage lockers.'에서 개인 소지품을 방치된 채로 두지 말고 물품들을 할당된 보관함에 두어야 한다고 했으므로 지문의 내용과 일치한다.

패러프레이징
leave ~ items in ~ lockers 물품들을 보관함에 두다 → Place ~ items in a locker 물품을 보관함에 넣다

어휘 obtain v. 받다, 얻다

168-171번은 다음 기사에 관한 문제입니다.

플라스틱 없는 미래를 구상하는 Keptics

2월 8일—168시애틀에 본사를 둔 글로벌 소비재 기업 Keptics는 친환경 청소 제품의 새로운 라인을 위해 시장을 평가하는 시범 프로그램의 시작을 발표했다. — [1] —. 제품들은 플라스틱 폐기물과 오염을 줄이기 위해 설계된 지속 가능한 포장재를 사용할 것이다. 3개월간의 프로그램은 3월 1일 시애틀에서 시작될 것이다.

참여하려면, 고객들은 온라인에서 Keptics Up 프로그램에 등록해야 한다. — [2] —. 169참가자들은 바꾸어 채워 넣을 수 있는 용기에 포장된 가정용 청소 제품 견본품들을 포함하는 수송품을 Keptics로부터 받을 것이다. 일단 용기의 내용물이 모두 소비되면, 171고객들은 Keptics에서 리필을 주문하거나 직접 리필하기 위해 여러 곳의 예정된 장소들 중 하나를 방문하면 된다. — [3] —.

Keptics 대표이사 Fiona Simpleton에 따르면, ¹⁷⁰그 프로그램은 회사가 비용을 주의 깊게 관찰할 수 있도록 시애틀에 한정될 것이다. — [4] —. 그러나, 만약 이것이 성공한다면, 내년 초에는 미국 전역의 다른 도시들에도 도입될 수 있다.

envision v. 구상하다, 상상하다 pilot program 시범 프로그램
evaluate v. 평가하다 sustainable adj. 지속 가능한
shipment n. 수송품 refillable adj. 바꾸어 채워 넣을 수 있는
container n. 용기 consume v. 소비하다, 다 써버리다
keep a close watch on ~을 주의 깊게 관찰하다

168 육하원칙 문제

문제 Keptics는 무엇을 할 계획인가?
(A) 새로운 제품 라인을 시험한다.
(B) 환경 단체를 설립한다.
(C) 브랜드 디자인을 업데이트한다.
(D) 보상 프로그램을 도입한다.

해설 Keptics가 무엇을(What) 할 계획인지를 묻는 육하원칙 문제이므로 질문의 핵심 어구인 Keptics planning to do와 관련하여, 'Keptics ~ has just announced the launch of a pilot program to evaluate the market for a new line of eco-friendly cleaning products.'에서 Keptics가 친환경 청소 제품의 새로운 라인을 위해 시장을 평가하는 시범 프로그램의 시작을 발표했다고 했으므로 (A)가 정답이다.

패러프레이징
evaluate the market for a new line of ~ products 제품의 새로운 라인을 위해 시장을 평가하다 → Test a new product line 새로운 제품 라인을 시험하다

어휘 start v. 설립하다, 시작하다

169 육하원칙 문제

문제 일부 Keptics 고객들은 무엇을 받을 것인가?
(A) 행사 초대장
(B) 온라인 소책자
(C) 견본품들
(D) 정기적인 수거 서비스

해설 일부 Keptics 고객들이 무엇을(What) 받을 것인지를 묻는 육하원칙 문제이므로 질문의 핵심 어구인 some Keptics customers receive와 관련하여, 'Participants will receive a shipment from Keptics that includes samples of its home cleaning products'에서 참가자들은 가정용 청소 제품 견본품들을 포함하는 수송품을 Keptics로부터 받을 것이라고 했으므로 (C)가 정답이다.

어휘 pickup n. 수거, 물건을 찾으러 감

170 육하원칙 문제

문제 Keptics는 왜 시애틀에서만 프로그램을 시작하고 있는가?
(A) 다른 도시들로부터 허가를 받아야 한다.
(B) 관련 비용을 관찰하기를 원한다.
(C) 원산지에서만 발견되는 재료들을 사용하고 있다.
(D) 다른 회사들과의 경쟁을 피하려고 하고 있다.

해설 Keptics가 왜(Why) 시애틀에서만 프로그램을 시작하고 있는지를 묻는 육하원칙 문제이므로 질문의 핵심 어구인 Keptics only launching a program in Seattle과 관련하여, 'the program will be limited to Seattle so that the company can keep a close watch on costs'에서 그 프로그램은 회사가 비용을 주의 깊게 관찰할 수 있도록 시애틀에 한정될 것이라고 했으므로 (B)가 정답이다.

패러프레이징
is ~ only launching a program in Seattle 시애틀에서만 프로그램을 시작하고 있다 → the program will be limited to Seattle 그 프로그램은 시애틀에 한정될 것이다

keep a close watch on costs 비용을 주의 깊게 관찰하다 → monitor ~ costs 비용을 관찰하다

어휘 permission n. 허가 monitor v. 관찰하다, 감시하다
associated adj. 관련된 locally adv. 원산지에서

171 문장 위치 찾기 문제

문제 [1], [2], [3], [4]로 표시된 위치 중, 다음 문장이 들어갈 곳으로 가장 적절한 것은?

"이 장소들은 다가오는 몇 주 내에 발표될 것이다."

(A) [1]
(B) [2]
(C) [3]
(D) [4]

해설 지문의 흐름상 주어진 문장이 들어가기에 가장 적절한 곳을 고르는 문제이다. These locations will be announced in the coming weeks에서 이 장소들은 다가오는 몇 주 내에 발표될 것이라고 했으므로, 주어진 문장 앞에 장소에 관한 내용이 있을 것임을 예상할 수 있다. [3]의 앞 문장인 'customers can order a refill from Keptics or visit one of several planned locations to refill it themselves'에서 고객들은 Keptics에서 리필을 주문하거나 직접 리필하기 위해 여러 곳의 예정된 장소들 중 하나를 방문하면 된다고 했으므로, [3]에 주어진 문장이 들어가면 여러 곳의 예정된 장소들이 몇 주 내에 발표될 것이라는 자연스러운 문맥이 된다는 것을 알 수 있다. 따라서 (C)가 정답이다.

어휘 coming adj. 다가오는

172-175번은 다음 온라인 채팅 대화문에 관한 문제입니다.

Jang-mi Bae [오후 2시 9분]
새로운 사무실 장소와 관련된 어떤 소식이라도 있나요? 만약 우리가 무언가를 찾지 못한다면 우리는 다음 달에 이곳의 임대 계약을 연장해야 해요.

Paul Knox [오후 2시 11분]
제가 어제 완벽하게 어울릴 것 같은 곳을 하나 봤어요. 그것은 Janus 타워라고 불리는 건물에 있어요.

Edward Watts [오후 2시 12분]
생활 편의 시설은 어때요? ^{172-A}체육관이 있나요? 지정된 주차장은요?

Paul Knox [오후 2시 15분]
^{172-A}그러한 것들은 있고 그 이상도 있어요. 이것은 또한 아주 새로운 냉난방 시스템을 갖추고 있어서, 우리에게 개조 비용을 절약하게 할 거예요. ¹⁷³가능성 있는 유일한 문제는 이것은 한 달에 6,500달러로 우리의 예산보다 높다는 거예요. 지금 지불하는 것보다 700달러 더 많아요.

Barbara Thompkins [오후 2시 16분]
¹⁷³우리는 좋은 한 해를 보냈죠. 만약 공공요금이 포함되어 있고 우리가 필요한 모든 것이 있다면, 저는 우리가 그것을 반드시 고려해야 한다고 생각해요.

Jang-mi Bae [오후 2시 16분]
일리가 있네요. ¹⁷³그래도, 저는 그것을 보고 싶어요. 방문 일정을 잡을 수 있을까요, Paul? ¹⁷⁴저는 금요일에 한가해요.

Paul Knox [오후 2시 18분]
물론이죠. 전화번호를 위해 제가 부동산 중개소의 모바일 앱을 확인해 볼게요.

Paul Knox [오후 2시 20분]
좋아요. ¹⁷⁴제가 부동산 중개인에게 전화했더니 그녀는 금요일 오전 11시에 우리를 만날 수 있다고 확인해 줬어요. 우리 모두 제 차를 타고 Janus 타워로 함께 가면 되겠어요.

Edward Watts [오후 2시 21분]

좋네요. ¹⁷⁴저도 그 시간에 가능해요.

Barbara Thompkins [오후 2시 21분]

¹⁷⁴저는 고객을 방문하느라 하루 종일 외출할 거예요.

Paul Knox [오후 2시 24분]

¹⁷⁵당신은 모바일 애플리케이션을 통해 사무실을 영상으로 볼 수도 있어요. 올 수 없는 사람은 대신에 그렇게 하면 되겠어요.

---

regarding prep. ~에 관련된, ~에 관하여 extend v. 연장하다
lease n. 임대 계약 amenity n. 생활 편의 시설
assign v. 지정하다, 할당하다 brand-new adj. 아주 새로운
definitely adv. 반드시 real estate agency 부동산 중개소
realtor n. 부동산 중개인

172 Not/True 문제

문제 Janus 타워에 대해 사실인 것은?

(A) 운동 시설을 포함한다.
(B) 저렴한 가구를 포함한다.
(C) 대중교통 근처에 위치해 있다.
(D) 시에 의해 소유되어 있다.

해설 질문의 핵심 어구인 Janus Tower와 관련된 내용을 지문에서 찾아 보기와 대조하는 Not/True 문제이다. (A)는 'Does it[Janus Tower] have a gym?'(2:12 P.M.)에서 Mr. Watts가 Janus 타워에 체육관이 있는지 묻자, 'It has those things and more.'(2:15 P.M.)에서 Mr. Knox가 그러한 것들이 있고 그 이상도 있다고 했으므로 지문의 내용과 일치한다. 따라서 (A)가 정답이다. (B), (C), (D)는 지문에 언급되지 않은 내용이다.

패러프레이징
gym 체육관 → workout facility 운동 시설

173 의도 파악 문제

문제 오후 2시 16분에, Ms. Bae가 "Valid point"라고 썼을 때, 그녀가 의도한 것 같은 것은?

(A) 회사가 더 높은 예산을 조달할 수 있다는 것에 동의한다.
(B) 단체가 잠재적인 문제를 고려해야 한다고 생각한다.
(C) 다른 직원들이 결정에 대해 협의되어야 한다고 느낀다.
(D) 부동산 중개인에게 도움을 요청하는 것이 현명하다고 생각한다.

해설 Ms. Bae가 의도한 것 같은 것을 묻는 문제이므로, 질문의 인용어구(Valid point)가 언급된 주변 문맥을 확인한다. 'The only potential issue is that it's above our budget at $6,500 a month.'(2:15 P.M.)에서 Mr. Knox가 가능성 있는 유일한 문제는 한 달에 6,500달러로 자신들의 예산보다 높다는 것이라고 했고, 'We've had a good year. If utilities are included and it has everything we need, I say we should definitely consider it.'(2:16 P.M.)에서 Ms. Thompkins가 좋은 한 해를 보냈다며 공공요금이 포함되어 있고 필요한 모든 것이 있다면 그것을 반드시 고려해야 한다고 생각한다고 하자, Ms. Bae가 'Valid point.'(일리가 있네요)라고 한 후, 'Still, I'd like to see it.'(2:16 P.M.)에서 그것을 보고 싶다고 한 것을 통해 Ms. Bae는 회사가 더 높은 예산을 조달할 수 있다는 것에 동의한다는 것을 알 수 있다. 따라서 (A)가 정답이다.

어휘 accommodate v. 조달하다, 수용하다 consult v. 협의하다, 상담하다

174 육하원칙 문제

문제 금요일에 얼마나 많은 사람들이 부동산 중개인과 동행할 것인가?

(A) 1
(B) 2
(C) 3
(D) 4

해설 금요일에 얼마나 많은(How many) 사람들이 부동산 중개인과

동행할 것인지를 묻는 육하원칙 문제이다. 질문의 핵심 어구인 accompanying the realtor on Friday와 관련하여, 'I'm free on Friday.'(2:16 P.M.)에서 Ms. Bae가 금요일에 한가하다고 했고, 'I called the realtor and she confirmed she can meet us on Friday at 11 A.M. We can all go to Janus Tower together in my car.'(2:20 P.M.)에서 Mr. Knox가 부동산 중개인에게 전화했더니 금요일 오전 11시에 만날 수 있다고 확인해 줬다며 모두 자신의 차를 타고 Janus 타워로 함께 가면 되겠다고 하자, 'I'm available at that time, too.'(2:21 P.M.)에서 Mr. Watts가 자신도 그 시간에 가능하다고 했다. 반면, 'I'm going to be out all day visiting a client.'(2:21 P.M.)에서 Ms. Thompkins가 고객을 방문하느라 하루 종일 외출할 것이라고 했으므로 Ms. Thompkins를 제외한 Ms. Bae, Mr. Knox, Mr. Watts 총 세 명이 금요일에 부동산 중개인과 동행할 것임을 알 수 있다. 따라서 (C)가 정답이다.

어휘 accompany v. 동행하다, 수반하다

175 육하원칙 문제

문제 온라인 채팅 대화문에 따르면, 사람들은 모바일 애플리케이션에서 무엇을 할 수 있는가?

(A) 건물로 가는 길을 찾는다.
(B) 사무실 공간을 찍은 영상을 본다.
(C) 가격 범위 내에서 대안을 찾는다.
(D) 장소 방문 일정을 잡는다.

해설 사람들이 모바일 애플리케이션에서 무엇을(what) 할 수 있는지를 묻는 육하원칙 문제이다. 질문의 핵심 어구인 mobile application과 관련하여, 'You can also see the office on video through the mobile application.'(2:24 P.M.)에서 Mr. Knox가 모바일 애플리케이션을 통해 사무실을 영상으로 볼 수도 있다고 했으므로 (B)가 정답이다.

어휘 alternative n. 대안, 대체재 range n. 범위

176-180번은 다음 광고와 온라인 후기에 관한 문제입니다.

Surf Shack으로 오세요

말리부 해변에 위치한, Surf Shack은 오셔서 바다의 멋진 전망을 즐길 수 있도록 여행객들과 현지인들을 모두 초대합니다. 몇몇 친구들을 위한 서핑하는 사람들의 천국으로 시작했던 것이 서핑 학교, 장비 상점, 그리고 식당으로 발전했습니다. ¹⁷⁶Surf Shack은 여러분이 일몰을 즐기며 파도 소리를 듣는 동안 훌륭한 요리와 음료를 제공합니다. 이것은 놓쳐서는 안 될 정말 특별한 경험입니다. 이것이 ^{177-B}라디오 방송국 말리부 102.5가 저희를 이 지역의 최고의 명소로 지정한 이유입니다.

Surf Shack은 장기적으로 공급되어온 재료들로 매일 신선한 스무디를 제공하는 전통을 가지고 있습니다. 저희는 현재 다음 조합으로 원 플러스 원 특별 메뉴를 운영하고 있습니다.

· ¹⁷⁹월요일 & 화요일: 바나나와 딸기
· 수요일 & 목요일: 파인애플과 코코넛
· 금요일 & 토요일: 사과와 배
· 일요일: 열대 지방 혼합 음료

¹⁷⁸오늘 555-9691로 전화하셔서 해변가 테이블을 예약하세요.

---

alike adv. 모두 spectacular adj. 멋진 paradise n. 천국, 낙원
sunset n. 일몰 truly adv. 정말, 참으로 name v. 지정하다, 임명하다
attraction n. 명소, 관광지 sustainably adv. 장기적으로, 지속 가능하게
source v. 공급하다, 제공하다
two-for-one 원 플러스 원(하나를 사면 하나를 더 주는 판매 방식)

Surf Shack

소개	식당	서핑	쇼핑	지점	후기

이름: Katerina Stokov
평점: 2/5

저는 최근 휴가에 로스앤젤레스를 방문했을 때 Surf Shack에 갔습니다. 저는 이전에 그곳에 한 번도 가본 적이 없는 몇몇의 현지 친구들과 함께 방문했습니다. 저희는 그 장소가 관광객들에게 잘 알려져 있다고 생각하지 않았기 때문에, 아름다운 해변가에서 비교적 조용한 오후를 즐길 것을 기대했습니다. [179]저희는 심지어 그들이 아마 가장 덜 바쁠 것 같은 화요일에 가기로 정했습니다.

저희가 도착했을 때, 그 장소가 관광객들로 붐비는 것을 알고 충격받았습니다. 저희가 해변가 테이블을 예약을 하지 않았던 것을 고려하면 운좋게도 식당에서 그것을 잡았습니다. [179]저는 특별 메뉴였던 스무디를 주문했고, 그것은 맛있었습니다. 그래도, 서비스가 느렸고, 테이블들이 정말 깨끗하지는 않았습니다. 전반적으로, [180]특히 인파로 인해, 제 경험은 그다지 좋지 않았고, 저는 누구에게도 그 장소를 추천할 수 없습니다.

look forward to ~을 기대하다   **relatively** adv. 비교적, 상대적으로
supposedly adv. 아마   **overall** adv. 전반적으로

176 동의어 찾기 문제

문제 광고에서, 1 문단의 세 번째 줄의 단어 "serves"는 의미상 –와 가장 가깝다.
(A) 시험하다
(B) 수행하다
(C) 제공하다
(D) 받아들이다

해설 광고의 serves를 포함한 문장 'Surf Shack serves excellent cuisine and drinks while you enjoy the sunset and listen to the waves.'에서 serves는 '제공하다'라는 뜻으로 사용되었다. 따라서 (C)가 정답이다.

177 Not/True 문제

문제 Surf Shack에 대해 언급된 것은?
(A) 지역 스포츠 학교와 합병했다.
(B) 라디오 방송국에 의해 추천되었다.
(C) 계절에 따라 메뉴를 바꾼다.
(D) 이전 서핑 챔피언들에 의해 소유된다.

해설 질문의 핵심 어구인 Surf Shack에 대해 묻는 Not/True 문제이므로 Surf Shack이 언급된 첫 번째 지문(광고)에서 관련 내용을 확인한다. (A)는 지문에 언급되지 않은 내용이다. (B)는 'radio station Malibu 102.5 has named us the top attraction in the area'에서 라디오 방송국 말리부 102.5가 자신들을 이 지역의 최고의 명소로 지정했다고 했으므로 지문의 내용과 일치한다. 따라서 (B)가 정답이다. (C)와 (D)는 지문에 언급되지 않은 내용이다.

어휘 **seasonally** adv. 계절에 따라, 계절적으로

178 육하원칙 문제

문제 광고에 따르면, 고객들은 어떻게 테이블을 예약할 수 있는가?
(A) 이메일을 보냄으로써
(B) 전화를 함으로써
(C) 모바일 앱을 사용함으로써
(D) 웹사이트를 방문함으로써

해설 고객들이 어떻게(how) 테이블을 예약할 수 있는지를 묻는 육하원칙 문제이므로 질문의 핵심 어구인 customers reserve a table이 언급된 광고에서 관련 내용을 확인한다. 첫 번째 지문(광고)의 'Call us at 555-9691 to reserve a beach table today.'에서 오늘 555-9691로 전화해서 해변가 테이블을 예약하라고 했으므로 (B)가 정답이다.

패러프레이징
Call 전화하다 → **making a phone call** 전화를 함

179 추론 문제 연계

문제 Ms. Stokov는 어떤 스투디 특별 메뉴를 주문했을 것 같은가?
(A) 바나나와 딸기
(B) 파인애플과 코코넛
(C) 사과와 배
(D) 열대 지방 혼합 음료

해설 질문의 핵심 어구인 smoothie special ~ Ms. Stokov ~ order에서 Ms. Stokov가 어떤 스무디 특별 메뉴를 주문했을 것 같은지를 묻고 있으므로 Ms. Stokov가 작성한 온라인 후기를 먼저 확인한다.
단서 1 두 번째 지문(온라인 후기)의 'We even chose to go on a Tuesday'와 'I ordered the smoothie that was on special offer'에서 Ms. Stokov가 화요일에 가기로 정했고 특별 메뉴였던 스무디를 주문했다고 했다. 그런데 화요일에 어떤 스무디가 제공되는지에 대해 제시되지 않았으므로 광고에서 관련 내용을 확인한다.
단서 2 첫 번째 지문(광고)의 'Monday & Tuesday: Banana and Strawberry'에서 화요일 특별 메뉴가 바나나와 딸기라는 것을 알 수 있다.
두 단서를 종합할 때, Ms. Stokov는 화요일 특별 메뉴인 바나나와 딸기 스무디를 주문했음을 알 수 있다. 따라서 (A)가 정답이다.

180 육하원칙 문제

문제 Ms. Stokov는 왜 Surf Shack에 불만족했는가?
(A) 종업원들이 불친절했다.
(B) 음식이 맛이 없었다.
(C) 경치가 광고된 것과 달랐다.
(D) 장소가 혼잡했다.

해설 Ms. Stokov가 왜(Why) Surf Shack에 불만족했는지를 묻는 육하원칙 문제이므로 질문의 핵심 어구인 Ms. Stokov dissatisfied with Surf Shack이 언급된 온라인 후기에서 관련 내용을 확인한다. 두 번째 지문(온라인 후기)의 'especially because of the crowds, my experience was not very good, and I cannot recommend the place to anyone'에서 특히 인파로 인해 경험이 그다지 좋지 않았고 누구에게도 그 장소를 추천할 수 없다고 했으므로 (D)가 정답이다.

패러프레이징
was ~ dissatisfied 불만족했다 → **experience was not very good** 경험이 그다지 좋지 않았다

어휘 **dissatisfy** v. 불만족하게 하다   **flavorless** adj. 맛이 없는

181-185번은 다음 공고와 기사에 관한 문제입니다.

Holton 센터 공고

Holton 센터는 연례 스탠퍼드 문학 축제를 위해 9월 19일에 휴관할 것입니다. [181]영국 전역에서 200개가 넘는 출판사들과 350명이 넘는 작가들이 참석할 것으로 예상됩니다. 이것은 오늘날 최고의 영국 작가들의 강연을 특별히 포함합니다. [183-C]초청된 분들 중에는 *East Kingdom*과 *The Gate*의 작가들이 있는데, 두 작품 모두 출간되어 비평가들의 굉장한 찬사를 받았습니다.

하루 내내, [182-B]작가들은 강연도 하고 그룹 토론에도 참여할 것입니다. 중앙 로비에서, 방문객들이 최신 책들을 할인하여 살 수 있는 부스를 출판사들이 마련할 것입니다. 일단 축제가 마무리되면, Lewistown 호텔에서 파티가 열릴 것인데, 그동안에 [182-C/D]참석자들은 유명한 작가들과 어울리고 그들의 책에 사인을 받을 수 있는 기회를 가질 것입니다. 일반 입장료는 파티를 포함하여 40달러이며, [184]작가 강연은 참석하는 데 추가적인 10달러가 됩니다.

acclaim n. 찬사, 호평   **set up** 마련하다, 설치하다   **title** n. 책, 서적
mingle v. 어울리다, 섞다

Margaret Davidson, 대담하면서 신선한 문학의 목소리
Charles Hagan 작성

[183-C]The Gate로 인해, Margaret Davidson은 내가 가장 좋아하는 젊은 작가들 중 한 명이 되었다. 30세의 New Music Monthly지 기자인 Ms. Davidson은 한때 유명한 기자였지만, [184]나는 스탠퍼드 문학 축제에서 그녀가 유쾌한 강연을 하는 것을 듣고 나서야 그녀의 책을 읽고 싶어졌다. 나는 그녀가 좋은 강연자인 만큼 좋은 작가라는 것을 알리게 되어 기쁘다. The Gate에서, 그녀는 5살에 R&B를 듣고 12살에 베이스를 연주하기 시작하면서, [185]처음 음악 저널리즘으로 그녀를 끌어들였던 경험에 대해 서술한다. 그 책은 세 개의 부분으로 나뉘는데, 첫 번째는 그녀의 어린 시절에 초점을 맞추고, 두 번째는 십 대 때 밴드에서 연주했던 시기에 초점을 맞추고, 그리고 마지막 부분은 음악 기자의 경력에 대한 것이다. 책의 끝에는 새로운 힙합 앨범에 대한 예리한 비평부터 펑크 그룹 Stone Age와의 여행에 대한 유머러스한 이야기에 이르는, New Music Monthly지 속 그녀의 글의 발췌들이 있다.

bold adj. 대담한 correspondent n. 기자, 통신원 journalist n. 기자
be inclined to ~하고 싶어지다, 마음이 기울다
hilarious adj. 유쾌한, 즐거운 excerpt n. 발췌, 인용
incisive adj. 예리한 account n. 이야기

181 추론 문제
문제 스태퍼드 문학 축제에 대해 암시되는 것은?
(A) 1년에 두 번 열린다.
(B) 한 국가의 작가들에 초점을 맞춘다.
(C) 주로 소설 작가들에 맞춰져 있다.
(D) 그다지 명성을 얻지 못했다.

해설 질문의 핵심 어구인 Stafford Literary Festival에 대해 추론하는 문제이므로 스태퍼드 문학 축제가 언급된 공고에서 관련 내용을 확인한다. 첫 번째 지문(공고)의 'Over 200 publishers and 350 writers from around the UK are expected to attend.'에서 영국 전역에서 200개가 넘는 출판사들과 350명이 넘는 작가들이 참석할 것으로 예상된다고 했으므로 스태퍼드 문학 축제는 한 국가의 작가들에 초점을 맞춘다는 것을 추론할 수 있다. 따라서 (B)가 정답이다.

어휘 gear v. 맞추다, 적합하게 하다 receive publicity 명성을 얻다

182 Not/True 문제
문제 사람들은 축제에서 무엇을 할 수 없는가?
(A) 특정 책들의 무료 사본을 받는다.
(B) 작가들의 강연을 듣는다.
(C) 참석한 작가들과 교류한다.
(D) 작가들의 사인을 받는다.

해설 질문의 핵심 어구인 people ~ do at the festival에 대해 묻는 Not/True 문제이므로 축제, 즉 스태퍼드 문학 축제가 언급된 첫 번째 지문(공고)에서 관련 내용을 확인한다. (A)는 지문에 언급되지 않은 내용이다. 따라서 (A)가 정답이다. (B)는 'writers will also be giving lectures'에서 작가들이 강연을 할 것이라고 했으므로 지문의 내용과 일치한다. (C)와 (D)는 'attendees will have the opportunity to mingle with noted writers and get their books signed'에서 참석자들은 유명한 작가들과 어울리고 그들의 책에 사인을 받을 수 있는 기회를 가질 것이라고 했으므로 지문의 내용과 일치한다.

패러프레이징
mingle with ~ writers 작가들과 어울리다 → Interact with writers 작가들과 교류하다
get ~ signed 사인을 받다 → Collect ~ signatures 사인을 받다

어휘 interact with ~와 교류하다, 상호작용하다

183 Not/True 문제 연계
문제 Ms. Davidson에 대해 언급된 것은?
(A) 두 편의 소설을 썼다.
(B) Mr. Hagan을 위해 책에 사인을 했다.
(C) 그녀의 작품은 비평가들로부터 호평을 받았다.
(D) 그녀의 경력은 여러 번 바뀌었다.

해설 두 지문의 내용을 종합해서 풀어야 하는 연계 문제이다. 질문의 핵심 어구인 Ms. Davidson과 관련된 내용을 지문에서 찾아 각 보기와 대조하는 Not/True 문제이므로 Ms. Davidson이 언급된 기사를 먼저 확인한다.
단서 1 두 번째 지문(기사)의 'With The Gate, Margaret Davidson has become one of my[Mr. Hagan] favourite young writers.'에서 The Gate로 인해 Margaret Davidson은 Mr. Hagan이 가장 좋아하는 젊은 작가들 중 한 명이 되었다고 했다. 그런데 The Gate에 대한 정보가 제시되지 않았으므로 공고에서 관련 내용을 확인한다.
단서 2 첫 번째 지문(공고)의 'Among those invited are the authors of East Kingdom and The Gate, both of which were released to spectacular critical acclaim.'에서 초청된 사람들 중에는 East Kingdom과 The Gate의 작가들이 있는데 두 작품 모두 출간되어 비평가들의 굉장한 찬사를 받았음을 확인할 수 있다.
두 단서를 종합할 때 Ms. Davidson의 작품인 The Gate가 비평가들로부터 호평을 받았음을 알 수 있다. 따라서 (C)가 정답이다.

패러프레이징
spectacular critical acclaim 비평가들의 굉장한 찬사 → was well received by critics 비평가들로부터 호평을 받았다

어휘 well received 호평을 받다

184 추론 문제 연계
문제 Mr. Hagan에 대해 추론될 수 있는 것은?
(A) 유명한 음악 기자이다.
(B) Ms. Davidson이 강연하는 것을 보기 위해 추가 요금을 지불했다.
(C) 밴드에서 연주하곤 했다.
(D) Lewistown 호텔에 머물렀다.

해설 질문의 핵심 어구인 Mr. Hagan이 작성한 기사를 먼저 확인한다.
단서 1 두 번째 지문(기사)의 'I wasn't inclined to read her [Ms. Davidson] book until I heard her give a hilarious talk at the Stafford Literary Festival'에서 Mr. Hagan은 스태퍼드 문학 축제에서 Ms. Davidson이 유쾌한 강연을 하는 것을 듣고 나서야 그녀의 책을 읽고 싶어졌다고 했다. 그런데 스태퍼드 문학 축제에서의 강연에 대한 정보가 제시되지 않았으므로 공고에서 관련 내용을 확인한다.
단서 2 첫 번째 지문(공고)의 'author lectures cost an additional $10 to attend'에서 작가 강연은 참석하는 데 추가적인 10달러가 든다는 것을 확인할 수 있다.
두 단서를 종합할 때, Mr. Hagan은 Ms. Davidson이 강연하는 것을 보기 위해 10달러의 추가 요금을 지불했다는 것을 알 수 있다. 따라서 (B)가 정답이다.

185 동의어 찾기 문제
문제 기사에서, 1문단 다섯 번째 줄의 단어 "drew"는 의미상 ~와 가장 가깝다.
(A) 끌어들였다
(B) 제시했다
(C) 만들었다
(D) 허용했다

해설 기사의 drew를 포함한 구절 'she writes about the experiences that drew her to music journalism in the first place'에서 drew가 '끌어들이다'라는 뜻으로 사용되었다. 따라서 (A)가 정답이다.

186-190번은 다음 편지, 이메일, 웹페이지 게시글에 관한 문제입니다.

Rick Houseman
119번지 Willow로
퀸즐랜드 주, 뉴질랜드 0600

Mr. Houseman께,

제 이름은 Matilda Gleeson이고, 퀸즐랜드 대학교에서 동문 사무국을 대표하여 편지를 씁니다. [186]저희는 퀸즐랜드 대학교의 엄선된 졸업생들이 저희 웹사이트를 위해 짧은 직업 약력을 제공해 주실 의향이 있는지 알아보기 위해 연락을 드리고 있습니다. 귀하가 세간의 이목을 끄는 환경 보호론자라는 점을 고려할 때, 저희는 귀하가 성공적인 퀸즐랜드 대학교 졸업생의 좋은 예시가 될 것으로 생각합니다.

만약 귀하가 관심이 있으시다면, [186/187]귀하의 경력을 설명하는 100단어 이하의 짧은 약력을 저희에게 보내주시기 바랍니다. [187]또한 귀하가 발표한 논문 샘플, 귀하에 관해 쓰여진 신문 기사, 그리고 최근 5년 이내에 촬영된 본인의 사진도 보내주시면 감사하겠습니다. 이것들을 gleeson22@qland.nz로 제출해 주시기 바랍니다. 감사드리며, 저는 귀하로부터 연락을 기다리고 있겠습니다.

Matilda Gleeson 드림
동문 사무국, 퀸즐랜드 대학교

on behalf of ~을 대표하여 alumni n. 동문, 동창생
selected adj. 엄선된 be willing to ~할 의향이 있다, 기꺼이 ~할 것이다
biography n. 약력, 자서전 high-profile adj. 세간의 이목을 끄는
conservationist n. 환경 보호론자

수신: Matilda Gleeson <gleeson22@qland.nz>
발신: Rick Houseman <rick.houseman@qlandwildlife.nz>
제목: 동문 약력
날짜: 5월 29일
첨부 파일: 파일1, 파일2, 파일3

Ms. Gleeson께,

동문 약력과 관련하여 저에게 연락해 주셔서 감사합니다. [187]저는 마지막 항목을 제외하고 당신이 요청한 모든 항목들을 첨부했습니다. 저는 내일 당신께 이것을 보내드리겠습니다. 저는 또한 학교 도서관 유지를 위해 동문 기금에 소액을 기부했습니다.

[188]당신이 웹사이트에 제 약력을 추가하실 때, 제게 페이지 링크를 보내서 알려주실 수 있나요? 저는 몇몇 친구들 및 가족과 그것을 공유하고 싶습니다. 또한, 제가 곧 약력을 업데이트해야 할 수도 있습니다. [190]저는 현재 뉴질랜드 보존 위원회와 그들의 부위원장의 역할을 하기 위해 논의 중입니다. 남은 것은 패널 면접을 하는 것뿐입니다. 당신께서 웹사이트에서 제 약력을 업데이트하실 수 있도록 며칠 내에 제가 그 자리를 얻게 될지 여부를 알려드리겠습니다.

Rick Houseman 드림

maintenance n. 유지, 보수 conservation n. 보존, 보호
commission n. 위원회 serve as ~의 역할을 하다
assistant chair 부위원장 undergo v. 하다, 받다, 겪다

퀸즐랜드 대학교

| 홈 | 입학 | 캠퍼스 생활 | 동문 | 공지사항 | 지원 |

동문 프로필
Rick Houseman

10년 전 퀸즐랜드 대학교 학사 과정을 졸업한 이후, Rick Houseman은 과학에 대한 전 세계의 지식을 발전시키기 위해 노력해 왔습니다. 그는 명망 있는 국립 자연 과학 학교에서 박사 학위를 받았으며 뉴질랜드의 야생동물에 대한 광범위한 학술 조사를 발표했습니다. [189]가장 최근 ⟳

에는, 키위새와 같은 독특한 동물의 서식지를 보존하는 것을 돕기 위해 뉴질랜드의 일부분을 야생동물 보호 구역으로 지정하는 새로운 법안의 통과를 보장하기 위해 노력했습니다. [190]현재, 그는 뉴질랜드 보존 위원회의 부위원장입니다.

profile n. 프로필, 인물 소개 undergraduate program 학사 과정
doctorate n. 박사 학위 research n. 학술 조사 passage n. 통과
legislation n. 법안 designate v. 지정하다 habitat n. 서식지

186 목적 찾기 문제

문제 Ms. Gleeson은 왜 Mr. Houseman에게 편지를 썼는가?
(A) 기부를 요청하기 위해
(B) 직책을 제안하기 위해
(C) 행사를 상기시키기 위해
(D) 몇몇 정보를 요청하기 위해

해설 Ms. Gleeson이 Mr. Houseman에게 편지를 쓴 목적을 묻는 목적 찾기 문제이므로 Ms. Gleeson이 작성한 편지의 내용을 확인한다. 첫 번째 지문(편지)의 'We are reaching out to selected graduates of Queensland University to see if they would be willing to contribute short professional biographies for our Web site.' 와 'please send us a short biography of 100 words or less describing your career'에서 퀸즐랜드 대학교의 엄선된 졸업생들이 웹사이트를 위해 짧은 직업 약력을 제공할 의향이 있는지 알아보기 위해 연락을 하고 있다고 한 후, 경력을 설명하는 100단어 이하의 짧은 약력을 보내줄 것을 요청하고 있으므로 (D)가 정답이다.

어휘 donation n. 기부, 기증

187 육하원칙 문제 연계

문제 Mr. Houseman은 내일 무엇을 보낼 것인가?
(A) 짧은 기사
(B) 사진
(C) 개인 프로필
(D) 연구 논문

해설 질문의 핵심 어구인 Mr. Houseman send tomorrow에서 Mr. Houseman이 내일 무엇(What)을 보낼 것인지를 묻고 있으므로 Mr. Houseman이 작성한 이메일을 먼저 확인한다.
단서 1 두 번째 지문(이메일)의 'I've attached all of the items you[Ms. Gleeson] requested except for the last one. I will send this to you tomorrow.'에서 마지막 항목을 제외하고 Ms. Gleeson이 요청한 모든 항목들을 첨부했다고 한 후, 내일 이것을 보내겠다고 했다. 그런데 마지막 항목이 무엇인지 제시되지 않았으므로 편지에서 관련 내용을 확인한다.
단서 2 첫 번째 지문(편지)의 'please send us a short biography of 100 words or less describing your career. In addition, we would appreciate it if you sent samples of papers you have published, newspaper articles written about you, and a photograph of yourself taken in the last five years.'에서 경력을 설명하는 100단어 이하의 짧은 약력, 발표한 논문 샘플, Mr. Houseman에 관해 쓰여진 신문 기사, 최근 5년 이내에 촬영된 본인의 사진을 보내주면 고맙겠다고 한 것을 확인할 수 있다.
두 단서를 종합할 때, Mr. Houseman은 Ms. Gleeson이 요청한 모든 항목들 중 마지막 항목인 사진을 내일 보낼 것임을 알 수 있다. 따라서 (B)가 정답이다.

188 육하원칙 문제

문제 Mr. Houseman은 Ms. Gleeson에게 무엇을 해달라고 요청하는가?
(A) 그의 약력에 개인 웹페이지 링크를 추가한다.
(B) 그에게 학교 운영에 대한 업데이트를 제공한다.
(C) 게시글이 작성되면 그에게 알린다.
(D) 동문 이메일 목록에 그를 추가한다.

해설 Mr. Houseman이 Ms. Gleeson에게 무엇(What)을 해달라고 요청하는지를 묻는 육하원칙 문제이므로 질문의 핵심 어구인 Mr. Houseman이 작성한 이메일에서 관련 내용을 확인한다. 두 번째 지문(이메일)의 'When you add my biography to the Web site, could you let me know by sending me a link to the page?'에서 웹사이트에 자신의 약력을 추가할 때 페이지 링크를 보내서 알려줄 수 있는지 물었으므로 (C)가 정답이다.

패러프레이징
let ~ know 알리다 → **Notify** 알리다

어휘 operation n. 운영 notify v. 알리다 post n. 게시글

189 육하원칙 문제

문제 웹페이지 게시글에 따르면, Mr. Houseman은 가장 최근에 무엇을 했는가?
(A) 텔레비전 프로그램에 출연했다.
(B) 대학 교수진에 합류했다.
(C) 새로운 법이 통과되는 것을 도왔다.
(D) 박사 학위 프로그램에 지원했다.

해설 Mr. Houseman이 가장 최근에 무엇(what)을 했는지를 묻는 육하원칙 문제이므로 질문의 핵심 어구인 most recently가 언급된 웹페이지 게시글에서 관련 내용을 확인한다. 세 번째 지문(웹페이지 게시글)의 'Most recently, he[Mr. Houseman] worked to ensure the passage of new legislation'에서 Mr. Houseman이 가장 최근에 새로운 법안의 통과를 보장하기 위해 노력했다고 했으므로 (C)가 정답이다.

패러프레이징
worked to ensure the passage of new legislation 새로운 법안의 통과를 보장하기 위해 노력했다 → **Helped pass a new law** 새로운 법이 통과되는 것을 도왔다

어휘 faculty n. 교수진, 교직원

190 추론 문제 연계

문제 Mr. Houseman에 대해 암시되는 것은?
(A) 퀸즐랜드 대학교에서 대학원 프로그램을 중퇴했다.
(B) 퀸즐랜드 지역의 도서관에서 일했다.
(C) 키위새에 관한 대학 논문을 썼다.
(D) 새로운 직책에 대한 패널 면접을 통과했다.

해설 질문의 핵심 어구인 Mr. Houseman이 작성한 이메일을 먼저 확인한다.

단서 1 두 번째 지문(이메일)의 'I am currently in talks with the New Zealand Conservation Commission to serve as their assistant chair. All that is left is to undergo a panel interview.'에서 Mr. Houseman이 현재 뉴질랜드 보존 위원회와 그들의 부위원장의 역할을 하기 위해 논의 중이라며 남은 것은 패널 면접을 하는 것뿐이라고 했다. 그런데 뉴질랜드 보존 위원회 부위원장의 역할을 맡게 되었는지에 대한 정보가 제시되지 않았으므로 웹페이지 게시글에서 관련 내용을 확인한다.

단서 2 세 번째 지문(웹페이지 게시글)의 'Presently, he[Mr. Houseman] is the assistant chair of the New Zealand Conservation Commission.'에서 현재 Mr. Houseman이 뉴질랜드 보존 위원회의 부위원장임을 확인할 수 있다. 두 단서를 종합할 때, Mr. Houseman이 새로운 직책인 뉴질랜드 보존 위원회 부위원장에 대한 패널 면접을 통과했음을 알 수 있다. 따라서 (D)가 정답이다.

어휘 drop out 중퇴하다 thesis n. 논문

191-195번은 다음 회람, 설문조사, 보고서에 관한 문제입니다.

수신: 고객 만족팀 직원
발신: Nick Christman, 고객 만족팀 관리자
제목: 3주년의 YourPage
날짜: 3월 22일

[192-D]오늘 일자로, YourPage는 3년 연속 운영해오고 있습니다. 그 기간 동안, [192-C]우리의 사용자층은 기하급수적으로 증가했습니다. 단지 지난 두 달 동안, 실제로, 우리는 사용자의 500퍼센트 증가를 경험했으며, 이는 우리를 가장 빠르게 성장하는 사회 연결망 사이트로 만들었습니다. 그것은 [191]우리 사이트에 대한 고객들의 경험이 어땠는지를 알아보기 위해 그들에 대한 설문조사를 실시할 때라는 것을 의미합니다. 우리는 얼마 동안은 이것을 사용해온 사람들에게 답변을 듣고 싶기 때문에, [193]1년도 더 전에 YourPage 프로필을 만든 사용자들에게 설문조사 요청을 보냅시다. 이는 또한 활동이 상당히 규칙적인 사람들이어야 합니다. [194]설문조사를 하는 것에 대한 혜택으로, 우리는 그들의 이름을 경품을 위한 추첨에 입력해줄 수 있습니다. 경품은 우리와 제휴된 회사들 중 하나의 신형 전자 기기가 될 것입니다.

as of ~ 일자로 exponentially adv. 기하급수적으로
social networking 사회 연결망 for a while 얼마 동안은, 잠시 동안
fairly adv. 상당히 raffle n. 추첨 (판매) affiliate v. 제휴하다

[193]YourPage: 설문조사

[193]이름: Pauline Carson
날짜: 4월 12일

1에서 5까지의 등급에서, 5가 최고점이라고 할 때, 당신은 YourPage에 대한 당신의 경험을 어떻게 평가하시겠습니까?
☐ 1   ☐ 2   ☐ 3   ☑ 4   ☐ 5

당신은 얼마나 자주 YourPage를 확인하십니까?
저는 평소 하루 종일 반복적으로 이것을 확인합니다. 저는 제가 지루하거나 제 친구들이 무엇을 하고 있는지 알아내고 싶을 때마다 이것을 합니다.

당신은 얼마나 자주 당신의 페이지에 메시지, 사진 또는 기타 콘텐츠를 게시하십니까?
저는 그렇게 자주 게시하지는 않습니다. 저는 아마도 일주일에 한두 번 정도 글을 올리는 것 같습니다. 하지만, 저는 다른 사람들의 게시물에 댓글을 다는 것을 정말 좋아합니다.

당신은 어떻게 YourPage에 대해 들었습니까?
몇몇 친구들을 통해

당신은 YourPage가 무엇이 개선되기를 바라십니까?
저는 프로필 페이지의 디자인이 서로 뒤죽박죽 섞인 여러 다른 정보로 인해, 조금 어수선하다고 생각합니다.

scale n. 등급, 규모 rank v. 평가하다 repeatedly adv. 반복적으로
catch up on (소식·정보를) 알아내다 cluttered adj. 어수선한

YourPage: 설문조사 결과

4월 한 달 동안, 우리는 5,000건이 넘는 설문조사 요청을 YourPage의 다양한 활성 사용자들에게 보냈습니다. [194]설문조사에 응한 사람들은 Silver Plus사 스마트폰을 위한 추첨에 참가되었는데, 이것들은 10명의 당첨자들에게 배부되었습니다. 대략 1,000명이 우리의 요청에 응답했습니다. 대부분(88 퍼센트)이 사이트에 대한 그들의 경험을 1에서 5까지의 등급에서, 5가 최고점이라고 할 때, 4 또는 5로 평가했습니다. 하지만, [195]사이트가 꽤 자주 종료되는 것과 혼란스러운 배치 때문에 프로필 페이지가 돌아다니기에 어렵다는 것을 포함하여, 몇몇 공통적인 비판이 있었습니다. 앞으로, 우리는 페이지를 닫히게 하는 컴퓨터 코드의 오류를 고치고 사용자들의 편의를 염두에 두고 페이지의 서식을 ➲

다시 설정함으로써 이러한 문제들을 처리하는 것이 중요합니다.

---

active user 활성 사용자　**enter into** ~에 참가하다
common adj. 공통적인, 일반적인　**criticism** n. 비판, 비난
navigate v. (인터넷·웹사이트를) 돌아다니다　**layout** n. 배치
going forward 앞으로, 장차　**reformat** v. 서식을 다시 설정하다

---

191 목적 찾기 문제

문제　회람의 목적은 무엇인가?
(A) 직원들의 수고를 칭찬하기 위해
(B) 지도부의 교체를 보고하기 위해
(C) 개선을 위한 제안을 요청하기 위해
(D) 정보를 모으기 위한 제안을 하기 위해

해설　회람의 목적을 묻는 목적 찾기 문제이므로 회람의 내용을 확인한다. 첫 번째 지문(회람)의 'it's time we conducted a survey of our customers to see how their experience with our site has been'에서 사이트에 대한 고객들의 경험이 어땠는지를 알아보기 위해 그들에 대한 설문조사를 실시할 때라고 했으므로 (D)가 정답이다.

192 Not/True 문제

문제　Mr. Christman이 YourPage에 대해 언급하는 것은?
(A) 주로 청소년들에 의해 사용된다.
(B) 지난 몇 달 동안 100명의 신규 사용자들을 유치했다.
(C) 급격히 더 인기를 얻고 있다.
(D) 1년 전에 출시되었다.

해설　Mr. Christman이 YourPage에 대해 언급한 것을 묻는 Not/True 문제이므로 Mr. Christman이 작성한 첫 번째 지문(회람)에서 관련 내용을 확인한다. (A)와 (B)는 지문에 언급되지 않은 내용이다. (C)는 'our[YourPage] user base has grown exponentially. In just the past two months, in fact, we have experienced a 500 percent increase in users, making us the fastest-growing social networking site.'에서 YourPage의 사용자층이 기하급수적으로 증가했고 단지 지난 두 달 동안 실제로 사용자의 500퍼센트 증가를 경험했으며 이는 가장 빠르게 성장하는 사회 연결망 사이트로 만들었다고 했으므로 지문의 내용과 일치한다. 따라서 (C)가 정답이다. (D)는 'As of today, YourPage has been operating for three straight years.'에서 오늘 일자로 YourPage가 3년 연속 운영해오고 있다고 했으므로 지문의 내용과 일치하지 않는다.

패러프레이징
user base has grown exponentially 사용자층이 기하급수적으로 증가했다 → **rapidly becoming more popular** 급격히 더 인기를 얻고 있다

193 추론 문제　연계

문제　Ms. Carson에 대해 추론될 수 있는 것은?
(A) 1년 넘게 YourPage를 사용해왔다.
(B) YourPage가 사용하기에 매우 쉽다고 생각한다.
(C) 추첨 상품에 당첨될 자격이 없다.
(D) 설문조사를 제시간에 제출하지 않았다.

해설　질문의 핵심 어구인 Ms. Carson이 작성한 설문조사를 먼저 확인한다. 단서 1 두 번째 지문(설문조사)의 'YourPage: Survey'와 'Name: Pauline Carson'에서 YourPage 설문조사에 응답한 사람이 Ms. Carson이라고 했다. 그런데 YourPage 설문조사의 대상자가 되기 위한 조건이 제시되지 않았으므로 회람에서 관련 내용을 확인한다. 단서 2 첫 번째 지문(회람)의 'let's send survey requests to users who made YourPage profiles over a year ago'에서 1년도 더 전에 YourPage 프로필을 만든 사용자들에게 설문조사 요청을 보내자고 한 것을 확인할 수 있다.
두 단서를 종합할 때, Ms. Carson이 1년 넘게 YourPage를 사용해왔으므로 설문조사의 대상자가 되었음을 알 수 있다. 따라서 (A)

가 정답이다.

어휘　**eligible** adj. 자격이 있는　**on time** 제시간에

194 추론 문제　연계

문제　Silver Plus사에 대해 암시되는 것은?
(A) 기업용 소프트웨어를 제작한다.
(B) 기술적인 문제들이 있어왔다.
(C) YourPage를 위한 설문조사를 만들었다.
(D) YourPage와 제휴하고 있다.

해설　질문의 핵심 어구인 Silver Plus가 언급된 보고서를 먼저 확인한다. 단서 1 세 번째 지문(보고서)의 'Those who took the survey were entered into a raffle for Silver Plus smartphones, which were distributed to 10 winners.'에서 설문조사에 응한 사람들은 Silver Plus사 스마트폰을 위한 추첨에 참가되었는데 이것들은 10명의 당첨자들에게 배부되었다고 했다. 그런데 Silver Plus사 스마트폰에 대한 정보가 제시되지 않았으므로 회람에서 관련 내용을 확인한다. 단서 2 첫 번째 지문(회람)의 'As an incentive for taking the survey, we[YourPage] could offer to enter their names into a raffle for prizes. The prizes could be brand-new electronic devices from one of the companies we are affiliated with.'에서 설문조사를 하는 것에 대한 혜택으로 YourPage가 참여자들의 이름을 경품을 위한 추첨에 입력해줄 수 있다고 했고 경품은 YourPage와 제휴된 회사들 중 하나의 신형 전자 기기가 될 것임을 확인할 수 있다.
두 단서를 종합할 때, 설문조사에 응한 사람들 중 일부는 YourPage와 제휴하고 있는 Silver Plus사 스마트폰을 경품으로 받았음을 알 수 있다. 따라서 (D)가 정답이다.

패러프레이징
are affiliated 제휴되다 → **has a partnership** 제휴하고 있다

195 육하원칙 문제

문제　보고서는 무엇을 할 것을 추천하는가?
(A) 해외 국가들에 사이트를 광고하는 것
(B) 웹사이트의 지속적인 문제들을 고치는 것
(C) 더 많은 피드백에 대한 추가 보상을 제공하는 것
(D) 더욱 면밀한 설문조사를 실시하는 것

해설　보고서가 무엇(What)을 할 것을 추천하는지를 묻는 육하원칙 문제이므로 report recommend doing과 관련된 내용이 언급된 보고서를 확인한다. 세 번째 지문(보고서)의 'there were some common criticisms, including that the site shut down fairly frequently and that profile pages were difficult to navigate because of the confusing layout. Going forward, it is important we address these problems'에서 사이트가 꽤 자주 종료되는 것과 혼란스러운 배치 때문에 프로필 페이지가 돌아다니기에 어렵다는 것을 포함하여 몇몇 공통적인 비판이 있었고 앞으로 이러한 문제들을 처리하는 것이 중요하다고 했으므로 (B)가 정답이다.

어휘　**persistent** adj. 지속적인　**in-depth** adj. 면밀한, 세심한

196-200번은 다음 공고와 두 이메일에 관한 문제입니다.

---

[198]제4회 보스턴 지도자 회담이 생방송될 것이다

[196-C]Jefferson 은행은 [196-A]제4회 연례 회담에 [196-C]두 명의 기조연설자들의 참여를 확보하였음을 발표하게 되어 자랑스럽게 생각하며, 이는 1월 17일과 18일로 예정되어 있습니다. SpitalGround사의 대표이사 Susanne Coerver는 그녀의 혁신적인 기업이 의료 서비스 부문을 변화시키고 있는 방식과 그녀가 경쟁적인 환경에서 그녀의 기업을 관리하는 방법에 대해 이야기할 것입니다. Moss Tech사의 최고 경영자인 Henry Moss는 성공적인 기업가가 되기 위해 무엇이 필요한지에 대한 통찰력으로 회담을 마무리할 것입니다. ➲

처음으로, [197]보스턴 지도자 회담은 온라인 애플리케이션을 통해 생방송으로도 재생될 것이며, [196-B]더 많은 청중에게 다가갈 수 있게 할 것입니다. 온라인으로 참여하는 표는 이틀간 220달러입니다. 하지만, [197]Jefferson 은행의 고객들은 무료로 리더십 기술에 대해 배우고, 연수회에 참여하고, 다른 온라인 고객들과 교류하도록 가상으로 행사에 초대됩니다. 가까운 Jefferson 은행 지점을 찾으시고, 회담 시간에 맞춰 고객이 되세요.

---

live adj. 생방송인, 실황인 **secure** v. 확보하다, 획득하다
innovative adj. 혁신적인 **health-care** n. 의료 서비스
insight n. 통찰력 **entrepreneur** n. 기업가 **enable** v. ~할 수 있게 하다
virtually adv. 가상으로 **in time for** ~하는 시간에 맞춰

수신: Allison Cruise <a.cruise@jeffersonbank.com>
발신: Preston Ali <p.ali@mosstechorg.com>
제목: 회담
날짜: 12월 28일

Ms. Cruise께,

저는 당신께 Mr. Moss가 예기치 못한 사업 문제로 인해 예정대로 회담에 참석할 수 없을 것임을 알리게 되어 유감입니다. 특히 [198]그는 작년의 행사에서 연설하며 정말 즐거운 시간을 가졌기 때문에, 그가 제게 그의 유감의 뜻을 전할 것을 요청하셨습니다.

그렇긴 하지만, [199-D]Mr. Moss가 그의 있어야 할 곳에 갈 누군가를 추천해드릴 수 있습니다. 그녀는 몇 년 전에 그녀와 Mr. Moss가 함께 설립했던 소프트웨어 서비스 회사인 Galacomms사의 대표이사입니다. 제가 그녀의 가능 여부에 대해 확인을 받자마자 당신께 그녀의 연락처를 보내드릴 수 있습니다. 당신은 이번 주말 전에 업데이트를 기대해도 됩니다. 다시 한번, 이러한 불편에 대한 저희의 사과를 받아주시길 바랍니다.

Preston Ali 드림
수석 비서
Moss Tech사

---

unforeseen adj. 예기치 못한 **regret** n. 유감의 뜻, 후회의 말
enjoyable adj. 즐거운 **take one's place** 있어야 할 곳에 가다
contact details 연락처

수신: Leonard Vega <l.vega@jeffersonbank.com>
발신: Allison Cruise <a.cruise@jeffersonbank.com>
제목: 회담
날짜: 1월 9일

Leonard께,

저는 원래 계획된 것보다 당신이 이틀 일찍 회담 장소로 가시길 바랍니다. 만약 당신이 그렇게 해야 한다면 새로운 항공편 예약을 진행해주세요.

당신이 아시다시피, 우리의 연사 인원에 변경이 있으며, 이러한 변경은 행사 장소에 게시된 모든 인쇄물에 반영되어야 합니다. 참고로, [199-D]새로운 연사의 이름은 Fiona Murphy이며, 그녀는 Galacomms사의 대표이사입니다. 당신이 행사 장소에 있는 동안, 모든 것이 원활하게 운영되는지 확실히 하기 위해 [200]생방송 재생 설정을 테스트해주세요.

당신의 도움에 감사드리고, 만약 질문이 있으시다면 제게 알려주십시오.

Alison 드림

---

lineup n. 인원, 구성 **reflect** v. 반영하다, 반사하다
smoothly adv. 원활하게, 순조롭게

---

196 Not/True 문제
문제 회담에 대해 사실이 아닌 것은?
(A) 이전에 개최된 적이 있다.

(B) 청중의 범위를 넓히고 있다.
(C) 금융 기관에 의해 주최될 것이다.
(D) 의료 서비스 산업에 초점을 맞출 것이다.

해설 질문의 핵심 어구인 summit에 대해 묻는 Not/True 문제이므로 회담과 관련된 내용이 언급된 첫 번째 지문(공고)을 확인한다. (A)는 'its fourth annual summit'에서 제4회 연례 회담이라고 했으므로 지문의 내용과 일치한다. (B)는 'enabling it[Summit] to reach a wider audience'에서 회담이 더 많은 청중에게 다가갈 수 있게 할 것이라고 했으므로 지문의 내용과 일치한다. (C)는 'Jefferson Bank is proud to announce that it has secured the participation of two keynote speakers'에서 Jefferson 은행은 두 명의 기조연설자들의 참여를 확보하였음을 발표하게 되어 자랑스럽게 생각한다고 했으므로 지문의 내용과 일치한다. (D)는 지문에 언급되지 않은 내용이다. 따라서 (D)가 정답이다.

패러프레이징
reach a wider audience 더 많은 청중에게 다가가다 → is expanding ~ audience reach 청중의 범위를 넓히고 있다
Bank 은행 → a financial institution 금융 기관

어휘 put on 개최하다 reach n. 범위; v. 다가가다, 닿다 host v. 주최하다
financial adj. 금융의, 재정적인 institution n. 기관, 협회

---

197 육하원칙 문제
문제 Jefferson 은행 고객들은 무엇을 하도록 권장되는가?
(A) 일부 콘텐츠를 무료로 재생한다.
(B) 더 높은 저축 이자율을 활용한다.
(C) 상금을 받기 위해 경연에 참가한다.
(D) 몇몇 상품을 위해 지점 장소를 방문한다.

해설 Jefferson 은행 고객들이 무엇(What)을 하도록 권장되는지를 묻는 육하원칙 문제이므로 질문의 핵심 어구인 Jefferson Bank customers encouraged to do와 관련된 내용이 언급된 공고를 확인한다. 첫 번째 지문(공고)의 'the Boston Leadership Summit will also be streamed live through an online application'과 'customers of Jefferson Bank are invited to virtually join the event to learn about leadership skills, partake in workshops, and interact with other online visitors free of charge'에서 보스턴 지도자 회담은 온라인 애플리케이션을 통해 생방송으로도 재생될 것이며 Jefferson 은행의 고객들은 무료로 리더십 기술에 대해 배우고 연수회에 참여하고 다른 온라인 고객들과 교류하도록 가상으로 행사에 초대된다고 했으므로 (A)가 정답이다.

패러프레이징
free of charge 무료로 → for free 무료로

어휘 interest n. 이자 merchandise n. 상품

---

198 추론 문제 연계
문제 Mr. Ali가 Mr. Moss에 대해 암시하는 것은?
(A) 다른 행사에서 연설하도록 초대되었다.
(B) 작년에 보스턴에 있었다.
(C) 온라인으로 연설을 시청할 것이다.
(D) 그의 회사에서 은퇴할 계획이다.

해설 질문의 핵심 어구인 Mr. Ali가 작성한 첫 번째 이메일을 먼저 확인한다.
단서 1 두 번째 지문(첫 번째 이메일)의 'he[Mr. Moss] had such an enjoyable time speaking at last year's event'에서 Mr. Moss가 작년의 행사에서 연설하며 정말 즐거운 시간을 가졌다고 했다. 그런데 작년의 행사에 대한 정보가 제시되지 않았으므로 행사에 대해 언급된 공고에서 관련 내용을 확인한다.
단서 2 첫 번째 지문(공고)의 'The 4th Boston Leadership Summit Is Going Live'에서 제4회 보스턴 지도자 회담이 생방송될 것이라고 했으므로 회담이 매년 보스턴에서 열린다는 것을 확인할 수 있다.
두 단서를 종합할 때, Mr. Moss가 작년에 보스턴에서 열린 회담에 참

석했다는 것을 알 수 있다. 따라서 (B)가 정답이다.

어휘 retire v. 은퇴하다

199 Not/True 문제 연계

문제 Fiona Murphy에 대해 언급된 것은?
(A) 일정 변경을 요청했다.
(B) Jefferson 은행의 고객이다.
(C) 항공편 예약의 확인이 필요하다.
(D) Mr. Moss와 함께 회사를 설립했다.

해설 두 지문의 내용을 종합해서 풀어야 하는 연계 문제이다. 질문의 핵심 어구인 Fiona Murphy와 관련된 내용을 지문에서 찾아 각 보기와 대조하는 Not/True 문제이므로 Fiona Murphy가 언급된 두 번째 이메일을 먼저 확인한다.
단서 1 세 번째 지문(두 번째 이메일)의 'the new speaker's name is Fiona Murphy, and she is the CEO of Galacomms'에서 새로운 연사의 이름이 Fiona Murphy이며 그녀는 Galacomms사의 대표이사라고 했다. 그런데 Galacomms사에 대한 정보가 제시되지 않았으므로 Galacomms사가 언급된 첫 번째 이메일에서 관련 내용을 확인한다.
단서 2 두 번째 지문(첫 번째 이메일)의 'Mr. Moss can recommend someone to take his place. She is the CEO of Galacomms, a software services company that she and Mr. Moss started together some years ago.'에서 Mr. Moss가 그의 있어야 할 곳에 갈 누군가를 추천했는데 그녀는 몇 년 전에 그녀와 Mr. Moss가 함께 설립했던 소프트웨어 서비스 회사인 Galacomms사의 대표이사임을 확인할 수 있다.
두 단서를 종합할 때, Fiona Murphy가 Mr. Moss와 함께 Galacomms사라는 회사를 설립했음을 알 수 있다. 따라서 (D)가 정답이다.

어휘 confirmation n. 확인

200 육하원칙 문제

문제 Ms. Cruise는 Mr. Vega에게 무엇을 해달라고 요청하는가?
(A) 생방송 재생 연결을 테스트한다.
(B) 연사 계약서를 수정한다.
(C) 새로운 행사 장소를 찾는다.
(D) 내부 소식지를 준비한다.

해설 Ms. Cruise가 Mr. Vega에게 무엇(What)을 해달라고 요청하는지를 묻는 육하원칙 문제이므로 질문의 핵심 어구인 Ms. Cruise가 Mr. Vega에게 작성한 두 번째 이메일에서 관련 내용을 확인한다. 세 번째 지문(두 번째 이메일)의 'please test the setup for the live stream'에서 생방송 재생 설정을 테스트해달라고 했으므로 (A)가 정답이다.

패러프레이징
test the setup for the live stream 생방송 재생 설정을 테스트하다 →
Test a live stream connection 생방송 재생 연결을 테스트하다

어휘 newsletter n. 소식지

TEST 2

LISTENING TEST
p.70

1 (D)	2 (D)	3 (B)	4 (C)	5 (A)
6 (B)	7 (B)	8 (A)	9 (B)	10 (C)
11 (C)	12 (C)	13 (A)	14 (C)	15 (B)
16 (C)	17 (A)	18 (C)	19 (B)	20 (A)
21 (A)	22 (A)	23 (C)	24 (B)	25 (A)
26 (B)	27 (A)	28 (B)	29 (A)	30 (C)
31 (A)	32 (A)	33 (D)	34 (B)	35 (A)
36 (A)	37 (D)	38 (A)	39 (B)	40 (C)
41 (A)	42 (B)	43 (B)	44 (C)	45 (C)
46 (B)	47 (B)	48 (A)	49 (B)	50 (C)
51 (B)	52 (A)	53 (A)	54 (A)	55 (B)
56 (D)	57 (B)	58 (C)	59 (D)	60 (D)
61 (B)	62 (A)	63 (D)	64 (A)	65 (B)
66 (A)	67 (B)	68 (A)	69 (A)	70 (C)
71 (D)	72 (B)	73 (B)	74 (C)	75 (A)
76 (D)	77 (B)	78 (D)	79 (D)	80 (B)
81 (B)	82 (B)	83 (C)	84 (A)	85 (A)
86 (B)	87 (B)	88 (B)	89 (B)	90 (C)
91 (A)	92 (B)	93 (A)	94 (D)	95 (D)
96 (C)	97 (B)	98 (B)	99 (A)	100 (B)

READING TEST
p.82

101 (D)	102 (A)	103 (B)	104 (A)	105 (A)
106 (B)	107 (A)	108 (C)	109 (B)	110 (A)
111 (D)	112 (A)	113 (A)	114 (A)	115 (C)
116 (A)	117 (A)	118 (B)	119 (B)	120 (C)
121 (D)	122 (A)	123 (D)	124 (C)	125 (B)
126 (B)	127 (D)	128 (D)	129 (C)	130 (C)
131 (C)	132 (A)	133 (C)	134 (D)	135 (D)
136 (A)	137 (C)	138 (B)	139 (C)	140 (A)
141 (B)	142 (C)	143 (D)	144 (B)	145 (C)
146 (C)	147 (C)	148 (B)	149 (D)	150 (D)
151 (B)	152 (A)	153 (D)	154 (A)	155 (B)
156 (D)	157 (C)	158 (D)	159 (B)	160 (D)
161 (D)	162 (B)	163 (C)	164 (D)	165 (B)
166 (C)	167 (C)	168 (A)	169 (D)	170 (C)
171 (C)	172 (B)	173 (C)	174 (D)	175 (A)
176 (B)	177 (B)	178 (C)	179 (C)	180 (C)
181 (D)	182 (A)	183 (B)	184 (C)	185 (D)
186 (A)	187 (B)	188 (B)	189 (D)	190 (C)
191 (C)	192 (C)	193 (D)	194 (C)	195 (B)
196 (D)	197 (B)	198 (A)	199 (B)	200 (D)

PART 1

1 🔊 호주식 발음

(A) He is wiping down a table.
(B) He is typing on a laptop.
(C) He is making a cup of coffee.
(D) He is wearing an apron.

wipe down ~을 구석구석 닦다　type[taip] 타자를 치다
apron[éiprən] 앞치마

해석　(A) 그는 테이블을 구석구석 닦고 있다.
(B) 그는 휴대용 컴퓨터로 타자를 치고 있다.
(C) 그는 커피 한잔을 만들고 있다.
(D) 그는 앞치마를 입고 있다.

해설　**1인 사진**
(A) [×] wiping down(~을 구석구석 닦고 있다)은 남자의 동작과 무관하므로 오답이다. 사진에 있는 테이블(table)을 사용하여 혼동을 주었다.
(B) [×] typing(타자를 치고 있다)은 남자의 동작과 무관하므로 오답이다. 사진에 있는 휴대용 컴퓨터(laptop)를 사용하여 혼동을 주었다.
(C) [×] making a cup of coffee(커피 한잔을 만들고 있다)는 남자의 동작과 무관하므로 오답이다. 사진에 있는 잔(cup)을 사용하여 혼동을 주었다.
(D) [○] 남자가 앞치마를 입고 있는 모습을 가장 잘 묘사한 정답이다.

2 🔊 영국식 발음

(A) The woman is swimming near a ship.
(B) The woman is waving her hand.
(C) The man is soaking his legs in the water.
(D) The man is pulling on a rope.

wave one's hand 손을 흔들다　soak[미 souk, 영 səuk] 담그다
pull on a rope 밧줄을 잡아당기다

해석　(A) 여자가 배 근처에서 수영하고 있다.
(B) 여자가 손을 흔들고 있다.
(C) 남자가 다리를 물에 담그고 있다.
(D) 남자가 밧줄을 잡아당기고 있다.

해설　**2인 이상 사진**
(A) [×] swimming(수영하고 있다)은 여자의 동작과 무관하므로 오답이다.
(B) [×] waving her hand(손을 흔들고 있다)는 여자의 동작과 무관하므로 오답이다.
(C) [×] 남자가 다리를 배 안에 둔 상태인데, 물에 담그고 있다고 잘못 묘사한 오답이다.
(D) [○] 남자가 밧줄을 잡아당기고 있는 모습을 가장 잘 묘사한 정답이다.

3 🔊 캐나다식 발음

(A) Some trees are lined up along a trail.
(B) The ornate building has several awnings.
(C) Some tables are stacked near a door.
(D) A sign has fallen down.

line up ~을 일렬로 세우다   trail[treil] 오솔길
ornate[ɔːrnéit] 화려하게 장식된   awning[ɔ́ːniŋ] 차양, 비 가리개
stack[stæk] 쌓다   fall down 쓰러지다, 굴러 떨어지다

해석 (A) 몇몇 나무들이 오솔길을 따라 일렬로 세워져 있다.
　　 (B) 화려하게 장식된 건물은 여러 개의 차양이 있다.
　　 (C) 몇몇 탁자들이 문 근처에 쌓여 있다.
　　 (D) 표지판이 쓰러져 있다.

해설 **사물 및 풍경 사진**
　　 (A) [×] 사진에 오솔길(trail)이 없으므로 오답이다.
　　 (B) [○] 화려하게 장식된 건물에 여러 개의 차양이 있는 모습을 가장 잘 묘사한 정답이다.
　　 (C) [×] 사진에서 탁자들은 보이지만, 쌓여 있는(are stacked) 모습은 아니므로 오답이다.
　　 (D) [×] 표지판이 서 있는 상태인데, 쓰러져 있다고 잘못 묘사한 오답이다.

4 🔊 호주식 발음

(A) The woman is making a purchase.
(B) The woman is folding some clothes.
(C) The woman has a bag on her back.
(D) The woman is ironing a shirt.

make a purchase 물건을 사다   fold[미 fould, 영 fəuld] 개다, 접다
iron[미 áiərn, 영 aiən] 다리다, 다리미질하다

해석 (A) 여자가 물건을 사고 있다.
　　 (B) 여자가 몇몇 옷을 개고 있다.
　　 (C) 여자가 등에 가방을 메고 있다.
　　 (D) 여자가 셔츠를 다리고 있다.

해설 **1인 사진**
　　 (A) [×] making a purchase(물건을 사고 있다)는 여자의 동작과 무관하므로 오답이다.
　　 (B) [×] folding(개고 있다)은 여자의 동작과 무관하므로 오답이다. 사진에 있는 옷(clothes)을 사용하여 혼동을 주었다.
　　 (C) [○] 여자가 등에 가방을 메고 있는 모습을 가장 잘 묘사한 정답이다.
　　 (D) [×] ironing(다리고 있다)은 여자의 동작과 무관하므로 오답이다. 사진에 있는 셔츠(shirt)를 사용하여 혼동을 주었다.

5 🔊 영국식 발음

(A) A man is giving a lecture.
(B) Some seats are unoccupied.
(C) Desks are arranged in a circle.
(D) A lecturer is pointing toward a student.

give a lecture 강의를 하다

---

unoccupied[미 ʌnάːkjəpàid, 영 ʌnɔ́kjəpàid] 비어 있는
arrange[əréindʒ] 배열하다   point toward ~을 가리키다

해석 (A) 한 남자가 강의를 하고 있다.
　　 (B) 몇몇 자리들이 비어 있다.
　　 (C) 책상들이 원형으로 배열되어 있다.
　　 (D) 한 강사가 한 학생을 가리키고 있다.

해설 **2인 이상 사진**
　　 (A) [○] 한 남자가 강의를 하고 있는 모습을 가장 잘 묘사한 정답이다.
　　 (B) [×] 사진에서 비어 있는(unoccupied) 자리를 확인할 수 없으므로 오답이다.
　　 (C) [×] 책상들이 일렬로 배열되어 있는 상태인데, 원형으로 배열되어 있다고 잘못 묘사한 오답이다.
　　 (D) [×] 강사가 한 학생을 가리키고 있는 것이 아니라 화이트보드를 가리키고 있으므로 오답이다.

6 🔊 미국식 발음

(A) Some desk drawers are open.
(B) A computer station is situated in a corner.
(C) Some binders have been placed on the ground.
(D) A lamp has been turned off.

drawer[drɔːr] 서랍   situate[sítʃuèit] 위치시키다
binder[báindər] (종이 등을 함께 묶는) 바인더   turn off ~을 끄다

해석 (A) 몇몇 책상 서랍들이 열려 있다.
　　 (B) 컴퓨터가 구석에 위치해 있다.
　　 (C) 몇몇 바인더들이 바닥에 놓여 있다.
　　 (D) 스탠드가 꺼져 있다.

해설 **사물 및 풍경 사진**
　　 (A) [×] 책상 서랍들이 닫혀 있는 상태인데, 열려 있다고 잘못 묘사한 오답이다.
　　 (B) [○] 컴퓨터가 방구석에 위치해 있는 모습을 가장 잘 묘사한 정답이다.
　　 (C) [×] 바인더들이 선반에 놓여 있는 상태인데, 바닥에 놓여 있다고 잘못 묘사한 오답이다.
　　 (D) [×] 스탠드가 켜져 있는 상태인데, 꺼져 있다고 잘못 묘사한 오답이다.

PART 2

7 🔊 캐나다식 발음 → 미국식 발음

Where did you purchase this coat?
(A) I can hang your jacket up.
(B) At a department store.
(C) There they are.

purchase[미 pə́ːrtʃəs, 영 pə́ːtʃəs] 사다   hang up (그림·옷 등을) 걸다
department store 백화점

해석 당신은 이 외투를 어디에서 샀나요?
　　 (A) 제가 당신의 재킷을 걸어드릴게요.
　　 (B) 백화점에서요.
　　 (C) 저기 그것들이 있네요.

해설 **Where 의문문**
　　 (A) [×] 질문의 coat(외투)와 관련 있는 jacket(재킷)을 사용하여 혼

동을 준 오답이다.
(B) [○] 백화점에서라며, 외투를 산 장소를 언급했으므로 정답이다.
(C) [×] 외투를 어디에서 샀는지를 물었는데, 이와 관련이 없는 저기 그것들이 있다는 내용으로 응답했으므로 오답이다.

8 호주식 발음 → 영국식 발음

> When was the last time that you ate at this restaurant?
> **(A) Three weeks ago, I think.**
> (B) They loved the salad.
> (C) Great, I'll meet you there.

해석 당신이 이 음식점에서 마지막으로 식사한 것이 언제였나요?
(A) 3주 전인 것 같아요.
(B) 그들은 그 샐러드를 좋아했어요.
(C) 좋아요, 거기에서 만나요.

해설 When 의문문
(A) [○] 3주 전인 것 같다며, 이 음식점에서 마지막으로 식사한 시점을 언급했으므로 정답이다.
(B) [×] 질문의 restaurant(음식점)과 관련 있는 salad(샐러드)를 사용하여 혼동을 준 오답이다.
(C) [×] 질문의 restaurant(음식점)을 나타낼 수 있는 there를 사용하여 혼동을 준 오답이다.

9 캐나다식 발음 → 영국식 발음

> Who made these blueprints for the sports stadium?
> (A) We joined a basketball club.
> **(B) Charles and I.**
> (C) Yes, thanks for the blueprints.

blueprint[blúːprint] 설계도, 계획 sports stadium 운동 경기장

해석 누가 운동 경기장을 위한 이 설계도들을 그렸나요?
(A) 우리는 농구 동호회에 가입했어요.
(B) Charles와 제가요.
(C) 네, 설계도들 고마워요.

해설 Who 의문문
(A) [×] 질문의 sports stadium(운동 경기장)과 관련 있는 basketball(농구)을 사용하여 혼동을 준 오답이다.
(B) [○] Charles와 자신이라며, 설계도들을 그린 사람을 언급했으므로 정답이다.
(C) [×] 의문사 의문문에 Yes로 응답했으며, 질문의 blueprints를 반복 사용하여 혼동을 준 오답이다.

10 미국식 발음 → 캐나다식 발음

> How frequently is the recycling picked up?
> (A) Let me show you how.
> (B) Only paper-based materials.
> **(C) Every other week.**

frequently[fríːkwəntli] 자주 recycling[riːsáikliŋ] 재활용품
pick up ~을 수거하다, 치우다 material[mətíəriəl] 자재, 물질
every other week 격주로

해석 재활용품은 얼마나 자주 수거되나요?
(A) 어떻게 하는지 제가 보여드릴게요.
(B) 오직 종이로 된 자재들만요.
(C) 격주로요.

해설 How 의문문
(A) [×] 재활용품이 얼마나 자주 수거되는지를 물었는데, 이와 관련이 없는 어떻게 하는지 보여주겠다는 내용으로 응답했으므로 오답이다.
(B) [×] 질문의 recycling(재활용품)과 관련 있는 paper-based materials(종이로 된 자재들)를 사용하여 혼동을 준 오답이다.
(C) [○] 격주로라며, 재활용품이 수거되는 빈도를 언급했으므로 정답이다.

11 호주식 발음 → 영국식 발음

> Who is scheduled to work the night shift this week?
> (A) Because I changed my schedule.
> (B) Shift it to the left.
> **(C) Ron Walters, I believe.**

be scheduled to ~하기로 예정되어 있다 night shift 야간 근무

해석 이번 주에 누가 야간 근무를 하기로 예정되어 있나요?
(A) 제가 일정을 바꿨기 때문이에요.
(B) 그것을 왼쪽으로 옮기세요.
(C) Ron Walters인 것 같아요.

해설 Who 의문문
(A) [×] 질문의 scheduled를 schedule로 반복 사용하여 혼동을 준 오답이다.
(B) [×] 질문의 shift((교대) 근무)를 '옮기다'라는 의미의 동사로 반복 사용하여 혼동을 준 오답이다.
(C) [○] Ron Walters인 것 같다며, 이번 주에 야간 근무를 하기로 예정된 사람을 언급했으므로 정답이다.

12 캐나다식 발음 → 호주식 발음

> Do you know how to use the Skysoft program?
> (A) We've never met.
> (B) I'll use this one, then.
> **(C) Try asking Carlos.**

해석 Skysoft 프로그램을 어떻게 사용하는지 아시나요?
(A) 우리는 만난 적이 없어요.
(B) 그럼, 저는 이걸 사용할게요.
(C) Carlos에게 물어보세요.

해설 조동사 의문문
(A) [×] Skysoft 프로그램을 사용하는 방법을 물었는데, 이와 관련이 없는 우리는 만난 적이 없다는 내용으로 응답했으므로 오답이다.
(B) [×] 질문의 use를 반복 사용하여 혼동을 준 오답이다.
(C) [○] Carlos에게 물어보라는 말로, Skysoft 프로그램을 어떻게 사용하는지 모른다는 것을 간접적으로 전달했으므로 정답이다.

13 호주식 발음 → 영국식 발음

> May I take my afternoon break a few minutes early?
> **(A) Sure, go ahead.**
> (B) There are a few missing parts.
> (C) You should have tried the soup.

break[breik] 휴식 (시간) missing[mísiŋ] 없어진
part[미 paːrt, 영 paːt] 부품

해석 제가 몇 분 일찍 오후 휴식을 취해도 될까요?
(A) 물론이죠, 그러세요.

(B) 없어진 부품들이 몇 개 있어요.
(C) 당신은 그 수프를 먹어봤어야 했어요.

해설 **요청 의문문**
(A) [○] Sure로 몇 분 일찍 오후 휴식을 취하고 싶다는 요청을 수락한 정답이다.
(B) [×] 질문의 a few를 반복 사용하여 혼동을 준 오답이다.
(C) [×] 몇 분 일찍 오후 휴식을 취해도 되는지를 물었는데, 이와 관련이 없는 그 수프를 먹어봤어야 했다는 내용으로 응답했으므로 오답이다.

14 ③ 호주식 발음 → 미국식 발음

> When does the clinic usually close?
> (A) It's across from Regions Park.
> (B) We have four nurses on staff.
> **(C) It shuts down at 7 o'clock.**

clinic[klínik] 병원 across from ~의 맞은편에
on (the) staff 직원으로 있는 shut down 문을 닫다

해석 병원은 보통 언제 문을 닫나요?
(A) 그곳은 Regions 공원의 맞은편에 있어요.
(B) 저희는 네 명의 간호사들이 직원으로 있어요.
(C) 그곳은 7시에 문을 닫아요.

해설 **When 의문문**
(A) [×] 병원이 문을 닫는 시점을 물었는데, 위치로 응답했으므로 오답이다.
(B) [×] 질문의 clinic(병원)과 관련 있는 nurses(간호사들)를 사용하여 혼동을 준 오답이다.
(C) [○] 7시에 문을 닫는다며, 병원이 문을 닫는 시간을 언급했으므로 정답이다.

15 ③ 호주식 발음 → 영국식 발음

> Which briefcase belongs to our client, Mr. Powell?
> (A) The meeting was very brief.
> **(B) This black one is his.**
> (C) I keep my files in it.

briefcase[brí:fkeis] 서류 가방 belong to ~의 것이다
brief[bri:f] (시간이) 짧은

해석 어느 서류 가방이 우리 고객인 Mr. Powell의 것인가요?
(A) 회의는 굉장히 짧았어요.
(B) 이 검은 것이 그의 것이에요.
(C) 저는 제 서류철들을 그것 안에 보관해요.

해설 **Which 의문문**
(A) [×] briefcase – brief의 유사 발음 어휘를 사용하여 혼동을 준 오답이다.
(B) [○] 검은 것이라며, Mr. Powell의 서류 가방이 어느 것인지를 언급했으므로 정답이다.
(C) [×] 질문의 briefcase(서류 가방)와 관련 있는 files(서류철들)를 사용하고, briefcase(서류 가방)를 나타낼 수 있는 it을 사용하여 혼동을 준 오답이다.

16 ③ 캐나다식 발음 → 미국식 발음

> Why did you show up to work late?
> (A) Just on Tuesdays and Thursdays.
> (B) It should be starting in a few minutes.   ○

> **(C) I was stuck in traffic.**

show up 도착하다, 나타나다 stuck in traffic 교통이 막힌

해석 당신은 왜 회사에 늦게 도착했나요?
(A) 화요일과 목요일에만요.
(B) 몇 분 내로 시작할 거예요.
(C) 교통이 막혀 있었어요.

해설 **Why 의문문**
(A) [×] 왜 회사에 늦게 도착했는지를 물었는데, 이와 관련이 없는 화요일과 목요일에만이라는 내용으로 응답했으므로 오답이다.
(B) [×] 질문의 late(늦게)와 관련 있는 in a few minutes(몇 분 내로)를 사용하여 혼동을 준 오답이다.
(C) [○] 교통이 막혀 있었다며, 회사에 늦게 도착한 이유를 언급했으므로 정답이다.

17 ③ 영국식 발음 → 캐나다식 발음

> Who is leading the weekend fitness class, Carl or Jane?
> **(A) Nobody has been assigned yet.**
> (B) Only gym members can apply.
> (C) Sometime next weekend.

lead[li:d] 이끌다 fitness class 운동 수업 assign[əsáin] 배정하다
apply[əplái] 신청하다

해석 누가 주말 운동 수업을 이끄나요, Carl인가요 Jane인가요?
(A) 아직 아무도 배정되지 않았어요.
(B) 체육관 회원들만 신청할 수 있어요.
(C) 다음 주말 중에요.

해설 **선택 의문문**
(A) [○] 아직 아무도 배정되지 않았다는 말로, Carl과 Jane 둘 다 선택하지 않은 정답이다.
(B) [×] 질문의 fitness class(운동 수업)와 관련 있는 gym(체육관)을 사용하여 혼동을 준 오답이다.
(C) [×] 질문의 weekend를 반복 사용하여 혼동을 준 오답이다.

18 ③ 미국식 발음 → 캐나다식 발음

> My plane leaves this evening.
> (A) Yes. One ticket, please.
> (B) Tomorrow morning as well.
> **(C) Enjoy your trip.**

해석 제 비행기는 오늘 저녁에 떠나요.
(A) 네. 티켓 한 장 주세요.
(B) 내일 아침에도요.
(C) 즐거운 여행을 하세요.

해설 **평서문**
(A) [×] 질문의 plane(비행기)과 관련 있는 ticket(티켓)을 사용하여 혼동을 준 오답이다.
(B) [×] 질문의 evening(저녁)과 관련 있는 morning(아침)을 사용하여 혼동을 준 오답이다.
(C) [○] 즐거운 여행을 하라는 말로, 오늘 저녁에 상대방이 여행을 떠나는 것을 격려했으므로 정답이다.

19 영국식 발음 → 호주식 발음

How is the parking garage renovation progressing?
(A) It's free to park on the street.
(B) I got busy with another project.
(C) Please take out the garbage.

parking garage 주차장 renovation[rènəvéiʃən] 수리, 혁신
progress[prəgrés] 진행되다 take out 가지고 나가다
garbage[gάːrbidʒ] 쓰레기

해석 주차장 수리는 어떻게 진행되고 있나요?
(A) 거리에 주차하는 것은 무료예요.
(B) 다른 프로젝트로 인해 바빴어요.
(C) 쓰레기를 가지고 나가세요.

해설 How 의문문
(A) [×] parking – park의 유사 발음 어휘를 사용하여 혼동을 준 오답이다.
(B) [○] 다른 프로젝트로 인해 바빴다는 말로, 주차장 수리가 진행되지 않고 있음을 간접적으로 전달했으므로 정답이다.
(C) [×] garage – garbage의 유사 발음 어휘를 사용하여 혼동을 준 오답이다.

20 호주식 발음 → 영국식 발음

Isn't it time for the movie to begin?
(A) Not quite yet.
(B) What a great opening scene.
(C) It doesn't end until Sunday.

scene[siːn] 장면

해석 영화가 시작할 시간이 아닌가요?
(A) 아직 아니에요.
(B) 멋진 첫 장면이네요.
(C) 일요일이 되어서야 끝이 나요.

해설 부정 의문문
(A) [○] 아직 아니라는 말로, 영화가 시작할 시간이 되지 않았음을 전달했으므로 정답이다.
(B) [×] 질문의 movie(영화)와 관련 있는 scene(장면)을 사용하여 혼동을 준 오답이다.
(C) [×] 질문의 begin(시작하다)과 반대 의미인 end(끝나다)를 사용하여 혼동을 준 오답이다.

21 캐나다식 발음 → 미국식 발음

The hole in the conference room wall must be fixed.
(A) I've already contacted a repairperson.
(B) The room is painted a nice color.
(C) Only half of the attendees are here.

hole[미 houl, 영 həul] 구멍 conference room 회의실
repairperson[미 ripέərpɜ̀ːrsn, 영 ripέəpɜ̀ːsn] 수리공
attendee[ətèndíː] 참석자

해석 회의실 벽에 있는 구멍이 수리되어야 해요.
(A) 제가 이미 수리공에게 연락했어요.
(B) 그 방은 멋진 색으로 페인트칠 되었어요.
(C) 참석자들의 절반만 여기 있어요.

해설 평서문
(A) [○] 이미 수리공에게 연락했다는 말로, 구멍이 수리되어야 하는 문

제점에 대한 해결책을 제시했으므로 정답이다.
(B) [×] 질문의 room을 반복 사용하여 혼동을 준 오답이다.
(C) [×] 질문의 conference(회의)와 관련 있는 attendees(참석자들)를 사용하여 혼동을 준 오답이다.

22 캐나다식 발음 → 영국식 발음

What kind of food should we order for the employee appreciation luncheon tomorrow?
(A) Rachel cannot eat seafood.
(B) We are expecting 50 attendees.
(C) I appreciate the service.

appreciation[əpriːʃiéiʃən] 감사, 감상 luncheon[lʌ́ntʃən] 오찬
expect[ikspékt] 예상하다, 기대하다 attendee[ətèndíː] 참석자

해석 내일 직원 감사 오찬을 위해 어떤 종류의 음식을 주문해야 하나요?
(A) Rachel은 해산물을 먹을 수 없어요.
(B) 저희는 50명의 참석자들을 예상하고 있어요.
(C) 서비스에 감사드려요.

해설 What 의문문
(A) [○] Rachel은 해산물을 먹을 수 없다며, 해산물을 주문할 수 없음을 간접적으로 전달했으므로 정답이다.
(B) [×] 질문의 luncheon(오찬)과 관련 있는 attendees(참석자들)를 사용하여 혼동을 준 오답이다.
(C) [×] appreciation – appreciate의 유사 발음 어휘를 사용하여 혼동을 준 오답이다.

23 영국식 발음 → 캐나다식 발음

Where is the security training session being held?
(A) Safety is an important consideration.
(B) On Monday at 3 P.M.
(C) Didn't you check the e-mail?

security[미 sikjúərəti, 영 sikjúəriti] 보안, 안전
training session 교육 (과정)
consideration[kənsìdəréiʃn] 고려 사항

해석 보안 교육은 어디에서 열리나요?
(A) 안전은 중요한 고려 사항이에요.
(B) 월요일 오후 3시예요.
(C) 당신은 이메일을 확인하지 않았나요?

해설 Where 의문문
(A) [×] security – Safety의 유사 발음 어휘를 사용하여 혼동을 준 오답이다.
(B) [×] 보안 교육이 어디에서 열리는지를 물었는데 시점으로 응답했으므로 오답이다. 질문의 Where를 When으로 혼동하여 When is the security training session being held?(보안 교육은 언제 열리나요?)로 생각해 정답으로 선택하지 않도록 주의한다.
(C) [○] 이메일을 확인하지 않았는지 되물어, 보안 교육이 열리는 장소는 이메일에서 확인할 수 있음을 간접적으로 전달했으므로 정답이다.

24 미국식 발음 → 영국식 발음

Should we go swimming on Saturday, or is it going to be too cold?
(A) I've never been to that beach.
(B) The weather will be nice all weekend.

(C) Let me grab you a jacket.

해석 우리는 토요일에 수영하러 갈까요, 아니면 너무 추울까요?
(A) 저는 그 해변에 가본 적이 없어요.
(B) 주말 내내 날씨가 좋을 거예요.
(C) 제가 당신께 재킷을 가져다드릴게요.

해설 선택 의문문
(A) [×] 질문의 swimming(수영)과 관련 있는 beach(해변)를 사용하여 혼동을 준 오답이다.
(B) [○] 주말 내내 날씨가 좋을 것이라는 말로, 토요일에 수영하러 갈 것을 간접적으로 선택했으므로 정답이다.
(C) [×] 질문의 too cold(너무 추운)와 관련 있는 jacket(재킷)을 사용하여 혼동을 준 오답이다.

25 3에 미국식 발음 → 호주식 발음

This jewelry shop is quite expensive.
(A) The prices seem reasonable to me.
(B) The gold earrings.
(C) Yes, we can stop by the store.

jewelry[dʒúːəlri] 보석   reasonable[ríːzənəbl] (가격이) 적당한, 합리적인
stop by ~에 들르다

해석 이 보석 가게는 가격이 꽤 비싸요.
(A) 저에게는 그 가격이 적당해 보이는데요.
(B) 금귀걸이요.
(C) 네, 우리는 그 가게를 들를 수 있어요.

해설 평서문
(A) [○] 자신에게는 그 가격이 적당해 보인다는 말로, 보석 가게의 가격에 대한 의견을 제시했으므로 정답이다.
(B) [×] 질문의 jewelry(보석)와 관련 있는 gold earrings(금귀걸이)를 사용하여 혼동을 준 오답이다.
(C) [×] 질문의 shop(가게)과 같은 의미인 store(가게)를 사용하여 혼동을 준 오답이다.

26 3에 캐나다식 발음 → 미국식 발음

Are any of these wood sculptures handmade?
(A) No, we don't have a fireplace.
(B) Yes, they all are.
(C) Well, let's make some more.

sculpture[미 skʌ́lptʃər, 영 skʌ́lptʃə] 조각품
handmade[hæ̀ndméid] 손으로 만든, 수제의
fireplace[미 fáiərplèis, 영 fáiəplèis] 벽난로

해석 이 나무 조각품들 중에 어느 것이라도 손으로 만든 게 있나요?
(A) 아뇨, 저희는 벽난로가 없어요.
(B) 네, 그것들 전부요.
(C) 음, 몇 개 더 만듭시다.

해설 Be동사 의문문
(A) [×] 질문의 wood(나무)와 관련 있는 fireplace(벽난로)를 사용하여 혼동을 준 오답이다.
(B) [○] Yes로 손으로 만든 조각품이 있음을 전달한 후, 그것들 전부라는 부연 설명을 했으므로 정답이다.
(C) [×] 질문의 made를 make로 반복 사용하여 혼동을 준 오답이다.

27 3에 미국식 발음 → 캐나다식 발음

Has a director been selected to oversee our regional branch?
(A) The search is ongoing.
(B) No, she originally managed the team.
(C) Please write down the directions.

director[미 diréktər, 영 diréktə] 책임자
oversee[미 ðuvərsíː, 영 ðuvəsíː] 감독하다   regional[ríːdʒənl] 지역의
branch[미 bræntʃ, 영 brɑːntʃ] 지점
ongoing[미 ɑ́ːngòuiŋ, 영 ɔ́ngòuiŋ] 계속되는   manage[mǽnidʒ] 감독하다
direction[dirékʃən] 지시 사항

해석 우리 지역의 지점을 감독할 책임자가 선정되었나요?
(A) 계속 찾고 있어요.
(B) 아뇨, 그녀가 원래 그 팀을 감독했어요.
(C) 지시 사항들을 적어주세요.

해설 조동사 의문문
(A) [○] 계속 찾고 있다며, 책임자가 선정되지 않았음을 간접적으로 전달했으므로 정답이다.
(B) [×] 질문의 oversee(감독하다)와 같은 의미인 manage(감독하다)를 사용하여 혼동을 준 오답이다.
(C) [×] director - directions의 유사 발음 어휘를 사용하여 혼동을 준 오답이다.

28 3에 호주식 발음 → 미국식 발음

Shouldn't the maintenance worker be here by now?
(A) Now is not a good time for me.
(B) He's waiting in the lobby.
(C) To maintain our current workforce.

maintenance[méintənəns] 정비, 유지   by now 지금쯤
current[미 kə́ːrənt, 영 kʌ́rənt] 현재의
workforce[미 wə́ːrkfɔːrs, 영 wə́ːkfɔːs] (모든) 직원

해석 정비 직원이 지금쯤 여기 와야 하지 않나요?
(A) 지금은 저한테 좋은 때가 아니에요.
(B) 그는 로비에서 기다리고 있어요.
(C) 우리의 현 직원을 유지하기 위해서요.

해설 부정 의문문
(A) [×] 질문의 now를 반복 사용하여 혼동을 준 오답이다.
(B) [○] 그가 로비에서 기다리고 있다는 말로, 정비 직원이 이미 와 있음을 전달했으므로 정답이다.
(C) [×] maintenance - maintain의 유사 발음 어휘를 사용하여 혼동을 준 오답이다.

29 3에 호주식 발음 → 미국식 발음

Did someone from the accounting department call in sick?
(A) Apparently, Kyle Alton has the flu.
(B) I didn't account for those costs.
(C) The hospital staff is extremely helpful.

accounting department 회계부서
call in sick 아파서 결근한다고 연락하다
apparently[əpǽrəntli] 듣자 하니   flu[fluː] 독감
account for ~의 지출 내역을 보고하다   extremely[ikstríːmli] 굉장히

해석 회계 부서의 누군가가 아파서 결근한다고 연락했나요?
(A) 듣자 하니, Kyle Alton이 독감에 걸렸대요.
(B) 저는 그 비용의 지출 내역을 보고하지 않았어요.
(C) 그 병원 직원은 굉장히 도움이 돼요.

해설 **조동사 의문문**
(A) [ㅇ] Kyle Alton이 독감에 걸렸다는 말로, Kyle Alton이 아파서 결근한다고 연락했음을 간접적으로 전달했으므로 정답이다.
(B) [x] accounting – account의 유사 발음 어휘를 사용하여 혼동을 준 오답이다.
(C) [x] 질문의 call in sick(아파서 결근한다고 연락하다)와 관련 있는 hospital(병원)을 사용하여 혼동을 준 오답이다.

30 ③3 영국식 발음 → 캐나다식 발음

There will be room for everyone on the shuttle bus, right?
(A) I expect the drive to take an hour.
(B) The subway was quite busy.
(C) I don't think there's enough space.

room[ru:m] 자리 expect[ikspékt] 예상하다 busy[bízi] 붐비는
space[speis] 자리, 공간

해석 셔틀 버스에 모든 사람을 위한 자리가 있을 거예요, 그렇죠?
(A) 저는 주행이 한 시간 걸릴 것으로 예상해요.
(B) 지하철이 꽤 붐볐어요.
(C) 저는 충분한 자리가 있을 거라고 생각하지 않아요.

해설 **부가 의문문**
(A) [x] 질문의 shuttle bus(셔틀 버스)와 관련 있는 drive(주행)를 사용하여 혼동을 준 오답이다.
(B) [x] 질문의 shuttle bus(셔틀 버스)와 관련 있는 subway(지하철)를 사용하여 혼동을 준 오답이다.
(C) [ㅇ] 충분한 자리가 있을 거라고 생각하지 않는다는 말로, 셔틀 버스에 모든 사람을 위한 자리가 없을 것임을 전달했으므로 정답이다.

31 ③3 호주식 발음 → 미국식 발음

Can you show me how to install this ceiling fan?
(A) In just a couple of minutes.
(B) Yes, Tom installed the door.
(C) I'm a big fan of you.

install[instɔ́:l] 설치하다 ceiling[síːliŋ] 천장 fan[fæn] 선풍기, 팬

해석 이 천장 선풍기를 어떻게 설치하는지 보여주실 수 있나요?
(A) 몇 분 후에요.
(B) 네, Tom이 그 문을 설치했어요.
(C) 저는 당신의 열혈 팬이에요.

해설 **요청 의문문**
(A) [ㅇ] 몇 분 후에라는 말로, 천장 선풍기를 어떻게 설치하는지 보여달라는 요청을 수락한 정답이다.
(B) [x] 질문의 install을 installed로 반복 사용하여 혼동을 준 오답이다.
(C) [x] 질문의 fan(선풍기)을 '팬'이라는 의미의 명사로 반복 사용하여 혼동을 준 오답이다.

PART 3

32-34 ③3 캐나다식 발음 → 미국식 발음

Questions 32-34 refer to the following conversation.

M: Hello. This is Nathan Green. ³²I'm calling in regard to the interview I had with your firm for a financial adviser position. I was told I'd be contacted within two weeks of the interview date. ³³But I haven't heard from anyone yet.

W: Oh, I'm so sorry, Mr. Green. ³³Our accounting director is still reviewing résumés at the moment. He plans to select someone later this afternoon.

M: I understand. When can I expect to hear back about the decision, then?

W: ³⁴One of our human resources staff will be letting candidates know tomorrow morning. You'll find out at that time.

in regard to ~에 대해 interview[미 íntərvjùː, 영 íntəvjùː] 면접
financial[finǽnʃəl] 재정의 adviser[미 ædváizər, 영 ədváizə] 고문
accounting[əkáuntiŋ] 회계 director[미 diréktər, 영 diréktə] 부장
review[rivjúː] 검토하다 résumé[미 rézəmèi, 영 rézjuːmei] 이력서
at the moment (바로) 지금 select[silékt] 선발하다
candidate[미 kǽndidèit, 영 kǽndidət] 지원자 find out 알게 되다

해석
32–34번은 다음 대화에 관한 문제입니다.
남: 안녕하세요. 저는 Nathan Green입니다. ³²당신의 회사에서 봤던 재정 고문직 면접에 대해 전화드립니다. 저는 면접일로부터 2주 안에 연락을 받을 것이라고 들었습니다. ³³하지만 아직 아무에게도 연락이 오지 않았습니다.
여: 아, 정말 죄송합니다, Mr. Green. ³³지금 저희 회계부장님이 아직 이력서들을 검토하고 계십니다. 그는 오늘 오후 늦게 사람을 선발할 예정이에요.
남: 그렇군요. 그럼, 결정사항에 대해서 언제쯤 연락이 올 것이라고 예상하면 되나요?
여: ³⁴저희 인사부 직원 중 한 명이 내일 아침에 지원자들에게 알려드릴 겁니다. 그때 알게 되실 거예요.

32 목적 문제
해석 남자는 왜 전화를 했는가?
(A) 면접에 대해 물어보기 위해
(B) 일자리 제의를 받아들이기 위해
(C) 만남을 마련하기 위해
(D) 프로젝트에 대해 의논하기 위해

해설 전화의 목적을 묻는 문제이므로, 대화의 초반을 반드시 듣는다. 남자가 "I'm calling in regard to the interview I had with your firm for a financial adviser position."이라며 여자의 회사에서 봤던 재정 고문직 면접에 대해 전화한다고 하였다. 따라서 (A)가 정답이다.

어휘 accept[미 æksépt, 영 əksépt] 받아들이다 job offer 일자리 제의 arrange[əréindʒ] 마련하다

33 이유 문제
해석 왜 지연이 있었는가?
(A) 지원서가 제출되지 않았다.
(B) 몇몇 팀원들이 휴가 중이다.
(C) 채용 위원회가 아직 모이지 않았다.
(D) 몇몇 서류들이 검토 중에 있다.

해설 질문의 핵심 어구(delay)와 관련된 내용을 주의 깊게 듣는다. 남자가 "But I haven't heard from anyone yet."이라며 아직 아무에게도 연락이 오지 않았다고 하자, 여자가 "Our accounting director is still reviewing résumés at the moment."라며 지금 회계부장이 아직 이력서들을 검토하고 있다고 하였다. 따라서 (D)가 정답이다.

패러프레이징
reviewing résumés 이력서들을 검토하고 있다 → Some documents are being reviewed 몇몇 서류들이 검토 중에 있다

어휘 application form 지원서 submit[səbmít] 제출하다
be on vacation 휴가 중이다 committee[kəmíti] 위원회

34 다음에 할 일 문제

해석 인사팀 직원은 내일 아침에 무엇을 할 것 같은가?
(A) 지원자들을 견학시킨다.
(B) 지원자들에게 연락한다.
(C) 이력서를 검토한다.
(D) 일자리를 광고한다.

해설 질문의 핵심 어구(tomorrow morning)가 언급된 주변을 주의 깊게 듣는다. 여자가 "One of our human resources staff will be letting candidates know tomorrow morning."이라며 인사부 직원 중 한 명이 내일 아침에 지원자들에게 결정사항을 알려줄 것이라고 하였다. 따라서 (B)가 정답이다.

패러프레이징
letting candidates know 지원자들에게 알려주다 → Contact applicants 지원자들에게 연락하다

어휘 applicant[æplikənt] 지원자 give a tour 견학을 시켜주다
look over ~을 검토하다
advertise[미 ædvərtàiz, 영 ædvətàiz] 광고하다

35-37 [3w] 영국식 발음 → 호주식 발음

Questions 35-37 refer to the following conversation.

W: Greg, ³⁵the publisher will release my book in two months, so I need a professional profile photo for the cover. It needs to be done as soon as possible. Can you do it?

M: I'm free today and tomorrow. ³⁶If you can come by, we can get it done in about an hour.

W: That sounds great. ³⁷I have a video call with representatives of a public relations firm scheduled for this afternoon, but I can stop by your studio tomorrow. I'll see you around 10 A.M.

publisher[미 pʌ́bliʃər, 영 pʌ́bliʃə] 출판사, 출판인
release[rilí:s] 출간(시)하다 professional[prəféʃənl] 전문적인
cover[미 kʌ́vər, 영 kʌ́və] 표지 as soon as possible 되도록 빨리
free[fri:] 한가한 come by 들르다
representative[rèprizéntətiv] 대표(자) public relations 홍보

해석
35-37번은 다음 대화에 관한 문제입니다.

여: Greg, ³⁵출판사가 제 책을 두 달 후에 출간할 것이라서, 표지에 넣을 전문 프로필 사진이 필요해요. 이것은 되도록 빨리 끝나야 해요. 당신이 해줄 수 있나요?
남: 저는 오늘과 내일 한가해요. ³⁶당신이 들를 수 있다면, 우리는 그것을 한 시간 정도 안에 끝낼 수 있어요.
여: 좋아요. ³⁷제가 오늘 오후에는 홍보 회사의 대표들과 화상 통화가 예정되어 있지만, 내일 당신의 스튜디오에 들를 수 있어요. 오전 10시 정도에 뵐게요.

35 화자 문제

해석 여자의 직업은 무엇인 것 같은가?
(A) 작가
(B) 출판업자
(C) 사진사
(D) 연기자

해설 대화에서 신분 및 직업과 관련된 표현을 놓치지 않고 듣는다. 여자가 "the publisher will release my book in two months"라며 출판사가 자신의 책을 두 달 후에 출간할 것이라고 한 말을 통해 여자가 작가임을 알 수 있다. 따라서 (A)가 정답이다.

어휘 profession[prəféʃn] 직업(종)

36 의도 파악 문제

해석 남자는 "저는 오늘과 내일 한가해요"라고 말할 때 무엇을 의도하는가?
(A) 작업을 수행할 것이다.
(B) 마감 기한을 연장할 것이다.
(C) 일정을 업데이트할 것이다.
(D) 하루 쉴 것이다.

해설 질문의 인용어구(I'm free today and tomorrow)가 언급된 주변을 주의 깊게 듣는다. 남자가 "If you can come by, we can get it[profile photo] done in about an hour."라며 여자가 들를 수 있다면 프로필 사진을 한 시간 정도 안에 끝낼 수 있다고 한 말을 통해 남자가 작업을 수행할 것임을 알 수 있다. 따라서 (A)가 정답이다.

어휘 perform[미 pərfɔ́:rm, 영 pəfɔ́:m] 수행하다 extend[iksténd] 연장하다
deadline[dédlain] 마감 기한 take a day off 하루 쉬다

37 다음에 할 일 문제

해석 여자는 오후에 무엇을 할 것인가?
(A) 워크숍에 참석한다.
(B) 발표를 한다.
(C) 사무실을 방문한다.
(D) 온라인 회의에 참여한다.

해설 질문의 핵심 어구(afternoon)가 언급된 주변을 주의 깊게 듣는다. 여자가 "I have a video call ~ scheduled for this afternoon"이라며 오늘 오후에 화상 통화가 예정되어 있다고 한 말을 통해 여자가 오후에 온라인 회의에 참여할 것임을 알 수 있다. 따라서 (D)가 정답이다.

패러프레이징
have a video call ~ scheduled 화상 통화가 예정되어 있다 → Join an online meeting 온라인 회의에 참여하다

어휘 attend[əténd] 참석하다

38-40 [3w] 호주식 발음 → 미국식 발음 → 영국식 발음

Questions 38-40 refer to the following conversation with three speakers.

M: ³⁸We've had fewer customers since that new deli opened across the street.

W1: Yeah, some of our regular customers have started eating there instead.

W2: We should do something to get them back. Do you have any ideas, Jason?

M: ³⁹How about reducing what we charge for appetizers and entrées?

W2: That won't do much. I mean, ⁴⁰we're already cheaper than the deli.

W1: ⁴⁰True. We've always been one of the neighborhood's most affordable restaurants. ○

M: Then, let's have a staff meeting with everyone tonight to discuss other ideas.

deli[déli] 조제 식품 판매점 **regular customer** 단골손님
appetizer[미 숍pitàizər, 영 숍pətaizə] 에피타이저(입맛을 돋구는 요리)
entrée[미 ɑ́:ntrei, 영 ɔ́ntrei] 주요리
neighborhood[néibərhùd] 동네, 주변
affordable[미 əfɔ́:rdəbl, 영 əfɔ́:dəbl] 저렴한

해석
38-40번은 다음 세 명의 대화에 관한 문제입니다.

남: ³⁸우리는 길 건너에 있는 새로운 조제 식품 판매점이 문을 열고 나서 손님들이 적어졌어요.
여1: 맞아요, 우리의 단골손님들 중 몇 명이 거기서 대신 먹기 시작했어요.
여2: 그들을 다시 오게 하려면 우리는 무언가를 해야 해요. Jason, 무슨 의견 있나요?
남: ³⁹에피타이저들과 주요리들의 가격을 낮추는 건 어떨까요?
여2: 그건 크게 도움이 안 될 거예요. 제 말은, ⁴⁰그 조제 식품 판매점보다 우리가 이미 더 저렴하잖아요.
여1: ⁴⁰맞아요. 우리는 항상 이 동네의 가장 저렴한 음식점들 중 하나였어요.
남: 그렇다면, 다른 의견들에 대해 의논하기 위해서 오늘 밤에 모두와 직원 회의를 가지죠.

38 문제점 문제
해석 무엇이 문제인가?
(A) 손님들이 줄었다.
(B) 업체가 문을 닫았다.
(C) 손님들이 항의했다.
(D) 음식의 질이 낮아졌다.

해설 대화에서 부정적인 표현이 언급된 주변을 주의 깊게 듣는다. 남자가 "We've had fewer customers since that new deli opened across the street."이라며 길 건너에 있는 새로운 조제 식품 판매점이 문을 열고 나서 손님들이 적어졌다고 하였다. 따라서 (A)가 정답이다.

패러프레이징
had fewer customers 손님들이 적어졌다 → Customers have decreased 손님들이 줄었다

어휘 **decrease**[dikrí:s] (크기·수 등이) 줄다 **complain**[kəmpléin] 항의하다

39 제안 문제
해석 남자는 무엇을 제안하는가?
(A) 새로운 주요리들을 선보이기
(B) 가격을 낮추기
(C) 직원을 더 고용하기
(D) 무료 에피타이저들을 제공하기

해설 남자의 말에서 제안과 관련된 표현이 언급된 다음을 주의 깊게 듣는다. 남자가 "How about reducing what we charge for appetizers and entrées?"라며 에피타이저들과 주요리들의 가격을 낮추자고 제안하였다. 따라서 (B)가 정답이다.

어휘 **introduce**[ìntrədjú:s] 선보이다, 소개하다

40 언급 문제
해석 여자들은 그들의 음식점에 대해 무엇을 언급하는가?
(A) 동네로 막 옮겨왔다.
(B) 최근에 요리법들을 변경했다.
(C) 비싸지 않은 음식을 제공한다.
(D) 2호점을 개점할 예정이다.

해설 여자들의 말에서 질문의 핵심 어구(restaurant)와 관련된 내용을 주의 깊게 듣는다. 여자2가 "we[restaurant]'re already cheaper than the deli"라며 그 조제 식품 판매점보다 자신들의 음식점이 더

저렴하다고 하자, 여자1이 "True. We've always been one of the neighborhood's most affordable restaurants."라며 여자2의 말이 맞다고 한 후, 항상 이 동네의 가장 저렴한 음식점들 중 하나였다고 하였다. 이를 통해 음식점이 비싸지 않은 음식들을 제공함을 알 수 있다. 따라서 (C)가 정답이다.

패러프레이징
have ~ been one of the ~ most affordable restaurants 가장 저렴한 음식점들 중 하나였다 → offers inexpensive dishes 비싸지 않은 음식들을 제공하다

어휘 **recipe**[미 résəpi, 영 résipi] 요리법
inexpensive[ìnikspénsiv] 비싸지 않은 **dish**[diʃ] 음식

41-43 [3a] 캐나다식 발음 → 미국식 발음

Questions 41-43 refer to the following conversation.

M: ⁴¹I've booked my flight to Spain for the trade exhibit next week, but I'm not sure where to stay. ⁴²This is my first time going to Barcelona, so I'm not familiar with the hotels there.
W: It's being held at the new convention center in the harbor district, right? I know of two hotels in the area . . . um, Hotel Costal is closer to the center, but ⁴³I'm concerned since it has higher rates. It's almost $200 for a room.
M: The company will reimburse me up to $250 per night, so ⁴³that's fine. Plus, I'd like to be near the event venue.

book[buk] 예약하다 **trade exhibit** 무역 전시회
be familiar with ~을 잘 알다 **harbor**[hɑ́:rbər] 항만
district[dístrikt] 지구, 지역 **rate**[reit] 요금
reimburse[미 rì:imbə́rs, 영 rì:imbə́:s] 상환하다 **up to** ~까지
venue[vénjuː] 장소

해석
41-43번은 다음 대화에 관한 문제입니다.

남: ⁴¹저는 다음 주 무역 전시회를 위해 스페인행 항공편을 예약했는데, 어디서 머무를지를 모르겠어요. ⁴²바르셀로나에 가는 게 이번이 처음이라, 저는 거기에 있는 호텔들을 잘 몰라요.
여: 그것은 항만 지구에 있는 새 컨벤션 센터에서 열리죠, 그렇죠? 제가 그 지역에 호텔 두 곳을 아는데... 음, Costal 호텔이 센터와 더 가깝지만, ⁴³요금이 더 높아서 우려되네요. 방 하나에 거의 200달러예요.
남: 회사가 일 박당 250달러까지 상환해줄 것이라서, ⁴³그건 괜찮아요. 게다가, 저는 행사 장소와 가까이 있고 싶어요.

41 다음에 할 일 문제
해석 다음 주에 무슨 일이 일어날 것인가?
(A) 여행 박람회
(B) 상점 개점
(C) 호텔 컨벤션
(D) 무역 박람회

해설 질문의 핵심 어구(next week)가 언급된 주변을 주의 깊게 듣는다. 남자가 "I've booked my flight to Spain for the trade exhibit next week"이라며 다음 주 무역 전시회를 위해 스페인행 항공편을 예약했다고 하였다. 따라서 (D)가 정답이다.

패러프레이징
trade exhibit 무역 전시회 → trade show 무역 박람회

42 주제 문제
해석 화자들은 주로 무엇에 대해 이야기하고 있는가?

(A) 항공편 일정
(B) 숙소 선택
(C) 행사 장소
(D) 전시회 날짜

해설 대화의 주제를 묻는 문제이므로, 대화의 초반을 반드시 듣는다. 남자가 "This is my first time going to Barcelona, so I'm not familiar with the hotels there."라며 바르셀로나에 가는 것이 이번이 처음이라 거기에 있는 호텔들을 잘 모른다고 한 후, 숙소 선택에 대한 내용으로 대화가 이어지고 있다. 따라서 (B)가 정답이다.

어휘 accommodation[미 əkàmədéiʃən, 영 əkɔ̀mədéiʃən] 숙소

43 의도 파악 문제
해설 남자는 왜 "회사가 일 박당 250달러까지 상환해줄 것이라"라고 말하는가?
(A) 제안을 거절하기 위해
(B) 우려를 해결하기 위해
(C) 제의를 하기 위해
(D) 불평에 대응하기 위해

해설 질문의 인용어구(The company will reimburse me up to $250 per night)가 언급된 주변을 주의 깊게 듣는다. 여자가 "I'm concerned since it[Hotel Costal] has higher rates. It's almost $200 for a room."이라며 Costal 호텔의 요금이 더 높아서 우려된다고 한 후, 방 하나에 거의 200달러라고 하자, 남자가 "that's fine"이라며 괜찮다고 한 말을 통해 여자의 우려를 해결하기 위함임을 알 수 있다. 따라서 (B)가 정답이다.

어휘 reject[ridʒékt] 거절하다 address[ədrés] 해결하다, 처리하다
respond[미 rispáːnd, 영 rispɔ́nd] 대응하다
complaint[kəmpléint] 불평

44-46 [호주식 발음 → 영국식 발음]

Questions 44-46 refer to the following conversation.

M: Janna, this is Martin Rodriguez. I'm calling to let you know that [44]my truck broke down on Freeway 76 near Exit 23 when I was plowing snow from the road. [44/45]I need to be picked up.

W: [45]I'll dispatch another one of our employees to get you right away. However, I won't be able to send a tow truck until tomorrow afternoon. [46]Is the vehicle blocking traffic where it's currently parked?

M: No, I managed to stop on the side of the road, so it should be fine here.

---

break down 고장 나다 freeway[fríːwei] 고속도로
plow[plau] 제설하다 pick up ~을 (차에) 태우다
dispatch[dispǽtʃ] (특별한 목적을 위해) 보내다
tow[미 tou, 영 təu] 견인; (자동차·보트를) 끌다
block[미 blɑk, 영 blɔk] 막다, 차단하다 manage[mǽnidʒ] 잘 처리하다

해석

44-46번은 다음 대화에 관한 문제입니다.

남: Janna, 저는 Martin Rodriguez예요. [44]제가 도로에서 제설을 하던 중 23번 출구 근처의 76번 고속도로에서 제 트럭이 고장이 난 것을 당신에게 알리기 위해 전화했어요. [44/45]저를 태우러 와주셔야 해요.

여: [45]당신을 데리러 우리 직원들 중 다른 한 명을 바로 보내드릴게요. 하지만, 저는 내일 오후나 되어야 견인 트럭을 보낼 수 있을 거예요. [46]차량이 현재 세워져 있는 곳에서 교통을 막고 있나요?

남: 아니요, 제가 도로변에 멈추도록 잘 처리해서, 여기에 있는 건 괜찮을 거예요.

---

44 문제점 문제
해석 남자의 문제는 무엇인가?
(A) 직원이 시간이 되지 않는다.
(B) 고속도로를 이용할 수 없다.
(C) 차량이 작동하지 않는다.
(D) 차고가 열려있지 않다.

해설 남자의 말에서 부정적인 표현이 언급된 주변을 주의 깊게 듣는다. 남자가 "my truck broke down ~. I need to be picked up."이라며 자신의 트럭이 고장이 났다고 한 후, 자신을 태우러 와주어야 한다고 하였다. 따라서 (C)가 정답이다.

패러프레이징
truck broke down 트럭이 고장 났다 → vehicle is not functioning 차량이 작동하지 않는다

어휘 available[əvéiləbl] 시간이 되는, 이용할 수 있는
highway[háiwèi] 고속도로 accessible[əksésəbl] 이용(접근) 가능한
function[fʌ́ŋkʃən] 작동하다

45 특정 세부 사항 문제
해석 여자는 무엇을 하기로 동의하는가?
(A) 메시지를 전달한다.
(B) 눈을 치운다.
(C) 직원을 보낸다.
(D) 응급요원에게 연락한다.

해설 대화에서 여자의 말을 주의 깊게 듣는다. 남자가 "I need to be picked up."이라며 자신을 태우러 와주어야 한다고 하자, 여자가 "I'll dispatch another one of our employees to get you right away."라며 남자를 데리러 직원들 중 다른 한 명을 바로 보내겠다고 하였다. 따라서 (C)가 정답이다.

어휘 forward[미 fɔ́ːrwərd, 영 fɔ́ːwəd] 전달하다
emergency personnel 응급요원

46 특정 세부 사항 문제
해석 여자는 무엇에 대해 물어보는가?
(A) 트럭이 견인될 수 있는지
(B) 교통이 막혀있는지
(C) 무엇이 지연을 초래했는지
(D) 언제 남자를 태우러 와야 하는지

해설 대화에서 여자의 말을 주의 깊게 듣는다. 여자가 남자에게 "Is the vehicle blocking traffic where it's currently parked?"라며 차량이 현재 세워져 있는 곳에서 교통을 막고 있는지 물었다. 따라서 (B)가 정답이다.

어휘 cause[kɔːz] 초래하다

47-49 [호주식 발음 → 미국식 발음]

Questions 47-49 refer to the following conversation.

M: Cindy, [47]could you drive some people to the employee retreat this weekend?

W: I thought we had hired a bus.

M: We reserved two, but the bus company just informed me that [48]one of the buses had an accident this morning, and their mechanic is out of town this week.

W: Oh, I see. I don't mind driving, and I have room for six others in my SUV.

M: You've made my job a lot easier. I really appreciate this.

W: If you need another vehicle, you should ask Bob Granger in marketing.

M: Do you think he'd be willing to drive?

W: Yes, and ⁴⁹he has a 15-passenger van.

---

retreat[ritríːt] 야유회　hire[미 haiər, 영 haiə] (단기간) 빌리다
inform[미 infɔ́ːrm, 영 infɔ́ːm] 알리다　mechanic[məkǽnik] 정비공
be out of town 출장 중이다　mind[maind] 상관하다, 개의하다
room[ruːm] 공간　be willing to 흔쾌히 ~하다

해석
47-49번은 다음 대화에 관한 문제입니다.

남: Cindy, ⁴⁷당신이 이번 주말에 몇몇 사람들을 직원 야유회까지 태워줄 수 있나요?

여: 저는 우리가 버스를 빌린 줄 알았어요.

남: 두 대를 빌렸는데, 버스 회사가 방금 저에게 ⁴⁸버스들 중 한 대가 오늘 아침에 사고가 났고, 그들의 정비공이 이번 주에 출장 중이라고 알려줬어요.

여: 아, 그렇군요. 저는 운전하는 것은 상관없고, 제 SUV에 여섯 명의 다른 사람들을 위한 공간이 있어요.

남: 당신 덕분에 일이 훨씬 수월해졌어요. 정말 고마워요.

여: 차량이 더 필요하다면, 마케팅팀의 Bob Granger에게 물어보세요.

남: 그가 흔쾌히 운전해줄 거라고 생각하나요?

여: 네, 그리고 ⁴⁹그는 15인승 밴을 가지고 있어요.

47 요청 문제
해석 남자는 여자에게 무엇을 하라고 요청하는가?
(A) 교통편을 제공한다.
(B) 목적지를 선택한다.
(C) 구입을 한다.
(D) 정보를 확인한다.

해설 남자의 말에서 요청과 관련된 표현이 언급된 다음을 주의 깊게 듣는다. 남자가 여자에게 "could you drive some people to the employee retreat this weekend?"라며 이번 주말에 몇몇 사람들을 직원 야유회까지 태워줄 수 있는지를 물었다. 이를 통해 남자가 여자에게 교통편을 제공해줄 것을 요청하고 있음을 알 수 있다. 따라서 (A)가 정답이다.

패러프레이징
drive 태워주다 → Provide transportation 교통편을 제공하다

어휘 destination[미 dèstənéiʃən, 영 dèstinéiʃən] 목적지, 도착지
verify[vérəfài] 확인하다, 검증하다

48 특정 세부 사항 문제
해석 오늘 아침에 무슨 일이 일어났는가?
(A) 버스가 파손되었다.
(B) 행사가 일정이 변경되었다.
(C) 정비공이 고용되었다.
(D) 예약이 확정되었다.

해설 질문의 핵심 어구(this morning)가 언급된 주변을 주의 깊게 듣는다. 남자가 "one of the buses had an accident this morning, and their mechanic is out of town this week"이라며 버스들 중 한 대가 오늘 아침에 사고가 났고 그들의 정비공이 이번 주에 출장 중이라고 한 말을 통해 버스가 파손되었음을 알 수 있다. 따라서 (A)가 정답이다.

어휘 reschedule[미 riːskédʒuːl, 영 rìːʃédʒuːl] 일정을 변경하다
confirm[미 kənfɔ́ːrm, 영 kənfɔ́ːm] 확정하다

49 언급 문제
해석 Bob Granger에 대해 무엇이 언급되는가?
(A) 전문 운전기사이다.
(B) 큰 차를 가지고 있다.

(C) 행사 주최자이다.
(D) 야유회 장소를 잘 안다.

해설 질문의 핵심 어구(Bob Granger)와 관련된 내용을 주의 깊게 듣는다. 여자가 "he[Bob Granger] has a 15-passenger van"이라며 Bob Granger가 15인승 밴을 가지고 있다고 하였다. 따라서 (B)가 정답이다.

어휘 automobile[ɔ̀ːtəməbíːl] 차(량)
organizer[미 ɔ́ːrgənàizər, 영 ɔ́ːgənaizə] 주최자, 조직자

50-52 3ꓮ 캐나다식 발음 → 영국식 발음

Questions 50-52 refer to the following conversation.

M: I was just in the conference room to set up for the board meeting this afternoon, and ⁵⁰I discovered that the projector won't turn on. I think it might be broken.

W: Oh, the projector isn't broken. ⁵¹I unplugged the power cord earlier today in order to use the outlet. I must have forgotten to plug it back in after recharging my cell phone.

M: I see. Well, I've never noticed an outlet in that room. ⁵²Can you tell me where it's located?

W: Sure. It's on the wall opposite the door. There's a table in front of it, which you'll have to move to plug in the cord.

---

set up ~을 준비하다, 세우다　board meeting 이사회 회의
discover[미 diskʌ́vər, 영 diskʌ́və] 알아내다, 발견하다　turn on 켜지다
broken[미 bróukən, 영 brɔ́ukən] 고장 난　unplug[ʌnplʌ́g] 플러그를 뽑다
power cord 전선　outlet[áutlet] 콘센트
recharge[미 riːtʃɑ́ːrdʒ, 영 riːtʃɑ́ːdʒ] (재)충전하다

해석
50-52번은 다음 대화에 관한 문제입니다.

남: 제가 방금 오늘 오후 이사회 회의를 준비하려고 회의실에 있었는데, ⁵⁰영사기가 켜지지 않는 것을 알았어요. 제 생각에 그것은 고장 난 것 같아요.

여: 아, 그 영사기는 고장 난 게 아니에요. ⁵¹제가 콘센트를 사용하려고 오늘 오전에 전선을 뽑았어요. 제가 제 핸드폰을 충전하고 나서 다시 그걸 꽂는 것을 잊어버린 게 분명해요.

남: 그렇군요. 음, 그 방에 콘센트가 있는지 전혀 몰랐어요. ⁵²그것이 어디 있는지 알려줄 수 있나요?

여: 그럼요. 문 반대편 벽에 있어요. 콘센트 앞에 테이블이 있는데, 전선을 꽂으려면 그것을 옮겨야 할 거예요.

50 문제점 문제
해석 남자는 무슨 문제를 언급하는가?
(A) 임무가 완료되지 않았다.
(B) 서류가 분실됐다.
(C) 기기가 작동하지 않는다.
(D) 사무실이 현재 사용되고 있다.

해설 남자의 말에서 부정적인 표현이 언급된 주변을 주의 깊게 듣는다. 남자가 "I discovered that the projector won't turn on"이라며 영사기가 켜지지 않는 것을 알았다고 하였다. 따라서 (C)가 정답이다.

패러프레이징
projector won't turn on 영사기가 켜지지 않는다 → device is not working 기기가 작동하지 않는다

어휘 assignment[əsáinmənt] (할당된) 임무　complete[kəmplíːt] 완료하다
lost[lɔːst] (물건이) 분실된　device[diváis] 기기, 장치
be in use 사용되고 있다

51 특정 세부 사항 문제

해석 여자는 오늘 오전에 무엇을 했는가?
(A) 영사기를 시험해봤다.
(B) 배터리를 충전했다.
(C) 전화기를 잃어버렸다.
(D) 회의에 참여했다.

해설 질문의 핵심 어구(earlier today)가 언급된 주변을 주의 깊게 듣는다. 여자가 "I unplugged the power cord earlier today ~. I must have forgotten to plug it back in after recharging my cell phone."이라며 오늘 오전에 전선을 뽑았다고 한 후, 핸드폰을 충전하고 나서 다시 그걸 꽂는 것을 잊어버린 게 분명하다고 한 말을 통해 여자가 오늘 오전에 배터리를 충전했음을 알 수 있다. 따라서 (B)가 정답이다.

어휘 **test**[test] 시험해보다(하다)
charge[미 tʃɑːrdʒ, 영 tʃɑːdʒ] 충전하다, 청구하다

52 특정 세부 사항 문제

해석 남자는 여자에게 무엇에 대해 물어보는가?
(A) 콘센트의 위치
(B) 전선의 길이
(C) 방의 크기
(D) 테이블의 높이

해설 대화에서 남자의 말을 주의 깊게 듣는다. 남자가 여자에게 "Can you tell me where it[outlet]'s located?"라며 콘센트가 어디 있는지 알려줄 수 있는지 물었다. 따라서 (A)가 정답이다.

어휘 **length**[미 leŋkθ, 영 leŋθ] 길이 **height**[hait] 높이

53-55 ③ 미국식 발음 → 캐나다식 발음 → 호주식 발음

Questions 53-55 refer to the following conversation with three speakers.

W: Chris, have you met Nick Walters, here? ⁵³He's just joined our company and will help us prepare the annual financial reports.

M1: Oh, that's great. It's nice to meet you, Nick. Have you worked for an investment bank like ours before?

M2: Yes, actually. I was a financial manager at Opus Investments for about five years.

M1: ⁵⁴That's quite a renowned corporation! Well, I'm glad to have you on the team. Is your desk on the ninth floor?

W: It is. He'll be sitting right next to me. ⁵⁵Let me lead you there now, Nick.

M2: All right, then. It was a pleasure meeting you, Chris.

join[dʒɔin] 입사하다, 참여하다 **financial**[finǽnʃəl] 회계의, 재정의
investment bank 투자 은행 **renowned**[rináund] 유명한
lead[liːd] 안내하다

해석

53-55번은 다음 세 명의 대화에 관한 문제입니다.

여: Chris, 여기 있는 Nick Walters를 만나신 적이 있나요? ⁵³그는 우리 회사에 막 입사했고 우리가 연례 회계 보고서들을 준비하는 데 도움을 줄 거예요.

남1: 아, 잘됐네요. Nick, 만나서 반가워요. 당신은 이전에 저희와 같은 투자 은행에서 일한 적이 있나요?

남2: 네, 실은 있어요. Opus Investments사에서 약 5년 동안 재무부장으로 있었어요.

남1: ⁵⁴그곳은 꽤 유명한 회사잖아요! 어쨌든, 당신을 팀에 두게 되어서 기뻐요. 당신의 자리는 9층에 있나요?

여: 맞아요. 그는 바로 제 옆에 앉을 거예요. ⁵⁵Nick, 그곳으로 제가 지금 안내할게요.

남2: 알겠어요, 그럼. Chris, 만나서 반가웠어요.

53 특정 세부 사항 문제

해석 여자에 따르면, 매년 무엇이 준비되는가?
(A) 회계 서류들
(B) 산업 협의회
(C) 교육 프로그램들
(D) 투자 계획

해설 여자의 말에서 질문의 핵심 어구(prepared every year)와 관련된 내용을 주의 깊게 듣는다. 여자가 "He[Nick Walters] ~ will help us prepare the annual financial reports."라며 Nick Walters가 연례 회계 보고서들을 준비하는 데 도움을 줄 것이라고 한 말을 통해 매년 회계 서류들이 준비됨을 알 수 있다. 따라서 (A)가 정답이다.

54 언급 문제

해석 Opus Investments사에 대해 무엇이 언급되는가?
(A) 유명한 회사이다.
(B) 9층에 있다.
(C) 신설 회사이다.
(D) 직원들을 이전시키고 있다.

해설 질문의 핵심 어구(Opus Investments)와 관련된 내용을 주의 깊게 듣는다. 남자1이 "That[Opus Investments]'s quite a renowned corporation!"이라며 Opus Investments사는 꽤 유명한 회사라고 하였다. 따라서 (A)가 정답이다.

어휘 **well-known**[미 wèlnóun, 영 wèlnə́un] 유명한, 잘 알려진
relocate[미 riːlóukeit, 영 rìːləukéit] 이전시키다, 이동하다

55 제안 문제

해석 여자는 무엇을 해주겠다고 제안하는가?
(A) 관리자들과의 회의를 준비한다.
(B) 동료를 업무 공간으로 안내한다.
(C) 회사 모임을 위한 자리를 배치한다.
(D) 생산 공장을 둘러보게 한다.

해설 여자의 말에서 제안과 관련된 표현이 언급된 다음을 주의 깊게 듣는다. 여자가 "Let me lead you there[Nick's desk] now, Nick."이라며 Nick에게 자리로 지금 안내하겠다고 하였다. 따라서 (B)가 정답이다.

어휘 **supervisor**[미 súːpərvàizər, 영 súːpəvaizə] 관리자, 감독관
arrange[əréindʒ] 배치하다 **gathering**[gǽðəriŋ] 모임
give a tour ~을 둘러보게 하다 **production facility** 생산 공장

56-58 ③ 호주식 발음 → 미국식 발음

Questions 56-58 refer to the following conversation.

M: Beth, I heard that you're giving a presentation at the Dumont Conference Center next week.

W: That's right. It's for a group of investors interested in one of our company's upcoming projects. ⁵⁶I'm a little worried, though. I've never been to the center. And I'm not sure what kind of audiovisual equipment is set up in the rooms.

M: Can't you just ask someone who works there?

W: ⁵⁷It's closed this week. I guess the lobby is being remodeled. ↻

M: Hmm . . . Maybe you should speak to Molly Martin in the research department. She attended a workshop at the center last month. So [58]she'll be able to give you the information you need. Her extension is 459.

investor[미 invéstər, 영 invéstə] 투자자 upcoming[ʌ́pkʌ̀miŋ] 곧 있을
audiovisual[미 ɔ̀ːdiouvíʒuəl, 영 ɔ̀ːdiəuvíʒuəl] 시청각의
set up ~을 설치하다 remodel[미 riːmáːdəl, 영 riːmɔ́ːdəl] 보수하다
extension[iksténʃən] 내선 번호

해석
56-58번은 다음 대화에 관한 문제입니다.

남: Beth, 당신이 다음 주에 Dumont 회의장에서 발표를 할 거라고 들었어요.

여: 맞아요. 우리 회사의 곧 있을 프로젝트들 중 하나에 관심이 있는 투자자 단체를 위한 거예요. [56]그렇지만, 저는 조금 걱정돼요. 저는 그 회의장에 가본 적이 없거든요. 그리고 회의실에 어떤 종류의 시청각 장비가 설치되어 있는지 모르겠어요.

남: 거기서 일하는 사람에게 그냥 물어보면 안 되나요?

여: [57]그곳은 이번 주에 문을 닫아요. 로비가 보수되고 있는 것 같아요.

남: 흠... 연구부에 있는 Molly Martin에게 이야기해보는 게 좋겠어요. 그녀는 지난달에 그 회의장에서 하는 워크숍에 참석했어요. 그러니 [58]당신이 필요한 정보를 그녀가 줄 수 있을 거예요. 그녀의 내선 번호는 459번이에요.

56 문제점 문제
해석 여자의 문제는 무엇인가?
(A) 발표를 볼 수 없다.
(B) 행사에 참석할 수 없다.
(C) 장비를 대여할 수 없다.
(D) 장소에 대해 잘 모른다.

해설 여자의 말에서 부정적인 표현이 언급된 다음을 주의 깊게 듣는다. 여자가 "I'm a little worried, though. I've never been to the center."라며 조금 걱정된다고 하며, 회의장에 가본 적이 없다고 한 말을 통해 여자가 장소에 대해 잘 모른다는 것을 알 수 있다. 따라서 (D)가 정답이다.

패러프레이징
have never been to the center 회의장에 가본 적이 없다
→ is unfamiliar with a venue 장소에 대해 잘 모른다

어휘 unfamiliar[미 ʌnfəmíliər, 영 ʌnfəmíliə] (~에 대해) 잘 모르는

57 이유 문제
해석 Dumont 회의장은 왜 이번 주에 문을 닫는가?
(A) 보수되고 있다.
(B) 로비가 청소되고 있다.
(C) 행사를 위해 준비되고 있다.
(D) 음향 시스템이 업그레이드되고 있다.

해설 질문의 핵심 어구(closed this week)가 언급된 주변을 주의 깊게 듣는다. 여자가 "It[Dumont Conference Center]'s closed this week. I guess the lobby is being remodeled."라며 Dumont 회의장은 이번 주에 문을 닫는다고 한 후, 로비가 보수되고 있는 것 같다고 하였다. 따라서 (A)가 정답이다.

어휘 renovate[rénəveit] 보수하다

58 방법 문제
해석 여자는 필요한 정보를 어떻게 얻을 수 있는가?
(A) 투자자와 만남으로써
(B) 워크숍에 참석함으로써
(C) 동료에게 전화함으로써

(D) 웹사이트를 방문함으로써

해설 질문의 핵심 어구(information ~ requires)와 관련된 내용을 주의 깊게 듣는다. 남자가 "she[Molly Martin]'ll be able to give you the information you need. Her extension is 459."라며 여자가 필요한 정보를 Molly Martin이 줄 수 있을 것이라고 한 후, 그녀의 내선 번호는 459번이라고 한 말을 통해 여자가 동료에게 전화함으로써 필요한 정보를 얻을 수 있음을 알 수 있다. 따라서 (C)가 정답이다.

어휘 coworker[미 kóuwə̀ːrkər, 영 kə́uwə̀ːkə] 동료

59-61 [음성] 캐나다식 발음 → 미국식 발음

Questions 59-61 refer to the following conversation.

M: [59]I'm trying to decide which of these boats would best suit my needs, but I can't. Would you mind giving me a recommendation?

W: Of course. [60]We offer over 20 different fishing boats, so I can understand why you're struggling to make up your mind. Are you interested in any specific features?

M: I'd like one that has fishing rod holders and a built-in cooler for food and drinks. It should also seat at least four people.

W: We have three models that meet those criteria. [61]Follow me, and I'll show them to you.

suit[suːt] ~에 적합하다 needs[niːdz] 필요, 요구
recommendation[미 rèkəmandéiʃən, 영 rèkəmendéiʃən] 추천
offer[미 ɔ́ːfər, 영 ɔ́fə] 팔려고 내놓다, 제공하다
struggle[strʌ́gl] 어려움을 겪다 make up one's mind 결정하다
specific[미 spisífik, 영 spəsífik] 구체적인, 특정한 fishing rod 낚싯대
built-in[bìltín] 내장된 seat[siːt] 수용하다, 앉히다
meet[miːt] (필요·요구 등을) 충족시키다
criterion[kraitíəriən] 기준(criteria의 단수형)

해석
59-61번은 다음 대화에 관한 문제입니다.

남: [59]저는 이 배들 중에 어떤 것이 제 필요에 가장 적합할지 결정하려고 하는데, 못하겠어요. 제게 추천 좀 해주시겠어요?

여: 물론이죠. [60]저희는 20대가 넘는 여러 가지 낚싯배들을 팔고 있어서, 고객님이 왜 결정하는 데 어려움을 겪고 계신지 이해할 수 있어요. 관심 있으신 구체적인 특징들이 있나요?

남: 저는 낚싯대 받침대들과 음식과 음료를 위한 내장된 냉장고가 있는 것을 원해요. 또한 최소한 4명은 수용할 수 있어야 해요.

여: 저희에게 그 기준들을 충족시키는 3개의 모델들이 있어요. [61]저를 따라오시면, 제가 그것들을 보여드릴게요.

59 특정 세부 사항 문제
해석 남자는 무엇에 도움이 필요한가?
(A) 좌석을 찾는 것
(B) 구매품을 반품하는 것
(C) 여행을 예약하는 것
(D) 제품을 선택하는 것

해설 질문의 핵심 어구(assistance)와 관련된 내용을 주의 깊게 듣는다. 남자가 "I'm trying to decide which of these boats would best suit my needs, but I can't. Would you mind giving me a recommendation?"이라며 이 배들 중에 어떤 것이 자신의 필요에 가장 적합할지 결정하려고 하는데 못하겠다고 한 후, 여자에게 추천해 줄 수 있는지 물었다. 따라서 (D)가 정답이다.

패러프레이징
decide which of ~ boats would best suit ~ needs 배들 중에

어떤 것이 필요에 가장 적합할지 결정하다 → **Selecting a product** 제품을 선택하는 것

어휘 assistance[əsístəns] 도움

60 화자 문제

해석 여자는 누구인 것 같은가?
(A) 여행 가이드
(B) 선장
(C) 손님
(D) 판매원

해설 대화에서 신분 및 직업과 관련된 표현을 놓치지 않고 듣는다. 여자가 "We offer over 20 different fishing boats, so I can understand why you're struggling to make up your mind."라며 자신의 가게가 20대가 넘는 여러 가지 낚싯배들을 팔고 있어서 남자가 왜 결정하는 데 어려움을 겪고 있는지 이해할 수 있다고 한 말을 통해 여자가 판매원임을 알 수 있다. 따라서 (D)가 정답이다.

어휘 tour guide 여행 가이드 captain[kǽptin] 선장
salesperson[미 séilzpə̀rːsn, 영 séilzpə̀ːsn] 판매원

61 다음에 할 일 문제

해석 남자는 다음에 무엇을 할 것 같은가?
(A) 탈것들을 살펴본다.
(B) 다른 매장을 방문한다.
(C) 시연을 본다.
(D) 음식을 주문한다.

해설 대화의 마지막 부분을 주의 깊게 듣는다. 여자가 남자에게 "Follow me, and I'll show them[models] to you."라며 자신을 따라오면 배 모델들을 보여주겠다고 한 말을 통해 남자가 다음에 탈것들을 살펴볼 것임을 알 수 있다. 따라서 (A)가 정답이다.

어휘 examine[igzǽmin] 살펴보다 demonstration[dèmənstréiʃən] 시연

62-64 〔3回〕영국식 발음 → 호주식 발음

Questions 62-64 refer to the following conversation and floor plans.

W: Hi. My name is Carla Farrow. [62]I have an appointment with Bruce Zimmerman, the accounting manager, at 3 P.M. We're meeting to discuss the annual tax report.
M: Oh, yes. He is expecting you. You can go right in to meet with him now. [63]He is already waiting in the meeting room. It's right next to the elevator.
W: Great. Is there a bathroom that I can use first?
M: Yes. There is one in the break room. [64]I'm going to bring some drinks in a few minutes. Would you like a coffee or water? We also have some sodas.
W: [64]Some water would be nice.

appointment[əpɔ́intmənt] 약속 accounting[əkáuntiŋ] 회계
annual[ǽnjuəl] 연간의, 연례의 break room 휴게실

해석

62-64번은 다음 대화와 평면도에 관한 문제입니다.

여: 안녕하세요. 제 이름은 Carla Farrow예요. [62]저는 오후 3시에 회계부장님 Bruce Zimmerman과 약속이 있어요. 저희는 연간 세금 보고서를 논의하기 위해 모일 거예요.
남: 아, 네. 그가 당신을 기다리고 있어요. 당신은 그를 만나러 지금 바로 들어가시면 됩니다. [63]그는 이미 회의실에서 기다리고 있어요. 그곳은 엘리베이터 바로 옆이고요.

여: 좋네요, 먼저 제가 사용할 수 있는 화장실이 있나요?
남: 네. 휴게실에 그것이 있습니다. [64]제가 몇 분 후에 음료를 가져갈 거예요. 커피나 물을 드릴까요? 저희는 탄산음료도 있어요.
여: [64]물이 좋겠어요.

62 특정 세부 사항 문제

해석 Mr. Zimmerman은 누구인 것 같은가?
(A) 부서장
(B) 인턴
(C) 접수 담당자
(D) 영업부장

해설 대화에서 신분 및 직업과 관련된 표현을 놓치지 않고 듣는다. 여자가 "I have an appointment with Bruce Zimmerman, the accounting manager, at 3 P.M."이라며 자신이 오후 3시에 회계부장 Bruce Zimmerman과 약속이 있다고 한 말을 통해 Mr. Zimmerman이 부서장임을 알 수 있다. 따라서 (A)가 정답이다.

어휘 receptionist[risépʃənist] 접수 담당자, 접수원

63 시각 자료 문제

해석 시각 자료를 보아라. 회의는 어디에서 열릴 것인가?
(A) 1호실
(B) 2호실
(C) 3호실
(D) 4호실

해설 제시된 평면도의 정보를 확인한 후 질문의 핵심 어구(meeting be held)와 관련된 내용을 주의 깊게 듣는다. 남자가 "He[Bruce Zimmerman] is already waiting in the meeting room. It's right next to the elevator."라며 Bruce Zimmerman이 이미 회의실에서 기다리고 있고 그곳은 엘리베이터 바로 옆에 있다고 하였으므로 4호실에서 회의가 열릴 것임을 평면도에서 알 수 있다. 따라서 (D)가 정답이다.

64 특정 세부 사항 문제

해석 여자는 곧 무엇을 받을 것인가?
(A) 음료
(B) 문서
(C) 방 열쇠
(D) 비밀번호

해설 질문의 핵심 어구(woman receive shortly)와 관련된 내용을 주의 깊게 듣는다. 남자가 "I'm going to bring some drinks in a few minutes. Would you like a coffee or water?"라며 자신이 몇 분 후에 음료를 가져갈 것이라며 커피나 물을 줄지 묻자, 여자가 "Some water would be nice."라며 물이 좋겠다고 하였다. 따라서 (A)가 정답이다.

패러프레이징
shortly 곧 → in a few minutes 몇 분 후에

어휘 shortly[ʃɔ́ːrtli] 곧, 금방 pass code 비밀번호, 암호

Questions 65-67 refer to the following conversation and table.

M: Good afternoon. My name is Ben Jenkins, and I'm checking out of Room 405. ⁶⁵Could I get my bill?

W: Certainly, Mr. Jenkins. I'll just pull up your information on the computer. Let's see . . . you canceled the last night of your booking, which means you were only here for one night, right?

M: That's correct.

W: And you didn't order any room service . . . So the total amount owed is $250 plus tax.

M: Oh, ⁶⁶that's unexpected. ⁶⁶/⁶⁷I thought the rate for my room was higher.

W: ⁶⁷It usually is. The regular price is $270 a night. But we're only charging you $250 as part of a special summer promotion.

bill[bil] 계산서　certainly[미 sə́:rtnli, 영 sə́:tənli] 물론이지요, 틀림없이
pull up ~을 가져오다, 서다　booking[búkiŋ] 예약
owe[미 ou, 영 əu] 지불할 의무가 있다
unexpected[ʌ̀nikspéktid] 예상 밖의
promotion[미 prəmóuʃən, 영 prəmə́uʃən] 판촉 활동

해석
65-67번은 다음 대화와 표에 관한 문제입니다.

남: 안녕하세요. 제 이름은 Ben Jenkins이고, 405호 방에서 체크아웃하려고 해요. ⁶⁵제 계산서를 받을 수 있을까요?

여: 물론입니다, Mr. Jenkins. 제가 컴퓨터에서 고객님의 정보를 가져오겠습니다. 어디 보자... 예약의 마지막 날 밤을 취소하셔서, 여기에 하룻밤만 계셨네요, 맞으시나요?

남: 맞아요.

여: 그리고 룸서비스 주문은 안 하셨네요... 그렇다면 지불하셔야 할 총금액은 250달러이며 세금은 별도입니다.

남: 아, ⁶⁶그건 예상 밖이네요. ⁶⁶/⁶⁷저는 제 객실 요금이 더 높은 줄 알았어요.

여: ⁶⁷보통은 그렇습니다. 정가는 일 박당 270달러입니다. 하지만 특별 여름 판촉 활동의 일환으로 250달러만 부과하고 있습니다.

객실 유형	정가
스탠더드	250달러
⁶⁷프리미엄	270달러
디럭스	300달러
리갈	350달러

65　요청 문제

해석　남자는 여자에게 무엇을 요청하는가?

(A) 환불
(B) 계산서
(C) 새로운 객실
(D) 할인

해설　남자의 말에서 요청과 관련된 표현이 언급된 다음을 주의 깊게 듣는다. 남자가 여자에게 "Could I get my bill?"이라며 자신의 계산서를 받을 수 있을지 물었다. 이를 통해 남자가 여자에게 계산서를 요청하고 있음을 알 수 있다. 따라서 (B)가 정답이다.

패러프레이징
bill 계산서 → statement 계산서

어휘　statement[stéitmənt] 계산서

66　이유 문제

해석　남자는 왜 놀라는가?

(A) 다른 가격을 예상하고 있었다.
(B) 객실이 좋지 않은 상태였다.
(C) 신용카드가 거절되었다.
(D) 늦은 체크아웃에 대한 비용이 부과되고 있다.

해설　질문의 핵심 어구(surprised)와 관련된 내용을 주의 깊게 듣는다. 남자가 "that[$250]'s unexpected. I thought the rate for my room was higher."라며 250달러는 예상 밖이라고 한 후, 자신의 객실 요금이 더 높은 줄 알았다고 하였다. 따라서 (A)가 정답이다.

패러프레이징
thought the rate ~ was higher 요금이 더 높은 줄 알았다
→ was expecting a different price 다른 가격을 예상하고 있었다

어휘　expect[ikspékt] 예상하다　decline[dikláin] 거절하다

67　시각 자료 문제

해석　시각 자료를 보아라. 남자는 어느 종류의 객실에 머물렀는가?

(A) 스탠더드
(B) 프리미엄
(C) 디럭스
(D) 리갈

해설　제시된 표의 정보를 확인한 후 질문의 핵심 어구(room ~ man stay in)와 관련된 내용을 주의 깊게 듣는다. 남자가 "I thought the rate for my room was higher."라며 자신의 객실 요금이 더 높은 줄 알았다고, 여자가 "It usually is. The regular price is $270 a night."라며 보통은 그렇다고 한 후, 정가는 일 박당 270달러라고 하였으므로, 남자는 정가가 270달러인 프리미엄 객실에 머물렀음을 표에서 알 수 있다. 따라서 (B)가 정답이다.

Questions 68-70 refer to the following conversation and transit map.

W: Hello. ⁶⁸I moved to this city recently, and I am wondering . . . How do I get to city hall? Can you help me?

M: Well, taking the 405 bus is the best way. However, ⁶⁹there's construction being done on the route between Kensington Avenue and Canterbury Avenue, so it is temporarily blocked. The bus will have to make a detour, which will take a lot of time.

W: Hmm . . . Is there a faster way? I actually don't have much time. City hall closes in an hour.

M: In that case, ⁷⁰taking a taxi might be a better idea.

W: How long will that take?

M: No more than about 30 minutes.

W: ⁷⁰I think I'll do that then. Thank you.

wonder[wʌ́ndər] 궁금하다　construction[kənstrʌ́kʃn] 건설, 공사
route[ru:t] 노선　temporarily[미 tèmpərérəli, 영 témpərerəli] 일시적으로
make a detour 우회하다

해석
68-70번은 다음 대화와 교통 체계 지도에 관한 문제입니다.

여: 안녕하세요. ⁶⁸제가 최근에 이 도시로 이사 왔는데, 저는 궁금해요... 시청에 어떻게 가나요? 저를 도와주실 수 있나요?

남: 음, 405번 버스를 타는 게 가장 좋은 방법이에요. 하지만, ⁶⁹Kensington 가와 Canterbury 가 사이의 노선에 진행 중인 공사가 있어서, 그것은 일시적으로 폐쇄돼요. 버스는 우회해야 할 것이고, 그것은 많은 시간이 걸

릴 거예요.

여: 흠... 더 빠른 방법이 있을까요? 전 사실 시간이 많지 않아요. 시청이 한 시간 후에 문을 닫아요.

남: 그렇다면, 70택시를 타는 게 더 좋은 생각일 거예요.

여: 그건 얼마나 걸릴까요?

남: 약 30분밖에 걸리지 않아요.

여: 70그러면 저는 그렇게 해야겠어요. 감사해요.

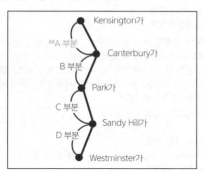

68 특정 세부 사항 문제

해석 여자는 최근에 무엇을 했는가?
(A) 새로운 도시로 이주했다.
(B) 일자리 제의를 받아들였다.
(C) 관공서를 방문했다.
(D) 통행권을 구입했다.

해설 여자가 최근에 한 일을 묻는 문제이므로, 질문의 핵심 어구(recently)가 언급된 주변을 주의 깊게 듣는다. 여자가 "I moved to this city recently"라며 최근에 이 도시로 이사 왔다고 하였다. 따라서 (A)가 정답이다.

패러프레이징
moved 이사 왔다 → Relocated 이주했다

어휘 government office 관공서 transit pass 통행권

69 시각 자료 문제

해석 시각 자료를 보아라. 어떤 부분이 일시적으로 폐쇄되는가?
(A) A 부분
(B) B 부분
(C) C 부분
(D) D 부분

해설 제시된 교통 체계 지도의 정보를 확인한 후 질문의 핵심 어구(temporarily closed)와 관련된 내용을 주의 깊게 듣는다. 남자가 "there's construction being done on the route between Kensington Avenue and Canterbury Avenue, so it is temporarily blocked"라며 Kensington가와 Canterbury가 사이의 노선에 진행 중인 공사가 있어서 그것이 일시적으로 폐쇄된다고 하였으므로, A 부분이 일시적으로 폐쇄된다는 것을 교통 체계 지도에서 알 수 있다. 따라서 (A)가 정답이다.

패러프레이징
is ~ blocked 폐쇄되다 → is ~ closed 폐쇄되다

어휘 segment[ségmənt] 부분, 영역

70 다음에 할 일 문제

해석 여자는 다음에 무엇을 할 것 같은가?
(A) 버스정류장으로 간다.
(B) 건설 현장을 점검한다.
(C) 택시를 탄다.
(D) 약속을 재조정한다.

해설 대화의 마지막 부분을 주의 깊게 듣는다. 남자가 "taking a taxi

might be a better idea"라며 택시를 타는 게 더 좋은 생각일 것이라고 하자, 여자가 "I think I'll do that then."이라며 그러면 그렇게 해야겠다고 한 말을 통해 여자가 다음에 택시를 탈 것임을 알 수 있다. 따라서 (C)가 정답이다.

어휘 inspect[inspékt] 점검하다, 검사하다

PART 4

71-73 [3M] 캐나다식 발음

Questions 71-73 refer to the following advertisement.

Are you anxious about the stuff that has accumulated in your home this winter? Don't worry about it! Let Stressless Cleaners take care of it for you. 71Our specialists can handle everything from tidying up your house to disposing of unwanted clothing and electronics devices. We can even help sort out stored items in garages and sheds. 72Until May 12, you can take advantage of our special spring cleaning offer. All customers who book a four-hour session will get 25 percent off. So, don't delay for another minute! 73Visit our Web site to arrange a date and time today.

anxious[éŋkʃəs] 염려하는, 걱정스러운
accumulate[미 əkjú:mjulèit, 영 əkjú:mjəlèit] 쌓이다
take care of ~을 처리하다 specialist[spéʃəlist] 전문가
handle[hǽndl] (일을) 처리하다 tidy up ~을 깔끔하게 정리하다
dispose of ~을 치우다 electronic device 전자 기기
sort out ~을 정리하다 store[미 stɔːr, 영 stɔː] 보관하다 shed[ʃed] 창고
take advantage of ~을 이용하다 spring cleaning 봄맞이 대청소
offer[미 ɔ́:fər, 영 ɔ́:fə] 할인 arrange[əréindʒ] 정하다

해석
71-73번은 다음 광고에 관한 문제입니다.

올 겨울 동안 집에 쌓인 물건들이 염려되시나요? 걱정하지 마세요! Stressless Cleaners가 당신을 위해 처리하게 해주세요. 71저희 전문가들은 당신의 집을 깔끔하게 정리하는 것부터 불필요한 옷과 전자 기기들을 치우는 것까지 모든 것을 처리해드립니다. 저희는 차고와 창고들에 보관된 물건들을 정리하는 것도 도와드릴 수 있습니다. 72 5월 12일까지, 봄맞이 대청소 특별 할인을 이용하실 수 있습니다. 4시간 작업을 예약하시는 모든 고객분들은 25퍼센트 할인을 받으실 것입니다. 그러니, 1분이라도 더 지체하지 마세요! 73날짜와 시간을 정하시려면 오늘 저희 웹사이트를 방문하세요.

71 주제 문제

해석 어떤 종류의 업체가 광고되고 있는가?
(A) 인테리어 디자인 회사
(B) 청소 회사
(C) 부동산 중개업체
(D) 가전 제품 소매점

해설 광고의 주제를 묻는 문제이므로, 지문의 초반을 반드시 듣는다. "Our specialists can handle everything from tidying up your house to disposing of unwanted clothing and electronics devices."라며 전문가들은 집을 깔끔하게 정리하는 것부터 불필요한 옷과 전자 기기들을 치우는 것까지 모든 것을 처리한다고 한 말을 통해 청소 회사가 광고되고 있음을 알 수 있다. 따라서 (B)가 정답이다.

어휘 real estate 부동산 retailer[미 ríːteilər, 영 ríːteilə] 소매점

72 특정 세부 사항 문제

해석 청자들은 5월 12일까지 무엇을 받을 수 있는가?
(A) 제품 샘플

(B) 무료 상담
(C) 상품권
(D) 할인된 서비스

해설 질문의 핵심 어구(until May 12)가 언급된 주변을 주의 깊게 듣는다. "Until May 12, you can take advantage of our special spring cleaning offer. All customers who book a four-hour session will get 25 percent off."라며 5월 12일까지 봄맞이 대청소 특별 할인을 이용할 수 있다고 한 후, 4시간 작업을 예약하는 모든 고객들은 25퍼센트 할인을 받을 것이라고 하였다. 따라서 (D)가 정답이다.

어휘 consultation[미 kànsəltéiʃən, 영 kɔ̀nsəltéiʃən] 상담
gift certificate 상품권

73 이유 문제
해석 청자들은 왜 웹사이트를 방문해야 하는가?
(A) 지불을 하기 위해
(B) 예약을 하기 위해
(C) 쿠폰을 다운로드하기 위해
(D) 설문지를 작성하기 위해

해설 질문의 핵심 어구(visit the Web site)와 관련된 내용을 주의 깊게 듣는다. "Visit our Web site to arrange a date and time today."라며 날짜와 시간을 정하려면 오늘 웹사이트를 방문하라고 하였다. 따라서 (B)가 정답이다.

패러프레이징
arrange a date and time 날짜와 시간을 정하다 → schedule an appointment 예약을 하다

어휘 make payment 지불하다 complete[kəmplíːt] 작성하다
questionnaire[미 kwèstʃənέər, 영 kwèstʃənέə] 설문지

74-76 [3어] 호주식 발음

Questions 74-76 refer to the following telephone message.

Hello, I'm calling for Janine Freeman. This is Jaehyun Kim from JetPeak Airlines. 74You filed a missing luggage claim for your flight on March 14. Well, your bag was found by one of our baggage handlers. It will be delivered to your home tomorrow afternoon. However, it appears that your suitcase has sustained some light damage. 75To receive compensation for the damage, you need to send completed application forms to our corporate office. After this call, 76I will e-mail the forms with instructions on how to fill them out. Please call me at 555-6793 if you have any questions.

file[fail] (서류 등을) 정식으로 제출하다 missing luggage 분실 수하물
claim[kleim] 청구서, 청구 baggage[bǽgidʒ] 수하물, 짐
handler[미 hǽndlər, 영 hǽndlə] 담당자, (직업적으로 무엇을) 취급하는 사람
sustain[səstéin] (피해를) 입다
compensation[미 kàmpənséiʃən, 영 kɔ̀mpənséiʃən] 변상, 보상
application form 신청서 instruction[instrʌ́kʃən] 설명

해석
74-76번은 다음 전화 메시지에 관한 문제입니다.

안녕하세요, 저는 Janine Freeman에게 전화드립니다. 저는 JetPeak 항공사의 Jaehyun Kim입니다. 74고객님께서는 3월 14일 항공편에 대한 분실 수하물 청구서를 제출하셨습니다. 음, 고객님의 가방이 저희 수하물 담당자들 중 한 명에 의해 발견됐습니다. 그것은 내일 오후 고객님 댁으로 배송될 것입니다. 하지만, 고객님의 여행 가방이 가벼운 손상을 입은 것으로 보입니다. 75손상에 대한 변상을 받으시려면, 고객님께서 작성된 신청서들을 저희 회사 사무실로 보내주셔야 합니다. 이 전화 후에, 76양식들과 함께 그것들을 어떻

게 작성하셔야 하는지에 대한 설명을 이메일로 보내드리겠습니다. 만약 질문이 있으시면 555-6793으로 제게 전화주시기 바랍니다.

74 주제 문제
해석 화자는 주로 무엇에 대해 이야기하고 있는가?
(A) 최신 정책
(B) 환불된 표
(C) 잃어버린 물건
(D) 결항된 항공편

해설 메시지의 주제를 묻는 문제이므로, 지문의 초반을 반드시 듣는다. "You filed a missing luggage claim for your flight on March 14."라며 청자가 3월 14일 항공편에 대한 분실 수하물 청구서를 제출했다고 한 후, 잃어버린 물건에 대한 내용으로 지문이 이어지고 있다. 따라서 (C)가 정답이다.

어휘 misplaced[mìspléist] 잃어버린

75 특정 세부 사항 문제
해석 Ms. Freeman은 변상을 받기 위해 무엇을 해야 하는가?
(A) 서류를 제출한다.
(B) 표를 제시한다.
(C) 수하물 담당자와 이야기한다.
(D) 손상된 제품을 반환한다.

해설 질문의 핵심 어구(receive compensation)가 언급된 주변을 주의 깊게 듣는다. "To receive compensation for the damage, you [Ms. Freeman] need to send completed application forms to our corporate office."라며 손상에 대한 변상을 받으려면 Ms. Freeman이 작성된 신청서들을 회사 사무실로 보내야 한다고 하였다. 따라서 (A)가 정답이다.

패러프레이징
send completed application forms to ~ office 작성된 신청서들을 사무실로 보내다 → Submit some paperwork 서류를 제출하다

어휘 submit[səbmít] 제출하다
paperwork[미 péipərwə̀ːrk, 영 péipəwə̀ːk] 서류

76 다음에 할 일 문제
해석 화자는 다음에 무엇을 할 것 같은가?
(A) 여행 가방을 살펴본다.
(B) 사무실에 간다.
(C) 결제를 확인한다.
(D) 이메일을 보낸다.

해설 지문의 마지막 부분을 주의 깊게 듣는다. "I will e-mail the forms with instructions on how to fill them out"이라며 화자가 양식들과 함께 그것들을 어떻게 작성해야 하는지에 대한 설명을 이메일로 보내겠다고 하였다. 따라서 (D)가 정답이다.

어휘 inspect[inspékt] 살펴보다
confirm[미 kənfə́ːrm, 영 kənfə́ːm] 확인하다

77-79 [3어] 캐나다식 발음

Questions 77-79 refer to the following introduction.

77I appreciate all of you attending the third annual seminar for writers on Gibbons Island. We have plenty of activities planned for the weekend that will help you develop your skills and get to know your fellow authors. But first, I'd like to introduce the keynote speaker for this year's retreat, Jill Holloway. You've probably heard her name. 78Ms. Holloway started out as a working mother who wrote in her free time and eventually became a best-selling novelist. ⁷⁹Today, she is going to talk for a few minutes about her career. Please join me in welcoming her to the stage.

---

plenty of 많은　get to know ~을 알게 되다
fellow[미 félou, 영 féləu] 동료의, 친구의　keynote speaker 기조연설자
free time 여가 시간　novelist[미 návəlist, 영 nɔ́vəlist] 소설가
career[미 kəríər, 영 kəríə] 경력

해석
77-79번은 다음 소개에 관한 문제입니다.

⁷⁷Gibbons섬에서 열리는 제3회 작가들을 위한 연례 세미나에 참석해주신 모든 분들께 감사드립니다. 저희는 이번 주말에 여러분의 기량을 발달시키고 동료 작가들을 알게 되는 데 도움을 줄 많은 활동들을 준비했습니다. 하지만 먼저, 올해 야유회의 기조연설자인 Jill Holloway를 소개하려고 합니다. ⁷⁸여러분은 아마 그녀의 이름을 들어보셨을 거예요. ⁷⁸Ms. Holloway는 여가 시간에 글을 쓰는 워킹맘으로 시작하여 결국 베스트셀러 소설가가 되었습니다. ⁷⁹오늘, 그녀가 그녀의 경력에 대해 잠시 이야기를 할 것입니다. 저와 함께 그녀를 무대로 맞아주세요.

77 장소 문제
해석 청자들은 어디에 있는 것 같은가?
(A) 퇴직 기념 파티에
(B) 글쓰기 워크숍에
(C) 미술 전시회에
(D) 시상식에

해설 지문에서 장소와 관련된 표현을 놓치지 않고 듣는다. "I appreciate all of you attending the third annual seminar for writers ~. We have plenty of activities planned ~ that will help you develop your skills and get to know your fellow authors."라며 제3회 작가들을 위한 연례 세미나에 참석해주어 고맙다고 한 후, 청자들의 기량을 발달시키고 동료 작가들을 알게 되는 데 도움을 줄 많은 활동들을 준비했다고 한 말을 통해 청자들이 글쓰기 워크숍에 있음을 알 수 있다. 따라서 (B)가 정답이다.

어휘 retirement[미 ritáiərmənt, 영 ritáiəmənt] 퇴직, 은퇴
exhibit[igzíbit] 전시회　award ceremony 시상식

78 의도 파악 문제
해석 화자는 "여러분은 아마 그녀의 이름을 들어보셨을 거예요"라고 말할 때 무엇을 의도하는가?
(A) Jill Holloway가 이전에 언급되었다.
(B) Jill Holloway가 이전의 행사에 참석했다.
(C) Jill Holloway가 최근에 상을 받았다.
(D) Jill Holloway가 유명하다.

해설 질문의 인용어구(You've probably heard her name)가 언급된 주변을 주의 깊게 듣는다. "Ms. Holloway started out as a working mother who wrote in her free time and eventually became a best-selling novelist."라며 Ms. Holloway가 여가 시간에 글을 쓰는 워킹맘으로 시작하여 결국 베스트셀러 소설가가 되었다고 한 말을 통해 Jill Holloway가 유명하다는 것을 알 수 있다. 따라서 (D)가 정답이다.

79 다음에 할 일 문제
해석 청자들은 다음에 무엇을 할 것 같은가?
(A) 책에 대해 토론한다.
(B) 세미나에 등록한다.
(C) 짧은 휴식을 가진다.
(D) 연설을 듣는다.

해설 지문의 마지막 부분을 주의 깊게 듣는다. "Today, she[Ms. Holloway] is going to talk for a few minutes about her career. Please

---

join me in welcoming her to the stage."라며 오늘 Ms. Holloway가 그녀의 경력에 대해 잠시 이야기를 할 것이라고 한 후, 함께 그녀를 무대로 맞아달라고 한 말을 통해 청자들이 다음에 연설을 들을 것임을 알 수 있다. 따라서 (D)가 정답이다.

어휘 brief[bri:f] 짧은　speech[spi:tʃ] 연설

80-82 [호] 호주식 발음

Questions 80-82 refer to the following excerpt from a meeting.

In order to stay competitive with other companies, ⁸⁰we're going to change our marketing approach. Right now, most of our advertising budget is spent on television commercials. Moving forward, however, we are going to invest more in online marketing. ⁸¹We've hired a new staff member, Mindy Lineman, to manage our accounts on social media. If you have any questions or suggestions regarding our approach, please direct them to her. Okay . . . our time is almost up, so ⁸²I'll conclude now. It looks like another team needs to use the conference room.

---

competitive[미 kəmpétətiv, 영 kəmpétitiv] 경쟁력 있는
approach[미 əpróutʃ, 영 əpróutʃ] 방법; 다가오다　budget[bʌ́dʒit] 예산
commercial[미 kəmə́:rʃəl, 영 kəmə́:ʃəl] 광고　invest[invést] 투자하다
manage[mǽnidʒ] 관리하다　account[əkáunt] 계정
regarding[미 rigá:rdiŋ, 영 rigá:diŋ] ~에 대해
direct[dirékt] (발언·비판 등을 남에게) 말하다
conclude[kənklú:d] 마치다

해석
80-82번은 다음 회의 발췌록에 관한 문제입니다.

다른 회사들에 비해 경쟁력을 유지하기 위해서, ⁸⁰우리는 마케팅 방법을 변경할 것입니다. 현재, 우리 광고 예산의 대부분이 텔레비전 광고들에 쓰입니다. 하지만, 앞으로는, 온라인 마케팅에 더 많이 투자할 것입니다. ⁸¹우리는 우리의 소셜 미디어 계정들을 관리하기 위해 새 직원인 Mindy Lineman을 채용했습니다. 우리의 방법에 대한 질문이나 제안이 있으면, 그녀에게 말씀하시기 바랍니다. 좋습니다... 시간이 거의 다 됐으니, ⁸²이제 마치겠습니다. 다른 팀이 회의실을 사용해야 하는 것 같네요.

80 주제 문제
해석 화자는 주로 무엇에 대해 이야기하고 있는가?
(A) 제품 평가
(B) 마케팅 전략
(C) 빈 일자리
(D) 근무 시간표

해설 회의의 주제를 묻는 문제이므로, 지문의 초반을 반드시 듣는다. "we're going to change our marketing approach"라며 마케팅 방법을 변경할 것이라고 한 후, 새로운 마케팅 전략에 대한 내용으로 지문이 이어지고 있다. 따라서 (B)가 정답이다.

어휘 review[rivjú:] 평가, 검토　strategy[strǽtədʒi] 전략
job opening 빈 (일)자리

81 특정 세부 사항 문제
해석 Mindy Lineman은 누구인 것 같은가?
(A) 회사 임원
(B) 사업 자문가
(C) 취업 지원자
(D) 신입 직원

해설 질문 대상(Mindy Lineman)의 신분 및 직업과 관련된 표현을 놓

치지 않고 듣는다. "We've hired a new staff member, Mindy Lineman"이라며 새 직원인 Mindy Lineman을 채용했다고 하였다. 따라서 (D)가 정답이다.

어휘 executive[미 igzékjutiv, 영 igzékjətiv] 임원, 경영진
consultant[kənsʌ́ltənt] 자문가, 상담가 job applicant 취업 지원자
hire[미 haiər, 영 haiə] 신입 직원

82 의도 파악 문제

해석 화자는 왜 "시간이 거의 다 됐으니"라고 말하는가?
(A) 회의 일정이 변경되어야 한다.
(B) 마감기한이 빠르게 다가오고 있다.
(C) 회의가 마칠 때가 되었다.
(D) 업무가 아직 완료되지 않았다.

해설 질문의 인용어구(our time is almost up)가 언급된 주변을 주의 깊게 듣는다. "I'll conclude now. It looks like another team needs to use the conference room."이라며 이제 마치겠다고 한 후, 다른 팀이 회의실을 사용해야 하는 것 같다고 한 말을 통해 회의가 마칠 때가 되었음을 알 수 있다. 따라서 (C)가 정답이다.

어휘 reschedule[미 ri:skédʒu:l, 영 ri:ʃédʒu:l] 일정을 변경하다
approach[미 əpróutʃ, 영 əpróutʃ] 다가오다
complete[kəmplí:t] 완료하다

83-85 [3세] 영국식 발음

Questions 83-85 refer to the following instruction.

For the last part of today's training session, I'd like to explain how to process a product return. When a customer brings an item back to our store, 83you should first check the receipt to find out when the purchase was made. Keep in mind that refunds cannot be issued after 10 days. Next, inspect the product carefully. 84If you see any damage, notify your supervisor immediately and let him or her decide whether a refund can be given. 85The final step is to have the customer fill out and sign a request form. It must include the reason for returning the item. That's it . . . Any questions?

training session 연수 (과정) process[미 práses, 영 próuses] 처리하다
find out ~을 알아보다 keep in mind ~을 명심하다 issue[íʃu:] 지급하다
notify[미 nóutəfài, 영 nə́utifài] 알리다 immediately[imí:diətli] 즉시
request form 신청서 include[inklú:d] 포함하다

해석
83-85번은 다음 설명에 관한 문제입니다.

오늘의 연수 마지막 순서로는, 반품을 처리하는 방법에 대해 설명해드리고자 합니다. 손님이 우리 매장에 상품을 다시 가져오면, 83여러분은 먼저 영수증을 확인하여 구매가 언제 이루어졌는지를 알아봐야 합니다. 10일이 지난 후에는 환불금이 지급될 수 없다는 것을 명심하세요. 그 다음, 상품을 자세히 살펴보세요. 84만약 어떤 손상이라도 발견할 경우, 즉시 상사에게 알려 환불금이 지급될 수 있는지를 결정하도록 해야 합니다. 85마지막 단계는 손님이 신청서를 작성하고 서명하도록 하는 것입니다. 그것은 반품하는 것에 대한 사유를 반드시 포함해야 합니다. 여기까지입니다... 질문 있으신가요?

83 특정 세부 사항 문제

해석 화자에 따르면, 무엇이 먼저 행해져야 하는가?
(A) 배송을 한다.
(B) 상품을 살펴본다.
(C) 날짜를 확인한다.
(D) 환불금을 지급한다.

해설 질문의 핵심 어구(done first)와 관련된 내용을 주의 깊게 듣는다. "you should first check the receipt to find out when the purchase was made"라며 먼저 영수증을 확인하여 구매가 언제 이루어졌는지를 알아봐야 한다고 하였다. 따라서 (C)가 정답이다.

패러프레이징
find out when the purchase was made 구매가 언제 이루어졌는지를 알아보다 → Confirm a date 날짜를 확인하다

어휘 examine[igzǽmin] 살펴보다

84 이유 문제

해석 청자들은 왜 상사에게 연락해야 하는가?
(A) 상품이 손상되었음을 알리기 위해
(B) 요청이 처리되었는지 확인하기 위해
(C) 일부 서류를 받기 위해
(D) 반품 사유를 제시하기 위해

해설 질문의 핵심 어구(contact a supervisor)와 관련된 내용을 주의 깊게 듣는다. "If you see any damage, notify your supervisor immediately"라며 만약 상품에 어떤 손상이라도 발견할 경우 즉시 상사에게 알리라고 하였다. 따라서 (A)가 정답이다.

어휘 report[미 ripɔ́:rt, 영 ripɔ́:t] 알리다, 보고하다
paperwork[미 péipərwə̀:rk, 영 péipəwə̀:k] 서류, 문서 업무

85 특정 세부 사항 문제

해석 청자들은 손님들에게 무엇을 하도록 요청해야 하는가?
(A) 양식을 작성한다.
(B) 구매를 한다.
(C) 지불을 취소한다.
(D) 계약서에 서명한다.

해설 질문의 핵심 어구(ask customers to do)와 관련된 내용을 주의 깊게 듣는다. "The final step is to have the customer fill out and sign a request form."이라며 마지막 단계가 손님이 신청서를 작성하고 서명하도록 하는 것이라고 하였다. 따라서 (A)가 정답이다.

어휘 complete[kəmplí:t] 작성하다 sign a contract 계약서에 서명하다

86-88 [3세] 미국식 발음

Questions 86-88 refer to the following broadcast.

You are listening to WZRL 95, and this is Kennedy Walker. 86And now for your local news. For those interested, the annual Summer Festival is being held this weekend at Marigold Park. The festival, sponsored by local business Marty's Cupcakes, will feature a variety of exciting events, including face painting, a relay race, and much more! 87Please keep in mind that there is limited parking on the streets near the park, so you should take a bus if possible. Now, 88we'll speak with Marty Peters, the owner of Marty's Cupcakes, and he'll tell us exactly how his bakery is getting involved in this year's festivities.

be sponsored by ~가 후원하다 feature[미 fí:tʃər, 영 fí:tʃə] 포함하다
a variety of 여러 가지의 keep in mind ~을 명심하다
limited[límitid] 한정된 festivity[festívəti] 축제 (행사)

해석
86-88번은 다음 방송에 관한 문제입니다.

여러분은 WZRL 95를 청취하고 계시며, 저는 Kennedy Walker입니다. 86그리고 지금은 여러분의 지역 뉴스 시간입니다. 관심 있으신 분들을 위해 말씀드리자면, 연례 여름 축제가 이번 주말에 Marigold 공원에서 열립니다. 지

역 업체 Marty's Cupcakes가 후원하는 이 축제는 페이스 페인팅, 이어달리기, 그 밖에 많은 것들을 포함하여 여러 가지 재미있는 행사들을 포함할 것입니다! ⁸⁷공원 근처의 거리들에는 주차 공간이 한정적임을 명심해서서, 가능하면 버스를 이용하시는 것이 좋겠습니다. 자, ⁸⁸Marty's Cupcakes의 업주인 Marty Peters와 이야기하도록 하죠, 그가 그의 제과점이 정확히 어떻게 올해 축제에 참여하게 될 것인지 알려줄 것입니다.

86 주제 문제

해석 방송은 주로 무엇에 대한 것인가?
(A) 교통 체증
(B) 지역 행사
(C) 새 음식점
(D) 학교 대회

해설 방송의 주제를 묻는 문제이므로, 지문의 초반을 반드시 듣는다. "And now for your local news. ~ the annual Summer Festival is being held this weekend at Marigold Park."라며 지역 뉴스 시간이라고 한 후, 연례 여름 축제가 이번 주말에 Marigold 공원에서 열린다고 하였다. 따라서 (B)가 정답이다.

어휘 traffic jam 교통 체증
competition [미 kàmpətíʃən, 영 kɔ̀mpətíʃən] 대회

87 요청 문제

해석 청자들은 무엇을 하도록 권고되는가?
(A) 대중교통을 이용한다.
(B) 주요 고속도로를 피한다.
(C) 행사에 일찍 등록한다.
(D) 자선 기부를 한다.

해설 지문의 중후반에서 요청과 관련된 표현이 포함된 문장을 주의 깊게 듣는다. "Please keep in mind that there is limited parking on the streets near the park, so you should take a bus if possible."이라며 공원 근처의 거리들에는 주차 공간이 한정적임을 명심하여 가능하면 버스를 이용하는 것이 좋겠다고 하였다. 따라서 (A)가 정답이다.

패러프레이징
take a bus 버스를 타다 → Use public transportation 대중교통을 이용하다

어휘 public transportation 대중교통 major [미 méidʒər, 영 méidʒə] 주요
charitable [tʃǽritəbl] 자선의

88 특정 세부 사항 문제

해석 청자는 다음에 누구로부터 들을 것인가?
(A) 일기 예보자
(B) 업체 주인
(C) 지역 정치인
(D) 유명한 요리사

해설 질문의 핵심 어구(hear from next)와 관련된 내용을 주의 깊게 듣는다. "we'll speak with Marty Peters, the owner of Marty's Cupcakes"라며 Marty's Cupcakes의 업주인 Marty Peters와 이야기하겠다고 하였다. 따라서 (B)가 정답이다.

어휘 weather forecaster 일기 예보자
politician [미 pàlitíʃən, 영 pɔ̀litíʃən] 정치인

89-91 [아이콘] 영국식 발음

Questions 89-91 refer to the following telephone message.

Good afternoon. This is Leslie Schwartz calling for Mr. Harvey Lynch. ⁸⁹I just wanted to follow up on the discussion we had last Tuesday about our company's product distribution to local grocery retailers. ⟳

⁹⁰I've gotten in touch with two major grocery sellers, and they have both expressed interest in our line of dairy products. I'm hoping you might be able to spare some time next week to join me when I meet with the owners of these businesses. ⁹¹They are interested in learning more about our product offerings and prices, so we should consider preparing a short presentation for them. Please call me back as soon as you receive this message at 555-2459.

---

follow up on ~을 끝까지 하다
distribution [미 dìstrəbjúːʃən, 영 dìstribjúːʃən] 유통
get in touch with ~와 연락하다 dairy product 유제품
spare [미 spɛər, 영 speə] (시간을) 내다 as soon as ~하자마자

해석
89-91번은 다음 전화 메시지에 관한 문제입니다.

안녕하세요. 저는 Mr. Harvey Lynch께 전화드리는 Leslie Schwartz입니다. ⁸⁹저는 지난 화요일에 지역 식료품상들로의 우리 회사의 제품 유통에 대해 가졌던 논의를 끝까지 하고 싶습니다. ⁹⁰저는 두 곳의 주요 식료품상들과 연락했는데, 그들 모두 우리의 유제품에 관심을 표했습니다. 저는 다음 주 중에 당신이 시간을 좀 내어서 이 업주들을 만날 때 저와 함께 했으면 합니다. ⁹¹그들이 우리의 제품과 가격에 대해 더 알아보는 것에 관심이 있으니, 그들을 위해 간단한 발표를 준비하는 것을 고려해보는 게 좋겠습니다. 이 메시지를 받자마자 555-2459로 제게 전화주시기 바랍니다.

89 목적 문제

해석 화자는 왜 전화를 했는가?
(A) 제품들을 주문하기 위해
(B) 대화를 이어나가기 위해
(C) 기한을 연장하기 위해
(D) 조언을 구하기 위해

해설 전화의 목적을 묻는 문제이므로, 지문의 초반을 반드시 듣는다. "I just wanted to follow up on the discussion we had last Tuesday"라며 지난 화요일에 가졌던 논의를 끝까지 하고 싶다고 한 말을 통해 화자가 대화를 이어나가기 위해 전화했음을 알 수 있다. 따라서 (B)가 정답이다.

패러프레이징
follow up on the discussion 논의를 끝까지 하다 → continue a conversation 대화를 이어나가다

어휘 extend a deadline 기한을 연장하다

90 특정 세부 사항 문제

해석 화자는 이미 무엇을 했는가?
(A) 샘플들을 배송했다.
(B) 사업 제안을 거절했다.
(C) 소매점에 연락했다.
(D) 가격표를 확인했다.

해설 질문의 핵심 어구(already done)와 관련된 내용을 주의 깊게 듣는다. "I've gotten in touch with two major grocery sellers"라며 두 곳의 주요 식료품상들과 연락했다고 하였다. 따라서 (C)가 정답이다.

패러프레이징
have gotten in touch with two ~ grocery sellers 두 곳의 식료품상들과 연락했다 → Contacted some retailers 소매점들에 연락했다

어휘 turn down ~을 거절하다 price list 가격표

91 이유 문제

해석 발표는 왜 준비되어야 하는가?
(A) 제품들에 대한 정보를 공유하기 위해
(B) 신입 사원을 소개하기 위해

(C) 새로운 서비스를 설명하기 위해
(D) 운송 과정을 설명하기 위해

해설 질문의 핵심 어구(presentation be prepared)와 관련된 내용을 주의 깊게 듣는다. "They[owners] are interested in learning more about our product offerings and prices, so we should consider preparing a short presentation for them."이라며 업주들이 제품과 가격에 대해 더 알아보는 것에 관심이 있으니 그들을 위해 간단한 발표를 준비하는 것을 고려하는 게 좋겠다고 한 말을 통해 제품들에 대한 정보를 공유하기 위해 발표가 준비되어야 함을 알 수 있다. 따라서 (A)가 정답이다.

어휘 recent hire 신입사원 describe[diskráib] 설명하다, 묘사하다
shipping[ʃípiŋ] 운송

92-94 🎧 캐나다식 발음

Questions 92-94 refer to the following broadcast.

> You're listening to *The Literary Hour* on 103 FM. This afternoon, I'll be interviewing ⁹²Judith Frost, who recently published the novel *Bright Lights*. ⁹³This is the final book in Frost's popular series **about the American film industry**. Before I start the interview, I should mention that ⁹⁴there have been some changes to Ms. Frost's book-signing schedule. Many people will likely be disappointed. ⁹⁴She will appear at Feldman's Books on Saturday, but all of her later appearances have been postponed. The schedule on her official Web site will be updated shortly. Now, I'd like to welcome Ms. Frost to the program.

publish[pʌ́bliʃ] 출간하다
appearance[미 əpíərəns, 영 əpíərəns] 출석, 등장

해석

92-94번은 다음 방송에 관한 문제입니다.

여러분은 103 FM의 *The Literary Hour*를 듣고 계십니다. 오늘 오후에, 저는 ⁹²최근에 소설 *Bright Lights*를 출간한 Judith Frost를 인터뷰할 것입니다. ⁹³이것은 미국 영화 산업에 대한 Frost의 인기 있는 시리즈물의 마지막 편입니다. 제가 인터뷰를 시작하기 전에, ⁹⁴Ms. Frost의 책 사인회 일정에 일부 변경 사항이 있음을 말씀드려야겠습니다. 많은 사람들이 실망할 것 같네요. ⁹⁴그녀는 토요일에 Feldman's Books에 나타날 것이지만, 그녀의 모든 이후 참석들이 연기되었습니다. 그녀의 공식 웹사이트에 있는 일정은 곧 업데이트될 것입니다. 자, Ms. Frost를 프로그램에 모시도록 하겠습니다.

92 특정 세부 사항 문제

해석 Judith Frost는 누구인 것 같은가?
(A) 문학 평론가
(B) 소설가
(C) 프로그램 진행자
(D) 영화감독

해설 질문 대상(Judith Frost)의 신분 및 직업과 관련된 표현을 놓치지 않고 듣는다. "Judith Frost, who recently published the novel *Bright Lights*"라며 최근에 소설 *Bright Lights*를 출간한 Judith Frost라고 한 말을 통해 Judith Frost가 소설가임을 알 수 있다. 따라서 (B)가 정답이다.

어휘 literary[lítərəri] 문학의 critic[krítik] 평론가, 비평가
host[미 houst, 영 həust] 진행자; 주최하다 film director 영화감독

93 언급 문제

해석 *Bright Lights*에 대해 무엇이 언급되는가?
(A) 전집의 일부이다.

(B) 영화로 만들어질 것이다.
(C) 기사에 특집으로 다뤄졌다.
(D) 아직 출간되지 않았다.

해설 질문의 핵심 어구(*Bright Lights*)와 관련된 내용을 주의 깊게 듣는다. "This[*Bright Lights*] is the final book in Frost's popular series"라며 *Bright Lights*는 Frost의 인기 있는 시리즈물의 마지막 편이라고 한 말을 통해 *Bright Lights*가 전집의 일부임을 알 수 있다. 따라서 (A)가 정답이다.

패러프레이징
final book in ~ series 시리즈물의 마지막 편 → **part of a collection** 전집의 일부

어휘 collection[kəlékʃən] 전집
feature[미 fíːtʃər, 영 fíːtʃə] (신문 등이) ~을 특집 기사로 다루다

94 의도 파악 문제

해석 화자는 "많은 사람들이 실망할 것 같네요"라고 말할 때 무엇을 의도하는가?
(A) 게스트가 인터뷰를 취소했다.
(B) 책 사인회 표의 입수 가능성이 제한적이다.
(C) 최근의 영화가 좋지 못한 비평을 받았다.
(D) 몇몇 행사들이 나중에 열릴 것이다.

해설 질문의 인용어구(Many people will likely be disappointed)가 언급된 주변을 주의 깊게 듣는다. "there have been some changes to Ms. Frost's book-signing schedule"이라며 Ms. Frost의 책 사인회 일정에 일부 변경 사항이 있다고 한 뒤, "She will appear at Feldman's Books on Saturday, but all of her later appearances have been postponed."라며 그녀가 토요일에 Feldman's Books에 나타날 것이지만 모든 이후 참석들이 연기되었다고 한 말을 통해 몇몇 행사들이 나중에 열릴 것임을 알 수 있다. 따라서 (D)가 정답이다.

어휘 availability[미 əvèiləbíləti, 영 əvèiləbíliti] 입수 가능, 유용성
limited[límitid] 제한된, 한정된

95-97 🎧 미국식 발음

Questions 95-97 refer to the following announcement and schedule.

> I am sorry to announce that we have had to cancel Jacklyn Parkerson's lecture next week. We barely sold any tickets, and it would just not be good for her reputation or ours. ⁹⁵I have already informed Ms. Parkerson and offered her a position on the panel. She will be able to speak for about 10 minutes at the beginning of the panel. **She is going to introduce corporate responsibility in the tech industry.** ⁹⁶She will receive the same fee as she is protected from any loss of compensation under her contract. ⁹⁷Could you put up a notice to let everyone know?

barely[béərli] 거의 ~하지 않다 reputation[rèpjutéiʃən] 명성, 평판
panel[pǽnl] 패널(토론회), 위원단
introduce[ìntrədúːs] 발표하다, 제출하다
corporate responsibility 기업의 책임
compensation[kàːmpənséiʃən] 보수, 급여, 보상
contract[kántrækt] 계약(서) put up 게시하다

해석

95-97번은 다음 공지와 일정표에 관한 문제입니다.

저는 우리가 다음 주 Jacklyn Parkerson의 강의를 취소해야 했다는 것을 알려드리게 되어 유감입니다. 우리는 표를 거의 팔지 못했고, 그것이 그녀 혹

은 우리의 명성에 좋지 않을 것입니다. ⁹⁵저는 이미 Ms. Parkerson에게 알렸고 그녀에게 패널 자리를 제안했습니다. 그녀는 패널 토론의 초반에 약 10분 동안 발표할 수 있을 것입니다. 그녀는 기술 산업에서 기업의 책임을 발표할 것입니다. ⁹⁶그녀는 그녀의 계약 하에 보수의 모든 손실로부터 보호받기 때문에 동일한 금액을 받을 것입니다. ⁹⁷모두가 알도록 여러분이 공지를 게시해 줄 수 있나요?

Horgen 문화 센터
강의 시리즈

시간	주제
오전 9시	급여 협상
오전 11시	기업 브랜딩
오후 4시	금융 범죄
⁹⁵오후 6시	패널 토론

95 시각 자료 문제

해석 시각 자료를 보아라. Ms. Parkerson은 언제 강연할 것 같은가?
(A) 오전 9시에
(B) 오전 11시에
(C) 오후 4시에
(D) 오후 6시에

해설 제시된 일정표의 정보를 확인한 후 질문의 핵심 어구(Ms. Parkerson) 가 언급된 주변을 주의 깊게 듣는다. "I have already informed Ms. Parkerson and offered her a position on the panel. She will be able to speak for about 10 minutes at the beginning of the panel."이라며 이미 Ms. Parkerson에게 알렸고 그녀에게 패널 자리를 제안했다고 하며, 그녀는 패널 토론의 초반에 약 10분 동안 발표할 수 있을 것이라고 하였으므로, Ms. Parkerson은 오후 6시에 강연을 할 것임을 일정표에서 알 수 있다. 따라서 (D)가 정답이다.

96 언급 문제

해석 화자는 Ms. Parkerson에 대해 무엇을 말하는가?
(A) 계약서에 서명하지 않았다.
(B) 그녀의 강의는 녹화될 것이다.
(C) 그녀의 보수는 변경되지 않을 것이다.
(D) 행사의 기조연설자이다.

해설 질문의 핵심 어구(Ms. Parkerson)와 관련된 내용을 주의 깊게 듣는다. "She[Ms. Parkerson] will receive the same fee as she is protected from any loss of compensation under her contract."라며 Ms. Parkerson은 그녀의 계약 하에 보수의 모든 손실로부터 보호받기 때문에 동일한 금액을 받을 것이라고 하였다. 따라서 (C)가 정답이다.

패러프레이징
compensation 보수 → payment 보수

97 요청 문제

해석 청자들은 무엇을 하도록 요청받는가?
(A) 강의를 복습한다.
(B) 공지를 게시한다.
(C) 유인물을 인쇄한다.
(D) 매표소를 연다.

해설 지문의 중후반에서 요청과 관련된 표현이 포함된 문장을 주의 깊게 듣는다. "Could you put up a notice to let everyone know?"라며 청자들에게 모두가 알도록 공지를 게시해 줄 수 있는지 물었다. 따라서 (B)가 정답이다.

패러프레이징
put up 게시하다 → Post 게시하다

어휘 review[rivjú:] 복습하다   handout[hǽndàut] 유인물

98-100 🔊 영국식 발음

Questions 98-100 refer to the following excerpt from a meeting and graph.

Let's take a few minutes to review the performance of the online service our company launched in May. As you know, ⁹⁸customers can use our Web site to book hotels and flights. Unfortunately, it hasn't attracted as many visitors as expected. Here, look at this graph. As you can see, ⁹⁹we achieved our goal of 5,000 visitors only once. That was in the month immediately after our television advertisement was released. However, this type of marketing campaign is too expensive to do every month. So, ¹⁰⁰I'd like you to come up with some other ideas on how to promote this service.

performance[미 pərfɔ́:rməns, 영 pəfɔ́:məns] 실적
launch[미 lɔːntʃ, 영 lɔːnʃ] 출시하다   attract[ətrǽkt] 끌어들이다
achieve[ətʃíːv] 달성하다   release[rilíːs] 공개하다, 발표하다
come up with ~을 제안하다, 생각해내다
promote[미 prəmóut, 영 prəmə́ut] 홍보하다

해석

98-100번은 다음 회의 발췌록과 그래프에 관한 문제입니다.

잠시 우리 회사가 5월에 출시한 온라인 서비스의 실적을 검토해보는 시간을 가지겠습니다. 여러분도 아시다시피, ⁹⁸고객들은 호텔들과 항공편들을 예약하기 위해서 우리의 웹사이트를 이용할 수 있습니다. 유감스럽게도, 이것은 예상했던 것만큼 많은 방문객들을 끌어들이지는 못했습니다. 여기, 이 그래프를 보십시오. 보시다시피, ⁹⁹우리는 우리의 목표치였던 5,000명의 방문객을 단 한 번만 달성했습니다. 그때는 우리의 텔레비전 광고가 공개된 직후의 달이었습니다. 하지만, 이런 종류의 마케팅 캠페인은 매달 진행하기에는 비용이 너무 많이 듭니다. 따라서, ¹⁰⁰저는 여러분이 이 서비스를 어떻게 홍보할 수 있을지에 대한 다른 방안들을 제안했으면 합니다.

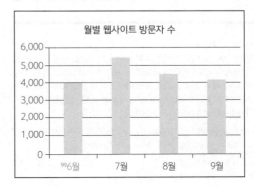

98 화자 문제

해석 화자는 어떤 종류의 업체에서 일하는 것 같은가?
(A) 연구 회사
(B) 여행사
(C) 온라인 소매점
(D) 운송 회사

해설 지문에서 신분 및 직업과 관련된 표현을 놓치지 않고 듣는다. "customers can use our Web site to book hotels and flights"라며 고객들이 호텔들과 항공편들을 예약하기 위해 자사의 웹사이트를 이용할 수 있다고 한 말을 통해 화자가 여행사에서 일한다는 것을 알 수 있다. 따라서 (B)가 정답이다.

어휘 research[미 risə́:rtʃ, 영 risə́:tʃ] 연구, 조사   travel agency 여행사

의 목적어 자리로 생각하여 목적격인 (C) them(그들을)을 선택하지 않도록 주의한다.

해석 직원 안내서는 직원들이 그들의 의료 보험을 어떻게 이용할 수 있는지에 관한 정보를 제공한다.

어휘 **employee handbook** 직원 안내서 **personnel** n. 직원들, 인원
take advantage of ~을 이용하다 **medical benefit** 의료 보험

104 명사 자리 채우기

해설 전치사(for)의 목적어 자리에 올 수 있는 것은 명사이므로 명사 contribution(기부금)의 복수형 (A) contributions가 정답이다. 동사 또는 분사 (B), 동사 (C)와 (D)는 명사 자리에 올 수 없다.

해석 요청 시, Global Awareness Foundation으로의 모든 기부금에 대해 공식 영수증이 발급될 수 있습니다.

어휘 **request** n. 요청; v. 요청하다 **official** adj. 공식적인 **receipt** n. 영수증
issue v. 발급하다, 발표하다

105 명사 어휘 고르기

해설 'Silent Moon은 최우수 영화상의 수상 후보 지명을 받았다'라는 문맥이므로 (A) nomination(수상 후보, 지명)이 정답이다. (B) subscription은 '신청, 구독', (C) destination은 '목적지, 목적', (D) creation은 '창조'라는 의미이다.

해석 감독 Phillip Anderson의 영화 Silent Moon은 올해 최우수 영화상의 수상 후보 지명을 받았다.

106 등위접속사 채우기

해설 '천 명이 넘는 요리사들과 많은 아마추어 요리사들'이라는 의미가 되어야 하므로 (B) and(그리고)가 정답이다.

해석 시애틀 음식 컨벤션은 천 명이 넘는 요리사들과 많은 아마추어 요리사들을 유치한 대성공이었다.

어휘 **success** n. (대)성공, 성과 **attract** v. 유치하다, 끌다
a large number of 많은

107 현재분사와 과거분사 구별하여 채우기

해설 수식 받는 명사(workforce)와 분사가 '숙련된 직원'이라는 의미의 수동 관계이므로 과거분사 (A) experienced가 정답이다. 참고로, 현재분사 (B) experiencing(경험하는)을 빈칸에 넣으면 '경험하는 직원'이라는 어색한 의미가 되므로 답이 될 수 없다.

해석 쇼핑 성수기 동안, Johnson's 스포츠 의류점은 숙련된 직원을 확보하기 위해 추가적인 직원 교육을 제공한다.

어휘 **peak season** 성수기 **ensure** v. 확보하다, 보장하다
workforce n. (모든) 직원

108 동사 관련 어구 완성하기

해설 '오직 15년 이상 근무한 직원들만 우수 근로자 상을 받을 자격이 있다'라는 문맥에서 빈칸 앞의 are과 빈칸 뒤의 to와 함께 쓰여 '~을 받을 자격이 있다'라는 의미의 어구를 이루는 동사 entitle의 p.p.형 (C) entitled가 정답이다. (be entitled to: ~을 받을 자격이 있다) (A) accountable은 '책임이 있는'으로 전치사 for와 함께 쓴다. (be accountable for: ~에 대해 책임이 있다), (B) modified는 '수정된', (D) important는 '중요한'이라는 의미이다.

해석 오직 15년 이상 근무한 직원들만 우수 근로자 상을 받을 자격이 있습니다.

어휘 **excellent** adj. 우수한

109 주어와 수일치하는 동사 채우기

해설 문장에 동사가 없으므로 동사 (B)와 (C)가 정답의 후보이다. 주어(The new recruitment process)가 단수이므로 단수 동사 (B) requires가 정답이다.

---

99 시각 자료 문제

해석 시각 자료를 보아라. 회사는 언제 텔레비전 광고를 진행했는가?
(A) 6월에
(B) 7월에
(C) 8월에
(D) 9월에

해설 제시된 그래프의 정보를 확인한 후 질문의 핵심 어구(run a television advertisement)와 관련된 내용을 주의 깊게 듣는다. "we achieved our goal of 5,000 visitors only once. That was in the month immediately after our television advertisement was released." 라며 목표치였던 5,000명의 방문객을 단 한 번만 달성했다고 한 후, 그 때는 텔레비전 광고가 공개된 직후의 달이었다고 하였으므로, 방문객이 5,000명을 넘은 7월 직전의 달인 6월에 텔레비전 광고를 진행했음을 그래프에서 알 수 있다. 따라서 (A)가 정답이다.

어휘 **run**[rʌn] 진행하다, 운영하다

100 요청 문제

해석 화자는 청자들에게 무엇을 하라고 요청하는가?
(A) 비용을 줄인다.
(B) 제안을 한다.
(C) 의견을 검토한다.
(D) 고객들에게 연락한다.

해설 지문의 중후반에서 요청과 관련된 표현이 포함된 문장을 주의 깊게 듣는다. "I'd like you to come up with some other ideas on how to promote this service"라며 청자들이 이 서비스를 어떻게 홍보할 수 있을지에 대한 다른 방안들을 제안했으면 한다고 하였다. 따라서 (B)가 정답이다.

패러프레이징
come up with ~ ideas 방안들을 제안하다 → Provide suggestions 제안을 하다

어휘 **feedback**[fíːdbæk] 의견

PART 5

101 형용사 자리 채우기

해설 빈칸은 be동사(is) 다음에 나온 주격 보어 자리이므로 명사 (A), 동명사 (C), 형용사 (D)가 정답의 후보이다. 빈칸 앞의 more와 빈칸 뒤의 than과 함께 쓰여 '온라인으로 홍보하는 것이 더 효과적이다'라는 의미가 되어야 하므로 주어(promoting ~ online)를 설명해주는 형용사 (D) effective(효과적인)가 정답이다.

해석 젊은 소비자들을 끌어들이기 위해서는, 신제품들을 온라인으로 홍보하는 것이 텔레비전에서 광고하는 것보다 더 효과적이다.

어휘 **attract** v. 끌어들이다, 매혹하다
effect n. 효과, 결과; v. (어떤 결과를) 가져오다

102 동사 어휘 고르기

해설 '다섯 개의 다른 언어들로 관광을 안내하는 가이드들'이라는 문맥이므로 (A) conduct(안내하다, 수행하다)가 정답이다. (B) receive는 '받다', (C) inspect는 '검사하다', (D) distribute는 '분배하다'라는 의미이다.

해석 Twins Excursions사는 다섯 개의 다른 언어들로 관광을 안내하는 면허증을 소지한 가이드들을 고용한다.

어휘 **excursion** n. (짧은) 여행 **licensed** adj. 면허증을 소지한, 허가된
tour n. 관광, 여행

103 격에 맞는 인칭대명사 채우기

해설 명사구(medical benefits) 앞에서 형용사처럼 쓰일 수 있는 인칭대명사는 소유격이므로 (B) their(그들의)가 정답이다. 전치사(of) 다음

해석 새로운 채용 절차는 모든 향후 입사 지원자들이 그들의 이력서를 이메일을 통해 제출하도록 요구한다.

어휘 recruitment n. 채용, 모집 job candidate 입사 지원자
via prep. ~을 통하여

110 부사 어휘 고르기
해설 '경기 침체가 반드시 실업률이 증가할 것임을 의미하는 것은 아니다'라는 문맥이므로 (A) necessarily(반드시, 필연적으로)가 정답이다. (B) expectedly는 '예상대로', (C) hesitantly는 '머뭇거리며', (D) consciously는 '의식적으로'라는 의미이다. 참고로, not necessarily는 '반드시 ~인 것은 아니다'라는 뜻의 표현이다.

해석 최근의 경기 침체가 반드시 실업률이 증가할 것임을 의미하는 것은 아니다.

어휘 economic downturn 경기 침체 unemployment rate 실업률

111 명사 자리 채우기
해설 전치사(of)의 목적어 자리에 올 수 있는 것은 명사이므로 명사 (D) encouragement(지지, 격려)가 정답이다. 부사 (A), 동사 (B), 동사 또는 분사 (C)는 명사 자리에 올 수 없다.

해석 환경에 특별한 관심이 있는 주민들의 지지의 결과로, 지방 정부는 도시 도처에 자전거 전용 도로를 만들고 있다.

어휘 as a result of ~의 결과로
environmentally conscious 환경에 특별한 관심이 있는
bicycle lane 자전거 전용 도로

112 전치사 채우기
해설 '예정된 날짜보다 최소 이틀 전에 예약을 재확인하다'라는 의미가 되어야 하므로 (A) prior to(~ 전에)가 정답이다. (B) provided that은 '오직 ~하는 경우에만', (C) among은 '~ 사이에', (D) since는 '~ 이래로'라는 의미이다.

해석 Foley 치과는 환자들이 예정된 날짜보다 최소 이틀 전에 예약을 재확인하도록 요청한다.

어휘 dental clinic 치과 reconfirm v. 재확인하다

113 'be동사 + p.p.' 채우기
해설 '계약을 제의받았다'라는 의미가 되기 위해서는 수동형 문장이 되어야 한다. 따라서 be동사(was)와 함께 수동형 동사를 만드는 p.p.형 (A) offered가 정답이다. (B)와 (C)는 동사로 쓰인 경우 be동사 다음에 올 수 없으며, 명사로 쓰이더라도 주어(Susan James)와 의미적으로 동격 관계를 이루지 못하므로 답이 될 수 없다. (D)는 be동사(was) 다음에 와서 능동 진행형을 만들 수 있지만, 이 문장에서는 '마침내 계약을 제공하고 있었다'라는 어색한 의미를 만든다.

해석 많은 출판사들로 원고를 보낸 후에, Susan James는 마침내 Spring Books사로부터 계약을 제의받았다.

어휘 manuscript n. 원고 dozens of 많은 contract n. 계약
offer v. 제의하다; n. 제안

114 형용사 어휘 고르기
해설 '높은 비용 때문에 컴퓨터 시스템을 업그레이드하는 것을 주저했다'라는 문맥이므로 (A) reluctant(주저하는)가 정답이다. (B) unanticipated는 '예상하지 않은', (C) acceptable은 '허용할 수 있는', (D) vulnerable은 '취약한'이라는 의미이다.

해석 Peramo사의 경영진은 높은 비용 때문에 컴퓨터 시스템을 업그레이드하는 것을 주저했다.

어휘 management n. 경영(진)

115 올바른 시제의 동사 채우기
해설 자금을 확보한 시점 이후에 발생한 일(개발자들을 채용하는 일)을 표현하기 위해서 미래 시제를 쓴다. 따라서 (C) will recruit가 정답이다. 참고로, 시간을 나타내는 부사절에서는 현재 시제가 미래를 나타내므로 현재 시제 동사 secures가 쓰였다.

해석 Telestar Computing사는 자금을 확보한 후에, 자사의 확장 계획들을 이행하도록 대규모의 개발자들을 채용할 것이다.

어휘 secure v. 확보하다 funding n. 자금 carry out ~을 이행하다

116 명사 어휘 고르기
해설 '결항된 항공편의 승객들은 그들의 불편에 대한 보상으로 전액 환불과 할인권을 받았다'라는 문맥이므로 (A) compensation(보상)이 정답이다. (B) presentation은 '제출, 발표', (C) motivation은 '동기부여, 자극', (D) admiration은 '존경, 감탄'이라는 의미이다.

해석 결항된 항공편의 승객들은 그들의 불편에 대한 보상으로 전액 환불과 500달러의 할인권을 받았다.

어휘 full refund 전액 환불 voucher n. 할인권, 상품권
inconvenience n. 불편

117 형용사 어휘 고르기
해설 '부정적인 평가들의 주된 이유는 수영장의 좋지 않은 상태이다'라는 문맥이므로 (A) principal(주된, 주요한)이 정답이다. (B) considerate는 '사려 깊은, 배려하는', (C) secure는 '안전한', (D) beneficial은 '유익한, 이로운'이라는 의미이다.

해석 Central Highland 체육관의 부정적인 평가들의 주된 이유는 수영장의 좋지 않은 상태이다.

어휘 negative adj. 부정적인 condition n. 상태, 조건

118 형용사 관용 표현 채우기
해설 '계획을 지지하다'라는 의미가 되어야 하므로 be supportive of(~을 지지하다)를 만드는 (B) supportive가 정답이다.

해석 최근 여론조사는 주민들이 새 공원을 위해 세금을 올리려는 시 의회의 계획을 지지한다는 것을 보여준다.

어휘 poll n. 여론조사 indicate v. 보여주다, 나타내다 support v. 지지하다
supportive adj. 지지하는

119 부사 자리 채우기
해설 동사(apologized)를 꾸미기 위해서는 부사가 와야 하므로 부사 (B) quickly(재빨리)가 정답이다. 명사 (A), 동사 (C), 동사 또는 분사 (D)는 동사를 꾸밀 수 없다.

해석 Mr. Cruise는 회사 주주들을 향한 연설 동안에 잘못 말한 것에 대해 재빨리 사과했다.

어휘 misspeak v. 잘못 말하다 shareholder n. 주주

120 명사 어휘 고르기
해설 '일련의 강의들을 주최할 것이다'라는 문맥이므로 (C) series(일련, 연속)가 정답이다. (A) gathering은 '모임, 수집', (B) means는 '수단, 방법', (D) conclusion은 '결론'이라는 의미이다.

해석 Killiam 공립 도서관은 여름 동안 지역 작가들에 의한 일련의 강의들을 주최할 것이다.

어휘 host v. 주최하다, 열다

121 부사절 접속사 채우기
해설 이 문장은 주어(representatives), 동사(will sign), 목적어(the contract)를 갖춘 완전한 절이므로 ____ an agreement is reached 는 수식어 거품으로 보아야 한다. 이 수식어 거품은 동사(is reached)가 있는 거품절이므로, 거품절을 이끌 수 있는 부사절 접속사 (A)와

(D)가 정답의 후보이다. '합의가 이뤄지자마자 계약서에 서명을 할 것이다'라는 의미가 되어야 하므로 (D) As soon as(~하자마자)가 정답이다. 참고로, (A) Not only는 상관접속사 but also와 짝을 이루는 상관접속사로, not only A but (also) B의 형태로 쓰여 'A뿐만 아니라 B도'라는 의미를 만든다.

해석 합의가 이뤄지자마자, 두 회사의 대표들은 계약서에 서명을 할 것이다.

어휘 agreement n. 합의, 협정 reach v. (목적을) 이루다, 도달하다
representative n. 대표 corporation n. 회사

122 부사 자리 채우기

해설 동사(reports)를 꾸미기 위해서는 부사가 와야 하므로 부사 (A) directly(직접적으로, 바로)가 정답이다. 형용사 또는 동사 (B), 동사 (C), 명사 (D)는 동사를 꾸밀 수 없다.

해석 지사장으로서, Ms. Nissim은 회사의 이사회에 직접 보고를 한다.

어휘 regional manager 지사장 board of directors 이사회

123 전치사 채우기

해설 '건물을 매입하는 것 대신에 사무 공간을 임대하기로 결정했다'라는 의미가 되어야 하므로 (D) instead of(~ 대신에)가 정답이다. (A) about은 '~에 대해', (B) on behalf of는 '~을 대표하여', (C) regarding은 '~에 관하여'라는 의미이다.

해석 Bolton사는 건물을 매입하는 것 대신에 새로운 지점을 위한 사무 공간을 임대하기로 결정했다.

어휘 rent v. 임대하다

124 재귀대명사 채우기

해설 빈칸 뒤의 명사(time)를 꾸밀 수 있는 소유격 인칭대명사 (A), 타동사(give)의 목적어 자리에 올 수 있는 소유대명사 (B), 재귀대명사 (C)와 (D) 모든 보기가 정답의 후보이다. give로 시작하는 절(give ~ workouts)은 명령문으로 주어 you가 생략되어 있는 문장이다. '운동 사이에 회복할 시간을 스스로에게 주어라'라는 의미가 되어야 하므로 주어(you)와 목적어가 동일할 때 목적어 자리에 올 수 있는 재귀대명사 (C) yourself가 정답이다. 소유격 인칭대명사 (A) your와 소유대명사 (B) yours를 쓸 경우 '회복할 너의 시간을 주어라/시간을 너의 것에게 주어라'라는 어색한 의미가 되므로 답이 될 수 없다. 재귀대명사 (D) itself는 주어와 같은 사물을 지칭할 때 쓴다.

해석 최상의 결과를 위해서는, 운동 사이에 회복할 시간을 스스로에게 주어라.

어휘 recover v. 회복하다 workout n. 운동

125 to 부정사의 동사원형 채우기

해설 '능가하기 위해'라는 의미가 되어야 하므로, 목적을 나타내는 to 부정사를 만들어야 한다. to 다음에는 동사원형이 와야 하므로 (B) surpass가 정답이다.

해석 Northpoint Cellular사는 자리를 확실히 잡은 다른 회사들을 능가하기 위해 새로운 무선 기술들에 많이 투자하고 있다.

어휘 heavily adv. 많이, 무겁게
well-established adj. 자리를 확실히 잡은, 안정된
surpass v. 능가하다

126 접속부사 채우기

해설 접속사 and가 절(Renewable energy ~ in recent years)과 절(more consumers ~ it)을 연결하고 있으며, '재생 에너지는 최근 몇 년 동안 더 저렴해졌고, 그러므로 더 많은 소비자들이 그것을 써 보려고 선택하고 있다'라는 의미가 되어야 하므로 (B) therefore(그러므로)가 정답이다. (A) otherwise는 '그렇지 않으면', (C) once는 '일단 ~하면', (D) instead는 '대신에'라는 의미이다.

해석 재생 에너지는 최근 몇 년 동안 더 저렴해졌고, 그러므로 더 많은 소비자들이 그것을 써 보려고 선택하고 있다.

어휘 renewable energy 재생 에너지
affordable adj. 저렴한

127 형용사 어휘 고르기

해설 '현실적인 대화와 그럴듯한 등장인물들을 높이 평가한 평론가들로부터 호의적인 평가를 받았다'라는 문맥이므로 (D) favorable(호의적인)이 정답이다. (A) defective는 '결함이 있는', (B) renewable은 '재생 가능한', (C) artificial은 '인위적인'이라는 의미이다.

해석 Joel Hardwick의 두 번째 소설은 그것의 현실적인 대화와 그럴듯한 등장인물들을 높이 평가한 평론가들로부터 호의적인 평가를 받았다.

어휘 praise v. 높이 평가하다, 칭찬하다 realistic adj. 현실적인
dialog n. 대화 believable adj. 그럴듯한
character n. 등장인물, 성격, 특징

128 현재분사와 과거분사 구별하여 채우기

해설 이 문장은 주어(The number ~ Edible Magazine), 동사(has increased)를 갖춘 완전한 절이므로, ____ that ~ publications는 수식어 거품으로 보아야 한다. 보기 중 수식어 거품이 될 수 있는 것은 분사 (C)와 (D)이다. 주절의 주어(The number of subscribers)와 분사구문이 '구독자 수가 넘다'라는 의미의 능동 관계이므로 현재분사 (D) exceeding이 정답이다. 수식어 거품이 될 수 없는 동사 (A)와 부사 (B)는 답이 될 수 없다.

해석 Edible지의 구독자 수는 다른 모든 요리 출판물들의 구독자 수를 넘어서면서 꾸준히 증가해 왔다.

어휘 subscriber n. 구독자 steadily adv. 꾸준히, 착실하게
culinary adj. 요리의, 음식의

129 전치사 채우기

해설 '판촉 활동의 셋째와 넷째 주 동안의 매출량'이라는 의미가 되어야 하므로 (C) during(~ 동안)이 정답이다.

해석 판촉 활동의 셋째와 넷째 주 동안의 매출량은 그것이 연장되어야 할지를 결정하기 위해 관찰될 것이다.

어휘 monitor v. (추적) 관찰하다, 감시하다
extend v. 연장하다, 늘이다

130 to 부정사 채우기

해설 이 문장은 주어(CanAir's frequent flyer program)와 동사(is designed)를 갖춘 완전한 절이므로, ____ passengers ~ airline은 부사 역할을 하는 수식어 거품으로 보아야 한다. 따라서 수식어 거품이 될 수 있는 to 부정사 (C) to reward가 정답이다. 이 경우 to reward는 목적(보상하기 위해서)을 나타내는 to 부정사이며, be designed to는 '~하기 위해 고안되다'라는 의미의 관용 표현이다. 명사 또는 동사 (A)와 (D), 형용사 (B)는 수식어 거품이 될 수 없다.

해석 CanAir사의 상용 고객 프로그램은 그 항공사의 비행기를 정기적으로 타는 승객들을 보상하기 위해 고안되었다.

어휘 frequent flyer 상용 고객 regularly adv. 정기적으로
fly v. 비행기를 타다, 날다
rewarding adj. 보람 있는, 돈을 많이 버는

PART 6

131-134번은 다음 편지에 관한 문제입니다.

Ms. Victoria Collins
645번지 Keystone가
벨뷰, 워싱턴 주 98007

Ms. Collins께,

¹³¹지난주에 귀하께서 상담을 위해 저희 가게에 계셨을 때, 귀하께서는 벨뷰 미술 협회의 자선 만찬 행사를 위한 특별한 옷이 필요할 것이라고 말씀하셨습니다.

¹³²저희는 방금 디자이너 Eleanor Harris의 여름 컬렉션의 여러 가지 옷들을 받았습니다. 특히, 귀하께서 관심이 있으실 수도 있는 파란색 이브닝 드레스를 갖고 있습니다. 이 제품은 저희 가게 외에 다른 곳에서는 사실 수 없습니다만, 스몰 사이즈입니다. ¹³³몸에 딱 맞도록 확실히 하기 위해 가벼운 수선이 행해질 수 있습니다.

¹³⁴귀하께서는 만찬이 5월에 열린다고 말씀하셨습니다. 날씨가 그때쯤에는 따뜻할 것이니, 이와 같은 가벼운 드레스는 그 행사에 완벽할 것입니다. 언제 들르실 수 있는지 알려주시기 바랍니다.

Miranda Hudson 드림
Dot 부티크

consultation n. 상담, 상의 **unique** adj. 특별한 **outfit** n. 옷
charity n. 자선 (단체) **exclusive** adj. 다른 곳에서는 살 수 없는, 독점적인

131 시간 표현과 일치하는 시제의 동사 채우기
해설 과거 시간 표현(last week)이 있으므로 과거 시제 (C) mentioned가 정답이다.

132 명사 어휘 고르기
해설 '디자이너의 여름 컬렉션의 여러 가지 옷들을 받았다'라는 문맥이므로 (A) assortment(여러 가지의 물건, 구색)가 정답이다. (B) estimate는 '추정, 견적서', (C) invitation은 '초대', (D) announcement는 '발표, 소식'이라는 의미이다.

133 알맞은 문장 고르기
해석 (A) 저희는 그 드레스가 너무 격식을 차린 것인지 염려됩니다.
　　 (B) 옷은 건조기에 넣으면 때때로 줄어들 수 있습니다.
　　 (C) 몸에 딱 맞도록 확실히 하기 위해 가벼운 수선이 행해질 수 있습니다.
　　 (D) 그것은 전국의 유명한 소매점에서 판매됩니다.
해설 빈칸에 들어갈 알맞은 문장을 고르는 문제이므로 주변 문맥 또는 전체 문맥을 파악한다. 앞부분에서 Ms. Collins가 관심이 있을 수도 있는 파란색 이브닝 드레스를 갖고 있다고 했고, 앞 문장 'This item is exclusive to our shop, but it is a size small.'에서 이 제품은 이 가게 외에 다른 곳에서는 살 수 없지만 스몰 사이즈라고 했으므로, 빈칸에는 몸에 딱 맞도록 확실히 하기 위해 가벼운 수선이 행해질 수 있다는 내용이 들어가야 함을 알 수 있다. 따라서 (C)가 정답이다.
어휘 **formal** adj. 격식을 차리는, 형식적인 **shrink** v. 줄어들다
　　 minor adj. 가벼운, 작은 **alteration** n. 수선, 변화
　　 fit n. 몸에 맞는 옷, 어울림 **retail store** 소매점

134 동사 어휘 고르기 주변 문맥 파악
해설 '만찬이 5월에 ___고 말했다'라는 문맥이므로 (B) discussed(논의하다), (C) canceled(취소하다), (D) held(열다)가 정답의 후보이다. 빈칸이 있는 문장만으로 정답을 고를 수 없으므로 주변 문맥이나 전체 문맥을 파악한다. 뒤 문장에서 '날씨가 그때쯤에는 따뜻할 것이니 이와 같은 가벼운 드레스는 그 행사에 완벽할 것이다(The weather will be warm by then, so a light dress such as this one will be perfect for the event.)'라고 했으므로 만찬이 5월에 열릴 것임을 알 수 있다. 따라서 (D) held가 정답이다.

135-138번은 다음 회람에 관한 문제입니다.

날짜: 12월 10일
수신: 전 직원

발신: Jonathan Carter, 최고 업무 집행 책임자
제목: 정책 변경사항

¹³⁵더 높은 효율성을 촉진하기 위해, 경영진은 내년에 직원 평가가 실시되는 방법을 변경하기로 결정했습니다. ¹³⁶1월부터, 팀원들은 매년 면밀한 평가에 참여해야 합니다. 이 과정은 그들의 성과의 모든 측면을 검토하는 것을 수반할 것입니다. ¹³⁷직원들은 그 결과를 기반으로 상여금을 받을 것입니다. 새로운 제도에 관한 추가적인 정보는 직원 수칙의 최신 버전에 포함되어 있습니다. ¹³⁸이 문서는 다음 주에 배부될 것입니다.

질문이 있으시면, 인사부장인 Dave Stewart에게 연락하시기 바랍니다.

COO n. 최고 업무 집행 책임자 **encourage** v. 촉진하다
carry out ~을 실시하다, 이행하다 **assessment** n. 평가
involve v. 수반하다, 포함하다 **aspect** n. 측면, 관점
performance n. 성과, 실적 **updated** adj. 최신의
employee manual 직원 수칙 **personnel** n. 인사부, 직원들

135 명사 어휘 고르기 전체 문맥 파악
해설 '더 높은 효율성을 촉진하기 위해, 경영진은 내년에 직원 ___가 실시되는 방법을 변경하기로 결정했다'라는 문맥이므로 모든 보기가 정답의 후보이다. 빈칸이 있는 문장만으로 정답을 고를 수 없으므로 주변 문맥이나 전체 문맥을 파악한다. 뒤 문장에서 '팀원들은 매년 평가(assessment)에 참여해야 한다'고 한 후, 지문 뒷부분에서 '이 과정은 그들의 성과의 모든 측면을 검토하는 것을 수반할 것이다(This process will involve examining all aspects of their performance)'라고 했으므로 직원 평가가 실시됨을 알 수 있다. 따라서 (D) evaluations(평가)가 정답이다.
어휘 **assignment** n. 과제, 임무 **registration** n. 등록

136 형용사 어휘 고르기 주변 문맥 파악
해설 '팀원들은 매년 ___한 평가에 참여해야 한다'라는 문맥이므로 모든 보기가 정답의 후보이다. 빈칸이 있는 문장만으로 정답을 고를 수 없으므로 주변 문맥이나 전체 문맥을 파악한다. 뒤 문장에서 '이 과정은 그들의 성과의 모든 측면을 검토하는 것을 수반할 것이다(This process will involve examining all aspects of their performance.)'라고 했으므로 평가가 면밀함을 알 수 있다. 따라서 (A) thorough(면밀한, 철저한)가 정답이다.
어휘 **temporary** adj. 일시적인, 임시의 **voluntary** adj. 자발적인
　　 selective adj. 선택적인

137 올바른 시제의 동사 채우기 주변 문맥 파악
해설 '직원들은 그 결과를 기반으로 상여금을 받는다'라는 문맥인데, 이 경우 빈칸이 있는 문장만으로는 올바른 시제의 동사를 고를 수 없으므로 주변 문맥이나 전체 문맥을 파악하여 정답을 고른다. 앞 문장에서 '이 과정은 그들의 성과의 모든 측면을 검토하는 것을 수반할 것이다(This process will involve examining all aspects of their performance.)'라고 했으므로 그 결과를 기반으로 상여금을 받는 시점은 미래임을 알 수 있다. 따라서 미래 시제 (C) will receive가 정답이다.

138 알맞은 문장 고르기
해석 (A) 이 과정은 이미 성과를 향상시켰습니다.
　　 (B) 이 문서는 다음 주에 배부될 것입니다.
　　 (C) 몇몇 직원들은 아직 평가되지 않았습니다.
　　 (D) 그러나, 이 결과들은 별로 놀랍지 않았습니다.
해설 빈칸에 들어갈 알맞은 문장을 고르는 문제이므로 주변 문맥 또는 전체 문맥을 파악한다. 앞 문장 'Additional information about the new system has been included in the updated version of the employee manual.'에서 새로운 제도에 관한 추가적인 정보는 직원 수칙의 최신 버전에 포함되어 있다고 했으므로, 빈칸에는 이 문서가 다음 주에 배부될 것이라는 내용이 들어가야 함을 알 수 있다. 따라서 (B)

가 정답이다.

어휘 **distribute** v. 배부하다

139-142번은 다음 광고에 관한 문제입니다.

> **Quinn Grill에서의 요리사 일자리**
>
> 저희는 훌륭한 명성을 가진 고급 식당이며, 5년 넘게 영업을 해왔습니다. ¹³⁹저희 고객층은 입소문과 평론가들로부터의 긍정적인 평가로 인해 이 기간 동안 빠르게 증가해 왔습니다. ¹⁴⁰저희가 주요 식사 공간을 확장하는 중이기 때문에, 경력이 있는 요리사들이 필요합니다. 모든 지원자들은 최소 2년의 식당에서 일한 경력이 있어야 합니다. 이는 다양하고 폭넓은 음식들을 요리하는 것을 포함해야 합니다. ¹⁴¹저희는 또한 몇 가지 다른 구체적인 요구 조건이 있습니다. ¹⁴²저희의 이상적인 지원자는 고도의 긴장을 요하는 환경을 감당하고, 다른 팀원들과 협력하며, 주말과 휴일을 포함하여 탄력적인 근무시간을 일할 수 있어야 할 것입니다.
>
> 여러분의 지원서, 이력서, 추천서를 Sophia Quinn에게 squinn@quinngrill.com으로 보내주시기 바랍니다.
>
> ---
>
> **vacancy** n. 일자리, 결원 **fine** adj. 고급의 **reputation** n. 명성, 평판
> **be in business** 영업을 하고 있다 **customer base** 고객층
> **rapidly** adv. 빠르게, 신속히 **critic** n. 평론가, 비평가
> **be in need of** ~이 필요하다 **experienced** adj. 경력(험)이 있는, 능숙한
> **ideal** adj. 이상적인, 완벽한 **handle** v. 감당하다, 처리하다
> **high-pressure** adj. 고도의 긴장을 요하는, 스트레스가 많은
> **collaborate** v. 협력하다 **reference letter** 추천서

139 올바른 시제의 동사 채우기 주변 문맥 파악

해설 '고객층이 이 기간 동안 빠르게 증가하다'라는 문맥인데, 이 경우 빈칸이 있는 문장만으로는 올바른 시제의 동사를 고를 수 없으므로 주변 문맥이나 전체 문맥을 파악하여 정답을 고른다. 앞 문장에서 '5년 넘게 영업을 해왔다(we have been in business for over five years)'라고 했으므로 과거 5년 전에 시작되어 현재에도 고객층이 증가하고 있음을 알 수 있다. 따라서 현재 완료 시제 (C) has grown이 정답이다.

어휘 **grow** v. 증가하다, 성장하다

140 부사절 접속사 채우기

해설 이 문장은 필수성분(we ~ cooks)을 갖춘 완전한 절이므로 ___ we ~ room은 수식어 거품으로 보아야 한다. 이 수식어 거품은 동사(are expanding)가 있는 거품절이므로, 거품절을 이끌 수 있는 부사절 접속사 (A), (C), (D)가 정답의 후보이다. '주요 식사 공간을 확장하는 중이기 때문에 경력이 있는 요리사들이 필요하다'라는 의미가 되어야 하므로 (A) Because(~이기 때문에)가 정답이다.

141 알맞은 문장 고르기

해석 (A) 모든 이들은 의무적인 식품 안전 과정을 통과했습니다.
(B) 저희는 또한 몇 가지 다른 구체적인 요구 조건이 있습니다.
(C) 면접 결과가 곧 게시될 것입니다.
(D) 손님들은 즉시 그들의 테이블로 안내되어야 합니다.

해설 빈칸에 들어갈 알맞은 문장을 고르는 문제이므로 주변 문맥 또는 전체 문맥을 파악한다. 앞부분에서 모든 지원자들은 최소 2년의 식당에서 일한 경력이 있어야 한다고 한 후, 뒤 문장 'Our ideal candidate will be able to handle a high-pressure environment, collaborate with other members of a team'에서 이상적인 지원자는 고도의 긴장을 요하는 환경을 감당하고 다른 팀원들과 협력할 수 있어야 할 것이라고 했으므로, 빈칸에는 몇 가지 다른 구체적인 요구 조건이 있다는 내용이 들어가야 함을 알 수 있다. 따라서 (B)가 정답이다.

어휘 **mandatory** adj. 의무적인 **show** v. 안내하다

142 형용사 자리 채우기

해설 명사(hours)를 꾸미기 위해서는 형용사가 와야 하므로 형용사 (C)

---

flexible(탄력적인, 융통성 있는)이 정답이다.

어휘 **flexibility** n. 융통성, 신축성 **flexibleness** n. 신축성 있음, 유연함

143-146번은 다음 편지에 관한 문제입니다.

> Sandra Ericta
> 임대주, Bristol 아파트
> 355번지 Main가
> 샌프란시스코, 캘리포니아 주 95125
>
> Ms. Ericta께,
>
> 이 편지는 제가 9월 30일에 Bristol 아파트 307호를 비울 것이라는 통지의 역할을 합니다. ¹⁴³저는 당신에게 제 임대 계약서에 따라 요구되는 30일 전의 통지를 드립니다.
>
> ¹⁴⁴저는 아파트가 양호한 상태에 있게 해야 할 의무가 있음을 이해하고 있습니다. 그렇지 않으면, 제 보증금을 잃을 것입니다. ¹⁴⁵당신이 언제 집을 점검하여 모든 것이 만족스러운지 확인하실 수 있는지 알려주시기 바랍니다. 저는 제가 이사를 나가고 열쇠를 당신에게 드린 후, 9월 30일에 제 보증금이 반환되었으면 좋겠습니다. ¹⁴⁶제가 같은 날에 제 은행 계좌 세부 정보를 드리겠습니다.
>
> 감사합니다.
>
> John Schroeder 드림
>
> ---
>
> **landlord** n. 임대주, 주인 **serve as** ~의 역할을 하다
> **vacate** v. 비우다, 떠나다 **rental contract** 임대 계약서
> **condition** n. 상태, 환경, 조건 **otherwise** adv. 그렇지 않으면
> **security deposit** 보증금 **move out** 이사를 나가다

143 현재분사와 과거분사 구별하여 채우기

해설 수식받는 명사(30 days' notice)와 분사가 '요구되는 30일 전의 통지'라는 의미의 수동 관계이므로 과거분사 (D) requested가 정답이다.

144 명사 어휘 고르기 주변 문맥 파악

해설 '아파트가 양호한 상태에 있게 해야 할 ___가 있다'라는 문맥이므로 (B) obligation(의무)과 (D) option(선택권)이 정답의 후보이다. 빈칸이 있는 문장만으로 정답을 고를 수 없으므로 주변 문맥이나 전체 문맥을 파악한다. 뒤 문장에서 '그렇지 않으면, 보증금을 잃을 것이다(Otherwise, I will lose my security deposit.)'라고 했으므로 편지 발신자인 Mr. Schroeder가 아파트가 양호한 상태에 있게 해야 할 의무가 있음을 알 수 있다. 따라서 (B) obligation이 정답이다.

어휘 **occupation** n. 직업, 업무 **inquiry** n. 문의

145 형용사 어휘 고르기

해설 '집을 점검하여 모든 것이 만족스러운지 확인하다'라는 문맥이 되어야 하므로 (C) satisfactory(만족스러운)가 정답이다.

어휘 **capable** adj. 유능한 **challenging** adj. 도전적인
appreciative adj. 감사하는

146 알맞은 문장 고르기

해석 (A) 세입자들은 열쇠를 복사하는 것이 금지되어 있습니다.
(B) 잘못된 금액이 송금된 것 같습니다.
(C) 제가 같은 날에 제 은행 계좌 세부 정보를 드리겠습니다.
(D) 저는 오늘 제 가구를 옮길 수 없을 것입니다.

해설 빈칸에 들어갈 알맞은 문장을 고르는 문제이므로 주변 문맥 또는 전체 문맥을 파악한다. 앞 문장 'I would like my deposit returned to me on September 30, after I have moved out and handed you the key.'에서 자신이 이사를 나가고 열쇠를 준 후 9월 30일에 보증금이 반환되었으면 좋겠다고 했으므로, 빈칸에는 이와 같은 날에 자신의 은행 계좌 세부 정보를 주겠다는 내용이 들어가야 함을 알 수

있다. 따라서 (C)가 정답이다.

어휘 tenant n. 세입자, 임차인 prohibit v. 금지하다
transfer v. 송금하다, 전달하다

PART 7

147-148번은 다음 광고에 관한 문제입니다.

새 아파트나 집으로 이제 막 이사 오셨나요? 당신의 집을 수리하는 데 도움이 필요하신가요? 그렇다면, 그저 전화만 하시면 되니 운이 좋습니다:

147Harold and Sons사
교외를 포함한 센터빌 지역에 서비스를 제공합니다
555-2398

147저희는 이들을 포함하여 폭넓은 서비스를 제공합니다:
기본 집 수리
가전제품, 조명, 고정 세간 설치
벽지 도배와 벽 페인트칠
가구 배치
타일 설치

Harold Clark는 25년 전에 그의 사업을 시작했고, 현재 그의 아들 Robert와 William이 그와 함께 일하며 홈 서비스들을 지역 주민들에게 제공하고 있습니다. 이 가문의 경력과 전문성은 비할 데가 없습니다. 1486월에 전화를 주시면, Harold and Sons사에서 어떠한 서비스의 구매에도 천장 선풍기나 조명 설비를 무료로 설치해드릴 것입니다.

---

fix up ~을 수리하다 be in luck 운이 좋다 greater adj. 교외를 포함한 lighting n. 조명 fixture n. 고정 세간(욕조·변기 등 이동할 수 없는 세간) installation n. 설치 wallpaper n. 벽지 arrangement n. 배치 lay v. 설치하다, 놓다 beyond comparison 비할 데 없는

147 추론 문제

문제 Harold and Sons사는 무슨 일을 하는 것 같은가?
(A) 집 인테리어를 위한 벽지 무늬를 디자인한다.
(B) 한 집에서 다른 집으로 가구를 옮긴다.
(C) 주택의 유지 보수 작업을 수행한다.
(D) 사무실 조명 설치를 전문으로 한다.

해설 질문의 핵심 어구인 Harold and Sons에 대해 추론하는 문제이다. 'Harold and Sons'와 'We provide a wide range of services, including: Basic home repairs, ~, Tile laying'에서 Harold and Sons사가 기본 집 수리, 타일 설치 등을 포함하여 폭넓은 서비스를 제공한다고 했으므로 주택의 유지 보수 작업을 수행한다는 것을 추론할 수 있다. 따라서 (C)가 정답이다.

어휘 conduct v. 수행하다 residential adj. 주택의, 주거의 maintenance n. 유지, 보수 specialize in ~을 전문으로 하다

148 육하원칙 문제

문제 고객들은 6월에 무엇을 받을 수 있는가?
(A) 상품권
(B) 무료 서비스
(C) 제품 샘플
(D) 새 회사 카탈로그

해설 고객들이 6월에 무엇을(What) 받을 수 있는지를 묻는 육하원칙 문제이다. 질문의 핵심 어구인 customers receive in June과 관련하여, 'If you call in the month of June, Harold and Sons will install a ceiling fan or light fixture for free with the purchase of any service.'에서 6월에 전화를 주면 Harold and Sons사에서 어떠한 서비스의 구매에도 천장 선풍기나 조명 설비를 무료로 설치해줄 것이라고 했으므로 (B)가 정답이다.

패러프레이징
install a ceiling fan or light fixture for free 천장 선풍기나 조명 설비를 무료로 설치하다 → A complimentary service 무료 서비스

어휘 complimentary adj. 무료의

149-150번은 다음 메시지 대화문에 관한 문제입니다.

Kelly Orville [오후 4시 30분]
자, 149-A/C우리는 다음 주 금요일에 Chez Mimi's 대신 Lococo's Grill에서 직원 회식을 갖기로 결정되었어요. 149-C그곳은 우리 사무실에서 훨씬 더 가까워요.

Nigel Wendt [오후 4시 31분]
훌륭한 선택이네요. 149-B저는 항상 거기서 식사해요. 150예약하기 위해 전화는 하셨나요? IT 부서의 몇몇 사람들이 결국 올 수 있다고 아까 제게 말해줬어요.

Kelly Orville [오후 4시 33분]
그렇게 할 셈이었는데, 150제가 오늘 정말 바빴어요. 몇 명의 IT 부서 직원들이 참석할 예정인가요? 그 식당은 많은 자리를 가지고 있어서, 더 많은 사람들이 오기를 원해도 분명히 우리 모두의 자리를 만들 수 있을 거예요.

Nigel Wendt [오후 4시 33분]
제가 알기로는, 7명이에요. 하지만 다시 한번 확인하셔야 할 거예요.

---

after all 결국 mean to ~할 셈이다 plenty of 많은 seat v. 자리를 만들다, 앉히다 double-check v. 다시 한번 확인하다

149 Not/True 문제

문제 Lococo's Grill에 대해 사실이 아닌 것은?
(A) 회사 모임들을 주최할 수 있다.
(B) Mr. Wendt에 의해 자주 방문된다.
(C) Chez Mimi's보다 직장에 더 가깝다.
(D) 주말에는 예약을 필요로 한다.

해설 질문의 핵심 어구인 Lococo's Grill과 관련된 내용을 지문에서 찾아 보기와 대조하는 Not/True 문제이다. (A)는 'we'll be having the staff dinner ~ at Lococo's Grill'(4:30 P.M.)에서 Lococo's Grill에서 직원 회식을 갖는다고 했으므로 지문의 내용과 일치한다. (B)는 'I eat there[Lococo's Grill] all the time.'(4:31 P.M.)에서 Mr. Wendt가 항상 Lococo's Grill에서 식사한다고 했으므로 지문의 내용과 일치한다. (C)는 'we'll be having the staff dinner ~ at Lococo's Grill instead of Chez Mimi's. It's much closer to our office.'(4:30 P.M.)에서 Chez Mimi's 대신 Lococo's Grill에서 직원 회식을 갖는데, 그곳이 사무실에서 훨씬 더 가깝다고 했으므로 지문의 내용과 일치한다. (D)는 지문에 언급되지 않은 내용이다. 따라서 (D)가 정답이다.

패러프레이징
eat there all the time 항상 거기서 식사하다 → It is frequently visited 자주 방문되다
much closer to ~ office 사무실에서 훨씬 더 가까운 → nearer to a workplace 직장에 더 가까운

어휘 workplace n. 직장

150 의도 파악 문제

문제 오후 4시 33분에, Ms. Orville이 "I've been meaning to"라고 썼을 때, 그녀가 의도한 것 같은 것은?
(A) 다른 부서의 직원들을 초대할 계획이다.
(B) 직원들이 얼마나 참석할지 모른다.
(C) 직원들에게 변경사항에 대해 알려줄 예정이다.
(D) 식당에 연락하지 않았다.

해설 Ms. Orville이 의도한 것 같은 것을 묻는 문제이므로, 질문의 인용

어구(I've been meaning to)가 언급된 주변 문맥을 확인한다. 'Have you called to make the reservation yet?'(4:31 P.M.)에서 Mr. Wendt가 식당을 예약하기 위해 전화는 했는지 묻자, Ms. Orville이 'I've been meaning to'(그렇게 할 셈이었는데)라고 한 후, 'but I've been really busy today'(4:33 P.M.)에서 오늘 정말 바빴다고 한 것을 통해, Ms. Orville이 바빠서 식당에 연락하지 않았다는 것을 알 수 있다. 따라서 (D)가 정답이다.

151-153번은 다음 기사에 관한 문제입니다.

> **Medallion사가 신입 사원들이 적응하도록 돕다**
>
> ¹⁵¹올해 초에, Medallion사는 직원들의 능력을 개발시키기 위한 직원 멘토링 프로그램을 만들었다. — [1] —. Medallion Mentoring이라고 불리는 이 프로그램은, 새로 채용된 사원들과 고위급 관리자들을 둘씩 조로 나누는데, 고위급 관리자들은 경력 발전 계획뿐만 아니라 일상 업무에 대한 조언을 제공한다. — [2] —. 인사부 담당자들은 신입 사원들에게 멘토들을 배정하고 일주일에 한 시간씩 두 번의 일정을 잡는다. — [3] —. 또한, ¹⁵²프로그램의 모든 멘토들은 이 시간 요건을 준수해야 한다.
>
> 이 프로그램이 시작하기까지는 한동안 시간이 걸렸지만, 참여는 서서히 증가하고 있다. ¹⁵³올해, 인사부 담당자들은 전사적으로 200명의 멘토들을 갖는 것을 목표하고 있다. — [4] —. Medallion사 회장 Sally Kay는 "현재 이 프로그램에 대한 관심이 훨씬 더 많아져서, 멘토로 자원하는 관리자들을 필요한 만큼 찾는 데 문제가 없을 것입니다"라고 말했다.
>
> pair v. 둘씩 조로 나누다, 짝을 짓다 senior-level adj. 고위급의
> day-to-day adj. 일상의 career n. 경력 strategy n. 계획, 전략
> coordinator n. 담당자, 진행자 assign v. 배정하다
> fulfill v. 준수하다, 충족시키다
> get ~ off the ground ~을 시작하다, 순조롭게 출발하다
> gradually adv. 서서히 aim to ~하는 것을 목표로 하다
> companywide adv. 전사적으로

151 추론 문제

문제 Medallion Mentoring 프로그램에 대해 암시되는 것은?
(A) 회사 웹사이트에서 크게 다루어졌다.
(B) 분기별로 구인 활동이 필요하다.
(C) 고위 경영진에게 지지받지 않았다.
(D) 확립된 지 12달이 채 되지 않았다.

해설 질문의 핵심 어구인 Medallion Mentoring program에 대해 추론하는 문제이다. 'Earlier this year, Medallion Corporation created a staff mentoring program to develop the skills of its employees.'에서 올해 초에 Medallion사가 직원들의 능력을 개발시키기 위한 직원 멘토링 프로그램을 만들었다고 했으므로 (D)가 정답이다.

어휘 feature v. (신문 등이) ~을 특종으로 크게 다루다, 포함하다
quarterly adv. 분기별 upper management 고위 경영진
establish v. 확립하다

152 육하원칙 문제

문제 멘토들은 무엇을 하도록 요구되는가?
(A) 최소한의 필수 시간을 충족시킨다.
(B) 퇴근 후 하루에 2시간 동안 자원 봉사를 한다.
(C) 지도를 받는 직원들의 가족들을 만난다.
(D) 담당자와 정기적인 상담 시간을 가진다.

해설 멘토들이 무엇을(What)을 하도록 요구되는지를 묻는 육하원칙 문제이다. 질문의 핵심 어구인 mentors required to do와 관련하여, 'all mentors in the program must fulfill this time requirement[two one-hour sessions per week]'에서 프로그램의 모든 멘토들은 일주일에 한 시간씩 두 번이라는 시간 요건을 준수해야 한다고 했으므로

(A)가 정답이다.

패러프레이징
fulfill ~ time requirement 시간 요건을 준수하다 → Meet a minimum number of necessary hours 최소한의 필수 시간을 충족시키다

어휘 meet v. 충족시키다 minimum adj. 최소한의 necessary adj. 필수의
get together ~를 만나다 counseling n. 상담

153 문장 위치 찾기 문제

문제 [1], [2], [3], [4]로 표시된 위치 중, 다음 문장이 들어갈 곳으로 가장 적절한 것은?
"이 목표는 10월까지 달성될 것으로 예상된다."
(A) [1]
(B) [2]
(C) [3]
(D) [4]

해설 지문의 흐름상 주어진 문장이 들어가기에 가장 적절한 곳을 고르는 문제이다. This goal is expected to be achieved by October에서 이 목표는 10월까지 달성될 것으로 예상된다고 했으므로, 주어진 문장 앞에 목표와 관련된 내용이 있을 것임을 예상할 수 있다. [4]의 앞 문장인 'This year, human resources coordinators aim to have 200 mentors companywide.'에서 올해 인사부 담당자들은 전사적으로 200명의 멘토들을 갖는 것을 목표하고 있다고 했으므로, [4]에 주어진 문장이 들어가면 전사적으로 200명의 멘토들을 갖는 목표가 10월까지 달성될 것으로 예상된다는 내용을 설명하는 자연스러운 문맥이 된다는 것을 알 수 있다. 따라서 (D)가 정답이다.

어휘 goal n. 목표 achieve v. 달성하다

154-155번은 다음 이메일에 관한 문제입니다.

> 수신: Leah Young <leahyoung@journeyon.com>
> 발신: Evan Harris <evanharris@smartmail.com>
> 날짜: 5월 9일
> 제목: 여행 보험
> 첨부: 영수증, 경찰 보고서
>
> Ms. Young께,
>
> ¹⁵⁴저는 예상치 못한 지출에 대한 상환을 요청하기 위해 이메일을 씁니다. 최근에, 저는 휴가로 멕시코에 여행을 갔습니다. 저는 Journey on Travel Insurance사를 통해 제 여행에 대한 보험을 들었습니다. 제 보험 증권번호는 4533906입니다.
>
> 저는 코수멜 섬에 있는 Fiesta 호텔에 방을 5박 동안 예약했습니다. ¹⁵⁵숙박 둘째 날, 누군가가 제 방에 접근해서 제 노트북 컴퓨터를 들고 갔습니다. 호텔 지배인이 남은 3박에 대한 환불금을 주었지만, 이것은 대체 컴퓨터를 구매할 비용이 되지 않습니다.
>
> 제가 알기로는, 이러한 유형의 상황에서 저는 귀사로부터 5,000달러까지의 보험 보장을 받을 자격이 있습니다. 제 노트북 컴퓨터의 총 비용은 2,300달러였습니다. 컴퓨터 영수증과 경찰 보고서의 사본들을 첨부하였습니다.
>
> Evan Harris 드림
>
> reimbursement n. 상환, 변제 unexpected adj. 예상치 못한
> insure v. 보험에 들다 gain access to ~에 접근하다
> remaining adj. 남은 come close to 거의 ~할 뻔하다
> cover v. (~에 충분한 돈이) 되다 replacement n. 대체
> be entitled to ~을 받을 자격이 있다 coverage n. 보장

154 목적 찾기 문제

문제 Mr. Harris는 왜 이메일을 썼는가?
(A) 보상을 요청하기 위해

(B) 예약을 하기 위해
(C) 호텔을 비판하기 위해
(D) 결제를 취소하기 위해

해설 Mr. Harris가 이메일을 쓴 목적을 묻는 목적 찾기 문제이므로 지문의 앞부분을 주의 깊게 확인한다. 'I am writing to request reimbursement for an unexpected expense.'에서 예상치 못한 지출에 대한 상환을 요청하기 위해 이메일을 쓴다고 했으므로 (A)가 정답이다.

어휘 compensation n. 보상 criticize v. 비판하다

155 육하원칙 문제
문제 이메일에 따르면, Fiesta 호텔에서 무슨 일이 있었는가?
(A) 손님의 객실 요금이 과잉 청구되었다.
(B) 전자 기기를 도난당했다.
(C) 개인 컴퓨터가 손상되었다.
(D) 환불 요청이 거부되었다.

해설 Fiesta 호텔에서 무슨(what) 일이 있었는지를 묻는 육하원칙 문제이다. 질문의 핵심 어구인 happened at Hotel Fiesta와 관련하여, 'On the second day of my visit, someone gained access to my room and took my laptop computer.'에서 숙박 둘째 날 누군가가 방에 접근해서 노트북 컴퓨터를 들고 갔다고 했으므로 (B)가 정답이다.

패러프레이징
someone ~ took ~ laptop computer 누군가가 노트북 컴퓨터를 들고 갔다 → An electronic device was stolen 전자 기기를 도난당했다

어휘 overcharge v. 과잉 청구하다 electronic adj. 전자의
device n. 기기 deny v. 거부하다

156-157번은 다음 웹페이지에 관한 문제입니다.

Delta의 엄청난 할인 혜택들
[156]지역 업체들에서의 특별 혜택들을 위한 당신의 정보원

저희는 가게, 음식점, 여행사, 미용실, 스파, 홈 서비스 업체들과 함께
Delta 지역의 소비자들을 위해
한 곳에서 모든 쇼핑을 할 수 있는 상점을 만들고자 합니다.
당신은 다른 어떤 곳에서도 이렇게 많은
할인 혜택들을 찾아볼 수 없을 것입니다.
[156]오늘 엄청난 할인 혜택을 찾아보세요!

상품 혹은 서비스 검색

업체 검색

이 웹사이트는 *Delta Times* 신문에 의해 제공되었습니다.

홈	쇼핑	홈 서비스	개인 서비스

할인 혜택 1번:
Hammerhead의 창문 청소
-주택 창문 청소 서비스 첫 이용 시 40달러 할인

할인 혜택 2번:
Scrub Masters의 타일과 환풍구 청소
-두 가지 서비스 모두 주문 시 정가의 20퍼센트 할인

할인 혜택 3번:
Bloom의 마당 서비스
-[157]6개월간의 주간 잔디 관리 서비스 선불 시, 25퍼센트 할인

할인 혜택 4번:
Swift Swipe의 카펫 청소
-최대 5개 방의 양탄자 청소 서비스 1회 10퍼센트 할인

다음 페이지에 계속. 여기를 누르세요! >>>

---

source n. 정보원, 출처 spa n. 스파, 온천, 휴양 시설
one-stop adj. 한 곳에서 다 할 수 있는 residential adj. 주택(용)의
air vent 환풍구 lawn n. 잔디 one-time adj. 1회만의, 한때 ~였던
rug n. 양탄자

---

156 목적 찾기 문제
문제 웹페이지의 목적은 무엇인가?
(A) 비슷한 서비스들의 가격을 비교하기 위해
(B) 지역 서비스업체들의 평가를 제공하기 위해
(C) 새로운 회사들을 소개하기 위해
(D) 업체들의 할인 제공을 광고하기 위해

해설 웹페이지의 목적을 묻는 목적 찾기 문제이므로 지문의 앞부분을 주의 깊게 확인한다. 'Your source for special deals at area businesses'에서 지역 업체들에서의 특별 혜택들을 위한 당신의 정보원이라고 한 후, 'Find a great deal today!'에서 오늘 엄청난 할인 혜택을 찾아보라고 했으므로 (D)가 정답이다.

어휘 compare v. 비교하다 enterprise n. 회사, 기업

157 육하원칙 문제
문제 조경 서비스에 얼마의 할인이 제공되고 있는가?
(A) 10퍼센트
(B) 20퍼센트
(C) 25퍼센트
(D) 40퍼센트

해설 조경 서비스에 얼마(How much)의 할인이 제공되고 있는지를 묻는 육하원칙 문제이다. 질문의 핵심 어구인 discount ~ offered on landscaping services와 관련하여, 'Six months of weekly lawn care services, prepaid, at 25 percent off'에서 6개월간의 주간 잔디 관리 서비스를 선불하면 25퍼센트 할인이라고 했으므로 (C)가 정답이다.

어휘 landscaping n. 조경

158-160번은 다음 편지에 관한 문제입니다.

4월 12일

Chad Steiner
1420번지 Elm가, 32호
매디슨, 위스콘신 주 53705

Mr. Steiner께,

이 편지는 Singing Vines 아파트의 모든 주민분들께 발송되었습니다. 여러분도 아시다시피, 이 건물의 주차장 내 자리들은 세입자분들을 위해 따로 마련되어 있습니다. 하지만, [158-D]저희는 이 규정을 무시하는 방문객들에 대해 몇 차례 항의를 받았습니다. [159]다음 주부터, 저희는 주차장에 주차되어 있는 모든 차량들을 확인할 것입니다. 만약 거주자 주차권이 유리창에 보여져 있지 않은 경우, 차량이 치워지도록 할 것입니다.

여러분의 손님들에게 그들이 건물 앞에 있는 Elm가에 하루 중 언제든지 무료로 주차할 수 있음을 알려주시기 바랍니다. 주차는 Boulder가와 Park로에도 가능하지만, 시간당 요금이 있습니다. [160]이 규정은 건물의 서쪽을 따라 이어지는 Devon 대로에서의 주차를 금지한다는 것을 알아두십시오.

만약 문의 사항이나 용건이 있으시면, 주저하지 마시고 제게 연락 주시기 바랍니다.

Rachel Solomon 드림
건물 관리자, Singing Vines 아파트

---

resident n. 주민, 거주자 **parking lot** 주차장
reserve v. (자리 등을) 따로 남겨 두다 **tenant** n. 세입자
complaint n. 항의, 불만 **regulation** n. 규정 **parking pass** 주차권
hourly adv. 시간당 **prohibit** v. 금지하다 **run** v. 이어지다

158 Not/True 문제

문제 Ms. Solomon은 무슨 문제를 언급하는가?
(A) 건물이 청소되지 않고 있다.
(B) 요금이 인상되었다.
(C) 차량에 긁힌 자국이 났다.
(D) 규정이 지켜지고 있지 않다.

해설 Ms. Solomon이 언급한 문제와 관련된 내용을 지문에서 찾아 보기와 대조하는 Not/True 문제이다. (A), (B), (C)는 지문에 언급되지 않은 내용이다. (D)는 'we have received several complaints about visitors ignoring this regulation'에서 Ms. Solomon이 규정을 무시하는 방문객들에 대해 몇 차례 항의를 받았다고 했으므로 지문의 내용과 일치한다. 따라서 (D)가 정답이다.

어휘 scratch v. 긁힌 자국을 내다

159 육하원칙 문제

문제 다음 주에 무슨 일이 일어날 것인가?
(A) 주차권이 발급될 것이다.
(B) 차량이 검사될 것이다.
(C) 세입자가 연락을 받을 것이다.
(D) 아파트가 보수될 것이다.

해설 다음 주에 무슨(What) 일이 일어날 것인지를 묻는 육하원칙 문제이다. 질문의 핵심 어구인 next week와 관련하여, 'Starting next week, we will be checking all automobiles parked in our lot.'에서 다음 주부터 주차장에 주차되어 있는 모든 차량들을 확인할 것이라고 했으므로 (B)가 정답이다.

어휘 issue v. 발급하다, 발표하다 examine v. 검사하다

160 육하원칙 문제

문제 방문객들이 주차하도록 허용되지 않는 곳은 어디인가?
(A) Elm가
(B) Boulder가
(C) Park로
(D) Devon 대로

해설 방문객들이 주차하도록 허용되지 않는 곳이 어디(Where)인지를 묻는 육하원칙 문제이다. 질문의 핵심 어구인 visitors not allowed to park와 관련하여, 'a city rule prohibits parking on Devon Boulevard'에서 시 규정이 Devon 대로에서의 주차를 금지한다고 했으므로 (D)가 정답이다.

161-163번은 다음 이메일에 관한 문제입니다.

수신: Marcy Sizemore <marcysizemore@fullerchemical.com>
발신: Shane Ellis <shaneellis@quantumlaboratories.com>
날짜: 1월 14일
제목: 축하합니다
첨부: 이력서

안녕하세요 Marcy,

[162]우리가 마지막으로 함께 일한 지 거의 10년이 되었지만, 제가 최근에 *Science News 월간지*에서 Fuller Chemical사 연구 개발 부서의 부사장으로의 당신의 승진에 대한 기사를 읽었을 때, [162]LabSure사에서 연구 보조원들로 같이 일했던 우리의 지난날들이 생각났습니다. 당신의 재능과 직업 의식 때문에, 저는 당신이 성공할 줄 알고 있었습니다. 당신의 승진을 축하합니다.

아시다시피, 저는 Quantum 연구소의 품질 보증 책임자로 있습니다. 저희에게는 다른 구직 기회들을 찾기 위해 우리 회사를 떠날 매우 유능한 연구원이 있습니다. 그녀를 잃게 되어 슬프지만, [161]당신의 회사에 적합한 자리가 있다면 그녀를 당신에게 추천하고 싶습니다. 당신은 그녀가 훌륭한 학력과 생물학 연구 분야에서 많은 경력을 갖고 있다는 것을 알게 될 것입니다. 당신이 검토할 수 있도록 그녀의 이력서를 첨부했습니다.

만일 비어있는 자리가 없다 해도, [163]그녀를 만나 직업에 관한 조언을 해주실 수 있을까요? 도움을 줄 의향이 있다면, 제게 알려주시기 바랍니다. 감사드리며, 새로운 직위에서 모든 것이 잘 되길 빕니다.

Shane Ellis 드림

promotion n. 승진 **vice president** 부사장 **assistant** n. 보조원
talent n. 재능 **work ethic** 직업 의식 **quality assurance** 품질 보증
talented adj. 유능한, 실력 있는 **seek out** ~을 찾다
employment opportunity 구직 기회 **suitable** sadj. 적합한
opening n. 빈자리, 공석 **impressive** adj. 훌륭한
educational background 학력 **a great deal of** 많은
biological adj. 생물학 **career advice** 직업에 관한 조언

161 목적 찾기 문제

문제 Mr. Ellis는 왜 이메일을 썼는가?
(A) 연구 프로젝트에 대한 도움을 요청하기 위해
(B) 그의 승진을 알리기 위해
(C) 투자 기회를 제의하기 위해
(D) 잠재 직원을 추천하기 위해

해설 Mr. Ellis가 이메일을 쓴 이유를 묻는 목적 찾기 문제이다. 특별히 이 문제는 지문의 중반에 목적 관련 내용이 언급되었음에 유의한다. 'I would like to recommend her[researcher] to you in case you have a suitable opening at your company'에서 이메일 수신자의 회사에 적합한 자리가 있다면 연구원을 추천하고 싶다고 했으므로 (D)가 정답이다.

어휘 investment n. 투자 potential adj. 잠재적인

162 육하원칙 문제

문제 Ms. Sizemore와 Mr. Ellis는 어떻게 서로를 아는가?
(A) 같은 회의에 참석했다.
(B) 직장 동료였다.
(C) 함께 아는 지인을 통해 만났다.
(D) 같은 학교를 다녔다.

해설 Ms. Sizemore와 Mr. Ellis가 어떻게(How) 서로를 아는지를 묻는 육하원칙 문제이다. 질문의 핵심 어구인 know each other와 관련하여, 'It has been nearly 10 years since we last worked together'에서 우리가 마지막으로 함께 일한 지 거의 10년이 되었다고 했고, 'I remembered our early days working together as research assistants for LabSure Corporation'에서 LabSure사에서 연구 보조원들로 같이 일했던 지난날들이 생각났다고 했으므로 (B)가 정답이다.

어휘 coworker n. 직장 동료 acquaintance n. 지인

163 육하원칙 문제

문제 Mr. Ellis는 Ms. Sizemore에게 무엇을 하도록 제안하는가?
(A) 일자리에 지원한다.
(B) 후보자를 제안한다.
(C) 만남을 갖는다.
(D) 고객에게 연락한다.

해설 Mr. Ellis가 Ms. Sizemore에게 무엇(What)을 하도록 제안하는지를 묻는 육하원칙 문제이다. 질문의 핵심 어구인 Mr. Ellis suggest that Ms. Sizemore do와 관련하여, 'would you mind meeting her[researcher] to offer career advice?'에서 Mr. Ellis가 Ms. Sizemore에게 연구원을 만나 직업에 관한 조언을 해줄 수 있는

지 물었으므로 (C)가 정답이다.

어휘 candidate n. 후보자, 지원자

164-167번은 다음 온라인 채팅 대화문에 관한 문제입니다.

Joy Saunders   [오후 2시 15분]
여러분 중에 출장비를 환급받는 데 어려움을 겪었던 분이 있나요? 최근에 다소 불평들이 있어서요.

Maurice Watts   [오후 2시 17분]
저는 문제를 겪었어요. 164-D제가 지난달에 무역 박람회를 위해 샌프란시스코에 갔을 때 지출했던 것의 적은 부분만을 환급받았어요. 그런데, 왜인지는 잘 모르겠어요. 저는 1,000달러 한도를 초과하지 않았고, 165해당 월의 첫째 주 금요일 전에 제 영수증들을 제출했어요. 그날이 마감일이잖아요, 그렇죠?

Joy Saunders   [오후 2시 18분]
맞아요. 회계팀에 문제가 무엇이었는지 물어보셨나요?

Maurice Watts   [오후 2시 19분]
네, 그런데 아직 답장을 받지 못했어요.

Jennifer Cole   [오후 2시 20분]
166저는 1월에 호텔에서 지불했던 600달러를 받는 데 거의 석 달을 기다려야 했어요. 제가 이유에 대해 물어봤을 때, 400달러가 넘는 경비는 회계팀에 미리 승인을 받아야 된다고 들었어요. 그렇지 않으면, 요청이 처리되기까지 몇 주가 걸릴 수도 있대요.

Charlie Pearson   [오후 2시 22분]
저는 교통수단에 500달러 넘게 썼는데 환급을 위해 그렇게 오래 기다릴 여유가 없어요.

Joy Saunders   [오후 2시 25분]
167회계부장에게 전화해서 일을 빨리 처리하기 위해 제가 무엇을 할 수 있는지 알아볼게요.

reimburse v. 환급하다   travel expense 출장비
complaint n. 불평, 불만 사항   run into ~을 겪다, 만나다
portion n. 부분, 일부   trade exhibition 무역 박람회
exceed v. 초과하다   limit n. 한도   explanation n. 이유, 설명
approve v. 승인하다   in advance 미리, 사전에   process v. 처리하다
afford to ~할 여유가 있다

164 Not/True 문제

문제 Mr. Watts에 대해 언급된 것은?
(A) 회계팀의 직원이다.
(B) 다른 지점으로 곧 전근을 갈 것이다.
(C) 무역 박람회를 준비하는 것을 도왔다.
(D) 최근에 출장을 갔다.

해설 질문의 핵심 어구인 Mr. Watts와 관련된 내용을 지문에서 찾아 보기와 대조하는 Not/True 문제이다. (A), (B), (C)는 지문에 언급되지 않은 내용이다. (D)는 'I went to San Francisco for the trade exhibition last month'(2:17 P.M.)에서 Mr. Watts가 지난달에 무역 박람회를 위해 샌프란시스코에 갔다고 했으므로 지문의 내용과 일치한다. 따라서 (D)가 정답이다.

어휘 transfer v. 전근 가다, 이동하다   organize v. 준비하다, 조직하다
trade show 무역 박람회

165 의도 파악 문제

문제 오후 2시 18분에, Ms. Saunders가 "That's correct"라고 썼을 때, 그녀가 의도한 것 같은 것은?
(A) 회계 부서는 보통 영수증을 복사한다.
(B) 마감일은 매달 첫째 주 금요일에 있다.
(C) 1,000달러의 한도는 어떠한 이유로도 초과될 수 없다.

(D) 한 팀원이 그녀의 비용을 제대로 설명했다.

해설 Ms. Saunders가 의도한 것 같은 것을 묻는 문제이므로, 질문의 인용 어구(That's correct)가 언급된 주변 문맥을 확인한다. 'I submitted my receipts before the first Friday of the month. That's the deadline, right?'(2:17 P.M.)에서 Mr. Watts가 해당 월의 첫째 주 금요일 전에 영수증들을 제출했다며 그날이 마감일이 맞는지 묻자, Ms. Saunders가 'That's correct'(맞아요)라고 한 것을 통해, 마감일이 매달 첫째 주 금요일에 있음을 알 수 있다. 따라서 (B)가 정답이다.

어휘 fall on (어떤 날이) ~에 있다, ~에 해당되다

166 육하원칙 문제

문제 Ms. Cole은 1월에 숙박 시설에 얼마를 지출했는가?
(A) 400달러
(B) 500달러
(C) 600달러
(D) 1,000달러

해설 Ms. Cole이 1월에 숙박 시설에 얼마(How much)를 지출했는지를 묻는 육하원칙 문제이다. 질문의 핵심 어구인 spend on accommodations in January와 관련하여, 'I had to wait almost three months to get the $600 I paid for a hotel in January.'(2:20 P.M.)에서 Ms. Cole이 1월에 호텔에서 지불했던 600달러를 받는 데 거의 석 달을 기다려야 했다고 했으므로 (C)가 정답이다.

어휘 accommodations n. 숙박 시설

167 추론 문제

문제 Ms. Saunders에 대해 추론될 수 있는 것은?
(A) 비행기 표 몇 장을 구매할 것이다.
(B) 환급 요청을 승인했다.
(C) 부서장에게 연락할 것이다.
(D) 경영진에 불만 사항을 제출했다.

해설 질문의 핵심 어구인 Ms. Saunders에 대해 추론하는 문제이다. 'Let me call the accounting manager and see what I can do to speed things up.'(2:25 P.M.)에서 Ms. Saunders가 회계부장에게 전화해서 일을 빨리 처리하기 위해 자신이 무엇을 할 수 있는지 알아보겠다고 했으므로 (C)가 정답이다.

168-171번은 다음 편지에 관한 문제입니다.

1월 28일

Eugene Lee
66번지 Westing로
윌밍턴, 델라웨어 주 19801

Mr. Lee께,

Hoyle 지역 극장에서는, 가능한 한 최고의 공연 예술 경험을 제공하고자 노력합니다. 비영리 단체로서, 저희는 지역 사회의 후원에 의존하고 있습니다. 따라서, 168저희는 저희의 후원자들께 정기적으로 기부해주실 것을 요청드립니다. — [1] —.

168귀하께서 기부금을 넣으실 수 있는 봉투가 동봉되어 있습니다. — [2] —. 어떠한 금액도 매우 환영될 것입니다. 171100달러 이상을 기부해주시는 분들께는 상당한 혜택들이 있습니다. — [3] —.

그리고 저희의 충실한 후원자분들께 감사를 표하기 위해, 저희는 올해 지금까지 중 가장 야심 찬 공연들을 몇 가지 무대에 올릴 예정입니다. — [4] —. 3월에, 저희는 169-DSearching for the Homeland라고 불리는 저명한 케냐인 극작가 David Kobo의 연극을 상연할 것입니다. 또한 6월에는, 지역 극작가 Steve Weller의 새 연극 공연을 3주간 열 것입니다. 그 다음, 이번 가을에는 고대 그리스 비극 시리즈를 공연할 것입니다.

¹⁷⁰월밍턴에서 무료 공연들을 제공하는 유일한 극장으로서, 귀하와 같은 분들에 의해 저희는 유지되고 있습니다. 따라서, 귀하의 지속적인 헌신에 감사드립니다.

Kathryn Little 드림
감독, ¹⁷⁰Hoyle 지역 극장

strive v. 노력하다 performing arts 공연 예술
nonprofit adj. 비영리적인 depend on ~에 의존하다 patron n. 후원자
periodically adv. 정기적으로, 주기적으로 make donations 기부하다
enclosed adj. 동봉된 appreciate v. 환영하다, 진가를 인정하다
substantial adj. 상당한 contribute v. 기부하다
stage v. 무대에 올리다; n. 무대 ambitious adj. 야심적인
put on a play 연극을 상연하다 famed adj. 저명한
playwright n. 극작가 classical adj. 고대 (그리스·로마)의
tragedy n. 비극 dedication n. 헌신

168 목적 찾기 문제

문제 편지의 목적은 무엇인가?
(A) 후원자로부터 자금을 요청하기 위해
(B) 새 극장을 홍보하기 위해
(C) 일정 변경을 알리기 위해
(D) 공연의 배우들을 구하기 위해

해설 편지의 목적을 묻는 목적 찾기 문제이다. 'we ask that our patrons periodically make donations'에서 후원자들에게 정기적으로 기부해줄 것을 요청한다고 한 후, 'Enclosed is an envelope into which you can place your donation.'에서 기부금을 넣을 수 있는 봉투가 동봉되어 있다고 했으므로 (A)가 정답이다.

패러프레이징
ask that ~ make donations 기부해줄 것을 요청하다 → solicit money 자금을 요청하다

어휘 solicit v. 요청하다 seek v. 구하다

169 Not/True 문제

문제 *Searching for the Homeland*에 대해 언급된 것은?
(A) 3주간 열릴 것이다.
(B) 그리스 비극을 바탕으로 한다.
(C) Steve Weller에 의해 감독되고 있다.
(D) 잘 알려진 예술가에 의해 쓰여졌다.

해설 질문의 핵심 어구인 *Searching for the Homeland*와 관련된 내용을 지문에서 찾아 보기와 대조하는 Not/True 문제이다. (A), (B), (C)는 지문에 언급되지 않은 내용이다. (D)는 'a play by the famed Kenyan playwright David Kobo called *Searching for the Homeland*'에서 *Searching for the Homeland*가 저명한 케냐인 극작가 David Kobo의 연극이라고 했으므로 (D)가 정답이다.

어휘 run v. 열리다, (얼마의 기간 동안) 계속되다 direct v. 감독하다

170 추론 문제

문제 Hoyle 지역 극장에 대해 암시되는 것은?
(A) 월밍턴 시외에 위치해 있다.
(B) 공연들에 학생 배우들을 쓴다.
(C) 입장에 요금을 부과하지 않는다.
(D) 주말과 공휴일에는 문을 닫는다.

해설 질문의 핵심 어구인 Hoyle Community Theater에 대해 추론하는 문제이다. 'As the only theater in Wilmington that offers free performances'와 'Hoyle Community Theater'에서 편지 발신자인 Hoyle 지역 극장이 월밍턴에서 무료 공연들을 제공하는 유일한 극장이라고 했으므로 Hoyle 지역 극장이 입장에 요금을 부과하지 않는다는 것을 추론할 수 있다. 따라서 (C)가 정답이다.

패러프레이징
offers free performances 무료 공연들을 제공하다 → does not charge money for admission 입장에 요금을 부과하지 않다

어휘 admission n. 입장 national holiday 공휴일

171 문장 위치 찾기 문제

문제 [1], [2], [3], [4]로 표시된 위치 중, 다음 문장이 들어갈 곳으로 가장 적절한 것은?

"이것들은 지역 내 음식점들의 상품권과 지역 콘서트들의 표를 포함합니다."

(A) [1]
(B) [2]
(C) [3]
(D) [4]

해설 지문의 흐름상 주어진 문장이 들어가기에 가장 적절한 곳을 고르는 문제이다. These include gift cards to restaurants in the area and tickets to local concerts에서 이것들은 지역 내 음식점들의 상품권과 지역 콘서트들의 표를 포함한다고 했으므로, 주어진 문장 앞에 제공되는 혜택들에 관한 내용이 있을 것임을 예상할 수 있다. [3]의 앞 문장인 'Substantial benefits are available to those who contribute $100 or more.'에서 100달러 이상을 기부하는 사람들에게는 상당한 혜택들이 있다고 했으므로, [3]에 주어진 문장이 들어가면 기부자들에게 제공되는 혜택들에 관한 내용을 설명하는 자연스러운 문맥이 된다는 것을 알 수 있다. 따라서 (C)가 정답이다.

172-175번은 다음 안내문에 관한 문제입니다.

도로 폐쇄

King가, Queen가와 Dundas가의 특정 구간들이 3월과 4월에 폐쇄될 것임을 알아두시기 바랍니다. ¹⁷²이 폐쇄는 긴 겨울 동안 손상된 이 도로들의 구간에 필요한 작업을 수행하기 위해 필수적입니다. ¹⁷³이 도로들은 모두 시내를 통과하는 주요 경로들이어서, 현재 상태로 남아 있어서는 안됩니다.

다음 일정을 알아두시기 바랍니다:

· 3월 6일에서 3월 20일 – Bathurst가와 University가 사이에 있는 ¹⁷⁴⁻ᴮKing가가 폐쇄될 것입니다.
· 3월 21일에서 4월 3일 – Ossington가와 Kensington가 사이에 있는 ¹⁷⁴⁻ᴬQueen가가 폐쇄될 것입니다.
· 4월 4일에서 4월 18일 – University가와 Young가 사이에 있는 ¹⁷⁴⁻ᶜDundas가가 폐쇄될 것입니다.

위에 나열된 모든 경로들을 위한 ¹⁷⁴⁻ᴰ우회로로 Royce가와 Church가를 이용하는 것을 권해드립니다. ¹⁷⁵주택가의 더 작은 도로들을 이용하기로 하실 경우, 항상 감소된 제한 속도를 준수하는 것을 기억하시기 바랍니다.

여러분의 인내와 양해에 감사드립니다.

토론토 공공 공사 위원회 드림

road closure 도로 폐쇄 section n. 구간, 부분 major adj. 주요한
route n. 경로 detour n. 우회로 residential adj. 주택지의
observe v. 준수하다, 관찰하다 speed limit 제한 속도
at all times 항상 committee n. 위원회

172 육하원칙 문제

문제 왜 몇몇 도로들이 폐쇄되고 있는가?
(A) 축제가 개최될 수 있도록 하기 위해
(B) 겨울이 지나 보수를 하기 위해
(C) 새 보도들을 만들기 위해
(D) 차선들을 추가하여 확장하기 위해

해설 왜(Why) 몇몇 도로들이 폐쇄되고 있는지를 묻는 육하원칙 문제이다. 질문의 핵심 어구인 some roads being closed와 관련하여, 'These closures are necessary to perform required work on parts of these roads that were damaged during the long winter.'에서 이 폐쇄는 긴 겨울 동안 손상된 도로들의 구간에 필요한 작업을 수행하기 위해 필수적이라고 했으므로 (B)가 정답이다.

어휘 take place 개최되다, 일어나다   sidewalk n. 보도

173 동의어 찾기 문제
문제 1문단 다섯 번째 줄의 단어 "condition"은 의미상 –와 가장 가깝다.
    (A) 요구 조건
    (B) 지역
    (C) 상태
    (D) 작업

해설 condition을 포함한 문장 'The roads are all major routes through the city, and they should not be left in their current condition.'에서 condition은 '상태'라는 뜻으로 사용되었다. 따라서 (C)가 정답이다.

174 Not/True 문제
문제 어떤 도로가 폐쇄되지 않을 것인가?
    (A) Queen가
    (B) King가
    (C) Dundas가
    (D) Royce가

해설 질문의 핵심 어구인 road ~ be closed와 관련된 내용을 지문에서 찾아 보기와 대조하는 Not/True 문제이다. (A)는 'Queen Street will be closed'에서 Queen가가 폐쇄될 것이라고 했으므로 지문의 내용과 일치한다. (B)는 'King Street will be closed'에서 King가가 폐쇄될 것이라고 했으므로 지문의 내용과 일치한다. (C)는 'Dundas Avenue will be closed'에서 Dundas가가 폐쇄될 것이라고 했으므로 지문의 내용과 일치한다. (D)는 'We suggest using Royce Avenue ~ as detours'에서 우회로로 Royce가를 이용하는 것을 권한다고 했으므로 지문의 내용과 일치하지 않는다. 따라서 (D)가 정답이다.

175 육하원칙 문제
문제 일부 운전자들은 무엇을 하도록 요청되는가?
    (A) 제한 속도를 지킨다.
    (B) 주요 도로들만 따라서 이동한다.
    (C) 정보를 위해 위원회에 연락한다.
    (D) 도로에 진입하기 위해 도로 요금소를 이용한다.

해설 일부 운전자들이 무엇(What)을 하도록 요청되는지를 묻는 육하원칙 문제이다. 질문의 핵심 어구인 some drivers asked to do와 관련하여, 'If you decide to use smaller residential streets, please remember to observe the reduced speed limit at all times.'에서 주택가의 더 작은 도로들을 이용하기로 할 경우 항상 감소된 제한 속도를 준수하는 것을 기억하라고 했으므로 (A)가 정답이다.

어휘 follow v. 지키다, 따르다   toll booth 도로 요금소

176-180번은 다음 회람과 양식에 관한 문제입니다.

¹⁷⁶수신: 전 직원
발신: Chase Milton
날짜: 12월 3일
제목: 직원 명절 선물
첨부: 선물 선택 카드

직원분들께,

아시다시피, 명절이 빠르게 다가오고 있습니다. ¹⁷⁶모든 분들께 올해 노고에 감사드리기 위해, Carrigan Foods사는 각 직원에게 칠면조, ⟳

햄, 또는 채식 식품 바구니를 제공할 것입니다. ¹⁷⁹육류 제품들은 12월 12일에 이용 가능할 것이지만, 바구니는 12월 16일에 준비될 것입니다.

¹⁷⁷각 직원은 단 하나의 선물을 선택하도록 허용된다는 점을 유념해주시기 바랍니다. 여러분의 선택을 나타내기 위해, 첨부된 카드를 작성하셔서 12월 6일 전에 여러분의 관리자에게 제출하십시오. 저희는 또한 여러분이 아무것도 받고 싶지 않을 경우에 이 품목들 중 하나를 노숙자들에게 음식을 제공하는 지역 푸드 뱅크로 보내는 선택사항을 포함해두었습니다.

여러분의 선물과 다가오는 명절을 즐기시기를 바랍니다.

Chase Milton 드림
회장, Carrigan Foods사

---

indicate v. 나타내다   turn in ~을 제출하다, 돌려주다
food bank 푸드 뱅크(가난한 사람들이 무료로 음식을 얻는 곳)
homeless n. 노숙자   coming adj. 다가오는, 다음의

Carrigan Foods사
직원 선물 선택 카드

보관 방법을 위해 귀하께서 받으신 식품 위의 라벨을 확인하세요. 모든 제품들은 냉장 또는 냉동된 상태로 보관되어야 합니다. 선물을 사무실이나 차 안에 오랜 시간 동안 내버려두지 않도록 ¹⁷⁸귀하의 근무시간이 끝났을 때 행정실에서 선물을 가져가시는 것이 권장됩니다.

만약 귀하의 선물이 나눠지도록 예정된 날에 근무하지 않으신다면, 동료분이 귀하를 위해 그것을 가져가도록 준비해주시기 바랍니다. 정해진 수령 일자가 지난 식품들을 저희가 가지고 있을 수 없음에 유의하십시오. 가져가지 않은 것들은 푸드 뱅크에 기부될 것입니다.

- -

¹⁷⁹이름: Selena Kim
직원 ID 번호: 1002532
^{180-D}부서: 마케팅
^{180-B}전화 내선번호: 7457

^{180-A}다음 선택사항들 중 하나를 선택해주십시오:
¹⁷⁹■ 냉동된 칠면조
☐ 냉동된 햄
☐ 채식 바구니

제 선물을 푸드 뱅크에 기부하고 싶습니다: 예 ☐ 아니오 ■

---

storage n. 보관, 저장   instruction n. 방법, 지시
refrigerated adj. 냉장한   frozen adj. 냉동된
administration office 행정실   shift n. 근무시간, 교대
distribute v. 나눠주다, 배포하다   arrange v. 준비하다, 배치하다
hold v. 가지고 있다, 붙들다   designated adj. 정해진, 지명된
give v. 기부하다, 주다

176 육하원칙 문제
문제 Carrigan Foods사는 무엇을 하려고 계획하고 있는가?
    (A) 명절 만찬을 준비한다.
    (B) 직원들에게 감사를 표한다.
    (C) 요리 기술에 대한 수업을 제공한다.
    (D) 몇몇 고객들에게 상품권을 보낸다.

해설 Carrigan Foods사가 무엇(What)을 하려고 계획하고 있는지를 묻는 육하원칙 문제이므로 질문의 핵심 어구인 Carrigan Foods planning to do와 관련된 내용이 언급된 회람을 확인한다. 첫 번째 지문(회람)의 'To: All employees'와 'To thank everyone for their hard work this year, Carrigan Foods will provide each employee with a turkey, ham, or basket of vegetarian food.'에서 Carrigan Foods사가 회람의 수신인인 전 직원에게 올해 노고에 감사하기 위해 각 직원에게 칠면조, 햄, 또는 채식 식품 바구니를 제공

할 것이라고 했으므로 (B)가 정답이다.

어휘 organize v. 준비하다, 조직하다 technique n. 기술, 기법
gift card 상품권

177 동의어 찾기 문제

문제 회람에서, 2문단 첫 번째 줄의 단어 "select"는 의미상 -와 가장 가깝다.
(A) 투표하다
(B) 선택하다
(C) 할당하다
(D) 선호하다

해설 회람의 select를 포함한 문장 'Please keep in mind that each employee is allowed to select only one gift.'에서 select는 '선택하다'라는 뜻으로 사용되었다. 따라서 '선택하다'라는 뜻을 가진 (B)가 정답이다.

178 육하원칙 문제

문제 양식에 따르면, 직원들은 무엇을 하도록 권고되는가?
(A) 지역 푸드 뱅크에 연락한다.
(B) 즉시 보관 장소로 간다.
(C) 업무를 마친 후에 물품을 얻는다.
(D) 미리 수령 시간을 정한다.

해설 직원들이 무엇을(what) 하도록 권고되는지를 묻는 육하원칙 문제이므로 질문의 핵심 어구인 employees advised to do와 관련된 내용이 언급된 양식을 확인한다. 두 번째 지문(양식)의 'It is recommended that you pick up your gift from the administration office when your shift has ended'에서 근무시간이 끝났을 때 행정실에서 선물을 가져가는 것이 권장된다고 했으므로 (C)가 정답이다.

패러프레이징
pick up your gift ~ when your shift has ended 근무시간이 끝났을 때 선물을 가져가다 → Claim an item after finishing work 업무를 마친 후에 물품을 얻다

어휘 claim v. 얻다, 주장하다

179 추론 문제 연계

문제 Ms. Kim은 언제 그녀의 선물을 받을 것 같은가?
(A) 12월 3일
(B) 12월 6일
(C) 12월 12일
(D) 12월 16일

해설 질문의 핵심 어구인 Ms. Kim이 작성한 양식을 먼저 확인한다.
단서 1 두 번째 지문(양식)의 'Name: Selena Kim'과 ■ Frozen turkey'에서 Ms. Kim이 냉동된 칠면조를 선택했음을 알 수 있다. 그런데 냉동된 칠면조를 언제 받을 수 있는지 제시되지 않았으므로 회람에서 관련 내용을 확인한다.
단서 2 첫 번째 지문(회람)의 'The meat products will be available on December 12'에서 육류 제품들은 12월 12일에 이용 가능함을 확인할 수 있다.
두 단서를 종합할 때, Ms. Kim이 선택한 냉동된 칠면조를 12월 12일에 받을 것임을 알 수 있다. 따라서 (C)가 정답이다.

180 Not/True 문제

문제 양식에서 요구되지 않은 정보는?
(A) 물품 선택
(B) 전화번호
(C) 수령 시간
(D) 부서명

해설 양식에 언급된 내용을 지문에서 찾아 보기와 대조하는 Not/True 문제이므로 두 번째 지문(양식)을 확인한다. (A)는 'Please pick one of

the following options[items]'에서 다음 물품들 중 하나를 선택해 달라고 했으므로 지문의 내용과 일치한다. (B)는 'Phone Extension: 7457'에서 전화 내선번호를 확인할 수 있으므로 지문의 내용과 일치한다. (C)는 지문에 언급되지 않은 내용이다. 따라서 (C)가 정답이다. (D)는 'Division: Marketing'에서 부서명을 확인할 수 있으므로 지문의 내용과 일치한다.

어휘 preference n. 선택, 선호

181-185번은 다음 공고와 이메일에 관한 문제입니다.

제15회 연례 도서 판매

[183]Ferris가에 있는 Carlton 도서관이 8월 2일 금요일에 제15회 연례 도서 판매를 개최합니다. 여러분이 가지고 있는 아무데나 놓여 있는 모든 책들을 안내 데스크에 있는 직원에게 가져다주십시오. [181-A/B/C]저희 직원이 이 책들에 찢어진 페이지, 물로 인한 손상, 또는 여백에 글씨가 없다는 것을 확실히 하기 위해 이것들을 확인할 것입니다. 만약 책들이 상태가 좋으면, 저희는 그것들을 적당한 가격에 구매할 것입니다.

또한, 저희는 도서관 2층에 판매 중인 엄청나게 다양한 중고 책들이 있습니다. 이들은 고대 시의 번역본에서부터 최신 베스트셀러에 이르는 모든 것을 포함합니다. [183]모든 종이 표지 책들은 5달러이고, 모든 두꺼운 표지 책들은 12달러입니다. 이 밖에도, 저희는 8달러의 대형 손가방, 20달러의 배낭, 11달러의 수첩을 포함하여 다양한 도서관 물품들을 팔고 있습니다.

[182]모든 판매로부터의 수익금은 아이들에게 교습을 제공하는 자선 단체인 Appleton 교육 협회에 기부될 것입니다. 도서 판매 행사에 대한 더 많은 정보를 위해서는, www.carltonsale.org를 방문해 주십시오.

---

lie around 아무데나 놓여 있다 margin n. 여백, 가장자리
be in good condition 상태가 좋다 reasonable adj. 적당한, 합리적인
on sale 판매 중인, 할인 중인 translation n. 번역(본)
ancient adj. 고대의 poetry n. 시 contemporary adj. 최신의, 현대의
paperback n. 종이 표지 책 proceeds n. 수익금
institute n. (교육·학술) 협회 charitable adj. 자선의, 자선을 베푸는
tutoring n. 교습

수신: <questions@appleton.org>
발신: Sally Fisher <sallyfisher44@fastmail.com>
제목: 자원봉사자 기회
날짜: 8월 4일
첨부: 이력서

관계자분께,

이틀 전에, [183]저는 Carlton 도서관의 도서 판매 행사에서 5달러짜리 물품을 사서 Appleton 교육 협회의 전단지를 받았습니다. [184-A]이전에 귀하의 기관에 대해 들어본 적이 없었지만, 그 전단지를 꼼꼼히 읽은 후, 저는 귀하께서 제공하시는 공헌들에 매우 관심 있게 되었습니다.

[184-C]저는 최근에 은퇴한 전직 고등학교 영어 선생님입니다. 하지만, 어느 정도 교육적인 일을 계속할 길을 찾고 있습니다. 저는 읽기와 쓰기에 어려움을 겪는 사람들을 가르쳤던 많은 경험이 있고, 그러한 유형의 일을 매우 즐깁니다. 따라서, 저는 귀하의 기관에 자원봉사나 시간제 근무 기회들이 있는지 궁금합니다.

[185]저는 목요일에는 지역 문화회관에서 자선 활동을 하지만, 일주일의 대부분의 날에는 시간이 있습니다. 제 이력서를 이 이메일에 첨부하였습니다. 곧 귀하로부터 답변을 듣기를 기대합니다.

Sally Fisher 드림

---

volunteer n. 자원봉사자 read over ~을 꼼꼼히 읽다
former adj. 이전의 retire v. 은퇴하다
be looking to do ~할 길을 찾고 있다 extensive adj. 많은, 폭넓은
struggle v. 어려움을 겪다, 애쓰다 available adj. 시간이 있는, 이용 가능한

181 Not/True 문제

문제 공고에 따르면, 도서관 직원이 중고 책에서 확인하지 않을 것은?
(A) 수분으로부터의 손상
(B) 찢어진 페이지
(C) 본문 옆의 필기
(D) 없어진 표지

해설 질문의 핵심 어구인 library staff ~ check used books for에 대해 묻는 Not/True 문제이므로 도서관 직원이 언급된 첫 번째 지문(공고)에서 관련 내용을 확인한다. (A), (B), (C)는 'Our staff will check these books[used books] to make sure that they don't have any torn pages, water damage, or writing in the margins.'에서 직원이 중고책들에 찢어진 페이지, 물로 인한 손상, 또는 여백에 글씨가 없다는 것을 확실히 하기 위해 책들을 확인할 것이라고 했으므로 지문의 내용과 일치한다. (D)는 지문에 언급되지 않은 내용이다. 따라서 (D)가 정답이다.

어휘 moisture n. 수분, 습기 rip v. 찢다 cover n. 표지, 덮개

182 육하원칙 문제

문제 도서 판매로 모인 돈은 무엇에 쓰일 것인가?
(A) 비영리 단체를 돕는 것
(B) 열람실을 개조하는 것
(C) 공립 학교들에 자금을 제공하는 것
(D) 새로운 잡지들을 광고하는 것

해설 도서 판매로 모인 돈이 무엇(What)에 쓰일 것인지를 묻는 육하원칙 문제이므로 질문의 핵심 어구인 the money raised by the book sale이 언급된 공고에서 관련 내용을 확인한다. 첫 번째 지문(공고)의 'The proceeds from all sales will be donated to the Appleton Institute, a charitable organization that provides tutoring to children.'에서 모든 판매로부터의 수익금은 아이들에게 교습을 제공하는 자선 단체인 Appleton 교육 협회에 기부될 것이라고 했으므로 (A)가 정답이다.

어휘 raise v. 모으다, 올리다 nonprofit adj. 비영리적인
reading room 열람실 public school 공립 학교
market v. 광고하다, (상품을) 내놓다

183 육하원칙 문제 연계

문제 Ms. Fisher가 Carlton 도서관에서 무엇을 구매했는가?
(A) 배낭
(B) 종이 표지 책
(C) 두꺼운 표지 책
(D) 수첩

해설 Ms. Fisher가 Carlton 도서관에서 무엇(What)을 구매했는지를 묻고 있으므로 Ms. Fisher가 보낸 이메일을 먼저 확인한다.
단서 1 두 번째 지문(이메일)의 'I bought a $5 item at the Carlton Library's book sale event'에서 Ms. Fisher가 Carlton 도서관의 도서 판매 행사에서 5달러짜리 물품을 샀다고 했다. 그런데 Carlton 도서관의 도서 판매 행사에서의 5달러짜리 물품이 무엇인지 제시되지 않았으므로 공고에서 관련 내용을 확인한다.
단서 2 첫 번째 지문(공고)의 'The Carlton Library ~ is holding its 15th Annual Book Sale'과 'All paperbacks are $5'에서 Carlton 도서관의 도서 판매 행사에서 종이 표지 책들이 5달러임을 확인할 수 있다.
두 단서를 종합할 때, Ms. Fisher가 Carlton 도서관의 도서 판매 행사에서 5달러짜리 종이 표지 책을 구매했다는 것을 알 수 있다. 따라서 (B)가 정답이다.

184 Not/True 문제

문제 Ms. Fisher가 그녀의 직업 경력에 대해 말하는 것은?
(A) 이전에 Appleton 교육 협회에서 근무했다.

(B) 어려움을 겪는 독자들을 돕기 위해 책들을 출간했다.
(C) 교육자로 근무했다.
(D) 도서관에서 영어 교습을 제공했다.

해설 질문의 핵심 어구인 her professional experience에 대해 묻는 Not/True 문제이므로 Ms. Fisher의 경력이 언급된 두 번째 지문(이메일)에서 관련 내용을 확인한다. (A)는 'I had never heard of your organization[Appleton Institute] before'에서 이전에 Appleton 교육 협회에 대해 들어본 적이 없었다고 했으므로 지문의 내용과 일치하지 않는다. (B)는 지문에 언급되지 않은 내용이다. (C)는 'I am a former high school English teacher who has recently retired.'에서 자신이 최근에 은퇴한 전직 고등학교 영어 선생님이라고 했으므로 지문의 내용과 일치한다. 따라서 (C)가 정답이다. (D)는 지문에 언급되지 않은 내용이다.

패러프레이징
a former ~ teacher who has recently retired 최근에 은퇴한 전직 선생님 → was employed as an educator 교육자로 고용되었다

어휘 experience n. 경력, 경험 educator n. 교육자

185 육하원칙 문제

문제 Ms. Fisher는 왜 목요일에 시간이 없는가?
(A) 어학 강의의 일정이 변경되었기 때문에
(B) 서점에서 일하기 때문에
(C) 독서회에서 주간 모임이 있기 때문에
(D) 자원봉사자 업무가 있기 때문에

해설 Ms. Fisher가 왜(Why) 목요일에 시간이 없는지를 묻는 육하원칙 문제이므로 질문의 핵심 어구인 Ms. Fisher not available on Thursdays와 관련된 내용이 언급된 이메일을 확인한다. 두 번째 지문(이메일)의 'I am available on most days of the week, although on Thursdays I perform charity work at a community center.'에서 Ms. Fisher가 일주일의 대부분의 날에는 시간이 있지만 목요일에는 지역 문화회관에서 자선 활동을 한다고 했으므로 (D)가 정답이다.

패러프레이징
perform charity work 자선 활동을 하다 → has a volunteer position 자원봉사자 업무가 있다

어휘 book club 독서회 position n. 업무, 일자리

186-190번은 다음 광고, 이메일, 양식에 관한 문제입니다.

RB 은행

[187]RB 은행에서 투자 계좌를 개설하고 저희의 특별 제공을 이용하세요. 2,500달러 이상을 예금할 시 60일의 무료 거래와 현금 혜택을 받으세요.*

· 2,500달러에서 49,999달러의 예금 시 100달러 혜택 + 무료 거래
· [187]50,000달러에서 99,999달러의 예금 시 250달러 혜택 + 무료 거래
· 100,000달러에서 249,999달러의 예금 시 500달러 혜택 + 무료 거래
· 250,000달러 이상의 예금 시 750달러 혜택 + 무료 거래

[186]왜 RB 은행을 선택하는가?

· 숨겨진 수수료 없는 적정한 가격 책정
· [186-D]모든 투자자를 위한 교육 자료
· [186-B]선택할 수 있는 다양한 투자 유형
· [186-C]투자 자문가들로부터의 24시간 계속되는 지원
· 데스크톱 컴퓨터와 모바일 기기를 위한 사용하기 쉬운 거래 소프트웨어

* 제공은 4월 30일까지 유효합니다. 기본 거래 수수료는 9.99달러입니다. 문의를 위해서는, 555-2975로 전화, 또는 info@rbbank.com으로 이메일을 보내시거나, 전국에 있는 저희의 60개 지점 중 하나를 방문하세요.

---

take advantage of ~을 이용하다 trading n. 거래, 매매
incentive n. 혜택, 장려금 deposit v. 예금하다; n. 예금, 보증금

fair adj. 적정한, 공평한　**pricing** n. 가격 책정　**hidden** adj. 숨겨진, 신비한
fee n. 수수료, 요금　**round-the-clock** adj. 24시간 계속의
financial adviser 투자 자문가　**valid** adj. 유효한
nationwide adj. 전국적인

수신: Beth Viola <b.viola@ambercrafts.com>
발신: Ron Campbell <r.campbell@rbbank.com>
제목: 귀하의 계좌
날짜: 4월 21일

Ms. Viola께,

[187]RB 은행에서 투자 계좌를 개설해주셔서 감사합니다. 귀하의 50,000달러의 예금이 어제 수령되었습니다. 귀하의 현금 보너스가 보내지는 데는 약 60일이 걸릴 것이라는 점을 유념하시기 바랍니다.

귀하의 다른 문의와 관련하여, 돈을 대출하기를 원하는 사업주들이 이용 가능한 두 가지 선택권이 있습니다. [188/189]첫 번째는 SBA 대출입니다. [189]이는 50명 미만의 직원들이 있는 회사들을 위한 것입니다. [188]4.9퍼센트의 이자율로 100,000달러까지 빌리실 수 있습니다. 다른 선택권은 CTA 대출입니다. 이는 50명 이상의 직원들이 있는 기업들에 의해서만 신청될 수 있습니다. [188]이 대출은 대출자가 3.9퍼센트의 이자율로 500,000달러까지 이용할 수 있습니다. 이 대출 프로그램들에 대한 추가적인 정보와 신청하는 방법에 대한 설명을 위해서는 저희 웹사이트를 방문해주시기 바랍니다.

Ron Campbell 드림
투자 자문가

---

borrow v. 대출하다, 빌리다　**loan** n. 대출　**interest rate** 이자율
borrower n. 대출자　**instruction** n. 설명

RB 은행

대출 신청서

회사 정보
[189]회사명: Amber Crafts사
[190]소유주: Beth Viola
주소: 527번지 Fairfax가, 로아노크, 버지니아 주 24016
전화번호: 555-2308
이메일: b.viola@ambercrafts.com

[189]대출 유형: SBA 대출
☑ RB 은행 개인 정보 보호 정책을 읽으셨으면 여기를 체크해주십시오.

[190]귀하의 신청서와 함께 귀사의 사업 허가증 사본을 포함하셔야 한다는 점을 유의해주시기 바랍니다.

privacy agreement 개인 정보 보호 정책　**business license** 사업 허가증

---

186 Not/True 문제

문제　RB 은행에 대해 언급되지 않은 것은?
(A) 업계에서 가장 낮은 수수료를 부과한다.
(B) 다양한 투자 선택권이 있다.
(C) 24시간 금융 지원을 제공한다.
(D) 투자자들을 위한 교육 자료를 제공한다.

해설　질문의 핵심 어구인 RB 은행에 대해 언급되지 않은 것을 묻는 Not/True 문제이므로 RB 은행이 언급된 첫 번째 지문(광고)에서 관련 내용을 확인한다. (A)는 지문에 언급되지 않은 내용이다. 따라서 (A)가 정답이다. (B)는 'Why choose RB Bank?'와 'Various investment types to choose from'에서 RB 은행을 선택하는 이유로 선택할 수 있는 다양한 투자 유형이라고 했으므로 지문의 내용과 일치한다. (C)는 'Round-the-clock support from financial advisers'에서 투자 자문가들로부터의 24시간 계속되는 지원이라고 했으므로 지문의 내용과 일치한다. (D)는 'Educational resources

---

for every investor'에서 모든 투자자를 위한 교육 자료라고 했으므로 지문의 내용과 일치한다.

패러프레이징
Various investment types to choose from 선택할 수 있는 다양한 투자 유형 → **a range of investment options** 다양한 투자 선택권
Round-the-clock support from financial advisers 투자 자문가들로부터의 24시간 계속되는 지원 → **24-hour financial support** 24시간 금융 지원
Educational resources for every investor 모든 투자자를 위한 교육 자료 → **learning materials for investors** 투자자들을 위한 교육 자료

어휘　**a range of** 다양한

187 육하원칙 문제 연계

문제　Ms. Viola는 투자 계좌를 개설하는 데 얼마의 현금을 받을 것인가?
(A) 100달러
(B) 250달러
(C) 500달러
(D) 750달러

해설　질문의 핵심 어구인 cash Ms. Viola receive for opening an investment account에서 Ms. Viola가 투자 계좌를 개설하는 데 얼마(How much)의 현금을 받을 것인지를 묻고 있으므로 Ms. Viola에게 보내진 이메일을 먼저 확인한다.
단서 1 두 번째 지문(이메일)의 'Thank you for opening an investment account with RB Bank. Your deposit of $50,000 was received yesterday. ~ your cash bonus to be released.'에서 Ms. Viola가 RB 은행에서 투자 계좌를 개설하여 50,000달러의 예금이 수령되었고, 현금 보너스가 보내진다고 했다. 그런데 얼마의 현금 보너스가 보내지는지 제시되지 않았으므로 광고에서 관련 내용을 확인한다.
단서 2 첫 번째 지문(광고)의 'Open an investment account with RB Bank ~. Get ~ a cash incentive when you deposit $2,500 or more.'에서 RB 은행에서 투자 계좌를 개설하고 2,500달러 이상을 예금할 시 현금 혜택을 받으라고 했고, '$250 incentive ~ with deposit of $50,000 to $99,999'에서 50,000달러에서 99,999달러를 예금 시 250달러의 혜택을 받을 수 있음을 확인할 수 있다.
두 단서를 종합할 때, Ms. Viola가 투자 계좌를 개설하여 50,000달러를 예금했으므로 현금 250달러를 받을 것임을 알 수 있다. 따라서 (B)가 정답이다.

188 육하원칙 문제

문제　이메일에 따르면, SBA 대출보다 CTA 대출의 유리한 점은 무엇인가?
(A) 더 많은 가입 보너스
(B) 더 낮은 이자율
(C) 더 긴 대출 기간
(D) 덜 복잡한 신청 절차

해설　SBA 대출보다 CTA 대출의 유리한 점이 무엇(what)인지를 묻는 육하원칙 문제이므로 질문의 핵심 어구인 CTA 대출과 SBA 대출이 언급된 이메일에서 관련 내용을 확인한다. 두 번째 지문(이메일)의 'The first is the SBA Loan.'과 'Up to $100,000 may be borrowed at a 4.9 percent interest rate.'에서 SBA 대출은 4.9퍼센트의 이자율로 돈을 빌릴 수 있다고 했고, 'The other option is the CTA Loan.'과 'For this loan, up to $500,000 is available to the borrower at a 3.9 percent interest rate.'에서 CTA 대출은 대출자가 3.9퍼센트의 이자율로 이용할 수 있다고 했으므로, SBA 대출보다 CTA 대출의 이자율이 더 낮음을 알 수 있다. 따라서 (B)가 정답이다.

어휘　**advantage** n. 유리한 점, 우위　**generous** adj. 많은, 후한
signup n. 가입　**borrowing** n. 대출　**complex** adj. 복잡한

189 추론 문제 연계

문제　Amber Crafts사에 대해 암시되는 것은?

(A) 소유주가 투자자들을 찾고 있다.
(B) 최근에 다른 지점을 열었다.
(C) 제품들이 여러 국가들에서 판매된다.
(D) 50명 미만의 직원들을 고용한다.

해설 질문의 핵심 어구인 Amber Crafts가 언급된 양식을 먼저 확인한다.
단서 1 세 번째 지문(양식)의 'Company Name: Amber Crafts'와
'Loan Type: SBA Loan'에서 Amber Crafts사가 SBA 대출을 신청
했다. 그런데 SBA 대출에 대한 정보가 제시되지 않았으므로 이메일에
서 관련 내용을 확인한다.
단서 2 두 번째 지문(이메일)의 'The first is the SBA Loan. This is
for companies with fewer than 50 employees.'에서 SBA 대출
이 50명 미만의 직원들이 있는 회사들을 위한 것임을 확인할 수 있다.
두 단서를 종합할 때, Amber Crafts사는 SBA 대출을 신청했으므
로 50명 미만의 직원들을 고용한다는 것을 알 수 있다. 따라서 (D)
가 정답이다.

어휘 look for ~를 찾다, 구하다   multiple adj. 여러, 다양한

190 육하원칙 문제

문제 Ms. Viola는 무엇을 제공하도록 요청되었는가?
(A) 인사 기록
(B) 재무 제표
(C) 경영 허가증
(D) 합법적인 계약서

해설 Ms. Viola가 무엇을(What) 제공하도록 요청되었는지를 묻는 육하원
칙 문제이므로 Ms. Viola가 작성한 양식에서 관련 내용을 확인한다.
세 번째 지문(양식)의 'Please note that you must include a copy
of your company's business license with your application.'에
서 신청서와 함께 회사의 사업 허가증 사본을 포함해야 한다는 점을
유의해달라고 했으므로 (C)가 정답이다.

패러프레이징
business license 사업 허가증 → An operating permit 경영 허가증

어휘 personnel records 인사 기록   financial statement 재무 제표
operating adj. 경영상의   permit n. 허가증; v. 허용하다
legal adj. 합법적인

191-195번은 다음 안내문, 광고, 편지에 관한 문제입니다.

> ## Empire 그룹에 대해
>
> 단 25년 이내에, Empire 그룹은 건설과 자금 조달에 능력이 있는 부동
> 산 개발의 선두 기업이 되었습니다.
>
> 현재, [191-C]Empire 그룹은 뉴욕, 샌프란시스코, 로스앤젤레스를 포함하
> 여 45개 도시에서 상업 및 주거 건설 프로젝트들을 수행하고 있습니다.
> 지난 2년 동안, Empire 그룹은 말레이시아, 캐나다, 독일에 사무 및 주
> 거용 건물들로 국제적 존재를 확고히 했습니다. 뿐만 아니라, 그룹은 미
> 국 내에 Blackwood사와 Le Clare사와 같은 대기업들에 의해 운영되
> 는 32개 호텔들을 건설했습니다.
>
> Empire Group사의 가장 최근의 사업 확장은 호주에서 이루어져 왔
> 습니다. 다른 지역들과 마찬가지로, [192]호주에서의 당사의 초기 목표는
> 대규모 인구의 고소득층 주민들이 있는 도시들에서 직원을 늘리는 것
> 입니다.
>
> leader n. 선두, 선도자   property n. 부동산, 재산
> experience n. 능력, 경험   financing n. 자금 조달
> carry out ~을 수행하다   commercial adj. 상업의
> residential adj. 주거의   establish v. 확고히 하다, 설립하다
> presence n. 존재, 영향력   operator n. 회사, 경영자
> initial adj. 초기의, 처음의   aim n. 목표, 목적   workforce n. 직원, 노동력
> population n. 인구

[192]Empire 그룹 호주지사는 몇 개의 정규직 자리를 채울 적격의 지원자
들을 찾고 있습니다.
지원하기 위해서는, 귀하의 이력서를 jobs@empiregroup.au로 이메
일을 보내주십시오.

비서
· [192]두 자리(브리즈번과 멜버른)
· 직무는 행정 지원을 제공하는 것을 포함합니다
· 출장을 가지 못할 사유가 없어야 합니다
· 기업체에서 2년 이상의 경력이 있는 대학 졸업생이 선호됩니다

[195]인사부 직원
· 두 자리(멜버른과 퍼스)
· 직무는 직원 관련 일들을 처리하고 채용 활동을 지원하는 것을 포함
합니다
· 3년 이상의 관련 경력과 함께 인적 자원 관리학 학위를 갖고 있어야
합니다
· [195]전문 자격증이 있는 지원자들에게 우선권이 주어집니다

계약 전문가
· 네 자리(시드니와 퍼스)
· 직무는 공급업체 관계를 관리하고 상업 계약을 성사시키는 것을 포
함합니다
· 5년 이상의 부동산 중개 경력과 함께 경영학 학위를 갖고 있어야 합
니다

[193]마케팅 직원
· [192]두 자리(브리즈번과 퍼스)
· 직무는 조사를 하고 광고 캠페인을 개발하는 것을 포함합니다
· [193-D]사무용 소프트웨어에 능하고 발표에 능숙해야 합니다
· [193-B]3년 이상의 부동산 중개 업무 경력이 있는 대학교 졸업생이어야
합니다

qualified adj. 적격의, 적임의   executive assistant 비서
duty n. 직무, 임무   willing adj. ~하지 못할 이유가 없는, 기꺼이 하는
priority n. 우선권   negotiate v. 성사시키다, 협상하다
real estate 부동산 중개업   proficient adj. 능한   adept at ~에 능숙한

Empire 그룹 호주지사
www.empiregroup.au

7월 14일

Ms. Chen께,

귀하의 지원과 면접 참여에 감사드립니다. [194]안타깝게도, 저희는 다른
지원자에게 일자리를 제공하기로 결정했습니다. [195]귀하께서 경력과 교
육 면에서는 저희의 기본 요구 조건들을 충족시키셨지만, 저희가 선택
한 지원자는 귀하께서 아직 취득하지 않으신 몇 개의 자격증들을 소유
하고 있습니다.

저희는 귀하의 잇따른 구직이 잘 되시기를 바라며 향후 Empire 그룹에
서의 다른 일자리들에 지원하시기를 권해드립니다. 회사가 아직 호주에
서 초기 단계에 있어 성장을 위한 추가 계획들이 있는데, 특히 귀하의 도
시인 멜버른에서 그렇습니다.

Leonora Mitchell 드림
채용 전문가

in terms of ~ 면에서   continued adj. 잇따른, 계속되는
early stage 초기 단계   further adj. 추가의, 그 이상의

191 Not/True 문제

문제 Empire 그룹에 대해 언급된 것은?
(A) 금융 서비스 회사로서 시작했다.
(B) 대부분의 사무소들이 유럽에 있다.
(C) 상업 및 주거용 건물들을 건설한다.

(D) 건설한 일부 호텔들이 다음 달에 개장할 것이다.

해설 질문의 핵심 어구인 Empire Group에 대해 묻는 Not/True 문제이므로 Empire 그룹과 관련된 내용이 언급된 첫 번째 지문(안내문)을 확인한다. (A)와 (B)는 지문에 언급되지 않은 내용이다. (C)는 'Empire Group carries out commercial and residential construction projects'에서 Empire 그룹이 상업 및 주거 건설 프로젝트들을 수행하고 있다고 했으므로 지문의 내용과 일치한다. 따라서 (C)가 정답이다. (D)는 지문에 언급되지 않은 내용이다.

192 추론 문제 연계

문제 브리즈번 시에 대해 추론될 수 있는 것은?
(A) 가장 많은 수의 지원 가능한 일자리가 있다.
(B) Empire 그룹의 호주 본사의 소재지이다.
(C) 많은 고소득 주민들이 있다.
(D) 다가오는 부동산 박람회의 장소이다.

해설 질문의 핵심 어구인 the city of Brisbane이 언급된 광고를 먼저 확인한다.
단서 1 두 번째 지문(광고)의 'Empire Group Australia is seeking qualified candidates to fill several full-time positions.'와 'Two positions (Brisbane and Melbourne)', 'Two positions (Brisbane and Perth)'에서 Empire 그룹 호주지사가 몇 개의 정규직 자리를 채울 지원자들을 찾고 있다고 했는데, 그 중 브리즈번 시가 포함되어 있다. 그런데 Empire 그룹 호주지사의 채용에 대한 정보가 제시되지 않았으므로 안내문에서 관련 내용을 확인한다.
단서 2 첫 번째 지문(안내문)의 'its[Empire Group] initial aim in Australia is to increase its workforce in cities that have a large population of upper-income residents'에서 호주에서의 Empire 그룹의 초기 목표가 대규모 인구의 고소득층 주민들이 있는 도시들에서 직원을 늘리는 것임을 확인할 수 있다.
두 단서를 종합할 때, Empire 그룹 호주지사가 직원을 채용하고자 하는 브리즈번 시에 많은 고소득 주민들이 있다는 것을 알 수 있다. 따라서 (C)가 정답이다.

어휘 job opening 일자리, (직장의) 빈 자리 exposition n. 박람회, 전시회

193 Not/True 문제

문제 광고된 마케팅 직무에 대해 사실인 것은?
(A) 매출 목표 초과에 대한 인센티브를 포함한다.
(B) 마케팅 학위를 가진 지원자들만 받는다.
(C) 때때로의 해외 출장이 필요하다.
(D) 뛰어난 컴퓨터 실력을 요구한다.

해설 질문의 핵심 어구인 marketing positions에 대해 묻는 Not/True 문제이므로 marketing positions에 대해 언급된 두 번째 지문(광고)에서 관련 내용을 확인한다. (A)는 지문에 언급되지 않은 내용이다. (B)는 'Marketing associate'와 'Must be college graduates with 3+ years of real estate work experience'에서 마케팅 직원 직무에 대해 경력만 언급하고 마케팅 학위는 언급하지 않았으므로 지문의 내용과 일치하지 않는다. (C)는 지문에 언급되지 않은 내용이다. (D)는 'Must be proficient in office software'에서 사무용 소프트웨어에 능해야 한다고 했으므로 지문의 내용과 일치한다. 따라서 (D)가 정답이다.

패러프레이징
be proficient in office software 사무용 소프트웨어에 능하다 → good computer skills 뛰어난 컴퓨터 실력

어휘 exceed v. 초과하다 be open to ~의 참가를 허가하고 있는
occasional adj. 때때로의, 가끔의

194 목적 찾기 문제

문제 Ms. Mitchell은 왜 편지를 썼는가?
(A) 합격자를 축하하기 위해
(B) 지원자에게 면접을 요청하기 위해

(C) 구직자를 불합격 처리하기 위해
(D) 이력에 대한 자세한 정보를 요구하기 위해

해설 Ms. Mitchell이 편지를 쓴 목적을 묻는 목적 찾기 문제이므로 Ms. Mitchell이 작성한 편지의 내용을 확인한다. 세 번째 지문(편지)의 'Unfortunately, we have decided to give the job to another applicant.'에서 안타깝게도 다른 지원자에게 일자리를 제공하기로 결정했다고 한 후, 불합격 사유에 대해 설명하고 있으므로 (C)가 정답이다.

어휘 successful applicant 합격자 invite v. 요청하다, 초대하다
reject v. 불합격으로 처리하다, 거절하다 detail n. 자세한 정보, 세부 사항
work history 이력

195 추론 문제 연계

문제 Ms. Chen은 어떤 직무에 지원했을 것 같은가?
(A) 비서
(B) 인사부 직원
(C) 계약 전문가
(D) 마케팅 직원

해설 질문의 핵심 어구인 position ~ Ms. Chen ~apply for에서 Ms. Chen이 어떤 직무에 지원했을 것 같은지를 묻고 있으므로 Ms. Chen에게 보내진 편지를 먼저 확인한다.
단서 1 세 번째 지문(편지)의 'Although you met our basic requirements in terms of experience and education, the applicant we selected has several certificates that you have not yet received.'에서 Ms. Chen이 경력과 교육 면에서는 기본 요구 조건들을 충족시켰지만, 선택된 지원자는 Ms. Chen이 아직 취득하지 않은 몇 개의 자격증들을 소유하고 있다고 했다. 그런데 자격증을 소유한 지원자가 선호되는 직무가 무엇인지 제시되지 않았으므로 광고에서 관련 내용을 확인한다.
단서 2 두 번째 지문(광고)의 'Human resources worker'와 'Priority given to candidates with professional certification'에서 인사부 직원 직무에서 전문 자격증이 있는 지원자들에게 우선권이 주어짐을 확인할 수 있다.
두 단서를 종합할 때, Ms. Chen이 인사부 직원 직무에 지원했기 때문에 전문 자격증이 있는 지원자에게 우선권이 주어졌다는 것을 알 수 있다. 따라서 (B)가 정답이다.

196-200번은 다음 웹페이지, 이메일, 브로슈어에 관한 문제입니다.

www.pps.org

필라델피아 보존 협회(PPS)를 후원하세요

196필라델피아 보존 협회의 활동 덕분에, 필라델피아에는 국내에서 진행 중인 가장 큰 공공미술 전시들 중 하나가 있습니다. 온갖 다양한 배경의 사람들이 언제든지 무료로 이 작품들을 접할 기회를 누릴 수 있습니다.

여러분께서 모든 사람들을 위해 공공미술을 보존하고자 하는 저희의 임무를 지원하실 수 있는 몇 가지 방법들이 여기 있습니다:
- 198PPS 개인 회원으로 가입하시고 PPS 특별 행사로의 사전 초청을 받으세요.
- PPS 기업 파트너가 되시고 귀사에서는 비용을 들이지 않고 저희의 연 2회의 만찬에 참석하세요.
- 여기를 클릭하셔서 얼마의 금액이든 일 회의 기부를 하세요. 197기부하실 때 무료 PPS 커피 머그잔을 얻으세요.

preservation n. 보존 thanks to ~ 덕분에
boast v. (자랑할 만한) ~을 가지고 있다, 자랑하다 ongoing adj. 진행 중인
collection n. 전시(회), 수집(품) background n. 배경, 출신
access n. 접촉 기회, 접근 mission n. 임무, 사명
advance adj. 사전의; v. 다가가다 semiannual adj. 연 2회의
banquet n. 만찬, 연회 at no cost 비용을 들이지 않고, 무료로

수신: Marilyn Johnson <m.johnson@pps.org>
발신: Dixie Piper <d.piper@solomon.edu>
제목: 수업 활동
날짜: 5월 2일

Ms. Johnson께,

198저는 최근에 필라델피아 보존 협회의 개인 회원으로 가입했고 귀하의 브로슈어에 나열된 셀프 가이드 투어들 중 하나에 제 6학년 미술 학급을 데려가는 데 관심이 있습니다. 가능하면, 199저는 학생들을 그들이 보는 것을 스케치할 수 있는 호수나 강 근처로의 투어에 데려가려고 싶습니다. 저희는 금요일 오전 9시부터 오후 12시까지 이 활동을 해서 소풍 점심으로 끝낼 수 있습니다. 199또한, 귀하의 셀프 가이드 투어들 중 하나가 그 옵션을 갖고 있는 것 같기 때문에 이 활동을 위해 자전거를 대여하고 싶습니다. 제가 구체적인 계획을 세울 수 있도록 귀하께서 어떻게 생각하시는지 알려주시기 바랍니다.

감사합니다,

Dixie Piper 드림

ideally adv. 가능하면, 이상적으로   **lead** v. 데리고 가다, 이끌다
end with ~으로 끝나다   **concrete** adj. 구체적인

필라델피아 보존 협회의 셀프 가이드 투어

셀프 가이드 투어는 필라델피아의 공공미술을 즐기기에 아주 좋은 방법입니다! 아래에 필라델피아 보존 협회에 의해 구성된 투어들 중 하나를 해보세요.

200-D자연 센터
200-A2시간짜리 투어
28,000평방미터의 손질이 잘 된 푸른 나무들 한복판에 위치한 현대 공공미술의 매력적인 작품들을 둘러보세요.(200-D정원은 오전 9시부터 오후 3시까지 주중에만 열려 있습니다.)

199/200-CKelly로
200-A2.5시간짜리 투어
199Schuylkill 강을 따라 가는 중에 수많은 야외 조각품들을 지나가면서 여유로운 투어를 해보세요.(199/200-C자전거 대여는 Floyd 홀에서 이용 가능합니다.)

필라델피아 미술관
1시간짜리 투어
미술관 주변 지역은 수많은 조각품들의 본고장입니다. 더 많은 미술품들을 위해서, 바로 이 미술관에 잠시 들르세요.(미술관 외부 구역은 월요일에는 대중에게 출입이 금지됩니다.)

리튼하우스 광장
1시간짜리 투어
필라델피아의 설립 이래 계속 존재하고 있는 아름다운 공원인 리튼하우스 광장에 있는 여러 가지 역사적인 조각품들을 보세요.

세부 사항은 www.pps.org를 방문하세요.

fascinating adj. 매력적인   **amid** prep. ~의 한복판에, 가운데에
well-tended adj. 손질이 잘 된   **greenery** n. 푸른 나무
ground n. 정원, 땅   **leisurely** adj. 여유로운, 한가한
a number of 수많은   **sculpture** n. 조각품   **on the way** 가는 중에
home n. 본고장, 고향
date back to ~ 이래 계속 존재하고 있다, 역사가 ~이나 되다
founding n. 설립, 수립

---

196 추론 문제

문제 필라델피아 보존 협회는 무엇을 하는 것 같은가?
(A) 지역 학생들에게 미술 교습을 제공한다.
(B) 시의 관광 산업을 관리한다.
(C) 근대 건물들의 보존에 자금을 댄다.
(D) 대중의 즐거움을 위해 미술품을 보존한다.

해설 질문의 핵심 어구인 Philadelphia Preservation Society에 대해 추론하는 문제이므로 필라델피아 보존 협회와 관련된 내용이 언급된 웹페이지를 확인한다. 첫 번째 지문(웹페이지)의 'Thanks to the work

---

of the Philadelphia Preservation Society, Philadelphia boasts one of the largest ongoing collections of public art in the country.'에서 필라델피아 보존 협회의 활동 덕분에 필라델피아에 국내에서 진행 중인 가장 큰 공공미술 전시들 중 하나가 있다고 했고, 'People from all backgrounds can enjoy access to these works at any time for free.'에서 온갖 다양한 배경의 사람들이 언제든지 무료로 이 작품들을 접할 기회를 누릴 수 있다고 했으므로, 필라델피아 보존 협회가 대중의 즐거움을 위해 미술품을 보존한다는 것을 추론할 수 있다. 따라서 (D)가 정답이다.

어휘 **tourist industry** 관광 산업   **modern** adj. 근대의, 현대의
maintain v. 보존하다, 유지하다   **artwork** n. 미술품

197 육하원칙 문제

문제 기부를 하는 사람들에게 무엇이 제공될 것인가?
(A) 멤버십 할인
(B) 무료 상품
(C) 정보가 있는 소책자
(D) 무료 체험 수업

해설 기부를 하는 사람들에게 무엇(What)이 제공될 것인지를 묻는 육하원칙 문제이므로 질문의 핵심 어구인 offered to those who give a donation과 관련된 내용이 언급된 웹페이지를 확인한다. 첫 번째 지문(웹페이지)의 'Get a free PPS coffee mug when you donate.'에서 기부할 때 무료 PPS 커피 머그잔을 얻으라고 했으므로 (B)가 정답이다.

패러프레이징
a free ~ coffee mug 무료 커피 머그잔 → A complimentary item 무료 상품

198 추론 문제 연계

문제 Ms. Piper에 대해 암시되는 것은?
(A) PPS 행사로의 초청을 받을 것이다.
(B) 최근에 현장 학습에 참여했다.
(C) 그녀의 단체를 위해 얼마간의 자금을 확보했다.
(D) PPS에 일 회의 기부를 할 것이다.

해설 질문의 핵심 어구인 Ms. Piper가 작성한 이메일을 먼저 확인한다.
단서 1 두 번째 지문(이메일)의 'I recently signed up as an individual member of the Philadelphia Preservation Society'에서 Ms. Piper가 최근에 필라델피아 보존 협회의 개인 회원으로 가입했다고 했다. 그런데 필라델피아 보존 협회의 개인 회원에 대한 정보가 제시되지 않았으므로 웹페이지에서 관련 내용을 확인한다.
단서 2 첫 번째 지문(웹페이지)의 'Join as a PPS individual member and receive advance invitations to PPS special events.'에서 PPS 개인 회원으로 가입하면 PPS 특별 행사로의 사전 초청을 받을 수 있음을 확인할 수 있다.
두 단서를 종합할 때, Ms. Piper가 PPS의 개인 회원으로 가입했으므로 PPS 특별 행사로의 사전 초청을 받을 것임을 알 수 있다. 따라서 (A)가 정답이다.

어휘 **field trip** 현장 학습   **secure** v. 확보하다, 획득하다

199 육하원칙 문제 연계

문제 Ms. Piper는 어떤 투어에 관심이 있는가?
(A) 자연 센터
(B) Kelly로
(C) 필라델피아 미술관
(D) 리튼하우스 광장

해설 질문의 핵심 어구인 Ms. Piper가 작성한 이메일을 먼저 확인한다.
단서 1 두 번째 지문(이메일)의 'I'd like to lead the students on a tour near a lake or river'에서 Ms. Piper가 학생들을 호수나 강 근처로의 투어에 데려가고 싶다고 했고, 'Also, I'd prefer to rent bikes

for this activity since one of your self-guided tours seemed to have that option.'에서 또한 셀프 가이드 투어들 중 하나가 그 옵션을 갖고 있는 것 같기 때문에 이 활동을 위해 자전거들을 대여하기를 원한다고 했다. 그런데 호수나 강 근처에서 할 수 있고 자전거를 대여할 수 있는 투어가 무엇인지 제시되지 않았으므로 브로슈어에서 관련 내용을 확인한다.

단서 2 세 번째 지문(브로슈어)의 'Kelly Drive'와 'Take a leisurely trip along the Schuylkill River', 'Bike rentals available'에서 Kelly로 투어가 Schuylkill 강을 따라 투어를 할 수 있고, 자전거 대여가 이용 가능함을 확인할 수 있다.

두 단서를 종합할 때, Ms. Piper는 강을 따라 투어를 할 수 있고 자전거 대여가 이용 가능한 Kelly로 투어에 관심이 있다는 것을 알 수 있다. 따라서 (B)가 정답이다.

200 Not/True 문제

문제 셀프 가이드 투어에 대해 언급된 것은?
(A) 각각 끝마치는 데 한 시간이 걸린다.
(B) 학생들과 단체들에게 할인된다.
(C) 모두 자전거를 타는 사람들에게 적합하다.
(D) 일부는 일주일의 특정 날에 이용이 불가능하다.

해설 질문의 핵심 어구인 self-guided tours에 대해 묻는 Not/True 문제이므로 셀프 가이드 투어가 언급된 세 번째 지문(브로슈어)에서 관련 내용을 확인한다. (A)는 '2-hour trip'과 '2.5-hour trip'에서 2시간짜리와 2.5시간짜리 투어가 있다고 했으므로 지문의 내용과 일치하지 않는다. (B)는 지문에 언급되지 않은 내용이다. (C)는 'Kelly Drive'와 'Bike rentals available'에서 Kelly로만 자전거 대여가 이용 가능하다고 했으므로 지문의 내용과 일치하지 않는다. (D)는 'Nature Center'와 'Grounds are open on weekdays only'에서 자연 센터의 정원이 주중에만 열려 있다고 했으므로 지문의 내용과 일치한다. 따라서 (D)가 정답이다.

패러프레이징
open on weekdays only 주중에만 열려 있는 → unavailable on certain days of the week 일주일의 특정 날에 이용이 불가능한

어휘 complete v. 끝마치다, 완료하다 suitable adj. 적합한, 알맞은

TEST 3

LISTENING TEST   p.112

1	(D)	2	(D)	3	(A)	4	(D)	5	(A)
6	(B)	7	(A)	8	(A)	9	(C)	10	(B)
11	(A)	12	(C)	13	(B)	14	(C)	15	(B)
16	(B)	17	(C)	18	(A)	19	(A)	20	(C)
21	(B)	22	(C)	23	(B)	24	(C)	25	(C)
26	(B)	27	(A)	28	(C)	29	(C)	30	(A)
31	(A)	32	(C)	33	(C)	34	(B)	35	(D)
36	(A)	37	(B)	38	(A)	39	(C)	40	(B)
41	(A)	42	(C)	43	(D)	44	(A)	45	(D)
46	(C)	47	(B)	48	(C)	49	(A)	50	(C)
51	(B)	52	(D)	53	(B)	54	(B)	55	(D)
56	(C)	57	(C)	58	(A)	59	(B)	60	(D)
61	(B)	62	(B)	63	(A)	64	(B)	65	(B)
66	(B)	67	(D)	68	(C)	69	(B)	70	(A)
71	(C)	72	(B)	73	(B)	74	(A)	75	(A)
76	(B)	77	(B)	78	(A)	79	(B)	80	(A)
81	(A)	82	(A)	83	(B)	84	(D)	85	(A)
86	(B)	87	(B)	88	(D)	89	(D)	90	(D)
91	(C)	92	(D)	93	(B)	94	(A)	95	(B)
96	(B)	97	(B)	98	(A)	99	(C)	100	(B)

READING TEST   p.124

101	(D)	102	(B)	103	(A)	104	(D)	105	(A)
106	(B)	107	(A)	108	(B)	109	(A)	110	(A)
111	(B)	112	(A)	113	(B)	114	(C)	115	(C)
116	(C)	117	(B)	118	(A)	119	(C)	120	(C)
121	(D)	122	(D)	123	(C)	124	(D)	125	(C)
126	(C)	127	(C)	128	(B)	129	(A)	130	(A)
131	(C)	132	(A)	133	(A)	134	(D)	135	(A)
136	(D)	137	(C)	138	(B)	139	(B)	140	(C)
141	(D)	142	(A)	143	(A)	144	(C)	145	(C)
146	(C)	147	(B)	148	(C)	149	(D)	150	(A)
151	(C)	152	(D)	153	(C)	154	(B)	155	(C)
156	(C)	157	(D)	158	(D)	159	(B)	160	(D)
161	(B)	162	(C)	163	(A)	164	(B)	165	(C)
166	(D)	167	(B)	168	(A)	169	(B)	170	(D)
171	(C)	172	(B)	173	(B)	174	(B)	175	(A)
176	(A)	177	(C)	178	(A)	179	(D)	180	(B)
181	(D)	182	(B)	183	(C)	184	(A)	185	(A)
186	(A)	187	(B)	188	(D)	189	(C)	190	(D)
191	(B)	192	(D)	193	(A)	194	(B)	195	(D)
196	(C)	197	(B)	198	(D)	199	(B)	200	(D)

PART 1

1 🔊 호주식 발음

(A) He is walking up some steps.
(B) He is relaxing in a lobby.
(C) He is drinking from a cup.
(D) He is reading a newspaper.

relax [riléks] 휴식을 취하다

해석 (A) 그는 계단을 걸어 올라가고 있다.
(B) 그는 로비에서 휴식을 취하고 있다.
(C) 그는 컵으로 마시고 있다.
(D) 그는 신문을 읽고 있다.

해설 **1인 사진**
(A) [×] 남자가 계단 위에 앉아 있는 상태인데, 계단을 걸어 올라가고 있다(walking up)는 동작으로 잘못 묘사한 오답이다.
(B) [×] 사진의 장소가 로비(lobby)가 아니므로 오답이다.
(C) [×] drinking(마시고 있다)은 남자의 동작과 무관하므로 오답이다. 사진에 있는 컵(cup)을 사용하여 혼동을 주었다.
(D) [○] 남자가 신문을 읽고 있는 모습을 가장 잘 묘사한 정답이다.

2 🔊 미국식 발음

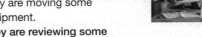

(A) They are looking at a computer.
(B) They are putting on safety gear.
(C) They are moving some equipment.
(D) They are reviewing some documents.

safety gear 안전장치

해석 (A) 그들은 컴퓨터를 보고 있다.
(B) 그들은 안전장치를 착용하고 있다.
(C) 그들은 몇몇 장비를 옮기고 있다.
(D) 그들은 몇몇 서류를 검토하고 있다.

해설 **2인 이상 사진**
(A) [×] 사람들이 서류를 보고 있는데, 컴퓨터를 보고 있다고 잘못 묘사한 오답이다.
(B) [×] putting on(착용하고 있다)은 사람들의 동작과 무관하므로 오답이다. 옷·모자·구두 등을 이미 입은 상태를 나타내는 wearing과 입고 있는 중이라는 동작을 나타내는 putting on을 혼동하지 않도록 주의한다.
(C) [×] moving(옮기고 있다)은 사람들의 동작과 무관하므로 오답이다.
(D) [○] 사람들이 몇몇 서류를 검토하고 있는 모습을 가장 잘 묘사한 정답이다.

3 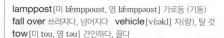 캐나다식 발음

(A) Some cars are parked along a street.
(B) A lamppost has fallen over.
(C) There are many vehicles driving by the building.
(D) A truck is being towed.

lamppost[미 lǽmppoust, 영 lǽmppəust] 가로등 (기둥)
fall over 쓰러지다, 넘어지다   vehicle[víːəkl] 차(량), 탈 것
tow[미 tou, 영 təu] 견인하다, 끌다

해석 (A) 몇몇 차들이 거리를 따라 주차되어 있다.
(B) 가로등 기둥이 쓰러져 있다.
(C) 건물을 지나는 많은 차들이 있다.
(D) 트럭이 견인되고 있다.

해설 **사물 및 풍경 사진**
(A) [○] 차들이 거리를 따라 주차되어 있는 모습을 가장 잘 묘사한 정답이다.
(B) [×] 가로등 기둥이 서 있는 상태인데, 쓰러져 있다고 잘못 묘사한 오답이다.
(C) [×] 차들이 주차되어 있는 상태인데, 건물을 지나고 있다고 잘못 묘사한 오답이다.
(D) [×] 사진에서 트럭이 견인되고 있는지(is being towed) 확인할 수 없으므로 오답이다.

4 호주식 발음

(A) A man is leaning against the bookcase.
(B) A picture is being displayed on the wall.
(C) A medical device is being plugged in.
(D) A man is resting his elbow on a desk.

lean against ~에 기대다   bookcase[búkkeis] 책장
display[displéi] 전시하다   medical device 의료 장비
plug in ~의 플러그를 꽂다   rest[rest] 얹다, 기대다   elbow[élbou] 팔꿈치

해석 (A) 한 남자가 책장에 기대어 있다.
(B) 그림이 벽에 전시되고 있다.
(C) 의료 장비의 플러그가 꽂히고 있다.
(D) 한 남자가 팔꿈치를 책상 위에 얹고 있다.

해설 **1인 사진**
(A) [×] 남자가 책장에 기대어 있는 것이 아니라 책상에 기대어 있으므로 오답이다.
(B) [×] 사진에서 벽에 전시되고 있는 그림(picture)을 확인할 수 없으므로 오답이다.
(C) [×] 사진에서 의료 장비는 보이지만, 플러그가 꽂히고 있는(is being plugged in) 모습은 아니므로 오답이다.
(D) [○] 남자가 팔꿈치를 책상 위에 얹고 있는 모습을 가장 잘 묘사한 정답이다.

5 미국식 발음

(A) A bicycle is positioned next to a building.
(B) Some lines are being painted on a road.
(C) A door is propped open.

(D) Some flowers are being planted in pots.

position[pəzíʃən] ~에 놓다, 두다   prop[미 prɑp, 영 prɔp] 받치다
plant[미 plænt, 영 plɑːnt] 심다

해석 (A) 자전거가 건물 옆에 놓여 있다.
(B) 길 위에 몇몇 선들이 그려지고 있다.
(C) 문이 밑을 받쳐 열려있다.
(D) 몇몇 꽃들이 화분에 심기고 있다.

해설 **사물 및 풍경 사진**
(A) [○] 자전거가 건물 옆에 놓여 있는 모습을 가장 잘 묘사한 정답이다.
(B) [×] 길 위에 선들이 이미 그려진 상태인데, 그려지고 있다(are being painted)는 동작으로 잘못 묘사한 오답이다.
(C) [×] 문이 닫혀 있는 상태인데, 열려있다고 잘못 묘사한 오답이다.
(D) [×] 몇몇 꽃들이 이미 화분에 심겨 있는 상태인데, 심기고 있다(are being planted)는 동작으로 잘못 묘사한 오답이다.

6 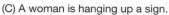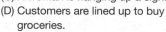 영국식 발음

(A) A man is removing his apron.
(B) Produce is in boxes at an outdoor market.
(C) A woman is hanging up a sign.
(D) Customers are lined up to buy groceries.

apron[éiprən] 앞치마   produce[prádjuːs] 농산물, 수확물
outdoor[áutdɔːr] 야외의, 옥외의   hang up ~을 걸다
line up 줄을 서다

해석 (A) 남자가 앞치마를 벗고 있다.
(B) 농산물이 야외 시장에서 상자 안에 들어 있다.
(C) 여자가 표지판을 걸고 있다.
(D) 손님들이 식료품을 사기 위해 줄을 서 있다.

해설 **2인 이상 사진**
(A) [×] 남자가 앞치마를 입은 상태인데, 벗고 있다고 잘못 묘사한 오답이다.
(B) [○] 농산물이 야외 시장에서 상자 안에 들어 있는 모습을 가장 잘 묘사한 정답이다.
(C) [×] hanging up(걸고 있다)은 여자의 동작과 무관하므로 오답이다. 사진에 있는 표지판(sign)을 사용하여 혼동을 주었다.
(D) [×] 사진에서 식료품을 사기 위해 줄을 서 있는 손님들을 확인할 수 없으므로 오답이다. 사진에 있는 식료품(groceries)을 사용하여 혼동을 주었다.

PART 2

7 미국식 발음 → 호주식 발음

Where is the locker room located?
(A) Across from the entrance.
(B) To change my clothes.
(C) It was donated.

locker room 탈의실   locate[미 lóukeit, 영 lə́ukeit] ~에 위치하다
across from ~의 맞은편에   entrance[éntrəns] 출입구
donate[미 dóuneit, 영 dəunéit] 기부하다

해석 탈의실은 어디에 위치해 있나요?
(A) 출입구의 맞은편에요.

(B) 제 옷을 갈아 입기 위해서요.
(C) 그것은 기부되었어요.

해설 **Where 의문문**
(A) [○] 출입구의 맞은편이라며, 탈의실의 위치를 언급했으므로 정답이다.
(B) [×] 질문의 locker room(탈의실)과 관련 있는 clothes(옷)를 사용하여 혼동을 준 오답이다.
(C) [×] located – donated의 유사 발음 어휘를 사용하여 혼동을 준 오답이다.

8 ⟨캐⟩ 캐나다식 발음 → 미국식 발음

> Why are you going to visit the shopping mall?
> **(A) I need a new shirt.**
> (B) In my shopping bag.
> (C) Because a customer took it.

customer[미 kʌ́stəmər, 영 kʌ́stəmə] 손님, 고객

해설 당신은 왜 쇼핑몰을 방문할 건가요?
(A) 저는 새로운 셔츠가 필요해요.
(B) 제 쇼핑백 안에요.
(C) 한 손님이 그것을 가져가기 때문이에요.

해설 **Why 의문문**
(A) [○] 새로운 셔츠가 필요하다며, 쇼핑몰을 방문하는 이유를 언급했으므로 정답이다.
(B) [×] 질문의 shopping을 반복 사용하여 혼동을 준 오답이다.
(C) [×] 질문의 shopping mall(쇼핑몰)과 관련 있는 customer(손님)를 사용하여 혼동을 준 오답이다.

9 ⟨미⟩ 미국식 발음 → 캐나다식 발음

> How often does the bus stop here?
> (A) On top of the car.
> (B) Do you have my bus pass?
> **(C) About every 30 minutes.**

on top of ~의 위에   bus pass 버스 승차권

해설 그 버스는 얼마나 자주 여기에 서나요?
(A) 자동차의 위에요.
(B) 당신이 제 버스 승차권을 가지고 있나요?
(C) 대략 30분마다요.

해설 **How 의문문**
(A) [×] 질문의 bus(버스)와 관련 있는 car(자동차)를 사용하여 혼동을 준 오답이다.
(B) [×] 질문의 bus(버스)와 관련 있는 bus pass(버스 승차권)를 사용하여 혼동을 준 오답이다.
(C) [○] 대략 30분마다라며, 버스가 오는 빈도를 언급했으므로 정답이다.

10 ⟨미⟩ 미국식 발음 → 호주식 발음

> When are you holding interviews for the receptionist position?
> (A) For the main reception desk.
> **(B) Within the next week.**
> (C) I'm excited to begin the job!

hold an interview 면접을 하다, 인터뷰를 하다
receptionist[risépʃənist] 접수 담당자   position[pəzíʃən] 직, (일)자리

해설 당신은 언제 접수 담당직에 대한 면접을 할 건가요?
(A) 주요 접수처를 위해서요.
(B) 다음 주 이내로요.
(C) 일을 시작하게 되어 신이 나요!

해설 **When 의문문**
(A) [×] receptionist – reception desk의 유사 발음 어휘를 사용하여 혼동을 준 오답이다.
(B) [○] 다음 주 이내로라며, 면접을 할 시기를 언급했으므로 정답이다.
(C) [×] 질문의 position(직)과 관련 있는 job(일)을 사용하여 혼동을 준 오답이다.

11 ⟨호⟩ 호주식 발음 → 미국식 발음

> Can I use your phone to make a brief call?
> **(A) Yes, no problem.**
> (B) No, in the telephone book.
> (C) A pretty short walk.

brief[bri:f] (시간이) 짧은   telephone book 전화번호부

해설 짧게 통화하기 위해 당신의 전화기를 사용할 수 있을까요?
(A) 네, 문제없어요.
(B) 아뇨, 전화번호부에요.
(C) 아주 잠깐 걸어요.

해설 **요청 의문문**
(A) [○] Yes로 전화기를 사용하고 싶다는 요청을 수락한 정답이다.
(B) [×] 질문의 phone(전화기)과 관련 있는 telephone book(전화번호부)을 사용하여 혼동을 준 오답이다.
(C) [×] 질문의 brief((시간이) 짧은)와 같은 의미인 short((시간이) 짧은)를 사용하여 혼동을 준 오답이다.

12 ⟨영⟩ 영국식 발음 → 캐나다식 발음

> Which banquet guests will be seated at the front table?
> (A) Well, these chairs should be moved.
> (B) This is a nice place for an event.
> **(C) Our company's board members.**

banquet[bǽŋkwit] 연회   seat[si:t] 앉다, 앉히다   board member 임원

해설 어떤 연회 손님들이 앞쪽 테이블에 앉을 건가요?
(A) 음, 이 의자들은 옮겨져야 해요.
(B) 이곳은 행사를 위한 좋은 장소네요.
(C) 우리 회사의 임원들이요.

해설 **Which 의문문**
(A) [×] 질문의 seated(앉은)와 관련 있는 chairs(의자들)를 사용하여 혼동을 준 오답이다.
(B) [×] 질문의 banquet(연회)과 관련 있는 event(행사)를 사용하여 혼동을 준 오답이다.
(C) [○] 회사의 임원들이라며, 앞쪽 테이블에 앉을 손님들을 언급했으므로 정답이다.

13 ⟨영⟩ 영국식 발음 → 미국식 발음

> What is the matter with your motorcycle?
> (A) That's the problem.
> **(B) The back tire has a hole.**
> (C) My brother is a mechanic, too.

motorcycle[미 móutərsàikl, 영 máutəsàikl] 오토바이
mechanic[məkǽnik] 정비사

해석 당신의 오토바이에 무슨 문제가 있나요?
(A) 그게 문제예요.
(B) 뒷바퀴에 구멍이 났어요.
(C) 제 남동생도 정비사예요.

해설 **What 의문문**
(A) [×] 질문의 matter(문제)와 같은 의미인 problem(문제)을 사용하여 혼동을 준 오답이다.
(B) [○] 뒷바퀴에 구멍이 났다며, 오토바이의 문제를 언급했으므로 정답이다.
(C) [×] 질문의 motorcycle(오토바이)과 관련 있는 mechanic(정비사)을 사용하여 혼동을 준 오답이다.

14 🔊 호주식 발음 → 영국식 발음

Who is responsible for updating the employee manual?
(A) Ms. Dunlap wrote the reports.
(B) Employees found it quite helpful.
(C) It has yet to be decided.

responsible for ~에 책임이 있는   manual[mǽnjuəl] 소책자
quite[kwait] 꽤   helpful[hélpfəl] 유용한, 도움이 되는

해석 누가 직원용 소책자를 업데이트하는 것에 책임이 있나요?
(A) Ms. Dunlap이 그 보고서들을 작성했어요.
(B) 직원들은 그것이 꽤 유용하다는 것을 알았어요.
(C) 그것은 아직 결정되지 않았어요.

해설 **Who 의문문**
(A) [×] 질문의 employee manual(직원용 소책자)과 관련 있는 report(보고서)를 사용하여 혼동을 준 오답이다.
(B) [×] 질문의 employee를 employees로 반복 사용하여 혼동을 주었고, employee manual(직원용 소책자)과 관련 있는 helpful(유용한)을 사용하여 혼동을 준 오답이다.
(C) [○] 그것은 아직 결정되지 않았다는 말로, 누가 업데이트하는 것에 책임이 있는지 모른다는 것을 간접적으로 전달했으므로 정답이다.

15 🔊 호주식 발음 → 미국식 발음

How large is the new couch in the waiting area?
(A) There's a furniture store nearby.
(B) Big enough for four people.
(C) I'll wait for you after the show.

couch[kautʃ] 소파   waiting area 대기실
furniture[미 fə́:rnitʃər, 영 fə́:nitʃə] 가구

해석 대기실에 있는 새로운 소파는 얼마나 큰가요?
(A) 근처에 가구점이 있어요.
(B) 네 사람이 앉기에 충분할 정도로 커요.
(C) 공연이 끝나고 당신을 기다릴게요.

해설 **How 의문문**
(A) [×] 질문의 couch(소파)와 관련 있는 furniture(가구)를 사용하여 혼동을 준 오답이다.
(B) [○] 네 사람이 앉기에 충분할 정도로 크다며, 소파의 크기를 언급했으므로 정답이다.
(C) [×] waiting – wait의 유사 발음 어휘를 사용하여 혼동을 준 오답이다.

16 🔊 호주식 발음 → 영국식 발음

Where is Peter right now?
(A) He is the supervisor.
(B) Weren't you just with him?
(C) That's the wrong number.

supervisor[미 súːpərvàizər, 영 súːpəvaizə] 감독관, 관리자

해석 Peter는 바로 지금 어디에 있나요?
(A) 그는 감독관이에요.
(B) 당신은 방금 그와 함께 있지 않았나요?
(C) 그것은 잘못된 번호예요.

해설 **Where 의문문**
(A) [×] 질문의 Peter를 나타낼 수 있는 He를 사용하여 혼동을 준 오답이다.
(B) [○] 방금 그와 함께 있지 않았는지를 되물어, Peter가 어디에 있는지 모른다는 것을 간접적으로 전달했으므로 정답이다.
(C) [×] 질문의 right(바로)의 다른 의미인 '옳은'과 반대 의미인 wrong(잘못된)을 사용하여 혼동을 준 오답이다.

17 🔊 캐나다식 발음 → 미국식 발음

This television came with a scratch on it.
(A) Our electronics are on sale.
(B) The colors match well.
(C) We can exchange it for you.

scratch[skrætʃ] 긁힌 자국
electronics[미 ilektrániks, 영 èlektrɔ́niks] 전자 기기   on sale 할인 중인
match[mætʃ] 어울리다, 일치하다   exchange[ikstʃéindʒ] 교환하다

해석 이 텔레비전은 긁힌 자국이 있는 상태로 왔어요.
(A) 저희의 전자 기기가 할인 중입니다.
(B) 색깔들이 잘 어울려요.
(C) 당신에게 그것을 교환해드릴 수 있습니다.

해설 **평서문**
(A) [×] 질문의 television(텔레비전)과 관련 있는 electronics(전자 기기)를 사용하여 혼동을 준 오답이다.
(B) [×] scratch – match의 유사 발음 어휘를 사용하여 혼동을 준 오답이다.
(C) [○] 그것을 교환해줄 수 있다는 말로, 텔레비전에 긁힌 자국이 있는 문제점에 대한 해결책을 제시했으므로 정답이다.

18 🔊 영국식 발음 → 캐나다식 발음

Would you empty the trashcan?
(A) Sure, just a second.
(B) Buy a black garbage can.
(C) Yes, I can fill it.

empty[émpti] 비우다   trashcan[trǽʃkæn] 쓰레기통
garbage can 쓰레기통   fill[fil] 채우다

해석 그 쓰레기통을 비워주실래요?
(A) 물론이죠, 잠시만요.
(B) 검은색 쓰레기통을 사세요.
(C) 네, 제가 그것을 채울게요.

해설 **요청 의문문**
(A) [○] Sure로 쓰레기통을 비워달라는 요청을 수락한 정답이다.
(B) [×] 질문의 trashcan(쓰레기통)과 같은 의미인 garbage can(쓰

레기통)을 사용하여 혼동을 준 오답이다.
(C) [×] 질문의 empty(비우다)와 반대 의미인 fill(채우다)을 사용하여 혼동을 준 오답이다.

19 3ช 미국식 발음 → 캐나다식 발음

Isn't it time to leave for the sales seminar?
(A) We're heading out right now.
(B) The instructor left them out.
(C) Next to the convention center.

sales[seilz] 영업 head out 출발하다
instructor[미 instrʌ́ktər, 영 instrʌ́ktə] 강사 leave out ~를 제외시키다
convention center 컨벤션 센터(회의 장소·숙박 시설 등이 집중된 종합 빌딩)

해석 영업 세미나로 떠날 시간 아닌가요?
(A) 우리는 지금 출발할 거예요.
(B) 강사가 그들을 제외시켰어요.
(C) 컨벤션 센터 옆에요.

해설 **부정 의문문**
(A) [ㅇ] 지금 출발할 것이라는 말로, 영업 세미나로 떠날 시간이 맞음을 간접적으로 전달했으므로 정답이다.
(B) [×] 질문의 seminar(세미나)와 관련 있는 instructor(강사)를 사용하여 혼동을 준 오답이다.
(C) [×] 질문의 seminar(세미나)와 관련 있는 convention center(컨벤션 센터)를 사용하여 혼동을 준 오답이다.

20 3ช 영국식 발음 → 호주식 발음

One of the firm's lawyers left a voice message for you.
(A) I work for a big law firm.
(B) All of the legal documentation.
(C) I'll listen to it now.

firm[미 fəːrm, 영 fəːm] 회사 lawyer[미 lɔ́iər, 영 lɔ́iə] 변호사
voice message 음성 메시지 legal[líːgəl] 법률의
documentation[미 dàkjumentéiʃən, 영 dɔ̀kjəmentéiʃən] 서류, 기록

해석 회사의 변호사들 중 한 명이 당신에게 음성 메시지를 남겼어요.
(A) 저는 큰 법률 회사에서 일해요.
(B) 모든 법률 서류요.
(C) 지금 그것을 들어볼게요.

해설 **평서문**
(A) [×] lawyers – law의 유사 발음 어휘를 사용하여 혼동을 준 오답이다.
(B) [×] 질문의 lawyers(변호사들)와 관련 있는 legal documentation(법률 서류)을 사용하여 혼동을 준 오답이다.
(C) [ㅇ] 지금 그것을 들어보겠다며, 음성 메시지를 확인할 것임을 전달했으므로 정답이다.

21 3ช 호주식 발음 → 영국식 발음

Do you know where the information desk is?
(A) That desk comes with drawers.
(B) I can show you if you'd like.
(C) Yes, the shopper was informed.

information desk 안내 데스크 come with ~이 딸려 있다
drawer[미 drɔːr, 영 drɔː] 서랍
informed[미 infɔ́ːrmd, 영 infɔ́ːmd] 알고 있는

해석 안내 데스크가 어디에 있는지 아시나요?
(A) 그 책상은 서랍들이 딸려 있어요.

(B) 원하시면 제가 안내해드릴게요.
(C) 네, 그 쇼핑객은 알고 있었어요.

해설 **의문사(Where)를 포함한 일반 의문문**
(A) [×] 질문의 desk를 반복 사용하여 혼동을 준 오답이다.
(B) [ㅇ] 원하면 안내해주겠다는 말로, 안내 데스크가 어디에 있는지 알고 있음을 간접적으로 전달했으므로 정답이다.
(C) [×] information – informed의 유사 발음 어휘를 사용하여 혼동을 준 오답이다.

22 3ช 캐나다식 발음 → 미국식 발음

Is Dr. Campbell available this afternoon?
(A) Most of our clinic's doctors.
(B) No, but you can keep them.
(C) I'm afraid his schedule is booked.

available[əvéiləbl] 시간이 있는 clinic[klínik] 병원
book[buk] 예약하다

해석 Dr. Campbell은 오늘 오후에 시간이 있나요?
(A) 저희 병원 의사들 대부분이요.
(B) 아뇨, 하지만 당신이 그것들을 가져도 돼요.
(C) 죄송합니다만 그의 일정은 예약되어 있어요.

해설 **Be동사 의문문**
(A) [×] 질문의 Dr. Campbell과 관련 있는 clinic(병원)을 사용하여 혼동을 준 오답이다.
(B) [×] Dr. Campbell이 오후에 시간이 있는지 물었는데, 이와 관련이 없는 당신이 그것들을 가져도 된다는 내용으로 응답했으므로 오답이다.
(C) [ㅇ] 죄송하지만 그의 일정은 예약되어 있다는 말로, Dr. Campbell이 오늘 오후에 시간이 없음을 간접적으로 전달했으므로 정답이다.

23 3ช 캐나다식 발음 → 영국식 발음

I would like to order a large pepperoni pizza.
(A) Actually, the smaller piece is mine.
(B) Where would you like it delivered?
(C) No, with extra cheese.

order[미 ɔ́ːrdər, 영 ɔ́ːdə] 주문하다 actually[ǽktʃuəli] 실은, 실제로
piece[piːs] 조각

해석 페퍼로니 피자 라지 사이즈를 주문하고 싶어요.
(A) 실은, 더 작은 조각이 제거예요.
(B) 어디로 그것을 배달 받고 싶으신가요?
(C) 아뇨, 치즈를 추가해서요.

해설 **평서문**
(A) [×] 질문의 pizza(피자)와 관련 있는 piece(조각)를 사용하여 혼동을 준 오답이다.
(B) [ㅇ] 어디로 배달 받고 싶은지를 되물어, 피자 주문에 대한 추가 정보를 요구한 정답이다.
(C) [×] 질문의 pizza(피자)와 관련 있는 cheese(치즈)를 사용하여 혼동을 준 오답이다.

24 3ช 캐나다식 발음 → 영국식 발음

Jane is moving out tomorrow, isn't she?
(A) Yes, yesterday afternoon.
(B) I can't move it alone.

(C) So far as I know.

---

move out 이사를 나가다 so far as ~하는 한

해석 Jane이 내일 이사를 나가죠, 그렇지 않나요?
(A) 네, 어제 오후에요.
(B) 저는 혼자서 그것을 옮길 수 없어요.
(C) 제가 아는 한 그래요.

해설 부가 의문문
(A) [×] 질문의 tomorrow(내일)와 관련 있는 yesterday(어제)를 사용하여 혼동을 준 오답이다.
(B) [×] 질문의 move(이사하다)를 '옮기다'라는 의미로 반복 사용하여 혼동을 준 오답이다.
(C) [○] 자신이 아는 한 그렇다는 말로, Jane이 내일 이사를 나감을 전달했으므로 정답이다.

25 [호주식 발음] 캐나다식 발음 → 호주식 발음

Did you find the correct part to fix the copier?
(A) Ten copies, please.
(B) Some factory machines.
(C) The component will arrive today.

---

part[미 pɑːrt, 영 pɑːt] 부품 copier[미 kɑ́piər, 영 kɔ́piə] 복사기
component[미 kəmpóunənt, 영 kəmpóunənt] 부품, 요소

해석 복사기를 고치기 위한 맞는 부품을 찾았나요?
(A) 열 부요.
(B) 몇몇 공장 기계들이요.
(C) 그 부품은 오늘 도착할 거예요.

해설 조동사 의문문
(A) [×] copier – copies의 유사 발음 어휘를 사용하여 혼동을 준 오답이다.
(B) [×] 질문의 copier(복사기)와 관련 있는 machines(기계들)를 사용하여 혼동을 준 오답이다.
(C) [○] 그 부품은 오늘 도착할 것이라는 말로, 복사기를 고치기 위한 맞는 부품을 찾았음을 간접적으로 전달했으므로 정답이다.

26 [영국식 발음] 영국식 발음 → 호주식 발음

The Internet doesn't seem to be working.
(A) That doesn't feel warm enough.
(B) Did you try restarting your laptop?
(C) Yes, I work out every day.

---

restart[미 riːstɑ́ːrt, 영 riːstɑ́ːt] 다시 시작하다
laptop[미 lǽptàp, 영 lǽptɔ̀p] 노트북 컴퓨터 work out 운동하다

해석 인터넷이 작동하지 않는 것 같아요.
(A) 그것은 충분히 따뜻하지 않아요.
(B) 당신의 노트북 컴퓨터를 다시 시작해봤나요?
(C) 네, 전 매일 운동해요.

해설 평서문
(A) [×] 인터넷이 작동하지 않는 것 같다는 문제점을 말했는데, 이와 관련이 없는 그것은 충분히 따뜻하지 않다는 내용으로 응답했으므로 오답이다.
(B) [○] 노트북 컴퓨터를 다시 시작해봤는지를 되물어, 인터넷이 작동하지 않는 문제점에 대한 해결책을 제시했으므로 정답이다.
(C) [×] working – work out의 유사 발음 어휘를 사용하여 혼동을 준 오답이다.

27 [영국식 발음] 영국식 발음 → 캐나다식 발음

Has the grocery store across the street closed down?
(A) It will in about a week.
(B) For the grand opening.
(C) You can store them here.

---

grocery store 식료품 가게 close down 문을 닫다, 폐점하다
grand opening 개점, 개장 store[미 stɔːr, 영 stɔː] 가게; 보관하다

해석 길 건너의 식료품 가게가 문을 닫았나요?
(A) 일주일 정도 후에 그럴 거예요.
(B) 개점을 위해서요.
(C) 여기에 그것들을 보관하셔도 돼요.

해설 조동사 의문문
(A) [○] 일주일 정도 후에 그럴 것이라며, 식료품 가게가 아직 문을 닫지 않았음을 전달한 후 폐점 시기에 대한 추가 정보를 제공했으므로 정답이다.
(B) [×] 질문의 closed down(문을 닫았다)과 반대 의미인 grand opening(개점)을 사용하여 혼동을 준 오답이다.
(C) [×] 질문의 store(가게)를 '보관하다'라는 의미의 동사로 반복 사용하여 혼동을 준 오답이다.

28 [미국식 발음] 미국식 발음 → 호주식 발음

Is Mr. Irving coming to the dinner, or will he join us another time?
(A) He joined the organization a year ago.
(B) The clock in the restaurant is broken.
(C) He should be here momentarily.

---

join[dʒɔin] 함께하다, 가입하다
organization[미 ɔ̀rgənizéiʃən, 영 ɔ̀gənaizéiʃən] 단체
broken[미 bróukən, 영 brɔ́ukən] 고장 난
momentarily[미 mòuməntérəli, 영 mə́uməntérəli] 금방

해석 Mr. Irving이 저녁 식사에 오나요, 아니면 그는 다음 번에 함께하나요?
(A) 그는 그 단체에 일 년 전에 가입했어요.
(B) 음식점의 시계가 고장이 났어요.
(C) 그는 여기에 금방 올 겁니다.

해설 선택 의문문
(A) [×] 질문의 join(함께하다)을 '가입하다'라는 의미로 반복 사용하여 혼동을 준 오답이다.
(B) [×] 질문의 dinner(저녁 식사)와 관련 있는 restaurant(음식점)을 사용하여 혼동을 준 오답이다.
(C) [○] 그는 여기에 금방 올 것이라는 말로, Mr. Irving이 저녁 식사에 올 것임을 선택했으므로 정답이다.

29 [캐나다식 발음] 캐나다식 발음 → 영국식 발음

The hotel we reserved has an outdoor pool, right?
(A) Thank you for making a reservation with us.
(B) No, the gathering took place indoors.
(C) Yes, I just checked that information online.

---

outdoor[미 àutdɔ́r, 영 àutdɔ́ː] 야외의 gathering[gǽðəriŋ] 모임
take place 열리다, 일어나다 indoors[미 indɔ́ːrz, 영 ìndɔ́ːz] 실내에서

해석 우리가 예약한 호텔에는 야외 수영장이 있죠, 그렇죠?
(A) 예약해주셔서 감사합니다.
(B) 아뇨, 그 모임은 실내에서 열렸어요.
(C) 네, 제가 방금 그 정보를 온라인에서 확인했어요.

해설 **부가 의문문**

(A) [×] 질문의 reserved(예약했다)를 '예약'이라는 의미의 명사 reservation으로 반복 사용하여 혼동을 준 오답이다.

(B) [×] 질문의 outdoor(야외의)와 관련 있는 indoors(실내에서)를 사용하여 혼동을 준 오답이다.

(C) [○] Yes로 예약한 호텔에 야외 수영장이 있음을 전달한 후, 방금 그 정보를 온라인에서 확인했다는 부연 설명을 했으므로 정답이다.

30 🔊 호주식 발음 → 영국식 발음

The number of people visiting our Web site increased in July.

(A) Our online marketing must be working.

(B) Let's count all of the letters.

(C) Between April and May.

increase[inkríːs] 증가하다   working[미 wə́ːrkiŋ, 영 wə́ːkiŋ] 효과가 있는   count[kaunt] 세다

해석 우리의 웹사이트를 방문하는 사람들의 수가 7월에 증가했어요.
(A) 우리의 온라인 마케팅이 효과가 있는 것이 분명해요.
(B) 모든 글자들을 세어봅시다.
(C) 4월과 5월 사이에요.

해설 **평서문**

(A) [○] 온라인 마케팅이 효과가 있는 것이 분명하다며, 웹사이트 방문자 수가 증가한 원인에 대해 언급했으므로 정답이다.

(B) [×] 질문의 number(수)와 관련 있는 count(세다)를 사용하여 혼동을 준 오답이다.

(C) [×] 질문의 July(7월)와 관련 있는 April and May(4월과 5월)를 사용하여 혼동을 준 오답이다.

31 🔊 미국식 발음 → 캐나다식 발음

Did any of the diners ask for some more food?

(A) No one said anything to me.

(B) The diner on Jefferson Street.

(C) I think it tastes very good.

diner[미 dáinər, 영 dáinə] 식사하는 사람, 식당   ask for ~을 필요로 하다

해석 식사하시는 분들 중에 음식을 좀 더 필요로 하는 사람이 있었나요?
(A) 아무도 저에게 어떤 말도 하지 않았어요.
(B) Jefferson가에 있는 식당이요.
(C) 굉장히 맛있는 것 같아요.

해설 **조동사 의문문**

(A) [○] 아무도 어떤 말도 하지 않았다며, 음식을 좀 더 필요로 하는 사람이 없었음을 간접적으로 전달했으므로 정답이다.

(B) [×] 질문의 diners(식사하는 사람들)를 '식당'이라는 의미의 diner로 반복 사용하여 혼동을 준 오답이다.

(C) [×] 질문의 food(음식)와 관련 있는 tastes(맛이 ~하다)를 사용하여 혼동을 준 오답이다.

PART 3

32-34 🔊 호주식 발음 → 영국식 발음

Questions 32-34 refer to the following conversation.

M: [32]Can you move the image of the car a little to the right? The text is blocking the vehicle's logo, which needs to be displayed on the cover of this magazine.

W: Sure. I'll also have to increase the size of the picture so the full car is in view. [33]Are there any other adjustments you think should be made? This is our last chance before we present the design in our meeting today.

M: Everything else looks good to me. However, [34]I think we should stop by Ms. Anderson's office briefly and see if she has any additional comments.

W: [34]All right. Let's go there now.

block[미 blɑk, 영 blɔk] 가리다, 막다   display[displéi] 보이다   cover[미 kʌ́vər, 영 kʌ́və] 표지   adjustment[ədʒʌ́stmənt] 수정   present[préznt] 발표하다, 제출하다   stop by ~에 들르다   briefly[bríːfli] 잠시   additional[ədíʃənl] 추가적인

32-34번은 다음 대화에 관한 문제입니다.

남: [32]차 사진을 오른쪽으로 조금 옮겨줄 수 있나요? 글자가 차의 로고를 가리고 있는데, 로고는 이 잡지의 표지에 보여야 해요.

여: 물론이죠. 차 전체가 보이도록 사진의 크기도 키워야겠어요. [33]당신이 생각하기에 해야 될 또 다른 수정이 있나요? 이번이 오늘 우리가 회의에서 디자인을 발표하기 전 마지막 기회예요.

남: 다른 것들은 괜찮아 보여요. 하지만, [34]저는 우리가 Ms. Anderson의 사무실에 잠시 들러서 그녀에게 추가적인 의견이 있는지 확인해야 한다고 생각해요.

여: [34]알겠어요. 지금 거기로 가요.

32 특정 세부 사항 문제

해석 화자들은 무엇을 작업하고 있는가?
(A) 차량 디자인
(B) 쇼윈도 상품 진열
(C) 출판물 표지
(D) 회사 웹사이트

해설 질문의 핵심 어구(working on)와 관련된 내용을 주의 깊게 듣는다. 남자가 여자에게 "Can you move the image of the car ~? The text is blocking the vehicle's logo, which needs to be displayed on the cover of this magazine."이라며 차 사진을 옮겨줄 수 있는지 물은 후, 글자가 차의 로고를 가리고 있는데 로고는 이 잡지의 표지에 보여야 한다고 한 말을 통해 화자들이 출판물 표지를 작업하고 있음을 알 수 있다. 따라서 (C)가 정답이다.

어휘 window display 쇼윈도의 상품 진열   publication[미 pʌ̀bləkéiʃən, 영 pʌ̀blikéiʃən] 출판물

33 특정 세부 사항 문제

해석 여자는 남자에게 무엇에 대해 물어보는가?
(A) 서류가 언제 출력되어야 하는지
(B) 사진이 왜 삭제되어야 하는지
(C) 초안에 변경이 더 필요한지
(D) 회의에 누가 참석할 것인지

해설 대화에서 여자의 말을 주의 깊게 듣는다. 여자가 남자에게 "Are there any other adjustments you think should be made?"라며 남자

가 생각하기에 해야 될 또 다른 수정이 있는지를 물었다. 따라서 (C)가
정답이다.

패러프레이징
any other adjustments ~ should be made 해야 될 또 다른 수정
→ requires more changes 변경이 더 필요하다

어휘 remove[rimúːv] 삭제하다 draft[미 dræft, 영 drɑːft] 초안

34 다음에 할 일 문제

해석 화자들은 다음에 무엇을 할 것 같은가?
(A) 디자인을 선택한다.
(B) 사무실을 방문한다.
(C) 차를 구매한다.
(D) 차량을 살펴본다.

해설 대화의 마지막 부분을 주의 깊게 듣는다. 남자가 "I think we
should stop by Ms. Anderson's office briefly"라며 자신들이
Ms. Anderson의 사무실에 잠시 들러야 한다고 생각한다고 하자, 여
자가 "All right. Let's go there now."라며 남자의 말에 알겠다고 한
후, 지금 거기로 가자고 하였다. 이를 통해 화자들이 사무실을 방문할
것임을 알 수 있다. 따라서 (B)가 정답이다.

어휘 examine[igzǽmin] 살펴보다

35-37 🔊 캐나다식 발음 → 영국식 발음

Questions 35-37 refer to the following conversation.

> M: ³⁵I need help making some bouquets for a wedding.
> ³⁶Andria was supposed to assist me with the flower
> arrangements, but she is sick today. So I'm behind
> schedule, and I'm not sure whether I will be able to
> prepare the order on time.
> W: No problem. ³⁷I can start bringing flowers and
> ribbons into the workroom. Or would you like me
> to do something else instead?
> M: I already have plenty of materials in there. It would
> be great if you could start bunching and tying red
> and white roses together. The bouquets should
> have roughly an even number of each color. I really
> appreciate the assistance!
>
> assist[əsíst] 돕다 flower arrangement 꽃꽂이
> behind schedule 일정보다 늦은 on time 제시간에
> workroom[미 wɔ́ːrkruːm, 영 wɔ́ːkruːm] 작업실
> material[mətíəriəl] 재료 bunch[bʌntʃ] 모으다 tie[tai] 묶다
> roughly[rʌ́fli] 거의 even[íːvən] 같은

해석
35-37번은 다음 대화에 관한 문제입니다.

남: ³⁵저는 결혼식을 위한 부케 몇 개를 만드는 데 도움이 필요해요. ³⁶Andria
가 꽃꽂이를 도와주기로 했었지만, 그녀는 오늘 아프대요. 그래서 저는 일
정보다 늦어져 있어서, 제시간에 그 주문을 준비할 수 있을지 모르겠어요.
여: 문제없어요. ³⁷제가 작업실로 꽃과 리본을 가져오기 시작할게요. 아니면
제가 대신 다른 것을 하기를 원하나요?
남: 거기 안에는 이미 많은 재료들이 있어요. 당신이 빨간 장미와 하얀 장미를
같이 모아서 묶기 시작하면 좋을 것 같아요. 부케에는 각 색상이 거의 같
은 수로 있어야 해요. 도움을 줘서 정말 고마워요!

35 화자 문제

해석 화자들은 어디에서 일하는 것 같은가?
(A) 사무용품점
(B) 식당
(C) 식료품점

(D) 꽃가게

해설 대화에서 신분 및 직업과 관련된 표현을 놓치지 않고 듣는다. 남자가 "I
need help making some bouquets for a wedding."이라며 결혼
식을 위한 부케 몇 개를 만드는 데 도움이 필요하다고 한 후, 부케 제작
에 대한 내용으로 대화가 이어지고 있다. 이를 통해 화자들이 꽃가게
에서 일한다는 것을 알 수 있다. 따라서 (D)가 정답이다.

어휘 office supplies 사무용품 grocery store 식료품점

36 이유 문제

해석 남자는 왜 일정보다 늦어져 있는가?
(A) 동료가 부재중이다.
(B) 주문이 변경되었다.
(C) 행사가 앞당겨졌다.
(D) 배송이 늦었다.

해설 질문의 핵심 어구(behind schedule)가 언급된 주변을 주의 깊게
듣는다. 남자가 "Andria was supposed to assist me with the
flower arrangements, but she is sick today. So I'm behind
schedule"이라며 Andria가 꽃꽂이를 도와주기로 했지만 그녀가
오늘 아파서 일정보다 늦어져 있다고 한 말을 통해 Andria가 부재중
임을 알 수 있다. 따라서 (A)가 정답이다.

어휘 unavailable[ʌnəvéiləbl] 부재중인, 이용할 수 없는 ahead[əhéd] 앞으로

37 제안 문제

해석 여자는 무엇을 해주겠다고 제안하는가?
(A) 물품들을 가져온다.
(B) 고객과 이야기한다.
(C) 약속을 정한다.
(D) 포장지를 벗긴다.

해설 여자의 말에서 남자를 위해 해주겠다고 언급한 내용을 주의 깊게 듣
는다. 여자가 "I can start bringing flowers and ribbons into the
workroom."이라며 작업실로 꽃과 리본을 가져오기 시작하겠다고 하
였다. 따라서 (A)가 정답이다.

패러프레이징
bringing flowers and ribbons 꽃과 리본을 가져오기 → Get some
supplies 물품들을 가져오다

어휘 set up ~을 정하다, 세우다 remove[rimúːv] 벗기다, 치우다
package[pǽkidʒ] 포장지, 상자

38-40 🔊 영국식 발음 → 캐나다식 발음 → 호주식 발음

Questions 38-40 refer to the following conversation with three speakers.

> W: ³⁸Did you two get the e-mail from the administrative
> team? I read through it this morning, and
> apparently our building's parking lot will be
> reserved for clients starting next week.
> M1: I never saw that. Where are employees supposed
> to leave their cars?
> M2: At the garage on Elm Street . . . ³⁹The company
> will cover the cost of parking passes. We just
> need to submit a receipt each month.
> W: Personally, I'm really unhappy about the policy.
> ⁴⁰That garage is three blocks away. Getting to the
> office is going to be really inconvenient.
> M1: Yeah, you're right. We should ask our manager
> whether there is another option for parking.
>
> administrative[미 ædmínəstrèitiv, 영 ədmínistrəitiv] 관리의
> read through ~을 꼼꼼히 읽다

apparently[əpǽrəntli] 보아 하니, 분명히 **parking lot** 주차장
reserve[미 rizə́:rv, 영 rizə́:v] (~용으로) 지정하다
cover[미 kʌ́vər, 영 kʌ́və] (경비·손실을) 부담하다 **parking pass** 주차권
submit[səbmít] 제출하다 receipt[risíːt] 영수증
personally[미 pə́:rsənəli, 영 pə́:sənəli] 개인적으로
inconvenient[미 ìnkənví:njənt, 영 ìnkənví:niənt] 불편한

해석

38-40번은 다음 세 명의 대화에 관한 문제입니다.

여: ³⁸두 분은 관리팀으로부터 이메일을 받으셨나요? 오늘 아침에 제가 그 것을 꼼꼼히 읽어봤는데, 보아하니 우리 건물의 주차장이 다음 주부터 고객들 전용으로 지정될 거래요.

남1: 전 그것을 전혀 보지 못했어요. 직원들은 차를 어디에 두어야 하죠?

남2: Elm가에 있는 주차장에요... ³⁹회사가 주차권 비용을 부담해줄 거예요. 우리는 매달 영수증을 제출하기만 하면 돼요.

여: 개인적으로, 저는 이 방침에 대해 정말 불만족스러워요. ⁴⁰그 주차장은 세 블록 떨어져 있어요. 사무실까지 가는 것이 정말 불편할 거예요.

남1: 네, 맞아요. 우리 부장님께 주차에 대한 다른 방안이 있는지 여쭤보도록 해요.

38 특정 세부 사항 문제

해석 여자는 오늘 아침에 무엇을 했는가?
(A) 메시지를 읽었다.
(B) 다른 부서를 방문했다.
(C) 영수증들을 검토했다.
(D) 이메일을 보냈다.

해설 질문의 핵심 어구(this morning)가 언급된 주변을 주의 깊게 듣는 다. 여자가 남자들에게 "Did you two get the e-mail from the administrative team? I read through it this morning"이라며 관리팀으로부터 이메일을 받았는지를 물은 후, 자신이 오늘 아침에 그것을 꼼꼼히 읽어봤다고 하였다. 따라서 (A)가 정답이다.

어휘 review[rivjúː] 검토하다

39 언급 문제

해석 회사에 대해 무엇이 언급되는가?
(A) 다른 건물로 옮길 것이다.
(B) 주차장을 확장할 것이다.
(C) 직원들에게 요금을 상환해줄 것이다.
(D) 고객들을 위한 특별 행사를 열 것이다.

해설 질문의 핵심 어구(company)가 언급된 주변을 주의 깊게 듣는다. 남자2가 "The company will cover the cost of parking passes." 라며 회사가 주차권 비용을 부담해줄 것이라고 하였다. 따라서 (C) 가 정답이다.

패러프레이징
cover the cost 비용을 부담해주다 → reimburse ~ for a fee 요금을 상환해주다

어휘 expand[ikspǽnd] 확장하다
reimburse[미 rìːimbə́ːrs, 영 rìːimbə́ːs] 상환하다

40 문제점 문제

해석 여자는 무엇에 대해 걱정하는가?
(A) 이용권의 비용
(B) 시설의 위치
(C) 벌금의 액수
(D) 주차장의 크기

해설 여자의 말에서 부정적인 표현이 언급된 주변을 주의 깊게 듣는다. 여자가 "That garage is three blocks away. Getting to the office is going to be really inconvenient."라며 그 주차장은 세 블록 떨어져 있다고 한 후, 사무실까지 가는 것이 정말 불편할 것이라고 한 말을 통해 여자가 시설의 위치에 대해 걱정하고 있음을 알 수 있다. 따라서

(B)가 정답이다.

어휘 fine[fain] 벌금

41-43 🎧 미국식 발음 → 호주식 발음

Questions 41-43 refer to the following conversation.

W: ⁴¹This is Jennifer Burke calling from Cool Fit, the nation's leading athletic wear store. May I please speak with Catherine Brady?

M: I'm Ms. Brady's personal assistant. ⁴²May I ask what the purpose of this call is? She's not interested in speaking with any telemarketers.

W: Oh no, sir. I'm simply calling to let her know that ⁴³her membership with our company will expire at the end of next month. She can easily renew it, however, by providing me with some basic information. If you could please connect me to her, I'll help her do that.

leading[líːdiŋ] 최고의, 선도적인 **athletic wear** 운동복
personal assistant 개인 비서 expire[미 ikspáiər, 영 ikspáiə] 만료되다
renew[rinjúː] 연장하다

해석

41-43번은 다음 대화에 관한 문제입니다.

여: ⁴¹저는 국내 최고의 운동복 매장인 Cool Fit사에서 전화 드리는 Jennifer Burke입니다. Catherine Brady와 이야기할 수 있을까요?

남: 저는 Ms. Brady의 개인 비서입니다. ⁴²이 전화의 목적이 무엇인지 여쭤 봐도 되겠습니까? 그녀는 텔레마케터와 이야기하는 데 관심이 없습니다.

여: 아, 아닙니다. 저는 그저 ⁴³저희 회사에서의 그녀의 멤버십이 다음 달 말에 만료된다는 것을 알려드리려고 전화 드렸습니다. 하지만, 저에게 몇몇 기본 정보를 제공해주시면, 그녀는 이것을 쉽게 연장하실 수 있습니다. 저를 그녀에게 연결해주신다면, 그것을 하실 수 있도록 제가 도와드리겠습니다.

41 화자 문제

해석 여자는 어디에서 일하는가?
(A) 옷 가게
(B) 운동 시설
(C) 가구점
(D) 잡지 회사

해설 대화에서 신분 및 직업과 관련된 표현을 놓치지 않고 듣는다. 여자가 "This is Jennifer Burke calling from Cool Fit, the nation's leading athletic wear store."라며 국내 최고의 운동복 매장인 Cool Fit사에서 전화하는 Jennifer Burke라고 한 말을 통해 여자가 옷 가게에서 일한다는 것을 알 수 있다. 따라서 (A)가 정답이다.

어휘 fitness[fítnis] 운동, 건강

42 특정 세부 사항 문제

해석 남자는 무엇을 알고 싶어 하는가?
(A) 제품의 가격
(B) 매장의 위치
(C) 전화의 이유
(D) 프로젝트의 목적

해설 대화에서 남자의 말을 주의 깊게 듣는다. 남자가 여자에게 "May I ask what the purpose of this call is?"라며 이 전화의 목적이 무엇인지 물어봐도 되는지 물었다. 따라서 (C)가 정답이다.

43 특정 세부 사항 문제

해석 여자에 따르면, 무엇이 곧 만료되는가?
(A) 쿠폰
(B) 출판물 구독
(C) 멤버십
(D) 임대 계약

해설 여자의 말에서 질문의 핵심 어구(expire soon)와 관련된 내용을 주의 깊게 듣는다. 여자가 "her[Ms. Brady] membership with our company will expire at the end of next month"라며 Ms. Brady의 멤버십이 다음 달 말에 만료된다고 하였다. 따라서 (C)가 정답이다.

어휘 publication[미 pÀbləkéiʃən, 영 pÀblikéiʃən] 출판물
subscription[səbskrípʃən] 구독

44-46 [3배속] 호주식 발음 → 미국식 발음

Questions 44-46 refer to the following conversation.

M: Hello. This is Gerald Short calling from Actercorp. ⁴⁴I attended your organization's recent seminar on sales planning at the Fairfield Hotel. ⁴⁵I just want to ask if you can provide me with the video recording of the presentation Raymond Eston gave on profit forecasting. I'd like to have it for reference.
W: Yes, Mr. Short, I can do that. ⁴⁶Shall I send it to the same e-mail address you used to register for last month's event?
M: Actually, ⁴⁶I think it would be better to send it to my personal account at gerryshort@usermail.net.

attend[əténd] 참석하다   forecasting[미 fɔ́ːrkæstiŋ, 영 fɔ́ːkɑːstiŋ] 예측
for reference 참고를 위해, 참고로
register[미 rédʒistər, 영 rédʒistə] 등록하다   account[əkáunt] 계정

해석
44-46번은 다음 대화에 관한 문제입니다.

남: 안녕하세요. 저는 Actercorp사에서 전화 드리는 Gerald Short입니다. ⁴⁴저는 Fairfield 호텔에서 열린 판매 전략에 대한 귀사의 최근 세미나에 참석했습니다. Raymond Eston이 수익 예측에 대해 했던 ⁴⁵발표의 영상 녹화물을 당신이 제게 주실 수 있는지 여쭤보고 싶습니다. 참고를 위해 갖고 싶어서요.
여: 네, Mr. Short, 그렇게 해드릴 수 있습니다. ⁴⁶지난달 행사에 등록하기 위해 사용하셨던 이메일 주소와 같은 데로 보내드리면 될까요?
남: 실은, ⁴⁶제 개인 계정인 gerryshort@usermail.net으로 보내주시는 것이 더 좋을 것 같습니다.

44 언급 문제

해석 남자는 세미나에 대해 무엇을 말하는가?
(A) 호텔에서 열렸다.
(B) 소수의 사람들이 참석했다.
(C) Actercorp사가 후원했다.
(D) 디지털 출판업에 중점을 두었다.

해설 남자의 말에서 질문의 핵심 어구(seminar)가 언급된 주변을 주의 깊게 듣는다. 남자가 "I attended your organization's recent seminar ~ at the Fairfield Hotel."이라며 Fairfield 호텔에서 열린 여자의 회사의 최근 세미나에 참석했다고 하였다. 따라서 (A)가 정답이다.

어휘 be sponsored by ~가 후원하다   focus on ~에 중점을 두다
publishing[pÀbliʃiŋ] 출판업

45 특정 세부 사항 문제

해석 남자는 여자가 무엇을 그에게 주기를 원하는가?
(A) 연락처 정보
(B) 신청서
(C) 지시 사항
(D) 미디어 파일

해설 대화에서 남자의 말을 주의 깊게 듣는다. 남자가 여자에게 "I just want to ask if you can provide me with the video recording of the presentation"이라며 발표의 영상 녹화물을 여자가 자신에게 줄 수 있는지 물어보고 싶다고 하였다. 따라서 (D)가 정답이다.

어휘 registration form 신청서   direction[dirékʃən] 지시, 방향

46 요청 문제

해석 남자는 무엇을 요청하는가?
(A) 새 계정을 만드는 것
(B) 연속 강의에 가는 것
(C) 다른 이메일 주소를 사용하는 것
(D) 물품을 직접 전달하는 것

해설 대화의 중후반에서 요청과 관련된 표현이 포함된 문장을 주의 깊게 듣는다. 여자가 남자에게 "Shall I send it to the same e-mail address you used to register for last month's event?"라며 지난달 행사에 등록하기 위해 사용했던 이메일 주소와 같은 데로 보내주면 되는지 묻자, 남자가 "I think it would be better to send it to my personal account"라며 자신의 개인 계정으로 보내주는 것이 더 좋을 것 같다고 하였다. 이를 통해 남자가 다른 이메일 주소를 사용하는 것을 요청하고 있음을 알 수 있다. 따라서 (C)가 정답이다.

어휘 lecture series 연속 강의   in person 직접

47-49 [3배속] 캐나다식 발음 → 미국식 발음

Questions 47-49 refer to the following conversation.

M: Hello. I want some information about trips to Asia. I'm interested in the cultural tours of Thailand and Vietnam I saw in your advertisements.
W: Sure. ⁴⁷Our most popular tour provides guests with an opportunity to learn how to make traditional crafts in Vietnam.
M: ⁴⁷Maybe that's not the best choice. I've always been interested in exotic cuisine.
W: OK. We also have a tour that includes cooking classes in Thailand. ⁴⁸Here are the pamphlets about it.
M: That's perfect. Can I book that for next month?
W: Yes. ⁴⁹Please give me a moment to open our booking system.

opportunity[미 àpərtjúːnəti, 영 ɔ̀pətjúːnəti] 기회
traditional[trədíʃənl] 전통의   craft[미 kræft, 영 krɑːft] 공예
exotic[미 igzátik, 영 igzɔ́tik] 이국적인   cuisine[kwizíːn] 요리, 음식
pamphlet[pǽmflət] 소책자, 팸플릿

해석
47-49번은 다음 대화에 관한 문제입니다.

남: 안녕하세요. 저는 아시아 여행에 대한 정보가 필요해요. 저는 당신의 광고에서 본 태국과 베트남의 문화 관광에 관심이 있어요.
여: 물론입니다. ⁴⁷저희의 가장 인기 있는 관광은 손님들에게 베트남의 전통 공예품들을 만드는 방법을 배울 수 있는 기회를 제공합니다.
남: ⁴⁷아마 그게 최선의 선택은 아닐 수도 있어요. 저는 항상 이국적인 요리에 관심이 있었거든요.

여: 알겠습니다. 저희는 태국에서의 요리 수업을 포함하는 관광도 있어요. ⁴⁸여기 그것에 대한 소책자가 있습니다.

남: 완벽하네요. 제가 그것을 다음 달로 예약할 수 있을까요?

여: 네. ⁴⁹저희의 예약 시스템을 열 테니 잠시 기다려주세요.

47 의도 파악 문제

해석 남자는 "저는 항상 이국적인 요리에 관심이 있었거든요"라고 말할 때 무엇을 의도하는가?
(A) 다른 선택지를 원한다.
(B) 비용에 대해 걱정하지 않는다.
(C) 태국 음식을 먹어본 적이 없다.
(D) 광고된 할인 상품을 선호한다.

해설 질문의 인용어구(I've always been interested in exotic cuisine)가 언급된 주변을 주의 깊게 듣는다. 여자가 "Our most popular tour provides guests with an opportunity to learn how to make traditional crafts in Vietnam."이라며 자신들의 가장 인기 있는 관광은 손님들에게 베트남의 전통 공예품들을 만드는 방법을 배울 수 있는 기회를 제공하는 것이라고 하자, 남자가 "Maybe that's not the best choice."라며 아마 그게 최선의 선택은 아닐 수도 있다고 한 말을 통해 남자가 다른 선택지를 원한다는 것을 알 수 있다. 따라서 (A)가 정답이다.

어휘 taste[teist] 먹다, 맛보다 deal[diːl] 할인 상품, 물건

48 특정 세부 사항 문제

해석 여자는 남자에게 무엇을 주는가?
(A) 쿠폰
(B) 일정표
(C) 책자
(D) 표

해설 질문의 핵심 어구(woman give to the man)와 관련된 내용을 주의 깊게 듣는다. "Here are the pamphlets about it[a tour that includes cooking classes in Thailand]."이라며 여기 태국에서의 요리 수업을 포함하는 관광에 대한 소책자가 있다고 한 말을 통해 여자가 남자에게 책자를 주었음을 알 수 있다. 따라서 (C)가 정답이다.

패러프레이징
pamphlets 소책자 → Brochures 책자

어휘 brochure[미 brouʃúər, 영 bróuʃə] (안내·광고용) 책자

49 다음에 할 일 문제

해석 여자는 다음에 무엇을 할 것 같은가?
(A) 예약 시스템을 확인한다.
(B) 여행 일정표를 업데이트한다.
(C) 컴퓨터를 재시동한다.
(D) 책을 보낸다.

해설 대화의 마지막 부분을 주의 깊게 듣는다. 여자가 "Please give me a moment to open our booking system."이라며 자신들의 예약 시스템을 열 테니 잠시 기다려달라고 하였다. 이를 통해 여자가 예약 시스템을 확인할 것임을 알 수 있다. 따라서 (A)가 정답이다.

패러프레이징
booking 예약 → reservation 예약

어휘 timetable[táimteibl] 일정표 reboot[ríːbuːt] 재시동하다

50-52 ㈜ 영국식 발음 → 호주식 발음

Questions 50-52 refer to the following conversation.

W: Excuse me. I'm staying in Room 232 with my husband, but we'd like to be moved.

M: May I ask the reason?   ○

W: Well, ⁵⁰our room is right by the elevator, and we heard people coming and going all last night.

M: I'm so sorry for the inconvenience.

W: ⁵⁰It was very annoying. We couldn't even sleep.

M: I see. Well, ⁵¹it looks like I can move you to Room 240 later today. But I'm afraid the other rooms are all booked. How does that sound?

W: Good—as long as it's the same price as our current room.

M: ⁵²Usually, it's $20 more. That's because it's a premium room, not a standard. But I'll waive the extra costs in this case.

inconvenience[미 ìnkənvíːnjəns, 영 ìnkənvíːnjəns] 불편
annoying[ənɔ́iiŋ] 거슬리는 waive[weiv] (규칙 등을) 적용하지 않다

해석
50-52번은 다음 대화에 관한 문제입니다.

여: 실례합니다. 제가 232호 방에 남편과 함께 머무르고 있는데, 저희를 옮겨주셨으면 해요.

남: 이유를 여쭤봐도 되겠습니까?

여: 음, ⁵⁰저희 방이 엘리베이터 바로 옆에 있는데, 어제 밤새도록 사람들이 드나드는 소리를 들었어요.

남: 불편을 겪게 해드려 정말 죄송합니다.

여: ⁵⁰이것은 매우 거슬렸어요. 저희는 잠도 잘 수 없었어요.

남: 알겠습니다. 음, ⁵¹제가 오늘 이따가 240호 방으로 옮겨드릴 수 있을 것 같네요. 유감스럽지만 다른 방들은 모두 예약이 찼습니다. 어떠신가요?

여: 좋아요. 지금 저희 방과 같은 가격이기만 하면요.

남: ⁵²보통, 이것은 20달러가 더 듭니다. 이는 스탠더드실이 아니라 프리미엄실이기 때문이에요. 하지만 제가 이번 경우에는 추가 비용을 적용하지 않겠습니다.

50 문제점 문제

해석 여자는 무슨 문제를 언급하는가?
(A) 시설에 비품들이 모자란다.
(B) 호텔 예약이 없어졌다.
(C) 방이 시끄러운 곳에 있다.
(D) 계산서가 정확하지 않다.

해설 여자의 말에서 부정적인 표현이 언급된 주변을 주의 깊게 듣는다. 여자가 "our room is right by the elevator, and we heard people coming and going all last night"라며 자신들의 방이 엘리베이터 바로 옆에 있는데 어제 밤새도록 사람들이 드나드는 소리를 들었다고 한 후, "It was very annoying. We couldn't even sleep."라며 이것은 매우 거슬려서 잠도 잘 수 없었다고 하였다. 이를 통해 방이 시끄러운 곳에 있음을 알 수 있다. 따라서 (C)가 정답이다.

어휘 be short on ~이 부족하다 supplies[səpláiz] 비품, 저장품
bill[bil] 계산서 inaccurate[미 inǽkjərit, 영 inǽkjərət] 정확하지 않은

51 추론 문제

해석 240호 방에 대해 무엇이 암시되는가?
(A) 오늘 밤에 예약이 되어있다.
(B) 유일하게 이용 가능한 방이다.
(C) 최근에 보수되었다.
(D) 복도 끝에 위치해 있다.

해설 질문의 핵심 어구(Room 240)가 언급된 주변을 주의 깊게 듣는다. 남자가 "it looks like I can move you to Room 240 later today. But I'm afraid the other rooms are all booked."라며 오늘 이따가 240호 방으로 옮겨줄 수 있을 것 같다고 한 후, 유감스럽지만 다른 방들은 모두 예약이 찼다고 한 말을 통해 240호 방이 유일하게 이용 가능한 방인 것을 알 수 있다. 따라서 (B)가 정답이다.

어휘 available[əvéiləbl] 이용 가능한 be located at ~에 위치해 있다

52 제안 문제

해석 남자는 무엇을 해주겠다고 제안하는가?
(A) 정식으로 이의를 제기한다.
(B) 수리를 요청한다.
(C) 관리자를 찾는다.
(D) 무료 업그레이드를 제공한다.

해설 남자의 말에서 여자를 위해 해주겠다고 언급한 내용을 주의 깊게 듣는다. 남자가 "Usually, it[Room 240]'s $20 more. That's because it's a premium room, not a standard. But I'll waive the extra costs in this case."라며 보통 240호 방은 20달러가 더 드는데 이는 스탠더드실이 아니라 프리미엄실이기 때문이라고 한 후, 하지만 이번 경우에는 추가 비용을 적용하지 않겠다고 한 말을 통해 남자가 무료 업그레이드를 제공할 것임을 알 수 있다. 따라서 (D)가 정답이다.

어휘 file[fail] (고소·신청 등을) 정식으로 제기하다
formal[미 fɔ́:rməl, 영 fɔ́:məl] 정식의 complaint[kəmpléint] 이의, 항의
supervisor[미 súːpərvaizer, 영 súːpəvaizə] 관리자

53-55 [듣기] 미국식 발음 → 호주식 발음

Questions 53-55 refer to the following conversation.

W: Hello. ⁵³I bought boots here yesterday, but I think I was overcharged. A sales clerk told me to speak to someone at the customer service desk. Here's my receipt.

M: Just a minute . . . Um, I don't see the problem. The amount you paid matches the price of that product.

W: But I belong to the Elite Loyalty Club, so shouldn't I receive a 10 percent discount?

M: Oh, ⁵⁴I'm sorry. That program was just launched last week, and our employees sometimes forget to ask whether customers are members.

W: You'll refund the amount that I was overcharged to my credit card, then?

M: Of course. ⁵⁵I just need you to fill out this form.

overcharge[미 òuvərtʃáːrdʒ, 영 əuvətʃáːdʒ] (금액을 너무 많이) 청구하다
match[mætʃ] 일치하다 belong to (클럽·조직에) 소속이다
launch[lɔːntʃ] 시작하다 fill out ~을 작성하다

해석
53-55번은 다음 대화에 관한 문제입니다.

여: 안녕하세요. ⁵³제가 어제 여기서 부츠를 샀는데, 금액이 더 청구된 것 같아요. 판매원이 저에게 고객 서비스 데스크에 있는 사람과 이야기하라고 했어요. 여기 제 영수증이 있어요.
남: 잠시만요... 음, 저는 무엇이 문제인지 모르겠습니다. 고객님께서 지불하신 금액은 그 상품의 가격과 일치합니다.
여: 하지만 저는 Elite Loyalty Club 소속인데, 그럼 10퍼센트 할인을 받아야 하지 않나요?
남: 아, ⁵⁴죄송합니다. 그 프로그램이 지난주에 막 시작되어서, 저희 직원들이 종종 고객님께서 회원이신지 여쭤보는 것을 잊어버립니다.
여: 그럼, 제 신용카드로 더 청구된 금액을 환불해주시는 건가요?
남: 물론입니다. ⁵⁵이 양식만 작성해주십시오.

53 장소 문제

해석 대화는 어디에서 일어나고 있는 것 같은가?
(A) 생산 공장에서
(B) 소매점에서
(C) 금융 기관에서
(D) 여행사에서

해설 대화에서 장소와 관련된 표현을 놓치지 않고 듣는다. 여자가 "I bought boots here yesterday ~. A sales clerk told me to speak to someone at the customer service desk."라며 어제 여기서 부츠를 샀다고 한 후, 판매원이 고객 서비스 데스크에 있는 사람과 이야기하라고 했다고 한 말을 통해 소매점에서 대화가 일어나고 있음을 알 수 있다. 따라서 (B)가 정답이다.

어휘 production facility 생산 공장 financial institution 금융 기관
travel agency 여행사

54 의도 파악 문제

해석 남자는 왜 "그 프로그램이 지난주에 막 시작되어서"라고 말하는가?
(A) 요청에 대한 우려를 나타내기 위해
(B) 실수를 해명하기 위해
(C) 새로운 서비스를 홍보하기 위해
(D) 지연에 대해 사과하기 위해

해설 질문의 인용어구(That program was just launched last week)가 언급된 주변을 주의 깊게 듣는다. 남자가 여자에게 "I'm sorry. ~ and our employees sometimes forget to ask whether customers are members."라며 죄송하다고 한 후, 직원들이 종종 고객들이 회원인지 물어보는 것을 잊어버린다고 한 말을 통해 실수를 해명하기 위함임을 알 수 있다. 따라서 (B)가 정답이다.

어휘 concern[미 kənsə́:rn, 영 kənsə́:n] 우려
promote[미 prəmóut, 영 prəmə́ut] 홍보하다 delay[diléi] 지연

55 요청 문제

해석 남자는 여자에게 무엇을 하라고 요청하는가?
(A) 신용카드를 제시한다.
(B) 나중에 다시 온다.
(C) 다른 상품을 착용해본다.
(D) 서류를 작성한다.

해설 남자의 말에서 요청과 관련된 표현이 언급된 다음을 주의 깊게 듣는다. 남자가 여자에게 "I just need you to fill out this form."이라며 이 양식만 작성해달라고 하였다. 따라서 (D)가 정답이다.

패러프레이징
fill out ~ form 양식을 작성하다 → Complete a document 서류를 작성하다

어휘 merchandise[미 má:rtʃəndàiz, 영 má:tʃəndaiz] 상품
complete[kəmplíːt] 작성하다

56-58 [듣기] 영국식 발음 → 캐나다식 발음 → 미국식 발음

Questions 56-58 refer to the following conversation with three speakers.

W1: ⁵⁶We are looking for someone to lend us a hand at the booth for our energy drink here at the Extreme Sports Expo. Have you done any promotional work like that?

M: Yes. I have worked at trade shows and have done food demonstrations.

W1: Great. I think you can start immediately as you already have experience. ⁵⁶Ms. Jones, could you show Sam where our booth is?

W2: Certainly. Follow me. ⁵⁷You will set up and restock the drinks.

M: It's a little chilly in here, Ms. Jones. Can I wear my coat?

W2: Actually, ⁵⁸I'll get the uniform you need to wear now. It includes a jacket. That should be sufficient.

lend a hand 도움을 주다
promotional [미 prəmóuʃənl, 영 prəmóuʃənl] 홍보의
demonstration[dèmənstréiʃən] 시연 set up 내놓다, 설치하다
restock[riːstáːk] 다시 채우다 chilly[tʃíli] 쌀쌀한, 냉랭한
sufficient[səfíʃənt] 충분한

해석
56-58번은 다음 세 명의 대화에 관한 문제입니다.

여1: 56저희는 여기 익스트림 스포츠 박람회의 에너지 음료 부스에서 저희에게 도움을 줄 사람을 찾고 있어요. 당신은 그런 홍보 업무를 해본 적이 있나요?

남: 네. 저는 무역 박람회에서 일한 적이 있고 음식 시연도 해봤어요.

여1: 좋네요. 당신은 이미 경험이 있으시니까 바로 시작할 수 있을 것 같네요. 56Ms. Jones, 우리 부스가 어디 있는지 Sam에게 보여주시겠어요?

여2: 물론이죠. 저를 따라오세요. 57당신은 음료를 내놓고 다시 채울 거예요.

남: 여기는 조금 쌀쌀하네요, Ms. Jones. 제 코트를 입어도 될까요?

여2: 사실, 58제가 지금 당신이 입어야 할 유니폼을 가져올 거예요. 그것은 재킷을 포함해요. 그러면 충분할 거예요.

56 장소 문제
해석 대화는 어디에서 일어나고 있는 것 같은가?
(A) 제조 시설에서
(B) 커피숍에서
(C) 박람회장에서
(D) 헬스장에서

해설 대화에서 장소와 관련된 표현을 놓치지 않고 듣는다. 여자1이 "We are looking for someone to lend us a hand at the booth for our energy drink here at the Extreme Sports Expo."라며 여기 익스트림 스포츠 박람회의 에너지 음료 부스에서 자신들에게 도움을 줄 사람을 찾고 있다고 한 후, "Ms. Jones, could you show Sam where our booth is?"라며 여자2[Ms. Jones]에게 부스가 어디 있는지 남자[Sam]에게 보여주라고 요청한 것을 통해 대화가 박람회장에서 일어나고 있음을 알 수 있다. 따라서 (C)가 정답이다.

패러프레이징
Expo 박람회 → exposition 박람회

어휘 exposition center 박람회장

57 특정 세부 사항 문제
해석 남자의 새로운 업무는 무엇으로 이루어져 있는가?
(A) 새로운 도구를 시연하는 것
(B) 부스를 세우는 것
(C) 음료들을 준비하는 것
(D) 온도를 확인하는 것

해설 질문의 핵심 어구(new assignment)와 관련된 내용을 주의 깊게 듣는다. 여자2가 남자에게 "You will set up and restock the drinks."라며 남자가 음료를 내놓고 다시 채울 것이라고 한 말을 통해 남자의 새로운 업무가 음료들을 준비하는 것으로 이루어져 있음을 알 수 있다. 따라서 (C)가 정답이다.

어휘 consist of ~으로 이루어지다 erect[irékt] 세우다, 설립하다
organize[미 ɔ́ːrɡənàiz, 영 ɔ́ːɡənaiz] 준비하다, 조직하다

58 다음에 할 일 문제
해석 Ms. Jones는 다음에 무엇을 할 것인가?
(A) 작업복을 제공한다.
(B) 매뉴얼을 출력한다.
(C) 지불금을 준비한다.
(D) 새로운 음료를 맛본다.

해설 대화의 마지막 부분을 주의 깊게 듣는다. 여자2[Ms. Jones]가 "I'll get the uniform you need to wear now"라며 남자가 입어야 할 유니폼을 가져올 것이라고 하였다. 따라서 (A)가 정답이다.

패러프레이징
uniform 유니폼 → work clothes 작업복

59-61 [3녀] 미국식 발음 → 캐나다식 발음

Questions 59-61 refer to the following conversation.

W: Doug, can you give me some help with this report? I'm trying to create a spreadsheet, but I'm not that familiar with this document format. 59My deadline is this weekend, so I'm kind of pressed for time.

M: Sure, Sarah. I can take a look at it. What are you having trouble with?

W: Well, 60I want to list these sales amounts from smallest to largest. But the data gets mixed up when I try to do it.

M: You just need to click on this green button. There . . . everything should be ordered how you want it now. Also, 61if you have similar issues with using this program, the Web site for the spreadsheet software offers lots of helpful tips.

format[미 fɔ́ːrmæt, 영 fɔ́ːmæt] 형식 familiar with ~에 익숙한
be pressed for time 시간에 쫓기다 take a look ~을 한 번 보다
list[list] (특정 순서로) 열거하다 mix up ~을 뒤섞다

해석
59-61번은 다음 대화에 관한 문제입니다.

여: Doug, 이 보고서에 도움을 좀 주실 수 있나요? 저는 스프레드시트를 만들려고 하는데, 이 문서 형식에 익숙지 않아요. 59제 마감일이 이번 주말이라서, 시간에 조금 쫓기고 있어요.

남: 물론이죠, Sarah. 제가 한 번 볼게요. 무엇에 어려움을 겪고 있나요?

여: 음, 60저는 이 매출액들을 제일 작은 것부터 큰 것 순으로 열거하고 싶어요. 하지만 제가 그렇게 하려고 하면 데이터가 뒤섞여요.

남: 이 녹색 버튼을 누르시기만 하면 돼요. 이렇게요... 이제 모든 게 당신이 원하는 것처럼 정렬이 됐을 거예요. 또, 61이 프로그램을 사용하는 데 비슷한 문제가 있을 경우에는, 스프레드시트 소프트웨어의 웹사이트가 유용한 정보들을 많이 제공해줘요.

59 언급 문제
해석 여자는 보고서에 대해 무엇을 말하는가?
(A) 그녀의 상사에 의해 만들어졌다.
(B) 이번 주에 제출되어야 한다.
(C) 정확하지 않은 정보를 포함한다.
(D) 회의를 위해 출력되어야 한다.

해설 여자의 말에서 질문의 핵심 어구(report)와 관련된 내용을 주의 깊게 듣는다. 여자가 "My deadline is this weekend"라며 마감일이 이번 주말이라고 하였다. 따라서 (B)가 정답이다.

어휘 include[inklúːd] 포함하다
inaccurate[미 inǽkjərit, 영 inǽkjərət] 정확하지 않은
gathering[ɡǽðəriŋ] 회의, 모임

60 특정 세부 사항 문제
해석 여자는 무엇을 하고 싶어 하는가?
(A) 복사를 한다.
(B) 계산을 한다.
(C) 웹사이트에 파일을 올린다.
(D) 수치들을 재배열한다.

해설 대화에서 여자의 말을 주의 깊게 듣는다. 여자가 "I want to list these sales amounts from smallest to largest"라며 이 매출액들을 제일 작은 것부터 큰 것 순으로 열거하고 싶다고 하였다. 따라서 (D)가 정답

이다.

패러프레이징

list ~ sales amounts from smallest to largest 매출액들을 제일 작은 것부터 큰 순으로 열거하다 → Rearrange some figures 수치들을 재배열하다

어휘 post[미 poust, 영 pəust] (웹사이트에 정보·사진을) 올리다
rearrange[rì:əréindʒ] 재배열하다   figure[미 fígjər, 영 fígə] 수치, 숫자

61 특정 세부 사항 문제

해석 남자에 따르면, 여자는 온라인에서 무엇을 찾을 수 있는가?
(A) 신청서
(B) 프로그램에 대한 도움
(C) 주문에 대한 정보
(D) 샘플 소프트웨어

해설 남자의 말에서 질문의 핵심 어구(online)와 관련된 내용을 주의 깊게 듣는다. 남자가 여자에게 "if you have similar issues with using this program, the Web site for the spreadsheet software offers lots of helpful tips"라며 이 프로그램을 사용하는 데 비슷한 문제가 있을 경우에는 스프레드시트 소프트웨어의 웹사이트가 유용한 정보들을 많이 제공해준다고 하였다. 따라서 (B)가 정답이다.

어휘 registration form 신청서   assistance[əsístəns] 도움

62-64 [3배] 영국식 발음 → 캐나다식 발음

Questions 62-64 refer to the following conversation and schedule.

W: Carl, ⁶²have you confirmed the agenda for our automotive engineering conference? Several industry executives will be there next month, so I want to make sure everything's well organized.

M: ⁶²Not yet. There's just one issue with the order of presentations. I was just informed that ⁶³the first speaker won't arrive until 12 P.M. I guess there was a problem with his train reservation, so he has to take a later one from Boston than originally planned.

W: Well, we'll need to switch his time with another speaker's, then. ⁶⁴Could you get in touch with one of the afternoon speakers? How about Fred Jones or Peter Wright?

M: OK. I'll give them both a call. Once I confirm the change, I'll update the schedule and e-mail it to you.

confirm[미 kənfə́:rm, 영 kənfə́:m] 확정하다
agenda[ədʒéndə] 의사 일정(회의 안건을 정해 놓은 차례)
automotive[미 ɔ̀:təmóutiv, 영 ɔ̀:təmə́utiv] 자동차의
conference[미 kɑ́nfərəns, 영 kɔ́nfərəns] 회의, 학회
executive[미 igzékjutiv, 영 igzékjətiv] 대표, 이사진
organized[미 ɔ́:rgənàizd, 영 ɔ́:gənaizd] (~하게) 계획된   issue[íʃu:] 문제
inform[미 infɔ́:rm, 영 infɔ́:m] 통지하다   originally[ərídʒənəli] 원래
switch[switʃ] 바꾸다   get in touch with ~와 연락하다

해석
62-64번은 다음 대화와 일정표에 관한 문제입니다.

여: Carl, ⁶²우리의 자동차 공학 기술 회의에 대한 의사 일정을 확정했나요? 다음 달에 여러 업계 대표들이 그곳에 있을 것이라서, 저는 모든 것이 잘 계획되어 있는지 확실히 하고 싶어요.

남: ⁶²아직이요. 발표 순서에만 문제가 하나 있어요. 저는 방금 ⁶³첫 번째 발표자가 오후 12시나 되어서야 도착할 것이라고 통지받았어요. 그의 열차 예

약에 문제가 있어서, 보스턴에서 원래 계획했던 것보다 더 늦게 출발하는 열차를 타야 하는 것 같아요.

여: 음, 그럼, 그의 시간을 다른 발표자의 것과 바꿔야겠네요. ⁶⁴당신이 오후 발표자들 중 한 명과 연락해볼 수 있나요? Fred Jones나 Peter Wright 는 어때요?

남: 알았어요. 제가 둘 다에게 전화해볼게요. 변경 사항을 확정하고 나면, 제가 일정표를 업데이트해서 당신에게 이메일로 보내드릴게요.

발표 일정표	
발표자	시간
⁶³John Foreman	오전 9:00 – 오전 10:30
Harry Garcia	오전 10:30 – 오후 12:00
Fred Jones	오후 1:30 – 오후 3:00
Peter Wright	오후 3:00 – 오후 4:30

62 주제 문제

해석 화자들은 주로 무엇에 대해 이야기하고 있는가?
(A) 행사 장소
(B) 발표 일정
(C) 신청의 마감기한
(D) 회의의 주제

해설 대화의 주제를 묻는 문제이므로, 대화의 초반을 주의 깊게 들은 후 전체 맥락을 파악한다. 여자가 남자에게 "have you confirmed the agenda for our automotive engineering conference?"라며 자동차 공학 기술 회의에 대한 의사 일정을 확정했는지 묻자, 남자가 "Not yet. There's just one issue with the order of presentations."라며 아직이라며 발표 순서에만 문제가 하나 있다고 한 후, 발표 일정에 대한 내용으로 대화가 이어지고 있다. 따라서 (B)가 정답이다.

63 시각 자료 문제

해석 시각 자료를 보아라. 누가 보스턴에서 올 것인가?
(A) John Foreman
(B) Harry Garcia
(C) Fred Jones
(D) Peter Wright

해설 제시된 일정표의 정보를 확인한 후 질문의 핵심 어구(Boston)가 언급된 주변을 주의 깊게 듣는다. 남자가 "the first speaker won't arrive until 12 P.M. ~ he has to take a later one[train] from Boston"이라며 첫 번째 발표자가 오후 12시나 되어서야 도착할 것이라고 한 후, 그가 보스턴에서 더 늦게 출발하는 열차를 타야 한다고 하였으므로, 첫 번째 발표자인 John Foreman이 보스턴에서 올 것임을 일정표에서 알 수 있다. 따라서 (A)가 정답이다.

64 요청 문제

해석 여자는 남자에게 무엇을 하라고 요청하는가?
(A) 추가 초대장들을 보낸다.
(B) 발표자들에게 연락한다.
(C) 장소 관리자와 만난다.
(D) 마감기한을 연장한다.

해설 여자의 말에서 요청과 관련된 표현이 언급된 다음을 주의 깊게 듣는다. 여자가 남자에게 "Could you get in touch with one of the afternoon speakers?"라며 오후 발표자들 중 한 명과 연락해볼 수 있는지 물었다. 따라서 (B)가 정답이다.

어휘 send out ~을 보내다, 발송하다   extend[iksténd] 연장하다

Questions 65-67 refer to the following conversation and map.

W: Good morning, Alan. ⁶⁵I saw that the city maintenance department put a sign on my front door about a plan to spray for weeds in Wrigley Park. Did you get the same one?

M: I did, and ⁶⁶I'm worried about it. The spray can be harmful to people's health.

W: I agree. Also, it's not necessary, since there aren't very many weeds growing in the park.

M: Well, there are some in ⁶⁷the area where the children usually play . . . you know, right between the stream and the picnic area.

W: True, but I'd still prefer not to have chemicals used there.

maintenance[méintənəns] 유지 (관리) sign[sain] 게시물, 간판
spray[sprei] 뿌리다; (살충제·향수 등의) 분무 weeds[wiːdz] 잡초
harmful[미 háːrmfəl, 영 háːmfəl] 해로운 stream[striːm] 개울
chemical[kémikəl] 화학 물질

해석

65-67번은 다음 대화와 지도에 관한 문제입니다.

여: 안녕하세요, Alan. ⁶⁵저는 도시 유지 관리부가 Wrigley 공원에 있는 잡초에 살충제를 뿌리려는 계획에 대해 제 대문에 게시물을 붙여둔 것을 봤어요. 당신도 같은 것을 받았나요?

남: 저도 받았는데, ⁶⁶그것에 대해 걱정돼요. 살충제를 뿌리는 것은 사람들의 건강에 해로울 수 있어요.

여: 저도 동의해요. 또한, 그 공원에 자라고 있는 잡초들이 그렇게 많지 않기 때문에, 필요하지 않아요.

남: 음, ⁶⁷아이들이 주로 노는 장소에 좀 있기는 해요... 그러니까, 개울과 소풍 구역 바로 그 사이에요.

여: 맞아요, 하지만 그래도 저는 거기에 화학 물질이 쓰이지 않으면 해요.

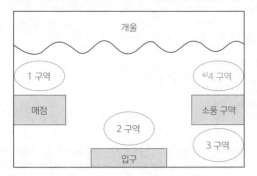

65 특정 세부 사항 문제

해석 여자는 최근에 무엇을 했는가?
(A) 새 문을 설치했다.
(B) 통지서를 읽었다.
(C) 잔디 관리 서비스를 신청했다.
(D) 정비원에게 연락했다.

해설 질문의 핵심 어구(recently do)와 관련된 내용을 주의 깊게 듣는다. 여자가 "I saw that the city maintenance department put a sign on my front door about a plan to spray for weeds in Wrigley Park."라며 도시 유지 관리부가 Wrigley 공원에 있는 잡초에 살충제를 뿌리려는 계획에 대해 대문에 게시물을 붙여둔 것을 봤다고 한 말을 통해 여자가 최근에 통지서를 읽었다는 것을 알 수 있다. 따라

서 (B)가 정답이다.

어휘 notification[미 nòutəfikéiʃən, 영 nèutifikéiʃən] 통지(서), 알림
lawn care 잔디 관리

66 문제점 문제

해석 남자는 왜 걱정하는가?
(A) 공무원들이 요청을 거절했다.
(B) 도시 계획이 부정적인 영향을 미칠 수 있다.
(C) 놀이 구역이 폐쇄되었다.
(D) 유지 관리 작업이 완료되지 않았다.

해설 남자의 말에서 부정적인 표현이 언급된 다음을 주의 깊게 듣는다. 남자가 "I'm worried about it[plan]. The spray can be harmful to people's health."라며 계획에 대해 걱정된다고 한 후, 살충제를 뿌리는 것은 사람들의 건강에 해로울 수 있다고 하였다. 따라서 (B)가 정답이다.

패러프레이징
harmful to people's health 사람들의 건강에 해로운 → have a negative impact 부정적인 영향을 미치다

어휘 official[əfíʃəl] 공무원 reject[ridʒékt] 거절하다
impact[ímpækt] 영향 close down 폐쇄하다

67 시각 자료 문제

해석 시각 자료를 보아라. 아이들은 주로 어디에서 노는가?
(A) 1 구역
(B) 2 구역
(C) 3 구역
(D) 4 구역

해설 제시된 지도의 정보를 확인한 후 질문의 핵심 어구(children usually play)가 언급된 주변을 주의 깊게 듣는다. 남자가 "the area where the children usually play ~, right between the stream and the picnic area"라며 아이들이 주로 노는 장소가 개울과 소풍 구역 바로 그 사이라고 하였으므로, 아이들이 주로 4 구역에서 노는 것을 지도에서 알 수 있다. 따라서 (D)가 정답이다.

Questions 68-70 refer to the following conversation and graph.

M: Michelle, can you look over the results of the customer questionnaires we released . . . the ones about our new speaker system, BeatBox 2?

W: I already did. ⁶⁸I was surprised to learn that it isn't as popular as the previous model, though. Look for yourself.

M: I see. I guess we need to figure out which aspect of the BeatBox 2 to improve upon first.

W: ⁶⁹The aspect with the worst customer satisfaction level can be easily adjusted, so let's discuss the second lowest first.

M: Yeah, that makes sense. ⁷⁰Can you give me a hard copy of this graph? I want to show it to our director this afternoon.

W: Sure thing.

look over ~을 검토하다
questionnaire[미 kwèstʃənéər, 영 kwèstʃənéə] 설문지
figure out ~을 알아내다 aspect[æspekt] 측면
improve[imprúːv] 개선하다 customer satisfaction 고객 만족
adjust[ədʒʌ́st] 조정하다, 조절하다 hard copy 출력물

68-70번은 다음 대화와 그래프에 관한 문제입니다.

남: Michelle, 우리가 배포했던 고객 설문지들의 결과를 검토해줄 수 있나요... 새로운 스피커 시스템인 BeatBox 2에 대한 것이요.

여: 이미 했어요. 그런데 ⁶⁸그것이 이전 모델만큼 인기가 많지 않다는 것을 알고 놀랐어요. 직접 보세요.

남: 그렇군요. BeatBox 2의 어떤 측면을 먼저 개선할지 알아내야겠네요.

여: ⁶⁹고객 만족도 수준이 가장 낮은 측면은 쉽게 조정될 수 있으니, 먼저 두 번째로 낮은 것부터 논의합시다.

남: 네, 맞는 말이에요. ⁷⁰제게 이 그래프의 출력물을 주실 수 있나요? 이것을 오늘 오후에 우리 이사님께 보여드리고 싶어요.

여: 물론이죠.

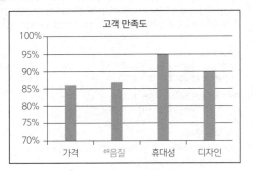

고객 만족도

| | 가격 | ⁶⁹음질 | 휴대성 | 디자인 |

68 이유 문제

해석 여자는 왜 놀랐는가?
(A) 회사가 기기의 생산을 중단했다.
(B) 스피커 시스템이 너무 비싸다.
(C) 제품이 상대적으로 인기가 없다.
(D) 회사가 회수를 발표했다.

해설 질문의 핵심 어구(surprised)가 언급된 주변을 주의 깊게 듣는다. 여자가 "I was surprised to learn that it[BeatBox 2] isn't as popular as the previous model"이라며 BeatBox 2가 이전 모델만큼 인기가 많지 않다는 것을 알고 놀랐다고 하였다. 따라서 (C)가 정답이다.

어휘 production[prədʌ́kʃən] 생산 device[diváis] 기기
relatively[rélətivli] 상대적으로 recall[rikɔ́ːl] 회수; 회수하다

69 시각 자료 문제

해석 시각 자료를 보아라. 어느 측면이 즉시 다뤄질 것 같은가?
(A) 가격
(B) 음질
(C) 휴대성
(D) 디자인

해설 제시된 그래프의 정보를 확인한 후 질문의 핵심 어구(aspect ~ be addressed immediately)와 관련된 내용을 주의 깊게 듣는다. 여자가 "The aspect with the worst customer satisfaction level can be easily adjusted, so let's discuss the second lowest first."라며 고객 만족도 수준이 가장 낮은 측면은 쉽게 조정될 수 있으니 먼저 두 번째로 낮은 것부터 논의하자고 하였으므로, 음질이 즉시 다뤄질 것임을 그래프에서 알 수 있다. 따라서 (B)가 정답이다.

어휘 portability[미 pɔ̀ːrtəbíləti, 영 pɔ̀ːtəbíləti] 휴대성

70 다음에 할 일 문제

해석 남자는 오늘 오후에 무엇을 할 것 같은가?
(A) 이사와 만난다.
(B) 고객들과 이야기한다.
(C) 도표들을 복사한다.
(D) 신제품을 시험해본다.

해설 질문의 핵심 어구(this afternoon)가 언급된 주변을 주의 깊게 듣는다. 남자가 여자에게 "Can you give me a hard copy of this graph? I want to show it to our director this afternoon."이라며 이 그래프의 출력물을 줄 수 있는지 물은 후, 이것을 오늘 오후에 이사에게 보여주고 싶다고 한 말을 통해 남자가 오늘 오후에 이사와 만날 것임을 알 수 있다. 따라서 (A)가 정답이다.

PART 4

71-73 [호주] 영국식 발음

Questions 71-73 refer to the following introduction.

Good morning, everyone. I'm delighted to introduce Mr. Juan Hernandez. ⁷¹Mr. Hernandez is taking over as the general manager of this branch of Homerson Bank. He has been employed by a number of financial firms during his 20 years in the industry. Most recently, ⁷²he led a training session for administrative workers at a major bank in New York. To allow Mr. Hernandez to get to know staff better, ⁷³a dinner is being held at Norman's Restaurant over on Rexford Drive this evening. You're all invited, so please try to make it.

delighted[diláitid] 기쁜 **take over as** ~직을 맡다
branch[미 brænʃ, 영 brɑːnʃ] 지점 **employ**[implɔ́i] 고용하다
a number of 많은 **training session** 연수 과정
administrative[미 ædmínəstrèitiv, 영 ədmínistrəitiv] 행정의
get to know ~을 알게 되다 **make it** 참석하다

71-73번은 다음 소개에 관한 문제입니다.

안녕하세요, 여러분. 저는 Mr. Juan Hernandez를 소개하게 되어 기쁩니다. ⁷¹Mr. Hernandez는 이 Homerson 은행 지점의 총 지점장직을 맡을 것입니다. 그는 이 업계에서의 20년 동안 많은 금융 회사들에 고용되어 왔습니다. 가장 최근에, ⁷²그는 뉴욕에 있는 한 주요 은행에서 행정 직원들을 위한 연수 과정을 이끌었습니다. Mr. Hernandez가 직원들을 더 잘 알게 되도록 하기 위해, ⁷³오늘 저녁에 Rexford로에 있는 Norman's 식당에서 만찬이 열립니다. 여러분 모두 초대되었으니, 참석하실 수 있도록 해주세요.

71 장소 문제

해석 청자들은 어디에 있는 것 같은가?
(A) 지역 문화 센터
(B) 직업소개소
(C) 금융 기관
(D) 관공서

해설 지문에서 장소와 관련된 표현을 놓치지 않고 듣는다. "Mr. Hernandez is taking over as the general manager of this branch of Homerson Bank."라며 Mr. Hernandez는 이 Homerson 은행 지점의 총 지점장직을 맡을 것이라고 한 말을 통해 청자들이 금융 기관에 있음을 알 수 있다. 따라서 (C)가 정답이다.

어휘 community center 지역 문화 센터
employment agency 직업소개소 financial institution 금융 기관
government office 관공서

72 특정 세부 사항 문제

해석 Mr. Hernandez는 뉴욕에서 무엇을 했는가?
(A) 직원을 면접했다.
(B) 워크숍을 이끌었다.
(C) 상을 받았다.
(D) 회사를 설립했다.

해설 질문의 핵심 어구(Mr. Hernandez do in New York)와 관련된 내용을 주의 깊게 듣는다. "he[Mr. Hernandez] led a training session ~ in New York"이라며 Mr. Hernandez가 뉴욕에서 연수 과정을 이끌었다고 하였다. 따라서 (B)가 정답이다.

패러프레이징
led a training session 연수 과정을 이끌었다 → conducted a workshop 워크숍을 이끌었다

어휘 interview [미 íntərvjùː, 영 íntəvjuː] 면접하다
conduct [kəndʌ́kt] 이끌다, 실시하다   found [faund] 설립하다

73 다음에 할 일 문제

해석 청자들은 오늘 저녁에 무엇을 할 것 같은가?
(A) 직원 오리엔테이션에 참석한다.
(B) 식당에서 모인다.
(C) 컨벤션 센터까지 운전해서 간다.
(D) 교육 과정을 듣는다.

해설 질문의 핵심 어구(this evening)가 언급된 주변을 주의 깊게 듣는다. "a dinner is being held at Norman's Restaurant ~ this evening. You're all invited, so please try to make it."이라며 오늘 저녁에 Norman's 식당에서 만찬이 열릴 것이라고 한 후, 청자들 모두 초대되었으니 참석할 수 있도록 하라고 한 말을 통해 청자들이 오늘 저녁에 식당에서 모일 것임을 알 수 있다. 따라서 (B)가 정답이다.

어휘 dining establishment 식당   training course 교육 과정

74-76 🔊 미국식 발음

Questions 74-76 refer to the following announcement.

This is an announcement for all passengers of Brava Airways Flight 788 to Madrid. 74Due to an unexpected technical malfunction with your aircraft, Flight 788 has been canceled. As Brava Airways does not have any other flights to Madrid this evening, 75the airline will be giving passengers hotel vouchers. We will also book everyone a replacement flight for tomorrow morning. 76Further information about the situation is available at our service desk near Gate 35. On behalf of Brava Airlines, we apologize for this inconvenience and thank you for choosing to travel with us.

passenger [미 pǽsəndʒər, 영 pǽsəndʒə] 승객
unexpected [ʌ̀nikspéktid] 예상치 못한   technical [téknikəl] 기술적인
malfunction [mælfʌ́ŋkʃən] 결함   aircraft [미 έərkræ̀ft, 영 έəkrɑːft] 비행기
voucher [미 váutʃər, 영 váutʃə] 이용권   replacement [ripléismənt] 대체
on behalf of ~을 대표(대신)하여
inconvenience [미 ìnkənvíːnjəns, 영 ìnkənvíːniəns] 불편

해석

74-76번은 다음 공지에 관한 문제입니다.

마드리드행 Brava 항공사 788 항공편의 모든 승객분들께 알립니다. 74비행기의 예상치 못한 기술적인 결함으로 인하여, 788 항공편이 결항되었습니다. Brava 항공사에는 오늘 저녁에 다른 마드리드행 항공편이 없기 때문에, 75항공사는 승객분들께 호텔 이용권을 드릴 것입니다. 저희는 또한 모든 분들께 내일 아침에 출발하는 대체 항공편을 예약해드릴 것입니다. 76상황에 대한 더 많은 정보는 35번 탑승구 근처의 저희 서비스 데스크에서 들으실 수 있습니다. Brava 항공사를 대표하여, 불편을 겪게 해드린 것에 대해 사과드리며 여행을 저희와 함께해주셔서 감사합니다.

74 이유 문제

해석 왜 결항이 있었는가?
(A) 비행기에 기술적인 결함이 있다.

(B) 기상 조건이 매우 심각하다.
(C) 보안 문제가 발생했다.
(D) 공항에 전기가 나갔다.

해설 질문의 핵심 어구(flight cancellation)와 관련된 내용을 주의 깊게 듣는다. "Due to an unexpected technical malfunction with your aircraft, Flight 788 has been canceled."라며 비행기의 예상치 못한 기술적인 결함으로 인하여 788 항공편이 결항되었다고 하였다. 따라서 (A)가 정답이다.

패러프레이징
technical malfunction 기술적인 결함 → mechanical issue 기술적인 문제

어휘 mechanical [məkǽnikəl] 기술적인, 기계적인
weather condition 기상 조건
severe [미 sivíər, 영 sivíə] (날씨·추위·더위 등이) 심각한

75 특정 세부 사항 문제

해석 특정 승객들에게 무엇이 제공될 것인가?
(A) 숙소 이용권
(B) 요금 할인
(C) 좌석 업그레이드
(D) 전액 환불

해설 질문의 핵심 어구(provided to certain passengers)와 관련된 내용을 주의 깊게 듣는다. "the airline will be giving passengers hotel vouchers"라며 항공사는 승객들에게 호텔 이용권을 줄 것이라고 하였다. 따라서 (A)가 정답이다.

어휘 accommodation [미 əkàmədéiʃən, 영 əkɔ̀mədéiʃən] 숙소, 숙박
fare [미 fɛər, 영 feə] 요금

76 특정 세부 사항 문제

해석 화자에 따르면, 서비스 데스크는 어디에 위치해 있는가?
(A) 탑승 수속 카운터 옆에
(B) 탑승구 근처에
(C) 식당 맞은편에
(D) 발권 사무소 옆에

해설 질문의 인용어구(service desk)가 언급된 주변을 주의 깊게 듣는다. "Further information about the situation is available at our service desk near Gate 35."라며 상황에 대한 더 많은 정보는 35번 탑승구 근처의 서비스 데스크에서 들을 수 있다고 한 말을 통해 서비스 데스크가 탑승구 근처에 있음을 알 수 있다. 따라서 (B)가 정답이다.

어휘 check-in [tʃékin] 탑승 수속

77-79 🔊 캐나다식 발음

Questions 77-79 refer to the following advertisement.

77Are you looking for a musical instrument that's just right for you? Then stop by Spark to browse our newly stocked selection of products. 78Spark's sales representatives are experts in various musical styles, and we promise excellent service. We're confident that our staff can assist you with any instrument-related questions or concerns you might have. And from now until the end of the month, we are offering a discount of up to 60 percent off select goods. 79Simply come down to 10 Westchester Street to take advantage of this spectacular limited-time deal.

look for ~을 찾다   stop by ~에 들르다   browse [brauz] 둘러보다
stock [미 stɑk, 영 stɔk] (상점 등에 물품을) 들여놓다

expert[미 ékspə:rt, 영 ékspə:t] 전문가　select[silékt] 선정된; 선정하다
take advantage of ~을 이용하다
spectacular[미 spektǽkjulər, 영 spektǽkjələ] 엄청난, 굉장한

해석

77-79번은 다음 광고에 관한 문제입니다.

⁷⁷당신에게 딱 맞는 악기를 찾고 계신가요? 그렇다면 Spark에 들러서 새로 들어온 저희의 엄선된 제품들을 둘러보세요. ⁷⁸Spark의 판매 직원들은 다양한 음악 스타일들에 있어 전문가들이며, 훌륭한 서비스를 약속 드립니다. 당신이 악기와 관련된 어떤 질문이나 용건이 있으셔도 저희 직원들이 도와드릴 수 있다고 자신합니다. 또한 지금부터 이번 달 말까지, 저희는 선정된 상품들에 대해 60퍼센트까지 할인을 해드리고 있습니다. ⁷⁹10번지 Westchester가에 오셔서 한정된 기간의 이 엄청난 할인 혜택을 이용해보세요.

77 특정 세부 사항 문제

해석　Spark는 어떤 종류의 업체인가?
(A) 부동산 중개 사무소
(B) 악기 매장
(C) 음악 학원
(D) 컨설팅 회사

해설　질문의 핵심 어구(Spark)가 언급된 주변을 주의 깊게 듣는다. "Are you looking for a musical instrument that's just right for you? Then stop by Spark to browse our newly stocked selection of products."라며 청자에게 딱 맞는 악기를 찾고 있는지 물은 후, 그렇다면 Spark에 들러서 새로 들어온 엄선된 제품들을 둘러보라고 한 말을 통해 Spark가 악기 매장임을 알 수 있다. 따라서 (B)가 정답이다.

어휘　real estate 부동산 중개업　academy[əkǽdəmi] 학원

78 언급 문제

해석　화자는 Spark의 직원들에 대해 무엇을 말하는가?
(A) 여러 종류의 음악을 잘 안다.
(B) 10년의 경력이 있다.
(C) 일주일 내내 현장에 있다.
(D) 개인 강습을 제공한다.

해설　질문의 핵심 어구(Spark's staff)와 관련된 내용을 주의 깊게 듣는다. "Spark's sales representatives are experts in various musical styles"라며 Spark의 판매 직원들은 다양한 음악 스타일에 있어 전문가들이라고 하였다. 따라서 (A)가 정답이다.

패러프레이징
experts in various musical styles 다양한 음악 스타일들에 있어 전문가들 → familiar with different kinds of music 여러 종류의 음악을 잘 아는

어휘　be familiar with 잘 알다　on site 현장의

79 방법 문제

해석　청자들은 어떻게 할인을 받을 수 있는가?
(A) 상담 전화에 연락함으로써
(B) 시설에 방문함으로써
(C) 웹페이지에 들어감으로써
(D) 판매원에게 이메일을 보냄으로써

해설　질문의 핵심 어구(receive a discount)와 관련된 내용을 주의 깊게 듣는다. "Simply come down to 10 Westchester Street to take advantage of this ~ deal."이라며 10번지 Westchester가에 와서 이 할인 혜택을 이용해보라고 하였다. 따라서 (B)가 정답이다.

어휘　hotline[미 hɑ́:tlain, 영 hɔ́tlain] 상담 전화

Questions 80-82 refer to the following talk.

Hi, everyone. My name is Kevin Baker, and I'm the director of the Mariposa Community Center. In just a moment, I'll be introducing tonight's special guest, ⁸⁰Gregory Smyth, who is the CEO of the Body First chain of fitness centers. He will be lecturing on the health benefits of exercise. Before that, however, I'd like to discuss an important issue with you. The city cut our funding by 30 percent. ⁸¹Our budget is no longer sufficient to operate the center, so it'd be nice if you could help us out. Any amount, great or small, will be appreciated, so please speak to me after the lecture if you are able to contribute. ⁸²OK, Mr. Smyth. You can now come up to the podium.

lecture[미 léktʃər, 영 léktʃə] 강의하다　cut[kʌt] 줄이다
funding[fʌ́ndiŋ] 재정 지원, 자금　budget[bʌ́dʒit] 예산(안)
sufficient[səfíʃənt] 충분한　operate[ɑ́pərèit] 운영하다, 경영하다
help out ~를 도와주다　contribute[kəntríbju:t] 기부하다, 기여하다
podium[미 póudiəm, 영 póudiəm] 연설대, 연단

해석

80-82번은 다음 담화에 관한 문제입니다.

안녕하세요, 여러분. 제 이름은 Kevin Baker이고, 마리포사 지역 문화 센터의 책임자입니다. 잠시 후에, 오늘 밤의 특별 손님인, ⁸⁰헬스클럽 체인점 Body First의 대표이사 Gregory Smyth를 소개해드리겠습니다. 그는 운동의 건강상의 이점들에 대해서 강의를 할 것입니다. 하지만, 그 전에, 저는 여러분들과 중요한 사안에 대해 논의하고자 합니다. 시에서 재정 지원을 30퍼센트 줄였습니다. ⁸¹저희의 예산이 센터를 운영하기에 더 이상 충분하지 않으므로, 여러분이 저희를 도와주실 수 있다면 좋겠습니다. 금액의 다소와 상관없이 감사히 받을 것이니, 기부하실 수 있으시다면 강연 후에 제게 말씀해주세요. ⁸²좋습니다, Mr. Smyth. 이제 연설대로 올라와 주십시오.

80 특정 세부 사항 문제

해석　Gregory Smyth는 누구인 것 같은가?
(A) 회사 경영 간부
(B) 공무원
(C) 전문 의료진
(D) 대학 교수

해설　질문 대상(Gregory Smyth)의 신분 및 직업과 관련된 표현을 놓치지 않고 듣는다. "Gregory Smyth, who is the CEO of the Body First chain of fitness centers"라며 Gregory Smyth가 헬스클럽 체인점 Body First의 대표이사라고 하였다. 따라서 (A)가 정답이다.

어휘　executive[igzékjutiv] 경영 간부, 경영진
government official 공무원, 정부 관계자

81 의도 파악 문제

해석　화자는 왜 "시에서 재정 지원을 30퍼센트 줄였습니다"라고 말하는가?
(A) 약간의 기부금을 요청하기 위해
(B) 일정 변경을 공지하기 위해
(C) 폐쇄의 이유를 제공하기 위해
(D) 몇몇 절약 방법을 제안하기 위해

해설　질문의 인용어구(The city cut our funding by 30 percent)가 언급된 주변을 주의 깊게 듣는다. "Our budget is no longer sufficient to operate the center, so it'd be nice if you could help us out. Any amount, great or small, will be appreciated"라며 예산이 센터를 운영하기에 더 이상 충분하지 않으므로 자신들을 도와줄 수 있다면 좋겠다며 금액의 다소와 상관없이 감사히 받겠다고 한 말을 통해

약간의 기부금을 요청하고 있다는 것을 알 수 있다. 따라서 (A)가 정답이다.

어휘 donation[dounéiʃən] 기부(금) closure[klóuʒər] 폐쇄, 휴업

82 다음에 할 일 문제

해석 다음에 무슨 일이 일어날 것인가?
(A) 발표자가 무대에 오를 것이다.
(B) 운동 수업이 시작될 것이다.
(C) 예산안이 공개될 것이다.
(D) 자선 모금운동이 논의될 것이다.

해설 지문의 마지막 부분을 주의 깊게 듣는다. "OK, Mr. Smyth. You can now come up to the podium."이라며 Mr. Smyth에게 이제 연설대로 올라와달라고 하였다. 따라서 (A)가 정답이다.

패러프레이징
come up to the podium 연설대로 올라오다 → take the stage 무대에 오르다

어휘 take the stage 무대에 오르다 release[rilí:s] 공개하다, 발표하다
charity drive 자선 모금운동

83-85 [3M] 캐나다식 발음

Questions 83-85 refer to the following excerpt from a meeting.

[83]I want to end our meeting by talking about how our line of tablet devices has been selling. The TabTech L2—our newest addition to the line—is doing very well. This is in large part thanks to [84]the successful promotional campaign that our partner On Point Solutions created for us. However, the TouchBolt's sales performance has decreased over the last three months. This decline is concerning as our analyses suggest that it should still be selling well. I would like each of you to spend the rest of the morning going over the customer reviews of the product posted on our Web site. [85]At 12:30 P.M., we'll meet again to talk about these comments. Maybe this will help us figure out the problem.

addition[ədíʃən] 새로 추가된 것 thanks to ~덕택에
promotional[미 prəmóuʃənl, 영 prəmə́uʃənl] 홍보의
decrease[dikrí:s] 감소하다 decline[dikláin] 감소
analysis[ənǽləsis] 분석 go over ~을 검토하다 review[rivjú:] 평가
post[미 poust, 영 pəust] (웹사이트에 정보 등을) 올리다
figure out ~을 알아내다

해석
83-85번은 다음 회의 발췌록에 관한 문제입니다.

[83]저는 우리의 태블릿 기기 라인이 어떻게 팔리고 있는지에 대해 이야기하는 것으로 회의를 마치고자 합니다. 라인에 가장 최근 추가된 TabTech L2는 아주 잘 팔리고 있습니다. 이는 [84]우리의 협력사인 On Point Solutions사가 우리를 위해 만들었던 성공적인 홍보 캠페인 덕이 아주 큽니다. 하지만, TouchBolt의 판매 실적은 지난 세 달 동안 감소해 왔습니다. 우리의 분석에 따르면 이것은 아직까지 잘 팔리고 있어야 하기 때문에 이러한 감소는 우려됩니다. 저는 여러분 각자가 오늘 아침에 남은 시간 동안 우리의 웹사이트에 올려져 있는 제품에 대한 고객 평가들을 검토했으면 합니다. [85]오후 12시 30분에, 우리는 다시 만나서 이 의견들에 대해 이야기할 것입니다. 어쩌면 이것이 우리가 문제를 해결하는 것을 도와줄 것입니다.

83 주제 문제

해석 화자는 주로 무엇에 대해 이야기하고 있는가?
(A) 설계 결함
(B) 판매 실적
(C) 광고 전략
(D) 부서 확장

해설 회의의 주제를 묻는 문제이므로, 지문의 초반을 반드시 듣는다. "I want to end our meeting by talking about how our line of tablet devices has been selling."이라며 태블릿 기기 라인이 어떻게 팔리고 있는지에 대해 이야기하는 것으로 회의를 마치고자 한다고 한 후, 판매 실적에 대한 내용으로 지문이 이어지고 있다. 따라서 (B)가 정답이다.

패러프레이징
how ~ devices has been selling 기기가 어떻게 팔리고 있는지
→ Sales performance 판매 실적

어휘 flaw[flɔ:] 결함 performance[미 pərfɔ́:rməns, 영 pəfɔ́:məns] 실적
strategy[strǽtədʒi] 전략 expansion[ikspǽnʃən] 확장

84 특정 세부 사항 문제

해석 화자에 따르면, On Point Solutions사는 무엇을 했는가?
(A) 부품들을 생산했다.
(B) 자금을 관리했다.
(C) 상품들을 유통했다.
(D) 캠페인을 만들었다.

해설 질문의 핵심 어구(On Point Solutions)가 언급된 주변을 주의 깊게 듣는다. "the successful promotional campaign ~ On Point Solutions created for us"라며 On Point Solutions사가 우리를 위해 만들었던 성공적인 홍보 캠페인이라고 한 말을 통해 On Point Solutions사가 캠페인을 만들었음을 알 수 있다. 따라서 (D)가 정답이다.

어휘 manufacture[미 mænjufǽktʃər, 영 mænjəfǽktʃə] 생산하다
distribute[distríbju:t] 유통하다

85 이유 문제

해석 회의는 왜 오늘 오후에 열릴 것인가?
(A) 고객 의견에 대해 논의하기 위해
(B) 기기의 기능을 시험해보기 위해
(C) 신제품을 계획하기 위해
(D) 재무 분석을 검토하기 위해

해설 질문의 핵심 어구(this afternoon)와 관련된 내용을 주의 깊게 듣는다. "At 12:30 P.M., we'll meet again to talk about these comments[customer reviews]."라며 오후 12시 30분에 다시 만나서 이 고객 평가들에 대해 이야기할 것이라고 하였다. 따라서 (A)가 정답이다.

패러프레이징
talk about these comments 이 의견들에 대해 이야기하다 → discuss customer feedback 고객 의견에 대해 논의하다

어휘 feature[미 fí:tʃər, 영 fí:tʃə] 기능

86-88 [3M] 호주식 발음

Questions 86-88 refer to the following instruction.

First of all, [86]I appreciate everyone coming in to help with the store's inventory. Now, [87]the store's storage area was reorganized yesterday. So, our first goal this evening is to transfer the necessary stock from the back room to the sales floor. After that, we'll need to count those products and then compare the actual numbers against what our records say. You've all

done this before. [88]So you know that if there are any inconsistencies between the two, you should report it to me or one of the other managers immediately. OK, let's get started.

---

appreciate[əprí:ʃièit] 감사하다 inventory[ínvəntɔ̀:ri] 재고
storage[stɔ́:ridʒ] 저장, 보관
reorganize[미 ri:ɔ́rgənaiz, 영 ri:ɔ́:gənaiz] 재정비하다
transfer[미 trænsfɔ́:r, 영 trænsfɔ́:] 옮기다 sales floor 매장
compare[미 kəmpέər, 영 kəmpέə] 비교하다
inconsistency[ìnkənsístənsi] 불일치 immediately[imí:diətli] 즉시

해석

86-88번은 다음 설명에 관한 문제입니다.

먼저, [86]매장의 재고를 정리하는 데 도움을 주러 온 모든 분들께 감사드립니다. 자, [87]어제 매장의 창고가 재정비되었습니다. 따라서, 오늘 저녁 우리의 첫 번째 목표는 필요한 재고품을 뒤쪽 방에서 매장으로 옮기는 것입니다. 그 후, 그 제품들을 세고 나서 우리의 기록에 따른 것과 실제 제품 수를 비교해봐야 합니다. 여러분은 모두 전에 이것을 해봤습니다. [88]따라서 여러분은 이 둘 사이에 일치하지 않는 것이 있을 경우, 저나 다른 관리자들 중 한 명에게 즉시 알려야 하는 것을 알고 있습니다. 좋습니다, 시작하죠.

86 목적 문제

해석 담화의 주요 목적은 무엇인가?
(A) 직원들에게 늦게까지 일하도록 요청하기 위해
(B) 매장 규정을 설명하기 위해
(C) 직원들에게 야유회에 대해 알리기 위해
(D) 업무를 설명하기 위해

해설 담화의 목적을 묻는 문제이므로, 지문의 초반을 주의 깊게 듣는다. "I appreciate everyone coming in to help with the store's inventory"라며 매장의 재고를 정리하는 데 도움을 주러 온 모든 사람들에게 고맙다고 한 후, 매장 재고 정리 순서에 대한 설명으로 지문이 이어지고 있다. 따라서 (D)가 정답이다.

어휘 inform[미 infɔ́:rm, 영 infɔ́:m] 알리다 outing[áutiŋ] 야유회
describe[diskráib] 설명하다, 묘사하다

87 특정 세부 사항 문제

해석 어제 무슨 일이 있었는가?
(A) 판촉 활동이 끝났다.
(B) 잃어버린 물품을 찾았다.
(C) 직원이 고용되었다.
(D) 창고가 정리되었다.

해설 질문의 핵심 어구(yesterday)가 언급된 주변을 주의 깊게 듣는다. "the store's storage area was reorganized yesterday"라며 어제 매장의 창고가 재정비되었다고 하였다. 따라서 (D)가 정답이다.

어휘 promotion[미 prəmóuʃən, 영 prəmóuʃən] 판촉 활동
misplaced[mìspléist] 잃어버린

88 의도 파악 문제

해석 화자는 "여러분은 모두 전에 이것을 해봤습니다"라고 말할 때 무엇을 의도하는가?
(A) 실수가 있었다.
(B) 절차가 익숙할 것이다.
(C) 프로젝트는 빨리 끝날 것이다.
(D) 변경 사항이 알려질 것이다.

해설 질문의 인용어구(You've all done this before)가 언급된 주변을 주의 깊게 듣는다. "So you know that if there are any inconsistencies between the two, you should report it to me or one of the other managers immediately."라며 청자들은 이 둘 사이에 일치하지 않는 것이 있을 경우 자신이나 다른 관리자들 중

한 명에게 즉시 알려야 하는 것을 알고 있다고 한 말을 통해 절차가 익숙할 것임을 알 수 있다. 따라서 (B)가 정답이다.

어휘 procedure[미 prəsí:dʒər, 영 prəsí:dʒə] 절차
announce[ənáuns] 알리다

89-91 🎧 영국식 발음

Questions 89-91 refer to the following announcement.

I've been asked by [89]the head of human resources, Philip Calandra, to notify everyone about some changes that have been made to our employee attendance system. [90]First, you should go to the main page of our intranet. Here, you can set up an account for the new system. Simply follow the steps on the screen to create an account. After that has been completed, [91]I suggest that you watch the training video in the upper left-hand corner of the page to learn more about how to log your work hours each day. Please feel free to contact me with any questions.

---

notify[미 nóutəfài, 영 nə́utifài] 알리다 attendance[ətέndəns] 출석
set up ~을 만들다, 설치하다 account[əkáunt] 계정
complete[kəmplí:t] 완료하다, 작성하다 log[lɔːg] 기록하다

해석

89-91번은 다음 공지에 관한 문제입니다.

저는 [89]인사부장인 Philip Calandra로부터 모든 분들께 직원 출결 시스템에 적용된 몇몇 변경 사항들에 대해 알려드리라는 요청을 받았습니다. [90]먼저, 여러분은 우리 인트라넷의 메인 페이지로 가셔야 합니다. 여기서, 여러분은 새 시스템을 위한 계정을 만드실 수 있습니다. 계정을 만들기 위해서는 화면에 있는 순서들을 따라 하시기만 하면 됩니다. 그것이 완료되면, 여러분의 근무 시간을 매일 기록할 수 있는 방법에 대해 더 알아보기 위해 [91]페이지 왼쪽 상단 가장자리에 있는 교육 동영상을 보는 것을 권해드립니다. 질문이 있으시면 언제든지 편하게 제게 연락주시기 바랍니다.

89 특정 세부 사항 문제

해석 Philip Calandra는 누구인가?
(A) 회사 이사
(B) 부서장
(C) 교육 강사
(D) 컴퓨터 기술자

해설 질문 대상(Philip Calandra)의 신분 및 직업과 관련된 표현을 놓치지 않고 듣는다. "the head of human resources, Philip Calandra"라며 Philip Calandra가 인사부장이라고 하였다. 따라서 (B)가 정답이다.

어휘 board member 이사
departmental[미 dipɑ̀:rtméntl, 영 dipɑ̀:tméntl] 부서의
instructor[미 instrʌ́ktər, 영 instrʌ́ktə] 강사
technician[tekníʃən] 기술자

90 요청 문제

해석 화자는 청자들에게 무엇을 먼저 하라고 요청하는가?
(A) 책자들을 배포한다.
(B) 출결 기록서에 서명한다.
(C) 직원 수칙을 다운로드한다.
(D) 웹사이트를 방문한다.

해설 지문의 중후반에서 요청과 관련된 표현이 포함된 문장을 주의 깊게 듣는다. "First, you should go to the main page of our intranet."이라며 먼저 청자들은 인트라넷의 메인 페이지로 가야 한다고 하였다. 따라서 (D)가 정답이다.

91 제안 문제

해석 화자는 무엇을 제안하는가?
(A) 계정을 삭제하는 것
(B) 세미나에 등록하는 것
(C) 동영상을 시청하는 것
(D) 설문지를 작성하는 것

해설 지문의 중후반에서 제안과 관련된 표현이 포함된 문장을 주의 깊게 듣는다. "I suggest that you watch the training video in the upper left-hand corner of the page"라며 페이지 왼쪽 상단 가장자리에 있는 교육 동영상을 보는 것을 권한다고 하였다. 따라서 (C)가 정답이다.

어휘 **delete**[dilíːt] 삭제하다 **register**[미 rédʒistər, 영 rédʒistə] 등록하다
survey[미 sə́rvei, 영 sə́:vei] (설문) 조사

92-94 ③ 캐나다식 발음

Questions 92-94 refer to the following telephone message.

Good morning, Ms. James. ⁹²My name is Carter Swain, and I am the owner of Swain Salon. I want to apologize for your unsatisfactory experience last week. My associate informed me about your complaint. The person who provided you the service is no longer working here, and ⁹³I can assure you all of my current employees are well-trained and knowledgeable about chemical-sensitivity issues. Therefore, ⁹⁴on top of providing you a full refund, I'd like to send you a coupon for $40 off your next visit. I will actually perform your treatment myself. So call me back at 555-4983, and I'll schedule an appointment for you.

unsatisfactory[ʌnsətisfǽktəri] 불만족스러운
complaint[kəmpléint] 불만, 불평 **assure**[əʃúər] 보장하다
well-trained 숙련의
knowledgeable[미 nɑ́lidʒəbl, 영 nɔ́lidʒəbl] 잘 아는, 박식한
on top of ~뿐 아니라, ~ 외에 **treatment**[tríːtmənt] 관리, 대우

해석
92-94번은 다음 전화 메시지에 관한 문제입니다.

좋은 아침입니다, Ms. James. ⁹²제 이름은 Carter Swain이고, 저는 Swain 미용실의 주인입니다. 저는 지난주 고객님의 불만족스러운 경험에 대해 사과하고 싶습니다. 제 동료가 고객님의 불만에 대해 제게 알려주었습니다. 고객님께 서비스를 제공한 사람은 더 이상 이곳에서 일하고 있지 않으며, ⁹³현재 제 모든 직원들은 화학 제품 민감성 문제에 대해 숙련되어 있고 잘 알고 있음을 보장할 수 있습니다. 따라서, ⁹⁴전액 환불을 해 드리는 것뿐 아니라, 저는 고객님께 다음 방문 시 40달러 할인 쿠폰을 보내드리고 싶습니다. 제가 실제로 직접 관리를 해드릴 것입니다. 그러니 555-4983으로 다시 전화 주시면, 제가 고객님을 위해 예약을 해드리겠습니다.

92 화자 문제

해석 화자는 어디에서 일하는 것 같은가?
(A) 콜 센터에서
(B) 직업소개소에서
(C) 화학 공장에서
(D) 미용실에서

해설 대화에서 신분 및 직업과 관련된 표현을 놓치지 않고 듣는다. "My name is Carter Swain, and I am the owner of Swain Salon."이

라며 화자가 자신의 이름은 Carter Swain이고 Swain 미용실의 주인이라고 하였다. 이를 통해 화자가 미용실에서 일한다는 것을 알 수 있다. 따라서 (D)가 정답이다.

패러프레이징
Salon 미용실 → beauty shop 미용실

어휘 **employment agency** 직업소개소

93 의도 파악 문제

해석 화자는 왜 "고객님께 서비스를 제공한 사람은 더 이상 이곳에서 일하고 있지 않으며"라고 말하는가?
(A) 더 많은 직원들이 고용될 필요가 있음을 암시하기 위해
(B) 문제가 다시 발생하지 않을 것임을 보장하기 위해
(C) 일부 서비스를 더 이상 사용할 수 없음을 보여주기 위해
(D) 예약 일정을 재조정할 것을 권하기 위해

해설 질문의 인용어구(The person who provided you the service is no longer working here)가 언급된 주변을 주의 깊게 듣는다. "I can assure you all of my current employees are well-trained and knowledgeable about chemical-sensitivity issues"라며 현재 모든 직원들이 화학 제품 민감성 문제에 대해 숙련되어 있고 잘 알고 있음을 보장할 수 있다고 한 말을 통해 문제가 다시 발생하지 않을 것임을 보장하기 위함임을 알 수 있다. 따라서 (B)가 정답이다.

어휘 **hire**[háiər] 고용하다 **guarantee**[gærəntíː] 보장하다

94 특정 세부 사항 문제

해석 청자는 무엇을 받을 것 같은가?
(A) 경제적 보상
(B) 추가 교육
(C) 무료 물품
(D) 가정 내 서비스

해설 질문의 핵심 어구(listener ~ receive)와 관련된 내용을 주의 깊게 듣는다. "on top of providing you a full refund, I'd like to send you a coupon for $40 off your next visit"라며 전액 환불을 해주는 것뿐 아니라 다음 방문 시 40달러 할인 쿠폰을 보내주고 싶다고 한 말을 통해 청자가 경제적 보상을 받을 것을 알 수 있다. 따라서 (A)가 정답이다.

어휘 **financial**[fainǽnʃəl] 경제적인 **compensation**[kɑ̀ːmpənséiʃən] 보상
complimentary[미 kɑ̀ːmpliméntəri, 영 kɔ̀mpliméntəri] 무료의

95-97 ③ 미국식 발음

Questions 95-97 refer to the following telephone message and schedule.

Good morning, Jim. This is Beth from CV Productions. I just got your e-mail about ⁹⁵the Mountain Music Festival we're holding this year to raise money for school art programs. ⁹⁶To answer your question, your band will be staying at Days Hotel, which is near the site of the performance. Oh . . . also, another thing. I just found out that the event schedule has been changed. Three bands will play on Saturday instead of Sunday. So you and the other members of The Black Hats will play first on Sunday night. ⁹⁷The band that was supposed to play before you will be the opening act on Saturday.

festival[미 féstəvəl, 영 féstivəl] 축제 **raise**[reiz] (돈·기부금을) 모으다
site[sait] 장소 **find out** ~을 알게 되다, 알아내다 **opening act** 개막 공연

해석
95-97번은 다음 전화 메시지와 일정표에 관한 문제입니다.

안녕하세요, Jim. 저는 CV Productions사의 Beth입니다. 저는 ⁹⁵우리가 올해 학교 예술 프로그램들을 위한 돈을 마련하기 위해 여는 Mountain 음악 축제에 대한 당신의 이메일을 방금 받았어요. ⁹⁶당신의 질문에 답하자면, 당신의 밴드는 Days 호텔에 머무르게 될 텐데, 호텔은 공연 장소 근처에 있어요. 아... 그리고, 하나가 더 있어요. 저는 행사 일정이 변경된 것을 방금 알게 됐어요. 3개의 밴드들이 일요일 대신 토요일에 공연을 할 거예요. 따라서 당신과 The Black Hats의 다른 멤버들은 일요일 밤에 첫 번째로 공연을 할 거예요. ⁹⁷당신들 전에 공연을 하기로 했던 밴드는 토요일에 개막 공연을 맡을 거예요.

Mountain 음악 축제 - 일정표	
토요일	오후 9:00 – The Early Birds
	오후 11:00 – Open Source
일요일	오후 7:00 – ⁹⁷Green Wave
	오후 9:00 – The Black Hats
	오후 11:00 – Cherry Blossom

95 언급 문제

해석 화자는 축제에 대해 무엇을 말하는가?
(A) 음악가에 의해 주최되었다.
(B) 자선 행사이다.
(C) 매년 열린다.
(D) 새로운 장소로 옮겨졌다.

해설 질문의 핵심 어구(festival)가 언급된 주변을 주의 깊게 듣는다. "the Mountain Music Festival we're holding this year to raise money for school art programs"라며 올해 학교 예술 프로그램들을 위한 돈을 마련하기 위해 여는 Mountain 음악 축제라고 한 말을 통해 축제가 자선 행사임을 알 수 있다. 따라서 (B)가 정답이다.

어휘 musician[mjuzíʃn] 음악가 charity event 자선 행사

96 특정 세부 사항 문제

해석 청자는 무엇에 대해 물어보았던 것 같은가?
(A) 장비
(B) 숙소
(C) 요금
(D) 교통

해설 질문의 핵심 어구(listener ~ ask about)와 관련된 내용을 주의 깊게 듣는다. "To answer your question, your band will be staying at Days Hotel"이라며 청자의 질문에 답하자면 청자의 밴드는 Days 호텔에 머무르게 될 것이라고 한 말을 통해 청자가 숙소에 대해 물어보았음을 알 수 있다. 따라서 (B)가 정답이다.

어휘 accommodation[미 əkàmədéiʃən, 영 əkɔ̀mədéiʃən] 숙소

97 시각 자료 문제

해석 시각 자료를 보아라. 어떤 밴드가 토요일 밤에 첫 번째로 공연할 것인가?
(A) Open Source
(B) Green Wave
(C) The Black Hats
(D) Cherry Blossom

해설 제시된 일정표의 정보를 확인한 후 질문의 핵심 어구(perform first on Saturday night)와 관련된 내용을 주의 깊게 듣는다. "The band that was supposed to play before you[The Black Hats] will be the opening act on Saturday."라며 The Black Hats 전에 공연을 하기로 했던 밴드는 토요일에 개막 공연을 맡을 것이라고 하였으므로, Green Wave가 토요일 밤에 첫 번째로 공연할 것임을 일정표에서 알 수 있다. 따라서 (B)가 정답이다.

패러프레이징
perform first 첫 번째로 공연하다 → be the opening act 개막 공연을 맡다

어휘 perform[미 pərfɔ́ːrm, 영 pəfɔ́ːm] 공연하다

98-100 〔캐나다식 발음〕

Questions 98-100 refer to the following talk and list of rooms.

⁹⁸The upcoming Chicago Restaurant Convention is the best opportunity we'll get for showcasing our new product. This will be the largest exposition of its kind in the country, and ⁹⁹it's coming just two weeks before we officially release the oven. Six of our staff members will be traveling with us to the exposition. ⁹⁹We'll be giving our presentation about the oven on the exposition's second day, July 23, so we'll travel there via bus on July 22. We've booked rooms at the Chicago Continental, one of the best hotels in the city. ¹⁰⁰Each staff member will be staying in a room with a king-sized bed.

upcoming[ʌ́pkʌmiŋ] 곧 있을, 다가오는
showcase[ʃóukeis] 소개하다, 전시하다; 공개 행사
exposition[èkspəzíʃən] 박람회, 전시회 officially[əfíʃəli] 공식적으로
via[váiə] ~을 이용하여

해석
98-100번은 다음 담화와 객실 목록에 관한 문제입니다.

⁹⁸곧 있을 시카고 식당 컨벤션은 저희의 신상품을 소개하기 위해 얻게 될 최고의 기회입니다. 이것은 국내에서 그런 종류 중 가장 큰 전시회가 될 것이며, ⁹⁹그것은 오븐을 공식적으로 출시하기 불과 2주 전에 있을 것입니다. 우리 직원들 중 여섯 명이 박람회에 우리와 함께 갈 것입니다. 박람회 둘째 날인 7월 23일에 ⁹⁹우리는 오븐에 대한 발표를 할 것이라서, 7월 22일에 버스를 이용하여 그곳에 갈 것입니다. 우리는 그 도시에서 가장 좋은 호텔들 중 하나인 시카고 컨티넨털에 객실을 예약했습니다. ¹⁰⁰직원마다 하나의 킹사이즈 침대가 있는 각 객실에 묵을 것입니다.

시카고 컨티넨털 스위트룸	
객실	침대의 종류
마스터 룸	1개의 싱글 보통 사이즈 침대
¹⁰⁰디럭스 룸	1개의 킹사이즈 침대
프리미엄 룸	2개의 보통 사이즈 침대
골드 룸	2개의 킹사이즈 침대

98 언급 문제

해석 화자는 시카고 식당 컨벤션에 대해 무엇을 말하는가?
(A) 상품을 광고할 좋은 기회를 제공한다.
(B) 참석자들에게 많은 입장료를 지불할 것을 요구한다.
(C) 매년 더 인기를 얻고 있다.
(D) 전 세계에서 참석자들을 끌어모은다.

해설 질문의 핵심 어구(Chicago Restaurant Convention)가 언급된 주변을 주의 깊게 듣는다. "The upcoming Chicago Restaurant Convention is the best opportunity we'll get for showcasing our new product."라며 곧 있을 시카고 식당 컨벤션은 신상품을 소개하기 위해 얻게 될 최고의 기회라고 하였다. 따라서 (A)가 정답이다.

패러프레이징
the best opportunity ~ for showcasing ~ product 상품을 소개하기 위한 최고의 기회 → a good chance to market a product

상품을 광고할 좋은 기회

어휘 **market**[미 mά:rkit, 영 mά:kit] 광고하다, 판매하다
admission[ədmíʃən] 입장, 입학

99 화자 문제

해석 화자는 어떤 분야에서 일하는 것 같은가?
(A) 접객
(B) 상업용 부동산
(C) 가전제품 제조
(D) 음식점 관리

해설 지문에서 신분 및 직업과 관련된 표현을 놓치지 않고 듣는다. "it[Chicago Restaurant Convention]'s coming just two weeks before we officially release the oven"이라며 시카고 식당 컨벤션은 오븐을 공식적으로 출시하기 불과 2주 전에 있을 것이라고 한 후, "We'll be giving our presentation about the oven"이라며 오븐에 대한 발표를 할 것이라고 한 말을 통해 화자가 가전제품 제조 분야에서 일하고 있음을 알 수 있다. 따라서 (C)가 정답이다.

어휘 **hospitality**[hὰspətǽləti] 접객, 접대, 환대
appliance[əpláiəns] 가전제품

100 시각 자료 문제

해석 시각 자료를 보아라. 직원들은 어떤 종류의 스위트룸에 묵을 것인가?
(A) 마스터 룸
(B) 디럭스 룸
(C) 프리미엄 룸
(D) 골드 룸

해설 제시된 객실 목록의 정보를 확인한 후 질문의 핵심 어구(employees staying in)와 관련된 내용을 주의 깊게 듣는다. "Each staff member will be staying in a room with a king-sized bed."라며 직원마다 하나의 킹사이즈 침대가 있는 각 객실에 묵을 것이라고 하였으므로 직원들이 디럭스 룸에 묵을 것임을 객실 목록에서 알 수 있다. 따라서 (B)가 정답이다.

PART 5

101 부사 자리 채우기

해설 동사(opposed)를 꾸미기 위해서는 부사가 와야 하므로 부사 (D) strongly(강력히)가 정답이다. 형용사 (A)와 (B), 명사 (C)는 동사를 꾸밀 수 없다.

해석 MYK사는 식당과 카페의 영업 시간을 규제하는 정부의 계획에 강력히 반대했다.

어휘 **oppose** v. 반대하다 **regulate** v. 규제하다, 단속하다
opening hour 영업 시간

102 전치사 채우기

해설 '관리자를 제외하고 아무도'라는 의미가 되어야 하므로 (B) except (~을 제외하고)가 정답이다. (A) within은 '~ 이내에', (C) across는 '~을 가로질러', (D) since는 '~ 이래로'라는 의미이다.

해석 관리자를 제외하고 아무도 상점의 비상 경보 장치를 정지시킬 수 없다.

어휘 **deactivate** v. 정지시키다, 비활성화시키다
alarm system 비상 경보 장치

103 부정대명사/형용사 채우기

해설 빈칸은 주어 자리로 명사가 와야 한다. '대부분이 프로젝트를 끝낼 수 있었다'라는 의미가 되어야 하므로 '대부분'을 의미하는 (A) most가 정답이다. (B) no는 형용사이므로 뒤에 명사 없이 혼자 주어 자리에 올 수 없으며, (C) each는 단수 동사와 쓰이는데 뒤에 복수 동사(were)가 왔으므로 답이 될 수 없다. (D) another는 이미 언급한 것 이외의

또 다른 하나를 의미하므로 문맥에 어울리지 않는다.

해석 연구원들은 새 프로그램에 대해 약간의 사소한 어려움들을 겪었지만, 대부분은 그들의 프로젝트를 끝낼 수 있었다.

어휘 **researcher** n. 연구원 **minor** adj. 사소한, 작은

104 명사 어휘 고르기

해설 '사무용품을 주문하기 전에 승인을 얻도록 요구된다'라는 문맥이므로 (D) permission(승인)이 정답이다. (A) distribution은 '분배, 유통', (B) confession은 '자백, 고백', (C) situation은 '상황, 환경'이라는 의미이다.

해석 직원들은 추가적인 사무용품을 주문하기 전에 승인을 얻도록 요구됩니다.

어휘 **obtain** v. 얻다 **office supply** 사무용품

105 격에 맞는 인칭대명사 채우기

해설 주어 자리에 올 수 있는 인칭대명사가 필요하므로 주격 (A) they(그들이)가 정답이다.

해석 투자자들은 그들이 회사의 재정 상태에 관한 정보에 접근할 수 없다고 항의했다.

어휘 **complain** v. 항의하다, 불평하다 **access** v. 접근하다, 이용하다
financial status 재정 상태

106 관계대명사 채우기

해설 관계절(attorneys ~ cases)에는 명사(attorneys)를 꾸며 주어 '회사의 변호사들'이라는 의미를 만드는 소유격 관계대명사가 필요하므로 (B) whose가 정답이다.

해석 Parker and Dean사는 회사의 변호사들이 민사와 형사 법률 소송 둘 다를 다루는 유일한 지역 법률 사무소이다.

어휘 **attorney** n. 변호사, 대리인 **deal with** ~을 다루다, 처리하다
civil adj. 민사상의, 시민의 **criminal** adj. 형사상의, 범죄의
legal adj. 법률의 **case** n. 소송 (사건)

107 명사 자리 채우기

해설 전치사(for)의 목적어 자리에 올 수 있는 것은 명사이므로 명사 (A) referral(소개)이 정답이다. 동사 (B), (C)와 동사 또는 분사 (D)는 명사 자리에 올 수 없다.

해석 환자는 Dr. Marple에게 안과 전문의의 소개를 요청했다.

어휘 **eye specialist** 안과 전문의 **refer** v. 참조하다, 언급하다

108 형용사 어휘 고르기

해설 '장관을 이루는 경치와 온화한 기후로, 산타로사는 휴양지로 매우 전도 유망한 장소이다'라는 문맥이므로 (B) promising(전도 유망한)이 정답이다.

해석 장관을 이루는 경치와 온화한 기후로, 산타로사는 휴양지로 매우 전도 유망한 장소이다.

어휘 **spectacular** adj. 장관을 이루는, 굉장한 **scenery** n. 경치
mild adj. 온화한, 포근한 **climate** n. 기후, 분위기 **resort** n. 휴양지
contribute v. 기부하다 **propose** v. 제안하다 **collect** v. 모으다

109 태에 맞는 동사 채우기

해설 문장에 동사가 없으므로 동사 (A), (B), (D)가 정답의 후보이다. '학위를 수여하다'라는 능동의 의미이고 뒤에 목적어(degrees)가 있으므로 능동태 동사 (A) grants가 정답이다.

해석 Southwest 대학은 공학부터 철학까지 매우 다양한 분야의 학위를 수여한다.

어휘 **a wide variety of** 매우 다양한 **field** n. 분야 **engineering** n. 공학
philosophy n. 철학 **grant** v. 수여하다, 승인하다

110 전치사 채우기

해설 '회의하기 전에 경비 보고서를 제출하라'는 의미가 되어야 하므로 (A) before(~ 전에)가 정답이다. (B) around은 '~ 주위에', (C) in front of는 '~ 앞에', (D) along은 '~을 따라'라는 의미이다.

해석 Ms. Thompson과 회의하기 전에 경비 보고서를 회계부서에 제출해주십시오.

어휘 expense report 경비 보고서 accounting department 회계부서

111 비교급 표현 채우기

해설 빈칸 뒤에 than이 왔으므로 함께 비교급 표현을 만드는 비교급 (B) lower가 정답이다.

해석 오래 계속된 가뭄은 저수지의 수위가 이전 그 어느 때보다 더 낮게 내려가도록 했다.

어휘 prolonged adj. 오래 계속되는, 장기적인 drought n. 가뭄
water level 수위 reservoir n. 저수지
lowly adj. (지위가) 낮은; adv. 초라하게

112 부사 자리 채우기

해설 동명사구(searching for new ways)를 꾸미기 위해서는 부사가 와야 하므로 (A) continually(끊임없이)가 정답이다. 형용사 (B), 동사 (C), 형용사 (D)는 동명사구를 꾸밀 수 없다.

해석 Peter Lee는 지난해를 젊은 소비자들에게 그의 소프트웨어를 광고하기 위한 새로운 방법들을 끊임없이 찾으며 보냈다.

어휘 market v. 광고하다, 팔다; n. 시장 continuous adj. 계속되는, 지속적인
continual adj. 거듭되는, 끊임없는

113 동사 어휘 고르기

해설 '부서 관리자의 주된 역할은 직원들이 회사의 정해진 목표들을 달성하는 쪽으로 나아가게 하는 것이다'라는 문맥이므로 (B) guide(나아가게 하다)가 정답이다. (A) adopt는 '채택하다, 도입하다', (C) initiate는 '시작하다, 개시하다', (D) establish는 '설립하다'라는 의미이다.

해석 부서 관리자의 주된 역할은 직원들이 회사의 정해진 목표들을 달성하는 쪽으로 나아가게 하는 것이다.

어휘 supervisor n. 관리자 stated adj. 정해진, 정기의

114 in/at/on 구별하여 채우기

해설 기간(two weeks) 앞에는 전치사 in(~ 후에)을 사용하므로 (C) in이 정답이다.

해석 지원자들은 회사의 결정을 약 2주 후에 통지 받을 것임을 유념해주시기 바랍니다.

어휘 applicant n. 지원자 notify v. 통지하다
approximately adv. 약, 거의

115 동사 어휘 고르기

해설 '더 밝은 색상과 더 큰 이미지들을 포함하도록 변경될 것이다'라는 문맥이므로 alter의 p.p.형 (C) altered(변경하다)가 정답이다. (A)의 partner는 '제휴하다, 협력하다', (B)의 practice는 '연습하다, 실행하다', (D)의 relieve는 '완화하다, 줄이다'라는 의미이다.

해석 요청하셨던 대로, 귀하의 웹사이트 디자인은 더 밝은 색상과 더 큰 이미지들을 포함하도록 변경될 것입니다.

어휘 request v. 요청하다; n. 요청 include v. 포함하다

116 to 부정사 채우기

해설 명사 a contract를 뒤에서 꾸밀 수 있는 과거분사 (B)와 to 부정사 (C)가 정답의 후보이다. '석유와 천연 가스를 공급하는 계약'이라는 문맥으로 보아 목적어(oil and natural gas)를 취하면서 명사(a contract)를 뒤에서 꾸밀 수 있는 to 부정사 (C) to supply가 정답이

다. 과거분사 (B) supplied는 뒤에 목적어를 취할 수 없으므로 답이 될 수 없다.

해석 Perot Petrochemicals사는 석유와 천연 가스를 공익 기업에 공급하는 계약을 맺었다.

어휘 sign a contract 계약을 맺다 natural gas 천연 가스
utility company 공익 기업

117 시간 표현과 일치하는 시제의 동사 채우기

해설 미래 시간 표현(by the end of next week)이 있으므로 미래 시제 (B) will be ready가 정답이다.

해석 저희 최신 텔레비전의 제품 설명서는 다음 주 말까지는 인쇄를 할 준비가 될 것입니다.

어휘 latest adj. 최신의 manual n. 설명서; adj. 수동의

118 부사 어휘 고르기

해설 '홍보 행사들을 돕기 위해 마케팅 팀원들을 매장에 정기적으로 보낼 것이다'라는 문맥이므로 (A) periodically(정기적으로)가 정답이다. (B) absently는 '무심코', (C) mistakenly는 '실수로', (D) formerly는 '예전에'라는 의미이다.

해석 저희는 홍보 행사들을 돕기 위해 마케팅 팀원들을 저희 매장에 정기적으로 보낼 것입니다.

119 병치 구문 채우기

해설 '지역 주민들을 만나고 정책들을 설명하느라 바쁘다'라는 의미로 보아, 등위접속사 and가 연결해야 하는 것은 be busy (in)의 목적어 두 개이다. and 앞에 동명사구 meeting local citizens가 왔으므로 and 뒤의 빈칸에도 동명사가 와야 한다. 따라서 (C) explaining이 정답이다. 참고로, be busy (in) -ing는 '~하느라 바쁘다'라는 의미의 관용 표현이다.

해석 선거운동 행사에서, 정치인은 지역 주민들을 만나고 그녀의 정책들을 설명하느라 바빴다.

어휘 campaign n. 선거운동 citizen n. 주민, 시민 policy n. 정책

120 부사절 접속사 채우기

해설 이 문장은 주어(All fees), 동사(must be received)를 갖춘 완전한 절이므로 ____ a bill ~ course는 수식어 거품으로 보아야 한다. 이 수식어 거품은 동사(has been issued)가 있는 거품절이므로, 거품절을 이끌 수 있는 부사절 접속사 (A)와 (C)가 정답의 후보이다. '모든 수업료는 청구서가 발급된 후에 한 달 이내로 수령되어야 한다'라는 의미가 되어야 하므로 (C) after(~ 후에)가 정답이다.

해석 모든 수업료는 강의에 대한 청구서가 발급된 후에 한 달 이내로 수령되어야 합니다.

어휘 fee n. 수업료, 보수 bill n. 청구서 issue v. 발급하다 course n. 강의

121 형용사 어휘 고르기

해설 '버스 정류장들이 더 접근하기 쉽게 만들기 위해 지역 도처에 그것들을 재배치하고 있다'라는 문맥이므로 (D) accessible(접근하기 쉬운, 이용하기 쉬운)이 정답이다. (A) increased는 '증가한', (B) adverse는 '불리한, 부정적인', (C) constructive는 '건설적인'이라는 의미이다.

해석 시의회는 버스 정류장들이 지역 주민들에게 더 접근하기 쉽게 만들기 위해 지역 도처에 그것들을 재배치하고 있다.

어휘 city council 시의회 relocate v. 재배치하다, 이동시키다
bus stop 버스 정류장 resident n. 주민

122 명사절 접속사 채우기

해설 동사(discussed)의 목적어 자리에 온 절(the new tax regulations ~ industry) 앞에는 명사절 접속사가 와야 하므로 (A), (B), (D)가 정

답의 후보이다. 이 명사절은 주어(the new tax regulations), 동사 (would affect), 목적어(the automobile industry)를 갖춘 완전한 절이므로 완전한 절을 이끄는 (D) how가 정답이다. 불완전한 절 앞에 오는 명사절 접속사 (A)와 복합관계대명사 (B)는 답이 될 수 없다.

해석 디트로이트 회계 협의회의 기조연설자는 새로운 세금 규정들이 자동차 산업에 어떻게 영향을 미칠지에 관해 논했다.

어휘 keynote speaker 기조연설자 regulation n. 규정, 제한
affect v. ~에 영향을 미치다 automobile n. 자동차

123 동사와 수일치하는 주어 채우기
해설 동사(is prohibited)가 단수이므로 뒤에 목적어(animals)를 가질 수 있으면서 단수 취급되는 동명사 (C) Feeding이 정답이다. 분사 또는 형용사 (B)는 뒤에 명사 animals를 꾸며 복수 동사가 와야 하므로 답이 될 수 없다.

해석 국가의 모든 국립 공원과 보호 구역 내에서는 동물들에게 먹이를 주는 것이 금지된다.

어휘 prohibit v. 금지하다, ~하지 못하게 하다 national park 국립 공원
conservation area 보호 구역 feed v. 먹이를 주다, 공급하다; n. 먹이

124 전치사 채우기
해설 동사 comply와 함께 쓰이는 전치사 (D) with가 정답이다.

해석 주택가 근처에 건설된 공장들은 엄격한 환경 보호 규정들에 따라야 한다.

어휘 residential area 주택가 comply v. (법·명령 등에) 따르다
strict adj. 엄격한 environmental adj. 환경 보호의, 환경의

125 현재분사와 과거분사 구별하여 채우기
해설 이 문장은 주어(The company), 동사(is known for), 목적어(its high-quality work)를 갖춘 완전한 절이므로, ____ the new Italian restaurant은 수식어 거품으로 보아야 한다. 보기 중 수식어 거품이 될 수 있는 것은 분사 (A)와 (C)이다. 분사의 수식을 받는 명사(The company)와 분사가 '회사가 짓다'라는 의미의 능동 관계이므로 현재분사 (C) building이 정답이다.

해석 새로운 이탈리아 음식점을 짓는 그 회사는 높은 수준의 작업으로 알려져 있다.

어휘 be known for ~으로 알려져 있다

126 동사 어휘 고르기
해설 '재무 평가가 마무리되면 보내질 것이다'라는 문맥이므로 finalize의 p.p.형 (C) finalized(마무리 짓다)가 정답이다. (A)의 nominate는 '(후보자로) 지명하다, 임명하다', (B)의 consume은 '소비하다', (D)의 misplace는 '잘못 두다'라는 의미이다.

해석 일단 재무 평가가 마무리되면, 그것은 Newfield Electronics사의 법무부로 보내질 것이다.

어휘 financial adj. 재무의 assessment n. 평가
legal department 법무부

127 동명사와 명사 구별하여 채우기
해설 문장에서 be동사(is) 앞에 위치한 ____ ~ Overland Resources는 주어 자리이다. 주어 자리 맨 앞에 오면서 뒤에 목적어(the merger ~ Overland Resources)를 가질 수 있는 것은 동명사이므로 (C) Approving이 정답이다. 명사 (D)는 뒤에 목적어를 가질 수 없다.

해석 Corus사와 Overland Resources사 간의 합병을 승인하는 것은 국가 공무원들에게 몇 주가 걸릴 것으로 예상된다.

어휘 merger n. 합병 government official 국가 공무원
approve v. 승인하다

128 동사 어휘 고르기
해설 '사무소 운영에 미치는 영향을 최소화하기 위해 주말에 이행될 것이다'라는 문맥이므로 (B) minimize(최소화하다)가 정답이다. (A) subtract는 '빼다, 공제하다', (C) disturb는 '방해하다', (D) consider는 '고려하다'라는 의미이다.

해석 Portman 빌딩의 보수는 사무소 운영에 미치는 영향을 최소화하기 위해 주말에 이행될 것이다.

어휘 carry out ~을 이행하다, 실시하다 effect n. 영향, 효과
operation n. 운영, 작업

129 전치사 채우기
해설 '국가 전역에 걸쳐'라는 의미가 되어야 하므로 (A) across(~의 전역에 걸쳐)가 정답이다.

해석 혹독한 겨울 폭풍 동안 국가 전역에 걸쳐 사상 최저 기온들이 보도되었다.

어휘 record low 사상 최저 report v. 보도하다, 알리다
severe adj. 혹독한, 극심한

130 형용사 어휘 고르기
해설 Although 이하의 부사절과 뒤 문장의 연결이 자연스러워야 한다. '다양한 주제에 관한 책들을 출판해 왔지만, 주된 초점은 유럽 역사이다'라는 문맥이므로 (A) main(주된, 가장 중요한)이 정답이다. (B) cooperative는 '협조하는', (C) convenient는 '편리한', (D) previous는 '이전의, 바로 앞의'라는 의미이다.

해석 Steven Harris가 다양한 주제에 관한 책들을 출판해 왔지만, 그의 주된 초점은 유럽 역사이다.

어휘 publish v. 출판하다 a variety of 다양한 focus n. 초점, 주안점

PART 6

131-134번은 다음 이메일에 관한 문제입니다.

수신: Linda Shute <lshute@plustech.com>
발신: Stanley Robinson <srobinson@midwayexhibitions.com>
제목: 사무용품 무역 박람회
날짜: 4월 23일

안녕하세요 Ms. Shute,

¹³¹저는 귀하께 최근의 예약 취소 때문에, 저희의 사무용품 무역 박람회에 전시 부스를 위한 자리가 하나 더 있다는 것을 알려드리고자 이메일을 씁니다. 저는 귀하께서 지난달의 신청 마감일을 놓친 것에 대해 얼마나 실망하셨는지를 기억하는데, 이제 등록하실 다시 한번의 기회가 있습니다. 그러나, 귀하께서는 가능한 한 빨리 귀하의 관심을 명시하셔야 합니다. ¹³²귀하께서는 참가하시기 위해 250달러의 요금을 내셔야 할 것입니다. ¹³³이는 은행 계좌 이체나 저희 사무실을 방문함으로써 이루어질 수 있습니다.

저는 귀하께서 참여하기를 강력히 권장합니다. ¹³⁴이것은 수년간 증가하는 팬들을 유치해오고 있는 행사이며 올해에도 다시 기록적인 수의 방문객을 끌어모을 것입니다.

Stanley Robinson 드림
고객 관리부

cancellation n. 예약 취소, 취소(된 것) recall v. 기억하다, 상기시키다
disappointed adj. 실망한 second chance 다시 한번의 기회
indicate v. 명시하다 following n. 팬들, 추종자들

131 전치사 채우기
해설 최근의 예약 취소는 전시 부스를 위한 자리가 하나 더 생긴 것의 원인이기 때문에 이유를 나타내는 전치사 (C) due to(~ 때문에)가 정답이

다. (A) in spite of는 '~에도 불구하고', (B) opposite는 '~의 맞은편에'라는 의미이다. (D) as long as는 절을 이끄는 접속사이므로 정답이 될 수 없다.

132 올바른 시제의 동사 채우기 전체 문맥 파악
해설 문장에 동사가 없으므로 동사 (A)와 (C)가 정답의 후보이다. '참가하기 위해 250달러의 요금을 내다'라는 문맥인데, 이 경우 빈칸이 있는 문장만으로는 올바른 시제의 동사를 고를 수 없으므로 주변 문맥이나 전체 문맥을 파악하여 정답을 고른다. 앞부분에서 '무역 박람회에 등록을 할 다시 한번의 기회가 있다(you now have a second chance to register)'고 했고, 앞 문장에서 가능한 한 빨리 관심을 명시해야 한다고 했으므로 박람회 참가를 위한 요금을 내는 시점은 미래임을 알 수 있다. 따라서 미래 시제 (A) will need가 정답이다.

133 알맞은 문장 고르기
해석 (A) 이는 은행 계좌 이체나 저희 사무실을 방문함으로써 이루어질 수 있습니다.
(B) 그 부스는 박람회 내내 많은 사람들에게 방문되었습니다.
(C) 전시하는 회사들이 이용할 수 있는 몇몇 빈자리들이 있습니다.
(D) 등록의 마감일이 상당히 조정되었습니다.

해설 빈칸에 들어갈 알맞은 문장을 고르는 문제이므로 주변 문맥 또는 전체 문맥을 파악한다. 앞 문장 'You (will need) to pay a fee of $250 to participate.'에서 참가하기 위해 250달러의 요금을 내야 할 것이라고 했으므로, 빈칸에는 요금은 은행 계좌 이체나 사무실을 방문함으로써 이루어질 수 있다는 내용이 들어가야 함을 알 수 있다. 따라서 (A)가 정답이다.

어휘 **bank transfer** 은행 계좌 이체 **widely** adv. 많은 사람들 사이에서, 널리 **opening** n. 빈자리 **significantly** adv. 상당히, 크게

134 관계사 자리 채우기
해설 이 문장은 주어(This), 동사(is), 보어(an event)를 갖춘 완전한 절이므로 _____ a growing following over the years는 수식어 거품으로 보아야 한다. 이 수식어 거품은 빈칸 앞의 명사(an event)를 수식하고 있으므로 명사를 수식할 수 있는 현재분사를 포함하는 (C)와 주격 관계대명사와 관계절의 동사를 포함하는 (D)가 정답의 후보이다. '수년간 증가하는 팬들을 유치해오고 있는 행사'라는 의미가 되어야 하므로 an event를 선행사로 갖는 관계절을 이끌면서 관계절 내에서 주어 역할을 할 수 있는 주격 관계대명사(which)와 관계절의 동사(has attracted)를 포함하는 (D) which has attracted가 정답이다. 현재분사를 포함하는 (C)는 수동태이므로 뒤에 목적어(a growing following)를 취할 수 없다. 동사 (A)와 (B)는 명사를 뒤에서 수식할 수 없다.

어휘 **attract** v. 유치하다, 끌다

135-138번은 다음 기사에 관한 문제입니다.

Edge Technologies사의 자유 근무시간 제도
Sarah Peterson 작성

6월 11일—Edge Technologies사의 최고 경영자 Gerald McCarthy가 그의 회사가 자유 근무시간 제도를 채택할 것이라고 발표했다. [135]그것이 이 제도를 완전히 시행하면, 모든 직원들은 그들의 일일 근무 일정을 조정하는 선택권을 가질 것이다. 예를 들어, 오전 9시 대신에 오전 7시에 오는 직원은 두 시간 일찍 갈 수 있을 것이다. [136]매일 근무한 총 시간은 여전히 동일할 것이다. 모든 사람들은 계속해서 사무실에서 하루 8시간 근무로 일해야 한다.

새로운 제도의 공식 목표는 모든 직원들이 더 나은 일과 삶의 균형을 발전시키도록 하는 것이다. [137]이렇게 해서, Mr. McCarthy는 그의 회사가 증진된 사기를 느끼기를 희망한다. [138]이 정책은 직원 직장 복리 후생 면에서 기술 회사들 사이에서 높아진 경쟁력에 대한 대응으로 고안되었다.

---

flextime n. 자유 근무시간 **adopt** v. 채택하다
put ~ into practice ~을 시행하다 **adjust** v. 조정하다
eight-hour day 하루 8시간 근무 **stated** adj. 공식의, 정해진
work-life balance 일과 삶의 균형 **morale** n. 사기, 의욕
competitiveness n. 경쟁력 **in terms of** ~ 면에서, 관하여
benefit n. 복리 후생, 혜택, 이익

135 명사와 수/인칭 일치된 대명사 채우기 주변 문맥 파악
해설 단수 동사(puts)가 온 것으로 보아, 단수 주어 (A)와 (C)가 정답의 후보이다. 빈칸이 있는 문장만으로 정답을 고를 수 없으므로 주변 문맥이나 전체 문맥을 파악한다. 앞 문장에서 그의 회사(his company)가 자유 근무시간 제도를 채택할 것이라고 했으므로 빈칸에 들어갈 대명사가 가리키게 되는 것은 company이다. 따라서 단수 사물명사(company)를 가리키는 대명사 (A) it이 정답이다.

136 알맞은 문장 고르기
해석 (A) 직원들은 집에서 빠진 시간을 자유롭게 보충할 수 있다.
(B) 매장은 계속 주말에 영업할 것이다.
(C) 일정은 더 이상 주 단위로 변경되지 않을 것이다.
(D) 매일 근무한 총 시간은 여전히 동일할 것이다.

해설 빈칸에 들어갈 알맞은 문장을 고르는 문제이므로 주변 문맥 또는 전체 문맥을 파악한다. 앞 문장 'For example, a staff member who comes in at 7:00 A.M. instead of 9:00 A.M. will be able to leave two hours earlier.'에서 오전 9시 대신에 오전 7시에 오는 직원은 두 시간 일찍 갈 수 있을 것이라고 예를 들었고, 뒤 문장 'Everyone must continue to work an eight-hour day at the office.'에서 모든 사람들은 계속해서 사무실에서 하루 8시간 근무로 일해야 한다고 했으므로, 빈칸에는 매일 근무한 총 시간은 여전히 동일할 것이라는 내용이 들어가야 함을 알 수 있다. 따라서 (D)가 정답이다.

어휘 **make up** 보충하다, 구성하다 **missing** adj. 빠진, 누락된, 없어진 **on a weekly basis** 주 단위로

137 접속부사 채우기 주변 문맥 파악
해설 빈칸이 콤마와 함께 문장의 맨 앞에 온 접속부사 자리이므로, 앞 문장과 빈칸이 있는 문장의 의미 관계를 파악하여 정답을 선택한다. 앞 문장에서 새로운 제도의 공식 목표는 직원들이 더 나은 일과 삶의 균형을 발전시키도록 하는 것이라고 했고, 빈칸이 있는 문장에서는 Mr. McCarthy는 그의 회사가 증진된 사기를 느끼기를 희망한다고 했으므로, 앞에서 말한 내용에 따른 결과를 언급하는 내용의 문장에서 사용되는 (C) In this way(이렇게 해서)가 정답이다.

어휘 **nevertheless** adv. 그럼에도 불구하고 **despite that** 그럼에도 불구하고

138 태에 맞는 동사 채우기
해설 주어(The policy)와 동사(create)가 '정책이 고안되다'라는 수동의 의미를 가지므로 수동태 동사 (B) was created가 정답이다.

어휘 **create** v. 고안하다, 창조하다

139-142번은 다음 광고에 관한 문제입니다.

Tree Doctor사

나무는 잘 돌봐지면 오래 살 수 있습니다. [139]당신의 나무들의 수명을 연장시키기 위해서는, 그들에게 제대로 된 관리를 제공해야 합니다. [140]Tree Doctor사의 직원들은 나무 관리의 광범위한 지식을 가지고 있습니다. 이는 그들이 모두 많은 경험을 가진 공인된 전문가들이기 때문입니다. 저희의 전문가들이 당신의 나무들의 상태를 평가하기 위해 당신의 소유지를 방문해드릴 수 있습니다. [141]구체적으로 말하자면, 그들은 병든 나뭇가지들과 뿌리들을 확인해드릴 것입니다. [142]그리고 만약 당신이 새로운 나무들을 심는 것을 고려하는 중이라면, 그들은 당신이 더할 계획인 나무들 중 어떤 것이 당신의 땅에서 잘 자랄지에 대해 조언을 해드릴

수 있습니다. 저희의 서비스들에 대해 더 알아보고 예약을 하시려면, www.treedoctor.com을 방문해 주십시오.

> **take care of** ~을 돌보다 **proper** adj. 제대로 된, 적절한
> **care** n. 관리, 보살핌, 관심 **certified** adj. 공인된, 증명된
> **professional** n. 전문가; adj. 전문적인 **a great deal of** 많은
> **property** n. 소유지, 건물, 부동산 **evaluate** v. 평가하다, 감정하다

139 to 부정사 채우기

해설 '나무들의 수명을 연장시키기 위해서'라는 의미가 되어야 하므로 목적을 나타내는 to 부정사 (B) To prolong이 정답이다.

어휘 prolong v. 연장시키다, 연장하다

140 형용사 어휘 고르기 주변 문맥 파악

해설 '직원들이 나무 관리의 ____한 지식을 가지고 있다'라는 문맥이므로 (A) prior(사전의), (C) extensive(광범위한, 폭넓은), (D) partial(부분적인, 불완전한)이 정답의 후보이다. 빈칸이 있는 문장만으로 정답을 고를 수 없으므로 주변 문맥이나 전체 문맥을 파악한다. 뒤 문장에서 '이는 그들이 모두 많은 경험을 가진 공인된 전문가들이기 때문이다(This is because they are all certified professionals with a great deal of experience.)'라고 했으므로 직원들이 광범위한 지식을 가지고 있음을 알 수 있다. 따라서 (C) extensive가 정답이다.

141 알맞은 문장 고르기

해석 (A) 그 결과, 그들은 다양한 치료법들에 대해 잘 알게 되었습니다.
(B) 특정 나무들은 이미 마당에서 제거되었습니다.
(C) 몇몇 비료들은 많은 종들에게 해롭습니다.
(D) 구체적으로 말하자면, 그들은 병든 나뭇가지들과 뿌리들을 확인해드릴 것입니다.

해설 빈칸에 들어갈 알맞은 문장을 고르는 문제이므로 주변 문맥 또는 전체 문맥을 파악한다. 앞 문장 'Our experts can visit your property to evaluate the condition of your trees.'에서 전문가들이 나무들의 상태를 평가하기 위해 소유지를 방문해줄 수 있다고 했으므로, 빈칸에는 구체적으로 말하자면 전문가들이 병든 나뭇가지들과 뿌리들을 확인해줄 것이라는 나무 상태 평가에 대한 구체적인 내용이 들어가야 함을 알 수 있다. 따라서 (D)가 정답이다.

어휘 be familiar with ~에 대해 잘 알다 a variety of 다양한
treatment n. 치료(법) yard n. 마당 fertilizer n. 비료
species n. 종 diseased adj. 병든, 병에 걸린 branch n. 나뭇가지
root n. 뿌리

142 올바른 시제의 동사 채우기

해설 새로운 나무들을 심는 것을 고려하는 중이라면 어떤 것이 당신의 땅에서 잘 자랄지에 대해 조언해줄 수 있다는 미래의 상황을 언급하는 문맥이므로 미래 시제 (A) will grow가 정답이다.

143-146번은 다음 이메일에 관한 문제입니다.

> 수신: Belle Rogers <brogers@smail.com>
> 발신: Aaron Cooper <aaroncooper@moneyphase.com>
> 제목: 환영합니다!
> 날짜: 1월 31일
>
> Ms. Rogers께,
>
> [143]저희 전체 회사를 대표하여, 저는 새로운 고객이 되신 귀하를 환영합니다. 저희는 귀하께서 귀하의 투자 포트폴리오를 관리하는 것에 대한 도움을 위해 저희 회사를 선택해주셔서 매우 기쁩니다.
>
> [144]저희는 귀하의 재정을 계획하는 것이 시간, 인내, 노력을 요한다는 것을 알고 있습니다. 선택할 수 있는 매우 다양한 투자 선택지들이 있고, 적합한 것들을 선택하는 것은 안내를 필요로 합니다. 귀하께서는 ⟳

저희가 전문적인 조언을 제공해드릴 것을 보장받으실 수 있습니다.

저희의 첫 회의를 언제 갖는 것이 편하실지 제게 알려주시기 바랍니다. [145]저희는 그때에 귀하의 단기 재정 목표들을 논의할 것입니다. [146]제게 555-1221로 연락하시거나 이 이메일로 답을 주시기 바랍니다. 다시 한번, 귀하를 환영하며 저희의 관계가 성공적이기를 바랍니다!

Aaron Cooper 드림

투자 분석가

> **on behalf of** ~을 대표(대신)하여 **manage** v. 관리하다, 운영하다
> **finance** n. 재정, 자금 **patience** n. 인내, 참을성
> **a wide variety of** 매우 다양한 **guidance** n. 안내, 지도
> **assure** v. 보장하다, 확신시키다 **expert** adj. 전문적인; n. 전문가

143 명사 어휘 고르기 주변 문맥 파악

해설 '새로운 ____이 된 귀하를 환영한다'라는 문맥이므로 모든 보기가 정답의 후보이다. 빈칸이 있는 문장만으로 정답을 고를 수 없으므로 주변 문맥이나 전체 문맥을 파악한다. 뒤 문장에서 '당신의 투자 포트폴리오를 관리하는 것에 대한 도움을 위해 자사를 선택해주어 매우 기쁘다(We are thrilled that you have chosen our company for assistance with managing your investment portfolio.)'라고 했으므로 이메일 수신자가 회사의 새로운 고객이 되었음을 알 수 있다. 따라서 (A) customer(고객)가 정답이다.

어휘 owner n. 소유주 vendor n. 판매자

144 동사 어휘 고르기 전체 문맥 파악

해설 '재정을 ____하는 것이 시간, 인내, 노력을 요한다'라는 문맥이므로 모든 보기가 정답의 후보이다. 빈칸이 있는 문장만으로 정답을 고를 수 없으므로 주변 문맥이나 전체 문맥을 파악한다. 뒤 문장에서 '선택할 수 있는 매우 다양한 투자 선택지들이 있고, 적합한 것들을 선택하는 것은 안내를 필요로 한다(There are a wide variety of investment options to choose from, and selecting the right ones requires guidance.)'고 했고, 뒷부분에서 '전문적인 조언을 제공해줄 것이다(we will provide you with expert advice)'라고 했으므로 재정을 계획하는 것을 알 수 있다. 따라서 (C) planning(계획하다)이 정답이다.

어휘 transfer v. 넘겨주다, 이동하다 decrease v. 줄이다, 줄다
cancel v. 취소하다

145 알맞은 문장 고르기

해석 (A) 저희는 이 제안들이 귀하의 수익을 올려줄 것이라 확신합니다.
(B) 저희는 귀하께서 저희에게 이메일로 보내신 재정 관련 조언에 감사드립니다.
(C) 저희는 그때에 귀하의 장단기 재정 목표들을 논의할 것입니다.
(D) 저희는 저희 약속의 일정을 변경해야 한다고 생각합니다.

해설 빈칸에 들어갈 알맞은 문장을 고르는 문제이므로 주변 문맥 또는 전체 문맥을 파악한다. 앞 문장 'Please let me know when it would be convenient to hold our first meeting.'에서 첫 회의를 언제 갖는 것이 편할지 알려달라고 했으므로, 빈칸에는 그때에 귀하의 장단기 재정 목표들을 논의할 것이라는 내용이 들어가야 함을 알 수 있다. 따라서 (C)가 정답이다.

어휘 reschedule v. 일정을 변경하다

146 상관접속사 채우기

해설 상관접속사 either와 맞는 짝인 (C) or가 정답이다. 참고로, either A or B가 동사구(contact me)와 동사구(reply to this e-mail)를 연결하고 있다.

PART 7

147-148번은 다음 공고에 관한 문제입니다.

> 브란덴부르크의 제3회 연례 겨울 축제 행사가 12월 2일에 열릴 것입니다. ^{147-B}Muller길을 따라 장식물들이 놓여질 것이고, Hastings가를 따라 얼음 조각품들이 있을 것이며, ^{147-C}Rossellini로와 Peters가의 교차로에 있는 스케이트장이 오전 8시부터 오후 6시까지 스케이트를 타는 사람들에게 개방될 것입니다. ^{147-D}이날 밤의 주요 행사는 Sterner길에 있는 큰 소나무의 점등일 것이며, 이는 오후 10시에 이루어질 것입니다. 그 후에, ^{147-A}브란덴부르크 악대가 다양한 휴일 노래들을 연주할 것입니다. ¹⁴⁸조명들은 새해 첫날까지 계속 켜져 있을 것이며, 그것들은 다음날 도시 공원 관리 직원들에 의해 치워질 것입니다.

decoration n. 장식(물) sculpture n. 조각(품)
ice rink 스케이트장, 아이스 링크 intersection n. 교차로
lighting n. 점등, 조명 brass band (관)악대 afterward adv. 그 후에

147 Not/True 문제
문제 겨울 축제 행사의 즐길거리가 아닌 것은?
(A) 음악 연주
(B) Peters가의 장식물
(C) 스케이트장의 운영
(D) 나무의 점등

해설 질문의 핵심 어구인 a feature of the Winter Festival Ceremony와 관련된 내용을 지문에서 찾아 보기와 대조하는 Not/True 문제이다. (A)는 'the Brandenburg Brass Band will play a variety of holiday songs'에서 브란덴부르크 악대가 다양한 휴일 노래들을 연주할 것이라고 했으므로 지문의 내용과 일치한다. (B)는 'Decorations will be placed along Muller Way'에서 장식물들이 Muller길을 따라 놓여질 것이라고 했으므로 Peters가의 장식물이라는 것은 지문의 내용과 일치하지 않는다. 따라서 (B)가 정답이다. (C)는 'the ice rink ~ will be open to skaters'에서 스케이트장이 스케이트를 타는 사람들에게 개방될 것이라고 했으므로 지문의 내용과 일치한다. (D)는 'The main event of the night will be the lighting of the large pine tree'에서 이날 밤의 주요 행사는 큰 소나무의 점등일 것이라고 했으므로 지문의 내용과 일치한다.

패러프레이징
play a variety of holiday songs 다양한 휴일 노래들을 연주하다
→ performance of some music 음악 연주
the ice rink ~ will be open 스케이트장이 개방될 것이다 → operation of a skating rink 스케이트장의 운영

어휘 feature n. (행사 등의) 즐길거리, 특색 operation n. 운영

148 육하원칙 문제
문제 새해 첫날 직후에 무슨 일이 일어날 것인가?
(A) 얼음 조각품들이 치워질 것이다.
(B) 도시 공원이 재개장할 것이다.
(C) 조명들이 치워질 것이다.
(D) 기념식이 열릴 것이다.

해설 새해 첫날 직후에 무슨(What) 일이 일어날 것인지를 묻는 육하원칙 문제이다. 질문의 핵심 어구인 after New Year's Day와 관련하여, 'The lights will stay up until New Year's Day, and they will be removed the next day'에서 조명들은 새해 첫날까지 계속 켜져 있을 것이며 다음날 치워질 것이라고 했으므로 (C)가 정답이다.

어휘 take down ~을 치우다

149-150번은 다음 편지에 관한 문제입니다.

> 5월 12일
>
> John Simon
> 772번지 North가
> 투손, 애리조나 주 85701
>
> Mr. Simon께,
>
> 세계 문화 재단에 의해 주최되는 Flagstaff에서의 만찬에서 연설을 하는 데 동의해주셔서 감사드립니다. ¹⁴⁹모든 사람들이 귀하께서 안데스 산맥 지역의 고대 문화에 대해 진행해오신 연구들에 대해 듣게 되어 기뻐하고 있습니다. 행사의 기조연설자이시기 때문에, ¹⁵⁰저희 재단의 회장인 Ernesto Paramo 바로 다음에 귀하께서 연설을 하실 것입니다. 그 후에, 대학생인 Will Meyer가 콜롬비아로의 최근 여행에 대해 그가 만든 영상을 보여줄 것이며, 이후 저녁 식사가 제공될 것입니다. 폐회사는 Robert Shelling에 의해 전해질 것인데, 그는 Flagstaff 문화원을 운영합니다.
>
> 귀하의 성함이 저희 초대자 명단에 추가되어 있으니, 귀하께서는 이곳에 와주시기만 하면 됩니다. 귀하와 함께하기를 기대합니다.
>
> Roberto Marquez 드림

organize v. 주최하다, 준비하다 conduct v. 진행하다
ancient adj. 고대의 keynote speaker 기조연설자
guest list 초대자 명단 show up ~에 오다, 나타나다

149 추론 문제
문제 Mr. Simon은 누구일 것 같은가?
(A) 재단의 장
(B) 워크숍 주최자
(C) 영화 제작자
(D) 연구원

해설 질문의 핵심 어구인 Mr. Simon에 대해 추론하는 문제이다. 'Everyone is excited to hear about the studies you've conducted about the ancient cultures of the Andes Mountains region.'에서 모든 사람들이 Mr. Simon이 안데스 산맥 지역의 고대 문화에 대해 진행해온 연구들에 대해 듣게 되어 기뻐하고 있다고 했으므로 Mr. Simon이 연구원이라는 것을 추론할 수 있다. 따라서 (D)가 정답이다.

어휘 head n. 장, 책임자 filmmaker n. 영화 제작자
researcher n. 연구원

150 육하원칙 문제
문제 누가 Mr. Simon보다 먼저 나서는가?
(A) Ernesto Paramo
(B) Will Meyer
(C) Robert Shelling
(D) Roberto Marquez

해설 누가(Who) Mr. Simon보다 먼저 나서는지를 묻는 육하원칙 문제이다. 질문의 핵심 어구인 precede Mr. Simon과 관련하여, 'you [Mr. Simon]'ll be giving your speech right after our organization's president, Ernesto Paramo'에서 재단의 회장인 Ernesto Paramo 바로 다음에 Mr. Simon이 연설을 할 것이라고 했으므로 (A)가 정답이다.

어휘 precede v. ~보다 먼저 나서다

151-152번은 다음 메시지 대화문에 관한 문제입니다.

> Tony Webb [오후 1시 15분]
> Dave Jonson이 다음 주에 떠난다는 것을 들었나요?

| Laura Hughes | [오후 1시 17분] |

네. 151-A/152그와 제가 오늘 아까 점심을 먹으러 나갔을 때, 152그가 새 일자리에 대한 제의를 받아들였다고 말했어요.

| Tony Webb | [오후 1시 19분] |

단지 그 혼자만이 아니에요. 152회사가 곧 더 많은 직원을 채용할까요?

| Laura Hughes | [오후 1시 21분] |

네. 인사부가 다음 주에 우리 부서를 위한 지원자들을 면접할 거예요. 151-B저는 새로 고용된 직원들을 위한 교육을 돕기로 했어요.

| Tony Webb | [오후 1시 21분] |

좋아요. 그래야 할 때죠. 151-D너무 적은 사람들로 우리의 모든 마케팅 기한을 지키기가 정말 어려웠어요.

| Laura Hughes | [오후 1시 22분] |

151-D저도 알아요. 제 직원 모두가 그것에 대해 걱정하고 있어요. 어쨌든, 제가 소식을 더 듣는 대로 알려줄게요.

---

offer n. 제의, 제안; v. 제의하다   **meet** v. (기한 등을) 지키다

---

151 Not/True 문제

문제 Ms. Hughes에 대해 사실이 아닌 것은?
(A) 최근에 동료와 함께 식사하러 갔다.
(B) 일을 위해 새 직원들을 예비 교육할 것이다.
(C) 다른 회사에서 일자리를 제의받았다.
(D) 마케팅 부서의 직원이다.

해설 질문의 핵심 어구인 Ms. Hughes와 관련된 내용을 지문에서 찾아 보기와 대조하는 Not/True 문제이다. (A)는 'When he[Dave Jonson] and I were out for lunch earlier today'(1:17 P.M.)에서 Ms. Hughes가 Dave Jonson과 오늘 아까 점심을 먹으러 나갔다고 했으므로 지문의 내용과 일치한다. (B)는 'I've agreed to help with the training for newly hired employees.'(1:21 P.M.)에서 Ms. Hughes가 새로 고용된 직원들을 위한 교육을 돕기로 했다고 했으므로 지문의 내용과 일치한다. (C)는 지문에 언급되지 않은 내용이다. 따라서 (C)가 정답이다. (D)는 'It's been really hard to meet all of our marketing deadlines with so few people'(1:21 P.M.)에서 Mr. Webb이 너무 적은 사람들로 우리의 모든 마케팅 기한을 지키기가 정말 어려웠다고 하자, 'I know. Everyone on my staff has been worried about that.'(1:22 P.M.)에서 Ms. Hughes가 자신도 안다고 하면서 자신의 직원 모두가 그것에 대해 걱정하고 있다고 했으므로 지문의 내용과 일치한다.

패러프레이징
help with the training for newly hired employees 새로 고용된 직원들을 위한 교육을 돕다 → prepare new employees 새 직원들을 예비 교육하다

어휘 **colleague** n. 동료   **prepare** v. 예비 교육하다, 준비시키다
position n. (일)자리

---

152 의도 파악 문제

문제 오후 1시 19분에, Mr. Webb이 "He's not the only one"이라고 썼을 때, 그가 의도한 것 같은 것은?
(A) 업무가 다른 사람에게 할당될 것이다.
(B) 교육 서류가 업데이트되어야 한다.
(C) 몇몇 지원자들이 선정되었다.
(D) 다른 팀원들이 사직했다.

해설 Mr. Webb이 의도한 것 같은 것을 묻는 문제이므로, 질문의 인용어구(He's not the only one)가 언급된 주변 문맥을 확인한다. 'When he[Dave Jonson] and I were out for lunch earlier today, he mentioned that he had accepted an offer of a new job.' (1:17 P.M.)에서 Ms. Hughes가 Dave Jonson과 오늘 아까 점심을 먹으러 나갔을 때 그가 새 일자리에 대한 제의를 받아들였다고 말

했다고 하자, Mr. Webb이 'He's not the only one'(단지 그 혼자만이 아니에요)이라고 한 후, 'Will the company hire more staff soon?'(1:19 P.M.)에서 회사가 곧 더 많은 직원을 채용할 것인지 묻는 말을 통해, 다른 팀원들이 사직했다는 것을 알 수 있다. 따라서 (D)가 정답이다.

어휘 **resign** v. 사직하다, 그만두다

153-154번은 다음 이메일에 관한 문제입니다.

수신: Mitchell O'Connor <moconnor@fastmail.com>
발신: Playback Streaming사 <support@playback.com>
제목: *Secrets of Paris*
날짜: 9월 19일

Mr. O'Connor께,

방송 콘텐츠 스트리밍 서비스 1위인 Playback Streaming사를 이용해 주셔서 감사합니다. 저희 기록은 귀하께서 최근에 153-CSam Marshall에 의해 감독되어 처음에 HistoryNow 채널에서 방영되었던 다큐멘터리 *Secrets of Paris*를 시청하셨다고 나타냅니다. 저희는 항상 저희 고객분들께 시청하신 것에 대한 평가를 작성하도록 권장하고 있습니다. 이를 하시려면, 의견을 말하고 싶은 영상 아래에 있는 버튼을 클릭만 하시면 됩니다. 특별 보상으로, 154100개 이상의 상영물을 평가해주시는 분들은 "프리미엄 이용자" 등급을 받으시는데, 이는 50달러 상당의 무료 영화들과 TV 쇼들을 받을 수 있도록 합니다.

다시 한번, 저희 서비스를 이용해주셔서 감사합니다.

Playback Streaming사 고객 지원 부서

---

media n. 방송   **direct** v. 감독하다   **air** v. 방영하다
encourage v. 권장하다   **review** n. 평가; v. 평가하다
beneath prep. ~ 아래에   **incentive** n. 보상, 장려책
award v. 주다, 수여하다   **status** n. 등급, 지위
eligible adj. (특정 조건이 맞아서) ~을 할 수 있는
complimentary adj. 무료의

---

153 Not/True 문제

문제 *Secrets of Paris*에 대해 언급된 것은?
(A) 유명한 책에 바탕을 둔다.
(B) 최우수 감독상을 받았다.
(C) 역사 채널에서 처음으로 방영되었다.
(D) 추가 비용으로 구매 가능하다.

해설 질문의 핵심 어구인 *Secrets of Paris*와 관련된 내용을 지문에서 찾아 보기와 대조하는 Not/True 문제이다. (A)와 (B)는 지문에 언급되지 않은 내용이다. (C)는 'the documentary *Secrets of Paris*, ~ first aired on the HistoryNow Channel'에서 처음에 HistoryNow 채널에서 방영되었던 다큐멘터리 *Secrets of Paris*라고 했으므로 지문의 내용과 일치한다. 따라서 (C)가 정답이다. (D)는 지문에 언급되지 않은 내용이다.

어휘 **be based on** ~에 바탕을 두다

---

154 육하원칙 문제

문제 고객들이 100개의 평가를 작성할 경우 무엇을 받을 수 있는가?
(A) 영화의 DVD 사본
(B) 추가 멤버십 포인트
(C) 1년간의 구독
(D) 무료 방송 콘텐츠

해설 고객들이 100개의 평가를 작성할 경우 무엇(What)을 받을 수 있는지를 묻는 육하원칙 문제이다. 질문의 핵심 어구인 customers receive if they write 100 reviews와 관련하여, 'those who review 100 items or more are ~ eligible to receive $50 worth of complimentary movies and TV shows'에서 100개 이상의 상

영물을 평가하는 사람들에게 50달러 상당의 무료 영화들과 TV 쇼들을 받을 수 있도록 한다고 했으므로 (D)가 정답이다.

패러프레이징
complimentary movies and TV shows 무료 영화들과 TV 쇼들 → Free media content 무료 방송 콘텐츠

어휘 copy n. 사본 yearlong adj. 1년간의 subscription n. 구독

155-157번은 다음 웹페이지에 관한 문제입니다.

브린클리 과학 센터를 탐험해보세요

과학의 경이로움을 대중과 함께 공유하는 데 전념하는 3층 높이의 박물관인 브린클리 과학 센터를 방문하는 데는 이유가 필요하지 않습니다. 저희 시설에서는, ¹⁵⁵⁻ᶜ음파와 토네이도부터 땅과 멀리 있는 행성들까지 모든 것에 대한 전시를 관람할 수 있습니다. 그러니, 여러분의 친구들과 가족들을 모두 데려오세요!

박물관 운영 시간
화요일–금요일: 오전 9시부터 오후 5시까지
토요일–일요일: 오전 9시부터 오후 6시까지
¹⁵⁵⁻ᴰ월요일에는 닫음

표 가격
일반 입장 10달러
학생 8달러
65세가 넘는 사람 6달러
¹⁵⁶⁻ᶜ브린클리 대학 학생들은 무료입장
6세 미만 어린이들은 무료입장

¹⁵⁶⁻ᴰ매달 첫 번째 화요일에, 모든 브린클리 주민들은 무료로 입장이 가능합니다. 거주 증명서 필요.

길 안내
자동차: 20번 고속도로에서, 60번 출구로 나가서 Grant로로 가십시오. 곧이어, ¹⁵⁷Lessing길 쪽으로 좌회전하십시오. 왼쪽 방향에 센터가 있을 것입니다.
지하철: Havel가 역의 2번 출구에서, Wallace가 쪽으로 우회전하십시오. 100미터 직진한 후 ¹⁵⁷Lessing길 쪽으로 우회전하십시오. 오른쪽 방향에 센터가 있을 것입니다.
버스: 80번과 125번 버스 모두 센터 바로 밖에 정차합니다.

---

explore v. 탐험하다 excuse n. 이유, 구실 story n. (건물의) 층
dedicated to ~에 전념하는 wonders n. 경이(로운 것)
exhibit n. 전시(품) sound wave 음파 distant adj. 멀리 있는
general adj. 일반적인 admission n. 입장, 입장료
admit v. 입장을 허락하다, 인정하다 proof of residence 거주 증명서

155 Not/True 문제
문제 브린클리 과학 센터에 대해 언급된 것은?
(A) 어린이들을 위한 특별한 공간이 있다.
(B) 많은 해외 관람객들을 끌어들인다.
(C) 기상과 관련된 전시가 있다.
(D) 휴일에는 닫는다.

해설 질문의 핵심 어구인 Brinkley Science Center와 관련된 내용을 지문에서 찾아 보기와 대조하는 Not/True 문제이다. (A)와 (B)는 지문에 언급되지 않은 내용이다. (C)는 'you can view exhibits on ~ tornadoes'에서 토네이도에 대한 전시를 관람할 수 있다고 했으므로 지문의 내용과 일치한다. 따라서 (C)가 정답이다. (D)는 'Closed on Mondays'에서 월요일에는 닫는다고 했으므로 지문의 내용과 일치하지 않는다.

패러프레이징
exhibits on ~ tornadoes 토네이도에 대한 전시 → weather-related exhibit 기상과 관련된 전시

어휘 attract v. 끌어들이다

156 육하원칙 문제
문제 누가 입장료를 절대 부과 받지 않는가?
(A) 노인들
(B) 6세 미만 어린이들의 부모들
(C) 브린클리 대학 학생들
(D) 브린클리 주민들

해설 누가(Who) 입장료를 절대 부과 받지 않는지를 묻는 육하원칙 문제이다. 질문의 핵심 어구인 never charged for admission과 관련하여, 'Free admission for students attending Brinkley College'에서 브린클리 대학 학생들은 무료입장이라고 했으므로 (C)가 정답이다. (D)는 'On the first Tuesday of every month, all residents of Brinkley are admitted for free.'에서 매달 첫 번째 화요일에 모든 브린클리 주민들이 무료로 입장이 가능하다고 했으므로 답이 될 수 없다.

패러프레이징
never charged for admission 입장료를 절대 부과 받지 않는 → Free admission 무료입장

157 추론 문제
문제 브린클리 과학 센터는 어디에 위치해 있는 것 같은가?
(A) Grant로에
(B) Havel가에
(C) Wallace가에
(D) Lessing길에

해설 질문의 핵심 어구인 Brinkley Science Center ~ located에 대해 추론하는 문제이다. 'turn left onto Lessing Way. The center will be on your left.'에서 Lessing길 쪽으로 좌회전하면 왼쪽 방향에 센터가 있을 것이라고 했고, 'turn right onto Lessing Way. The center will be on your right.'에서 Lessing길 쪽으로 우회전하면 오른쪽 방향에 센터가 있을 것이라고 했으므로 브린클리 과학 센터가 Lessing길에 위치해 있다는 것을 추론할 수 있다. 따라서 (D)가 정답이다.

158-160번은 다음 구인 광고에 관한 문제입니다.

전임 매장 직원을 찾고 있는 Heimart

Heimart는 가정용품과 가전제품을 저렴한 가격에 제공하는 것을 전문으로 하는 선도적인 유럽 소매업체입니다. — [1] —. ¹⁵⁸⁻ᴬ뉴욕, 시카고, 그리고 로스앤젤레스에서 저희의 첫 번째 미국 매장들의 성공 이후, ¹⁵⁸⁻ᴰ저희는 미국의 다른 주요 도시들에 있는 새로운 지점들에 충원할 것을 기대하고 있습니다.

¹⁵⁹매장 직원으로서, 당신은 새로운 재고의 하역, 선반 채우기, 매장을 항상 깨끗하고 정돈된 상태로 유지하는 것과 같은 일상적인 작업을 수행할 책임이 있을 것입니다. — [2] —. 성과에 따라, 다른 직무를 해볼 기회가 제공될 수도 있습니다. 여러분은 금전 등록기를 다루는 방법, 고객 서비스에서 일하는 방법 등을 배울 수 있습니다. — [3] —.

지원자들은 21세 이상이어야 하며 유사한 직무에 이전 경험이 있어야 합니다. ¹⁶⁰직원들은 유연한 일정으로 근무할 의향이 있어야 합니다. — [4] —. 합격자들은 경쟁력 있는 시간당 임금, 의료 보험, 정기 상여금, 그리고 지속적인 직업 훈련을 받을 것입니다.

지원하려면, jobs@heimart.com으로 이메일을 보내십시오.

---

full-time adj. 전임의 store associate 매장 직원
leading adj. 선도적인 specialize in ~을 전문으로 하다
appliance n. 가전제품 look to ~을 기대하다, 기다리다
be responsible for ~에 책임이 있다 carry out 수행하다
routine adj. 일상적인 unload v. 하역하다, 짐을 내리다
orderly adj. 정돈된 register n. (금전) 등록기
be willing to ~할 의향이 있다, 기꺼이 ~할 것이다 flexible adj. 유연한
successful candidate 합격자 competitive adj. 경쟁력 있는
wage n. 임금, 급료

158 Not/True 문제

문제 Heimart에 대해 언급된 것은?
(A) 첫 번째 미국 매장을 열 것이다.
(B) 다양한 사무용 가구를 취급한다.
(C) 가정배달 서비스를 제공하고 있다.
(D) 몇몇 도시들에 일자리가 있다.

해설 질문의 핵심 어구인 Heimart와 관련된 내용을 지문에서 찾아 보기와 대조하는 Not/True 문제이다. (A)는 'the success of our first American stores in New York, Chicago, and Los Angeles'에서 뉴욕, 시카고, 그리고 로스앤젤레스에서 첫 번째 미국 매장들이 성공했다고 했으므로 지문의 내용과 일치하지 않는다. (B)와 (C)는 지문에 언급되지 않은 내용이다. (D)는 'we are looking to fill positions at new locations in other major US cities'에서 미국의 다른 주요 도시들에 있는 새로운 지점들에 충원할 것을 기대하고 있다고 했으므로 지문의 내용과 일치한다. 따라서 (D)가 정답이다.

어휘 carry v. 취급하다

159 육하원칙 문제

문제 매장 직원의 책무는 무엇인가?
(A) 일정을 조정하는 것
(B) 제품 공급업체를 찾는 것
(C) 청결을 유지하는 것
(D) 주문품을 배달하는 것

해설 매장 직원의 책무가 무엇(What)인지를 묻는 육하원칙 문제이다. 질문의 핵심 어구인 responsibility of the store associate와 관련하여, 'As a store associate, you will be responsible for carrying out routine tasks, such as ~ keeping the store clean and orderly at all times.'에서 매장 직원으로서 매장을 항상 깨끗하고 정돈된 상태로 유지하는 것과 같은 일상적인 작업을 수행할 책임이 있다고 했으므로 (C)가 정답이다.

패러프레이징
keeping ~ clean 깨끗하게 유지하는 것 → Maintaining cleanliness 청결을 유지하는 것

어휘 arrange v. 조정하다　maintain v. 유지하다

160 문장 위치 찾기 문제

문제 [1], [2], [3], [4]로 표시된 위치 중, 다음 문장이 들어갈 곳으로 가장 적절한 것은?

"이것은 때때로 이른 아침 및 야간 교대를 포함합니다."

(A) [1]
(B) [2]
(C) [3]
(D) [4]

해설 지문의 흐름상 주어진 문장이 들어가기에 가장 적절한 곳을 고르는 문제이다. This includes early morning and night shifts on occasion에서 이것이 때때로 이른 아침 및 야간 교대를 포함한다고 했으므로, 주어진 문장 앞에 근무 시간과 관련된 내용이 있을 것임을 예상할 수 있다. [4]의 앞 문장인 'Employees should be willing to work on a flexible schedule.'에서 직원들은 유연한 일정으로 근무할 의향이 있어야 한다고 했으므로, [4]에 주어진 문장이 들어가면 직원들은 유연한 일정으로 일할 의향이 있어야 하며 이것은 때때로 이른 아침 및 야간 교대를 포함한다는 내용을 설명하는 자연스러운 문맥이 된다는 것을 알 수 있다. 따라서 (D)가 정답이다.

어휘 shift n. 교대(조)　on occasion 때때로

161-163번은 다음 회람에 관한 문제입니다.

수신: Brumfield사의 전 직원
발신: Fred Sears, 인사부장

날짜: 5월 10일
제목: 개조 작업

아시다시피, ¹⁶¹⁻ᴮBrumfield사는 다음 주부터 한 달 동안의 4층 개조 작업을 진행할 것입니다. ¹⁶¹⁻ᶜ이는 현재 그곳에서 근무하고 있는 마케팅 부서 직원들에게 자리 문제를 야기합니다. ¹⁶²저희는 원래 그들을 건물 다른 층들에 있는 여러 이용 가능한 자리에 앉히는 것을 검토했었습니다. 하지만, 고심 끝에, 저희는 이것이 좋은 방안이 아니라고 결론지었습니다. 마케팅 직원들은 전화상으로 많은 이야기를 하는 것이 요구되기 때문에, ¹⁶²그들을 이런 식으로 배치하는 것은 정숙이 필요한 업무들을 하는 다른 부서 직원들에게 성가실 수 있습니다.

그러므로, ¹⁶¹⁻ᶜ/¹⁶³저희는 건물의 2층에 있는 대회의실에 그 팀을 위한 임시 작업 공간을 만들기로 결정했습니다. IT 부서는 필요한 컴퓨터들과 인쇄기들을 내일 그곳에 설치할 것입니다. ¹⁶³3층에 직원 휴게실 옆에 있는 더 작은 회의실이 다음 한 달 정도 동안 다른 부서 직원들이 이용할 수 있는 유일한 회의실이 될 것입니다.

감사합니다.

aware adj. 알고 있는　undergo v. 진행하다　create v. 야기하다, 만들다
space n. 자리, 공간　look into ~을 검토하다　seat v. 앉히다, 수용하다
consideration n. 고심, 고려　conclude v. 결론짓다
arrange v. 배치하다　bothersome adj. 성가신, 번거로운
silence n. 정숙　temporary adj. 임시의　break room 휴게실

161 Not/True 문제

문제 Brumfield사에 대해 언급된 것은?
(A) 마케팅팀을 확장하고 있다.
(B) 사무실을 개조할 것이다.
(C) IT 부서를 이동시킬 것이다.
(D) 컴퓨터들을 업그레이드하고 있다.

해설 질문의 핵심 어구인 Brumfield Co.와 관련된 내용을 지문에서 찾아 보기와 대조하는 Not/True 문제이다. (A)는 지문에 언급되지 않은 내용이다. (B)는 'Brumfield Co. will be undergoing a month-long renovation of its fourth floor starting next week'에서 Brumfield사는 다음 주부터 한 달 동안의 4층 개조 작업을 진행할 것이라고 했으므로 지문의 내용과 일치한다. 따라서 (B)가 정답이다. (C)는 'This creates a space problem for the marketing department employees currently working there[fourth floor].'에서 현재 4층에서 근무하고 있는 마케팅 부서 직원들에게 자리 문제를 야기한다고 했고, 'we have decided to create a temporary work area for the team ~ on the second floor of the building'에서 건물의 2층에 마케팅 팀을 위한 임시 작업 공간을 만들기로 결정했다고 한 것에서, IT 부서가 아닌 마케팅 부서를 이동시킬 것임을 알 수 있으므로 지문의 내용과 일치하지 않는다. (D)는 지문에 언급되지 않은 내용이다.

어휘 expand v. 확장하다　relocate v. 이동시키다

162 육하원칙 문제

문제 마케팅 직원들은 왜 여러 층에 걸쳐 흩어지지 않을 것인가?
(A) 대부분의 업무들을 함께 해야 한다.
(B) 중요한 발표를 준비하고 있다.
(C) 다른 직원들에게 지장을 줄 것이다.
(D) 서로 프로젝트들에 대해 논의해야 한다.

해설 마케팅 직원들이 왜(Why) 여러 층에 걸쳐 흩어지지 않을 것인지를 묻는 육하원칙 문제이다. 질문의 핵심 어구인 marketing staff not be spread out over several floors와 관련하여, 'We initially looked into seating them[marketing staff] in various available workstations on the other floors of the building.'에서 원래 마케팅 직원들을 건물 다른 층들에 있는 여러 이용 가능한 자리에 앉히는 것을 검토했다고 했고, 'arranging them in this way would be bothersome to other department members whose jobs require silence'에서 그들을 이런 식으로 배치하는 것은 정숙이 필요한 업무들을 하는 다른 부서 직원들에게 성가실 수 있다고 했으므로 (C)가 정답이다.

패러프레이징
bothersome to other department members 다른 부서 직원들에게 성가신 → **disruptive to other workers** 다른 직원들에게 지장을 주는

어휘 **spread out** 널리 흩어지게 하다 **assignment** n. (할당된) 업무 **disruptive** adj. 지장을 주는

163 추론 문제

문제 대회의실에 대해 추론될 수 있는 것은?
(A) 일부 직원들은 이용할 수 없을 것이다.
(B) 인쇄실 옆에 위치해 있다.
(C) 지난달에 새로 단장되었다.
(D) 직원 휴게실로 사용되어 왔다.

해설 질문의 핵심 어구인 main conference room에 대해 추론하는 문제이다. 'we have decided to create a temporary work area for the team[marketing team] in the main conference room on the second floor of the building'에서 건물의 2층에 있는 대회의실에 마케팅 팀을 위한 임시 작업 공간을 만들기로 결정했다고 했고, 'The smaller meeting room ~ will be the only one available for members of other departments to use'에서 더 작은 회의실이 다른 부서 직원들이 이용할 수 있는 유일한 회의실이 될 것이라고 했으므로 대회의실을 일부 직원들은 이용할 수 없을 것임을 추론할 수 있다. 따라서 (A)가 정답이다.

어휘 **unavailable** adj. 이용할 수 없는 **refurbish** v. 새로 단장하다 **lounge** n. 휴게실

164-167번은 다음 메시지 대화문에 관한 문제입니다.

> Carol Medina [오전 11시 41분]
> ¹⁶⁴저는 회사의 연례 송년회를 계획 중이에요. 도움을 좀 얻을 수 있으면 정말 좋겠어요.
>
> Annie Sanders [오전 11시 42분]
> 제가 기꺼이 도와드릴게요. 제가 무엇을 하길 원하세요?
>
> Carol Medina [오전 11시 43분]
> 저는 아직 파티를 열 장소를 찾지 못했어요. ¹⁶⁵당신이 적합한 연회장을 구해주실 수 있나요? 우리는 12월 22일자로 한 곳을 예약해야 해요.
>
> Annie Sanders [오전 11시 43분]
> ¹⁶⁵물론이죠. 올해에는 몇 명이 참석할 건가요?
>
> Carol Medina [오전 11시 44분]
> 그건 말씀드리기 어려워요. 각 직원은 한 명의 손님을 초대할 수 있어요. 그래서, 우리는 모든 직원들에게 연락해서 그들이 파티에 누군가를 데려올 예정인지 물어봐야 해요.
>
> Vincent Bryce [오전 11시 45분]
> 제가 지금 그것을 할 수 있어요. 제가 그냥 회사의 모든 사람들에게 이메일을 보낼게요. 내일 점심까지 예상하는 손님 수를 두 분에게 알려드릴게요.
>
> Annie Sanders [오전 11시 46분]
> 완벽해요. 음식은 어떻게 하나요? ¹⁶⁶제가 음식 공급 업체들도 찾아보기를 원하시나요?
>
> Carol Medina [오전 11시 47분]
> 필요 없어요. ¹⁶⁶Bellwood Fine Foods사는 훌륭한 메뉴와 적당한 가격을 가지고 있어요. ¹⁶⁷우리는 지난 6년 넘게 그들을 자주 이용해오고 있어요.

year-end party 송년회 **could use** ~을 얻을 수 있으면 좋겠다

---

lend a hand 도움을 주다 **look for** ~을 찾다, 구하다 **suitable** adj. 적합한 **banquet hall** 연회장 **intend to** ~할 예정이다 **catering** n. 음식 공급 **reasonable** adj. (가격이) 적당한

164 목적 찾기 문제

문제 Ms. Medina는 왜 동료들에게 연락했는가?
(A) 다가오는 행사를 알리기 위해
(B) 음식에 대한 조언을 요청하기 위해
(C) 업무에 대한 도움을 요청하기 위해
(D) 프로젝트에 관심을 표현하기 위해

해설 Ms. Medina가 동료들에게 연락한 목적을 묻는 목적 찾기 문제이므로 지문의 앞부분을 주의 깊게 확인한다. 'I'm planning the company's annual year-end party. I could really use some help.'(11:41 A.M.)에서 Ms. Medina가 회사의 연례 송년회를 계획 중인데 도움을 얻을 수 있으면 좋겠다고 했으므로 (C)가 정답이다.

패러프레이징
help 도움 → **assistance** 도움

어휘 **assistance** n. 도움

165 육하원칙 문제

문제 Ms. Sanders는 무엇을 하기로 동의하는가?
(A) 참석자 수를 확인한다.
(B) 음식 공급 업체에 연락한다.
(C) 장소를 구한다.
(D) 초대장을 보낸다.

해설 Ms. Sanders가 무엇(What)을 하기로 동의하는지를 묻는 육하원칙 문제이다. 질문의 핵심 어구인 Ms. Sanders agree to do와 관련하여, 'Could you look for a suitable banquet hall?'(11:43 A.M.)에서 Ms. Medina가 Ms. Sanders에게 적합한 연회장을 구해줄 수 있는지 묻자, 'Sure.'(11:43 A.M.)에서 Ms. Sanders가 그러겠다고 했으므로 (C)가 정답이다.

패러프레이징
look for a suitable banquet hall 적합한 연회장을 구하다 → **Find a venue** 장소를 구하다

어휘 **attendance** n. 참석자 (수), 참석 **caterer** n. 음식 공급 업체 **venue** n. 장소

166 의도 파악 문제

문제 오전 11시 47분에, Ms. Medina가 "No need"라고 썼을 때, 그녀가 의도한 것 같은 것은?
(A) 메뉴를 바꾸는 것에 대해 물어볼 것이다.
(B) 손님들의 수를 알고 있다.
(C) 이미 홀의 이용 가능성을 확인했다.
(D) 특정 음식 공급 업체를 이용할 것이다.

해설 Ms. Medina가 의도한 것 같은 것을 묻는 문제이므로, 질문의 인용어구(No need)가 언급된 주변 문맥을 확인한다. 'Would you like me to look for catering companies as well?'(11:46 A.M.)에서 Ms. Sanders가 자신이 음식 공급 업체들도 찾아보기를 원하는지 묻자, Ms. Medina가 'No need'(필요 없어요)라고 한 후, 'Bellwood Fine Foods has excellent menu options and reasonable prices.'(11:47 A.M.)에서 Bellwood Fine Foods사가 훌륭한 메뉴와 적당한 가격을 가지고 있다고 한 것을 통해, Ms. Medina가 특정 음식 공급 업체를 이용할 것임을 알 수 있다. 따라서 (D)가 정답이다.

어휘 **availability** n. 이용 가능성, 이용 할 수 있음

167 추론 문제

문제 Bellwood Fine Foods사에 대해 암시되는 것은?
(A) 소규모 단체를 위한 파티를 전문으로 한다.
(B) 여러 해 동안 영업 중이다.

(C) 한정된 수의 메뉴 옵션을 제공한다.
(D) 최근에 가격을 인하했다.

해설 질문의 핵심 어구인 Bellwood Fine Foods에 대해 추론하는 문제이다. 'We've used them[Bellwood Fine Foods] often over the past six years.'(11:47 A.M.)에서 지난 6년 넘게 Bellwood Fine Foods사를 자주 이용해오고 있다고 했으므로 Bellwood Fine Foods사가 여러 해 동안 영업 중이라는 것을 추론할 수 있다. 따라서 (B)가 정답이다.

어휘 specialize in ~을 전문으로 하다 be in business 영업 중이다
limited adj. 한정된

168-171번은 다음 기사에 관한 문제입니다.

공사 소식

East Parsons, 6월 3일—오늘 기자회견에서, 교통국장 Claudia Rittora가 새 지하철 노선인 초록 노선이 9월부터 공사를 진행할 것이라고 발표했다. 이 노선은 Peterson과 Forest Falls 교외 지역들로의 운항을 제공할 것이다. ¹⁶⁸이것은 Pew가, Jackson가, Crispin 대로의 정류장들을 포함할 것이며, 그 후에는 시내로 운행하는 빨강 노선과 합류할 것이다. — [1] —.

Ms. Rittora는 ¹⁶⁹교외에 지하철 노선을 만드는 결정은 도시로 통근해야 하는 사람들로부터 일어난 많은 불만들에 대응하여 이루어졌다고 말했다. — [2] —. 외진 지역들로 가는 버스는 단지 몇 개뿐이며, 그것들은 모두 드문 간격으로 운행한다. 한때는 외곽 교외들까지 이어져 Jackson가와 Wellford가를 따라 정류장들이 있는 전차 노선이 있었다. 하지만, ^{170-C/171}그것은 운영하는 데 비용이 매우 많이 들었으며, ^{170-D/171}많지 않은 사람들이 그것을 이용했다. — [3] —.

새 지하철 노선은 교외 지역들의 인구가 크게 증가했기 때문에 더 성공적일 것이다. — [4] —. 초록 노선은 하루 24시간, 일주일 내내 운행할 것이며, 열차들은 매 10분마다 역에 도착할 것이다. 더 많은 것을 알아보고 싶은 이들은 www.eastparsonscity.gov로 가면 된다.

press conference 기자회견 commissioner n. 국장
undergo v. 진행하다, 겪다 service to ~로의 운항
suburban adj. 교외의 neighborhood n. 지역, 이웃
merge v. 합류하다 downtown adv. 시내로; n. 시내 suburb n. 교외
in response to ~에 대응하여 commute v. 통근하다
outlying adj. 외진 infrequent adj. 드문 interval n. 간격
tram n. 전차 extend to ~까지 이어지다 outer adj. 외곽의
costly adj. 많은 비용이 드는

168 동의어 찾기 문제

문제 1문단 다섯 번째 줄의 단어 "merge"는 의미상 -와 가장 가깝다.
(A) 합쳐지다
(B) 쌓이다
(C) 돌아오다
(D) 거래하다

해설 merge를 포함한 문장 'It will include stops at Pew Street, Jackson Avenue, and Crispin Boulevard, after which it will merge with the Red Line that runs downtown.'에서 merge는 '합류하다'라는 뜻으로 사용되었다. 따라서 '합쳐지다'라는 뜻을 가진 (A)가 정답이다.

169 육하원칙 문제

문제 새 지하철 노선은 왜 만들어질 것인가?
(A) 시내에 사는 사람들의 통근 시간을 단축시키기 위해
(B) 외진 지역들로부터의 불만을 처리하기 위해
(C) 새로 지어진 지역사회의 주민들을 수용하기 위해
(D) 버스 운행의 취소를 보완하기 위해

해설 새 지하철 노선이 왜(Why) 만들어질 것인지를 묻는 육하원칙 문제이다. 질문의 핵심 어구인 the new subway line be constructed와 관련하여, 'the decision to build a subway line in the suburbs was made in response to the many complaints that have been made by people who must commute to the city'에서 교외에 지하철 노선을 만드는 결정은 도시로 통근해야 하는 사람들로부터 일어난 많은 불만들에 대응하여 이루어졌다고 했으므로 (B)가 정답이다.

패러프레이징
was made in response to the many complaints 많은 불만들에 대응하여 이루어졌다 → address ~ dissatisfaction 불만을 처리하다

어휘 commuting time 통근 시간 address v. 처리하다, 다루다
dissatisfaction n. 불만 accommodate v. 수용하다
compensate v. 보완하다, 보상하다 cancellation n. 취소, 중지
bus service 버스 운행

170 Not/True 문제

문제 전차 노선에 대해 언급된 것은?
(A) 하루에 24시간 운행 가능했다.
(B) 사기업이 소유했다.
(C) 건설하는 데 비용이 많이 들었다.
(D) 적은 수의 사람들에게 이용되었다.

해설 질문의 핵심 어구인 tram line과 관련된 내용을 지문에서 찾아 보기와 대조하는 Not/True 문제이다. (A)와 (B)는 지문에 언급되지 않은 내용이다. (C)는 'it[tram line] was very costly to operate'에서 전차 노선이 운영하는 데 비용이 매우 많이 들었다고 했지 건설 비용에 대해서는 알 수 없으므로 지문의 내용과 일치하지 않는다. (D)는 'not many people used it[tram line]'에서 많지 않은 사람들이 전차 노선을 이용했다고 했으므로 지문의 내용과 일치한다. 따라서 (D)가 정답이다.

어휘 operational adj. 운행 가능한

171 문장 위치 찾기 문제

문제 [1], [2], [3], [4]로 표시된 위치 중, 다음 문장이 들어갈 곳으로 가장 적절한 것은?
"그 결과, 시에서 20년 전에 이 운행을 중단하기로 결정했다."
(A) [1]
(B) [2]
(C) [3]
(D) [4]

해설 지문의 흐름상 주어진 문장이 들어가기에 가장 적절한 곳을 고르는 문제이다. As a result, the city decided to end this service 20 years ago에서 그 결과 시에서 20년 전에 이 운행을 중단하기로 결정했다고 했으므로, 주어진 문장 앞에 이전에 운행되었던 교통 시설의 운행이 중단된 이유에 관한 내용이 언급된 부분이 있을 것임을 예상할 수 있다. [3]의 앞 문장인 'it[tram line] was very costly to operate, and not many people used it'에서 전차 노선은 운영하는 데 비용이 매우 많이 들었으며, 많지 않은 사람들이 이용했다고 했으므로, [3]에 주어진 문장이 들어가면 시에서 전차 노선의 운행을 중단한 이유를 설명하는 자연스러운 문맥이 된다는 것을 알 수 있다. 따라서 (C)가 정답이다.

172-175번은 다음 양식에 관한 문제입니다.

*THE NORTHWEST LEDGER*지

¹⁷²성함: Mohammed Abbar
구독: ■ 일간   □ 주간   □ 주 2회
주소: 155번지 Winateka로, 타코마, 워싱턴 주 98401

¹⁷²제가 원하는 것은:
□ 구독을 변경합니다   ■ 구독을 취소합니다   ○

만약 구독을 변경하신다면, 서비스를 선택해주십시오:
□ 일간   □ 주간   □ 주 2회

만약 취소하신다면, 사유를 제시해주십시오:
□ 다른 주소지로 이사를 갑니다.
□ 구독료를 지불할 여유가 없습니다.
□ 내용의 질에 만족하지 않습니다.
■ 기타

기타 사유일 경우, 상세히 기술해주십시오:

> 저는 일간 지역 소식을 위해 *The Northwest Ledger*지에 의존했었습니다. 하지만 [173]최근 몇 년간, 저는 TacomaToday.com과 다른 웹사이트들로부터 대신 소식을 받아오고 있습니다. 게다가, 제가 전보다 더 바빠져서, 앉아서 큰 신문지를 읽을 가능성이 더 적어졌습니다.

[174]*THE NORTHWEST LEDGER*지를 개선하기 위한 의견:

> 귀사의 신문은 주로 국내 스포츠 리그의 보도를 제공합니다. [174]저는 우리 지역 리그 야구 및 하키팀들을 다룬 기사들이 더 많아야 한다고 생각합니다. 음식점 후기들도 더 많아져야 합니다.

이 양식을 제출하시면, [175]귀하의 서비스는 변경되거나 중단됩니다. 이것이 완료되었음을 확인해드리기 위해, 귀하께서는 위에 명시하신 주소로 편지를 받으실 것입니다. 만약 이 편지를 받지 못하신다면, subscriptions@northwestledger.com으로 저희에게 연락하시기 바랍니다.

subscription n. 구독   **daily** adj. 일간의; n. 일간지
weekly adj. 주간의; n. 주간지   **semiweekly** adj. 주 2회의
rely on ~에 의존하다   **be less likely to** ~할 가능성이 더 적다
coverage n. 보도   **story** n. 기사, 이야기
devoted to ~을 다룬, ~에 헌신하는   **discontinue** v. 중단하다
confirm v. 확인해주다, 확인하다

172 목적 찾기 문제

문제 Mr. Abbar는 왜 양식을 작성했는가?
(A) 주간 우편물을 신청하기 위해
(B) 신문을 받아보는 것을 중단하기 위해
(C) 우편물 발송 주소를 변경하기 위해
(D) 기사들에 대해 불평하기 위해

해설 Mr. Abbar가 양식을 작성한 목적을 묻는 목적 찾기 문제이므로 지문의 앞부분을 주의 깊게 확인한다. 'NAME: Mohammed Abbar'와 'I WOULD LIKE TO: ■ Cancel my subscription'에서 Mr. Abbar가 구독을 취소하고 싶다고 했으므로 (B)가 정답이다.

패러프레이징
Cancel ~ subscription 구독을 취소하다 → stop getting a newspaper 신문을 받아보는 것을 중단하다

어휘 **sign up for** ~을 신청하다   **mailing** n. 우편물
mailing address 우편물 발송 주소

173 추론 문제

문제 Mr. Abbar에 대해 추론될 수 있는 것은?
(A) 최근에 타코마로 이사했다.
(B) 소설 출판물들을 읽는 것을 즐긴다.
(C) 구독을 연장하고 싶어 한다.
(D) 온라인 뉴스원들을 선호한다.

해설 질문의 핵심 어구인 Mr. Abbar에 대해 추론하는 문제이다. 'in recent years, I have been getting news from TacomaToday.com and other Web sites instead'에서 최근 몇 년간 TacomaToday.com과 다른 웹사이트들로부터 대신 소식을 받아오고 있다고 했으므로 (D)가 정답이다.

어휘 **fiction** n. 소설   **publication** n. 출판물   **renew** v. 연장하다, 갱신하다
news source 뉴스원, 뉴스의 출처

174 추론 문제

문제 *The Northwest Ledger*지에 대해 암시되는 것은?
(A) 논평란이 없다.
(B) 한정된 지역 스포츠란을 가지고 있다.
(C) 일일 단위로 발행되지 않는다.
(D) 온라인 버전이 있다.

해설 질문의 핵심 어구인 The Northwest Ledger에 대해 추론하는 문제이다. 'SUGGESTIONS FOR IMPROVING THE NORTHWEST LEDGER:'와 'I think there should be more stories devoted to our local league baseball and hockey teams.'에서 The Northwest Ledger지를 개선하기 위한 의견으로 지역 리그 야구 및 하키팀들을 다룬 기사들이 더 많아야 한다고 생각한다고 했으므로 The Northwest Ledger지가 한정된 지역 스포츠란을 가지고 있다는 것을 추론할 수 있다. 따라서 (B)가 정답이다.

어휘 **section** n. (신문 등의) 난, 부분   **limited** adj. 한정된
on a daily basis 일일 단위로, 매일

175 추론 문제

문제 Mr. Abbar는 무엇을 받을 것 같은가?
(A) 확인 편지
(B) 상품권
(C) 전액 환불
(D) 무료 도서

해설 질문의 핵심 어구인 Mr. Abbar ~ receive에 대해 추론하는 문제이다. 'your service will be changed or discontinued. To confirm that this has been done, you will receive a letter'에서 서비스가 변경되거나 중단되는데, 이것이 완료되었음을 확인해주기 위해 Mr. Abbar가 편지를 받을 것이라고 했으므로 Mr. Abbar가 확인 편지를 받을 것임을 추론할 수 있다. 따라서 (A)가 정답이다.

어휘 **confirmation** n. 확인   **complimentary** adj. 무료의

176-180번은 다음 이메일과 제품 설명서에 관한 문제입니다.

> 수신: Angelica Lucci <angelica@craincameras.com>
> 발신: Brad Farley <brad@craincameras.com>
> 제목: 제품 설명서
> 날짜: 1월 28일
>
> Angelica께,
>
> 저는 우리의 새로운 Selector 디지털카메라의 홍보물을 작성하는 일을 맡았는데, 구체적으로 말하면, 우리의 온라인 쇼핑 사이트에서 제품의 사진들 옆에 나올 글입니다. 하지만, 저는 이 담당 업무의 특정 측면에서 약간의 어려움을 겪고 있습니다. [176/178]저는 우리의 이전 모델인 ProViewer에는 포함되지 않았던 이 카메라의 기능들에 초점을 맞추고 싶습니다. [176]당신이 두 카메라 모델의 제품 담당 책임자이니, 이와 관련해 저를 도와주실 수 있을까요? 예를 들어, 저는 ProViewer가 얼굴 인식 기술을 포함했는지 알고 싶습니다. 또한, 그것이 4기가바이트의 저장 용량을 가지고 있었나요? 만약 그렇지 않다면, 이러한 기능들을 Selector의 제품 설명서에서 강조하려고 합니다. 저는 Selector의 새로운 동영상 기능에 대해서도 조금 혼란스럽습니다. 그것에 대해 제게 더 알려주실 수 있을까요? 시간이 있으실 때 제 질문들에 대한 답을 알려주시기 바랍니다. 감사합니다!
>
> Brad Farley 드림

assign v. 맡기다, 배정하다   **publicity material** 홍보물
aspect n. 측면, 양상, 관점   **assignment** n. 담당 업무, 배정
feature n. 기능, 특징   **product manager** 제품 담당 책임자

face-detection n. 얼굴 인식　storage n. 저장　capacity n. 용량, 능력　highlight v. 강조하다

CRAIN CAMERAS사의 새로운 SELECTOR 디지털카메라

[177]전문가 및 아마추어 사진작가들 둘 다에게 완벽한, 새로운 Selector 카메라는 모든 면에서 뛰어납니다. [178]저희의 이전 모델들과 같이, Selector는 4기가바이트까지 사진들을 저장할 수 있고 다양한 조명 상태에서 사용될 수 있습니다. 그러나, 더 다용도이고, 사용하기 쉽고, 정교하게 만들기 위해 저희는 많은 새로운 기능들을 추가했습니다.

■ Selector는 사람 얼굴의 가장 선명한 이미지를 만들어내기 위해 초점을 자동으로 조정하는 얼굴 인식 기술을 가지고 있습니다.
■ 저희는 Selector가 재충전될 필요 없이 최고 20시간 동안 지속될 수 있도록 배터리 수명을 늘렸습니다.
■ [179-D]Selector는 최고 30분 길이의 동영상을 촬영할 수 있습니다. 이 동영상들이 높은 해상도를 가지고 있기 때문에, 이들은 매우 상세합니다. [179-B]그들은 또한 거의 모든 동영상 편집 소프트웨어를 이용하여 다양한 형식으로 전환될 수 있습니다.

이 밖에도, [180]모든 상품들에는 카메라를 올려놓을 수 있는 접이식 삼각대가 딸려 있습니다. 이 삼각대는 조정 가능하여, 여러분이 낮고 높은 각도 모두에서 사진을 찍을 수 있도록 합니다.

professional adj. 전문가의, 능숙한　alike adv. 둘 다, 비슷하게
lighting n. 조명　versatile adj. 다용도의, 다재다능한
accessible adj. 사용하기 쉬운, 접근할 수 있는
sophisticated adj. 정교한, 고성능의, 세련된
adjust v. 조정하다, 적응하다
last v. 지속되다　recharge v. (재)충전하다
shoot v. 촬영하다, 사진을 찍다　detailed adj. 상세한
be converted into ~으로 전환되다　come with ~이 딸려 있다
foldout adj. 접이식의　tripod n. 삼각대　mount v. 올려놓다, 오르다

176 목적 찾기 문제

문제　Mr. Farley는 왜 이메일을 썼는가?
(A) 제품에 대한 정보를 요청하기 위해
(B) 고객 문의에 대한 후속 조치를 하기 위해
(C) 문서가 교정되도록 요청하기 위해
(D) 마케팅 전략을 제안하기 위해

해설　Mr. Farley가 이메일을 쓴 목적을 묻는 목적 찾기 문제이므로 Mr. Farley가 작성한 이메일의 내용을 확인한다. 첫 번째 지문(이메일)의 'I'd like to focus on the features of this camera that were not included in our previous model ~.'에서 Mr. Farley가 이전 모델에는 포함되지 않았던 이 카메라의 기능들에 초점을 맞추고 싶다고 했고, 'Since you're the product manager for both camera models, could you help me with this?'에서 이메일 수신자에게 두 카메라 모델의 제품 담당 책임자이니 이와 관련해 도와줄 수 있는지 물었으므로 (A)가 정답이다.

어휘　follow up 후속 조치를 하다　proofread v. 교정하다

177 동의어 찾기 문제

문제　제품 설명서에서, 1문단 첫 번째 줄의 단어 "outstanding"은 의미상 -와 가장 가깝다.
(A) 명백한
(B) 기한이 지난
(C) 뛰어난
(D) 의미 있는

해설　제품 설명서의 outstanding을 포함한 문장 'Perfect for professional and amateur photographers alike, the new Selector camera is outstanding in every way.'에서 outstanding은 '뛰어난'이라는 뜻으로 사용되었다. 따라서 '뛰어난'이라는 뜻을 가

진 (C)가 정답이다.

178 추론 문제 연계

문제　ProViewer에 대해 암시되는 것은?
(A) 4기가바이트까지 데이터를 저장할 수 있다.
(B) 전문가들 사이에서 매우 인기있다.
(C) 약 일 년 전에 출시되었다.
(D) 자동으로 대상에 초점을 맞춘다.

해설　질문의 핵심 어구인 ProViewer가 언급된 이메일을 먼저 확인한다.
　단서1　첫 번째 지문(이메일)의 'our previous model, the ProViewer'에서 ProViewer가 이전 모델이라고 했다. 그런데 이전 모델에 대한 정보가 제시되지 않았으므로 제품 설명서에서 관련 내용을 확인한다.
　단서2　두 번째 지문(제품 설명서)의 'As with our earlier models, the Selector can store up to four gigabytes of photographs'에서 이전 모델들이 4기가바이트까지 사진들을 저장할 수 있음을 확인할 수 있다.
두 단서를 종합할 때, 이전 모델인 ProViewer가 4기가바이트까지 사진들을 저장할 수 있다는 것을 알 수 있다. 따라서 (A)가 정답이다.

어휘　release v. 출시하다

179 Not/True 문제

문제　제품 설명서에서 Selector의 동영상 기능에 대해 말하는 것은?
(A) 추가 요금으로 추가될 수 있다.
(B) 특정한 소프트웨어 프로그램을 필요로 한다.
(C) 장면을 온라인 계정으로 보낸다.
(D) 30분짜리 동영상 촬영을 할 수 있게 한다.

해설　질문의 핵심 어구인 Selector's video feature에 대해 묻는 Not/True 문제이므로 Selector의 동영상 기능이 언급된 두 번째 지문(제품 설명서)에서 관련 내용을 확인한다. (A)는 지문에 언급되지 않은 내용이다. (B)는 'They[videos] can also be converted into various formats using almost any video-editing software.'에서 동영상들이 거의 모든 동영상 편집 소프트웨어를 이용하여 다양한 형식으로 전환될 수 있다고 했으므로 지문의 내용과 일치하지 않는다. (C)는 지문에 언급되지 않은 내용이다. (D)는 'The Selector can shoot videos of up to 30 minutes in length.'에서 Selector가 최고 30분 길이의 동영상을 촬영할 수 있다고 했으므로 지문의 내용과 일치한다. 따라서 (D)가 정답이다.

패러프레이징
shoot videos of up to 30 minutes in length 최고 30분 길이의 동영상을 촬영하다 → allows for filming of half-hour videos 30분짜리 동영상 촬영을 할 수 있게 하다

어휘　footage n. 장면

180 육하원칙 문제

문제　제품 설명서에 따르면, Selector에 무엇이 딸려 있는가?
(A) 추가 배터리
(B) 조정 가능한 삼각대
(C) 휴대용 케이스
(D) 다양한 렌즈

해설　Selector에 무엇(what)이 딸려 있는지를 묻는 육하원칙 문제이므로 질문의 핵심 어구인 Selector come with가 언급된 제품 설명서에서 관련 내용을 확인한다. 두 번째 지문(제품 설명서)의 'all units come with a foldout tripod ~. The tripod is adjustable'에서 모든 상품들에는 접이식 삼각대가 딸려 있고 이는 조정 가능하다고 했으므로 (B)가 정답이다.

어휘　a selection of 다양한

181-185번은 다음 공고와 이메일에 관한 문제입니다.

West Carver 주민들께 드리는 공고

이번 주에, 몇몇 거리들이 3일간의 푸에르토리코 문화 축제를 위해 폐쇄될 것입니다:

- ¹⁸³Madeline가의 100에서 800 블록이 무용수들과 악대가 있는 푸에르토리코 행진을 위해, 7월 2일 금요일 오전 8시부터 오후 12시까지 폐쇄될 것입니다.

- MacDunn가의 200에서 500 블록이 ¹⁸¹⁻ᴬ전통 음악 공연을 위해, 7월 3일 토요일 오전 11시부터 오후 5시까지 폐쇄될 것입니다.

- Harrison가의 300에서 600 블록이 ¹⁸¹⁻ᴮ물 미끄럼틀과 다른 축제 놀이기구들을 특별히 포함하는 오락의 날을 위해, 7월 4일 일요일 오후 2시부터 오후 10시까지 폐쇄될 것입니다.

노래, 춤, ¹⁸¹⁻ᶜ경품 추첨을 포함한 더 많은 활동들은 Carver 공원에서 7월 3일과 4일 오전 9시와 오후 11시 사이에 열릴 것입니다.

¹⁸²만약 마을을 걸어서 돌아다니는 것을 어렵게 하는 장애가 있으시다면, 저희는 services@sanmiguel.gov로 정부 직원에게 연락하시기를 권장합니다. 여러분이 관심 있으신 행사로 데려다드릴 준비가 마련될 것입니다.

---

marching band 악대 fun and games 오락, 재미
feature v. 특별히 포함하다 ride n. 놀이기구 raffle for ~의 추첨
disability n. 장애 arrangement n. 준비

수신: Lucy Garcia <lgarcia@puertoricanfestival.com>
발신: Michael Gomez <mgomez@fastmail.com>
제목: 몇 가지 질문들
날짜: 7월 3일

Ms. Garcia께,

제 이름은 Michael Gomez이며, West Carver 동네의 주민입니다. 어제, ¹⁸³저는 제 집이 위치한 거리를 따라 지나가는 대형 행진 소리를 들었고 그것이 무엇인지 알아보기 위해 온라인으로 검색했습니다. ¹⁸⁴저는 푸에르토리코의 이전 주민이기 때문에, 지역 주민들이 제 문화유산을 기념하는 것을 돕는 데 관심이 있습니다. 귀하께서 아직 자원봉사자들을 받고 계신가요? 저는 동네 주변에 포스터들을 붙이고, 참가자들을 특정 행사들로 안내하거나, 활동들을 위한 천막을 설치할 수 있습니다. ¹⁸⁵또한 제가 트럭을 가지고 있어서, 비품들을 싣고 가져다 놓을 수 있습니다. 제가 이 행사를 도울 수 있는 방법이 있으면 제게 알려주시기 바랍니다.

귀하로부터 답변이 오기를 기대합니다.

Michael Gomez 드림

---

celebrate v. 기념하다 heritage n. 문화유산, 전통
put up ~을 붙이다, 게시하다 attendee n. 참가자
set up ~을 설치하다, 세우다 pick up ~을 싣다, 태우다
drop off ~을 가져다 놓다, 내려주다 assist v. 돕다, 도움이 되다

---

181 Not/True 문제
문제 공고에 나열된 즐길거리가 아닌 것은?
(A) 음악 공연
(B) 수상 놀이기구
(C) 상품 추첨
(D) 시식 행사

해설 질문의 핵심 어구인 an attraction에 대해 묻는 Not/True 문제이므로 an attraction과 관련된 내용이 언급된 첫 번째 지문(공고)을 확인한다. (A)는 'a performance of traditional music'에서 전통 음악 공연이라고 했으므로 지문의 내용과 일치한다. (B)는 'a waterslide'에서 물 미끄럼틀이라고 했으므로 지문의 내용과 일치한다. (C)는 'a

---

raffle for gifts'에서 경품 추첨이라고 했으므로 지문의 내용과 일치한다. (D)는 지문에 언급되지 않은 내용이다. 따라서 (D)가 정답이다.

어휘 attraction n. 즐길거리, 끌림, 명소 prize drawing 상품 추첨

182 육하원칙 문제
문제 주민들은 언제 국가 공무원에게 연락해야 하는가?
(A) 표를 구매할 수 없을 때
(B) 걸어서 장소에 갈 수 없을 때
(C) 파티에 대해 더 많이 알아보고 싶을 때
(D) 행사의 영상들을 보고 싶을 때

해설 주민들이 언제(When) 국가 공무원에게 연락해야 하는지를 묻는 육하원칙 문제이므로 질문의 핵심 어구인 residents contact a government official이 언급된 공고에서 관련 내용을 확인한다. 첫 번째 지문(공고)의 'If you have any disabilities that make it difficult to walk around town, we encourage you to contact a government representative'에서 만약 마을을 걸어서 돌아다니는 것을 어렵게 하는 장애가 있다면 정부 직원에게 연락하기를 권장한다고 했으므로 (B)가 정답이다.

패러프레이징
difficult to walk around town 마을을 걸어서 돌아다니는 것이 어려운
→ cannot get to a location on foot 걸어서 장소에 갈 수 없다

어휘 get to ~에 가다, (단계에) 이르다 on foot 걸어서, 도보로

183 추론 문제 연계
문제 Mr. Gomez에 대해 암시되는 것은?
(A) 이전에 공연을 했다.
(B) 가족들이 West Carver를 방문 중이다.
(C) 집이 Madeline가에 위치해 있다.
(D) 새로운 동네로 이사할 것이다.

해설 질문의 핵심 어구인 Mr. Gomez가 작성한 이메일을 먼저 확인한다.
단서 1 두 번째 지문(이메일)의 'I heard a large parade passing down the street my house is situated on'에서 Mr. Gomez가 자신의 집이 위치한 거리를 따라 지나가는 대형 행진 소리를 들었다고 했다. 그런데 행진이 진행되었던 거리가 어디인지 제시되지 않았으므로 공고에서 관련 내용을 확인한다.
단서 2 첫 번째 지문(공고)의 'Madeline Street will be closed ~ for a Puerto Rican parade'에서 Madeline가가 푸에르토리코 행진을 위해 폐쇄될 것임을 확인할 수 있다.
두 단서를 종합할 때, Madeline가에서 행진이 진행되었으므로 Mr. Gomez의 집이 Madeline가에 위치해 있다는 것을 알 수 있다. 따라서 (C)가 정답이다.

184 육하원칙 문제
문제 Mr. Gomez는 왜 축제에서 자원 봉사를 하고 싶어 하는가?
(A) 이전에 푸에르토리코에서 살았다.
(B) 창고에 여분의 장식품들이 있다.
(C) 전통 음식을 요리하는 것을 즐긴다.
(D) 비영리 단체에서 일하고 싶어 한다.

해설 Mr. Gomez가 왜(Why) 축제에서 자원 봉사를 하고 싶어 하는지를 묻는 육하원칙 문제이므로 질문의 핵심 어구인 Mr. Gomez want to volunteer at the festival이 언급된 이메일에서 관련 내용을 확인한다. 두 번째 지문(이메일)의 'As I am a former resident of Puerto Rico, I'm interested in helping local residents celebrate my heritage. Are you still accepting volunteers?'에서 Mr. Gomez가 푸에르토리코의 이전 주민이기 때문에 지역 주민들이 자신의 문화유산을 기념하는 것을 돕는 데 관심이 있다고 한 후, 아직 자원봉사자들을 받고 있는지 물었으므로 (A)가 정답이다.

어휘 decoration n. 장식품, 장식 storage n. 창고, 저장
cuisine n. 요리, 음식 nonprofit adj. 비영리적인

185 육하원칙 문제

문제 Mr. Gomez는 무엇을 하는 것을 제안하는가?
(A) 그의 차량으로 물품들을 나른다.
(B) 온라인에 광고를 게시한다.
(C) 특정 거리들을 차단한다.
(D) 공원의 쓰레기를 청소한다.

해설 Mr. Gomez가 무엇(What)을 하는 것을 제안하는지를 묻는 육하원칙 문제이므로 질문의 핵심 어구인 Mr. Gomez offer to do와 관련된 내용이 언급된 이메일을 확인한다. 두 번째 지문(이메일)의 'I also have a truck, so I can pick up and drop off supplies.'에서 Mr. Gomez가 트럭을 가지고 있어서 비품들을 싣고 가져다 놓을 수 있다고 했으므로 (A)가 정답이다.

패러프레이징
pick up and drop off supplies 비품들을 싣고 가져다 놓다
→ Transport items 물품들을 나르다

어휘 transport v. 나르다, 운송하다 block off ~을 차단하다, 막다

186-190번은 다음 안내문, 초대장, 편지에 관한 문제입니다.

Opal 미술관
방문객 알림

[186]Opal 미술관의 방문객들은 Fairfield 주차장, Morrison 주차장, Gosling 주차장의 세 가지 주차 선택지가 있습니다. Gosling 주차장은 저희 행사에서 가장 가까운 반면, Morrison 주차장은 미술관의 정문으로의 가장 가까운 출입을 제공합니다.

반드시 자동 기계로부터 주차권을 받으세요. 요금은 나가실 때 이 기계들 중 하나에서 신용카드나 현금으로 지불될 수 있습니다. 미술관 회원으로서 할인을 받으시려면, [187]Gosling 주차장에 있는 기계에 귀하의 Opal 미술관 회원 카드를 스캔하세요.

[189]시간	비회원 요금	[189]회원 요금
1시간 미만	10달러	8달러
1-2시간	12달러	10달러
2-3시간	14달러	12달러
3-4시간	16달러	14달러
[189]4시간 이상	20달러	[189]18달러

문의를 위해서는, 미술관의 관리실에 555-6698로 전화해주시기 바랍니다.

garage n. 주차장, 차고 access n. 출입, 접근 front entrance 정문
automated adj. 자동의, 자동화된 payable adj. 지불할 수 있는
administrative office 관리실

---

[189]Ms. Kerry Fulton,
Opal 미술관의 장기간 회원으로서
6월 5일 금요일, [189]오후 5-10시에
Crystal 홀에서 개최되는 분기별 행사인
예술가와의 만찬에
당신을 정식으로 초대합니다.

이번 봄에, [188-D]저희 미술관은 국제적으로 호평을 받고 있는 조각가 Alexandra Galanos와 [190]그녀의 최신 전시 *Crossing the Road*를 소개하는 [188-D]5시간의 만찬 행사를 개최할 것인데, [190]이 전시의 제막식이 6월 12일에 Alabaster 별관에서 거행될 것입니다. [188-B]만찬은 정확히 오후 8시에 나올 것이며, 뒤이어 Ms. Galanos의 연설이 이어지고 이후 박물관 관장 Darrell Finn의 발표가 있을 것입니다.

이번 행사에서 즐거운 시간을 보내시기 바랍니다. 미술관에 대한 지속적인 지원에 감사드립니다.

---

longtime adj. 장기간의, 오랜 formally adv. 정식으로, 공식적으로
quarterly adj. 분기별의 acclaimed adj. 호평을 받고 있는
sculptor n. 조각가 exhibit n. 전시(품)
unveil v. ~의 제막식을 거행하다, 공개하다 wing n. 별관, 부속 건물
promptly adv. 정확히, 즉석에서 announcement n. 발표

---

[190]6월 12일

Darrell Finn
Opal 미술관, 관장실
400번지 Morrison가
트렌턴, 뉴저지 주 08618

Mr. Finn께,

저는 지난주 행사의 성공에 대해 귀하를 칭찬하고 싶습니다. 귀하의 연설은 감동적이었고 제가 귀하의 기관의 회원인 것을 자랑스럽게 여기도록 하였습니다.

또한, [190]제가 오늘 Ms. Galanos의 전시 개막식에 참석했다고 말씀드리고 싶습니다. [190]저는 조각품들뿐만 아니라 전시가 열렸던 장소에 이루어진 개조에도 감명을 받았습니다.

감사드리며, 향후 미술관 행사들을 기대합니다.

Kerry Fulton 드림

---

commend v. 칭찬하다, 추천하다 inspiring adj. 감동시키는, 격려하는
impressed adj. 감명을 받은

186 목적 찾기 문제

문제 안내문의 목적은 무엇인가?
(A) 주차를 위한 선택지를 제시하기 위해
(B) 몇몇 새로운 요금을 알려주기 위해
(C) 몇몇 안전 주의를 제공하기 위해
(D) 박물관 회원권을 홍보하기 위해

해설 안내문의 목적을 묻는 목적 찾기 문제이므로 안내문의 내용을 확인한다. 첫 번째 지문(안내문)의 'Visitors to the Opal Museum of Art have three parking options: the Fairfield Lot, the Morrison Lot, and the Gosling Garage.'에서 Opal 미술관의 방문객들은 Fairfield 주차장, Morrison 주차장, Gosling 주차장의 세 가지 주차 선택지가 있다고 했으므로 (A)가 정답이다.

어휘 reminder n. 주의, 상기시켜 주는 것
membership n. 회원권, 회원 자격

187 추론 문제

문제 Gosling 주차장에 대해 암시되는 것은?
(A) 가장 비싼 주차 선택지이다.
(B) 카드를 스캔하는 기기가 있다.
(C) 미술관의 입구와 가장 가깝다.
(D) 시 행사를 위해 최근에 폐쇄되었다.

해설 질문의 핵심 어구인 Gosling Garage에 대해 추론하는 문제이므로 Gosling 주차장이 언급된 안내문에서 관련 내용을 확인한다. 첫 번째 지문(안내문)의 'scan your Opal Museum of Art membership card at a machine in the Gosling Garage'에서 Gosling 주차장에 있는 기계에 Opal 미술관 회원 카드를 스캔하라고 했으므로 Gosling 주차장에 카드를 스캔하는 기기가 있다는 것을 추론할 수 있다. 따라서 (B)가 정답이다.

188 Not/True 문제

문제 Ms. Galanos에 대해 언급된 것은?
(A) 이전에 Opal 미술관을 방문했다.
(B) 조각에 대한 강의를 할 것이다.
(C) Mr. Finn과 계약을 맺었다.

(D) 행사에서 연설을 할 것이다.

해설 질문의 핵심 어구인 Ms. Galanos에 대해 묻는 Not/True 문제이므로 Ms. Galanos가 언급된 두 번째 지문(초대장)에서 관련 내용을 확인한다. (A), (B), (C)는 지문에 언급되지 않은 내용이다. (D)는 'our museum will hold a five-hour dinner event'에서 5시간의 만찬 행사를 개최할 것이라고 했고, 'Dinner will be ~ followed by a speech from Ms. Galanos'에서 만찬에 뒤이어 Ms. Galanos의 연설이 이어진다고 했으므로 지문의 내용과 일치한다. 따라서 (D)가 정답이다.

패러프레이징
a speech 연설 → make some remarks 연설을 하다

어휘 sign a contract 계약을 맺다   make remarks 연설하다
gathering n. 행사, 모임

189 육하원칙 문제 연계

문제 Ms. Fulton이 행사 내내 머물렀다면 주차에 얼마를 지불했는가?
(A) 10달러
(B) 14달러
(C) 18달러
(D) 20달러

해설 질문의 핵심 어구인 Ms. Fulton pay for parking if she stayed for the entire event에서 Ms. Fulton이 행사 내내 머물렀다면 주차에 얼마(How much)를 지불했는지를 묻고 있으므로 Ms. Fulton에게 보내진 초대장을 먼저 확인한다.
단서 1 두 번째 지문(초대장)의 'Ms. Kerry Fulton, As a longtime member of the Opal Museum of Art, You are formally invited to Dinner with the Artist'와 '5–10 P.M.'에서 Opal 미술관의 회원인 Ms. Fulton이 행사에 초대되었고, 행사 시간이 오후 5–10시라고 했다. 그런데 Opal 미술관의 주차 비용에 대한 정보가 제시되지 않았으므로 주차 비용이 언급된 안내문에서 관련 내용을 확인한다.
단서 2 첫 번째 지문(안내문)의 'Period, 4 or more hours', 'Member Fee, $18'에서 Opal 미술관의 주차 안내에서 4시간 이상의 회원 요금이 18달러임을 확인할 수 있다.
두 단서를 종합할 때, Opal 미술관의 회원인 Ms. Fulton이 행사 시간인 5시간 내내 머물렀다면 주차 비용이 18달러였음을 알 수 있다. 따라서 (C)가 정답이다.

어휘 entire adj. 내내, 전체의

190 육하원칙 문제 연계

문제 편지에 따르면, Ms. Fulton이 6월 12일에 감명받았던 것은 무엇인가?
(A) Ms. Galanos의 유익한 강의
(B) 다시 칠해진 Crystal 홀
(C) Mr. Finn의 시설 견학
(D) 개선된 Alabaster 별관

해설 질문의 핵심 어구인 Ms. Fulton impressed with on June 12에서 Ms. Fulton이 6월 12일에 감명받았던 것이 무엇(what)인지를 묻고 있으므로 Ms. Fulton이 보낸 편지를 먼저 확인한다.
단서 1 세 번째 지문(편지)의 'June 12'와 'I attended the opening of Ms. Galanos's exhibit today. I was impressed with ~ the renovations that were made in the area where the exhibition was held.'에서 Ms. Fulton이 6월 12일에 Ms. Galanos의 전시 개막식에 참석했는데 전시가 열렸던 장소에 이루어진 개조에 감명을 받았다고 했다. 그런데 Ms. Galanos의 전시가 열렸던 장소가 어디인지 제시되지 않았으므로 초대장에서 관련 내용을 확인한다.
단서 2 두 번째 지문(초대장)의 'her[Ms. Galanos] latest exhibit ~ which will be unveiled in the Alabaster Wing on June 12'에서 Ms. Galanos의 최신 전시의 제막식이 6월 12일에 Alabaster 별관에서 거행될 것임을 확인할 수 있다.
두 단서를 종합할 때, Ms. Galanos의 전시의 제막식이 Alabaster 별관에서 거행되었으므로 Ms. Fulton이 6월 12일에 개조로 인해 개

선된 Alabaster 별관에 감명받았음을 알 수 있다. 따라서 (D)가 정답이다.

어휘 informative adj. 유익한   tour n. 견학, 관광

191-195번은 다음 웹페이지, 이메일, 후기에 관한 문제입니다.

www.sbntc.com

프로그램 일정	연락처	다음 쇼

사업가들을 필요로 합니다!

당신은 새로운 제품이나 아이디어를 가진 사업가 또는 발명가입니까? 만약 그렇다면, 사파이어 방송 네트워크(SBN)가 당신을 찾고 있습니다! [191-B]저희 방송망은 인기 있는 미국 텔레비전 프로그램인 *Lion's Den*의 판권을 매입했고, SBN 스튜디오에서 싱가포르를 기반으로 하는 버전을 제작할 계획입니다. [191-A/D]참가자들은 쇼 동안에 그들의 제품이나 아이디어를 그 지역에서 저명한 네 명의 기업가 패널에게 발표할 것입니다. 각 발표 후에, 패널 위원들이 질문을 하고 그들이 그 제품이나 아이디어에 투자하고 싶은지를 결정할 것입니다. 그들은 그들 자신의 자금을 제공할 것입니다. [194]SBN은 이번 시즌에 총 12개 에피소드들을 제작할 것입니다.

캐스팅은 2월 8일부터 2월 10일까지 싱가포르에 있는 SBN 스튜디오에서 열릴 것입니다. 여기를 클릭하셔서 온라인 신청서를 작성하세요. [191-C]오디션의 자격을 얻은 분들만이 연락을 받을 것입니다.

call for ~을 필요로 하다   entrepreneur n. (특히 모험적인) 사업가, 기업가
businessperson n. 기업가   inventor n. 발명가
network n. 네트워크, 방송망   right n. 판권, 권리
prominent adj. 저명한, 중요한   casting n. 캐스팅, 배역 선정
qualify for ~의 자격을 얻다

수신: Susan Tsang <susantsang@rubydevelopments.com>
발신: Dennis Ping <dping@sbntc.com>
제목: *Lion's Den Asia*
날짜: 1월 29일

Ms. Tsang께,

귀하께서 저희 프로그램에 투자자로서 출연하시는 데 관심이 있으셔서 매우 기쁩니다. 저희는 이미 Chanchai Akkarat 회장과 Deepa Sidhu 회장을 쇼에 고용했습니다. [193]Trinity Manufacturing사의 최고경영자 Mi-young Choi가 네 번째 자리를 맡는 것을 고려 중이지만 아직 그녀의 업무 일정이 쇼에 참여하기 위해 조정될 수 있는지를 확인해야 합니다.

제작은 4월 초에 시작하지만, [192]저는 여러분이 맡으신 일들에 대해 더 상세히 논의하기 위해 그 전에 귀하와 다른 패널 위원들을 만나고 싶습니다. 따라서, 저는 귀하께 3월 28일에 시내에 있는 저희 싱가포르 사무소에서 저희와의 회의에 참석해주시기를 요청드리겠습니다.

다시 한번 저희 프로그램의 일원이 되는 데 동의해주신 것에 매우 감사드립니다!

Dennis Ping 드림
제작자, *Lion's Den Asia*

appear v. 출연하다, 나타나다   investor n. 투자자
responsibility n. 맡은 일, 책무   in detail 상세히
downtown adj. 시내에 있는; adv. 도심에서   part n. 일원, 부분

---

http://www.couchtvreviewer.com/realitytv/lionsdenasia/

[193/194]텔레비전 프로그램: *Lion's Den Asia*   [194]방송망: SBN
방송 시간: 매주 수요일 오후 8시   [194]후기 작성자: Abdul
Hassan ➡

저는 원작 *Lion's Den* 쇼의 열렬한 팬입니다. 그래서, 아시아판이 제작되고 있다는 소식을 들었을 때, 매우 들떴습니다. [194]저는 쇼의 처음 여섯 개의 에피소드들을 보았고, 그것들은 저를 실망시키지 않았습니다. 진행자 Rajiv Sunder는 매우 유쾌하고, 모든 패널 위원들은 정말 흥미롭습니다. [193]Mi-young Choi는 특히 재치 있는데, 종종 발표자들에게 예상 밖의 질문들을 합니다. 그리고 Chanchai Akkarat는 그 이외에는 진지한 프로그램에 약간의 유머를 더합니다. 저는 또한 Susan Tsang이 쇼의 사업가 참가자들에게 빈번한 제의들을 하는 것을 높이 평가합니다. 그에 반해, [195]패널 위원 Deepa Sidhu가 지금까지 단 세 명의 사업가들에게만 투자가 되는 것을 제의한 것이 저는 다소 우려됩니다. 저는 그녀가 돈을 투자하는 것에 더 열린 마음을 가져야 한다고 생각합니다. 하지만 전반적으로, 쇼의 이 버전이 미국 버전만큼 만족스럽다고 생각합니다.

original adj. 원작의, 최초의 host n. 진행자, 주최자
charming adj. 유쾌한, 매력적인 clever adj. 재치 있는, 현명한
unexpected adj. 예상 밖의, 돌발적인
appreciate v. 높이 평가하다, 감사하다 frequent adj. 빈번한, 잦은
in contrast 그에 반해서 so far 지금까지
open to ~에 대해 열린 마음을 가진

191 Not/True 문제

문제 *Lion's Den*에 대해 사실이 아닌 것은?
(A) 지역 기업가들을 출연시킨다.
(B) 싱가포르에서 처음 방송되었다.
(C) 쇼 참가자들을 위한 오디션을 연다.
(D) 참가자들에 의한 발표들을 포함한다.

해설 질문의 핵심 어구인 *Lion's Den*에 대해 묻는 Not/True 문제이므로 *Lion's Den*이 언급된 첫 번째 지문(웹페이지)에서 관련 내용을 확인한다. (A)와 (D)는 'Participants will present their product or idea to a panel of four prominent businesspeople from the region during the show.'에서 참가자들은 쇼 동안에 그들의 제품이나 아이디어를 그 지역에서 저명한 네 명의 기업가 패널에게 발표할 것이라고 했으므로 지문의 내용과 일치한다. (B)는 'Our network has purchased the rights to the popular American television program *Lion's Den*, and we plan to produce a version based in Singapore at the SBN studios.'에서 인기 있는 미국 텔레비전 프로그램인 *Lion's Den*의 판권을 매입하여 SBN 스튜디오에서 싱가포르를 기반으로 하는 버전을 제작할 계획이라고 했으므로 지문의 내용과 일치하지 않는다. 따라서 (B)가 정답이다. (C)는 'Only those who qualify for auditions will be contacted.'에서 오디션의 자격을 얻은 사람들만이 연락을 받을 것이라고 했으므로 지문의 내용과 일치한다.

패러프레이징
businesspeople from the region 지역의 기업가들 → regional entrepreneurs 지역 기업가들
Participants will present their product or idea 참가자들은 그들의 제품이나 아이디어를 발표할 것이다 → presentations by contestants 참가자들에 의한 발표

어휘 feature v. 출연시키다, 특징으로 삼다 contestant n. 참가자

192 육하원칙 문제

문제 Mr. Ping은 왜 3월 28일에 회의를 마련했는가?
(A) 일부 아이디어에 대한 승인을 얻기 위해
(B) 발표자들에 대한 보수를 협상하기 위해
(C) 투자자들에게 생산 팀을 소개하기 위해
(D) 패널 구성원들의 의무를 논의하기 위해

해설 Mr. Ping이 왜(Why) 3월 28일에 회의를 마련했는지를 묻는 육하원칙 문제이므로 Mr. Ping이 작성한 이메일에서 관련 내용을 확인한다. 두 번째 지문(이메일)의 'I would like to meet with you and

the other members of our panel before then to discuss your responsibilities in more detail. Therefore, I will require you to attend a meeting ~ on March 28.'에서 패널 위원들이 맡은 일들에 대해 더 상세히 논의하기 위해 3월 28일에 회의에 참석해주기를 요청한다고 했으므로 (D)가 정답이다.

패러프레이징
discuss ~ responsibilities 맡은 일들에 대해 논의하다 → discuss the obligations 의무를 논의하다

어휘 arrange v. 마련하다, 미리 준비하다 secure v. 얻다
approval n. 승인 negotiate v. 협상하다, 성사시키다
compensation n. 보수, 보상 obligation n. 의무, 책무

193 추론 문제 연계

문제 Ms. Choi는 무엇을 했을 것 같은가?
(A) 쇼에 출연하기 위해 일정을 변경했다.
(B) 패널 자리를 위해 몇몇 기업가들을 면접했다.
(C) 지역 텔레비전 방송망의 매입을 성사시켰다.
(D) 제조 회사의 공동 경영자와 제휴했다.

해설 질문의 핵심 어구인 Ms. Choi가 언급된 이메일을 먼저 확인한다.
단서 1 두 번째 지문(이메일)의 'Mi-young Choi ~ still has to see if her work schedule can be adjusted to join the show[*Lion's Den Asia*].'에서 Ms. Choi가 아직 그녀의 업무 일정이 *Lion's Den Asia* 쇼에 참여하기 위해 조정될 수 있는지 확인해야 한다고 했다. 그런데 Ms. Choi가 *Lion's Den Asia* 쇼에 출연했는지 제시되지 않았으므로 후기에서 관련 내용을 확인한다.
단서 2 세 번째 지문(후기)의 'TELEVISION PROGRAM: *Lion's Den Asia*'와 'Mi-young Choi is especially clever, often asking presenters unexpected questions.'에서 Ms. Choi가 *Lion's Den Asia*에 출연했음을 확인할 수 있다.
두 단서를 종합할 때, Ms. Choi가 *Lion's Den Asia*에 출연했으므로 쇼에 출연하기 위해 일정을 변경했다는 것을 알 수 있다. 따라서 (A)가 정답이다.

어휘 partner with ~와 제휴하다 associate n. 공동 경영자, 제휴자, 동료

194 추론 문제 연계

문제 Mr. Hassan에 대해 암시되는 것은?
(A) 오디션에 대해 이메일로 연락을 받았다.
(B) *Lion's Den Asia*의 에피소드 중 절반을 보지 않았다.
(C) *Lion's Den Asia*가 원작보다 덜 재미있었다고 생각한다.
(D) 이전에 참여한 투자자들 중 한 명을 직접 만났다.

해설 질문의 핵심 어구인 Mr. Hassan이 작성한 후기를 먼저 확인한다.
단서 1 세 번째 지문(후기)의 'TELEVISION PROGRAM: *Lion's Den Asia*', 'NETWORK: SBN', 'REVIEWER: Abdul Hassan'과 'I have watched the first six episodes of the show'에서 Mr. Hassan이 SBN 방송망의 *Lion's Den Asia* 쇼의 처음 여섯 개의 에피소드들을 봤다고 했다. 그런데 SBN 방송망의 *Lion's Den Asia*의 전체 에피소드가 몇 개인지 제시되지 않았으므로 웹페이지에서 관련 내용을 확인한다.
단서 2 첫 번째 지문(웹페이지)의 'SBN will produce a total of 12 episodes for this season[*Lion's Den Asia*].'에서 SBN이 *Lion's Den Asia*에 총 12개 에피소드들을 제작할 것임을 확인할 수 있다.
두 단서를 종합할 때, Mr. Hassan이 *Lion's Den Asia*의 총 12개 에피소드 중 절반을 보지 않았다는 것을 알 수 있다. 따라서 (B)가 정답이다.

어휘 personally adv. 직접

195 육하원칙 문제

문제 Mr. Hassan은 어떤 패널 위원에 대한 우려를 나타내는가?
(A) Chanchai Akkarat
(B) Susan Tsang

(C) Mi-young Choi
(D) Deepa Sidhu

해설 　Mr. Hassan이 어떤(Which) 패널 위원에 대한 우려를 나타내는지를 묻는 육하원칙 문제이므로 질문의 핵심 어구인 Mr. Hassan express concern about과 관련된 내용이 언급된 후기를 확인한다. 세 번째 지문(후기)의 'I'm a bit worried that panel member Deepa Sidhu has only offered to be an investor for three of the entrepreneurs so far'에서 Mr. Hassan이 패널 위원 Deepa Sidhu가 지금까지 단 세 명의 사업가들에게만 투자자가 되는 것을 제의한 것이 다소 우려된다고 했으므로 (D)가 정답이다.

어휘 　express concern 우려를 나타내다

196-200번은 다음 기사, 광고, 이메일에 관한 문제입니다.

> *Richmond Sun*지
>
> **건강에 좋은 패스트푸드가 다가온다**
>
> 프레데릭스버그, 7월 9일—196-B국내 최초 유기농 패스트푸드 식당인 Fresh Goods가 다음 달에 95번 고속도로에서 개업한다. 소유주 Libby Hawkins는 그것이 수백 개 중 최초로 여행자들에게 빠르고, 건강에 좋으며, 저렴한 음식을 제공하는 곳이 되기를 희망한다.
>
> Ms. Hawkins는 20년 전에 자신의 농장을 운영하기 시작한 이래로 유기농 제품들의 지지자로 지내왔다. 현재, 196-C그녀의 농장은 버지니아 주의 가장 큰 우유 및 치즈 생산업체들 중 하나이다. 본인이 여행을 자주하는 사람인 197그녀는 휴게소에서 판매되는 건강에 좋은 음식이 부족하다는 것을 인지했을 때 197/200Fresh Goods를 열기로 결정했다.
>
> 200현재, 그녀는 Fresh Goods에 유기농 재료들을 공급할 농장들의 네트워크를 확립하는 데 노력을 들이고 있다. 참가 농장주들은 그들의 생산품들에 대한 유기농 인증과 적정 가격을 받는 것을 기대할 수 있다. 하지만, 재료들의 신선도를 보장하기 위해, 200이 네트워크의 일원이 될 농장들은 이 식당으로부터 50마일보다 더 멀리 있을 수 없다.

on the way 다가오는, 도중에　organic adj. 유기농의
proprietor n. 소유주, 경영자　affordable adj. 저렴한, 알맞은
supporter n. 지지자, 후원자　lack n. 부족한 것, 부족
rest stop 휴게소　work on ~에 노력을 들이다
certification n. 인증, 보증　fair price 적정 가격
ingredient n. 재료, 성분　part n. 일원, 부분

> **제4회** 198-A연례 Culpeper 추수감사제
> 198-B9월 8일 금요일부터 9월 10일 일요일까지
>
> **9월 8일: 논의**
> 오후 5시 · Spotswood 호텔 커피점, 215번지 Davis가
> 버지니아 식품 협동조합(VFC) 이사 Emmett Ashby와 함께함
> 더 많은 세부사항은 www.vfc.org에 있음
>
> **9월 9일: 농장 투어**
> 오전 11시-오후 1시 · Westover 농장, 15384번지 Mill로
> 오후 1시-3시 · Whisper Hill 사육장, 899번지 Yowell로
> 오후 3시-5시 · Salt Cedar 부화장, 11452번지 Maple로
>
> **9월 10일: 농산물 직판장**
> 198-D현지에서 기른 재료들로 준비된 지역사회 식사 시간인
> Great Meal이 이어짐
> 누구나 함께 나눌 요리를 가져올 수 있음(선택적)
> 오후 2시-4시 30분 · 농산물 직판장
> 오후 5시 · Great Meal
> 199농산물 직판장과 Great Meal 모두 308번지 Chandler가의
> Kingsbrook 공원에서 열릴 것임

harvest festival 추수감사제　cooperative n. 협동조합; adj. 협동하는
field n. 사육장　hatchery n. 부화장　farmer's market 농산물 직판장 ◐

---

dish n. 요리, 접시　optional adj. 선택적인

> 수신: Marvin Cooper <m.cooper@harrisonburg.net>
> 발신: Libby Hawkins <l.hawkins@freshgoods.com>
> 제목: 만남
> 날짜: 8월 29일
>
> Mr. Cooper께,
>
> 200최근에 제 농장 네트워크의 일원이 되어주신 것과 제 식당에 닭고기를 공급하기로 결정해주신 것에 감사드립니다. 또한, 당신이 제게 이메일로 보낸 문의에 관해서, 저는 다가오는 Culpeper 추수감사제에서 기꺼이 당신을 만나고 싶습니다. 저는 당신의 농장인 Salt Cedar 부화장의 투어에 합류할 수 없을 것이지만, 199그 다음날 Great Meal 전에 약간의 시간을 할애하여 농산물 직판장에서 당신의 부스에 잠시 들를 수 있습니다. 문제가 있으면, 제게 555-2498로 전화하시면 됩니다. 감사드리며, 곧 뵙겠습니다!
>
> Libby Hawkins 드림

spare time 시간을 할애하다

---

196 Not/True 문제

문제 　Ms. Hawkins의 농장에 대해 언급된 것은?
(A) 내년에 확장할 예정이다.
(B) 95번 고속도로 근처에 위치해 있다.
(C) 유제품들을 생산한다.
(D) 전국적으로 식당들에 공급한다.

해설 　질문의 핵심 어구인 Ms. Hawkins's farm에 대해 묻는 Not/True 문제이므로 Ms. Hawkins의 농장이 언급된 첫 번째 지문(기사)에서 관련 내용을 확인한다. (A)는 지문에 언급되지 않은 내용이다. (B)는 'The country's first organic fast food restaurant, Fresh Goods, opens next month on Interstate 95.'에서 Fresh Goods가 95번 고속도로에서 개업한다고 했지 Ms. Hawkins의 농장이 95번 고속도로에 위치한 것이 아니므로 지문의 내용과 일치하지 않는다. (C)는 'her[Ms. Hawkins] farm is one of Virginia's biggest producers of milk and cheese'에서 Ms. Hawkins의 농장이 버지니아 주의 가장 큰 우유 및 치즈 생산업체들 중 하나라고 했으므로 지문의 내용과 일치한다. 따라서 (C)가 정답이다. (D)는 지문에 언급되지 않은 내용이다.

패러프레이징
one of ~ biggest producers of milk and cheese 가장 큰 우유 및 치즈 생산업체들 중 하나 → produces dairy products 유제품들을 생산하다

어휘 　dairy product 유제품　nationwide adv. 전국적으로; adj. 전국적인

197 육하원칙 문제

문제 　Ms. Hawkins가 식당을 개업하도록 한 것은 무엇인가?
(A) 식품업 잡지에 게재된 기사
(B) 일부 장소에서 건강에 좋은 음식 선택권의 이용 불가
(C) 이전 동료들 중 한 명으로부터의 추천
(D) 제품들을 위한 시장을 찾아야 할 필요성

해설 　Ms. Hawkins가 식당을 개업하도록 한 것이 무엇(What)인지를 묻는 육하원칙 문제이므로 질문의 핵심 어구인 caused Ms. Hawkins to open her restaurant과 관련된 내용이 언급된 기사를 확인한다. 첫 번째 지문(기사)의 'she decided to open Fresh Goods when she noticed the lack of healthy dishes sold at rest stops'에서 Ms. Hawkins는 휴게소에서 판매되는 건강에 좋은 음식이 부족하다는 것을 인지했을 때 Fresh Goods를 열기로 결정했다고 했으므로 (B)가 정답이다.

패러프레이징
the lack of healthy dishes sold at rest stops 휴게소에서 판매되는

건강에 좋은 음식이 부족하다는 것 → **The unavailability of healthy food options at some locations** 일부 장소에서 건강에 좋은 음식 선택권의 이용 불가

어휘 **publish** v. 게재하다, 출판하다 **unavailability** n. 이용 불가능 **former** adj. 이전의

198 Not/True 문제

문제 Culpeper 추수감사제에 대해 사실인 것은?
(A) 주로 일 년에 두 번 개최된다.
(B) 일주일 동안 계속된다.
(C) 정부가 후원한다.
(D) 현지 식품을 포함한다.

해설 질문의 핵심 어구인 the Culpeper Harvest Festival에 대해 묻는 Not/True 문제이므로 Culpeper 추수감사제가 언급된 두 번째 지문(광고)에서 관련 내용을 확인한다. (A)는 'Annual Culpeper Harvest Festival'에서 연례 Culpeper 추수감사제라고 했으므로 지문의 내용과 일치하지 않는다. (B)는 'Friday, September 8, to Sunday, September 10'에서 9월 8일 금요일부터 9월 10일 일요일까지 열린다고 했으므로 지문의 내용과 일치하지 않는다. (C)는 지문에 언급되지 않은 내용이다. (D)는 'Followed by the Great Meal ~ prepared with locally grown ingredients'에서 현지에서 기른 재료로 준비된 Great Meal이 이어진다고 했으므로 지문의 내용과 일치한다. 따라서 (D)가 정답이다.

어휘 **be sponsored by** ~가 후원하다

199 육하원칙 문제 연계

문제 Ms. Hawkins는 어디에서 Mr. Cooper를 만나고 싶어 하는가?
(A) Spotswood 호텔에서
(B) Kingsbrook 공원에서
(C) Salt Cedar 부화장에서
(D) Westover 농장에서

해설 질문의 핵심 어구인 Ms. Hawkins want to meet Mr. Cooper에서 Ms. Hawkins가 어디(Where)에서 Mr. Cooper를 만나고 싶어 하는지를 묻고 있으므로 Ms. Hawkins가 보낸 이메일을 먼저 확인한다.
[단서 1] 세 번째 지문(이메일)의 'I can spare some time ~ to stop by your[Mr. Cooper] booth at the Farmer's Market'에서 Ms. Hawkins가 농산물 직판장에서 Mr. Cooper의 부스에 잠시 들를 수 있다고 했다. 그런데 농산물 직판장이 어디에서 열리는지 제시되지 않았으므로 광고에서 관련 내용을 확인한다.
[단서 2] 두 번째 지문(광고)의 'Both the Farmer's Market and the Great Meal will be held at Kingsbrook Park'에서 농산물 직판장이 Kingsbrook 공원에서 열릴 것임을 확인할 수 있다.
두 단서를 종합할 때, Ms. Hawkins가 Mr. Cooper를 농산물 직판장이 열리는 Kingsbrook 공원에서 만나고 싶어 함을 알 수 있다. 따라서 (B)가 정답이다.

200 추론 문제 연계

문제 Mr. Cooper에 대해 추론될 수 있는 것은?
(A) Great Meal에서 몇몇 요리를 제공할 것이다.
(B) 그의 시설은 10년 넘게 운영되고 있다.
(C) 축제에 처음으로 참가한다.
(D) 그의 농장은 Fresh Goods의 50마일 이내에 있다.

해설 질문의 핵심 어구인 Mr. Cooper에게 보내진 이메일을 먼저 확인한다.
[단서 1] 세 번째 지문(이메일)의 'Thank you for recently becoming a member of my network of farms'에서 Ms. Hawkins가 Mr. Cooper에게 최근에 자신의 농장 네트워크의 일원이 되어준 것에 고맙다고 했다. 그런데 Ms. Hawkins의 농장 네트워크의 일원에 대한 정보가 제시되지 않았으므로 기사에서 관련 내용을 확인한다.
[단서 2] 첫 번째 지문(기사)의 'she[Ms. Hawkins] decided to open Fresh Goods'와 'Currently, she is working on establishing

a network of farms that will supply organic ingredients for Fresh Goods.'에서 Fresh Goods를 열기로 한 Ms. Hawkins가 Fresh Goods에 유기농 재료들을 공급할 농장들의 네트워크를 확립하는 데 노력을 들이고 있다고 했고, 'farms that will be part of this network can be no farther than 50 miles from the restaurant[Fresh Goods]'에서 이 네트워크의 일원이 될 농장들은 Fresh Goods로부터 50마일보다 더 멀리 있을 수 없음을 확인할 수 있다.
두 단서를 종합할 때, Mr. Cooper가 Ms. Hawkins의 농장 네트워크의 일원이 되었으므로 그의 농장이 Fresh Goods의 50마일 이내에 있다는 것을 알 수 있다. 따라서 (D)가 정답이다.

어휘 **operate** v. 운영하다, 작동하다

TEST 4

LISTENING TEST   p.154

1	(D)	2	(A)	3	(C)	4	(A)	5	(B)
6	(C)	7	(C)	8	(C)	9	(A)	10	(C)
11	(A)	12	(B)	13	(A)	14	(C)	15	(C)
16	(C)	17	(C)	18	(B)	19	(C)	20	(B)
21	(A)	22	(A)	23	(A)	24	(B)	25	(B)
26	(B)	27	(B)	28	(B)	29	(A)	30	(B)
31	(B)	32	(B)	33	(A)	34	(C)	35	(B)
36	(A)	37	(C)	38	(D)	39	(A)	40	(C)
41	(D)	42	(C)	43	(D)	44	(B)	45	(A)
46	(C)	47	(D)	48	(C)	49	(D)	50	(D)
51	(D)	52	(B)	53	(C)	54	(C)	55	(B)
56	(A)	57	(D)	58	(A)	59	(B)	60	(A)
61	(A)	62	(D)	63	(B)	64	(D)	65	(A)
66	(B)	67	(B)	68	(B)	69	(D)	70	(D)
71	(B)	72	(B)	73	(C)	74	(C)	75	(D)
76	(B)	77	(D)	78	(B)	79	(C)	80	(D)
81	(D)	82	(A)	83	(B)	84	(B)	85	(D)
86	(C)	87	(A)	88	(B)	89	(B)	90	(C)
91	(B)	92	(B)	93	(A)	94	(C)	95	(C)
96	(C)	97	(B)	98	(A)	99	(B)	100	(B)

READING TEST   p.166

101	(C)	102	(A)	103	(D)	104	(B)	105	(C)
106	(C)	107	(B)	108	(A)	109	(B)	110	(C)
111	(D)	112	(D)	113	(D)	114	(B)	115	(D)
116	(B)	117	(D)	118	(B)	119	(A)	120	(D)
121	(C)	122	(D)	123	(C)	124	(D)	125	(B)
126	(A)	127	(B)	128	(B)	129	(A)	130	(C)
131	(D)	132	(D)	133	(C)	134	(D)	135	(B)
136	(C)	137	(A)	138	(A)	139	(B)	140	(D)
141	(A)	142	(A)	143	(C)	144	(C)	145	(D)
146	(B)	147	(C)	148	(D)	149	(C)	150	(D)
151	(C)	152	(C)	153	(A)	154	(C)	155	(C)
156	(A)	157	(D)	158	(C)	159	(C)	160	(B)
161	(B)	162	(B)	163	(C)	164	(C)	165	(C)
166	(D)	167	(C)	168	(C)	169	(B)	170	(C)
171	(D)	172	(C)	173	(D)	174	(B)	175	(C)
176	(D)	177	(B)	178	(D)	179	(B)	180	(C)
181	(B)	182	(B)	183	(A)	184	(D)	185	(B)
186	(D)	187	(C)	188	(B)	189	(D)	190	(B)
191	(B)	192	(C)	193	(D)	194	(D)	195	(C)
196	(C)	197	(A)	198	(C)	199	(C)	200	(A)

PART 1

1 🔊 캐나다식 발음

(A) He is rolling up his sleeves.
(B) He is removing items from a container.
(C) He is sitting on a bed.
(D) He is facing away from some boxes.

roll up one's sleeves 소매를 걷어 올리다   remove [rimú:v] 치우다
container [미 kəntéinər, 영 kəntéinə] 용기
face away ~에서 고개를 돌리다

해석 (A) 그는 소매를 걷어 올리고 있다.
(B) 그는 용기에서 물건들을 치우고 있다.
(C) 그는 침대 위에 앉아 있다.
(D) 그는 몇몇 상자들에서 고개를 돌리고 있다.

해설 1인 사진
(A) [×] 남자가 이미 소매를 걷어 올린 상태인데, 걷어 올리고 있다(is rolling up)는 동작으로 잘못 묘사한 오답이다.
(B) [×] removing(치우고 있다)은 남자의 동작과 무관하므로 오답이다. 사진에 있는 용기(container)를 사용하여 혼동을 주었다.
(C) [×] 남자가 서 있는 상태인데, 앉아 있다고 잘못 묘사한 오답이다.
(D) [○] 남자가 몇몇 상자들에서 고개를 돌리고 있는 모습을 가장 잘 묘사한 정답이다.

2 🔊 호주식 발음

(A) The man is lifting a load with a work truck.
(B) The man is labeling some packages.
(C) The man is climbing up the scaffolding.
(D) The man is getting out of the vehicle.

lift [lift] 들어 올리다   load [미 loud, 영 ləud] 화물, 짐
label [léibəl] 라벨을 붙이다   package [pǽkidʒ] 상자
climb up ~ (위)에 오르다   scaffolding [skǽfəldiŋ] 발판
get out of (차량 등에서) 내리다

해석 (A) 남자가 작업용 트럭으로 화물을 들어 올리고 있다.
(B) 남자가 몇몇 상자들에 라벨을 붙이고 있다.
(C) 남자가 발판 위에 오르고 있다.
(D) 남자가 차량에서 내리고 있다.

해설 1인 사진
(A) [○] 남자가 작업용 트럭으로 화물을 들어 올리고 있는 모습을 가장 잘 묘사한 정답이다.
(B) [×] labeling(라벨을 붙이고 있다)은 남자의 동작과 무관하므로 오답이다. 사진에 있는 상자들(packages)을 사용하여 혼동을 주었다.
(C) [×] climbing up(~ 위에 오르고 있다)은 남자의 동작과 무관하므로 오답이다.
(D) [×] 남자가 차량에 타고 있는 상태인데, 내리고 있다(is getting out of)는 동작으로 잘못 묘사한 오답이다.

3 [미국식 발음]

(A) The man is riding in an elevator.
(B) A bucket is being emptied.
(C) The man is cleaning some tiles.
(D) A sign is being carried away.

---

ride in ~을 타다   empty[émpti] 비우다   carry away ~을 운반하다

해석 (A) 남자가 승강기를 타고 있다.
　　(B) 양동이가 비워지고 있다.
　　(C) 남자가 타일들을 청소하고 있다.
　　(D) 표지판이 운반되고 있다.

해설 **1인 사진**
　　(A) [×] 남자가 승강기 밖에 있는 상태인데, 타고 있다고 잘못 묘사한
　　　　　오답이다.
　　(B) [×] 사진에서 양동이는 보이지만, 비워지고 있는(is being
　　　　　emptied) 모습은 아니므로 오답이다.
　　(C) [○] 남자가 타일들을 청소하고 있는 모습을 가장 잘 묘사한 정답
　　　　　이다.
　　(D) [×] 표지판이 세워져 있는 상태인데, 운반되고 있다고 잘못 묘사
　　　　　한 오답이다.

4 [영국식 발음]

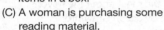

**(A) Some books have been left on
a shelf.**
(B) A woman is inspecting some
items in a box.
(C) A woman is purchasing some
reading material.
(D) Some products have been wrapped.

---

inspect[inspékt] 검사하다, 조사하다   reading material 읽을거리
wrap[ræp] 포장하다, ~을 싸다

해석 (A) 몇 권의 책들이 선반 위에 놓여 있다.
　　(B) 한 여자가 상자 안의 몇몇 물건들을 검사하고 있다.
　　(C) 한 여자가 몇몇 읽을거리를 사고 있다.
　　(D) 몇몇 제품들이 포장되어 있다.

해설 **2인 이상 사진**
　　(A) [○] 몇 권의 책들이 선반 위에 놓여 있는 모습을 가장 잘 묘사한
　　　　　정답이다.
　　(B) [×] 사진에 상자(box)가 없으므로 오답이다.
　　(C) [×] 사진에 몇몇 읽을거리를 사고 있는(purchasing some
　　　　　reading material) 여자가 없으므로 오답이다.
　　(D) [×] 사진에서 제품들은 보이지만, 포장되어 있는지(have been
　　　　　wrapped) 확인할 수 없으므로 오답이다.

5 [호주식 발음]

(A) A computer monitor has been
turned on.
**(B) There are windows on one side
of the wall.**
(C) Books have been spread out on the desks.
(D) One of the keyboards is being used.

---

turn on ~을 켜다   spread out 펼쳐지다

해석 (A) 컴퓨터 화면이 켜져 있다.
　　(B) 한쪽 벽면에 창문들이 있다.
　　(C) 책들이 책상들 위에 펼쳐져 있다.
　　(D) 키보드들 중 한 대가 사용되고 있다.

해설 **사물 및 풍경 사진**
　　(A) [×] 컴퓨터 화면이 꺼져 있는 상태인데, 켜져 있다고 잘못 묘사한
　　　　　오답이다.
　　(B) [○] 한쪽 벽면에 창문들이 있는 모습을 가장 잘 묘사한 정답이다.
　　(C) [×] 사진에 책들(Books)이 없으므로 오답이다.
　　(D) [×] 사진에서 키보드는 보이지만, 사용되고 있는(is being used)
　　　　　모습은 아니므로 오답이다.

6 [미국식 발음]

(A) Some trees are being trimmed.
(B) Some lamps are hanging from a
fence.
(C) A garden gate has been shut.
(D) A lawn is being watered.

---

trim[trim] 다듬다, 손질하다   shut[ʃʌt] 닫다   lawn[lɔːn] 잔디

해석 (A) 몇몇 나무들이 다듬어지고 있다.
　　(B) 몇몇 조명들이 울타리에 매달려 있다.
　　(C) 정원 출입구가 닫혀 있다.
　　(D) 잔디에 물이 뿌려지고 있다.

해설 **사물 및 풍경 사진**
　　(A) [×] 사진에서 나무들은 보이지만, 다듬어지고 있는(are being
　　　　　trimmed) 모습은 아니므로 오답이다.
　　(B) [×] 사진에서 울타리에 매달려 있는 조명들을 확인할 수 없으므로
　　　　　오답이다.
　　(C) [○] 정원 출입구가 닫혀 있는 모습을 가장 잘 묘사한 정답이다.
　　(D) [×] 사진에서 잔디는 보이지만, 물이 뿌려지고 있는(is being
　　　　　watered) 모습은 아니므로 오답이다.

PART 2

7 [캐나다식 발음 → 호주식 발음]

What time does this restaurant close?
(A) We have no more tables available.
(B) Mostly Italian food.
(C) Usually around 10 P.M.

---

available[əvéiləbl] 이용할 수 있는

해석 이 음식점은 몇 시에 문을 닫나요?
　　(A) 이용하실 수 있는 테이블들이 더 없습니다.
　　(B) 대부분 이탈리아 음식이요.
　　(C) 보통 오후 10시쯤이요.

해설 **What 의문문**
　　(A) [×] 질문의 restaurant(음식점)과 관련 있는 tables(테이블들)를
　　　　　사용하여 혼동을 준 오답이다.
　　(B) [×] 질문의 restaurant(음식점)과 관련 있는 food(음식)를 사용하
　　　　　여 혼동을 준 오답이다.
　　(C) [○] 보통 오후 10시쯤이라며, 음식점이 문을 닫는 시간을 언급했
　　　　　으므로 정답이다.

8 영국식 발음 → 캐나다식 발음

Where do you think you lost your wallet?
(A) I don't think it's the right size.
(B) You didn't pay for the ticket.
(C) At the movie theater, I believe.

wallet [미 wάlit, 영 wɔ́lit] 지갑 pay for ~의 값을 지불하다

해석 어디에서 당신의 지갑을 잃어버린 것 같나요?
(A) 그것은 알맞은 사이즈인 것 같지 않아요.
(B) 당신은 티켓 값을 지불하지 않았어요.
(C) 영화관에서인 것 같아요.

해설 Where 의문문
(A) [x] 어디에서 지갑을 잃어버린 것 같은지를 물었는데, 이와 관련이 없는 그것은 알맞은 사이즈인 것 같지 않다는 내용으로 응답했으므로 오답이다.
(B) [x] 질문의 wallet(지갑)과 관련 있는 pay for(~의 값을 지불하다)를 사용하여 혼동을 준 오답이다.
(C) [o] 영화관에서인 것 같다며, 지갑을 잃어버린 것 같은 장소를 언급했으므로 정답이다.

9 미국식 발음 → 호주식 발음

Who forgot to put away the paint brushes?
(A) I think it was Fidel.
(B) Thanks, I meant to paint it.
(C) Beside those bushes.

put away ~을 치우다 paint brush 페인트 붓 bush [buʃ] 풀숲, 덤불

해석 누가 페인트 붓들을 치우는 것을 잊었나요?
(A) Fidel인 것 같아요.
(B) 고마워요, 저는 그것을 페인트칠할 셈이었어요.
(C) 그 풀숲 옆에서요.

해설 Who 의문문
(A) [o] Fidel인 것 같다며, 페인트 붓들을 치우는 것을 잊어버린 인물을 언급했으므로 정답이다.
(B) [x] 질문의 paint(페인트)를 '페인트칠하다'라는 의미의 동사로 반복 사용하여 혼동을 준 오답이다.
(C) [x] brushes - bushes의 유사 발음 어휘를 사용하여 혼동을 준 오답이다.

10 캐나다식 발음 → 영국식 발음

Why did you order a different computer chair?
(A) You'll get another reminder.
(B) Use these order forms.
(C) My current one gives me back pain.

order [미 ɔ́ːrdər, 영 ɔ́ːdə] 주문하다; 주문
reminder [미 rimáindər, 영 rimáində] 상기시켜 주는 편지(것)
current [미 kə́ːrənt, 영 kʌ́rənt] 지금의 back [bæk] 등
pain [pein] 아픔, 통증

해석 당신은 왜 다른 컴퓨터 의자를 주문했나요?
(A) 당신은 상기시켜 주는 다른 편지를 받을 겁니다.
(B) 이 주문 양식들을 이용하세요.
(C) 지금의 제 것은 등을 아프게 해요.

해설 Why 의문문
(A) [x] 질문의 different(다른)와 같은 의미의 another(다른)를 사용

하여 혼동을 준 오답이다.
(B) [x] 질문의 order(주문하다)를 '주문'이라는 의미의 명사로 반복 사용하여 혼동을 준 오답이다.
(C) [o] 지금의 것은 등을 아프게 한다며, 다른 컴퓨터 의자를 주문한 이유를 언급했으므로 정답이다.

11 호주식 발음 → 영국식 발음

When do you leave work today?
(A) In a couple of hours.
(B) I was working on a proposal.
(C) Leave the check here.

leave work 퇴근하다 a couple of 두어, 몇몇의
proposal [미 prəpóuzəl, 영 prəpɔ́uzəl] 제안서 check [tʃek] 수표

해석 오늘 언제 퇴근하나요?
(A) 두어 시간 후에요.
(B) 저는 제안서를 작업하고 있었어요.
(C) 수표를 여기에 두세요.

해설 When 의문문
(A) [o] 두어 시간 후라며, 퇴근할 시점을 언급했으므로 정답이다.
(B) [x] 질문의 work(직장)를 '작업하고 있었다'라는 의미의 동사 was working으로 반복 사용하여 혼동을 준 오답이다.
(C) [x] 질문의 leave(떠나다)를 '두다'라는 의미로 반복 사용하여 혼동을 준 오답이다.

12 미국식 발음 → 호주식 발음

What impressed you the most about the novel?
(A) Yes, it was written by Jason Crawford.
(B) The main character.
(C) Oh, I found it at a local bookstore.

impress [imprés] 깊은 인상을 주다 novel [미 nάvəl, 영 nɔ́vəl] 소설
main character 주인공 local [미 lóukəl, 영 lɔ́ukəl] 지역의, 현지의

해석 그 소설에서 무엇이 당신에게 가장 깊은 인상을 주었나요?
(A) 네, 그것은 Jason Crawford에 의해 쓰여졌어요.
(B) 주인공이요.
(C) 아, 저는 그것을 지역 서점에서 발견했어요.

해설 What 의문문
(A) [x] 의문사 의문문에 Yes로 응답했으므로 오답이다.
(B) [o] 주인공이라며, 그 소설에서 가장 깊은 인상을 준 것을 언급했으므로 정답이다.
(C) [x] 질문의 novel(소설)과 관련 있는 bookstore(서점)를 사용하여 혼동을 준 오답이다.

13 캐나다식 발음 → 미국식 발음

Can we practice for Friday's presentation now?
(A) After lunch would be better for me.
(B) My soccer team practices daily.
(C) Last Saturday night.

practice [præktis] 연습하다 daily [déili] 매일

해석 금요일의 발표를 지금 연습해도 될까요?
(A) 저는 점심 이후가 더 좋아요.
(B) 제 축구팀은 매일 연습해요.
(C) 지난 토요일 밤이요.

해설 **제안 의문문**
(A) [o] 점심 이후가 더 좋다는 말로, 지금 연습을 하자는 제안을 간접적으로 거절한 정답이다.
(B) [x] 질문의 practice를 practices로 반복 사용하여 혼동을 준 오답이다.
(C) [x] 질문의 Friday(금요일)와 관련 있는 Saturday(토요일)를 사용하여 혼동을 준 오답이다.

14 🔊 미국식 발음 → 캐나다식 발음

Which company should we hire to print our flyers?
(A) Print enough for everyone.
(B) To post them around the neighborhood.
(C) The same one we used last time.

hire[미 haiər, 영 haiə] 고용하다 flyer[미 fláiər, 영 fláiə] 광고지, 전단지
post[미 poust, 영 pəust] (안내문 등을) 게시하다
neighborhood[미 néibərhùd, 영 néibəhud] 인근 (지역)

해석 우리의 광고지들을 인쇄하기 위해 어느 업체를 고용해야 할까요?
(A) 모두를 위해 충분히 인쇄하세요.
(B) 그것들을 인근 지역에 게시하기 위해서요.
(C) 우리가 지난번에 이용했던 곳과 같은 곳이요.

해설 **Which 의문문**
(A) [x] 질문의 print를 반복 사용하여 혼동을 준 오답이다.
(B) [x] 질문의 flyers(광고지들)를 나타낼 수 있는 them을 사용하여 혼동을 준 오답이다.
(C) [o] 지난번에 이용했던 곳과 같은 곳이라는 말로, 광고지들을 인쇄하기 위해 고용할 업체를 언급했으므로 정답이다.

15 🔊 미국식 발음 → 호주식 발음

When can I expect my merchandise to arrive?
(A) You can save the rest for later.
(B) Yes, according to experts.
(C) No later than March 12.

merchandise[미 mə́ːrtʃəndàiz, 영 mə́ːtʃəndàiz] (구매한) 물품
save[seiv] 남겨두다 rest[rest] 나머지 according to ~에 따르면
expert[미 ékspəːrt, 영 ékspəːt] 전문가 no later than 늦어도 ~까지

해석 언제 제가 구매한 물품이 도착할 것으로 예상하면 되나요?
(A) 다음을 위해 나머지를 남겨두셔도 돼요.
(B) 네, 전문가들에 따르면요.
(C) 늦어도 3월 12일까지요.

해설 **When 의문문**
(A) [x] 구매한 물품이 언제 도착할 것으로 예상하면 되는지를 물었는데, 이와 관련이 없는 다음을 위해 나머지를 남겨둬도 된다는 내용으로 응답했으므로 오답이다.
(B) [x] 의문사 의문문에 Yes로 응답했으므로 오답이다.
(C) [o] 늦어도 3월 12일까지라며, 물품이 도착할 것으로 예상되는 시점을 언급했으므로 정답이다.

16 🔊 호주식 발음 → 미국식 발음

Who told you about the board of directors' election results?
(A) I received my test results.
(B) Tell Sam about these suggestions.
(C) My manager made an announcement.

board of directors 경영진, 이사회 election[ilékʃən] 선거
suggestion[səgdʒéstʃən] 의견, 제안
make an announcement 발표를 하다

해석 누가 당신에게 경영진의 선거 결과에 대해 알려주었나요?
(A) 저는 제 검사 결과를 받았어요.
(B) Sam에게 이 의견들을 알려주세요.
(C) 제 부장님이 발표했어요.

해설 **Who 의문문**
(A) [x] 질문의 results를 반복 사용하여 혼동을 준 오답이다.
(B) [x] 질문의 told를 tell로 반복 사용하여 혼동을 준 오답이다.
(C) [o] 자신의 부장이 발표했다며, 선거 결과에 대해 알려준 인물을 언급했으므로 정답이다.

17 🔊 영국식 발음 → 캐나다식 발음

Have you decided on the location of the fashion show?
(A) The clothing line is amazing.
(B) Will you be relocating?
(C) Ashley is handling that.

decide on ~을 결정하다
relocate[미 riːlóukeit, 영 riːləukéit] 전근하다, 이전하다
handle[hǽndl] 처리하다, 다루다

해석 당신은 패션쇼 장소를 결정했나요?
(A) 그 의류 제품은 굉장해요.
(B) 당신은 전근할 건가요?
(C) Ashley가 그것을 처리하고 있어요.

해설 **조동사 의문문**
(A) [x] 질문의 fashion show(패션쇼)와 관련 있는 clothing line(의류 제품)을 사용하여 혼동을 준 오답이다.
(B) [x] location – relocating의 유사 발음 어휘를 사용하여 혼동을 준 오답이다.
(C) [o] Ashley가 그것을 처리하고 있다는 말로 자신이 담당자가 아니라는 간접적인 응답을 했으므로 정답이다.

18 🔊 미국식 발음 → 영국식 발음

I'd like to book a flight from Baltimore to San Francisco.
(A) Sorry, I haven't been there.
(B) I can help with that.
(C) Pick it up at the gate.

book[buk] 예약하다 flight[flait] 항공편 pick up ~을 찾아가다
gate[geit] 탑승구

해석 저는 볼티모어에서 출발하는 샌프란시스코행 항공편을 예약하고 싶어요.
(A) 죄송하지만, 전 그곳에 가본 적이 없어요.
(B) 제가 그것을 도와드릴게요.
(C) 탑승구에서 그것을 찾아가세요.

해설 **평서문**
(A) [x] 항공편을 예약하고 싶다고 했는데, 이와 관련이 없는 그곳에 가본 적이 없다는 내용으로 응답했으므로 오답이다.
(B) [o] 그것을 도와주겠다는 말로, 항공편을 예약하고 싶다는 요청을 수락한 정답이다.
(C) [x] 질문의 flight(항공편)와 관련 있는 gate(탑승구)를 사용하여 혼동을 준 오답이다.

19 〔호〕 호주식 발음 → 영국식 발음

Are the training participants in the conference room?
(A) The train leaves at 10 A.M.
(B) We can make room for the equipment.
(C) It has been canceled.

---

participant[미 pɑːrtísəpənt, 영 pɑːtísipənt] 참가자
conference room 회의실   room[ruːm] 공간, 자리
equipment[ikwípmənt] 장비

해석 교육 참가자들은 회의실에 있나요?
(A) 그 기차는 오전 10시에 떠나요.
(B) 우리는 장비를 위한 공간을 만들 수 있어요.
(C) 그것은 취소되었어요.

해설 **Be동사 의문문**
(A) [×] training – train의 유사 발음 어휘를 사용하여 혼동을 준 오답이다.
(B) [×] 질문의 room(실, 방)을 '공간, 자리'라는 의미로 반복 사용하여 혼동을 준 오답이다.
(C) [○] 그것이 취소되었다는 말로 교육 참가자들이 회의실에 있지 않음을 간접적으로 전달했으므로 정답이다.

20 〔호〕 호주식 발음 → 미국식 발음

How much will it cost to repair the delivery van?
(A) They offer free delivery.
(B) Shouldn't we just replace it?
(C) The rental costs $30 a day.

---

van[væn] 승합차, 밴   replace[ripléis] 교체하다, 대체하다
rental[réntl] 사용료, 임대료

해석 배달용 승합차를 수리하는 데 비용이 얼마나 많이 들까요?
(A) 그들은 무료 배달을 제공해요.
(B) 그냥 교체해야 하지 않을까요?
(C) 사용료는 하루에 30달러예요.

해설 **How 의문문**
(A) [×] 질문의 delivery를 반복 사용하여 혼동을 준 오답이다.
(B) [○] 그냥 교체해야 하지 않을지를 되물어, 배달용 승합차를 수리하는 데 비용이 많이 든다는 것을 간접적으로 전달했으므로 정답이다.
(C) [×] 질문의 cost를 costs로 반복 사용하여 혼동을 준 오답이다.

21 〔호〕 호주식 발음 → 영국식 발음

Hasn't our latest speaker model been selling well?
(A) Yes, but only in certain states.
(B) I'll speak to her now.
(C) Profits from a manufacturing firm.

---

latest[léitist] 최신의   state[steit] 국가   profit[미 práfit, 영 prɔ́fit] 수익
manufacturing firm 제조 회사

해석 우리의 최신 스피커 모델은 잘 팔리고 있지 않나요?
(A) 네, 하지만 일부 국가에서만요.
(B) 제가 그녀에게 지금 이야기를 할게요.
(C) 제조 회사로부터의 수익이요.

해설 **부정 의문문**
(A) [○] Yes로 최신 스피커 모델이 잘 팔리고 있음을 전달한 후, 일부 국가들에서만이라는 부연 설명을 했으므로 정답이다.

(B) [×] speaker – speak의 유사 발음 어휘를 사용하여 혼동을 준 오답이다.
(C) [×] 질문의 selling(팔리고 있는)과 관련 있는 Profits(수익)를 사용하여 혼동을 준 오답이다.

22 〔호〕 캐나다식 발음 → 미국식 발음

I don't think we were sent the correct books.
(A) Oh, these are the novels I ordered.
(B) A textbook publisher.
(C) Send a sample by today.

---

novel[미 návəl, 영 nɔ́vəl] 소설(책)   textbook[미 tékstbuk] 교과서
publisher[미 pʌ́bliʃər, 영 pʌ́bliʃə] 출판사, 출판인

해석 우리가 맞는 책들을 받은 것 같지 않아요.
(A) 아, 이것들은 제가 주문했던 소설책들이에요.
(B) 교과서 출판사요.
(C) 오늘까지 샘플을 보내세요.

해설 **평서문**
(A) [○] 자신이 주문했던 소설책들이라는 말로, 맞는 책들을 받았음을 간접적으로 전달했으므로 정답이다.
(B) [×] 질문의 books(책들)와 관련 있는 textbook(교과서)을 사용하여 혼동을 준 오답이다.
(C) [×] 질문의 sent를 send로 반복 사용하여 혼동을 준 오답이다.

23 〔호〕 영국식 발음 → 캐나다식 발음

How will I finish our report while you're on vacation?
(A) Mandy can help.
(B) At a popular resort.
(C) I wish I could go.

---

be on vacation 휴가 중이다

해석 당신이 휴가 중일 동안 제가 어떻게 우리 보고서를 마무리할 수 있나요?
(A) Mandy가 도와줄 수 있어요.
(B) 인기 있는 리조트에서요.
(C) 제가 갈 수 있었으면 좋겠어요.

해설 **How 의문문**
(A) [○] Mandy가 도와줄 수 있다며, 자신이 휴가 중일 동안 Mandy에게 도움을 받아 보고서를 마무리할 수 있음을 간접적으로 전달했으므로 정답이다.
(B) [×] 질문의 vacation(휴가)과 관련 있는 resort(리조트)를 사용하여 혼동을 준 오답이다.
(C) [×] 휴가 중일 동안 어떻게 보고서를 마무리할 수 있는지를 물었는데, 이와 관련이 없는 자신이 갈 수 있었으면 좋겠다는 내용으로 응답했으므로 오답이다.

24 〔호〕 미국식 발음 → 캐나다식 발음

Is our food going to be delivered soon, or will it take a while longer?
(A) It was surprisingly spicy.
(B) I can call and find out.
(C) As soon as you cook it.

---

take[teik] (시간이) 걸리다
surprisingly[미 sərpráiziŋli, 영 səpráiziŋli] 놀라울 정도로
spicy[spáisi] 매운   find out ~을 알아내다   as soon as ~하자마자

해석 우리 음식이 곧 배달될 건가요, 아니면 시간이 좀 더 걸릴까요?

(A) 그것은 놀라울 정도로 매웠어요.
(B) 제가 전화해서 알아볼게요.
(C) 당신이 그것을 요리하자마자요.

해설 **선택 의문문**

(A) [×] 질문의 food(음식)와 관련 있는 spicy(매운)를 사용하여 혼동을 준 오답이다.
(B) [○] 자신이 전화해서 알아보겠다는 말로, 음식이 언제 배달될 것인지 모른다는 간접적인 응답을 했으므로 정답이다.
(C) [×] 질문의 food(음식)와 관련 있는 cook(요리하다)을 사용하고, 질문의 soon을 반복 사용하여 혼동을 준 오답이다.

25 🔊 영국식 발음 → 호주식 발음

Our ferry has arrived at the dock.
(A) Lock the doors when you're done.
(B) OK, I'll grab my luggage.
(C) After the boat tour.

ferry[féri] 여객선, 나룻배 dock[미 dɑk, 영 dɔk] 부두
lock[미 lɑk, 영 lɔk] 잠그다 grab[græb] (급히) 가져오다
luggage[lʌ́gidʒ] 짐

해석 우리 여객선이 부두에 도착했어요.
(A) 끝나면 문들을 잠그세요.
(B) 알았어요, 제 짐을 가져올게요.
(C) 보트 투어 후에요.

해설 **평서문**

(A) [×] dock – lock의 유사 발음 어휘를 사용하여 혼동을 준 오답이다.
(B) [○] OK로 여객선이 부두에 도착했음을 알았다고 한 후, 짐을 가져오겠다는 부연 설명을 했으므로 정답이다.
(C) [×] 질문의 ferry(여객선)와 관련 있는 boat(보트)를 사용하여 혼동을 준 오답이다.

26 🔊 호주식 발음 → 영국식 발음

Would you bring this document to the head of the finance team?
(A) Some official documents.
(B) I think he already has a copy of it.
(C) Yes, we met with the CEO.

document[미 dɑ́kjumənt, 영 dɔ́kjumənt] 문서 finance team 재무팀
official[əfíʃəl] 공식적인

해석 이 문서를 재무팀장에게 가져다줄래요?
(A) 몇몇 공식 문서들이요.
(B) 그가 이미 그것의 사본을 가지고 있는 것 같은데요.
(C) 네, 우리는 대표이사와 만났어요.

해설 **요청 의문문**

(A) [×] 질문의 document를 documents로 반복 사용하여 혼동을 준 오답이다.
(B) [○] 그가 이미 그것의 사본을 가지고 있는 것 같다는 말로, 문서를 재무팀장에게 가져다달라는 요청을 간접적으로 거절한 정답이다.
(C) [×] 질문의 head((조직의) 장)와 관련 있는 CEO(대표이사)를 사용하여 혼동을 준 오답이다.

27 🔊 캐나다식 발음 → 미국식 발음

The event's date has changed again, hasn't it?
(A) Yes, it was a success.

○

(B) I'm afraid so.
(C) You never sign up for the event.

sign up for ~에 등록하다

해석 그 행사의 날짜가 또 바뀌었어요, 그렇지 않나요?
(A) 네, 그것은 성공이었어요.
(B) 유감스럽지만 그런 것 같아요.
(C) 당신은 그 행사에 한 번도 등록하지 않네요.

해설 **부가 의문문**

(A) [×] 질문의 event(행사)를 나타낼 수 있는 it을 사용하여 혼동을 준 오답이다.
(B) [○] 유감스럽지만 그런 것 같다는 말로, 행사의 날짜가 또 바뀌었음을 전달했으므로 정답이다.
(C) [×] 질문의 event를 반복 사용하여 혼동을 준 오답이다.

28 🔊 캐나다식 발음 → 영국식 발음

Isn't our new factory going to be built in Jacksonville?
(A) On the plant floor.
(B) According to our manager.
(C) Yes, my house is being built.

plant[미 plænt, 영 plɑːnt] 공장 floor[미 flɔːr, 영 flɔː] 작업장, 바닥
according to ~에 따르면

해석 우리의 새로운 공장은 Jacksonville에 지어질 예정이 아닌가요?
(A) 공장 작업장에서요.
(B) 우리의 관리자에 따르면요.
(C) 네, 제 집이 지어지고 있는 중이에요.

해설 **부정 의문문**

(A) [×] 질문의 factory(공장)와 같은 의미인 plant(공장)를 사용하여 혼동을 준 오답이다.
(B) [○] 관리자에 따르면이라는 말로, 새로운 공장이 Jacksonville에 지어질 예정임을 간접적으로 전달했으므로 정답이다.
(C) [×] 질문의 built를 반복 사용하여 혼동을 준 오답이다.

29 🔊 캐나다식 발음 → 영국식 발음

We missed the shipping deadline for a customer last week.
(A) Mr. Clemens already informed me.
(B) No, he arrived last week.
(C) Be sure not to miss the talk.

shipping[ʃípiŋ] 배송, 선적 deadline[dédlain] 마감일
inform[미 infɔ́ːrm, 영 infɔ́ːm] 알리다 be sure to 반드시 ~을 하다
miss[mis] (못 보고·듣고) 놓치다 talk[tɔːk] 강연

해석 우리는 지난주에 고객을 위한 배송 마감일을 놓쳤어요.
(A) Mr. Clemens가 저에게 이미 알려줬어요.
(B) 아뇨, 그는 지난주에 도착했어요.
(C) 그 강연을 반드시 놓치지 마세요.

해설 **평서문**

(A) [○] Mr. Clemens가 자신에게 이미 알려줬다는 말로, 배송 마감일을 놓친 것을 알고 있음을 전달했으므로 정답이다.
(B) [×] 질문의 last week를 반복 사용하여 혼동을 준 오답이다.
(C) [×] 질문의 missed를 miss로 반복 사용하여 혼동을 준 오답이다.

Did you change your e-mail address?
(A) Sorry, I'm out of change.
(B) It's the same as before.
(C) Thanks for sending me the message.

change[tʃeindʒ] 바꾸다; 잔돈 be out of ~이 떨어지다

해석 당신은 이메일 주소를 바꿨나요?
(A) 죄송하지만, 저는 잔돈이 떨어졌어요.
(B) 그것은 이전과 같아요.
(C) 제게 메시지를 보내줘서 고마워요.

해설 **조동사 의문문**
(A) [×] 질문의 change(바꾸다)를 '잔돈'이라는 의미의 명사로 반복 사용하여 혼동을 준 오답이다.
(B) [○] 이전과 같다는 말로, 이메일 주소를 바꾸지 않았음을 전달했으므로 정답이다.
(C) [×] 질문의 e-mail(이메일)과 관련 있는 message(메시지)를 사용하여 혼동을 준 오답이다.

The lights were turned off in the garage, right?
(A) We turned it into a kitchen.
(B) I made sure to double-check.
(C) Yes, this color is much lighter.

light[lait] 전등; 밝은 turn off ~을 끄다
garage[미 gəráːdʒ, 영 gǽrɑːʒ] 차고 turn into ~으로 바꾸다
make sure to 확실하게 ~하다 double-check[dʌ̀bəltʃék] 재확인하다

해석 차고의 전등들은 꺼졌죠, 그렇죠?
(A) 우리는 그것을 주방으로 바꿨어요.
(B) 제가 확실하게 재확인했어요.
(C) 네, 이 색상이 훨씬 더 밝네요.

해설 **부가 의문문**
(A) [×] 질문의 turned를 반복 사용하여 혼동을 준 오답이다.
(B) [○] 자신이 확실하게 재확인했다는 말로, 차고의 전등들이 꺼졌음을 간접적으로 전달했으므로 정답이다.
(C) [×] lights – lighter의 유사 발음 어휘를 사용하여 혼동을 준 오답이다.

PART 3

32-34 [3에] 캐나다식 발음 → 미국식 발음

Questions 32-34 refer to the following conversation.

M: Good afternoon. ³²This is Woodbridge Medical Facility. How may I assist you?
W: Hello. May I please speak with Dr. Anderson? This is one of his patients, Jennifer Ford.
M: I'm so sorry, Ms. Ford, but Dr. Anderson is in the staff cafeteria having lunch right now. ³³I can take down a message for him, if you'd like.
W: Yes, please. I'd just like to let him know that ³⁴my back pain has improved. So, I won't need a refill of the medication he prescribed me last month.

medical facility 의료시설 assist[əsíst] 돕다 take down ~을 적다 ○

---

pain[pein] 통증 improve[imprúːv] 나아지다, 개선하다
refill[ríːfil] 보충, 보충용 물건
medication[미 mèdəkéiʃən, 영 mèdikéiʃən] 약, 약물
prescribe[priskráib] 처방하다

해석
32-34번은 다음 대화에 관한 문제입니다.
남: 안녕하세요. ³²여기는 Woodbridge 의료시설입니다. 어떻게 도와드릴까요?
여: 안녕하세요. Dr. Anderson과 이야기할 수 있을까요? 저는 그의 환자들 중 한 명인 Jennifer Ford예요.
남: 정말 죄송합니다, Ms. Ford, 하지만 Dr. Anderson은 지금 직원 식당에서 점심을 드시고 계십니다. ³³원하신다면, 제가 그를 위한 메시지를 적어드리겠습니다.
여: 네, 그렇게 해주세요. 저는 그저 ³⁴제 허리 통증이 나아졌다는 것을 그에게 알려드리려고 해요. 그래서, 저는 지난달에 그가 저에게 처방해준 약의 보충이 필요 없을 거예요.

32 화자 문제
해석 남자는 누구인 것 같은가?
(A) 점원
(B) 접수 담당자
(C) 약사
(D) 의사

해설 대화에서 신분 및 직업과 관련된 표현을 놓치지 않고 듣는다. 남자가 "This is Woodbridge Medical Facility. How may I assist you?"라며 여기는 Woodbridge 의료시설이라고 한 후, 여자에게 어떻게 도와줄지 물은 것을 통해 남자가 접수 담당자임을 알 수 있다. 따라서 (B)가 정답이다.

어휘 cashier[미 kæʃíər, 영 kæʃíə] 점원
receptionist[risépʃənist] 접수 담당자
pharmacist[미 fáːrməsist, 영 fáːməsist] 약사

33 제안 문제
해석 남자는 무엇을 해주겠다고 제안하는가?
(A) 메모를 적는다.
(B) 문자 메시지를 보낸다.
(C) 약을 처방한다.
(D) 예약을 미룬다.

해설 남자의 말에서 여자를 위해 해주겠다고 언급한 내용을 주의 깊게 듣는다. 남자가 여자에게 "I can take down a message for him, if you'd like."라며 원한다면 자신이 메시지를 적어주겠다고 하였다. 따라서 (A)가 정답이다.

패러프레이징
take down a message 메시지를 적다 → Write a note 메모를 적다

어휘 postpone[미 poustpóun, 영 pəustpə́un] 미루다

34 언급 문제
해석 여자에 대해 무엇이 언급되는가?
(A) 늦게 도착할 것이다.
(B) 지난달에 허리를 다쳤다.
(C) 상태가 나아졌다.
(D) 지불금이 받아지지 않았다.

해설 대화에서 여자와 관련된 내용을 주의 깊게 듣는다. 여자가 "my back pain has improved"라며 자신의 허리 통증이 나아졌다고 하였다. 따라서 (C)가 정답이다.

어휘 expect to ~할 것(셈)이다 condition[kəndíʃən] 상태

35-37 [음성] 호주식 발음 → 영국식 발음

Questions 35-37 refer to the following conversation.

M: Hello. ³⁵You've reached Delta Card. How can I help you today?

W: Hi. This is Lauren O'Day. ³⁵/³⁶I'm calling about my recent credit card bill. ³⁶There's a $125 fee that I didn't expect.

M: OK . . . ³⁶That's the annual fee for your account. It covers services such as credit protection, our rewards program, and our hotel discount program.

W: ³⁷I'm sure this is a mistake. I've had this card for over a year, and ³⁷I've never had to pay this before.

M: The fee is waived for the first 12 months as part of our promotion for new account holders. It's all explained in your cardholder's agreement.

W: Oh . . . I wasn't aware of that. I should have looked at it closer.

---

credit card 신용카드 annual fee 연회비
account[əkáunt] 신용 거래, 계좌
cover[미 kʌ́vər, 영 kʌ́və] 포함하다, (경비·손실을) 부담하다
reward[미 riwɔ́ːrd, 영 riwɔ́ːd] 보상
waive[weiv] (규칙 등을) 적용하지 않다
promotion[미 prəmóuʃən, 영 prəmə́uʃən] 판촉 활동
account holder 계좌 소지자 agreement[əgríːmənt] 계약서, 합의서

해석
35-37번은 다음 대화에 관한 문제입니다.

남: 안녕하세요. ³⁵당신은 Delta 카드사로 연락 주셨습니다. 제가 오늘 어떻게 도와드릴까요?

여: 안녕하세요. 저는 Lauren O'Day라고 합니다. ³⁵/³⁶저는 제 최근 신용카드 청구서에 대해 전화드려요. ³⁶제가 예상하지 못한 125달러의 요금이 있어서요.

남: 그렇군요. ³⁶그건 고객님의 신용 거래에 대한 연회비입니다. 그것은 신용 보호, 저희의 보상 프로그램 및 호텔 할인 프로그램과 같은 서비스 비용을 포함합니다.

여: ³⁷저는 이것이 실수라고 확신해요. 제가 이 카드를 1년 넘게 가지고 있었는데, ³⁷이전에 이것을 지불해야 했던 적이 없었거든요.

남: 그 요금은 신규 계좌 소지자들을 위한 저희의 판촉 활동의 일환으로 첫 12개월 동안에는 적용되지 않습니다. 그것은 고객님의 카드 소지자 계약서에 모두 설명이 되어 있습니다.

여: 아... 그건 몰랐어요. 제가 그것을 더 자세히 봤어야 했네요.

35 화자 문제

해석 남자는 어디에서 일하는 것 같은가?
(A) 법률 사무소에서
(B) 금융 기관에서
(C) 소매점에서
(D) 보안 회사에서

해설 대화에서 신분 및 직업과 관련된 표현을 놓치지 않고 듣는다. 남자가 여자에게 "You've reached Delta Card. How can I help you today?"라며 Delta 카드사로 연락 주었다고 한 후, 오늘 어떻게 도와줄지 묻자, 여자가 "I'm calling about my recent credit card bill."이라며 최근 신용카드 청구서에 대해 전화한다고 하였다. 이를 통해 남자가 금융 기관에서 일한다는 것을 알 수 있다. 따라서 (B)가 정답이다.

어휘 law office 법률 사무소 financial institution 금융 기관
retail outlet 소매점 security[sikjúərəti] 보안의; 보안

36 언급 문제

해석 여자의 신용카드에 대해 무엇이 언급되는가?
(A) 정기적인 회비가 있다.
(B) 캐시백 보상을 제공한다.
(C) 호텔 숙박에 대한 비용이 청구되었다.
(D) 1년간 유효하다.

해설 질문의 핵심 어구(woman's credit card)와 관련된 내용을 주의 깊게 듣는다. 여자가 "I'm calling about my recent credit card bill. There's a $125 fee that I didn't expect."라며 자신의 최근 신용카드 청구서에 대해 전화한다며 예상하지 못한 125달러의 요금이 있다고 하자, 남자가 "That's the annual fee for your account."라며 그것은 여자의 신용 거래에 대한 연회비라고 하였다. 따라서 (A)가 정답이다.

패러프레이징
annual fee 연회비 → regular fee 정기적인 회비

어휘 valid[vǽlid] 유효한, 타당한

37 의도 파악 문제

해석 여자는 왜 "제가 이 카드를 1년 넘게 가지고 있었는데"라고 말하는가?
(A) 교체를 요청하기 위해
(B) 서비스에 대한 만족을 표현하기 위해
(C) 요금에 대한 의문을 제기하기 위해
(D) 무료 상품을 요청하기 위해

해설 질문의 인용어구(I've had this card for over a year)가 언급된 주변을 주의 깊게 듣는다. 여자가 "I'm sure this[annual fee] is a mistake."라며 연회비가 실수라고 확신한다고 한 후, "I've never had to pay this before"라며 이전에 이것을 지불해야 했던 적이 없었다고 한 말을 통해 요금에 대한 의문을 제기하기 위함임을 알 수 있다. 따라서 (C)가 정답이다.

어휘 replacement[ripléismənt] 교체, 대체

38-40 [음성] 캐나다식 발음 → 미국식 발음 → 호주식 발음

Questions 38-40 refer to the following conversation with three speakers.

M1: ³⁸I think we should upgrade our office lights.

W: I agree. ³⁹Our current ones are way too bright. I find them distracting.

M2: So, Mark, what kind of lighting do you have in mind?

M1: Well, I read about ones that automatically adjust their brightness when it gets darker outside.

M2: That sounds good, but are they within our budget?

M1: Our office is fairly large, so installing them certainly wouldn't be cheap.

W: We should keep in mind that if the new lights help increase worker productivity, they would be worth the cost.

M2: Let's see what the other managers think about the idea. ⁴⁰I'll bring this up at the weekly meeting on Thursday.

---

upgrade[미 ʌ̀pgréid, 영 ʌ́pgreid] 개선하다
distracting[distrǽktiŋ] 집중할 수 없게 하는, 마음을 산란케 하는
lighting[láitiŋ] 조명 have in mind ~을 생각하다, 염두에 두다
automatically[미 ɔ̀ːtəmǽtikəli, 영 ɔ̀ːtəmǽtikli] 자동으로
adjust[ədʒʌ́st] 조절하다 brightness[bráitnis] 밝기
budget[bʌ́dʒit] 예산 fairly[미 fέərli, 영 fέəli] 꽤, 상당히

해석

38-40번은 다음 세 명의 대화에 관한 문제입니다.

남1: ³⁸저는 우리의 사무실 조명을 개선해야 한다고 생각해요.

여: 동의해요. ³⁹현재의 것들은 너무 밝아요. 그것들은 집중할 수 없게 해요.

남2: 그래서, Mark, 어떤 종류의 조명을 생각하고 있나요?

남1: 음, 저는 밖이 어두워지면 자동으로 밝기를 조절하는 것들에 대해 읽어본 적이 있어요.

남2: 그거 괜찮은데요, 하지만 그것들이 우리의 예산 범위 안에 있나요?

남1: 우리 사무실이 꽤 커서, 그것들을 설치하는 것은 분명 싸진 않을 거예요.

여: 우리는 새 조명들이 직원의 생산성을 높이는 데 도움이 된다면, 비용을 들일 가치가 있다는 것을 명심해야 해요.

남2: 다른 부장들은 이 의견에 대해 어떻게 생각하는지 알아보죠. ⁴⁰제가 목요일에 있을 주간 회의에서 이것을 얘기해볼게요.

38 주제 문제

해석 화자들은 주로 무엇에 대해 이야기하고 있는가?
(A) 소프트웨어 개선
(B) 생산성 감소
(C) 제품 출시
(D) 사무실 개선

해설 대화의 주제를 묻는 문제이므로, 대화의 초반을 반드시 듣는다. 남자1이 "I think we should upgrade our office lights."라며 사무실 조명을 개선해야 한다고 생각한다고 한 후, 사무실 개선에 대한 내용으로 대화가 이어지고 있다. 따라서 (D)가 정답이다.

어휘 decline [dikláin] 감소   launch [lɔːntʃ] 출시, 개시

39 언급 문제

해석 여자는 사무실 조명에 대해 무엇을 언급하는가?
(A) 너무 강하다.
(B) 너무 많은 전기를 사용한다.
(C) 부실하게 설치되었다.
(D) 낡았다.

해설 여자의 말에서 질문의 핵심 어구(office lights)와 관련된 내용을 주의 깊게 듣는다. 여자가 "Our current ones[office lights] are way too bright. I find them distracting."이라며 현재의 사무실 조명은 너무 밝다고 한 후, 그것들은 집중할 수 없게 한다고 하였다. 따라서 (A)가 정답이다.

어휘 electricity [ilèktrísəti] 전기
poorly [미 púərli, 영 pɔ́ːli] 부실하게, 좋지 못하게   out of date 낡은

40 다음에 할 일 문제

해석 다음 주 목요일에 무슨 일이 일어날 것인가?
(A) 조명이 수리될 것이다.
(B) 새로운 공간이 개방될 것이다.
(C) 정기 회의가 열릴 것이다.
(D) 예산 삭감이 발표될 것이다.

해설 질문의 핵심 어구(next Thursday)가 언급된 주변을 주의 깊게 듣는다. 남자2가 "I'll bring this up at the weekly meeting on Thursday."라며 목요일에 있을 주간 회의에서 이것을 얘기해보겠다고 한 말을 통해 다음 주 목요일에 정기 회의가 열릴 것임을 알 수 있다. 따라서 (C)가 정답이다.

어휘 regular [미 régjulər, 영 régjələr] 정기적인   budget cut 예산 삭감
announce [ənáuns] 발표하다

41-43 🔊 미국식 발음 → 캐나다식 발음

Questions 41-43 refer to the following conversation.

W: Hello, Greg. This is Carol from Westfield International. I want to tell you that ⁴¹I received the catalog you sent me on behalf of your firm yesterday. I have some questions about the CrystalSet.

M: Yes, that's our latest tablet. What are you curious about in particular?

W: Well, ⁴²I'm wondering if it comes in multiple sizes. The catalog says it's 10 inches wide, but we'd like something bigger for our staff.

M: Right now, that's the only version available. However, a larger model will be launched in early summer. ⁴³If you want, I can call again when I have more details about the exact release date.

해석

41-43번은 다음 대화에 관한 문제입니다.

여: 안녕하세요, Greg. 저는 Westfield International사의 Carol입니다. ⁴¹당신이 회사를 대표해서 제게 보내주신 카탈로그를 어제 받았다는 것을 알려드리고 싶어요. 저는 CrystalSet에 대해 질문이 몇 개 있어요.

남: 네, 그건 저희의 최신 태블릿이네요. 특별히 어떤 것에 대해 궁금하신가요?

여: 음, ⁴²저는 이것이 다양한 크기로 나오는지 궁금해요. 카탈로그에는 이것이 10인치 넓이라고 쓰여 있는데, 저희는 직원들을 위해 더 큰 것을 원해요.

남: 현재로서는, 그것이 이용 가능한 유일한 버전이에요. 하지만, 초여름에 더 큰 모델이 출시될 거예요. ⁴³원하신다면, 제가 정확한 출시일에 대한 정보를 더 알게 될 때 다시 전화를 드릴게요.

41 특정 세부 사항 문제

해석 어제 무엇이 배송되었는가?
(A) 대체 부품
(B) 전자 기기
(C) 개인적인 편지
(D) 제품 목록

해설 질문의 핵심 어구(delivered yesterday)와 관련된 내용을 주의 깊게 듣는다. 여자가 "I received the catalog you sent me on behalf of your firm yesterday"라며 남자가 회사를 대표해서 자신에게 보내준 카탈로그를 어제 받았다고 한 말을 통해 어제 제품 목록이 배송되었음을 알 수 있다. 따라서 (D)가 정답이다.

어휘 replacement [ripléismənt] 대체, 교체   part [미 pɑːrt, 영 pɑːt] 부품
electronic device 전자 기기

42 특정 세부 사항 문제

해석 여자는 남자에게 무엇에 대해 물어보는가?
(A) 제품 출시일
(B) 출판물의 가격
(C) 물건의 크기
(D) 태블릿의 무게

해설 대화에서 여자의 말을 주의 깊게 듣는다. 여자가 남자에게 "I'm

wondering if it[tablet] comes in multiple sizes"라며 태블릿이 다양한 크기로 나오는지 궁금하다고 하였다. 따라서 (C)가 정답이다.

어휘 **publication**[미 pʌ̀bləkéiʃən, 영 pʌ̀blikéiʃən] 출판물 **weight**[weit] 무게

43 제안 문제
해석 남자는 무엇을 해주겠다고 제안하는가?
(A) 재무 정보를 공유한다.
(B) 다음에 다시 전화한다.
(C) 상사에게 확인한다.
(D) 다른 모델들을 제안한다.

해설 남자의 말에서 여자를 위해 해주겠다고 언급한 내용을 주의 깊게 듣는다. 남자가 여자에게 "If you want, I can call again when I have more details about the exact release date."라며 원한다면 정확한 출시일에 대한 정보를 더 알게 될 때 다시 전화를 주겠다고 하였다. 따라서 (B)가 정답이다.

어휘 **share**[미 ʃɛər, 영 ʃeə] 공유하다 **financial**[finǽnʃəl] 재무의
call back 다시 전화를 하다
supervisor[미 súːpərvàizər, 영 súːpəvàizə] 상사, 관리자

44-46 [호주식 발음 → 영국식 발음]

Questions 44-46 refer to the following conversation.

M: ⁴⁴Here are copies of the reports that we'll need for our presentation on the firm's accounting procedures.

W: Thanks. I don't know about you, but ⁴⁵I'm a bit nervous about tomorrow. I've never spoken in front of such a large group. And many of the managers I report to will be there.

M: If you want, ⁴⁶we can stay a bit later than usual tonight to practice our parts. Doing that should make tomorrow a lot easier.

W: All right. ⁴⁶That's a really good idea. I'll meet you in the main conference room at 7 P.M.

accounting [əkáuntiŋ] 회계
procedure [미 prəsíːdʒər, 영 prəsíːdʒə] 절차
report [미 ripɔ́ːrt, 영 ripɔ́ːt] 보고하다 **practice** [prǽktis] 연습하다

해석
44-46번은 다음 대화에 관한 문제입니다.

남: ⁴⁴여기 회사의 회계 절차에 대한 우리의 발표에 필요할 보고서들의 사본이에요.
여: 고마워요. 당신은 어떨지 모르겠지만, ⁴⁵저는 내일에 대해 조금 긴장돼요. 저는 그렇게 큰 단체 앞에서 발표해본 적이 없어요. 그리고 제가 보고를 드리는 많은 부장님들이 거기에 계실 거예요.
남: 원한다면, ⁴⁶우리의 부분들을 연습하기 위해 오늘 밤에 평소보다 조금 더 늦게까지 남아있을 수 있어요. 그렇게 하면 내일 훨씬 더 편할 거예요.
여: 좋아요. ⁴⁶그거 정말 좋은 생각이네요. 오후 7시에 대회의실에서 당신을 만날게요.

44 특정 세부 사항 문제
해석 남자에 따르면, 화자들은 무엇을 할 것인가?
(A) 보고서를 작성한다.
(B) 발표를 한다.
(C) 회계 장부를 검토한다.
(D) 영사기를 설치한다.

해설 대화에서 남자의 말을 주의 깊게 듣는다. 남자가 "Here are copies of the reports that we'll need for our presentation on the firm's accounting procedures."라며 회사의 회계 절차에 대한 자신들의

발표에 필요할 보고서들의 사본들이라고 한 말을 통해 화자들이 발표를 할 것임을 알 수 있다. 따라서 (B)가 정답이다.

어휘 **account**[əkáunt] (회계) 장부, 계정 **set up** ~을 설치하다

45 문제점 문제
해석 여자는 왜 걱정하는가?
(A) 업무에 대해 자신감이 없다.
(B) 회의에 참석할 수 없다.
(C) 서류를 잘못 두었다.
(D) 계산 실수를 했다.

해설 여자의 말에서 부정적인 표현이 언급된 다음을 주의 깊게 듣는다. 여자가 "I'm a bit nervous about tomorrow. I've never spoken in front of such a large group."이라며 내일에 대해 조금 긴장된다고 한 후, 그렇게 큰 단체 앞에서 발표해본 적이 없다고 한 말을 통해 여자가 업무에 대해 자신감이 없음을 알 수 있다. 따라서 (A)가 정답이다.

어휘 **confident**[미 kɑ́nfədənt, 영 kɔ́nfidənt] 자신감 있는
misplace[mìspléis] 잘못 두다
calculation[미 kælkjuléiʃən, 영 kælkjəléiʃən] 계산

46 다음에 할 일 문제
해석 화자들은 오늘 저녁에 무엇을 할 것인가?
(A) 수치들을 검토한다.
(B) 상사들과 만난다.
(C) 직장에 늦게까지 남는다.
(D) 세미나를 위한 자리를 예약한다.

해설 질문의 핵심 어구(this evening)와 관련된 내용을 주의 깊게 듣는다. 남자가 "we can stay a bit later than usual tonight to practice our parts"라며 자신들의 부분들을 연습하기 위해 오늘 밤에 평소보다 조금 더 늦게까지 남아있을 수 있다고 하자, 여자가 "That's a really good idea. I'll meet you in the main conference room at 7 P.M."이라며 남자의 말에 정말 좋은 생각이라고 한 후, 오후 7시에 대회의실에서 만나자고 하였다. 이를 통해 화자들이 오늘 저녁에 직장에 늦게까지 남을 것임을 알 수 있다. 따라서 (C)가 정답이다.

어휘 **look over** ~을 검토하다 **figure**[미 fígjər, 영 fígə] 수치, 숫자

47-49 [캐나다식 발음 → 영국식 발음 → 미국식 발음]

Questions 47-49 refer to the following conversation with three speakers.

M: ⁴⁷I'd like to invite the two of you to a birthday party I'm having this Saturday evening at my home.

W1: I'm definitely interested in joining.

W2: Me too. I'm supposed to meet a friend for dinner that night, but I can do it another time.

M: Great. Do you know where I live?

W2: It's the blue house on Briar Lane, isn't it?

M: Actually, I moved a few months back. ⁴⁸My new house is at 321 Folgers Drive. It's across the street from Janes Park.

W1: Sounds good. When should we arrive? And I'll bring snacks to share.

M: The party starts at 7 P.M., Laura. And . . . ⁴⁹Kelly, will you bring over some drinks to the party, then?

definitely[미 défənitli, 영 définətli] 당연히, 분명히 **join**[dʒɔin] 참석하다
actually[ǽktʃuəli] 실은, 실제로 **share**[미 ʃɛər, 영 ʃeə] 나누다

해석
47-49번은 다음 세 명의 대화에 관한 문제입니다.

남: ⁴⁷저는 두 분을 이번 주 토요일 저녁에 저희 집에서 열리는 생일파티에 초대하고 싶어요.

여1: 저는 당연히 참석하고 싶어요.

여2: 저도요. 저는 그날 밤에 저녁 식사를 하러 친구와 만나기로 했는데, 다른 때에 하면 돼요.

남: 좋아요. 제가 어디 사는지 아시나요?

여2: Briar로에 있는 파란색 집이죠, 아닌가요?

남: 실은, 저는 몇 달 전에 이사했어요. ⁴⁸제 새 집은 321번지 Folgers로에 있어요. Janes 공원의 길 건너편이에요.

여1: 좋아요. 저희가 언제 도착해야 하나요? 그리고 제가 나눠 먹을 과자를 가져갈게요.

남: 파티는 오후 7시에 시작해요, Laura. 그리고... ⁴⁹Kelly, 그러면 당신이 음료수 몇 개를 파티에 가져와 줄래요?

47 주제 문제

해석 대화는 주로 무엇에 대한 것인가?
(A) 회사 만찬
(B) 주택 공개
(C) 자원 행사
(D) 사적인 모임

해설 대화의 주제를 묻는 문제이므로, 대화의 초반을 반드시 듣는다. 남자가 "I'd like to invite the two of you to a birthday party I'm having ~ at my home."이라며 여자들을 자신의 집에서 열리는 생일파티에 초대하고 싶다고 한 후, 사적인 모임에 대한 내용으로 대화가 이어지고 있다. 따라서 (D)가 정답이다.

어휘 house showing (매각이나 임대를 위한) 주택 공개
volunteer[미 vὰləntíər, 영 vɔ̀ləntíə] 자원의; 자원봉사자
gathering[gǽðəriŋ] 모임

48 특정 세부 사항 문제

해석 남자에 따르면, 무엇이 Folgers로에 위치해 있는가?
(A) 백화점
(B) 직장
(C) 주택
(D) 슈퍼마켓

해설 남자의 말에서 질문의 핵심 어구(Folgers Drive)가 언급된 주변을 주의 깊게 듣는다. 남자가 "My new house is at 321 Folgers Drive."라며 자신의 새 집은 321번지 Folgers로에 있다고 하였다. 따라서 (C)가 정답이다.

패러프레이징
house 집 → residence 주택

어휘 department store 백화점
workplace[미 wə́ːrkpleis, 영 wə́ːkpleis] 직장
residence[미 rézədəns, 영 rézidəns] 주택

49 특정 세부 사항 문제

해석 남자는 Kelly에게 무엇을 가져오라고 요청하는가?
(A) 책
(B) 선물
(C) 디저트
(D) 음료

해설 남자의 말에서 질문의 핵심 어구(Kelly ~ bring)가 언급된 주변을 주의 깊게 듣는다. 남자가 "Kelly, will you bring over some drinks to the party, then?"이라며 Kelly에게 음료수 몇 개를 파티에 가져와 달라고 하였다. 따라서 (D)가 정답이다.

패러프레이징
drinks 음료수 → Beverages 음료

50-52 🔊 호주식 발음 → 영국식 발음

Questions 50-52 refer to the following conversation.

M: Good afternoon, and welcome to Clothing Works. What can I help you with today?

W: Hello. ⁵⁰I just purchased this dress for a business conference I'm going to in Frankfurt tomorrow. Unfortunately, it looks like the salesperson who assisted me forgot to remove the security tag at the checkout counter.

M: I'm sorry about that. I can go ahead and remove it for you. ⁵¹I'll just need to see your receipt for the item.

W: Oh, yes. Here it is. Just so you know, I'm in a bit of a hurry. ⁵²I've got to catch the shuttle bus to the airport hotel in 30 minutes.

---

conference[미 kάnfərəns, 영 kɔ́nfərəns] 회의
salesperson[미 séilzpə̀ːrsən, 영 séilzpə̀ːsən] 판매원 assist[əsíst] 돕다
remove[rimúːv] 제거하다 security[sikjúərəti] 보안
checkout counter 계산대 be in a hurry 서두르다
catch[kætʃ] (버스·기차 등을 시간 맞춰) 타다

해석
50-52번은 다음 대화에 관한 문제입니다.

남: 안녕하세요, Clothing Works에 오신 것을 환영합니다. 오늘 무엇을 도와드릴까요?

여: 안녕하세요. ⁵⁰저는 방금 전에 내일 프랑크푸르트에서 있을 업무 회의를 위해 이 드레스를 구매했어요. 공교롭게도, 저를 도와줬던 판매원이 계산대에서 보안 태그를 제거하는 것을 잊어버린 것 같아요.

남: 죄송합니다. 제가 바로 제거해드리겠습니다. ⁵¹물품의 영수증만 좀 확인해보겠습니다.

여: 아, 네. 여기 있어요. 사실, 저는 조금 서둘러야 해요. ⁵²저는 30분 후에 공항 호텔까지 가는 셔틀 버스를 타야 하거든요.

50 이유 문제

해석 여자는 왜 프랑크푸르트로 갈 것인가?
(A) 친척을 방문하기 위해
(B) 시설을 점검하기 위해
(C) 디자이너를 만나기 위해
(D) 회의에 참석하기 위해

해설 질문의 핵심 어구(Frankfurt)가 언급된 주변을 주의 깊게 듣는다. 여자가 "I just purchased this dress for a business conference I'm going to in Frankfurt tomorrow."라며 내일 프랑크푸르트에서 있을 업무 회의를 위해 이 드레스를 구매했다고 한 말을 통해 여자가 회의에 참석하기 위해 프랑크푸르트로 갈 것임을 알 수 있다. 따라서 (D)가 정답이다.

어휘 relative[rélətiv] 친척 inspect[inspékt] 점검하다

51 요청 문제

해석 남자는 여자에게 무엇을 하라고 요청하는가?
(A) 매니저와 이야기한다.
(B) 다른 지점에 간다.
(C) 보호용 태그를 제거한다.
(D) 구매 증명서를 제시한다.

해설 남자의 말에서 요청과 관련된 표현이 언급된 다음을 주의 깊게 듣는다. 남자가 "I'll just need to see your receipt for the item."이라며 물품의 영수증만 좀 확인해보겠다고 한 말을 통해 남자가 여자에게 구매 증명서를 제시할 것을 요청하고 있음을 알 수 있다. 따라서 (D)가 정답이다.

receipt for the item 물품의 영수증 → proof of purchase 구매 증명서

어휘 **branch**[미 bræntʃ, 영 brɑːntʃ] 지점 **protective**[prətéktiv] 보호용의
proof of purchase 구매 증명서

52 다음에 할 일 문제

해석 여자는 30분 후에 무엇을 할 것 같은가?
(A) 약속을 잡는다.
(B) 셔틀 버스를 탄다.
(C) 소매점으로 돌아온다.
(D) 비행기에 탑승한다.

해설 질문의 핵심 어구(half an hour)와 관련된 내용을 주의 깊게 듣는다.
여자가 "I've got to catch the shuttle bus to the airport hotel in
30 minutes."라며 30분 후에 공항 호텔까지 가는 셔틀 버스를 타야
한다고 하였다. 따라서 (B)가 정답이다.

어휘 **schedule**[미 skédʒuːl, 영 ʃédʒuːl] 일정을 잡다 **get on** ~을 타다
retail outlet 소매점 **board**[미 bɔːrd, 영 bɔːd] 탑승하다

53-55 [2M] 미국식 발음 → 캐나다식 발음

Questions 53-55 refer to the following conversation.

W: ⁵³I'm interested in traveling abroad to Lima for my
upcoming vacation period. I've looked at several
tour packages on your Web site, but I'm not sure
which one would be best for me. I want some
guided tours, but I'd also like a bit of freedom to
explore on my own.
M: ⁵⁴Then I recommend going with the Peru Adventure
package. That one has the most flexible itinerary.
W: How much does that one cost?
M: Here are the price details for all of our packages.
Also, ⁵⁵if you sign up for a membership today, you'll
be able to get a discounted rate on your trip.

abroad[əbrɔ́ːd] 해외에 **upcoming**[ʌ́pkʌ̀miŋ] 다가오는
guided tour 가이드가 있는 여행 **freedom**[fríːdəm] 자유
explore[미 iksplɔ́ːr, 영 iksplɔ́ː] 답사하다 **flexible**[fléksəbl] 유연한
itinerary[aitínərèri] 여행 일정(표) **rate**[reit] 가격, 요금

해석
53-55번은 다음 대화에 관한 문제입니다.

여: ⁵³저는 다가오는 휴가 기간 동안 리마로 해외 여행을 가는 것에 관심이 있
어요. 제가 당신의 웹사이트에 있는 여러 여행 상품들을 살펴봤는데, 어떤
것이 저한테 가장 좋을지 모르겠어요. 저는 가이드가 있는 여행도 조금 원
하지만, 저 혼자 답사할 수 있는 자유도 조금 있으면 좋겠어요.
남: ⁵⁴그렇다면 저는 페루 어드벤처 상품으로 하시는 것을 추천해드려요. 그
상품이 가장 유연한 여행 일정을 가지고 있어요.
여: 그 상품은 비용이 얼마나 들까요?
남: 여기에 저희의 모든 상품들에 대한 가격 정보가 있습니다. 또한, ⁵⁵오늘 회
원권을 신청하시면, 여행에 할인된 가격을 받으실 수 있습니다.

53 특정 세부 사항 문제

해석 여자는 무엇을 고려하고 있는가?
(A) 여름방학 아르바이트를 수락하는 것
(B) 여행 가이드로 일하는 것
(C) 해외로 여행을 가는 것
(D) 여행 계획을 변경하는 것

해설 질문의 핵심 어구(woman considering)와 관련된 내용을 주의 깊게
듣는다. 여자가 "I'm interested in traveling abroad to Lima for
my upcoming vacation period."라며 다가오는 휴가 기간 동안 리

마로 해외 여행을 가는 것에 관심이 있다고 하였다. 따라서 (C)가 정답
이다.

어휘 **summer job** 여름방학 아르바이트
accept[미 æksépt, 영 əksépt] 수락하다, 받아들이다
tour guide 여행 가이드 **overseas**[미 ðuvərsíːz, 영 ðuvəsíːz] 해외로

54 이유 문제

해석 남자는 왜 페루 어드벤처 상품을 추천하는가?
(A) 고급스러운 호텔 방을 포함한다.
(B) 그녀의 돈을 절약해줄 것이다.
(C) 더 많은 유연성을 제공한다.
(D) 무료 상품이 딸려있을 것이다.

해설 질문의 핵심 어구(Peru Adventure package)가 언급된 주변을 주
의 깊게 듣는다. 남자가 "Then I recommend going with the Peru
Adventure package. That one has the most flexible itinerary."
라며 페루 어드벤처 상품으로 하는 것을 추천한다고 한 후, 그 상품이 가
장 유연한 여행 일정을 가지고 있다고 하였다. 따라서 (C)가 정답이다.
패러프레이징
has the most flexible itinerary 가장 유연한 여행 일정을 가지고 있다
→ offers more flexibility 더 많은 유연성을 제공하다

어휘 **save**[seiv] (비용·시간·노력 등을) 절약하다
flexibility[미 flèksəbíləti, 영 flèksəbíliti] 유연성
come with ~이 딸려있다
complimentary[미 kɑ̀mpləméntəri, 영 kɔ̀mpliméntəri] 무료의

55 특정 세부 사항 문제

해석 남자에 따르면, 회원권은 무슨 혜택을 제공하는가?
(A) 여행 보험
(B) 할인된 가격
(C) 무료 안내서
(D) 추가 관광지

해설 남자의 말에서 질문의 핵심 어구(benefit ~ membership provide)
와 관련된 내용을 주의 깊게 듣는다. 남자가 여자에게 "if you sign up
for a membership today, you'll be able to get a discounted
rate on your trip"이라며 오늘 회원권을 신청하면 여행에 할인된 가
격을 받을 수 있다고 하였다. 따라서 (B)가 정답이다.

어휘 **insurance**[inʃúərəns] 보험 **reduced**[ridjúːst] 할인된, 감소된
guidebook[gáidbuk] 안내서 **additional**[ədíʃənl] 추가적인
destination[미 dèstənéiʃən, 영 dèstinéiʃən] 관광지, 목적지

56-58 [2M] 호주식 발음 → 미국식 발음

Questions 56-58 refer to the following conversation.

M: ⁵⁶I've got a shipment of computer hardware devices
for Alicia Carson. They're from TechnicStore. ⁵⁶Where
would you like me to put the package?
W: Oh, thanks. ⁵⁷Please just place it on top of the desk
right near the window there. I appreciate it.
M: Certainly. Could you please sign this form indicating
your acceptance of the delivery? It's required by the
sender in order to confirm that you've successfully
received the items.
W: OK . . . Yes . . . it looks like everything listed here
is in the package. ⁵⁸I'll go ahead and do that, then.

shipment[ʃípmənt] 배송품, 수송 **package**[pǽkidʒ] 소포
place[pleis] 놓다 **indicate**[índikèit] 나타내다
acceptance[미 ækséptəns, 영 əkséptəns] 받아들임, 수락
confirm[미 kənfə́ːrm, 영 kənfə́ːm] 확인하다

56-58번은 다음 대화에 관한 문제입니다.

남: ⁵⁶저는 Alicia Carson을 위한 컴퓨터 하드웨어 기기 배송품을 가지고 있습니다. 이것들은 TechnicStore에서 온 거예요. ⁵⁶제가 이 소포를 어디에 놓기를 원하시나요?

여: 아, 고마워요. ⁵⁷그것을 그냥 저쪽 창문 바로 근처에 있는 책상 위에다 놓아주세요. 감사합니다.

남: 물론이죠. 이 양식에 당신이 배달물을 받았음을 나타내도록 서명을 해주실 수 있나요? 당신이 물품들을 잘 받았다는 것을 확인하기 위해서 발신인에게 필요하거든요.

여: 알겠습니다... 네... 여기 나열된 모든 것이 소포 안에 있는 것 같네요. 그럼, ⁵⁸제가 어서 서명을 하도록 할게요.

56 화자 문제

해석　남자는 누구인 것 같은가?
(A) 배달원
(B) 개인 비서
(C) 컴퓨터 프로그래머
(D) 사무장

해설　대화에서 신분 및 직업과 관련된 표현을 놓치지 않고 듣는다. 남자가 "I've got a shipment of computer hardware devices for Alicia Carson."이라며 Alicia Carson을 위한 컴퓨터 하드웨어 기기 배송품을 가지고 있다고 한 후, "Where would you like me to put the package?"라며 여자에게 소포를 어디에 놓기를 원하는지 물은 것을 통해 남자가 배달원임을 알 수 있다. 따라서 (A)가 정답이다.

어휘　assistant[əsístənt] 비서

57 요청 문제

해석　여자는 남자에게 무엇을 하라고 말하는가?
(A) 새 주소로 소포를 보낸다.
(B) 상자의 내용물을 확인한다.
(C) 서비스 카운터에 들른다.
(D) 책상 위에 배송품을 놓는다.

해설　여자의 말에서 요청과 관련된 표현이 언급된 다음을 주의 깊게 듣는다. 여자가 남자에게 "Please just place it[package] on top of the desk"라며 소포를 책상 위에다 놓아달라고 하였다. 따라서 (D)가 정답이다.

어휘　contents[kántents] 내용물　stop by ~에 들르다

58 다음에 할 일 문제

해석　여자는 다음에 무엇을 할 것 같은가?
(A) 서류에 서명을 한다.
(B) 구매한 상품들의 목록을 살펴본다.
(C) 최초 발신인에게 연락한다.
(D) 또 다른 하드웨어를 주문한다.

해설　대화의 마지막 부분을 주의 깊게 듣는다. 여자가 "I'll go ahead and do that[sign]"이라며 어서 서명을 하겠다고 하였다. 따라서 (A)가 정답이다.

어휘　signature[미 sígnətʃər, 영 sígnətʃə] 서명　look over ~을 살펴보다
original[ərídʒənəl] 최초의, 원래의　place an order 주문하다

59-61 〔3ω〕 영국식 발음 → 캐나다식 발음

Questions 59-61 refer to the following conversation.

W: Hi, Walter. ⁵⁹I thought you were visiting our branch in Toronto this week.

M: ⁵⁹That's right. I flew out there on Monday and got back yesterday. ⁶⁰I had to interview some　◯

candidates for the manager position. The current head of the branch . . . um, Peter Greer . . . he has decided to resign.

W: How did it go?

M: Well, a couple of candidates look promising, but none of them are ideal. I'm going to recommend that we promote someone else.

W: Interesting. Do you have anyone in mind?

M: Well, ⁶¹the assistant manager is the most obvious choice, but she has requested a transfer to our Vancouver office. So, ⁶¹I'm thinking of recommending the head of the sales team instead.

---

fly out 비행기로 가다　candidate[kǽndidət] 후보자
current[미 kə́:rənt, 영 kʌ́rənt] 현재의　resign[rizáin] 사임하다
promising[미 prámisiŋ, 영 prɔ́misiŋ] 유망한
ideal[미 aidí:əl, 영 aidíəl] 완벽한
promote[미 prəmóut, 영 prəmə́ut] 승진시키다, 촉진하다
have in mind ~을 생각하다, 염두에 두다
obvious[미 ɑ́bviəs, 영 ɔ́bviəs] 명백한, 분명한
transfer[미 trænsfə́:r, 영 trænsfə́:] 전근, 이동

59-61번은 다음 대화에 관한 문제입니다.

여: 안녕하세요, Walter. ⁵⁹저는 당신이 이번 주에 토론토에 있는 우리 지점에 방문하는 줄 알았어요.

남: ⁵⁹맞아요. 저는 월요일에 비행기로 거기에 갔다가 어제 돌아왔어요. ⁶⁰저는 지점장 직위를 위해 몇몇 후보자들을 면접해야 했어요. 현재 지점장... 음, Peter Greer... 그가 사임하기로 결정했어요.

여: 어떻게 됐나요?

남: 음, 두어 명의 후보자들이 유망해 보이지만, 그들 중 누구도 완벽하지는 않아요. 저는 다른 사람을 승진시키는 것을 제안할 거예요.

여: 흥미롭네요. 생각하고 있는 사람이 있나요?

남: 음, ⁶¹부지점장이 가장 명백한 선택이겠지만, 그녀는 밴쿠버 사무소로 전근을 요청했어요. 그래서, ⁶¹저는 대신 영업팀장을 추천하는 것을 생각 중이에요.

59 특정 세부 사항 문제

해석　남자는 이번 주 초에 무엇을 했는가?
(A) 팀장과 이야기를 했다.
(B) 출장을 갔다.
(C) 워크숍에 참석했다.
(D) 승진을 요청했다.

해설　질문의 핵심 어구(earlier in the week)와 관련된 내용을 주의 깊게 듣는다. 여자가 "I thought you were visiting our branch in Toronto this week."라며 남자가 이번 주에 토론토에 있는 지점에 방문하는 줄 알았다고 하자, 남자가 "That's right. I flew out there on Monday and got back yesterday."라며 여자의 말에 맞다고 한 후, 월요일에 비행기로 거기에 갔다가 어제 돌아왔다고 하였다. 이를 통해 남자가 이번 주 초에 출장을 갔음을 알 수 있다. 따라서 (B)가 정답이다.

어휘　participate[미 pɑ:rtísəpèit, 영 pɑ:tísipèit] 참여하다
promotion[미 prəmóuʃən, 영 prəmə́uʃən] 승진

60 이유 문제

해석　면접은 왜 진행되었는가?
(A) 지점장이 사임할 것이다.
(B) 지점이 확장될 것이다.
(C) 부서에 직원이 부족하다.
(D) 일자리 제의가 거절되었다.

해설　질문의 핵심 어구(interviews conducted)와 관련된 내용을 주의

깊게 듣는다. 남자가 "I had to interview some candidates for the manager position. The current head of the branch ~ has decided to resign."이라며 지점장 직위를 위해 몇몇 후보자들을 면접해야 했다고 한 후, 현재 지점장이 사임하기로 결정했다고 하였다. 따라서 (A)가 정답이다.

어휘 **expand**[ikspǽnd] 확장되다
understaffed[미 ʌ̀ndərstǽft, 영 ʌ̀ndəstάːft] 직원이 부족한
job offer 일자리 제의 **turn down** ~을 거절하다

61 의도 파악 문제

해석 남자는 왜 "그녀는 밴쿠버 사무소로 전근을 요청했어요"라고 말하는가?
(A) 선택지를 왜 이용할 수 없는지 설명하기 위해
(B) 직위의 중요성을 강조하기 위해
(C) 다른 지점을 추천하기 위해
(D) 여자가 결정을 하도록 격려하기 위해

해설 질문의 인용어구(she has requested a transfer to our Vancouver office)가 언급된 주변을 주의 깊게 듣는다. 남자가 "the assistant manager is the most obvious choice"라며 부지점장이 가장 명백한 선택이겠지만이라고 한 후, "I'm thinking of recommending the head of the sales team instead"라며 대신 영업팀장을 추천하는 것을 생각 중이라고 하였으므로, 선택지를 왜 이용할 수 없는지 설명하기 위함임을 알 수 있다. 따라서 (A)가 정답이다.

어휘 **unavailable**[ʌ̀nəvéiləbl] 이용할 수 없는 **stress**[stres] 강조하다
importance[미 impɔ́ːrtəns, 영 impɔ́ːtəns] 중요성
encourage[미 inkə́ːridʒ, 영 inkʌ́ridʒ] 격려하다
make a decision 결정을 하다

62-64 [3회] 영국식 발음 → 호주식 발음

Questions 62-64 refer to the following conversation and product list.

> W: I was really surprised by the sales figures for our latest watch line. They've sold better than we expected.
> M: So was I. ⁶²The watch with the round face is doing especially well. Although it was released most recently, it has sold the most this year.
> W: Yes, that is quite surprising. ⁶³Unfortunately, we're running out of that model now.
> M: Can't we make more of them?
> W: I've contacted our factory supervisor, and she is planning to increase production.
> M: That's good. ⁶⁴With the holiday season coming up, demand will probably increase even more.
> W: Exactly. Watches are always popular gifts.
>
> **sales figures** 매출액 **face**[feis] (시계의) 앞면
> **run out of** ~이 없어지다, ~을 바닥내다
> **demand**[미 dimǽnd, 영 dimάːnd] 수요; 요구하다

해석
62-64번은 다음 대화와 상품 목록에 관한 문제입니다.

여: 저는 우리의 최신 시계 제품의 매출액에 정말 놀랐어요. 그것들은 우리가 예상했던 것보다 더 잘 팔렸어요.
남: 저도 그랬어요. ⁶²동그란 앞면을 가진 시계가 특히 잘 팔리고 있어요. 그건 가장 최근에 출시되었음에도 불구하고, 올해 가장 많이 팔렸어요.
여: 네, 그건 꽤 놀라워요. ⁶³안타깝게도, 우린 지금 그 모델이 없어지고 있네요.
남: 우리가 그것들을 더 만들 수 없나요?
여: 제가 공장 관리자에게 연락했는데, 그녀는 생산을 늘리는 것을 계획하

고 있어요.
남: 그거 좋네요. ⁶⁴휴가철이 다가오면서, 수요는 아마도 훨씬 더 늘어날 거예요.
여: 맞아요. 시계는 항상 인기 있는 선물이죠.

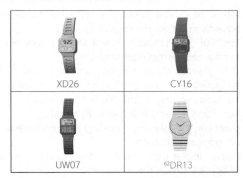

62 시각 자료 문제

해석 시각 자료를 보아라. 어떤 모델이 가장 최근에 출시되었는가?
(A) XD26
(B) CY16
(C) UW07
(D) DR13

해설 제시된 상품 목록의 정보를 확인한 후 질문의 핵심 어구(most recently released)가 언급된 주변을 주의 깊게 듣는다. 남자가 "The watch with the round face is doing especially well. Although it was released most recently, it has sold the most this year."라며 동그란 앞면을 가진 시계가 특히 잘 팔리고 있고 가장 최근에 출시되었음에도 불구하고 올해 가장 많이 팔렸다고 하였으므로, DR13 모델이 가장 최근에 출시되었음을 상품 목록에서 알 수 있다. 따라서 (D)가 정답이다.

63 문제점 문제

해석 여자는 무슨 문제를 언급하는가?
(A) 새 시계에 대한 평가는 부정적이었다.
(B) 한 품목의 재고가 떨어져 가고 있다.
(C) 공장에서 생산이 정지되었다.
(D) 관리자가 직원을 구하는 데 어려움을 겪고 있다.

해설 여자의 말에서 부정적인 표현이 언급된 다음을 주의 깊게 듣는다. 여자가 "Unfortunately, we're running out of that model[The watch with the round face] now."라며 안타깝게도 지금 동그란 앞면을 가진 시계 모델이 없어지고 있다고 하였다. 따라서 (B)가 정답이다.

어휘 **negative**[négətiv] 부정적인 **run low** 떨어져 가다, 고갈되다
shut down 정지시키다 **have trouble -ing** ~하는 데 어려움을 겪다

64 이유 문제

해석 남자는 왜 매출이 증가할 것으로 예상하는가?
(A) 일부 품목이 할인되었다.
(B) 시계가 점점 더 인기를 얻고 있다.
(C) 외부 마케팅 회사가 고용되었다.
(D) 휴가철이 다가오고 있다.

해설 질문의 핵심 어구(sales to increase)와 관련된 내용을 주의 깊게 듣는다. 남자가 "With the holiday season coming up, demand will probably increase even more."라며 휴가철이 다가오면서 수요가 아마도 훨씬 더 늘어날 것이라고 하였다. 따라서 (D)가 정답이다.

Questions 65-67 refer to the following conversation and graph.

W: Alton, have you finished editing the latest job advertisement for the engineer position?
M: Yes. But ^{65}I still need to post it online. I'm planning to take care of that right after lunch.
W: ^{66}We need to hire another employee as soon as possible as we can't continue with the mall construction project until we find someone.
M: Yes, filling this role is a priority right now.
W: Have you thought about posting the advertisement on industry job boards?
M: I have. In the past, ^{67}we got the highest number of applications in the month that we uploaded job listings to a site that targets engineers. So, I'm going to publish it there.

edit[édit] 편집하다 latest[léitist] 최신의
job advertisement 구인 광고
post[미 poust, 영 pəust] (웹사이트에 정보·사진을) 게시하다
take care of ~을 처리하다 fill[fil] (어떤 일자리에 사람을) 채우다
priority[prai5:rəti] 우선순위 job board 구인란
application[미 æpləkéiʃən, 영 æplikéiʃən] 지원서 job listing 구인 목록
target[미 tá:rgit, 영 tá:git] 대상으로 삼다 publish[pʌbliʃ] 게시하다

해석

65-67번은 다음 대화와 그래프에 관한 문제입니다.

여: Alton, 엔지니어직을 위한 최신 구인 광고를 편집하는 것을 끝냈나요?
남: 네. 하지만 ^{65}아직 그것을 온라인에 게시해야 해요. 저는 그것을 점심 직후에 처리하려고 해요.
여: ^{66}우리는 누군가를 구하고 나서야 쇼핑몰 건축 프로젝트를 계속할 수 있기 때문에 다른 직원을 되도록 빨리 채용해야 해요.
남: 맞아요, 지금은 이 직무를 채우는 것이 우선순위예요.
여: 광고를 업계 구인란에 게시하는 것을 생각해봤나요?
남: 해봤어요. 과거에, ^{67}우리가 엔지니어 대상의 사이트에 구인 목록을 올렸던 달에 가장 많은 수의 지원서를 받았어요. 그래서, 저는 거기에 광고를 게재할 거예요.

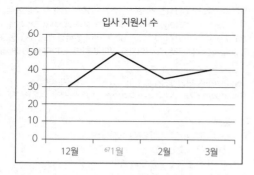

65 특정 세부 사항 문제

해석 남자는 아직 무엇을 해야 하는가?
(A) 광고를 게시한다.
(B) 면접을 준비한다.
(C) 최근 지원자들에게 연락한다.
(D) 신입 사원들을 교육한다.

해설 질문의 핵심 어구(still need to do)와 관련된 내용을 주의 깊게 듣는다. 남자가 "I still need to post it[job advertisement] online"이

라며 아직 구인 광고를 온라인에 게시해야 한다고 하였다. 따라서 (A)가 정답이다.

어휘 applicant[ǽplikənt] 지원자 train[trein] 교육하다

66 이유 문제

해석 여자에 따르면, 채용 결정은 왜 시급한가?
(A) 회의가 다가오고 있다.
(B) 프로젝트가 보류되어 있다.
(C) 주요 직원이 그만두었다.
(D) 팀이 재편성되었다.

해설 여자의 말에서 질문의 핵심 어구(hiring decision urgent)와 관련된 내용을 주의 깊게 듣는다. 여자가 "We need to hire another employee as soon as possible as we can't continue with the mall construction project until we find someone."이라며 누군가를 구하고 나서야 쇼핑몰 건축 프로젝트를 계속할 수 있기 때문에 다른 직원을 되도록 빨리 채용해야 한다고 하였다. 따라서 (B)가 정답이다.

어휘 approach[미 əpróutʃ, 영 əpráutʃ] 다가오다 on hold 보류된
key[ki:] 주요한 quit[kwit] 그만두다
reorganize[미 ri:5:rgənaiz, 영 ri:5:gənaiz] 재편성하다

67 시각 자료 문제

해석 시각 자료를 보아라. 채용 공고는 언제 웹사이트에 광고되었는가?
(A) 12월에
(B) 1월에
(C) 2월에
(D) 3월에

해설 제시된 그래프의 정보를 확인한 후 질문의 핵심 어구(job openings advertised on the Web site)와 관련된 내용을 주의 깊게 듣는다. 남자가 "we got the highest number of applications in the month that we uploaded job listings to a site that targets engineers"라며 엔지니어 대상의 사이트에 구인 목록을 올렸던 달에 가장 많은 수의 지원서를 받았다고 하였으므로, 채용 공고는 1월에 웹사이트에 광고되었음을 그래프에서 알 수 있다. 따라서 (B)가 정답이다.

Questions 68-70 refer to the following conversation and seating chart.

M: Good morning. ^{68}I'm checking in for my flight to Oakland. ^{69}Here's my passport.
W: Thank you. Do you have any luggage besides that carry-on bag?
M: No, that's it. I'm going on a short trip.
W: OK. I'll finish confirming your reservation, then. Hmm . . . It appears that the seat you originally booked has been reassigned. ^{70}Two passengers traveling with a baby need the cot area that is located in front of the seat. I apologize for the inconvenience.
M: In that case, ^{70}can I move to a window seat?
W: ^{70}Yes, I'll put you in the same row as you were, just on the other side of the aisle.

check in 탑승 수속을 밟다 passport[미 pǽspɔ:rt, 영 pá:spɔ:t] 여권
luggage[lʌgidʒ] 짐 carry-on bag 휴대용 가방
reassign[ri:əsáin] 다시 배정하다, 다시 맡기다
cot[미 kɑt, 영 kɔt] 아기 침대 in that case 그렇다면, 그런 경우라면
row[미 rou, 영 rəu] 줄, 열 aisle[ail] 통로, 복도

해석

68-70번은 다음 대화와 좌석 배치도에 관한 문제입니다.

남: 안녕하세요. ⁶⁸저는 오클랜드행 항공편을 위한 탑승 수속을 하려고 해요. ⁶⁹여기 제 여권이 있어요.

여: 감사합니다. 그 휴대용 가방 외에 다른 짐이 있으십니까?

남: 아니요, 이게 다예요. 저는 짧은 여행을 가려고 해요.

여: 알겠습니다. 그럼, 제가 고객님의 예약 확인을 완료하겠습니다. 흠... 고객님이 원래 예약하셨던 좌석이 다시 배정된 것으로 보이네요. ⁷⁰아기와 함께 가시는 승객 두 분이 좌석 앞에 위치한 아기 침대 구역을 필요로 하세요. 불편을 겪게 해드려 죄송합니다.

남: 그렇다면, ⁷⁰창가 자리로 옮겨가도 될까요?

여: ⁷⁰네, 제가 고객님을 원래와 같은 줄에서 통로 반대편으로만 옮겨 드리겠습니다.

68 장소 문제

해석 화자들은 어디에 있는 것 같은가?
(A) 여객선 항구에
(B) 공항에
(C) 기차역에
(D) 버스 정류장에

해설 장소와 관련된 표현을 놓치지 않고 듣는다. 남자가 "I'm checking in for my flight to Oakland."라며 오클랜드행 항공편을 위한 탑승 수속을 하려고 한다고 한 말을 통해 화자들이 공항에 있음을 알 수 있다. 따라서 (B)가 정답이다.

어휘 ferry[féri] 여객선 port[pɔːrt] 항구

69 특정 세부 사항 문제

해석 남자는 여자에게 무엇을 주는가?
(A) 신용카드
(B) 분실품 신고서
(C) 짐
(D) 신분증

해설 질문의 핵심 어구(give to the woman)와 관련된 내용을 주의 깊게 듣는다. 남자가 여자에게 "Here's my passport."라며 여기 자신의 여권이 있다고 하였다. 따라서 (D)가 정답이다.

패러프레이징
passport 여권 → identification 신분증

어휘 missing-item 분실품
identification[미 aidèntifəkéiʃən, 영 aidèntifikéiʃən] 신분증

70 시각 자료 문제

해석 시각 자료를 보아라. 어떤 좌석이 남자에게 주어질 것인가?
(A) A-1
(B) A-2
(C) A-3
(D) A-4

해설 제시된 좌석 배치도의 정보를 확인한 후 질문의 핵심 어구(seat ~ given)와 관련된 내용을 주의 깊게 듣는다. 여자가 "Two passengers ~ need the cot area that is located in front of the seat."라며 승객 두 명이 좌석 앞에 위치한 아기 침대 구역을 필요로 한다고 하자, 남자가 여자에게 "can I move to a window seat?"라며 창가 자리로 옮겨가도 되는지 물었고, 여자가 "Yes, I'll put you in the same row as you were, just on the other side of the aisle."이라며 남자를 원래와 같은 줄에서 통로 반대편으로만 옮겨주겠다고 하였으므로, 아기 침대 앞 좌석들과 같은 줄에 있으며 통로 반대편의 창가 자리

인 A-4 좌석이 남자에게 주어질 것임을 좌석 배치도에서 알 수 있다. 따라서 (D)가 정답이다.

PART 4

71-73 [3] 호주식 발음

Questions 71-73 refer to the following recorded message.

Thank you for calling the Gramsfield City Library. ⁷¹Our facility is currently closed for renovations. We will reopen on Tuesday, February 23, at 9 A.M. ⁷²During our temporary closure, checked-out library materials may be returned through the book drop slot on the right side of the building. All late fee payments made on our Web site will be processed normally. As for books that were placed on reserve before February 23, they may be picked up at the circulation desk when the library reopens. ⁷³Should you have any urgent issues, please call 555-6632. Have a nice day.

renovation[rènəvéiʃən] 수리, 보수 temporary[témpərèri] 임시의
closure[미 klóuʒər, 영 klóuʒə] 폐쇄 check out (도서관 등에서) 대출하다
book drop 도서 반환통 process[미 práses, 영 próuses] 처리하다
normally[미 nɔ́ːrməli, 영 nɔ́ːməli] 정상적으로
pick up (어디에서) ~을 찾다, 찾아오다 circulation desk 대출대
urgent[미 ə́ːrdʒənt, 영 ə́ːdʒənt] 급한

해석

71-73번은 다음 녹음 메시지에 관한 문제입니다.

Gramsfield 시립 도서관에 전화주셔서 감사드립니다. ⁷¹저희 시설은 현재 수리로 인해 문을 닫았습니다. 저희는 2월 23일 화요일 오전 9시에 다시 문을 열 것입니다. ⁷²임시 폐쇄 동안, 대출된 도서관 자료들은 건물의 오른쪽에 있는 도서 반환통을 통해 반환될 수 있습니다. 웹사이트상에서 지불되는 모든 연체료는 정상적으로 처리될 것입니다. 2월 23일 전에 예약된 책들의 경우, 도서관이 다시 문을 열면 대출대에서 찾아가실 수 있습니다. ⁷³급한 용건이 있으시면, 555-6632로 전화주시기 바랍니다. 좋은 하루 되십시오.

71 이유 문제

해석 시설은 왜 문을 닫았는가?
(A) 휴일이 기념되고 있다.
(B) 건물이 수리되고 있다.
(C) 기기가 점검되어야 한다.
(D) 시스템이 업데이트되어야 한다.

해설 질문의 핵심 어구(facility closed)가 언급된 주변을 주의 깊게 듣는다. "Our facility is currently closed for renovations."라며 시설은 현재 수리로 인해 문을 닫았다고 하였다. 따라서 (B)가 정답이다.

어휘 celebrate[séləbrèit] 기념하다 repair[미 ripɛ́ər, 영 ripéə] 수리하다
inspect[inspékt] 점검하다

72 특정 세부 사항 문제

해석 화자에 따르면, 청자들은 폐쇄 동안 무엇을 할 수 있는가?
(A) 책들을 반환한다.
(B) 자료들을 찾아간다.
(C) 대출 카드를 갱신한다.
(D) 다른 지점들에 간다.

해설 질문의 핵심 어구(during a closure)와 관련된 내용을 주의 깊게 듣는다. "During our temporary closure, checked-out library materials may be returned through the book drop slot on the right side of the building."이라며 임시 폐쇄 동안 대출된 도서관 자료들은 건물의 오른쪽에 있는 도서 반환통을 통해 반환될 수 있다고 하

였다. 따라서 (A)가 정답이다.

어휘 renew[rinjúː] 갱신하다 library card (도서관) 대출 카드

73 방법 문제

해석 청자들은 어떻게 급한 용건들을 처리할 수 있는가?
(A) 직원을 만남으로써
(B) 전화를 겲으로써
(C) 온라인 양식을 작성함으로써
(D) 이메일을 보냄으로써

해설 질문의 핵심 어구(urgent issues)가 언급된 주변을 주의 깊게 듣는다. "Should you have any urgent issues, please call 555-6632." 라며 급한 용건이 있으면 555-6632로 전화를 달라고 하였다. 따라서 (B)가 정답이다.

어휘 address[ədrés] (어려운 문제 등을) 처리하다 dial a number 전화 걸다

74-76 [3ʰ] 미국식 발음

Questions 74-76 refer to the following instruction.

My name is Cameron Bell. [74]For today's training session, I'll be showing you all how to use our company's accounting software, NextBook. You'll see that the software is already loaded on the computers in front of you, and [75]an ID number is required to log in to the program. I'll give each of you those numbers in just a moment. But before we start using NextBook, [76]my assistant is going to pass out these instruction manuals for your reference. Keep these with you throughout the morning, as I'll be referring to them multiple times.

training session 교육 (과정) pass out (물건을) 나누어 주다
instruction manual 사용 안내서 for reference 참고를 위한
refer to 인용하다, 언급하다

해석

74-76번은 다음 설명에 관한 문제입니다.

제 이름은 Cameron Bell입니다. [74]오늘 교육에서는, 여러분 모두에게 회사의 회계 소프트웨어인 NextBook을 사용하는 방법을 알려드릴 것입니다. 여러분은 앞에 있는 컴퓨터에 그 소프트웨어가 이미 로딩이 되어 있으며, [75]프로그램에 로그인하는 데 ID 번호가 필요하다는 것을 보실 수 있을 겁니다. 제가 곧 여러분 각자에게 그 번호들을 드리겠습니다. 하지만 우리가 NextBook을 사용하는 것을 시작하기 전에, [76]제 비서가 여러분들의 참고를 위한 이 사용 안내서들을 나눠드릴 것입니다. 제가 그것들을 여러 번 인용할 것이기 때문에, 오전 내내 가지고 계시기 바랍니다.

74 화자 문제

해석 화자는 누구인 것 같은가?
(A) 컴퓨터 수리공
(B) 연구 분석가
(C) 회사 교육자
(D) 판매원

해설 지문에서 신분 및 직업과 관련된 표현을 놓치지 않고 듣는다. "For today's training session, I'll be showing you all how to use our company's new accounting software, NextBook."이라며 오늘 교육에서는 청자들 모두에게 회사의 회계 소프트웨어인 NextBook을 사용하는 방법을 알려줄 것이라고 한 말을 통해 화자가 회사 교육자임을 알 수 있다. 따라서 (C)가 정답이다.

어휘 analyst[ǽnəlist] 분석가 trainer[미 tréinər, 영 tréinə] 교육자, 훈련사
sales representative 판매원

75 언급 문제

해석 화자는 NextBook에 대해 무엇을 말하는가?
(A) 수 개월 전에 업데이트되었다.
(B) 컴퓨터에 로딩되는 데 시간이 좀 걸린다.
(C) 회장에 의해 승인되었다.
(D) 이용하려면 특별한 번호가 필요하다.

해설 질문의 핵심 어구(NextBook)와 관련된 내용을 주의 깊게 듣는다. "an ID number is required to log in to the program[NextBook]"이라며 NextBook에 로그인하는 데 ID 번호가 필요하다고 하였다. 따라서 (D)가 정답이다.

패러프레이징
ID number is required to log in 로그인하는 데 ID 번호가 필요하다
→ requires a special code to access 이용하려면 특별한 번호가 필요하다

어휘 approve[əprúːv] 승인하다 code[미 koud, 영 kəud] 번호, 암호
access[ǽkses] 이용하다, 접근하다

76 특정 세부 사항 문제

해석 비서는 무엇을 나눠줄 것인가?
(A) 신청서들
(B) 교육 자료들
(C) 사무 장비
(D) 전자 기기들

해설 질문의 핵심 어구(assistant pass out)가 언급된 주변을 주의 깊게 듣는다. "my assistant is going to pass out these instruction manuals for your reference"라며 비서가 참고를 위한 사용 안내서들을 나눠줄 것이라고 하였다. 따라서 (B)가 정답이다.

어휘 application form 신청서 electronic device 전자 기기

77-79 [3ʰ] 영국식 발음

Questions 77-79 refer to the following broadcast.

Good afternoon. This is Arlene Vickers, and I've got your traffic report. The unexpectedly heavy snow that began falling at 6 A.M. is still being cleared by city snow plows. [77]A representative of the transportation department, John Harris, said that the work will likely take a couple of hours to complete. [78]Motorists are urged to drive carefully, especially when crossing the Harborview Bridge as ice has reportedly formed on it. And if you were planning on taking the Park Expressway into the downtown area, you may want to reconsider. [79]The snowy conditions have resulted in several accidents, bringing traffic to a standstill. Use Kensington Street or Fourth Avenue instead.

traffic report 교통 정보 unexpectedly[ʌ̀nikspéktidli] 예상외로
heavy snow 폭설 snow plow 제설차
urge[미 əːrdʒ, 영 əːdʒ] 강력히 권고하다
reportedly[미 ripɔ́ːrtidli, 영 ripɔ́ːtidli] 알려진 바에 따르면
form[미 fɔːrm, 영 fɔːm] 형성되다 expressway[ikspréswèi] 고속도로
downtown[dáuntàun] 시내
reconsider[미 rìːkənsídər, 영 rìːkənsídə] 재고하다
result in (결과적으로) ~을 야기하다, 낳다 standstill[stǽndstil] 정체, 정지

해석

77-79번은 다음 방송에 관한 문제입니다.

안녕하세요. 저는 Arlene Vickers이며, 교통 정보를 가지고 왔습니다. 오전 6시에 내리기 시작한 예상 외의 폭설이 아직도 도시 제설차로 치워지고 있습니다. [77]교통부 직원인 John Harris는 작업은 완료하는 데 두 시간 정도 걸릴

것 같다고 말했습니다. ⁷⁸운전자들은 조심해서 운전을 하도록 강력히 권고되는데, 알려진 바에 따르면 Harborview 다리 위에 얼음이 형성되어 있기 때문에 이 다리를 건널 때 특히 조심해야 합니다. 또한 Park 고속도로를 이용하여 시내로 가실 계획이었다면, 재고하셔야겠습니다. ⁷⁹눈이 많이 내리는 날씨가 여러 사고들을 야기하여, 교통이 정체되도록 했습니다. Kensington가나 4번가를 대신 이용하십시오.

77 특정 세부 사항 문제

해석 John Harris는 누구인 것 같은가?
(A) 기자
(B) 일기 예보자
(C) 제설차 운전자
(D) 공무원

해설 지문에서 질문 대상(John Harris)의 신분 및 직업과 관련된 표현을 놓치지 않고 듣는다. "A representative of the transportation department, John Harris"라며 교통부 직원인 John Harris라고 한 말을 통해 John Harris가 공무원임을 알 수 있다. 따라서 (D)가 정답이다.

어휘 journalist[미 dʒə́:rnəlist, 영 dʒə́:nəlist] 기자
weather forecaster 일기 예보자
operator[미 ápərèitər, 영 ɔ́pərèitə] (기계 등의) 운전자
public official 공무원

78 언급 문제

해석 Harborview 다리에 대해 무엇이 언급되는가?
(A) 사고 현장이다.
(B) 얼음으로 뒤덮여 있다.
(C) 시내로 가는 유일한 길이다.
(D) 눈이 완전히 치워져 있다.

해설 질문의 핵심 어구(Harborview Bridge)가 언급된 주변을 주의 깊게 듣는다. "Motorists are urged to drive carefully, especially when crossing the Harborview Bridge as ice has reportedly formed on it."이라며 운전자들은 조심해서 운전을 하도록 강력히 권고되는데, 알려진 바에 따르면 Harborview 다리 위에 얼음이 형성되어 있기 때문에 이 다리를 건널 때 특히 조심해야 한다고 한 말을 통해 Harborview 다리가 얼음으로 뒤덮여 있음을 알 수 있다. 따라서 (B)가 정답이다.

패러프레이징
ice has ~ formed 얼음이 형성되어 있다 → frozen over 얼음으로 뒤덮여 있는

어휘 site[sait] 현장 freeze over 얼음으로 뒤덮이다
completely[kəmplí:tli] 완전히

79 의도 파악 문제

해석 화자는 "재고하셔야겠습니다"라고 말할 때 무엇을 의도하는가?
(A) 행사는 연기될 수도 있다.
(B) 신호등이 제대로 작동하지 않는다.
(C) 다른 길이 이용되어야 한다.
(D) 최근의 보도는 확인되지 않았다.

해설 질문의 인용어구(you may want to reconsider)가 언급된 주변을 주의 깊게 듣는다. "The snowy conditions have resulted in several accidents, bringing traffic to a standstill. Use Kensington Street or Fourth Avenue instead."라며 눈이 많이 내리는 날씨가 여러 사고들을 야기하여 교통이 정체되도록 했다고 한 후, Kensington가나 4번가를 대신 이용하라고 한 말을 통해 다른 길이 이용되어야 한다는 것을 알 수 있다. 따라서 (C)가 정답이다.

어휘 postpone[미 poustpóun, 영 pəustpə́un] 연기하다
traffic light 신호등 properly[미 prápərli, 영 prɔ́pəli] 제대로
alternative[미 ɔːltə́:rnətiv, 영 ɔːltə́:nətiv] 다른, 대안의
route[ru:t] 길, 경로

Questions 80-82 refer to the following excerpt from a meeting.

Starting from next week, we will begin planning a TV advertising campaign for a major Taiwanese beverage manufacturer, Refresh. ⁸⁰A representative from the firm will be visiting our headquarters next Friday to discuss how the company wants its brand portrayed in the advertisements. ⁸¹I've asked the research team to put together a short presentation on work that we've done for similar organizations in the past. As usual, Peter Zimmer will lead the design team, and he'll be present at the meeting as well. ⁸²If anyone has a question about their role for the upcoming campaign, please contact me at extension 567 at any time.

beverage[bévəridʒ] 음료
manufacturer[미 mænjufǽktʃərər, 영 mǽnjəfǽktʃərər] 제조업체
representative[rèprizéntətiv] 대표(자)
headquarters[미 hédkwɔ̀:rtərz, 영 hédkwɔ̀:təz] 본사
portray[미 pɔːrtréi, 영 pɔːtréi] 묘사하다, 그리다
put together (이것저것을 모아) 준비하다, 만들다 as usual 여느 때처럼
lead[li:d] 이끌다 extension[iksténʃən] 내선번호

해석
80-82번은 다음 회의 발췌록에 관한 문제입니다.

다음 주부터, 우리는 대만의 주요 음료 제조업체인 Refresh사를 위한 텔레비전 광고 캠페인을 기획하기 시작할 것입니다. ⁸⁰다음 주 금요일에 그 회사의 대표가 당사의 브랜드가 광고에 어떻게 묘사되기를 원하는지 의논하기 위해 우리 본사를 방문할 것입니다. ⁸¹저는 연구팀에 우리가 과거에 비슷한 조직들을 위해 했던 작업에 대한 짧은 발표를 준비할 것을 요청했습니다. 여느 때처럼, Peter Zimmer가 디자인팀을 이끌 것이며, 그는 회의에도 참석할 것입니다. ⁸²곧 있을 이 캠페인을 위한 자신의 역할에 대해 질문이 있으신 분은, 언제든지 내선번호 567번으로 제게 연락주시기 바랍니다.

80 다음에 할 일 문제

해석 화자는 다음 주에 무슨 일이 일어날 것이라고 말하는가?
(A) 제조 공장이 문을 열 것이다.
(B) 음료 제품이 출시될 것이다.
(C) 텔레비전 광고가 완성될 것이다.
(D) 고객이 회사에 올 것이다.

해설 질문의 핵심 어구(next week)와 관련된 내용을 주의 깊게 듣는다. "A representative from the firm will be visiting our headquarters next Friday"라며 다음 주 금요일에 그 회사의 대표가 본사를 방문할 것이라고 하였다. 따라서 (D)가 정답이다.

패러프레이징
A representative from the firm will be visiting ~ headquarters 그 회사의 대표가 본사를 방문할 것이다 → A client will come to an office 고객이 회사에 올 것이다

어휘 manufacturing plant 제조 공장 release[rilí:s] 출시하다
commercial[미 kəmə́:rʃəl, 영 kəmə́:ʃəl] 광고

81 요청 문제

해석 화자는 연구팀에게 무엇을 하라고 요청했는가?
(A) 소비자들을 조사하는 것을 시작한다.
(B) 보고서를 수정한다.
(C) 온라인으로 결과들을 공유한다.
(D) 간단한 발표를 준비한다.

해설 지문의 중후반에서 요청과 관련된 표현이 포함된 문장을 주의 깊게 듣

는다. "I've asked the research team to put together a short presentation on work"라며 연구팀에 작업에 대한 짧은 발표를 준비할 것을 요청했다고 하였다. 따라서 (D)가 정답이다.

패러프레이징
put together a short presentation 짧은 발표를 준비하다
→ Prepare a brief presentation 간단한 발표를 준비하다

어휘 **survey**[미 sərvéi, 영 sə:véi] (설문) 조사하다
make a correction 수정하다, 정정하다

82 이유 문제

해석 청자들은 왜 화자에게 연락할 것인가?
(A) 질문을 하기 위해
(B) 일정을 조정하기 위해
(C) 참석을 확정하기 위해
(D) 일에 지원하기 위해

해설 질문의 핵심 어구(contact the speaker)와 관련된 내용을 주의 깊게 듣는다. "If anyone has a question about their role for the upcoming campaign, please contact me"라며 곧 있을 캠페인을 위한 자신의 역할에 대해 질문이 있는 사람은 화자에게 연락을 달라고 하였다. 따라서 (A)가 정답이다.

어휘 **coordinate**[미 kouɔ́:rdəneit, 영 kəuɔ́:dineit] 조정하다
confirm[미 kənfə́:rm, 영 kənfə́:m] 확정하다
attendance[əténdəns] 참석, 출석   **volunteer for** ~에 지원하다

83-85 [3에] 호주식 발음

Questions 83-85 refer to the following introduction.

I'd like to ask you all to please welcome Gerald Kramer, the new senior director of Hampton Insurance. [83]Mr. Kramer has significant experience overseeing workers at major insurance providers. [84]He has also lived and worked abroad, achieving near-native proficiency in Spanish. That's a major reason why Mr. Kramer was brought on—to aid us in assisting our many Spanish-speaking clients. One of his main tasks will be to provide further professional development in language skills for all staff going forward. To celebrate the fact that Mr. Kramer is now joining our office, [85]we will be holding a casual staff get-together next Friday evening at 7 P.M.

---

senior director 선임 이사   **significant**[signífikənt] 상당한, 중요한
oversee[미 òuvərsí:, 영 ə̀uvəsí:] 감독하다   **achieve**[ətʃí:v] 성취하다
proficiency[prəfíʃənsi] 유창함, 능숙   **aid**[eid] 돕다
going forward 앞으로   **celebrate**[séləbrèit] 기념하다
casual[kǽʒuəl] 비격식적인, 가벼운
get-together[미 géttəgèðər, 영 géttəgèðə] 모임

해석
83-85번은 다음 소개에 관한 문제입니다.

저는 여러분 모두가 Hampton 보험사의 새 선임 이사인 Gerald Kramer를 환영해주셨으면 합니다. [83]Mr. Kramer는 주요 보험 회사들에서 직원들을 감독하는 데 상당한 경력이 있습니다. [84]그는 또한 해외에서 거주하고 근무하여, 스페인어에 있어 모국어에 가까운 유창함을 성취하였습니다. 그것이 바로 Mr. Kramer를 데려오게 된 주된 이유입니다. 즉, 우리가 스페인어를 사용하는 우리의 많은 고객들에게 도움이 되는 것을 돕기 위함입니다. 그의 주 업무들 중 하나는 앞으로 모든 직원의 언어 실력에 있어서 더 큰 전문적인 성장을 제공하는 것이 될 것입니다. Mr. Kramer가 이제부터 우리 회사와 함께 하는 것을 기념하기 위해, [85]우리는 다음 주 금요일 저녁 오후 7시에 비격식적인 직원 모임을 가질 것입니다.

83 특정 세부 사항 문제

해석 Mr. Kramer는 무엇을 하는 데 많은 경력이 있는가?
(A) 보험 상품들을 판매하기
(B) 직원들을 관리하기
(C) 고객 불만사항을 처리하기
(D) 회사 합병을 처리하기

해설 질문의 핵심 어구(have a lot of experience)와 관련된 내용을 주의 깊게 듣는다. "Mr. Kramer has significant experience overseeing workers at major insurance providers."라며 Mr. Kramer는 주요 보험 회사들에서 직원들을 감독하는 데 상당한 경력이 있다고 하였다. 따라서 (B)가 정답이다.

어휘 **handle**[hǽndl] 처리하다, 다루다
merger[미 mə́:rdʒər, 영 mə́:dʒə] (조직체·사업체의) 합병

84 언급 문제

해석 화자는 Mr. Kramer에 대해 무엇을 언급하는가?
(A) 강연을 하고 싶어 한다.
(B) 다른 나라에 거주했다.
(C) 다른 제의들을 거절했다.
(D) 비서를 고용할 것이다.

해설 질문의 핵심 어구(Mr. Kramer)와 관련된 내용을 주의 깊게 듣는다. "He[Mr. Kramer] has also lived ~ abroad"라며 Mr. Kramer는 또한 해외에서 거주했다고 하였다. 따라서 (B)가 정답이다.

어휘 **give a talk** 강연하다   **refuse**[rifjú:z] 거절하다

85 다음에 할 일 문제

해석 다음 주 금요일에 무슨 일이 일어날 것 같은가?
(A) 어학 수업
(B) 무역 박람회
(C) 영업 회의
(D) 비격식적 모임

해설 질문의 핵심 어구(next Friday)가 언급된 주변을 주의 깊게 듣는다. "we will be holding a casual staff get-together next Friday evening at 7 P.M."라며 다음 주 금요일 저녁 오후 7시에 비격식적인 직원 모임을 가질 것이라고 하였다. 따라서 (D)가 정답이다.

패러프레이징
casual staff get-together 비격식적인 직원 모임 → An informal gathering 비격식적 모임

어휘 **trade fair** 무역 박람회
informal[미 infɔ́:rməl, 영 infɔ́:məl] 비격식적인, 비공식의
gathering[gǽðəriŋ] 모임

86-88 [3에] 캐나다식 발음

Questions 86-88 refer to the following speech.

[86]Thank you all for attending the annual shareholders' meeting for Freemont Industries. I am pleased to be here, representing Freemont as its CEO for the last 15 years. For those who don't know, [87]the magazine *BizSurprise* just named us one of Canada's most successful businesses in its most recent monthly edition. That's a huge honor, and it has motivated us to work even harder to maintain our standing in the coming years. But before I discuss future plans, CFO for Freemont Jennifer Harvey will be presented with a special award in recognition of her hard work. [88]Ms. Harvey, please join me on the stage and say a few words.

해석

86-88번은 다음 연설에 관한 문제입니다.

⁸⁶Freemont Industries사의 연례 주주회의에 참석해주셔서 모두 감사드립니다. 저는 지난 15년 동안 Freemont사의 대표이사로서 당사를 대표하여 이 자리에 나와 기쁩니다. 모르시는 분들을 위해, ⁸⁷BizSurprise지는 최신 월간호에서 저희를 캐나다의 가장 성공한 사업체들 중 하나로 명명했습니다. 그것은 엄청난 영광이며, 저희가 앞으로 몇 년간 저희의 지위를 유지하기 위해 더 열심히 일할 수 있도록 동기를 주었습니다. 하지만 제가 앞으로의 계획들에 대해 이야기하기 전에, Freemont사의 재무 담당 최고 책임자인 Jennifer Harvey가 그녀의 노고에 대한 표창으로 특별상을 수여받겠습니다. ⁸⁸Ms. Harvey, 무대에 저와 함께하셔서 몇 마디 해주시기 바랍니다.

86 청자 문제

해석 청자들은 누구인 것 같은가?
(A) 회사 회장들
(B) 은행원들
(C) 회사 주주들
(D) 잡지 편집자들

해설 지문에서 신분 및 직업과 관련된 표현을 놓치지 않고 듣는다. "Thank you all for attending the annual shareholders' meeting for Freemont Industries."라며 Freemont Industries사의 연례 주주회의에 참석해줘서 모두 감사하다고 한 말을 통해 청자들이 회사 주주들임을 알 수 있다. 따라서 (C)가 정답이다.

어휘 bank teller 은행원 stakeholder[미 stéikhòuldər, 영 stéikhèuldə] 주주 editor[미 édətər, 영 édɪtə] 편집자

87 추론 문제

해석 BizSurprise지에 대해 무엇이 암시되는가?
(A) 월간호를 출간한다.
(B) 대표이사를 인터뷰하고 싶어 한다.
(C) 기업 박람회들을 후원한다.
(D) 더 많은 작가들을 채용해야 한다.

해설 질문의 핵심 어구(BizSurprise)가 언급된 주변을 주의 깊게 듣는다. "the magazine BizSurprise just named us one of Canada's most successful businesses in its most recent monthly edition"이라며 BizSurprise지는 최신 월간호에서 화자의 회사를 캐나다의 가장 성공한 사업체들 중 하나로 명명했다고 한 말을 통해 BizSurprise지가 월간호를 출간한다는 것을 알 수 있다. 따라서 (A)가 정답이다.

어휘 publish[pʌ́bliʃ] 출간하다, 발행하다 sponsor[미 spάnsər, 영 spɔ́nsə] 후원하다 fair[미 fɛər, 영 feə] 박람회

88 요청 문제

해석 화자는 Ms. Harvey에게 무엇을 하라고 요청하는가?
(A) 상을 수여한다.
(B) 연설을 한다.
(C) 우승자에게 박수를 친다.
(D) 자리에 앉는다.

해설 지문의 중후반에서 요청과 관련된 표현이 포함된 문장을 주의 깊게 듣는다. "Ms. Harvey, please ~ say a few words."라며 Ms. Harvey에게 몇 마디 해달라고 하였다. 따라서 (B)가 정답이다.

89-91 🎧 캐나다식 발음

Questions 89-91 refer to the following excerpt from a meeting.

Over the past several months, ⁸⁹/⁹⁰we in the City Recreation Department have noticed that many of our public parks have had an unusually large amount of litter. ⁹⁰In one way, this is to be expected. It is tourist season, after all. Still, having empty bags and bottles on the ground makes our parks unattractive to visitors. We need to come up with solutions. ⁹¹One idea I have is to conduct an advertising campaign that informs people about the importance of keeping our parks clean. We could put up posters to remind people to properly dispose of waste. ⁹¹I was also thinking about running radio ads highlighting the importance of cleaning up litter. If anyone has other ideas, please feel free to suggest them now.

해석

89-91번은 다음 회의 발췌록에 관한 문제입니다.

지난 몇 달 동안, ⁸⁹/⁹⁰우리 도시 휴양 부서는 우리의 여러 국립 공원들에 비정상적으로 많은 양의 쓰레기가 있다는 것을 인지했습니다. ⁹⁰어떤 면에서, 이것은 당연합니다. 어쨌든, 지금은 관광 철입니다. 그럼에도 불구하고, 땅에 빈 봉지와 병이 있는 것은 우리 공원을 방문객들에게 매력적이지 않게 만듭니다. 우리는 해결책을 생각해 낼 필요가 있습니다. ⁹¹제가 가지고 있는 한 아이디어는 사람들에게 공원을 깨끗하게 유지하는 것의 중요성을 알리는 광고 캠페인을 진행하는 것입니다. 우리는 사람들에게 쓰레기를 제대로 처리할 것을 상기시키기 위해 포스터를 붙일 수 있습니다. ⁹¹저는 또한 쓰레기를 치우는 것의 중요성을 강조하는 라디오 광고를 내는 것에 대해 생각하고 있었습니다. 만약 누군가 다른 아이디어가 있으시다면, 지금 편하게 제안해주십시오.

89 화자 문제

해석 화자는 누구인 것 같은가?
(A) 라디오 진행자
(B) 시 직원
(C) 관광 안내원
(D) 광고 책임자

해설 지문에서 신분 및 직업과 관련된 표현을 놓치지 않고 듣는다. "we in the City Recreation Department have noticed that many of our public parks have had an unusually large amount of litter"라며 화자가 속한 도시 휴양 부서는 자신들의 여러 국립 공원들에 비정상적으로 많은 양의 쓰레기가 있다는 것을 인지했다고 한 말을 통해 화자가 시 직원임을 알 수 있다. 따라서 (B)가 정답이다.

어휘 host[미 houst, 영 həust] 진행자 executive[igzékjutiv] 책임자, 경영자

90 의도 파악 문제

해석 화자는 왜 "어쨌든, 지금은 관광 철입니다"라고 말하는가?
(A) 공원 근처에 왜 관광버스가 많은지 나타내기 위해

(B) 특정 날짜까지 수리가 완료되어야 함을 나타내기 위해
(C) 공원에 왜 많은 쓰레기가 있는지 설명하기 위해
(D) 판촉 행사를 개최하는 것을 권장하기 위해

해설 질문의 인용어구(It is tourist season, after all)가 언급된 주변을 주의 깊게 듣는다. "we ~ have noticed that many of our public parks have had an unusually large amount of litter. In one way, this is to be expected."라며 여러 국립 공원들에 비정상적으로 많은 양의 쓰레기가 있다는 것을 인지했다며, 어떤 면에서 이것이 당연하다고 하였다. 따라서 (C)가 정답이다.

어휘 note[nout] 나타내다, 표시하다 certain[sə́:rtn] 특정한

91 제안 문제

해석 화자는 무엇을 제안하는가?
(A) 쓰레기봉투를 나눠주는 것
(B) 광고를 내는 것
(C) 임시 직원을 모집하는 것
(D) 청소 회사에 부탁하는 것

해설 지문의 중후반에서 제안과 관련된 표현이 포함된 문장을 주의 깊게 듣는다. "One idea I have is to conduct an advertising campaign that informs people about the importance of keeping our parks clean."이라며 화자가 가지고 있는 한 아이디어는 사람들에게 공원을 깨끗하게 유지하는 것의 중요성을 알리는 광고 캠페인을 진행하는 것이라고 한 후, "I was also thinking about running radio ads highlighting the importance of cleaning up litter."라며 쓰레기를 치우는 것의 중요성을 강조하는 라디오 광고를 내는 것에 대해 생각하고 있었다고 하였다. 따라서 (B)가 정답이다.

어휘 hand out 나눠주다 temporary[témpərèri] 임시의
speak to ~에게 부탁하다

92-94 🎧 호주식 발음

Questions 92-94 refer to the following announcement.

As a reminder, a new overtime policy will be implemented on Friday. ⁹²All overtime will have to be approved in advance by a supervisor. If you have any questions, ⁹³speak with Rhonda Levy in human resources. She's covering for her supervisor, Brittany Jacobs, who's on leave. OK, let's turn to project schedules. The company wants to release the SDX Digital Camera in mid-July now, so ⁹⁴I need the marketing plan by June 10 instead of June 23. I know . . . we have only five people. ⁹⁴So, Sandra and Debbie, I'm going to assign some of your team members to this project, but I'll extend your team's deadlines in return.

reminder[미 rimáindər, 영 rimáində] 상기시키는 것
overtime[미 óuvərtàim, 영 óuvətaim] 초과 근무의; 초과 근무
implement[ímpləmənt] 시행하다
approve[əprú:v] 승인하다 in advance 사전에
cover for (자리를 비운 사람의 일을) 대신하다 be on leave 휴가 중이다
assign[əsáin] 배정하다 extend[iksténd] 연장하다 in return 대신에

해석
92-94번은 다음 공지에 관한 문제입니다.

상기시켜드리자면, 새로운 초과 근무 정책이 금요일에 시행될 것입니다. ⁹²모든 초과 근무는 상사에게 사전에 승인되어야 할 것입니다. 만약 질문이 있으시다면, ⁹³인사부의 Rhonda Levy와 이야기하십시오. 그녀는 휴가 중인 그녀의 상사인 Brittany Jacobs의 일을 대신하고 있습니다. 좋습니다, 프로젝트 일정으로 넘어가죠. 회사가 이제 SDX 디지털카메라를 7월 중순에 출

시하기를 원하기 때문에, ⁹⁴저는 6월 23일 대신 6월 10일까지 마케팅 계획이 필요합니다. 저도 압니다... 우리는 다섯 명뿐입니다. ⁹⁴그래서, Sandra와 Debbie, 제가 여러분의 팀원들 중 몇 명을 이 프로젝트에 배정할 것인데, 대신 여러분 팀의 마감일을 연장해드리겠습니다.

92 특정 세부 사항 문제

해석 화자에 따르면, 무엇이 승인되어야 하는가?
(A) 휴가
(B) 추가 근무 시간
(C) 제품 디자인
(D) 경영진 변경

해설 질문의 핵심 어구(approved)가 언급된 주변을 주의 깊게 듣는다. "All overtime will have to be approved in advance by a supervisor."라며 모든 초과 근무는 상사에게 사전에 승인되어야 할 것이라고 하였다. 따라서 (B)가 정답이다.

패러프레이징
overtime 초과 근무 → Additional work 추가 근무

어휘 time off 휴가, 휴식 work hours 근무 시간

93 특정 세부 사항 문제

해석 Brittany Jacobs는 누구인 것 같은가?
(A) 인사과 직원
(B) 판매원
(C) 사진 촬영 전문가
(D) 교육 강사

해설 지문에서 질문 대상(Brittany Jacobs)의 신분 및 직업과 관련된 표현을 놓치지 않고 듣는다. "speak with Rhonda Levy in human resources. She's covering for her supervisor, Brittany Jacobs"라며 인사부의 Rhonda Levy와 이야기하라고 한 후, 그녀는 그녀의 상사인 Brittany Jacobs의 일을 대신하고 있다고 한 말을 통해 Brittany Jacobs가 인사과 직원임을 알 수 있다. 따라서 (A)가 정답이다.

패러프레이징
human resources 인사부 → personnel 인사과

어휘 photography[fətágrəfi] 사진 촬영, 사진술 expert[ékspə:rt] 전문가

94 의도 파악 문제

해석 화자는 "우리는 다섯 명뿐입니다"라고 말할 때 무엇을 의도하는가?
(A) 중요한 결정이 합의에 이를 수 없다.
(B) 회사가 곧 더 많은 직원들을 채용할 것이다.
(C) 업무를 완료하기 위해 일부 도움이 필요하다.
(D) 몇몇 직원들이 초과근무를 해야 한다.

해설 질문의 인용어구(we have only five people)가 언급된 주변을 주의 깊게 듣는다. "I need the marketing plan by June 10 instead of June 23"라며 6월 23일 대신 6월 10일까지 마케팅 계획이 필요하다고 한 후, "So, Sandra and Debbie, I'm going to assign some of your team members to this project"라며 그래서 Sandra와 Debbie의 팀들 중 몇 명을 이 프로젝트에 배정할 것이라고 한 말을 통해 업무를 완료하기 위해 일부 도움이 필요하다는 것을 알 수 있다. 따라서 (C)가 정답이다.

95-97 🎧 미국식 발음

Questions 95-97 refer to the following telephone message and price list.

Mr. Harrison, ⁹⁵this is Beth Williams calling from Viva Rentals at the Dallas International Airport regarding your inquiry. To respond to your first question, we're open from 6 A.M. until 11 P.M. daily, so your 9 P.M. ⊙

arrival time won't be a problem. ⁹⁶You also mentioned that you would like to reserve a minivan because you are traveling with four coworkers. Unfortunately, we don't have any available for the date you arrive, but we do have another type of vehicle that can seat five people comfortably. I'll e-mail you some information now. Once you've made your choice, ⁹⁷please visit our Web site to reserve your vehicle.

inquiry [inkwáiəri] 문의　respond [미 rispánd, 영 rispónd] 답하다
arrival time 도착 시각
coworker [미 kóuwə̀:rkər, 영 kóuwə̀:kə] 직장 동료
seat [si:t] (건물·차량 등이) 수용하다, ~ 명의 좌석을 가지다
comfortably [미 kʌ́mfərtəbli, 영 kʌ́mftəbli] 수월하게, 편안하게

해석

95-97번은 다음 전화 메시지와 가격표에 관한 문제입니다.

Mr. Harrison, ⁹⁵저는 댈러스 국제 공항에 있는 Viva Rentals에서 고객님의 문의에 대해 전화드리는 Beth Williams입니다. 고객님의 첫 번째 질문에 답해드리자면, 저희는 매일 오전 6시부터 오후 11시까지 열려있기 때문에, 고객님의 오후 9시 도착 시각은 문제가 되지 않을 것입니다. ⁹⁶고객님은 또한 네 명의 직장 동료들과 이동할 것이기 때문에 미니밴을 예약하고 싶다고 하셨습니다. 유감스럽게도, 저희에게 고객님께서 도착하시는 날짜에는 이용 가능한 것이 없지만, 다섯 명을 수월하게 수용할 수 있는 다른 종류의 차량이 있습니다. 제가 몇몇 정보를 지금 이메일로 보내드리겠습니다. 고객님께서 선택을 하시면, ⁹⁷저희의 웹사이트에 방문하셔서 차량을 예약해주시기 바랍니다.

Viva Rentals		
종류	수용 인원	일일 요금
스포츠카	2명	32.00달러
세단	4명	22.00달러
⁹⁶SUV	6명	28.00달러
미니밴	8명	34.00달러

95 목적 문제

해석　화자는 왜 전화를 하고 있는가?
(A) 예약을 확정하기 위해
(B) 특가 상품을 제공하기 위해
(C) 몇몇 질문에 답을 하기 위해
(D) 상점 위치를 제공하기 위해

해설　전화의 목적을 묻는 문제이므로, 대화의 초반을 반드시 듣는다. "this is Beth Williams calling from Viva Rentals ~ regarding your inquiry"라며 Viva Rentals에서 청자의 문의에 대해 전화하는 Beth Williams라고 한 말을 통해 화자가 몇몇 질문에 답을 하기 위해 전화하고 있음을 알 수 있다. 따라서 (C)가 정답이다.

96 시각 자료 문제

해석　시각 자료를 보아라. 청자는 어떤 차량을 선택할 것 같은가?
(A) 스포츠카
(B) 세단
(C) SUV
(D) 미니밴

해설　제시된 가격표의 정보를 확인한 후 질문의 핵심 어구(vehicle ~ choose)와 관련된 내용을 주의 깊게 듣는다. "You also mentioned that you would like to reserve a minivan ~. Unfortunately, we don't have any available for the date you arrive, but we do have another type of vehicle that can seat five people comfortably."라며 청자가 미니밴을 예약하고 싶다고 했다고 한 후, 유감스럽게도 그 날짜에는 이용 가능한 것이 없지만 다섯 명을 수월하

게 수용할 수 있는 다른 종류의 차량이 있다고 하였으므로, 청자가 다섯 명 이상을 수용할 수 있는 SUV를 선택할 것임을 가격표에서 알 수 있다. 따라서 (C)가 정답이다.

97 특정 세부 사항 문제

해석　청자는 무엇을 하도록 안내되는가?
(A) 차량을 제시간에 반납한다.
(B) 온라인 예약을 한다.
(C) 여행 날짜를 확인한다.
(D) 양식을 직접 제출한다.

해설　질문의 핵심 어구(instructed to do)와 관련된 내용을 주의 깊게 듣는다. "please visit our Web site to reserve your vehicle"이라며 웹사이트에 방문해서 차량을 예약해달라고 하였다. 따라서 (B)가 정답이다.

패러프레이징
visit ~ Web site to reserve 웹사이트에 방문해서 예약하다 →
Make an online booking 온라인 예약을 하다

어휘　return [미 ritə́:rn, 영 ritə́:n] 반납하다　on time 제시간에
verify [미 vérəfài, 영 vérifài] 확인하다　in person 직접

98-100 [3m] 영국식 발음

Questions 98-100 refer to the following broadcast and map.

In local business news, ⁹⁸Western Development announced that it took over its former rival, Bedford Properties. Jill Myers, president of Western Development, said that the acquisition will provide her company with the resources needed to launch several new developments. ⁹⁹The most significant of these will be the building of a large shopping mall. Construction will begin on June 3. Moreover, Ms. Myers stated that Western Development is relocating to a larger office. ¹⁰⁰The company has rented a building on Oak Street next to City Hall to serve as its new headquarters. The transition is expected to be complete by May 25.

take over (기업 등을) 인수하다　former [미 fɔ́:rmər, 영 fɔ́:mə] 이전의
acquisition [æ̀kwizíʃən] 인수　resource [미 rí:sɔ:rs, 영 rí:sɔ:s] 자원, 자산
launch [lɔ:ntʃ] 시작하다　significant [signífikənt] 중요한
state [steit] (정식으로) 말하다　rent [rent] 임대하다
serve [미 sə:rv, 영 sə:v] (특히 특정한 용도로) 쓸 수 있다, 쓰일 수 있다
transition [trænzíʃən] 이전, 이동, 이행

해석

98-100번은 다음 방송과 지도에 관한 문제입니다.

지역 경제 뉴스로는, ⁹⁸Western Development사가 이전의 경쟁업체였던 Bedford Properties사를 인수했다고 발표했습니다. Western Development사의 회장인 Jill Myers는 이 인수가 그녀의 회사에 여러 새로운 개발을 시작하는 데 필요한 자원들을 제공할 것이라고 말했습니다. ⁹⁹이들 중 가장 중요한 것은 대형 쇼핑몰의 건축일 것입니다. 공사는 6월 3일에 시작합니다. 또한, Ms. Myers는 Western Development사가 더 큰 사무실로 이전할 것이라고 말했습니다. ¹⁰⁰회사는 새로운 본사로 쓰기 위해 시청 옆에 있는 Oak가의 건물을 임대했습니다. 이 이전은 5월 25일까지 완료될 예정입니다.

	건물 A			시립 도서관
¹⁰⁰건물 B	시청	Ocean가	건물 C
Oak가			
백화점	건물 D		지하철역

98 주제 문제

해설 방송은 주로 무엇에 대한 것인가?
(A) 회사 인수
(B) 건물 구입
(C) 행사 장소
(D) 토지 개발

해설 방송의 주제를 묻는 문제이므로, 지문의 초반을 주의 깊게 듣는다. "Western Development announced that it took over its former rival, Bedford Properties"라며 Western Development사가 이전의 경쟁업체였던 Bedford Properties사를 인수했다고 발표했다고 한 후, 회사 인수에 대한 내용으로 지문이 이어지고 있다. 따라서 (A)가 정답이다.

패러프레이징
took over ~ former rival 이전의 경쟁업체를 인수했다 → A corporate acquisition 회사 인수

어휘 property[미 prάpərti, 영 prόpəti] 건물, 재산

99 다음에 할 일 문제

해설 6월 3일에 무슨 일이 일어날 것인가?
(A) 회사가 이전할 것이다.
(B) 프로젝트가 시작할 것이다.
(C) 경영자가 은퇴할 것이다.
(D) 사무실이 다시 문을 열 것이다.

해설 질문의 핵심 어구(June 3)가 언급된 주변을 주의 깊게 듣는다. "The most significant of these[developments] will be the building of a large shopping mall. Construction will begin on June 3."라며 개발 중 가장 중요한 것은 대형 쇼핑몰의 건축일 것이라고 한 후, 공사는 6월 3일에 시작한다고 한 말을 통해 6월 3일에 프로젝트가 시작할 것임을 알 수 있다. 따라서 (B)가 정답이다.

어휘 executive[igzékjutiv] 경영자, 임원   retire[미 ritáiər, 영 ritáiə] 은퇴하다

100 시각 자료 문제

해설 시각 자료를 보아라. Western Development사는 어떤 건물을 임대했는가?
(A) 건물 A
(B) 건물 B
(C) 건물 C
(D) 건물 D

해설 제시된 지도의 정보를 확인한 후 질문의 핵심 어구(rent)가 언급된 주변을 주의 깊게 듣는다. "The company has rented a building on Oak Street next to City Hall to serve as its new headquarters."라며 회사는 새로운 본사로 쓰기 위해 시청 옆에 있는 Oak가의 건물을 임대했다고 하였으므로, Western Development사가 건물 B를 임대했음을 지도에서 알 수 있다. 따라서 (B)가 정답이다.

PART 5

101 시간 표현과 일치하는 시제의 동사 채우기

해설 과거 시간 표현(recently)이 있으므로 과거 시제 (C) purchased가 정답이다.

해설 Sanders Industries사는 최근에 자사의 생산량을 두 배로 만들게 해줄 최첨단 기계를 구입했다.

어휘 high-tech adj. 최첨단의   double v. 두 배로 만들다   output n. 생산량

102 동사와 수일치하는 주어 채우기

해설 빈칸은 주어 자리이므로 주어가 될 수 있는 대명사 (A)와 (B)가 정답의 후보이다. 동사(is pleased)가 단수이므로 단수 취급되는 수량 표현 (A) Each가 정답이다. (B) All은 of 뒤의 명사에 동사를 수일치시

켜야 하므로 복수 동사와 쓰여야 한다. (C) Other와 (D) Their own은 형용사이므로 명사가 와야 하는 주어 자리에 올 수 없다.

해설 설문 조사를 받았던 각 직원은 은퇴 프로그램의 확대에 만족한다.

어휘 survey v. (설문) 조사하다, 점검하다   be pleased with ~에 만족하다
expansion n. 확대   retirement n. 은퇴

103 명사 자리 채우기

해설 소유격(the train's) 다음에 올 수 있는 것은 명사이므로 명사 (D) departure가 정답이다. 동사 (A)와 (C), 동사 또는 분사 (B)는 명사 자리에 올 수 없다.

해설 폭설은 기차의 출발을 네 시간 이상 지연시켰다.

어휘 heavy snowfall 폭설   delay v. 지연시키다, 미루다
depart v. 출발하다   departure n. 출발, 떠남

104 빈도 부사 채우기

해설 '일 년 내내 관광객들로 가득 차기 때문에 항상 붐빈다'라는 의미가 되어야 하므로 (B) always(항상)가 정답이다. 잠시 후에 어떤 일이 일어날 것이라는 문맥, 또는 잠시 후에 어떤 일이 일어났다는 상황에 쓰이는 시간 부사 (D) soon(곧)을 정답으로 선택하지 않도록 주의해야 한다.

해설 Shoreline 식당은 그 지역이 일 년 내내 관광객들로 가득 차기 때문에 항상 붐빈다.

어휘 busy adj. 붐비는, 바쁜   be filled with ~으로 가득 차다
year-round adv. 일 년 내내   exactly adv. 정확히

105 부정대명사/형용사 채우기

해설 빈칸은 주어 자리로 명사가 와야 하므로 지시대명사 (A), (B), (C)가 정답의 후보이다. '대부분의 새로운 사업들은 5년 안에 실패하지만 몇몇은 매우 성공적으로 된다'는 의미가 되어야 하므로 (C) some(몇몇)이 정답이다. (A) any(무엇이든지)와 (B) these(이것들)는 '대부분의 새로운 사업들은 5년 안에 실패하지만 무엇이든지/이것들은 매우 성공적이게 된다'는 어색한 의미를 만들기 때문에 답이 될 수 없다.

해설 대부분의 새로운 사업들은 5년 안에 실패하지만, 몇몇은 매우 성공적이게 된다.

어휘 fail v. 실패하다

106 동사 어휘 고르기

해설 '집이 부동산 중개인에게 평가되도록 했다'라는 문맥이므로 assess의 p.p.형 (C) assessed(평가하다)가 정답이다. (A)의 perform은 '수행하다, 실시하다', (B)의 appear는 '나타나다', (D)의 outline은 '윤곽을 그리다'라는 의미이다.

해설 Ms. Wang은 그녀의 집을 팔려고 내놓기 전에 그것이 부동산 중개인에게 평가되도록 했다.

어휘 real estate agent 부동산 중개인   offer for sale ~을 팔려고 내놓다

107 현재분사와 과거분사 구별하여 채우기

해설 수식받는 명사(seats)와 분사가 '좌석이 예약되다'라는 의미의 수동 관계이므로 과거분사 (B) reserved가 정답이다.

해설 시상식에는 수상자들의 가족과 동료들을 위해 예약된 30개의 좌석이 있습니다.

어휘 recipient n. (어떤 것을) 받는 사람   coworker n. 동료
awards ceremony 시상식

108 명령문의 동사 자리 채우기

해설 전치사구(In order to ~ security) 뒤에 나온 문장이 주어가 없는 명령문이므로, 명령문의 동사로 사용되는 동사원형 (A) include가 정답이다.

해설 귀하의 계정 보안을 유지하기 위해, 비밀번호에 최소한 하나의 숫자와

하나의 문자를 포함하십시오.

어휘 maintain v. 유지하다, 지속하다 account n. 계정, 계좌
security n. 보안, 경비

109 형용사 어휘 고르기
해설 'Findera 건설사는 국제적 인지도를 높이기 위해 베트남 주택 시장의 급속한 성장을 기회로 활용했다'라는 문맥이므로 (B) rapid(급속한, 빠른)가 정답이다. (A) best는 '최고의', (C) original은 '원래의', (D) adverse는 '부정적인, 불리한'이라는 의미이다.

해석 Findera 건설사는 국제적 인지도를 높이기 위해 베트남 주택 시장의 급속한 성장을 기회로 활용했다.

어휘 take advantage of ~을 기회로 활용하다 profile n. 인지도

110 현재분사와 과거분사 구별하여 채우기
해설 수식받는 명사(ending)와 분사가 '아주 신나는 결말'이라는 의미의 능동 관계이므로 현재분사 (C) thrilling이 정답이다. 참고로, thrill과 같은 감정동사의 현재분사와 과거분사를 구별할 때, 주어가 감정을 느끼면 과거분사 p.p., 주어가 감정의 원인이면 현재분사 -ing를 쓴다. 이 경우 주어(ending)가 신나게 하는 원인이므로 현재분사(thrilling)를 써야 한다.

해석 많은 평론가들이 감독 John Parker의 최신 액션 영화의 아주 신나는 결말에 대해 그를 칭찬했다.

어휘 critic n. 평론가 praise v. 칭찬하다 ending n. 결말, 끝
thriller n. 스릴러물 thrill n. 전율, 스릴; v. 신나게 만들다

111 시간 표현과 일치하는 시제의 동사 채우기
해설 미래 시간 표현(The upcoming sale)이 있으므로 미래 시제 (D) will save가 정답이다. (A)는 복수 동사이므로 답이 될 수 없다.

해석 Westside Electronics사의 다가오는 할인 판매는 쇼핑객들이 텔레비전에 많은 돈을 절약하게 해줄 것이다.

어휘 upcoming adj. 다가오는, 이번의 a great deal of 많은
save v. 절약하다, 구하다

112 형용사 어휘 고르기
해설 '새 컴퓨터 모델에 결함이 있는 부품들이 들어있다는 것을 알아낸 후에 그것을 회수했다'라는 문맥이므로 (D) defective(결함이 있는)가 정답이다. (A) functional은 '실용적인, 기능적인', (B) adjustable은 '조정 가능한', (C) portable은 '휴대용의, 이동하기 쉬운'이라는 의미이다.

해석 RubioTech사는 새 컴퓨터 모델에 결함이 있는 부품들이 들어있다는 것을 알아낸 후에 그것을 회수했다.

어휘 recall v. 회수하다, 상기하다 discover v. 알아내다
contain v. ~이 들어있다, 억누르다 component n. 부품, 요소

113 동명사 채우기
해설 전치사(Before)의 목적어 자리에는 명사 (A)와 (B), 동명사 (D)가 올 수 있다. 명사(Carla Evans)를 목적어로 취하면서 전치사의 목적어 자리에 올 수 있는 동명사 (D) contacting이 정답이다. 명사 앞에 다른 명사가 연결어나 전치사 없이 바로 올 수 없으므로 명사 (A)와 (B)는 답이 될 수 없다.

해석 면접 일정을 잡기 위해 Carla Evans에게 연락하기 전에, Mr. Harris는 그녀의 이력서에 있는 정보를 확인했다.

어휘 schedule v. 일정을 잡다 verify v. 확인하다, 입증하다
résumé n. 이력서 contact n. 연락; v. 연락하다

114 to 부정사 채우기
해설 동사 need 다음에는 to 부정사가 와야 하므로 (B) to register가 정답이다. 동사원형 (A), 동명사 (C), 동사 또는 분사 (D)는 동사 need

다음에 올 수 없다.

해석 회의에 참석할 계획인 분들은 최소한 7일 전에 미리 등록해야 합니다.

어휘 attend v. 참석하다 in advance 미리, 앞서 register v. 등록하다

115 부사 어휘 고르기
해설 '주문품을 잘못하여 엉뚱한 주소로 보냈다'라는 문맥이므로 (D) accidentally(잘못하여, 뜻하지 않게)가 정답이다. (A) generously는 '관대하게', (B) mutually는 '상호간에, 공통으로', (C) productively는 '생산적으로'라는 의미이다.

해석 TriGem Chemicals사는 고객의 주문품을 잘못하여 엉뚱한 주소로 보냈었다는 것을 시인했다.

어휘 admit v. 시인하다, 인정하다, 자백하다

116 명사 어휘 고르기
해설 '제품 배송은 계약 조건에 따라 3일 이내에 완료되어야 한다'라는 문맥이므로 (B) contract(계약)가 정답이다. (A) figure는 '수치, 인물', (C) research는 '조사, 연구', (D) concept는 '개념, 관념'이라는 의미이다.

해석 제품 배송은 계약 조건에 따라 3일 이내에 완료되어야 한다.

어휘 terms n. 조건, 용어

117 전치사 채우기
해설 '15퍼센트만큼 증가했다'라는 의미가 되어야 하므로 (D) by(~만큼)가 정답이다.

해석 XL550 태블릿의 매출은 운영 체제의 새로운 버전이 출시된 이후에 15퍼센트만큼 증가했다.

어휘 increase v. 증가하다 operating system 운영 체제
release v. 출시하다

118 강조 부사 채우기
해설 비교급(higher) 앞의 빈칸에는 비교급을 강조하는 부사가 와야 하므로 (B) much가 정답이다. (A) very나 (D) so는 형용사나 부사를 꾸미는 역할을 하며 비교급을 강조하지 못한다. (C) more는 'more + 원급'의 형태로 비교급을 만든다. 참고로, very는 최상급을 강조할 때 'the + very + 최상급'의 형태로 쓰임을 알아두자.

해석 Ice River 국립공원의 10월 방문자 수는 이전 달보다 훨씬 더 높았다.

어휘 previous adj. 이전의

119 동사 관련 어구 완성하기
해설 '관리직용 구내식당이 직원 휴게실로 전환되다'라는 문맥에서 빈칸 뒤의 전치사 into와 함께 쓰여 '~으로 전환하다'라는 의미의 어구를 이루는 convert의 p.p.형 (A) converted가 정답이다. (convert A into B: A를 B로 전환하다) (B)의 convince는 '확신시키다, 설득하다', (C)의 consent는 '동의하다', (D)의 conceal은 '감추다, 숨기다'라는 의미이다.

해석 회사의 관리직용 구내식당은 개조 동안에 직원 휴게실로 전환될 것이다.

어휘 executive adj. 관리직의; n. 임원 cafeteria n. 구내식당
lounge n. 휴게실 renovation n. 개조, 보수

120 형용사 자리 채우기
해설 빈칸은 be동사(is) 다음에 나온 주격 보어 자리이므로 명사 (A)와 (B), 현재분사 (C), 형용사 (D) 모든 보기가 정답의 후보이다. '국가들이 화석 연료 사용을 제한하면서 그들의 경제 규모를 계속해서 늘릴 수 있을지는 논란의 여지가 있다'라는 의미가 되어야 하므로 형용사 (D) debatable(논란의 여지가 있는)이 정답이다. 단수 명사(A)는 관사와 함께 쓰여야 하고 복수 명사 (B)는 단수 동사 is와 함께 쓸 수 없다. 동사 debate의 현재분사 (C) debating(논의하고 있는)을 쓴다고 하

더라도, 주어 It이 빈칸 이하의 '국가들이 화석 연료 사용을 제한하면서 그들의 경제 규모를 계속해서 늘릴 수 있을지(whether countries ~ fossil fuel use)'를 지칭하므로 It이 논의하는 주체가 될 수 없기 때문에 답이 될 수 없다.

해석 국가들이 화석 연료 사용을 제한하면서 그들의 경제 규모를 계속해서 늘릴 수 있을지는 논란의 여지가 있다.

어휘 fossil fuel 화석 연료

121 부사 어휘 고르기

해설 '처음에 해외로 확장하려고 계획했었지만 대신에 국내 매출량을 늘리는 데 집중하기로 결정했다'라는 문맥이므로 (C) initially(처음에)가 정답이다. (A) negatively는 '부정적으로', (B) currently는 '지금, 현재', (D) rarely는 '드물게'라는 의미이다.

해석 Poole Automotive사는 처음에 해외로 확장하려고 계획했었지만 대신에 국내 매출량을 늘리는 데 집중하기로 결정했다.

어휘 expand v. 확장하다 overseas adv. 해외로 increase v. 늘리다
domestic adj. 국내의

122 전치사 채우기

해설 '호텔들 사이에서'라는 의미가 되어야 하므로 (D) among(~ 사이에)이 정답이다. (A) before는 '~ 앞에', (B) toward는 '~ 쪽으로', (C) onto는 '~ (위)로'라는 의미이다.

해석 일 박에 단 50달러인 Warren 호텔은 그 지역 내 많은 호텔들 사이에서 특가품으로 여겨진다.

어휘 consider v. 여기다, 생각하다 bargain n. 특가품, 싼 물건; v. 흥정하다

123 형용사 어휘 고르기

해설 '복리 후생 제도에 대해 더 알아보는 데 관심이 있는 지원자들'이라는 문맥이므로 (C) interested(관심이 있는)가 정답이다.

해석 회사의 복리 후생 제도에 대해 더 알아보는 데 관심이 있는 지원자들은 저희의 웹사이트를 방문하시면 됩니다.

어휘 find out ~을 알아보다, 발견하다 benefits package 복리 후생 제도
obsess v. 강박감을 갖다 display v. 전시하다
stimulate v. 자극하다

124 동사 관련 어구 완성하기

해설 '최신 전자레인지와 이전 모델들을 구분 짓다'라는 문맥에서 빈칸 뒤의 전치사 from과 함께 쓰여 '~을 구분 짓다'라는 의미의 어구를 이루는 (D) differentiate가 정답이다. (differentiate A from B: A와 B를 구분 짓다, 구별하다) (A) concentrate는 '집중하다, 전념하다'로 전치사 on과 함께 쓴다. (concentrate on: ~에 집중하다) (B) handle은 '다루다', (C) designate는 '지정하다'라는 의미이다.

해석 자사의 최신 전자레인지와 이전 모델들을 구분 짓기 위해, Langford Appliances사는 중대한 마케팅 캠페인을 시작했다.

어휘 microwave n. 전자레인지 launch v. 시작하다, 출시하다
major adj. 중대한, 주요한

125 명사 어휘 고르기

해설 '중심가 위치에 대한 회원들의 선호에 근거하여 Debran 센터를 택했다'라는 문맥이므로 (B) preference(선호, 선호도)가 정답이다. (A) performance는 '성과, 공연', (C) collection은 '수집, 무리', (D) exception은 '예외, 반대'라는 의미이다.

해석 소매업자 협회는 중심가 위치에 대한 회원들의 선호에 근거하여 회의를 위한 장소로 Debran 센터를 택했다.

어휘 association n. 협회, 연합 based on ~에 근거하여
central adj. 중심(가)의

126 부사절 접속사 자리 채우기

해설 이 문장은 필수성분(Mr. Cooper made appointments)을 갖춘 완전한 절이므로 ____ he ~ job은 수식어 거품으로 보아야 한다. 이 수식어 거품은 동사(had decided)가 있는 거품절이므로, 거품절을 이끌 수 있는 부사절 접속사 (A) Once(~하자마자)가 정답이다. 전치사 (B), 부사 (C)와 (D)는 거품절을 이끌 수 없다.

해석 새로운 직장을 구하기로 결심하자마자, Mr. Cooper는 몇몇 채용정보 회사들과 만날 약속을 했다.

어휘 make an appointment with ~와 만날 약속을 하다
recruitment agency 채용정보 회사

127 관계사 자리 채우기

해설 이 문장은 주어(Pacer Industries), 동사(purchased), 목적어(a factory)를 갖춘 완전한 절이므로, ____ produces ~ components는 수식어 거품으로 보아야 한다. 따라서 보기 중 수식어 거품을 이끌 수 있는 관계사 (B) that이 정답이다. 이 수식어 거품은 앞의 명사(a factory)를 뒤에서 꾸미는 역할을 하는 관계절이다. 대명사 (A) it은 수식어 거품을 이끌 수 없다. 명사절 접속사 (C) what과 (D) whether는 주어, 목적어, 보어 자리에 오는 명사절을 이끄는 접속사이므로 관계사 자리에 올 수 없다.

해석 Pacer Industries사는 중국 내 다양한 전자 부품들을 생산하는 공장을 매입했다.

어휘 a wide range of 다양한 electronic component 전자 부품

128 비교급 표현 채우기

해설 '더 짧은 시간을 일할 수 있다면'이라는 의미가 되어야 하므로 비교급 (B) shorter가 정답이다. 부사 (A)와 동사 (C)는 명사(hours)를 수식할 수 없다. '최상급 + 명사' 앞에는 주로 the나 소유격이 와야 하므로 (D)는 답이 될 수 없다.

해석 최근 여론 조사는 대부분의 직장인들이 더 짧은 시간을 일할 수 있다면 임금 삭감을 받아들일 것이라는 점을 시사한다.

어휘 poll n. 여론 조사, 투표 suggest v. 시사하다, 암시하다
take a pay cut 임금 삭감을 받아들이다 shortly adv. 곧
shorten v. 단축하다

129 관계대명사 채우기

해설 선행사(anyone)가 사람이며, 빈칸에 들어갈 관계대명사가 관계절(____ stays there ~ month) 안에서 주어 역할을 해야 한다. 따라서 주격 사람 관계대명사 (A) who가 정답이다.

해석 Paxton 호텔은 한 달에 4박 이상을 그곳에서 머무르는 누구에게나 20퍼센트의 할인을 제공한다.

130 동사 어휘 고르기

해설 '기부금들은 국립 고대 미술관을 위한 재정 지원을 제공한다'라는 문맥이므로 (C) provide(제공하다)가 정답이다. (A) notify는 '알리다', (B) interpret는 '해석하다, 설명하다', (D) confront는 '맞서다'라는 의미이다.

해석 Lumour사로부터의 기부금은 국립 고대 미술관을 위한 재정 지원을 제공한다.

어휘 donation n. 기부금, 기부 funding n. 재정 지원, 자금
ancient adj. 고대의

PART 6

131-134번은 다음 기사에 관한 문제입니다.

체인점인가 자영업체인가?

4월 11일—사업가가 직면하는 어려운 결정 사항 하나는 체인점을 여느냐 아니면 자영업체를 여느냐이다. ¹³¹두 가지 선택 모두 장점과 단점을 가지고 있다. 체인점 소유주는 브랜드 인지도를 향상시키는 데에 몇 년을 보낼 필요가 없고 본사로부터 지원을 받는다. ¹³²한편, 자영업체를 여는 사람들은 제품들을 선택할 더 많은 자유를 가지고 그것들의 가격을 어떻게 정할지를 결정할 수 있다. 고려해야 할 또 다른 요소는 초기 투자이다. ¹³³비록 가맹점을 운영하는 것은 단지 적은 초기 투자금을 필요로 하지만, 일부 수익이 회사의 본사에 지급되어야 한다. ¹³⁴그에 반해서, 자영업체 소유주는 높은 창업 비용이 있겠지만 모든 수익을 가질 것이다.

franchise n. 체인점 entrepreneur n. 사업가
face v. 직면하다, 마주보다 brand recognition 브랜드 인지도
headquarters n. 본사 set v. 정하다 initial adj. 초기의
in contrast 그에 반해서

131 알맞은 문장 고르기
해석 (A) 대부분의 사람들은 국제적인 체인점에서 쇼핑하는 것을 선호한다.
(B) 많은 업체들이 영업의 첫 해에 손해를 본다.
(C) 시중에 나와있는 몇몇 브랜드들은 값이 상당히 비싸게 매겨져 있다.
(D) 두 가지 선택 모두 장점과 단점을 가지고 있다.

해설 빈칸에 들어갈 알맞은 문장을 고르는 문제이므로 주변 문맥 또는 전체 문맥을 파악한다. 앞 문장 'A difficult decision that an entrepreneur faces is whether to open a franchise or an independent business.'에서 사업가가 직면하는 어려운 결정 사항 하나는 체인점을 여느냐 아니면 자영업체를 여느냐라고 했고, 빈칸 뒤에서 체인점 소유주와 자영업체 소유주가 갖는 장점과 단점을 설명하고 있으므로, 빈칸에는 두 가지 선택 모두 장점과 단점을 가지고 있다는 내용이 들어가야 함을 알 수 있다. 따라서 (D)가 정답이다.

어휘 lose money 손해를 보다 operation n. 영업, 운용
on the market 시중에 나와있는 significantly adv. 상당히, 현저히
overpriced adj. (제 가치보다) 값이 비싸게 매겨진, 너무 비싼

132 격에 맞는 인칭대명사 채우기
해설 명사(prices) 앞에서 형용사처럼 쓰일 수 있는 인칭대명사는 소유격이므로 (D) their(그것들의)가 정답이다.

133 부사절 접속사 채우기
해설 이 문장은 필수성분(some profits ~ headquarters)을 갖춘 완전한 절이므로 _____ running a franchise ~ investment는 수식어 거품으로 보아야 한다. 이 수식어 거품은 동사(requires)가 있는 거품절이므로, 거품절을 이끌 수 있는 부사절 접속사 (B)와 (C)가 정답의 후보이다. '비록 가맹점을 운영하는 것은 단지 적은 초기 투자금을 필요로 하지만 일부 수익이 회사의 본사에 지급되어야 한다'라는 의미가 되어야 하므로 (C) Although(비록 ~이지만)가 정답이다.

어휘 except prep. ~을 제외하고

134 동사 어휘 고르기 주변 문맥 파악
해설 '그에 반해서, 자영업체 소유주는 모든 수익을 _____ 할 것이다'라는 문맥이므로 모든 보기가 정답의 후보이다. 빈칸이 있는 문장만으로 정답을 고를 수 없으므로 주변 문맥이나 전체 문맥을 파악한다. 앞 문장에서 '가맹점을 운영하는 것은 일부 수익이 회사의 본사에 지급되어야 한다(some profits must be paid to the corporate headquarters)'라고 했으므로 그에 반해서 자영업체 소유주는 모든 수익을 가질 것임을 알 수 있다. 따라서 (D) keep(자기 것으로 갖다)이 정답이다.

어휘 estimate v. 추정하다, 평가하다 waste v. 낭비하다
eliminate v. 없애다, 제거하다

135-138번은 다음 공고에 관한 문제입니다.

모든 고객분들께:

저희는 Hamby-Russ사가 Carmona사와 합병했다는 것을 알리게 되어 기쁩니다. ¹³⁵이번 달 초에, 시애틀에 있는 저희 본사는 Hamby-Russ & Carmona사라는 이름으로 운영하기 시작했습니다.

¹³⁶이 합병은 거의 10개월간 계획되어 왔습니다. 이 기간 동안, 두 회사는 쇼핑객들에게 이용 가능한 최고의 오락 제품들을 제공하기 위한 전략을 만들기 위해 대대적으로 협상했습니다. 저희의 조직 구조에 대해 말씀드리자면, 그것은 조정되는 중입니다. ¹³⁷하지만, 저희는 기존의 모든 직원들은 유지할 것입니다. 그 결과, 여러분은 이전에 두고 있었던 동일한 판매원들과 함께 일을 처리하실 수 있을 것입니다. 저희의 전화번호들도 바뀌지 않을 것입니다. ¹³⁸어떠한 문의라도 주저하지 말고 저희 행정팀에 555-3438로 연락주십시오.

merge v. 합병하다 operate v. 운영하다
under the name ~이라는 이름으로 negotiate v. 협상하다
extensively adv. 대대적으로 recreational adj. 오락의, 기분 전환의
as for ~에 대해 말하자면 organizational structure 조직 구조
adjust v. 조정하다 original adj. 기존의, 원래의
salesperson n. 판매원 administrative adj. 행정의

135 전치사 채우기
해설 '이번 달 초에'라는 의미를 만들기 위해서 At the start of the month가 와야 하므로 (B) At(~에)이 정답이다. (A) While은 부사절 접속사로, 주어와 동사가 있는 절을 이끈다.

136 알맞은 문장 고르기
해석 (A) 저희는 운영을 완전히 중단하는 것이 최선일 것이라고 결정했습니다.
(B) 봄 쇼핑 시즌은 저희의 연중 가장 바쁜 시기입니다.
(C) 이 합병은 거의 10개월간 계획되어 왔습니다.
(D) 합의가 마무리되면 발표가 될 것입니다.

해설 빈칸에 들어갈 알맞은 문장을 고르는 문제이므로 주변 문맥 또는 전체 문맥을 파악한다. 앞부분에서 Hamby-Russ사가 Carmona사와 합병했다고 했고, 뒤 문장 'During this time, both companies negotiated extensively to develop a strategy for providing shoppers with the best recreational products available.'에서 이 기간 동안 두 회사가 쇼핑객들에게 이용 가능한 최고의 오락 제품들을 제공하기 위한 전략을 만들기 위해 대대적으로 협상했다고 했으므로, 빈칸에는 이 합병이 거의 10개월간 계획되어 왔다는 협상 기간에 대한 내용이 들어가야 함을 알 수 있다. 따라서 (C)가 정답이다.

어휘 cease v. 중단하다 entirely adv. 완전히 agreement n. 합의
finalize v. 마무리하다

137 동사 어휘 고르기 주변 문맥 파악
해설 '기존의 모든 직원들은 _____ 할 것이다'라는 문맥이므로 모든 보기가 정답의 후보이다. 빈칸이 있는 문장만으로 정답을 고를 수 없으므로 주변 문맥이나 전체 문맥을 파악한다. 뒤 문장에서 '그 결과, 이전에 두고 있었던 동일한 판매원들과 함께 일을 처리할 수 있을 것이다(As a result, you will be able to work with the same salespeople that you had before.)'라고 했으므로 기존의 모든 직원들을 유지할 것임을 알 수 있다. 따라서 (A) maintain(유지하다)이 정답이다.

어휘 transfer v. 이동하다, 옮기다 replace v. 교체하다, 대신하다
dismiss v. 해고하다, 해산시키다

138 조동사 다음에 동사원형 채우기
해설 조동사(Do) 다음에는 동사원형 (A) 또는 (B)가 와야 한다. '주저하지

말고 연락달라'는 능동의 의미가 되어야 하므로 능동태 (A) hesitate가 정답이다.

어휘 hesitate v. 주저하다, 망설이다

139-142번은 다음 고객 후기에 관한 문제입니다.

139마이애미로 가는 최근 여행을 위해, 저는 EZ Auto사를 통해 자동차 대여를 계획해두었습니다. 저는 이 회사가 경쟁사들보다 여행자들을 위한 더 낮은 일일 요금을 가지고 있기 때문에 이 회사를 선택했습니다. 그러나, 제가 공항 근처에 있는 EZ Auto사 지점에 도착했을 때, 제가 예약했었던 SUV를 이용할 수 없었습니다. 140보아하니, 날짜에 착오가 있었습니다. 부지에 트럭 하나가 있어서, 저는 대신 그것을 대여해달라고 요청했습니다. 141하지만 저는 그 더 큰 차량에 대해 전액을 지불해야 할 것이라고 통지받았고, 그것은 SUV의 전액보다 더 높았습니다. EZ Auto사 직원은 그들의 실수에 대해 보상하기 위해 저에게 추가적인 요금 없이 업그레이드를 제공해주었어야 했습니다. 142따라서, 저는 이 회사의 서비스를 향후에 다시 이용하지 않기로 결심했습니다.

recent adj. 최근의 arrange v. 계획하다, 정리하다
competitor n. 경쟁사 unavailable adj. 이용할 수 없는 lot n. 부지
compensate v. 보상하다

139 명사 어휘 고르기 전체 문맥 파악

해설 '자동차 ____를 계획해두었다'라는 문맥이므로 모든 보기가 정답의 후보이다. 빈칸이 있는 문장만으로 정답을 고를 수 없으므로 주변 문맥이나 전체 문맥을 파악한다. 뒤 문장에서 '회사가 여행자들을 위한 더 낮은 일일 요금(lower daily rates for travelers)을 가지고 있다'고 했고, 뒷부분에서 '예약했었던 SUV를 이용할 수 없었다(the SUV I had reserved was unavailable)'라고 했으므로 자동차 대여를 계획해두었음을 알 수 있다. 따라서 (B) rental(대여)이 정답이다.

어휘 repair n. 수리, 보수 inspection n. 점검 delivery n. 배달

140 알맞은 문장 고르기

해석 (A) 그들은 네비게이션 시스템에 대한 제 신청 기록을 갖고 있지 않았습니다.
(B) 유감스럽게도, 다른 차량들이 없었습니다.
(C) 보아하니, 날짜에 착오가 있었습니다.
(D) 저는 이미 환불을 요청했습니다.

해설 빈칸에 들어갈 알맞은 문장을 고르는 문제이므로 주변 문맥 또는 전체 문맥을 파악한다. 앞 문장 'the SUV I had reserved was unavailable'에서 자신이 예약했었던 SUV를 이용할 수 없었다고 했으므로 빈칸에는 예약 차량을 이용할 수 없었던 이유인 날짜에 착오가 있었다는 내용이 들어가야 함을 알 수 있다. 따라서 (C)가 정답이다. (B)는 뒤 문장 'As there was a truck on the lot, I asked to rent it instead.'에서 부지에 트럭 하나가 있어서 대신 그것을 대여해달라고 요청했다고 했으므로 답이 될 수 없다.

어휘 apparently adv. 보아하니, 듣자 하니

141 태에 맞는 동사 채우기

해설 주절에 동사가 없으므로 동사 (A), (B), (D)가 정답의 후보이다. 주어(I)와 동사(inform)가 '내가 통지를 받다'라는 수동의 의미를 가지므로 수동태 동사 (A) was informed가 정답이다. 참고로, inform은 목적어를 2개 갖는 4형식 동사이므로, 이 문장은 능동태 문장이 수동태 문장이 되면서 간접 목적어(I)가 주어로 오고 직접 목적어(that ~ vehicle)가 동사 뒤에 남은 형태이다.

어휘 inform v. 통지하다, 알리다

142 to 부정사 채우기

해설 동사 decide(have decided) 다음에는 to 부정사가 와야 하므로 (A) to use가 정답이다.

143-146번은 다음 회람에 관한 문제입니다.

발신: Diane Langston, 영업부장
수신: 모든 직원들
날짜: 9월 23일
제목: 가을 마라톤 거리 폐쇄

연례 Renfield 가을 마라톤이 이번 주 금요일에 열립니다. 143행사 동안 일부 인근 거리가 폐쇄될 수 있음을 유의하십시오. 144Sandy Brook로와 우리 건물 옆 주차장은 오전 9시부터 오후 2시까지 들어갈 수 없을 것입니다. 그래서 만약 여러분이 평소에 운전해서 출근한다면, 여러분은 다른 계획을 세워야 합니다. 145예를 들어, 29번가에 여러분이 사용할 수 있는 주차장이 있습니다. 이곳은 사무실에서 걸어서 단 5분이 걸립니다. 여러분은 또한 Davis로로 가는 버스도 탈 수 있는데, 그곳은 여기에서 두 블록 떨어져 있습니다. 여러분은 모든 버스 노선을 온라인으로 조회할 수 있습니다. 146도움이 더 필요하시면, 제게 알려주시면 됩니다.

take place 열리다, 발생하다 garage n. 주차장, 차고
normally adv. 평소에 assistance n. 도움

143 다른 명사를 수식하는 명사 채우기

해설 '인근 거리'라는 복합 명사의 의미이므로 복합 명사를 만드는 명사 (C) neighborhood가 정답이다.

어휘 neighborly adj. 사교성 있는, 친절한 neighbor n. 이웃, 주변 사람
neighborliness n. 이웃 사람다움, 이웃 사랑

144 형용사 어휘 고르기 주변 문맥 파악

해설 'Sandy Brook로와 우리 건물 옆 주차장은 오전 9시부터 오후 2시까지 ____할 것입니다'라는 문맥이므로 (A) safe(안전한)와 (C) inaccessible(들어갈 수 없는)이 정답의 후보이다. 빈칸이 있는 문장만으로 정답을 고를 수 없으므로 주변 문맥이나 전체 문맥을 파악한다. 앞 문장에서 '행사 동안 일부 거리가 폐쇄될 수 있음을 유의하십시오(Be aware that some ~ streets may be closed during the event.)'라고 했고, 뒤 문장에서 '그래서 만약 평소에 운전해서 출근한다면 다른 계획을 세워야 합니다(So if you normally drive to work, you should make other plans.)'라고 했으므로 Sandy Brook로와 건물 옆 주차장은 오전 9시부터 오후 2시까지 들어갈 수 없을 것임을 알 수 있다. 따라서 형용사 (C) inaccessible이 정답이다.

어휘 vulnerable adj. 취약한, 연약한 acceptable adj. 용인되는

145 알맞은 문장 고르기

해석 (A) 만약 여러분이 재택 근무를 할 수 있다면, 저는 그렇게 하는 것을 추천합니다.
(B) 다행히도, 우리는 일시적인 불편함만 겪었을 뿐입니다.
(C) 사무실은 마라톤이 끝난 후에 문을 열 것입니다.
(D) 예를 들어, 29번가에 여러분이 사용할 수 있는 주차장이 있습니다.

해설 빈칸에 들어갈 알맞은 문장을 고르는 문제이므로 주변 문맥 또는 전체 문맥을 파악한다. 앞 문장 'So if you normally drive to work, you should make other plans.'에서 만약 평소에 운전해서 출근한다면 다른 계획을 세워야 한다고 했고, 뒤 문장 'It is only a five-minute walk from the office.'에서 이곳은 사무실에서 걸어서 단 5분이 걸린다고 했으므로, 빈칸에는 예를 들어 29번가에 사용할 수 있는 주차장이 있다는 내용이 들어가야 함을 알 수 있다. 따라서 (D)가 정답이다.

어휘 telecommute v. 재택 근무하다

146 if 없는 가정법

해설 '도움이 더 필요하면, 제게 알려주시면 됩니다'라는 의미가 되어야 하므로 (B) Should you need가 정답이다. 'Should + 주어 + 동사원형'은 '~이라면'의 의미이고, 이는 가정법 미래 문장 'If + 주어 + should + 동사원형'에서 If가 생략되면서 주어와 조동사(should)의

도치가 일어난 것이다. 참고로, 가정법 미래 문장에서 If가 생략되는 경우, 'Should + 주어 + 동사원형, 주어 + will(can, may, should) + 동사원형'의 형태를 만든다.

PART 7

147-148번은 다음 온라인 후기에 관한 문제입니다.

https://www.oakridge.com/customerreviews

고객 이름: Ruth Bell
평점: ★
날짜: 4월 3일
제목: Lucas 커피 테이블

2월 10일에 저는 Oakridge Furniture사에서 커피 테이블을 주문했습니다. 전반적으로, 이 가구에 만족합니다. 디자인이 매우 멋지고 현대적이며, 147-C테이블은 제 새 아파트의 거실에 딱 맞는 크기입니다. 147-A조립하는 것도 매우 쉬웠습니다. 148제가 이 회사에 다섯 개 중에 단 한 개의 별만 주는 이유는 제 주문품이 도착하는 데에 예상보다 훨씬 더 오래 걸렸기 때문입니다. 저는 원래 3월 8일에 그것이 배송될 것이라고 들었지만, 3월 26일이 되어서야 제 집에 배달되었습니다. 회사의 배달 시스템에 기술적인 오류가 있어 테이블이 잘못된 주소로 배송이 되었던 것 같습니다. 저는 이 과실에 대한 사과와 심지어 할인까지도 받았어야 했지만, 그렇지 못했습니다. 그렇기 때문에, 저는 Oakridge Furniture사에서 다시 물건을 사지 않을 것 같습니다.

order v. 주문하다; n. 주문품 overall adv. 전반적으로
assemble v. 조립하다 originally adv. 원래
drop off (물건을) 배달하다 distribution n. 배달, 유통
result in (결과적으로) ~이 되다

147 Not/True 문제

문제 Ms. Bell에 대해 언급된 것은?
(A) 테이블을 조립할 수 없었다.
(B) 가구 한 점을 반품할 것이다.
(C) 새 거주지로 이사했다.
(D) 새 아파트를 찾고 있다.

해설 질문의 핵심 어구인 Ms. Bell과 관련된 내용을 지문에서 찾아 보기와 대조하는 Not/True 문제이다. (A)는 'It was also very easy to assemble.'에서 조립하는 것이 매우 쉬웠다고 했으므로 지문의 내용과 일치하지 않는다. (B)는 지문에 언급되지 않은 내용이다. (C)는 'the table is just the right size for the living room of my new apartment'에서 테이블이 새 아파트의 거실에 딱 맞는 크기라고 한 것에서 Ms. Bell이 새 거주지로 이사했음을 알 수 있으므로 지문의 내용과 일치한다. 따라서 (C)가 정답이다. (D)는 지문에 언급되지 않은 내용이다.

어휘 residence n. 거주지, 주택

148 육하원칙 문제

문제 Ms. Bell은 왜 회사에 좋지 않은 평가를 주는가?
(A) 물품이 더 이상 재고가 없다.
(B) 사과 편지가 너무 늦게 보내졌다.
(C) 상품이 운송 중에 파손되었다.
(D) 배송이 예정대로 도착하지 않았다.

해설 Ms. Bell이 왜(Why) 회사에 좋지 않은 평가를 줬는지를 묻는 육하원칙 문제이다. 질문의 핵심 어구인 a poor review와 관련하여, 'The reason that I am giving this company only one star out of a possible five is that my order took much longer than expected to arrive.'에서 Ms. Bell이 이 회사에 다섯 개 중에 단 한

개의 별만 주는 이유는 주문품이 도착하는 데에 예상보다 훨씬 더 오래 걸렸기 때문이라고 했으므로 (D)가 정답이다.

패러프레이징
a poor review 좋지 않은 평가 → only one star out of a possible five 다섯 개 중에 단 한 개의 별
took much longer than expected to arrive 도착하는 데에 예상보다 훨씬 더 오래 걸렸다 → did not arrive on schedule 예정대로 도착하지 않았다

어휘 be in stock 재고가 있다 package n. 상품, 소포
in transit 운송 중에 on schedule 예정대로

149-150번은 다음 메시지 대화문에 관한 문제입니다.

Mia Heilig [오후 2시 37분]
안녕하세요, Chantal. 제 비행기가 날씨가 좋지 않아 방금 연착됐어요. 그래서, 149-A제가 몬트리올에 언제 도착할지 확실하지 않아요.

Chantal Lacroix [오후 2시 39분]
얼마나 연착이 되죠? 150그래도 여기에 오늘 밤에는 오시는 거죠, 그렇죠?

Mia Heilig [오후 2시 45분]
가능성이 없어 보여요. 제 출발 시간이 3시간 뒤로 미뤄져서, 149-C/150덴버에서의 연결편 비행기를 놓치게 될 거예요. 이용 가능한 다음 것을 타야 할텐데, 150그게 언제가 될지 모르겠어요.

Chantal Lacroix [오후 2시 47분]
유감이네요. 어쨌든, 149-D덴버에 도착하시면 저에게 연락하셔서 새로 바뀐 도착 시간을 말씀해주세요. 알게 되는 즉시 제가 저희 운전 기사와 필요한 준비를 해둘게요.

delay v. 연착하다; n. 연착 departure time 출발 시간
push back (시간 등을) 미루다 mean v. (결국) ~하게 되다, 뜻하다
connecting flight 연결편 비행기 available adj. 이용 가능한
arrival time 도착 시간 arrangement n. 준비

149 Not/True 문제

문제 Ms. Heilig에 대해 사실인 것은?
(A) 몬트리올에서 출발했다.
(B) Ms. Lacroix를 태우러 갈 것이다.
(C) 여러 비행기를 탈 것이다.
(D) 덴버에서 Ms. Lacroix에게 연락했다.

해설 질문의 핵심 어구인 Ms. Heilig와 관련된 내용을 지문에서 찾아 보기와 대조하는 Not/True 문제이다. (A)는 'I'm not sure when I'll be arriving in Montreal'(2:37 P.M.)에서 몬트리올에 언제 도착할지 확실하지 않다고 했으므로 지문의 내용과 일치하지 않는다. (B)는 지문에 언급되지 않은 내용이다. (C)는 'I'll miss my connecting flight in Denver. I'll have to get the next available one'(2:45 P.M.)에서 연결편 비행기를 타야 한다고 했으므로 지문의 내용과 일치한다. 따라서 (C)가 정답이다. (D)는 'call me when you get to Denver'(2:47 P.M.)에서 Ms. Lacroix가 Ms. Heilig에게 덴버에 도착하면 연락하라고 했으므로 지문의 내용과 일치하지 않는다.

어휘 pick up ~를 (차에) 태워 가다 multiple adj. 여러, 다수의

150 의도 파악 문제

문제 오후 2시 45분에, Ms. Heilig가 "It's not looking good"이라고 썼을 때, 그녀가 의도한 것 같은 것은?
(A) 티켓을 교환할 수 없다.
(B) 환불을 받지 못할 수도 있다.
(C) 운전 기사에게 연락할 수 없다.
(D) 오늘 밤에 도착하지 못할 수도 있다.

해설 Ms. Heilig가 의도한 것 같은 것을 묻는 문제이므로, 질문의 인용어구(It's not looking good)가 언급된 주변 문맥을 확인한다. 'You'll still be getting here tonight, right?'(2:39 P.M.)에서 Ms. Lacroix가 Ms. Heilig에게 여기에 오늘 밤에는 오는 게 맞는지 묻자 Ms. Heilig가 'It's not looking good'(가능성이 없어 보여요)이라고 한 후, 'I'll miss my connecting flight in Denver. I'll have to get the next available one, but I don't know when that will be.'(2:45 P.M.)에서 덴버에서의 연결편 비행기를 놓치게 될 것이라고 한 후, 이용 가능한 다음 것을 타야 할텐데 그게 언제가 될지 모르겠다고 한 것을 통해, Ms. Heilig가 오늘 밤에 도착하지 못할 수도 있다는 것을 알 수 있다. 따라서 (D)가 정답이다.

어휘 exchange v. 교환하다 refund n. 환불

151-152번은 다음 광고에 관한 문제입니다.

Video Marketing사
372번지 Highland가
모빌, 앨라배마 주 36575
555-8230

[151-C]Video Marketing사에서는, 아이디어 창출, 대본 작성, 캐스팅, 연출, 촬영, 편집을 포함하여, 당신의 사업을 위한 다양한 영상 제작 서비스들을 제공합니다.

저희는 모든 유형 및 규모의 단체들을 위한 영상들을 제작합니다. 마케팅 캠페인, 제품 설명회, 혹은 교육 워크숍들을 위한 영상들이 필요하시다면 저희에게 연락하세요. 저희는 영상 제작 과정의 모든 단계에 대해 잘 알고 있는 다양한 전문가들을 고용합니다. 물론, 저희의 촬영 장비와 무대 소품들은 이용할 수 있는 최상의 품질입니다.

[152]11월 1일부터 12월 31일까지, 저희는 소규모 사업주들을 위한 특별 겨울 할인 혜택을 제공해 드립니다. 단 2,000달러에, 당신의 기업을 위한 30초짜리 영상을 만들어드릴 것입니다. 그 다음, 저희 온라인 마케팅 팀이 당신의 영상을 소셜 미디어 사이트들에 홍보하는 방법에 대한 팁들을 드릴 것입니다. 이것은 당신이 텔레비전 방송국들에 비용이 많이 드는 방송 시간을 위해 지불해야 할 필요 없이 당신의 광고가 많은 시청자들에게 보여지도록 할 것입니다. 이 할인 혜택이나 전반적으로 저희 회사에 대한 더 많은 정보를 얻으시려면, www.videomarketing enterprise.com으로 저희 웹사이트를 방문하세요.

generation n. 창출, 발생 script n. 대본 directing n. 연출
filming n. 촬영 editing n. 편집
product demonstration 제품 설명회 professional n. 전문가
knowledgeable adj. 잘 아는 not to mention ~은 물론이고
props n. 소품 promote v. 홍보하다 audience n. 시청자
costly adv. 비용이 많이 드는 airtime n. 방송 시간
television network 방송국 in general 전반적으로

---

151 Not/True 문제

문제 Video Marketing사에 대해 언급된 것은?
(A) 몇 안 되는 직원들만 있다.
(B) 영화 제작자들을 위한 워크숍을 진행한다.
(C) 다양한 서비스들을 제공한다.
(D) 영상 제작 장비를 판매한다.

해설 질문의 핵심 어구인 Video Marketing Enterprise와 관련된 내용을 지문에서 찾아 보기와 대조하는 Not/True 문제이다. (A)와 (B)는 지문에 언급되지 않은 내용이다. (C)는 'At Video Marketing Enterprise, we offer various video production services for your business, including idea generation, script writing, casting, directing, filming, and editing.'에서 Video Marketing사에서는 아이디어 창출, 대본 작성, 캐스팅, 연출, 촬영, 편집을 포함하여 다양한 영상 제작 서비스들을 제공한다고 했으므로 지문의 내용과 일치한다. 따라서 (C)가 정답이다. (D)는 지문에 언급되지 않은 내용이다.

어휘 filmmaker n. 영화 제작자 a wide range of 다양한

152 육하원칙 문제

문제 11월 1일부터 12월 31일까지 무슨 일이 일어날 것인가?
(A) 웹사이트가 업데이트될 것이다.
(B) 회사가 확장될 것이다.
(C) 판촉 활동이 열릴 것이다.
(D) 소셜 미디어 플랫폼이 출시될 것이다.

해설 11월 1일부터 12월 31일까지 무슨(What) 일이 일어날 것인지를 묻는 육하원칙 문제이다. 질문의 핵심 어구인 from November 1 to December 31과 관련하여, 'From November 1 to December 31, we are offering a special winter deal for small business owners.'에서 11월 1일부터 12월 31일까지 소규모 사업주들을 위한 특별 겨울 할인 혜택을 제공한다고 했으므로 (C)가 정답이다.

패러프레이징
offering a special ~ deal 특별 할인 혜택을 제공하다 → A promotion will be held 판촉 활동이 열릴 것이다

어휘 expand v. 확장하다 promotion n. 판촉 활동, 홍보
launch v. 출시하다

153-154번은 다음 이메일에 관한 문제입니다.

수신: 모든 강사들
발신: Adam Fitzpatrick
　　　<afitzpatrick@hardingbusinessinstitute.com>
제목: 최신 정보
[153]날짜: 6월 17일

안녕하세요 여러분,

여러분도 아마 아시다시피, [153]어제의 태풍으로 인해 Farley 건물의 지하실이 지난밤에 침수되었습니다. 따라서, 우리는 지하실에서 열리는 모든 수업들을 임시로 옆 건물 Sherman 센터로 옮길 것입니다. 여기 임시 방 배정 목록이 있습니다:

수업	강사	방
당신의 신생 기업에 투자자들 유치하기	Mark Helling	200
브랜드 상품화 101	Jesse Weiner	205
상급 재무 회계	Helen Boucher	207
소셜 미디어를 이용한 마케팅	Megan Davis	210

여러분의 수업 시간들은 동일하게 유지될 것이며, 학생들은 오늘 오후에 이 상황에 대해 이메일로 통지받을 것입니다. Farley 건물의 관리인인 [154]Alfred King은 침수된 방들이 다음 3일 동안 깨끗이 치워지고 보수될 것이라고 저에게 알렸습니다. 그는 방들이 다음 주 월요일에 다시 사용 가능할 것이라고 말했습니다.

문의 사항이 있으시면 저에게 연락주십시오.

Adam Fitzpatrick 드림
총장, Harding 경영 전문 교육기관

basement n. 지하실 flood v. 침수시키다 typhoon n. 태풍
temporarily adv. 임시로 meet v. (수업 등이) 열리다, 모이다
assignment n. 배정 advanced adj. 상급의, 선진의
financial accounting 재무 회계 notify v. 통지하다
clean out 깨끗이 치우다 available adj. (사용) 가능한

---

153 육하원칙 문제

문제 회람에 따르면, 6월 16일에 무슨 일이 일어났는가?
(A) 폭풍이 발생했다.
(B) 몇몇 수업들이 취소되었다.
(C) 몇몇 시험들이 채점되었다.

(D) 강사 한 명이 휴가를 갔다.

해설 6월 16일에 무슨(what) 일이 일어났는지를 묻는 육하원칙 문제이다. 질문의 핵심 어구인 June 16과 관련하여, 'Date: June 17'에서 회람이 작성된 날짜가 6월 17일임을 알 수 있고, 'yesterday's typhoon'에서 어제의 태풍이라고 했으므로 6월 16일에 태풍이 발생했음을 알 수 있다. 따라서 (A)가 정답이다.

어휘 storm n. 폭풍 correct v. 채점하다, 정정하다

154 육하원칙 문제

문제 Mr. King은 Mr. Fitzpatrick에게 무엇을 말했는가?
(A) Sherman 센터의 2층이 열려있다.
(B) 마케팅 관련 수업은 예정대로 열릴 수 있다.
(C) 수해는 보수하는 데 너무 많은 비용이 든다.
(D) Farley 건물 지하실은 다음 주에 사용 가능할 것이다.

해설 Mr. King이 Mr. Fitzpatrick에게 무엇을(What) 말했는지를 묻는 육하원칙 문제이다. 질문의 핵심 어구인 Mr. King tell Mr. Fitzpatrick과 관련하여, 'Alfred King ~ informed me that the flooded rooms ~ will be available for use again next Monday.'에서 Mr. King이 회람의 작성자 Mr. Fitzpatrick에게 침수된 방들이 다음 주 월요일에 다시 사용 가능할 것이라고 알렸다고 했으므로 (D)가 정답이다.

어휘 as scheduled 예정대로 water damage 수해

155-157번은 다음 공고에 관한 문제입니다.

공고

[155]Thomas Anderson 시장의 재활용 계획을 지지하는 Bristol 시의회는 Sanders Waste Management사와의 계약을 올해 말까지 끝내기로 합의했습니다. 그 시점부터, 모든 폐기물은 Perry Waste and Recycling사에 의해 처리될 것입니다.

[156-A]이 재활용 계획의 결과로, Bristol 주민들은 1월 1일부터 그들의 쓰레기를 분리하도록 요청될 것입니다. 금속, 유리, 그리고 종이는 녹색 쓰레기통에 넣게 되는 반면, 일반 쓰레기는 검은색 쓰레기통에 넣게 될 것입니다. 새로운 쓰레기통은 자세한 소책자와 함께 이번 주에 배달될 것입니다. [157]주민들은 인쇄된 지침서를 주의 깊게 검토할 것이 권고됩니다.

mayor n. 시장 initiative n. 계획 conclude v. 끝내다, 마치다 contract n. 계약 separate v. 분리시키다 bin n. 쓰레기통 along with ~과 함께 pamphlet n. 소책자

---

155 목적 찾기 문제

문제 공고의 목적은 무엇인가?
(A) 의회 회의를 요청하기 위해
(B) 프로젝트에 대한 지원을 표명하기 위해
(C) 서비스 변경을 알리기 위해
(D) 프로그램의 성공을 보고하기 위해

해설 공고의 목적을 묻는 목적 찾기 문제이다. 'The Bristol City Council ~ has agreed to conclude its contract with Sanders Waste Management by the end of the year. From that point on, all waste will be handled by Perry Waste and Recycling.'에서 Bristol 시의회가 Sanders Waste Management사와의 계약을 올해 말까지 끝내기로 합의했고 그 시점부터 모든 폐기물이 Perry Waste and Recycling사에 의해 처리될 것이라고 했으므로 (C)가 정답이다.

어휘 call for ~을 요청하다 report v. 보고하다

156 Not/True 문제

문제 재활용 계획에 대해 언급된 것은?
(A) 다음 해에 시행될 것이다.

(B) 이전 시장에 의해 제안되었다.
(C) 의회 의원에 의해 관리될 것이다.
(D) 더 큰 캠페인의 일부이다.

해설 질문의 핵심 어구인 recycling initiative와 관련된 내용을 지문에서 찾아 보기와 대조하는 Not/True 문제이다. (A)는 'As a result of this recycling initiative, Bristol residents will be asked to separate their trash beginning January 1.'에서 재활용 계획의 결과로 Bristol 주민들은 1월 1일부터 그들의 쓰레기를 분리하도록 요청될 것이라고 했으므로 지문의 내용과 일치한다. 따라서 (A)가 정답이다. (B), (C), (D)는 지문에 언급되지 않은 내용이다.

어휘 take effect 시행되다

157 육하원칙 문제

문제 Bristol 주민들은 무엇을 하도록 권장되는가?
(A) 쓰레기를 더 자주 버린다.
(B) 한 종류의 쓰레기통을 사용한다.
(C) 시의회 회의에 참석한다.
(D) 서류를 읽는다.

해설 Bristol 주민들이 무엇을(What) 하도록 권장되는지를 묻는 육하원칙 문제이다. 질문의 핵심 어구인 Bristol residents encouraged to do와 관련하여, 'Residents are advised to review the printed guidelines carefully.'에서 주민들은 인쇄된 지침서를 주의 깊게 검토할 것이 권고된다고 했으므로 (D)가 정답이다.

패러프레이징
are ~ encouraged 권장되다 → are advised 권고되다
review the printed guidelines 인쇄된 지침서를 검토하다 → Read a document 서류를 읽다

어휘 dispose of ~을 버리다, 처분하다

158-161번은 다음 기사에 관한 문제입니다.

---
*On the Loose Again*이 Goldwin 극장에서 개봉될 예정이다

[158-A/C/160-A]인기 있는 코미디 *On the Loose*의 속편인 *On the Loose Again*이 5월 16일에 Goldwin 극장에서 개봉될 것이다. [158-C]두 영화 모두의 주연인 Max Walter와 Elena Marconi가 참석할 것이며, 영화가 상영되기 전에 간단한 사진 촬영이 있을 것이다. [159]극장이 열자마자 레드 카펫 행사가 시작될 것이며, 영화는 한 시간 뒤인 오후 6시부터 오후 8시까지 상영될 것이다. 영화 직후에는 출연진 및 제작진과의 질의응답 시간이 있을 것이다. 마지막으로, 오후 8시 30분에는 사인회가 열릴 것이다.

*On the Loose Again*은 이전 영화가 끝났던 부분에서 계속 이어진다. 이 영화는 탈주범과 그의 아내를 그리는데 그들은 경찰을 피하려고 시도하면서 미국 남부 전역에 걸쳐 이동한다. [160-A/B]*Above Ground*와 *Special Investigations*를 포함해 수많은 인기 텔레비전 시리즈들도 제작한 감독 Jamie Moya가 [160-A]원작 영화의 감독 Richard Weber의 뒤를 이었다. 첫 번째 영화가 꽤 흥행했기 때문에, *On the Loose Again*은 많은 관객들을 끌어들일 것으로 예상된다. [161]시사회를 위한 표를 구하고 싶은 사람들은 www.goldwintheater.com/tickets를 방문하거나 555-3716으로 전화하여 그것들을 상당히 미리 구입해야 할 것이다.

premiere v. 개봉되다; n. 시사회 sequel to ~의 속편 star n. 주연 be in attendance 참석하다 photo shoot 사진 촬영 question and answer session 질의응답 시간 cast n. 출연진 feature v. (특징을) 그리다, 특별히 포함하다 escaped adj. 탈출한 criminal n. 범죄자 numerous adj. 수많은 replace v. ~의 뒤를 잇다, 대신하다 draw v. 끌어들이다 obtain v. 구하다, 얻다 well adv. 상당히, 꽤 in advance 사전에, 미리

---

158 Not/True 문제

문제 *On the Loose Again*에 대해 사실인 것은?
(A) 시리즈의 세 번째 영화이다.
(B) 청소년들 사이에서 특히 인기가 있다.
(C) 첫 번째 영화와 동일한 배우들을 주연으로 한다.
(D) 긍정적인 평가들을 받았다.

해설 질문의 핵심 어구인 *On the Loose Again*과 관련된 내용을 지문에서 찾아 보기와 대조하는 Not/True 문제이다. (A)는 'On the Loose Again, the sequel to the popular comedy *On the Loose*'에서 *On the Loose Again*이 *On the Loose*의 속편이라고 했으므로 지문의 내용과 일치하지 않는다. (B)는 지문에 언급되지 않은 내용이다. (C)는 'On the Loose Again, the sequel to the popular comedy *On the Loose*'와 'The stars of both films—Max Walter and Elena Marconi—'에서 *On the Loose*와 그 속편 *On the Loose Again* 두 영화 모두의 주연인 Max Walter와 Elena Marconi라고 한 것에서 *On the Loose Again*에 첫 번째 영화와 동일한 배우들이 주연함을 알 수 있으므로 지문의 내용과 일치한다. 따라서 (C)가 정답이다. (D)는 지문에 언급되지 않은 내용이다.

어휘 review n. 평가

159 동의어 찾기 문제

문제 1문단 여섯 번째 줄의 단어 "shown"은 의미상 –와 가장 가깝다.
(A) 노출된
(B) 보고된
(C) 수행된
(D) 상영된

해설 shown을 포함한 문장 'The red carpet event will begin as soon as the theater opens, and the film will be shown one hour later, from 6 p.m. to 8 p.m.'에서 shown은 '상영된'이라는 뜻으로 사용되었다. 따라서 (D)가 정답이다.

160 Not/True 문제

문제 Mr. Moya에 대해 언급된 것은?
(A) *On the Loose*의 감독이었다.
(B) 텔레비전 작품으로 알려져 있다.
(C) Ms. Marconi의 친구이다.
(D) *On the Loose Again*의 대본을 썼다.

해설 질문의 핵심 어구인 Mr. Moya와 관련된 내용을 지문에서 찾아 보기와 대조하는 Not/True 문제이다. (A)는 'On the Loose Again, the sequel to ~ *On the Loose*'와 'Director Jamie Moya ~ replaced Richard Weber, the director of the original movie.'에서 Jamie Moya가 원작 영화인 *On the Loose*의 감독 Richard Weber의 뒤를 이었다고 했으므로 지문의 내용과 일치하지 않는다. (B)는 'Director Jamie Moya, who has also produced numerous popular television series'에서 수많은 인기 텔레비전 시리즈들도 제작한 감독 Jamie Moya라고 했으므로 지문의 내용과 일치한다. 따라서 (B)가 정답이다. (C)와 (D)는 지문에 언급되지 않은 내용이다.

패러프레이징
has ~ produced numerous popular television series 수많은 인기 텔레비전 시리즈들을 제작했다 → is known for ~ work in television 텔레비전 작품으로 알려져 있다

어휘 be known for ~으로 알려져 있다 script n. 대본

161 육하원칙 문제

문제 기사는 사람들에게 무엇을 하라고 권고하는가?
(A) 오후 8시까지 극장에 간다.
(B) 표를 일찍 구입한다.
(C) 사진 촬영에 참여한다.
(D) 온라인으로 추첨에 참가한다.

해설 기사가 사람들에게 무엇(What)을 하라고 권고하는지를 묻는 육하원칙 문제이다. 질문의 핵심 어구인 advise people to do와 관련하여, 'Those wishing to obtain tickets to the premiere should buy them well in advance'에서 시사회를 위한 표를 구하고 싶은 사람들은 그것들을 상당히 미리 구입해야 할 것이라고 했으므로 (B)가 정답이다.

어휘 raffle n. 추첨, 복권

162-165번은 다음 온라인 채팅 대화문에 관한 문제입니다.

Robin Underwood [오후 8시 30분]
안녕하세요, 여러분. 제가 신규 체육관 회원들을 끌어들일 수 있는 방법을 찾아낸 것 같아요.

Franklin Bates [오후 8시 31분]
기쁘네요. ¹⁶²⁻ᴮ우리는 길 아래쪽에 최근에 개장한 헬스장에 많은 고객들을 잃었어요. 당신의 계획이 무엇인가요?

Robin Underwood [오후 8시 33분]
¹⁶³6개월 회원권을 신청하는 신규 회원들에게 한 달 치 요금을 적용하지 않고 1년 회원권일 경우 두 달 치 요금을 적용하지 않을 수 있어요.

Norma Flores [오후 8시 34분]
다른 많은 체육관들에 비슷한 판촉 활동들이 있어요. ¹⁶³아마 우리는 더 많은 걸 해야 할 거예요.

Robin Underwood [오후 8시 35분]
그게 바로 제가 우리 기존 회원들에게 우리를 친구들에게 추천하는 걸 권장하는 것도 계획하고 있는 이유예요. ¹⁶⁴다른 사람을 여기에 등록하도록 하는 회원들은 선물로 무료 체육관 가방을 받을 거예요.

Franklin Bates [오후 8시 37분]
그건 아마 효과가 있을 것 같네요. ¹⁶⁵제가 이 정보를 우리 웹사이트에 추가하기를 원하시나요? 제가 가르치는 첫 번째 운동 수업이 내일 오후 1시가 되어서야 있어서, 점심 전에 이것을 할 시간이 있을 거예요.

Robin Underwood [오후 8시 38분]
그거 좋을 것 같네요. Norma, 이 새 정책에 관한 안내문들을 체육관 안에 게시해줄 수 있나요?

Norma Flores [오후 8시 38분]
물론이죠. 제가 다른 직원들에게도 알려서 그들이 우리 고객들에게 알려줄 수 있도록 할게요.

come up with (해답·돈 등을) 찾아내다   attract v. 끌어들이다
waive v. (규칙 등을) 적용하지 않다, (권리 등을) 포기하다
sign up 등록하다   existing adj. 기존의   put up ~을 게시하다
notice n. 안내문   notify v. 알리다

---

162 Not/True 문제

문제 Ms. Underwood가 일하고 있는 체육관에 대해 언급된 것은?
(A) 두 번째 지점을 개장했다.
(B) 새로운 경쟁자가 있다.
(C) 다른 위치로 옮길 것이다.
(D) 2개월 회원권을 제공한다.

해설 질문의 핵심 어구인 gym where Ms. Underwood works와 관련된 내용을 지문에서 찾아 보기와 대조하는 Not/True 문제이다. (A)는 지문에 언급되지 않은 내용이다. (B)는 'We've lost a lot of customers to the fitness center that recently opened down the street.'(8:31 P.M.)에서 길 아래쪽에 최근에 개장한 헬스장에 많은 고객들을 잃었다고 했으므로 지문의 내용과 일치한다. 따라서 (B)가 정답이다. (C)와 (D)는 지문에 언급되지 않은 내용이다.

패러프레이징
the fitness center that recently opened 최근에 개장한 헬스장
→ a new competitor 새로운 경쟁자

어휘 competitor n. 경쟁자

163 의도 파악 문제

문제 오후 8시 34분에, Ms. Flores가 "Lots of other gyms have similar promotions"라고 썼을 때, 그녀가 의도한 것 같은 것은?
(A) 제안을 따라 하고 싶어 한다.
(B) 제안에 동의한다.
(C) 계획에 대해 확신이 없다.
(D) 몇 가지 세부 사항을 확인할 필요가 있다.

해설 Ms. Flores가 의도한 것 같은 것을 묻는 문제이므로, 질문의 인용어구(Lots of other gyms have similar promotions)가 언급된 주변 문맥을 확인한다. 'We can waive one month's fee for new members who sign up for a six-month membership and two months' fees if it's an annual membership.'(8:33 P.M.)에서 Ms. Underwood가 6개월 회원권을 신청하는 신규 회원에게 한 달 치 요금을 적용하지 않고 1년 회원권일 경우 두 달 치 요금을 적용하지 않는 계획을 설명하자, Ms. Flores가 'Lots of other gyms have similar promotions'(다른 많은 체육관에 비슷한 판촉 활동들이 있어요)라고 한 후, 'Maybe we need to do more.'(8:34 P.M.)에서 아마 더 많은 걸 해야 할 것이라고 한 것을 통해, Ms. Flores가 계획에 대해 확신이 없다는 것을 알 수 있다. 따라서 (C)가 정답이다.

어휘 imitate v. 따라 하다, 본받다 doubtful adj. 확신이 없는

164 육하원칙 문제

문제 일부 기존 회원들은 무엇을 받을 자격이 있을 것인가?
(A) 상품권
(B) 요금 인하
(C) 회원권 상향
(D) 무료 물품

해설 일부 기존 회원들이 무엇(What)을 받을 자격이 있을 것인지를 묻는 육하원칙 문제이다. 질문의 핵심 어구인 some existing members be eligible to receive와 관련하여, 'Members[existing members] who get someone else to sign up here will receive a free gym bag as a gift.'(8:35 P.M.)에서 다른 사람을 등록하도록 하는 기존 회원들은 선물로 무료 체육관 가방을 받을 것이라고 했으므로 (D)가 정답이다.

어휘 be eligible to ~할 자격이 있다 gift certificate 상품권 reduction n. 인하 complimentary adj. 무료의

165 추론 문제

문제 Mr. Bates는 내일 아침에 무엇을 할 것 같은가?
(A) 안내문들을 출력한다.
(B) 운동 수업을 지도한다.
(C) 웹사이트를 업데이트한다.
(D) 직원들과 회의한다.

해설 질문의 핵심 어구인 Mr. Bates ~ do tomorrow morning에 대해 추론하는 문제이다. 'Would you like me to add this information to our Web site? The first exercise class I teach isn't until 1:00 P.M. tomorrow, so I'll have time to do it before lunch.'(8:37 P.M.)에서 Mr. Bates가 자신이 정보를 웹사이트에 추가하기를 원하는지 물으며 자신이 가르치는 첫 번째 운동 수업이 내일 오후 1시가 되어서야 있어서 점심 전에 이것, 즉 정보를 웹사이트에 추가하는 것을 할 시간이 있을 것이라고 했으므로 Mr. Bates가 내일 아침에 웹사이트를 업데이트할 것임을 추론할 수 있다. 따라서 (C)가 정답이다.

패러프레이징
add ~ information 정보를 추가하다 → Update 업데이트하다

166-168번은 다음 안내문에 관한 문제입니다.

> **직장 보건 연구 협회**
>
> www.whra.org
>
> [166]직장 보건 연구 협회(WHRA)는 제5회 연례 직장 보건 학회를 10월 10일과 11일에 WHRA 기관에서 엽니다. 연구 단체들의 연합체인 WHRA는 직원들의 복지를 주요 목표로 삼아왔습니다.
>
> 올해의 학회는 참석자들에게 수면, 영양, 운동이 어떻게 직장에서의 생산성에 영향을 주는지에 대한 최신 정보를 제공할 것입니다. [167-B]강의 주제들과 발표자들에 대한 추가적인 세부 사항은 8월 7일에 확정되어 www.whra.org/events에 게시될 것입니다.
>
> [167-D]등록하시려면, 온라인 신청서를 작성해주시기 바랍니다. [167-A]만약 WHRA 회원이시라면, 양일 모두 참석하는 것의 총 비용에서 30퍼센트 할인을 받을 것입니다. 등록 시에 회원 번호를 제공할 준비를 해주시기 바랍니다. 회원 신청을 하고 싶으시다면, 사이트의 회원 페이지를 방문해주십시오.
>
> [168]등록은 8월 1일에 시작하여 9월 15일에 끝납니다. 등록을 취소하고 싶으시다면, 9월 21일까지 rebecca.smith@whra.org로 이메일을 보내주시기 바랍니다. 이 날짜 이후로는, 환불금이 주어지지 않을 것입니다. 질문 및 문의 사항이 있으시면, fifthconference@whra.org로 이메일을 보내시면 됩니다.
>
> workplace n. 직장 association n. 협회 alliance n. 연합체, 동맹
> well-being n. 복지 primary adj. 주요한 latest adj. 최신의
> nutrition n. 영양 productivity n. 생산성
> finalize v. 확정하다, 마무리 짓다
> grant v. (인정하여 정식으로) 주다, 승인하다

166 추론 문제

문제 WHRA에 대해 암시되는 것은?
(A) 새 연구 프로젝트를 시작할 것이다.
(B) 최근에 설립되었다.
(C) 해외 사무소들을 운영한다.
(D) 이전에 학회들을 주최했었다.

해설 질문의 핵심 어구인 WHRA에 대해 추론하는 문제이다. 'The Workplace Health Research Association (WHRA) is holding its Fifth Annual Workplace Health Conference'에서 직장 보건 연구 협회(WHRA)가 제5회 연례 직장 보건 학회를 연다고 했으므로 WHRA가 이전에 학회들을 주최했었다는 것을 추론할 수 있다. 따라서 (D)가 정답이다.

어휘 establish v. 설립하다 operate v. 운영하다 overseas adv. 해외에 host v. 주최하다

167 Not/True 문제

문제 행사에 대해 언급되지 않은 것은?
(A) 참석자들은 할인을 받을 자격이 있을 수 있다.
(B) 행사 계획이 온라인상에 게시될 것이다.
(C) 참석하려면 회원 자격이 요구된다.
(D) 참가자들은 웹사이트에서 등록할 수 있다.

해설 질문의 핵심 어구인 event와 관련된 내용을 지문에서 찾아 보기와 대조하는 Not/True 문제이다. (A)는 'If you are a member of WHRA, you will receive 30 percent off'에서 WHRA 회원이라면 30퍼센트 할인을 받을 것이라고 했으므로 지문의 내용과 일치한다. (B)는 'Additional details about lecture topics and presenters will be ~ posted on www.whra.org/events'에서 강의 주제와 발표자들에 대한 추가적인 세부 사항은 웹사이트에 게시될 것이라고 했으므로 지문의 내용과 일치한다. (C)는 지문에 언급되지 않은 내용이다. 따라서 (C)가 정답이다. (D)는 'To register, please fill out the online registration form.'에서 등록하려면 온라인 신청서를 작성해달라고 했으므로 지문의 내용과 일치한다.

패러프레이징
receive 30 percent off 30퍼센트 할인을 받다 → qualify for a discount 할인을 받을 자격이 있다
Additional details about lecture topics and presenters 강의 주제들과 발표자들에 대한 추가적인 세부 사항 → A program 행사 계획

어휘 qualify for ~의 자격을 얻다 program n. 행사 계획

168 육하원칙 문제
문제 참가자들은 어떤 날짜까지 등록해야 하는가?
(A) 8월 1일
(B) 8월 7일
(C) 9월 15일
(D) 9월 21일

해설 참가자들이 어떤(what) 날짜까지 등록해야 하는지를 묻는 육하원칙 문제이다. 질문의 핵심 어구인 date ~ participants register와 관련하여, 'Registration ~ ends on September 15.'에서 등록이 9월 15일에 끝난다고 했으므로 (C)가 정답이다.

169-171번은 다음 기사에 관한 문제입니다.

Stanton의 임대 부동산 수요가 계속해서 상승하다

지난 10년간 Stanton의 취업 시장이 양호해왔기 때문에, [169]임대 주택에 대한 수요가 꾸준히 상승세로 오르고 있다. — [1] —. 시내의 상업 지역에서 일하는 사람들은 시내에서 살기를 원하며, 시장 조사는 이들이 시내에 있는 비싼 집을 소유하기 위해 많은 대출을 하는 것보다 차라리 아파트를 임대하고 싶어 한다고 밝혔다. — [2] —. 개발업자들은 이러한 추세를 이용하여, 고층 아파트 건물들을 그 지역 안과 주변에 건설하고 있다. — [3] —. 많은 새 아파트 단지들이 지어지고 있긴 하지만, [171]Stanton 내 세대들에 대한 높은 수요 때문에 월 임대료는 계속해서 상승하고 있다. — [4] —. [170]부동산 전문가들은 수요가 충족되기 전까지는 이 동향이 몇 해간 더 지속될 것이라고 예상한다.

property n. 부동산 demand n. 수요 need n. 수요, 필요
rental housing 임대 주택 climb v. 오르다 steadily adv. 꾸준히
upward adv. 위쪽으로 business district 상업 지역
market survey 시장 조사 take out a loan ~을 대출하다
real estate 집, 부동산 take advantage of ~을 이용하다
trend n. 추세 high-rise adj. 고층의 expert n. 전문가
predict v. 예상하다 pattern n. 동향 satisfy v. 충족시키다

---

169 주제 찾기 문제
문제 기사는 주로 무엇에 대한 것인가?
(A) 고층 건물들의 인기
(B) 지역 내 높은 임대 주택 수요
(C) 도심 부동산의 하락하는 가격
(D) 예상되는 시외의 성장 동향

해설 기사가 주로 무엇에 대한 것인지를 묻는 주제 찾기 문제이다. 'the need for rental housing has climbed steadily upward'에서 임대 주택에 대한 수요가 꾸준히 상승세로 오르고 있다고 한 후, Stanton 내 높은 임대 주택 수요에 대해 설명하고 있으므로 (B)가 정답이다.

패러프레이징
the need for rental housing has climbed steadily upward 임대 주택에 대한 수요가 꾸준히 상승세로 오르고 있다 → High rental housing demand 높은 임대 주택 수요

어휘 popularity n. 인기 multi-story adj. 고층의, 여러 층의
urban adj. 도심의 forecast v. 예상하다 suburb n. 시외, 교외

170 추론 문제
문제 Stanton의 임대 주택 시장에 대해 암시되는 것은?
(A) 이미 정점에 이르렀다.
(B) 상당히 둔화될 것으로 예상된다.
(C) 당분간 현재의 상승을 유지할 것이다.
(D) 높은 실업률에 영향을 받고 있다.

해설 질문의 핵심 어구인 Stanton's rental housing market에 대해 추론하는 문제이다. 'Real estate experts predict that the pattern will continue for a few more years before demand is satisfied.'에서 부동산 전문가들은 수요가 충족되기 전까지는 이 동향, 즉 임대 주택 수요의 상승세가 몇 해간 더 지속될 것이라고 예상한다고 했으므로 (C)가 정답이다.

어휘 peak n. 정점 considerably adv. 상당히
unemployment n. 실업(률)

171 문장 위치 찾기 문제
문제 [1], [2], [3], [4]로 표시된 위치 중, 다음 문장이 들어갈 곳으로 가장 적절한 것은?
"하지만, 높아지는 비용은 사람들이 임대하는 것을 막지 못했다."
(A) [1]
(B) [2]
(C) [3]
(D) [4]

해설 지문의 흐름상 주어진 문장이 들어가기에 가장 적절한 곳을 고르는 문제이다. However, the rising costs have not prevented people from renting에서 하지만 높아지는 비용은 사람들이 임대하는 것을 막지 못했다고 했으므로, 주어진 문장 앞에 높아지는 비용에 관한 내용이 언급된 부분이 있을 것임을 예상할 수 있다. [4]의 앞 문장인 'monthly rental fees continue to rise due to high demand for units in Stanton'에서 Stanton 내 세대들에 대한 높은 수요 때문에 월 임대료는 계속해서 상승하고 있다고 했으므로, [4]에 주어진 문장이 들어가면 월 임대료가 계속해서 상승하고 있음에도 사람들이 계속 임대를 하려고 한다는 자연스러운 문맥이 된다는 것을 알 수 있다. 따라서 (D)가 정답이다.

패러프레이징
monthly rental fees continue to rise 월 임대료가 계속해서 상승하고 있다 → rising costs 높아지는 비용

어휘 prevent v. 막다, 예방하다

172-175번은 다음 회람에 관한 문제입니다.

날짜: 5월 5일
수신: 전 직원
발신: Joel Smith, 인사부장
제목: 복리 후생

안녕하세요 여러분,

관리자들 사이에서 기업의 복리 후생 제도에 대한 많은 논의가 있었습니다. [172-B]Smartech사가 처음 문을 열었을 때, 저희는 직원들에게 기본적인 건강 보험만을 제공할 수 있었습니다. — [1] —.

하지만, [172-D]3년 전에 회사가 설립된 이래로, [172-A]저희는 상당한 매출 성장을 경험해왔습니다. — [2] —. 따라서, 저희는 직원 복리 후생 제도를 개선하기로 결정했습니다. [175]7월 1일부터, 기본적인 치아 관리가 제공될 것입니다. — [3] —. [173]직원들은 또한 더 많은 치과 보험 보장을 위해 추가 비용을 지불하는 선택권을 가질 것입니다. 이를 이용하시려면, 신청서를 작성하기만 해서 인사부로 그것을 가져오십시오.

[174]이 혜택 변경에 대한 정보가 있는 최신 직원 안내서가 다음 주에 모든 직원들에게 발송될 것입니다. — [4] —. 질문이 있으시면, j.smith@smartech.com으로 제게 이메일을 보내주시거나 제 사무실에 들 ○

러주시기 바랍니다. 감사합니다.

Joel Smith 드림

---

employee benefits 복리 후생 benefits package 복리 후생 제도
health insurance 건강 보험 found v. 설립하다 significant adj. 상당한
revenue n. 매출 dental adj. 치아의, 치과의
coverage n. (보험 등의) 보장 take advantage of (기회 등을) 이용하다
updated adj. 최신의

172 Not/True 문제

문제 Smartech사에 대해 언급되지 않은 것은?
(A) 매출이 증가했다.
(B) 설립 이래로 건강 보험을 제공해왔다.
(C) 직원들은 연간 보너스를 받는다.
(D) 3년 전에 설립되었다.

해설 질문의 핵심 어구인 Smartech와 관련된 내용을 지문에서 찾아 보기와 대조하는 Not/True 문제이다. (A)는 'we have experienced significant revenue growth'에서 상당한 매출 성장을 경험해왔다고 했으므로 지문의 내용과 일치한다. (B)는 'When Smartech first opened, we could only provide basic health insurance to employees.'에서 Smartech사가 처음 문을 열었을 때 직원들에게 기본적인 건강 보험만을 제공할 수 있었다고 했으므로 지문의 내용과 일치한다. (C)는 지문에 언급되지 않은 내용이다. 따라서 (C)가 정답이다. (D)는 'Since the company was founded three years ago'에서 3년 전에 회사가 설립되었다고 했으므로 지문의 내용과 일치한다.

패러프레이징
have experienced significant revenue growth 상당한 매출 성장을
경험했다 → revenues have increased 매출이 증가했다

어휘 founding n. 설립

173 육하원칙 문제

문제 직원들은 어떻게 추가적인 보험 보장을 얻을 수 있는가?
(A) 관리자에게 연락함으로써
(B) 온라인에서 선택권을 고름으로써
(C) 의료 진단서를 제출함으로써
(D) 추가적인 요금을 지불함으로써

해설 직원들이 어떻게(How) 추가적인 보험 보장을 얻을 수 있는지를 묻는 육하원칙 문제이다. 질문의 핵심 어구인 acquire additional insurance coverage와 관련하여, 'Employees will also have the option of paying extra for more dental insurance coverage.'에서 직원들이 더 많은 치과 보험 보장을 위해 추가 비용을 지불하는 선택권을 가질 것이라고 했으므로 (D)가 정답이다.

어휘 acquire v. 얻다 option n. 선택권
medical report 의료 진단서, 진료 보고

174 육하원칙 문제

문제 다음 주에 무슨 일이 일어날 것인가?
(A) 정책이 시행될 것이다.
(B) 문서가 배부될 것이다.
(C) 계약이 협의될 것이다.
(D) 직원 회의 일정이 잡힐 것이다.

해설 다음 주에 무슨(What) 일이 일어날 것인지를 묻는 육하원칙 문제이다. 질문의 핵심 어구인 next week과 관련하여, 'An updated employee manual ~ will be sent to all staff members next week.'에서 최신 직원 안내서가 다음 주에 모든 직원들에게 발송될 것이라고 했으므로 (B)가 정답이다.

패러프레이징
An updated employee manual ~ will be sent 최신 직원 안내서가
발송될 것이다 → A document will be distributed 문서가 배부될 것이다

어휘 implement v. 시행하다 distribute v. 배부하다
negotiate v. 협의하다

175 문장 위치 찾기 문제

문제 [1], [2], [3], [4]로 표시된 위치 중, 다음 문장이 들어갈 곳으로 가장 적절한 것은?

"이는 중대한 치과 진료가 아닌 정기 검진과 세정의 비용을 부담할 것입니다."

(A) [1]
(B) [2]
(C) [3]
(D) [4]

해설 지문의 흐름상 주어진 문장이 들어가기에 가장 적절한 곳을 고르는 문제이다. This will cover the costs of regular checkups and cleaning but not major dental work에서 이는 중대한 치과 진료가 아닌 정기 검진과 세정의 비용을 부담할 것이라고 했으므로, 주어진 문장 앞에 치과 정기 검진과 세정의 비용을 부담하는 것에 관한 내용이 언급된 부분이 있을 것임을 예상할 수 있다. [3]의 앞 문장인 'Starting July 1, basic dental care will be provided.'에서 7월 1일부터 기본적인 치아 관리가 제공될 것이라고 했으므로, [3]에 주어진 문장이 들어가면 7월 1일부터 기본적인 치아 관리가 제공될 것이지만 이는 중대한 치과 진료가 아닌 정기 검진과 세정의 비용만 부담할 것이라는 자연스러운 문맥이 된다는 것을 알 수 있다. 따라서 (C)가 정답이다.

어휘 cover v. (경비를) 부담하다, 덮다 regular checkup 정기 검진

176-180번은 다음 기사와 양식에 관한 문제입니다.

Launch Technologies사가 노트북 컴퓨터를 회수하다

5월 13일의 기자 회견에서, Launch Technologies사의 최고경영자 Jasmine Hong은 [176]회사가 Edge XL과 Glide 780 두 가지 자사 노트북 컴퓨터의 회수를 발표했다고 말했다. [177]지난해 동안 75만대가 넘는 이 모델들이 판매되어, 이 회수를 회사가 이전에 했던 다른 어떤 회수보다도 더 크게 만들었다.

Ms. Hong에 따르면, [180]Edge XL에는 결함이 있는 전원 케이블이 있다. 이 부품은 컴퓨터가 작동되고 있을 때 과열하기 쉬우며, 몇몇 경우에는 노트북 컴퓨터가 불붙게 했다. "이것의 사례들로 보고된 것은 조금밖에 없었지만, 저희는 고객들의 안전을 매우 진지하게 생각합니다. 그것이 바로 저희가 이 노트북 컴퓨터를 구입했던 모든 분들께 즉시 그것을 반환하도록 요청하고 있는 이유입니다"라고 Ms. Hong은 말했다. 회사는 동시에 Glide 780을 회수하기로 결정했는데 갑자기 그것을 멈추게 만드는 결점이 있는 하드 드라이브가 있기 때문이다.

[178]둘 중 어떤 모델이든 소유하고 있는 고객들은 전액 환불과 모든 Launch Technologies사의 제품에 사용될 수 있는 200달러 상품권을 받을 자격이 있다.

recall v. 회수하다; n. 회수 press conference 기자 회견
issue v. 발표하다; n. 사안 defective adj. 결함이 있는, 불완전한
component n. 부품, 구성 요소 be prone to ~하기 쉽다
overheat v. 과열하다; n. 과열 catch on fire 불붙다
take ~ seriously ~을 진지하게 생각하다 instance n. 사례
at the same time 동시에
faulty adj. 결점이 있는, 불완전한 shut down 멈추다, 정지하다
unexpectedly adv. 갑자기, 뜻밖에 be eligible to ~할 자격이 있다

---

[180]제품 반환 양식
Launch Technologies사
2839번지 Cumberland로
Wheeling, 웨스트버지니아 주 26003

■ 고객 정보   날짜: 5월 14일

[179/180]이름: Garret Brewer 이메일: gbrewer@breweraccounting.com

전화번호: 555-4119		집 주소: 990번지 Park로, 314호, 콜럼버스, 오하이오 주 43203

180제품명	수량	180사유
Edge XL	7	제조사로부터 회수된 제품

■ 의견

179저는 제가 소유한 회사에서 일하는 직원들에 의해 사용되도록 이 컴퓨터들을 구입했습니다. 분명히, 이들을 반환해야 하는 것은 상당히 불편한 일입니다. 제가 즉시 대체품들을 주문할 수 있도록 환불 요청이 5월 16일까지 처리되기를 바랍니다. 제게 지불되어야 할 금액은 기존 구매를 할 때 제가 사용했던 기업 신용카드로 환불되어야 합니다. 추가적인 정보가 필요하시면, 위에 제공된 번호로 제게 연락하시면 됩니다. 감사합니다.

obviously adv. 분명히 **significant** adj. 상당한 **process** v. 처리하다
replacement n. 대체품, 후임자 **owe** v. 지불할 의무가 있다
reach v. (특히 전화로) 연락하다

176 동의어 찾기 문제

문제 기사에서, 1문단 세 번째 줄의 단어 "issued"는 의미상 ~와 가장 가깝다.
(A) 결정했다
(B) 배부했다
(C) 인정했다
(D) 발표했다

해설 기사의 issued를 포함한 구절 'the company has issued a recall for two of its laptops'에서 issued는 '발표하다'라는 뜻으로 사용되었다. 따라서 (D)가 정답이다.

177 추론 문제

문제 Launch Technologies사에 대해 추론될 수 있는 것은?
(A) 지난달에 노트북 컴퓨터를 출시했다.
(B) 이전에 제품들을 회수했다.
(C) 10년보다 더 전에 설립되었다.
(D) 최근에 새로운 최고경영자를 고용했다.

해설 질문의 핵심 어구인 Launch Technologies에 대해 추론하는 문제이므로 Launch Technologies사가 언급된 기사에서 관련 내용을 확인한다. 첫 번째 지문(기사)의 'these models ~ making this recall larger than any others the company has ever had before'에서 이 모델들이 이 회수를 회사가 이전에 했던 다른 어떤 회수보다도 더 크게 만들었다고 했으므로 Launch Technologies사가 이전에 제품들을 회수했다는 것을 추론할 수 있다. 따라서 (B)가 정답이다.

어휘 **establish** v. 설립하다 **decade** n. 10년

178 육하원칙 문제

문제 Edge XL과 Glide 780의 구매자들은 무엇을 받을 것인가?
(A) 무료 소프트웨어 프로그램
(B) 컴퓨터 부대용품에 대한 할인
(C) 무료 수리 서비스
(D) 향후 구매에 대한 포인트

해설 Edge XL과 Glide 780의 구매자들이 무엇(What)을 받을 것인지를 묻는 육하원칙 문제이므로 질문의 핵심 어구인 buyers of the Edge XL and the Glide 780 receive가 언급된 기사에서 관련 내용을 확인한다. 첫 번째 지문(기사)의 'Customers who own either model[Edge XL or Glide 780] are eligible to receive ~ a $200 voucher that can be used for any Launch Technologies product.'에서 Edge XL과 Glide 780 중 어떤 모델이든 소유하고 있는 고객들은 모든 Launch Technologies사의 제품에 사용될 수 있는 200달러 상품권을 받을 자격이 있다고 했으므로 (D)가 정답이다.

패러프레이징
a $200 voucher that can be used for any ~ product 모든 제품에 사용될 수 있는 200달러 상품권 → Credit for a future purchase 향후 구매에 대한 포인트

어휘 **accessory** n. 부대용품, 장신구 **complimentary** adj. 무료의

179 추론 문제

문제 Mr. Brewer는 누구일 것 같은가?
(A) 제품 검사자
(B) 사업체 소유주
(C) 컴퓨터 기술자
(D) 공장 근로자

해설 질문의 핵심 어구인 Mr. Brewer에 대해 추론하는 문제이므로 Mr. Brewer가 작성한 양식에서 관련 내용을 확인한다. 두 번째 지문(양식)의 'Name: Garret Brewer'와 'I purchased these computers to be used by the staff working at the company I own.'에서 Mr. Brewer가 자신이 소유한 회사에서 일하는 직원들에 의해 사용되도록 컴퓨터를 구입했다고 했으므로 Mr. Brewer가 사업체 소유주라는 것을 추론할 수 있다. 따라서 (B)가 정답이다.

어휘 **inspector** n. 검사자

180 추론 문제 연계

문제 Mr. Brewer에 의해 구입된 기기에 대해 암시되는 것은?
(A) 교체 부품들이 딸려 있다.
(B) 예고 없이 꺼진다.
(C) 작동되는 동안 뜨거워진다.
(D) 하드 드라이브의 업그레이드를 필요로 한다.

해설 질문의 핵심 어구인 the devices purchased by Mr. Brewer가 언급된 양식을 먼저 확인한다.

단서 1 두 번째 지문(양식)의 'Product Return Form', 'Name: Garret Brewer', 'Product Name, Edge XL'과 'Reason, Product recalled by manufacturer'에서 Mr. Brewer가 Edge XL이 제조사로부터 회수된 제품이기 때문에 제품 반환 양식을 작성했다고 했다. 그런데 Edge XL이 제조사로부터 회수되는 이유가 제시되지 않았으므로 기사에서 관련 내용을 확인한다.

단서 2 첫 번째 지문(기사)의 'the Edge XL has a defective power cable. This component is prone to overheating when the computer is running'에서 Edge XL에는 결함이 있는 전원 케이블이 있는데, 이 부품은 컴퓨터가 작동되고 있을 때 과열하기 쉬움을 확인할 수 있다.

두 단서를 종합할 때, Mr. Brewer에 의해 구입되어 반환되려는 기기인 Edge XL은 작동되는 동안 뜨거워진다는 것을 알 수 있다. 따라서 (C)가 정답이다.

패러프레이징
overheating when the computer is running 컴퓨터가 작동되고 있을 때 과열하다 → become hot while being operated 작동되는 동안 뜨거워지다

어휘 **come with** ~이 딸려 있다 **replacement component** 교체 부품
without warning 예고 없이

181-185번은 다음 웹페이지와 온라인 후기에 관한 문제입니다.

Captain Jack's Seafood

소개	메뉴	위치	후기

브리지포트 해변에 위치한, Captain Jack's Seafood는 10년보다 더 전에 Jack Hoult에 의해 설립되었는데, 그는 자신의 해산물 요리 전문 식당을 여는 것을 꿈꿨던 지역의 어부였습니다. 이 식당은 초기에 근처 해산물 음식점들로부터의 많은 경쟁에 직면했습니다. 하지만, 신선하고 잘 준비된 요리들을 제공하는 것에 대한 Mr. Hoult의 헌신은 ⟳

Captain Jack's Seafood를 인기 있는 음식점으로 만들었습니다. 실제로, 181-B*Food & Drink*지는 잡지의 많은 기사들에서 Captain Jack's Seafood를 브리지포트에서 최고의 해산물 요리 전문 식당이라고 말했습니다.

Captain Jack's Seafood는 랍스타와 게살 케이크 같은 이곳의 특색인 해산물 요리들로 알려져 있습니다. 그리고 182이곳의 맛있는 음료들은 주민들이 특히 좋아하는 것들입니다. 적정 가격에 제공되는 183몇 개의 일간 특별 메뉴를 드셔보세요:

183목요일 – 게살 케이크　　　　금요일 – 피시 앤 칩스
　　토요일 – 튀긴 오징어　　　　일요일 – 랍스터

184오후 6시 이전에 도착하시면, 다음 방문에 대한 쿠폰도 받으실 겁니다. 예약이 권장됩니다. 자리를 예약하시려면, 555-2243으로 전화하십시오.

found v. 설립하다, 만들다　**face** v. 직면하다, 향하다
competition n. 경쟁　**early years** 초기에　**dedication** n. 헌신, 전념
eatery n. 음식점, 식당　**name** v. 말하다, 이름을 붙이다
favorite n. 특히 좋아하는 것; adj. 아주 좋아하는
special n. 특별 메뉴; adj. 특별한　**reasonable price** 적정 가격

Captain Jack's Seafood

소개	메뉴	위치	후기

이름: Carmen Vasquez
평점: ★★★☆☆

저는 지난주에 깜짝 놀랄 것을 기대하면서 Captain Jack's Seafood에 갔습니다. 제 친구들이 제게 그곳이 시내에서 가장 훌륭한 해산물 음식점이며 메뉴에 선택 가능한 것들이 많이 있다고 알려주었습니다. 183/184하지만 제가 그곳에 갈 때, 목요일 오후 5시밖에 되지 않았음에도 불구하고 30분의 대기가 있었습니다. 식당 밖에서 한동안 서 있은 후에, 저는 마침내 자리에 앉았습니다. 하지만 종업원이 제게 메뉴판을 주기까지 또 10분이 걸렸습니다. 183저는 칵테일과 오늘의 특별 메뉴를 주문했는데, 그 뒤에 종업원은 제 음식을 가져오기 전에 또 40분 동안 보이지 않았습니다.

전반적으로, 저는 Captain Jack's Seafood에 별 세 개를 주고 싶습니다. 음식과 음료들은 훌륭했고, 분위기가 아주 안락해 보였습니다. 185하지만 직원들은 손님들의 요구를 더 빠르고 효율적으로 처리하는 법을 익힐 필요가 있습니다.

amazed adj. 깜짝 놀란　**selection** n. 선택 가능한 것들, 선택
disappear v. 보이지 않게 되다　**beverage** n. 음료
atmosphere n. 분위기　**welcoming** adj. 안락해 보이는, 환영하는
efficiently adv. 효율적으로

181 Not/True 문제
문제 Captain Jack's Seafood에 대해 언급된 것은?
(A) 메뉴가 최근에 변경되었다.
(B) 한 출판물에 의해 인정받았다.
(C) 요리사들이 대부분 어부들이다.
(D) 여러 지점들이 있다.

해설 질문의 핵심 어구인 Captain Jack's Seafood에 대해 묻는 Not/True 문제이므로 Captain Jack's Seafood와 관련된 내용이 언급된 첫 번째 지문(웹페이지)을 확인한다. (A)는 지문에 언급되지 않은 내용이다. (B)는 '*Food & Drink Magazine* has named Captain Jack's Seafood in many of its articles as the best seafood restaurant in Bridgeport'에서 *Food & Drink*지가 잡지의 많은 기사들에서 Captain Jack's Seafood를 브리지포트에서 최고의 해산물 요리 전문 식당이라고 말했다고 했으므로 지문의 내용과 일치한다. 따라서 (B)가 정답이다. (C)와 (D)는 지문에 언급되지 않은 내용이다.

어휘 **publication** n. 출판물, 발표　**mostly** adv. 대부분, 거의

182 육하원칙 문제
문제 웹페이지에 따르면, 주민들은 Captain Jack's Seafood에서 무엇을 특히 즐기는가?
(A) 멋진 주변 전망들
(B) 맛있는 음료들
(C) 예의 바른 종업원들
(D) 건강에 좋은 음식 선택권들

해설 주민들이 Captain Jack's Seafood에서 무엇(what)을 특히 즐기는지를 묻는 육하원칙 문제이므로 질문의 핵심 어구인 locals especially enjoy at Captain Jack's Seafood가 언급된 웹페이지에서 관련 내용을 확인한다. 첫 번째 지문(웹페이지)의 'its delicious drinks are favorites among locals'에서 Captain Jack's Seafood의 맛있는 음료들은 주민들이 특히 좋아하는 것들이라고 했으므로 (B)가 정답이다.

패러프레이징
locals especially enjoy 주민들이 특히 즐기다 → favorites among locals 주민들이 특히 좋아하는 것들

어휘 **surrounding** adj. 주변의, 둘러싸는　**view** n. 전망, 관점
tasty adj. 맛있는　**polite** adj. 예의 바른

183 추론 문제 연계
문제 Ms. Vasquez는 무슨 요리를 주문했을 것 같은가?
(A) 게살 케이크
(B) 피시 앤 칩스
(C) 튀긴 오징어
(D) 랍스터

해설 질문의 핵심 어구인 Ms. Vasquez ~ order에서 Ms. Vasquez가 무슨 요리를 주문했을 것 같은지를 묻고 있으므로 Ms. Vasquez가 작성한 온라인 후기를 먼저 확인한다.
단서 1 두 번째 지문(온라인 후기)의 'When I got there[Captain Jack's Seafood] ~ on Thursday.'에서 Ms. Vasquez가 Captain Jack's Seafood에 갔을 때가 목요일이라고 했고, 'I ordered ~ the special of the day'에서 오늘의 특별 메뉴를 주문했다고 했다. 그런데 Ms. Vasquez가 주문한 목요일의 특별 메뉴가 무엇인지 제시되지 않았으므로 웹페이지에서 관련 내용을 확인한다.
단서 2 첫 번째 지문(웹페이지)의 'Try one of several daily specials'와 'Thursdays – Crab Cakes'에서 Captain Jack's Seafood에서 목요일에는 특별 메뉴로 게살 케이크가 제공됨을 확인할 수 있다.
두 단서를 종합할 때, Ms. Vasquez가 목요일에 오늘의 특별 메뉴인 게살 케이크를 주문했다는 것을 알 수 있다. 따라서 (A)가 정답이다.

184 추론 문제 연계
문제 Ms. Vasquez에 대해 추론될 수 있는 것은?
(A) 식품 잡지를 구독한다.
(B) 야외 테이블에 앉았다.
(C) 최근에 Bridgeport로 이사했다.
(D) 나중의 사용을 위한 쿠폰을 받았다.

해설 질문의 핵심 어구인 Ms. Vasquez가 작성한 온라인 후기를 먼저 확인한다.
단서 1 두 번째 지문(온라인 후기)의 'When I got there, however, there was a 30-minute wait, despite it being only 5 P.M. on Thursday.'에서 Ms. Vasquez가 Captain Jack's Seafood에 갔을 때 목요일 오후 5시밖에 되지 않았음에도 불구하고 30분의 대기가 있었다고 했다. 그런데 오후 5시에 도착할 경우 어떻게 되는지 제시되지 않았으므로 웹페이지에서 관련 내용을 확인한다.
단서 2 첫 번째 지문(웹페이지)의 'Arrive before 6 P.M., and you will also receive a coupon for your next visit.'에서 오후 6시 이전에 도착하면 다음 방문에 대한 쿠폰을 받을 수 있음을 확인할 수 있다.

두 단서를 종합할 때, Ms. Vasquez가 오후 6시 이전에 도착했으므로 나중의 사용을 위한 쿠폰을 받았음을 알 수 있다. 따라서 (D)가 정답이다.

어휘 subscribe v. 구독하다

185 동의어 찾기 문제

문제 온라인 후기에서, 2문단 세 번째 줄의 단어 "address"는 의미상 ~와 가장 가깝다.
(A) (법·명령 등에) 따르다
(B) 기록하다
(C) ~에게 말을 걸다
(D) ~을 처리하다

해설 온라인 후기의 address를 포함한 문장 'But the staff members need to learn how to address their customers' needs more quickly and efficiently.'에서 address가 '처리하다'라는 뜻으로 사용되었다. 따라서 (D)가 정답이다.

186-190번은 다음 두 이메일과 일정표에 관한 문제입니다.

수신: Tom Gonzales <t.gonzales@gomail.com>
발신: Cecilia Wiggins <c.wiggins@topsmile.net>
제목: 갑작스러운 변경사항
날짜: 5월 25일

Mr. Gonzales께,

[186]귀하께서 구강 건강 진단을 요청하셨던 날짜에 Dr. Makata가 시간이 없을 것임을 알려드리게 되어 유감입니다. 저는 귀하께서 이 예약을 4월 12일에 하신 것으로 알고 있습니다. 하지만, [187/188-C]Dr. Makata가 동료를 대신해서 일을 봐달라는 요청을 받아서 [187]귀하의 일정이 잡혀있는 그날에 엘패소에서의 학회에 있을 것입니다. [188-A]그녀는 6월 16일이 되어서야 진료실로 돌아올 예정입니다. 저희가 혹시 귀하의 예약을 그 다음 주로 옮길 수 있을까요? [186]제가 귀하께서 선호하시는 시간인 오전 10시로 예약을 잡아드릴 수 있습니다. 제게 알려주시기 바랍니다.

Cecilia Wiggins 드림

regret v. 유감으로 생각하다 available adj. 시간이 있는 oral adj. 구강의
checkup n. 건강 진단 fill in for ~를 대신해서 일을 봐주다
not ... until ~ ~이(나) 되어서야 …하다 due adj. ~할 예정인

[187/189]제15회 남부 지역 치과 학회
6월 12일부터 14일, Bamba 호텔, [187]엘패소, 텍사스 주

[187/189]6월 14일 토요일 일정

시간	행사	장소	[188-D]연사
[189]오전 8시 –11시 30분	[189]워크숍: 치아 사진 촬영 및 디지털 처리	[189]Javelina 홀	Dr. Stephen Gentry
오전 9시 –11시 30분	강의: 치아 수술을 위한 도구 선택	Oryx실	Dr. Warren Francis
오전 11시 30분 –오후 1시 30분	점심 시간		
오후 1시 30분 –2시 30분	워크숍: 환자 고객 서비스에서의 우수함	Javelina 홀	Dr. Janine Kirst
오후 1시 30분 –3시	회의: 신규 치과 의사들을 위한 재무 전략들	Oryx실	Dr. Heather Wallace
[188-B]오후 2시 –4시 30분	[188-B]강의: 환자 보험과 관련된 사안들	Finch실	[187/188-B/D]Dr. Noemi Makata

알림: 회원들은 어떠한 강의나 회의에도 무료로 참가할 수 있습니다. 그러나, [189]워크숍을 참가하는 데에는 요금이 부과될 수 있습니다. 취소될 경우에는 모든 요금이 환불될 수 있습니다.

---

regional adj. 지역의 dental adj. 치과의, 치아의 processing n. 처리
material n. 도구, 재료 excellence n. 우수함, 탁월 strategy n. 전략
issue n. 사안, 문제 surrounding adj. 관련된, 둘러싸는
free of charge 무료로 in the event of ~의 경우에는

수신: Kyle Green <k.green@srdc.org>
발신: Larry Ayala <l.ayala@bamba.com>
제목: 귀하의 우려사항
[189]날짜: 6월 13일

Mr. Green께,

저희는 저희 기술자들에게 Javelina 홀에 있는 에어컨을 점검해달라고 요청했습니다. 유감스럽게도, 그것은 수리가 필요할 것이며, 이것이 끝나는 가장 빠른 시점은 내일 아침입니다. 불편에 대해 사과드리는데, 이는 [189]저희가 내일 점심시간 이전에 그 홀에서 열리는 남부 지역 치과 학회의 행사를 취소해야 할 것임을 의미합니다. 그건 그렇고, [190]제가 뷔페 음식의 온도에 대한 귀하의 우려사항과 관련해서 Ms. Lopez와 이야기했습니다. 그녀는 점심 시간이 끝날 때까지 남겨진 모든 음식들이 식지 않도록 확실히 할 것입니다. 추가적인 도움이 필요하시면, 제 휴대전화 번호 555-4106으로 제게 연락하시면 됩니다.

Larry Ayala 드림
Bamba 호텔

concern n. 우려, 걱정 inconvenience n. 불편 temperature n. 온도
make sure 확실히 하다 keep warm ~이 식지 않도록 하다
further adj. 추가의 assistance n. 도움

186 추론 문제

문제 Ms. Wiggins는 누구일 것 같은가?
(A) 시설 소유주
(B) 행사 진행자
(C) 학회 연사
(D) 병원 접수 담당자

해설 질문의 핵심 어구인 Ms. Wiggins에 대해 추론하는 문제이므로 Ms. Wiggins가 보낸 이메일에서 관련 내용을 확인한다. 첫 번째 지문(이메일)의 'I regret to inform you that Dr. Makata will not be available on the date you requested for your oral health checkup.'에서 Ms. Wiggins가 이메일 수신자에게 구강 건강 진단을 요청했던 날짜에 Dr. Makata가 시간이 없을 것임을 알려주게 되어 유감이라고 했고, 'I could schedule an appointment for your preferred time'에서 선호하는 시간으로 예약을 잡아줄 수 있다고 했으므로 Ms. Wiggins가 병원 접수 담당자라는 것을 추론할 수 있다. 따라서 (D)가 정답이다.

어휘 coordinator n. 진행자 clinic n. 병원, 진료
receptionist n. 접수 담당자

187 육하원칙 문제 연계

문제 Mr. Gonzales는 Dr. Makata와 언제 만나기로 되어 있었는가?
(A) 4월 12일에
(B) 5월 25일에
(C) 6월 14일에
(D) 6월 16일에

해설 질문의 핵심 어구인 Mr. Gonzales supposed to meet with Dr. Makata에서 Mr. Gonzales가 Dr. Makata와 언제(When) 만나기로 되어 있었는지를 묻고 있으므로 Mr. Gonzales에게 보내진 이메일을 먼저 확인한다.
[단서 1] 첫 번째 지문(이메일)의 'Dr. Makata ~ will be at a conference in El Paso on the day scheduled for you [Mr. Gonzales]'에서 Dr. Makata가 Mr. Gonzales의 일정이 잡혀있는 그날에 엘패소에서의 학회에 있을 것이라고 했다. 그런데

Dr. Makata가 엘패소에서의 학회에 참가하는 날이 언제인지 제시되지 않았으므로 일정표에서 관련 내용을 확인한다.

단서 2 두 번째 지문(일정표)의 '15th Southern Regional Dental Conference', 'El Paso'와 'Schedule for Saturday, June 14', 'Dr. Noemi Makata'에서 엘패소의 제15회 남부 지역 치과 학회의 6월 14일 일정에 Dr. Makata가 참가함을 확인할 수 있다.

두 단서를 종합할 때, Dr. Makata가 엘패소에서의 학회에 6월 14일에 참가하므로 Mr. Gonzales가 Dr. Makata와 만나기로 되어 있었던 날이 6월 14일이었다는 것을 알 수 있다. 따라서 (C)가 정답이다.

188 Not/True 문제

문제 Dr. Makata에 대해 언급되지 않은 것은?
(A) 6월 16일에 직장에 복귀할 것이다.
(B) 오전 워크숍에 참석할 것이다.
(C) 동료를 대신하여 일을 도울 것이다.
(D) 행사에서 연설할 것이다.

해설 질문의 핵심 어구인 Dr. Makata에 대해 언급되지 않은 것을 묻는 Not/True 문제이므로 Dr. Makata가 언급된 이메일과 일정표 모두에서 관련 내용을 확인한다. (A)는 첫 번째 지문(이메일)의 'She [Dr. Makata] is not due back in the office until June 16.'에서 Dr. Makata가 6월 16일이 되어서야 진료실로 돌아올 예정이라고 했으므로 지문의 내용과 일치한다. (B)는 두 번째 지문(일정표)의 '2:00-4:30 P.M., Lecture, Dr. Noemi Makata'에서 Dr. Makata가 오후 강의에 참석함을 알 수 있으므로 지문의 내용과 일치하지 않는다. 따라서 (B)가 정답이다. (C)는 첫 번째 지문(이메일)의 'Dr. Makata was asked to fill in for a colleague'에서 Dr. Makata가 동료를 대신해서 일을 봐달라는 요청을 받았다고 했으므로 지문의 내용과 일치한다. (D)는 두 번째 지문(일정표)의 'Speaker'와 'Dr. Noemi Makata'에서 Dr. Makata가 연사라고 했으므로 지문의 내용과 일치한다.

어휘 be present 참석하다 associate n. 동료

189 추론 문제 연계

문제 남부 지역 치과 학회에 대해 추론될 수 있는 것은?
(A) Dr. Francis의 강의가 취소될 것이다.
(B) 점심에 추가적인 식사 선택사항들이 있을 것이다.
(C) Dr. Kirst의 행사가 연기될 수도 있다.
(D) 일부 워크숍 참가자들에게 환불이 될 것이다.

해설 질문의 핵심 어구인 the Southern Regional Dental Conference가 언급된 두 번째 이메일을 먼저 확인한다.

단서 1 세 번째 지문(이메일)의 'Date: June 13'과 'we will have to cancel the event for the Southern Regional Dental Conference being held in that hall[Javelina Hall] before lunchtime tomorrow'에서 이메일 발신 날짜가 6월 13일이고, 내일 점심시간 이전에 Javelina 홀에서 열리는 남부 지역 치과 학회의 행사를 취소해야 할 것이라고 했다. 그런데 6월 14일 점심시간 이전에 Javelina 홀에서 열리는 학회 행사에 대한 정보가 제시되지 않았으므로 일정표에서 관련 내용을 확인한다.

단서 2 두 번째 지문(일정표)의 '15th Southern Regional Dental Conference', 'Schedule for ~ June 14'과 '8:00-11:30 A.M., Workshop, Javelina Hall'에서 6월 14일 오전 8시부터 11시 30분까지 Javelina 홀에서 열리는 학회 행사가 워크숍이며, 'a fee may be charged for attending a workshop. All fees may be refunded in the event of cancellation.'에서 워크숍을 참가하는 데에는 요금이 부과될 수 있는데, 취소될 경우에는 모든 요금이 환불될 수 있음을 확인할 수 있다.

두 단서를 종합할 때, Javelina 홀에서 열리는 오전 워크숍이 취소될 것이므로 일부 워크숍 참가자들에게 환불이 될 것임을 알 수 있다. 따라서 (D)가 정답이다.

190 육하원칙 문제

문제 Mr. Green의 우려사항은 무엇인가?
(A) 공간이 너무 붐빌 수도 있다.
(B) 음식이 식을 것이다.
(C) 관리자와 이야기할 수 없을 것이다.
(D) 자료들이 늦게 배부될 수도 있다.

해설 Mr. Green의 우려사항이 무엇(What)인지를 묻는 육하원칙 문제이므로 질문의 핵심 어구인 Mr. Green's concern이 언급된 두 번째 이메일에서 관련 내용을 확인한다. 세 번째 지문(이메일)의 'I spoke to Ms. Lopez regarding your[Mr. Green] concern about the temperature of the buffet food. She will make sure that any dishes left out are kept warm'에서 이메일 발신자가 뷔페 음식의 온도에 대한 Mr. Green의 우려사항과 관련해서 남겨진 모든 음식들이 식지 않도록 확실히 할 것이라고 했으므로 Mr. Green의 우려사항이 음식이 식을 수도 있다는 것임을 알 수 있다. 따라서 (B)가 정답이다.

어휘 crowded adj. 붐비는, 복잡한 distribute v. 배부하다, 나누어주다

191-195번은 다음 광고지, 이메일, 후기에 관한 문제입니다.

---

[193]Billings 호텔에서의 Thumping Thursdays

훌륭한 음악, 음식, 와인을 위해 퇴근 후에 Gordon's Grill에서 저희와 함께 하세요! 라이브 음악을 즐기는 동안 베란다에 있는 의자를 차지하거나 잔디 위에 앉으세요. 저희는 저녁 식사를 위해 오후 5시부터 오후 10시까지 열려 있습니다. 라이브 음악 공연들의 날짜와 음악가들은 아래에 적혀 있습니다. [191]만약 날씨가 좋으면, 모든 공연들은 오후 6시부터 오후 8시까지 진행될 것입니다. 시 규정들에 의해, 주류들은 잔디에서 허용되지 않습니다. 더 많은 세부 사항을 위해 www.billingshotel.com을 방문하세요.

7월 10일: Mister Misty	[193]8월 14일: Roxy Blues
7월 17일: Elder Lake	8월 21일: Terry Crank
[193]7월 24일: Roxy Blues	8월 28일: Mister Misty
7월 31일: Mister Misty	[193]9월 4일: Roxy Blues
8월 7일: Elder Lake	[194]9월 11일: Mister Misty

take a seat 앉다, 착석하다 lawn n. 잔디 per prep. ~에 의해, ~당
regulation n. 규정, 규제 alcoholic beverage 주류

수신: Walt Galvin <galvinw@stompmail.com>
발신: Pauline Eagan <eaganp@bluemail.com>
제목: 할 수 있는 공연들
날짜: 7월 4일

Walt,

제가 Billings 호텔의 행사 관리자인 Dena Harris에게 제 명함을 남기고 갔던 때를 기억하시나요? 음, [192/193]그녀가 오늘 제게 연락해서 당신과 Deacon Delta의 당신 동료 멤버들이 Thumping Thursdays라는 호텔 행사에서 공연할 의향이 있는지 물어봤습니다. 듣자하니, [193]그녀가 원래 Roxy Blues와 출연 계약을 했었지만, 그들이 에든버러에 있는 블루스 축제에서 공연하도록 초청되었을 때 빠지게 됐다고 합니다. 그녀는 당신들이 그들의 모든 할당된 시간대를 대신해주기를 원합니다. 현재, [192]제가 당신의 밴드가 Cowhead Lounge에서 매주 금요일 밤에만 공연하도록 일정을 잡아두었으니, [193]이 공연들을 위한 시간이 충분히 있을 것입니다. 제가 이미 Ms. Harris에게 Deacon Delta가 그 행사를 위한 시간이 있다고 말해두었으니, 이 일을 할 수 있음을 확정해주시기 바랍니다.

Pauline 드림

business card 명함 apparently adv. 듣자하니, 보자하니
book v. ~와 출연 계약을 하다, 예약하다 back out 빠지다, 취소하다
cover v. (자리를 비운 사람의 일을) 대신하다 timeslot n. (할당된) 시간대

plenty of 충분한, 많은

TRIP TALES
www.triptales.com

홈 > 숙박 시설 후기 > Billings 호텔 후기

미시시피 주의 꿈 ★★★★☆
¹⁹⁴Isabel Calhoun이 9월 20일에 게시함

¹⁹⁴저는 이번 달 초에 이 호텔에서 열렸던 친구의 결혼식에 참석하는 동안 여기서 3박 4일간 머물렀습니다. 방들은 단순했지만 편안했고 무료 와이파이를 포함하고 있었습니다. 저는 호텔의 다른 식당인 Gordon's Grill의 음식을 더 선호하긴 했지만, Polk Room의 조식 뷔페는 괜찮았습니다. ¹⁹⁴호텔에는 또한 제가 그곳에서 식사했던 첫날 밤에 Mister Misty라는 훌륭한 블루스 밴드가 있었습니다. 근처에는, 할 것과 볼 것들이 많았습니다. ¹⁹⁵이 전체 여행에 관한 제 유일한 불만사항은 제 창문 바깥의 공사 소음으로 인해 오전 8시에 깨게 되는 것이었습니다. 저는 나중에 이것이 호텔이 새로운 건물을 짓고 있는 중이기 때문에 발생했다는 것을 알게 됐습니다. 전반적으로, 호텔이 좋은 가치와 많은 즐거움을 제공했기에, 저는 다른 여행자들, 특히 블루스 음악을 즐기는 사람들에게 이곳을 매우 추천합니다.

---

decent adj. 괜찮은, 알맞은　**entire** adj. 전체의
discover v. 알다, 발견하다　**wing** n. 건물
overall adv. 전반적으로; adj. 전체의　**value** n. (가격·비용 대비) 가치
particularly adv. 특히

---

191 육하원칙 문제

문제　광고지에 따르면, 무엇이 주최자들이 음악 행사를 취소하도록 할 수 있는가?
(A) 시 규정들
(B) 좋지 못한 날씨
(C) 진행 중인 수리
(D) 다른 행사 예약

해설　무엇(what)이 주최자들이 음악 행사를 취소하도록 할 수 있는지를 묻는 육하원칙 문제이므로 질문의 핵심 어구인 cause organizers to cancel a musical event와 관련된 내용이 언급된 광고지를 확인한다. 첫 번째 지문(광고지)의 'All performances[music performances] will run ~ if the weather permits.'에서 만약 날씨가 좋으면 모든 공연들이 진행될 것이라고 했으므로 날씨가 좋지 않으면 주최자들이 음악 행사를 취소할 수 있음을 알 수 있다. 따라서 (B)가 정답이다.

어휘　**inclement** adj. (날씨가) 좋지 못한　**ongoing** adj. 진행 중인

---

192 추론 문제

문제　Ms. Eagan은 누구일 것 같은가?
(A) 행사 관리자
(B) 식당 소유주
(C) 밴드 매니저
(D) 아마추어 음악가

해설　질문의 핵심 어구인 Ms. Eagan에 대해 추론하는 문제이므로 Ms. Eagan이 작성한 이메일에서 관련 내용을 확인한다. 두 번째 지문(이메일)의 'she contacted me today to ask if you and your fellow members of Deacon Delta would be willing to play at a hotel event ~'에서 Ms. Eagan이 이메일 수신자와 Deacon Delta의 동료 멤버들이 호텔 행사에서 공연할 의향이 있는지 묻는 연락을 받았다고 했고, 'I only have your band[Deacon Delta] scheduled to perform on Friday nights'에서 Ms. Eagan이 Deacon Delta 밴드가 매주 금요일 밤에만 공연하도록 일정을 잡아두었다고 했으므로, Ms. Eagan이 Deacon Delta 밴드의 매니저라는 것을 추론할 수 있다. 따라서 (C)가 정답이다.

---

193 추론 문제 연계

문제　Deacon Delta에 대해 암시되는 것은?
(A) 에든버러에서의 콘서트 일정을 변경해야 할 수도 있다.
(B) 과거에 Roxy Blues와 공연했었다.
(C) 음악 축제의 출연을 위해 오디션을 봤다.
(D) Billings 호텔에서 세 번의 공연 일정이 잡힐 수도 있다.

해설　질문의 핵심 어구인 Deacon Delta의 멤버에게 보내진 이메일을 먼저 확인한다.
단서 1 두 번째 지문(이메일)의 'she contacted me today to ask if you and your fellow members of Deacon Delta would be willing to play at a hotel event called Thumping Thursdays'에서 Deacon Delta가 Thumping Thursdays라는 호텔 행사에서 공연할 의향이 있는지 묻는 연락을 받았다고 했고, 'she had originally booked Roxy Blues, but they backed out ~. She'd like you[Deacon Delta] to cover all of their timeslots.'와 'you'll have plenty of time for these performances'에서 Deacon Delta가 원래 출연하기로 했던 Roxy Blues의 모든 할당된 시간대를 대신해주기를 원하며, Deacon Delta가 이 공연들을 위한 시간이 충분히 있을 것이라고 했다. 그런데 원래 Roxy Blues가 Thumping Thursdays에서 공연하기로 한 날이 언제인지 제시되지 않았으므로 광고지에서 관련 내용을 확인한다.
단서 2 첫 번째 지문(광고지)의 'Thumping Thursdays at the Billings Hotel'과 'July 24: Roxy Blues', 'August 14: Roxy Blues', 'September 4: Roxy Blues'에서 Billings 호텔에서의 Thumping Thursdays에서 Roxy Blues가 세 번 공연하기로 되어 있음을 확인할 수 있다.
두 단서를 종합할 때, Roxy Blues가 Billings 호텔에서 세 번의 공연을 하기로 되어 있었으므로 Deacon Delta가 Billings 호텔에서 세 번의 공연 일정이 잡힐 수도 있다는 것을 알 수 있다. 따라서 (D)가 정답이다.

어휘　**spot** n. 출연, 자리

---

194 추론 문제 연계

문제　Ms. Calhoun은 Mister Misty의 공연을 언제 봤을 것 같은가?
(A) 7월 10일에
(B) 8월 28일에
(C) 9월 4일에
(D) 9월 11일에

해설　질문의 핵심 어구인 Ms. Calhoun ~ see Mister Misty's performance에서 Ms. Calhoun이 본 Mister Misty의 공연을 묻고 있으므로 Ms. Calhoun이 작성한 후기를 먼저 확인한다.
단서 1 세 번째 지문(후기)의 'Posted September 20 by Isabel Calhoun'과 'I stayed at this hotel[Billings Hotel] earlier this month'에서 Ms. Calhoun이 9월 초에 Billings 호텔에 머물렀다고 했고, 'The hotel also had a great blues band called Mister Misty on the first night I ate there.'에서 자신이 있었을 때 호텔에 Mister Misty라는 블루스 밴드가 있었다고 했다. 그런데 Mister Misty가 9월 초에 공연한 날짜가 언제인지 제시되지 않았으므로 광고지에서 관련 내용을 확인한다.
단서 2 첫 번째 지문(광고지)의 'September 11: Mister Misty'에서 9월 11일에 Mister Misty의 공연이 있었음을 확인할 수 있다.
두 단서를 종합할 때, Ms. Calhoun이 9월 초에 Billings 호텔에 머물렀으므로 Mister Misty의 공연을 9월 11일에 봤다는 것을 알 수 있다. 따라서 (D)가 정답이다.

---

195 육하원칙 문제

문제　Ms. Calhoun은 Billings 호텔에 대해 무엇을 싫어했는가?
(A) 그녀의 방이 장식된 방식
(B) 제공 중인 선택 가능한 적은 음식
(C) 일부 공사로 인한 소란

(D) 관광지로부터의 거리

해설 Ms. Calhoun이 Billings 호텔에 대해 무엇(What)을 싫어했는지를 묻는 육하원칙 문제이므로 질문의 핵심 어구인 Ms. Calhoun dislike about the Billings Hotel과 관련된 내용이 언급된 후기를 확인한다. 세 번째 지문(후기)의 'My only complaint about this entire trip was getting woken up at 8 A.M. by construction noise outside my window.'에서 이 전체 여행에 관한 Ms. Calhoun의 유일한 불만 사항은 창문 바깥의 공사 소음으로 인해 오전 8시에 깨게 되는 것이었 다고 했으므로 Ms. Calhoun은 Billings 호텔에 대해 일부 공사로 인 한 소란을 싫어했음을 알 수 있다. 따라서 (C)가 정답이다.

패러프레이징
construction noise 공사 소음 → The disturbances caused by some work 일부 공사로 인한 소란

어휘 decorate v. 장식하다 food items 음식물
disturbance n. 소란, 소동

196-200번은 다음 광고, 웹페이지, 공지에 관한 문제입니다.

Glider로 여러분의 자기관리를 개선하세요

Glider는 모든 신체 부위에 작용하는 다기능 마사지 도구입니다. 고주파 진동은 스트레스와 통증을 완화하고 신체 회복을 돕습니다. 196-CGlider 는 또한 그것의 사용에 대한 통계를 기록하고 실시간 정보와 프로그램 제 안을 제공하는 스마트 기기입니다. Glider는 Glider 온라인 애플리케이 션과 동기화하며, 여러분의 일상 건강 추적기처럼 기능합니다.

Glider는 이미 전문 운동선수들과 스포츠 전문 상담소에서 사용되고 있 습니다. 당신의 기기를 지금 주문하시고, 수천 명의 만족한 고객들 중 한 명이 되어 보세요. 만약 여러분이 신규 고객이라면, Glider에 10퍼센트 할인을 받으실 것입니다. www.gliderdevice.net을 확인하세요. 저희 는 또한 도매 고객들을 환영합니다. 198D이번 9월에, 도매 협력 업체가 되 어 여러분의 주문에 20퍼센트 할인을 받으세요.

multifunctional adj. 다기능의 high-frequency n. 고주파
vibration n. 진동 statistics n. 통계 (자료) sync v. 동기화하다
function v. 기능하다 wellness n. 건강
clinic n. 전문 상담소, 클리닉 wholesale adj. 도매의, 대규모의; n. 도매
account n. 고객, 거래처

Glider
www.gliderdevice.net

홈	쇼핑	정보	제휴	지원

도매 정보
197Glider는 도매 주문이 가능합니다. 건강 전문 상담소, 운동 스튜디오 또는 스포츠 단체에서 기기를 사용하고 홍보해 보세요. 현장에서 기기를 홍보하는 것 외에, 197저희는 여러분이 소셜 미디어 페이지에 이것을 게 재하기를 추천합니다. 기기에 대한 홍보용 게시물을 업로드하는 것은 당 신에게 무료 액세서리를 받을 자격을 줄 것입니다.

199문의사항에 대해서는, Brianna Perez에게 b.perez@glider device.net으로 직접 연락해주세요. 여러분이 기기를 올바르게 사용하 는 방법에 대해 그녀에게 직접 배울 것입니다. 이것은 어떤 새로운 도매 고객에게라도 제공되는 무료 서비스입니다.

partnership n. 제휴, 협력 available adj. 이용할 수 있는
workout n. 운동 apart from ~ 외에, ~을 제외하고
on-site adv. 현장에서 feature v. 게재하다; n. 특징
entitle to ~에게 자격을 주다 instruct v. 가르치다, 지시하다

Pursuit 필라테스 직원 공지
198,9월 14일 주간

198/199Pursuit 필라테스는 지난주 Glider 마사지 기기의 공식 도매 ⟳

협력 업체가 되었습니다. 개인적인 경험을 통해, 저는 이 기기가 매우 효 과적이고 우리의 고객들이 그것을 정기적으로 사용함으로써 이익을 얻 을 것이라고 말할 수 있습니다.

199이러한 진전과 관련하여, 각 강사는 9월 30일 오후 7시의 강습회에 참석하는 것이 요구될 것입니다. Glider 담당자가 기기의 올바른 사용에 대해 우리에게 직접 가르쳐줄 것입니다. 200수반된 Glider 소프트웨어 애 플리케이션을 강습회 전에 다운로드하십시오. 마지막으로, 저는 우리 고 객들이 스튜디오에서 Glider 기기를 직접 구매할 수 있도록 모두가 장려 하기를 바랍니다. 우리는 구매 전에 그들이 시험 삼아 해볼 수 있는 전시 모델을 접수처에 둘 것입니다.

official adj. 공식적인 in connection with ~에 관하여
development n. 진전, 성장, 발전 workshop n. 강습회
accompany v. 수반하다, 함께 ~하다 reception n. 접수처

196 Not/True 문제

문제 Glider에 대해 사실인 것은?
(A) 시리즈 중 가장 최신 모델이다.
(B) 건강 전문가에 의해 고안되었다.
(C) 사용자들에게 실시간 의견을 제공한다.
(D) 30일간의 환불 보증이 딸려 있다.

해설 질문의 핵심 어구인 Glider에 대해 묻는 Not/True 문제이므로 Glider 에 대해 언급된 첫 번째 지문(광고)에서 관련 내용을 확인한다. (A) 와 (B)는 지문에 언급되지 않은 내용이다. (C)는 'The Glider is ~ a smart device, recording statistics on its use and providing live information and program suggestions.'에서 Glider는 그것의 사 용에 대한 통계를 기록하고 실시간 정보와 프로그램 제안을 제공하는 스마트 기기라고 했으므로 지문의 내용과 일치한다. 따라서 (C)가 정 답이다. (D)는 지문에 언급되지 않은 내용이다.

패러프레이징
live information 실시간 정보 → live feedback 실시간 의견

어휘 series n. 시리즈, 연속물 come with ~이 딸려 있다 warranty n. 보증

197 육하원칙 문제

문제 도매 고객들은 무엇을 하도록 권장되는가?
(A) 소셜 미디어에 기기를 홍보한다.
(B) 정기적으로 주문을 한다.
(C) 공식 인증을 취득한다.
(D) 2년 약정을 체결한다.

해설 도매 고객들이 무엇(What)을 하도록 권장되는지를 묻는 육하원칙 문 제이므로 질문의 핵심 어구인 wholesale customers encouraged to do에 대해 언급된 웹페이지에서 관련 내용을 확인한다. 두 번째 지 문(웹페이지)의 'The Glider is available for wholesale orders.' 와 'we recommend that you feature it on your social media page'에서 Glider가 도매 주문이 가능하며 소셜 미디어 페이지에 이 것을 게재하기를 추천한다고 했으므로 (A)가 정답이다.

패러프레이징
feature ~ on ~ social media page 소셜 미디어 페이지에 게재하다 →
Promote ~ on social media 소셜 미디어에 홍보하다

어휘 on a regular basis 정기적으로 certificate n. 인증, 증명서
commitment n. 약정, 계약

198 추론 문제 연계

문제 Pursuit 필라테스에 대해 추론될 수 있는 것은?
(A) 온라인 수업을 연다.
(B) 이전에 다른 마사지 도구들을 구입했다.
(C) 20퍼센트 할인을 받았다.
(D) 회원 수가 늘어났다.

해설 질문의 핵심 어구인 Pursuit Pilates가 언급된 공지를 먼저 확인한다.

므로 (A)가 정답이다.

단서 1 세 번째 지문(공지)의 'Week of September 14'와 'Pursuit Pilates became an official wholesale partner of the Glider massage device last week.'에서 9월 14일 주간 공지에서 Pursuit 필라테스가 지난주 Glider 마사지 기기의 공식 도매 협력 업체가 되었다고 했다. 그런데 9월 14일 이전 주에 공식 도매 협력 업체가 된 것의 혜택이 무엇인지 제시되지 않았으므로 광고에서 관련 내용을 확인한다.

단서 2 첫 번째 지문(광고)의 'This September, become a wholesale partner and receive 20 percent off your order.'에서 이번 9월에 도매 협력 업체가 되면 주문에 20퍼센트 할인을 받을 수 있음을 확인할 수 있다.

두 단서를 종합할 때, Pursuit 필라테스가 9월 14일 이전 주에 Glider 마사지 기기의 공식 도매 협력 업체가 되었으므로 20퍼센트 할인을 받았음을 알 수 있다. 따라서 (C)가 정답이다.

199 추론 문제 연계

문제 Brianna Perez에 대해 암시되는 것은?
(A) 소프트웨어 공학 학위가 있다.
(B) Glider의 공동 설립자들 중 한 명이다.
(C) 9월 30일에 모이는 것을 동의했다.
(D) Pursuit 필라테스에서 정기적으로 운동한다.

해설 질문의 핵심 어구인 Brianna Perez가 언급된 웹페이지를 먼저 확인한다.

단서 1 두 번째 지문(웹페이지)의 'For inquiries, please contact Brianna Perez directly ~. You will be instructed by her personally on how to use the device correctly. This is a free service offered to any new wholesale account.'에서 문의사항에 대해서는 Brianna Perez에게 직접 연락해달라고 하며 기기를 올바르게 사용하는 방법에 대해 그녀에게 직접 배울 것이며 이것은 어떤 새로운 도매 고객에게라도 제공되는 무료 서비스라고 했다. 그런데 새로운 도매 고객에게 Brianna Perez가 언제 기기 사용법을 가르쳐 주는지에 대한 세부 정보가 제시되지 않았으므로 공지에서 관련 내용을 확인한다.

단서 2 세 번째 지문(공지)의 'Pursuit Pilates became an official wholesale partner of the Glider massage device ~.'와 'In connection with this development, each instructor is being asked to attend a workshop on September 30 at 7 P.M. A Glider representative will instruct us directly on the correct use of the device.'에서 Pursuit 필라테스가 Glider 마사지 기기의 공식 도매 협력 업체가 되었고 이러한 진전과 관련하여 각 강사는 9월 30일 오후 7시의 강습회에 참석하는 것이 요구될 것이며 Glider 담당자가 기기의 올바른 사용에 대해 직접 가르쳐줄 것임을 확인할 수 있다.

두 단서를 종합할 때, Pursuit 필라테스에 기기 사용법에 대한 강습을 위해 Glider 담당자인 Brianna Perez가 9월 30일에 모이는 것을 동의했음을 알 수 있다. 따라서 (C)가 정답이다.

어휘 **degree** n. 학위 **cofounder** n. 공동 설립자

200 육하원칙 문제

문제 Pursuit 필라테스의 직원들은 무엇을 하도록 요청되는가?
(A) 프로그램을 다운로드한다.
(B) 기기를 설치한다.
(C) 영업 회의에 참석한다.
(D) 새로운 팀원을 교육한다.

해설 Pursuit 필라테스의 직원들이 무엇(What)을 하도록 요청되는지를 묻는 육하원칙 문제이므로 질문의 핵심 어구인 employees at Pursuit Pilates asked to do에 대해 언급된 공지에서 관련 내용을 확인한다. 세 번째 지문(공지)의 'Please download the accompanying Glider software application before the workshop.'에서 수반된 Glider 소프트웨어 애플리케이션을 강습회 전에 다운로드하라고 했으

TEST 5

LISTENING TEST

1 (D)	2 (A)	3 (D)	4 (B)	5 (A)
6 (B)	7 (C)	8 (B)	9 (B)	10 (B)
11 (C)	12 (C)	13 (A)	14 (B)	15 (B)
16 (A)	17 (A)	18 (C)	19 (C)	20 (B)
21 (C)	22 (C)	23 (C)	24 (B)	25 (B)
26 (A)	27 (B)	28 (C)	29 (A)	30 (A)
31 (B)	32 (B)	33 (B)	34 (C)	35 (A)
36 (C)	37 (A)	38 (B)	39 (B)	40 (D)
41 (D)	42 (B)	43 (B)	44 (C)	45 (A)
46 (D)	47 (D)	48 (A)	49 (B)	50 (D)
51 (C)	52 (B)	53 (B)	54 (B)	55 (A)
56 (D)	57 (A)	58 (D)	59 (A)	60 (C)
61 (B)	62 (D)	63 (B)	64 (D)	65 (D)
66 (A)	67 (A)	68 (A)	69 (D)	70 (C)
71 (D)	72 (A)	73 (B)	74 (D)	75 (C)
76 (A)	77 (C)	78 (D)	79 (B)	80 (B)
81 (D)	82 (C)	83 (A)	84 (B)	85 (C)
86 (B)	87 (D)	88 (B)	89 (C)	90 (D)
91 (D)	92 (A)	93 (C)	94 (C)	95 (C)
96 (B)	97 (A)	98 (C)	99 (B)	100 (A)

READING TEST

p.208

101 (A)	102 (C)	103 (A)	104 (C)	105 (A)
106 (D)	107 (D)	108 (B)	109 (D)	110 (B)
111 (A)	112 (A)	113 (A)	114 (B)	115 (D)
116 (C)	117 (C)	118 (B)	119 (D)	120 (A)
121 (A)	122 (C)	123 (C)	124 (B)	125 (D)
126 (A)	127 (B)	128 (A)	129 (D)	130 (D)
131 (B)	132 (B)	133 (D)	134 (B)	135 (B)
136 (D)	137 (D)	138 (D)	139 (D)	140 (A)
141 (C)	142 (C)	143 (D)	144 (A)	145 (B)
146 (A)	147 (B)	148 (C)	149 (C)	150 (A)
151 (D)	152 (D)	153 (C)	154 (B)	155 (C)
156 (B)	157 (D)	158 (C)	159 (C)	160 (C)
161 (C)	162 (B)	163 (D)	164 (C)	165 (B)
166 (A)	167 (D)	168 (B)	169 (B)	170 (A)
171 (C)	172 (D)	173 (B)	174 (C)	175 (C)
176 (B)	177 (A)	178 (C)	179 (B)	180 (C)
181 (A)	182 (A)	183 (C)	184 (B)	185 (B)
186 (C)	187 (B)	188 (B)	189 (A)	190 (C)
191 (C)	192 (D)	193 (A)	194 (D)	195 (D)
196 (D)	197 (A)	198 (B)	199 (C)	200 (A)

PART 1

1 🔊 호주식 발음

(A) She is holding up a car hood.
(B) She is writing on a clipboard.
(C) She is repairing a motorcycle.
(D) She is speaking on the phone.

hold up ~을 떠받치다 repair[미 ripέər, 영 ripéə] 수리하다

해석 (A) 그녀는 자동차 후드를 떠받치고 있다.
(B) 그녀는 클립보드에 글을 쓰고 있다.
(C) 그녀는 오토바이를 수리하고 있다.
(D) 그녀는 전화로 이야기하고 있다.

해설 **1인 사진**
(A) [×] holding up(~을 떠받치고 있다)은 여자의 동작과 무관하므로 오답이다. 사진에 있는 자동차 후드(car hood)를 사용하여 혼동을 주었다.
(B) [×] writing(글을 쓰고 있다)은 여자의 동작과 무관하므로 오답이다.
(C) [×] 사진에 오토바이(motorcycle)가 없으므로 오답이다.
(D) [○] 여자가 전화로 이야기하고 있는 모습을 가장 잘 묘사한 정답이다.

2 🔊 영국식 발음

(A) Some people are sitting on a log.
(B) Some people are hiking up a hill.
(C) A man is pouring liquid into a cup.
(D) A woman is tying her shoelace.

log[미 lɔːg, 영 lɒg] 통나무 pour[미 pɔːr, 영 pɔː] 따르다, 붓다
liquid[líkwid] 액체 tie[tai] 묶다, 매다 shoelace[ʃúːleis] 신발 끈

해석 (A) 몇몇 사람들이 통나무 위에 앉아 있다.
(B) 몇몇 사람들이 언덕 위를 하이킹하고 있다.
(C) 한 남자가 액체를 컵에 따르고 있다.
(D) 한 여자가 신발 끈을 묶고 있다.

해설 **2인 이상 사진**
(A) [○] 몇몇 사람들이 통나무 위에 앉아 있는 모습을 가장 잘 묘사한 정답이다.
(B) [×] hiking(하이킹하고 있다)은 사람들의 동작과 무관하므로 오답이다.
(C) [×] pouring(따르고 있다)은 남자의 동작과 무관하므로 오답이다. 사진에 있는 컵(cup)을 사용하여 혼동을 주었다.
(D) [×] tying(묶고 있다)은 여자의 동작과 무관하므로 오답이다. 사진에 있는 신발 끈(shoelace)을 사용하여 혼동을 주었다.

3 🔊 캐나다식 발음

(A) The man is resting his arm on a table.
(B) Some flowers are arranged in a vase.

TEST 5 Part 1 **167**

TEST **5** 인강으로 끝내는 해커스 토익 실전 LC+RC 1

(C) Pillows are stacked on the floor.
(D) A television is mounted on the wall.

rest[rest] 얹다, 기대다 pillow[미 pílou, 영 píləu] 베개
mount[maunt] 고정시키다, 올려놓다

해석 (A) 남자가 팔을 탁자 위에 얹고 있다.
(B) 몇몇 꽃들이 꽃병에 꽂혀 있다.
(C) 베개들이 바닥에 쌓여 있다.
(D) 텔레비전이 벽에 고정되어 있다.

해설 1인 사진
(A) [×] 남자가 팔을 뻗고 있는 상태인데, 탁자 위에 얹고 있다고 잘못 묘사한 오답이다.
(B) [×] 사진에 꽃(flowers)이 없으므로 오답이다. 사진에 있는 꽃병 (vase)을 사용하여 혼동을 주었다.
(C) [×] 베개들이 소파 위에 놓여 있는 상태인데, 바닥에 쌓여 있다고 잘못 묘사한 오답이다.
(D) [○] 텔레비전이 벽에 고정되어 있는 모습을 가장 잘 묘사한 정답 이다.

4 🔊 호주식 발음

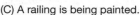

(A) A worker is climbing onto a platform.
(B) A worker is spraying water with a hose.
(C) A railing is being painted.
(D) A ladder is attached to a wall.

climb onto ~ 위로 기어오르다
platform[미 plǽtfɔːrm, 영 plǽtfɔːm] 플랫폼, 단상 spray[sprei] 뿌리다
railing[réiliŋ] 난간 attach to ~에 붙이다

해석 (A) 한 인부가 플랫폼 위로 기어오르고 있다.
(B) 한 인부가 호스로 물을 뿌리고 있다.
(C) 난간이 칠해지고 있다.
(D) 사다리가 벽에 붙어 있다.

해설 1인 사진
(A) [×] climbing onto(~ 위로 기어오르고 있다)는 사진 속 인부의 동작과 무관하므로 오답이다.
(B) [○] 인부가 호스로 물을 뿌리고 있는 모습을 가장 잘 묘사한 정답이다.
(C) [×] 사진에 난간(railing)이 없으므로 오답이다.
(D) [×] 사진에 사다리(ladder)가 없으므로 오답이다.

5 🔊 영국식 발음

(A) A vehicle is passing by a storefront.
(B) A passenger is stepping off a bus.
(C) A train track leads into a tunnel.
(D) A roof is being installed on a shop.

vehicle[미 víːikl, 영 víəkl] 차량, 탈것
storefront[미 stɔ́ːrfrʌ̀nt, 영 stɔ́ːfrʌnt] 상점 앞, 상점 정면
passenger[미 pǽsəndʒər, 영 pǽsəndʒə] 승객 step off ~에서 내리다
lead into ~로 이어지다 install[instɔ́ːl] 설치하다

해석 (A) 차량 한 대가 상점 앞을 지나가고 있다.
(B) 한 승객이 버스에서 내리고 있다.
(C) 열차 선로가 터널로 이어진다.
(D) 지붕이 상점에 설치되고 있다.

해설 2인 이상 사진
(A) [○] 차량 한 대가 상점 앞을 지나가고 있는 모습을 가장 잘 묘사한 정답이다.
(B) [×] 사진에서 버스에서 내리고 있는 승객을 확인할 수 없으므로 오답이다.
(C) [×] 사진에서 열차 선로가 터널로 이어지는지 확인할 수 없으므로 오답이다.
(D) [×] 사진에서 지붕은 보이지만, 설치되고 있는(is being installed) 모습은 아니므로 오답이다.

6 🔊 미국식 발음

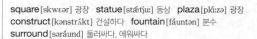

(A) A square is covered with fallen leaves.
(B) There is a statue in a plaza.
(C) A building is being constructed.
(D) A fountain is surrounded by a fence.

square[skwɛər] 광장 statue[stǽtʃuː] 동상 plaza[plάːzə] 광장
construct[kənstrʌ́kt] 건설하다 fountain[fáuntən] 분수
surround[səráund] 둘러싸다, 에워싸다

해석 (A) 광장이 떨어진 나뭇잎으로 덮여 있다.
(B) 광장에 동상이 있다.
(C) 건물이 건설되고 있다.
(D) 분수가 울타리에 둘러싸여 있다.

해설 사물 및 풍경 사진
(A) [×] 사진에 떨어진 나뭇잎(fallen leaves)이 없으므로 오답이다. 사진에 있는 광장(square)을 사용하여 혼동을 주었다.
(B) [○] 광장에 동상이 있는 모습을 가장 잘 묘사한 정답이다.
(C) [×] 사진에서 건물은 보이지만, 건설되고 있는(is being constructed) 모습은 아니므로 오답이다.
(D) [×] 사진에 분수(fountain)가 없으므로 오답이다. 사진에 있는 울타리(fence)를 사용하여 혼동을 주었다.

PART 2

7 🔊 캐나다식 발음 → 미국식 발음

Who is your supervisor?
(A) Yes, I respect our supervisor.
(B) For a new project.
(C) The man standing over there.

supervisor[미 súːpərvàizər, 영 súːpəvàizə] 관리자, 감독관
respect[rispékt] 존경하다

해석 누가 당신의 관리자인가요?
(A) 네, 전 우리의 관리자를 존경해요.
(B) 새로운 프로젝트를 위해서요.
(C) 저쪽에 서 있는 남자요.

해설 Who 의문문
(A) [×] 질문의 supervisor를 반복 사용하여 혼동을 준 오답이다.
(B) [×] 질문의 supervisor(관리자)와 관련 있는 project(프로젝트)를 사용하여 혼동을 준 오답이다.
(C) [○] 저쪽에 서 있는 남자라며, 자신의 관리자가 누구인지를 언급 했으므로 정답이다.

When is this tree going to be removed?
(A) John planted a pine tree.
(B) Before the end of the week.
(C) We moved the furniture.

remove[rimú:v] 치우다, 없애다　pine tree 소나무
furniture[미 fɔ́:rnitʃər, 영 fɔ́:nitʃə] 가구

해석　이 나무는 언제 치워질 예정인가요?
(A) John이 소나무 한 그루를 심었어요.
(B) 이번 주말 전에요.
(C) 우리는 가구를 옮겼어요.

해설　When 의문문
(A) [×] 질문의 tree를 반복 사용하여 혼동을 준 오답이다.
(B) [○] 이번 주말 전이라며, 나무가 치워질 시점을 언급했으므로 정답이다.
(C) [×] removed – moved의 유사 발음 어휘를 사용하여 혼동을 준 오답이다.

What job did you apply for?
(A) We appreciate your application.
(B) Computer technician.
(C) Come after the interview.

apply for ~에 지원하다　appreciate[əprí:ʃièit] 고마워하다
application[미 æpləkéiʃən, 영 æplikéiʃən] 지원
technician[tekníʃən] 기술자

해석　어느 일자리에 지원하셨나요?
(A) 지원해주셔서 감사합니다.
(B) 컴퓨터 기술자요.
(C) 면접 이후에 오세요.

해설　What 의문문
(A) [×] apply for(~에 지원하다)와 관련 있는 application(지원)을 사용하여 혼동을 준 오답이다.
(B) [○] 컴퓨터 기술자라며, 어느 일자리에 지원했는지를 언급했으므로 정답이다.
(C) [×] 질문의 job(일자리)과 관련 있는 interview(면접)를 사용하여 혼동을 준 오답이다.

Why is Ms. Albright leaving our department?
(A) Oh, not until next month.
(B) To work at headquarters.
(C) Yes, we're ready to go.

department[미 dipá:rtmənt, 영 dipá:tmənt] 부서
headquarters[미 hédkwɔ̀:rtərz, 영 hédkwɔ̀:təz] 본사

해석　Ms. Albright는 왜 우리 부서를 떠나나요?
(A) 아, 다음 달이나 되어서요.
(B) 본사에서 일하기 위해서요.
(C) 네, 우리는 떠날 준비가 되었어요.

해설　Why 의문문
(A) [×] Ms. Albright가 부서를 떠나는 이유를 물었는데, 시점으로 응답했으므로 오답이다.

(B) [○] 본사에서 일하기 위해서라며, Ms. Albright가 부서를 떠나는 이유를 언급했으므로 정답이다.
(C) [×] 의문사 의문문에 Yes로 응답했으므로 오답이다. 질문의 leaving(떠나다)과 같은 의미인 go(떠나다)를 사용하여 혼동을 주었다.

Who is able to train the new cashier?
(A) The train is behind schedule.
(B) From one of the clerks.
(C) Clarence, the day manager.

train[trein] 교육하다; 기차　cashier[미 kæʃíər, 영 kæʃíə] 계산원
behind schedule 예정보다 늦게　clerk[미 klə:rk, 영 klɑ:k] 점원, 직원

해석　누가 신입 계산원을 교육할 수 있나요?
(A) 기차가 예정보다 늦네요.
(B) 점원들 중 한 명으로부터요.
(C) 주간 매니저인 Clarence요.

해설　Who 의문문
(A) [×] 질문의 train(교육하다)을 '기차'라는 의미의 명사로 반복 사용하여 혼동을 준 오답이다.
(B) [×] 질문의 cashier(계산원)와 관련 있는 clerks(점원들)를 사용하여 혼동을 준 오답이다.
(C) [○] 주간 매니저인 Clarence라며, 신입 계산원을 교육할 수 있는 사람을 언급했으므로 정답이다.

Where did you buy this briefcase?
(A) To carry my work files.
(B) Some amazing accessories.
(C) Through an online retailer.

briefcase[brí:fkeis] 서류 가방　carry[kǽri] 가지고 다니다
retailer[미 rí:teilər, 영 rí:teilə] 소매업체

해석　당신은 이 서류 가방을 어디에서 샀나요?
(A) 제 업무용 서류철들을 가지고 다니기 위해서요.
(B) 몇몇 멋진 액세서리요.
(C) 온라인 소매업체를 통해서요.

해설　Where 의문문
(A) [×] 서류 가방을 산 장소를 물었는데, 서류 가방을 산 이유로 응답했으므로 오답이다.
(B) [×] 질문의 briefcase(서류 가방)와 관련 있는 accessories(액세서리)를 사용하여 혼동을 준 오답이다.
(C) [○] 온라인 소매업체를 통해서라며, 서류 가방을 산 장소를 언급했으므로 정답이다.

How much do the brown shoes cost?
(A) They're on sale for $50.
(B) Whichever color you want.
(C) The shop specializes in footwear.

cost[kɔ:st] (값이) ~이다　on sale 판매되는
specialize[spéʃəlàiz] 전문으로 하다
footwear[미 fútwɛər, 영 fútwɛə] 신발

해석　그 갈색 신발은 값이 얼마예요?

(A) 50달러에 판매되고 있어요.
(B) 당신이 원하는 색상이면 무엇이든지요.
(C) 그 가게는 신발을 전문으로 해요.

해설 **How 의문문**
(A) [ㅇ] 50달러에 판매되고 있다며, 신발의 가격을 언급했으므로 정답
이다.
(B) [×] 질문의 brown(갈색)과 관련 있는 color(색상)를 사용하여 혼
동을 준 오답이다.
(C) [×] 질문의 shoes(신발)와 같은 의미인 footwear(신발)를 사용하
여 혼동을 준 오답이다.

14 호주식 발음 → 미국식 발음

This bakery sells fresh bread daily, right?
(A) No, a sales representative.
(B) Yes, that's correct.
(C) The bread has been sliced.

fresh[freʃ] 갓 만든 daily[déili] 매일 sales representative 판매 직원
slice[slais] 얇게 썰다

해석 이 빵집은 매일 갓 만든 빵을 판매해요, 그렇죠?
(A) 아뇨, 판매 직원이요.
(B) 네, 맞아요.
(C) 빵이 얇게 썰려 있어요.

해설 **부가 의문문**
(A) [×] 질문의 sells(판매하다)와 관련 있는 sales representative(판
매 직원)를 사용하여 혼동을 준 오답이다.
(B) [ㅇ] Yes로 이 빵집이 매일 갓 만든 빵을 판매함을 전달했으므로 정
답이다.
(C) [×] 질문의 bread를 반복 사용하여 혼동을 준 오답이다.

15 호주식 발음 → 영국식 발음

Why do you want images of the venue?
(A) Here is the camera.
(B) For a business pamphlet.
(C) I imagine it was hard.

image[ímidʒ] 사진, 그림 venue[vénjuː] 장소
pamphlet[pǽmflət] 소책자 imagine[imǽdʒin] ~이라고 생각하다

해석 당신은 왜 그 장소의 사진을 원하나요?
(A) 여기 카메라가 있어요.
(B) 회사 소책자를 위해서요.
(C) 그것이 어려웠을 거라고 생각해요.

해설 **Why 의문문**
(A) [×] 질문의 images(사진)와 관련 있는 camera(카메라)를 사용하
여 혼동을 준 오답이다.
(B) [ㅇ] 회사 소책자를 위해서라며, 그 장소의 사진을 원하는 이유를
언급했으므로 정답이다.
(C) [×] images – imagine의 유사 발음 어휘를 사용하여 혼동을 준
오답이다.

16 캐나다식 발음 → 미국식 발음

Who is organizing the park cleanup?
(A) I've never heard about that.
(B) Across from a dry cleaner.
(C) Should I park nearby?

organize[미 ɔ́ːrɡənàiz, 영 ɔ́ːɡənàiz] 준비하다, 계획하다
cleanup[klínʌp] 대청소 across from ~의 맞은편에

해석 누가 공원 대청소를 준비하고 있나요?
(A) 금시초문이에요.
(B) 드라이클리닝 가게 맞은편에요.
(C) 제가 근처에 주차해야 하나요?

해설 **Who 의문문**
(A) [ㅇ] 금시초문이라는 말로, 누가 공원 대청소를 준비하고 있는지 모
른다는 간접적인 응답을 했으므로 정답이다.
(B) [×] cleanup – cleaner의 유사 발음 어휘를 사용하여 혼동을 준
오답이다.
(C) [×] 질문의 park(공원)를 '주차하다'라는 의미의 동사로 반복 사
용하여 혼동을 준 오답이다.

17 영국식 발음 → 캐나다식 발음

I'd like to order an appetizer before dinner.
(A) That's a good idea.
(B) The order is for Table 3.
(C) Because my meal is cold.

order[미 ɔ́ːrdər, 영 ɔ́ːdə] 주문하다; 주문
appetizer[미 ǽpitàizər, 영 ǽpətàizə] 에피타이저(식욕을 돋구는 것)
meal[miːl] 음식

해석 저녁 식사 전에 에피타이저를 주문하고 싶어요.
(A) 좋은 생각이에요.
(B) 그 주문은 3번 테이블 것이에요.
(C) 제 음식이 차갑기 때문이에요.

해설 **평서문**
(A) [ㅇ] 좋은 생각이라는 말로, 저녁 식사 전에 에피타이저를 주문하고
싶다는 의견에 동의했으므로 정답이다.
(B) [×] 질문의 order(주문하다)를 '주문'이라는 의미의 명사로 반복
사용하여 혼동을 준 오답이다.
(C) [×] 질문의 dinner(저녁 식사)와 관련 있는 meal(음식)을 사용하
여 혼동을 준 오답이다.

18 미국식 발음 → 캐나다식 발음

Would you tell Mark about tomorrow's presentation?
(A) They didn't say anything.
(B) An informative speech.
(C) No problem.

presentation[prèzəntéiʃən] 발표
informative[미 infɔ́ːrmətiv, 영 infɔ́ːmətiv] 유익한 speech[spiːtʃ] 강연

해석 Mark에게 내일 발표에 대해 말해 줄래요?
(A) 그들은 아무 말도 하지 않았어요.
(B) 유익한 강연이요.
(C) 문제없어요.

해설 **요청 의문문**
(A) [×] 질문의 tell(말하다)과 같은 의미인 say(말하다)를 사용하여 혼
동을 준 오답이다.
(B) [×] 질문의 presentation(발표)과 관련 있는 speech(강연)를 사
용하여 혼동을 준 오답이다.
(C) [ㅇ] 문제없다는 말로, Mark에게 발표에 대해 말해달라는 요청을
수락한 정답이다.

19 영국식 발음 → 호주식 발음

> Do you need any help, or can you finish filing these records yourself?
> (A) I guess so.
> (B) Oh, you don't need to call her.
> (C) I'll be fine. Thanks.

file[fail] 정리하다 record[미 rékərd, 영 rékəd] 기록 (문서)

해석 도움이 필요한가요, 아니면 혼자서 이 기록 문서 정리를 끝낼 수 있나요?
(A) 그런 것 같아요.
(B) 아, 그녀에게 전화하지 않으셔도 돼요.
(C) 괜찮을 것 같아요. 고마워요.

해설 선택 의문문
(A) [×] 도움이 필요한지 아니면 혼자서 기록 문서 정리를 끝낼 수 있는지를 물었는데, 이와 관련이 없는 그런 것 같다는 내용으로 응답했으므로 오답이다.
(B) [×] 질문의 need를 반복 사용하여 혼동을 준 오답이다.
(C) [o] 괜찮을 것 같다는 말로, 혼자서 기록 문서 정리를 끝낼 수 있다는 것을 선택했으므로 정답이다.

20 호주식 발음 → 영국식 발음

> My notebook is missing again.
> (A) We missed you, too.
> (B) I saw it beside the photocopier.
> (C) The receptionist found some keys.

missing[mísiŋ] 없어진 miss[mis] 그리워하다 beside[bisáid] ~ 옆에
photocopier[미 fóutəkàpiər, 영 fə́utəukɔ̀piə] 복사기
receptionist[risépʃənist] 접수 담당자

해석 제 공책이 또 없어졌어요.
(A) 우리도 당신을 그리워했어요.
(B) 저는 그것을 복사기 옆에서 봤어요.
(C) 접수 담당자가 몇몇 열쇠를 찾았어요.

해설 평서문
(A) [×] missing – missed의 유사 발음 어휘를 사용하여 혼동을 준 오답이다.
(B) [o] 그것을 복사기 옆에서 봤다는 말로, 상대방이 찾고 있는 공책의 위치를 전달한 정답이다.
(C) [×] 질문의 missing(없어진)과 관련된 found(찾았다)를 사용하여 혼동을 준 오답이다.

21 캐나다식 발음 → 미국식 발음

> What is the dress code for the year-end gathering?
> (A) The retirement celebration.
> (B) He's giving a special address.
> (C) Business casual should be fine.

gathering[gǽðəriŋ] 모임
retirement[미 ritáiərmənt, 영 ritáiəmənt] 퇴직
celebration[sèləbréiʃən] 기념 행사 give an address 연설을 하다

해석 연말 모임의 드레스 코드는 무엇인가요?
(A) 퇴직 기념 행사요.
(B) 그가 특별 연설을 할 거예요.
(C) 비즈니스 캐주얼이면 괜찮을 거예요.

해설 What 의문문
(A) [×] 질문의 year-end gathering(연말 모임)과 관련 있는 celebration(기념 행사)을 사용하여 혼동을 준 오답이다.
(B) [×] dress – address의 유사 발음 어휘를 사용하여 혼동을 준 오답이다.
(C) [o] 비즈니스 캐주얼이면 괜찮을 거라며, 연말 모임의 드레스 코드를 언급했으므로 정답이다.

22 미국식 발음 → 호주식 발음

> Where is the closest bathroom to the conference room?
> (A) The conference is about sales tactics.
> (B) It starts at 1:30 P.M.
> (C) There's a floor plan near the elevator.

tactic[tǽktik] 전략, 전술 floor plan 층별 안내도, 평면도

해석 회의실에서 가장 가까운 화장실은 어디인가요?
(A) 그 회의는 판매 전략에 관한 것이에요.
(B) 그것은 오후 1시 30분에 시작해요.
(C) 엘리베이터 근처에 층별 안내도가 있어요.

해설 Where 의문문
(A) [×] 질문의 conference를 반복 사용하여 혼동을 준 오답이다.
(B) [×] 회의실에서 가장 가까운 화장실이 어디인지를 물었는데 시점으로 응답했으므로 오답이다. conference(회의)와 관련 있는 starts at 1:30 P.M.(오후 1시 30분에 시작한다)을 사용하여 혼동을 주었다.
(C) [o] 엘리베이터 근처에 층별 안내도가 있다며, 회의실에서 가장 가까운 화장실이 어디인지 모른다는 것을 간접적으로 전달했으므로 정답이다.

23 캐나다식 발음 → 영국식 발음

> Our athletic footwear line will launch next year.
> (A) We're standing in line near the entrance.
> (B) Only 20 athletes attended.
> (C) Yes. It is expected to do well.

athletic[æθlétik] 운동용의 footwear[미 fútwɛər, 영 fútweə] 신발
launch[lɔːntʃ] 출시하다 entrance[éntrəns] 출입구
athlete[ǽθliːt] 운동선수 attend[əténd] 참가하다
expect[ikspékt] 기대하다

해석 저희의 운동용 신발 라인이 내년에 출시될 거예요.
(A) 우리는 출입구 근처에서 줄을 서 있어요.
(B) 스무 명의 운동선수들만 참가했어요.
(C) 네. 그것은 잘 될 것으로 기대돼요.

해설 평서문
(A) [×] 질문의 line((상품) 라인)을 '줄'이라는 의미로 반복 사용하여 혼동을 준 오답이다.
(B) [×] athletic – athletes의 유사 발음 어휘를 사용하여 혼동을 준 오답이다.
(C) [o] Yes로 내년에 운동용 신발 라인이 출시될 예정이라는 것을 알고 있다고 전달한 후, 잘 될 것으로 기대된다는 부연 설명을 했으므로 정답이다.

24 영국식 발음 → 캐나다식 발음

> Can I purchase tickets for the concert at the venue?
> (A) It's a really good band.   ○

(B) They must be ordered online.
(C) No, I saw them live in concert.

purchase [미 pə́:rtʃəs, 영 pə́:tʃəs] 구매하다   venue [vénju:] 현장, 장소

해석   현장에서 콘서트 티켓들을 구매할 수 있나요?
(A) 정말 훌륭한 밴드예요.
(B) 그것들은 온라인으로 주문되어야 해요.
(C) 아뇨, 저는 그들을 콘서트에서 라이브로 봤어요.

해설   **조동사 의문문**
(A) [×] 질문의 concert(콘서트)와 관련 있는 band(밴드)를 사용하여 혼동을 준 오답이다.
(B) [○] 그것들은 온라인으로 주문되어야 한다며, 현장에서 콘서트 티켓들을 구매할 수 없음을 간접적으로 전달했으므로 정답이다.
(C) [×] 질문의 concert를 반복 사용하여 혼동을 준 오답이다.

25 〔호〕 호주식 발음 → 미국식 발음

Is the front door locked, or do I need to take care of that?
(A) Take as many as you want.
(B) I'll go find out.
(C) No, that's my bike lock.

lock [미 lɑk, 영 lɔk] 잠그다; 자물쇠   take care of ~을 처리하다
find out 알아내다   bike [baik] 자전거

해석   현관문이 잠겼나요, 아니면 제가 그것을 처리해야 하나요?
(A) 당신이 원하는 만큼 가져가세요.
(B) 제가 가서 알아볼게요.
(C) 아뇨, 그것은 제 자전거 자물쇠예요.

해설   **선택 의문문**
(A) [×] 현관문이 잠겼는지 아니면 자신이 처리해야 하는지를 물었는데, 이와 관련이 없는 원하는 만큼 가져가라는 내용으로 응답했으므로 오답이다.
(B) [○] 가서 알아보겠다는 말로, 현관문이 잠겼는지 모른다는 간접적인 응답을 했으므로 정답이다.
(C) [×] 질문의 locked(잠긴)를 '자물쇠'라는 의미의 명사 lock으로 반복 사용하여 혼동을 준 오답이다.

26 〔캐〕 캐나다식 발음 → 영국식 발음

The city library is closed for repairs until next month.
(A) I heard about that recently.
(B) Check your library card.
(C) April is actually the best time to travel.

library [미 láibrèri, 영 láibrəri] 도서관   repair [미 ripɛ́ər, 영 ripéə] 수리
library card (도서관의) 대출 카드

해석   시립 도서관이 수리를 위해 다음 달까지 문을 닫아요.
(A) 그것에 대해 최근에 들었어요.
(B) 대출 카드를 확인하세요.
(C) 4월이 사실 여행하기에 가장 좋은 시기예요.

해설   **평서문**
(A) [○] 그것에 대해 최근에 들었다는 말로, 시립 도서관이 문을 닫는다는 것을 알고 있음을 전달했으므로 정답이다.
(B) [×] 질문의 library를 반복 사용하여 혼동을 준 오답이다.
(C) [×] 질문의 month(달)와 관련 있는 April(4월)을 사용하여 혼동을 준 오답이다.

27 〔호〕 호주식 발음 → 미국식 발음

Aren't we supposed to bring food to Charlie's party?
(A) There aren't enough gloves.
(B) Everything will be provided.
(C) I suppose he will show up.

be supposed to ~해야 하다   provide [prəváid] 제공하다
suppose [미 səpóuz, 영 səpə́uz] ~이라고 생각하다
show up (예정된 곳에) 나타나다

해석   우리는 Charlie의 파티에 음식을 가져가야 하지 않나요?
(A) 장갑이 충분히 없어요.
(B) 모든 것이 제공될 거예요.
(C) 그가 나타날 거라고 생각해요.

해설   **부정 의문문**
(A) [×] 파티에 음식을 가져가야 하지 않을지를 물었는데, 이와 관련이 없는 장갑이 충분히 없다는 내용으로 응답했으므로 오답이다.
(B) [○] 모든 것이 제공될 거라는 말로, 음식을 가져갈 필요가 없음을 간접적으로 전달했으므로 정답이다.
(C) [×] supposed to – suppose의 유사 발음 어휘를 사용하여 혼동을 준 오답이다.

28 〔미〕 미국식 발음 → 캐나다식 발음

Can I get a ride with you to the theater?
(A) The performance got great reviews.
(B) Did you enjoy the movie, too?
(C) I've got room in my car.

get a ride (탈것에) 타다   theater [미 θí:ətər, 영 θíətə] 극장
performance [미 pərfɔ́:rməns, 영 pəfɔ́:məns] 공연
room [ru:m] 자리, 공간

해석   제가 당신과 함께 차를 타고 극장에 갈 수 있을까요?
(A) 그 공연은 훌륭한 평들을 받았어요.
(B) 당신도 그 영화를 즐겼나요?
(C) 제 차에 자리가 있어요.

해설   **요청 의문문**
(A) [×] 질문의 theater(극장)와 관련 있는 performance(공연)를 사용하여 혼동을 준 오답이다.
(B) [×] 질문의 theater(극장)와 관련 있는 movie(영화)를 사용하여 혼동을 준 오답이다.
(C) [○] 차에 자리가 있다는 말로, 함께 차를 타고 극장에 가고 싶다는 요청을 간접적으로 수락한 정답이다.

29 〔호〕 호주식 발음 → 미국식 발음

Didn't you say you have to work over the holiday weekend?
(A) Yes, but Rachel is going to cover my shift.
(B) Over by the cabinet.
(C) No, Friday was the delivery date.

cover [미 kʌ́vər, 영 kʌ́və] 대신하다   shift [ʃift] (교대) 근무 시간
cabinet [kǽbənit] 캐비닛   delivery [dilívəri] 배송, 배달

해석   당신은 주말 연휴에 일해야 한다고 하지 않았나요?
(A) 네, 그런데 Rachel이 제 근무 시간을 대신할 거예요.
(B) 저쪽 캐비닛 옆에요.
(C) 아뇨, 금요일이 배송일이었어요.

해설 **부정 의문문**

(A) [○] Yes로 그렇게 말했음을 전달한 후, Rachel이 자신의 근무 시
간을 대신할 것이라서 주말 연휴에 일할 필요가 없어졌다는
부연 설명을 했으므로 정답이다.

(B) [×] 질문의 over를 반복 사용하여 혼동을 준 오답이다.

(C) [×] 질문의 weekend(주말)와 관련 있는 Friday(금요일)를 사용
하여 혼동을 준 오답이다.

30 🎧 영국식 발음 → 캐나다식 발음

> When can I come over to collect the sales report?
> **(A) How about Wednesday afternoon?**
> (B) Sales have been really strong.
> (C) It's a large collection.

strong[strɔːŋ] 오름세의, 강세의

해석 제가 언제 영업 보고서를 받으러 오면 되나요?

(A) 수요일 오후는 어때요?
(B) 매출이 정말 오름세네요.
(C) 그것은 상당한 수집품이네요.

해설 **When 의문문**

(A) [○] 수요일 오후는 어떤지를 되물어, 영업 보고서를 받으러 오면
되는 시점에 대한 상대방의 의견을 묻는 정답이다.

(B) [×] 질문의 sales를 반복 사용하여 혼동을 준 오답이다.

(C) [×] collect – collection의 유사 발음 어휘를 사용하여 혼동을 준
오답이다.

31 🎧 호주식 발음 → 미국식 발음

> Will we be holding the customer appreciation day
> event at Albertville Park?
> (A) You can park behind the building.
> **(B) We don't have the budget for it this year.**
> (C) I really appreciate all your hard work.

해석 우리는 Albertville 공원에서 고객 감사의 날 행사를 개최할 건가요?

(A) 당신은 건물 뒤에 주차하시면 돼요.
(B) 우리는 올해 그것을 위한 예산이 없어요.
(C) 저는 당신의 모든 노고에 정말 감사드려요.

해설 **조동사 의문문**

(A) [×] 질문의 Park(공원)를 '주차하다'라는 의미의 동사 park로 반
복 사용하여 혼동을 준 오답이다.

(B) [○] 올해 그것을 위한 예산이 없다며, 고객 감사의 날 행사를 개최
하지 않을 것임을 간접적으로 전달했으므로 정답이다.

(C) [×] appreciation – appreciate의 유사 발음 어휘를 사용하여
혼동을 준 오답이다.

PART 3

32-34 🎧 호주식 발음 → 미국식 발음

Questions 32-34 refer to the following conversation.

> M: Welcome to Golden Touch Restaurant. Will you be
> dining alone tonight?
> W: Oh, no . . . I'm not here to eat. ³²I believe I lost my
> wallet here earlier. I had lunch with some business
> partners at a long table by the window. I had my
> wallet when I paid for the bill, but I later realized ○

> it was missing from my purse. ³³Would you ask
> your staff members if they've found it?
> M: I'm sorry to hear that. We have a lost and found
> basket in the manager's office. ³⁴If you could tell
> me what the wallet looks like, I'll check the basket.

dine[dain] (잘 차린) 식사를 하다   business partner 동업자
realize[ríːəlàiz] 알아차리다   missing[mísiŋ] 없어진
lost and found 분실물 보관(소)

해석
32-34번은 다음 대화에 관한 문제입니다.

남: Golden Touch 식당에 오신 것을 환영합니다. 오늘 밤에 혼자 식사하
십니까?

여: 아, 아니요... 저는 식사하러 온 게 아니에요. ³²여기서 아까 제 지갑을 잃
어버린 것 같아요. 저는 창문 옆에 긴 테이블에서 동업자들 몇 명과 함께
점심을 먹었어요. 계산서를 지불할 때까지만 해도 제가 지갑을 가지고 있
었는데, 나중에 그것이 제 핸드백에서 없어진 것을 알아차렸어요. ³³당신
이 직원들에게 혹시 그것을 발견했는지 물어봐 주실 수 있나요?

남: 안타깝네요. 저희는 지배인의 사무실에 분실물 보관 바구니가 있습니다.
³⁴지갑이 어떻게 생겼는지 제게 말씀해주시면, 제가 바구니를 확인해보
겠습니다.

32 문제점 문제

해석 여자의 문제는 무엇인가?

(A) 예약하는 것을 잊어버렸다.
(B) 개인 소지품을 잃어버렸다.
(C) 집에 지갑을 놓고 왔다.
(D) 식사에 대해 불만족스럽다.

해설 여자의 말에서 부정적인 표현이 언급된 다음을 주의 깊게 듣는다. 여자
가 "I believe I lost my wallet here[restaurant] earlier."라며 식당
에서 아까 지갑을 잃어버린 것 같다고 하였다. 따라서 (B)가 정답이다.

어휘 make a reservation 예약하다   personal belonging 개인 소지품

33 특정 세부 사항 문제

해석 여자는 남자가 무엇을 하기를 원하는가?

(A) 다른 테이블로 옮겨준다.
(B) 몇몇 직원들에게 이야기한다.
(C) 계산서에서 요금을 제해준다.
(D) 점심 메뉴를 가져다준다.

해설 대화에서 여자의 말을 주의 깊게 듣는다. 여자가 남자에게 "Would
you ask your staff members if they've found it[wallet]?"이라
며 직원들에게 혹시 지갑을 발견했는지 물어봐 줄 수 있는지 물었다.
따라서 (B)가 정답이다.

어휘 remove[rimúːv] 제거하다, 없애다

34 다음에 할 일 문제

해석 여자는 다음에 무엇을 할 것 같은가?

(A) 자리에 앉는다.
(B) 직장으로 돌아간다.
(C) 물건을 묘사한다.
(D) 주문을 한다.

해설 대화의 마지막 부분을 주의 깊게 듣는다. 남자가 여자에게 "If you
could tell me what the wallet looks like, I'll check the basket."
이라며 지갑이 어떻게 생겼는지 말해주면 바구니를 확인해보겠다고
한 말을 통해 여자가 다음에 물건을 묘사할 것임을 알 수 있다. 따라서
(C)가 정답이다.

패러프레이징
tell ~ what the wallet looks like 지갑이 어떻게 생겼는지 말하다 →
Describe an item 물건을 묘사하다

어휘 take a seat 자리에 앉다 describe[diskráib] 묘사하다
place an order 주문하다

35-37 🎧 캐나다식 발음 → 영국식 발음 → 호주식 발음

Questions 35-37 refer to the following conversation with three speakers.

M1: Did you two see our office lobby? It looks amazing.

W: Yeah, ³⁵the new sofas and chairs are great. Very modern. They're a huge improvement over our previous furniture.

M2: I wonder, though, about the cost. They look expensive. Seeing as how our profits were down last year, can we afford them?

M1: Actually, ³⁶the company's finances improved last quarter. Brandon is planning to announce the news at this afternoon's staff meeting.

M2: Oh, I can't attend that because I have to go see a client. ³⁷Let me know what he says tomorrow.

W: ³⁷Sure, I can do that.

---

amazing[əméiziŋ] 굉장한 modern[미 mɑ́dərn, 영 mɔ́dən] 현대적인
improvement[imprúːvmənt] 발전, 개선
wonder about ~에 대해 궁금해하다 seeing as ~을 고려하면
profit[미 prɑ́fit, 영 prɔ́fit] 수익, 이익
afford[미 əfɔ́ːrd, 영 əfɔ́ːd] (~을 살 금전적·시간적) 여유가 되다
finance[fáinæns] 재정, 자금 quarter[미 kwɔ́ːrtər, 영 kwɔ́ːtə] 분기
announce[ənáuns] 알리다, 발표하다 attend[əténd] 참석하다

해석

35-37번은 다음 세 명의 대화에 관한 문제입니다.

남1: 두 분은 우리 사무실 로비를 보셨나요? 굉장해 보이던데요.

여: 네, ³⁵새 소파와 의자들은 정말 좋아요. 아주 현대적이에요. 그것들은 전에 있던 가구들에 비하면 엄청난 발전이에요.

남2: 저는, 그런데, 비용이 궁금해요. 그것들은 비싸 보여요. 우리 수익이 작년에 낮았던 것을 고려했을 때, 우리가 그것들을 살 여유가 되나요?

남1: 사실, ³⁶회사의 재정 상태가 지난 분기에 개선되었어요. Brandon이 오늘 오후의 직원 회의에서 이 소식을 알릴 예정이에요.

남2: 아, 저는 고객을 만나러 가야 하기 때문에 그곳에 참석하지 못해요. ³⁷그가 뭐라고 하는지 내일 제게 알려주세요.

여: ³⁷물론이죠, 그렇게 할게요.

35 특정 세부 사항 문제

해석 무엇이 교체되었는가?

(A) 좌석들
(B) 접수처
(C) 로비 테이블들
(D) 서류 정리함

해설 질문의 핵심 어구(replaced)와 관련된 내용을 주의 깊게 듣는다. 여자가 "the new sofas and chairs are great"라며 새 소파와 의자들은 정말 좋다고 한 말을 통해 좌석들이 교체되었음을 알 수 있다. 따라서 (A)가 정답이다.

어휘 replace[ripléis] 교체하다 seating[síːtiŋ] 좌석
reception desk 접수처 filing cabinet 서류 정리함

36 특정 세부 사항 문제

해석 회사는 최근에 무엇을 하였는가?

(A) 대출을 신청했다.
(B) 물품을 돌려보냈다.
(C) 수익을 늘렸다.

(D) 직원들을 채용했다.

해설 질문의 핵심 어구(recently do)와 관련된 내용을 주의 깊게 듣는다. 남자1이 "the company's finances improved last quarter"라며 회사의 재정 상태가 지난 분기에 개선되었다고 한 말을 통해 회사가 최근에 수익을 늘렸음을 알 수 있다. 따라서 (C)가 정답이다.

어휘 apply for ~을 신청하다, 등록하다 loan[미 loun, 영 ləun] 대출
merchandise[미 mə́ːrtʃəndàiz, 영 mə́ːtʃəndàiz] 물품
increase[inkríːs] 늘리다, 증대시키다

37 특정 세부 사항 문제

해석 여자는 무엇을 하기로 동의하는가?

(A) 회의를 간추려 말해준다.
(B) 고객들에게 연락한다.
(C) 의견들을 제안한다.
(D) 예산안을 검토한다.

해설 대화에서 여자의 말을 주의 깊게 듣는다. 남자2가 "Let me know what he says tomorrow."라며 그가 회의에서 뭐라고 하는지 내일 알려달라고 하자, 여자가 "Sure, I can do that."이라며 남자2의 말에 물론이라며 그렇게 하겠다고 하였다. 이를 통해 여자가 회의 내용을 간추려 말해주기로 동의했음을 알 수 있다. 따라서 (A)가 정답이다.

어휘 summarize[sʌ́məràiz] 간추려 말하다 look over ~을 검토하다
budget[bʌ́dʒit] 예산안, 예산

38-40 🎧 캐나다식 발음 → 미국식 발음

Questions 38-40 refer to the following conversation.

M: Jane, I've got a problem. ³⁸I'm supposed to get together with David Corey from Grandoff Industries at 3 P.M. But our CEO just asked me to meet with her at the same time.

W: Can you reschedule one of your appointments?

M: Um, ³⁹I'm actually wondering if you'd be willing to meet with Mr. Corey instead. He has some questions about the revised estimate for the warehouse. Your team created it.

W: OK. That'll be fine. ⁴⁰I'll look over the cost analysis now to prepare. I want to make sure I'm ready to answer his questions.

---

get together with ~와 만나다
reschedule[미 riːskédʒuːl, 영 riːʃédʒuːl] 일정을 변경하다
wonder[미 wʌ́ndər, 영 wʌ́ndə] 궁금하다
revised[riváizd] 수정된, 변경된 estimate[éstimət] 견적서
warehouse[미 wérhaus, 영 wéəhaus] 창고 look over ~을 검토하다
analysis[ənǽləsis] 분석 결과

해석

38-40번은 다음 대화에 관한 문제입니다.

남: Jane, 제게 문제가 생겼어요. ³⁸저는 오후 3시에 Grandoff Industries사의 David Corey와 만나기로 되어 있었어요. 그런데 저희 대표이사님이 방금 제게 같은 시간에 만나자고 요청하셨어요.

여: 당신의 약속들 중 하나의 일정을 변경할 수 있나요?

남: 음, ³⁹저는 사실 당신이 Mr. Corey를 대신 만나줄 수 있을지 궁금해요. 그는 창고의 수정된 견적서에 대해 몇 가지 질문이 있대요. 당신의 팀이 그것을 제작했잖아요.

여: 네, 괜찮을 거예요. ⁴⁰준비하기 위해 지금 비용 분석 결과를 검토할게요. 그의 질문들에 답할 준비가 되어있도록 확실히 해두고 싶어요.

38 문제점 문제

해석 남자의 문제는 무엇인가?

(A) 고객에게 연락할 수 없다.
(B) 일정 충돌이 있다.
(C) 약속에 대해 잊어버렸다.
(D) 마감 기한을 놓쳤다.

해설 남자의 말에서 부정적인 표현이 언급된 주변을 주의 깊게 듣는다. 남자가 "I'm supposed to get together with David Corey ~ at 3 P.M. But our CEO just asked me to meet with her at the same time."이라며 오후 3시에 David Corey와 만나기로 되어 있었는데 대표이사가 방금 같은 시간에 만날 것을 요청했다고 하였다. 따라서 (B)가 정답이다.

어휘 conflict[kánflikt] 충돌, 상충; (계획 등이) ~과 겹치다
miss[mis] 놓치다

39 의도 파악 문제
해설 남자는 왜 "당신의 팀이 그것을 제작했잖아요"라고 말하는가?
(A) 그녀가 돕기로 동의했음을 상기시키기 위해
(B) 그녀가 프로젝트를 잘 알고 있음을 내비치기 위해
(C) 높이 평가되는 직원이 된 것에 대해 그녀를 칭찬하기 위해
(D) 문제가 있음을 그녀에게 나타내기 위해

해설 질문의 인용어구(Your team created it)가 언급된 주변을 주의 깊게 듣는다. 남자가 "I'm actually wondering if you'd be willing to meet with Mr. Corey instead. He has some questions about the revised estimate for the warehouse."라며 여자가 Mr. Corey를 자기 대신 만나줄 수 있을지 궁금하다고 한 후, 그가 창고의 수정된 견적서에 대해 몇 가지 질문이 있다고 한 말을 통해 여자가 프로젝트를 잘 알고 있음을 내비치기 위함을 알 수 있다. 따라서 (B)가 정답이다.

어휘 commend[kəménd] 칭찬하다 valued[vǽljuːd] 높이 평가되는, 소중한

40 다음에 할 일 문제
해설 여자는 다음에 무엇을 할 것 같은가?
(A) 대표이사와 만난다.
(B) 프로젝트를 취소한다.
(C) 공장을 방문한다.
(D) 서류를 검토한다.

해설 대화의 마지막 부분을 주의 깊게 듣는다. 여자가 "I'll look over the cost analysis now to prepare."라며 준비하기 위해 지금 비용 분석 결과를 검토하겠다고 하였다. 따라서 (D)가 정답이다.

패러프레이징
look over the cost analysis 비용 분석 결과를 검토하다 → Review a document 서류를 검토하다

어휘 cancel[kǽnsəl] 취소하다 review[rivjúː] 검토하다

41-43 [영국식 발음 → 호주식 발음]
Questions 41-43 refer to the following conversation.

W: ⁴¹We have quite a few people going to the team retreat at The Learning Camp. I hope there's plenty of parking available.
M: ⁴¹Why not pay for a bus to take us? It's a long enough drive to make it worthwhile.
W: No, I don't think we have enough people for that. There are only 21 people from our company attending the event. ⁴²I wonder if any of our staff own a large van. Then some people can ride together.
M: We could rent two vans from Hart Street Car Rental. Each holds about a dozen people. That way, ◯

everybody could leave their cars at the office. ⁴³I'll call them to ask about prices.

quite[kwait] 꽤 retreat[ritríːt] 야유회 plenty of 많은
available[əvéiləbl] 이용 가능한
worthwhile[미 wɜ̀ːrθwáil, 영 wɜ̀ːθwáil] ~할 가치가 있는
rent[rent] 빌리다 hold[미 hould, 영 həuld] (사람·사물을) 수용하다

해석
41-43번은 다음 대화에 관한 문제입니다.
여: ⁴¹The Learning Camp에서 하는 팀 야유회에 가는 사람들이 꽤 있어요. 저는 이용할 수 있는 주차 공간이 많길 바라요.
남: ⁴¹우리를 데려갈 수 있는 버스 비용을 내는 건 어때요? 그만한 가치가 있을 만큼 충분히 긴 주행이에요.
여: 아니요, 그렇게 할 만큼 충분한 사람들이 있는 것 같지는 않아요. 우리 회사에서 행사에 참여하는 사람들은 21명뿐이에요. ⁴²저는 직원들 중 누구라도 큰 밴을 소유한 사람이 있는지 궁금해요. 그럼 몇몇 사람들이 함께 타고 갈 수 있을 거예요.
남: 우리는 Hart Street 자동차 대여점에서 밴 두 대를 빌릴 수 있을 거예요. 각각 12명 정도의 사람들을 수용해요. 그렇게 하면, 모든 사람들이 차를 회사에 두고 갈 수 있을 거예요. ⁴³제가 그들에게 전화해서 가격에 대해 물어볼게요.

41 주제 문제
해석 화자들은 주로 무엇에 대해 이야기하고 있는가?
(A) 야유회의 경비
(B) 밴을 위한 주차 공간
(C) 캠프장까지 가는 길 안내
(D) 행사로 가는 운송 수단

해설 대화의 주제를 묻는 문제이므로, 대화의 초반을 반드시 듣는다. 여자가 "We have quite a few people going to the team retreat ~. I hope there's plenty of parking available."이라며 팀 야유회에 가는 사람들이 꽤 있다고 한 후, 이용할 수 있는 주차 공간이 많길 바란다고 하자, 남자가 "Why not pay for a bus to take us?"라며 자신들을 데려갈 수 있는 버스 비용을 내는 건 어떤지 물은 후, 행사로 가는 운송 수단에 대한 내용으로 대화가 이어지고 있다. 따라서 (D)가 정답이다.

어휘 expense[ikspéns] 경비, 비용 directions[dirékʃənz] 길 안내

42 특정 세부 사항 문제
해석 여자는 무엇에 대해 알고 싶어 하는가?
(A) 셔틀 버스가 얼마나 비용이 들지
(B) 직원이 밴을 가지고 있는지
(C) 대여 차량을 누가 운전할 것인지
(D) 주차장이 어디에 위치해 있는지

해설 대화에서 여자의 말을 주의 깊게 듣는다. 여자가 "I wonder if any of our staff own a large van."이라며 직원들 중 누구라도 큰 밴을 소유한 사람이 있는지 궁금하다고 하였다. 따라서 (B)가 정답이다.

어휘 rental[réntl] 대여의 parking garage 주차장

43 다음에 할 일 문제
해석 남자는 다음에 무엇을 할 것 같은가?
(A) 버스를 탄다.
(B) 전화를 한다.
(C) 행사에 등록한다.
(D) 가격을 비교한다.

해설 대화의 마지막 부분을 주의 깊게 듣는다. 남자가 "I'll call them[Hart Street Car Rental] to ask about prices."라며 Hart Street 자동차 대여점에 전화해서 가격에 대해 물어보겠다고 한 말을 통해 남자가 다음에 전화를 할 것임을 알 수 있다. 따라서 (B)가 정답이다.

어휘 bus ride 버스 탑승 register for ~에 등록하다
　　　compare[미 kəmpéər, 영 kəmpéə] 비교하다

44-46 〔캐〕 캐나다식 발음 → 영국식 발음

Questions 44-46 refer to the following conversation.

M: So, ⁴⁴how should we spend our final day in Hawaii?
　　We can go on a guided hike in the mountains from
　　2 P.M. to 5 P.M. That sounds fun. Or we could take
　　beginner surfing lessons.
W: ⁴⁵I don't want to choose until Rachel gets back
　　from the spa, since she should have a say, too.
M: Fair enough. When is she going to return?
W: At 11 o'clock, so in about an hour.
M: Well, ⁴⁶why don't you look this over in the
　　meantime? It's a pamphlet that I picked up in the
　　reception area. It details the day trips offered by
　　the resort.

spend[spend] (시간을) 보내다 go on a hike 하이킹 가다
beginner[미 biɡínər, 영 biɡínə] 초보자 get back 돌아오다
spa[spa:] 온천 have a say 발언권이 있다
fair enough (생각이나 제안이) 좋다, 괜찮다 look over ~을 살펴보다
in the meantime 그동안에 reception area 로비
detail[díːteil] 상세히 알리다 day trip 당일 여행

해석
44-46번은 다음 대화에 관한 문제입니다.

남: 자, ⁴⁴하와이에서의 우리의 마지막 날을 어떻게 보내야 할까요? 우리는
　　오후 2시부터 오후 5시까지 가이드가 있는 산으로의 하이킹을 갈 수 있
　　어요. 재미있을 것 같네요. 아니면 우리는 초보자 서핑 수업을 들을 수
　　도 있어요.
여: 저는 그녀에게도 발언권이 있기 때문에, ⁴⁵Rachel이 온천에서 돌아오고
　　나면 선택하고 싶어요.
남: 좋아요. 그녀는 언제 돌아오나요?
여: 11시에 올 것이니까, 한 시간 이내로요.
남: 음, ⁴⁶그동안 이것을 살펴보고 있는 건 어때요? 제가 로비에서 가져온 팸
　　플릿이에요. 이것은 리조트에 의해 제공되는 당일 여행들에 대해 상세히
　　알려주고 있어요.

44 주제 문제
해석 대화는 주로 무엇에 관한 것인가?
　　(A) 호텔 방을 선택하기
　　(B) 휴가를 준비하기
　　(C) 활동을 정하기
　　(D) 여행 비용을 지불하기

해설 대화의 주제를 묻는 문제이므로, 대화의 초반을 반드시 듣는다. 남자
　　가 "how should we spend our final day in Hawaii?"라며 하와이
　　에서의 마지막 날을 어떻게 보내야 할지 물은 후, "We can go on a
　　guided hike in the mountains ~. Or we could take beginner
　　surfing lessons."라며 두 가지 활동 선택권을 언급하였다. 따라서
　　(C)가 정답이다.

어휘 select[silékt] 선택하다

45 언급 문제
해석 Rachel에 대해 무엇이 언급되는가?
　　(A) 온천에 갔다.
　　(B) 서핑 수업에 관심이 있다.
　　(C) 하와이에 거주한다.
　　(D) 11시에 회의가 있다.

해설 질문의 핵심 어구(Rachel)가 언급된 주변을 주의 깊게 듣는다. 여자가
　　"I don't want to choose until Rachel gets back from the spa"
　　라며 Rachel이 온천에서 돌아오고 나면 선택하고 싶다고 하였다. 따
　　라서 (A)가 정답이다.

46 특정 세부 사항 문제
해석 남자는 여자에게 무엇을 주는가?
　　(A) 여행 가방
　　(B) 기념품
　　(C) 열쇠
　　(D) 책자

해설 질문의 핵심 어구(give to the woman)와 관련된 내용을 주의 깊
　　게 듣는다. 남자가 여자에게 "why don't you look this over in the
　　meantime? It's a pamphlet that I picked up in the reception
　　area."라며 그동안 이것을 살펴보고 있는 건 어떤지 물은 후, 자신이
　　로비에서 가져온 팸플릿을 주었다. 따라서 (D)가 정답이다.

패러프레이징
pamphlet 팸플릿 → brochure 책자

어휘 souvenir[미 sùːvəníər, 영 sùːvəníə] 기념품

47-49 〔미〕 미국식 발음 → 캐나다식 발음

Questions 47-49 refer to the following conversation.

W: Hello, Mr. Smith. This is Elaine Fredericks from
　　Cortez Coffee. I'm wondering if you've received
　　your monthly order as my records don't indicate
　　whether you have.
M: ⁴⁷Our coffee shop got everything on time as usual.
　　And ⁴⁸the free samples of Honduran coffee that you
　　gave us to try out really impressed our customers. I
　　plan to purchase some with my next order.
W: That's good news. I can send a shipment of only
　　those coffee beans today if you don't want to wait
　　a full month until your next scheduled delivery.
M: I suppose that would work. ⁴⁹Please mail four
　　boxes.

indicate[índikèit] (글로) 명시하다 on time 제때에
as usual 평상시처럼 impress[imprés] 깊은 인상을 주다
shipment[ʃípmənt] 배송품, 수송품 mail[meil] (우편으로) 보내다

해석
47-49번은 다음 대화에 관한 문제입니다.

여: 안녕하세요, Mr. Smith. 저는 Cortez 커피의 Elaine Fredericks입니다.
　　저희 기록이 고객님께서 월간 주문품을 받으셨는지를 명시하지 않아서 그
　　것을 받으셨는지 궁금합니다.
남: ⁴⁷저희 커피숍은 평상시처럼 모든 것을 제때에 받았어요. 그리고 ⁴⁸당신
　　이 시험해보라고 주셨던 무료 Honduran 커피 샘플들은 저희 고객들에
　　게 정말 깊은 인상을 줬어요. 저는 제 다음 주문에 몇 개를 구매할 계획
　　이에요.
여: 잘됐네요. 고객님의 예정된 다음 배송까지 한 달을 기다리는 것을 원치 않
　　으시면 제가 오늘 그 커피콩들의 배송품만 보내드릴 수 있어요.
남: 그렇게 하면 될 것 같네요. ⁴⁹네 상자를 보내주세요.

47 화자 문제
해석 남자는 누구인 것 같은가?
　　(A) 청소 업체 소유주
　　(B) 상점 회계장부 담당자
　　(C) 배송 트럭 기사
　　(D) 카페 운영자

해설 대화에서 신분 및 직업과 관련된 표현을 놓치지 않고 듣는다. 남자가 "Our coffee shop got everything on time as usual."이라며 자신의 커피숍은 평상시처럼 모든 것을 제때에 받았다고 한 말을 통해 남자가 카페 운영자임을 알 수 있다. 따라서 (D)가 정답이다.

어휘 cleaning[klíːniŋ] 청소　bookkeeper[búkkìːpər] 회계장부 담당자

48 특정 세부 사항 문제

해석 배송품과 함께 무엇이 보내졌는가?
(A) 샘플 상품들
(B) 수정된 청구서
(C) 사무용품들
(D) 특별 쿠폰

해설 질문의 핵심 어구(sent with a shipment)와 관련된 내용을 주의 깊게 듣는다. 남자가 "the free samples of Honduran coffee that you gave us to try out really impressed our customers"라며 여자가 시험해보라고 줬던 무료 Honduran 커피 샘플들은 고객들에게 정말 깊은 인상을 줬다고 한 말을 통해 샘플 상품들이 배송품과 함께 보내졌음을 알 수 있다. 따라서 (A)가 정답이다.

어휘 revise[riváiz] 수정하다　office supply 사무용품

49 요청 문제

해석 남자는 여자에게 무엇을 하라고 요청하는가?
(A) 이메일을 작성한다.
(B) 상자 몇 개를 보낸다.
(C) 할인권을 사용한다.
(D) 상품 몇 개를 반품한다.

해설 남자의 말에서 요청과 관련된 표현이 언급된 다음을 주의 깊게 듣는다. 남자가 여자에게 "Please mail four boxes."라며 네 상자를 보내달라고 하였다. 따라서 (B)가 정답이다.

패러프레이징
mail ~ boxes 상자를 보내다 → Send some packages 상자 몇 개를 보내다

어휘 package[pǽkidʒ] 상자, 소포
voucher[미 váutʃər, 영 váutʃə] 할인권, 상품권

50-52 [호] 호주식 발음 → 미국식 발음

Questions 50-52 refer to the following conversation.

M: Excuse me, ⁵⁰can you show me where the new novels are shelved?

W: ⁵⁰They're right next to the checkout area. Are you looking for any title in particular?

M: Two, actually. *The Old Bride* by Phyllis McNeal and *Voting for Peanuts* by . . . um . . . I forget the author's name.

W: It's Dale Daniels, if I'm not mistaken. But I'm afraid we're sold out of that one. ⁵¹/⁵²It was recently featured on a famous talk show and after that, it sold quickly.

M: ⁵²Of course. I heard it was popular. Well, when will more copies be available?

W: Just a moment. Let me check now.

novel[미 nάvəl, 영 nɔ́vəl] 소설　shelve[ʃelv] 선반에 놓다
checkout[tʃékaut] 계산대　look for ~을 찾다　title[táitl] 서적, 제목
in particular 특별히, 특히　actually[ǽktʃuəli] 실은
mistaken[mistéikən] 잘못 알고 있는　sold out 다 팔린
feature[미 fíːtʃər, 영 fíːtʃə] (신문·잡지 등이) ~을 특집으로 다루다

해석 50-52번은 다음 대화에 관한 문제입니다.

남: 실례합니다, ⁵⁰새로 나온 소설들이 어디에 있는 선반에 놓여있는지 알려 주시겠어요?

여: ⁵⁰그것들은 계산대 구역 바로 옆에 있어요. 특별히 찾으시는 서적이 있나요?

남: 실은, 두 개예요. Phyllis McNeal의 *The Old Bride*와 *Voting for Peanuts*는... 음... 작가의 이름을 잊어버렸네요.

여: 제가 잘못 알고 있는 게 아니라면, Dale Daniels에요. 하지만 안타깝게도 그것은 다 팔렸어요. ⁵¹/⁵²최근에 유명한 토크쇼에서 특집으로 다뤄지고 난 후, 그것은 빠르게 판매되었어요.

남: ⁵²그렇겠죠. 그것이 인기가 있다고 들었어요. 그렇다면, 언제 더 많은 책들이 구매 가능할까요?

여: 잠시만요. 제가 지금 확인해볼게요.

50 장소 문제

해석 대화는 어디에서 일어나고 있는 것 같은가?
(A) 서점에서
(B) 도서관에서
(C) 출판 박람회에서
(D) 방송국 스튜디오에서

해설 대화에서 장소와 관련된 표현을 놓치지 않고 듣는다. 남자가 여자에게 "can you show me where the new novels are shelved?"라며 새로 나온 소설들이 어디에 있는 선반에 놓여있는지 알려달라고 하자, 여자가 "They're right next to the checkout area."라며 그것들은 계산대 구역 바로 옆에 있다고 하였다. 이를 통해 서점에서 대화가 일어나고 있음을 알 수 있다. 따라서 (A)가 정답이다.

어휘 bookstore[미 búkstɔːr, 영 búkstɔː] 서점　publishing[pʌ́bliʃiŋ] 출판
expo[미 ékspou, 영 ékspəu] 박람회, 전시회

51 언급 문제

해석 여자는 *Voting for Peanuts*에 대해 무엇을 말하는가?
(A) *The Old Bride* 이후에 출간되었다.
(B) 안내 데스크 뒤 선반에 놓여있다.
(C) 매체에서 알려졌다.
(D) 토크쇼 진행자에 의해 쓰여졌다.

해설 여자의 말에서 질문의 핵심 어구(*Voting for Peanuts*)와 관련된 내용을 주의 깊게 듣는다. 여자가 "It[*Voting for Peanuts*] was recently featured on a famous talk show"라며 최근에 *Voting for Peanuts*가 유명한 토크쇼에서 특집으로 다뤄졌다고 하였다. 따라서 (C)가 정답이다.

패러프레이징
featured on a ~ talk show 토크쇼에서 특집으로 다뤄졌다
→ publicized in the media 매체에서 알려졌다

어휘 publicize[미 pʌ́bləsàiz, 영 pʌ́blisàiz] 알리다, 관심받다
media[míːdiə] (신문·텔레비전 등의) 매체
host[미 houst, 영 həust] 진행자

52 의도 파악 문제

해석 남자는 왜 "그것이 인기가 있다고 들었어요"라고 말하는가?
(A) 흥분을 표현하기 위해
(B) 놀랍지 않음을 나타내기 위해
(C) 결정 사항을 설명하기 위해
(D) 신간 도서를 추천하기 위해

해설 질문의 인용어구(I heard it was popular)가 언급된 주변을 주의 깊게 듣는다. 여자가 "It[*Voting for Peanuts*] was recently featured on a famous talk show and after that, it sold quickly."라며 최근에 *Voting for Peanuts*가 유명한 토크쇼에서 특집으로 다뤄지고 난 후 빠르게 판매되었다고 하자, 남자가 "Of course. ~ Well, when will more copies be available?"이라며 여자의 말에 그렇겠다고 하며 언제 더 많은 책들이 구매 가능할지 물었다. 이를 통해 남자가 놀랍

지 않음을 나타내기 위함임을 알 수 있다. 따라서 (B)가 정답이다.

어휘 **indicate**[índikèit] 나타내다　**recommend**[rèkəménd] 추천하다

53-55 [캐] 캐나다식 발음 → 미국식 발음

Questions 53-55 refer to the following conversation.

M: Have you seen the documentary called *Help Yourself*? ⁵³It focuses on ways to treat and prevent illnesses with healthy food and supplements.
W: No, I haven't, but I've read positive reviews about it.
M: ⁵⁴I found it informative and consistent with our nutritional consultation services. I wonder if we can buy a copy of it and play it in the waiting room.
W: I bet the movie can be downloaded for a fee online.
M: True. But before we show the film, ⁵⁵you should watch it as well to make sure you find it appropriate.
W: I'll do that this weekend, and then we can discuss if we want to show it here.

---

focus on ~에 집중하다　**treat**[tri:t] 치료하다
prevent[privént] 예방하다　**illness**[ílnis] 질병
supplement[미 sʌ́pləmənt, 영 sʌ́plimənt] 보조식품　**review**[rivjú:] 평가
informative[미 infɔ́:rmətiv, 영 infɔ́:mətiv] 유익한
consistent[kənsístənt] ~과 일치하는　**nutritional**[nju:tríʃənl] 영양의
consultation[미 kʌ̀nsəltéiʃən, 영 kʌ̀nsʌltéiʃən] 상담
bet[bet] ~이 분명하다　**appropriate**[미 əpróupriət, 영 əpróupriət] 적절한

해석
53-55번은 다음 대화에 관한 문제입니다.

남: *Help Yourself*라는 다큐멘터리를 보신 적 있나요? ⁵³그것은 건강한 음식과 보조식품들로 질병들을 치료하고 예방하는 방법들을 집중적으로 다뤄요.
여: 아니요, 저는 아직 안 봤지만, 그것에 대한 긍정적인 평가들을 읽었어요.
남: ⁵⁴저는 그것이 유익하고 우리의 영양 상담 서비스와도 맥락이 일치한다고 생각해요. 우리가 그것의 복사물을 사서 대기실에서 틀 수 있을지 궁금해요.
여: 그 영화는 분명히 온라인에서 요금을 주고 다운로드될 수 있을 거예요.
남: 맞아요. 하지만 그 영화를 보여주기 전에, ⁵⁵그것이 적절하다고 생각되는지 확실히 하기 위해 당신도 그것을 봐야 해요.
여: 이번 주말에 그렇게 할게요, 그 후에 우리가 그것을 여기서 보여주기를 원하는지에 대해 논의할 수 있을 거예요.

53 언급 문제

해석 남자는 *Help Yourself*에 대해 무엇을 말하는가?
　(A) 올해 촬영되었다.
　(B) 지역 극장에서 상영하고 있다.
　(C) 유명한 배우를 출연시킨다.
　(D) 식품 선택에 대해 다룬다.

해설 질문의 핵심 어구(*Help Yourself*)와 관련된 내용을 주의 깊게 듣는다. 남자가 "It[*Help Yourself*] focuses on ways to treat and prevent illnesses with healthy food and supplements."라며 *Help Yourself*는 건강한 음식과 보조식품들로 질병들을 치료하고 예방하는 방법들을 집중적으로 다룬다고 하였다. 따라서 (D)가 정답이다.

어휘 **film**[film] 촬영하다
feature[미 fí:tʃər, 영 fí:tʃə] (배우를) ~으로 출연(주연)시키다
well-known[미 wèlnóun, 영 wèlnóun] 유명한　**deal with** ~을 다루다

54 특정 세부 사항 문제

해석 화자들은 어떤 종류의 서비스를 제공하는 것 같은가?
　(A) 제품 광고
　(B) 영양 상담

　(C) 영상 판매
　(D) 진로 조언

해설 질문의 핵심 어구(type of service)와 관련된 내용을 주의 깊게 듣는다. 남자가 "I found it[documentary] ~ consistent with our nutritional consultation services."라며 다큐멘터리가 화자들의 영양 상담 서비스와도 맥락이 일치한다고 생각한다고 한 말을 통해 화자들이 영양 상담 서비스를 제공함을 알 수 있다. 따라서 (B)가 정답이다.

어휘 **advertising**[미 ǽdvərtàiziŋ, 영 ǽdvətàiziŋ] 광고(업)
career[미 kəríər, 영 kəríə] 진로, 경력

55 제안 문제

해석 남자는 무엇을 제안하는가?
　(A) 다큐멘터리를 보기
　(B) 다른 방에서 기다리기
　(C) 광고를 촬영하기
　(D) 자료들을 온라인에 업로드하기

해설 남자의 말에서 제안과 관련된 표현이 언급된 다음을 주의 깊게 듣는다. 남자가 여자에게 "you should watch it[documentary] as well to make sure you find it appropriate"라며 다큐멘터리가 적절하다고 생각되는지 확실히 하기 위해 여자도 그것을 봐야 한다고 하였다. 따라서 (A)가 정답이다.

어휘 **commercial**[미 kəmə́:rʃəl, 영 kəmə́:ʃəl] 광고
material[mətíəriəl] 자료, 재료

56-58 [영] 영국식 발음 → 미국식 발음 → 호주식 발음

Questions 56-58 refer to the following conversation with three speakers.

W1: Macy, ⁵⁶I think we could cut costs by stopping the water bottle deliveries to our offices and installing a filtration system instead.
W2: Right. That would also reduce plastic waste.
W1: We should ask if it's in the budget. ⁵⁷There's Andrew, the accounting department manager . . . Andrew, is there money to purchase a water filtration system in the budget?
M: I think so. Those systems cost a lot, but it would cut costs in the long term.
W1: Thanks. ⁵⁸Then, I will do some research and get a few estimates.
W2: ⁵⁸I also have some time. Let's have a look now.

---

install[instɔ́:l] 설치하다　**filtration system** 여과 장치
in the long term 장기적으로　**estimate**[éstəmèit] 견적(액)

해석
56-58번은 다음 세 명의 대화에 관한 문제입니다.

여1: Macy, ⁵⁶우리는 사무실에 물병 배달을 중단하고 대신에 여과 장치를 설치함으로써 비용을 줄일 수 있을 것 같아요.
여2: 맞아요. 그것은 또한 플라스틱 쓰레기를 줄일 거예요.
여1: 우리는 그것이 예산 내에 있는지 물어봐야 해요. ⁵⁷회계부장 Andrew가 있네요... Andrew, 예산 내에 정수기를 살 돈이 있나요?
남: 그런 것 같아요. 그러한 장치들은 비용이 많이 들지만, 장기적으로는 비용을 절감할 거예요.
여1: 감사해요. ⁵⁸그럼, 제가 조사를 좀 해서 견적을 몇 개 받아볼게요.
여2: ⁵⁸저도 시간이 좀 있어요. 지금 한번 봐요.

56 주제 문제

해석 대화는 주로 무엇에 대한 것인가?
　(A) 캠페인을 시작하는 것

(B) 공공시설에 대한 비용을 절약하는 것
(C) 환경오염을 방지하는 것
(D) 새로운 물 공급원을 시도하는 것

해설 대화의 주제를 묻는 문제이므로, 지문의 초반을 주의 깊게 듣는다. 여자1이 "I think we could cut costs by stopping the water bottle deliveries to our offices and installing a filtration system instead"라며 사무실에 물병 배달을 중단하고 대신에 여과 장치를 설치함으로써 비용을 줄일 수 있을 것 같다고 한 후, 새로운 물 공급원을 시도하는 것, 즉 정수기 설치에 대한 내용으로 대화가 이어지고 있다. 따라서 (D)가 정답이다.

어휘 launch[lɔ:ntʃ] 시작하다, 개시하다

57 화자 문제

해석 남자는 어느 부서에서 일하는가?
(A) 회계
(B) 배송
(C) 인적 자원
(D) 정비

해설 지문에서 신분 및 직업과 관련된 표현을 놓치지 않고 듣는다. 여자1이 "There's Andrew, the accounting department manager ~."라며 회계부장 Andrew가 있다고 한 말을 통해 남자가 회계 부서에서 일한다는 것을 알 수 있다. 따라서 (A)가 정답이다.

어휘 accounting[əkáuntiŋ] 회계 human resources 인적 자원
maintenance[méintənəns] 정비, 보수

58 특정 세부 사항 문제

해석 여자들은 무엇을 하기로 결정하는가?
(A) 회의를 재조정한다.
(B) 일부 배달품을 가지러 간다.
(C) 새로운 장치를 주문한다.
(D) 가격 견적을 몇 개 받아본다.

해설 질문의 핵심 어구(women decide to do)와 관련된 내용을 주의 깊게 듣는다. 여자1이 "Then, I will do some research and get a few estimates."라며 자신이 조사를 좀 해서 견적을 몇 개 받아보겠다고 하자, 여자2가 "I also have some time. Let's have a look now."라며 자신도 시간이 좀 있다며 지금 한번 보자고 하였다. 따라서 (D)가 정답이다.

패러프레이징
get a few estimates 견적을 몇 개 받아보다 → Get some price quotes 가격 견적을 몇 개 받아보다

어휘 quote[kwout] 견적

59-61 🎧 영국식 발음 → 캐나다식 발음

Questions 59-61 refer to the following conversation.

W: My family is in town, and ⁵⁹I'm trying to figure out something fun to do with them. I've taken them to the museums, shopping areas, and parks. I can't think of anything else that they might enjoy.
M: ⁶⁰Why don't you see the new musical at the Central Arts Center? It features country songs performed in the style of rock.
W: Maybe I will. That sounds interesting. Do you know if there are shows on weekends?
M: There definitely are some on Saturdays, but I'm not sure about Sundays. ⁶¹I'll text the Web site address to you now so you can check.

figure out ~을 생각해내다

feature[fíːtʃər] 특별히 포함하다, 특징으로 삼다
definitely[미 défənitli, 영 définətli] 확실히

해석
59-61번은 다음 대화에 관한 문제입니다.

여: 제 가족이 시내에 있는데, ⁵⁹그들과 함께 할 재미있는 무언가를 생각해내려 하고 있어요. 저는 그들을 박물관, 쇼핑 지역, 그리고 공원에 데려갔었어요. 그들이 즐길 수 있을 만한 또 다른 것을 생각해낼 수가 없네요.
남: ⁶⁰Central 아트 센터에서 하는 새로운 뮤지컬을 보는 것은 어때요? 그곳은 록 스타일로 연주되는 컨트리 노래를 특별히 포함해요.
여: 아마도 그래야겠네요. 재미있겠어요. 혹시 주말에도 공연이 있는지 알고 계신가요?
남: 토요일에는 확실히 있는데, 일요일은 잘 모르겠어요. ⁶¹제가 당신이 확인할 수 있도록 지금 웹사이트 주소를 문자로 보내드릴게요.

59 특정 세부 사항 문제

해석 여자는 무엇을 하려고 하는가?
(A) 오락거리를 계획한다.
(B) 친구에게 그녀와 함께할 것을 설득한다.
(C) 지역 행사를 홍보한다.
(D) 박물관 표를 산다.

해설 질문의 핵심 어구(trying to do)와 관련된 내용을 주의 깊게 듣는다. 여자가 "I'm trying to figure out something fun to do with them[family]"이라며 자신의 가족과 함께 할 재미있는 무언가를 생각해내려 하고 있다고 하였다. 따라서 (A)가 정답이다.

패러프레이징
figure out something fun 재미있는 무언가를 생각해내다 → Plan some entertainment 오락거리를 계획하다

어휘 entertainment[èntərtéinmənt] 오락, 즐거움, 여흥
convince[kənvíns] 설득하다
promote[미 prəmóut, 영 prəmə́ut] 홍보하다

60 제안 문제

해석 남자는 무엇을 제안하는가?
(A) 공원에 소풍을 가는 것
(B) 쇼핑센터를 방문하는 것
(C) 공연을 관람하는 것
(D) 교외 여행을 가는 것

해설 남자의 말에서 제안과 관련된 표현이 언급된 다음을 주의 깊게 듣는다. 남자가 "Why don't you see the new musical at the Central Arts Center?"라며 Central 아트 센터에서 하는 새로운 뮤지컬을 보는 게 어떤지 물었다. 따라서 (C)가 정답이다.

패러프레이징
see the ~ musical 뮤지컬을 보다 → Watching a performance 공연을 관람하는 것

어휘 countryside[kʌ́ntrisaid] 교외, 전원 지역

61 다음에 할 일 문제

해석 남자는 무엇을 할 것이라고 말하는가?
(A) 건물 주소에 대해 문의한다.
(B) 온라인 링크를 공유한다.
(C) 공연 시간을 확인한다.
(D) 명소 몇 군데를 나열한다.

해설 대화의 마지막 부분을 주의 깊게 듣는다. 남자가 "I'll text the Web site address to you now so you can check."이라며 여자가 확인할 수 있도록 지금 웹사이트 주소를 문자로 보내겠다고 하였다. 따라서 (B)가 정답이다.

패러프레이징
text the Web site address 웹사이트 주소를 문자로 보내다 → Share an online link 온라인 링크를 공유하다

어휘 inquire[미 inkwáiər, 영 inkwáiə] 문의하다
share[미 ʃɛər, 영 ʃeə] 공유하다 attraction[ətrǽkʃn] 명소, 명물

62-64 🎧 미국식 발음 → 호주식 발음

Questions 62-64 refer to the following conversation and business card.

> W: ⁶²I'm here to pick up the business cards your shop printed for me. My name is Helga Kim.
>
> M: Yes, Ms. Kim. I have your completed order right here. Please look them over and make sure the information is correct.
>
> W: Hmm . . . It looks like there's an error. ⁶³The operational hours and contact information are fine. However, the number "31" was incorrectly printed as "37."
>
> M: Oh, my apologies. ⁶⁴I'll fix that part and print new ones for you right away, which should only take about 10 minutes.

pick up (어디에서) ~을 찾다, 찾아오다 order[미 ɔ́ːrdər, 영 ɔ́ːdə] 주문품
look over ~을 살펴보다 error[미 érər, 영 érə] 오류
contact information 연락처

해석
62-64번은 다음 대화와 명함에 관한 문제입니다.

여: ⁶²저는 당신의 가게가 출력한 명함들을 찾으러 왔어요. 제 이름은 Helga Kim이에요.

남: 네, Ms. Kim. 바로 여기 완성된 주문품이 있습니다. 그것들을 살펴보시고 정보가 맞는지 확인해보세요.

여: 흠... 오류가 하나 있는 것 같네요. ⁶³운영 시간과 연락처는 괜찮아요. 하지만, 숫자 "31"이 "37"로 잘못 출력되었어요.

남: 아, 사과드립니다. ⁶⁴제가 바로 그 부분을 고쳐서 새 것을 출력해드릴 텐데, 이것은 10분 정도 밖에 걸리지 않을 거예요.

Helga's 드라이클리닝
Helga Kim, 사장

전화번호: 555-6922
일일 운영 시간: 오전 9시-오후 7시
⁶³거리 주소: 37번지 Pine로
이메일 주소: helga@cleanwiz.net

---

62 목적 문제

해석 여자는 왜 가게에 방문하는가?
(A) 금액을 확인하기 위해
(B) 항의를 하기 위해
(C) 재료들을 고르기 위해
(D) 물건들을 가지러 오기 위해

해설 대화의 목적을 묻는 문제이므로, 대화의 초반을 반드시 듣는다. 여자가 "I'm here to pick up the business cards your shop printed for me."라며 남자의 가게가 출력한 명함들을 찾으러 왔다고 하였다. 따라서 (D)가 정답이다.

패러프레이징
pick up the business cards 명함들을 찾으러 오다 → collect some items 물건들을 가지러 오다

어휘 verify[미 vérəfài, 영 vérifài] 확인하다
make a complaint 항의하다, 불평하다
collect[kəlékt] 가지러 오다(가다)

63 시각 자료 문제

해석 시각 자료를 보아라. 어떤 정보에 오류가 있는가?
(A) 전화번호
(B) 거리 주소
(C) 일일 운영 시간
(D) 이메일 주소

해설 잘못된 정보를 묻는 문제이므로, 제시된 명함의 정보를 확인한 후 이와 일치하지 않는 내용이 있는지 주의 깊게 듣는다. 여자가 "The operational hours and contact information are fine. However, the number "31" was incorrectly printed as "37.""이라며 운영 시간과 연락처는 괜찮다고 한 후, 하지만 숫자 "31"이 "37"로 잘못 출력되었다고 하였으므로, 거리 주소에 오류가 있음을 명함에서 알 수 있다. 따라서 (B)가 정답이다.

어휘 contain[kəntéin] 들어있다, 포함하다

64 특정 세부 사항 문제

해석 무엇이 완료되는 데 10분이 걸릴 것인가?
(A) 옷들을 세탁하기
(B) 복사기를 고치기
(C) 양식을 작성하기
(D) 새 명함들을 출력하기

해설 질문의 핵심 어구(10 minutes)가 언급된 주변을 주의 깊게 듣는다. 남자가 "I'll fix that part and print new ones[business cards] for you right away, which should only take about 10 minutes."라며 바로 그 부분을 고쳐서 새 명함들을 출력해줄 텐데 이것은 10분 정도 밖에 걸리지 않을 것이라고 하였다. 따라서 (D)가 정답이다.

어휘 garment[미 gáːrmənt, 영 gáːmənt] 옷
photocopier[미 fóutoukàpiər, 영 fə́utəukɔ̀piər] 복사기
fill out ~을 작성하다 card[kɑːrd] 명함

65-67 🎧 영국식 발음 → 캐나다식 발음

Questions 65-67 refer to the following conversation and list.

> W: Hi. ⁶⁵I'm calling about the booking my company made at your facilities for our upcoming conference. I'm wondering if it's possible to make some last-minute changes.
>
> M: Possibly. What specific changes?
>
> W: Well, 200 people ended up registering . . . that's 100 more than we were expecting. I'm not sure if the original room we booked is large enough.
>
> M: Hmm . . . yes, we'll have to move your event to another space, since ⁶⁶the room you originally booked can seat only 100 people. Luckily, all of our other rooms are free, so we can easily relocate you.
>
> W: Great. ⁶⁷We'll also need to double our catering order to provide meals to all the extra attendees.

make a change ~을 변경하다
last-minute[미 lǽstmìnit, 영 làstmínit] 마지막 순간의
specific[미 spisífik, 영 spəsífik] 구체적인 end up (결국) ~하게 되다
original[ərídʒənl] 원래의 seat[siːt] 수용하다 luckily[lʌ́kili] 다행히
double[dʌ́bl] ~을 두 배로 하다 catering[kéitəriŋ] 음식 제공
attendee[ətèndíː] 참석자

해석
65-67번은 다음 대화와 목록에 관한 문제입니다.

여: 안녕하세요. ⁶⁵저는 곧 있을 회의를 위해 당신의 시설에 저희 회사가 한 예약에 대해 연락 드려요. 마지막 순간에 몇 가지를 변경하는 것이 가능

한지 궁금해요.

남: 아마도요. 구체적으로 어떤 변경인가요?

여: 음, 200명이 등록하게 되었어요... 이건 저희가 예상하던 것보다 100명이 더 많아요. 저희가 예약했던 원래의 방이 충분히 큰지 모르겠어요.

남: 흠... 네, ⁶⁶원래 예약하셨던 방은 100명만 수용할 수 있어서, 행사를 다른 장소로 옮겨야 할 것 같네요. 다행히, 저희의 다른 모든 방들이 비어 있기 때문에, 쉽게 옮겨드릴 수 있어요.

여: 좋아요. ⁶⁷저희는 또한 모든 추가 참석자들에게 식사를 제공하기 위해 음식 주문을 두 배로 해야 할 거예요.

회의실	최대 수용 인원
⁶⁶Majesty 홀·············100명	
Throne 홀·············150명	
Scepter 홀·············200명	
Royalty 홀·············250명	

65 목적 문제

해석 여자는 왜 전화를 하고 있는가?
(A) 행사에 등록하기 위해
(B) 회의 발표자에 대해 문의하기 위해
(C) 시설의 위치를 물어보기 위해
(D) 예약을 업데이트하기 위해

해설 전화의 목적을 묻는 문제이므로, 대화의 초반을 반드시 듣는다. "I'm calling about the booking my company made at your facilities for our upcoming conference. I'm wondering if it's possible to make some last-minute changes."라며 곧 있을 회의를 위해 남자의 시설에 자신의 회사가 한 예약에 대해 연락을 한다고 한 후, 마지막 순간에 몇 가지를 변경하는 것이 가능한지 궁금하다고 하였다. 따라서 (D)가 정답이다.

패러프레이징
make some ~ changes 몇 가지를 변경하다 → update a reservation 예약을 업데이트하다

어휘 sign up for ~에 등록하다

66 시각 자료 문제

해석 시각 자료를 보아라. 여자는 원래 어떤 방을 예약했었는가?
(A) Majesty 홀
(B) Throne 홀
(C) Scepter 홀
(D) Royalty 홀

해설 제시된 목록의 정보를 확인한 후 질문의 핵심 어구(originally booked)가 언급된 주변을 주의 깊게 듣는다. 남자가 "the room you originally booked can seat only 100 people"이라며 원래 예약했던 방은 100명만 수용할 수 있다고 하였으므로, 여자가 원래 Majesty 홀을 예약했었음을 목록에서 알 수 있다. 따라서 (A)가 정답이다.

67 요청 문제

해석 여자는 무엇을 요청하는가?
(A) 추가 음식
(B) 발표 장비
(C) 변경된 방 목록
(D) 추가 손님 입장권

해설 여자의 말에서 요청과 관련된 표현이 언급된 다음을 주의 깊게 듣는다. 여자가 "We'll also need to double our catering order to provide meals to all the extra attendees."라며 모든 추가 참석자들에게 식사를 제공하기 위해 음식 주문을 두 배로 해야 할 것이라고 하였다. 따라서 (A)가 정답이다.

패러프레이징
double ~ catering order 음식 주문을 두 배로 하다 →
Additional food 추가 음식

68-70 ③w 캐나다식 발음 → 미국식 발음

Questions 68-70 refer to the following conversation and service options.

M: Hello. Thank you for calling Velco. This is Marvin. How may I help you?

W: Hi. My name is Sandra Smith. ⁶⁸I'd like to change my phone plan.

M: Will this be a temporary change?

W: No, it will be ongoing. ⁶⁸Starting this month, I need to make regular calls to new clients in other countries.

M: Um . . . You currently have the Gold Plan. ⁶⁹I'd recommend switching to a different plan. There is one that includes free international calling.

W: Great. I'll do that then.

M: OK. ⁷⁰I'll change your plan now. You should be able to make free calls in about an hour.

plan[plæn] 요금제, 제도   temporary[témpəreri] 일시적인
ongoing[á:ngouiŋ] 계속하고 있는   starting[stá:rtiŋ] ~ 부터
regular[régjulər] 잦은, 정기적인   switch[switʃ] 바꾸다
international[미 intərnǽʃnəl, 영 intənǽʃnəl] 국제(상)의, 국제적인

해석
68-70번은 다음 대화와 서비스 옵션에 관한 문제입니다.

남: 안녕하세요. Velco사에 전화해 주셔서 감사합니다. 저는 Marvin입니다. 제가 어떻게 도와드릴까요?

여: 안녕하세요. 제 이름은 Sandra Smith예요. ⁶⁸저는 제 전화 요금제를 변경하고 싶어요.

남: 이것은 일시적인 변경일까요?

여: 아니요, 계속일 거예요. ⁶⁸이번 달부터, 저는 다른 나라에 있는 새로운 고객들에게 잦은 전화를 해야 해요.

남: 음... 고객님은 현재 골드 플랜을 가지고 계시네요. ⁶⁹저는 다른 요금제로 바꾸는 것을 추천합니다. 무료 국제 전화를 포함하는 것이 있습니다.

여: 좋아요. 그럼 그걸로 할게요.

남: 알겠습니다. ⁷⁰지금 고객님의 요금제를 변경하겠습니다. 고객님은 약 한 시간 후에 무료 통화를 하실 수 있을 겁니다.

	브론즈 요금제	실버 요금제	골드 요금제	⁶⁹플래티넘 요금제
무료 국내 전화	v	v	v	v
무료 국제 전화				v
무제한 메시지		v	v	v
무제한 인터넷			v	v

68 이유 문제

해석 여자는 왜 그녀의 서비스 요금제를 바꾸고 싶어 하는가?
(A) 새로운 사업 관계를 맺었다.
(B) 추가 전화선이 필요하다.
(C) 스마트폰으로 업그레이드하기를 원한다.
(D) 국제 출장을 갈 것이다.

해설 질문의 핵심 어구(change ~ service plan)와 관련된 내용을 주의 깊게 듣는다. 여자가 "I'd like to change my phone plan."이라며 전화 요금제를 변경하고 싶다고 한 후, "Starting this month, I need to make regular calls to new clients in other countries."라며 이번 달부터 다른 나라에 있는 새로운 고객들에게 잦은 전화를 해야 한다고 하였다. 따라서 (A)가 정답이다.

어휘 establish[istǽbliʃ] 맺다, 확립하다 relationship[riléiʃnʃip] 관계
additional[ədíʃənl] 추가적인

69 시각 자료 문제

해석 시각 자료를 보아라. 남자는 어떤 요금제를 추천하는가?
(A) 브론즈 요금제
(B) 실버 요금제
(C) 골드 요금제
(D) 플래티넘 요금제

해설 제시된 서비스 옵션의 정보를 확인한 후 질문의 핵심 어구(recommend)가 언급된 주변을 주의 깊게 듣는다. 남자가 여자에게 "I'd recommend switching to a different plan. There is one that includes free international calling."이라며 다른 요금제로 바꾸는 것을 추천하며 무료 국제 전화를 포함하는 것이 있다고 하였으므로, 남자가 플래티넘 요금제를 추천한다는 것을 서비스 옵션에서 알 수 있다. 따라서 (D)가 정답이다.

70 다음에 할 일 문제

해석 남자는 다음에 무엇을 할 것 같은가?
(A) 경품을 제공한다.
(B) 대금을 징수한다
(C) 계정을 업데이트한다.
(D) 전화를 건다.

해설 지문의 마지막 부분을 주의 깊게 듣는다. 남자가 "I'll change your plan now."라며 지금 여자의 요금제를 변경하겠다고 한 말을 통해 남자가 계정을 업데이트할 것임을 알 수 있다. 따라서 (C)가 정답이다.

어휘 free gift 경품 payment[péimənt] 대금, 지불금

PART 4

71-73 🎧 영국식 발음

Questions 71-73 refer to the following telephone message.

> This is Lindsay Kruger calling for Tyler Sharp. Mr. Sharp, I'm sorry to inform you that ⁷¹I won't be able to meet with you tomorrow to listen to your sales proposal. ⁷²Unfortunately, a personal matter with a relative has come up, and I'll be taking the day off. I would like to reschedule the meeting for later this week—perhaps Thursday. As I'll be out of the office for the rest of today as well, ⁷³please leave a message with my assistant at 555-7558 to let me know if this will work for you. I apologize again for the cancellation and hope to hear back from you soon.
>
> **sales proposal** 매매 제안(서) **relative**[rélətiv] 친척
> **come up** 생기다, 발생하다 **take a day off** 하루 쉬다
> **reschedule**[미 ri:skédʒu:l, 영 ri:ʃédʒu:l] 일정을 변경하다
> **perhaps**[미 pərhǽps, 영 pəhǽps] 될 수 있는 한, 가능하면
> **assistant**[əsístənt] 비서

해석

71-73번은 다음 전화 메시지에 관한 문제입니다.

저는 Tyler Sharp께 전화드리는 Lindsay Kruger입니다. Mr. Sharp, ⁷¹제가 내일 당신의 매매 제안을 듣기 위해 당신과 회의할 수 없을 것임을 알려드리게 되어 죄송합니다. ⁷²안타깝게도, 친척과 관련된 개인적인 일이 생겨서, 저

는 그날 쉴 것입니다. 저는 이번 주 후반, 될 수 있는 한 목요일로 회의 일정을 변경하고 싶습니다. 오늘 남은 시간에도 제가 사무실에 없을 것이기 때문에, ⁷³이것이 당신에게도 괜찮을지 제게 알려주시기 위해서는 555-7558로 제 비서에게 메시지를 남겨주시기 바랍니다. 취소에 대해 다시 한번 사과드리며 당신으로부터 곧 다시 연락 오기를 바라겠습니다.

71 특정 세부 사항 문제

해석 내일 무엇이 논의되기로 되어 있었는가?
(A) 근무 일정
(B) 프로젝트 취소
(C) 취업 기회
(D) 매매 제안

해설 질문의 핵심 어구(tomorrow)가 언급된 주변을 주의 깊게 듣는다. "I won't be able to meet with you tomorrow to listen to your sales proposal"이라며 내일 매매 제안을 듣기 위해 청자와 회의할 수 없을 것이라고 하였다. 따라서 (D)가 정답이다.

패러프레이징
sales proposal 매매 제안 → **sales proposition** 매매 제안

어휘 **proposition**[pràpəzíʃən] 제안, 제의

72 이유 문제

해석 회의는 왜 연기되어야 하는가?
(A) 가족 관련 일이 처리되어야 한다.
(B) 항공편이 초과 예약되었다.
(C) 직원이 해외로 출장 중이다.
(D) 사무장이 몸이 좋지 않다.

해설 질문의 핵심 어구(a meeting be postponed)와 관련된 내용을 주의 깊게 듣는다. "Unfortunately, a personal matter with a relative has come up, and I'll be taking the day off. I would like to reschedule the meeting for later this week ~."이라며 안타깝게도 친척과 관련된 개인적인 일이 생겨서 그날 쉴 것이라고 한 후, 이번 주 후반으로 회의 일정을 변경하고 싶다고 하였다. 따라서 (A)가 정답이다.

패러프레이징
a personal matter with a relative 친척과 관련된 개인적인 일 → **A family matter** 가족 관련 일

어휘 **postpone**[미 poustpóun, 영 pəustpóun] 연기하다, 미루다
handle[hǽndl] 처리하다 **ill**[il] 몸이 안 좋은, 아픈

73 요청 문제

해석 화자는 청자에게 무엇을 하라고 요청하는가?
(A) 사무실에 들른다.
(B) 비서에게 연락한다.
(C) 휴대전화로 전화한다.
(D) 이메일을 보낸다.

해설 지문의 중후반에서 요청과 관련된 표현이 포함된 문장을 주의 깊게 듣는다. "please leave a message with my assistant ~ to let me know if this will work for you"라며 이것, 즉 회의 일정 변경이 청자에게도 괜찮을지 알려주기 위해서는 화자의 비서에게 메시지를 남겨주기 바란다고 하였다. 따라서 (B)가 정답이다.

어휘 **stop by** ~에 들르다

74-76 🎧 미국식 발음

Questions 74-76 refer to the following news report.

> Now it's time for Radio ZPS's morning traffic update. Due to an accident that took place 30 minutes ago, ⁷⁴Lincoln Bridge has been closed to vehicles and pedestrians. Although nobody was injured, a railing ◑

was damaged and is currently being fixed. **Also,** [75]the vehicles involved in the accident need to be towed from the scene before the bridge will once again be accessible. This should be taken care of within the hour. **For the time being, however,** [76]I encourage commuters to cross the Hubert River by using West Bridge.

---

traffic update 교통 속보   pedestrian[pədéstriən] 보행자
be injured 부상당하다   railing[réiliŋ] 난간
involve[미 inválv, 영 invólv] (상황·사건·활동에 사람을) 연루(관련)시키다
tow[미 tou, 영 təu] 견인하다   scene[siːn] 현장, 상황
accessible[əksésəbl] 이용 가능한   take care of ~을 처리하다, 돌보다
for the time being 당분간
commuter[미 kəmjúːtər, 영 kəmjúːtə] 통근자

해석
74-76번은 다음 뉴스 보도에 관한 문제입니다.

지금은 라디오 ZPS의 아침 교통 속보 시간입니다. 30분 전에 일어났던 사고 때문에, [74]Lincoln 다리가 차량과 보행자들에게 폐쇄되어 있습니다. 아무도 부상당하지 않았지만, 난간이 손상되어 현재 수리되고 있는 중입니다. 또한, [75]사고에 연루된 차량들은 다리가 다시 이용 가능해지기 전에 현장에서 견인되어야 합니다. 이는 한 시간 내에 처리될 것입니다. 그러나, 당분간 [76]저는 통근자들께 West 다리를 이용하여 Hubert 강을 건너시기를 권해드립니다.

74 특정 세부 사항 문제
해석   무엇이 아직도 일어나고 있는가?
(A) 달리기 경주
(B) 표지판 설치
(C) 건물 건설
(D) 다리 보수

해석   질문의 핵심 어구(still taking place)와 관련된 내용을 주의 깊게 듣는다. "Lincoln Bridge has been closed to vehicles and pedestrians. ~ a railing was damaged and is currently being fixed."라며 Lincoln 다리가 차량과 보행자들에게 폐쇄되어 있다고 한 후, 난간이 손상되어 현재 수리되고 있는 중이라고 하였다. 따라서 (D)가 정답이다.

어휘   sign[sain] 표지판, 간판   installation[instəléiʃən] 설치

75 다음에 할 일 문제
해석   한 시간 내에 무슨 일이 일어날 것 같은가?
(A) 추가 최신 정보가 제공될 것이다.
(B) 지역사회 행사가 시작될 것이다.
(C) 구역에서 차량들이 옮겨질 것이다.
(D) 병원이 문을 다시 열 것이다.

해석   질문의 핵심 어구(within the hour)가 언급된 주변을 주의 깊게 듣는다. "the vehicles involved in the accident need to be towed from the scene ~. This should be taken care of within the hour."라며 사고에 연루된 차량들은 현장에서 견인되어야 한다고 한 후, 이는 한 시간 내에 처리될 것이라고 하였다. 따라서 (C)가 정답이다.

패러프레이징
the vehicles ~ need to be towed from the scene 차량들이
현장에서 견인되어야 하다 → Cars will be moved from an area
구역에서 차량들이 옮겨질 것이다

어휘   further[미 fə́ːrðər, 영 fə́ːðə] 추가의
update[미 ʌ́pdeit, 영 ʌpdéit] 최신 정보

76 제안 문제
해석   화자는 무엇을 제안하는가?

(A) 다른 경로를 이용하기
(B) 통근을 일찍 시작하기
(C) 대중교통을 이용하기
(D) 교차로를 피하기

해석   지문의 중후반에서 제안과 관련된 표현이 포함된 문장을 주의 깊게 듣는다. "I encourage commuters to cross the Hubert River by using West Bridge"라며 통근자들에게 West 다리를 이용하여 Hubert 강을 건너기를 권한다고 하였다. 따라서 (A)가 정답이다.

어휘   commute[kəmjúːt] 통근   public transport 대중교통
intersection[미 intərsékʃən, 영 intəsékʃən] 교차로

77-79   [호주] 캐나다식 발음

Questions 77-79 refer to the following announcement.

Good morning, everyone. As scientific consultants, [77]you've been asked to come here today to discuss my company's plan to open a factory. [78]We've found a location that could be ideal, but . . . uh . . . Actually, it's near a residential area. [78/79]I'm worried that our plant might have a negative impact on the natural surroundings and local residents as it will produce some chemical waste. [79]Therefore, we have to develop a strategy for disposing of the waste properly so that it cannot get into the local rivers. That's where you all come in. I want your ideas on how such a system might be developed.

---

consultant[kənsʌ́ltənt] 고문   ideal[미 aidíːəl, 영 aidíəl] 이상적인, 완벽한
plant[미 plænt, 영 plɑːnt] 공장   impact[ímpækt] 영향
surrounding[səráundiŋ] 환경, 주변   chemical waste 화학 폐기물
dispose[미 dispóus, 영 dispə́uz] 처리하다   get into ~에 들어가다
come in (일·사업 등에) 참여(참가)하다, 관여하다

해석
77-79번은 다음 공지에 관한 문제입니다.

좋은 아침입니다, 여러분. 과학계 고문들로서, [77]여러분은 공장을 열고자 하는 제 회사의 계획에 대해 논의하기 위해 오늘 이곳에 오도록 요청받으셨습니다. [78]저희는 이상적일 수 있는 장소를 찾았습니다만, 그런데... 어... 실은, 그곳은 주거 지역 근처입니다. [78/79]저는 공장이 일부 화학 폐기물을 배출할 것이기 때문에 자연환경과 지역 주민들에게 부정적인 영향을 줄까 봐 걱정됩니다. [79]따라서, 저희는 그 폐기물을 제대로 처리할 전략을 개발하여 그것이 지역 하천들로 들어갈 수 없도록 해야 합니다. 바로 이 부분에 여러분 모두가 참여합니다. 저는 이러한 시스템이 어떻게 개발될 수 있을지에 대한 여러분의 아이디어를 원합니다.

77 특정 세부 사항 문제
해석   회사는 무엇을 하려고 계획하고 있는가?
(A) 본사를 이전한다.
(B) 몇몇 화학 제품들을 주문한다.
(C) 새 공장을 연다.
(D) 몇몇 직원들을 전근시킨다.

해석   질문의 핵심 어구(company planning to do)와 관련된 내용을 주의 깊게 듣는다. "you've been asked to come here today to discuss my company's plan to open a factory"라며 청자들이 공장을 열고자 하는 화자의 회사의 계획에 대해 논의하기 위해 오늘 이곳에 오도록 요청받았다고 한 것을 통해 회사가 새 공장을 여는 것을 계획하고 있음을 알 수 있다. 따라서 (C)가 정답이다.

패러프레이징
factory 공장 → plant 공장

어휘   transfer[미 trænsfə́ːr, 영 trænsfə́ː] 전근시키다, 옮기다

78 의도 파악 문제

해석 화자는 왜 "실은, 그곳은 주거 지역 근처입니다"라고 말하는가?
(A) 잠재적인 우려를 떨쳐 버리기 위해
(B) 편리한 위치를 강조하기 위해
(C) 시설을 옮기는 것을 제안하기 위해
(D) 복잡한 요인을 지적하기 위해

해설 질문의 인용어구(Actually, it's near a residential area)가 언급된 주변을 주의 깊게 듣는다. "We've found a location that could be ideal"이라며 이상적일 수 있는 장소를 찾았다고 한 후, "I'm worried that our plant might have a negative impact on the natural surroundings and local residents ~."라며 자연환경과 지역 주민들에게 부정적인 영향을 줄까 봐 걱정된다고 하였으므로 공장을 여는 것과 관련된 복잡한 요인을 지적하기 위함임을 알 수 있다. 따라서 (D)가 정답이다.

어휘 **dismiss**[dismís] 떨쳐 버리다, 일축하다 **highlight**[háilait] 강조하다
point out ~을 지적하다, 주목하다

79 특정 세부 사항 문제

해석 화자는 무엇에 대해 걱정하는가?
(A) 재무 비용
(B) 환경 오염
(C) 생산 일정
(D) 정부 정책

해설 질문의 핵심 어구(concerned)와 관련된 내용을 주의 깊게 듣는다. "I'm worried that our plant might have a negative impact on the natural surroundings ~ as it will produce some chemical waste. Therefore, we have to develop a strategy for disposing of the waste properly so that it cannot get into the local rivers."라며 공장이 일부 화학 폐기물을 배출할 것이기 때문에 자연환경에 부정적인 영향을 줄까 봐 걱정되므로 그 폐기물을 제대로 처리할 전략을 개발하여 그것이 지역 하천들로 들어갈 수 없도록 해야 한다고 하였다. 따라서 (B)가 정답이다.

패러프레이징
a negative impact on the natural surroundings 자연환경에 부정적인 영향 → Environmental pollution 환경 오염

어휘 **financial**[fainǽnʃəl] 재무의, 재정의
environmental pollution 환경 오염 **policy**[미 pɑ́ləsi, 영 pɔ́ləsi] 정책

80-82 [2] 호주식 발음

Questions 80-82 refer to the following instruction.

[80]I'm here today to share some tips on job hunting. As a professional recruiter, I've seen thousands of résumés and job applications, so I can tell you what's effective and what's not. [81]I know what you might be thinking . . . how hard can it be to apply for a job? You'd be surprised. [81]Many people make very basic mistakes, such as not proofreading their résumés and cover letters. However, even [82]one incorrectly spelled word can leave a bad impression on a hiring manager. I'll be teaching you how to catch things like these so that you can best position yourself for success.

job hunting 구직 **recruiter**[미 rikrú:tər, 영 rikrú:tə] 채용 담당자
résumé[미 rézumei, 영 rézju:mei] 이력서
application[미 æpləkéiʃən, 영 æplikéiʃən] 지원서
proofread[prú:fri:d] 교정을 보다 **spell**[spel] 맞춤법에 맞게 글을 쓰다
leave a bad impression 나쁜 인상을 남기다
position[pəzíʃən] 선전하다, 두다

해석
80-82번은 다음 설명에 관한 문제입니다.

[80]저는 오늘 구직에 대한 몇 가지 팁을 공유하기 위해 이 자리에 있습니다. 전문적인 채용 담당자로서, 저는 수천 개의 이력서와 입사 지원서들을 봐서, 여러분께 무엇이 효과적이고 무엇이 그렇지 않은지 말씀드릴 수 있습니다. [81]여러분들이 무슨 생각을 하실지 압니다... 취업 원서를 내는 게 얼마나 어렵겠어요? 여러분은 아마 놀랄 것입니다. [81]많은 사람들이 그들의 이력서와 자기소개서를 교정보지 않는 것과 같은 아주 기본적인 실수들을 합니다. 하지만, 심지어 [82]맞춤법에 맞지 않게 쓴 한 개의 단어가 채용 담당자에게 나쁜 인상을 남길 수 있습니다. 제가 여러분들께 이와 같은 것들을 잡아내는 방법을 가르쳐드려서 여러분들이 성공을 위해 자신을 가장 잘 선전할 수 있도록 해드리겠습니다.

80 주제 문제

해석 화자는 주로 무엇에 대해 이야기하고 있는가?
(A) 업무 관계에 대한 조언
(B) 구직자들을 위한 지도
(C) 진로 선택하기
(D) 실무 교육 수행하기

해설 설명의 주제를 묻는 문제이므로, 지문의 초반을 반드시 듣는다. "I'm here today to share some tips on job hunting."이라며 오늘 구직에 대한 몇 가지 팁을 공유하기 위해 이 자리에 있다고 한 후, 구직자들을 지도하는 내용으로 지문이 이어지고 있다. 따라서 (B)가 정답이다.

어휘 **guidance**[gáidns] 지도, 안내 **job seeker** 구직자
career path 진로, 진로 계획
pursue[미 pərsú:, 영 pəsjú:] 수행하다, 추구하다 **job training** 실무 교육

81 의도 파악 문제

해석 화자는 "여러분은 아마 놀랄 것입니다"라고 말할 때 무엇을 의도하는가?
(A) 서류에 오류가 거의 없다.
(B) 절차가 더 복잡해졌다.
(C) 필요조건이 비교적 새롭다.
(D) 문제가 쉽게 발생한다.

해설 질문의 인용어구(You'd be surprised)가 언급된 주변을 주의 깊게 듣는다. "I know what you might be thinking . . . how hard can it be to apply for a job?"이라며 취업 원서를 내는 것이 얼마나 어렵겠냐고 생각할 것이라고 한 후, "Many people make very basic mistakes"라며 많은 사람들이 아주 기본적인 실수들을 한다고 하였으므로, 문제가 쉽게 발생한다는 것을 알 수 있다. 따라서 (D)가 정답이다.

어휘 **process**[미 prɑ́ses, 영 prɔ́uses] 절차, 과정
requirement[미 rikwáiərmənt, 영 rikwáiəmənt] 필요조건

82 특정 세부 사항 문제

해석 화자에 따르면, 무엇이 나쁜 인상을 남길 수 있는가?
(A) 긴 자기소개서
(B) 불충분한 경력
(C) 맞춤법 실수
(D) 부적절한 복장

해설 질문의 핵심 어구(leave a bad impression)가 언급된 주변을 주의 깊게 듣는다. "one incorrectly spelled word can leave a bad impression on a hiring manager"라며 맞춤법에 맞지 않게 쓴 한 개의 단어가 채용 담당자에게 나쁜 인상을 남길 수 있다고 하였다. 따라서 (C)가 정답이다.

패러프레이징
incorrectly spelled word 맞춤법에 맞지 않게 쓴 단어 → Spelling mistakes 맞춤법 실수

어휘 **insufficient**[insəfíʃənt] 불충분한 **spelling**[spéliŋ] 맞춤법
inappropriate[미 inəpróupriət, 영 inəprɔ́upriət] 부적절한
attire[미 ətáiər, 영 ətáiə] 복장

Questions 83-85 refer to the following speech.

⁸³As the manager of CRT Center, I'm happy to see that so many people have come to celebrate the grand opening of the complex. ⁸⁴This venue will be the new location for all games played by our city's amateur baseball team, the Dallas Snakes. Throughout the afternoon, fans will be able to explore the complex, including the field, general seating area, and luxury suites. But before you head inside, I want to give special thanks to the residents of the Dallas community. ⁸⁵I'd also like to express my gratitude to Mayor Kent Berkley for providing such overwhelming support for the construction of the facility. Without his help, it wouldn't have been possible to build this state-of-the-art complex.

grand opening 개장, 개점
complex [미 kámpleks, 영 kɔ́mpleks] 복합 건물
explore [미 iksplɔ́:r, 영 iksplɔ́:] 답사하다   field [fi:ld] 경기장
luxury suite 호화 특별 관람석   give thanks to ~에게 감사하다
express gratitude 감사의 뜻을 표하다   mayor [미 méiər, 영 meə] 시장
overwhelming [미 ðuvərhwélmiŋ, 영 ðuvəwélmiŋ] 엄청난, 압도적인
state-of-the-art [미 stèitəvðiáːrt, 영 stèitəvðiáːt] 최첨단의

해석

83-85번은 다음 연설에 관한 문제입니다.

⁸³CRT 센터의 운영자로서, 저는 이 복합 건물의 개장을 기념하기 위해 이렇게 많은 분들이 오신 것을 볼 수 있어 기쁩니다. ⁸⁴이 장소는 시의 아마추어 야구 팀인 Dallas Snakes가 하는 모든 경기들을 위한 새로운 장소가 될 것입니다. 오후 내내, 팬들은 경기장, 일반 좌석 구역, 호화 특별 관람석들을 포함하여 복합 건물을 답사할 수 있을 것입니다. 하지만 내부로 향하기 전에, 댈러스 지역사회의 주민들께 특별한 감사를 드리고 싶습니다. ⁸⁵또한 시장 Kent Berkley께 시설의 건설을 위해 이처럼 엄청난 지원을 제공해주신 것에 대해 감사의 뜻을 표하고 싶습니다. 그의 지원이 없었다면, 이 최첨단 복합 건물을 세우는 것이 불가능했을 것입니다.

83 화자 문제

해석 화자는 누구인 것 같은가?
(A) 시설 운영자
(B) 국가 공무원
(C) 전문 운동 선수
(D) 기업 투자자

해설 지문에서 신분 및 직업과 관련된 표현을 놓치지 않고 듣는다. "As the manager of CRT Center, I'm happy to see that so many people have come to celebrate the grand opening of the complex."라며 화자가 CRT 센터의 운영자로서 이 복합 건물의 개장을 기념하기 위해 이렇게 많은 사람들이 온 것을 볼 수 있어 기쁘다고 한 말을 통해 화자가 시설 운영자임을 알 수 있다. 따라서 (A)가 정답이다.

어휘 government official 국가 공무원   athlete [金θli:t] 운동 선수
investor [미 invéstər, 영 invéstə] 투자자

84 특정 세부 사항 문제

해석 CRT 센터는 무엇을 위해 쓰일 것인가?
(A) 자선 경매
(B) 스포츠 경기
(C) 산업 협의회
(D) 지역사회 모임

해설 질문의 핵심 어구(CRT Center be used for)와 관련된 내용을 주의 깊게 듣는다. "This venue[CRT Center] will be the new location for all games played by our city's amateur baseball team"이라며 CRT 센터는 시의 아마추어 야구 팀이 하는 모든 경기들을 위한 새로운 장소가 될 것이라고 하였다. 따라서 (B)가 정답이다.

패러프레이징
games played by ~ baseball team 야구 팀이 하는 경기들
→ Sporting events 스포츠 경기

어휘 charity [tʃǽrəti] 자선   auction [ɔ́:kʃən] 경매
sporting event 스포츠 경기   gathering [gǽðəriŋ] 모임, 집회

85 언급 문제

해석 Kent Berkley에 대해 무엇이 언급되는가?
(A) 일부 공사를 감독했다.
(B) 최근에 시장과 만났다.
(C) 프로젝트를 지원했다.
(D) 연설을 할 계획이다.

해설 질문의 핵심 어구(Kent Berkley)가 언급된 주변을 주의 깊게 듣는다. "I'd also like to express my gratitude to Mayor Kent Berkley for providing such overwhelming support for the construction of the facility."라며 시장 Kent Berkley에게 시설의 건설을 위해 이처럼 엄청난 지원을 제공해준 것에 대해 감사의 뜻을 표하고 싶다고 하였다. 따라서 (C)가 정답이다.

패러프레이징
providing ~ support for the construction of the facility 시설의 건설을 위해 지원을 제공한 것 → supported a project 프로젝트를 지원했다

어휘 oversee [미 ðuvərsíː, 영 ðuvəsíː] 감독하다

Questions 86-88 refer to the following telephone message.

Hi, Sheena? It's John Murray. ⁸⁶I'm a student in your Tuesday guitar class. ⁸⁷I was wondering if you have any recommendations for an electric guitar. Since you've been playing for years, I figured that you'd be the best person to ask. I'm considering buying one, and I want to make sure I choose something that's right for me. I need a guitar that's affordable and not too heavy as I'll be carrying it around pretty frequently. ⁸⁸As for a brand, there isn't a specific one that I like more than another . . . so I'm flexible. Please give me a callback when you get a chance. Thanks!

figure [미 fígjər, 영 fígə] 생각하다, 판단하다
affordable [미 əfɔ́:rdəbl, 영 əfɔ́:dəbl] (가격이) 적당한, 알맞은
frequently [frí:kwəntli] 자주   as for ~에 관해서는
flexible [fléksəbl] 융통성 있는, 유연한   callback [kɔ́:lbæk] 답신 전화

해석

86-88번은 다음 전화 메시지에 관한 문제입니다.

안녕하세요, Sheena? John Murray입니다. ⁸⁶저는 당신의 화요일 기타 수업의 학생입니다. ⁸⁷저는 당신이 추천해주실 만한 전자 기타가 있는지 궁금합니다. 당신이 다년간 연주해 왔기 때문에, 당신이 물어보기에 가장 알맞은 사람이라고 생각했습니다. 저는 전자 기타를 사는 것을 생각 중인데, 제게 맞는 것으로 고르는 것을 확실히 하고 싶습니다. 가격이 적당하고 너무 무겁지 않은 기타가 필요한데 제가 꽤 자주 그것을 가지고 다닐 것이기 때문입니다. ⁸⁸브랜드에 관해서는, 다른 것에 비해 더 좋아하는 특정한 것이 없습니다... 그래서 저는 융통성이 있습니다. 기회가 될 때 제게 답신 전화를 주시기 바랍니다. 감사합니다!

86 청자 문제

해석 청자는 누구인 것 같은가?
(A) 콘서트 주최자
(B) 음악 강사
(C) 학교 사무관
(D) 상점 주인

해설 지문에서 신분 및 직업과 관련된 표현을 놓치지 않고 듣는다. "I'm a student in your Tuesday guitar class."라며 자신이 청자의 화요일 기타 수업의 학생이라고 한 말을 통해 청자가 음악 강사임을 알 수 있다. 따라서 (B)가 정답이다.

어휘 instructor[미 instrʌ́ktər, 영 instrʌ́ktə] 강사
secretary[sékrətèri] (기관 등의) 사무관, 비서

87 목적 문제

해석 메시지의 주요 목적은 무엇인가?
(A) 질문에 답하기 위해
(B) 연주자를 예약하기 위해
(C) 수업에 등록하기 위해
(D) 의견을 구하기 위해

해설 메시지의 목적을 묻는 문제이므로, 지문의 초반을 주의 깊게 들은 후 전체 맥락을 파악한다. "I was wondering if you have any recommendations for an electric guitar."라며 청자가 추천해줄 만한 전자 기타가 있는지 궁금하다고 한 후, 의견을 구하는 내용으로 지문이 이어지고 있다. 따라서 (D)가 정답이다.

어휘 performer[미 pərfɔ́ːrmər, 영 pəfɔ́ːmə] 연주자

88 의도 파악 문제

해석 화자는 왜 "저는 융통성이 있습니다"라고 말하는가?
(A) 한가한 일정을 가지고 있다.
(B) 브랜드 선호가 없다.
(C) 수업을 받을 시간이 있다.
(D) 여러 연주자를 좋아한다.

해설 질문의 인용어구(I'm flexible)가 언급된 주변을 주의 깊게 듣는다. "As for a brand, there isn't a specific one that I like more than another"라며 브랜드에 관해서는 다른 것에 비해 더 좋아하는 특정한 것이 없다고 한 말을 통해 브랜드 선호가 없음을 알 수 있다. 따라서 (B)가 정답이다.

어휘 open[미 óupən, 영 ə́upən] 한가한, 약속이 없는
preference[préfərəns] 선호(도)   available[əvéiləbl] 시간이 있는

89-91 🎧 영국식 발음

Questions 89-91 refer to the following speech.

It's been a pleasure to spend 25 years as creative director for Magique Perfume House. ⁸⁹Now that I'm retiring, I'd like to briefly reflect on my working life. One of my greatest achievements and memories was working with so many of you to market the Evening Rose line of perfume. ⁹⁰That campaign played a key role in expanding our company into international markets. I still think of it as a highlight of my career. However, ⁹¹the experience I value the most was getting the chance to get to know you all better. You're such wonderful people, and I'll miss interacting with you so often.

creative director 광고 제작 감독   retire[미 ritáiər, 영 ritáiə] 은퇴하다
briefly[bríːfli] 잠시, 간단히   reflect on ~을 돌이켜보다 ⊙

---

market[미 máːrkit, 영 máːkit] 광고하다   line[lain] 제품, 종류
play a key role 핵심적인 역할을 하다   highlight[háilait] 가장 중요한 부분
career[미 kəríər, 영 kəríə] 직장 생활   value[vǽljuː] 소중하게 생각하다
interact[intərǽkt] 교류하다, 소통하다

해석
89-91번은 다음 연설에 관한 문제입니다.

Magique Perfume House의 광고 제작 감독으로서 25년을 보내어 기뻤습니다. ⁸⁹제가 은퇴하기 때문에, 잠시 제 직장 생활을 돌이켜보고자 합니다. 저의 가장 훌륭한 성과 및 추억들 중 하나는 Evening Rose 향수 제품을 광고하기 위해 많은 여러분들과 함께 일했던 것입니다. ⁹⁰그 캠페인은 우리 회사가 국제 시장으로 확장하는 데 핵심적인 역할을 했습니다. 저는 아직도 그것이 제 직장 생활의 가장 중요한 부분이라고 생각합니다. 하지만, ⁹¹제가 가장 소중하게 생각하는 경험은 여러분 모두를 더 잘 알게 되는 기회를 갖게 된 것이었습니다. 여러분은 매우 훌륭한 사람들이며, 저는 여러분과 자주 교류했던 것을 그리워할 것입니다.

89 장소 문제

해석 청자들은 어디에 있는 것 같은가?
(A) 채용 면접에
(B) 무역 박람회에
(C) 은퇴 기념 행사에
(D) 명절 파티에

해설 지문에서 장소와 관련된 표현을 놓치지 않고 듣는다. "Now that I'm retiring, I'd like to briefly reflect on my working life."라며 화자가 은퇴하기 때문에 잠시 자신의 직장 생활을 돌이켜보고자 한다는 말을 통해 청자들이 은퇴 기념 행사에 있음을 알 수 있다. 따라서 (C)가 정답이다.

어휘 recruitment[rikrúːtmənt] 채용, 신규 모집   trade show 무역 박람회
retirement[미 ritáiərmənt, 영 ritáiəmənt] 은퇴
celebration[sèləbréiʃən] 기념 행사

90 특정 세부 사항 문제

해석 화자에 따르면, 캠페인은 왜 중요했는가?
(A) 외국 언론의 관심을 끌었다.
(B) 상을 받았다.
(C) 새로운 기술을 이용했다.
(D) 회사가 확장하는 데 기여했다.

해설 질문의 핵심 어구(a campaign significant)와 관련된 내용을 주의 깊게 듣는다. "That campaign played a key role in expanding our company into international markets."라며 그 캠페인은 회사가 국제 시장으로 확장하는 데 핵심적인 역할을 했다고 하였다. 따라서 (D)가 정답이다.

패러프레이징
played a key role in expanding ~ company into international markets 회사가 국제 시장으로 확장하는 데 핵심적인 역할을 했다 → helped grow a business 회사가 확장하는 데 기여했다

어휘 attract media attention 언론의 관심을 끌다

91 언급 문제

해석 화자는 무엇을 가장 소중하게 생각한다고 말하는가?
(A) 직원들의 헌신
(B) 프로젝트의 목적
(C) 해외 경험
(D) 동료들과의 관계

해설 질문의 핵심 어구(values the most)가 언급된 주변을 주의 깊게 듣는다. "the experience I value the most was getting the chance to get to know you all better"라며 자신이 가장 소중하게 생각하는 경험은 모두를 더 잘 알게 되는 기회를 갖게 된 것이었다고 하였다. 따라서 (D)가 정답이다.

어휘 purpose[미 pə́ːrpəs, 영 pə́ːpəs] 목적

92-94 🎧 미국식 발음

Questions 92-94 refer to the following report.

Yesterday afternoon, 92the Harlington County School Board formally announced plans to build a second high school. There is currently only one high school in the district, and that institution alone is no longer able to meet the demands of the local community. The new one will serve students living in the western part of the district. Ultimately, both facilities will accommodate roughly 2,000 students. 93During the announcement, school board chair Yolanda Moya said that construction of the school will take place over 10 months—from April to January. Given how many classrooms are overcrowded at the moment, 94most students and parents approve of this government project.

county school 공립학교 formally[미 fɔ́ːrməli, 영 fɔ́ːməli] 공식적으로
district[dístrikt] 지역 institution[ìnstətjúːʃən, 영 ìnstitjúːʃən] 기관, 단체
meet[miːt] 충족시키다
serve[미 səːrv, 영 səːv] (요구·필요 등을) 충족시키다
ultimately[미 ʌ́ltəmətli, 영 ʌ́ltimətli] 결과적으로
accommodate[미 əkɑ́mədèit, 영 əkɔ́mədeit] 수용하다
roughly[rʌ́fli] 대략 given[gívən] ~을 고려해볼 때
overcrowded[미 òuvərkráudid, 영 əuvəkráudid] 혼잡한
approve of ~에 찬성하다, 승인하다

해석
92-94번은 다음 보도에 관한 문제입니다.

어제 오후, 92Harlington 공립학교 위원회가 두 번째 고등학교를 세우려는 계획안을 공식적으로 발표했습니다. 현재 지역에는 하나의 고등학교만 있어, 이 기관 하나만으로는 더 이상 지역 사회의 수요들을 충족시킬 수 없게 되었습니다. 새로운 학교는 지역의 서부에 살고 있는 학생들의 수요를 충족시킬 것입니다. 결과적으로, 두 시설들은 대략 2,000명의 학생들을 수용할 것입니다. 93발표 중에, 학교 위원회장인 Yolanda Moya는 학교의 건설이 4월부터 1월까지 10개월에 걸쳐 진행될 것이라고 말했습니다. 현재 얼마나 많은 교실들이 혼잡한지를 고려하여, 94대부분의 학생들과 학부모들이 이 정부 프로젝트에 찬성합니다.

92 주제 문제

해석 보도는 주로 무엇에 대한 것인가?
(A) 추가적인 학교를 설립하는 것
(B) 교사들을 교육하는 것
(C) 새 교장을 임명하는 것
(D) 현재의 교육 과정을 확대시키는 것

해설 보도의 주제를 묻는 문제이므로, 지문의 초반을 반드시 듣는다. "the Harlington County School Board formally announced plans to build a second high school"이라며 Harlington 공립학교 위원회가 두 번째 고등학교를 세우려는 계획안을 공식적으로 발표했다고 한 후, 추가적인 학교 설립에 대한 내용으로 지문이 이어지고 있다. 따라서 (A)가 정답이다.

어휘 establish[istǽbliʃ] 설립하다 appoint[əpɔ́int] 임명하다
principal[미 prínsəpəl, 영 prínsipəl] 교장, 학장
expand[ikspǽnd] 확대시키다
curriculum[미 kəríkjuləm, 영 kəríkjələm] 교육 과정

93 특정 세부 사항 문제

해석 Yolanda Moya는 어제 무엇을 발표했는가?

(A) 사무실의 위치
(B) 프로그램의 규모
(C) 개발의 비용
(D) 프로젝트의 기간

해설 질문의 핵심 어구(Yolanda Moya announce yesterday)와 관련된 내용을 주의 깊게 듣는다. "During the announcement, ~ Yolanda Moya said that construction of the school will take place over 10 months"라며 발표 중에 Yolanda Moya는 학교의 건설이 10개월에 걸쳐 진행될 것이라고 말했다고 하였다. 따라서 (D)가 정답이다.

패러프레이징
construction of the school will take place over 10 months
학교의 건설이 10개월에 걸쳐 진행될 것이다 → The length of a project 프로젝트의 기간

어휘 size[saiz] 규모 length[미 leŋkθ, 영 leŋθ] 기간

94 언급 문제

해석 일부 학부모들에 대해 무엇이 언급되는가?
(A) 아이들이 이동되는 것을 원하지 않는다.
(B) 지난주에 사안에 대해 투표했다.
(C) 정부 계획안을 받아들인다.
(D) 비용이 낮아져야 한다고 생각한다.

해설 질문의 핵심 어구(parents)가 언급된 주변을 주의 깊게 듣는다. "most ~ parents approve of this government project"라며 대부분의 학부모들이 이 정부 프로젝트에 찬성한다고 하였다. 따라서 (C)가 정답이다.

어휘 relocate[미 riːlóukeit, 영 riːləukéit] 이동하다
expense[ikspéns] 비용 lower[미 lóuər, 영 lə́uə] 낮추다

95-97 🎧 영국식 발음

Questions 95-97 refer to the following talk and form.

95Thank you for stopping for this brief demonstration of Joytone Industries' newest electric keyboard, the TouchFone 1000. As you can see, 96the device has a variety of buttons on the front panel. These buttons control different sound effects, of which there are over 100. Moreover, the TouchFone 1000 is our most energy-efficient keyboard. Lastly, since 97the TouchFone 1000 is our lightest model yet, it is easy to transport. Right now, I'll hand out some flyers that include technical details about this product. Anyone who's interested in trying the device is free to experiment with this one.

brief[briːf] 간략한, 짧은 demonstration[dèmənstréiʃən] 시연회, 시연
electric[iléktrik] 전자의 a variety of 여러 가지의
control[미 kəntróul, 영 kəntrául] 조절하다
energy-efficient[미 énərdʒifíʃənt, 영 énədʒifíʃənt] 에너지 효율이 좋은
technical[téknikəl] 기술적인
transport[미 trænspɔ́rt, 영 trænspɔ́ːt] 옮기다, 나르다
hand out ~을 나누어주다

해석
95-97번은 다음 담화와 양식에 관한 문제입니다.

95Joytone Industries사의 최신 전자 키보드인 TouchFone 1000의 간략한 시연회를 위해 들러주셔서 감사합니다. 여러분께서 보시다시피, 96이 기기는 전면 패널에 여러 가지의 버튼이 있습니다. 이 버튼들은 다양한 음향 효과들을 조절하는데, 이들은 100가지가 넘습니다. 게다가, TouchFone 1000은 에너지 효율이 가장 좋은 키보드입니다. 마지막으로, 97TouchFone 1000은

TEST 5 Part 4 **187**

TEST 5

안 권으로 끝내는 해커스 토익 실전 LC+RC 1

현재까지 저희의 가장 가벼운 모델이기 때문에, 옮기기가 쉽습니다. 지금, 제가 이 제품에 대한 기술적인 세부 사항들을 포함한 몇몇 전단지들을 나눠드릴 것입니다. 이 기기를 사용해보고 싶으신 분은 이것으로 시험해보셔도 됩니다.

제품 사양	
제품 무게	가격
⁹⁷20파운드	2,000달러
25파운드	1,750달러
28파운드	1,000달러
35파운드	2,200달러

95 주제 문제

해석 어떤 종류의 제품이 설명되고 있는가?
(A) 청소 용품
(B) 디지털 프린터
(C) 악기
(D) 평면 스크린 텔레비전

해설 담화의 주제를 묻는 문제이므로, 지문의 초반을 반드시 듣는다. "Thank you for stopping for this brief demonstration of ~ electric keyboard"라며 전자 키보드의 간략한 시연회를 위해 들러줘서 감사하다고 한 말을 통해 악기가 설명되고 있음을 알 수 있다. 따라서 (C)가 정답이다.

어휘 appliance[əpláiəns] 용품   musical instrument 악기
flat screen 평면 스크린(의)

96 특정 세부 사항 문제

해석 화자에 따르면, 무엇이 전면 패널에 있는가?
(A) 표시 화면
(B) 조작 버튼
(C) 전원 스위치
(D) 경고 표시기

해설 질문의 핵심 어구(on the front panel)가 언급된 주변을 주의 깊게 듣는다. "the device has a variety of buttons on the front panel. These buttons control different sound effects"라며 이 기기는 전면 패널에 여러 가지의 버튼이 있다고 한 후, 이 버튼들은 다양한 음향 효과들을 조절한다고 한 말을 통해 조작 버튼이 전면 패널에 있음을 알 수 있다. 따라서 (B)가 정답이다.

패러프레이징
buttons control different sound effects 버튼들이 다양한 음향 효과들을 조절한다 → Control buttons 조작 버튼

어휘 display screen 표시 화면   warning[미 wɔ́ːrniŋ, 영 wɔ́ːniŋ] 경고, 주의
indicator[미 índikèitər, 영 índikèitə] 표시기

97 시각 자료 문제

해석 시각 자료를 보아라. TouchFone 1000은 얼마인가?
(A) 2,000달러
(B) 1,750달러
(C) 1,000달러
(D) 2,200달러

해설 제시된 양식의 정보를 확인한 후 질문의 핵심 어구(TouchFone 1000)가 언급된 주변을 주의 깊게 듣는다. "the TouchFone 1000 is our lightest model yet"이라며 TouchFone 1000은 현재까지 가장 가벼운 모델이라고 하였으므로, 가장 가벼운 제품이 TouchFone 1000이며 이것이 2000달러임을 양식에서 알 수 있다. 따라서 (A)가 정답이다.

98-100 [2세] 호주식 발음

Questions 98-100 refer to the following tour information and map.

Welcome to Dwyers' Sweets. I'm Raymond Watts, the factory's manager. ⁹⁸We've been making candy at this location for 100 years. You may be surprised to learn that most of our candies start off with the same base, cooked sugar, as you can see here. ⁹⁹When we get to the flavoring department in the next area, we'll show you how we give each type of candy its individual taste. Using this basic technique, we produce more than 150 varieties of candy that are sold around the world. ¹⁰⁰When we finish our tour, we'll give you some of our best-selling products to try.

start off with ~으로부터 시작하다   base[beis] 주성분, 주재료
flavoring[fléivəriŋ] 향료, 조미료
individual[ìndəvídʒuəl] 각기 다른, 각각의   try[trai] 먹어 보다, 입어 보다

해석
98-100번은 다음 관광 안내와 지도에 관한 문제입니다.

Dwyers' Sweets에 오신 것을 환영합니다. 저는 공장 관리자 Raymond Watts입니다. ⁹⁸저희는 이 장소에서 100년 동안 사탕을 만들어 왔습니다. 여러분은 저희 사탕의 대부분이 이곳에서 보실 수 있는 것처럼, 조리된 설탕이라는 동일한 주성분으로부터 시작한다는 것을 알게 되시면 놀랄지도 모릅니다. ⁹⁹우리가 다음 구역에 있는 향료 부문에 가면, 저희는 여러분께 어떻게 각 종류의 사탕에 각기 다른 맛을 내게 하는지를 보여드리겠습니다. 이 기본적인 기술을 사용하여, 저희는 전 세계에서 판매되는 150가지가 넘는 종류의 사탕을 생산합니다. ¹⁰⁰우리가 관광을 마칠 때, 저희는 가장 잘 팔리는 제품들 중 몇 가지를 먹어 보도록 드릴 겁니다.

생산 체계

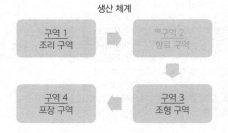

98 특정 세부 사항 문제

해석 Dwyers' Sweets의 특징은 무엇인가?
(A) 100가지 종류의 사탕을 생산한다.
(B) 두 번째 지점을 열었다.
(C) 100년 된 시설을 운영한다.
(D) 가족 기업으로 남아있다.

해설 질문의 핵심 어구(characteristic of Dwyers' Sweets)와 관련된 내용을 주의 깊게 듣는다. "We've been making candy at this location for 100 years."라며 이 장소에서 100년 동안 사탕을 만들어 왔다고 하였다. 따라서 (C)가 정답이다.

어휘 remain[riméin] ~으로 남다, 남아있다
family-owned business 가족 기업

99 시각 자료 문제

해석 시각 자료를 보아라. 투어 단체는 다음에 어디로 갈 것인가?
(A) 구역 1
(B) 구역 2
(C) 구역 3

(D) 구역 4

해설 제시된 지도의 정보를 확인한 후 질문의 핵심 어구(tour group go next)와 관련된 내용을 주의 깊게 듣는다. "When we get to the flavoring department in the next area, we'll show you how we give each type of candy its individual taste."라며 다음 구역에 있는 향료 부문에 가면 어떻게 각 종류의 사탕에 각기 다른 맛을 내게 하는지를 보여주겠다고 하였으므로, 투어 단체는 다음에 향료 구역인 구역 2로 갈 것임을 지도에서 알 수 있다. 따라서 (B)가 정답이다.

100 특정 세부 사항 문제

해석 청자들은 관광 후에 무엇을 받을 것인가?
(A) 사탕의 샘플들
(B) 가장 잘 팔리는 것들의 목록
(C) 해외 매장들의 위치
(D) 상품권들

해설 질문의 핵심 어구(receive after the tour)와 관련된 내용을 주의 깊게 듣는다. "When we finish our tour, we'll give you some of our best-selling products[candies] to try."라며 관광을 마칠 때 가장 잘 팔리는 사탕들 중 몇 가지를 먹어 보도록 준다고 하였다. 따라서 (A)가 정답이다.

어휘 gift voucher 상품권

PART 5

101 의미 구별하여 명사 채우기

해설 '신분증을 제시하다'라는 의미이므로 명사 (A) identification(신분증)이 정답이다. (B) identity(신분)를 쓰면 '신분을 제시하다'라는 어색한 의미가 된다.

해석 방문객들은 연구소에 들어가거나 기밀을 다루는 구역들에 접근할 때 신분증을 제시해야 한다.

어휘 research facility 연구소 access v. 접근하다, 들어가다
sensitive adj. 기밀을 다루는, 민감한 identification n. 신분증, 식별
identity n. 신분, 신원

102 형용사 어휘 고르기

해설 '요식업으로 확장되었지만 주된 중심은 여전히 패션이다'라는 문맥이므로 (C) primary(주된, 주요한)가 정답이다. (A) high는 '높은', (B) multiple은 '복합의, 다수의', (D) outside는 '외부의'라는 의미이다.

해석 Orex사는 요식업으로 확장되었지만, 주된 중심은 여전히 패션이다.

어휘 focus n. 중심, 주안점 expand v. 확장되다, 발전하다
restaurant business 요식업

103 태에 맞는 동사 채우기

해설 주어(Mr. Kurtz)가 만족감을 느끼므로 수동태를 써야 한다. be동사(was)와 함께 수동태 동사를 만드는 p.p.형 (A) pleased가 정답이다. be동사 다음에는 보어로 명사 (D)도 올 수 있지만 'Mr. Kurtz가 만족이다'라는 어색한 의미를 만들기 때문에 (D)는 답이 될 수 없다.

해석 Mr. Kurtz는 계약 협상에 매우 만족해했는데, 그 계약 협상은 15퍼센트의 임금 인상의 결과를 낳았다.

어휘 contract n. 계약 negotiation n. 협상, 협의
result in ~의 결과를 낳다 please v. 만족시키다, 기쁘게 하다

104 those 채우기

해설 문장의 주어 자리가 비어 있고, 빈칸 뒤에 관계절(who ~ Web site)이 나오므로, 관계절의 수식을 받아 '회사 웹사이트를 통해 이력서를 제출하는 사람들'을 나타내는 (C) those가 정답이다. 관계대명사 (B)와 (D)는 앞에 선행사가 있어야 하므로 답이 될 수 없다.

해석 회사 웹사이트를 통해 이력서를 제출하는 사람들만 그 인턴직에 고려될 것입니다.

어휘 submit v. 제출하다 résumé n. 이력서 consider v. 고려하다

105 부사 자리 채우기

해설 동명사(selling)를 꾸미기 위해서는 부사가 와야 하므로 부사 (A) exclusively(오로지, 전적으로)가 정답이다. 명사 (B), 동사 (C), 형용사 (D)는 동명사를 꾸밀 수 없다.

해석 Pete's Produce는 오로지 유기농 과일과 채소들을 판매하는 것으로 유명하다.

어휘 be well-known for ~으로 유명하다 organic adj. 유기농의
exclusion n. 제외, 배제 exclude v. 제외하다, 배제하다
exclusive adj. 배타적인, 독점적인, 고급의

106 시간 표현과 일치하는 시제의 동사 채우기

해설 과거 완료 시제와 함께 쓰이는 표현 'By the time + 과거 동사(opened)'가 왔으므로 과거 완료 시제 (D) had established가 정답이다.

해석 SolarTech사가 유럽에 첫 공장을 열었을 때쯤, 당사는 이미 미국과 아시아에 시설들을 설립했었다.

어휘 facility n. 시설, 설비 establish v. 설립하다, 수립하다

107 부사 자리 채우기

해설 동사(work)를 꾸미기 위해서는 부사가 와야 하므로 부사 (D) routinely(일상적으로, 정기적으로)가 정답이다. 동사 또는 분사 (A), 명사 또는 형용사 (B), 명사 (C)는 동사를 꾸밀 수 없다.

해석 Flemwell 백화점의 직원들은 바쁜 연휴 기간 동안에는 일상적으로 야근한다.

어휘 work overtime 야근하다 route v. (~을 경유하여) 보내다
routine n. 일상; adj. 일상적인

108 전치사 채우기

해설 '공항 도처에 자동 탑승 수속 기계를 사용하다'라는 의미가 되어야 하므로 (B) throughout(~ 도처에)이 정답이다.

해석 Air East사 승객들은 공항 도처에 자동 탑승 수속 기계를 사용하도록 권고받는다.

어휘 be advised to do ~하도록 권고받다 automated adj. 자동의
check-in n. 탑승 수속

109 동사 어휘 고르기

해설 '무제한의 문자 전송과 데이터 사용을 제공하는 요금제를 신청함으로써 예기치 않은 요금을 피할 수 있다'라는 문맥이므로 (D) avoid(피하다)가 정답이다. (A) prepare는 '준비하다', (B) shorten은 '단축하다', (C) comply는 '따르다'라는 의미이다. 참고로, (A) prepare가 '예기치 않은 요금에 대비하다'라는 의미로 쓰이려면 전치사 for와 함께 쓰여야 한다.

해석 고객들은 무제한의 문자 전송과 데이터 사용을 제공하는 휴대전화 요금제를 신청함으로써 예기치 않은 요금을 피할 수 있다.

어휘 unexpected adv. 예기치 않은 fee n. 요금 cellular adj. 휴대전화의
unlimited adj. 무제한의 usage n. 사용

110 to 부정사의 in order to 채우기

해설 이 문장은 주어(Employees), 동사(must contact), 목적어(the human resources department)를 갖춘 완전한 절이므로 ____ request a leave of absence는 수식어 거품으로 보아야 한다. 따라서 동사(request)가 있는 거품절을 이끌면서 '휴가를 신청하기 위해'라는 목적을 나타내는 (B) in order to가 정답이다. 참고로, to 부정사가 목적을 나타낼 때는 to 대신 in order to나 so as to를 쓸 수

있다. 부사 (A)와 (D)는 수식어 거품이 될 수 없다. 전치사 (C)는 동사가 없는 거품구를 이끌기 때문에 답이 될 수 없다.

해석 직원들은 휴가를 신청하기 위해 인사부에 연락해야 한다.

어휘 contact v. 연락하다 leave of absence 휴가

111 명사 어휘 고르기

해설 '임대 계약의 조건에 따르면 세입자는 1개월 전에 알려야 한다'라는 문맥이므로 (A) terms(조건)가 정답이다. (B)의 right는 '권리', (C)의 cause는 '이유', (D)의 sign은 '기호, 신호'라는 의미이다.

해석 임대 계약의 조건에 따르면, 세입자는 이사를 나가기에 앞서 1개월 전에 알려야 한다.

어휘 under prep. (합의·법률 등) ~에 따르면
lease agreement 임대 계약 tenant n. 세입자
give a month's notice 1개월 전에 알리다
move out (살던 집에서) 이사를 나가다

112 의문사 채우기

해설 be동사(is)의 보어 자리에 온 절(the name ~ announced) 앞에 명사절 접속사를 채우는 문제이다. 빈칸 다음에 주어(the name ~ CEO), 동사(will be announced)를 갖춘 완벽한 절이 왔으며, '새로운 최고경영자의 이름이 발표되는 때'라는 의미가 되어야 하므로 (A) when(~하는 때)이 정답이다. 빈칸 뒤에 완전한 절이 왔으므로 불완전한 절을 이끄는 (B)와 (D)는 답이 될 수 없다.

해석 이번 주 수요일은 Zoltek Engineering사의 새로운 최고경영자의 이름이 발표되는 때이다.

어휘 announce v. 발표하다

113 현재분사와 과거분사 구별하여 채우기

해설 이 문장은 주어(Athletes), 동사(participated in), 목적어(the World Tennis Tournament)를 갖춘 완전한 절이므로, ___ more than 50 countries는 수식어 거품으로 보아야 한다. 보기 중 수식어 거품이 될 수 있는 것은 분사 (A)와 (B)이다. 분사의 수식을 받는 명사(Athletes)와 분사가 '대표하는 운동 선수들'이라는 의미의 능동 관계이므로 현재분사 (A) representing이 정답이다. 참고로, held last year in Guangzhou는 목적어(the World Tennis Tournament)를 꾸며 주는 수식어 거품이다.

해석 50개가 넘는 국가들을 대표하는 운동 선수들이 작년에 광저우에서 열렸던 세계 테니스 경기에 참가했다.

어휘 athlete n. 운동 선수 participate in ~에 참가하다
tournament n. 경기 represent v. 대표하다
representation n. 표현, 대표

114 명사 어휘 고르기

해설 '시골에서 도시 지역으로의 거주자들의 이전'이라는 문맥이므로 (B) relocation(이전)이 정답이다. (A) arrangement는 '배열, 합의', (C) environment는 '환경', (D) discovery는 '발견'이라는 의미이다.

해석 시골에서 도시 지역으로의 거주자들의 지속적인 이전은 마닐라에 주택 부족을 야기해 왔다.

어휘 continued adj. 지속적인 resident n. 거주자 rural adj. 시골의
urban adj. 도시의 create v. 야기하다
housing shortage 주택 부족

115 동사 어휘 고르기

해설 '세부 사항은 발표 후에 알려지기 시작할 것이다'라는 문맥이므로 (D) emerge(알려지다, 나타나다)가 정답이다. (A) compile은 '편집하다', (B) include는 '포함하다', (C) appoint는 '임명하다, 정하다'라는 의미이다. 참고로, 빈칸 뒤에 목적어가 없으므로 빈칸에는 자동사 emerge만 올 수 있음을 알아두자.

해석 다가오는 교육 워크숍에 대한 세부 사항은 발표 후에 알려지기 시작할 것이다.

어휘 following prep. ~ 후에

116 전치사 채우기

해설 '2월 첫째 주까지'라는 의미가 되어야 하므로 (C) until(~까지)이 정답이다. (A) about은 '~에 관하여', (B) towards는 '~ 쪽으로', (D) except는 '~ 외에는'이라는 의미이다.

해석 잠재적 회사 합병에 관한 모든 논의들은 2월 첫째 주까지 보류되었다.

어휘 potential adj. 잠재적인 merger n. 합병 put on hold 보류하다

117 형용사 자리 채우기

해설 명사(candidate)를 꾸며 줄 수 있는 형용사 (C) inadequate(부적당한)가 정답이다. 부사 (A), 명사 (B)와 (D)는 명사를 꾸밀 수 없다.

해석 Mr. Ross는 전문적인 경험이 부족했기 때문에 마케팅 직에 부적당한 지원자로 여겨졌다.

어휘 consider v. 여기다 candidate n. 지원자 lack v. ~이 부족하다
professional adj. 전문적인; n. 전문가 inadequately adv. 불충분하게
inadequacy n. 부적당함, 부족 inadequateness n. 불충분함

118 형용사 어휘 고르기

해설 Although 이하의 부사절과 뒤 문장의 연결이 자연스러워야 한다. '참여는 전적으로 자발적이지만 직원 참여가 매우 높다'라는 문맥이므로 (B) voluntary(자발적인)가 정답이다. (A) precise는 '정확한', (C) significant는 '중요한', (D) persistent는 '끈기 있는, 끊임없는'이라는 의미이다.

해석 HPS사의 사회적 책임 위원회에의 참여는 전적으로 자발적이지만, 직원 참여가 매우 높다.

어휘 social responsibility 사회적 책임 committee n. 위원회
purely adv. 전적으로 involvement n. 참여, 관여

119 to 부정사 채우기

해설 동사 allow의 목적격 보어 자리에는 to 부정사가 와야 하므로 (D) to return이 정답이다.

해석 도서관의 정문 옆에 설치된 새로운 수납함들은 시설이 문을 닫은 후에도 이용자들이 자료들을 반납할 수 있도록 한다.

어휘 place v. 설치하다, 놓다; n. 장소 main entrance 정문
patron n. 이용자 material n. 자료

120 부사 어휘 고르기

해설 Because 이하의 부사절과 뒤 문장의 연결이 자연스러워야 한다. '분기별로 발행되기 때문에, 구독자들은 일 년에 네 번씩 최신 정보를 얻는다'라는 문맥이므로 (A) quarterly(분기별로)가 정답이다. (B) properly는 '적절히', (C) constantly는 '끊임없이', (D) recently는 '최근에'라는 의미이다.

해석 SharpBiz지가 분기별로 발행되기 때문에, 구독자들은 일 년에 네 번씩 주요 경제 뉴스에 대한 최신 정보를 얻는다.

어휘 an update on ~에 대한 최신 정보
essential adj. 주요한, 필수의; n. 필수적인 것

121 명사 자리 채우기

해설 타동사(have)의 목적어 자리에 올 수 있는 것은 명사이므로 명사 (A) influence(영향)가 정답이다. 빈칸 앞에 형용사(greater)가 있는 것도 명사 자리를 알려 주는 단서가 된다. 형용사 (B), 동사 또는 분사 (C), 동사 (D)는 명사 자리에 올 수 없다.

해석 최근 조사들에 따르면, 텔레비전에서의 광고들이 신문과 잡지에 있는 광고들보다 소비자들에게 더 큰 영향을 미친다.

어휘 advertisement n. 광고

122 전치사 채우기
해설 '해외 확장의 상황에 관하여 성명을 발표할 것이다'라는 의미가 되어야 하므로 (C) regarding(~에 관하여)이 정답이다. (A) behind는 '~ 뒤에', (B) beyond는 '~ 너머', (D) within은 '~ 안에'라는 의미이다.

해석 Edgecom사는 오늘 자사의 해외 확장의 상황에 관하여 성명을 발표할 것이다.

어휘 issue a statement 성명을 발표하다 status n. 상황, 지위
overseas adj. 해외의; adv. 해외로 expansion n. 확장

123 동사 어휘 고르기
해설 '월별 모바일 데이터 할당량을 초과한 고객들은 추가 요금을 받을 것이다'라는 문맥이므로 (B) incur((손해 등을) 받다, 발생시키다)가 정답이다. (A) replace는 '대체하다', (C) switch는 '바꾸다', (D) possess는 '소유하다'라는 의미이다.

해석 월별 모바일 데이터 할당량을 초과한 고객들은 추가 요금을 받을 것이다.

어휘 allocation n. 할당량, 할당

124 명사 어휘 고르기
해설 '여름 할인 판매는 다양한 새 신발들을 구매하는 데 좋은 기회가 될 것이다'라는 문맥이므로 (A) opportunity(기회)가 정답이다. (B) contribution은 '기여', (C) appearance는 '출연, 외모', (D) restoration은 '복원'이라는 의미이다.

해석 Mayfield Footwear사의 여름 할인 판매는 쇼핑객들이 다양한 새 신발들을 구매하는 데 좋은 기회가 될 것이다.

어휘 purchase v. 구입하다; n. 구매 a variety of 다양한

125 부사절 접속사 채우기
해설 이 문장은 필수성분(Software products ~ purchase)을 갖춘 완전한 절이므로 ____ they are ~ receipt는 수식어 거품으로 보아야 한다. 이 수식어 거품은 동사(are accompanied)가 있는 거품절이므로, 거품절을 이끌 수 있는 부사절 접속사 (B), (C), (D)가 정답의 후보이다. '오직 영수증 원본과 함께 있는 경우에만 환불될 수 있다'라는 의미가 되어야 하므로 (D) as long as(오직 ~하는 경우에만)가 정답이다. (B) although는 '~이긴 하지만', (C) so that은 '~할 수 있도록'이라는 의미이므로 이 문맥에 어울리지 않는다.

해석 Digital Age사의 소프트웨어 제품들은 오직 영수증 원본과 함께 있는 경우에만 구매 한달 이내에 환불될 수 있다.

어휘 refund v. 환불하다; n. 환불 accompany v. ~과 함께 있다, 동반하다
original receipt 영수증 원본

126 주어와 수일치하는 동사 채우기
해설 문장에 동사가 없으므로 동사 (A)와 (D)가 정답의 후보이다. 주어(The revised environmental regulations)가 복수이므로 복수 동사 (D) are aimed가 정답이다. 참고로, be aimed at은 '~을 목표로 삼다'라는 의미의 관용 표현이다.

해석 개정된 환경 규제는 지역 공장들로부터 방출되는 온실가스의 양을 줄이는 것을 목표로 삼는다.

어휘 revised adj. 개정된, 수정된 environmental adj. 환경의
regulation n. 규제 greenhouse gas 온실가스 emit v. 방출하다

127 상관접속사 채우기
해설 상관접속사 but also와 맞는 짝인 (B) Not only가 정답이다. 참고로, 이 문장은 부정어(Not)가 문장 맨 앞에 와서 주어와 동사가 도치된 문장이다.

해석 구매자들은 그 집의 가격을 마음에 들어 했을 뿐만 아니라, 그것의 위치

또한 높이 평가했다.

어휘 appreciate v. ~을 높이 평가하다, 감사하다

128 사람명사 추상명사 구별하여 채우기
해설 전치사(for)의 목적어 자리에 올 수 있는 것은 명사이므로 명사 (A)와 (D)가 정답의 후보이다. '재정 지원에 자격을 얻으려면'이라는 의미이므로 추상명사 (A) assistance(지원, 원조)가 정답이다. 사람명사 (D)가 '조수로서 자격을 얻으려면'이라는 의미를 나타내기 위해서는 'To qualify as a financial assistant'와 같이 쓰여야 하기 때문에 답이 될 수 없다.

해석 재정 지원에 자격을 얻으려면, 학생들은 매 학기에 재정 지원 요청서를 제출해야 한다.

어휘 qualify v. 자격을 얻다 financial adj. 재정의
funding n. 재정 지원, 자금 request n. 요청(서); v. 요청하다
term n. 학기

129 동사 어휘 고르기
해설 '수익이 감소할 것으로 예상하기 때문에 예상 매출액을 줄였다'라는 문맥이므로 reduce의 과거형 (C) reduced(줄이다)가 정답이다. (A)의 overtake는 '추월하다', (B)의 connect는 '연결하다', (D)의 compliment는 '칭찬하다'라는 의미이다.

해석 Nesbit Software사는 올해 수익이 감소할 것으로 예상하기 때문에 예상 매출액을 줄였다.

어휘 sales projections 예상 매출(액) revenue n. 수익, 매출
decrease v. 감소하다

130 형용사 어휘 고르기
해설 '이전 노트북 컴퓨터 모델은 최신 노트북 컴퓨터 모델보다 인기가 있었다'라는 문맥이므로 (D) previous(이전의)가 정답이다. (A) various는 '다양한', (B) relative는 '상대적인', (C) customary는 '관례적인'이라는 의미이다.

해석 Core Electronics사에서 출시된 이전 노트북 컴퓨터 모델은 당사의 최신 노트북 컴퓨터 모델보다 훨씬 더 소비자들에게 인기가 있었다.

어휘 release v. 출시하다, 발표하다 latest adj. 최신의

PART 6

131-134번은 다음 이메일에 관한 문제입니다.

수신: Allan White <a.white@trytek.com>
발신: Joseph Winfield <j.winfield@trytek.com>
날짜: 3월 12일
제목: 예비 교육 세미나

Allan께,

새로운 인턴들을 위한 우리의 예비 교육 세미나에 대한 계획이 순조롭게 진행되고 있음을 전하게 되어 기쁩니다. 그러나, 한 가지 중요한 사항이 아직 해결되지 않고 있습니다. [131]우리는 아직 마케팅 부서의 누군가가 하는 간단한 발표의 일정을 잡아야 하는데, 저는 세미나에 참여하고 싶어 하는 누구에게도 연락을 받지 않았습니다. [132]직원들은 이것이 너무 많은 시간이 걸릴 것이라 생각할지도 모릅니다. [133]그러니, 모든 사람들에게 발표자는 인턴들의 일상적인 업무들에 대해 단 10분간만 연설할 것이라는 점을 알려주시기 바랍니다. [134]또한, 당신은 모두에게 세미나 참석자들은 그들의 시간과 노력에 대한 보상으로 200달러를 받을 것이라는 점을 상기시켜야 합니다.

감사합니다,

Joe 드림
---

planning n. 계획 orientation n. 예비 교육
proceed v. 진행되다, 나아가다 smoothly adv. 순조롭게
detail n. (세부)사항; v. 상세히 알리다 unresolved adj. 미해결의
duty n. 업무, 임무 remind v. 상기시키다 contributor n. 참석자, 원인
compensation n. 보상

131 조동사 다음에 동사원형 채우기

해설 빈칸 앞 would와 함께 조동사처럼 쓰이는 표현 'would like to + 동사원형'의 형태를 만들어 '참여하고 싶다'라는 의미를 만드는 (D) like to participate가 정답이다. 참고로, 'would like to + 동사원형'은 '~하고 싶다'라는 의미이다. (B)는 'would have + p.p.'의 형태를 만들어 '참여하고 싶었을 것이다'라는 어색한 의미를 만들기 때문에 답이 될 수 없다.

132 알맞은 문장 고르기

해석 (A) 발표자들은 이미 연설을 예행 연습하는 것을 시작했습니다.
(B) 직원들은 이것이 너무 많은 시간이 걸릴 것이라 생각할지도 모릅니다.
(C) 새로운 구성원들 또한 그들의 경험에 대해 연설하기 위해 참가했습니다.
(D) 참가는 명시된 직원들에게 의무입니다.

해설 빈칸에 들어갈 알맞은 문장을 고르는 문제이므로 주변 문맥 또는 전체 문맥을 파악한다. 앞 문장 'We still need to schedule a short presentation ~, but I have not heard from anyone'에서 간단한 발표의 일정을 잡아야 하는데 누구에게도 연락을 받지 않았다고 했고, 뒤 문장 'So, please let everyone know that the presenter will talk ~ for only 10 minutes.'에서 그러니 모든 사람들에게 발표자는 단 10분간만 연설할 것이라는 점을 알려주라고 했으므로 빈칸에는 직원들은 발표가 너무 많은 시간이 걸릴 것이라 생각할지도 모른다는 내용이 들어가야 함을 알 수 있다. 따라서 (B)가 정답이다.

어휘 rehearse v. 예행 연습을 하다 join v. 참가하다, 결합하다
mandatory adj. 의무적인 specified adj. 명시된

133 형용사 어휘 고르기 전체 문맥 파악

해설 '발표자는 인턴들의 ____ 업무들에 대해 연설할 것이다'라는 문맥이므로 (B) momentary(순간적인), (C) regular(일상적인), (D) ongoing(계속 진행 중인)이 정답의 후보이다. 빈칸이 있는 문장만으로 정답을 고를 수 없으므로 주변 문맥이나 전체 문맥을 파악한다. 앞부분에서 새로운 인턴들을 위한 예비 교육 세미나에 대한 계획이 진행되고 있다고 했으므로 발표자가 인턴들의 일상적인 업무들에 대해 연설할 것임을 알 수 있다. 따라서 (C) regular가 정답이다.

어휘 momentary adj. 순간적인, 순식간의 ongoing adj. 계속 진행 중인

134 접속부사 채우기 주변 문맥 파악

해설 빈칸이 콤마와 함께 문장의 맨 앞에 온 접속부사 자리이므로, 앞 문장과 빈칸이 있는 문장의 의미 관계를 파악하여 정답을 선택한다. 앞 문장에서 모든 사람들에게 발표자는 단 10분간만 연설할 것이라는 점을 알려주라고 했고, 빈칸이 있는 문장에서는 모두에게 세미나 참석자들은 200달러를 받을 것이라는 점을 상기시켜야 한다고 했으므로, 앞 문장에서 언급된 내용에 추가 정보를 덧붙이는 내용의 문장에서 사용되는 (B) In addition(또한)이 정답이다.

어휘 unfortunately adv. 안타깝게도 namely adv. 즉
nevertheless adv. 그럼에도 불구하고

135-138번은 다음 광고에 관한 문제입니다.

Madison Woodworks사
1987년 설립

¹³⁵집이나 사무실을 개조할 것을 계획하고 계십니까? Madison

Woodworks사의 정교하게 공들여 만들어진 제품들로 여러분의 새로운 인테리어를 보완하세요. 30년이 넘는 기간 동안, 저희는 체스터필드 자치주 전역의 가정과 기업에 양질의 수공예 제품을 공급해 왔습니다. 여러분이 전통적인 스타일을 좋아하든 현대적인 스타일을 좋아하든, 여러분은 저희 가게에서 다가올 수년간 동안 즐길만한 것을 찾으실 것이라고 확신합니다. ¹³⁶만약 여러분이 더 개인화된 제품들을 선호하신다면, 특별한 식탁, 책상 또는 의자를 제작하는 것에 대해 저희의 내부 디자이너들 중 한 명에게 문의하세요. 오늘 맨체스터의 627번지 Stockport로에 있는 저희 가게에 들러 보세요. ¹³⁷7월 말까지 이미 만들어져 있는 모든 가구에 대한 할인을 기회로 이용하세요. 여러분은 온라인으로도 저희의 카탈로그를 보실 수 있습니다. ¹³⁸저희의 전체 소장품을 둘러보시려면 www.madisonwoodworks.com을 방문하세요.

complement v. 보완하다, 보충하다 finely adv. 정교하게
craft v. 공들여 만들다 handmade adj. 수공예의
contemporary adj. 현대적인 consult v. 문의하다
take advantage of ~을 이용하다
ready-made adj. 이미 만들어져 있는, 기성품의

135 동사 어휘 고르기 주변 문맥 파악

해설 '집이나 사무실을 ____ 할 것을 계획하고 계십니까?'라는 문맥이므로 모든 보기가 정답의 후보이다. 빈칸이 있는 문장만으로 정답을 고를 수 없으므로 주변 문맥이나 전체 문맥을 파악한다. 뒤 문장에서 'Madison Woodworks사의 정교하게 공들여 만들어진 제품들로 새로운 인테리어를 보완하세요(Complement your new interior with finely crafted items from Madison Woodworks.)'라고 했으므로 집이나 사무실을 개조할 것을 계획하고 있는지를 묻고 있음을 알 수 있다. 따라서 (B) renovate(개조하다)가 정답이다.

어휘 leave v. 떠나다, 출발하다 finance v. 자금을 대다
promote v. 홍보하다, 촉진하다

136 현재분사와 과거분사 구별하여 채우기

해설 수식받는 명사(items)와 분사가 '개인화된 제품들'이라는 의미의 수동 관계이므로 과거분사 (D) personalized가 정답이다.

어휘 personalize v. 개인화하다

137 명사 어휘 고르기 전체 문맥 파악

해설 '7월 말까지 이미 만들어져 있는 모든 ____에 대한 할인을 기회로 이용하세요'라는 문맥이므로 모든 보기가 정답의 후보이다. 빈칸이 있는 문장만으로 정답을 고를 수 없으므로 주변 문맥이나 전체 문맥을 파악한다. 앞부분에서 '특별한 식탁, 책상 또는 의자를 제작하는 것에 대해 내부 디자이너들 중 한 명에게 문의하세요(consult one of our in-house designers about creating a unique table, desk, or chair)'라고 했으므로 7월 말까지 이미 만들어져 있는 모든 가구에 대한 할인을 기회로 이용하라는 것임을 알 수 있다. 따라서 (C) furniture(가구)가 정답이다.

어휘 fabric n. 섬유 gadget n. 도구 structure n. 건축물

138 알맞은 문장 고르기

해석 (A) 기술자 팀이 여러분의 집에서 제품을 점검할 예정입니다.
(B) 만약 여러분이 저희에게 이 보증서를 주신다면 제품들은 교체될 수 있습니다.
(C) 그것을 조립하려면 포함된 사용 설명서와 몇몇 간단한 도구들을 이용하세요.
(D) 저희의 전체 소장품을 둘러보시려면 www.madisonwoodworks.com을 방문하세요.

해설 빈칸에 들어갈 알맞은 문장을 고르는 문제이므로 주변 문맥 또는 전체 문맥을 파악한다. 앞 문장 'You can also view our catalog online.'에서 온라인으로도 카탈로그를 볼 수 있다고 했으므로, 빈칸에는 전체 소장품을 둘러보려면 홈페이지를 방문하라는 내용이 들어가야 함을 알

수 있다. 따라서 (D)가 정답이다.

어휘 **inspect** v. 점검하다, 검사하다 **assemble** v. 조립하다
browse v. 둘러보다 **entire** adj. 전체의 **collection** n. 소장품, 수집품

139-142번은 다음 회람에 관한 문제입니다.

수신: 전 직원
발신: Jason Fraser, 인사부
날짜: 8월 5일
제목: 전문성 개발 강의

¹³⁹경영진은 이번 가을부터 Hearthstone Appliances사의 직원들이
그들의 업무 분야와 관련 있는 대학 강의들에 대해 재정적 지원을 받을
자격이 있을 것임을 알리게 되어 기쁩니다. 참여하는 직원들은 전체 수업
료의 50퍼센트를 환급받을 것입니다. ¹⁴⁰이 금액은 그들이 선택한 프로
그램들의 성공적인 수료 하에 지급될 것입니다.

¹⁴¹공인된 교육 기관에 의해 진행되는 강의를 수강하는 직원들만이 재정
지원을 받을 수 있습니다. 또한, 특정 개인들이 참여하지 못하게 할 수도
있는 몇몇 다른 제약들이 있습니다. ¹⁴²따라서, 저희는 강의에 등록하기
전에 인사부 직원과의 회의 일정을 잡기를 강력히 권고합니다.

management n. 경영진 **academic** adj. 대학의, 학업의
related to ~과 관련 있는 **responsibility** n. 업무, 책임
reimburse v. 환급하다 **tuition fee** 수업료
deliver v. (강연 등을) 하다, 배달하다 **approved** adj. 공인된, 승인된
funding n. 재정 지원, 자금 **restriction** n. 제약, 규제

139 형용사 관용 표현 채우기

해설 '재정적 지원을 받을 자격이 있다'라는 의미가 되어야 하므로 be
eligible to do(~할 자격이 있다)를 만드는 (A) eligible이 정답이다.

어휘 **prominent** adj. 중요한 **social** adj. 사회적인
preferable adj. 선호되는

140 알맞은 문장 고르기

해석 (A) 이 금액은 그들이 선택한 프로그램들의 성공적인 수료 하에 지급
될 것입니다.
(B) 지사장들은 최소한 20시간의 교육을 지도하도록 요구됩니다.
(C) 학교 직원들은 교재와 다른 용구들에 할인을 받을 것입니다.
(D) 일자리에 대한 지원서들은 인사부에서 수집될 것입니다.

해설 빈칸에 들어갈 알맞은 문장을 고르는 문제이므로 주변 문맥 또는 전
체 문맥을 파악한다. 앞 문장 'Participating employees will be
reimbursed for 50 percent of their total tuition fees.'에서 참여
하는 직원들은 전체 수업료의 50퍼센트를 환급받을 것이라고 했으므
로 빈칸에는 이 금액은 프로그램들의 성공적인 수료 하에 지급될 것이
라는 환급 조건에 대한 내용이 들어가야 함을 알 수 있다. 따라서 (A)
가 정답이다.

어휘 **completion** n. 수료, 완성 **district manager** 지사장
be required to do ~하도록 요구되다 **lead** v. 지도하다, 이끌다
material n. 용구, 재료 **application** n. 지원(서), 적용
job opening 일자리

141 현재분사와 과거분사 구별하여 채우기

해설 이 문장은 주어(employees), 동사(may receive), 목적어(funding)
를 갖춘 완전한 절이므로, ___ a class ~ institution은 수식어 거
품으로 보아야 한다. 보기 중 수식어 거품이 될 수 있는 것은 현재
분사 (C)와 과거분사 (D)이다. 수식 받는 명사(employees)와 분
사가 '직원들이 강의를 수강하다'라는 의미의 능동 관계이므로 현재
분사 (C) taking이 정답이다. 참고로, delivered by an approved
educational institution은 a class를 꾸며 주는 수식어 거품이다.

142 접속부사 채우기 주변 문맥 파악

해설 빈칸이 콤마와 함께 문장의 맨 앞에 온 접속부사 자리이므로, 앞 문장
과 빈칸이 있는 문장의 의미 관계를 파악하여 정답을 선택한다. 앞 문
장에서 특정 개인들이 참여하지 못하게 할 수도 있는 몇몇 다른 제약
들이 있다고 했고, 빈칸이 있는 문장에서는 강의에 등록하기 전에 인
사부 직원과의 회의 일정을 잡기를 강력히 권고한다고 했으므로, 원인
에 대한 결과를 나타내는 문장에서 사용되는 (C) Consequently(따
라서)가 정답이다.

어휘 **likewise** adv. 마찬가지로 **afterward** adv. 그 후
for instance adv. 예를 들어

143-146번은 다음 공고에 관한 문제입니다.

PEN AND PAPER: 저희의 개업일을 알립니다

11월 1일에 오셔서 저희와 함께 개업을 축하해주세요. ¹⁴³Pen and
Paper는 모든 종류의 업소용 장비, 문구류, 그리고 다른 사무용품들을
공급하는 소매점입니다.

¹⁴⁴저희는 여러분이 작업 공간을 위해 필요로 하는 것이 무엇이든, 저희
상점에서 찾을 수 있을 것임을 확신합니다. 저희 직원들에게 찾고 있는
것을 말씀만 해주시면, 그들이 여러분에게 고르실 수 있는 다양한 선택권
들을 제공해드릴 것입니다. 제본 서비스뿐만 아니라, 저희는 브로슈어와
명함과 같은 다양한 인쇄 작업들도 수행합니다.

¹⁴⁵그날 저희 상점에 오시는 고객 누구나를 위한 온갖 증정품들이 있을
것입니다. 뿐만 아니라, 100번째 손님은 100달러 상품권을 받을 것입니
다. ¹⁴⁶이는 저희 상점 내부에 있는 어떤 것에도 쓰일 수 있습니다. 그
러니, 이 특별 행사를 위해 550번지 Emerald가에서 꼭 저희와 함께
하세요!

grand opening 개업, 개장 **stationery** n. 문구류
office supplies 사무용품 **workspace** n. 작업 공간
a range of 다양한 **in addition to** ~뿐만 아니라 **business card** 명함
giveaway n. 증정품; adj. 헐값의 **gift card** 상품권

143 다른 명사를 수식하는 명사 채우기

해설 '소매점'이라는 복합 명사의 의미이므로 복합 명사를 만드는 명사 (D)
establishment가 정답이다. 분사 (C)를 빈칸에 넣으면 '설립된 소매'
라는 어색한 의미가 되어 버린다.

어휘 **establish** v. 설립하다 **establishment** n. 상점

144 동사 어휘 고르기 주변 문맥 파악

해설 '작업 공간을 위해 필요로 하는 것이 무엇이든, 상점에서 ___할 수 있
을 것이다'라는 문맥이므로 모든 보기가 정답의 후보이다. 빈칸이 있
는 문장만으로 정답을 고를 수 없으므로 주변 문맥이나 전체 문맥을 파
악한다. 뒤 문장에서 '찾고 있는 것을 말만 해주면 다양한 선택권들을
제공할 것이다(Just tell ~ what you are looking for, and they'll
provide you with a range of options)'라고 했으므로 필요로 하는
것을 상점에서 찾을 수 있음을 알 수 있다. 따라서 (A) find(찾다)가 정
답이다.

어휘 **deliver** v. 배달하다 **repair** v. 수리하다, 바로잡다
exchange v. 교환하다

145 선행사와 수일치하는 주격 관계절의 동사 채우기

해설 주격 관계절(who ~ on that day)의 동사가 없으므로 동사 (A),
(B), (C)가 정답의 후보이다. 주격 관계사(who)의 선행사(any
customer)가 단수이고, '고객이 오다'라는 능동의 의미가 맞으므로
능동태 단수 동사 (B) enters가 정답이다.

146 알맞은 문장 고르기

해석 (A) 이는 저희 상점 내부에 있는 어떤 것에도 쓰일 수 있습니다.

(B) 개업에 저희 회사의 최고경영자가 참석하실 것입니다.
(C) 저희 상점의 보수가 완료되었습니다.
(D) 저희는 내일 경품의 당첨자를 발표할 것입니다.

해설 빈칸에 들어갈 알맞은 문장을 고르는 문제이므로 주변 문맥 또는 전체 문맥을 파악한다. 앞 문장 'the 100th customer will receive a $100 gift card'에서 100번째 손님은 100달러 상품권을 받을 것이라고 했으므로 빈칸에는 이 상품권이 상점 내부에 있는 어떤 것에도 쓰일 수 있다는 내용이 들어가야 함을 알 수 있다. 따라서 (A)가 정답이다.

어휘 complete v. 완료하다

PART 7

147-148번은 다음 설문지에 관한 문제입니다.

Petra's Grill

고객에게 가능한 최고의 식사 경험을 제공하는 것이 저희의 사명이기에, 저희는 고객 의견을 환영합니다. 이 간단한 설문지를 작성하셔서 출구 옆에 있는 박스 안에 넣어주시기 바랍니다. 감사합니다!

귀하께서는 신속한 서비스를 제공받으셨습니까?
---네   -X-아니오

귀하의 음식의 질을 어떻게 평가하시겠습니까?
---훌륭함   -X-매우 좋음   ---만족스러움   ---안 좋음

귀하의 메인 음식은 무엇이었습니까?
구운 치킨과 이탈리안 드레싱을 곁들인 야채 샐러드

음식은 가격만큼의 가치가 있었습니까?
-X-네   ---아니오

Petra's Grill에 얼마나 자주 방문하십니까?
---자주   ---가끔   ---거의 안 옴   147-X-첫 방문이었음

의견
저는 반드시 이곳이 덜 바쁠 때 올 것이기 때문에 147이곳으로의 저의 다음 방문은 더 좋을 것이라고 생각합니다. 제 종업원은 친절하고 공손했지만, 다른 여러 테이블들을 담당하고 있었어서, 148저를 알아차리고 메뉴판을 가져다주는 데 매우 오랜 시간이 걸렸습니다.

questionnaire n. 설문지 mission n. 사명, 임무 dining n. 식사
prompt adj. 신속한 rate v. 평가하다 server n. (서빙 담당) 종업원
deal with ~을 처리하다, 대하다 polite adj. 공손한

147 추론 문제

문제 설문지에서 추론될 수 있는 것은?
(A) 식당은 주로 이탈리아 요리를 제공한다.
(B) 고객은 Petra's Grill에서 두 번째 식사를 할 의향이 있다.
(C) 음식점은 최근에 개조되었다.
(D) 고객 의견을 반영하기 위해 메뉴가 바뀌었다.

해설 설문지에서 추론될 수 있는 것을 묻는 추론 문제이다. 이 문제는 질문에 핵심 어구가 없으므로 각 보기의 핵심 어구와 관련된 내용을 지문에서 확인한다. '-X-This was my first visit'에서 고객이 Petra's Grill에 첫 방문이라고 한 후, 'I think my next visit here will be better'에서 다음 방문은 더 좋을 것이라고 생각한다고 했으므로 고객이 Petra's Grill에서 두 번째 식사를 할 의향이 있다는 것을 추론할 수 있다. 따라서 (B)가 정답이다.

어휘 primarily adv. 주로 serve v. (음식을) 제공하다 cuisine n. 요리
intend to ~할 의향이 있다

148 육하원칙 문제

문제 고객은 식당에서 무슨 문제가 있었는가?
(A) 음식이 왔을 때 식어 있었다.

(B) 즉시 이용할 수 있는 테이블들이 없었다.
(C) 종업원에게 알아차려지는 데 시간이 얼마간 걸렸다.
(D) 메뉴판에 있는 품목들이 너무 비쌌다.

해설 고객이 식당에서 무슨(What) 문제가 있었는지를 묻는 육하원칙 문제이다. 질문의 핵심 어구인 problem ~ the customer have와 관련하여, 'it took a very long time for her[server] to notice me and bring over a menu'에서 종업원이 자신을 알아차리고 메뉴판을 가져다주는 데 매우 오랜 시간이 걸렸다고 했으므로 (C)가 정답이다.

패러프레이징
took a very long time ~ to notice 알아차리는 데 매우 오랜 시간이 걸렸다 → took a while to be acknowledged 알아차려지는 데 시간이 얼마간 걸렸다

어휘 acknowledge v. 알아차렸음을 알리다, (사실임을) 인정하다
overpriced adj. 너무 비싼

149-151번은 다음 공고에 관한 문제입니다.

6월 4일은 밀링턴 주립 공원이 대중에게 처음 문을 연 지 50주년을 기념하는 날입니다. 이 중요한 시점을 축하하고 지역의 야생동물을 보호하려는 저희의 노력을 지지해주신 것에 대해 감사의 뜻을 전하기 위하여, 149레저 차량 한 대당 55달러, 차량 한 대당 35달러, 오토바이 한 대당 25달러, 149/150보행자 혹은 자전거 이용객 한 명당 10달러의 일반 입장료가 6월 4일부터 6월 10일까지 적용되지 않을 것입니다. 이 면제는 입장료에만 적용되며 단체 여행, 야영장, 보트나 낚시 도구와 같은 장비 대여에 대한 요금에는 적용되지 않을 알아두시기 바랍니다. 또한, 151이 기간 동안 공원에 입장하셨지만 6월 11일이나 그 이후까지 머무실 경우, 나가실 때 요금이 청구될 것입니다.

mark v. 기념하다; n. 표시 in honor of ~을 축하하여
milestone n. 중요한 시점 wildlife n. 야생동물 entry fee 입장료
pedestrian n. 보행자 waive v. 적용하지 않다, 포기하다
exemption n. 면제 entrance fee 입장료 organized tour 단체 여행
camping site 야영장 fishing gear 낚시 도구 charge v. 청구하다

149 주제 찾기 문제

문제 공고의 주제는 무엇인가?
(A) 시설의 주차 규정에 대한 변경
(B) 기관의 환경 보호 노력
(C) 휴양지의 일시적 무료입장
(D) 주립 공원에서 열린 기념일 연회

해설 공고의 주제가 무엇인지를 묻는 주제 찾기 문제이다. 특별히 이 문제는 지문의 중반에 주제 관련 내용이 언급되었음에 유의한다. 'our[Millington State Park] regular entry fees ~ will be waived from June 4 until June 10'에서 밀링턴 주립 공원의 일반 입장료가 6월 4일부터 6월 10일까지 적용되지 않을 것이라고 했으므로 (C)가 정답이다.

패러프레이징
entry fees ~ will be waived from June 4 until June 10 입장료가 6월 4일부터 6월 10일까지 적용되지 않을 것이다 → Temporary free admission 일시적 무료입장
Park 공원 → a recreational area 휴양지

어휘 regulation n. 규정, 규제 environmental adj. 환경 보호의, 환경의
admission n. 입장 recreational area 휴양지

150 육하원칙 문제

문제 자전거를 타고 공원에 입장하는 데 얼마가 드는가?
(A) 10달러
(B) 25달러
(C) 35달러
(D) 55달러

해설 자전거를 타고 공원에 입장하는 데 얼마(How much)가 드는지를 묻는 육하원칙 문제이다. 질문의 핵심 어구인 cost to enter the park on a bicycle과 관련하여, 'entry fees of ~ $10 per ~ cyclist'에서 입장료가 자전거 이용객 한 명당 10달러라고 했으므로 (A)가 정답이다.

151 추론 문제

문제 밀링턴 주립 공원에 대해 암시되는 것은?
(A) 차량 내 사람 수를 기준으로 방문객들에게 요금을 청구한다.
(B) 단체 여행은 대규모 그룹들에게 할인된다.
(C) 대중으로부터 정기적으로 재정적 지원을 요청한다.
(D) 방문객들은 며칠간 머무를 수 있다.

해설 질문의 핵심 어구인 Millington State Park에 대해 추론하는 문제이다. 'if you enter the park during this period but stay until June 11 or later'에서 이 기간 동안 공원에 입장하였지만 6월 11일이나 그 이후까지 머무를 경우라고 했으므로 밀링턴 주립 공원에 방문객들이 며칠간 머무를 수 있다는 것을 추론할 수 있다. 따라서 (D)가 정답이다.

패러프레이징
stay until June 11 or later 6월 11일이나 그 이후까지 머무르다 →
stay for multiple days 며칠간 머무르다

어휘 based on ~을 기준으로   regularly adv. 정기적으로

152-153번은 다음 메시지 대화문에 관한 문제입니다.

Brad Lee	오전 9시 34분

저는 방금 우리가 관리하는 건물들 중 하나의 세입자로부터 전화를 받았어요. 그녀는 5번가에 있는 Plaza Tower의 202호에 있어요.

Sara Godfrey	오전 9시 35분

¹⁵²그녀가 로비의 보수 작업으로 인한 소음 때문에 화가 났나요? 이번 주에 그 건물의 거주자들로부터 많은 항의를 받아 왔어요.

Brad Lee	오전 9시 36분

아니요, 그게 아니에요. 그녀가 시애틀에 있는 회사에서 일자리를 제안받았대요. 그 일이 다음 주부터 시작해서, 그녀는 이번 달에 방에서 이사를 나가야 할 거예요. 하지만 그녀는 1년의 임대 계약을 했대요. ¹⁵³그녀는 위약금을 물어야 할 것인지를 알고 싶어 해요.

Sara Godfrey	오전 9시 38분

확실히 알 수 없어요. ¹⁵³그녀는 이번 달 말까지 새로운 세입자를 찾아야 해요. 그렇지 않으면, 그녀는 지불해야 할 거예요.

Brad Lee	오전 9시 39분

실은, 그녀가 그녀의 남동생이 그 방에 관심이 있다고 했어요. 제가 그에게 이번 주에 신청서를 작성하라고 말할게요. 그러고 나서, 소유주와 이야기해볼게요.

tenant n. 세입자   property n. 건물, 재산   complaint n. 항의, 불평
resident n. 거주자   move out 이사를 나가다
apartment n. 방, 아파트   lease agreement 임대 계약
penalty n. 위약금, 벌금

152 추론 문제

문제 Plaza Tower에 대해 암시되는 것은?
(A) 시애틀에 있는 회사에 의해 소유된다.
(B) 1년 이내에 지어졌다.
(C) 몇 개의 빈 방들이 있다.
(D) 현재 보수되고 있는 중이다.

해설 질문의 핵심 어구인 Plaza Tower에 대해 추론하는 문제이다. 'Is she[tenant] upset about the noise from the renovation work in the lobby? I've gotten a lot of complaints from the residents of that building[Plaza Tower] this week.'(9:35 A.M.)에서 Ms. Godfrey가 세입자가 로비의 보수 작업으로 인한 소음 때문

에 화가 났는지 물은 후, 이번 주에 Plaza Tower의 거주자들로부터 많은 항의를 받아 왔다고 했으므로 Plaza Tower가 현재 보수되고 있는 중이라는 것을 추론할 수 있다. 따라서 (D)가 정답이다.

어휘 be owned by ~에 의해 소유되다   vacant adj. 비어 있는

153 의도 파악 문제

문제 오전 9시 38분에, Ms. Godfrey가 "That depends"라고 썼을 때, 그녀가 의도한 것 같은 것은?
(A) 계약서는 아직 서명되지 않았다.
(B) 건물주는 연락하기가 어렵다.
(C) 새로운 세입자를 찾으면 위약금이 적용되지 않을 것이다.
(D) 특정 날짜 이후에는 한 가구를 사용할 수 없을 수도 있다.

해설 Ms. Godfrey가 의도한 것 같은 것을 묻는 문제이므로, 질문의 인용어구(That depends)가 언급된 주변 문맥을 확인한다. 'She[tenant] wants to know if she will have to pay a penalty.'(9:36 A.M.)에서 Mr. Lee가 세입자가 위약금을 물어야 할 것인지를 알고 싶어 한다고 하자, Ms. Godfrey가 'That depends.'(확실히 알 수 없어요)라고 한 후, 'She has until the end of the month to find a new tenant. Otherwise, she will have to pay.'(9:38 A.M.)에서 이번 달 말까지 새로운 세입자를 찾지 않으면 지불해야 할 것이라고 한 말을 통해, 새로운 세입자를 찾으면 위약금이 적용되지 않을 것임을 알 수 있다. 따라서 (C)가 정답이다.

어휘 agreement n. 계약서   waive v. (규칙 등을) 적용하지 않다, 생략하다
unit n. 한 가구, 단위

154-156번은 다음 이메일에 관한 문제입니다.

수신: Diana Mansfield <dmans@timemail.com>
발신: Herbal Greens사 고객 지원 부서 <cs@herbalgreens.com>
날짜: 8월 2일
제목: 회원

Ms. Mansfield께,

저희는 고객님께서 지난 몇 달 동안 저희로부터 여러 번 주문하셨으나, 아직 ¹⁵⁵⁻ᴮ저희 웹사이트에서 회원으로 가입하지 않으신 것을 알게 되었습니다. ─ [1] ─. 등록하지 않아도 저희의 상품들을 구매하시는 것이 여전히 가능하지만, ¹⁵⁴회원이 되어야 하는 많은 이유들이 있습니다.

우선, ¹⁵⁶고객님께서 구매를 하실 때마다 고객님의 물건 발송 주소, 전화번호, 신용카드 세부 정보들을 더 이상 입력할 필요가 없을 것입니다. ─ [2] ─. 또한 주간 판촉 행사들에 대한 최신 정보들도 받아보실 것인데, 이는 고객님이 회원이 아니면 알지 못할 엄청난 할인 혜택들을 확인하실 수 있도록 합니다. ─ [3] ─. 게다가, ¹⁵⁵⁻ᴮ오직 회원들만 고객 마일리지를 쌓을 수 있습니다. 고객님께서 가입하신다면, ¹⁵⁵⁻ᴰ고객님은 주문하실 때마다 쓰는 총 금액의 10퍼센트를 얻으실 것입니다. ¹⁵⁵⁻ᴬ이 마일리지를 고객님의 다음 구매의 비용에 보태거나 나중에 사용할 수 있도록 모으실 수 있습니다. ─ [4] ─.

계정을 만드는 데는 2분이 채 걸리지 않으며 아무 비용도 들지 않습니다. 저희는 고객님께서 오늘 가입하셔서 Herbal Greens사의 회원 혜택들을 이용하시기를 권해드립니다.

Clay Lewis 드림
Herbal Greens사 고객 지원 부서

place an order 주문하다   sign up for ~에 가입하다, 등록하다
numerous adj. 많은   shipping address 물건 발송 주소
otherwise adv. 그렇지 않으면   build up ~을 쌓다
put toward (비용의 일부를) 보태다, 주다   accumulate v. 모으다
take advantage of ~을 이용하다

154 목적 찾기 문제

문제 이메일의 목적은 무엇인가?

(A) 온라인 계정을 어떻게 개설하는지 설명하기 위해
(B) 회원이 되도록 고객을 설득하기 위해
(C) 고객에게 비밀번호를 변경하도록 요청하기 위해
(D) 회원 업그레이드 혜택을 설명하기 위해

해설 이메일의 목적을 묻는 목적 찾기 문제이다. 'there are numerous reasons to become a member'에서 회원이 되어야 하는 많은 이유들이 있다고 한 후, 회원이 될 경우 받을 수 있는 혜택들을 알려주고 있으므로 (B)가 정답이다.

어휘 set up ~을 개설하다, 세우다   convince v. 설득하다
describe v. 설명하다

155 Not/True 문제

문제 고객 마일리지에 대해 언급되지 않은 것은?
(A) 물품들을 구매하는 데 사용될 수 있다.
(B) 웹사이트의 회원들만 얻을 수 있다.
(C) 일정 시간이 지나면 만료된다.
(D) 매번 주문의 비용이 지불될 때마다 얻어진다.

해설 질문의 핵심 어구인 loyalty credit과 관련된 내용을 지문에서 찾아 보기와 대조하는 Not/True 문제이다. (A)는 'You can put this credit toward the cost of your next purchase'에서 마일리지를 다음 구매의 비용에 보탤 수 있다고 했으므로 지문의 내용과 일치한다. (B)는 'a membership on our Web site'와 'only members can build up loyalty credit'에서 오직 웹사이트에서의 회원들만 고객 마일리지를 쌓을 수 있다고 했으므로 지문의 내용과 일치한다. (C)는 지문에 언급되지 않은 내용이다. 따라서 (C)가 정답이다. (D)는 'you will earn 10 percent of the total amount you spend whenever you place an order'에서 주문할 때마다 쓰는 총 금액의 10퍼센트를 얻을 것이라고 했으므로 지문의 내용과 일치한다.

패러프레이징
whenever ~ place an order 주문할 때마다 → each time an order is paid for 매번 주문의 비용이 지불될 때마다

어휘 expire v. 만료되다   acquire v. 얻다, 획득하다

156 문장 위치 찾기 문제

문제 [1], [2], [3], [4]로 표시된 위치 중, 다음 문장이 들어갈 곳으로 가장 적절한 것은?
"이 정보는 고객님께서 계산하실 준비가 되었을 때 자동으로 필요한 항목들에 입력될 것입니다."
(A) [1]
(B) [2]
(C) [3]
(D) [4]

해설 지문의 흐름상 주어진 문장이 들어가기에 가장 적절한 곳을 고르는 문제이다. This information will be automatically inputted into the necessary fields when you are ready to check out에서 이 정보는 계산할 준비가 되었을 때 자동으로 필요한 항목에 입력될 것이라고 했으므로, 주어진 문장 앞에 정보에 대한 내용이 언급된 부분이 있을 것임을 예상할 수 있다. [2]의 앞 문장인 'you will no longer be required to enter your shipping address, telephone number, and credit card details each time you make a purchase'에서 구매를 할 때마다 물건 발송 주소, 전화번호, 신용카드 세부 정보들을 더 이상 입력할 필요가 없다고 했으므로, [2]에 주어진 문장이 들어가면 구매를 할 때마다 물건 발송 주소, 전화번호, 신용카드 세부 정보들을 입력할 필요 없이 자동으로 입력될 것이라는 자연스러운 문맥이 된다는 것을 알 수 있다. 따라서 (B)가 정답이다.

어휘 automatically adv. 자동으로   input v. 입력하다   field n. 항목
check out 계산하다

Tam Bakery – 시내 최고의 케이크들!

생일, 결혼 혹은 다른 중요한 행사를 계획하고 계신가요? 당신의 특별한 행사를 기념하기 위해 완벽한 케이크를 원하신다면, Harbor가와 Elm가의 모퉁이에 있는 Tam Bakery를 방문하세요. 저희의 뛰어난 케이크 제작자들은 저렴하면서도 맛있는 예술 작품을 만들어드릴 수 있습니다. 157-B그들은 당신이 받는 케이크가 당신이 구상했던 것이 되도록 하기 위해 당신과 긴밀하게 작업할 것입니다. 게다가, 157-A저희는 최고의 재료들만 사용하며 채식주의자와 저지방 선택권들도 제공합니다. 5월 15일부터 6월 15일까지, 158저희의 10주년을 기념하기 위해 157-C/158모든 주문 제작 케이크들의 가격을 10퍼센트 내릴 것입니다. 그러니, 지체하지 마시고 어서 들르셔서 당신의 완벽한 케이크를 계획하기 시작하세요.

Tam Bakery와 저희가 제공하는 제품들에 대한 더 많은 정보를 위해서는, www.tambakery.com을 방문해주세요.

---

occasion n. 행사   talented adj. 뛰어난   affordable adj. 저렴한
ensure v. (반드시) ~하게 하다, 보장하다   envision v. 구상하다, 상상하다
vegan n. 채식주의자   low-fat adj. 저지방의
anniversary n. 주년(기념일)   stop by ~에 들르다

157 Not/True 문제

문제 Tam Bakery의 케이크들에 대해 언급되지 않은 것은?
(A) 고품질의 재료들로 만들어질 수 있다.
(B) 고객에 의해 구상될 수 있다.
(C) 할인된 가격에 구입될 수 있다.
(D) 행사 장소로 배달될 수 있다.

해설 질문의 핵심 어구인 Tam Bakery's cakes와 관련된 내용을 지문에서 찾아 보기와 대조하는 Not/True 문제이다. (A)는 'we use only the best ingredients'에서 최고의 재료들만 사용한다고 했으므로 지문의 내용과 일치한다. (B)는 'They will work closely with you to ensure that the cake you receive is the one you envisioned.'에서 고객이 받는 케이크가 고객이 구상했던 것이 되도록 하기 위해 고객과 긴밀하게 작업할 것이라고 했으므로 지문의 내용과 일치한다. (C)는 'we are reducing the prices of all custom cakes by 10 percent'에서 모든 주문 제작 케이크들의 가격을 10퍼센트 내릴 것이라고 했으므로 지문의 내용과 일치한다. (D)는 지문에 언급되지 않은 내용이다. 따라서 (D)가 정답이다.

어휘 high-quality adj. 고품질의   at a discount 할인된 가격에
venue n. 장소

158 추론 문제

문제 Tam Bakery에 대해 암시되는 것은?
(A) 제품을 온라인에서 판매한다.
(B) 다른 지점을 열 것이다.
(C) 여러 해 동안 영업을 해왔다.
(D) 웹사이트에 요리법들을 포함하고 있다.

해설 질문의 핵심 어구인 Tam Bakery에 대해 추론하는 문제이다. 'we are reducing the prices ~ to celebrate our 10th anniversary'에서 10주년을 기념하기 위해 가격을 내릴 것이라고 했으므로 Tam Bakery가 여러 해 동안 영업을 해왔다는 것을 추론할 수 있다. 따라서 (C)가 정답이다.

어휘 branch n. 지점   be in business 영업을 하다   recipe n. 요리법

9월 7일—Brytwells 백화점의 대변인이 오늘, 31년 만에 처음으로, 159회사가 로고를 변경할 것이라고 발표했다. 고객들에게 굉장히 친숙한 고전적인 빨간색과 노란색의 디자인은 더 현대적인 것으로 바뀌게 ↻

된다. 이는 160-C최고경영자 Marcus Cathwell의 회사의 이미지를 갱신하기 위한 더 폭넓은 노력의 일환인데, 그는 Jackson Stevens가 두 달 전 퇴임하자 그의 자리로 승진했다.

지금까지 20년이 넘도록, Brytwells는 더 많은 종류를 더 저렴한 가격에 제공하는 새로운 백화점들과의 치열한 경쟁에 직면해 왔다. 매해 몇몇 매장들의 폐점이 발생했고, 161다음 12개월 이내에 또 다른 5곳이 운영을 중단할 예정이다. Mr. Cathwell은 Brytwells 브랜드가 한참 전에 갱신이 행해졌어야 한다고 인정하면서 새로운 로고는 회사에 적용되는 다른 변화들과 잘 부합할 것임을 확신한다고 말한다. 162-A이들은 새로운 현대적인 매장 배치와 젊은 사람들을 위한 15개의 의류 브랜드들의 도입을 포함한다.

162-CBrytwells가 첫 매장을 열었던 국내의 북동쪽 지역에 위치한 Brytwells 지점들은 10월에 가장 먼저 이 로고를 사용하기 시작할 것이다. 162-D전국의 다른 Brytwells 매장들은 가을이 끝나기 전에 새로운 회사 이미지를 도입할 것이다.

spokesperson n. 대변인 familiar with ~에 친숙한
replace v. 바꾸다, 대체하다 modern adj. 현대적인
move up into ~으로 승진하다 retire v. 퇴임하다 decade n. 10년
face v. (상황에) 직면하다 stiff adj. 치열한 variety n. 많은 종류, 다양성
closure n. 폐점 result v. 일어나다 be set to ~하도록 예정되어 있다
cease v. 중단하다 operation n. 운영 acknowledge v. 인정하다
overdue adj. 벌써 행해졌어야 할 fit in ~과 부합하다, 맞다
contemporary adj. 현대의 layout n. 배치
adopt v. 도입하다, 채택하다

159 주제 찾기 문제
문제 기사는 주로 무엇에 대한 것인가?
(A) 새로운 매장의 로고를 위한 아이디어
(B) 전국적 체인 점포의 폐점
(C) 회사 상징에 대한 변화들
(D) 소매점들간의 경쟁

해설 기사가 주로 무엇에 대한 것인지를 묻는 주제 찾기 문제이므로 지문의 앞부분을 주의 깊게 확인한다. 'the company will change its logo'에서 회사가 로고를 변경할 것이라고 한 후, 로고 변경과 그에 관한 변화들을 설명하고 있으므로 (C)가 정답이다.

어휘 symbol n. 상징 retailer n. 소매점

160 Not/True 문제
문제 Mr. Cathwell에 대해 언급된 것은?
(A) 평면도를 제작했다.
(B) 3월에 고용되었다.
(C) 최근에 승진되었다.
(D) 회사를 설립했다.

해설 질문의 핵심 어구인 Mr. Cathwell과 관련된 내용을 지문에서 찾아 보기와 대조하는 Not/True 문제이다. (A)와 (B)는 지문에 언급되지 않은 내용이다. (C)는 'CEO Marcus Cathwell, who moved up into his position when Jackson Stevens retired two months ago'에서 최고경영자 Marcus Cathwell은 Jackson Stevens가 두 달 전 퇴임하자 그의 자리로 승진했다고 했으므로 지문의 내용과 일치한다. 따라서 (C)가 정답이다. (D)는 지문에 언급되지 않은 내용이다.

패러프레이징
moved up into ~ two month ago 두 달 전 승진했다 →
was recently promoted 최근에 승진되었다

어휘 floor plan 평면도 found v. 설립하다

161 추론 문제
문제 내년에 무슨 일이 일어날 것 같은가?
(A) Brytwells는 새로운 웹사이트를 출시할 것이다.

(B) Brytwells는 모든 지점들에서 가격을 낮출 것이다.
(C) Brytwells의 여러 매장들이 폐업할 것이다.
(D) Brytwells의 최고경영자가 자리에서 사임할 것이다.

해설 질문의 핵심 어구인 next year에 대해 추론하는 문제이다. 'another five[five stores] are set to cease operations within the next 12 months'에서 다음 12개월 이내에 또 다른 5개의 매장들이 운영을 중단할 예정이라고 했으므로 내년에 Brytwells의 여러 매장들이 폐업할 것임을 추론할 수 있다. 따라서 (C)가 정답이다.

패러프레이징
cease operations 운영을 중단하다 → close down 폐업하다

어휘 launch v. 출시하다, 공개하다 close down 폐업하다
resign v. 사임하다

162 Not/True 문제
문제 Brytwells에 대해 언급되지 않은 것은?
(A) 젊은 사람들을 위한 더 많은 상품들을 판매하기 시작할 것이다.
(B) 본점이 이전할 것이다.
(C) 북동쪽 지역에 첫 매장을 열었다.
(D) 전국에 걸쳐 지점들을 가지고 있다.

해설 질문의 핵심 어구인 Brytwells와 관련된 내용을 지문에서 찾아 보기와 대조하는 Not/True 문제이다. (A)는 'These[changes] include ~ the introduction of 15 clothing brands for young people.'에서 회사에 적용되는 다른 변화들은 젊은 사람들을 위한 15개의 의류 브랜드들의 도입을 포함한다고 했으므로 지문의 내용과 일치한다. (B)는 지문에 언급되지 않은 내용이다. 따라서 (B)가 정답이다. (C)는 'the northeastern region of the nation, where Brytwells opened its initial store'에서 Brytwells가 첫 매장을 열었던 국내의 북동쪽 지역이라고 했으므로 지문의 내용과 일치한다. (D)는 'Other Brytwells stores across the country'에서 전국의 다른 Brytwells 매장들이라고 했으므로 지문의 내용과 일치한다.

패러프레이징
introduction of ~ clothing brands for young people 젊은 사람들을 위한 의류 브랜드들의 도입 → begin selling more products for young people 젊은 사람들을 위한 더 많은 상품들을 판매하기 시작하다

어휘 relocate v. 이전하다

163-165번은 다음 공고에 관한 문제입니다.

공고

Hopewell 제작사가 7월 8일에 *A New Life*의 장면을 촬영할 것입니다. 이 장편 영화는 Christina Harvey와 Mike Mann에게 주연을 맡기며 Herbert Mercer에 의해 감독되고 있습니다.

16318세 이상이라면 누구나 단역 배우로 오디션을 보도록 권해집니다. 165-D단역 배우들을 위한 오디션은 West Newton 고등학교에서 7월 1일에 정오부터 오후 8시까지 열릴 것이며, 164모든 참가자들은 운전면허증, 여권, 혹은 사진이 포함된 다른 종류의 공식적인 신분증을 가져와야 합니다.

163/165-C단역 배우들은 쇼핑몰에서 이루어지는 짧은 장면을 위해 주로 군중들로 활용될 것입니다. 165-A촬영은 10시간에서 12시간이 걸릴 것이며 많은 서 있기와 기다림을 수반할 것입니다. 음식은 제공될 것이며, 165-B마지막에 작은 경품들의 추첨이 있을 것입니다. 급여는 시간당 9달러입니다.

film v. 촬영하다 scene n. 장면 feature-length adj. 장편의
star v. 주연을 맡기다, 주연하다 invite v. 권하다, 안내하다
extra n. 단역 배우 driver's license 운전면허증 official adj. 공식적인
identification n. 신분증 primarily adv. 주로 crowd n. 군중
sequence n. 장면 shoot n. 촬영 involve v. 수반하다
wait around (특별히 하는 일 없이) 그냥 기다리다 raffle n. 추첨

163 육하원칙 문제

문제 공고에 따르면, Hopewell 제작사는 사람들에게 무엇을 하라고 권하고 있는가?
(A) 출장 연회팀에서 일한다.
(B) 장비를 설치한다.
(C) 촬영장 견학을 안내한다.
(D) 장면에 출연한다.

해설 Hopewell 제작사가 사람들에게 무엇을(what) 하라고 권하고 있는지를 묻는 육하원칙 문제이다. 질문의 핵심 어구인 Hopewell Productions encouraging people to do와 관련하여, 'Anyone over the age of 18 is invited to audition as an extra.'에서 18세 이상이라면 누구나 단역 배우로 오디션을 보도록 권해진다고 한 후, 'Extras will be used primarily as crowd members for a short sequence'에서 단역 배우들은 짧은 장면을 위해 주로 군중들로 활용될 것이라고 했으므로 (D)가 정답이다.

어휘 **catering** n. 출장 연회 **set up** ~을 설치하다 **conduct** v. 안내하다
set n. 촬영장

164 육하원칙 문제

문제 참가자들은 West Newton 고등학교에 무엇을 가져와야 하는가?
(A) 입출금 내역서
(B) 이력서와 자기소개서
(C) 신분증명서
(D) 공연의 녹화물

해설 참가자들이 West Newton 고등학교에 무엇(What)을 가져와야 하는지를 묻는 육하원칙 문제이다. 질문의 핵심 어구인 participants bring to West Newton High School과 관련하여, 'all participants must bring a driver's license, a passport, or some other type of official photo identification'에서 모든 참가자들은 운전면허증, 여권, 혹은 사진이 포함된 다른 종류의 공식적인 신분증을 가져와야 한다고 했으므로 (C)가 정답이다.

패러프레이징
a driver's license, a passport, or some other type of official photo identification 운전면허증, 여권, 혹은 사진이 포함된 다른 종류의 공식적인 신분증 → A form of identification 신분증명서

어휘 **bank statement** (은행 계좌의) 입출금 내역서 **cover letter** 자기소개서
recording n. 녹화(음)(된 것)

165 Not/True 문제

문제 촬영에 대해 언급된 것은?
(A) 며칠 동안 계속될 것이다.
(B) 경품 추첨을 포함할 것이다.
(C) 대부분 야외에서 진행할 것이다.
(D) 정오에 시작할 것이다.

해설 질문의 핵심 어구인 shoot과 관련된 내용을 지문에서 찾아 보기와 대조하는 Not/True 문제이다. (A)는 'The shoot will take 10 to 12 hours'에서 촬영은 10시간에서 12시간이 걸릴 것이라고 했으므로 지문의 내용과 일치하지 않는다. (B)는 'a raffle for small prizes will be held at the end'에서 마지막에 작은 경품들의 추첨이 있을 것이라고 했으므로 지문의 내용과 일치한다. 따라서 (B)가 정답이다. (C)는 'Extras will be used ~ for a short sequence that takes place in a mall.'에서 단역 배우들은 쇼핑몰에서 이루어지는 짧은 장면을 위해 활용될 것이라고 했으므로 지문의 내용과 일치하지 않는다. (D)는 'The casting call ~ will take place ~ from noon'에서 오디션이 정오부터 열릴 것이라고 했지 촬영이 정오에 시작하는 것은 아니므로 지문의 내용과 일치하지 않는다.

패러프레이징
a raffle for small prizes 작은 경품들의 추첨 → a prize drawing 경품 추첨

어휘 **last** v. 계속되다 **prize drawing** 경품 추첨

166-169번은 다음 이메일에 관한 문제입니다.

수신: Pingvillian 호텔 예약 부서 <rsvn@pingvillianhotel.com>
발신: Alice Rolstin <alirol@alertmail.com>
날짜: 9월 10일
제목: 숙박

관계자분께,

저는 166-A/D온라인 여행사 Frewel.com을 통해 당신의 호텔에 하나의 방을 예약한 것에 대해 이메일을 씁니다. 저는 두 가지 요청 사항이 있습니다. — [1] —. 먼저, 제 남편과 저는 늦은 체크인이 필요할 것입니다. 166-C저희는 치앙마이에 9월 17일 오후 11시 30분에 도착할 것입니다. 169만약 당신의 웹페이지에 나와 있는 정보가 정확하다면 저희는 호텔에 자정쯤에 도착할 것입니다. — [2] —.

또한, 당신은 저희가 9월 25일에 퇴실하기로 되어 있다는 것을 아실 것입니다. 하지만, 집으로 가는 항공편이 변경되어서, 166-C저희는 24일 오후 8시 30분에 떠날 것입니다. — [3] —. 167처음에 계획했던 것처럼 25일 밤을 당신의 호텔에서 보내지 않을 것이기 때문에, 저희의 마지막 날 예약을 취소하고 대신 24일 오후 6시 정도에 퇴실해도 될지 궁금합니다. — [4] —. 168퇴실 시간이 정오인 것을 알지만, 저희가 공항으로 가는 택시를 타는 때까지 머무를 수 있다면 정말 도움이 될 것 같습니다.

시간을 내주셔서 감사드리며, Pingvillian 호텔에서 머무를 것을 기대합니다.

Alice Rolstin 드림

in regard to ~에 대하여 **travel agency** 여행사
late check-in 늦은 체크인(자정 이후에 하는 체크인) **land** v. 도착하다
midnight n. 자정 **accurate** adj. 정확한
be supposed to ~하기로 되어 있다 **check out** (호텔 등에서) 퇴실하다
depart v. 떠나다, 출발하다 **look forward to** ~을 기대하다

166 Not/True 문제

문제 Ms. Rolstin에 대해 사실인 것은?
(A) 웹사이트를 통해 예약을 했다.
(B) 예정보다 일찍 호텔에 도착할 것이다.
(C) 다음 달까지 치앙마이에 머무를 것이다.
(D) Pingvillian 호텔에 두 개의 방을 예약했다.

해설 질문의 핵심 어구인 Ms. Rolstin과 관련된 내용을 지문에서 찾아 보기와 대조하는 Not/True 문제이다. (A)는 'the reservation I made ~ through ~ Frewel.com.'에서 Frewel.com을 통해 예약한 것이라고 했으므로 지문의 내용과 일치한다. 따라서 (A)가 정답이다. (B)는 지문에 언급되지 않은 내용이다. (C)는 'We should be landing in Chiang Mai ~ on September 17.'과 'we will be departing ~ on the 24th'에서 치앙마이에 9월 17일에 도착하여 24일에 떠날 것이라고 했으므로 지문의 내용과 일치하지 않는다. (D)는 'the reservation I made for a room at your hotel'에서 호텔에 하나의 방을 예약했다고 했으므로 지문의 내용과 일치하지 않는다.

167 동의어 찾기 문제

문제 2문단 세 번째 줄의 단어 "originally"는 의미상 -와 가장 가깝다.
(A) 유일하게
(B) 완전히
(C) 다르게
(D) 처음에

해설 originally를 포함한 구절 'Since we won't be spending the night of the 25th at your hotel as originally planned, I was wondering if we could cancel our reservation for the final day'에서 originally가 '처음에'라는 뜻으로 사용되었다. 따라서 (D)가 정답이다.

168 육하원칙 문제

문제 Ms. Rolstin은 무엇을 요청하는가?
(A) 보상 할인권
(B) 늦은 퇴실 시간
(C) 공항까지의 운전
(D) 추가 숙박

해설 Ms. Rolstin이 무엇을(What) 요청하는지를 묻는 육하원칙 문제이다. 질문의 핵심 어구인 Ms. Rolstin ask for와 관련하여, 'I know your check-out time is noon, but if we could stay until it is time for us to get a taxi to the airport, it would really be helpful.'에서 Ms. Rolstin이 퇴실 시간이 정오인 것을 알지만 공항으로 가는 택시를 타는 때까지 머무를 수 있다면 정말 도움이 될 것 같다고 했으므로 (B)가 정답이다.

어휘 compensation n. 보상   voucher n. 할인권, 상품권

169 문장 위치 찾기 문제

문제 [1], [2], [3], [4]로 표시된 위치 중, 다음 문장이 들어갈 곳으로 가장 적절한 것은?

"그것에는 공항에서 택시를 타는 것이 15분에서 20분 정도만 걸린다고 쓰여있습니다."

(A) [1]
(B) [2]
(C) [3]
(D) [4]

해설 지문의 흐름상 주어진 문장이 들어가기에 가장 적절한 곳을 고르는 문제이다. It says getting a taxi from the airport only takes about 15 to 20 minutes에서 그것에는 공항에서 택시를 타는 것이 15분에서 20분 정도만 걸린다고 쓰여있다고 했으므로, 주어진 문장 앞에 공항에서 택시를 탔을 때 걸리는 시간이 쓰여 있는 곳에 관한 내용이 있을 것임을 예상할 수 있다. [2]의 앞 문장인 'I believe we will arrive at the hotel by midnight if the information on your Web page is accurate.'에서 만약 웹페이지에 나와 있는 정보가 정확하다면 호텔에 자정쯤에 도착할 것이라고 했으므로, [2]에 주어진 문장이 들어가면 웹페이지에 공항에서 택시를 타면 15분에서 20분 정도만 걸린다고 쓰여있으므로 호텔에 자정쯤에 도착할 것이라는 자연스러운 문맥이 된다는 것을 알 수 있다. 따라서 (B)가 정답이다.

170-171번은 다음 기사에 관한 문제입니다.

폐수처리장 건설이 여전히 불확실하다

Komlossy에 폐수처리장을 건설하려는 지역 정부의 계획에 대중들이 다소 반신반의해 왔다. 만약 시의 수질관리 공무원들이 이 건설 프로젝트를 승인할 경우, 지역 내 주거용 및 상업용 부동산 소유자들은 그 비용을 충당하기 위해 더 많은 세금을 내야 할 것이다. 이 시스템은 건설하는 데 5천 2백만 달러가 들 것이며, 운영 및 유지에 차후 매달 42만 달러가 들 것으로 추정된다. 일부 납세자들은 현재 사용되고 있는 훨씬 저렴한 시스템을 사용하는 것을 멈추기를 꺼려하지만, 다수는 이 새로운 시스템이 추가되는 비용의 가치가 있다고 생각한다. 적어도, 170그것은 어떠한 오염물질도 이전 것처럼 근처 강과 호수들에 들어가도록 하지는 않을 것이다. 171이 사안은 11월 6일 Komlossy의 수질관리 이사회 회의에서 심도 있게 논의될 것이다.

proposal n. 계획, 제안 **wastewater treatment center** 폐수처리장
uncertainty n. 반신반의, 불확실성 **municipal** adj. 시의, 지방 자치제의
approve v. 승인하다 **residential** adj. 주거(용)의
commercial adj. 상업(용)의 **subsequent** adj. 차후의
taxpayer n. 납세자 **be reluctant to** ~을 꺼리다 **majority** n. 다수
at the very least 적어도 **permit** v. (어떤 일을) 가능하게 하다
contaminant n. 오염물질 **issue** n. 사안, 주제 **in depth** 심도 있게

170 추론 문제

문제 현재 폐수 시스템에 대해 암시되는 것은?
(A) 수질 오염의 한 원인이 된다.
(B) 운영하는 데 비용이 매우 많이 든다.
(C) 작년에 설치되었다.
(D) 대부분의 주민들에게 선호된다.

해설 질문의 핵심 어구인 current wastewater system에 대해 추론하는 문제이다. 'it[new system] will not permit any contaminants to enter nearby rivers and lakes, as the old one does'에서 새로운 시스템은 어떠한 오염물질도 이전 것처럼 근처 강과 호수들에 들어가도록 하지는 않을 것이라고 했으므로 현재 폐수 시스템은 수질 오염의 한 원인이 된다는 것을 추론할 수 있다. 따라서 (A)가 정답이다.

패러프레이징
permit ~ contaminants to enter nearby rivers and lakes 오염물질이 근처 강과 호수들에 들어가도록 하다 → contributes to water pollution 수질 오염의 한 원인이 되다

어휘 contribute v. ~의 한 원인이 되다, 기여하다   water pollution 수질 오염

171 육하원칙 문제

문제 기사에 따르면, 11월에 무슨 일이 일어날 것인가?
(A) 시의 새로운 시설 건설 공사가 시작될 것이다.
(B) 시민들은 하수처리장을 지을 것인지를 가결할 것이다.
(C) 시의 사안이 회의에서 검토될 것이다.
(D) 도시 전체에 새로운 세금제가 시행될 것이다.

해설 11월에 무슨(what) 일이 일어날 것인지를 묻는 육하원칙 문제이다. 질문의 핵심 어구인 November와 관련하여, 'The issue[construction of wastewater treatment center] will be discussed in depth at Komlossy's Water Quality Control Board meeting on November 6.'에서 폐수처리장 건설 사안은 11월 6일 Komlossy의 수질관리 이사회 회의에서 심도 있게 논의될 것이라고 했으므로 (C)가 정답이다.

어휘 vote on ~을 가결하다   sewage n. 하수   implement v. 시행하다

172-175번은 다음 온라인 채팅 대화문에 관한 문제입니다.

Soomin Park [오후 6시 38분]
계획에 변경이 생겼어요. 172Ms. Lawson이 방금 저에게 6월 4일에 우리 서비스를 더 이상 필요로 하지 않을 것이라고 문자를 보냈어요. 그녀의 결혼식 날짜가 9월 16일로 옮겨져서, 우리 사진관이 그녀의 식과 피로연을 위한 사진 촬영을 그날 대신 해주길 원해요.

Lauren Jean [오후 6시 41분]
그건 문제가 되겠는걸요. 그때 저는 다른 고객의 행사를 하루 종일 담당할 거예요. 게다가, 이제 우리는 6월 4일에 아무 작업도 예약되어 있지 않네요.

Taylor Morgan [오후 6시 43분]
173그녀의 결혼식이 9월 16일에도 같은 장소에서 같은 시간에 있나요? 그렇다면, 제가 할 수 있어요. 저는 오후 내내 한가할 거예요.

Soomin Park [오후 6시 44분]
고마워요, Taylor. 173시간과 장소는 전에 요청했던 것과 같아요. 174저는 Ms. Lawson에게 우리가 6월 4일에 다른 예약을 받게 되면, 그녀의 보증금을 9월 16일자 청구서로 옮겨줄 것이라고 했어요. 174/175그렇지 않다면, 그녀는 보증금을 잃게 될 거예요.

Lauren Jean [오후 6시 45분]
그거 말이 되네요. 175우리는 그날 우리를 고용하고 싶어 했던 몇몇 다른 잠재 고객들을 거절했었잖아요. 지금 와서 생각해보니, 그들 중 몇 명은 아직 사진작가를 필요로 할지도 몰라요.

Soomin Park [오후 6시 45분]
정말요? 시간이 있으시면, 그들과 연락을 해보세요.

photography n. 사진 촬영 reception n. 피로연 cover v. 담당하다
transfer v. 옮기다 deposit n. 보증금 prospective adj. 잠재적인
get in touch with ~와 연락하다

172 육하원칙 문제

문제 Ms. Lawson은 왜 Ms. Park에게 연락했는가?
(A) 사진관에서의 사진 촬영을 계획하기 위해
(B) 할인 요금을 협상하기 위해
(C) 장소 변경을 알리기 위해
(D) 예약 일정을 변경하기 위해

해설 Ms. Lawson이 왜(Why) Ms. Park에게 연락했는지를 묻는 육하원칙 문제이다. 질문의 핵심 어구인 Ms. Lawson contact Ms. Park과 관련하여, 'Ms. Lawson just texted me to say she will no longer be requiring our services on June 4. Her wedding date has been moved to September 16, and she wants our studio to do the photography ~ on that day instead.'(6:38 P.M.)에서 Ms. Lawson이 방금 Ms. Park에게 6월 4일에 서비스를 더 이상 필요로 하지 않을 것이라고 문자를 보냈다고 한 후, 그녀의 결혼식 날짜가 9월 16일로 옮겨져서 사진 촬영을 그날 대신 해주길 원한다고 했으므로 (D)가 정답이다.

어휘 arrange v. 계획하다 photo shoot 사진 촬영 negotiate v. 협상하다 notify v. 알리다 reschedule v. 일정을 변경하다

173 추론 문제

문제 Ms. Lawson의 결혼식에 대해 추론될 수 있는 것은?
(A) 야외 장소에서 열릴 것이다.
(B) Mr. Morgan에 의해 촬영될 것이다.
(C) 전액 지불되었다.
(D) 한 달 후에 일어날 것이다.

해설 질문의 핵심 어구인 Ms. Lawson's wedding에 대해 추론하는 문제이다. 'Is her[Ms. Lawson] wedding still going to be at the same place and time on September 16? If so, I can do it.'(6:43 P.M.)에서 Mr. Morgan이 Ms. Lawson의 결혼식이 9월 16일에도 같은 장소에서 같은 시간에 있는지 물은 후, 그렇다면 자신이 할 수 있다고 하자, 'The time and venue are the same as previously requested.'(6:44 P.M.)에서 Ms. Park이 시간과 장소는 전에 요청했던 것과 같다고 했으므로 Ms. Lawson의 결혼식이 Mr. Morgan에 의해 촬영될 것임을 추론할 수 있다. 따라서 (B)가 정답이다.

어휘 pay in full 전액을 지불하다

174 육하원칙 문제

문제 6월 4일에 사진관이 예약을 받지 못하면 무슨 일이 일어날 것인가?
(A) Ms. Park이 새 계약서 초안을 작성할 것이다.
(B) Ms. Jean은 결혼식에 참석할 여유가 있을 것이다.
(C) Ms. Lawson은 지불했던 돈을 잃을 것이다.
(D) Mr. Morgan이 장소에 출입할 수 없을 것이다.

해설 6월 4일에 사진관이 예약을 받지 못하면 무슨(What) 일이 일어날 것인지를 묻는 육하원칙 문제이다. 질문의 핵심 어구인 happen if the studio cannot make a booking for June 4와 관련하여, 'I told Ms. Lawson that if we[studio] get another booking for June 4, we will transfer her deposit to her bill for September 16. If not, she will lose the deposit.'(6:44 P.M.)에서 Ms. Park이 Ms. Lawson에게 6월 4일에 사진관이 다른 예약을 받게 되면 그녀의 보증금을 9월 16일자 청구서로 옮겨줄 것이고, 그렇지 않다면 그녀는 보증금을 잃게 될 것이라고 했으므로 (C)가 정답이다.

어휘 draft v. 초안을 작성하다

175 의도 파악 문제

문제 오후 6시 45분에, Ms. Jean이 "That makes sense"라고 썼을 때, 그

녀가 의도한 것 같은 것은?
(A) 다른 고객들에 대한 불평을 하고 싶어 한다.
(B) 계좌를 확인할 계획이다.
(C) 결정이 합리적이라고 생각한다.
(D) 보증금이 환불되어야 한다고 생각한다.

해설 Ms. Jean이 의도한 것 같은 것을 묻는 문제이므로, 질문의 인용어구(That makes sense)가 언급된 주변 문맥을 확인한다. 'If not, she[Ms. Lawson] will lose the deposit.'(6:44 P.M.)에서 Ms. Park이 사진관이 6월 4일에 다른 예약을 받지 못하면 Ms. Lawson은 보증금을 잃게 될 것이라고 하자, Ms. Jean이 'That makes sense.'(그거 말이 되네요)라고 한 후, 'We turned down several other prospective clients who wanted to hire us for that day.'(6:45 P.M.)에서 그날 자신들을 고용하고 싶어 했던 몇몇 다른 잠재 고객들을 거절했었다고 한 것을 통해 Ms. Jean이 그 결정이 합리적이라고 생각한다는 것을 알 수 있다. 따라서 (C)가 정답이다.

어휘 complain v. 불평하다 account n. 계좌 reasonable adj. 합리적인

176-180번은 다음 광고와 기사에 관한 문제입니다.

워터타운 음악 축제

¹⁷⁸6월 5일 토요일부터 6월 6일 일요일까지, 워터타운 시가 모든 음악 애호가가 분명히 즐길 행사를 개최합니다! ¹⁷⁶⁻ᶜ워터타운 음악 축제는 Kayla Swank, Sienna Hanson, Tristan Woodlawn을 포함하여 인근 지역의 가수들이 출연하는 이틀간의 축하 행사가 될 것입니다. ¹⁷⁶⁻ᴮ/¹⁷⁸공연들은 Morton 경기장 바깥과 안 모두에 설치되어 있는 여러 무대 위에서 이루어질 것입니다. ¹⁷⁷티켓은 모든 공연장과 식당의 이용을 허용할 것입니다. 성인은 입장에 30달러가 부과될 것이고, 10살 이하의 어린이는 무료로 올 수 있습니다.

축제는 New Wave사가 후원하는데, 이는 거의 30년간 영업 중인 음악 및 도서 소매업체입니다. ¹⁷⁹Darrell Lane의 전국 투어 콘서트의 무대 뒤 출입증을 얻는 기회를 위해 복합 단지의 입구 옆에 있는 New Wave사의 부스를 지나치지 마세요. 더 많은 정보와 표 구매를 위해서는, www.watertownmusicfest.com을 방문하세요.

surely adv. 분명히, 확실히 vocalist n. 가수 surrounding adj. 인근의
set up ~을 설치하다 arena n. 경기장 access n. 이용, 접근
dining facility 식당 entry n. 입장 be sponsored by ~가 후원하다
be in business 영업 중이다 complex n. 복합 단지
win v. 얻다, 이기다 backstage pass 무대 뒤 출입증
nationwide adj. 전국적인

엄청난 인기의 지역 축제

Marcus Cooper 작성

6월 10일—이번 달 초에 있었던 워터타운 음악 축제는 시의 주요 행사였다. ¹⁷⁸올해, 음악가들은 이틀에 걸쳐 2만 명 이상의 청중들을 불러모았다. 이를 가능하도록 도왔던 것은 장소의 변경이었다. 이번 6월의 장소는 작년 Westfield 경기장보다 추가적인 무대들이 설치되도록 더 많은 공간을 허용했다.

지역의 식당 소유주 Nancy Welsh는 이 축제가 그녀의 온 가족에게 엄청나게 인기가 있었다고 말했다. "제 세 명의 어린 자녀들이 뛰어다닐 충분한 공간이 있었고, 저는 모든 멋진 음악을 즐기면서 많은 즐거운 시간을 보냈습니다"라고 Ms. Welsh가 언급했다. ¹⁷⁹"저는 심지어 New Wave사가 후원하는 경품 행사에 참여했는데, 결과적으로 제가 8월에 가려고 이미 계획 중이었던 콘서트의 무대 뒤 출입증을 얻게 되었습니다!"

이번 6월에 참석하지 못했던 사람들은 ¹⁸⁰⁻ᶜ축제의 스마트폰 애플리케이션을 다운로드해서 내년의 행사에 대한 최신 정보를 알아둘 수 있다.

major adj. 엄청난, 주요한 draw in ~을 불러모으다

incredibly adv. 엄청나게 plenty of 충분한, 많은
take part in ~에 참여하다 giveaway n. 경품
result in 결과적으로 ~이 되다 make it ~에 참석하다, 성공하다

176 Not/True 문제

문제 워터타운 음악 축제에 대해 언급된 것은?
(A) 10년이 넘는 기간 동안 개최되었다.
(B) 실내와 야외 공연장이 있을 것이다.
(C) 국제적인 유명 인사들이 출연할 것이다.
(D) 다른 행사 때문에 연기되었다.

해설 질문의 핵심 어구인 the Watertown Music Festival에 대해 묻는 Not/True 문제이므로 워터타운 음악 축제가 언급된 첫 번째 지문(광고)에서 관련 내용을 확인한다. (A)는 지문에 언급되지 않은 내용이다. (B)는 'Performances will be given on multiple stages that have been set up both outside and within the Morton Arena.'에서 공연들이 Morton 경기장 바깥과 안 모두에 설치되어 있는 여러 무대 위에서 이루어질 것이라고 했으므로 지문의 내용과 일치한다. 따라서 (B)가 정답이다. (C)는 'The Watertown Music Festival will be a ~ celebration featuring vocalists from the surrounding region'에서 워터타운 음악 축제는 인근 지역의 가수들이 출연하는 축하 행사라고 했으므로 지문의 내용과 일치하지 않는다. (D)는 지문에 언급되지 않은 내용이다.

어휘 international adj. 국제적인 celebrity n. 유명 인사

177 동의어 찾기 문제

문제 광고에서, 1문단 여덟 번째 줄의 단어 "grant"는 의미상 ~와 가장 가깝다.
(A) 허용하다
(B) 서명하다
(C) 조사하다
(D) 요청하다

해설 광고의 grant를 포함한 문장 'Tickets will grant access to all performance areas and dining facilities.'에서 grant가 '허용하다'라는 뜻으로 사용되었다. 따라서 (A)가 정답이다.

178 추론 문제 연계

문제 Westfield 경기장에 대해 암시되는 것은?
(A) 매년 축제 장소로 사용된다.
(B) 여름 동안 폐쇄될 것이다.
(C) Morton 경기장보다 덜 넓다.
(D) 식사 공간을 포함하도록 개조될 것이다.

해설 질문의 핵심 어구인 the Westfield Arena가 언급된 기사를 먼저 확인한다.
단서 1 두 번째 지문(기사)의 'This year, musical artists drew in more than 20,000 audience members ~. What helped make this possible was the change of venue. This June's location allowed more space ~ than Westfield Arena did last year.'에서 올해 2만 명 이상의 청중들을 불러모으는 것을 가능하도록 도왔던 것은 장소의 변경이었는데, 이번 6월의 장소가 작년 Westfield 경기장보다 더 많은 공간을 허용했기 때문이라고 했다. 그런데 이번 6월의 행사 장소가 어디인지 제시되지 않았으므로 광고에서 관련 내용을 확인한다.
단서 2 첫 번째 지문(광고)의 'From ~ June 5 through ~ June 6, the city of Watertown is hosting an event'에서 6월 5일부터 6월 6일까지 워터타운 시가 행사를 개최한다고 했고, 'Performances will be given ~ both outside and within the Morton Arena.'에서 공연들이 Morton 경기장 바깥과 안 모두에서 이루어질 것이라고 했으므로 6월의 행사 장소가 Morton 경기장임을 확인할 수 있다.
두 단서를 종합할 때, Westfield 경기장이 Morton 경기장보다 덜 넓다는 것을 알 수 있다. 따라서 (C)가 정답이다.

어휘 close down ~을 폐쇄하다 spacious adj. 넓은

179 육하원칙 문제 연계

문제 Ms. Welsh는 8월에 어떤 가수를 볼 계획인가?
(A) Kayla Swank
(B) Darrell Lane
(C) Sienna Hanson
(D) Tristan Woodlawn

해설 Ms. Welsh가 8월에 어떤(Which) 가수를 볼 계획인지를 묻는 육하원칙 문제이므로 질문의 핵심 어구인 performer ~ Ms. Welsh plan to see in August와 관련된 내용이 언급된 기사를 먼저 확인한다.
단서 1 두 번째 지문(기사)의 '"I[Ms. Welsh] even took part in a prize giveaway sponsored by New Wave, which resulted in me winning backstage passes to a concert I was already planning on attending in August!"'에서 Ms. Welsh가 New Wave사가 후원하는 경품 행사에 참여했는데, 결과적으로 자신이 8월에 가려고 이미 계획 중이었던 콘서트의 무대 뒤 출입증을 얻게 되었다고 했다. 그런데 New Wave사의 경품 행사에서 제공하는 무대 뒤 출입증이 어떤 가수를 위한 것인지 제시되지 않았으므로 광고에서 관련 내용을 확인한다.
단서 2 첫 번째 지문(광고)의 'Be sure not to miss New Wave's booth ~ for a chance to win backstage passes to a concert on Darrell Lane's nationwide tour.'에서 New Wave사의 부스에서 Darrell Lane의 전국 투어 콘서트의 무대 뒤 출입증을 얻는 기회가 있음을 확인할 수 있다.
두 단서를 종합할 때, Ms. Welsh가 참여한 행사에서 Darrell Lane의 콘서트의 무대 뒤 출입증이 경품으로 제공되므로 Ms. Welsh가 8월에 Darrell Lane을 볼 계획이라는 것을 알 수 있다. 따라서 (B)가 정답이다.

180 Not/True 문제

문제 스마트폰 어플리케이션에 대해 언급된 것은?
(A) 이번 6월에 몇몇 디자인 변화가 있을 것이다.
(B) Ms. Welsh의 자녀들에 의해 다운로드되었다.
(C) 다음 축제에 대한 세부사항들을 포함할 것이다.
(D) 작년에 지역 잡지에서 소개되었다.

해설 질문의 핵심 어구인 the smartphone application에 대해 묻는 Not/True 문제이므로 스마트폰 어플리케이션이 언급된 두 번째 지문(기사)에서 관련 내용을 확인한다. (A)와 (B)는 지문에 언급되지 않은 내용이다. (C)는 'keep up to date with information on next year's event by downloading the festival's smartphone application'에서 축제의 스마트폰 어플리케이션을 다운로드해서 내년의 행사에 대한 최신 정보를 알아둘 수 있다고 했으므로 스마트폰 어플리케이션이 다음 축제에 대한 세부사항들을 포함할 것임을 알 수 있다. 따라서 (C)가 정답이다. (D)는 지문에 언급되지 않은 내용이다.
패러프레이징
information on next year's event 내년의 행사에 대한 정보
→ details about a subsequent festival 다음 축제에 대한 세부사항들

어휘 undergo v. 겪다, 진행하다 subsequent adj. 다음의

181-185번은 다음 양식과 이메일에 관한 문제입니다.

매매 계약서

이 계약서는 11월 5일에 ¹⁸¹댄빌의 City Street Motors사(Blaine Ritter가 대리함)로부터 Grace Huang으로의 중고차 판매를 나타냅니다. 모든 당사자는 이 계약서에 기술된 대로 판매에 합의했습니다. 이 계약서는 구매자와 판매자 양측에 의해 해지되지 않는 한 유효합니다.

제조사 및 모델: Merriton Motors사, Juniper
외부 및 내부 색상: 파란색, 회색

차량 식별 번호: XCN138004832738
판매가: 14,000달러
[185]지불 방법: ■ 현금   □ 수표   □ 신용카드

판매자는 차량의 사고 및 수리 내역에 관한 모든 정보를 양도했습니다. 구매자는 차량을 현 상태 그대로 구매하기로 합의했으며, 계약서에 서명이 되면, 발견되는 어떠한 결함으로 인해서도 이 거래를 취소할 수 없을 것입니다. [182-B/C/D]판매자는 서명을 할 때 자동차 판매의 공식 영수증과 함께, 구매자에게 두 개의 차 열쇠와 최근의 차량 검사 기록을 제공할 것입니다.

판매자 대리인 서명 _____
구매자 서명 _____

sales contract 매매 계약(서)   represent v. 나타내다, 대표하다
used car 중고차   party n. 당사자   outline v. 기술하다; n. 윤곽
valid adj. 유효한   terminate v. 해지하다, 끝나다
identification number 식별 번호   pay in full 전액을 지불하다
release v. 양도하다, 놓아주다   as is (어떤 조건·상태이건) 있는 그대로
defect n. 결함

수신: Blaine Ritter <blaineritter@citystreetmotors.com>
발신: Grace Huang <gracehuang@huangdesign.com>
날짜: 11월 2일
제목: 계약서 검토

Mr. Ritter께,

Juniper 세단의 계약서를 작성해주셔서 감사합니다. 저는 그런 좋은 차를 구매하게 되어 기쁩니다. [183-C]제 원래 차는 수리될 수 없어서, 제가 특히 이 새로운 차를 갖기를 간절히 바라게 만들었습니다. 저는 계약서에 관해 질문이 하나 있습니다. 어제 우리가 얘기했을 때, [184]우리는 11월 6일에 만나기로 약속했습니다. 하지만 계약서에는 판매 일자가 11월 5일이라고 쓰여있습니다. 이 날짜가 정정되어야 하지 않습니까? 변경을 부탁드리며 제가 도착하기 전에 정정된 서류를 준비해주시기 바랍니다.

저는 오전 10시에 당신의 지점을 방문할 계획입니다. 제 친구가 저를 그곳에 내려줄 것이니, 제의에 감사드리지만 당신이 저를 태워주실 필요가 없습니다. [185]제가 도착할 때 지불할 준비가 되어 있도록 City Street Motors사에 가는 길에 은행에 들르겠습니다.

당신의 도움에 감사드리며, [185]11월 6일에 당신과의 만남을 기대합니다.

Grace Huang 드림

eager adj. 간절히 바라는, 열렬한   correct v. 정정하다
drop off ~를 차에서 내려주다

181 추론 문제

문제 Blaine Ritter는 어디에서 일할 것 같은가?
(A) 자동차 판매 대리점
(B) 대여 사무소
(C) 법률 사무소
(D) 차량 부품 상점

해설 질문의 핵심 어구인 Blaine Ritter에 대해 추론하는 문제이므로 Blaine Ritter가 언급된 첫 번째 지문(양식)에서 관련 내용을 확인한다. 첫 번째 지문(양식)의 'the sale of a used car by City Street Motors of Danville (represented by Blaine Ritter)'에서 댄빌의 City Street Motors사를 Blaine Ritter가 대리하여 중고차 판매를 한다고 한 후, 중고차 판매와 관련된 조건을 설명하고 있으므로 Blaine Ritter가 자동차 판매 대리점에서 일한다는 것을 추론할 수 있다. 따라서 (A)가 정답이다.

어휘 dealership n. 판매 대리점   law office 법률 사무소
vehicle part 차량 부품

182 Not/True 문제

문제 양식에 따르면, 판매자가 제공할 것이 아닌 것은?
(A) 보험 서식
(B) 검사 결과
(C) 열쇠 세트
(D) 지불 증명서

해설 질문의 핵심 어구인 the seller ~ provide에 대해 묻는 Not/True 문제이므로 판매자가 제공하는 것이 언급된 첫 번째 지문(양식)에서 관련 내용을 확인한다. (A)는 지문에 언급되지 않은 내용이다. 따라서 (A)가 정답이다. (B), (C), (D)는 'The seller will provide two keys for the car and recent automobile inspection records ~, along with an official receipt for the sale of the automobile.'에서 판매자가 자동차 판매의 공식 영수증과 함께 두 개의 차 열쇠와 최근의 차량 검사 기록을 제공할 것이라고 했으므로 지문의 내용과 일치한다.

패러프레이징
an official receipt for the sale of the automobile 자동차 판매의 공식 영수증 → Proof of payment 지불 증명서

어휘 proof n. 증명(서)

183 Not/True 문제

문제 Ms. Huang의 현재 차량에 대해 언급된 것은?
(A) 페인트칠이 되어야 한다.
(B) 새 부품이 필요하다.
(C) 수리될 수 없다.
(D) 너무 작다.

해설 질문의 핵심 어구인 Ms. Huang's current vehicle에 대해 묻는 Not/True 문제이므로 Ms. Huang이 작성한 이메일에서 관련 내용을 확인한다. (A)와 (B)는 지문에 언급되지 않은 내용이다. (C)는 'My old car cannot be repaired'에서 Ms. Huang이 자신의 원래 차는 수리될 수 없다고 했으므로 지문의 내용과 일치한다. 따라서 (C)가 정답이다. (D)는 지문에 언급되지 않은 내용이다.

패러프레이징
cannot be repaired 수리될 수 없다 → is unfixable 수리될 수 없다

어휘 component n. 부품, 요소

184 육하원칙 문제

문제 Ms. Huang은 계약서에 무슨 문제가 있는가?
(A) 이름의 철자가 틀리다.
(B) 서명이 누락되었다.
(C) 날짜가 맞지 않는다.
(D) 가격이 정확하지 않다.

해설 Ms. Huang이 계약서에 무슨(What) 문제가 있는지를 묻는 육하원칙 문제이므로 질문의 핵심 어구인 problem ~ Ms. Huang have with the contract에 대해 언급된 이메일에서 관련 내용을 확인한다. 두 번째 지문(이메일)의 'we agreed to meet on November 6. But the contract says that the sale date is November 5.'에서 Ms. Huang과 판매자가 11월 6일에 만나기로 약속했지만, 계약서에는 판매 일자가 11월 5일이라고 쓰여있다고 했으므로 (C)가 정답이다.

어휘 misspell v. 철자가 틀리다   incorrect adj. 맞지 않는, 부정확한
inaccurate adj. 부정확한, 오류가 있는

185 추론 문제 연계

문제 Ms. Huang은 왜 11월 6일에 은행을 방문할 것 같은가?
(A) 수표를 찾기 위해
(B) 송금을 하기 위해
(C) 돈을 인출하기 위해
(D) 신용카드를 신청하기 위해

해설 질문의 핵심 어구인 Ms. Huang visit a bank on November 6에서 Ms. Huang이 왜 11월 6일에 은행을 방문할 것 같은지를 묻고 있으므로 Ms. Huang이 작성한 이메일을 먼저 확인한다.

단서 1 두 번째 지문(이메일)의 'I will stop by the bank on the way to City Street Motors so that I'll be prepared to make the payment when I arrive.'와 'I look forward to meeting with you on November 6'에서 Ms. Huang이 11월 6일에 도착할 때 지불할 준비가 되어 있도록 City Street Motors사에 가는 길에 은행에 들르겠다고 했다. 그런데 Ms. Huang이 어떤 방법으로 지불할 것인지 제시되지 않았으므로 양식에서 관련 내용을 확인한다.

단서 2 첫 번째 지문(양식)의 'Payment Method: ■ Cash'에서 Ms. Huang의 지불 방법이 현금임을 확인할 수 있다.

두 단서를 종합할 때, Ms. Huang이 11월 6일에 현금을 인출하기 위해 은행을 방문할 것임을 알 수 있다. 따라서 (C)가 정답이다.

어휘 pick up ~을 찾다 wire transfer 송금 withdraw v. 인출하다
apply for ~을 신청하다

186-190번은 다음 웹페이지, 이메일, 문자 메시지에 관한 문제입니다.

---

http://www.fairviewest.com/home

| 홈 | 건물들 | 홈 디자인 | 방문 예약 |

Fairview Estates에서 당신의 꿈의 집을 알아보세요!

아름다운 포틀랜드에 위치한 Fairview Estates가 지금 영업 중입니다! 저희의 아름다운 건물들을 보시고 186-B"방문 예약"을 클릭하셔서 방문 일정을 세워보세요.

189Fairview Estates는 침실이 두 개, 세 개, 네 개인 주택들을 포함합니다. 위의 "홈 디자인"을 클릭하셔서 저희 모델 하우스의 사진들을 보세요. 각 주택에는 부엌, 식사 공간, 거실, 두 개의 욕조가 완비된 욕실이 딸려 있습니다. 186-A모든 주택들은 실내 차고를 갖고 있습니다. 189침실이 두 개인 세대들은 하나의 차량 공간을 갖고 있는 반면, 다른 세대들은 두 대의 차량을 수용할 수 있는 차고를 갖고 있습니다. 그리고 186-C단지에는 여러분과 여러분의 가족들의 안전을 보장하기 위해 경비원이 24시간 있습니다.

186-D각 주택 당 865달러의 연간 관리비가 구내의 유지를 위해 청구됩니다.

property n. 건물, 부동산, 재산 discover v. 알아내다, 발견하다
be open for business 영업 중이다 arrange v. 일정을 세우다
show home 모델 하우스 come with ~이 딸려 있다
full bathroom 욕조가 완비된 욕실 garage n. 차고
complex n. 단지, 복합 건물 security guard 경비원 loved one 가족
management fee 관리비 maintenance n. 유지, 보수
ground n. 구내, 땅

수신 Fairview Estates사 관리사무소 <inquiries@fairviewest.com>
발신 Mona Sawyer <monasawyer@genmail.com>
제목 방문 예약
날짜 3월 2일

안녕하세요,

187제가 새 일자리를 제의받아서 여기 시카고의 제 현재 집에서 이사를 해야 합니다. 제 집의 매매를 방금 완료해서, 새 집을 구매할 것을 생각하고 있습니다. 저는 3월 8일에 도착할 것이고, 당신의 건물을 보고 모델 하우스들을 둘러보는 것에 관심이 있습니다. 남편과 저는 두 아이가 있어서, 저희는 세 개의 침실이 필요합니다. 하지만 188저희가 여분의 방을 재택 사무실로 바꾸는 것을 고려하고 있기 때문에 침실이 네 개인 세대도 보여주시기 바랍니다. 저희가 빨리 집을 얻어야 하기에 곧 답변을 듣기를 바랍니다. 이 이메일로 답변을 하거나 제게 555-2833으로 문자 메시지를 보내시면 됩니다.

Mona Sawyer 드림

position n. (일)자리 look to ~을 생각해보다

발신: Andrew Kraft (555-5121)
수신: Mona Sawyer (555-2833)
수신됨: 3월 10일, 오후 2시 10분

저는 저희의 내일 약속을 위한 몇 가지 세부사항을 알려드리고자 합니다. 오전 10시에 관리사무소에서 당신을 만나려 합니다. 187당신이 오전 8시에 당신의 회계사 사무소를 들러야 한다고 말씀하셨기 때문에 이 시간이 당신에게 괜찮을 것이라 생각합니다. 서류 작업을 거친 후에, 당신께 열쇠들과 189침실이 네 개인 당신의 새로운 집의 보안 암호를 드리겠습니다. 지연이 없도록 하기 위해, 190당신의 은행 대출 계약서 사본을 반드시 함께 가지고 와주시겠습니까? 감사합니다.

administrative office 관리사무소 go through ~을 거치다, 검토하다
paperwork n. 서류 작업 code n. 암호 loan agreement 대출 계약서

---

186 Not/True 문제

문제 Fairview Estates에 대해 사실이 아닌 것은?
(A) 세대들이 모두 주차를 위한 실내 공간을 가지고 있다.
(B) 방문자들이 집을 보기 위한 예약을 할 수 있게 한다.
(C) 구내가 밤에만 경비원에 의해 지켜진다.
(D) 세입자들에게 관리비를 내도록 요구한다.

해설 질문의 핵심 어구인 Fairview Estates에 대해 묻는 Not/True 문제이므로 Fairview Estates가 언급된 첫 번째 지문(웹페이지)에서 관련 내용을 확인한다. (A)는 'All homes have indoor garages.'에서 모든 주택들은 실내 차고를 갖고 있다고 했으므로 지문의 내용과 일치한다. (B)는 'arrange for a tour by clicking on "BOOK VISIT"'에서 "방문 예약"을 클릭해서 방문 일정을 세워보라고 했으므로 지문의 내용과 일치한다. (C)는 'the complex has a 24-hour security guard available'에서 단지에는 경비원이 24시간 있다고 했으므로 지문의 내용과 일치하지 않는다. 따라서 (C)가 정답이다. (D)는 'An annual management fee of $865 per home is charged for the maintenance of the grounds.'에서 각 주택 당 865달러의 연간 관리비가 구내의 유지를 위해 청구된다고 했으므로 지문의 내용과 일치한다.

패러프레이징
garages 차고 → spaces for parking 주차를 위한 공간
arrange for a tour 방문 일정을 세우다 → make reservations to view homes 집을 보기 위한 예약을 하다
management fee ~ per home is charged 각 주택 당 관리비가 청구되다 → requires tenants to pay for the cost of maintenance 세입자들에게 관리비를 내도록 요구하다

어휘 tenant n. 세입자 protect v. 지키다, 보호하다
cost of maintenance 관리비

187 육하원칙 문제 연계

문제 Ms. Sawyer는 왜 이사할 것인가?
(A) 가족이 너무 커져서 현재 주택에 맞지 않게 되었다.
(B) 최근에 회계 분야 직장을 얻었다.
(C) 남편이 더 큰 재택 사무실을 필요로 한다.
(D) 시카고에 있는 집에 초과 지불하고 있다.

해설 Ms. Sawyer가 왜(Why) 이사할 것인지를 묻는 육하원칙 문제이므로 Ms. Sawyer가 보낸 이메일에서 관련 내용을 확인한다.

단서 1 두 번째 지문(이메일)의 'I have been offered a new position and I have to move from my current place here in Chicago.'에서 Ms. Sawyer가 새 일자리를 제의받아서 시카고의 현재 집에서 이사를 해야 한다고 했다. 그런데 제의받은 일자리가 무엇인지 제시되지 않았으므로 문자 메시지에서 관련 내용을 확인한다.

단서 2 세 번째 지문(문자 메시지)의 'you[Ms. Sawyer] mentioned you need to stop by your accounting office at 8 A.M.'에서 Ms. Sawyer가 자신의 회계사 사무소를 들러야 함을 확인할 수 있다. 두 단서를 종합할 때, Ms. Sawyer가 새 일자리를 제의받았고 자신의 회계사 사무소를 들러야 한다고 했으므로 최근에 회계 분야 직장을 얻었다는 것을 알 수 있다. 따라서 (B)가 정답이다.

어휘 relocate v. 이사하다, 이동하다 outgrow v. 너무 커져서 맞지 않게 되다
residence n. 주택 overpay v. 초과 지불하다

188 육하원칙 문제

문제 Ms. Sawyer는 왜 침실이 네 개인 모델 하우스를 보고 싶어 하는가?
(A) 추가적인 주차 공간이 필요하다.
(B) 업무 공간을 마련하는 것을 고려 중이다.
(C) 많은 손님들을 초대할 계획을 하고 있다.
(D) 자녀를 위한 넓은 놀이 공간을 원한다.

해설 Ms. Sawyer가 왜(Why) 침실이 네 개인 모델 하우스를 보고 싶어 하는지를 묻는 육하원칙 문제이므로 질문의 핵심 어구인 Ms. Sawyer가 보낸 이메일에서 관련 내용을 확인한다. 두 번째 지문(이메일)의 'please show us the four-bedroom unit as well because we are considering turning the extra bedroom into a home office'에서 Ms. Sawyer가 여분의 방을 재택 사무실로 바꾸는 것을 고려하고 있기 때문에 침실이 네 개인 세대를 보여달라고 했으므로 (B)가 정답이다.

패러프레이징
turning ~ into a home office 재택 사무실로 바꾸는 것 → setting up a work space 업무 공간을 마련하는 것

어휘 parking spot 주차 공간 set up ~을 마련하다, 세우다
work space 업무 공간

189 추론 문제 연계

문제 Ms. Sawyer가 선택한 집에 대해 암시되는 것은?
(A) 여러 차량을 위한 차고를 포함한다.
(B) 현재 세입자들이 살고 있다.
(C) 단지의 정문 옆에 위치해 있다.
(D) 작은 벽장이 딸려 있다.

해설 질문의 핵심 어구인 Ms. Sawyer's chosen home과 관련된 내용이 언급된 문자 메시지를 먼저 확인한다.
단서 1 세 번째 지문(문자 메시지)의 'your[Ms. Sawyer] new four-bedroom home'에서 Ms. Sawyer의 새로운 집이 침실이 네 개인 집이라고 했다. 그런데 침실이 네 개인 집에 대한 다른 정보가 제시되지 않았으므로 부동산에 대해 언급된 웹페이지에서 관련 내용을 확인한다.
단서 2 첫 번째 지문(웹페이지)의 'Fairview Estates includes two-, three-, and four-bedroom homes.'와 'The two-bedroom units include a single-vehicle space, while the others have garages that can accommodate two cars.'에서 침실이 네 개인 집은 두 대의 차량을 수용할 수 있는 차고를 갖고 있음을 확인할 수 있다. 두 단서를 종합할 때, Ms. Sawyer가 선택한 침실이 네 개인 집은 여러 차량을 위한 차고를 포함한다는 것을 알 수 있다. 따라서 (A)가 정답이다.

어휘 multiple adj. 여러, 다수의 situate v. 위치시키다
storage closet 벽장

190 육하원칙 문제

문제 Mr. Kraft는 무엇을 요청하는가?
(A) 서명된 임대 계약서
(B) 초기 보증금
(C) 금융 서류 사본
(D) 아파트 출입 암호

해설 Mr. Kraft가 무엇(What)을 요청하는지를 묻는 육하원칙 문제이므로 질문의 핵심 어구인 Mr. Kraft가 보낸 문자 메시지에서 관련 내용을 확인한다. 세 번째 지문(문자 메시지)의 'could you please make sure to bring a copy of your bank loan agreement with you?'에서 Mr. Kraft가 은행 대출 계약서 사본을 반드시 함께 가지고 와달라고 했으므로 (C)가 정답이다.

패러프레이징
a copy of ~ bank loan agreement 은행 대출 계약서 사본
→ A financial document copy 금융 서류 사본

어휘 housing contract 임대 계약(서) initial adj. 초기의
access n. 출입, 접근; v. 들어가다

191-195번은 다음 광고, 이메일, 주문 양식에 관한 문제입니다.

¹⁹²New Leaf 식료품점: 저렴한 가격의 천연 농산물!

가공 또는 유전자 변형의 식품이 적고, 농약이 없는 건강한 식단을 유지하는 것은 어려운 일일 수 있습니다! 라벨에 있는 모든 정보를 읽는 것은 많은 시간이 걸리고, 어떤 제품들이 천연이고 유기농인지 조사하는 것은 지루할 수 있습니다. 자, New Leaf 식료품점이 이곳 킹스턴에 왔으니 그것은 이제 과거의 문제입니다. 저희는 하나의 큰 차이점을 가진 포괄적인 서비스를 제공하는 식료품점을 운영합니다. 저희는 ¹⁹²오직 천연이고 유기농인 제품들만 저희 상점에서 판매된다는 점을 보장합니다. 제품에 대한 저희의 엄격한 요건들은 여러분이 저희 상점에서 사는 것이 무엇이든 여러분과 여러분의 가족에게 안전하다는 것을 확신할 수 있도록 합니다. ¹⁹¹저희의 주간 특별 상품들과 다른 할인들을 www.newleafgrocers.com에서 확인하세요! 또는 월요일부터 금요일 오전 8시부터 오후 8시까지, 주말에는 오전 11시에서 오후 6시에 694번지 Victoria가로 저희를 방문하세요.

produce n. 농산물 affordable adj. (가격이) 저렴한, 적정한
diet n. 식단 low in ~이 적은 process v. 가공하다
genetically modified 유전자 변형의 free of ~이 없는
pesticide n. 농약 time-consuming adj. (많은) 시간이 걸리는
tedious adj. 지루한 full-service adj. 포괄적인 서비스를 제공하는
rest assured ~라고 확신하다 special n. 특별 상품; adj. 특별한
offer n. 할인, 제공; v. 제공하다

수신	Rob Dawson <robdawson@selectcereals.com>
발신	Ariana Septus <arianas@newleafgrocers.com>
제목	주문
날짜	5월 2일
첨부 파일	주문 양식

Mr. Dawson께,

¹⁹³라스베이거스의 Eco-Food 박람회 동안에 귀사의 부스에서 귀하를 만나 매우 즐거웠습니다. 귀하께서 제게 주셨던 Select Cereals사 제품들의 샘플 몇 개를 제 동료들과 함께 나누어 먹었는데, 그들 또한 그것들을 즐겼습니다. ¹⁹²Select Cereals사의 식품들이 New Leaf 식료품점에서 판매되는 제품에 대한 모든 기준을 충족하기에, 저희는 귀하의 씨리얼들을 고객들에게 시험해보고 나서 첫 주문을 하고 싶습니다. ¹⁹⁴저희는 첨부된 주문 양식에서 가장 많은 양을 요청한 제품의 정기 배송에 관심이 있습니다. 앞으로의 배송은 같은 양일 것이고, 저희는 그것들이 매달 마지막 주 중에 도착하기를 바랍니다. 귀하의 다른 제품들이 저희 손님들에게 인기가 있다는 것이 입증되면, 저희는 그것들 또한 정기적인 주문을 할 여지가 있습니다.

시간을 내주셔서 감사하며, 추가 정보가 필요하시면 알려주십시오.

Ariana Septus 드림

colleague n. 동료 test out ~을 시험해보다 place an order 주문하다
regular adj. 정기의, 정기적인 be open to ~의 여지가 있다

[194]SELECT CEREALS사
주문 양식

고객 성함: Ariana Septus
[194/195]회사: New Leaf 식료품점

전화 번호: (613) 555-2039
이메일: arianas@newleafgro cers.com

[195]지불 방법: 회사 수표

배송 주소: 694번지 Victoria가, 킹스턴 온타리오 주

[194]제품	상자 당 가격*	[194]상자 수량	총액
Bran Cereal with Blueberries	24.00달러	2	48.00달러
Oat Cereal with Honey	20.00달러	3	60.00달러
Corn Cereal with Fruit and Nuts	24.00달러	2	48.00달러
[194]Multigrain Cereal with Raisins	22.00달러	[194]4	88.00달러

소계: 244.00달러
판매세: 24.40달러
배송 및 취급 비용: 56.00달러
총 주문액: 324.40달러

*각 상자에는 시리얼 5상자가 들어있습니다. 신용카드나 은행 이체로 지불할 수 있습니다. [195]회사 수표로의 지불도 허용되지만, 귀하의 은행에 의해 승인되고 금액이 저희 계좌로 예치되어야 주문품이 발송될 것입니다.

contain v. 들어있다, 포함하다 **acceptable** adj. 허용되는
clear v. 승인하다 **deposit** v. 예치하다 **account** n. 계좌

191 육하원칙 문제

문제 광고에 따르면, 상점의 웹사이트에서 무엇을 확인할 수 있는가?
(A) 상점으로 가는 길 안내
(B) 휴일 휴업의 일정표
(C) 특별 판촉 상품들에 대한 세부사항
(D) 제품 성분들의 목록

해설 상점의 웹사이트에서 무엇을(what) 확인할 수 있는지를 묻는 육하원칙 문제이므로 광고에서 관련 내용을 확인한다. 첫 번째 지문(광고)의 'Check out our weekly specials and other offers at www. newleafgrocers.com!'에서 상점의 주간 특별 상품들과 다른 할인들을 웹사이트에서 확인하라고 했으므로 상점의 웹사이트에서 특별 판촉 상품들에 대한 세부사항을 확인할 수 있음을 알 수 있다. 따라서 (C)가 정답이다.

어휘 **closure** n. 휴업, 폐쇄 **ingredient** n. 성분, 재료

192 추론 문제 연계

문제 Select Cereals사에 대해 암시되는 것은?
(A) 유기농 제품들의 다양성을 확대하기를 바란다.
(B) 식품들이 전문점에서만 판매된다.
(C) 매년 라스베이거스 음식 박람회에 참가한다.
(D) 제품들이 천연으로 자란 재료들로 만들어졌다.

해설 질문의 핵심 어구인 Select Cereals가 언급된 이메일을 먼저 확인한다. 단서 1 두 번째 지문(이메일)의 'As food items from Select Cereals meet all the criteria for merchandise sold at New Leaf Grocers'에서 Select Cereals사의 식품들이 New Leaf 식료품점에서 판매되는 제품에 대한 모든 기준을 충족한다고 했다. 그런데 New Leaf 식료품점에서 판매되는 제품들에 대한 기준이 무엇인지 제시되지 않았으므로 광고에서 관련 내용을 확인한다. 단서 2 첫 번째 지문(광고)의 'New Leaf Grocers'와 'only natural,

organic products are sold in our establishment'에서 오직 천연이고 유기농인 제품들만 New Leaf 식료품점에서 판매됨을 확인할 수 있다.
두 단서를 종합할 때, Select Cereals사의 제품들이 천연으로 자란 재료들로 만들어졌다는 것을 알 수 있다. 따라서 (D)가 정답이다.

어휘 **range** n. 다양성, 범위 **specialty store** 전문점

193 추론 문제

문제 Mr. Dawson에 대해 암시되는 것은?
(A) 식료업 행사에서 회사를 대표했다.
(B) 동료들에게 제품 샘플 몇 개를 발송했다.
(C) 출장 중에 구매 양식을 작성했다.
(D) New Leaf 식료품점의 정기 공급자이다.

해설 질문의 핵심 어구인 Mr. Dawson에 대해 추론하는 문제이므로 Mr. Dawson에게 보내진 이메일에서 관련 내용을 확인한다. 두 번째 지문(이메일)의 'I very much enjoyed meeting with you at your company booth during the Eco-Food Fair in Las Vegas.'에서 라스베이거스의 Eco-Food 박람회 동안에 Mr. Dawson의 회사 부스에서 Mr. Dawson을 만나 매우 즐거웠다고 했으므로 Mr. Dawson이 식료업 행사에서 회사를 대표하여 부스에 있었다는 것을 추론할 수 있다. 따라서 (A)가 정답이다.

어휘 **represent** v. 대표하다 **mail** v. 발송하다; n. 우편 **fill out** ~을 작성하다
supplier n. 공급자

194 육하원칙 문제 연계

문제 Select Cereals사는 어떤 제품을 New Leaf 식료품점에 정기적으로 배송할 것인가?
(A) Bran Cereal with Blueberries
(B) Oat Cereal with Honey
(C) Corn Cereal with Fruit and Nuts
(D) Multigrain Cereal with Raisins

해설 Select Cereals사가 어떤(Which) 제품을 New Leaf 식료품점에 정기적으로 배송할 것인지를 묻고 있으므로 정기 배송에 대한 내용이 언급된 이메일을 먼저 확인한다.
단서 1 두 번째 지문(이메일)의 'We[New Leaf Grocers] are interested in regular delivery of the product we requested the greatest amount of on the attached order form.'에서 New Leaf 식료품점이 주문 양식에서 가장 많은 양을 요청한 제품의 정기 배송에 관심이 있다고 했다. 그런데 가장 많은 양을 요청한 제품이 무엇인지 제시되지 않았으므로 주문 양식에서 관련 내용을 확인한다.
단서 2 세 번째 지문(주문 양식)의 'SELECT CEREALS, Order Form', 'Company: New Leaf Grocers'와 'ITEM, Multigrain Cereal with Raisins', 'QUANTITY OF CASES, 4'에서 New Leaf 식료품점이 Select Cereals사의 주문 양식에서 가장 많이 요청한 제품이 Multigrain Cereal with Raisins임을 확인할 수 있다.
두 단서를 종합할 때, New Leaf 식료품점에 Multigrain Cereal with Raisins가 정기적으로 배송될 것임을 알 수 있다. 따라서 (D)가 정답이다.

195 추론 문제

문제 주문 양식에 따르면, New Leaf 식료품점에 대해 암시되는 것은?
(A) 오트밀 시리얼보다 옥수수 시리얼을 더 많이 원한다.
(B) 영수증이 고객들에게 이메일로 전달된다.
(C) 다음 주문에 배송비를 낼 필요가 없을 것이다.
(D) 지불이 처리되고 난 이후에 주문품이 보내질 것이다.

해설 질문의 핵심 어구인 New Leaf Grocers에 대해 추론하는 문제이므로 New Leaf 식료품점이 언급된 주문 양식에서 관련 내용을 확인한다. 세 번째 지문(주문 양식)의 'Company: New Leaf Grocers'와 'Payment method: Company Check'에서 New Leaf 식료품점의

지불 방법이 회사 수표라고 했고, 'Payment by company check is also acceptable, but the order will not ship until the check has been cleared by your bank and the money has been deposited in our account.'에서 회사 수표로의 지불도 허용되지만 주문품은 은행에 의해 승인되고 금액이 계좌로 예치되어야 발송될 것이라고 했으므로 New Leaf 식료품점의 주문품이 지불이 처리되고 난 이후에 보내질 것이라는 것을 추론할 수 있다. 따라서 (D)가 정답이다.

패러프레이징
order will not ship until the check has been cleared ~ and the money has been deposited 주문품은 승인되고 금액이 예치되어야 발송될 것이다 → order will be sent after a payment has been processed 지불이 처리되고 난 이후에 주문품이 보내질 것이다

어휘 oat n. 오트밀　process v. 처리하다, 가공하다; n. 과정

196-200번은 다음 기사, 이메일, 편지에 관한 문제입니다.

세금 혜택 프로그램을 고려 중인 정부
Evan Proust 작성
1월 3일

[196]몇몇 뉴사우스웨일스 주 공무원들이 어제 회담을 열었고 새로운 세금 혜택 프로그램을 제안했다. 그들이 말하기를 그것이 만약 승인된다면, [196]이 프로그램은 주거 건물 및 제조 시설 소유주들이 태양 전지판을 위한 수리 비용에 대해 세금을 내는 것을 면제해줄 것이다. 그러나, [200]전지판들로 생성된 모든 미사용 에너지의 판매에 대해서는 12퍼센트의 세금이 계속해서 부과될 것이다.

[197]이 프로그램은 1월이 끝나기 전에 환경 보호국에 의해 투표로 결정될 것이다. 프로그램이 승인된다면, 주택 및 사업체 소유주들은 환경 보호국의 웹사이트에서 등록을 신청할 수 있을 것이다.

incentive n. 혜택, 장려책　hold discussion 회담을 열다
propose v. 제안하다　exempt v. 면제하다; adj. 면제되는
residential adj. 주거의　solar panel 태양 전지판
generate v. 생성하다, 일으키다　enrollment n. 등록, 기재

수신: Patty Kindale <patkin@eastonmanufacturing.co.au>
발신: Rich Ward <richward@eastonmanufacturing.co.au>
제목: 새로운 임무
날짜: 2월 10일

Patty,

우리가 지난주에 논의했던 사안과 관련하여 이메일을 씁니다. [197]저는 당신이 태양열 전지판을 사용하는 우리의 각 건물들에 관해서 우리가 최근에 승인된 세금 혜택 프로그램에 신청하기 위해 필요한 서류를 준비해주었으면 합니다. 신청을 위한 필요조건들은 시설의 종류에 따라 다를 수 있으니, 환경 보호국의 웹페이지에서 그 세부사항들을 재확인해주시기 바랍니다. 이것이 어쩌면 많은 양의 일이라는 것을 알지만, 우리가 가능한 한 빨리 이 프로그램에 등록하는 것이 정말 중요합니다. 저는 Jerry Headley와 Brianne O'Neil에게도 당신이 이 준비를 하는 것을 도우라고 요청해두었습니다. 저는 가능하면, 모든 신청 서류들이 금요일까지 준비되었으면 좋겠습니다. 만약 그것이 절대로 충분한 시간이 되지 않는다면, 이 일을 위해 더 합당한 마감일을 알려주시기 바랍니다. [198]그리고 이 업무에 추가적인 도움이 필요하면, 제 비서 Vera Santos 또한 당신을 돕도록 할 수 있습니다.

감사합니다,

Rich 드림

documentation n. 서류　property n. 건물
double-check v. 재확인하다　potentially adv. 어쩌면, 잠재적으로
enroll in ~에 등록하다　preparation n. 준비, 대비
simply adv. 절대로, 간단히　reasonable adj. 합당한, 이성적인
deadline n. 마감일, 최종 기한　assistant n. 비서, 보조

3월 28일

Rich Ward
회계부장
Easton Manufacturing사
44번지 Grahame가
Blaxland, 뉴사우스웨일스 2774

Mr. Ward께,

[199]이 편지는 새로 시행된 정부의 태양 에너지 세금 혜택 프로그램에 대한 귀사의 신청들이 승인되었음을 확인해 드립니다. 귀사는 4월 1일부터 각 제조 시설들에 대한 세금 혜택에 자격을 얻게 될 것입니다.

[200]그러나, 귀사 건물들 중 세 개가 태양 전지판들로 생성되는 초과 에너지량을 가지고 있음을 알게 되었고, 이 에너지는 귀사가 지역 회사들에게 판매해오고 있는 것입니다. 이 관행과 관련된 세금 혜택 프로그램의 정책은 변경되지 않았음을 명심하시기 바랍니다.

이 프로그램에 참여하고 뉴사우스웨일스의 청정하고 안전한 에너지 생산에 기여해주셔서 감사합니다.

Fred Dionne 드림
환경 보호국

verify v. 확인하다, 입증하다　implement v. 시행하다; n. 도구
excess adj. 초과한　take part in ~에 참여하다

---

196 육하원칙 문제

문제 기사에 따르면, 어제 공무원들은 무엇을 했는가?
(A) 관공서들에 대한 새로운 지침을 만들었다.
(B) 태양 전지판에 대한 세금을 없애자는 제안을 거부했다.
(C) 지역 사회를 위한 태양 전지판을 구매하는 계약을 제안했다.
(D) 일부 부동산 소유주들에게 혜택을 주는 계획을 논의했다.

해설 어제 공무원들이 무엇(what)을 했는지를 묻는 육하원칙 문제이므로 기사에서 관련 내용을 확인한다. 첫 번째 지문(기사)의 'Several New South Wales government officials held discussions yesterday and proposed a new tax incentive program.'에서 몇몇 뉴사우스웨일스 주 공무원들이 어제 회담을 열었고 새로운 세금 혜택 프로그램을 제안했다고 했고, 'this program will exempt residential building and manufacturing facility owners from paying taxes on repair costs for solar panels'에서 이 프로그램은 주거 건물 및 제조 시설 소유주들이 태양 전지판을 위한 수리 비용에 대해 세금을 내는 것을 면제해줄 것이라고 했으므로 어제 공무원들이 일부 부동산 소유주들에게 혜택을 주는 계획을 논의했음을 알 수 있다. 따라서 (D)가 정답이다.

어휘 guideline n. 지침　government office 관공서
reject v. 거부하다, 거절하다　deal n. 계약, 거래, 협정

197 추론 문제 연계

문제 세금 혜택 프로그램에 대해 암시되는 것은?
(A) 1월에 정부에 의해 승인되었다.
(B) 개인적으로 소유된 사업체들에게만 적용된다.
(C) 지역에 외국 제조사들을 유치해 왔다.
(D) 내년부터 신청될 수 있다.

해설 질문의 핵심 어구인 tax incentive program이 언급된 기사를 먼저 확인한다.
단서 1 첫 번째 지문(기사)의 'The program[tax incentive program] will be voted on by the department of environmental protection before the end of January. Should the program be approved, residence and business owners will be able to apply for enrollment'에서 세금 혜택 프로그램이 1월이 끝나기 전에 환경 보호국에 의해 투표로 결정될 것이고, 프로그램이 승인된다면 주택 및 사업체 소유주들이 등록을 신청할 수 있을

것이라고 했다. 그런데 이 프로그램이 승인되었는지 제시되지 않았으므로 이메일에서 관련 내용을 확인한다.

[단서 2] 두 번째 지문(이메일)의 'I'd like you to prepare the documentation we need to apply for the recently approved tax incentive program'에서 이메일 발신자가 최근에 승인된 세금 혜택 프로그램에 신청하기 위해 필요한 서류를 준비해달라고 요청함을 확인할 수 있다.

두 단서를 종합할 때, 세금 혜택 프로그램의 신청이 진행되고 있으므로 세금 혜택 프로그램이 1월이 끝나기 전에 환경 보호국에 의해 투표로 결정되어 승인되었다는 것을 알 수 있다. 따라서 (A)가 정답이다.

어휘 **apply to** ~에 적용되다 **privately** adv. 개인적으로, 은밀히
attract v. 유치하다

198 육하원칙 문제

문제 Mr. Ward는 Ms. Kindale에게 무엇을 해주겠다고 제안하는가?
(A) 프로젝트를 위한 추가적인 자금을 제공한다.
(B) Vera Santos를 업무에 배정한다.
(C) 도움이 되는 자료들을 보내준다.
(D) Jerry Headley에게 시설을 점검하도록 요청한다.

해설 Mr. Ward가 Ms. Kindale에게 무엇(What)을 해주겠다고 제안하는지를 묻는 육하원칙 문제이므로 Mr. Ward가 작성한 이메일에서 관련 내용을 확인한다. 두 번째 지문(이메일)의 'And should you [Ms. Kindale] need extra help with this task, I can have my assistant Vera Santos help you out as well.'에서 Mr. Ward가 이 업무에 추가적인 도움이 필요하면 자신의 비서 Vera Santos 또한 Ms. Kindale을 돕도록 할 수 있다고 했으므로 (B)가 정답이다.

어휘 **assign** v. 배정하다, 임명하다 **inspect** v. 점검하다, 조사하다

199 목적 찾기 문제

문제 편지는 왜 쓰여졌는가?
(A) 연구의 결과들을 알리기 위해
(B) 건설 제안을 승인하기 위해
(C) 프로그램에 대한 적격성을 확인해주기 위해
(D) 세금 납부의 수령을 확인해주기 위해

해설 편지가 쓰여진 목적을 묻는 목적 찾기 문제이므로 편지의 내용을 확인한다. 세 번째 지문(편지)의 'This letter serves to verify that your company's applications for the government's newly implemented solar energy tax benefit program have been approved.'에서 이 편지가 새로 시행된 정부의 태양 에너지 세금 혜택 프로그램에 대한 신청들이 승인되었음을 확인해준다고 했으므로 (C)가 정답이다.

어휘 **confirm** v. 확인해주다, 공식화하다, 승인하다 **eligibility** n. 적격(성), 적임

200 추론 문제 연계

문제 Easton Manufacturing사의 일부 시설들에 대해 암시되는 것은?
(A) 12퍼센트의 세금이 부과될 수 있다.
(B) 예상보다 더 많은 전력을 필요로 한다.
(C) 2월 10일에 생산 수준을 줄였다.
(D) 운영을 재개하기 전에 수리가 필요하다.

해설 질문의 핵심 어구인 some of Easton Manufacturing's facilities가 언급된 편지를 먼저 확인한다.
[단서 1] 세 번째 지문(편지)의 'I did notice ~ that three of your [Easton Manufacturing] buildings have an excess amount of energy generated by solar panels, which you have been selling to local firms.'에서 Easton Manufacturing사의 건물들 중 세 개가 태양 전지판들로 생성되는 초과 에너지량을 가지고 있으며 이 에너지를 지역 회사들에게 판매해오고 있다고 했고, 'Please keep in mind that the tax incentive program's policy regarding this practise has not changed.'에서 이 관행과 관련한 세금 혜택 프로

그램의 정책은 변경되지 않았음을 명심하라고 했다. 그런데 이 관행과 관련하여 변경되지 않은 세금 혜택 프로그램의 정책이 무엇인지 제시되지 않았으므로 기사에서 관련 내용을 확인한다.
[단서 2] 첫 번째 지문(기사)의 'a 12 percent tax will continue to be charged for the sale of any unused energy generated by the panels'에서 전지판들로 생성된 모든 미사용 에너지의 판매에 대해서는 12퍼센트의 세금이 계속해서 부과될 것임을 확인할 수 있다.

두 단서를 종합할 때, Easton Manufacturing사가 초과 생산되는 에너지를 지역 회사들에 판매하고 있으므로 미사용 에너지 판매에 대해 12퍼센트의 세금이 부과될 수 있음을 알 수 있다. 따라서 (A)가 정답이다.

어휘 **be in need of** ~을 필요로 하다 **electricity** n. 전력, 전기
anticipate v. 예상하다 **cut back on** ~을 줄이다
renovation n. 수리, 혁신 **resume** v. 재개하다
operation n. 운영, 사업

MEMO

5천 개가 넘는
해커스토익 무료 자료!

대한민국에서 공짜로 토익 공부하고 싶으면 | 해커스영어 Hackers.co.kr ▾ | 검색

RC 정수진 RC 이상길

강의도 무료

베스트셀러 1위 토익 강의 150강 무료 서비스,
누적 시청 1,900만 돌파!

3,730제 무료

문제도 무료

토익 RC/LC 풀기, 모의토익 등
실전토익 대비 문제 3,730제 무료!

LC 한승태 RC 김동영

최신 특강도 무료

2,400만뷰 스타강사의
압도적 적중예상특강 매달 업데이트!

공부법도 무료

**토익 고득점 달성팁, 비법노트,
점수대별 공부법 무료 확인**

전원 무료

*미션 달성 시

가장 빠른 정답까지!

615만이 선택한 해커스 토익 정답!
시험 직후 가장 빠른 정답 확인

더 많은 토익무료자료
보기 ▶

327만이 선택한 외국어학원
1위 해커스어학원

토익 단기졸업 달성을 위한 해커스 약점관리 프로그램

자신의 약점을 정확히 파악하고 집중적으로 보완하는 것이야말로
토익 단기졸업의 필수코스입니다.

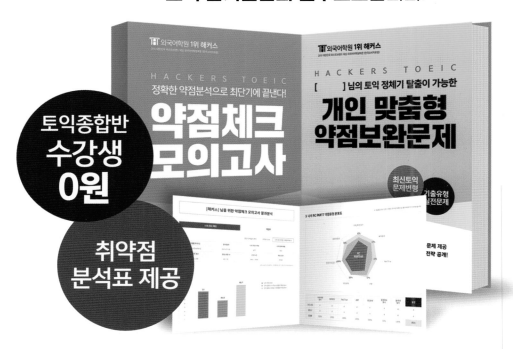

토익종합반 수강생 0원

취약점 분석표 제공

STEP 01
약점체크 모의고사 응시

*비매품

최신 토익 출제경향을 반영한
약점체크 모의고사 응시

STEP 02
토익 취약점 분석표 확인

파트별 취약점 분석표를 통해
객관적인 실력 파악

STEP 03
개인별 맞춤 보완문제 증정

최대 180제 제공

*PDF

영역별 취약 부분에 대한
보완문제로 취약점 극복

지금 바로 신청하고
토익 취약점 완벽 극복 ▶